The New American

WEBSTER
HANDY
COLLEGE
DICTIONARY

**Includes Abbreviations, Geographical Names
Foreign Words and Phrases**

Revised and Updated

ALBERT and LOY MOREHEAD
Editors

A SIGNET BOOK from
NEW AMERICAN LIBRARY
TIMES MIRROR

SIGNET TRADEMARK REG. U.S. PAT. OFF. AND FOREIGN COUNTRIES
REGISTERED TRADEMARK—MARCA REGISTRADA
HECHO EN CHICAGO, U.S.A.

SIGNET, SIGNET CLASSICS, MENTOR, PLUME AND MERIDIAN BOOKS
are published by The New American Library, Inc.,
1301 Avenue of the Americas, New York, New York 10019

78 79 80 81

PRINTED IN THE UNITED STATES OF AMERICA

CONTENTS

Prepared and Edited by

The National Lexicographic Board

ALBERT H. MOREHEAD, *Chairman and General Editor*
WALDEMAR VON ZEDTWITZ, *President*
LOY C. MOREHEAD, *Vice President & Secretary;* LOYD F. GEHRES, SALVATORE RAMONDINO, *Vice Presidents;* DONALD D. WOLF, WILLIAM C. CAMPBELL, GEORGE H. COPELAND, JACK LUZZATTO.

Staff for The New American Handy College Dictionary

ALBERT *and* LOY MOREHEAD, *Editors*

GEOFFREY MOTT-SMITH, *Managing Editor.* WILLIAM T. ATWOOD, WILLIAM C. CAMPBELL, JACK LUZZATTO, RICHARD HOWARD, *Associate Editors.* JANE McDOWELL, *Drawings.* (Incorporating in part *The New American Webster Dictionary,* LOYD F. GEHRES, *Editor-in-Chief.*)

Consultants

JOHN G. ALBRIGHT
Head, Department of Physics
University of Rhode Island

HAROLD C. VORIS, M.D.
Clinical Professor of Surgery
Loyola University

PAUL HENLE
Professor and Chairman
Department of Philosophy
University of Michigan

The Rev. EMIL G. KRAELING
Professor (retired)
Union Theological Seminary

MARIO A. PEI
Professor of Romance Philology
Columbia University

Capt. R. S. BARNABY, U.S.N. Ret.
Chief, Aeronautics Section
Franklin Institute, Philadelphia

WATSON B. MILLER
Member, Subversive Activities
Control Board

HOWARD DWIGHT SMITH
University Architect
Ohio State University

ELMO N. STEVENSON
President
Southern Oregon College

Brother AMANDUS LEO, F.S.C.
Dean of Engineering
Manhattan College

The Rev. JUVENAL D. LALOR, O.F.M.
President
St. Bonaventure University

BENJAMIN E. MAYS
President, Morehouse College

CLAUDE COLLIER MARION
Professor of Agriculture
Maryland State College

CHESTER L. VINCENT
Professor of Horticulture
State College of Washington

LOUIS S. CHASE, M.D.
Assistant Professor of Psychiatry
Tufts Medical School

The Rev. PATRICK J. FLYNN, C.S.P.
The Rev. JOHN J. KEATING, C.S.P.
Paulist Information Center

DONALD J. HART
Dean, School of Business
Administration, University of Idaho

LLOYD R. WYLIE
Professor of Astronomy
Wittenberg College

ANGUS M. WOODBURY
Head, Department of Vertebrate
Zoölogy, University of Utah

The Rev. MORRIS N. KERTZER
American Jewish Committee

EDWIN J. POLLOCK
Sports Editor, Philadelphia Bulletin

JOHN MILTON FOGG, JR.
Professor of Botany
and Vice-President
University of Pennsylvania

CLAUDE E. ZOBELL
Professor of Microbiology
Scripps Institution of Oceanography
University of California

HOW TO USE THIS DICTIONARY

This dictionary supplies the spelling, syllabication, pronunciation and meaning of the most useful words of the English language as it is spoken in the United States. Abbreviations, foreign words and phrases, and the names and descriptions of places may be found in the pages following the main vocabulary.

Words are not listed separately when they are identical in spelling and pronunciation and differ only in etymology.

SPELLING

Where a word may correctly be spelled in more than one way, we have generally preferred the simplest way. Space does not permit us to include every spelling for which there is authority. The user of this dictionary may rely upon finding a correct way to spell his word, but it will not necessarily be *the only* correct way.

SYLLABICATION

Each word in its first spelling is divided into syllables, either by stress marks or by dots. The syllable preceding the mark (') is primarily stressed; a syllable preceding the mark (") receives secondary stress. The dots should not be confused with hyphens. When a word is to be hyphenated in spelling, it is marked with a bold, long hyphen (-).

It is not conventionally proper to divide a word, at the end of a line, at any place except where a stress mark, dot or hyphen appears. Even where the dictionary shows a division into syllables, it is not good style to leave a single letter of a word on one line; for example, words like *abound*, *alike*, *glossy*, should not be divided between lines.

GUIDE TO PRONUNCIATION

a	as in fat	ů	as in pull	ngg	as in finger
ā	as in fate	e	as in comm*a*,	nk	as in ink (pronounced *ingk*)
ä	as in far		label,		
å	as in fall		pupil,		
à	as in ask		censor,		
ā	as in dare		focus		
e	as in met	b	as in but	p	as in pen
ē	as in mete	ch	as in chair	r	as in rat
ẽ	as in her	d	as in day	s	as in sit, this
è	as in maybe	f	as in fill	sh	as in she
i	as in pin	g	as in go	t	as in to
ī	as in pine	h	as in hat	th	as in thin
o	as in not	hw	as in when	*th*	as in then
ō	as in note	j	as in joke	v	as in van
oo	as in spoon	k	as in keep	w	as in win
ô	as in or	kt	as in act	y	as in yet
oi	as in oil	l	as in late	z	as in zone, quiz
ow	as in owl	m	as in man	zh	as in azure
u	as in tub	n	as in nod	ö	as in Ger. *schön*
ū	as in mute	ng	as in sing	ü	as in Fr. *tu*
				ǹ	as in Fr. *bon*
				kh	as in blockhouse

The criterion for pronunciation is the best usage in regions where there is no marked peculiarity of speech and in normal conversation rather than in formal speech.

Where the respelling of a word for pronunciation would be in all respects the same as the original spelling, the word is not respelled.

Most of the diacritical marks are self-explanatory, but some suggest comment:

ə (the upside-down e, called the schwa) marks the a in comma e in label i in pupil o in censor u in focus	Any unaccented vowel tends to become an "uh" sound. The use of the ə does not mean you must not pronounce the actual vowel; with meticulous speakers the original vowel sound remains recognizable. Say *char·i·ty* if you wish, but with equal confidence—and much more company—you may say *char·ə·ty*. The schwa is also used to indicate certain "lost" vowel sounds, as in the word *garden*, where the *n* is merely a nasal utterance following the gard-.
à as in ask	However you pronounce *ask*, *laugh*, *aunt*—with the *a* as in *cat*, or as in *father*, or somewhere in between—that is how you should render this à.
ô as in corn, horn, torn	Traditionally, dictionaries say that the sound of *o* in *corn*, *horn*, *morn* is different from the sound of *o* in *worn*, *torn*, *sworn*; that *horse* and *hoarse*, *border* and *boarder*, *born* and *borne*, are not pronounced the same. We do not make this distinction. In the few regions where it is made, the *r* is not pronounced.
ê to represent the *y* in story	The terminal *y* is rendered as short *i* in other dictionaries. Along with the writers of popular songs, we hear it, from coast to coast, as an unstressed long *e*.
nk as in ink	This is actually pronounced *ngk*; but since it is never pronounced any other way, it seems unnecessary to respell a word each time *nk* occurs.

Compound words are not respelled for pronunciation if each element is pronounced elsewhere in the dictionary. A derivative form is respelled for pronunciation only to the extent necessary: *odd'i·ty* (-ə·tē).

INFLECTIONAL FORMS

In the formation of plurals, inflection of verbs, and comparison of adjectives and adverbs, only irregular forms are specified in the dictionary. In the absence of specific exception, it should be assumed that the following rules apply.

PLURAL FORMS OF NOUNS

1. Usually, form the plural by adding -*s* to the singular noun. The -*s* is pronounced *z*, unless *s* is easier.

2. Usually add -*es* to a singular noun ending in a sibilant sound. The -*es* then forms a new syllable, pronounced -*iz*. Thus: *dresses* (dres'iz), *matches* (mach'iz).

If the singular noun ends in a sibilant but has a silent terminal *e*, add only -*s*, but the new syllable still occurs: *base*, *bases* (bās'iz).

3. When a noun ends in *y* preceded by a consonant, the plural form is -*ies*: *dairy*, *dairies* (dâr'ēz). But when the terminal *y* is preceded by a vowel, add merely -*s*: *day*, *days*.

4. The plural form of a noun ending in a consonant and *o* is -*oes*: *hero*, *heroes* (hir'ōz). But when a vowel precedes the terminal *o* add merely -*s*: *radio radios* (rā'dē·ōz").

POSSESSIVE FORMS

1. To form the possessive, add *'s* to a singular noun or to a plural noun not ending in *s*: a *man's* voice, the *horse's* mouth, the *fish's* tail, *men's* lives. The pronunciation follows the rules for regular plurals: *fish's* is the same as *fishes* (fish'ĭz).

2. To form the possessive of a plural noun ending in *s*, add the apostrophe (') alone: the *workers'* wages.

3. The foregoing rules apply also to proper names: *John's* book, John *Harris's* house, the *Smiths'* party. It is incorrect to write *the Harris' ages* instead of *Harrises'*.

4. The possessive forms of pronouns are usually irregular and are given in the dictionary.

INFLECTION OF REGULAR VERBS

1. The present indicative tense uses the infinitive in all cases except third person singular, which is regularly formed the same as the plurals of nouns (see preceding paragraphs). Thus: *to like, I like you like, we like, they like,* but *he, she,* or *it likes.*

2. The past tense (preterit) is formed by adding *-d* or *-ed* to the infinitive, according as the latter does or does not end with *e*. The *-ed* forms a new syllable after *d* or *t*, and is pronounced *-id:* to want, *wanted* (wŏnt'ĭd); to end, *ended* (en'dĭd). In other cases the *-d* or *-ed* does not form a new syllable and is pronounced *d* or *t*, whichever is easier: to play, *played* (plād); to match, *matched* (macht). A terminal *y* preceded by a consonant changes to *-ied:* to bury, *bur'ied.*

3. The past participle is the same as the preterit.

4. The present participle is formed by adding *-ing* to the infinitive, from which the terminal *e* (if any) is dropped. Thus: to jump, *jump'ing;* to hate, *hat'ing;* to grapple. *grap'pling;* to bury, *bur'y-ing.*

5. A consonant preceded by a short vowel is doubled: to can, *canned* (kand), *can'ning.* (These forms are regularly given in the dictionary.)

6. Many of the fundamental verbs are irregular, as *be, have, go, run, make,* etc. All forms of the auxiliary verbs *be* and *have* are given in the text under the infinitives. The forms of the other irregular verbs are given after the infinitive, in square brackets [ ], in the order: preterit, past participle, present participle. When the preterit and past participle are the same form, it is not repeated. When only one syllable is shown, it replaces the last syllable only of the word previously spelled out: *fit* [fĭt'ted, -ting].

7. Regular and irregular verbs alike form their other tenses as follows. *Present perfect:* add the past participle to the present indicative of *have.* (Thus: to go, I have gone.) *Past perfect:* or *pluperfect:* add the past participle to the preterit of *have.* (Thus: to go, I had gone.) *Present progressive:* add the present participle to the present indicative of *be.* (Thus: to go, I am going.) *Past progressive:* add the present participle to the preterit of *be.* (Thus: to go, I was going.) *Passive voice:* add the past participle to the appropriate tense of *be.* (Thus: to call, I am called, I was called, I have been called, I had been called, etc.) *Future tense:* add the infinitive to the appropriate tense of *will* or *shall.* (Thus: to call, I will call, I shall call, I shall be called, etc.) *Subjunctive mood:* add the infinitive to *would* or *should* (active voice) or the past participle to the subjunctive form of *be* (passive voice). (Thus: to call, if I should call, if I should be called.) *Imperative mood:* use the infinitive. (Thus: to go, Go!)

COMPARISON OF ADJECTIVES AND ADVERBS

1. The main vocabulary lists only the positive forms of adjectives and adverbs. The regular formation of the comparative is to add -*r* or -*er* to the positive; of the superlative, to add -*st* or -*est* (according as the positive does or does not end in *e*). A consonant preceded by a short vowel is doubled: *mad, mad'der, mad'dest*. For words ending in *y*, the forms are -*ier*, -*iest*. Often the regular formation makes for awkward pronunciation; in such a case, for the comparative, precede the positive by *more*; for the superlative, precede it by *most*. In general, this alternative is followed for words of three or more syllables.

2. For adjectives and adverbs compared irregularly, the text appends the comparative and superlative in square brackets [ ]: good [bet'ter, best].

THE FORMATION OF ADDITIONAL WORDS

1. Unlike other small dictionaries, this dictionary lists hundreds of prefixes, suffixes, and other word elements from which additional words can be formed and the meanings of other words can be inferred.

2. The adjectival forms ending in -*ful*, -*some*, -*like*, and -*less* are generally omitted from the dictionary.

3. Adverbs are regularly formed from adjectives by the addition of -*ly*: bright, *bright'ly*. When the adjective ends in -*y*, this letter regularly changes to *i*, making the terminal -*ily*: heavy, *heav'i·ly*. When the adjective ends in -*le* preceded by a consonant, the adverb is formed by changing the final *e* to *y*: idle, *i'dly*. Virtually all regular adverbial forms are omitted from the dictionary.

4. Nouns of agency are regularly formed by adding -*er* to a verb: *to pound; pound'er*, one who or that which pounds. The rules follow those for forming the comparatives of adjectives: *to bury, bur'i·er; to pine, pin'er; to dig, dig'ger*. Most of the regular forms are omitted from the dictionary. Such nouns when formed by adding -*or*, -*ist*, -*eer*, etc. are given in the dictionary.

AMERICAN AND BRITISH SPELLINGS

The preferred spellings in this dictionary follow American usage. In the following cases British usage differs:

1. Many nouns such as *honor, armor* (U.S.) are spelled *honour, armour* (Brit.). Similar variation between *o* and *ou* occurs in a few other words, as *molt* (U.S.), *moult* (Brit.); *smolder* (U.S.), *smoulder* (Brit.).

2. Most verbs ending in -*ize* (U.S.) are spelled -*ise* (Brit.): *realize* (U.S.), *realise* (Brit.).

3. Many words ending in -*er* (U.S.) are spelled -*re* (Brit.): *center, fiber* (U.S.), *centre, fibre* (Brit.).

4. In forms of verbs ending in *l* preceded by a short vowel, the *l* is not usually doubled (U.S.) and is usually doubled (Brit.): *traveled, traveling, traveler* (U.S.), *travelled, travelling, traveller* (Brit.).

A

A, a (ā) first letter of the English alphabet. —*adj., indef. art.* one; any.

a- *pref.* **1,** not. **2,** in, on. **3,** an intensive, as in *arouse.*

AA (ā′ā′) *n.* antiaircraft fire.

aard′vark″ (ärd′värk″) *n.* an African ant-eating mammal; groundhog.

ab- *pref.* away from; off.

a″ba·cá′ (ä″bä-kä′) *n.* a Philippine palm; its fiber, used in making hemp.

a·back′ (ə-bak′) *adv.* toward the rear. —**taken aback,** disconcerted.

ab′a·cus (ab′ə-kəs) *n.* a calculating device consisting of beads strung on rods in a frame.

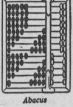

Abacus

a·baft′ (ə-baft′) *adv. & prep.* (*Naut.*) toward the stern; behind.

ab″a·lo′ne (ab″-ə-lō′nē) *n.* a large snail abundant on the Pacific coast.

a·ban′don (ə-ban′dən) *v.t.* give up; leave; forsake; cast away. —*n.* freedom from restraint. —**a·ban′doned,** *adj.* reckless; dissolute. —**a·ban′don·ment,** *n.*

a·base′ (ə-bās′) *v.t.* reduce in rank or estimation. —**a·base′ment,** *n.*

a·bash′ (ə-bash′) *v.t.* make ashamed or dispirited; embarrass.

a·bate′ (ə-bāt′) *v.t.* beat down; reduce; moderate. —*v.i.* diminish; lessen. —**a·bate′ment,** *n.*

ab″at·toir′ (ab″ə-twär′) *n.* slaughterhouse.

ab·bé′ (á-bā′) *n.* a French ecclesiastic.

ab′bess (ab′es) *n.* the head of a convent.

ab′bey (ab′ē) *n.* a monastery or convent.

ab′bot (ab′ət) *n.* the head of a monastery. —**ab′ba·cy** (ab′ə-sē) *n.*

ab·bre″vi·ate′ (ə-brē′vē·āt′) *v.t.* shorten by omission of some parts.

ab·bre″vi·a′tion (-ā′shən) *n.* **1,** abridgment. **2,** a shortened form, esp. of a word.

ab′di·cate″ (ab′də-kāt″) *v.i. & t.* renounce or relinquish an office, power, or right. —**ab″di·ca′tion,** *n.* —**ab′di·ca″tor,** *n.*

ab′do·men (ab′də-mən) *n.* the lower part of the human body, between thorax and pelvis. —**ab·dom′i·nal** (ab-dom′i-nəl) *adj.*

ab·duct″ (ab-dukt′) *v.t.* carry away by force; kidnap. —**ab·duc′tion,** *n.* —**ab·duc′tor,** *n.*

a·beam′ (ə-bēm′) *adv.* at right angles to the keel of a ship; in a sideward direction.

a·bed′ (ə-bed′) *adv.* in bed.

a·bele′ (ə-bēl′) *n.* the white poplar tree.

Ab″er·deen″ An′gus (ab′ər-dēn″ ang′gəs) one of a breed of hornless beef cattle.

ab·er·rant (ab-er′ənt) *adj.* straying from the right course; wandering. —**ab·er′rance, ab·er′ran·cy,** *n.*

ab″er·ra′tion (ab″ə-rā′shən) *n.* **1,** departure from a normal course. **2,** deviation from truth or moral rectitude. **3,** apparent displacement of a heavenly body, due to its motion relative to the earth. **4,** any disturbance of light rays that prevents accurate focusing.

a·bet′ (ə-bet′) *v.t.* [**a·bet′ted, -ting**] encourage; aid by approval, esp. in bad conduct. —**a·bet′ment,** *n.* —**a·bet′ter, a·bet′tor,** *n.*

a·bey′ance (ə-bā′əns) *n.* temporary suspension or inactivity.

ab·hor′ (ab-hôr′) *v.t.* [**-horred′, -hor′ring**] regard with extreme repugnance; detest.

ab·hor′rence (ab-hor′əns) *n.* strong hatred; detestation. —**ab·hor′rent,** *adj.* detestable; disgusting.

a·bide′ (ə-bīd′) *v.i.* [*pret. & p.p.* **a·bode′**] **1,** remain, continue. **2,** dwell. **3,** stand firm. —*v.i. & t.* [**a·bid′ed**] put up with; tolerate.

a·bil′i·ty (ə-bil′ə-tē) *n.* **1,** state of being able; possession of qualities necessary. **2,** competence; skill; a particular talent.

-a·bil′i·ty *suf.* marking noun forms of adjectives ending in *-able.*

ab′ject (ab′jekt) *adj.* **1,** low in condition or estimation; hopeless. **2,** servile; despicable. —**ab·ject′ness,** *n.*

ab·jure′ (ab-jûr′) *v.t.* renounce solemnly or on oath; repudiate; forswear. —**ab′ju·ra′tion,** *n.*

ab′la·tive (ab′lə-tiv) *n. & adj.* a grammatical case denoting agency, place, etc., in certain inflected languages, as Latin.

a·blaze′ (ə-blāz′) *adv. & adj.* **1,** on fire. **2,** brilliantly lighted up. **3,** very excited; angry.

a′ble (ā′bəl) *adj.* [**a′bler, a′blest**] **1,** having the means or power to be or act. **2,** having marked intellectual qualifications; talented. —**a′ble·bod″ied,** *adj.* of strong body; physically competent.

fat, fāte, fär, fâre, fâll, ásk; met, hē, hēr, maybē; pin, pīne; not, nōte, ôr, tool tub, cūte, pùll; label; oil, owl; go, chip, she, thin, *then,* sing, ink; *see p. 6*

11

-a·ble (ə-bəl) *suf.* denoting ability, liability, tendency.

a·bloom' (ə-bloom') *adv. & adj.* in blossom.

ab·lu'tion (ab-loo'shən) *n.* washing; cleansing, esp. ceremonial.

ab'ne·gate" (ab'nə-gāt") *v.t.* renounce or deny oneself (own rights or powers). —**ab"ne·ga'tion,** *n.*

ab·nor'mal (ab-nôr'məl) *adj.* not ordinary; unusual; deviating from a type or standard. —**ab"nor·mal'i·ty** (ab"nôr-mal'ə-tē) *n.* the state or an instance of being abnormal.

a·board' (ə-bôrd') *adv. & prep.* on board (a ship, train or other conveyance).

a·bode' (ə-bōd') *n.* **1,** dwelling place. **2,** sojourn; continuance. —*v.* pret. & p.p. of *abide.*

a·bol'ish (ə-bol'ish) *v.t.* put an end to; annul; destroy. —**a·bol'ish·ment,** *n.*

ab"o·li'tion (ab"ə-lish'ən) *n.* **1,** destruction; annulment. **2,** the extinction of Negro slavery. —**ab"o·li'tion·ism,** *n.* advocacy of abolition, esp. of Negro slavery. —**ab"o·li'tion·ist,** *n.*

A-'bomb" (ā'bom") *n.* atom bomb.

a·bom'i·na·ble (ə-bom'i-nə-bəl) *adj.* detestable; abhorrent.

a·bom'i·nate" (ə-bom'ə-nāt") *v.t.* hate extremely; abhor; detest.

a·bom"i·na'tion (-nā'shən) *n.* **1,** intense aversion. **2,** a detestable quality, act, or condition.

ab"o·rig'i·nal (ab"ə-rij'i-nəl) *adj.* **1,** pert. to earliest times or conditions; primitive. **2,** indigenous.

ab"o·rig'i·nes (-nēz) *n.pl.* [*sing.* -ne (-nē)] earliest inhabitants.

a·bort' (ə-bôrt') *v.i.* **1,** miscarry in giving birth. **2,** remain rudimentary; fail to develop. —**a·bor'tive,** *adj.*

a·bor'tion (ə-bôr'shən) *n.* **1,** untimely birth. **2,** any fruit or product in a state of arrested development.

a·bound' (ə-bownd') *v.i.* be plentiful or prevalent; be filled (with).

a·bout' (ə-bowt') *adv.* **1,** in every direction; all around. **2,** near in time or place; approximately. **3,** on the point of; in readiness. **4,** at work; astir. —*prep.* **1,** in regard to. **2,** near to. **3,** on the outside of; surrounding. —**a·bout-"face',** *n.* reversal of attitude or position.

a·bove' (ə-buv') *adv. & prep.* **1,** in a higher place than; superior to. **2,** greater in quantity or degree (than). —*adj.* forementioned.

a·bove'board" *adj. & adv.* without deceit.

ab"ra·ca·dab'ra (ab"rə-kə-dab'rə) *n.* a cabalistic word-charm.

a·brade' (ə-brād') *v.t. & t.* wear away by friction.

a·bra'sion (ə-brā'zhən) *n.* **1,** act or result of abrading. **2,** a scraped spot.

a·bra'sive (-siv) *n.* any material for abrading, grinding, or polishing. —*adj.* tending to wear down; rough.

a·breast' (ə-brest') *adj. & adv.* side by side; to the same degree.

a·bridge' (ə-brij') *v.t.* **1,** shorten, as by omission and condensation. **2,** cut off; curtail. —**a·bridg'ment,** *n.*

a·broad' (ə-brâd') *adv.* **1,** in a foreign country; absent. **2,** in circulation; astir.

ab'ro·gate" (ab'rə-gāt") *v.t.* repeal or annul by authoritative act. —**ab"ro·ga'tion,** *n.*

ab·rupt' (ə-brupt') *adj.* **1,** changing or terminating suddenly; discontinuous. **2,** precipitous. —**ab·rupt'ness,** *n.*

ab'scess (ab'ses) *n.* localized collection of pus in the body tissues. —*v.i.* form an abscess.

ab·scond' (ab-skond') *v.i.* hide or depart suddenly, esp. to avoid legal process.

ab'sence (ab'səns) *n.* **1,** state or period of being away. **2,** lack.

ab'sent (ab'sənt) *adj.* not present; not in a certain place; away. —*v.t.* (ab-sent') keep (oneself) away; withdraw.

ab"sen·tee' (ab"sən-tē') *n.* one who is absent, as from his job. —*adj.* without being present. —**ab"sen·tee'ism,** *n.*

ab'sent-mind"ed *adj.* preoccupied; forgetful. —**ab'sent-mind"ed·ness,** *n.*

ab'sinthe (ab'sinth) *n.* a liqueur made from wormwood and brandy.

ab'so·lute" (ab'sə-loot") *adj.* **1,** unqualified; unlimited. **2,** perfect; complete. **3,** positive; fixed; entirely determined; irrevocable. —**ab'so·lute'ness,** *n.* —**absolute кero,** the temperature at which (in theory) all thermal motion ceases, about —459.6 F. —**the Absolute,** God.

ab"so·lu'tion (ab"sə-loo'shən) *n.* **1,** act of absolving. **2,** forgiveness of sins; remission of punishment for sins.

ab'so·lut·ism (ab'sə-loo-tiz-əm) *n.* **1,** advocacy of autocratic government. **2,** any doctrine held without reservations.

ab·solve' (ab-solv') *v.t.* **1,** pardon; free from penalty. **2,** release from an obligation.

ab·sorb' (ab-sôrb') *v.t.* **1,** suck up a liquid; take in; assimilate. **2,** swallow, engulf, or engross completely. —**ab·sorbed',** *adj.* preoccupied.

ab·sorb'ent (-ənt) *adj.* readily sucking up. —**ab·sorb'en·cy,** *n.*

ab·sorb'ing *adj.* very interesting.

ab·sorp'tion (ab-sôrp'shən) *n.* 1, act of absorbing; assimilation. 2, preoccupation. —**ab·sorp'tive,** *adj.*

ab·stain' (ab-stān') *v.i.* refrain (usually, from pleasurable action).

ab·ste'mi·ous (ab-stē'mē-əs) *adj.* moderate, temperate, esp. as to food and drink. —**ab·ste'mi·ous·ness,** *n.*

ab·sten'tion (ab-sten'shən) *n.* act of abstaining. —**ab·sten'tious,** *adj.*

ab'sti·nence (ab'sti-nəns) *n.* self-restraint in satisfaction of appetite. —**ab'sti·nent,** *adj.*

ab·stract' (ab-strakt') *v.t.* 1, consider in general terms. 2, take away; steal. 3, (ab'strakt) reduce to a summary; epitomize. —*n.* (ab'strakt) 1, a summary or inventory. 2, the essential aspects of a subject. —*adj.* (ab'strakt) conceived in general or theoretical terms. —**ab·stract'ed,** *adj.* inattentive; preoccupied.

ab·strac'tion (ab-strak'shən) *n.* 1, act of abstracting. 2, state of being preoccupied or inattentive. 3, an abstract idea, concept, etc.

ab·struse' (ab-stroos') *adj.* 1, difficult to comprehend. 2, profound. —**ab·struse'ness,** *n.*

ab·surd' (ab-sērd') *adj.* contrary to common sense or sound judgment; logically impossible; ridiculous.

ab·surd'i·ty (-ə-tē) *n.* quality of being absurd; something that is absurd.

a·bun'dance (ə-bun'dəns) *n.* copious supply or quantity; plenteousness. —**a·bun'dant,** *adj.*

a·buse' (ə-būz') *v.t.* 1, put to a wrong or bad use; misapply. 2, do wrong to; injure; violate; defile. 3, attack with contumelious language; revile. —*n.* (-būs') improper use; injury; insult. —**a·bus'ive** (-būs'iv) *adj.*

a·but' (ə-but') *v.t.* [**a·but'ted, -ting**] rest against; be contiguous to.

a·but'ment (-mənt) *n.* 1, a junction. 2, a supporting base.

a·bys'mal (ə-biz'məl) *adj.* like an abyss; immeasurably deep or low.

a·byss' (ə-bis') *n.* bottomless pit; gulf; any deep, immeasurable space.

a·ca'cia (ə-kā'shə) *n.* 1, (*cap.*) a genus of shrubby plants. 2, gum arabic. 3, the locust tree.

ac"a·dem'ic (ak"ə-dem'ik) *adj.* 1, conforming to set rules or traditions; conventional. 2, pert. to a college or other institution of higher learning. 3, theoretical. —**ac"a·dem'i·cal·ly,** *adv.*

a·cad'e·mi'cian (ə-kad"ə-mish'ən) *n.* a member of a society for the promotion of an art or science.

a·cad'e·my (ə-kad'ə-mē) *n.* 1, a school for instruction in a particular art or science. 2, a private college-preparatory school. 3, an association of adepts for the promotion of an art or science

Def. 1   *Acanthus*   Def. 2

a·can'thus (ə-kan'thəs) *n.* 1, a spiny shrub of Europe and Africa. 2, a conventionalized representation of its leaf, used as an ornament in architecture.

ac'a·rid (ak'ə-rid) *n.* a mite or tick.

ac·cede' (ak-sēd') *v.i.* 1, give assent; yield. 2, come into possession of; attain.

ac·cel'er·ate" (ak-sel'ə-rāt") *v.i.* increase in speed. —*v.t.* cause to move or develop faster.

ac·cel'er·a'tion (ak-sel"ə-rā'shən) *n.* 1, act of accelerating. 2, increase in speed; the rate of such increase.

ac·cel'er·a"tor (ak-sel'ə-rā"tər) *n.* 1, a pedal for opening and closing the throttle of an automobile. 2, a substance for hastening a chemical reaction.

ac'cent (ak'sent) *n.* 1, special emphasis; stress placed on a particular syllable in uttering a word. 2, manner of utterance; peculiarity of pronunciation, *as a foreign accent.* 3, a mark attached to a letter, syllable or musical note, to show pronunciation, stress, octave, etc. —*v.t.* (also ak-sent') 1, utter with emphasis. 2, mark to show stress, etc.

ac·cen'tu·ate" (ak-sen'choo-āt") *v.t.* stress; emphasize. —**ac·cen'tu·a'tion,** *n.*

ac·cept' (ak-sept') *v.t. & i.* 1, receive with approval; take in a formal way. 2, agree to; give credence to. —**ac·cept'a·ble,** *adj.* worthy of approval.

ac·cept'ance (ak-sep'təns) *n.* 1, act of accepting; approval. 2, (*Com.*) a bill one has agreed to pay later.

ac'cess (ak'ses) *n.* 1, means of approach or admission. 2, condition of being approachable. —**ac·ces'si·ble,** *adj.*

ac·ces'sion (ak-sesh'ən) *n.* 1, attainment of a right or office. 2, something added; increment. 3, agreement; consent.

ac·ces'so·ry (ak-ses'ə-rē) n. 1, an added and subordinate part. 2, (Law) one who aids or abets a felony without being present at its commission. —adj. 1, belonging to. 2, contributory.

ac·ciac"ca·tu'ra (ät-chäk"kə-too'rə) n. (Music) a grace note half a step below its principal.

ac'ci·dent (ak'si-dənt) n. 1, an unfortunate occurrence; mishap; catastrophe. 2, any chance or fortuitous event.

ac"ci·den'tal (-den'təl) adj. 1, happening by chance. 2, subsidiary.

ac·cip'i·ter (ak-sip'ə-tər) n. a long-tailed hawk.

ac·claim' (ə-klām') v.t. 1, applaud. 2, proclaim with general approval.

ac"cla·ma'tion (ak"lə-mā'shən) n. a demonstration of joy or approval; election by such a demonstration. —ac·clam'a·to·ry (ə-klam'ə-tôr-ē) adj.

ac·cli'mate (ə-klī'mət) v.t. & i. accustom or become accustomed to a new climate or environment. Also, ac·cli'ma·tize" (-mə-tīz). —ac"cli·ma'tion, ac·cli"ma·ti·za'tion, n.

ac·cliv'i·ty (ə-kliv'ə-tē) n. an upward slope.

ac"co·lade" (ak"ə-lād') n. a ceremony conferring honor, as knighthood.

ac·com'mo·date" (ə-kom'ə-dāt') v.t. 1, make suitable; adapt. 2, do a kindness to; serve; furnish. —v.i. come into adjustment or conformance. —ac·com'mo·dat"ing, adj. obliging.

ac·com"mo·da'tion (ə-kom"ə-dā'shən) n. 1, adaptation. 2, readiness to serve. 3, anything that supplies a want. 4, (pl.) lodgings.

ac·com'pa·ni·ment (ə-kum'pə-nē-mənt) n. 1, something subordinate added to a principal thing. 2, (Music) harmony supplied to support solo voices.

ac·com'pa·ny (ə-kum'pə-nē) v.t. 1, go with; be associated with. 2, (Music) give harmonic support to (a voice, etc.). —ac·com'pa·nist, n.

ac·com'plice (ə-kom'plis) n. an associate in a crime.

ac·com'plish (ə-kom'plish) v.t. 1, bring to pass; do; complete. 2, achieve; gain. —ac·com'plished, adj. talented; skillful. —ac·com'plish·ment, n. performance; attainment.

ac·cord' (ə-kôrd') v.i. be in harmony; agree. —v.t. 1, bring into agreement; adjust. 2, render; concede. —n. agreement. —ac·cord'ance, n. —ac·cord'ant, adj.

ac·cord'ing (ə-kôr'ding) adv. 1, (with to or as) in conformance with; in proportion to. 2, (with to) as said by. —ac·cord'ing·ly, adv. so; hence; consequently.

ac·cor'di·on (ə-kôr'dē-ən) n. a keyboard wind instrument with metal reeds, operated by a bellows. —adj. pleated like the bellows of an accordion. —ac·cor'di·on·ist, n.

Accordion

ac·cost' (ə-kåst') v.t. approach and speak to; address.

ac·count' (ə-kownt') n. 1, a record of pecuniary transactions. 2, enumeration. 3, explanatory statement; recital of facts. 4, advantage. —v.i. 1, keep records, esp. of money. 2, give explanation. —v.t. impute. —ac·count'a·ble, adj. 1, able to be explained. 2, liable. 3, responsible.

ac·count'ant (-ənt) n. one who practices accounting. —ac·count'an·cy, n.

ac·count'ing n. 1, the keeping and auditing of financial records. 2, a statement of transactions; account.

ac·cou'ter·ments (ə-koo'tər-mənts) n.pl. personal clothing; equipment, esp. of a soldier.

ac·cred'it (ə-kred'it) v.t. 1, accept as true; believe. 2, ascribe or attribute to. 3, confer authority upon; certify.

ac·crete' (ə-krēt') v.i. grow together; adhere. —v.t. add to.

ac·cre'tion (ə-krē'shən) n. act or result of accreting; increase; an added part.

ac·cru'al (ə-kroo'əl) n. that which accrues; in accounting, an amount entered on the books but payable or receivable in the future.

ac·crue' (ə-kroo') v.i. happen in due course; result from natural growth.

ac·cu'mu·late" (ə-kū'mū-lāt") v.t. collect or bring together; amass. —v.i. increase in size, quantity, or number. —ac·cu"mu·la'tion, n. —ac·cu'mu·la·tive, adj.

ac'cu·ra·cy (ak'yū-rə-sē) n. correctness; precision.

ac'cu·rate (ak'yū-rət) adj. correct; true; in exact conformity with a standard. —ac'cu·rate·ness, n.

ac·curs'ed (ə-kēr'səd) adj. doomed to misfortune; detestable. Also, ac·curst'. —ac·curs'ed·ness, n.

ac"cu·sa'tion (ak"yū-zā'shən) n. 1, act of accusing. 2, a charge of wrongdoing.

ac·cu'sa·tive (ə-kū'zə-tiv) n. & adj. a grammatical case denoting the direct object of a verb.

ac·cuse' (ə-kūz') v.t. charge with guilt or blame.

ac·cus'tom (ə-kus'təm) v.t. familiarize by custom or use. —accus'tomed, adj. 1, customary; usual. 2, wonted.

ace (ās) n. 1, a playing card or face of a die marked with a single pip. 2, a point won without contest, as in tennis. 3, an expert; adept. 4, a very small quantity or degree. 5, a fighter pilot who has downed five or more enemy planes. —adj. of highest rank or proficiency; excellent.

ac'er·bate' (as'ər-bāt') v.t. embitter; exasperate.

a·cerb'i·ty (ə-sėr'bə-tē) n. 1, sourness of taste. 2, harshness of temper or expression.

ac'er·ose' (as'ə-rōs') adj. shaped like a needle.

ac'et·an'i·lide (as'i-tan'ə-lid) n. a compound used to reduce fever or relieve pain.

ac'e·tate' (as'ə-tāt') n. (Chem.) a salt of acetic acid. —acetate cellulose, a thermoplastic compound.

a·ce'tic (ə-sē'tik) adj. pert. to vinegar.

ac'e·tone' (as'ə-tōn') n. a distillate of acetates, used as a solvent.

a·cet'y·lene (ə-set'ə-lin) n. a gas used as an illuminant and to produce a very hot flame.

ache (āk) n. continued pain. —v.i. 1, suffer enduring pain. 2, (Colloq.) yearn.

a·chieve' (ə-chēv') v.t. & i. execute successfully; accomplish.

a·chieve'ment (-mənt) n. act or result of achieving; consummation; a notable deed.

A·chil'les heel (ə-kil'ēz) a vulnerable spot.

ach''ro·mat'ic (ak''rə-mat'ik) adj. free from coloration, as achromatic lens, one that transmits light without decomposing it. —ach''ro·mat'i·cal·ly, adv.

ac'id (as'id) n. 1, any substance with a sour taste. 2, (Chem.) a compound in which hydrogen can be replaced by a metal. —adj. —a·cid'i·ty, n.

ac''i·doph'i·lus milk (as''i-dof'ə-ləs) a fermented milk used medicinally.

ac''i·do'sis (as''i-dō'sis) n. excess acidity of the blood.

a·cid'u·lous (ə-sid'ū-ləs) adj. somewhat acid; slightly sour.

-a·cious (ā-shəs) suf. forming adjectives from nouns ending in -acity.

-a·ci·ty (as-ə-tē) suf. the quality of being, or a tendency to be (the root word).

ack (ak) n. (Brit.) the letter A. —ack'ack'', n. antiaircraft fire.

ac·knowl'edge (ak-nol'ij) v.t. 1, admit the existence or truth of. 2, give evidence of recognizing or realizing; certify the receipt of. —ac·knowl'edg·ment, n.

ac'me (ak'mē) n. the top or highest point.

ac'ne (ak'nē) n. a pimply skin eruption.

ac'o·lyte' (ak'ə-līt') n. 1, a novice esp. in a religious order. 2, an attendant; assistant.

ac'o·nite' (ak'ə-nīt') n. 1, a plant, monkshood or wolfbane. 2, a medicinal tincture of this plant.

a'corn (ā'kôrn) n. the nut of the oak tree.

Acorns

a·cous'tic (ə-koos'tik) adj. pert. to sound, hearing, or acoustics. —a·cous'ti·cal·ly, adv.

a·cous'tics (ə-koos'tiks) n.pl. the science of sound; sound-reflecting properties.

ac·quaint' (ə-kwānt') v.t. make familiar with; inform.

ac·quaint'ance (-əns) n. 1, personal knowledge. 2, a person known only slightly. —ac·quaint'ance·ship, n.

ac''qui·esce' (ak''wē-es') v.i. consent; agree. —ac·qui·es'cence, n. —ac·qui·es'cent, adj. yielding; submissive.

ac·quire' (ə-kwīr') v.t. obtain; gain. —ac·quire'ment, n.

ac''qui·si'tion (ak''wə-zish'ən) n. 1, the act of acquiring. 2, something acquired.

ac·quis'i·tive (ə-kwiz'ə-tiv) adj. tending to acquire; avaricious; grasping. —ac·quis'i·tive·ness, n.

ac·quit' (ə-kwit') v.t. [ac·quit'ted, -ting] 1, pronounce not guilty; release, as from an obligation. 2, discharge or pay, as a debt. —acquit oneself, behave.

ac·quit'tal (-əl) n. act or result of acquitting; exoneration.

a'cre (ā'kər) n. a measure of area, 43,560 sq. ft. —a'cre·age, n.

ac'rid (ak'rid) adj. sharp or biting to the tongue; pungent; severe. —a·crid'i·ty, ac'rid·ness, n.

ac''ri·mo'ny (ak'rə-mō'nē) n. bitterness of temper or expression. —ac''ri·mo'ni·ous, adj.

ac'ro·bat (ak'rə-bat) n. a gymnastic performer. —ac''ro·bat'ic, adj. —ac''ro·bat'i·cal·ly, adv.

ac''ro·bat'ics (-iks) n. sing. & pl. the feats of an acrobat; agility.

ac'ro·nym'' (ak'rə-nim') n. a word

made from the initial letters of a term or phrase, as *WAC*.

ac'ro-pho'bi-a (ak'rə-fō'bē-ə) *n.* fear of high places.

a-crop'o-lis (ə-krop'ə-lis) *n.* 1, a settlement located on an eminence. 2, (*cap.*) the citadel of Athens.

a-cross' (ə-krâs') *prep.* from side to side of; transverse to; on the other side of. —*adv.* from side to side; crosswise.

a-cros'tic (ə-krâs'tik) *n. & adj.* a composition in which the initial letters of lines form a word or phrase.

a-cryl'ic (ə-kril'ik) *adj.* pert. to an acid used in certain plastics, as lucite and plexiglass.

act (akt) *v.i.* 1, do something; exert energy or force in any way. 2, exert influence; operate. 3, perform on the stage. —*v.t.* do; perform; transact; represent by action. —*n.* 1, anything done; an exertion of energy or force; deed. 2, a law, ordinance, decree, or judgment, etc. 3, individual performance in a varied program. 4, a main division of a play. —**act'ing,** *adj.* 1, functioning. 2, serving temporarily.

ACTH *n.* a pituitary derivative used in combating rheumatic fever, arthritis, etc.

ac-tin'ic (ak-tin'ik) *adj.* pert. to chemical reactions caused by radiant energy as in a photographic emulsion by sunlight. —**ac-tin'i-cal-ly,** *adv.*

ac-tin'i-um (ak-tin'ē-əm) *n.* a radioactive chemical element resembling the rare earths, no. 89, symbol Ac.

ac'tion (ak'shən) *n.* 1, something done; an exertion of energy or force; act. 2, state of being active; continued influence; behavior; conduct. 3, a sequence of events; the main story of a play or narrative; a battle. 4, an operating mechanism, as of a watch. 5, a legal proceeding. —**ac'tion-a-ble,** *adj.* giving ground for a lawsuit.

ac'ti-vate'' (ak'tə-vāt') *v.t.* make active; hasten action; put into operation. —**ac'ti-va'tion,** *n.* —**ac'ti-va'tor,** *n.*

ac'tive (ak'tiv) *adj.* 1, engaged in action; busy; brisk; agile. 2, having the power to function, operate, or influence. 3, (*Gram.*) denoting the verb-form of action performed by the subject. —**ac'tive-ness,** *n.*

ac-tiv'i-ty (ak-tiv'ə-tē) *n.* 1, state of being active. 2, a function; event.

ac'tor (ak'tər) *n.* one who acts, esp. a stage-player. —**ac'tress,** *n.fem.*

ac'tu-al (ak'choo-əl) *adj.* 1, of real existence. 2, now existing; present.

ac'tu-al'i-ty (ak'choo-al'ə-tē) *n.* 1, real existence. 2, something real. 3, (*pl.*) actual circumstances; realities.

ac'tu-ar-y (ak'choo-er-ē) *n.* one who calculates insurance risks. —**ac'tu-ar'i-al,** *adj.*

ac'tu-ate'' (ak'choo-āt') *v.t.* put or incite into action. —**ac'tu-a'tion,** *n.*

a-cu'men (ə-kū'mən) *n.* mental acuteness; keenness of perception or insight.

a-cute' (ə-kūt') *adj.* 1, sharp-pointed; intense; shrill. 2, keen in perception or penetration; susceptible of slight impressions; discriminating. —**acute accent,** the mark ('), as in the French **é.** —**acute angle** (*Geom.*) one of less than 90°. —**a-cute'ness,** *n.*

-a-cy (ə-sē) *suf.* forming nouns denoting quality or state.

ad *n.* (*Colloq.*) advertisement.

ad- *pref.* denoting addition, direction, or tendency.

ad'age (ad'ij) *n.* a pithy saying; proverb.

a-da'gio (ə-dä'zhō) *adj. & adv.* (*Music*) slow. —*n.* a movement in slow time. —**adagio dance,** a dance, usually for two, characterized by much posturing.

ad'a-mant'' (ad'ə-mant') *adj.* hard; hard-hearted; unyielding. —*n.* any extremely hard mineral, as diamond.

Ad'am's apple the prominent formation of thyroid cartilage at the front of a man's throat.

a-dapt' (ə-dapt') *v.t.* make suitable; alter to fit. —**a-dapt'a-ble,** *adj.* easy to adapt; readily able to conform. —**ad''ap-ta'tion** (ad'əp-tā'shən) *n.*

add (ad) *v.t.* 1, increase by attaching more; annex. 2, unite in one sum or aggregate. —*v.i.* 1, supply as an addition. 2, perform arithmetical addition.

ad'dend (ad'end) *n.* a number to be added.

ad-den'dum (ə-den'dəm) *n.* [*pl.* -da (-də)] something that is added, as the appendix of a book.

ad'der (ad'ər) *n.* any of several common vipers.

Adder

ad'dict (ad'ikt) *n.* one who has a confirmed habit, as the overuse of drugs. —**ad-dict'-ed,** *adj.* —**ad-dic'tion,** *n.*

ad-di'tion (ə-dish'ən) *n.* 1, the act or process of adding or uniting. 2, the arithmetical operation of finding a sum, expressed by the symbol +. 3, anything added. —**ad-di'tion-al,** *adj.* added; extra.

ad'dle (ad'əl) *v.t. & i.* make or become muddled or confused.

ad-dress' (ə-dres') *v.t.* 1, speak or write to. 2, direct attention to. 3, direct for transmission. 4, pay court to as a lover. —n. 1, a formal utterance in speech or writing directed to a body of persons. 2, the place where a person lives or may be reached. 3, personal bearing; manner of speech. —ad·dress'ee (-ē) n.

ad·duce' (ə-dūs') v.t. bring forward as a reason or explanation; cite as evidence.

ad'e·noid" (ad'ə-noid") n. (usually pl.) a swollen lymphatic tissue in the pharynx that often impedes breathing. —ad'e·noid'al, adj.

ad'ept (ad'ept) n. one who has attained proficiency. —adj. (ə-dept') skilful; expert. —a·dept'ness, n.

ad'e·quate (ad'i-kwət) adj. equal to requirement or occasion; sufficient; suitable. —ad'e·qua·cy (-kwə-sē) n.

ad·here' (ad-hir') v.t. 1, stick fast; become joined. 2, hold closely, as to an idea or course; be devoted. —ad·her'ence, n.

ad·her'ent (-ənt) n. one who follows a leader or supports a cause.

ad·he'sion (ad-hē'zhən) n. adherence between unlike particles.

ad·he'sive (ad-hē'siv) adj. sticky; tenacious; adhering. —n. that which sticks. —ad·he'sive·ness, n.

a·dieu' (ə-dū') (Fr.) interj. & n. [pl. -dieus'; -dieux' (-dūz')] farewell; goodbye.

a·dios' (ä-dyäs') interj. (Sp.) goodbye.

ad'i·pose" (ad'i-pōs") adj. fatty. —n. body fat, esp. on the kidneys. —ad'i·pos'i·ty (-pos'ə-tē) n.

ad'it n. an entrance or passageway.

ad·ja'cent (ə-jā'sənt) adj. lying near, close, or contiguous; adjoining. —ad·ja'cen·cy (-sən-sē) n.

ad'jec·tive (aj'ek-tiv) n. (Gram.) a word used to qualify, limit, or define a noun, as: a large tree.

ad·join' (ə-join') v.t. & i. be adjacent; be in contact; abut.

ad·journ' (ə-jėrn') v.t. & i. 1, suspend a sitting till another day, as of a legislature or court. 2, defer; postpone. —ad·journ'ment, n.

ad·judge' (ə-juj') v.t. 1, decide by judicial opinion; pronounce, decree, or award formally. 2, judge; deem.

ad·ju'di·cate' (ə-joo'di-kāt') v.t. & i. adjudge; determine judicially. —ad·ju'di·ca'tion, n. —ad·ju'di·ca"tor, n.

ad'junct (a'junkt) n. something added to another. —adj. additional, esp. in a subordinate sense.

ad·jure' (ə-jūr') v.t. command, charge, or bind earnestly and solemnly. —ad'ju·ra'tion(aj'ə-rā'shən) n.

ad·just' (ə-just') v.t. 1, make to fit or conform; adapt. 2, put in order; regulate. 3, bring to a satisfactory

result; settle. —ad·just'ment, n.

ad·ju·tant (aj'ə-tənt) n. 1, a military executive officer or aide. 2, an assistant. 3, an East Indian stork.

Adjutant

ad-lib' v.t. & i. [-libbed', -lib'bing] (Colloq.) improvise (lines or action not in the script of a play).

ad·min'is·ter (ad-min'əs-tər) v.t. 1, manage as an agent; conduct; superintend. 2, make application of; supply; dispense. —v.i. (with to) bring aid.

ad·min"is·tra'tion (-strā'shən) n. 1, conduct. 2, any body of men entrusted with ultimate executive powers. —ad·min·is·tra"tive, adj.

ad·min'is·tra"tor (ad-min'i-strā"tər) n. one who administers; executor. —ad·min'is·tra"trix (-triks) n. fem.

ad'mi·ra·ble (ad'mə-rə-bəl) adj. worthy of admiration; excellent. —ad'mi·ra·ble·ness, n.

ad'mi·ral (ad'mə-rəl) n. 1, a naval officer of highest rank. 2, the commander of a fleet.

ad'mi·ral·ty (ad'mə-rəl-tē) n. 1, the office of admiral. 2, the administration of a navy. 3, maritime law.

ad"mi·ra'tion (ad'mə-rā'shən) n. act of admiring; approval.

ad·mire' (ad-mīr') v.t. regard with approbation, esteem, or affection. —v.i. (Dial.) wish (to). —ad·mir'er, n. one who admires; (Colloq.) a suitor.

ad·mis'si·ble (ad-mis'ə-bəl) adj. that may be conceded or allowed. —ad·mis"si·bil'i·ty, n.

ad·mis'sion (ad-mish'ən) n. 1, the act of entering or admitting, or being allowed to enter. 2, entrance fee. 3, an acknowledgment or confession that something is true.

ad·mit' v.t. & i. [-mit'ted, -ting] 1, allow to enter; give means or right of entry. 2, concede as valid; acknowledge to be true. —ad·mit'tance (-əns) n. permission or right to enter.

ad·mix'ture (ad-miks'chər) n. 1, the act of mixing or mingling, esp. of different substances. 2, something added; ingredient.

ad·mon'ish v.t. 1, reprove mildly. 2, warn against something; exhort, guide. —ad·mon'ish·ment, n.

ad"mo·ni'tion (ad'mə-nish'ən) n. reproof; advice; warning. —ad·mon'i·to·ry (ad-mon'ə-tōr-ē) adj.

a·do' (ə-doo') n. action; bustle; trouble.

a·do'be (ə-dō'bē) *n.* a sun-dried block of mud used in rude building.

ad"o·les'cence (ad"ə-les'əns) *n.* the age of human life between puberty and adulthood, from about 14 to 25 (men) or 12 to 21 (women).

ad"o·les'cent (-ənt) *adj.* of or characteristic of adolescence. —*n.* an adolescent boy or girl.

a·dopt' (ə-dopt') *v.t.* 1, take or receive as one's own. 2, (of a council or legislature) vote to accept. —**a·dop'tion**, *n.*

a·dor'a·ble (ə-dôr'ə-bəl) *adj.* worthy of the utmost love or admiration. —**a·dor'a·ble·ness**, *n.*

ad"o·ra'tion (ad"ə-rā'shən) *n.* act of adoring or worshiping.

a·dore' (ə-dôr') *v.t.* 1, regard with utmost love, esteem, or respect. 2, worship as divine.

a·dorn' (ə-dôrn') *v.t.* decorate; dress with ornaments; embellish. —**a·dorn'ment**, *n.*

ad·re'nal (ə-drē'nəl) *adj.* near or on the kidneys; of the adrenal glands.

ad·ren'a·lin (ə-dren'ə-lin) *n.* a drug used to stimulate heart action.

a·drift' (ə-drift') *adv. & adj.* floating at random; not moored; swayed by any chance impulse.

a·droit' (ə-droit') *adj.* dextrous; skillful; ingenious. —**a·droit'ness**, *n.*

ad·sorp'tion (ad-sôrp'shən) *n.* condensation of a gas on the surface of a solid. —**ad·sorb'**, *v.t.*

ad'u·late" (ad'ū-lāt") *v.t.* show feigned devotion to; flatter servilely. —**ad"u·la'tion**, *n.*

ad'ult *n.* a person or animal grown to full size and strength. —*adj.* (ə·dult') full-grown; mature; legally of age.

a·dul'ter·ant (ə-dul'tər-ənt) *n.* a baser ingredient. —*adj.* serving to adulterate.

a·dul'ter·ate" (ə-dul'tə-rāt") *v.t.* debase by addition or substitution of inferior ingredients; make impure. —**a·dul'ter·a'tion**, *n.*

a·dul'ter·er (ə-dul'tər-ər) *n.* one who commits adultery. —**a·dul'ter·ess** (-əs) *n.fem.*

a·dul'ter·y (ə-dul'tə-rē) *n.* illicit relations between a married person and another than his lawful spouse. —**a·dul'ter·ous**, *adj.*

ad·um'brate (ad-um'brāt) *v.t.* give a faint shadow or outline of; foreshadow. —**ad"um·bra'tion**, *n.*

ad·vance' (ad-väns') *v.t.* 1, bring forward; raise; enhance; promote. 2, supply beforehand; furnish on credit. —*v.i.* 1, move forward. 2, make progress; improve; increase in quantity or price. —*n.* 1, forward movement; a step forward; an improvement. 2, money or goods supplied beforehand or on credit. 3, the foremost part, as of an army. —**ad·vance'ment**, *n.*

ad·van'tage (ad-vån'tij) *n.* 1, any favorable circumstance. 2, benefit; gain; profit. 3, superiority. —**ad"van·ta'geous** (ad"vən-tā'jəs) *adj.*

ad'vent *n.* 1, arrival. 2, (*cap.*) the coming of Christ into the world.

ad"ven·ti'tious (ad"vən-tish'əs) *adj.* not intrinsic to the subject; accidentally or casually acquired; foreign.

ad·ven'ture (ad-ven'chər) *n.* 1, a remarkable occurrence; a noteworthy event; a hazardous enterprise. 2, activity of a hazardous or exciting nature. —*v.t. & i.* embark upon; take the risk of; dare. —**ad·ven'tur·er**, *n.* a bold person; explorer; soldier of fortune. —**ad·ven'tur·ess**, *n.fem.* (*Derogatory*) a female adventurer; a social climber. —**ad·ven'tur·ous**, *adj.* 1, risky. 2, daring.

ad'verb (ad'vėrb) *n.* (*Gram.*) a word used to qualify, clarify, limit or extend a verb or adjective, or another adverb. —**ad·ver'bi·al**, *adj.*

ad'ver·sar·y (ad'vər-ser-ē) *n.* an opponent in a contest; enemy.

ad·verse' (ad-vėrs') *adj.* 1, contrary in purpose or effect; opposite. 2, harmful to one's interests; unfortunate.

ad·ver'si·ty (ad-vėr'sə-tē) *n.* ill fortune; an unfortunate happening.

ad·vert' (ad-vėrt') *v.i.* (with *to*) refer; turn attention.

ad'ver·tise" (ad'vər-tīz") *v.t. & i.* 1, make public announcement of; give information concerning. 2, praise or otherwise promote, as in selling wares.

ad"ver·tise'ment (-mənt) *also,* ad-vėr'tiz-mənt) *n.* a paid notice in a publication.

ad'ver·tis"ing (ad'vər-tīz"ing) *n.* the art and practice of promoting enterprises by paid public notices.

ad·vice' (ad-vīs') *n.* 1, counsel as to a course of action; suggestion. 2, information; communication of news.

ad·vis'a·ble (ad-vī'zə-bəl) *adj.* wise to do. —**ad·vis"a·bil'i·ty**, *n.*

ad·vise' (ad-vīz') *v.t.* 1, give counsel to; offer an opinion to. 2, urge as wise or prudent; recommend. 3, give information to. —*v.i.* take or offer advice. —**ad·vised'**, *adj.* considered, as in ill-advised. —**ad·vise'ment**, *n.* consideration.

ad·vi'so·ry (ad-vī'zə-rē) *adj.* giving advice; consultative.

ad'vo·ca·cy (ad'və-kə-sē) *n.* act of advocating; espousal; support.

ad'vo·cate'' (ad'və-kāt') *v.t.* plead in favor of; defend in argument; support. —*n.* (-kət) one who pleads or espouses a cause.

adz *n.* a cutting tool, comprising a blade fixed at right angles to a handle, used for rough trimming.

Adz

ae- see *e-*.

ae'gis (ē'jis) *n.* egis.

a'er·ate (ā'ər-āt') *v.t.* 1, expose freely to air. 2, charge with air, carbon dioxide, or other gas. —**a''er·a'tion,** *n.* —**a'er·a''tor,** *n.*

aer'i·al (ar'ē-əl) *adj.* 1, of, produced by, or inhabiting air. 2, high in the air. 3, light in weight or substance; visionary. 4, graceful; ethereal. —*n.* a radio antenna. —**aer'i·al·ist,** *n.* a trapeze acrobat.

aer'ie (ār'ē; ir'ē) *n.* 1, an eagle's nest. 2, a dwelling on a height.

aer'o- (ār-ə; e·ir'ə-) *pref.* pert. to 1, air; 2, gas; 3, airplane.

aer'o·naut'' (ār-ə-) *n.* one who flies in the air; a balloonist.

aer''o·nau'tics (-nȧ'tiks) *n.* 1, flight in aircraft. 2, the art or science of flying. —**aer'o·nau'tic,** *adj.* —**aer''o·nau'ti·cal·ly,** *adv.*

aer'o·sol (-sol) *n.* 1, a gas bearing another substance. 2, a container that discharges such a gas.

aer'o·stat (-stat) *n.* lighter-than-air aircraft.

a·far' (ə-fär') *adv.* from a distance; far away.

af'fa·ble (af'ə-bəl) *adj.* easy to approach (esp. of one in high station); courteous; gracious. —**af''fa·bil'i·ty,** *n.*

af·fair' (ə-fār') *n.* 1, a matter, action, business, or concern requiring attention and effort. 2, a particular event or performance. 3, an involvement of love. 4, (*pl.*) pecuniary interests or relations.

af·fect' (ə-fekt') *v.t.* 1, produce an effect or change on; influence. 2, impress deeply. 3, make a show of; feign; imitate; adopt; assume the character of.

af''fec·ta'tion (af''ek-tā'shən) *n.* artificiality of manner; pretension to qualities not actually possessed.

af·fect'ed *adj.* 1, influenced; impaired. 2, artificial in manner or conduct. 3, moved by emotion.

af·fect'ing *adj.* pitiful.

af·fec'tion (ə-fek'shən) *n.* 1, good will; love. 2, the result, act, or state of being influenced. —**af·fec'tion·ate** (-ət) *adj.* loving; warm-hearted.

af·fi'ance (ə-fī'əns) *v.t.* bind in promise of marriage; betroth.

af''fi·da'vit (af''i-dā'vit) *n.* (*Law*) a written and sworn declaration of alleged facts.

af·fil'i·ate'' (ə-fil'ē-āt') *v.t. & t.* bring into association; unite in action and interest; join with. —*n.* (-ē-ət) an associate; a branch organization. —**af·fil'i·a'tion,** *n.*

af·fin'i·ty (ə-fin'ə-tē) *n.* 1, a natural liking for, or attraction to, a person or thing. 2, inherent likeness or agreement between things.

af·firm' (ə-fėrm') *v.t.* 1, assert positively; declare to be a fact. 2, confirm; ratify. —*v.i.* (*Law*) declare solemnly, in lieu of swearing upon oath. —**af''fir·ma'tion** (af''ər-mā'shən) *n.*

af·firm'a·tive (ə-fėr'mə-tiv) *adj.* positive in form, not negative. —*n.* 1, a word or phrase expressing assent, agreement, or affirmation. 2, the side favoring a proposition.

af·fix' (ə-fix') *v.t.* 1, add or append. 2, fasten or attach. —*n.* (af'iks) that which is added or attached.

af·fla'tus (ə-flā'təs) *n.* mental force or inspiration, evinced by religious, poetical, or oratorical expression.

af·flict' (ə-flikt') *v.t.* distress with mental or bodily pain; torment.

af·flic'tion (ə-flik'shən) *n.* 1, distress; pain. 2, a cause of distress; an ill or disease. —**af·flic'tive,** *adj.*

af'flu·ence (af'loo-əns) *n.* 1, an abundant supply, as of material wealth. 2, a flowing toward, as of a tributary watercourse.

af'flu·ent (af'loo-ənt) *adj.* 1, flowing freely. 2, rich; wealthy.

af·ford' (ə-fōrd') *v.t.* 1, be able; have the means. 2, yield; produce; furnish.

af·fray' (ə-frā') *n.* a noisy quarrel; brawl; disturbance.

af·front' (ə-frunt') *n.* a personally offensive act or word; an open manifestation of disrespect or contumely. —*v.t.* insult openly; make ashamed or confused.

Afghan

Af'ghan (af'gan) *n.* 1, a native of Afghanistan. 2, a breed of hound. 3, (*l.c.*) a kind of woolen blanket or shawl.

a·field' (ə-fēld') *adv.* abroad; off the beaten track; away from home.

a·fire' (ə-fīr') *adv. & adj.* burning.

a·flame' (ə-flām') *adv. & adj.* on fire.

a·float' (ə-flōt') *adv. & adj.* 1, borne on the water. 2, moving about; in circulation.

a·foot' (ə-fut') *adv. & adj.* 1, walking. 2, in progress.

a·fore'said (ə-fôr'sed) *adj.* which was mentioned previously.

a·fore'thought" (ə-fôr'thȧt') *adj.* premeditated.

a·foul' (ə-fowl') *adv. & adj.* in a state of collision or entanglement.

a·fraid' (ə-frād') *adj.* impressed with fear or apprehension.

Af'ri·can (af'ri-kən) *adj.* pert. to Africa, its inhabitants, or their languages. —*n.* a native of Africa; a Negro.

aft *adv.* (*Naut.*) in, near, or toward the stern of a ship.

af'ter (ȧf'tər) *prep.* 1, later in time; subsequent to. 2, behind in place; in the rear of; below in rank. 3, in pursuit of; with desire for. 4, according to; in proportion to; in imitation of. —*adv. & adj.* 1, later in time. 2, behind or below in place. 3, (*Naut.*) aft.

af'ter·birth" *n.* the placenta.

af'ter·math" *n.* what comes after; the consequences.

af"ter·noon' *n. & adj.* the part of the day from noon to night.

af'ter·thought" *n.* a belated idea or act.

af'ter·ward (-wərd) *adv.* later in time; subsequently. Also, **af'ter·wards**.

a·gain' (ə-gen') *adv.* 1, once more; another time; anew. 2, in addition; moreover. 3, back; in the opposite direction.

a·gainst' (ə-genst') *prep.* 1, in an opposite direction to. 2, in contact with; toward; upon. 3, adverse or hostile to. 4, in provision for; in exchange for.

a·gape' (ə-gāp'; ə-gap') *adv. & adj.* with the mouth wide open.

a'gar (ā'gär) *n.* a gelatinous culture medium made from certain seaweeds.

ag'ate (ag'ət) *n.* 1, a variety of quartz. 2, a child's marble made of agate or of glass in imitation of agate. 3, (*Printing*) 5½-point type.

a·ga've (ə-gā'vē) *n.* a genus of plants found chiefly in Mexico; the century plant.

age (āj) *n.* 1, the length of time during which a being or thing has existed. 2, the lifetime of an indi-vidual; duration of existence. 3, a particular period of history; the people and events of an era. 4, (*Colloq.*) a long time. —*v.i.* grow old. —*v.t.* 1, bring to maturity. 2, make old. —**age'less**, *adj.* unchanging.

-age (ij) *suf.* forming nouns denoting condition, effect, result, etc.

a'ged (ā'jed) *adj.* 1, old; having lived a long time. 2, (ājd) having the age of, as *aged twenty years.*

a'gen·cy (ā'jən-sē) *n.* 1, a means of producing effects or exerting power; an instrument. 2, the office and duties of an agent. 3, a commercial or government office furnishing a particular public service.

a·gen'da (ə-jen'də) *n.pl.* [*sing.* -dum] items of business to be brought before a council, etc.

a'gent (ā'jənt) *n.* 1, a person acting on behalf of another. 2, a representative, as of a commercial firm or government bureau; an official. 3, an active cause, as (*Chem.*) a substance that produces a reaction.

ag·glom'er·ate" (ə-glom'ə-rāt') *v.t. & t.* collect in a mass. —*adj.* (-ət) piled together; in a dense cluster. —*n.* a cluster, as of rock fragments. —**ag·glom'er·a'tion**, *n.*

ag·glu'ti·nate" (ə-gloo'tə-nāt') *v.t. & t.* unite or cause to adhere, as with glue. —*adj.* adhering by or as by glue. —**ag·glu'ti·na'tion**, *n.*

ag'gran·dize" (ag'rən-dīz') *v.t.* 1, make greater in power, wealth, or rank; widen in scope; extend. 2, magnify; exaggerate. —**ag·gran'-dize·ment** (ə-gran'diz-mənt) *n.*

ag'gra·vate" (ag'rə-vāt') *v.t.* 1, intensify; make more serious or troublesome. 2, (*Colloq.*) irritate; provoke. —**ag"gra·va'tion**, *n.*

ag'gre·gate" (ag'ri-gāt') *v.t.* 1, collect into a sum, mass, or body. 2, amount to (a number). —*v.i.* come together. —*n.* (ag'rə-gət) 1, gross amount. 2, (*Geol.*) rock formed of a mixture of different minerals. —*adj.* (-gət) total; combined. —**ag'-gre·ga'tion**, *n.*

ag·gress' (ə-gres') *v.i.* begin a quarrel.

ag·gres'sion (ə-gresh'ən) *n.* 1, an act of hostility; an assault or encroachment. 2, offensive action in general.

ag·gres'sive (ə-gres'iv) *adj.* 1, tending to attack or be hostile. 2, vigorous. —**ag·gres'sive·ness**, *n.*

ag·gres'sor (ə-gres'ər) *n.* one who begins a quarrel or starts a war without adequate provocation.

ag·grieved' (ə-grēvd') *p. adj.* offended; having cause to feel vexed. —**ag·grieve'**, *v.t.*

a·ghast' (ə-gȧst') *adj.* struck with amazement; filled with sudden fright and horror.

ag'ile (aj'əl) *adj.* able to move quickly; active; nimble.

a·gil'i·ty (ə-jil'ə-tē) *n.* ability to move quickly; nimbleness.

ag'i·tate (aj'ə-tāt") *v.t.* 1, force into violent motion; shake briskly; perturb. 2, call attention to by speech or writing. —*v.i.* engage in discussion or debate. —**ag"i·ta'tion**, *n.* —**ag'i·ta"tor,** *n.*

a·glow' (ə-glō') *adj.* glowing.

ag'nate (ag'nāt) *adj.* related on the father's side. —*n.* a kinsman on the father's side.

ag·nos'tic (ag-nos'tik) *n.* one who holds that ultimate causes (as God) are unknowable. —*adj.* holding this view. —**ag·nos'ti·cal·ly**, *adv.* —**ag·nos'ti·cism** (ag-nos'ti-siz-əm) *n.*

a·go' (ə-gō') *adv.* & *adj.* in past time.

a·gog' (ə-gog') *adj.* & *adv.* in a state of excitement, curiosity, or eager desire.

-agon *suf.* denoting a plane geometrical figure, as *pentagon.*

a·gon'ic (ə-gon'ik) *adj.* not forming an angle.

ag'o·nize" (ag'ə-nīz") *v.i.* suffer violent anguish. —*v.t.* distress with extreme pain.

ag'o·ny (ag'ə-nē) *n.* 1, extreme and prolonged mental or bodily pain. 2, the death struggle.

a·gou'ti (ə-goo'tē) *n.* a rabbitlike rodent of Central and So. Amer.

a·grar'i·an (ə-grâr'ē-ən) *adj.* 1, pert. to land or property rights in land. 2, agricultural; rural. —*n.* one who favors an equal division of landed property.

a·gree' (ə-grē') *v.i.* 1, give assent; consent. 2, be of one opinion or mind; arrive at a settlement. 3, be consistent; harmonize. 4, be similar; correspond; coincide. —*v.t.* concede.

a·gree'a·ble (-ə-bəl) *adj.* 1, pleasing to the mind or senses. 2, conformable; willing to consent. —**a·gree'a·ble·ness,** *n.*

a·gree'ment (-mənt) *n.* 1, concord; harmony. 2, a contract; bargain.

ag'ri·cul"ture (ag'ri-kul'chər) *n.* the cultivation of the ground to raise food; husbandry; farming. —**ag"ri·cul'tur·al,** *adj.* —**ag"ri·cul'tur·ist,** *n.*

a·ground' (ə-grownd') *adj.* & *adv.* on the ground; stranded.

a'gue (ā'gū) *n.* a malarial fever marked by intermittent paroxysms of chills and sweating.

ah (ä) *interj.* of understanding, agreement, or almost any emotion.

a·ha' (ä-hä') *interj.* of surprise, triumph, or contempt.

a·head' (ə-hed') *adv.* 1, in or to the front; in advance. 2, forward; onward.

a·hem' (ə-hem') *interj.* to attract attention, as by an affected cough.

a·hoy' (ə-hoi') *interj.* used to attract attention of persons at a distance.

aid (ād) *v.t.* 1, give support or relief to; help. 2, promote the accomplishment of; facilitate. —*n.* 1, assistance; support. 2, he who or that which gives help.

aide (ād) *n.* (*Mil.*) a secretarial assistant to an officer. Also, **aide'-de-camp.**

ai'grette (ā'gret) *n.* a plume of feathers worn on the head.

ail (āl) *v.t.* affect with pain. —*v.i.* feel pain; be unwell.

ai'ler·on (ā'lə-ron) *n.* a hinged flap in the wing of an airplane, controlling its horizontal position.

ail'ment (-mənt) *n.* illness; malady.

aim (ām) *v.t.* point at something; fix in a certain direction, as *aim a gun.* —*v.i.* (with an infinitive) strive toward; intend. —*n.* 1, the direction in which something is aimed. 2, the act of aiming. 3, the thing aimed at; target; intention; purpose. —**aim'less,** *adj.* without purpose or direction.

ain't (ānt) vulgar form of am not, is not, are not, has not, have not.

air (âr) *n.* 1, the earth's atmosphere; the particular mixture of nitrogen, oxygen, etc. of which it is composed. 2, a light breeze. 3, space; scope. 4, utterance abroad; publication. 5, outward appearance; personal mien or bearing. 6, (*pl.*) affected manners. 7, a tune; a principal melody. —*v.t.* 1, expose to the air; let air into; ventilate. 2, bring to public notice; proclaim. —*adj.* 1, operated by compressed air, as *air brake.* 2, for or by aircraft, as *air base, air raid.*

air'borne" (-bôrn") *adj.* supported by the air.

air'coach" *n.* a low-priced air passenger transport service.

air conditioning a system of indoor ventilation and temperature control. Also, **air cooling.**

air'craft" (âr'kraft") *n.* any type of machine that flies in the air, whether lighter or heavier than air.

air'drome" (-drōm") *n.* airport.

Aire'dale" (âr'dāl") *n.* a breed of large terriers.

air'field" (âr'fēld") *n.* a place leveled and surfaced on which aircraft alight; an airport.

Airedale

air'foil'' (âr'foil'') n. any surface on an aircraft used for steering, lifting, etc., by the flow of air upon it.

air force the branch of the military forces controlling aircraft.

air lift use of aircraft as the sole means of transportation to a place.

air'line'' n. a company furnishing air transport on fixed schedules.

air'man (-mən) n. [pl. -men] aviator.

air'plane'' (âr'plān'') n. a motor-driven aircraft heavier than air.

air'port'' (âr'pôrt'') n. an airfield having some attendant facilities for handling aircraft and their passengers, and freight.

air'ship'' (âr'ship'') n. a motor-driven aircraft lighter than air.

air'tight'' adj. 1, sealed against air. 2, (of an argument, etc.) flawless.

air'y (âr'ē) adj. 1, like air; unsubstantial. 2, open to a free current of air; well-ventilated. 3, flimsy; unreal; visionary. 4, light in manner or movement; sprightly. 5, affectedly lofty; pretentious. —air'i-ness, n.

aisle (īl) n. a passageway giving access, as to the seats in a church.

a-jar' (ə-jär') adv. & adj. partly open (said of a door).

a-kim'bo (ə-kim'bō) adv. & adj. in a sharp bend (said of the arms when the hands are placed on the hips and the elbows are extended sideward).

a-kin' (ə-kin') adj. 1, related by blood. 2, similar in nature.

-al (əl) suf. pertaining to.

al'a-bas''ter (al'ə-bas''tər) n. a marblelike mineral, often white, used for ornamental purposes. —adj. like alabaster; white.

a-lac'ri-ty (ə-lak'rə-tē) n. cheerful willingness; eager promptitude.

a'lar (ā'lər) adj. having wings; pert. to wings.

a-larm' (ə-lärm') n. 1, a warning of approaching danger; an urgent summons; a signal for attention. 2, any mechanical device for giving such a signal. 3, sudden fear; apprehension of danger. —v.t. 1, fill with anxiety or apprehension; frighten. 2, give notice of danger to; rouse.

a-larm'ist (-ist) n. one disposed to expect or prophesy calamity.

a-las' (ə-lås') interj. of sorrow or pity.

a'late (ā'lāt) adj. having wings or membranes like wings.

alb n. a white robe worn by a priest.

al'ba-tross'' (al'bə-trâs'') n. a web-footed seabird of the petrel family.

al-be'it (al-bē'it) conj. although; notwithstanding that.

al-bi'no (al-bī'nō) n. [pl. -nos] a person or animal having a whitish coloring. —al'bi-nism (al'bə-niz-əm) n.

al'bum (al'bəm) n. a book of blank leaves for the insertion of photographs, stamps, phonograph records, or the like.

al-bu'men (al-bū'mən) n. the white of an egg.

al-bu'min (al-bū'min) n. a protein occurring in the body.

al'che-my (al'kə-mē) n. the doctrines and processes of early and medieval chemists. —al'che-mist, n.

al'co-hol'' (al'kə-hâl'') n. 1, a liquid, ethyl hydrate, derived by fermentation or distillation from organic substances. 2, any intoxicating liquor containing alcohol.

al''co-hol'ic (-hol'ik) adj. of or containing alcohol. —n. one suffering from alcoholism. —al''co-hol'i-cal-ly, adv.

al'co-hol-ism (-iz-əm) n. addiction to excessive drinking of alcoholic liquors; dipsomania.

al'cove (al'kōv) n. a covered recess, bay, or niche.

al'der (âl'dər) n. any of numerous shrubs and trees abundant in temperate climates.

al'der-man (âl'dər-mən) n. [pl. -men] a municipal official; in the U.S. he usually represents a ward in a legislative body.

Al'der-ney (âl'dər-nē) n. one of a breed of dairy cattle.

ale (āl) n. a beverage made from malt, similar to beer but containing more alcohol.

a-lem'bic (ə-lem'bik) n. a beaker.

a-lert' (ə-lêrt') adj. 1, vigilantly attentive; watchful. 2, brisk; nimble. —v.t. warn of or activate for impending danger. —n. 1, a warning signal. 2, a state of vigilant readiness. —a-lert'ness, n.

ale'wife (āl'wif') n. a No. Amer. fish similar to the shad.

Alewife

a-lex'i-a (ə-lek'sē-ə) n. loss of the faculty of understanding written language.

al-fal'fa (al-fal'fə) n. a forage plant extensively cultivated in the U.S.; lucerne.

al'ga (al'gə) n. [pl. al'gae (-jē)]

any of a numerous class of plants that grow in sea and fresh water.

al'ge·bra (al'jə-brə) *n.* **1,** a branch of mathematics concerned with generalizing the arithmetic operations and analyzing equations. **2,** any system of compact notation for dealing with generalizations. —**al'·ge·bra'ic** (-brā'ik) *adj.* —**al'ge·bra'i·cal·ly,** *adv.*

a'li·as (ā'lē-əs) *n.* an assumed name.

al'i·bi'' (al'ə-bī'') *n.* (*Law*) a plea of having been elsewhere at the time an offense is alleged to have been committed; (*Colloq.*) any excuse.

a'li·dade'' (al'ə-dād'') *n.* a straight edge attached to a telescope or a graduated circle, for sighting or measuring angles.

al'ien (āl'yən) *adj.* **1,** not residing in the country of one's citizenship. **2,** different in nature; foreign; adverse or hostile. —*n.* one who is estranged or excluded; a foreigner.

al'ien·a·ble (āl'yə-nə-bəl) *adj.* capable of being sold or transferred.

al'ien·ate'' (āl'yə-nāt'') *v.t.* **1,** repel or turn away in feeling; estrange. **2,** *Law,* transfer title or property to another. —**al'ien·a'tion,** *n.*

a'li·n·ist (āl'yən-ist) *n.* a psychiatrist, esp. one who pronounces upon legal insanity.

a·light' (ə-līt') *v.i.* **1,** dismount. **2,** disembark after a flight. —*adv. & adj.* glowing with light or fire.

a·lign' (ə-līn') *v.t. & i.* form into a line; straighten. Also, **a·line'.** —**a·lign'ment,** *n.*

a·like' (ə-līk') *adv.* in the same manner, form, or degree; in common; equally. —*adj.* having resemblance; similar; having no marked difference.

al'i·ment (al'ə-mənt) *n.* anything that nourishes or sustains; food; support. —**al'i·men·ta·ry** (al'ə-men'tə-rē) **canal,** the entire food passage.

al'i·mo''ny (al'ə-mō'nē) *n.* an allowance directed to be paid by a man to his former wife after divorce.

a·live' (ə-līv') *adj.* **1,** living; existent. **2,** active; animated. **3,** open to impressions; susceptible. **4,** filled with living things.

al'ka·li'' (al'kə-lī'') *n.* (*Chem.*) any of numerous substances that have the power of neutralizing acids and forming salts; a base. —**al'ka·line** (-līn) *adj.* —**al''ka·lin'i·ty** (-lin'ə-tē) *n.*

al'ka·loid (al'kə-loid) *n.* any of certain compounds of nitrogen.

all (âl) *adj. & pron.* the whole quantity or number of (as to substance, extent, degree, duration, etc.). —*adj.* every; any. —*adv.* wholly; entirely. —*n.* a totality of things or qualities.

Al'lah (ä'lä) *n.* (*Moslem*) God.

all-''a·round' *adj.* versatile; complete. Also, **all-''round'.**

al·lay' (a-lā') *v.t.* **1,** make quiet or calm; pacify. **2,** make less violent; mitigate.

al''le·ga'tion (al''ə-gā'shən) *n.* **1,** act of alleging. **2,** an assertion or plea.

al·lege' (ə-lej') *v.t.* **1,** declare positively. **2,** assert without proof.

al·le'giance (ə-lē'jəns) *n.* **1,** the obligation of a person to his state or government. **2,** fidelity to a person or principle; devotion.

al''le·go'ry (al'ə-gôr'ē) *n.* the discussion or representation of a subject, not directly stated, through another analogous to it. —**al''le·gor'i·cal** (al'ə-gôr'i-kəl) *adj.*

al·le'gro (ə-lā'grō) *adj.* (*Music*) brisk; lively.

al''le·lu'ia (al''ə-loo'yə) *n., interj.* praise ye the Lord.

al·ler'gic (ə-lêr'jik) *adj.* having an allergy (to something); (*Colloq.*) averse.

al'ler·gy (al'ər-jē) *n.* abnormal sensitiveness to certain foods or substances.

al·le'vi·ate'' (ə-lē'vē-āt'') *v.t.* remove in part; lessen; mitigate. —**al·le''vi·a'tion,** *n.*

al'ley (al'ē) *n.* **1,** a narrow passageway; a back street. **2,** a long, narrow rink for sports, as bowling. **3,** a large playing-marble.

al·li'ance (ə-lī'əns) *n.* **1,** state of being allied or joined together, as in marriage or political confederation. **2,** the aggregate of persons or parties allied. **3,** the instrument of an alliance, as a treaty. **4,** kinship; similarity.

al·lied' (ə-līd') *adj.* **1,** joined together by compact or treaty. **2,** similar or related.

al''li·ga'tor (al'ə-gā'tər) *n.* a large lizardlike reptile, akin to the crocodile. —**alligator pear,** avocado.

Alligator

al·lit''er·a'tion (ə-lit'ə-rā'shən) *n.* repetition of the same initial letter or sound in two or more nearby words, as *foolish fancy.*

al'lo·cate'' (al'ə-kāt'') *v.t.* set apart for a particular purpose; allot; assign. —**al''lo·ca'tion,** *n.*

al·lop'a·thy (ə-lop'ə-thē) *n.* treatment of disease by the agents that produce effects different from the symptoms of the disease. —**al''lo·path'ic,** *adj.* —**al''lo·path'i·cal·ly,** *adv.*

al·lot' (ə-lot') *v.t.* [al·lot'ted, al-lot'ting] **1,** distribute as by lot; parcel out; apportion. **2,** set apart; appoint; assign for a particular purpose.

al·lot'ment (-mənt) *n.* **1,** act of allotting; distribution. **2,** a portion or share; an assigned quantity.

al'lo·trope' (al'ə-trōp') *n.* any of several different physical forms in which a chemical element may occur, as coal or diamond, both carbon. —al'lo·trop'ic, *adj.* —al'lo·trop'i·cal·ly, *adv.* —al·lot'ro·py, al·lot'ro·pism, *n.*

all-"out' *adj.* with full vigor.

al·low' (ə-low') *v.t.* **1,** permit; grant; yield; assign. **2,** admit; concede. **3,** make provision (for); take into account. **4,** (*Dial.*) aver; believe.

al·low'ance (ə-low'əns) *n.* **1,** a share or allotment, esp. of money granted to defray expenses. **2,** an addition or deduction, as the allowable difference from prescribed dimensions in machining. **3,** admission or acceptance; sanction.

al·loy' (al'oi) *n.* **1,** a mixture of two or more metals, intimately fused. **2,** an admixture; a deleterious component; taint. —*v.t.* (ə-loi') **1,** mix. **2,** debase by admixture.

all right 1, in good condition; correct; correctly; unharmed. **2,** expression of assent or agreement; very well; yes.

all'spice' (âl'spīs") *n.* the berry of a W. I. tree; pimento.

al·lude' (ə-lood') *v.i.* (with *to*) refer casually or indirectly.

al·lure' (ə-lûr') *v.t.* attract by some proposed pleasure or advantage; entice. —*n.* charm. —al·lure'ment, *n.* —al·lur'ing, *adj.* tempting; charming.

al·lu'sion (ə-loo'zhən) *n.* a casual reference; a slight or incidental mention. —al·lu'sive (-siv) *adj.*

al·lu'vi·um (ə-loo'vē-əm) *n.* [*pl.* -a (-ə)] a deposit of sand formed by flowing water. —al·lu'vi·al, *adj.*

al·ly' (ə-lī') *v.t. & i.* join together; combine with; associate. —*n.* one joined with another in a common enterprise; a confederate.

al'ma ma'ter (âl'mə-mä'tər) one's school or college.

al'ma·nac" (âl'mə-nak") *n.* a yearly calendar showing the times of certain events, as the rising and setting of the sun and moon, the changes of the sun and moon, the tides, dates of holidays, etc.

al·might'y (âl-mī'tē) *adj.* **1,** supremely powerful; of boundless sufficiency. **2,** (*Colloq.*) extreme. —*n.* (*cap.*) God.

al'mond (ä'mənd) *n.* **1,** a tree found in subtropical climates. **2,** the edible kernel of its fruit. **3,** the color of the kernel, light brown. **4,** anything shaped like an almond kernel.

Almond

Shell   Nut

al'mon·er (al'mən-ər) *n.* a giver of alms. —al'mon·ry (-rē) *n.*

al'most (âl'mōst) *adv.* nearly all; for the most part; very nearly; all but.

alms (ämz) *n.pl.* what is given to the poor or needy; anything bestowed in charity. —alms'house", *n.* poorhouse.

al'oe (al'ō) *n.* **1,** an African plant used in making drugs and fiber. **2,** the American century plant. **3,** (*pl.*) a bitter purgative drug made from the juice of the aloe.

a·loft' (ə-lâft') *adv. & adj.* in the air; above the ground; (*Naut.*) in the upper rigging.

a·lo'ha (ə-lō'ə) (*Hawaiian*) *interj.* of well-wishing, used as both a greeting and a farewell.

a·lone' (ə-lōn') *adj.* apart from or to the exclusion of other persons or things; solitary; single. —*adv.* solely; only.

a·long' (ə-lâng') *prep.* in a longitudinal direction through, over, or by the side of. —*adv.* **1,** lengthwise. **2,** onward. **3,** in company; together.

a·long'side *adv. & prep.* along or by the side of; beside.

a·loof' (ə-loof') *adv.* at a distance, but within view; withdrawn. —*adj.* reserved; indifferent. —a·loof'ness, *n.*

a·loud' (ə-lowd') *adv.* audibly; with the natural tone of the voice as distinguished from whispering.

alp *n.* a high mountain.

al·pac'a (al-pak'ə) *n.* **1,** a domesticated sheeplike ruminant of South America. **2,** its hair; a fabric made from the hair. **3,** any glossy fabric made in imitation of alpaca.

al'pha (al'fə) *n.* the first letter of the Greek alphabet (A, α), corresponding to English a.

al'pha·bet" (al'fə-bet") *n.* the letters of a language in their customary order. —al'pha·bet'i·cal (-i-kəl) *adj.* in that order. —al'pha·bet·ize" (-bə-tīz") *v.t.* put into alphabetical order.

al'pine (al'pīn) *adj.* **1,** mountainous; high; elevated. **2,** (*cap.*) pert. to the Alps.

al·read'y (âl-red'ē) *adv.* previously to the present or a specified time.

al'so (ál'sō) *adv.* in addition; too; likewise; further.

al'tar (ál'tər) *n.* a structure, as a block of stone or a table, at which religious rites are performed.

al'ter (ál'tər) *v.t.* make some change in; cause to vary; modify. —*v.i.* become different; change. —**al'ter·a'tion,** *n.*

al'ter·ca'tion (ál'tər-kā'shən) *n.* an angry or noisy dispute; wrangle.

al'ter·nate (ál'tər-nāt') *v.i.* 1, follow one another in time or place reciprocally. 2, move or change in turn from one place or condition to another. —*v.t.* do or perform in turns, or in succession. —*adj.* (-nət) 1, following by turns, recurrently or in succession. 2, every other one of a series. —*n.* (-nət) a person authorized to take the place of another in his absence. —**al'ter·na'tion,** *n.*

alternating current electric current that reverses its direction of flow, usually 120 times per second.

al·ter'na·tive (ál-tẽr'nə-tiv) *n.* one of a set of mutually exclusive choices or possibilities. —*adj.* 1, affording a choice. 2, mutually exclusive.

al·though' (ál-thō') *conj.* in spite of the fact that; even admitting that.

al·tim'e·ter (al-tim'ə-tər) *n.* an instrument for measuring altitudes.

al'ti·tude' (al'ti-tood') *n.* the distance upward, esp. from sea level to a point in the atmosphere; height.

al'to (al'tō) *adj.* (*Music*) higher than tenor. —*n.* [*pl.* -tos] (*Music*) 1, a high male or low female voice. 2, a part in the range of such a voice. 3, any of several instruments.

al'to·geth'er (ál'tə-geth'ər) *adv.* wholly; entirely.

al'tru·ism (al'troo-iz-əm) *n.* regard for the welfare of others; benevolent practices. —**al'tru·ist,** *n.* —**al'tru·is'tic,** *adj.* —**al'tru·is'ti·cal·ly,** *adv.*

al'um (al'əm) *n.* any of numerous bitter, astringent compounds used in drugs and dyes.

a·lu'mi·num (ə-loo'mə-nəm) *n.* a metallic chemical element, much used in alloys because of its light weight, no. 13, symbol Al. Also (*Brit.*) **al'u·min'i·um** (al-ū-min'ē-əm).

a·lum'nus (ə-lum'nəs) *n.* [*pl.* -ni (-nī)] a graduate or former student of a school or college. —**a·lum'na** [*pl.* -nae (-nē)] *n. fem.*

al'ways (ál'wēz) *adv.* 1, throughout all time; uninterruptedly. 2, at every recurring time.

am *v.* 1st person sing. of *be.*

a·mal'gam (ə-mal'gəm) *n.* 1, an alloy of mercury with another metal. 2, any mixture or compound.

a·mal'ga·mate' (ə-mal'gə-māt') *v.t. & i.* 1, mix or come together;

blend; unite. 2, combine with a metal. —**a·mal'ga·ma'tion,** *n.*

a·man'u·en'sis (ə-man'ū-en'sis) *n.* [*pl.* -ses (-sēz)] a person who writes what another dictates; a secretary.

am'a·ranth (am'ə-ranth) *n.* any of various flowering plants.

am'a·ryl'lis (am'ə-ril'is) *n.* 1, a bulbous plant, the belladonna lily. 2, (*cap.*) a shepherdess.

a·mass' (ə-mas') *v.t.* collect in a mass or heap; bring together in great amount.

am'a·teur' (am'ə-chûr') *n.* 1, one who pursues an activity for pleasure instead of for material gain. 2, one who is unskillful; a dilettante. —*adj.* not professional. —**am'a·teur'ish,** *adj.* unskillful. —**am'a·teur·ism,** *n.*

am'a·tive (am'ə-tiv) *adj.* loving.

am'a·to'ry (am'ə-tôr'ē) *adj.* pert: to lovemaking.

a·maze' (ə-māz') *v.t.* cause to feel great astonishment, surprise, or wonder. —**a·maze'ment,** *n.*

am'a·zon" (am'ə-zon") *n.* a large and strong, or quarrelsome, woman.

am·bas'sa·dor (am-bas'ə-dər) *n.* a diplomatic agent of highest rank. —**am·bas'sa·dor'i·al** (-dôr'ē-əl) *adj.* —**am·bas'sa·dress,** *n. fem.*

am'ber (am'bər) *n.* 1, a mineralized resin on which rubbing produces a negative electric charge. 2, the pale yellow color of amber. —*adj.* like amber; yellow.

am'ber·gris" (am'bər-grēs") *n.* a morbid secretion of the sperm whale, prized for making perfume.

am·bi- *pref.* meaning both, or on both sides. Also, **am·phi-.**

am"bi·dex'trous (am"bi-deks'-trəs) *adj.* apt with both hands. —**am"bi·dex·ter'i·ty,** *n.*

am·bi·gu'i·ty (am-bi-gū'ə-tē) *n.* state of being ambiguous; double meaning.

am·big'u·ous (am-big'ū-əs) *adj.* of doubtful purport; open to various interpretations; having a double meaning.

am'bit *n.* boundary; compass;

am·bi'tion (am-bish'ən) *n.* eager desire for distinction, power, or fame.

am·bi'tious (am-bish'əs) *adj.* having much ambition; eager for success.

am·biv'a·lence (am-biv'ə-ləns) *n.* mixed or conflicting feelings. —**am·biv'a·lent,** *adj.*

am'ble (am'bəl) *v.i.* move easily and gently, like a walking horse.

am·bro'sia (am-brō'zhə) *n.* in Greek legend, the food of the gods. —**am·bro'sial** (-zhəl) *adj.*

am·bu·lance (am'bū-ləns) *n.* a vehicle for carrying the sick or wounded.

am·bu·late (am'bū-lāt) *v.i.* move about from place to place. —am'bu·la'tion, *n.* —am'bu·lant, am'bu·la·to'ry (-tôr'ē) *adj.*

am·bus·cade (am'bəs-kād') *n. & v.* ambush.

am·bush (am'bûsh) *v.t.* attack unexpectedly from a hidden position. —*n.* 1, the act of lying concealed for a surprise attack. 2, a place of concealment.

a·me·ba (ə-mē'bə) *n.* a one-celled animal that continually changes shape to engulf and absorb its food. Also, a·moe·ba.

Ameba

a·mel·io·rate (ə-mēl'yə-rāt') *v.t. & i.* make or become better, more satisfactory, or more tolerable. —a·mel'io·ra'tion, *n.* —a·mel'io·ra·tive, *adj.*

a·men (ā'men') *interj. & adv.* be it so (an expression of invocation or endorsement at the end of a prayer). —*n.* an expression of fervent assent.

a·me·na·ble (ə-mē'nə-bəl) *adj.* 1, disposed to yield; submissive. 2, liable, as to control or claim. —a·me'na·bil'i·ty, a·me'na·ble·ness, *n.*

a·mend (ə-mend') *v.t.* 1, make better; correct; improve. 2, alter. —*v.i.* become better; reform. —*n. (pl.)* compensation for loss or injury; recompense.

a·mend'ment (-mənt) *n.* 1, correction; improvement. 2, a change, as in a law; *(cap.)* a change in the Constitution of the U. S.

a·men·i·ty (ə-men'ə-tē) *n.* 1, the quality of being pleasant or agreeable. 2, *(pl.)* pleasant aspects; conveniences.

A·mer·i·can (ə-mer'i-kən) *adj. & n.* pert. to any country of the Western Hemisphere, esp. the U. S. its people, customs, etc. —American plan, a system whereby a hotel's charge includes room and meals.

am·e·thyst (am'ə-thist) *n.* 1, a bluish variety of quartz used in making ornaments. 2, a violet sapphire. 3, a light purple or violet color.

a·mi·a·ble (ā'mē-ə-bəl) *adj.* 1, pleasing; lovable. 2, friendly; kindly. —a'mi·a·bil'i·ty, a'mi·a·ble·ness, *n.*

am·i·ca·ble (am'i-kə-bəl) *adj.* exhibiting friendliness; peaceable; harmonious. —am'i·ca·bil'i·ty, *n.*

a·mid (ə-mid') *prep.* in the midst of; surrounded by. Also, a-midst'.

a·mid·ships (ə-mid'ships) *adv.* midway of the length of a ship.

Am·ish (äm'ish) *adj.* of a certain sect of Mennonites.

a·miss (ə-mis') *adv.* in a faulty manner; out of proper course or order. —*adj.* improper; faulty.

am·i·ty (am'ə-tē) *n.* friendship; pleasant relations, esp. between nations.

am·me·ter (am'mē'tər) *n.* an instrument for measuring amperes.

am·mo·ni·a (ə-mōn'yə) *n.* 1, a gaseous compound of nitrogen and hydrogen. 2, a solution of this gas in water. —am·mo'ni·ate' (-āt') *v.t.*

am·mu·ni·tion (am'ū-nish'ən) *n.* materials used in discharging firearms, etc., as bullets, explosives, etc.

am·ne·sia (am-nē'zhə) *n.* loss of memory. —am·ne'sic (-zik) *adj.*

am·nes·ty (am'nəs-tē) *n.* a general pardon for a whole class of offenses against a government.

a·moe·ba (ə-mē'bə) *n.* ameba.

a·mok (ə-mok') *adv.* amuck.

a·mong (ə-mung') *prep.* 1, in the midst of; in association with; in the class or group of. 2, with or by the whole of. 3, to each of.

a·mon·til·la·do (ə-mon'tə-lä'dō) *n.* a dry sherry.

am·o·rous (am'ə-rəs) *adj.* 1, inclined to love; loving. 2, indicating or conveying love. —am'o·rous·ness, *n.*

a·mor·phous (ə-môr'fəs) *adj.* 1, having no determinate form; of irregular shape. 2, of no particular kind; heterogeneous. —a·mor'phous·ness, *n.*

am·or·tize (am'ər-tīz') *v.t.* extinguish (a debt) by means of a sinking fund. —am'or·ti·za'tion, *n.*

a·mount (ə-mownt') *n.* 1, the sum of two or more quantities. 2, a sum quantity, value, or import, viewed as a whole. —*v.i.* (with to) add up; reach in quantity or degree.

a·mour (ä-môr') *n.* a love affair.

am·per·age (am'pir-ij) *n.* the measure of a current in amperes.

am·pere (am'pir) *n.* a unit of electromotive force, one volt acting against the resistance of one ohm.

am·per·sand (am'pər-sand') *n.* the character &: and.

am·phet·a·mine (am-fet'ə-mēn) *n.* a drug used to relieve nasal congestion.

am·phib·i·an (am-fib'ē-ən) *n.* an amphibious animal, plant, or airplane.

am·phib·i·ous (am-fib'ē-əs) *adj.* capable of living or operating both on land and in water.

am·phi·the·a·ter (am'fə-thē'ə-tər) *n.* a circular or oval arena for sports, surrounded by tiers of seats on a sloping gallery.

---

am'ple (am'pəl) *adj.* **1,** large in extent or amount; copious. **2,** plentifully sufficient. —**am'ple·ness,** *n.*

am'pli·fi'er (am'plə-fī'ər) *n.* a device for increasing the amplitude of electrical impulses.

am'pli·fy' (am'plə-fī') *v.t.* make larger in extent or importance; enlarge. —**am'pli·fi·ca'tion,** *n.*

am'pli·tude' (am'pli-tood') *n.* **1,** extension in space; largeness. **2,** (of a wave) the distance or magnitude of a crest or trough from the mean value. —**amplitude modulation,** a system of radio transmission.

am'pu·tate' (am'pū-tāt') *v.t.* cut off (a limb). —**am'pu·ta'tion,** *n.* —**am'pu·tee',** *n.*

a·muck' (ə-muk') *adv.* in a frenzied manner. —**run amuck,** indiscriminately attack everyone encountered.

am'u·let (am'ū-let) *n.* an object superstitiously worn to bring good luck, avert illness, etc.

a·muse' (ə-mūz') *v.t.* excite pleasure or mirth in; entertain; divert.

a·muse'ment (-mənt) *n.* **1,** pleasurable interest; mirth. **2,** that which amuses; a pastime.

an *adj.* a: the indefinite article, used before a word beginning with a vowel sound.

a·nab'a·sis (ə-nab'ə-sis) *n.* [*pl.* **-ses** (-sēz)] a long march by a military force.

a·nach'ro·nism (ə-nak'rə-niz-əm) *n.* an error in respect to dates or the order of historical events. —**a·nach'ro·nis'tic** (-nis'tik) *adj.* —**a·nach'ro·nis'ti·cal·ly,** *adv.*

an'a·con'da (an'ə-kon'də) *n.* any large snake; boa constrictor.

an'a·gram' (an'ə-gram') *n.* a word or phrase formed from another by transposition of the letters.

a'nal (ā'nəl) *adj.* pert. to the anus.

an'al·ge'sia (an'əl-jē'zhə) *n.* inability of a part to feel pain.

an'al·ge'sic (an'əl-jē'zik) *n.* a remedy to relieve pain. —*adj.* relieving pain.

a·nal'o·gous (ə-nal'ə-gəs) *adj.* corresponding; similar.

an'a·logue (an'ə-log) *n.* something analogous to another.

a·nal'o·gy (ə-nal'ə-jē) *n.* similarity or agreement between one thing and another; resemblance; comparison.

a·nal'y·sis (ə-nal'ə-sis) *n.* [*pl.* **-ses** (-sēz)] **1,** the separation of a complex material or conception into its elements. **2,** determination of causes from results; induction. **3,** an abstract; summary.

an'a·lyst (an'ə-list) *n.* **1,** one who analyzes. **2,** a psychoanalyst.

an·a·lyt'i·cal (an-ə-lit'i-kəl) *adj.* being or pert. to analysis. Also, **an·a·lyt'ic.**

an'a·lyze' (an'ə-līz') *v.t.* **1,** separate into its elements; determine the constituents of. **2,** examine critically.

an'a·pest' (an'ə-pest') *n.* a foot in poetry, two unstressed syllables followed by a stressed one. —**an'a·pes'tic,** *adj.*

an'arch·ism (an'ər-kiz-əm) *n.* the political doctrine that all governments should be abolished.

an'arch·ist (an'ər-kist) *n.* **1,** a social rebel; insurrectionist. **2,** a believer in anarchism. —**an'ar·chis'tic,** *adj.*

an'arch·y (an'ər-kē) *n.* **1,** general disorder from lack of government. **2,** anarchism. —**an·ar'chic** (an-ärk'-ik), **an·ar'chi·cal,** *adj.*

a·nath'e·ma (ə-nath'ə-mə) *n.* **1,** a denunciation, accompanied by excommunication, by an ecclesiastical authority. **2,** any solemn execration or curse. **3,** something accursed.

a·nat'o·my (ə-nat'ə-mē) *n.* **1,** the structure of an animal or plant body. **2,** the science of structure; the art of dissecting bodies to determine their structure. —**an'a·tom'i·cal,** *adj.*

-ance (-əns) *suf.* same as **-ence.**

an'ces·tor (an'ses-tər) *n.* a foregoing person or organism (usually deceased) from whom one is descended; forebear; progenitor. —**an'ces·tress,** *n. fem.*

an·ces'tral (an-ses'trəl) *adj.* pert. to ancestry or an ancestor.

an'ces·try (an'ses-trē) *n.* a series of ancestors; line of descent.

an'chor (ang'kər) *n.* **1,** a device for securing a vessel to the ground under water by means of a cable. **2,** any device that holds in place, gives security or stability. —*v.t.* fix firmly in place. —*v.i.* drop anchor.

Anchor

an'chor·age (-ij) *n.* a place suitable for anchoring.

an'cho·vy (an'chō-vē) *n.* a small fish similar to the herring.

an'cient (ān'shənt) *adj.* **1,** having existed in the remote past. **2,** very old.

an'cil·lar'y (an'sə-ler'ē) *adj.* serving in a subordinate or auxiliary capacity. —*n.* (*pl.*) (*Mil.*) auxiliary forces, as of supply, transport, etc.

-an·cy (ən-sē) *suf.* same as **-ence,** **-ency.**

and *conj.* in addition; also; too.

an·dan'te (an-dan'tē) *adj.* (*Music*) moderately slow.

and'i'ron (and'ī'ərn) *n.* one of a pair of iron stands used to support wood burned in an open hearth.

an'ec·dote' (an'ek-dōt') n. a short narrative of an occurrence.

a·ne'mi·a (ə-nē'mē-ə) n. quantitative deficiency of blood. —**a·ne'mic**, adj. —**a·ne'mi·cal·ly**, adv.

an"e·mom'e·ter (an"ə-mom'ə-tər) n. a device for measuring the velocity of the wind.

a·nem'o·ne (ə-nem'ə-nē) n. 1, a wild flower. 2, a small sea animal.

a·nent' (ə-nent') prep. (Archaic) in regard to; concerning.

an'er·oid" (an'ər-oid") adj. using no fluid.

an"es·the'sia (an"əs-thē'zhə) n. (Med.) loss of feeling, esp. as induced by certain drugs.

an"es·thet'ic (-thet'ik) n. a drug that induces anesthesia.

an·es'the·tist (ə-nes'thə-tist) n. one who administers an anesthetic.

an·es'the·tize" (ə-nes'thə-tīz") v.t. administer an anesthetic to.

a·new' (ə-nū') adv. once more; again; in a new form.

an'gel (ān'jəl) n. 1, an attendant of God, esp. a messenger. 2, a kindly woman. 3, (Colloq.) a financial backer. —**an·gel'ic** (an-jel'ik) adj. —**an·gel'i·cal·ly**, adv.

an'ger (ang'gər) n. a strong emotion of displeasure and resentment; wrath. —v.t. excite to anger.

an·gi'na pec'to·ris (an-jī'nə pek'tə-ris) a spasm in the chest, symptom of a heart disease.

an'gle (ang'gəl) n. 1, an enclosure or space formed by two intersecting lines or planes. 2, (Geom.) that proportion of a circular arc intercepted by such lines. 3, an angular projection; a corner. 4, a point of view; an aspect or phase. —v.t. & i. form into an angle. —v.t. 1, fish with hook and line. 2, try to obtain by artful means. —**an'gler**, n. a fisherman. —**an'gling**, n. the art of fishing.

an'gle·worm" n. an earthworm.

An'gli·can (ang'gli-kən) adj. pert. to the Church of England.

An'gli·cism (ang'glə-siz-əm) n. something peculiarly English.

an'gli·cize" (ang'gli-sīz") v.t. adapt to English form or custom.

An'glo- (ang'glō) pref. pert. to England or the English.

An'glo-Sax'on (-sak'sən) adj. & n. pert. to the early Germanic inhabitants of England, their language, or their descendants.

An·go'ra (ang-gôr'ə) n. 1, a long-haired domestic cat. 2, a breed of long-haired goat. 3, a fabric (usually called mohair) woven from the hair of a goat.

an'gry (ang'grē) adj. 1, feeling anger; expressive of anger; tempestuous. 2, sore; inflamed.

an'guish (ang'gwish) n. acute bodily or mental distress; extreme pain. —v.t. & i. afflict with pain; suffer anguish.

an'gu·lar (ang'gū-lər) adj. 1, having or forming angles, corners, or projections. 2, bony; gaunt. 3, stiff in manner. —**an·gu·lar'i·ty** (-lar'ə-tē) n.

an'il n. a West Indian shrub that yields indigo.

an'i·line (an'ə-lin) n. a liquid used in making dyes, perfumes, etc.

an"i·mad·ver'sion (an"ə-mad-vēr'zhən) n. 1, a slurring remark; blame. 2, unfavorable bias.

an'i·mal (an'ə-məl) n. 1, any living thing not a plant. 2, any animal other than man. 3, a brutish person. —adj. 1, belonging to the realm or nature of animals. 2, pert. to the bodily appetites or functions of man. —**an"i·mal'i·ty** (-mal'ə-tē) n.

an"i·mal'cule" (an"i-mal'kūl') n. a minute animal.

an'i·mate" (an'ə-māt") v.t. 1, give life to. 2, infuse with vigor or liveliness. 3, incite to action. —adj. (-mət) having life; lively. —**an'i·mat"ed**, adj. full of spirit; vigorous. —**an"i·ma'tion**, n.

an"i·mos'i·ty (an"ə-mos'ə-tē) n. active enmity; hatred; ill-will.

an'i·mus (an'ə-məs) n. 1, animosity. 2, a grudge.

an'ise (an'is) n. a Mediterranean plant whose seed (aniseed) is used in making drugs, perfumes, and liqueurs.

an"i·sette' (an"i-set') n. an anise-flavored liqueur.

an'kle (ang'kəl) n. the joint connecting the foot with the leg.

ank'let (ang'klet) n. 1, a low sock that reaches just above the ankle. 2, a bracelet or other ornament worn on the lower leg.

an'nals (an'əlz) n. pl. 1, a history of events recorded year by year. 2, historical records generally.

an·neal' (ə-nēl') v.t. treat (glass, metals, etc.) by heating and gradually cooling, which toughens the substance and removes brittleness.

an·nex' (ə-neks') v.t. 1, attach at the end; affix. 2, unite or join, esp. a smaller thing to a larger. —n. (an'eks) something annexed, as a subsidiary building; a supplement. —**an"nex·a'tion**, n.

an·ni'hi·late" (ə-nī'ə-lāt") v.t. destroy utterly; reduce to nothing. —**an·ni"hi·la'tion**, n.

an"ni·ver'sa·ry (an"ə-vēr'sə-rē) n. 1, the annually recurring date of a past event. 2, the celebration of such a date. —adj. recurring each year.

an'no·tate (an'ō-tāt') *v.t.* & *i.* furnish with explanatory or critical notes; comment upon in notes —**an'no·ta'tion**, *n.*

an·nounce' (ə-nowns') *v.t.* make known formally; give notice of; publish; proclaim.

an·nounce'ment (-mənt) *n.* 1, act of announcing. 2, what is announced; a formal notice.

an·noun'cer (ə-nown'sər) *n.* one who announces, esp. commercials, news, etc. on radio.

an·noy' (ə-noi') *v.t.* & *i.* be troublesome or vexatious to; irk and harass. —**an·noy'ance**, *n.*

an'nu·al (an'ū-əl) *adj.* 1, occurring or returning once a year. 2, lasting or continuing one year. —*n.* 1, a plant or animal whose natural term of life is one year or season. 2, a book published once a year, or covering the events of a year.

an·nu'i·ty (ə-nū'ə-tē) *n.* a periodical payment of money, usually a fixed amount in each year.

an·nul' (ə-nul') *v.t.* [-nulled', -nul'ling] make null or void; abolish. —**an·nul'ment**, *n.*

an'nu·lar (an'ū-lər) *adj.* having the form of a ring.

an·nun'ci·a'tion (ə-nun'sē-ā'shən) *n.* (usually *cap.*) 1, the announcement by Gabriel to Mary that she would bear Jesus. 2, a feast day commemorating this.

an'ode (an'ōd) *n.* the positive pole of a battery; an electrode that emits positive ions.

an'o·dyne' (an'ə-dīn') *n.* & *adj.* 1, a drug that relieves pain. 2, anything that relieves mental pain or distress.

a·noint' (ə-noint') *v.t.* pour oil upon, as in a religious ceremony. —**a·noint'ment**, *n.*

a·nom'a·ly (ə-nom'ə-lē) *n.* deviation from the common rule; something abnormal or irregular. —**a·nom'a·lous**, *adj.*

a·non' (ə-non') *adv.* (*Archaic*) in a short time; soon.

an''o·nym'i·ty (an''ə-nim'ə-tē) *n.* state of being anonymous.

a·non'y·mous (ə-non'ə-məs) *adj.* lacking the name of the author, composer, contributor, etc.; from an unacknowledged source.

a·noph'e·les' (ə-nof'ə-lēz') *n.* [*pl.* -les''] the mosquito that carries malaria.

an·oth'er (ə-nuth'ər) *adj.* 1, one more; an additional. 2, a different; of distinct kind. —*pron.* one additional, or a different, person or thing.

an'swer (an'sər) *n.* 1, a reply or response. 2, the solution of a problem. —*v.t.* & *i.* 1, make a reply or response (to). 2, serve or suit. 3, atone (for). —**an'swer·a·ble**, *adj.* 1, capable of being answered. 2, liable (with *for*).

ant *n.* a small insect that lives in communities.

Ant

-ant (ent) *suf.* 1, denoting a doer or agent. 2, forming participial adjectives; equivalent to *-ing*.

ant·ac'id (ant-as'id) *n.* & *adj.* a drug or reagent for neutralizing acids.

an·tag'o·nism (an-tag'ə-niz-əm) *n.* mutual resistance or opposition of two forces in action.

an·tag'o·nist (an-tag'ə-nist) *n.* an active opponent. —**an·tag'o·nis'tic**, *adj.* opposed; unfriendly; hostile. —**an·tag'o·nis'ti·cal·ly**, *adv.*

an·tag'o·nize'' (an-tag'ə-nīz'') *v.t.* incur the ill will of; make hostile.

ant·arc'tic (an-tärk'tik) *adj.* near or at the South Pole. —*n.* (*cap.*) the South Polar regions.

an'te (an'tē) *n.* a compulsory bet made by a card player before seeing his cards. —*v.t.* & *i.* [-ted (-tēd), -te·ing] make such a bet.

an·te- (an-tē) *pref.* meaning before.

an''te·ce'dent (an''tē·sē'dənt) *adj.* existing or going before, in time or place. —*n.* 1, (*Gram.*) the noun or phrase for which a pronoun stands. 2, (*Math., Logic*) the first of two correlative parts, as the first term of a ratio. 3, (*pl.*) one's origin, previous associations, or avowed principles. —**an''te·ce'dence**, *n.*

an''te·cham''ber *n.* a room leading into another; waiting room.

an''te·date'' (an'tē·dāt') *v.t.* 1, precede in time. 2, date before the true time. 3, ascribe to an earlier time.

an''te·lope'' (an'tə·lōp'') *n.* a horned ruminant related to cattle.

an·ten'na (an-ten'ə) *n.* 1, a conducting wire from which radio waves are sent or received. 2, [*pl.* -nae (-ē)] one of the appendages occurring in pairs on the head of an insect, also called *feelers*.

an·te'ri·or (an-tir'ē-ər) *adj.* 1, situated at the front; placed before. 2, (of a human or animal body) toward the front; toward the head.

an''te·room'' (an'tē·room'') *n.* a smaller room giving access to a larger; waiting room; reception room.

an'them (an'thəm) *n.* 1, a sacred hymn. 2, a song of devotion or patriotism.

an'ther (an'thər) *n.* (*Bot.*) the part of a stamen bearing pollen.

an·thol'o·gist (an-thol'ə-jist) *n.* the compiler of an anthology.

an·thol'o·gy (an-thol'ə-jē) *n.* a collection in one volume of writings of various authors.

an'thra·cite (an'thrə-sīt) *n.* hard coal. —*adj.* coal-black.

an'thrax (an'thraks) *n.* a malignant bacterial disease of cattle and man.

an'thro·poid" (an'thrə-poid") *adj.* resembling man.

an·thro·pol'o·gy (an"thrə-pol'ə-jē) *n.* **1**, the general science of man. **2**, the science of man's origin, early development and culture. —*an"thro·pol'o·gist, n.*

an·ti- *pref.* against; opposed to.

an"ti·bi·ot'ic (an"ti-bī-ot'ik) *n.* a substance derived from certain organisms that tends to destroy harmful organisms.

an"ti·bod"y (an'ti-bod'ē) *n.* an immunizing agent within the human body that counteracts malignant bacteria.

an'tic (an'tik) *n.* (chiefly *pl.*) escapade; (*pl.*) ludicrous behavior; capers.

An'ti·christ" (an'tē-krīst") *n.* the personification of the force of evil.

an·tic'i·pate" (an-tis'ə-pāt") *v.t.* **1**, expect; foresee. **2**, realize beforehand. **3**, be ahead of time or of another; forestall. —*an·tic'i·pa'tion, n.* —*an·tic'i·pa·to'ry* (-tôr'ē) *adj.*

an"ti·cli'max (an"ti-klī'maks) *n.* an abrupt descent in style or subject from lofty ideas or expression; ludicrous contrast with what has preceded. —*an"ti·cli·mac'tic* (-klī-mak'tik) *adj.*

an'ti·dote" (an'ti-dōt") *n.* **1**, a drug that counteracts the effect of a poison. **2**, any remedy against disease or injurious influence.

an'ti·freeze" (an'tē-frēz") *n.* a substance that reduces the freezing point of water.

an"ti·his'ta·mine" (an"tē-his'tə-mēn") *n.* a medicine used in treatment of allergic reactions.

an"ti·log'a·rithm (an"tē-log'ə-rith-əm) *n.* the number of which a given number is the logarithm.

an"ti·mo"ny (an'tə-mō"nē) *n.* a metallic chemical element, no. 51, symbol Sb.

an"ti·pas'to (än'tē-päs'tō) *n.* (*It.*) an appetizer; hors d'oeuvres.

an·tip'a·thy (an-tip'ə-thē) *n.* dislike. —*an"ti·pa·thet'ic* (an"tē-pə-thet'ik) *adj.* —*an"ti·pa·thet'i·cal·ly, adv.*

an·tiph'o·ny (an-tif'ə-nē) *n.* **1**, alternate singing by two parts of a choir. **2**, a composition arranged to be so chanted. —*an·tiph'o·nal, adj.*

an·tip'o·des (an-tip'ə-dēz) *n.pl.*

places diametrically opposite each other on the earth. —*an·tip'o·dal, adj.*

an"ti·quar"y (an'ti-kwâr"ē) *n.* a collector of or expert on antiques or matters ancient. —*an"ti·quar'i·an* (-kwâr'ē-ən) *n. & adj.*

an"ti·quat·ed (an'ti-kwā-tid) *adj.* grown old; obsolete.

an·tique' (an-tēk') *adj.* belonging to former times; old-fashioned. —*n.* a relic of antiquity.

an·tiq'ui·ty (an-tik'wə-tē) *n.* **1**, ancient times; former ages. **2**, the quality of being ancient.

an"ti·Se·mit'ic (an"tē-sə-mit'ik) *adj.* prejudiced against Jews. —*an"ti·Sem'ite* (-sem'īt) *n.*

an"ti·sep'tic (an"ti-sep'tik) *adj. & n.* destructive of microörganisms that cause disease. —*an"ti·sep'ti·cal·ly, adv.* —*an"ti·sep'sis, n.*

an"ti·so'cial (an"tē-sō'shəl) *adj.* not inclined to seek or enjoy the company of others.

an·tith'e·sis (an-tith'ə-sis) *n.* [*pl.* -ses (-sēz)] **1**, direct opposition; marked contrast. **2**, what is directly opposite. —*an"ti·thet'i·cal* (an"ti-thet'i-kəl) *adj.*

an"ti·tox'in (an"ti-tok'sin) *n.* a substance that counteracts a toxin or poison.

ant'ler (ant'lər) *n.* one of the branching horns of an animal of the deer family.

an'to·nym (an'tə-nim) *n.* a word meaning exactly the opposite of a given word.

an'trum (an'trəm) *n.* a cavity; hole.

a'nus (ā'nəs) *n.* the posterior opening of the alimentary canal.

an'vil (an'vəl) *n.* **1**, a heavy iron block on which metalwork is laid for beating. **2**, a bone of the ear.

anx·i'e·ty (ang-zī'ə-tē) *n.* **1**, uneasiness of mind from care or apprehension. **2**, concern or solicitude.

anx'ious (ank'shəs) *adj.* **1**, full of anxiety; worried. **2**, earnestly desirous. —*anx'ious·ness, n.*

an'y (en'ē) *adj. & pron.* one, or some, indiscriminately from a larger number. —*adv.* to whatever extent; in whatever degree; at all.

an'y·bod"y *pron.* any person.

an'y·how" *adv.* **1**, in any way. **2**, in any case.

an'y·one" *pron.* any person.

an'y·thing" *pron.* any thing, fact, or deed.

an'y·way" *adv.* **1**, in any way. **2**, in any case; nevertheless.

an'y·where" *adv.* in or to any place.

a·or'ta (ā-ôr'tə) *n.* the chief artery of the human body, issuing from the heart.

a·pace' (ə-pās') *adv.* speedily.

a·pache' *n.* **1,** (ə-päsh') (*Fr.*) a Parisian rowdy or gangster. **2,** (ə-pach'ē) (*cap.*) a certain American Indian tribe or member of it.

a·part' (ə-pärt') *adv.* **1,** with parts separated; in pieces. **2,** at one side; separately from: aside from.

A·part'heid" (ə-pärt'hāt") *n.* segregation of races in South Africa.

a·part'ment (ə-pärt'mənt) *n.* **1,** a set of rooms designed for tenancy as a unit. **2,** a single room.

ap'a·thet'ic (ap'ə-thet'ik) *adj.* lacking feeling; expressing or being apathy. —**ap'a·thet'i·cal·ly,** *adv.*

ap'a·thy (ap'ə-thē) *n.* lack of feeling; absence of emotion; indifference.

ape (āp) *n.* **1,** any of several anthropoid animals, the gorilla, chimpanzee, orangutan, or gibbon. **2,** an imitator; a mimic. —*v.t.* imitate.

ap'er·ture (ap'ər-chûr) *n.* an opening; hole; gap.

a'pex (ā'peks) *n.* the highest point of anything; top; peak; climax.

a·pha'sia (ə-fā'zhə) *n.* loss of the faculty of understanding written or spoken language. —**a·pha'sic,** *adj.*

a'phid (ā'fid) *n.* a plant louse.

aph'o·rism (af'ə-riz-əm) *n.* a concise statement of a principle.

aph"ro·dis'i·ac (af"rə-diz'ē-ak) *adj. & n.* stimulating sexual desire.

a'pi·ar''y (ā'pē-ār"ē) *n.* a place where bees are kept.

ap'i·cal (ap'ə-kəl) *adj.* being or pert. to an apex.

a·piece' (ə-pēs') *adv.* for each.

ap'ish (ā'pish) *adj.* apelike.

a·plomb' (ə-plom') *n.* self-confidence; assurance of manner.

ap'o- *pref.* from; away from.

a·poc'a·lypse (ə-pok'ə-lips) *n.* **1,** a revelation. **2,** (*cap.*) the book Revelation in the New Testament of the Bible. —**a·poc'a·lyp'tic** (-lip'tik) *adj.* —**a·poc'a·lyp'ti·cal·ly,** *adv.*

A·poc'ry·pha (ə-pok'rə-fə) *n. pl.* certain books of the Old Testament whose canonicity is disputed.

a·poc'ry·phal (ə-pok'rə-fəl) *adj.* **1,** of doubtful authorship or authenticity. **2,** spurious.

ap'o·gee (ap'ə-jē) *n.* the point of greatest distance, in an orbit.

a·pol'o·get'ic (ə-pol"ə-jet'ik) *adj.* expressing regret; constituting an apology. —**a·pol'o·get'i·cal·ly,** *adv.*

a·pol'o·gist (ə-pol'ə-jist) *n.* one who seeks to justify a cause.

a·pol'o·gize" (ə-pol'ə-jīz") *v.t.* offer an excuse; express regret.

a·pol'o·gy (ə-pol'ə-jē) *n.* **1,** an expression of regret for a slight or

---

injury. **2,** something said or written in defense or vindication.

ap'o·plex''y (ap'ə-plek"sē) *n.* sudden loss of consciousness or mobility from rupture of a blood vessel in the brain. —**ap'o·plec'tic,** *adj.* —**ap'o·plec'ti·cal·ly,** *adv.*

a·pos'ta·sy (ə-pos'tə-sē) *n.* total desertion of one's professed principles, faith, or party. —**a·pos'tate"** (-tāt") *n. & adj.*

a pos·te'ri·o'ri (ā'pos-tir'ē-ôr"ē) (*Lat.*) from later; after observing what has occurred.

a·pos'tle (ə-pos'əl) *n.* **1,** (*cap.*) one of the twelve disciples chosen by Christ to preach the gospel. **2,** a pioneer of any great moral reform. —**ap'os·tol'ic** (ap'ə-stol'ik) *adj.* —**ap'os·tol'i·cal·ly,** *adv.*

a·pos'tro·phe (ə-pos'trə-fē) *n.* **1,** a mark of punctuation (') indicating the omission of one or more letters. **2,** a direct address to a person or persons, interpolated in a speech or writing. —**a·pos'tro·phize"** (-fīz") *v.t.*

a·poth'e·car''y (ə-poth'ə-ker"ē) *n.* one who deals in drugs; pharmacist.

ap'o·thegm (ap'ə-them) *n.* a short, pithy, instructive saying; a maxim.

a·poth"e·o'sis (ə-poth"ē-ō'sis) *n.* [*pl.* **-ses** (-sēz)] glorified personification of a principle or idea.

ap·pall' (ə-pâl') *v.t.* fill with fear or horror. Also, **ap·pal'.**

ap"pa·ra'tus (ap"ə-rā'təs) *n.* all the equipment used for some purpose.

ap·par'el (ə-par'əl) *n.* **1,** clothing, esp. outer garments. **2,** outward aspect; guise. —*v.t.* clothe.

ap·par'ent (ə-par'ənt) *adj.* **1,** in plain view; capable of being clearly perceived; obvious. **2,** seeming in appearance, not necessarily real.

ap"pa·ri'tion (ap"ə-rish'ən) *n.* a ghostly appearance; specter; phantom.

ap·peal' (ə-pēl') *v.i.* **1,** call for aid, sympathy, or mercy; make an earnest entreaty. **2,** resort. **3,** be attractive; excite interest. —*v.i. & t.* (*Law*) apply for review to a higher court. —*n.* **1,** a call or entreaty for aid, etc. **2,** attractiveness. **3,** (*Law*) application for review. —**ap·peal'ing,** *adj.* arousing admiration or sympathy.

ap·pear' (ə-pir') *v.i.* **1,** become visible. **2,** seem to be. **3,** be known; be obvious. **4,** come into public view; be published. **5,** (*Law*) come formally before a tribunal.

ap·pear'ance (-əns) *n.* **1,** act of appearing. **2,** outward look; aspect; semblance. **3,** a coming to a place; presence. **4,** (*pl.*) indications; circumstances.

ap·pease' (ə-pēz') *v.t.* **1,** allay (anger or strife); placate, esp. by concession. **2,** satisfy (an appetite or demand). —**ap·pease'ment,** *n.* act of

---

tub, cūte, pŭll; label; oil, owl; go, chip, she, thin, *then*, sing, ink; *see p. 6*

appeasing; partial submission to a threatening nation.

ap·pel'lant (ə-pel'ənt) n. one who appeals. —adj. appellate.

ap·pel'late (-ət) adj. (Law) 1, concerned with an appeal. 2, having the duty to hear appeals.

ap"pel·la'tion (ap"ə-lā'shən) n. 1, the word by which a thing or person is called; name; title. 2, the act of naming.

ap·pend' (ə-pend') v.t. add; attach; subjoin.

ap·pend'age (-ij) n. an added and subordinate part.

ap"pen·dec'to·my (ap"ən-dek'tə-mē) n. removal of the vermiform appendix.

ap·pen"di·ci'tis (a-pen"də-sī'tis) n. (Pathol.) inflammation of the vermiform appendix.

ap·pen'dix (ə-pen'diks) n. [pl. -dix·es, -di·ces" (-də-sēz")] a section added but not essential to a document or book. —vermiform appendix, a sac attached to the human intestine.

ap"per·tain' (ap"ər-tān') v.i. belong as a part or member; belong by association or normal relation.

ap'pe·tite' (ap'ə-tīt") n. 1, craving for food. 2, any strong desire. 3, inclination to satisfy a want.

ap'pe·tiz"er (ap'ə-tīz"ər) n. a snack to whet the appetite.

ap'pe·tiz"ing adj. appealing to the appetite or taste.

ap·plaud' (ə-plâd') v.t. & i. 1, show approval of; commend; praise. 2, acclaim by clapping the hands.

ap·plause' (ə-plâz') n. 1, act of applauding. 2, a loud expression of approval, as by handclapping.

ap'ple (ap'əl) n. an edible fruit, or the tree on which it grows.

ap'ple·sauce" n. 1, a sauce of boiled apples. 2, (Slang) nonsense.

ap·pli'ance (ə-plī'əns) n. 1, a tool or utensil for a particular use. 2, act of applying or putting to use.

ap'pli·ca·ble (ap'li-kə-bəl) adj. capable of being applied; suitable; relevant. —ap"pli·ca·bil'i·ty, n.

Apple

ap'pli·cant (ap'li-kənt) n. one who applies, as for a job.

ap"pli·ca'tion (ap"li-kā'shən) n. 1, the act of applying. 2, something applied, as a salve. 3, relevance; bearing. 4, a request or petition. 5, close attention; diligence.

ap'pli·ca"tor (ap'li-kā"tər) n. a utensil for applying something.

ap"pli·qué (ap"li-kā') adj. added by sewing, pasting, cementing, etc. —n. ornamentation so added.

ap·ply' (ə-plī') v.t. 1, bring into physical contact; lay on. 2, put to use; bring into operation. 3, devote to a particular purpose. 4, give earnestly. —v.i. 1, be applicable or pertinent. 2, request or appeal.

ap·point' (ə-point') v.t. 1, nominate or assign; designate. 2, fix by decree; prescribe. 3, provide with necessary equipment; rig. —ap·poin'tive, adj. done or filled by appointment.

ap·point'ment (ə-point'mənt) n. 1, the act of appointing. 2, an office held by a person appointed. 3, an agreement to meet at a stipulated time. 4, (pl.) furnishings; equipment.

ap·por'tion (ə-pôr'shən) v.t. divide and allot proportionally. —ap·por'tion·ment, n.

ap'po·site (ap'ə-zit) adj. applicable; suitable; well-adapted. —ap"po·si'tion, n.

ap·prais'al (ə-prā'zəl) n. act or result of appraising; estimate.

ap·praise' (ə-prāz') v.t. estimate the quality or value of, esp. in money. —ap·prais'er, n. one who estimates the value of property.

ap·pre'ci·a·ble (ə-prē'shə-ə-bəl) adj. capable of being estimated; large or intense enough to be perceived.

ap·pre'ci·ate' (ə-prē'shē-āt') v.t. 1, recognize the worth of; esteem duly. 2, be fully conscious of. 3, raise in value. —v.i. rise in value. —ap·pre"ci·a'tion, n. —ap·pre'ci·a·tive, adj. duly grateful.

ap"pre·hend' (ap"rē-hend') v.t. 1, seize physically; take into custody; arrest. 2, grasp mentally; understand. 3, have fear of; anticipate.

ap"pre·hen'sion (ap"rē-hen'shən) n. 1, act of apprehending. 2, result of apprehending; arrest; understanding.

ap"pre·hen'sive (-siv) adj. uneasy or fearful about future events. —ap"pre·hen'sive·ness, n.

ap·pren'tice (ə-pren'tis) n. one who works under tutelage to learn a trade. —ap·pren'tice·ship, n.

ap·prise' (ə-prīz') v.t. give notice; inform.

ap·proach' (ə-prōch') v.t. & i. 1, draw near to; advance toward. 2, be similar to in quality or degree. 3, make advances or proposals to. —n. 1, the act of approaching. 2, method or means of access; avenue. 3, nearness; proximity.

ap"pro·ba'tion (ap"rə-bā'shən) n. approval; commendation.

ap·pro'pri·ate (ə-prō'prē-āt) *v.t.* 1, allot (money) for a specific use. 2, take possession of. —*adj.* (-ət) suitable; applicable. —**ap·pro'pri·ate·ness,** *n.*

ap·pro'pri·a'tion (-ā'shən) *n.* 1, money set aside for a specific purpose. 2, act of appropriating.

ap·prov'al (ə-proov'əl) *n.* act or effect of approving; commendation; approbation.

ap·prove' (ə-proov') *v.t.* 1, pronounce good; admit the propriety or excellence of. 2, sanction officially; ratify. —*v.i.* judge favorably; be pleased.

ap·prox'i·mate (ə-prok'sə-mət) *adj.* 1, nearly correct or precise. 2, close together; very similar in form or degree. —*v.i.* (-māt') be nearly like. —**ap·prox'i·mate·ly,** *adv.* nearly; about. —**ap·prox'i·ma'tion,** *n.*

ap·pur'te·nance (ə-pēr'tə-nəns) *n.* 1, (*Law*) a right or privilege belonging to a property. 2, an accessory part; appendage. 3, (*pl.*) furnishings; apparatus. —**ap·pur'te·nant,** *adj.*

a'pri·cot' (ā'prə-kot') *n.* 1, the fruit of a tree resembling the plum and peach. 2, the apricot tree. 3, a light orange color.

A'pril (ā'prəl) *n.* the fourth month of the year.

a pri·o'ri (ā'prē-ôr'ē) (*Lat.*) from before; before knowing what will occur.

a'pron (ā'prən) *n.* 1, an outer garment worn to protect the clothing. 2, any protective shield or flange.

ap'ro·pos' (ap'rə-pō') *adv.* 1, to the purpose; opportunely. 2, (with *of*) in reference to.—*adj.* appropriate.

apse (aps) *n.* an alcove or recess, usually semicircular and vaulted.

apt *adj.* 1, suited to its purpose. 2, quick in learning. 3, having a tendency; inclined. —**apt'ness,** *n.*

ap'ti·tude (ap'ti-tood) *n.* fitness; innate ability.

aq'ua·ma·rine' (ak'wə-mə-rēn') *n.* 1, a bluish-green color. 2, semiprecious stone.

aq'ua·plane' (ak'wə-plān') *n.* a board towed behind a motorboat for carrying a surf-rider. —*v.i.* ride on such a board.

a·quar'i·um (ə-kwâr'ē-əm) *n.* a tank or building in which are kept living aquatic animals and plants.

A·quar'i·us (ə-kwâr'ē-əs) *n.* a constellation, the Water Bearer (see *zodiac*).

a·quat'ic (ə-kwat'ik) *adj.* 1, pert. to water. 2, living or done in water. —**a·quat'i·cal·ly,** *adv.*

aq'ua·tint (ak'wə-tint) *n.* 1, a method of engraving. 2, a print so made.

aq'ue·duct' (ak'wi-dukt') *n.* an artificial channel or conduit for con-

ducting water from one place to another.

a'que·ous (ā'kwē-əs) *adj.* like water; containing or formed by water.

aq'ui·line (ak'wə-lin) *adj.* 1, pert. to the eagle. 2, (of a nose) like an eagle's beak.

ar'a·besque' (ar'ə-besk') *n.* a style of fanciful decoration.

Ar'a·bic (ar'ə-bik) *adj.* pert. to Arabia, or its language, or to *Arabic numerals:* 0, 1, 2, 3, etc.

Arabesque

ar'a·ble (ar'ə-bəl) *adj.* fit for plowing and tillage. —**ar'a·bil'i·ty,** *n.*

Ar·a·ma'ic (ar-ə-mā'ik) *n. & adj.* a Semitic language, used by Jesus.

ar'bi·ter (är'bi-tər) *n.* 1, one who has power to judge and decide. 2, arbitrator; umpire.

ar'bi·trar'y (är'brə-trâr'ē) *adj.* 1, not regulated by fixed rule or law. 2, despotic. 3, capricious; unreasonable. —**ar'bi·trar'i·ness,** *n.*

ar'bi·trate' (är'bi-trāt') *v.t.* 1, act as a formal umpire between contestants; mediate. 2, submit to arbitration. —**ar'bi·tra'tion,** *n.* settlement of a dispute by lay judges, out of court. —**ar'bi·tra'tor,** *n.*

ar'bor (är'bər) *n.* 1, a bower formed by foliage trained over a lattice. 2, a shaft or supporting bar in a machine. Also, ar'bour. —**ar·bo're·al** (-bôr'ē-əl) *adj.* pert. to or living in trees.

arbor vi'tae (vī'tē) an evergreen tree; the red cedar.

ar·bu'tus (är-bū'təs) *n.* 1, any of several evergreen shrubs with scarlet berries. 2, a creeping vine with fragrant white and pink flowers.

arc (ärk) *n.* 1, a segment of a circle. 2, any bow-shaped curve. 3, a spark or luminescence caused by a flow of current across a gap between two electrical terminals.

ar·cade' (är-kād') *n.* a roofed passageway; a covered avenue lined with shops.

arch (ärch) *n.* 1, a building structure in the shape of a curve concave from below, supported at its extremities. 2, anything that resembles an arch. —*v.t.* 1, span with an arch. 2, curve like an arch. —*adj.* 1, chief; preëminent. 2, sly; roguish.

arch- *pref.* first; chief.

ar'chae·ol'o·gy (är'kē-ol'ə-jē) *n.* the study of past cultures through their surviving relics. —**ar'chae·o·log'i·cal,** *adj.* —**ar'chae·ol'o·gist,** *n.*

ar·cha'ic (är-kā'ik) *adj.* **1.** of an earlier period; antiquated. **2.** (*Lexic.*) not in current usage, but familiar in surviving earlier literature.

arch'an"gel (ärk'-) *n.* a chief angel.

arch'bish"op (ärch'-) *n.* a bishop of highest rank.

arch'duke' (ärch'-) *n.* title of former Austrian royal princes.

arch'er (är'chər) *n.* **1.** one who uses a bow and arrow. **2.** (*cap.*) the constellation of Sagittarius. —**arch'er·y** (-ē) *n.*

ar'che·type" (är'ki-tīp") *n.* an original model; prototype.

ar"chi·pel'a·go' (är"kə-pel'ə-gō") *n.* a group of many islands.

ar'chi·tect' (är'kə-tekt') *n.* **1.** one who designs buildings. **2.** the planner or maker of anything.

ar"chi·tec'ture (-tek'chər) *n.* **1.** the designing of buildings. **2.** style of building. —**ar"chi·tec'tur·al,** *adj.*

ar'chives (är'kīvz) *n.pl.* **1.** documents preserved for their political or historical value. **2.** the place where such documents are kept.

arch'way' (ärch'wā) *n.* an entrance or passage under an arch.

arc'tic (ärk'tik) *adj.* near or at the North Pole. —*n.* (*cap.*) the North Polar regions.

ar'dent (är'dənt) *adj.* **1.** fervent in feeling; intense; passionate. **2.** burning; fiery; glowing. —**ar'den·cy,** *n.*

ar'dor (är'dər) *n.* **1.** intensity of feeling; zeal; passion. **2.** fiery heat. Also, **ar'dour.**

ar'du·ous (är'dū-əs) *adj.* requiring prolonged effort; wearisome. —**ar'du·ous·ness,** *n.*

are (är) *v.* 1st person pl. of *be.*

ar'e·a (är'ē-ə) *n.* **1.** amount of surface; extent in general; scope. **2.** a region or tract.

a·re'na (ə-rē'nə) *n.* the enclosure in which an athletic contest is held.

aren't (ärnt) *contraction* are not.

ar'gent (är'jənt) *adj.* like silver, esp. in color.

ar'gon (är'gon) *n.* a colorless, odorless, inert gaseous element present in air, no. 18, symbol A.

ar'go·sy (är'gə-sē) *n.* a merchant vessel or fleet carrying a rich cargo.

ar'got (är'gō) *n.* the slang or cant of a particular class, as of thieves.

ar'gue (är'gū) *v.i.* engage in intellectual dispute. —*v.t.* **1.** state reasons for and against; discuss. **2.** maintain; seek to prove.

ar'gu·ment (är'gū-mənt) *n.* **1.** discussion of a controversial nature; debate. **2.** a statement or chain of reasoning tending to induce belief. **3.** an abstract or summary of a writing or speech. —**ar"gu·men·ta'tion,** *n.*

ar·gu·men'ta·tive (är-gyə-men'tə-tiv) *adj.* disposed to argue; contentious.

ar'gy·rol' (är'ji-röl") *n.* (*T.N.*) an antiseptic containing silver.

a'ri·a (ä'rē-ə) *n.* **1.** a vocal solo, with or without accompaniment. **2.** any tune.

ar'id *adj.* **1.** lacking moisture; parched with heat. **2.** uninteresting. —**a·rid'i·ty** (ə-rid'ə-tē) *n.*

Ar'i·es (är'ēz) *n.* a northern constellation, the Ram (see *zodiac*).

a·rise' (ə-rīz') *v.i.* [a·rose', a·ris'en (-riz'ən)] **1.** come into being or action. **2.** get up; move upward.

ar"is·toc'ra·cy (är"is-tok'rə-sē) *n.* **1.** government by a privileged upper class. **2.** any class having special privileges or considered superior.

a·ris'to·crat (ə-ris'tə-krat) *n.* a member of the aristocracy, or one who behaves like a nobleman. —**a·ris"to·crat'ic,** *adj.* —**a·ris"to·crat'i·cal·ly,** *adv.*

a·rith'me·tic (ə-rith'mə-tik) *n.* the art of computation, the most elementary branch of mathematics. —**a·rith"me·ti'cian** (-tish'ən) *n.*

ar"ith·met'i·cal (ar"ith-met'i-kəl) *adj.* of or by arithmetic. Also, **ar"ith·met'ic.**

ark (ärk) *n.* **1.** the vessel built by Noah to save those chosen from the Flood; a large boat or building. **2.** the chest containing the Covenant (between God and the Jews).

arm (ärm) *n.* **1.** the upper limb of the human body, extending from shoulder to hand. **2.** anything like an arm in form or position. **3.** range of authority; power. **4.** a branch, esp. of military forces. **5.** (usually *pl.*) a weapon. —*v.t.* & *i.* equip with arms; provide what is necessary for security or defense.

ar·ma'da (är-mä'də) *n.* a fleet of warships.

ar"ma·dil'lo (är"mə-dil'ō) *n.* [*pl.* -los] a So. and Central Amer. mammal having hard scales.

Armadillo

ar'ma·ment (är'mə-mənt) *n.* **1.** the totality of weapons with which a military unit is armed. **2.** the act of arming.

ar'ma·ture (är'mə-chūr) *n.* **1.** defensive armor; protective covering. **2.** a supporting or connecting member.

arm'chair' n. a chair with side arms.

arm'ful' n. 1, as much as the arms can hold. 2, (Colloq.) a stout or shapely girl.

ar'mi·stice (är'mi-stis) n. a temporary suspension of hostilities; truce.

ar'mor (är'mər) n. 1, any covering worn for protection against offensive weapons. 2, anything that protects.

ar·mor'i·al (är-mōr'ē-əl) adj. pert· to heraldic bearings.

ar'mor·y (är'mə-rē) n. a place for storing or manufacturing weapons.

arm'pit' n. the hollow under the arm at the shoulder.

ar'my (är'mē) n. 1, a large body of men trained for war on land, excluding naval and (usually) air forces. 2, any large body of persons.

ar'ni·ca (är'ni-kə) n. a medicinal tincture used on wounds and bruises.

a·ro'ma (ə-rō'mə) n. an agreeable odor; fragrance. —ar'o·mat'ic (ar'ə-mat'ik) adj. —ar'o·mat'i·cal·ly, adv.

a·round' (ə-rownd') prep. & adv. 1, on all sides; encircling. 2, from place to place; here and there. 3, (Colloq.) near at hand; approximately. 4, rotating.

a·rouse' (ə-rowz') v.t. excite into action; awaken; put in motion.

ar·peg'gi·o (är-pej'yō) n. (Music) the sounding of the notes of a chord in succession instead of simultaneously.

ar·raign' (ə-rān') v.t. 1, (Law) call into court to answer a charge. 2, accuse. —ar·raign'ment, n.

ar·range' (ə-rānj') v.t. 1, put in proper order. 2, come to an agreement; settle. 3, make preparation; plan. 4, (Music) adapt for performance by particular voices or instruments. —ar·range'ment, n.

ar'rant (ar'ənt) adj. 1, manifest; notorious. 2, downright; thorough.

ar·ray' (ə-rā') n. 1, regular order or arrangement; an orderly assemblage. 2, a display. 3, raiment or apparel. —v.t. 1, place in order or in a display. 2, dress; bedeck.

ar·rears' (ə-rirz') n.pl. that which is overdue, as an unpaid debt.

ar·rest' (ə-rest') v.t. 1, take (a person) into custody; seize; capture. 2, stop forcibly; check or hinder. —n. 1, detention under legal warrant. 2, capture; restraint; stoppage. —ar·rest'ing, adj. striking.

ar·riv'al (ə-rī'vəl) n. 1, the act, fact, or time of arriving at a place. 2, a person or thing that arrives.

ar·rive' (ə-rīv') v.i. 1, reach a certain point. 2, come; occur. 3, attain a position of eminence or success.

ar'ro·gant (ar'ə-gənt) adj. aggressively haughty. —ar'ro·gance, n.

ar'ro·gate' (ar'ə-gāt') v.t. assume, demand, or appropriate unduly or presumptuously. —ar'ro·ga'tion, n.

ar'row (ar'ō) n. 1, a rodlike missile weapon to be shot from a bow. 2, an angular sign, like the head of an arrow, used to point direction.

ar'row·head' (-hed') n. 1, a hard, pointed tip for an arrow. 2, a wedge-shaped mark.

ar·roy'o (ə-roi'ō) n. a small gulch or ravine.

ar'se·nal (är'sə-nəl) n. a manufactory or storehouse for military arms and supplies.

ar'se·nic (är'sə-nik) n. 1, a volatile chemical element, no. 33, symbol As. 2, a poison derived therefrom. —ar·sen'i·cal (-sen'i-kəl) adj.

ar'son (är'sən) n. the malicious burning of a building.

art (ärt) n. 1, any system of rules and traditional methods for the practice of a craft, trade, or profession; the application of knowledge and skill. 2, works designed to give intellectual pleasure, as music, sculpture, and esp. pictorial representation. 3, skillful workmanship. 4, cunning; guile.

ar·te'ri·o·scle·ro'sis (är-tir'ē-ō-skle-rō'sis) n. a thickening of the blood vessels.

ar'ter·y (är'tə-rē) n. 1, any of the large vessels that convey blood from the heart to another part of the body. 2, a main channel of conveyance or transportation. —ar·te'ri·al (-tir'ē-əl) adj.

ar·te'sian well (är-tē'zhən) a deep well in which water rises by subsurface pressure.

art'ful (ärt'fəl) adj. 1, crafty; wily· 2, skillful. —art'ful·ness, n.

ar·thri'tis (är-thrī'tis) n. inflammation of a joint. —ar·thrit'ic (-thrit'ik) adj.

ar'ti·choke' (är'ti-chōk') n. a thistlelike plant with an edible head.

ar'ti·cle (är'tə-kəl) n. 1, a separate item; a separate portion of anything. 2, a literary composition on a specific topic. 3, (Gram.) a word used before a noun, marking its application. —definite article, the. —indefinite article, a or an.

ar·tic'u·late' (är-tik'ū-lāt') v.t. & i. 1, say or speak distinctly, with clear separation of syllables. 2, unite by joints. —adj. (-lət) 1, able to speak; expressive. 2, having joints; segmented. 3, clear; distinct. —ar·tic'u·la'tion, n.

ar'ti·fice (är'tə-fis) n: 1, a crafty device. 2, trickery.

ar'ti·fi'cial (är'tə-fish'əl) adj. 1, man-made; contrived by human skill. 2, assumed; pretended; fictitious. 3, full of affectation. —ar'ti·fi'ci·al'i·ty (är'ti-fish'ē-al'ə-tē) n.

artificial satellite any object or device propelled by rockets beyond the atmosphere and caused to revolve in an orbit.

ar·til·ler·y (är-til′ə-rē) *n.* 1, all heavy, mounted firearms; cannons. 2, troops servicing such firearms.

ar·ti·san (är′tə-zən) *n.* one skilled in an industrial craft.

art·ist (är′tist) 1, one who pursues a pictorial art, esp. a painter. 2, a performer in an art of entertainment. 3, a person of special skill. —ar·tis′tic, *adj.* —ar·tis′ti·cal·ly, *adv.* —art′ist·ry (-rē) *n.*

art·less (ärt′ləs) *adj.* simple and natural; free from guile; sincere. —art′less·ness, *n.*

-ar·y (er-ē) *suf.* forming adjectives: pertaining to.

Ar′yan (är′yən) *adj. & n.* 1, European or Asiatic (in race). 2, (incorrectly) gentile; Nordic. Also, **Ar′i·an** (ar′ē-ən).

as (az) *adv.* in that degree; to that extent; so far. —*conj.* 1, to the same degree or extent; in similar manner. 2, at the same time. 3, because. 4, for example. —*pron.* that or who.

as″a·fet′i·da (as″ə-fet′i-də) *n.* a herb or a pungent drug made from it.

as·bes′tos (az-bes′təs) *n.* a mineral used for fireproofing.

as·cend (ə-send′) *v.i.* go upward; rise. —*v.t.* climb; mount.

as·cend′ant (ə-sen′dənt) *adj.* 1, rising. 2, dominant. —*n.* (with *the*) superiority. —as·cend′an·cy, *n.*

as·cen′sion (ə-sen′shən) *n.* a rising, esp. (*cap.*) of Christ into heaven.

as·cent (ə-sent′) *n.* 1, act of ascending; a climbing or moving upward; rise. 2, an upward slope.

as″cer·tain′ (as″ər-tān′) *v.t.* find out by examination; determine. —as″cer·tain′ment, *n.*

as·cet′ic (ə-set′ik) *adj.* extreme in self-restraint or self-denial. —*n.* a recluse or hermit. —as·cet′i·cal·ly, *adv.* —as·cet′i·cism (-i-siz-əm) *n.*

a·scor′bic acid (ə-skôr′bik) vitamin O, used to combat scurvy.

as′cot (as′kət) *n.* a broad necktie folded like a scarf.

as·cribe (ə-skrīb′) *v.t.* attribute to a cause or source; impute. —as·crip′tion (ə-skrip′shən) *n.*

a·sep′tic (ā-sep′tik) *adj.* free of germs that cause disease or decay. —a·sep′ti·cal·ly, *adv.*

a·sex′u·al (ā-sek′shoo-əl) *adj.* not having or involving sex.

ash *n.* 1, the incombustible residue that remains after burning. 2, (*pl.*) human remains. 3, a hardwood tree. —**ash tray**, a dish for tobacco ashes.

a·shamed (ə-shāmd′) *adj.* feeling guilty; abashed.

ash′en (ash′ən) *adj.* 1, pale; gray. 2, pert. to the ash tree.

a·shore (ə-shôr′) *adj.* to or on land, not water.

Ash Wednesday the Wednesday on which Lent begins.

ash′y (ash′ē) *adj.* pale as ashes. —ash′i·ness, *n.*

A′si·at′ic (ā″zhē-at′ik) *adj.* pert. to Asia or its inhabitants. —*n.* a native of Asia. Also, **A′sian** (ā′zhən). —**Asiatic flu** or **Asian flu**, a mild form of influenza, usually lasting 5 days.

a·side (ə-sīd′) *adv.* 1, on or to one side; apart or separately. 2, out of consideration or regard. —*n.* (*Stage*) ~~a private remark to the audience.~~

as″i·nine″ (as′ə-nīn″) *adj.* obtusively silly; stupid. —as″i·nin′i·ty (-nin′ə-tē) *n.*

ask (ȧsk) *v.t. & i.* 1, put a question (to); interrogate. 2, seek to obtain; request. 3, inquire (about). 4, invite.

a·skance′ (ə-skans′) *adv.* distrustfully; from the side, as a glance.

a·skew′ (ə-skū′) *adv.* in an oblique position; out of line; awry.

a·slant′ (ə-slȧnt′) *adj. & adv.* slanting; oblique.

a·sleep′ (ə-slēp′) *adv. & adj.* 1, sleeping; numb. 2, inactive.

asp *n.* a poisonous snake.

as·par′a·gus (ə-spar′ə-gəs) *n.* a plant having edible shoots.

as′pect (as′pekt) *n.* 1, one of the ways in which a thing may be viewed or contemplated. 2, outward appearance; facial expression. 3, view.

as′pen (as′pən) *adj.* tremulous; quivering. —*n.* a poplar tree.

as·per′i·ty (as-per′ə-tē) *n.* harshness of temper; severity.

as·perse′ (ə-spērs′) *v.t.* make false or foul charges against; slander. —as·per′sion (-zhən) *n.*

as′phalt (as′fȧlt) *n.* a bituminous substance used for paving, etc.

as′pho·del (as′fə-del) *n.* a plant of the lily family.

as·phyx′i·a (as-fik′sē-ə) *n.* extreme lack of oxygen; suffocation.

as·phyx′i·ate″ (as-fiks′ē-āt″) *v.t. & i.* kill or die by deprivation of oxygen; suffocate. —as·phyx″i·a′tion, *n.*

as′pic (as′pik) *n.* a clear jelly made of meat or vegetables.

as′pi·rate″ (as′pə-rāt″) *v.t.* pronounce with an audible emission of breath. —*n. & adj.* (-rət) the sound represented by h.

as″pi·ra′tion (as″pə-rā′shən) *n.* 1, desire; ambition. 2, breathing.

as·pire′ (ə-spīr′) *v.i.* be ardently desirous, esp. for something spiritual. —as·pir′ant, *n.*

as'pi·rin (as'pə-rin) *n.* a drug used to relieve pain and reduce fever.

ass (as) *n.* 1, a horselike beast of burden; the donkey. 2, a stupid person; a fool.

as·sail' (ə-sāl') *v.t.* attack; belabor with entreaties or abuse. —**as·sail'ant**, *n.* attacker.

as·sas'sin (ə-sas'in) *n.* one who kills another by secret assault.

as·sas'si·nate'' (ə-sas'ə-nāt') *v.t.* kill violently and treacherously. —**as·sas''si·na'tion**, *n.*

as·sault' (ə-sâlt') *v.t.* attack by physical means; assail with argument, abuse. —*n.* an attack.

as·say' (ə-sā') *v.t.* test; analyze, esp. metallic ore.

as·sem'blage (ə-sem'blij) *n.* persons or things assembled.

as·sem'ble (ə-sem'bəl) *v.t.* 1, bring together in one place. 2, fit together. —*v.i.* come together; congregate.

as·sem'bly (ə-sem'blē) *n.* 1, act of bringing or coming together. 2, a group; congregation. 3, a legislative body.

as·sent' (ə-sent') *v.i.* express agreement or approval; concur. —*n.* (as'ent) agreement; acquiescence.

as·sert' (ə-sērt') *v.t.* 1, state as true; declare; aver. 2, claim and defend.

as·ser'tion (ə-sēr'shən) *n.* 1, act of asserting. 2, statement; claim; affirmation.

as·ser'tive (-tiv) *adj.* positive; overbearing. —**as·ser'tive·ness**, *n.*

as·sess' (ə-ses') *v.t.* 1, estimate the value of (property) as a basis for taxation. 2, impose a tax, charge or fine. —**as·sess'ment**, *n.* —**as·ses'sor**, *n.*

as'set (as'et) *n.* 1, anything advantageous. 2, (usually *pl.*) items of property available; total resources.

as·sev'er·ate'' (ə-sev'ə-rāt') *v.t.* aver solemnly and positively. —**as·sev''er·a'tion**, *n.*

as''si·du'i·ty (as''i-dū'ə-tē) *n.* quality of being assiduous; diligence.

as·sid'u·ous (ə-sij'oo-əs) *adj.* diligent; attentive; unremitting. —**as·sid'u·ous·ness**, *n.*

as·sign' (ə-sīn') *v.t.* 1, set apart; allot; transfer. 2, appoint, as to office or duties. 3, specify; designate; ascribe; refer. —*n.* (*Law*) [also, **as'sign·ee'** (as''ə-nē')] one to whom property is transferred.

as''sig·na'tion (as''ig-nā'shən) *n.* an appointment for an illicit love meeting.

as·sign'ment (-mənt) *n.* 1, act of assigning. 2, something assigned to be done; task; mission. 3, a document attesting to a transfer of interest.

as·sim'i·late'' (ə-sim'ə-lāt') *v.t.* 1, take in and incorporate; absorb and digest. 2, make similar; bring into conformity; adapt. —*v.i.* assimilate something. —**as·sim''i·la'tion**, *n.*

as·sist' (ə-sist') *v.t.* give help; aid; —*v.i.* be present; attend.

as·sist'ance (-əns) *n.* act of assisting; help; aid.

as·sist'ant (-ənt) *n.* a helper.

as·size' (ə-sīz') *n.* 1, a session of a legislature. 2, (*pl.*) a term of sittings of an English court.

as·so''ci·ate'' (ə-sō'shē-āt') *v.t.* 1, link together in some conceptual relationship. 2, join in partnership; combine in a union. —*v.i.* consort together; unite. —*n.* (-ət) 1, a partner, confederate, or companion. 2, anything that usually accompanies another. —*adj.* (-ət) 1, allied; concomitant. 2, having subordinate membership.

as·so''ci·a'tion (ə-sō''sē-ā'shən) *n.* 1, act of associating. 2, state of being associated; partnership; combination. 3, a society, league, etc.

as'so·nance (as'ə-nəns) *n.* resemblance in spoken sound, without strict rhyme. —**as'so·nant**, *adj.*

as·sort' (ə-sôrt') *v.t.* separate and distribute according to kind; classify; arrange.

as·sort'ment (-mənt) *n.* 1, act of assorting. 2, a diversified group or collection.

as·suage' (ə-swāj') *v.t.* lessen; mitigate; pacify. —**as·suage'ment**, *n.*

as·sume' (ə-soom') *v.t.* 1, take for granted without proof. 2, take upon oneself; undertake. 3, take the appearance of; pretend to possess. 4, take for oneself; appropriate.

as·sump'tion (ə-sum'shən) *n.* 1, act of assuming. 2, a supposition or hypothesis. 3, (*cap.*) bodily acceptance into heaven, esp. of the Virgin Mary.

as·sur'ance (ə-shûr'əns) *n.* 1, an earnest statement intended to give confidence. 2, freedom from doubt. 3, boldness; impudence. 4, a promise or pledge; surety. 5, insurance.

as·sure' (ə-shûr') *v.t.* 1, make sure or certain; make secure or stable. 2, make confident; convince.

as'ter (as'tər) *n.* any of many species of common flowers having colored petals around a yellow disk.

as'ter·isk (as'tər-isk) *n.* a symbol (*) used in printing.

a·stern' (ə-stērn') *adv. & adj.* (*Naut.*) to the rear; behind.

as'ter·oid'' (as'tər-oid') *n.* any of the many small planets located chiefly between Mars and Jupiter.

asth'ma (az'mə) *n.* a disorder of respiration, marked by labored breathing. —**asth·mat'ic** (-mat'ik) *adj.* —**asth·mat'i·cal·ly**, *adv.*

a·stig'ma·tism (ə-stig'mə-tiz-əm) *n.* defect of the eye producing imperfect focus. —**as″tig·mat′ic** (as″-tig-mat′ik) adj.

a·stir′ (ə-stẽr′) adv. & adj. on the move; active; out of bed.

as·ton′ish (ə-ston′ish) v.t. strike with wonder; surprise; amaze. —**as·ton′ish·ment,** n.

as·tound′ (ə-stownd′) v.t. strike with amazement; astonish greatly.

as′tral (as′trəl) adj. 1, pert. to the stars; stellar. 2, star-shaped.

a·stray′ (ə-strā′) adv. & adj. away from the proper path; wandering.

a·stride′ (ə-strīd′) prep. with one leg on each side of.

as·tringe′ (ə-strinj′) v.t. contract; draw together. —**as·trin′gen·cy,** n.

as·trin′gent (ə-strin′jənt) n. a substance used to contract the bodily tissues and so diminish discharge, as of blood. —adj. 1, tending to constrict. 2, severe; austere.

as′tro·labe″ (as′trə-lāb″) n. an astronomical instrument.

as·trol′o·gy (ə-strol′ə-jē) n. the study of the supposed influence of the stars and planets on human affairs. —**as·trol′o·ger** (-jər) n.

as′tro·naut (as′trə-nât) n. the pilot of a space ship.

as″tro·nom′i·cal (as″trə-nom′i-kəl) adj. 1, pert. to astronomy. 2, huge.

as·tron′o·my (ə-stron′ə-mē) n. the general science of all celestial bodies. —**as·tron′o·mer,** n.

as·tute′ (ə-stoot′) adj. keen in discernment; sagacious; cunning. —**as·tute′ness,** n.

a·sun′der (ə-sun′dər) adv. & adj. into separate parts; in a position apart.

a·sy′lum (ə-sī′ləm) n. 1, an institution for the care of the insane or afflicted. 2, any place of refuge.

at prep. used in many idiomatic phrases to imply local or relative position, direction of motion or activity, time, order, condition, circumstance, etc.

at′a·brine (at′ə-brin) n. (T.N.) a drug used against malaria.

at′a·vism (at′ə-viz-əm) n. reversion to distant hereditary traits or characteristics. —**at″a·vis′tic** (-vis′tik) adj. —**at″a·vis′ti·cal·ly,** adv.

ate (āt) v. pret. of eat.

at″el·ier′ (at′əl-yā′) n. a studio; workshop.

a′the·ism (ā′thē-iz-əm) n. the doctrine that there is no God. —**a′the·ist,** n. —**a″the·is′tic** (-is′tik) adj. —**a″the·is′ti·cal·ly,** adv.

ath″e·nae′um (ath″ə-nē′əm) n. an institution of learning; a library.

a·the′ni·um (a-thē′nē-əm) n. a chemical element, No. 99.

ath′lete (ath′lēt) n. one who engages in exercises of physical agility and strength. —**athlete′s foot,** a fungous skin disease.

ath·let′ic (ath-let′ik) adj. 1, like an athlete; strong. 2, pert. to athletics. —**ath·let′i·cal·ly,** adv.

ath·let′ics (-iks) n.pl. sports requiring physical prowess.

a·thwart′ (ə-thwôrt′) adv. & prep. 1, from side to side; crosswise. 2, perversely.

-a′tion (ā′shən) suf. forming nouns denoting the act, process, result, effect, or cause (of the root word).

at′las (at′ləs) n. a bound collection of maps.

at′mos·phere″ (at′məs-fir″) n. 1, the entire gaseous envelope of the earth; the air. 2, a unit of pressure, about 15 pounds per square inch. 3, environment; predominant aspect or mood. —**at″mos·pher′ic** (-fer′ik) adj. —**at″mos·pher′i·cal·ly,** adv.

at·oll′ (at′ol; ə-tol′) n. an island enclosing a lagoon.

at′om (at′əm) n. 1, the smallest particle having the properties of a specific chemical element. 2, anything extremely small. —**a·tom′ic** (ə-tom′ik) adj. —**a·tom′i·cal·ly,** adv.

atom bomb a bomb caused to explode by fission of the nuclei of its atoms. Also, **atomic bomb.**

Atom Bomb Explosion

at′om·ize″ (at′ə-mīz″) v.t. reduce to bits, esp. to spray. —**at′om·iz″er,** n. a device for reducing liquid to a fine spray.

a·tone′ (ə-tōn′) v.i. make amends for sin or error. —**a·tone′ment,** n.

a·top′ (ə-top′) adv. & prep. on top of.

a·tro′cious (ə-trō′shəs) adj. extremely wicked, criminal, or cruel; heinous. —**a·tro′cious·ness,** n.

a·troc′i·ty (ə-tros′ə-tē) n. an atrocious act; wickedness.

at′ro·phy (at′rə-fē) n. a wasting away or arrested development, from defective nutrition. —v.i. waste away.

at′ro·pine (at′rə-pin) n. a medicinal drug derived from belladonna.

at·tach′ (ə-tach′) v.t. 1, fasten; affix. 2, appoint; assign. 3, (Law) seize by legal authority. 4, bind by ties of affection or interest.

at·ta·ché′ (at″ə-shā′) *n.* a minor diplomatic officer.

at·tach′ment (ə-tach′mənt) *n.* **1**, act of attaching; state of being attached. **2**, something added, as a part to a machine.

at·tack′ (ə-tak′) *v.t.* **1**, fall upon with force or violence; assault; assail. **2**, begin to work upon; begin to affect. —*n.* **1**, a violent onset or assault, the offensive in a military conflict. **3**, a seizure or illness.

at·tain′ (ə-tān′) *v.t.* reach or achieve; accomplish.

at·tain′der (-dər) *n.* nullification of civil rights of one convicted of a high crime.

at·tain′ment (-mənt) *n.* **1**, act of attaining. **2**, an acquired personal ability, honor, etc.

at·taint′ (ə-tānt′) *v.t.* disgrace; taint.

at′tar (at′ər) *n.* an essential oil of roses.

at·tempt′ (ə-tempt′) *v.t.* make an effort to do; endeavor; undertake. —*n.* an effort to do something.

at·tend′ (ə-tend′) *v.t. & i.* **1**, be present at. **2**, go with; accompany. **3**, take care of; minister to; serve. **4**, listen to; heed. —**at·tend′ance**, *n.*

at·tend′ant (-ənt) *n.* one who attends another. —*adj.* attending.

at·ten′tion (ə-ten′shən) *n.* **1**, direction of the mind to an object of sense or thought. **2**, observant care; notice. **3**, an act of care, civility, or courtesy. **4**, (*Mil.*) a certain prescribed erect posture.

at·ten′tive (-tiv) *adj.* **1**, observant; intent. **2**, polite; (*Colloq.*) wooing. —**at·ten′tive·ness**, *n.*

at·ten′u·ate (ə-ten′ū-āt″) *v.t. & i.* **1**, make or become thin. **2**, weaken in force; lessen in quantity, value, or degree. —**at·ten″u·a′tion**, *n.*

at·test′ (ə-test′) *v.t.* **1**, bear witness to; declare to be true or genuine. **2**, give proof or evidence of. —**at″tes·ta′tion** (at″es-tā′shən) *n.*

at′tic (at′ik) *n.* a room directly under the roof; a garret.

at·tire′ (ə-tīr′) *v.t.* dress; clothe; adorn. —*n.* clothing; apparel.

at′ti·tude″ (at′ə-tood″) *n.* **1**, a position or manner indicative of feeling, opinion, or intention toward a person or thing. **2**, a bodily posture; position.

at·tor′ney (ə-tĕr′nē) *n.* **1**, a lawyer. **2**, one empowered to transact business for another; an agent. —**attorney general**, the chief law officer and legal head of a state or nation.

at·tract′ (ə-trakt′) *v.t.* **1**, draw toward (itself) by inherent physical force; cause to cohere with. **2**, invite; allure.

at·trac′tion (ə-trak′shən) *n.* **1**, act of attracting; power to attract.

at·trac′tive (-tiv) *adj.* appealing; likable; good-looking. —**at·trac′tive·ness**, *n.*

at·trib′ute (ə-trib′ūt) *v.t.* consider as belonging, as a possession, quality, or cause; ascribe; impute. —*n.* (at′ri-būt″) characteristic; anything attributed, as a property, quality, or cause. —**at″tri·bu′tion** (at″rə-bū′shən) *n.*

at·tri′tion (ə-trish′ən) *n.* the act of wearing away, or of being worn down, by friction; abrasion.

at·tune′ (ə-toon′) *v.t.* make harmonious.

au′burn (â′bĕrn) *n.* a reddish-brown color.

auc′tion (âk′shən) *n.* a public sale in which goods are sold to the highest bidder. —*v.t.* sell by auction. —**auc′tion·eer′** (-ir′) *n.*

au·da′cious (â-dā′shəs) *adj.* **1**, bold; daring; intrepid. **2**, unrestrained; impudent.

au·dac′i·ty (â-das′ə-tē) *n.* boldness; impudence.

au′di·ble (â′də-bəl) *adj.* loud enough to be heard. —**au″di·bil′i·ty**, *n.*

au′di·ence (â′dē-əns) *n.* **1**, an assembly of hearers or spectators; the persons reached by a publication, radio, etc. **2**, a formal interview; a hearing. **3**, liberty or opportunity of being heard.

au′di·o (â′dē-ō″) *adj.* pert. to audible sound waves. —*n.* radio.

au′di·on (â′dē-on″) *n.* a vacuum tube used in radio.

au′dit (â′dit) *n.* an official examination and verification of accounts or dealings. —*v.t. & i.* examine and certify accounts.

au·di′tion (â-dish′ən) *n.* **1**, the sense or act of hearing. **2**, a hearing or performance for test purposes, as by a musician. —*v.t. & i.* perform, or cause to perform, as a test.

au′di·tor (â′di-tər) *n.* **1**, a hearer; listener. **2**, one who audits accounts.

au″di·to′ri·um (â″də-tôr′ē-əm) *n.* a large room, space, or building for containing an audience or spectators.

au′di·to·ry (â′də-tôr′ē) *adj.* pert. to the sense or organs of hearing.

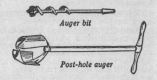

Auger bit

Post-hole auger

au′ger (â′gər) *n.* a tool for boring holes.

aught (ât) *n.* **1,** anything whatever. **2,** naught. —*adv.* in any respect; at all.

aug·ment' (ag-ment') *v.t.* cause to increase; add to. —*v.i.* increase. —aug'men·ta'tion, *n.*

au'gur (â'gər) *v.t. & i.* **1,** predict from omens; foretell. **2,** be a sign of; presage. —*n.* a prophet.

au'gu·ry (â'gyû-rè) *n.* **1,** prophecy divination. **2,** an omen.

au·gust' (â-gust') *adj.* highly dignified; imposing; eminent.

Au'gust (â'gəst) *n.* the eighth month of the year.

auk (âk) *n.* a diving bird found in northern regions.

aunt (ânt) *n.* **1,** the sister of one's father or mother. **2,** the wife of one's uncle.

au'ra (â'rə) *n.* **1,** a supposed force or imponderable matter emanating from a body and surrounding it like an atmosphere. **2,** a distinctive character or quality.

au'ral (â'rəl) *adj.* pert. to the ear or to hearing.

au're·ole" (ôr'è-ōl") *n.* a halo or nimbus.

au"re·o·my'cin (ôr'è-ō-mi'sin) *n.* an antibiotic used in treatment of certain virus diseases.

au'ri·cle (â'rə-kəl) *n.* **1,** the outer ear. **2,** one of the chambers of the heart. —au·ric'u·lar (â-rik'yə-lər) *adj.*

au·rif'er·ous (â-rif'ər-əs) *adj.* containing gold.

au·ro'ra (â-rôr'ə) *n.* **1,** morning twilight; the dawn of anything. **2,** an atmospheric phenomenon causing night lights in polar regions, aurora bo"re·a'lis (bôr'è-al'is) in the north, aurora aus·tra'lis (â-strā'lis) in the south.

aus'pice (â'spis) *n.* **1,** (*pl.*) favoring influence; protection or patronage. **2,** a favorable circumstance.

aus·pi'cious (â-spish'əs) *adj.* well-omened; betokening success. —aus·pi'cious·ness, *n.*

aus·tere' (â-stir') *adj.* **1,** severely simple; unadorned. **2,** serious; morally strict. **3,** harsh; stern; rigorous.

aus·ter'i·ty (âs-ter'ə-tè) *n.* **1,** state of being austere; harshness. **2,** simplicity in living.

aus'tral (â'strəl) *adj.* southern; lying in the southern hemisphere.

au'tar·chy (â'tär-kè) *n.* **1,** absolute power; autocracy. **2,** self-government. **3,** economic self-sufficiency (of a country). —au·tar'chic (â-tär'kik) *adj.*

au·then'tic (â-then'tik) *adj.* **1,** actually of the ascribed authorship or origin; genuine. **2,** duly authorized. —au·then'ti·cal·ly, *adv.* —au·then·tic'i·ty (-tis'ə-tè) *n.*

au·then'ti·cate" (â-then'ti-kāt") *v.t.* make valid; attest to the genuineness of. —au·then'ti·ca'tion, *n.*

au'thor (â'thər) *n.* **1,** the originator or creator of anything. **2,** one who writes literary works. —au'thor·ess, *n.fem.* —au'thor·ship, *n.*

au·thor'i·tar'i·an (ə-thor'ə-tär'è-ən) *adj.* favoring rule by absolute authority. —*n.* an advocate of such rule.

au·thor'i·ta'tive (-tā'tiv) *adj.* based on authority; authentic.

au·thor'i·ty (ə-thor'ə-tè) *n.* **1,** the right to govern, control, or command. **2,** a person or group having such right. **3,** power or influence derived from reputation. **4,** an expert on a subject; an accepted source of information or counsel.

au"thor·i·za'tion (â"thə-ri-zā'-shən) *n.* act or result of authorizing; authority to act.

au'thor·ize" (â'thə-rīz") *v.t.* give authority, warrant, or legal power to; empower (a person).

au'to (â'tō) *n.* automobile.

au·to- (â-tō) *pref.* meaning self.

au"to·bi·og'ra·phy (â"tə-bī-og'rə-fè) *n.* a biography of a person written by himself. —au"to·bi"o·graph'i·cal, *adj.*

au·toc'ra·cy (â-tok'rə-sè) *n.* government by an absolute monarch.

au'to·crat" (â'tə-krat") *n.* one who rules by inherent right, subject to no restrictions. —au"to·crat'ic, *adj.* au"to·crat'i·cal·ly, *adv.*

au"to·gi'ro (â"-tə-jī'rō) *n.* a propeller-driven air craft supported in flight by a windmill-like rotor.

Autogiro

au'to·graph" (â'tə-grâf") *n.* **1,** one's own signature. **2,** one's own handwriting.

au'to·mat" (â'tə-mat") *n.* a restaurant where food is vended by automatic coin-machines.

au"to·mat'ic (â"tə-mat'ik) *adj.* **1,** having the power of self-motion. **2,** operated by self-acting machinery. **3,** following inevitably as a consequence. **4,** done without volition; reflex; habitual. —*n.* an automatic pistol. —au"to·mat'i·cal·ly, *adv.*

au·tom'a·ton" (â-tom'ə-ton")*n.*[*pl.* -ta (-tä)] **1,** a machine actuated to operate for some time without external guidance; a mechanical figure actuated by concealed machinery. **2,** a person who acts in a monotonous routine manner.

au'to·mo·bile" (â'tə-mə-bēl") *n.* a vehicle propelled by a self-contained engine and designed to travel on ordinary roads. —*adj.* (-mō'bəl) self-propelled.

au·to·mo·tive (â"tə-mō'tiv) *adj.* **1**, pert. to self-propelled vehicles, esp. automobiles. **2**, self-propelling.

au·ton·o·my (â-ton'ə-mē) *n.* self-government; independence. —**au·ton'o·mous,** *adj.*

au·top'sy (â'top'sē) *n.* dissection and inspection of a dead body to discover the cause of death.

au·tumn (â'təm) *n.* the third season of the year, between summer and winter; also called *fall.* —**au·tum'nal** (â-tum'nəl) *adj.*

aux·il'ia·ry (ag-zil'yə-rē) *adj.* **1**, giving help or support. **2**, subordinate; additional.

a·vail' (ə-vāl') *v.i. & t.* have force or efficacy; serve. —**avail oneself of,** make use of.

a·vail'a·ble (-ə-bəl) *adj.* obtainable; at one's disposal. —**a·vail"a·bil'i·ty,** *n.*

av'a·lanche' (av'ə-lanch') *n.* the sudden fall of a mass of ice and debris down the side of a mountain.

a·vant·'garde' (ə-vän'gärd') *n. & adj.* (Fr.) vanguard.

av'a·rice (av'ə-ris) *n.* inordinate desire for wealth; greed; covetousness. —**av"a·ri'cious** (-rish'əs) *adj.*

a·vast' (ə-vast') *interj.* (Naut.) stop! hold!

av'a·tar (av'ə-tär") *n.* (Hindu) incarnation of a deity.

Ave Maria (ä'və-mä-rē'ə) a prayer, the Hail Mary, from Luke 1:28,42 and other sources.

a·venge' (ə-venj') *v.t.* exact satisfaction or vengeance for or on behalf of.

av'e·nue" (av'ə-nū") *n.* **1**, a wide street. **2**, any roadway of approach, passageway, or means of access.

a·ver' (ə-vēr') *v.t.* [a·verred', a·ver'ring] declare in a positive manner; affirm with confidence.

av'er·age (av'ər-ij) *n.* **1**, the mean value of a series of quantities, determined by dividing their sum by their number. **2**, any mean, typical, or normal number, quantity, degree, quality, etc. —*adj.* intermediate, typical, or normal. —*v.t.* **1**, determine an average of. **2**, result in an average of.

a·verse' (ə-vērs') *adj.* **1**, disposed against; reluctant. **2**, turned away from in position.

a·ver·sion (ə-vēr'zhən) *n.* **1**, dislike. **2**, that which is disliked.

a·vert' (ə-vērt') *v.t.* **1**, ward off; prevent. **2**, turn away.

a'vi·ar"y (ā'vē-er"ē) *n.* an enclosure in which birds are kept.

a'vi·a'tion (ā"vē-ā'shən) *n.* the art or science of flying in the air,

esp. in heavier-than-air aircraft.

a'vi·a"tor (ā'vē-ā"tər) *n.* a member of an aircraft's operating crew, esp. a pilot.

av'id *adj.* eager.

a·vid'i·ty (ə-vid'ə-tē) *n.* eagerness.

av"o·ca'do (av"ə-kä'dō) *n.* [*pl.* -dos] *n.* a tropical American fruit: the alligator pear.

av"o·ca'tion (av"ə-kā'shən) *n.* an occupation pursued for pleasure or diversion; a hobby.

a·void' (ə-void') *v.t.* keep away from; shun; refrain from. —**a·void'ance,** *n.*

av"oir·du·pois' (av"ər-də-poiz') *n.* the system of weights in which the ounce, pound and ton are used.

a·vouch' (ə-vowch') *v.t.* **1**, vouch for; guarantee. **2**, acknowledge frankly.

a·vow' (ə-vow') *v.t.* declare openly; admit or confess frankly; acknowledge. —**a·vow'al** (-əl) *n.*

a·vun'cu·lar (ə-vung'kū-lər) *adj.* like or pert. to an uncle.

a·wait' (ə-wāt') *v.t.* **1**, wait for; look for and expect. **2**, lie in store for.

a·wake' (ə-wāk') *v.i. & t.* [-woke', -waked', -wak'ing] **1**, wake up. **2**, call into being or action; bestir. —*adj.* **1**, not sleeping. **2**, alert; vigilant.

a·wak'en (ə-wā'kən) *v.i. & t.* awake. —**a·wak'en·ing,** *n.* a sudden awareness or excitement.

a·ward' (ə-wôrd') *v.t.* bestow as a prize or reward, or as something due. —*n.* **1**, anything awarded. **2**, a decision of a judge or arbiter.

a·ware' (ə-wâr') *adj.* conscious (of); informed; cognizant.

a·wash' (ə-wosh') *adv. & adj.* (Naut.) just at water level.

a·way' (ə-wā') *adv.* **1**, from this place; off; apart; aside. **2**, out of one's presence, possession, or attention. —*adj.* **1**, absent. **2**, distant.

awe (â) *n.* fear mingled with admiration or reverence. —*v.t.* inspire with awe.

a·weigh' (ə-wā') *adj.* of an anchor, raised so that a ship may sail.

awe'some (-səm) *adj.* inspiring awe. —**awe'some·ness,** *n.*

awe'struck' *adj.* feeling awe.

aw'ful (â'fəl) *adj.* **1**, inspiring reverential fear. **2**, (Colloq.) extremely bad or unpleasant. —*adv.* (Colloq.) very. —**aw'ful·ness,** *n.*

a·while' (ə-hwīl') *adv.* for a short time.

awk'ward (âk'wərd) *adj.* **1**, lacking dexterity or skill; clumsy. **2**, graceful; uncouth. **3**, ill-adapted for use. **4**, difficult to handle or deal with; requiring caution. **5**, embarrassing. —**awk'ward·ness,** *n.*

awl (âl) *n.* a tool for punching small holes in leather, wood, etc.

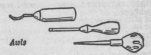

Awls

awn'ing (ă'ning) *n.* a movable cloth stretched above a door or window as protection from the sun's rays.

a·woke' (ə-wōk') *v.* pret. of *awake.*

a·wry' (ə-rī') *adv. & adj.* away from a true direction or position; askew; perverse.

ax (aks) *n.* a cutting tool or weapon, comprising a heavy-bladed head fixed to a handle. —*v.t.* 1, trim with an ax. 2, (*Slang*) discharge from employment; injure. Also, **axe.**

ax'i·om (ak'sē-əm) *n.* 1, a proposition deemed to be self-evident and assumed without proof. 2, a universal proposition, amply proved, easily verifiable, or generally accepted. —**ax″i·o·mat'ic** (-mat'ik) *adj.* —**ax″i·o·mat'i·cal·ly,** *adv.*

ax'is (ak'sis) *n.* [*pl.* **-es** (-sēz)] 1, the line about which a rotating body turns. 2, the line with respect to which a body or structure is symmetrical. 3, a principal supporting member. 4, (*cap.*) the military alliance of Germany and Italy in World War II. —**ax'i·al** (ak'sē-əl) *adj.*

ax'le (ak'səl) *n.* the pin or shaft on which a wheel turns, or which turns with it on a bearing.

aye (ī) *adv. & n.* 1, yes. 2, always. Also, **ay.**

Ayr'shire (âr'shər) *n.* one of a breed of dairy cattle.

a·zal'ea (ə-zāl'yə) *n.* a plant bearing brightly-colored flowers.

az'i·muth (az'ə-məth) *n.* 1, an angle measured clockwise from north to south. 2, (*Astron.*) this angle measured on a horizon circle.

Az'tec (az'tek) *adj.* pert. to an aboriginal American Indian group.

az'ure (azh'ər) *adj. & n.* sky blue.

B

B, b (bē) second letter of the English alphabet.

baa (bää) *v.t.* [**baaed, baa'ing**] *& n.* bleat.

bab'ble (bab'əl) *v.i.* 1, talk idly; chatter. 2, utter words imperfectly; prattle. —*v.t.* utter incoherently.

babe (bāb) *n.* 1, baby. 2, (*Slang*) girl.

Ba'bel (bā'bəl) *n.* confused and overpowering sound; discord.

ba·boon' *n.* any of several large monkeys.

ba'by (bā'bē) *n.* 1, a very young child; infant. 2, a childish person. 3, the youngest child. 4, (*Slang*) pet (term of endearment). —*adj.* 1, suited for a baby; infantile. 2, small. —*v.t.* pamper. —**ba'by·hood,** *n.*

ba'by·sit' *v.i.* act as a temporary nurse for a child. —**ba'by·sit'ter,** *n.*

bac″ca·lau're·ate (bak″ə-lôr'ē-ət) *adj.* pert. to or designating an address given before a graduating class.

bach'e·lor (bach'ə-lər) *n.* 1, an unmarried man. 2, recipient of a college degree. —**bach'e·lor·hood,** *n.*

ba·cil'lus (bə-sil'əs) *n.* [*pl.* **-li** (-lī)] a rod-shaped bacterium.

back (bak) *n.* 1, the spinal, posterior, or dorsal side or surface of an animal. 2, the rear or hind part of anything. 3, support or stiffening in general. 4, a player and his position in certain athletic games, as football. —*v.t.* 1, furnish with a back; support or favor. 2, cause to move backward. —*v.i.* go backward. —*adv.* 1, toward the rear. 2, toward the past.

back'bite″ (bak'bīt″) *v.t. & i.* speak evil of (an absent person).

back'bone″ (bak'bōn″) *n.* 1, the human spine or vertebral column; any similar supporting or stiffening member. 2, firmness; resolution.

back'fire″ *n.* 1, a premature explosion in a gasoline engine. 2, a fire set to check a forest fire. 3, a result opposite to what was intended. —*v.i.* produce a backfire.

back'gam″mon (bak'gam″ən) *n.* a game played by moving pieces on a board in accordance with casts of dice.

back'ground″ (bak'grownd″) *n.* 1, the more distant objects and planes of sight in a view or picture. 2, antecedent events and circumstances, in relation to a person or later event.

back'hand″ (bak'hand″) *n.* writing that slopes to the left. —*adj.* performed with the hand turned back outward, as a backhand stroke in tennis.

back'hand″ed *adj.* 1, backhand. 2, oblique in meaning; ironic.

back'slide″ (bak'slīd″) *v.i.* abandon religious principles or practices.

back'stairs″ (bak'stārz″) *adj.* indirect; underhand; secret.

back'ward (bak'wərd) *adv.* [also, **back'wards**] *& adj.* 1, toward the back or rear. 2, with back foremost; reverse. 3, in reverse order. 4, toward or in past time. —*adj.* 1, late in time; slow; unprogressive. 2, reluctant; shy.

back'woods" (bak'wûdz") *adj.* primitive; uncultivated.

ba'con (bā'kən) *n.* meat from the back and sides of the hog, salted and dried.

bac·te'ri·a (bak-tir'ē-ə) *n. pl.* [*sing.* -um] vegetable microörganisms that cause fermentation, decay, disease, etc. —**bac·te'ri·al,** *adj.*

bad *adj.* [worse, worst] 1, wicked; vicious. 2, not good; defective; not valid. 3, hurtful; noxious. 4, unfavorable; unfortunate. 5, sick. —*n.* any thing or condition that is bad. —**bad'ness,** *n.*

bade (bad) *v.* pret. of *bid.*

badge (baj) *n.* a token, mark, or device worn to show allegiance, honors, etc.

badg'er (baj'ər) *n.* a carnivorous mammal prized for its fur. —*v.t.* pester; harass.

bad'i·nage' (bad'ə-näzh') *n.* playful banter; raillery.

bad'lands" *n.pl.* a barren region with eroded rock formations.

bad'ly (-lē) *adv.* 1, with bad effect. 2, (*Colloq.*) very much.

bad'min·ton (bad'min-tən) *n.* an outdoor game similar to tennis.

baf'fle (baf'əl) *v.t.* disconcert by interposing obstacles; frustrate; confuse. —*n.* an obstacle. —**baf'fle·ment,** *n.*

bag *n.* 1, a portable receptacle made of a flexible material, capable of being closed at the mouth. 2, a suitcase. 3, anything formed like or serving the purpose of a bag. 4, the contents of a bag; an amount taken or collected. —*v.t.* [bagged, bag'ging] capture. —*v.i.* 1, swell out; bulge. 2, hang loosely.

bag"a·telle' (bag'ə-tel') *n.* 1, anything trifling. 2, a game played by striking balls with a cue.

bag'gage (bag'ij) *n.* 1, containers, as trunks, suitcases, etc., used by a traveler. 2, a saucy young woman.

bag'gy (bag'ē) *adj.* bulging; hanging loosely. —**bag'gi·ness,** *n.*

bag'pipe" (bag'pīp") *n.* a Scottish musical instrument with several reed pipes, one melodic and the rest drones, actuated by a wind bag.

bah (bä) *interj.* of disgust or contempt.

bail' (bāl) *n.* (*Law*) security given to obtain the temporary release of a prisoner. —*v.t.* grant or obtain release of a prisoner in bail.

bail'iff (bā'lif) *n.* a deputy officer of a court of law.

bail'i·wick (bāl'ə-wik) *n.* an area of jurisdiction, activity, or influence.

bail out 1, remove (water) from a boat with a bucket or pump. 2,

jump from an airplane with a parachute.

bait (bāt) *n.* 1, a lure placed on a fishhook or in a trap. 2, any device of allurement. —*v.t.* 1, place bait on or in. 2, torment; tease.

baize (bāz) *n.* a feltlike woolen fabric.

bake (bāk) *v.t. & i.* 1, cook by dry heat. 2, harden by heat. —*v.i.* become baked.

bak'er (bā'kər) *n.* one whose business is baking bread. —**baker's dozen,** thirteen.

bak'er·y (bā'kə-rē) *n.* a baker's shop or plant.

bal'ance (bal'əns) *n.* 1, an instrument for weighing. 2, equal distribution of weight; a state of equilibrium; harmonious arrangement of parts. 3, mental stability; good judgment. 4, equality between two sides of an account. 5, an excess or remainder. —*v.t.* 1, bring into balance or equilibrium. 2, arrange in harmonious form. 3, weigh; estimate; compare. 4, equalize two sides of an account. —*v.i.* come into equilibrium; be harmonious.

bal·brig'gan (bal-brig'ən) *n.* unbleached cotton, used chiefly for underwear.

bal'co·ny (bal'kə-nē) *n.* 1, a platform projecting from a wall, having an outer railing or parapet. 2, an elevated tier of seats in a theater.

bald (bâld) *adj.* 1, destitute of hair or other natural covering. 2, bare; unadorned. 3, undisguised. —**bald'ness,** *n.*

bal'der·dash" (bâl'dər-dash") *n.* a nonsensical jumble of words.

bale (bāl) *n.* a large bundle of merchandise, closely compressed and bound. —*v.t.* pack into bales.

ba·leen' (bə-lēn') *n.* a flexible, bony substance from a whale; whalebone.

bale'ful (bāl'fəl) *adj.* menacing; malign. —**bale'ful·ness,** *n.*

balk (bâk) *n.* 1, an obstacle; a check or defeat. 2, a blunder or failure. 3, (*Baseball*) a penalizable feint by the pitcher. 4, a heavy wooden timber. —*v.t.* hinder; thwart. —*v.i.* stop at an obstacle; refuse to act or continue. —**balk'y,** *adj.*

ball (bâl) *n.* 1, any round or roundish body; sphere; globe. 2, any of various games played with balls, as football, baseball. 3, (*Baseball*) a pitch not struck at by the batter and ruled to be too high, low, or wide. 4, a solid projectile fired from a gun. 5, a social assembly for dancing. 6, (*Slang*) a highball. —*v.t.* (with *up*) (*Slang*) disarrange; confuse.

bal'lad (bal'əd) *n.* a simple narrative poem; a sentimental song.

bal'last (bal'əst) *n.* 1, heavy material carried to increase stability or decrease buoyancy. 2, crushed stone, etc., forming the bed of a railroad.

bal·le·ri′na (bal′ə-rē′nə) *n.* a female ballet dancer.

bal′let (bal′ā) *n.* **1,** a theatrical pantomime of dancing and music. **2,** a stylized form of solo and group dancing. **3,** a troupe of professional dancers.

bal·let′o·mane (ba-let′ō-mān) *n.* an enthusiastic spectator of ballet dancing.

bal·lis′tics (bə-lis′tiks) *n.* the science of the motion of projectiles.

bal·loon′ (bə-loon′) *n.* **1,** an airship that derives its lift from a large bag inflated with a gas lighter than air. **2,** an inflated rubber bag, used as a child's toy. **3,** (in cartoons) a loop enclosing words represented as issuing from the mouth of a speaker. —*v.t.* swell out. —**bal·loon′ist,** *n.*

bal′lot (bal′ət) *n.* **1,** a ticket or other device for marking an individual vote. **2,** the casting of ballots; the whole number of votes recorded. —*v.i.* **1,** vote by ballot. **2,** draw lots.

ball′point″ pen a fountain pen with a minute ball bearing for a point.

ball′room″ *n.* a room for dancing.

bal′ly·hoo″ (bal′ė-hoo″) *n.* (*Slang*) crude or blatant advertising. —*v.t.* promote by ballyhoo.

balm (bäm) *n.* **1,** any of various aromatic resinous substances. **2,** anything that soothes or mitigates pain.

balm′y *adj.* **1,** mild. **2,** fragrant. **3,** (*Slang*) mildly insane. —**balm′i·ness,** *n.*

ba·lo′ney (bə-lō′nē) *n.* **1,** (*Slang*) nonsense; humbug. **2,** (*Colloq.*) a sausage named for Bologna, Italy.

bal′sa (bâl′sə) *n.* a tree having exceedingly light wood.

bal′sam (bâl′səm) *n.* **1,** balm. **2,** transparent turpentine. **3,** any plant or tree yielding balsam.

bal′us·ter (bal′ə-stər) *n.* an ornamental upright post giving support to a rail.

bal″us·trade′ (bal″ə-strād′) *n.* a row of balusters topped by a rail.

bam·boo′ *n.* **1,** a woody tropical grass. **2,** its hollow stem.

Baluster

bam·boo′zle (bam-boo′zəl) *v.t.* deceive by trickery; mystify.

ban *v.t.* [**banned, ban′ning**] forbid; prohibit. —*n.* **1,** prohibition. **2,** denunciation.

ba′nal (bā′nəl) *adj.* commonplace; trite. —**ba·nal′i·ty** (bə-nal′ə-tē) *n.*

ba·nan′a (bə-nan′ə) *n.* a tropical fruit.

band *n.* **1,** a flat strip of flexible material, used to bind, confine, trim, or ornament. **2,** a stripe; a zone marked off from adjacent areas. **3,** a company of persons traveling or acting together. **4,** a group of musicians playing together, esp. a group not including stringed instruments. —*v.t. & i.* unite.

band′age (ban′dij) *n.* cloth used to bind up a wound.

ban·dan′na (ban-dan′ə) *n.* a large colored handkerchief.

band′box″ (band′boks″) *n.* a hat box; a small compartment or room.

ban·deau′ (ban-dō′) *n.* a band worn on the head.

ban′dit *n.* a robber, esp. one of a band of marauders. —**ban′dit·ry,** *n.*

band′stand″ *n.* a platform on which a musical band plays.

band′wag″on *n.* **1,** a vehicle carrying a musical band in a parade. **2,** (*Slang*) the successful side, as in an election.

ban′dy (ban′dē) *v.t.* strike, throw, or pass back and forth; give and take. —*adj.* crooked. —**ban′dy-leg″ged,** *adj.* having bowlegs.

bane (bān) *n.* **1,** a deadly poison. **2,** anything that destroys or spoils. —**bane′ful,** *adj.* very inimical.

bang *n.* **1,** a loud, explosive noise, of a gun, etc. **2,** (*Colloq.*) energy; spirit. **3,** (*Slang*) thrill. **4,** (usually *pl.*) a fringe of short, evenly-cut hairs over the forehead. —*v.t.* knock about; drub; slam. —*v.i.* **1,** strike violently. **2,** make a sudden, loud noise. —*adv.* suddenly; loudly.

ban′gle (bang′gəl) *n.* an ornamental bracelet without a clasp.

ban′ish *v.t.* put in exile; drive away; dismiss. —**ban′ish·ment,** *n.*

ban′is·ter (ban′is-tər) *n.* a baluster or balustrade.

ban′jo (ban′jō) *n.* [*pl.* -**jos**] a musical stringed instrument with a circular head. —**ban′jo·ist,** *n.*

bank *n.* **1,** a long pile or ridge, as of earth. **2,** a slope; the border of a watercourse. **3,** an elevated plateau in the sea or a river; a shoal. **4,** lateral inclination. **5,** a tier, as of keys on an organ. **6,** an institution for receiving and lending money; the quarters of such an institution. **7,** a store, fund, reserve, or depository. —*v.t.* **1,** provide with or form into a bank. **2,** give a lateral inclination to. **3,** cover up (a fire). **4,** deposit in a bank. —*v.i.* **1,** act as a banker. **2,** depend or rely (on).

bank′er (-ər) *n.* one who conducts or works in a bank. —**bank′ing,** *n.*

bank′note″ *n.* a piece of paper money.

bank′rupt *n.* (*Law*) one who is adjudged insolvent. —*adj.* unable to pay debts; bereft. —*v.t.* make bankrupt. —**bank′rupt·cy** (-sē) *n.*

ban′ner (ban′ər) *n.* **1,** a flag, pennant, or other device emblematic of a country, faith, etc. **2,** anything displayed as a profession of principles. **3,** a headline extending across the full width of a newspaper. —*adj.* foremost; leading.

banns (banz) *n. pl.* notice of an intended marriage.

ban′quet (bang′kwit) *n.* a rich entertainment of food and drink.

ban′shee″ (ban′shē″) *n.* a wailing spirit that heralds death.

ban′tam (ban′təm) *n.* **1,** a small-sized variety of chicken. **2,** any small animal. —*adj.* very small.

ban′tam-weight″ *n.* a boxer of 112 to 118 pounds.

ban′ter (ban′tər) *n.* playful talk; good-humored raillery. —*v.t. & i.* make fun of; chaff.

ban′yan (ban′yən) *n.* an E. Ind. fig tree.

ban·zai′ (bän′zä′ē) *interj.* (*Jap.*) may he (it) live 10,000 years!

bap′tism (bap′tiz-əm) *n.* a sacrament of the Christian church, signalized by sprinkling with or immersion in water. —**bap·tis′mal** (-tiz′məl) *adj.*

Bap′tist *n.* a member of a certain Christian denomination.

bap·tize′ (-tīz′) *v.t.* **1,** administer baptisr_ to. **2,** christen; name.

bar (bär) *n.* **1,** a rod used as an obstruction or guard. **2,** anything that obstructs. **3,** a band or stripe; anything of oblong shape. **4,** a room where liquors are sold: barroom. **5,** lawyers as a whole; the legal profession. **6,** any tribunal. **7,** (*Music*) a vertical line marking the division between measures; a measure. —*v.t.* **1,** [**barred, bar′ring**] **1,** shut out; exclude. **2,** block; close. —*prep.* except.

barb (bärb) *n.* **1,** a pointed part projecting backward, as on a fishhook. **2,** a beardlike growth or member. —**barbed,** *adj.* **1,** having a hooked point. **2,** spiteful.

bar·bar′i·an (bär-bâr′ē-ən) *n.* a man in a primitive, savage, or uncivilized state. —*adj.* uncivilized.

bar·bar′ic (bär-bar′ik) *adj.* **1,** of or like barbarians. **2,** magnificent but crude. —**bar·bar′i·cal·ly,** *adv.*

bar·bar′i·ty (bär-bar′ə-tē) *n.* **1,** brutality; cruelty. **2,** crudeness.

bar′bar·ous (bär′bə-rəs) *adj.* **1,** uncultured; crude. **2,** brutal; cruel. —**bar′bar·ous·ness,** *n.*

bar′be·cue″ (bär′bə-kū″) *n.* a social gathering where animal carcasses are roasted whole. —*v.t.* broil or roast (a carcass) whole.

bar′ber (bär′bər) *n.* one whose occupation is to shave the beard,

cut and dress the hair. —*v.t.* trim or dress the facial hair of.

bar·bette′ (bär-bet′) *n.* (*Mil.*) a gun platform or housing.

bar′bi·tal″ (bär′bə-tal″) *n.* a sleep-producing drug.

bar·bit′u·rate″ (bär-bit′yû-rāt″) *n.* one of various sedative drugs.

bar′ca·role″ (bär′kə-rōl″) *n.* a boating song.

bard (bärd) *n.* poet; minstrel.

bare (bâr) *adj.* **1,** without clothing or covering; naked; nude. **2,** without usual furniture or equipment. **3,** bald; unadorned. **4,** open to view; not concealed. **5,** scarcely or just sufficient. —*v.t.* lay open to view; denude; strip. —**bare′ness,** *n.*

bare′back″ *adv. & adj.* without a saddle.

bare′faced″ (-fāst″) *adj.* shameless.

bare′foot″ *adj.* with bare feet.

bare′ly (-lē) *adv.* **1,** only; just. **2,** openly; nakedly.

bar′gain (bär′gən) *n.* **1,** an agreement as to sale or exchange of goods. **2,** an advantageous purchase. —*v.i.* discuss terms of sale; haggle.

barge (bärj) *n.* **1,** an unpowered boat for transporting goods. **2,** any capacious, slow-moving, or ceremonial vessel. —*v.i.* **1,** move in a slow, heavy manner. **2,** (with *in*) (*Colloq.*) intrude. **3,** (with *into*) (*Colloq.*) collide with.

bar′i·tone″ (bar′ə-tōn″) *n. & adj.* **1,** a male voice intermediate between bass and tenor. **2,** a musical instrument having analogous range.

bar′i·um (bâr′ē-əm) *n.* a chemical element, no. 56, symbol Ba.

bark (bärk) *n.* **1,** the abrupt cry of a dog. **2,** any similar cry or sound by an animal or person. **3,** the outer covering of the stems of woody plants. **4,** a small three-masted ship. —*v.i.* **1,** utter a harsh sound like the bark of a dog. **2,** speak gruffly; make a clamor. —*v.t.* remove bark from; rub off the skin of.

bark′er (bär′kər) *n.* (*Colloq.*) a person who urges passers-by to enter a theater, etc.

bar′ley (bär′lē) *n.* a cereal plant widely cultivated for food and the making of liquors.

barn (bärn) *n.* an outbuilding of a farm, used for storing grain and housing cattle and horses.

bar′na·cle (bär′nə-kəl) *n.* a small marine crustacean that attaches itself tenaciously to rocks and ships.

barn′storm″ (bärn′stôrm″) *v.i.* (*Colloq.*) tour rural areas, lecturing or performing publicly.

ba·rom′e·ter (bə-rom′ə-tər) *n.* an instrument for measuring atmospheric pressure.

---

tub, cūte, pŭll; label; oil, owl; go, chip, she, thin, *then*, sing, ink; *see p. 6*

bar'on (bar'ən) n. 1, a nobleman of the lowest rank of peerage. 2, a powerful person in industry, business, or finance. —**bar'on·ess**, n. fem. —**ba·ro'ni·al** (bə·rō'nē·əl), adj.

bar'on·age (-ij) n. 1, the whole body of barons. 2, a baron's rank.

bar'on·et' (bar'ə·net') n. a hereditary noble below a baron and above a knight. —**bar'on·et·cy** (-sē) n. his rank.

bar'o·ny (bar'ə·nē) n. the estate or rank of a baron.

ba·roque' (bə·rōk') n. a style of architecture and ornamentation characterized by grotesque or exaggerated forms. —adj. in this style.

bar'rack (bar'ək) n. (usually pl.) a large building for lodging soldiers.

Barracuda

bar'ra·cu'da (bar'ə·koo'də) n. a large, fierce tropical game fish.

bar·rage' (bə·räzh') n. 1, (Mil.) a barrier of sustained artillery fire. 2, a sustained flow.

bar'rel (bar'əl) n. 1, a cylindrical vessel of wooden staves bound together with hoops. 2, any similar container or part, as the tube of a gun. —barrel organ, a hand organ.

bar'ren (bar'ən) adj. 1, incapable of producing offspring; sterile. 2, unproductive; unprofitable. 3, destitute of interest or attraction. —**bar'ren·ness**, n.

bar·rette' (bə·ret') n. a clasp for a girl's hair.

bar'ri·cade' (bar'ə·kād') n. 1, a hastily-made fortification against the advance of any enemy. 2, any temporary barrier. —v.t. block.

bar'ri·er (bar'ē·ər) n. 1, any fence or structure erected to bar passage. 2, any natural obstacle to passage or communication. 3, anything that hinders or prevents progress, access, etc. 4, a limit or boundary.

bar'ris·ter (bar'is·tər) n. (Brit.) a lawyer who tries cases in court.

bar'row (bar'ō) n. 1, a frame with handles, for carrying a load; a wheelbarrow. 2, a heap, esp. a burial mound.

bar'ter (bär'tər) v.i. & t. exchange goods without the use of money. —n. this method of exchange.

bas'al (bā'səl) adj. basic. —basal metabolism, rate of expenditure of energy by the body at rest.

ba·salt' (bə·sâlt') n. a dark, dense, igneous rock.

base (bās) n. 1, the bottom of anything, considered as its support. 2, a fundamental principle; foundation. 3, the starting point of action or reckoning; the first ingredient of a concoction. 4, a principal seat of direction or supply; a depot. —v.t. 1, place on a foundation; found. 2, establish as a fact or conclusion. —adj. 1, morally low; mean in spirit. 2, low in rank; inferior in value. —**base'ness**, n.

base'ball' (bās'bâl') n. an athletic game in which a ball is batted to advance runners around a circuit of bases; the ball used in this game.

base'ment (bās'mənt) n. a story of a building below the entrance level, usually underground.

bash'ful (bash'fəl) adj. timorous in approach to other persons; diffident; shy. —**bash'ful·ness**, n.

bas'ic (bā'sik) adj. 1, pert. to a base or standard. 2, fundamental. —**bas'i·cal·ly**, adv.

bas'il (baz'əl) n. an herb used as flavoring.

ba·sil'i·ca (bə·sil'i·kə) n. a church or other building with a broad nave flanked by rows of columns.

bas'i·lisk (bas'ə·lisk) n. 1, a fabulous creature supposed to kill by its breath or look. 2, a tropical lizard.

ba'sin (bā'sən) n. 1, a shallow, circular vessel for holding liquids. 2, a lowland.

ba'sis (bā'sis) n. [pl. -ses (-sēz)] 1, a fundamental principle; foundation; groundwork. 2, principal ingredient.

bask (bàsk) v.i. thrive as the object of benign influence, as warmth, etc.

bas'ket (bas'kit) n. 1, a container woven of pliable reeds, etc. 2, the contents or capacity of a basket. 3, (Basketball) a wire hoop supporting an open net, fixed to a backboard; the score for throwing the ball through the hoop.

bas'ket·ball' (bas'kit·bâl') n. an indoor athletic game in which the object is to throw an inflated leather ball through a hoop or basket; the ball used in this game.

Basque (bàsk) n. 1, a people of N Spain, or their language. 2, (l.c.) a tight blouse.

bas·re·lief' (bä'rə·lēf') n. sculpture with the figures projecting only slightly from the surface; low relief.

bass (bās) adj. (Music) low in pitch or range. —n. 1, [also, bas'so] a man who sings bass. 2, a bass instrument, esp. the bass viol.

bass (bas) n. 1, a perchlike food fish. 2, a tree, the basswood or linden.

bas'set (bas'it) n. a hound dog with short legs and long body.

bas′si·net′ (bas″i-net′) n. a hooded basket used as a baby's cradle.

bas′so (bas′ō) n. bass.

bas·soon′ (ba-soon′) n. a musical instrument, the baritone of the double-reed wind family.

bassoon

bas′tard (bas′tėrd) n. an illegitimate child. —adj. 1, of illegitimate birth. 2, spurious; impure.

bas′tard·ize′ (-īz) v.t. 1, make a bastard of. 2, adulterate; debase.

bas′tar·dy (-dē) n. act of begetting a bastard.

baste (bāst) v.t. 1, sew with temporary stitches. 2, moisten (meat) while cooking. 3, beat with a stick.

bas·tille′ (bas-tēl′) n. a prison, esp. one conducted oppressively.

bas″ti·na′do (bas″ti-nā′dō) n. punishment by beating the feet with a stick; the stick used.

bas′tion (bas′chen) n. 1, a walled fortification projecting from a main rampart. 2, a fortified sector.

bat n. 1, a heavy club or cudgel. 2, the club used to strike the ball in certain games. 3, a nocturnal flying mammal. 4, (Slang) a spree. —v.t. & i. [bat′ted, -ting] strike with a bat; have a turn at batting.

batch (bach) n. 1, a quantity prepared for, or produced by, one operation. 2, a quantity or group from a larger aggregation.

bate (bāt) v.t. lessen or restrain.

bath (bàth) n. 1, a washing of the body in water. 2, equipment for a bath: the fluid or a bathtub.

bathe (bāth) v.t. & i. 1, take or administer a bath. 2, immerse or be immersed in a liquid.

bath′house″ n. a seaside building where bathers disrobe.

ba′thos (bā′thos) n. 1, a ludicrous descent from the elevated to the commonplace. 2, mawkish pathos.

bath′robe″ n. a loose robe worn instead of clothing.

bath′room″ n. a room containing bathing and other toilet facilities.

bath′tub″ n. a tub in which a person lies to bathe.

bath′y·sphere″ (bath′is-fir″) n. an apparatus lowered into deep waters for observation from a spherical compartment. —bath′y·scaphe″ (-skāf″) n. a bathysphere with a wedge-shaped underportion to permit greater descent.

ba·tik′ (bä-tēk′) n. a method of printing colors on cloth, by covering with wax portions to be unprinted.

ba·tiste′ (bə-tēst′) n. a plain, thin cotton fabric.

ba·ton′ n. 1, a staff or club carried as a symbol of authority. 2, a wand used in conducting an orchestra.

bat·tal′ion (bə-tal′yen) n. (Mil.) a body of troops, of variable number but usually less than a regiment.

bat′ten (bat′en) v.i. feed gluttonously; grow fat; thrive. —v.t. 1, fatten. 2, furnish with battens. 3, (Naut.) cover with tarpaulins secured by battens. —n. a light strip of wood; slat.

bat′ter (bat′ėr) v.t. & i. beat persistently; pound violently. —n. 1, a mixture of flour, eggs, etc. for making bread or pastry; any mixture of similar consistency. 2, one who wields a bat, as in baseball.

bat′ter·y (bat′ė-rē) n. 1, a device for producing an electric current or storing electricity. 2, a unit of artillery; a group of guns. 3, a set of similar machines or devices. 4, (Baseball) the pitcher and catcher together. 5, (Law) the unlawful beating of another.

bat′ting (bat′ing) n. cotton or wool in matted sheets for quilts or bedcovers.

bat′tle (bat′el) n. a fight, hostile encounter, or engagement between opposing forces. —v.t. & i. engage in battle; struggle; contend. —battle royal, a fight in which each of several contestants opposes each other.

bat′tle·dore″ (-dôr″) n. the racket used in badminton.

bat′tle·field″ n. the field or place where a battle is fought. Also, bat′tle·ground″.

bat′tle·ment (-ment) n. a parapet on a fort, castle, etc. having openings for shooting through.

bat′tle·ship″ (bat′el-ship″) n. the most heavily armed type of warship.

bau′ble (bâ′bel) n. a trinket of little value.

baux′ite (bâk′sīt) n. the ore from which aluminum is derived.

bawd′y (bâ′dē) adj. lewd; indecent. —bawd′i·ness, n.

bawl (bâl) v.t. & i. shout clamorously; cry vehemently; wail. —bawl out (Colloq.) scold.

bay (bā) n. 1, a recess in a shore; an inlet; a large cove or small gulf. 2, a turret projecting outward from a wall; a niche or alcove. 3, a compartment of space. 4, any of several trees, as laurel. 5, the deep-toned bark of a hunting dog. 6, a horse of reddish-brown color. —v.i. bark with a deep, prolonged sound. —at bay, trapped, as by hunting dogs.

bay′o·net (bā′ə-net) n. a steel weapon for stabbing or slashing, attached to the barrel of a rifle. —v.t. stab with a bayonet.

bay′ou (bī′oo) *n.* a cove of a lake; a sluggish watercourse.

bay window a group of windows projecting from a room in a floor-level recess.

ba·zaar′ (bə-zär′) *n.* 1, a market place. 2, a sale of miscellaneous goods for charitable purposes.

ba·zoo′ka (bə-zoo′kə) *n.* (*Mil.*) a tubular rocket launcher portable by one or two men.

be (bē) *v.i.* [*present indicative*: I am; you are (*Archaic*, thou art); he is; we, you, they are; *pret.* I, he was; we, you, they were; *p.p.* been (bin); be′ing] 1, (as substantive) exist; live; have reality; occur; take place; remain in a condition. 2, (as copulative) a link between a subject and a predicate, as I *am* here; an element in participial and infinitive phrases, as it is *being* done; we wish to *be* informed. 3, (as auxiliary) used with a participle to form a progressive, as he is *reading*; we *have been* waiting; used to indicate passive voice, as it *was* repaired.

be- *pref.* 1, affect with, as *becloud.* 2, take off or away, as *behead.*

beach (bēch) *n.* the part of a shore washed by the tide or waves. —*v.t.* run or haul (a boat) upon a beach. —**beach wagon,** a station wagon.

beach′comb″er (-kō″mər) *n.* an outcast living on a tropical beach.

beach′head″ *n.* a position on an enemy shore.

bea′con (bē′kən) *n.* 1, a lighthouse, signal buoy, or other fixed marker that guides ships or aircraft. 2, anything that warns or guides.

bead (bēd) *n.* 1, a small ball pierced with a hole for stringing with others. 2, (*pl.*) a necklace or rosary. 3, a drop of liquid; a bubble, as in froth. 4, any small globular body or mass. —*v.t.* ornament with beads.

bea′dle (bē′dəl) *n.* a minor official having disciplinary duties.

bea′gle (bē′gəl) *n.* a small, long-eared hunting dog.

beak (bēk) *n.* 1, the horny bill of a bird. 2, the snout, jaws, or similar part of any animal.

beak′er (bē′kər) *n.* a glass vessel.

Beagle

beam (bēm) *n.* 1, a horizontal supporting member. 2, a lever or piston. 3, the greatest width of a ship. 4, a bundle of parallel rays of light; a focused train of electronic waves. —*v.t. & i.* 1, emit rays; form like a beam of light. 2, smile radiantly.

bean (bēn) *n.* 1, the edible seed of a leguminous plant. 2; any oval or roundish seed, berry, nut, or lump. 3, a plant producing seed in the shape of beans. 4, (*Slang*) head; (*pl.*) money; spirit. —*v.t.* (*Slang*) strike on the head.

bear (bār) *v.t.* [**bore, borne**] 1, hold up; support; carry; convey. 2, put up with; accept; endure; sustain. 3, bring forward; render. 4, possess; show; exercise. 5, give birth to. 6, produce by natural growth. —*v.i.* 1, remain firm; be patient. 2, press; have effect or reference. 3, move or tend in a specific direction; be situated. 4, produce offspring, fruit, etc. —*n.* 1, a large omnivorous mammal, covered with heavy fur. 2, a person likened to a bear, as gruff, clumsy, predatory, etc. 3, a trader in financial stocks who sells short in the belief prices will go down. —**Great Bear, Little Bear,** two constellations.

beard (bird) *n.* 1, the growth of hair on the face of a man, esp. the chin. 2, a tuft of hair, bristle, etc.

bear′ing (bār′ing) *n.* 1, the manner in which a person bears or comports himself; carriage; behavior. 2, the act or capability of producing offspring, fruit, etc. 3, a supporting member of a structure or machine; a fixed part supporting a moving part. 4, the relation of parts; mode of connection; implication. 5, the compass direction of one object from another. 6, (*pl.*) position; orientation.

bear′ish *adj.* 1, surly. 2, pessimistic. —**bear′ish·ness,** *n.*

beast (bēst) *n.* 1, any four-footed animal. 2, a brutal, coarse, or otherwise beastlike human. —**beast′ly** (-lē) *adj.* very unpleasant.

beat (bēt) *v.t.* [**beat, beat′en, beat′ing**] 1, strike repeatedly. 2, move repeatedly; flutter; (*Music*) mark time by strokes. 3, dash with force. 4, overcome; vanquish; surpass; baffle. 5, (*Slang*) swindle. —*v.i.* 1, strike repeated blows; strike (against). 2, throb; pulsate. —*n.* 1, a stroke, blow, or throb. 2, a series of regular strokes, as the ticking of a watch. 3, accent or stress. 4, an assigned or habitual course of travel. 5, (*Slang*) publication of a news story in advance of rival newspapers.

be·at′i·fy″ (bē-at′ə-fī″) *v.t.* 1, make supremely happy. 2, (*Rom. Cath. Ch.*) declare to be blessed and therefore worthy of certain honors. —**be″a·tif′ic** (bē″ə·tif′ik) *adj.* —**be·at″i·fi·ca′tion,** *n.*

be·at′i·tude″ (bē·at′ə·tūd″) *n.* 1, blessedness; bliss. 2, (*cap.*) any of Jesus's statements on blessedness in the Sermon on the Mount.

beau (bō) *n.* 1, a male lover; swain; 2, a man fussy of his dress; a fop.

beau′te·ous (bū′tē·əs) *adj.* beautiful. —**beau′te·ous·ness,** *n.*

beau·ti′cian (bū·tish′ən) *n.* one who owns or works in a beauty parlor.

---

beau'ti·ful (bū'ti-fəl) *adj.* having beauty; lovely.

beau'ti·fy" (bū'ti-fī") *v.t. & i.* make er become beautiful. —**beau'ti·fi·ca'tion,** *n.*

beau'ty (bū'tē) *n.* 1, the quality of an object of sense or thought that arouses admiration, approval, or pleasure. 2, a particular trait, grace, or charm that pleases. 3, an object possessing beauty, esp. a woman.

bea'ver (bē'vər) *n.* 1, an amphibious rodent prized for its fur. 2, a hat made of beaver fur; a man's high silk hat. 3, a heavy woolen cloth.

be·calm' (bē-käm') *v.t.* make calm or still. —**be·calmed',** *adj.* (*Naut.*) motionless, by lack of wind.

Beaver

be·cause' (bē-kâz') *conj.* for the reason that; since. —*adv.* (with *of*) by reason; on account.

beck (bek) *n.* a beckoning gesture.

beck'on (bek'ən) *v.i. & i.* 1, signal to approach by a gesture of the hand or head. 2, lure; entice.

be·cloud' (bē-klowd') *v.t.* obscure; make unclear.

be·come' (bē-kum') *v.t.* [-came', -com'ing] change (into a state or condition); come into being as. —*v.i.* befit in appearance; grace. —**be·com'ing,** *adj.* attractive; appropriate.

bed *n.* 1, an article of furniture, on which one sleeps. 2, any place of rest or repose. 3, any bottom layer or foundation; the ground in which plants are grown; the bottom of a body of water; the lowest layer of a road. —*v.i.* [bed'ded, bed'ding] 1, shelter. 2, seat firmly in a substance. —*v.i.* go to bed.

bed'bug" *n.* a small blood-sucking insect that infests beds.

bed'cham"ber *n.* a room for sleeping.

bed'clothes" *n. pl.* the sheets, covers, etc. placed on a bed.

bed'ding *n.* bedclothes.

be·deck' (bē-dek') *v.t.* decorate; hang ornaments on.

be·dev'il (bē-dev'əl) *v.t.* torment maliciously; confuse. —**be·dev'il·ment,** *n.*

bed'lam (bed'ləm) *n.* 1, wild uproar and confusion. 2, a lunatic asylum.

be·drag'gled (bē-drag'əld) *adj.* untidy or soiled, as clothes; unkempt.

bed'rid"den (bed'rid"ən) *adj.* not strong or well enough to rise from bed.

bed'room" *n.* a room designed to be slept in.

bed'spread" *n.* an outer cover for a bed, usually decorative.

bed'stead" *n.* the framework of a bed.

bed'time" *n.* the time one goes to bed.

bee (bē) *n.* 1, any of a family of insects that live in colonies and gather honey. 2, a social gathering.

beech (bēch) *n.* a smooth-barked tree found in temperate regions. —**beech'en,** *adj.*

beef (bēf) *n.* 1, the meat of a bovine animal. 2, [*pl.* **beeves**] a steer, bull or cow. 3, (*Colloq.*) muscle; flesh. 4, (*Colloq.*) a complaint. —*v.i.* (*Colloq.*) complain. —**beef'eat"er,** *n.* (*Slang*) an English soldier. —**beef'steak",** *n.* a slice from the best cuts of beef. —**beef'y** (-ē) *adj.* brawny.

bee'line" (bē'līn") *n.* a direct line.

been (bin) *v.* p.p. of *be.*

beer (bir) *n.* 1, an alcoholic beverage made from grain. 2, any fermented nonalcoholic beverage.

bees'wax" (bēz'waks") *n.* wax secreted by bees to make honeycomb.

beet (bēt) *n.* a plant with a dark red fleshy root, used as food or to produce sugar.

bee'tle (bē'təl) *n.* 1, any of an order of insects. 2, a heavy mallet or pestle. 3, (*Slang*) a slow racehorse. —*v.t.* beat; ram. —*v.i.* jut out.

beeves (bēvz) *n. pl.* of *beef.*

be·fall' (bē-fâl') *v.t.* happen; occur. —*v.i.* happen to.

be·fit' (bē-fit') *v.t.* [-fit'ted, -ting] be suitable for; be appropriate to.

be·fogged' (bē-fogd') *adj.* in a fog; bewildered or muddled.

be·fore' (bē-fôr') *prep.* 1, earlier than; previous to. 2, in the future. 3, ahead of in position; in front of. 4, in precedence of; in preference to. 5, in the presence of. —*conj.* 1, previous to the time when. 2, rather than. —*adv.* 1, ahead; in advance. 2, previously; sooner. —**be·fore'hand",** *adv.* in advance of a usual or appointed time.

be·foul' (bē-fowl') *v.t.* make foul.

be·friend' (bē-frend') *v.t.* act as a friend to; aid; favor.

be·fud'dle (bē-fud'əl) *v.t.* stupefy with liquor; muddle; confuse.

beg *v.t. & i.* [begged, beg'ging] 1, ask as alms; live by asking alms. 2, ask as a favor.

be·get' (bē-get') *v.t.* [-got', -get'ting] 1, procreate; generate (of the male parent). 2, produce as an effect. —**be·got'ten,** *adj.* sired; fathered.

beg'gar (beg'ər) *n.* 1, one who begs. 2, one who is very poor. 3, fellow;

rogue. —*v.t.* **1**, make a beggar of; impoverish. **2**, exhaust the resources of. —**beg′gar·y,** *n.*

be·gin′ (bė-gin′) *v.t. & i.* [**-gan′, -gin′ning**] **1**, take the first step in an action; commence; start. **2**, come into existence; arise. —**be·gin′ner,** *n.* one just beginning to learn or do something; a novice. —**be·gin′ning,** *n.* **1**, a start or starting point; an early stage. **2**, origin; source.

be·go′ni·a (bi-gō′nė-ȧ) *n.* a tropical plant having showy flowers.

be·grime′ (bė-grīm′) *v.t.* soil.

be·grudge′ (bė-gruj′) *v.t.* **1**, be disinclined to give or allow. **2**, be envious of another's possession of.

be·guile′ (bė-gīl′) *v.t.* **1**, delude with guile; deceive. **2**, amuse; divert; pass (time). —**be·guile′ment,** *n.*

be·half′ (bė-hâf′) *n.* interest; favor.

be·have′ (bė-hāv′) *v.i.* **1**, conduct oneself or itself; act or operate. **2**, comport oneself properly.

be·hav′ior (bė-hāv′yėr) *n.* manner of behaving; deportment; habits or tendencies.

be·head′ (bė-hed′) *v.t.* cut off the head of.

be·he·moth (bē′ȧ-mȧth; bȧ-hē′-) *n.* a huge, powerful person or animal.

be·hest′ (bė-hest′) *n.* a command.

be·hind′ (bė-hīnd′) *prep.* **1**, at the back of; in the rear of; on the farther side of; beyond. **2**, less advanced than; inferior to. **3**, later than. —*adv.* **1**, toward the back or rear. **2**, in arrears; slow.

be·hind′hand″ *adv.* late; in arrears.

be·hold′ (bė-hōld′) *v.t.* [**-held′, -hold′ing**] observe with care; look at; see. —*interj.* look!

be·hold′en (bė-hōl′dȧn) *adj.* held by an obligation; grateful.

be·hoof′ (bė-hoof′) *n.* advantage.

be·hoove′ (bė-hoov′) *v.t.* (with expletive *it*) be fitting or necessary.

beige (bāzh) *n.* a light tan color.

be′ing (bē′ing) *n.* **1**, existence; life. **2**, a creature; a human.

be·la′bor (bė-lā′bėr) *v.t.* **1**, beat soundly; thump. **2**, assail persistently, as with criticism.

be·lat′ed (bė-lā′tid) *adj.* coming late or too late.

be·lay′ (bė-lā′) *v.t.* fasten (a rope) by winding it around a pin or cleat. —*interj.* stop! desist!

belch *v.i.* **1**, eject wind noisily from the stomach through the mouth; eructate. **2**, issue in spurts. —*v.t.* eject violently; emit spasmodically. —*n.* an eructation; a burst, as of smoke, etc.

be·lea′guer (bė-lē′gėr) *v.t.* surround, as in laying siege to.

bel′fry (bel′frė) *n.* **1**, a tower for a bell. **2**, the part of a steeple or other structure in which a bell is hung.

be·lie′ (bė-lī′) *v.t.* **1**, give a false representation of. **2**, show to be false; contradict.

be·lief′ (bė-lēf′) *n.* **1**, the act of believing; faith. **2**, an accepted opinion.

be·lieve′ (bė-lēv′) *v.t.* **1**, accept as true. **2**, give credence to.

be·lit′tle (bė-lit′al) *v.t.* make lower in importance; disparage.

Church bell   Doorbell   Bell jar

bell (bel) *n.* **1**, a hollow metal device giving forth a resonant or tinkling sound when struck. **2**, a cup-shaped object suggesting a bell. **3**, a nautical unit of time. —*v.i.* swell out. —*v.t.* attach a bell to.

bel′la·don′na (bel′ȧ-don′ȧ) *n.* a medicinal herb.

bell′boy″ (bel′boi″) *n.* an attendant in a hotel. Also (*Colloq.*) **bell′hop″.**

belle (bel) *n.* a beautiful woman, a favorite of admirers.

bel′li·cose″ (bel′ȧ-kōs″) *adj.* warlike; pugnacious. —**bel·li·cos′i·ty** (-kos′ȧ-tė) *n.*

bel·lig′er·ent (bȧ-lij′ėr-ȧnt) *adj.* **1**, pert. to war. **2**, given to waging war; bellicose. **3**, at war. —*n.* a country at war. —**bel·lig′er·ence,** *n.*

bel′low (bel′ō) *v.i. & t.* make a loud, hollow noise; roar. —*n.* a loud outcry.

bel′lows (bel′ōz) *n.* **1**, an instrument for producing a current of air, a kind of box with collapsible sides. **2**, something resembling a bellows.

bell′weth″er (-weth″ėr) *n.* a sheep (usually wearing a bell) that leads the flock.

bel′ly (bel′ė) *n.* **1**, the part of a vertebrate animal between its breast and groin; the abdomen; the stomach. **2**, the inside of anything. —*v.i. & t.* bulge.

be·long′ (bė-lâng′) *v.i.* **1**, (with *to*) be a property or concern (of). **2**, have place (in).

be·lov'ed (bė-luv'id) *adj.* greatly loved. —*n.* one greatly loved.

be·low' (bė-lō') *adv.* **1,** in a lower place; beneath. **2,** at a later point in a writing. —*prep.* **1,** lower than, in position or direction; under; beneath. **2,** inferior to.

belt *n.* **1,** a flexible band worn around the waist. **2,** a similar endless loop. **3,** a stripe; a zone. —*v.t.* **1,** gird. **2,** beat, as with a belt.

be·mused' (bė-mūzd') *adj.* **1,** confused. **2,** lost in thought.

bench *n.* **1,** a long seat. **2,** the office of judge; the judiciary. **3,** a stout table; workbench. **4,** a shelf.

bend *v.t.* [*pret. & p.p.* **bent**] **1,** put a curve or crook in. **2,** turn in a different direction. **3,** force into submission. —*v.i.* become curved or crooked. —*n.* **1,** a curve or crook. **2,** (*pl.*) a disease caused by rapid emergence from compression.

be·neath' (bė-nēth') *adv.* in a lower place, condition, rank, etc.; underneath. —*prep.* below.

ben'e·dict (ben'ə-dikt) *n.* a bridegroom.

ben'e·dic'tion (ben'ə-dik'shən) *n.* **1,** the act of pronouncing a blessing. **2,** a blessing.

ben'e·fac'tion (ben'ə-fak'shən) *n.* **1,** the doing of good. **2,** a benefit conferred, esp. a charitable donation. —**ben'e·fac'tor,** *n.*

ben'e·fice (ben'ə-fis) *n.* an ecclesiastical position providing a living.

be·nef'i·cent (bə-nef'i-sənt) *adj.* conferring benefit; charitable. —**be·nef'i·cence,** *n.*

ben'e·fi'cial (ben'ə-fish'əl) *adj.* **1,** helpful; profitable. **2,** pert. to a benefit.

ben'e·fi'ci·ar·y (ben'ə-fish'ē-er-ē) *n.* a recipient of benefits.

ben'e·fit (ben'ə-fit) *n.* **1,** advantage; profit. **2,** an act of kindness. **3,** an activity, as a theatrical performance, to raise money for a charitable purpose. —*v.i.* [-**fit'ted,** -**ting**] derive a benefit (from). —*v.t.* be beneficial to.

be·nev'o·lent (bə-nev'ə-lənt) *adj.* manifesting a desire to do good; kind. —**be·nev'o·lence,** *n.*

be·night'ed (bė-nī'tid) *adj.* in a state of mental darkness; in deep ignorance.

be·nign' (bė-nīn') *adj.* **1,** of a kind disposition; gracious. **2,** favorable; propitious. —**be·nig'ni·ty** (bė-nig'nə-tē) *n.*

be·nig'nant (bė-nig'nənt) *adj.* kindly; benign. —**be·nig'nan·cy,** *n.*

ben'i·son (ben'i-sən) *n.* a blessing.

bent *adj.* **1,** curved or crooked. **2,** determined; resolved. —*n.* tendency; inclination. —*v.* pret. & p.p. of *bend.*

ben'zene (ben'zēn) *n.* a volatile liquid derived from coal, used as a solvent and fuel.

ben'zine (ben'zēn) *n.* a volatile liquid obtained from petroleum, used in cleaning, etc.

ben'zo·ate (ben'zō-ət) *n.* a salt obtained from benzoin, used as a food preservative.

ben'zo·in (ben'zō-in) *n.* a fragrant resin used in perfumes and drugs.

ben'zol (ben'zōl) *n.* a form of benzene used as a motor fuel, etc.

be·queath' (bė-kwēth') *v.t.* dispose of (property) by will.

be·quest' (bė-kwest') *n.* a legacy.

be·rate' (bė-rāt') *v.t.* scold.

be·reave' (bė-rēv') *v.t.* [*pret. & p.p.* often **be·reft'**] take away from, esp. by death. —**be·reave'ment,** *n.*

be·reft' (bė-reft') *adj.* deprived; destitute.

be·ret' (bə-rā') *n.* a round, soft, visorless cap.

ber'i·ber'i (ber'ē-) *n.* a vitamin-deficiency disease.

Beret

ber'ry (ber'ē) *n.* **1,** any small pulpy fruit. **2,** a dry kernel, as of coffee. —*v.i.* **1,** produce berries. **2,** gather berries.

ber'serk (bėr'sėrk) *adj.* in a frenzy; amuck.

berth (bėrth) *n.* **1,** a sleeping compartment; bunk. **2,** a storage space; a dock. **3,** a job. —*v.i. & t.* enter or place in a berth.

ber'yl (ber'əl) *n.* **1,** a mineral occurring in many colors, prized as a gem. **2,** a blue-green color.

be·ryl'li·um (bə-ril'ē-əm) *n.* a metallic chemical element, no. 4, symbol Be.

be·seech' (bė-sēch') *v.t.* ask urgently; entreat; implore; solicit.

be·seem' (bė-sēm') *v.t.* be fit for or worthy of.

be·set' (bė-set') *v.t.* [**be·set', -set'ting**] attack from all sides; assail; harass.

be·shrew' (bė-shroo') *v.t.* put a curse on.

be·side' (bė-sīd') *prep.* **1,** at the side of; near. **2,** in addition to. **3,** apart from; not connected with. —*adv.* besides.

be·sides' (bė-sīdz') *adv.* **1,** moreover; further. **2,** in addition. **3,** otherwise; else. —*prep.* beside.

be·siege' (bė-sēj') *v.t.* **1,** lay siege to. **2,** harass, as with demands, etc.

be·smirch' (bė-smėrch') *v.t.* soil; sully the honor of.

be'som (bē'zəm) *n.* a broom of twigs.

be·sot'ted (bė-sot'id) *adj.* **1,** stupefied, as with drink. **2,** addicted to drink. —**be·sot'**, *v.i.*

be·speak' (bė-spēk') *v.t.* [**be·spoke'**, **be·spo'ken**] **1,** show; indicate. **2,** order in advance.

best *adj.* **1,** superlative of *good.* **2,** largest. —*adv.* **1,** superlative of *well.* **2,** with most advantage or success. **3,** most fully. —*n.* the utmost; the highest quality. —*v.t.* defeat; surpass.

bes'tial (bes'chəl) *adj.* **1,** like a beast; brutal. **2,** pert. to beasts. —**bes·tial'i·ty** (-chal'ə-tē) *n.*

be·stir' (bė-stēr') *v.t. & i.* [-**stirred'**, -**stir'ring**] agitate; rouse.

be·stow' (bė-stō') *v.t.* **1,** give; confer as a gift. **2,** deposit; consign. —**be·stow'al**, *n.*

be·stride' (bė-strīd') *v.t.* [**be·strode'**, **be·strid'den**] **1,** sit astride of; straddle. **2,** step over or across.

bet *v.t. & i.* [**bet**, **bet'ting**] pledge as forfeit upon some contingency; wager. —*n.* **1,** a wager. **2,** the stake.

be'ta (bā'tə) *n.* the second letter of the Greek alphabet (B, β).

be·take' (bė-tāk') *v.t.* [-**took'**, -**tak'ing**] take (oneself) to a place; go.

be·think' (bė-think') *v.t.* [*pret. & p.p.* -**thought'**] remind (oneself); recall.

be·tide' (bė-tīd') *v.i. & t.* come to pass; happen (to).

be·times' (bė-tīmz') *adv.* (*Archaic*) early; soon.

be·to'ken (bė-tō'kən) *v.t.* be a token or visible sign of; indicate.

be·tray' (bė-trā') *v.t.* **1,** deliver treacherously to an enemy. **2,** be unfaithful in (a trust). **3,** reveal unconsciously. —**be·tray'al**, *n.*

be·troth' (bė-trâth') *v.t.* engage to take or give in marriage. —**be·troth'al**, *n.*

bet'ter (bet'ər) *adj.* **1,** comparative of *good.* **2,** larger. **3,** improved in health. —*adv.* comparative of *well.* —*v.t.* **1,** improve. **2,** surpass. —*n.* **1,** something or someone superior. **2,** [also, **bet'tor**] one who bets. —**bet'ter·ment**, *n.* act or effect of bettering; improvement.

be·tween' (bė-twēn') *prep.* **1,** in the space that separates (two things). **2,** intermediate in time, quantity, or degree. **3,** in joint interest or action of. **4,** involving; concerning. —*adv.* intermediate in space, time, etc.

be·twixt' (bė-twikst') *prep.* between.

bev'el (bev'əl) *n.* **1,** an angle other than a right angle between two lines or surfaces. **2,** an instrument for measuring or cutting a bevel.

—*v.t. & i.* cut or slant obliquely. —*adj.* oblique.

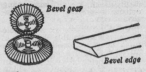

Bevel gear

Bevel edge

bev'er·age (bev'ər-ij) *n.* any liquid fit for drinking.

bev'y (bev'ė) *n.* a flock of birds or girls.

be·wail' (bė-wāl') *v.t. & i.* mourn aloud (for).

be·ware' (bė-wār') *v.i. & t.* be wary (of), cautious, or vigilant.

be·wil'der (bė-wil'dər) *v.t.* lead into perplexity; confuse. —**be·wil'der·ment**, *n.*

be·witch' (bė-wich') *v.t.* **1,** please extremely; charm; fascinate. **2,** cast a spell upon. —**be·witch'ing**, *adj.*

be·yond' (bė-yond') *prep. & adv.* **1,** on the other side of; farther on than. **2,** more than; superior to. **3,** outside the reach or limits of.

bez'el (bez'əl) *n.* a beveled face or part.

bi- *pref.* two; twice; once in every two.

bi'as (bī'əs) *n.* **1,** an oblique line or direction. **2,** prejudice. —*v.t.* prejudice; warp. —*adj. & adv.* oblique; unbalanced.

bib *n.* a cloth worn over the breast to protect the clothing.

Bi'ble (bī'bəl) *n.* **1,** the collection of sacred writings of the Christian religion, comprising the Old and New Testaments. **2,** (*l.c.*) any book regarded as authoritative. —**Bib'li·cal** (bib'li-kəl) *adj.*

bib'li·og'ra·phy (bib'lė-og'rə-fė) *n.* **1,** classification of books. **2,** a list of books. —**bib'li·o·graph'i·cal**, *adj.*

bib'li·o·phile' (bib'lė-ō-fīl') *n.* a lover of books.

bib'u·lous (bib'yə-ləs) *adj.* addicted to drinking liquor. —**bib'u·lous·ness**, *n.*

bi·cam'er·al (bī-kam'ər-əl) *adj.* (of a legislature) comprising two houses.

bi·car'bon·ate of soda (bī-kär'bə-nət) a white, crystalline, alkaline substance, commonly called *baking soda.*

bi'ceps (bī'seps) *n.* a muscle having a double origin at one end, esp. that on the upper arm.

bi·chlor'ide (bī-klôr'īd) *n.* a compound in which each molecule contains two atoms of chlorine.

bick′er (bik′ər) v.i. & n. engage in a petulant quarrel; wrangle.

bi·cus′pid (bī-kus′pid) adj. having two cusps or points. —n. a double-pointed tooth.

bi′cy·cle (bī′sik-əl) n. a vehicle having two wheels in line.

bid v.t. 1, [bade, bid′den, -ding] command; invite. 2, [pret. & p.p. bid] offer a price of. —v.i. make an offer. —n. 1, an amount or thing offered. 2, an effort. 3, an invitation. —bid′der, n.

bide (bīd) v.t. & i. pause; await.

bi·en′ni·al (bī-en′ē-əl) adj. happening every two years.

bier (bir) n. a framework on which a coffin is laid before burial.

biff (bif) v.t. (Colloq.) strike sharply. —n. a blow.

bi·fo′cal (bī-fō′kəl) adj. having two lenses. —n. (pl.) eyeglasses having lenses for near and far vision.

big adj. [big′ger, -gest] 1, large in size, extent, degree, etc. 2, important. 3, generous, tolerant.

big′a·mist (big′ə-mist) n. one who commits bigamy.

big′a·my (big′ə-mē) n. the crime of having two wives or husbands at the same time. —big′a·mous, adj.

big′horn″ n. a wild sheep of the Rocky Mountains.

bight (bīt) n. 1, a bend, as of a coastline; a bay. 2, a loop in rope.

big′ot (big′ət) n. a person intolerant of creeds, opinions, etc. other than his own. —big′ot·ry (-rē) n.

big′wig″ n. (Colloq.) a high-ranking person.

bike (bīk) n. (Colloq.) bicycle.

bi·lat′er·al (bī-lat′ər-əl) adj. having two sides.

bile (bīl) n. 1, a secretion of the liver. 2, ill nature; peevishness.

bilge (bilj) n. 1, the bulging or broadest part, as of a ship or barrel. 2, (Slang) buncombe; obscenity. —bilge water, evil-smelling water that collects in the hold of a ship.

bil′ious (bil′yəs) adj. having an excess of bile. —bil′ious·ness, n.

-bil′i·ty (bil′ə-tē) suf. forming nouns of adjectives ending in -able and -ible.

bilk v.t. defraud; swindle.

bill (bil) n. 1, an account of money owed. 2, a written order to pay money. 3, a piece of paper money. 4, a proposed law. 5, a list or public notice: handbill. 6, the horny beak of a bird. —v.t. 1, enter on a bill; send a bill to. 2, engage or schedule on a theatrical program. —bill and coo, make love sentimentally. —bill of fare, a list of dishes available in a restaurant. —bill of sale, a document transferring possession. —Bill of Rights, constitutional law guaranteeing civil liberties.

bill′board″ (bil′bōrd″) n. a large board for posting of advertisements.

bil′let (bil′it) n. 1, a sleeping space or lodging, esp. for a soldier or sailor. 2, assignment; job. 3, a ticket; a written note [also, bi″lā″]. 4, a stick of wood, esp. for fuel. —v.i. assign to a lodging or place.

bil′liards (bil′yərdz) n. a game played with balls driven by cues on a rectangular table. —bil′liard, n. a scoring shot in this game; carom.

bill′ing n. 1, act of sending or listing on a bill. 2, advertisement of a performer's name on a program.

bil′lings·gate″ (bil′ingz-gāt″) n. coarse and abusive language.

bil′lion (bil′yən) n. 1, (U.S.) a thousand millions: also (Brit.) mil′liard. 2, (Brit.) a million millions.

bil′low (bil′ō) n. a large sea wave; any similar surging mass. —v.i. surge like a sea wave. —bil′low·y, adj.

bil′ly (bil′ē) n. a small bludgeon, esp. a policeman's club.

bil′ly-goat″ n. a male goat.

bi·met′al·lism (bī-met′ə-liz-əm) n. use of both gold and silver as a monetary standard.

bin n. a storage compartment.

bi′na·ry (bī′nə-rē) adj. 1, having two parts or components. 2, based on the radix 2.

bind (bīnd) v.t. [pret. & p.p. bound] 1, make fast with a band; fasten; cause to cohere. 2, form a border on. 3, obligate; compel. —v.i. 1, stick fast; cohere. 2, be obligatory.

bind′er (bīn′dər) n. 1, one who binds. 2, a device for binding; a cover in which loose pages are held. 3, an adhesive; cement. —bind′er·y, n. a place where books are bound.

bind′ing (bīn′ding) n. 1, that which binds: the cover of a bound book; a reinforcing strip; etc.

binge (binj) n. (Slang) spree.

bin′go (bing′gō) n. a game based on lotto. —interj. a cry of triumph.

bin′na·cle (bin′ə-kəl) n. the stand that holds a ship's compass.

bi·noc′u·lar (bə-nok′yə-lər) adj. having or requiring two eyes. —n. (pl.) a telescope or microscope with two eyepieces.

bi·no′mi·al (bī-nō′mē-əl) adj. having two parts. —n. an algebraic expression, as a + b.

bi·og′ra·phy (bī-og′rə-fē) n. 1, a history of the life of a person. 2, such histories collectively. —bi″o·graph′i·cal, adj.

bi·ol·o·gy (bī-ol'ə-jē) *n.* the general science of the structure and processes of living organisms. —**bi'o·log'i·cal**, *adj.* —**bi·ol'o·gist**, *n.*

bi·par·ti·san (bī-pär'ti·zən) *adj.* representing or involving two parties.

bi'ped (bī'ped) *n.* a two-footed animal.

bi'plane" (bī'plān") *n.* an airplane with two wings in tier.

birch (bėrch) *n.* a tree having smooth bark, often white; its wood.

bird (bėrd) *n.* any feather-covered vertebrate animal whose forelimbs form wings. —**bird's-'eye'**, *adj.* general; cursory, as a view.

bird'ie (bėr'dē) *n.* (*Golf*) a score on a hole of one under par.

birth (bėrth) *n.* 1, act of being born. 2, the bringing forth of offspring. 3, lineage; descent. 4, the origin or inception of anything.

birth'day" *n.* the day of one's birth, or any anniversary of it.

birth'mark" *n.* a congenital blemish on the body.

birth'place" *n.* the place where one was born.

birth'right" *n.* inheritance.

bis'cuit (bis'kit) *n.* 1, (*U.S.*) a small, soft cake made from leavened dough. 2, (*Brit.*) a flat, hard cake made from unleavened dough; a cracker. 3, anything in the shape of a biscuit. 4, plastic material in process of shaping, molding, or baking.

bi·sect' (bī-sekt') *v.t.* 1, cut into two parts. 2, divide into two equal parts. —**bi·sec'tion**, *n.*

bish'op (bish'əp) *n.* 1, a high officer of a church. 2, a chess piece. —**bish'op·ric** (-rik) *n.* the diocese or office of a bishop; see.

bis'muth (biz'məth) *n.* a metallic element, no. 83, symbol Bi.

bi'son (bī'sən) *n.* a large animal of the ox family; the buffalo.

bisque (bisk) *n.* 1, a thickened soup. 2, unglazed porcelain. 3, a handicap allowed a weaker player.

bis'tro (bis'trō) *n.* a small café.

Bison

bit *n.* 1, a small piece or quantity of anything. 2, any small coin; a money value of 12½ cents. 3, the mouthpiece of a horse's bridle. 4, the essential part of a cutting tool. —*v.* pret. of *bite.*

bitch (bich) *n.* 1, a female of the dog family. 2, a malicious woman. 3, (*Slang*) a complaint. —*v.i.* (*Slang*) complain. —*v.t.* (*Slang*) bungle; spoil.

bite (bīt) *v.t.* [bit, bit'ten, bit'ing] 1, grip or pierce with the teeth. 2, sting. 3, take firm hold of. 4, eat into; corrode. —*v.i.* 1, take a bait; accept something deceptive. 2, take hold; act with effect. —*n.* 1, the act of biting. 2, a wound made by biting. 3, a piece bitten off. 4, a small quantity of food.

bit'ten (bit'ən) *v.* p.p. of *bite.*

bit'ter (bit'ər) *adj.* 1, having a harsh taste. 2, hard to bear; disagreeable. 3, cruel; sarcastic. —*n.* (*pl.*) a liquor having a bitter taste. —**bit'ter·ness**, *n.*

bit'tern (bit'ərn) *n.* a No. Amer. heron.

bi·tu'men (bi-tū'mən) *n.* any of a class of natural substances such as petroleum and asphalt. —**bi·tu'mi·nous**, *adj.*

bi'valve" (bī'valv") *n.* a mollusk having two shells, as the oyster. —*adj.* two-shelled.

biv'ou·ac" (biv'oo-ak") *n.* an unsheltered encampment or camp. —*v.i.* [biv'ou·acked", -ack"ing] encamp without shelter.

bi·zarre" (bi-zär') *adj.* odd; whimsical; grotesque. —**bi·zarre'ness**, *n.*

blab *v.t.* [blabbed, blab'bing] utter thoughtlessly; disclose. —*v.i.* talk indiscreetly.

black (blak) *n.* the color of coal; strictly, the absence of all color or of all illumination. —*adj.* 1, entirely or relatively dark. 2, dismal; wicked; calamitous. —*v.t.* put blacking on.

black'a·moor" (blak'ə·mûr") *n.* a Negro.

black'ball" *v.t.* reject.

black'ber"ry *n.* a thorny vine, or its fruit.

black'bird" *n.* any of various birds having dark plumage.

black'board" *n.* a slate bulletin board.

black'en (-ən) *v.t. & i.* make or become black.

black'guard (blag'ərd) *n.* a scoundrel. —**black'guard·ly**, *adj.*

black'head" *n.* 1, a secretion of fatty matter in a skin follicle. 2, a disease of poultry.

black'ing *n.* shoe polish;

Blackjack

black'jack" (blak'jak") *n.* 1, a club with a heavy head and a short elastic shaft. 2, card game: *twenty-one.* —*v.t.* 1, hit with a blackjack. 2, coerce.

black'leg" n. 1, a disease of cattle. 2, a strikebreaker; scab. 3, a swindler; a crooked gambler.

black'list" n. a list of persons in disfavor. —v.t. vote against (a candidate for club membership).

black'mail" n. extortion of a bribe for silence. —v.t. threaten exposure unless paid.

black market the selling of goods in violation of legal restrictions. —**black mar"ket-eer"**, one who sells goods on the black market.

black'out" n. 1, the extinguishing of lights as a protection against enemy airplanes. 2, unconsciousness; a faint. 3, loss of memory.

black sheep a disgraceful member of a family or group.

black'smith" (blak'smith") n. a worker in iron, esp. a horseshoer.

black'thorn" n. a prickly shrub.

black widow a kind of poisonous spider.

blad'der (blad'ər) n. 1, a body sac in which urine is retained. 2, any elastic sac or bag.

blade (blād) n. 1, the sharpened part of a cutting or piercing weapon or tool; the weapon or tool itself, esp. a sword. 2, the leaf of a plant; the broad part of a leaf. 3, any broad thin part, as of an oar. 4, a gay or rakish fellow.

blame (blām) v.t. charge with an error or fault. —n. imputation of error or fault; censure. —**blame'wor"thy**, adj. culpable.

blanch (blanch) v.t. make white or pale. —v.i. become pale.

bland adj. 1, suave. 2, affable; kindly. 3, mild; balmy. 4, oily; nonirritating or nonstimulating (of foods or medicines). —**bland'ness**, n.

blan'dish v.t. coax or cajole with flattery or caresses. —**blan'dish·ment**, n.

blank adj. 1, empty; bare; void of something usual or necessary to completeness. 2, not written or printed on. 3, showing no emotion; unresponsive. 4, complete; unmitigated. 5, white or pale. —n. 1, a space from which something is absent or omitted; a vacancy. 2, a printed form or space not filled out by writing. 3, a rough-fashioned wood or metal part to be finished by tooling. —v.t. 1, (with out) make blank. 2, (Colloq.) keep an opponent in a game from scoring. —**blank'ness**, n.

blan'ket (blang'kit) n. 1, a large piece of heavy cloth, used as a bed-covering. 2, any extensive or close covering, as of snow. —adj. widespread; comprehensive. —v.t. cover with or as with a blanket.

blare (blâr) v.i. give out a brazen sound; bellow. —v.t. sound loudly; proclaim. —n. 1, a trumpet's sound. 2, blatancy in sound, color, etc.

blar'ney (blär'nē) n. wheedling talk; cajolery. —v.t. & i. flatter; cajole.

bla·sé' (blä-zā') adj. satiated with pleasure; bored.

blas·pheme' (blas-fēm') v.t. speak irreverently of God or sacred things. —v.i. 1, speak impiously of (God, etc.) 2, speak evil of; revile. —**blas'phe·my** (-fə-mē) n.

blast (blåst) n. 1, a forcible stream or sudden gust of air. 2, the blowing of a horn, whistle, etc.; the sound of a wind instrument. 3, an explosion; a charge of explosives. 4, a blight. —v.t. 1, shatter with explosives. 2, ruin; destroy; cause to shrivel.

bla'tant (blā'tənt) adj. 1, offensively loud-voiced; noisy. 2, obtrusive. —**bla'tan·cy** (-tən-sē) n.

blaze (blāz) n. 1, flame or fire. 2, any dazzling display; brilliant sunlight; a bright flame; a hot glow. 3, a sudden outburst of fire, passion, etc. 4, a white spot on the face of a horse, cow, etc. 5, a mark made on a tree to indicate a path or boundary. 6, (pl.) (Slang) hell. —v.i. burst into flame; burn brightly; shine. —v.t. 1, exhibit vividly; proclaim. 2, mark with a blaze.

blaz'er (blā'zər) n. 1, a bright-colored coat for sports wear. 2, a pan for use over a flame. 3, (Colloq.) anything intensely hot or bright.

bla'zon (blā'zən) v.t. 1, depict or describe in heraldic terms. 2, adorn. 3, display; proclaim. —n. 1, a coat of arms. 2, pompous display. —**bla'zon·ry**, n.

bleach (blēch) v.t. & i. make or become white, pale, or colorless. —n. a bleaching agent.

bleach'ers (blē'chərz) n. pl. unsheltered seats on a playing field.

bleak (blēk) adj. 1, desolate and windswept. 2, cold; piercing. 3, cheerless; dreary. —**bleak'ness**, n.

blear (blir) v.t. dim (the eyes) with tears, etc. —adj. (of the eyes) sore or dimmed. —**blear'y**, adj.

bleat (blēt) n. the cry of a sheep, goat, or calf. —v.i. utter such a cry.

bled v. pret. & p.p. of **bleed**.

bleed (blēd) v.i. [bled] 1, emit blood. 2, exude fluid. 3, flow out; run together. 4, feel pity, sorrow, or anguish. —v.t. 1, cause to lose blood, sap, etc.; make flow; drain out. 2, (Colloq.) extort money from, as by overcharge or blackmail. 3, (Printing) allow (a picture) to run off the page; trim (a page) so as to cut into the printing.

blem'ish v.t. deface; mar; damage. —n. defect; flaw; stain.

blench v.i. draw back; flinch; quail.

blend v.t. **1,** mix inseparably. **2,** mix so as to obtain a desired combination of qualities. —v.i. **1,** combine into a harmonious whole. **2,** pass imperceptibly into one another. —n. **1,** the act of blending. **2,** something formed by blending; a smooth mixture; a harmonious whole.

bless (bles) v.t. **1,** consecrate by a religious rite. **2,** invoke God's favor upon. **3,** make happy, fortunate, or prosperous. **4,** praise; extol. —**bless'ed** (-ed), **blessed,** or **blest,** adj. —**bless'ed** event, the birth of a child.

bless'ing n. **1,** a short prayer for divine approval. **2,** a fortunate occurrence. **3,** benediction; approval.

blew (bloo) v. pret. of **blow.**

blight (blīt) n. **1,** any widespread disease of plants. **2,** any similar malignant and destructive influence. —v.t. **1,** cause to wither or decay. **2,** ruin; frustrate.

blimp n. an airship with a non-rigid gas bag.

Blimp

blind (blīnd) adj. **1,** lacking or having lost the sense of sight. **2,** lacking in discernment; unable to understand or judge. **3,** irrational; undiscriminating; heedless. **4,** out of sight; hidden; unlighted. **5,** having no opening or outlet. **6,** done without seeing. —v.t. **1,** deprive of sight. **2,** make obscure; conceal. **3,** impair the perception or judgment of. —n. **1,** something that obstructs vision or excludes light. **2,** something that masks a purpose or action. **3,** a rude shelter for hunters. —**blind alley,** a street blocked at one end; an impasse. —**blind date,** an engagement with a stranger. —**blind'ness,** n.

blind'fold" n. a bandage over the eyes.

blink v.i. **1,** wink rapidly and repeatedly. **2,** shine unsteadily; glimmer. —v.t. **1,** catch sight of. **2,** regard with indifference; ignore. —n. **1,** a wink or gleam. **2,** a glance or glimpse.

blink'er n. **1,** an intermittent signal light. **2,** (pl.) shades for horses' eyes.

bliss (blis) n. **1,** supreme happiness; spiritual joy. **2,** gladness. —**bliss'ful,** adj.

blis'ter (blis'tər) n. **1,** a vesicle on the skin. **2,** any similar swelling, as in a coat of paint; an air bubble in a metal casting. —v.t. **1,** raise a blister on. **2,** vituperate; mortify. —v.i. become blistered.

blithe (blīth) adj. merry; joyous; glad; light-hearted. —**blithe'ness,** n. —**blithe'some** (-səm) adj. merry; gay.

blitz (blits) n. **1,** a violent and highly mobile attack by combined military forces of different types. **2,** any sudden or overwhelming onslaught. —v.t. attack with a blitz.

blitz'krieg" (blits'krēg") n. (Ger.) lightning warfare; blitz.

bliz'zard (bliz'ərd) n. **1,** a heavy fall of snow. **2,** a violent windstorm with sleet or dry snow.

bloat (blōt) v.t. **1,** cause to swell or distend. **2,** make vain or conceited. **3,** cure (fish) by smoking. —v.i. puff up; dilate. —n. a dietary ailment of cattle, sheep, and horses.

bloat'er (-ər) n. a fish cured by salting and smoking, like herring.

blob n. a small globe of liquid; a drop, bubble, or lump.

bloc (blok) n. a group of legislators, often of several parties, acting together for a particular interest.

block (blok) n. **1,** a solid mass of stone, wood, metal, etc. **2,** a solid mass used as a table for heavy work; a form on which something is molded or shaped. **3,** a base on which an engraving is mounted for printing. **4,** a platform, as that mounted by an auctioneer. **5,** a case containing one or more pulleys, for rigging rope tackles. **6,** an obstruction; the condition of being obstructed. **7,** the area of a town bounded by two intersecting pairs of two adjacent streets. **8,** a portion or section treated as a unit. **9,** a section of a railway, allotted for signaling purposes. —v.t. **1,** mount on or fit with a block. **2,** (usually with out) plan or sketch roughly. **3,** obstruct; check.

block·ade' (blok-ād') n. **1,** the barring of entrance to and exit from a place, esp. a port or coast. **2,** any obstruction of passage or progress. —v.t. shut up or obstruct by a blockade.

block'bust"er n. a large explosive aerial bomb.

block'head" (blok'hed") n. a stupid person.

block'house" n. a house of heavy timber used as a fort.

blond adj. [fem. **blonde** (blond)] light-colored, esp. as to hair and skin. —n. a person with light hair and fair skin. —**blond'ness,** n.

blood (blud) n. **1,** the fluid that circulates in the arteries and veins of animals. **2,** any vital fluid; the sap or juice of plants. **3,** descent; lineage; racial heritage. **4,** a person of high spirit; a rake. —**blood bank,** a supply of whole blood or plasma. —**blood count,** a count of red and white blood cells per unit of volume. —**blood relation,** a person related by birth. —**blood vessel,** any vein or artery.

blood'hound" n. a keen-scented tracking dog.

blood'less adj. 1, done without bloodshed. 2, pale. 3, lacking courage.

blood'shed" n. slaughter.

blood'shot" adj. (of eyes) streaked with red.

blood'suck"er n. 1, a leech. 2, an extortioner.

blood'thirst"y adj. eager to kill. —**blood'thirst"i·ness**, n.

blood'y (blud'ē) adj. 1, covered with blood; gory. 2, marked by great bloodshed. 3, (Brit.) a vulgar expletive. —**blood'i·ness**, n.

bloom n. 1, the flower of a plant. 2, the state of blossoming; a flourishing condition. 3, a rosy glow or other evidence of youth or good health. 4, a powdery deposit or coating, as on plums, cabbage leaves, etc. 5, a rough-rolled ingot of steel. —v.i. 1, produce blossoms. 2, flourish; be in good health. 3, glow with color. —**bloom'er**, n. a blunder.

bloom'ers (bloo'mərz) n. pl. loose trousers gathered at the knees, for women.

bloom'ing adj. confounded: an expletive of little or no meaning.

blos'som (blos'əm) n. 1, the flower of a plant. 2, the state of bearing flowers. —v.i. 1, produce blossoms. 2, become mature; develop.

blot n. 1, a spot or stain, as of ink on paper. 2, an erasure or obliteration. 3, a blemish, as upon character or reputation. —v.t. [blot'ted, -ting] 1, stain; spatter. 2, efface; obliterate. 3, dry with a blotter. —v.i. form a stain; become stained.

blotch (bloch) n. a large irregular spot or blot. —v.t. blot; blur.

blot'ter (blot'ər) n. 1, a piece of absorbent paper used to remove excess ink. 2, a journal book, esp. as used in a police station.

blouse (blows) n. 1, a loose garment worn on the upper body, esp. by women and children. 2, an outer garment reaching to the knees, often belted, worn by both sexes in Russia and elsewhere.

blow (blō) v.i. [blew, blown (blōn), blow'ing] 1, produce a current of air. 2, be carried about by or as by wind. 3, make a whistling sound; give out sound. 4, breathe hard; pant. 5, (with up or out) explode. 6, (with over) subside. 7, (Colloq.) boast. 8, produce flowers; blossom. —v.t. 1, drive by a current of air. 2, force air into or through, in order to clear, cause to sound, inflate, etc. 3, scatter or shatter, as by exploding. 4, (with up) inflate; enlarge. 5, (Slang) squander. —n. 1, a blast of air; a gale of wind. 2, a stroke with the hand; a thump. 3, a sudden shock or calamity.

blow'out" n. 1, a sudden escape of air or liquid, as from a ruptured tire, steam pipe, etc. 2, (Colloq.) a spree.

blow'pipe" n. a pipe through which air is forced.

blub'ber (blub'ər) n. the fat of whales. —v.i. weep with a contorted face. —v.t. say tearfully.

blu'cher (bloo'kər) n. 1, a shoe in which tongue and upper are cut from one piece. 2, a short boot.

bludg'eon (bluj'ən) n. a heavy-headed club. —v.t. 1, hit with a bludgeon. 2, bully; coerce.

blue (bloo) n. 1, the color of the clear sky; a hue between green and violet in the spectrum. 2, (Poetic) the sky; the sea. —adj. 1, of blue color; azure. 2, (of the skin) livid, as from cold or fear. 3, depressed; despondent. 4, dismal; unpromising. 5, strict in morals; puritanic. —v.t. make blue; dye blue.

blue'bell" (bloo'bel") n. any of various plants having blue bell-shaped flowers.

blue'ber"ry n. the small, bluish, edible fruit of various shrubs.

blue'bird" n. a blue songbird of eastern U.S.

blue'blood" n. (Colloq.) an aristocrat.

blue'bon"net n. the state flower of Texas.

blue'bot"tle (bloo'bot"əl) n. 1, a large fly of blue-green color. 2, any of several plants with blue flowers; the cornflower.

blue'fish" n. any of various edible fishes.

blue'jack"et n. a sailor.

blue'print" (bloo'print") n. 1, a photographic process that produces a print with white lines on a blue field. 2, such a print. 3, any detailed plan. —v.t. make a blueprint of.

blues (blooz) n. 1, a style of mournful jazz music. 2, a feeling of despondency.

bluff (bluf) v.t. & i. mislead by a pretense of strength, influence, etc. —n. 1, the act of bluffing. 2, a broad, steep, face of a hill or headland. —adj. 1, somewhat abrupt in manner; rough and hearty; frank. 2, having a broad front or face.

blu'ing (bloo'ing) n. a bluish dye used to whiten clothes after washing.

blun'der (blun'dər) n. a gross or stupid mistake. —v.i. 1, make such a mistake. 2, move blindly or clumsily. —v.t. confuse; bungle.

blun'der·buss" (-bus") n. a musket with flaring mouth.

blunt *adj.* 1, having a rounded or thick point or edge; not sharp. 2, rough in manner or speech; abrupt; plain-spoken. —*v.t.* make blunt; impair the force or keenness of. —blunt'ness, *n.*

blur (blẽr) *v.t.* [blurred, blur'ring] 1, make indistinct; obscure without effacing. 2, sully; stain. 3, dim the perception or susceptibility of. —*v.i.* become indistinct. —*n.* 1, a blot, smudge, or smear. 2, a confused appearance. —blur'ry, *adj.* —blur'ri-ness, *n.*

blurb (blẽrb) *n.* a laudatory advertisement, esp. of a book.

blurt (blẽrt) *v.t.* utter suddenly; divulge inadvertently.

blush *v.i.* 1, become red in the face from shame or embarrassment. 2, be ashamed. 3, become red or rosy. —*n.* 1, a reddening of the face. 2, a pink tinge.

blus'ter (blus'tər) *v.i.* 1, be loud and boastful; swagger; utter empty menaces. 2, roar. —*n.* boastful utterance.

bo'a (bō'ə) *n.* 1, any of various large snakes that kill by constricting. 2, a long neckpiece worn by women.

boar (bōr) *n.* 1, the wild hog. 2, an uncastrated domesticated hog.

board (bōrd) *n.* 1, a long, thin cut of timber. 2, a flat slab of wood used for some specific purpose, as for ironing, posting notices, playing games, etc. 3, a table, esp. for food. 4, provision for daily meals. 5, a group of officials acting together. 6, border; edge. —*v.t.* 1, cover with boards. 2, furnish with daily meals. —*v.i.* be supplied with daily meals. —board'ing house, a lodging house where meals are served.

boast (bōst) *v.i.* 1, speak vaingloriously or exaggeratedly of one's own worth, property, deeds, etc. 2, speak with laudable pride. —*v.t.* 1, speak of with vanity or exultation. 2, take pride in possessing. —*n.* 1, something boasted of. 2, bragging speech. —boast'ful, *adj.*

boat (bōt) *n.* 1, a vessel for transport on water, esp. a small one moved by oars. 2, an open dish, as for gravy. —*v.i.* & *t.* go or transport by boat.

boat'swain (bō'sən; bōt'swān") *n.* a superior seaman in charge of anchors, cables, etc.

bob *n.* 1, a jerk; jerking motion. 2, any small dangling object: a weight on a plumb line; a float on a

Boa Constrictor

fishing line. 3, a style of short haircut. 4, a kind of sled. 5, (*Brit.*) a shilling. —*v.i.* [bobbed, bob'bing] move jerkily; go up and down quickly. —*v.t.* 1, cut short. 2, hit lightly.

bob'bin (bob'in) *n.* a reel or spool for holding thread, yarn, or wire.

bob'by (bob'ē) *n.* a policeman.

bobby pin a clip for the hair.

bobby socks ankle-length socks. Also, bobby sox. —bobby sox'er (sok'sər) a teen-age girl.

bob'cat" *n.* an Amer. wildcat.

bob'o-link" (bob'ə-link") *n.* an American songbird.

bob'white" (bob'hwit") *n.* an American quail or partridge.

bock (bok) *n.* a dark beer, usually the first brew of the spring season.

bode (bōd) *v.t.* & *i.* be an omen (of); portend; betoken.

bod'ice (bod'is) *n.* 1, a laced outer garment covering the upper body, worn by women. 2, a close-fitting waist or body of a gown.

bod'i-ly (bod'ə-lē) *adj.* pert. to the body; corporeal.

bod'kin *n.* 1, a blunt needle for drawing tape through a hem or loop. 2, an awl for making holes in cloth, etc. 3, (*Obs.*) a dagger.

bod'y (bod'ē) *n.* 1, the physical structure of an animal. 2, the main portion of this structure, excluding the head, appendages, etc. 3, the main part of anything; a vehicle exclusive of wheels, etc.; a speech or treatise exclusive of introduction, appendix, etc. 4, anything existing in three-dimensional space; a solid; anything having inertia or mass. 5, weight, density, consistency, or other attribute of a solid. 6, a group of persons or things collectively. **bod'y-guard"** *n.* a private guard; an escort.

Boer (bōr) *n.* a So. Afr. native of Dutch descent.

bog *n.* an area of wet and spongy ground; marsh. —*v.t.* & *i.* [bogged, bog'ging] sink in a bog; flounder among obstacles.

bo'gey (bō'gē) *n.* (*Golf*) a score of par on a hole (*Brit.*) or one over par (*U.S.*).

bo'gie (bō'gē) *n.* bogy.

bo'gus (bō'gəs) *adj.* counterfeit; spurious; sham.

bo'gy (bō'gē) *n.* a troublesome imp; hobgoblin; anything that annoys. Also, bo'gie.

Bo-he'mi-an (bō-hē'mē-ən) *adj.* pert. to Bohemia or Bohemians, or the Czech language. —*n.* (*l.c.*) One who lives a gay, unconventional life.

boil *v.i.* 1, change from liquid to gas under the influence of heat.

2, be agitated, as by bubbles of gas rising to the surface of a heated liquid; be excited, esp. by anger. —*v.t.* **1,** cause to boil. **2,** cook by boiling. **3,** (with *down*) abridge; condense. —*n.* **1,** the act or condition of boiling. **2,** an inflammatory and suppurating sore on the skin. —**boil′er,** *n.* a vessel in which a liquid is boiled, esp. a tank in which water is converted to steam to operate an engine or furnish heat.

bois′ter·ous (boi′stər-əs) *adj.* **1,** noisy and violent; clamorous. **2,** coarse and unrestrained. —**bois′terous·ness,** *n.*

bold (bōld) *adj.* **1,** daring; brave; courageous. **2,** overstepping usual bounds; forward; impudent. **3,** requiring or exhibiting courage. **4,** standing out to view; conspicuous. **5,** steep; abrupt. —**bold′ness,** *n.*

bole *n.* the trunk of a tree.

bo·le′ro (bō-lār′ō) *n.* [*pl.* -ros] **1,** a lively Spanish dance in triple time. **2,** a short close-fitting jacket reaching only to the waist.

boll (bōl) *n.* a pod or seed vessel of cotton, flax, and other plants. —**boll weevil,** a beetle infesting cotton bolls.

bo·lo′gna (bə-lōn′yə) *n.* a variety of sausage.

Bol′she·vik (bol′shə-vik) *n.* [*pl.* -vi′ki (-vē′kē)] a member of the controlling Communist party in Russia. —**Bol′she·vism,** *n.* the doctrines of this party. —**Bol′she·vist,** *n.*

bol′ster (bōl′stər) *n.* **1,** a long cylindrical pillow. **2,** anything resembling a bolster, used to pad or prop. —*v.t.* prop up; support.

bolt (bōlt) *n.* **1,** a metal pin, usually threaded at one end to receive a nut. **2,** the movable pin or bar of a lock that engages the fixed socket or frame. **3,** an arrow used in a crossbow. **4,** a bundle or roll, as of cloth or wallpaper. **5,** a stream of lightning; thunderbolt. **6,** a sudden spring; the act of running away; desertion of a political party or candidate. —*v.t.* & *i.* **1,** fasten with a bolt. **2,** run away from; desert. **3,** swallow (food) hastily. —*adv.* abruptly; stiffly.

bomb (bom) *n.* **1,** an explosive missile, not fired from a gun. **2,** a mass of lava ejected from a volcano. —*v.t.* & *i.* hurl bombs at or on.

bom·bard′ (bom-bärd′) *v.t.* **1,** attack with bombs. **2,** attack with artillery. **3,** assail violently. —*n.* the earliest type of cannon.

bom′bast *n.* high-sounding, extravagant, or stilted words. —**bombas′tic,** *adj.* —**bom·bas′ti·cal·ly,** *adv.*

bomb′er (bom′ər) *n.* an airplane used to drop bombs.

bomb′shell″ *n.* **1,** a bomb. **2,** a sudden and devastating event.

bomb′sight″ *n.* a device for aiming bombs dropped by aircraft.

bo′na-fide″ (bō′nə-fīd″) (*Lat.*) in good faith; without fraud. —*adj.* made in good faith; genuine.

bo·nan′za (bō-nan′zə) *n.* **1,** a rich mass of ore. **2,** any lucky find or profitable enterprise.

bon′bon″ *n.* a piece of candy.

bond *n.* **1,** anything that binds, fastens, or confines. **2,** something that unites people; a cause of union. **3,** something that constrains action; an obligation or duty. **4,** a written promise or obligation to pay money, perform a duty, etc.; an insurance agreement. **5,** an interest-bearing certificate of indebtedness of a corporation or government. **6,** a substance for compacting particles into a solid mass. **7,** a close-compacted variety of paper. —*v.t.* **1,** put under bond. **2,** place a bonded debt upon. **3,** form into a compact mass. —*v.i.* hold together; adhere solidly.

bond′age (bon′dij) *n.* **1,** involuntary servitude; slavery. **2,** the state of being under obligation, restraint, or captivity.

bonds′man (bondz′mən) *n.* [*pl.* -men] a surety.

bone (bōn) *n.* **1,** any of the pieces of which the skeleton of a vertebrate is composed. **2,** the hard tissue of which the skeleton is made. **3,** any of various similar hard substances, as ivory. **4,** something made of bone or the like; a domino; a die; a strip of whalebone or metal for stiffening a corset. —*v.t.* **1,** remove the bones from. **2,** put bone or bones into. —*v.i.* (*Slang*) study hard; cram. —**bone′-head″,** *n.* a stupid person.

bon′fire″ (bon′fīr″) *n.* a fire built in the open.

bon′i·face″ (bon′i-fās″) *n.* the keeper of an inn.

bon′net (bon′it) *n.* **1,** a covering for the head worn by women and children, usually tied with ribbons under the chin. **2,** protective cover; the hood of an automobile.

Bonnet

bon′ny (bon′ē) *adj.* pretty.

bo′nus (bō′nəs) *n.* a sum of money given over and above what is required to be paid.

bon′y (bō′nē) *adj.* **1,** of, like, or full of bones. **2,** thin. —**bon′i·ness,** *n.*

boo *interj.* expressing contempt or disapproval, or used to frighten. —*v.t.* show contempt for; disapprove. —*v.i.* utter a boo.

---

boo'by (boo'bè) n. 1, a stupid person. 2, the contestant who finishes lowest or last in a game. 3, any of various gannets. —**booby hatch** (Colloq.) a mental institution. —**booby trap,** a stratagem to deceive the unwary; a hidden explosive or mine.

boo'dle (boo'dəl) n. money fraudulently obtained in public service. —v.t. obtain money by corruption.

boo'gie-woo'gie (bû'gè-wû'gè) n. a form of jazz music.

book (bûk) n. 1, a written or printed composition of considerable length. 2, a number of sheets of paper bound together. 3, a similar bundle of tickets, stamps, tobacco leaves, etc. 4, (cap.) the Bible. 5, a written record; the script of a play; the libretto of an opera. —v.t. & i. 1, enter in a book; record. 2, engage place for; engage the services of; schedule.

book'case'' n. a set of shelves for books.

book'ie (-è) n. bookmaker.

book'keep''ing (bûk'kē''ping) n. the theory and practice of keeping records of money transactions.

book'let (-lət) n. a book having few pages and often no cover.

book'mak''er n. one who accepts bets, esp. on horse races.

book'worm'' n. 1, an insect larva that feeds on bookbindings. 2, a person devoted to books and reading.

boom n. 1, a prolonged hollow sound. 2, a rapid heightening or increase of interest, activity, popularity, prices, etc. 3, a spar used to extend the foot of certain kinds of sails. 4, the movable arm of a derrick. 5, a barrier set up in water, of logs, chains, etc. —v.t. 1, say or give forth with a prolonged resonant sound. 2, promote vigorously. —v.i. 1, make a booming sound. 2, swell in magnitude; flourish.

boom'er·ang'' (boo'mə-rang'') n. 1, a missile weapon of the Australian aborigines, which returns to the thrower if it misses the target. 2, a scheme or enterprise that recoils with injurious effect.

boon n. 1, a benefit enjoyed; something to be thankful for. 2, a favor asked. —adj. convivial.

boor (bûr) n. 1, one who is rude, unmannerly, or clownish. 2, a rustic. —**boor'ish,** adj.

boost v.t. 1, shove upward; lift from below; raise. 2, aid by speaking well of; promote. —n. 1, an upward shove. 2, an act of assistance or promotion.

boost'er (-ər) n. 1, a device to increase applied power. 2, a zealous supporter.

boot n. 1, a foot covering that reaches high above the ankle, usually to the knee. 2, (Brit.) a shoe that covers the ankle. 3, any of several kinds of protective covering; a footband for a horse; an apron for the driver's seat of a vehicle. 4, a blow with the foot; a kick. 5, (Slang) dismissal. —v.t. 1, kick. 2, (Slang) dismiss. 3, (Colloq.) bungle. 4, put boots on. —**to boot,** in addition.

boot'black'' n. one who shines shoes.

booth n. 1, a temporary structure as for the display of wares, for voting, etc. 2, a small room or compartment, as for projecting motion pictures.

boot'leg'' n. liquor transported or sold illegally. —v.t. & i. [-legged'', -leg''ging] deal in (liquor or other commodity) unlawfully. —adj. made, transported or sold illegally. —**boot'leg''ger,** n.

boo'ty (boo'tè) n. 1, spoil taken from an enemy in war; anything seized by violence. 2, any prize or gain.

booze (booz) n. (Colloq.) intoxicating liquor. —v.i. drink immoderately. —**booz'y,** adj.

bop n. a type of jazz music.

bo·rac'ic acid (bə-ras'ik) boric acid.

bo'rax (bôr'əks) n. a white crystalline mineral used as a flux and cleansing agent.

bor'der (bôr'dər) n. 1, a side or edge; limit or boundary. 2, a line separating two countries, etc.; the area near such a line; frontier. 3, something marking a boundary; an ornamental strip; a frame of lines. —v.t. 1, enclose or adorn with a border. 2, be a boundary to. 3, lie at the boundary of; adjoin. —v.i. touch upon; abut; approach closely.

bore (bôr) v.t. 1, pierce or gouge out with an auger or drill. 2, penetrate forcibly. 3, weary or annoy by tedious iteration, dullness, etc.—v.i. 1, make a hole with a rotary cutting instrument. 2, advance by persistent thrusting. —n. 1, a hole made by or as if by boring. 2, the internal diameter of a circular hole or a hollow cylinder; the caliber of a gun. 3, a tiresome or annoying person. 4, a cause of ennui. 5, a periodic and forceful flow of tidal water through a narrow channel.

bo're·al (bôr'è-əl) adj. 1, pert. to the north wind. 2, northern.

bore'dom (-dəm) n. state of being bored; ennui.

bor'ic (bôr'ik) adj. containing boron. —**boric acid,** a substance obtained from borax, used in solution as a mild antiseptic and eye wash.

born (bôrn) adj. 1, brought forth by birth. 2, congenital.

borne (bōrn) v. p.p. of *bear.* —*adj.* 1, carried. 2, endured.

bo'ron (bōr'on) n. a chemical element, no. 5, symbol B.

bor'ough (bẽr'ō) n. 1, an incorporated municipality smaller than a city. 2, one of the administrative divisions of a city, as in New York.

bor'row (bor'ō) v.t. 1, obtain temporary possession or use of; take (a thing) on pledge to return it or an equivalent. 2, take and adopt (words, ideas) from a foreign source. 3, transfer (units) in arithmetical subtraction. —v.i. receive a loan.

borsch (bôrsh) n. a beet soup. Also, **borsht** (bôrsht).

bosh n. utter nonsense; nothing.

bos'om (būz'əm) n. 1, the human breast. 2, the enclosure formed by the breast and arms; embrace. 3, the breast as the supposed seat of tender emotions. 4, the part of a garment that covers the breast. —*adj.* intimate; familiar. —v.t. 1, embrace; cherish. 2, conceal.

boss (bâs) n. 1, an overseer of workmen; superintendent; manager. 2, one who controls a political party. 3, a rounded protuberance, knob, stud, or enlarged part. —v.t. be the boss of; manage; direct. —v.i. 1, be boss. 2, be domineering. —*adj.* chief; master. —**boss'y,** *adj.*

bot'a·ny (bot'ə-nē) n. 1, the general science of plant life. 2, the plants of a region. —bo·tan'i·cal (bə-tan'i-kəl) *adj.* —bot'a·nist (bot'ə-nist) n.

botch (boch) v.t. spoil by unskillful work; bungle. —n. a poorly-done piece of work.

both (bōth) *adj. & pron.* the one and the other (of two); the pair or couple together. —*adv. & conj.* including the two; equally; alike.

both'er (both'ər) v.t. & i. give trouble to; annoy; pester; bewilder. —n. 1, someone or something that bothers. 2, the state of being annoyed or worried. —*interj.* [also (*Colloq.*) **both'er·a'tion**] expressing mild vexation or perplexity. —**both'er·some** (-səm) *adj.* causing trouble; perplexing.

bot'tle (bot'əl) n. 1, a vessel for holding liquids, usually of glass. 2, the contents or capacity of a bottle. 3, intoxicating liquor. —v.t. 1, put in a bottle. 2, (often with *up*) shut in; restrain forcibly. —**bot'tle·neck'**, n. a point at which progress is retarded.

bot'tom (bot'əm) n. 1, the lowest or deepest part of anything; the base, foundation, or root; the under side. 2, the ground under any body of water. 3, the hull of a ship; the part of the hull below the wales; a ship generally. 4, the buttocks. 5, the fundamental aspect; basic principles.

—*adj.* 1, lowest; undermost. 2, fundamental. —v.t. 1, furnish with a bottom. 2, use as a base. 3, get to the bottom of; fathom. —v.i. 1, be based; rest. 2, run aground.

bot'u·lism (boch'ə-liz-əm) n. poisoning due to a toxin produced by certain bacteria in preserved foods.

bou'doir (boo'dwär) n. a woman's bedroom or private sitting room.

bough (bow) n. a branch of a tree.

bought (bât) v. pret. & p.p. of *buy.*

bouil'lon (būl'yon) n. a clear soup, the liquid from boiling meat, etc.

boul'der (bōl'dər) n. a large detached rock.

boul'e·vard' (būl'ə-värd″) n. a broad street, esp. one shaded by trees or used as a promenade.

bounce (bowns) v.i. 1, spring back like an elastic ball; recoil. 2, move with a spring or leap. —v.t. 1, cause to spring or rebound. 2, (*Slang*) eject or dismiss summarily. —n. 1, a rebound; a sudden leap. 2, elasticity or resilience. 3, (*Slang*) expulsion or dismissal. 4, bluster; impudence.

bound (bownd) v.i. 1, jump; move by leaps. 2, bounce back; rebound. —v.t. 1, cause to bounce or leap. 2, be the boundary of; limit. 3, name the boundaries of. —n. 1, a jump, leap, or rebound. 2, a limiting line or boundary. 3, something that binds or restrains. 4, (*pl.*) territory near a boundary, or enclosed by it. —*adj.* 1, made fast by a band or bond; tied; fettered. 2, under obligation or compulsion. 3, destined; determined; resolved. 4, traveling (to); destined (for).

bound'a·ry (bown'də-rē) n. a bounding line; something that marks a limit.

bound'er (bown'dər) n. (*Colloq.*) a vulgar, ill-bred person; an upstart.

boun'te·ous (bown'tē-əs) *adj.* bountiful. —**boun'te·ous·ness,** n.

boun'ti·ful (bown'tē-fəl) *adj.* 1, generous in giving. 2, plentiful; abundant. —**boun'ti·ful·ness,** n.

boun'ty (bown'tē) n. 1, liberality in giving; generosity. 2, a favor given benevolently. 3, a premium offered by a government to encourage a certain activity, as the destruction of pests.

bou·quet' (bō·kā′; boo-) n. 1, a bunch of flowers. 2, the characteristic aroma of a wine.

Bour'bon (bûr'bən) n. 1, name of a French royal family. 2, (bẽr'bən) a whiskey made from corn.

bour·geois' (bûr-zhwä′) n. a person of the middle class; a tradesman, or one owning property. —*adj.* middle-class. —**bour'geoi·sie'** (-zē) n.

bourne (bûrn) n. 1, boundary;

limit. **2,** goal; destination. Also, bourn.

bout *v.t.* (bowt) *n.* **1,** a contest between two persons, esp. of physical strength or endurance. **2,** a period of struggle, as against illness. **3,** a turn or round, as of work.

bo'vine (bō'vīn) *adj.* **1,** of the family that includes the ox; oxlike. **2,** stolid; dull. —*n.* a bovine animal.

bow *v.i.* **1,** bend; curve; stoop. **2,** tend; turn; yield; submit. **3,** bend the body or head in salutation, worship, etc. —*v.t.* **1,** cause to bend, stoop, or turn. **2,** force to submit; subdue. —*n.* **1,** a bend of the body or head in salutation, etc. **2,** the forward end of a ship.

bow (bō) *n.* **1,** a weapon for shooting arrows, comprising a long elastic stick bent in a curve by a string attached to both ends. **2,** a device in similar form, for playing a musical stringed instrument. **3,** a knot in cord or ribbon having one or more prominent loops. **4,** a bend or curve. **5,** something curved; a rainbow; an ear-piece to hold eyeglasses in place. —*adj.* bent like a bow; curved. —*v.t. & i.* **1,** bend; curve. **2,** use a bow (in playing an instrument).

bow'el (bow'əl) *n.* **1,** the intestine of an animal; (*pl.*) the entire alimentary canal below the stomach. **2,** (*pl.*) the inner parts of anything.

bow'er (bow'ər) *n.* **1,** a shelter made with boughs or vines. **2,** (*Poetic*) a rustic cottage; a boudoir. **3,** a playing-card jack.

bow'ie knife (bō'ē) a dagger-like hunting knife.

Bowie Knife

bowl (bōl) *n.* **1,** a deep dish or basin; a large drinking-cup: **2,** something bowl-shaped; a rounded hollow in the ground; the container of a spoon or tobacco-pipe. **3,** a stadium for athletic contests, etc. **4,** a ball used in bowls or bowling. —*v.i.* **1,** play at bowls or bowling. **2,** move with rapid easy motion. —*v.t.* **1,** roll or trundle. **2,** (with *over* or *down*) knock down; upset; disconcert. —**bowl'ing,** *n.* a game of knocking down pins with a ball.

bowl'der (bōl'dər) *n.* boulder.

bow'leg'' (bō'leg'') *n.* **1,** an outward curvature of the leg. **2,** a leg so curved. —**bow'leg''ged,** *adj.*

bowls (bōlz) *n.sing.* an outdoor game of rolling balls toward a goal.

bow'man (bō'mən) *n.* [*pl.* -men] a soldier armed with a bow and arrows.

box (boks) *n.* **1,** a container, case, or receptacle, esp. one that is rectangular. **2,** a compartment or cell of a larger enclosure; a space in a theater barred off by curtains or rails. **3,** a small shelter; a country-house for temporary use; a booth for sentries, railroad workers, etc. **4,** a housing or casing; a protective part. **5,** a socket, pit, or hollow part. **6,** an area marked out by a border, esp. rectangular; a bordered section of printed matter on a newspaper; a place where the batter stands in baseball. **7,** a blow with the hand. **8,** an evergreen shrub; its wood. —*v.i.* **1,** put in a box. **2,** enclose; confine; house. **3,** strike with the hand, esp. the ear. **4,** engage in a fist-fight or boxing match. —*v.t.* **1,** fight with the fists; **2,** fight cautiously; spar. —**box office,** a ticket booth in a theater.

box'er (bok'sər) *n.* **1,** one who fights with his fists; a pugilist; **2,** a large smooth-coated dog.

box'ing (bok'sing) *n.* fighting with the fists; pugilism.

boy (boi) *n.* **1,** a male child, esp. before the beginning of youth. **2,** any male person, regarded familiarly or as immature. **3,** a male servant. —**boy'hood''**, *n.* —**boy'ish**, *adj.* like a boy, in manner or appearance.

boy'cott (boi'kot) *v.t.* combine with others to abstain from buying, using, patronizing, etc. (a business, product, etc.), as a means of coercing or intimidating. —*n.* **1,** the act of boycotting. **2,** an instance of boycotting.

bra (brä) *n.* brassiere;

Brace and bit

brace (brās) *n.* **1,** something that holds parts together or in place. **2,** something that makes strong, rigid, firm, or steady. **3,** a piece of timber strengthening a framework; a wire band to straighten the teeth; a truss or support for weak body joints; a bitstock for holding bits or drills. **4,** (*pl.*) trouser suspenders. **5,** a symbol { } for joining printed lines or musical staves. **6,** a pair or couple. —*v.t.* **1,** join, fix, or strengthen with a brace. **2,** make steady, firm, or tight; increase the tension of. **3,** stimulate; fortify in resolution. —*v.i.* (with *up*) fortify one's resolution or vigor.

brace'let (brās'lət) *n.* **1,** an ornamental band worn on the arm. **2,** any similar circlet or shackle; a handcuff.

brachi-al (brā'kē-əl) *adj.* **1,** pert. to the arm, foreleg, wing, or other forelimb of a vertebrate. **2,** like an arm.

bracket (brak'it) *n.* **1,** a supporting piece for a shelf; a small shelf on such a piece. **2**, one of a pair of marks ([ ]) used like a parenthesis; a mark ([ ]) grouping several items. **3**, a group of persons of similar condition, esp. taxpayers. —*v.t.* **1**, support by a bracket. **2**, enclose in brackets. **3**, group persons in or as in a bracket. **4**, of gunfire, straddle.

brack′ish (brak′ish) *adj*. (of water) salty; stale. —**brack′ish·ness**, *n.*

brad *n.* a small, slender nail.

brae (brā) *n.* (*Scot.*) a slope; hillside.

brag *v.i.* [bragged, brag′ging] boast; swagger. —*n.* a boast.

brag″ga·do′ci·o (brag″ə-dō′shē-ō″) *n.* [*pl.* -os″ (-ōz″)] **1**, vain boasting. **2**, a braggart.

brag′gart (brag′ərt) *n.* a boastful person.

Brah′man (brä′mən) *n.* [*pl.* -mans] **1**, a member of the priestly and highest caste of Hindus. **2**, (*Colloq.*) a member of an old and prominent family in Boston. Also, **Brah′min.** —**Brah′man·ism**, *n.*

braid (brād) *v.t.* **1**, interlace three strands, as of hair; plait. **2**, weave, as a rug, by braiding. —*n.* **1**, ornamental tape. **2**, a length of braided hair.

Braille (brāl) *n.* a system of raised printing, read by touch, for the blind.

brain (brān) *n.* **1**, a mass of nerve matter in the skull; the organ of thought, consciousness, and body control. **2**, (often *pl.*) intelligence. —*v.t.* kill by beating out the brain.

brain′sick″ *adj.* crazy. —**brain′sick″ness**, *n.*

brain′storm″ *n.* a sudden aberration or inspiration.

brain trust a group of expert advisers. —**brain′trust″er**, *n.*

brain′y (brā′nē) *adj.* intelligent. —**brain′i·ness**, *n.*

braise (brāz) *v.t.* of meat, brown and stew slowly.

brake (brāk) *n.* **1**, a device for slowing or stopping a vehicle or machine. **2**, fig., a retarding influence. **3**, a thicket. —*v.t.* apply a brake.

brake′man (-mən) *n.* [*pl.* -men] an assistant to a railroad conductor.

bram′ble (bram′bəl) *n.* a thorny shrub. —**bram′bly**, *adj.*

bran *n.* the outer coat of wheat or other grains, used as a breakfast cereal and flour.

branch (brănch) *n.* **1**, a limb; a bough. **2**, an offshoot or subdivision. **3**, a stream or small river. —*v.i.* put forth branches; diverge.

brand *n.* **1**, a piece of burning wood; an ember. **2**, an identifying mark made with a hot iron; the

iron implement so used. **3**, any identifying mark. **4**, an article identified by a brand. **5**, quality as indicated by a brand. **6**, a mark of infamy; stigma. —*v.t.* mark with, or as with, a brand; stigmatize. —**brand new**, unused.

bran′dish *v.t.* flourish; wave.

bran′dy (bran′dē) *n.* an alcoholic liquor distilled from wine, cider, etc. —*v.t.* flavor with or steep in brandy. —**bran′died** (-dēd) *adj.*

brash *adj.* **1**, reckless; impetuous. **2**, impudent. —**brash′ness**, *n.*

brass (brās) *n.* **1**, an alloy of copper and zinc. **2**, a brass wind instrument; such instruments collectively. **3**, (*Colloq.*) assurance; impudence. **4**, (*Slang*) persons in authority, esp. *Mil.*: *brass hats.*

bras′sard (bras′ärd) *n.* **1**, a mourning band on the sleeve. **2**, a badge or identifying mark worn on the arm.

brass′ie (-ē) *n.* a brass-soled golf club.

bras·siere′ (brə-zir′) *n.* a woman's undergarment, a band having cups to support the breasts.

brass′y (-ē) *adj.* **1**, having a metallic sound. **2**, (*Colloq.*) impudent. —**brass′i·ness**, *n.*

brat *n.* an unruly or spoiled child.

bra·va′do (brə-vä′dō) *n.* **1**, swaggering defiance; boastful truculence. **2**, a bully.

brave (brāv) *adj.* **1**, courageous. **2**, splendid; handsome. —*n.* an American Indian warrior. —*v.t.* face with courage; defy. —**brave′ness**, *n.* —**brav′er·y**, *n.* courage.

bra′vo (brä′vō) *interj.* Well done! —*n.* a thug; assassin.

brawl (brâl) *n.* **1**, a noisy quarrel. **2**, a wild, noisy party. —*v.i.* **1**, quarrel noisily. **2**, carouse.

brawn (brân) *n.* **1**, powerful muscles; muscular strength. **2**, flesh of the boar. —**brawn′y**, *adj.*

bray (brā) *n.* the harsh cry of an ass, or a sound resembling it. —*v.i.* make such a sound. —*v.t.* pound; crush to powder.

braze (brāz) *v.t.* **1**, join with a solder containing brass. **2**, make of or cover with brass.

bra′zen (brā′zən) *adj.* **1**, made of brass. **2**, giving forth the sound of vibrating brass. **3**, impudent; shameless. —*v.t.* (with *out*) face with impudence. —**bra′zen·ness**, *n.*

bra′zier (brā′zhər) *n.* **1**, a worker in brass. **2**, a vessel in which coal or charcoal is burned.

bra·zil′ (brə-zil′) *n.* a red dye from various tropical trees.

breach (brēch) *n.* 1, a break or separation; a violation, as of a law; a quarrel. 2, a gap broken in a wall or the like. 3, an interruption. —*v.t.* make a break in.

bread (bred) *n.* 1, a food made of flour or meal and generally leavening, baked in loaves. 2, food in general. —*v.t.* cover with bread crumbs.

bread'fruit" (bred'froot") *n.* a pulpy fruit of a tree found in the So. Seas, baked for food.

bread'stuff" *n.* grain, flour, or meal used to make bread.

breadth (bredth) *n.* 1, the measure of an object from side to side; width. 2, liberality; freedom from narrowness. 3, wide extent; broadness.

bread'win"ner (bred'win"ər) *n.* the principal working member and supporter of a family.

break (brāk) *v.t.* [broke, bro'ken, break'ing] 1, shatter violently; rupture; crack. 2, interrupt; destroy the continuity of. 3, destroy the integrity of; change into smaller units, as *break* a dollar bill. 4, tame; train. 5, violate, as a law. 6, be first to tell, as news. 7, demote, as an officer. 8, weaken; soften, as a fall. 9, exceed or surpass, as a record. 10, (*Law*) enter by force with criminal intent. 11, render bankrupt or penniless. 12, (with *down*) separate into component parts; analyze. 13, (with *off*) discontinue. —*v.i.* 1, be shattered, ruptured, or cracked. 2, change gait (of a horse), tone (of a voice), etc. 3, discharge, as a sore. 4, begin suddenly, as day. 5, (with *in*) force one's way. 6, (with *down*) succumb to illness or emotion. 7, (with *up*) disband; separate. —*n.* 1, a breach; a fracture. 2, an interruption; a gap; a suspension. 3, a sudden change.

break'down" *n.* 1, a collapse, as from illness. 2, an analysis.

break'er *n.* a breaking wave.

break'fast (brek'fəst) *n.* the first meal of the day.

break'neck" (brāk'nek") *adj.* dangerously fast.

break-'up" *n.* disintegration; ruin.

break'wa"ter (brāk'wä"tər) *n.* a sea wall to protect a harbor, swimming area, etc.

bream (brēm) *n.* [*pl.* bream] any of several American food fishes.

breast (brest) *n.* 1, the front of the upper body, enclosing the lungs; the chest. 2, a mammary gland or the flesh covering it. 3, the chest regarded as the seat of human emotion. —*v.t.* 1, push against with the breast. 2, face courageously.

breast'pin *n.* a brooch.

breast'work" *n.* a protective wall, as of earth.

breath (breth) *n.* 1, the air inhaled or exhaled in a respiration. 2, a respiration. 3, a light breeze. 4, ability to breathe. 5, a faint scent. 6, a trifle; a trivial speech.

breathe (brēth) *v.i.* 1, draw air into and expel it from the lungs; live. 2, pause; rest. —*v.t.* 1, inhale and exhale. 2, speak softly; whisper. 3, allow to rest. —**breath'er** (brē'thər) *n.* a short rest.

breath'less (breth'ləs) *adj.* 1, panting. 2, in suspense; thrilled; astounded. —**breath'less-ness**, *n.*

breath'tak"ing (breth'tā"king) *adj.* rendering one breathless, as from astonishment, fright, etc.

breech (brēch) *n.* the rear part of anything, esp. a gun; the buttocks.

breech'cloth" *n.* a garment wrapped around the buttocks.

breech'es (brich'iz) *n.* 1, short pants, reaching from waist to knee. 2, (*Colloq.*) trousers.

breed (brēd) *v.t.* [*pret. & p.p.* bred] 1, beget; produce offspring. 2, cause to produce offspring; mate. 3, bring up; rear. —*v.i.* beget; produce; be produced. —*n.* a distinctive race or kind. —**breed'ing**, *n.* 1, genetic strain or background. 2, gentility.

breeze (brēz) *n.* a light wind. —*v.i.* 1, blow lightly. 2, (*Colloq.*) travel fast without great effort.

breez'y (brē'zē) *adj.* 1, mildly windy. 2, fresh; airy; (*Colloq.*) pert. —**breez'i-ness**, *n.*

breth'ren (breth'rin) *n.pl.* 1, brothers. 2, associates.

breve (brēv) *n.* 1, (*Music*) a whole note (see *note*). 2, (*Print.*) a diacritical mark (˘)

bre-vet' (brə-vet') *n.* formerly, a temporary commission of high military rank. —*v.t.* [bre-vet'ted, -vet'-ting] promote by brevet.

bre'vi-ar-y (brē'vē-er-ē) *n.* a book of daily prayers.

brev'i-ty (brev'ə-tē) *n.* shortness; terseness.

brew (broo) *v.t.* 1, produce by fermenting grains, as ale. 2, steep, as tea. —*n.* the beverage so produced.

brew'er (-ər) *n.* a maker of beer. —**brew'er-y** (brōr'ē) *n.* a place where beer or ale is brewed.

bri'ar (brī'ər) *n.* brier.

bribe (brīb) *n.* a gift or promise given unethically in return for a favor. —*v.t.* make or offer a bribe. —**brib'er-y** (brī'bər-ē) *n.*

bric-'a-brac" (brik'ə-brak") *n.* unusual small objects of art; knickknack.

brick (brik) *n.* **1,** a rectangular block of molded and baked, or dried, clay. **2,** any solid resembling a brick. **3,** (*Colloq.*) a good fellow. —*adj.* made of brick. —*v.t.* (often with *up*) build with bricks. —**brick′bat″,** *n.* a brick or piece of a brick.— **brick′lay″er,** *n.* one who builds with brick.

brid′al (brī′dəl) *adj.* pert. to a bride, her wedding, attendants, etc.

bride (brīd) *n.* a woman at, or immediately before or after, her wedding.

bride′groom″ *n.* a man at, or immediately before or after, his wedding.

brides′maid″ (brīdz′-) *n.* an unmarried attendant on a bride.

bridge (brij) *n.* **1,** a pathway spanning a stream, valley, or road; anything that spans a gap. **2,** the bony structure of the nose. **3,** a raised platform on a ship. **4,** a device for raising the strings of a stringed instrument from the sounding board. **5,** a device for measuring electrical resistance. **6,** a card game. **7,** a device for holding false teeth in place. —*v.t.* build a bridge across; cross; span. —**bridge′head″,** *n.* a position held on the enemy's shore of a river.

bri′dle (brī′dəl) *n.* **1,** the head part of a harness for a horse, etc. **2,** a restraint. —*v.t.* restrain; check. —*v.i.* toss the head, in contempt, deprecation, etc. —**bridle path,** a road reserved for horseback riders.

brief (brēf) *adj.* short; terse; succinct. —*n.* a concise summary. —*v.t.* **1,** condense. **2,** give brief instructions to. —**brief′ness,** *n.*

brief′case″ *n.* a leather bag for carrying documents; portfolio.

bri′er (brī′ər) *n.* **1,** a thorny shrub. **2,** a root used for making pipes for smoking.

brig *n.* **1,** a square-rigged sailing ship. **2,** a ship's jail.

bri·gade′ (bri-gād′) *n.* **1,** a military unit, two or more regiments. **2,** an organized body of persons.

brig″a·dier′ (brig″ə-dir′) *n.* [in the U.S. Army, **brigadier general**] an officer ranking next above colonel.

brig′and (brig′ənd) *n.* a robber; highwayman.

brig′an·tine (brig′an-tēn; -tīn) *n.* a type of two-masted sailing vessel.

bright (brīt) *adj.* **1,** having the quality of reflecting light; shining; glowing; clear. **2,** sunny; fair. **3,** clever; mentally alert. **4,** vivacious; happy. —**bright′en** (-ən) *v.t. & i.* make or become bright. —**bright′ness,** *n.*

bril′liance (bril′yəns) *n.* **1,** sparkling appearance; luster; magnificence. **2,** outstanding mental superiority; vivacity. —**bril′liant,** *adj.*

brim *n.* the edge; a projecting rim. —**brim′ful″,** *adj.* as full as can be.

brim′stone″ (brim′stōn″) *n.* sulphur. —*adj.* greenish yellow.

brin′dled (brin′dəld) *adj.* gray or brownish streaked with darker colors.

brine (brīn) *n.* **1,** a strong solution of salt in water. **2,** the sea. — **brin′y,** *adj.*

bring *v.t.* [*pret. & p.p.* **brought** (brât)] **1,** carry or conduct to where the speaker is (so distinguished from *take*); fetch. **2,** produce; yield. **3,** (often with *around*) induce; persuade. **4,** command as a price. **5,** (with *up*) rear, as a child.

brink *n.* an edge, as of a cliff or the like; verge.

brisk *adj.* lively; quick; swift; vivacious. —**brisk′ness,** *n.*

bris′ket *n.* a cut of meat from the breast.

bris′ling (bris′ling) *n.* a small herring; a size or grade of sardine.

bris′tle (bris′əl) *n.* a stiff hair. —*v.i.* stand erect, as fur on a frightened cat; evince resentment. — **bris′tly,** *adj.*

bris′tling (bris′ling) *adj.* **1,** stubbly; prickly. **2,** resentful.

Brit′ish *adj.* pert. to Great Britain, its people, customs, etc.

brit′tle (brit′əl) *adj.* **1,** fragile; easily snapped apart; crisp. **2,** highstrung; lacking strength. —**brit′tleness,** *n.*

broach (brōch) *n.* **1,** a tool for piercing. **2,** a brooch. —*v.t.* **1,** pierce; open. **2,** introduce, as a subject.

broad (brâd) *adj.* **1,** wide. **2,** of great extent; widespread. **3,** liberal; inclusive. **4,** indelicate; plainspoken. **5,** pronounced openly and sustained, as the *broad a* in father.

broad′cast″ (brâd′kåst″) *adj.* widely published, disseminated, or scattered. —*n.* a widely disseminated radio program. —*v.t. & i.* [*pret. & p.p.* **-cast″** or **-cast″ed**] publish or spread widely.

broad′cloth″ (brâd′klåth″) *n.* **1,** a fine, smooth-finish woolen cloth. **2** a cotton material with a silky luster.

broad′loom″ *n.* carpeting fabric woven on a wide loom.

broad′mind″ed *adj.* free from prejudice or bigotry; liberal.

broad′side″ (brâd′sīd″) *n.* **1,** the side of a ship above the water line. **2,** a simultaneous discharge of all guns on one side of a warship; fig., any concerted attack. **3,** (*Colloq.*) a large printed sheet.

broad'sword" n. a sword with a broad blade.

bro·cade' (brō-kād') n. a rich silken fabric with a raised pattern.

broc'co·li (brok'ə-lē) n. a vegetable with edible stalks and flower heads.

bro·chure' (brō-shūr') n. a pamphlet.

bro'gan (brō'gən) n. a heavy leather boot.

brogue (brōg) n. 1, a dialectal pronunciation of English, esp. that of the Irish. 2, a low shoe.

broil v.t. & i. cook by direct exposure to an open fire, as on a grill. —n. a portion of meat, esp. mixed meats, cooked by broiling.

broil'er (-ər) n. 1, a pan, oven, or stove holding a grill for broiling. 2, a young fowl to be broiled.

broke (brōk) v. pret. of **break**. —adj. (Slang) without money; penniless.

bro'ken (brō'kən) adj. 1, rough or hilly, as terrain. 2, shattered; cracked; not in repair. 3, imperfectly spoken, as a language. 4, infirm; in poor health. 5, violated, as a vow. 6, tamed to obedience; crushed in spirit. —v. p.p. of **break**.

bro'ken-heart'ed (brō'kən-här'tid) adj. disappointed to the point of despair.

bro'ker (brō'kər) n. an agent who buys or sells property, esp. stocks and bonds on commission. —bro'ker·age (-ij) n. 1, a broker's business or office. 2, a commission paid to a broker.

bro'mide (brō'mīd) n. 1, a compound of bromine, used as a sedative. 2, (Colloq.) a trite remark.

bro·mid'ic (brō-mid'ik) adj. (Colloq.) trite. —bro·mid'i·cal·ly, adv.

bro'mine (brō'mēn) n. a reddish-brown chemical element, no. 35, symbol Br.

bron'chi (brong'kī) n. [sing. -chus (-kəs)] the two main branches of the windpipe. —bron'chi·al (brong'kē-əl) adj.

bron·chi'tis (brong-kī'təs) n. inflammation in the bronchial tubes.

bron'cho·scope" (brong'kə-skōp") n. a tubular instrument that can penetrate to the bronchi or lungs, for inspection or treatment.

bron'co (brong'kō) n. in the western U. S., a small horse, esp. when half-broken. Also, **bron'cho**.

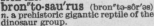

Bronco

bron'to·sau'rus (bron'tə-sôr'əs) n. a prehistoric gigantic reptile of the dinosaur group.

bronze (bronz) n. 1, an alloy of copper and tin. 2, the color brown with tinges of red and yellow. —v.t. & i. make or become this color, esp. (of men) by suntanning. —adj. of this color.

brooch (brōch) n. an ornamental pin.

brood n. the young hatched in one nest or of one mother. —v.t. & i. 1, sit (on eggs). 2, ponder moodily. —brood'er, n. 1, a heated device for raising baby chicks. 2, a moody person. —brood'y, adj. preoccupied.

brook (bruk) n. a small stream. —v.t. bear; put up with.

broom n. 1, a brush for sweeping. 2, a shrub of the pea family. —broom'stick", n. the handle of a broom.

broth (brāth) n. a thin soup.

broth'el (broth'əl) n. a house where illicit lovemaking is afforded.

broth'er (bruth'ər) n. 1, a male relative having the same parents as another. 2, a fellow man. 3, a member of a religious order.

broth'er·hood" (bruth'ər-hud") n. 1, fellowship. 2, a fraternity of men; its members collectively.

broth'er-in-law" n. [pl. broth'ers-] 1, the brother of one's spouse. 2, the husband of one's sister.

broth'er·ly (-lē) adj. sympathetic; kind; befitting a brother. —broth'er·li·ness, n.

brough'am (broo'əm) n. 1, a carriage with a straight front. 2, a similar body for a chauffeur-driven automobile.

brought (brât) v. pret. & p.p. of **bring**.

brow n. 1, the forehead. 2, the edge of the top of a cliff or hill.

brow'beat" (brow'bēt") v.t. bully; intimidate.

brown n. a shade between orange and black. —adj. of this color. —v.t. & i. make or become brown. —brown shirt, a Nazi. —brown study, a reverie.

brown'ie (brow'nē) n. 1, a good-natured elf supposed to do chores at night. 2, a kind of cookie. 3, (cap.) a junior Girl Scout.

browse (browz) n. twigs, tender shoots, etc., as food for animals. —v.i. 1, feed on or crop twigs, leaves, etc.; graze. 2, read idly here and there, as in a book or library.

bru'in (broo'in) n. a bear, from a name given a bear in fairy tales.

bruise (brooz) n. an injury caused by a blow that discolors but does not break the skin. —v.t. inflict such an injury upon. —**bruis′er**, *n.* a fight; a powerful-looking man.

bruit (broot) *v.t.* make known publicly, as by rumor.

brum′ma·gem (brum′ə-jəm) *adj.* cheap; spurious.

brunch *n.* (*Slang*) breakfast eaten at or near lunch time.

bru·nette′ (broo-net′) *adj.* (*fem.*) having dark eyes and hair. —*n.* a brunette person. Also, **bru·net′**.

brunt *n.* the main force of an attack or shock; the principal burden.

brush *n.* 1, a thicket; scrub. 2, lopped-off branches of trees. 3, an implement with hair bristles, wire, etc., attached to a handle or back, for painting, scrubbing, etc. 4, a bushy tail. 5, a light touch; a graze. 6, a minor conflict; a skirmish. —*v.t.* 1, sweep, rub, clean, etc. with a brush. 2, remove with or as with a brush. 3, touch lightly in passing. —*v.i.* 1, (with *by*) sweep past. 2, (with *up*) practice; refresh one's memory.

brusque (brusk) *adj.* abrupt; curt. —**brusque′ness**, *n.*

Brus′sels sprout (brus′əlz) a vegetable whose edible buds resemble miniature cabbage heads.

bru′tal (broo′təl) *adj.* cruel. —**bru·tal′i·ty** (-tal′ə-tē) *n.*

brute (broot) *n.* 1, a beast. 2, a savage, cruel person. —*adj.* like a beast; not sensitive or reasoning.

brut′ish (broo′tish) *adj.* like an animal; stupid; savage. —**brut′ish·ness**, *n.*

bry′o·ny (brī′ə-nē) *n.* a vine of the gourd family.

bub′ble (bub′əl) *n.* 1, a thin film of liquid holding gas or air. 2, a small bead of gas or air in a liquid. 3, an unsound project or idea. —*v.i.* give forth bubbles; boil; effervesce; be aerated, esp. with a gurgling sound, as a brook. —**bubble gum**, chewing gum that stretches to a strong film.

bu′bo (bū′bō) *n.* an inflammatory swelling of a lymph gland, esp. in the groin. —**bu·bon′ic** (-bon′ik), *adj.* —**bubonic plague**, a deadly, epidemic disease, marked by inflammation of the lymphatic glands.

buc′ca·neer′ (buk′ə-nir′) *n.* a pirate.

buck (buk) *n.* 1, the male of various animals. 2, a fop. 3, (*Slang*) a dollar. 4, a sawhorse. —*v.i.* 1, make a sudden, twisting leap, said of a horse. 2, (*Colloq.*) demur; suddenly object. —*v.t.* 1, throw off by bucking. 2, (*Colloq.*) go against. 3, in Amer. football, charge into (the opponents' line).

buck′board″ (buk′bôrd″) *n.* a light horsedrawn wagon.

buck′et (buk′it) *n.* 1, a vessel for carrying water or other fluids, usually in the shape of an inverted truncated cone; a pail. 2, a scoop, as on a dredge. —**bucket shop**, a fraudulent stockbroker's office.

buck′eye″ (buk′ī″) *n.* 1, a tree or its inedible nutlike seed. 2, (*Cap.*) a native of Ohio.

buck fever a beginner's fear.

buck′le (buk′əl) *n.* 1, a clasp for joining loose ends, as of a belt or strap. 2, a bend or kink in metal. —*v.t.* 1, fasten with a buckle. 2, crumple; bend. —*v.i.* 1, (often with *down*) apply oneself with vigor. 2, crumple; warp.

buck′ler (buk′lər) *n.* a round shield carried on the arm.

buck′ram (buk′rəm) *n.* a coarse, stiffened fabric, used in bookbinding, millinery, etc.

buck′saw″ (buk′sâ″) *n.* a saw blade set in a large quadrangular frame.

buck′shot″ *n.* a large size of shot used in hunting.

buck′skin″ (buk′skin″) *n.* 1, leather made of deer or sheep skin. 2, (*pl.*) garments made of buckskin.

buck′thorn″ (buk′thôrn″) *n.* any of various shrubs and trees with prickly branches.

buck′tooth″ (buk′tooth″) *n.* a tooth that sticks out. —**buck′-toothed″**, *adj.*

buck′wheat″ (buk′hwēt″) *n.* a cereal plant whose seeds are ground into flour; this flour.

bu·col′ic (bū-kol′ik) *adj.* pastoral; rustic. —*n.* a poem dealing with simple country life. —**bu·col′i·cal·ly**, *adv.*

bud *n.* 1, an undeveloped swelling on a plant that may open into a leaf or flower. 2, a person or thing in an early stage of development. 3, a debutante. —*v.i.* [**bud′ded**, -**ding**] sprout.

Bud′dha (bûd′ə) *n.* 1, the title of saint, in Buddhism. 2, a conventionalized statue of Gautama Buddha, founder of Buddhism.

Bud′dhism (bûd′iz-əm) *n.* an Asiatic religion that teaches self-denial. —**Bud′dhist** (-ist) *n.* & *adj.*

bud′dy (bud′ē) *n.* (*Colloq.*) a friend; pal.

budge (buj) *v.t.* & *i.* move; stir.

budg′et (buj′it) *n.* an estimate of future financial income and outgo. —*v.t.* plan (expenditures) by making a budget. —**budg′et·ar·y** (-er-ē) *adj.*

buff (buf) *n.* 1, a dull-yellow leather; a military coat made of it. 2, a dull-yellowish color. —*v.t.* polish by vigorous rubbing with a soft substance.

buf'fa·lo" (buf'ə-lō") *n.* a kind of wild ox, esp. the Amer. bison.

buff'er (buf'ər) *n.* 1, a polisher. 2, anything that serves to deaden the shock of striking forces.

buf'fet (buf'it) *n.* a slap; any blow. —*v.t.* 1, beat. 2, contend against.

buf·fet' (bə-fā') *n.* 1, a sideboard; a public refreshment counter. 2, food set out for guests to help themselves. —*adj.* served informally.

buf·foon' (bə-foon') *n.* a clownish jester. —**buf·foon'e·ry** (-ə-rē) *n.* the pranks or behavior of a buffoon.

bug *n.* 1, one of an order of insects that suck vital fluids. 2, (*Colloq.*) any crawling insect. 3, (*Slang*) a disease germ. 4, (*Slang*) a fanatic; a zealot.

bug'a·boo" (bug'ə-boo") *n.* a fancied object of terror. Also, **bug'bear"**.

Buggy

bug'gy (bug'ē) *n.* a single-seated, horsedrawn vehicle for two persons, open but with a folding top.

bu'gle (bū'gəl) *n.* a trumpetlike brass wind instrument. —**bu'gler,** *n.*

build (bild) *v.t.* [*pret. & p.p.* built (bilt)] 1, construct; fashion; erect. 2, found. 3, increase and strengthen. —*v.i.* construct something, esp. a house. —*n.* bodily figure or shape; form; make or brand of manufacture. —**build'ing,** *n.* any architectural structure, as a house.

bulb *n.* 1, the rounded underground stem of certain plants, as the lily, onion, etc. 2, anything shaped like a bulb, as the lamp of an electric light. —**bulb'ous,** *adj.*

bulge (bulj) *n.* an outward swelling; a rounded protuberance. —*v.t. & i.* swell outward.

bulk *n.* 1, extent or volume, as of massed substance. 2, an aggregate; a large quantity. 3, the major part. —*v.i.* loom large. —**bulk'y,** *adj.*

bulk'head" (bulk'hed") *n.* a wall or compartment protruding from a main body, as to protect it.

bull (bul) *n.* 1, the male of any animal of the ox family, and of various other large animals. 2, one who tries to raise the price of stocks. 3, a papal edict. 4, a ludicrous blunder in language.

bull'dog" (bul'dâg") *n.* a powerful short-haired dog. —*adj.* tenacious; stubborn. —*v.t. & i.* in western U. S., throw (a calf steer) by twisting its neck.

Bulldog

bull'doze" (bul'dōz") *v.t.* coerce; bully; frighten. —**bull'doz"er,** *n.* a tractor-driven pushing blade for clearing land, building roads, etc.

bul'let (bul'ət) *n.* a small missile to be fired from a firearm.

bul'le·tin (bul'ə-tən) *n.* 1, a short, official news report. 2, a periodical journal, as of an organization.

bull'fight" *n.* a combat between a man and a bull, held in an arena for spectators' amusement.

bull'finch" (bul'finch") *n.* any of various finches.

bull'frog" (bul'frog") *n.* an Amer. frog with a bellowing croak.

bull'head"ed (bul'hed"id) *adj.* obstinate. —**bull'head"ed·ness,** *n.*

bul'lion (bul'yən) *n.* uncoined gold or silver.

bull market a rising trend in stock prices.

bull'ock (bul'ək) *n.* an ox; steer.

bull's-'eye" (bulz'ī") *n.* 1, a thick disk of glass in a deck, roof, etc. 2, a convex lens for concentrating rays of light. 3, the center of a target; a shot that reaches it.

bul'ly (bul'ē) *n.* a tormentor of those smaller or weaker. —*v.t.* hector with threats and bluster. —*adj. & interj.* (*Colloq.*) fine; first-rate.

bul'rush" (bul'rush") *n.* 1, any of various rushes or reedy plants. 2, (*Bib.*) the papyrus plant.

bul'wark (bul'wərk) *n.* 1, a wall for defense; rampart. 2, any means of protection.

bum (*Slang*) *v.i.* [bummed, bum'ming] loaf; beg. —*v.t.* get by sponging or begging. —*n.* a worthless fellow; a beggar. —*adj.* worthless.

bum'ble·bee" (bum'bəl-bē") *n.* a large, hairy, humming bee.

bump *n.* 1, a thump; collision. 2, a swelling caused by a blow; any rounded elevation or protuberance.

—*v.t.* strike together or against.
—*v.i.* 1, collide heavily. 2, jolt along.
—**bump off** (*Slang*) kill; murder.

bump′er (bum′pər) *n.* 1, a device, as a protective bar or pad, to deaden the shock of a collision. 2, a glass filled to the top. —*adj.* (*Colloq.*) very large.

bump′kin *n.* an awkward fellow.

bump′tious (bump′shəs) *adj.* (*Colloq.*) ebullient; brash.

bun *n.* 1, a sweetened biscuit. 2, a wad of coiled hair as part of a hair-dress.

bu′na (boo′nə) *n.* a synthetic rubber.

bunch *n.* a cluster of things of the same kind growing, grouped, or fastened together. —*v.t. & i.* make into or form a bunch.

bun′combe (bung′kəm) *n.* (*Colloq.*) humbug; nonsense. Also, **bunk′um**.

bun′dle (bun′dəl) *n.* 1, articles packed together; a pack; a package. 2, (*Colloq.*) a large quantity. —*v.t.* 1, tie in a package. 2, (with *off*) dispose of hurriedly. —*v.i.* 1, (often with *off*) depart hurriedly. 2, lie in the same bed without undressing.

bung *n.* a stopper for the hole in a cask; the hole itself: *bunghole*.

bun′ga·low (bung′gə-lō″) *n.* a one-story house.

bun′gle (bung′gəl) *v.t. & i.* perform clumsily. —**bung′ler,** *n.*

bun′ion (bun′yən) *n.* a chronic enlargement of the first joint of the big toe.

bunk *n.* 1, a frame built against a wall for use as a bed. 2, buncombe. —*v.i.* (with *together*) share the same bed.

bunk′er (bung′kər) *n.* 1, a bin for storage, esp. a ship's coal bin. 2, in golf, a sand pit.

bun′ny (bun′ē) *n.* a rabbit.

Bun′sen burner (bun′sən) a burner producing a single jet of hot flame produced by mixture of gas with air.

bunt *v.t. & i.* 1, butt. 2, in baseball, tap (the ball) without swinging the bat. —*n.* a hit so made.

bun′ting *n.* 1, a light fabric, esp. used for flags, streamers, etc. 2, a small songbird. 3, an infant's outer garment.

buoy (boi) *n.* 1, an anchored float to guide navigation. 2, a life-saving device. —*v.t.* (often with *up*) keep from sinking; hence, sustain morally; encourage.

buoy′an·cy (boi′ən-sē) *n.* 1, ability to float. 2, lightheartedness. —**buoy′ant,** *adj.*

bur (bėr) *n.* any rough, prickly seed covering. Also, **burr**.

bur′den (bėr′dən) *n.* 1, something carried; a load. 2, something borne with difficulty, as care, grief, etc. 3, an encumbrance. 4, a main theme; a refrain. —*v.t.* 1, load. 2, encumber; tax. Also, **bur′then** (bėr′thən). —**bur′den·some,** *adj.*

bu′reau (byûr′ō) *n.* 1, a chest of drawers; a dresser. 2, an executive branch or office of a government or business.

bu·reauc′ra·cy (byû-rok′rə-sē) *n.* control or great influence in government by minor officials.

bu′reau·crat″ (byûr′ə-krat″) *n.* a jobholder in a bureaucracy. —**bu′reau·crat′ic,** *adj.* —**bu′reau·crat′i·cal·ly,** *adv.*

burg (bėrg) *n.* (*Colloq.*) a town.

bur′geon (bėr′jən) *v.i.* sprout buds.

-burg′er (bėr′gər) *suf.* patty (pert. to newly developed dishes, as *fish-burger, shrimpburger,* etc.).

bur′gess (bėr′jis) *n.* 1, a municipal official or councilman. 2, a full voting citizen.

burgh (bėrg) *n.* town; borough.

bur′glar (bėr′glər) *n.* one who breaks into a house with intent to rob. —**bur′glar·ize** (-īz″) *v.t.* break into and rob. —**bur′gla·ry,** *n.*

bur′go·mas″ter (bėr′gō-mås″tər) *n.* a mayor, in Ger. and Dutch towns.

Bur′gun·dy (bėr′gən-dē) *n.* any of various wines from Burgundy, France.

bur′i·al (ber′ē-əl) *n.* interment; the act of burying or state of being buried.

bur′lap (bėr′lap) *n.* a coarse fabric of hemp or jute, used for bags, etc.

bur·lesque′ (bėr-lesk′) *n.* 1, an imitation of a literary or dramatic work for comic effect; a parody. 2, a theatrical entertainment characterized by coarse comedy. —*v.t.* caricature; parody.

bur′ly (bėr′lē) *adj.* stout; brawny. —**bur′li·ness,** *n.*

burn (bėrn) *v.t.* [**burned** or **burnt,** **burn′ing**] 1, destroy by fire. 2, scorch; injure by heat or radiation. 3, produce by fire. 4, consume as fuel. 5, inflame. —*v.i.* 1, be on fire. 2, become charred or scorched. 3, suffer from too much heat or radiation. 4, become inflamed, as with emotion. —*n.* an injury caused by fire, heat, or radiation.

bur′nish (bėr′nish) *v.t.* make bright by polishing, esp. metal.

bur·noose' (bĕrnoos') n. a hooded cloak worn by Arabs.

burr (bĕr) n. 1, a roughness left by a tool in cutting metal, wood, etc. 2, a bur. 3, a guttural pronunciation of the letter r. 4, a dentist's drill. —v.t. 1, make rough or jagged. 2, pronounce with a burr.

bur'ro (bẽr'ō) n. [pl. -ros] a small donkey.

Burnoose

bur'row (bẽr'ō) n. a hole dug in the ground by an animal. —v.t. into the ground.

bur'sa (bẽr'sə) n. a sac between body joints.

bur'sar (bẽr'sər) n. a treasurer.

bur·si'tis (bẽr-sī'tis) n. inflammation of the bursa.

burst (bẽrst) v.i. [burst, bursting] 1, break from internal pressure; explode. 2, break or give way. 3, (with a prep.) display (sudden emotion). 4, appear or go suddenly. —v.t. rupture. —n. 1, an outburst. 2, an explosion. 3, a rush; a spurt.

bur'y (bẽr'ē) v.t. 1, put underground; inter; entomb. 2, cover or conceal from sight or attention. 3, wholly engage (oneself), as in thought.

bus n. 1, a large public motor vehicle: omnibus. 2, (Slang) any automobile.

bus'boy" n. a waiter's assistant in a restaurant.

bush (bûsh) n. 1, a low, woody shrub. 2, uncleared land; scrub. 3, brush. —bushed, adj. (Colloq.) fatigued; worn out.

bush'el (bûsh'əl) n. a unit of dry measure; four pecks.

bu'shi·do" (boo'shē-dō") n. the chivalric code of the Jap. gentry and officer class.

bush'ing (bûsh'ing) n. a metal lining in which an axle or shaft turns.

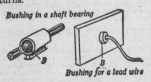

Bushing in a shaft bearing

Bushing for a lead wire

bush'man (bûsh'mən) n. [pl. -men] a member of a savage aboriginal tribe in Australia or (often cap.) Africa.

bush'mas"ter (bûsh'màs"tər) n. a poisonous snake of tropical Amer.

bush'whack"er (bûsh'hwak"ər) n. (Colloq.) a backwoodsman; a hillbilly.

bush'y (-ē) adj. formed like a bush; dense in growth, as a beard. —bush'iness, n.

busi'ness (biz'nəs) n. 1, occupation; calling. 2, a commercial enterprise; a company. 3, commercial pursuits in general; capital engaged in trade or industry. 4, industrial activity; the condition of businessmen collectively. 5, duty; aim. 6, affair; a matter of interest or concern. 7, in the theater, action illustrative of the script.

busi'ness·like" adj. methodical.

busi'ness·man" n. [pl. -men"] a man engaged in business.

bus'kin n. a short soft boots

buss (bus) v.t. kiss.

bust n. 1, a sculptured likeness of the head and shoulders of a person. 2, the human chest or bosom. 3, (Colloq.) a failure. 4, (Colloq.) a spree. —v.t. (Colloq.) burst; fail. —bust'ed, adj. (Colloq.) out of money.

bus'tard (bus'tərd) n. a large cranelike bird.

bus'tle (bus'əl) v.i. be fussily busy. —n. 1, stir; ado. 2, a pad under the back of a woman's skirt.

bus'y (biz'ē) adj. 1, actively occupied. 2, crowded with activity, as a busy day. —v.t. keep occupied. —bus'y·ness, n.

bus'y·bod"y (biz'ē-bod"ē) n. a prying or meddling person.

but adv. only. —prep. except; besides. —conj. 1, unless. 2, nevertheless; though. 3, on the contrary. 4, whether.

butch'er (bûch'ər) n. 1, one who slaughters animals for food and dresses meat for market; a seller of meat. 2, one who kills brutally. —v.t. 1, kill and dress for food. 2, murder wantonly. 3, botch, spoil. —butch'er·y, n. slaughter.

but'ler (but'lər) n. a manservant, usually the head servant of a large household.

butt (but) n. 1, a wine cask. 2, the thicker end of anything, as of a tool, log, etc. 3, a target; the object of criticism, a joke, etc. 4, a push with the head. —v.t. 1, strike something with the head. 2, collide. 3, abut. —v.t. strike with the head.

butte (būt) n. a steep-sided hill;

but'ter (but'ər) n. 1, a fatty substance made by churning cream. 2, any butterlike substance. —v.t. 1, spread with butter. 2, (Colloq.) (with up to) flatter; ingratiate oneself with. —but'ter·y, adj.

but′ter·cup″ (but′ər-kup″) *n.* a meadow plant with yellow flowers.

but′ter·fly″ (but′ər-flī″) *n.* **1,** an insect with broad, brilliantly colored wings. **2,** (*Colloq.*) a gay, fickle woman.

but′ter·milk″ (but′ər-milk″) *n.* the mildly acid liquid left after butter is churned.

but′ter·nut″ (but′ər-nut″) *n.* the Amer. white walnut; the tree; its oily fruit.

but′ter·scotch″ (but′ər-skoch″) *n.* a hard candy.

but′tocks (but′əks) *n. pl.* the fleshy part of the hips; the rump.

but′ton (but′ən) *n.* **1,** a knob or disk used on clothes as an ornament or a fastener. **2,** any buttonlike object or device. —*v.t. & i.* fasten with buttons.

but′ton·hole″ (but′ən-hōl″) *n.* the loop or slit for a button. —*v.t.* **1,** make such a slit in. **2,** (*Colloq.*) detain in conversation.

but′tress (but′ris) *n.* **1,** masonry built against a wall or building for strength and support. **2,** any prop. —*v.t.* prop; brace.

bux′om (buk′səm) *adj.* plump; healthy. —**bux′om·ness,** *n.*

buy (bī) *v.t.* [bought (bât), buy′ing]. **1,** obtain in exchange for money; purchase. **2,** obtain by any sacrifice. **3,** bribe. —**buy′er,** *n.* a purchaser; a departmental manager in a store.

buzz (buz) *n.* **1,** a humming sound, as of bees. **2,** a confused murmur. **3,** (*Slang*) a telephone call. —*v.i.* **1,** (*Slang*) swoop down upon in an airplane, as a prank. **2,** enlighten privately. —*v.t.* **1,** make a humming sound. **2,** (*Colloq.*) be very active. —**buzz bomb,** a bomb self-propelled by a rocket or jet engine.

buz′zard (buz′ərd) *n.* **1,** a hawklike bird. **2,** an Amer. vulture.

buzz′saw″ *n.* a circular saw.

by (bī) *prep.* **1,** beside; near. **2,** along; over. **3,** past and beyond. **4,** through the action or agency of. **5,** in or to the amount of. **6,** before; no later than. —*adv.* **1,** near; beside. **2,** aside. **3,** past.

Buzzard

by- (bī) *pref.* **1,** secondary. **2,** out of the way. **3,** near.

bye (bī) *n.* **1,** in a tournament, an idle round in which a competitor nevertheless advances. **2,** goodbye.

by′gone″ (bī′gon″) *adj.* of times past; former. —*adv.* past. —*n.* (*pl.*) deeds done in the past.

by′law″ (bī′lâ″) *n.* a regulation or rule adopted by a corporation or organization.

by-′line″ (bī′līn″) *n.* the line naming the author of a story or article.

by-′pass″ (bī′pas″) *n.* an alternative route, as a road or pipe. —*v.t.* avoid and progress beyond.

by′path″ *n.* **1,** a side or private road. **2,** an indirect route or course; a detour.

by-′prod′uct (bī′prod″əkt) *n.* a secondary product, produced incidentally to the manufacture of something else.

by′stand′er (bī′stan″dər) *n.* a spectator.

by′way″ (bī′wā″) *n.* a side road.

by′word″ (bī′wẽrd″) *n.* **1,** a proverb; a motto or slogan. **2,** a pet expression.

C

C, c (sē) the third letter of the English alphabet.

cab (kab) *n.* **1,** a horse-drawn or motor vehicle for public hire. **2,** the driver's compartment of a truck or locomotive.

ca·bal′ (kə-bal′) *n.* **1,** a secret scheme or intrigue. **2,** a group of secret plotters.

cab′a·la (kab′ə-lə) *n.* any occult science. —**cab″a·lis′tic,** *adj.*

ca·ba′ña (kə-bä′nyə) *n.* **1,** a small cabin. **2,** a private bathhouse.

cab″a·ret′ (kab″ə-rā′) *n.* a restaurant that provides entertainment.

cab′bage (kab′ij) *n.* a vegetable plant having edible leaves formed into a thick compact head.

cab′in (kab′in) *n.* **1,** cottage; hut. **2,** a room in a ship or airplane.

cab′i·net (kab′i-nət) *n.* **1,** a piece of furniture used as a cupboard. **2,** a small meeting room. **3,** an advisory council. —*adj.* **1,** pert. to a council. **2,** of a certain small size.

ca′ble (kā′bəl) *n.* **1,** a thick, strong rope or chain. **2,** a number of wires for conducting electricity, bound together in a cylindrical sheath. **3,** [also, **ca′ble·gram″**] a telegram sent by submarine cable. **4,** (*Naut.*) a unit of length. —*v.t. & i.* furnish with cables; communicate by cable.

ca·boose′ (kə-boos′) *n.* a car on a freight train fitted for use of the crew.

cab″ri·o·let′ (kab″rē-ə-lā′) *n.* **1,** a light, two-wheeled carriage. **2,** an automobile with a folding top.

ca·ca'o (kə-kä'ō) n. a tropical evergreen tree whose seeds are the source of cocoa and chocolate.

cache (kash) n. 1, a place of storage or concealment, esp. underground. 2, a store of provisions, treasure, etc. so concealed. —v.t. hide.

cack'le (kak'əl) n. 1, the shrill repeated cry of a goose or hen. 2, silly chatter; noisy laughter.

ca·coph'o·ny (kə-kof'ə-nē) n. a combination of discordant sounds; dissonance. —ca·coph'o·nous, adj.

cac'tus (kak'təs) n. [pl. -ti (-tī)] a leafless spiny desert plant.

cad (kad) n. an ill-bred or contemptible person. —cad'dish, adj.

ca·dav'er (kə-dav'ər) n. a dead body; corpse. —ca·dav'er·ous, adj.

cad'die (kad'ē) n. a boy engaged to carry the clubs of a golf player. —v.i. act as a caddie. Also, cad'dy.

cad'dy (kad'ē) n. a small can or chest for holding tea, etc.

ca'dence (kā'dəns) n. 1, rhythmic flow. 2, a fall in pitch or tempo. 3, (Music) a sequence of chords expressing conclusion, finality, or repose. 4, the beat or rate of a rhythm.

ca·den'za (kə-den'zə) n. a passage in showy style for a soloist in a concerto.

ca·det' (kə-det') n. 1, a young man in training for army service. 2, a younger son.

cadge (kaj) v.t. peddle or beg.

cad'mi·um (kad'mē-əm) n. a metallic chemical element, no. 48, symbol Cd.

ca'dre (kā'dər) n. a permanently organized group of persons forming the framework of a larger unit.

ca·du'ce·us (kə-doo'sē-əs) n. [pl. -i' (-ī')] a winged staff: symbol of the medical profession.

cae'cum (sē'kəm) n. the inner end of the large intestine, to which the vermiform appendix is attached.

Cae·sar'e·an (si-zâr'ē-ən) adj. pert. to Caesarean operation or section, delivery of a baby by cutting into the womb.

cae·su'ra (sē-zhûr'ə) n. a natural break or pause, due to sense, in a line of poetry.

Caduceus

ca·fé' (ka-fā') n. a restaurant or barroom.

caf''e·te'ri·a (kaf'ə-tir'ē-ə) n. a self-service restaurant.

caf'feine (kaf'ēn) n. a bitter alkaloid having a stimulating effect.

cage (kāj) n. an enclosure made of wires or bars. —v.t. put in a cage.

cag'y (kā'jē) adj. (Colloq.) wary; shrewd. Also, cage'y.

ca·hoots' (kə-hoots') n. pl. (Colloq.) secret partnership.

cairn (kârn) n. 1, a heap of stones, erected as a monument. 2, a small dog of a terrier breed.

cais'son (kā'sən) n. 1, a large boxlike structure with an open bottom, used in submarine excavation. 2, a floating structure used as a dock, etc. 3, a wagon for ammunition.

cai'tiff (kā'tif) n. (Archaic) a wicked or mean person.

ca·jole' (kə-jōl') v.t. & i. persuade by flattery; wheedle. —ca·jol'er·y, n.

cake (kāk) n. 1, a sweet food baked from dough. 2, any loaflike mass, as of soap.

cake'walk' n. a dance.

cal'a·bash' (kal'ə-bash') n. any of various gourds or gourd trees.

cal'a·boose' (kal'ə-boos') n. (Slang) a jail.

cal'a·mine' (kal'ə-mīn') n. a white mineral, an ore of zinc, used medicinally.

ca·lam'i·ty (kə-lam'ə-tē) n. a great misfortune or cause of distress; disaster. —ca·lam'i·tous, adj.

cal·car'e·ous (kal-kâr'ē-əs) adj. containing calcium carbonate; chalky.

cal'ci·fy' (kal'sə-fī') v.t. & i. harden or become hard by deposit of calcium. —cal''ci·fi·ca'tion, n.

cal'ci·mine' (kal'sə-mīn') n. a thin water-soluble paint, usually white. —v.t. whitewash. Also, kal'so·mine'.

cal'cine (kal'sīn) v.t. heat in order to fuse, crumble, oxidize, etc. —cal''ci·na'tion, n.

cal'ci·um (kal'sē-əm) n. a chemical element, no. 20, symbol Ca, found in bone, chalk, lime, etc.

cal'cu·late' (kal'kū-lāt') v.t. 1, ascertain by mathematics; compute. 2, plan. 3, (Colloq.) intend; guess. —v.i. reckon. —cal'cu·la·ble, adj. —cal''cu·la'tion, n. —cal'cu·la''tor, n.

cal'cu·lus (kal'kū-ləs) n. 1, (Math.) any system of computation or analysis by a specialized algebraic notation. 2, a small stone, as a gallstone.

cal'dron (kâl'drən) n. a large kettle. Also, caul'dron.

cal'en·dar (kal'ən-dər) n. 1, any system of division of time. 2, a table of days, weeks, and months. **3**, a list, register, or catalog; a list of cases to be tried in a court. —*v.t.* enter in a calendar; register.

ca·len·du·la (kə-len'jə-lə) *n.* any of various flowering plants including the marigold.

calf (kăf) *n.* [*pl.* **calves** (kăvz)] **1**, the young of certain animals, as cow, elephant, seal, whale. **2**, calfskin leather. **3**, the thick fleshy part of the human leg, below the knee.

cal'i·ber (kal'ə-bər) *n.* **1**, diameter, esp. of the hollow inside of a cylinder. **2**, capacity of mind; degree of importance. Also, **cal'i·bre.**

cal'i·brate" (kal'ə-brāt") *v.t.* mark (a measuring instrument) with graduations; verify or rectify. —**cal"i·bra'tion,** *n.*

cal'i·co" (kal'ə-kō") *n.* a printed cotton cloth.

cal'i·per (kal'ə-pər) *n.* (usually *pl.*) a measuring instrument for determining diameters. —*v.t. & i.* measure with calipers.

ca'liph (kā'lif) *n.* title of a sovereign in Mohammedan countries.

cal"is·then'ics (kal"əs-then'iks) *n. pl.* light gymnastics.

calk (kâk) *v.t.* make (a boat, boiler, tank, etc.) watertight. —*n.* a metal spike or spur on the bottom of a shoe. Also, **caulk.**

call (kâl) *v.t.* **1**, utter loudly; announce; proclaim. **2**, attract or demand the attention of; summon. **3**, give a name to; designate; characterize. **4**, telephone to. —*v.i.* **1**, shout. **2**, make a short visit. —*n.* **1**, a cry or shout. **2**, the characteristic cry of an animal or bird; the note of a bugle or horn. **3**, a notice, summons, or invitation. **4**, a short visit.

cal'la (kal'ə) *n.* [also, **calla lily**] a plant with a large white flower and bright yellow spadix.

cal·lig'ra·phy (kə-lig'rə-fē) *n.* fancy handwriting.

call'ing *n.* **1**, profession or vocation. **2**, act of summoning, etc.

cal·li'o·pe (kə-lī'ə-pē) *n.* a musical instrument employing steam whistles.

cal·los'i·ty (kə-los'ə-tē) *n.* **1**, a hardened part; a callus. **2**, a callous condition.

cal'lous (kal'əs) *adj.* **1**, hard; hardened. **2**, unfeeling; unkind. —**cal'lous·ness,** *n.*

cal'low (kal'ō) *adj.* very immature. —**cal'low·ness,** *n.*

cal'lus (kal'əs) *n.* a hardened or thickened part of the skin.

calm (käm) *adj.* **1**, quiet; still. **2**, serene; tranquil. —*n.* the state of being calm. —*v.t. & i.* quiet. —**calm'ness,** *n.*

cal'o·mel" (kal'ə-mel") *n.* a medicine, mercurous chloride, used as a purgative.

cal'o·rie (kal'ə-rē) *n.* a measure of heat, and of the energy-producing property of food. —**ca·lor'ic** (kə-lôr'ik) *adj.*

cal'u·met" (kal'ū-met") *n.* an Indian ceremonial tobacco pipe.

ca·lum'ni·ate" (kə-lum'nē-āt") *v.t.* slander. —**ca·lum"ni·a'tion,** *n.*

cal'um·ny (kal'əm-nē) *n.* a false accusation of crime or misconduct; slander. —**ca·lum'ni·ous,** *adj.*

Cal'va·ry (kal'və-rē) *n.* **1**, a picture or sculpture of the scene of the Crucifixion. **2**, (*cap.*) the place where Christ was crucified.

calve (kăv) *v.i.* bear a calf.

calves (kăvz) *n. pl.* of *calf.*

Cal'vin·ism (kal'vin-iz-əm) *n.* the theological doctrines of John Calvin; Presbyterianism. —**Cal'vin·ist,** *n.* —**Cal"vin·is'tic,** *adj.*

ca'lyx (kā'liks) *n.* the outermost envelope of a flower; the sepals.

cam (kam) *n.* an eccentric wheel or part for converting rotary motion into linear or irregular motion.

ca"ma·ra'de·rie (kä"mə-rä'də-rē) *n.* comradeship.

cam'ber (kam'bər) *n.* a slight curve or arch.

cam'bric (kām'brik) *n.* a closely-woven fabric of cotton or linen. —**cambric tea,** hot water, cream, and sugar.

came (kām) *v.* pret. of *come.*

cam'el (kam'əl) *n.* a large ruminant quadruped used in Asia and Africa as a beast of burden.

ca·mel'lia (kə-mēl'yə) *n.* an evergreen plant bearing red or white flowers.

ca·mel'o·pard" (kə-mel'ə-pärd") *n.* the giraffe.

Camels
Arabian   Bactrian

Cam'em·bert" (kam'əm-bâr") *n.* a soft-ripening cheese.

cam'e·o" (kam'ē-ō") *n.* a stone or shell decorated with raised carving.

cam'er·a (kam'ər-ə) *n.* **1**, a photographic apparatus for recording an image on a sensitized surface. **2**, the private chamber of a judge.

cam'i·sole" (kam'ə-sōl") *n.* **1**, a woman's underwaist. **2**, a straight jacket.

cam'o·mile" (kam'ə-mīl") *n.* a herb used to make a medicinal tea.

cam'ou·flage (kam'ə-fläzh″) *n.* 1, (*Mil.*) disguise of objects that cannot be wholly concealed. 2, any disguise; false pretense. —*v.t.* disguise.

camp (kamp) *n.* 1, a place for the erection of temporary shelters. 2, a group of temporary lodgings, as for lumbermen. 3, a cabin in the wilderness. 4, fig., a group or sect. —*v.i.* 1, live in a camp. 2, (with *on*) follow persistently; haunt.

cam·paign' (kam-pān′) *n.* 1, military operations during one season or in a definite enterprise. 2, a series of activities directed to a single purpose, as for election to public office.

cam″pa·ni'le (kam″pə-nē'lē) *n.* a bell tower.

cam·pan'u·la (kam-pan'yə-lə) *n.* the bellflower.

cam'phor (kam'fər) *n.* 1, a vegetable or synthetic gum used in medicine, plastics, etc. 2, an oriental tree. —**cam'phor·at″ed** (-ā″tid) *adj.*

cam'pus (kam'pəs) *n.* the grounds of a college or university.

can (kan) *aux. v.* [*pret.* **could**] 1, have the ability or power to; be able to. 2, (*Colloq.*) may; have permission to. —*n.* a metal container or receptacle. —*v.t.* [**canned** (kand), **can'ning**] 1, seal in a container. 2, (*Colloq.*) dismiss from employment.

ca·nal' (kə-nal′) *n.* 1, an artificial waterway for navigation or irrigation. 2, any channel, duct, or passage conveying or containing a fluid.

can'a·pé (kan'ə-pē) *n.* a small piece of bread or toast bearing a morsel of appetizing food.

ca·nard' (kə-närd′) *n.* a false story; a hoax.

ca·nar'y (kə-när'ē) *n.* 1, a songbird, widely domesticated as a household pet. 2, a light yellow color.

ca·nas'ta (kə-näs'tə) *n.* a card game based on rummy.

can'can (kan'kan) *n.* a posturing dance with high kicking.

can'cel (kan'səl) *v.t.* 1, draw lines across (something written) so as to deface. 2, make void; annul. 3, compensate for; offset; neutralize. —**can″cel·la'tion,** *n.*

can'cer (kan'sər) *n.* a malignant tumor; any evil that grows and spreads. —**can'cer·ous,** *adj.*

Can'cer (kan'sər) *n.* a northern constellation, the Crab (see *zodiac*).

can″de·la'brum (kan″də-lä'brəm) *n.* [*pl.* **-bra** (-brə), **-brums**] an ornamental branched candlestick.

can'did (kan'did) *adj.* outspoken; frank. —**can'did·ness,** *n.*

can'di·date″ (kan'də-dāt″) *n.* one who seeks an office or honor. —**can'di·da·cy** (-də-sē) *n.*

can'dle (kan'dəl) *n.* a rod of wax, tallow, or paraffin with an embedded wick, burned to give sustained light. —*v.t.* examine (esp. eggs) by holding between the eye and a light. —**candle power,** a measure of illumination.

can'dle·stick″ *n.* a holder for a candle.

can'dor (kan'dər) *n.* frankness; sincerity. Also, **can'dour.**

can'dy (kan'dē) *n.* any of a variety of confections containing sugar. —*v.t.* 1, cook with much sugar or syrup. 2, make agreeable.

cane (kān) *n.* 1, a walking stick. 2, the woody stem of certain plants, as sugar cane, bamboo. 3, pliable woody fibers. —*v.t.* 1, flog with a cane. 2, make or weave with cane. —**cane'brake″,** *n.* a thicket of canes.

ca'nine (kā'nīn) *adj.* pert. to dogs. —*n.* 1, any dog or member of the dog family. 2, a long, pointed tooth.

can'is·ter (kan'is-tər) *n.* a small can or box; a caddy.

can'ker (kang'kər) *n.* an ulcerous sore, esp. in the mouth. —*v.t. & i.* infect or become infected with canker; fig. poison or corrupt slowly. —**can'ker·ous,** *adj.*

can'na (kan'ə) *n.* a tropical flowering plant.

can'ner (kan'ər) *n.* one who cans food for preservation. —**can'ner·y,** *n.* a place where foods are canned.

can'ni·bal (kan'ə-bəl) *n.* 1, a person who eats human flesh. 2, any animal that eats the flesh of its own kind. —**can'ni·bal·ism,** *n.* —**can'ni·bal·is'tic,** *adj.* —**can'ni·bal·is'ti·cal·ly,** *adv.*

can'non (kan'ən) *n.* 1, a large, mounted gun for hurling projectiles. 2, (*Brit.*) a carom in billiards. —*v.i.* discharge cannons. —**can'non·ry,** *n.*

can″non·ade' (kan″ə-nād″) *n.* concentrated cannon fire. —*v.t. & i.* bombard.

can'not (kan'ot) *v.* can not.

can'ny (kan'ē) *adj.* wary; prudent; sagacious. —**can'ni·ness,** *n.*

Canoe

ca·noe' (kə-noo′) *n.* a light, round-bottomed boat pointed at both ends, propelled by paddling. —*v.i.* go in a canoe. —**ca·noe'ist,** *n.*

can'on (kan'ən) *n.* **1**, any rule, law, or body of law, esp. ecclesiastical. **2**, genuine books, esp. of the Bible. **3**, a church officer. —**ca·non'i·cal** (kə-non'i-kəl) *adj.* —**can'on·ize** (-nīz") *v.t.* designate as a saint.

ca'ñon (kan'yən) *n.* canyon.

can'o·py (kan'ə-pē) *n.* a suspended covering over a bed, entrance, etc.

cant (kant) *n.* **1**, insincere speech or writing, esp. conventional pretense to high ideals or aims. **2**, the special vocabulary or speech of a profession or class, as the whine of beggars; argot. **3**, a tilt, slant, or obliquity. **4**, a salient angle. —*v.i.* **1**, utter cant. **2**, tilt; list. —*v.t.* **1**, make oblique; bevel. **2**, tip; upset.

can't (kant) *contraction* cannot.

can'ta·loupe" (kan'tə-lōp") *n.* a variety of muskmelon.

can·tan'ker·ous (kan-tang'kər-əs) *adj.* perverse in disposition; cross; ill-natured. —**can·tan'ker·ous·ness,** *n.*

can·ta'ta (kən-tä'tə) *n.* a choral composition, sacred or secular.

can·teen' (kan-tēn') *n.* **1**, a shop, bar, or recreation hall in a military camp, barracks, etc. **2**, a portable container for water.

can'ter (kan'tər) *n.* a gait of a horse; an easy gallop. —*v.i.* ride at a canter.

can'ti·cle (kan'tə-kəl) *n.* a spoken or chanted nonmetrical hymn.

can'ti·lev"er (kan'tə-lev"ər; -lē"vər) *adj.* supported at one end.

can'to (kan'tō) *n.* a main division of a long poem.

can'ton (kan'tən) *n.* a subdivision of a country; a small district.

can·ton'ment (kan-ton'mənt) *n.* a military camp, esp. a large one.

can'tor (kan'tər) *n.* the singing leader in a cathedral or synagogue.

can'vas (kan'vəs) *n.* **1**, a heavy cloth of hemp or flax. **2**, something made of canvas, esp. a sail, a tent, or an oil painting.

can'vass (kan'vəs) *v.t.* **1**, traverse (a district) for purposes of questioning or solicitation. **2**, examine; discuss. —*v.i.* solicit votes, opinions, etc. —*n.* **1**, a campaign of soliciting votes, opinions, etc. **2**, examination; investigation; discussion.

can'yon (kan'yən) *n.* a narrow valley with steep sides; a ravine. Also, **ca'ñon.**

cap (kap) *n.* **1**, a covering for the head. **2**, something resembling a cap, esp. a covering for an opening. **3**, the head or top; the acme. **4**, a noise-making or explosive device. —*v.t.* [**capped, cap'ping**] **1**, cover with a cap. **2**, complete; bring to a climax; surpass.

ca'pa·ble (kā'pə-bəl) *adj.* **1**, (with *of*) having the ability, capacity, inclination, etc. **2**, competent; efficient. —**ca"pa·bil'i·ty,** *n.*

ca·pa'cious (kə-pā'shəs) *adj.* capable of holding much; roomy. —**ca·pa'cious·ness,** *n.*

ca·pac'i·ty (kə-pas'ə-tē) *n.* **1**, the power of receiving or containing. **2**, cubic contents; volume. **3**, ability; power to act. **4**, function; role.

ca·par'i·son (kə-par'i-sən) *n.* **1**, an ornamental covering for a horse. **2**, equipment; clothing. —*v.t.* equip; bedeck.

cape (kāp) *n.* **1**, a loose outer garment, covering the shoulders. **2**, a piece of land jutting from the coast into a sea or lake.

ca'per (kā'pər) *v.i.* leap or skip about; frolic. —*n.* **1**, a leap or skip. **2**, a prank. **3**, a plant whose bud is used for seasoning; the pickled bud.

cap·il·lar"y (kap'ə-ler"ē) *adj.* **1**, pert. to a tube of small bore. **2**, pert. to the surface tension of a liquid. **3**, resembling hair. —*n.* a minute tube or vessel.

cap'i·tal (kap'ə-təl) *n.* **1**, the city that is the official seat of the government of a country or of a subdivision. **2**, a capital letter. **3**, the head of a pillar. **4**, wealth used in trade; the net worth of a business. **5**, the owners of capital wealth, collectively. —*adj.* **1**, principal; most important. **2**, excellent. **3**, pert. to the seat of government. **4**, (of letters) of the large size used at the beginnings of sentences. **5**, (of a crime) punishable by death. —**capital ship,** a warship of largest size.

cap'i·tal·ism (-iz-əm) *n.* the economic system in which the ownership and exploitation of wealth are left largely in private hands.

cap'i·tal·ist *n.* **1**, one with wealth invested for profit. **2**, one who favors capitalism. —**cap"i·tal·is'tic,** *adj.* —**cap'i·tal·is·ti·cal·ly,** *adv.*

cap'i·tal·ize (-īz") *v.t.* **1**, provide capital for; use as capital. **2**, use to advantage. **3**, begin with a capital letter.

cap'i·tol (kap'ə-təl) *n.* the chief office building of a government.

ca·pit'u·late" (kə-pich'ə-lāt") *v.t.* surrender on stipulated terms. —**ca·pit"u·la'tion,** *n.*

ca'pon (kā'pon) *n.* a castrated rooster.

ca·price' (kə-prēs') *n.* **1**, a sudden change of mind or humor; a whim. **2**, fickleness. —**ca·pri'cious** (-prē'shəs) *adj.*

Cap"ri·corn" (kap'ri-kôrn") *n.* a constellation, the Goat (see *zodiac*).

cap·size' (kap-sīz') *v.i. & t.* overturn; upset (esp. of a boat).

cap′stan (kap′stən) *n.* a type of windlass, a drum rotating on an upright axle, manually operated.

cap′sule (kap′səl) *n.* **1,** a gelatin case enclosing a dose of medicine. **2,** a small casing or envelope.

cap′tain (kap′tən) *n.* **1,** one in authority; chief; leader. **2,** (*Mil.*) a rank between lieutenant and major. **3,** (*Naval*) a rank between commander and commodore or admiral. **4,** the master of any ship. —*v.t.* command.

cap′tion (kap′shən) *n.* a headline or title.

cap′tious (kap′shəs) *adj.* faultfinding; hypercritical. —**cap′tiousness,** *n.*

cap′ti·vate″ (kap′ti-vāt″) *v.t.* enthrall by charm; fascinate. —**cap′ti·va′tion,** *n.*

cap′tive (kap′tiv) *n.* a prisoner. —*adj.* captured; held prisoner. —**cap·tiv′i·ty** (kap-tiv′ə-tē) *n.*

cap′tor (kap′tər) *n.* one who captures.

cap′ture (kap′chər) *v.t.* take prisoner; seize. —*n.* **1,** act of capturing. **2,** who or what is captured.

cap·u·chin (kap′yū-shin) *n.* **1,** a long-tailed South American monkey. **2,** a hooded cloak. **3,** (*cap.*) an order of Franciscan monks.

car (kär) *n.* **1,** automobile. **2,** any of a variety of vehicles. **3,** an elevator. **4,** a compartment for passengers or freight.

ca″ra·ba′o (kär″ə-bä′ō) *n.* a large animal of the ox family; a water buffalo.

car′a·cul (kar′ə-kəl) *n.* the curly fleece of the Astrakhan sheep.

ca·rafe′ (kə-raf′) *n.* a glass water bottle; decanter.

car′a·mel (kar′ə-məl) *n.* **1,** burnt sugar, as used for flavoring. **2,** a kind of candy.

car′at (kar′ət) *n.* **1,** a unit of weight for precious stones. **2,** a measure of purity of gold. Also, **kar′at.**

car′a·van″ (kar′ə-van″) *n.* **1,** a group of travelers banded together for safety, esp. in desert regions of Asia and Africa. **2,** a large covered wagon; van.

car″a·van′sa·ry (kar″ə-van′sə-rē) *n.* an inn for caravan travelers.

car′a·way″ (kar′ə-wā″) *n.* a pungent seed used as a flavoring.

car′bide (kär′bīd) *n.* a chemical compound, esp. calcium carbide, used to make acetylene gas.

Carbine

car′bine (kär′bīn) *n.* a short-barreled rifle.

car″bo·hy′drate (kär″bō-hī′drāt) *n.* a class of compounds of carbon, hydrogen, and oxygen, important in foods, as sugar and starch.

car·bol′ic (kär-bol′ik) *adj.* pert. to carbolic acid, or phenol, a disinfectant.

car′bon (kär′bən) *n.* **1,** a chemical element, no. 6, symbol C, that occurs pure as diamond and graphite, impurely as coal, and in compounds to form organic substances. **2,** a rod of carbon used as an electrode. **3,** [carbon paper] a piece of paper backed with black preparation, for making duplicate copies; a copy so made. —**carbon dioxide,** dry ice. —**carbon tetrachloride** (tet″rə-klôr′id) a noninflammable liquid used in fire extinguishers and as a solvent in cleaning fluids. —**car·bon′ic** (-bon′ik) *adj.*

car′bon·ate″ (kär′bə-nāt″) *v.t.* charge (water) with carbonic acid gas. —**carbonated water,** soda water.

Car″bo·run′dum (kär″bə-run′dəm) *n.* (*T.N.*) an abrasive made of silicon and carbon.

car′bun·cle (kär′bung-kəl) *n.* **1,** a garnet, or its color. **2,** a circumscribed inflammation exuding pus.

car′bu·re″tor (kär′bə-rā″tər) *n.* a device for vaporizing a fuel to produce a combustible gas.

car′cass (kär′kəs) *n.* the dead body of an animal.

car″ci·no′ma (kär″sə-nō′mə) *n.* (*Med.*) a malignant growth in body tissues; cancer.

card (kärd) *n.* **1,** a piece of thick paper or thin pasteboard, usually rectangular and printed, as *calling card, membership card, greeting card.* **2,** one of a set of such pieces printed for playing games: *playing card;* (*pl.*) any game played with such cards. **3,** a program of events; a bill of fare. **4,** (*Colloq.*) an amusing person. **5,** a brush or other implement for combing fibers. —*v.t.* **1,** comb (fibers). **2,** list; schedule.

card′board″ *n.* thin stiff pasteboard.

car′di·ac″ (kär′dē-ak″) *adj.* **1,** pert. to the heart. **2,** pert. to the upper part of the stomach.

car′di·gan (kär′də-gən) *n.* a close-fitting wool jacket.

car′di·nal (kär′də-nəl) *adj.* **1,** of first importance; chief; fundamental. **2,** deep red. —*n.* **1,** a member of the Sacred College of the Rom. Cath. Church. **2,** a No. Amer. finch. **3,** a deep red color. —**cardinal numbers,** one, two, etc., as distinguished from first, second, etc.

car″di·o·graph″ (kär′dē-ə-graf″) *n.* an instrument for recording heart action. —**car″di·o·graph′ic,** *adj.*

care (kār) *n.* **1,** attention; heed; solicitude; anxiety. **2,** a cause of worry, etc. **3,** protection; charge. —*v.i.* **1,** be concerned, etc. **2,** provide (for). **3,** have an inclination (to) or affection (for).

ca·reen' (kə-rēn') *v.i.* sway or lean to one side, as a ship.

ca·reer' (kə-rir') *n.* **1,** a general course of action, esp. progress in a lifework. **2,** a calling pursued as a lifework. **3,** speed. —*v.i.* run or move at full speed.

care'free' *adj.* free of anxiety or worry.

care'ful (kār'fəl) *adj.* employing care; cautious. —**care'ful·ness,** *n.*

care'less (kār'lis) *adj.* **1,** inattentive; negligent; reckless. **2,** unworried. —**care'less·ness,** *n.*

ca·ress' (kə-res') *v.t.* touch with the hand to express affection. —*n.* an act of affection.

car'et (kar'ət) *n.* the mark (∧) used to show where to insert additional matter in a written or printed line.

care'tak'er *n.* a watchman or janitor.

care'worn' *n.* showing fatigue, etc. from worry.

car'fare' *n.* the charge for a ride on a streetcar, bus, etc.

car'go (kär'gō) *n.* the goods or merchandise carried by a ship.

car'i·bou' (kar'ə-boo') *n.* a No. Amer. reindeer.

car'i·ca·ture (kar'i-kə-chŭr') *n.* a picture or verbal description that ludicrously exaggerates the characteristics of the thing depicted. —*v.t.* make a caricature of. —**car'i·ca·tur'ist,** *n.*

car'ies (kār'ēz) *n.* decay, esp. of teeth.

car'il·lon' (kar'ə-lon') *n.* a set of bells tuned to play melodies.

car'load' *n.* capacity or contents of a railroad freight car.

car·min'a·tive (kär-min'ə-tiv) *adj.* tending to reduce flatulence.

car'mine (kär'min) *n. & adj.* a purplish-red color.

car'nage (kär'nij) *n.* the slaughter of many; a massacre.

car'nal (kär'nəl) *adj.* pert. to the body; not spiritual. —**car·nal'i·ty,** *n.*

car·na'tion (kär-nā'shən) *n.* **1,** a fragrant flower. **2,** a shade of pink. —*adj.* pink.

car·nel'ian (kär-nēl'yən) *n.* a reddish, semi-precious stone.

car'ni·val (kär'nə-vəl) *n.* **1,** riotous revelry. **2,** the feasting season immediately preceding Lent. **3,** an amusement park set up temporarily.

car'ni·vore' (kär'nə-vôr') *n.* any animal living chiefly on flesh. —**car·niv'o·rous** (-niv'ə-rəs) *adj.*

car'ol (kar'əl) *n.* a song of joy, esp. one sung at Christmas. —*v.i. & t.* sing joyously; celebrate in song.

car'om (kar'əm) *n.* **1,** (*Billiards*) a shot in which the cue ball is made to strike two other balls. **2,** any glancing blow or rebound. —*v.i.* rebound.

ca·rot'id (kə-rot'id) *n.* an artery leading to the head.

ca·rouse' (kə-rowz') *v.i.* drink freely; revel noisily. —**ca·rous'al,** *n.*

carp (kärp) *v.i.* find fault. —*n.* any of several fresh-water food fishes.

car'pal (kär'pəl) *adj.* pert. to the wrist.

car'pel (kär'pəl) *n.* (*Bot.*) a seed vessel in the pistil.

car'pen·ter (kär'pən-tər) *n.* a builder or repairer of wooden structures. —**car'pen·try,** *n.*

car'pet (kär'pit) *n.* a heavy cloth floor covering. —*v.t.* cover with, or as with carpet. —**car'pet·ing,** *n.* such fabric.

car'pet·bag'ger (-bag'ər) *n.* one who carries all his possessions in one bag, esp. a Northerner in the South after the Civil War.

car'riage (kar'ij) *n.* **1,** a wheeled vehicle for the conveyance of persons. **2,** any part of a machine or apparatus that carries another part. **3,** manner of carrying one's person; posture. **4,** the act of carrying, conveying, or transporting.

car'ri·er (kar'ē-ər) *n.* **1,** a company, as a railroad, engaged in public transportation. **2,** a naval vessel designed to carry airplanes.

car'ri·on (kar'ē-ən) *n.* dead and putrefying flesh.

car'rot (kar'ət) *n.* a plant having an edible orange-yellow root.

car'rou·sel' (kar'ə-sel') *n.* a merry-go-round.

car'ry (kar'ē) *v.t.* **1,** transport from place to place; convey. **2,** bear the weight of; support. **3,** adopt (a bill or motion); obtain election from (an electorate). **4,** be possessed of. **5,** transfer. —*v.i.* **1,** reach a distance, as a voice or missile. **2,** be adopted, as by a vote. **3,** (with *on*) display emotion. **4,** (with *on*) continue. —*n.* **1,** distance traversed. **2,** a portage.

cart (kärt) *n.* a two-wheeled vehicle.

cart'age (kär'tij) *n.* **1,** conveyance in a cart. **2,** a fee therefore.

car·tel' (kär-tel') *n.* a syndicate formed to seek a business monopoly.

cart'er (-ər) *n.* a truckman.

car'ti·lage (kär'tə-lij) n. a firm, elastic substance in the body; gristle. —**car"ti·lag'i·nous** (-laj'i-nəs) adj.

car·tog'ra·phy (kär-tog'rə-fē) n. the art and science of making maps. **car·tog'ra·pher,** n. —**car"to·graph'ic,** adj. —**car"to·graph'i·cal·ly,** adv.

car'ton (kär'tən) n. a cardboard box, usually large.

car·toon' (kär-toon') n. a drawing, often in caricature, made as a commentary on current events, or to illustrate a joke or narrative. —**car·toon'ist,** n.

car'tridge (kär'trij) n. 1, a cylindrical metal or cardboard case holding a charge of powder and shot. 2, any similar sealed container.

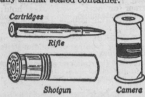

Cartridges

Rifle

Shotgun   Camera

carve (kärv) v.t. & t. cut with an edged tool, esp. with skill.

car"y·at'id (kar'ē-at'id) n. a sculptured figure of a woman used as a supporting column.

ca·sa'ba (kə-sä'bə) n. a variety of muskmelon. Also, **cas·sa'ba.**

cas·cade' (kas-kād') n. 1, a waterfall; a series of waterfalls. 2, something likened to waterfalls.

cas·ca'ra (kas-kar'ə) n. 1, a kind of buckthorn. 2, a laxative made from its bark.

case (kās) n. 1, that which happens; actual circumstances. 2, a particular instance among like instances. 3, a question, problem, or state of things requiring discussion or decision; a cause of legal action. 4, a statement of facts and reasons relevant to a decision. 5, an instance of disease; a patient. 6, (Gram.) one of the categories in the inflection of nouns, as nominative case. 7, an outer covering or sheath; a box or receptacle. —v.t. 1, put in a case; enclose; 2, (Slang) survey, as for criminal intent. —upper case, capital (letters). —lower case, small (letters).

ca'se·in (kā'sē·in) n. a protein precipitated from milk.

case'ment (kās'mənt) n. a hinged frame for a glass window.

cash (kash) n. 1, currency; specie. 2, immediate payment. —v.t. exchange (a check, etc.) for cash. —cash in (Colloq.) 1, terminate a speculation, usually with profit. 2,

die. —cash register, a machine that holds and records money received.

cash'ew (kash'oo) n. a tropical American tree or its fruit, a small edible nut.

cash·ier' (ka-shir') n. an employee or officer who receives money, makes change, etc.; a treasurer. —v.t. dismiss in disgrace.

cash'mere (kash'mir) n. 1, a fabric made from the hair of Kashmir goats. 2, a twilled wool fabric.

ca·si'no (kə-sē'nō) n. [pl. -nos] 1, a building or room for indoor games. 2, [also, cas·si'no] a card game.

cask (kåsk) n. 1, a barrel for holding liquids. 2, its capacity.

cas'ket (kås'kit) n. 1, a small box, esp. for jewels. 2, a coffin.

cas·sa'va (kə-sä'və) n. a tropical plant cultivated for its starchy roots.

cas'se·role" (kas'ə-rōl") n. a baking dish with a cover.

cas'sia (kash'ə) n. 1, a Chinese tree, or cinnamon obtained from it. 2, a tropical tree or its pulpy pods, which yield senna.

cas'sock (kas'ək) n. a long, close-fitting clerical coat.

cas'so·war"y (kas'ə-wâr"ē) n. a large, flightless bird of Australia.

cast (kåst) v.t. [pret. & p.p. cast] 1, throw; hurl; fling. 2, throw off; shed. 3, plan; contrive; arrange; compute. 4, select actors for (a play); assign (an actor) to a rôle. 5, pour (molten metal, plaster, etc.) into a mold; make by this process. —v.i. 1, throw. 2, calculate; conjecture. —n. 1, a throw. 2, what is cast; something molded [also, cast'ing]. 3, the list of actors in a play. 4, tendency; expression; tinge. 5, a computation.

cas"ta·net' (kas'tə-net') n. a shell of hard wood, used in pairs as clappers to provide a rhythmic beat.

cast'a·way" (kast'ə-wā") n. a person marooned, as by shipwreck.

caste (kåst) n. 1, one of the hereditary social classes among the Hindus. 2, any group united by its social position.

Castanets

cas·tel·lat"ed (kas'tə-lā"tid) adj. built like a castle; having turrets and battlements. —**cas"tel·la'tion,** n.

cast'er (kås'tər) n. 1, one who or that which casts. 2, a small wheel attached to the leg of a piece of furniture. 3, a small cruet or shaker

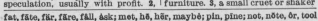

cas'ti·gate (kas'tə-gāt") *v.t.* **1,** criticize severely. **2,** punish; correct. —**cas'ti·ga'tion,** *n.*

cas'tile (kas'tēl) *n.* soap made with olive oil and soda.

cast-'i'ron (kåst'ī"ərn) *adj.* **1,** made of cast iron, an alloy of iron, carbon, etc. **2,** inflexible. **3,** hardy.

cas'tle (kås'əl) *n.* **1,** a fortified residence of feudal times. **2,** a fortress. **3,** an imposing building. **4,** a chess piece, the rook.

cas'tor oil (kas'tər) thick oil obtained from a bean (*castor bean*), used as a cathartic or lubricant.

cas'trate (kas'trāt) *v.t.* emasculate. —**cas·tra'tion,** *n.*

cas'u·al (kazh'ū-əl) *adj.* **1,** happening by chance; offhand. **2,** careless; negligent. **3,** occasional; irregular. —*n.* **1,** a worker employed only irregularly. **2,** a casualty. —**cas'u·al·ness,** *n.*

cas'u·al·ty (kazh'ū-əl-tē) *n.* **1,** an accident involving bodily injury or death. **2,** a person injured accidentally. **3,** (*Mil.*) a soldier lost through enemy action.

cas'u·ist·ry (kazh'oo-is-trē) *n.* specious reasoning. —**cas'u·ist,** *n.*

cat (kat) *n.* **1,** a domesticated animal of the feline family. **2,** any feline animal, as lion, tiger, etc. **3,** (*Colloq.*) a spiteful woman. **4,** a whip formed of several thongs: *cat-o'nine tails.* —**cat nap,** a short sleep.

cat'a·clysm (kat'ə-kliz-əm) *n.* a violent, usually destructive upheaval. —**cat'a·clys'mic,** *adj.* —**cat'a·clys'mi·cal·ly,** *adv.*

cat'a·comb" (kat'ə-kōm") *n.* (usually *pl.*) an underground burial vault.

cat'a·lep"sy (kat'ə-lep"sē) *n.* a morbid condition of muscular rigidity, loss of sensation, etc. —**cat'a·lep'tic,** *adj.*

cat'a·log" (kat'ə-låg") *n.* a list of separate items; a register; a series of explanatory notes. —*v.t.* **1,** list. **2,** describe in explanatory notes. Also, **catalogue.**

ca·tal'pa (kə-tal'pə) *n.* a flowering tree of Asia and America.

ca·tal'y·sis (kə-tal'y-sis) *n.* acceleration of a chemical reaction by a substance which itself remains unaffected. —**cat'a·lyst** (kat'ə-list) *n.* the substance used in catalysis.

cat'a·mount" (kat'ə-mownt") *n.* a wild animal of the feline family; the cougar; the lynx.

cat'a·pult" (kat'ə-pult") *n.* a contrivance for hurling; a launching device for airplanes. —*v.t.* hurl by recoil. —*v.i.* leap suddenly.

cat'a·ract" (kat'ə-rakt") *n.* **1,** a large or spectacular waterfall; any

furious downpour of water. **2,** a disease of the eye, characterized by opacity of the lens.

ca·tarrh' (kə-tär') *n.* inflammation of the mucous membrane, esp. in the nose and throat. —**ca·tarrh'al,** *adj.*

ca·tas'tro·phe (kə-tas'trə-fē) *n.* a sudden or extreme disaster. —**cat'a·stroph'ic** (kat'ə-strof'ik) *adj.* —**cat'a·stroph'i·cal·ly,** *adv.*

cat'boat" (kat'bōt") *n.* a small sailboat.

catch (kach) *v.t.* [**caught**] **1,** capture after pursuing; seize. **2,** overtake; intercept; reach. **3,** halt; check. **4,** entrap; deceive. **5,** get; receive; incur. **6,** understand; perceive. **7,** (*Colloq.*) see or hear (a performer or act). —*v.i.* take hold; become entangled. —*n.* **1,** the act of catching. **2,** a device for stopping or checking motion. **3,** what is caught. **4,** (*Colloq.*) something desirable to catch, as a matrimonial prospect. **5,** a trick; ruse.

catch'up (kech'əp) *n.* a sauce of tomatoes and spices. Also, **cat'sup, ketch'up.**

catch'y (kach'ē) *adj.* quick to win attention and favor.

cat'e·chism (kat'ə-kiz-əm) *n.* a series of questions and the answers to them. —**cat'e·chize"** ('-kīz") *v.t.*

cat'e·gor'i·cal (kat'ə-gôr'i-kəl) *adj.* **1,** stated unconditionally; explicit. **2,** pert. to a category.

cat'e·go"ry (kat'ə-gôr'ē) *n.* a comprehensive division or class.

ca'ter (kā'tər) *v.i.* make provision, as of food, service, etc. —**ca'ter·er,** *n.* a purveyor of food.

cat'er·cor"nered (kat'ər-kôr"nərd) *adj.* diagonal.

cat'er·pil'lar (kat'ər-pil"ər) *n.* the wormlike larva of a moth or butterfly. —*adj.* (*T.N.*) moving on treads, as some tractors.

cat'er·waul" (kat'ər-wâl") *v.i.* howl or screech like a cat. —*n.* such a sound.

cat'fish" (kat'fish") *n.* any of many smooth-skinned, blunt-headed fishes.

ca·thar'sis (kə-thär'sis) *n.* **1,** (*Med.*) purgation. **2,** any cleansing or release, as of pent-up emotions. —**ca·thar'tic** (-tik) *adj.* & *n.*

ca·the'dral (kə-thē'drəl) *n.* **1,** the principal church in a diocese. **2,** any imposing church edifice.

cath'e·ter (kath'ə-tər) *n.* a tube used to drain the bladder.

cath'ode (kath'ōd) n. the negative pole of an electric current.

cath'o·lic (kath'ə-lik) adj. 1, universal in extent, character, or application. 2, (cap.) pert. to the Roman Catholic Church, or to any of certain other Christian churches. —n. (cap.) a member of a Catholic church. —Ca·thol'i·cism (kə-thol'ə-siz-əm) n. —cath'o·lic'i·ty (-lis'ə-tē) n. universality.

cat'nip (kat'nip) n. a plant of the mint family, relished by cats.

cat's-'paw'' (kats'på'') n. a dupe.

cat'tail'' (kat'tāl'') n. a marsh plant with velvety spikes of brown flowers.

cat'tle (kat'əl) n. 1, bovine animals. 2, livestock generally.

cat'ty (kat'ē) adj. malicious. Also, cat'tish. —cat'ti·ness, n.

cat'walk'' (kat'wåk'') n. a narrow suspended path, as on a ship.

Cau·ca'sian (kä-kā'zhən) adj. & n. "white" in race.

cau'cus (kä'kəs) n. a meeting of the leaders of a political party. —v.i. meet to discuss party policy.

cau'dal (kä'dəl) adj. 1, like a tail. 2, at or near the tail.

caught (kåt) v. pret. & p.p. of catch.

caul'dron (kål'drən) n. caldron.

cau'li·flow''er (kä'lə-flow''ər) n. 1, a plant whose flower forms a compact head. 2, the edible flower.

caulk (kåk) v.t. calk.

cau·sa'tion (kä-zā'shən) n. effect of causing; cause. —caus'a·tive (käz'ə-tiv) adj.

cause (käz) n. 1, that which produces an effect or a result. 2, the reason or motive for an action. 3, a subject of discussion or debate; a case for judicial decision. 4, a doctrine, view, or side of a question. —v.t. make occur or be; bring about. —caus'al, adj.

cause'way'' n. a raised road; a paved highway.

caus'tic (kås'tik) adj. 1, capable of burning, corroding, or destroying animal tissue. 2, severely critical or sarcastic. —n. a caustic substance. —caus'ti·cal·ly, adv.

cau'ter·ize'' (kä'tər-īz'') v.t. burn with a hot iron or a caustic, as morbid flesh. —cau'ter·i·za'tion, n.

cau'tion (kä'shən) n. 1, prudence in regard to danger; wariness. 2, a warning of danger. —v.t. warn; admonish.

cau'tious (-shəs) adj. wary. —cau'tious·ness, n.

cav'al·cade'' (kav'əl-kād'') n. a procession of persons on horseback or in carriages.

cav''a·lier' (kav''ə-lir') n. 1, a horseman; knight. 2, a courtly or gallant person; a man who escorts a woman. —adj. haughty; disdainful.

cav'al·ry (kav'əl-rē) n. military troops that serve on horseback. —mechanized cavalry, troops serving in motor vehicles.

cave (kāv) n. a hollow place in a hillside, esp. a natural underground cavity of large size. —v.i. (with in) collapse.

cav'ern (kav'ərn) n. a cave.

cav'ern·ous (-əs) adj. 1, containing caves. 2, hollow; gaping.

cav'i·ar'' (kav'ē-är'') n. roe of fish, esp. sturgeon, prepared as a relish.

cav'il (kav'əl) v.i. find fault without good reason; carp. —n. a captious objection.

cav'i·ty (kav'ə-tē) n. any hollow place or space.

ca·vort' (kə-vôrt') v.i. prance about; caper.

caw (kå) n. the call of a crow, or any similar sound.

cay·enne' (kī-en') n. a red pepper.

cay·use' (kī-ūs') n. an Indian pony.

cease (sēs) v.i. 1, stop doing an action; desist; come to rest. 2, come to an end. —v.t. discontinue. —cease'less, adj. without stopping.

ce'dar (sē'dər) n. any of several coniferous trees.

cede ((sēd) v.t. yield and surrender to another; grant.

ce·dil'la (sə-dil'ə) n. a mark (ç) indicating that a c is pronounced as s.

ceil'ing (sē'ling) n. 1, the interior overhead surface, as of a room. 2, the maximum altitude an aircraft can reach, or from which it has clear visibility of the earth. —ceiling price, a maximum established by law.

cel'e·brate'' (sel'ə-brāt'') v.t. 1, commemorate (a day or event) with festivities, ceremonies, etc. 2, perform (rites). 3, make known with honor or praise; extol. —v.i. make merry. —cel'e·brant, n. —cel'e·bra'tion, n.

ce·leb'ri·ty (sə-leb'rə-tē) n. a famous person.

ce·ler'i·ty (sə-ler'ə-tē) n. rapidity of motion; swiftness.

cel'er·y (sel'ə-rē) n. a plant whose stalks are used as a food.

ce·les'tial (sə-les'chəl) adj. 1, pert. to the sky. 2, heavenly; divine.

cel'i·ba·cy (sel'ə-bə-sē) n. the state of being unmarried. —cel'i·bate, adj. & n.

cell (sel) n. 1, one of many like rooms, as in a prison. 2, any small room. **3,** a group forming a unit in an organization, political party, etc. **4,** the structural unit of organic life. **5,** a device for producing an electric current chemically.

cel'lar (sel'ər) *n.* a room or rooms under a building, partly or wholly underground.

cel'lo (chel'ō) *n.* [*pl.* -los] a musical instrument of the violin family. —**cel'list,** *n.*

cel'lo·phane" (sel'ə-fān") *n.* a transparent plastic sheeting.

cel'lu·lar (sel'ū-lər) *adj.* pert. to, or consisting of, cells.

cel'lu·loid" (sel'yə-loid") *n.* a nitrocellulose plastic compound.

cel'lu·lose" (sel'yə-lōs") *n.* the chief constituent of the cell walls of all plants, used in making plastic fibers, feed, fertilizers, etc.

Celt'ic (sel'tik) *adj.* pert. to the Celts, a people including the Irish, Welsh, Gaels, and Bretons. —*n.* a Celtic language. Also, **Kelt'ic.**

ce·ment' (si-ment') *n.* **1,** any of various adhesive plastic substances. **2,** pulverized limestone and clay, used in making concrete; Portland cement. —*v.t. & i.* join; bind.

cem'e·ter"y (sem'ə-ter"ē) *n.* a burial ground.

cen'o·taph" (sen'ə-taf") *n.* an empty tomb as a memorial to someone buried elsewhere.

cen'ser (sen'sər) *n.* a vessel or pan in which incense is burned.

cen'sor (sen'sər) *n.* **1,** one empowered to judge the fitness of manuscripts, communications, etc. for publication. **2,** one who censures; a faultfinder. —*v.t.* judge critically; examine for fitness; delete as unsuitable. —**cen'sor·ship,** *n.*

cen·sor'i·ous (sen-sôr'ē-əs) *adj.* faultfinding; carping. —**cen·sor'i·ous·ness,** *n.*

cen'sure (sen'shər) *v.t.* reprove. —*n.* reproof.

cen'sus (sen'səs) *n.* registration and enumeration of the population.

cent (sent) *n.* in U. S. coinage, a copper coin worth .01 dollar.

cen'taur (sen'tôr) *n.* a mythological animal, half horse and half man.

cen'te·nar"i·an (sen"tə-nâr'ē-ən)*n.* a person aged 100 or more years.

cen'te·nar"y (sen'tə-ner"ē) *adj.* pert. to or consisting of 100. —*n.* a 100-year period.

Centaur

cen·ten'ni·al (sen-ten'ē-əl) *n. & adj.* the 100th anniversary.

cen'ter (sen'tər) *n.* **1,** the point equidistant from all extremities; the mid-point. **2,** the area near the middle. **3,** a pivot or axis. **4,** a principal object. **5,** position of a player in various games. **6,** a political party of moderate views. —*v.i. & t.* be or place at the center. Also, **cen'tre.**

cen'ti- (sen'tə) *pref.* **1,** 100. **2,** 1/100th. —**cen'ti·gram,** *n.* 1/100th gram. —**cen'ti·me"ter,** *n.* 1/100th meter.

cen'ti·grade" (sen'tə-grād") *adj.* pert. to the thermometer on which boiling and freezing points of water are 100° and 0° respectively.

cen'ti·pede" (sen'tə-pēd") *n.* any of various insects having many legs.

cen'tral (sen'trəl) *adj.* in the center; conveniently located. —*n.* a telephone operator.

cen·trif'u·gal (sen-trif'yə-gəl) *adj.* radiating or flying off or out, from a center.

cen'tri·fuge" (sen'tri·fūj") *n.* a machine that whirls a mixture to separate its ingredients.

cen·trip'e·tal (sen-trip'ə-təl) *adj.* progressing or stressed toward, or held to, the center.

cen·tu'ri·on (sen-tyûr'ē-ən) *n.* in ancient Rome, a military officer of medium rank, commanding 100 men.

cen·tu'ri·um (sen-tyûr'ē-əm) *n.* a chemical element, no. 100.

cen'tu·ry (sen'chə-rē) *n.* **1,** a period of 100 years. **2,** 100 of anything.

ce·phal'ic (sə-fal'ik) *adj.* pert. to the head or skull.

ce·ram'ics (sə-ram'iks) *n. pl.* **1,** clay or porcelain objects. **2,** the art or manufacture of such objects.

ce're·al (sir'ē-əl) *adj.* pert. to edible grain or seeds. —*n.* a food prepared from corn, wheat, etc.

cer"e·bel'lum (ser"ə-bel'əm) *n.* the rear lobe of the brain.

cer'e·bral (ser'ə-brəl) *adj.* pert. to the cerebrum or brain. —**cerebral palsy,** a crippling disease, characterized by paralysis or spasms, due to brain injury.

cer'e·brum (ser'ə-brəm) *n.* the front portion of the brain.

cere'ment (sir'mənt) *n.* **1,** the cloth in which a body is wrapped for embalming. **2,** (*pl.*) grave clothes.

cer"e·mo'ni·al (ser"ə-mō'nē-əl) *adj.* pert. to or being a ceremony or rite; formal. —*n.* rite.

cer'e·mo"ny (ser'ə-mō"nē) *n.* **1,** a formal occasion; rite. **2,** usages of politeness. —**cer"e·mo'ni·ous,** *adj.*

ce·rise' (sə-rēs') *adj.* cherry red.

ce'ri·um (sir'ē·əm) *n.* a metallic chemical element of the rare-earth group, no. 58, symbol Ce.

cer'tain (sēr'tən) *adj.* **1,** sure to occur; inevitable. **2,** established as true or sure. **3,** free from doubt; confident. **4,** definite; specified. **5,** unspecified in amount, degree or identity; some. —**cer′tain·ty,** *n.*

cer·tif′i·cate (sẽr-tif′i-kət) *n.* **1,** a document of attestation. **2,** a written testimonial as to status, qualifications, etc. **3,** a banknote, bond, or similar financial document. —*v.t.* (-kāt′) certify by such a document. —**cer′ti·fi·ca′tion,** *n.*

cer′ti·fy (sẽr′tə-fī′) *v.t.* attest to the truth or validity of.

cer′ti·tude (sẽr′tə-tūd″) *n.* certainty; complete freedom from doubt.

ce·ru′le·an (sə-roo′lē-ən) *adj.* sky-blue; light blue.

cer′vix (sẽr′viks) *n.* **1,** the neck. **2,** a necklike part. —**cer′vi·cal,** *adj.*

ces·sa′tion (se-sā′shən) *n.* ceasing or discontinuance of action or motion.

ces′sion (sesh′ən) *n.* the act of ceding; transfer of rights or property; surrender.

cess′pool (ses′pool″) *n.* a pit for the reception of sewage.

ce·ta′cean (sə-tā′shən) *adj.* pert. to whales.

chafe (chāf) *v.t.* **1,** abrade or roughen by friction. **2,** vex; annoy.

chaff (chaf) *n.* **1,** the residue left from threshing grain. **2,** finely-chopped straw for cattle food. **3,** gentle banter; raillery. —*v.t. & i.* tease; banter.

cha·grin′ (shə-grin′) *n.* mental disquiet or grief; self-dissatisfaction. —*v.t.* render crestfallen.

chain (chān) *n.* **1,** a connected series of links of metal or other material. **2,** something that binds, restrains, or fetters. **3,** (*pl.*) bondage. **4,** a series of connected phenomena, events, objects, etc. **5,** a measuring instrument, 66 feet long (surveyor's chain) or 100 feet long (engineer's chain). —*v.t.* fasten with a chain; unite; restrain. —**chain gang,** a group of prisoners chained together. —**chain reaction,** a series in which each effect causes the next one. —**chain store,** one of a group of retail stores owned and managed by the same company.

chair (chãr) *n.* **1,** a seat with a back, for one person. **2,** a presiding officer (**chair′man**) or his office. **3,** a position of authority; a professorship, as, the *chair* of physics.

chaise (shāz) *n.* **1,** an open horse-drawn vehicle; shay. **2,** [also, chaise longue (lăng)] an armchair whose seat extends to form a couch.

chal·ced′o·ny (kal-sed′ə-nē) *n.* a variety of quartz; a semiprecious stone.

cha·let′ (sha-lā′) *n.* a style of country house, with a wide heavy roof.

chal′ice (chal′is) *n.* a cup-shaped vessel from which the wine is administered at communion.

chalk (chȧk) *n.* **1,** a soft whitish variety of limestone. **2,** a crayon or cube of such substance. —*v.t.* **1,** treat with chalk. **2,** (with *up*) write; score; earn.

chal′lenge (chal′inj) *n.* **1,** a call to battle or debate. **2,** a demand for explanation or identification. **3,** an objection. —*v.t.* **1,** invite to battle or debate. **2,** demand explanation of. etc. **3,** take exception to; object to.

cham′ber (chām′bər) *n.* **1,** a room, esp. an inner or secluded room; a bedroom. **2,** a legislative body or its meeting place. **3,** any enclosed space, hollow, or cavity. **4,** (*pl.*) a private office or apartment, esp. of a judge or lawyer. **5,** a pot used as a urinal.

cham′ber·lain (chām′bər-lin) *n.* **1,** one responsible for the management of rooms. **2,** a supervisory official; treasurer; guardian.

cham′ber·maid″ *n.* a girl servant who takes care of bedrooms.

cham′bray (sham′brā) *n.* a kind of gingham.

cha·me′le·on (kə-mē′lē·ən) *n.* a lizardlike reptile that can adapt its coloration to that of its surroundings.

cham′fer (cham′fer) *n.* a bevel on the edge of a board or other solid, usually of 45°. —*v.t.* bevel.

cham′ois (sham′ē) *n.* **1,** a Europ. antelope. **2,** its skin, or similar soft leather.

champ *v.t. & i.* bite into small pieces; munch; chew. —*n.* champion.

Chamois

cham·pagne′ (sham-pān′) *n.* a sparkling white wine.

cham′pi·on (cham′pē-ən) *n.* **1,** the winner of a contest. **2,** one who defends a person or a cause. —*adj.* first among all competitors; pre-eminent. —*v.t.* defend; support. —**cham′pi·on·ship,** *n.* **1,** supremacy. **2,** support or defense.

chance (chȧns) *n.* **1,** accident; fortuity. **2,** hazard; risk. **3,** a favorable contingency; an opportunity. **4,** an unexpected event. **5,** (often *pl.*) probability; likelihood. —*v.i. & t.* **1,** occur by accident. **2,** hazard.

chan′cel (chȧn′səl) *n.* an enclosed space about the altar of a church.

chan′cel·lor (chȧn′sə-lər) *n.* **1,** the judge in a court of equity or chancery. 2, a high or the highest officer of certain universities, courts, etc.

chan'cer·y (chăn'sə-rē) n. 1, a court of equity. 2, an office of public records. 3, [also, **chan·cel·ler·y** (-lə-rē)] the court or office of a chancellor. —**in chancery,** in a helpless or embarrassing position.

chan''de·lier' (shan'də-lir') n. a branched cluster of lights hung from a ceiling.

chan'dler (chăn'dlər) n. 1, a dealer in specific supplies, provisions, etc. 2, a maker of candles.

change (chānj) v.t. 1, make different; alter. 2, replace by another; substitute. 3, give and take reciprocally; exchange. —v.i. become different; pass from one condition or state to another. —n. 1, alteration; modification; transformation. 2, substitution; exchange. 3, variety; novelty. 4, money of small denomination; coins. —**change'ling,** n. a child secretly substituted for another. —**change of life,** menopause.

chan'nel (chan'əl) n. 1, the bed of a waterway; a navigable waterway. 2, a means of access; a route. 3, a furrow or groove. 4, a frequency band, as in radio. 5, (pl.) (Mil. Slang) the prescribed routing of an application or order. —v.t. 1, direct into a particular course. 2, cut or form a channel in.

chan'son (shän'sən) n. (Fr.) a song.

chant (chănt) n. 1, a simple song in which an indefinite number of syllables are intoned on each note, as in canticle-singing. 2, any monotonous song or singing. —v.t. & i. sing; intone in a monotonous manner.

chant'ey (chant'tē) n. a tune sung, esp. by sailors, to set the rhythm of united physical labor.

chan''ti·cleer' (chan'tə-klir') n. a cock; a male fowl.

chan'try (chăn'trē) n. a chapel attached to a church; used for minor services.

cha·os (kā'os) n. the absence of form or order; utter confusion. —**cha·ot'ic** (-ot'ik) adj. —**cha·ot'i·cal·ly,** adv.

chap v.t. & i. [chapped, chap'ping] (of the skin) split in clefts; crack and roughen. —n. fellow; a familiar term for a man or boy.

chap''ar·ral' (chap''ə-ral') n. a dense thicket.

cha·peau' (shä-pō') n. (Fr.) [pl. -peaux' (-pō')] a hat.

chap'el (chap'əl) n. 1, a small church; a subordinate place of worship in a church. 2, a room for religious services in a school; the services held there.

chap'er·on'' (shap'e-rōn'') n. an older, usually married, woman accom-

panying younger unmarried women. —v.t. & i. attend as a chaperon.

chap'lain (chap'lin) n. a clergyman serving a special group, as a legislature, army, navy, etc.

chap'let (chap'lit) n. 1, a wreath, as of flowers, worn on the head. 2, a string of beads.

chaps n. pl. seatless riding breeches worn by American cowboys.

chap'ter (chap'tər) n. 1, a main division of a book or treatise. 2, a council; assemblage. 3, a branch of an association, fraternity, etc.

char (chär) v.t. [charred, char'ring] burn to charcoal; scorch. —v.i. 1, become charcoal. 2, do menial household tasks. —**char''wom''an,** n. a domestic servant hired by the day.

char'ac·ter (kar'ik-tər) n. 1, the aggregate of properties and qualities that distinguishes one person or thing from another. 2, a trait. 3, good qualities. 4, a person, esp. (Colloq.) an odd one; an actor or rôle in a play. 5, a mark made in writing, printing, etc.

char''ac·ter·is'tic (-is'tik) n. a distinguishing quality or trait. —adj. typical. —**char''ac·ter·is'ti·cal·ly,** adv.

char'ac·ter·ize (-īz) v.t. describe in terms of characteristics. —**char''ac·ter·i·za'tion,** n.

cha·rade' (shə-rād') n. (often pl.) a game of pantomime acting to convey words and their syllables.

char'coal'' (chär'kōl'') n. the residue of wood or other organic material reduced to carbon by imperfect combustion.

chard (chärd) n. a spinachlike vegetable: Swiss chard.

charge (chärj) v.t. 1, put a load on or in; fill or occupy with something to be carried or retained. 2, command; enjoin. 3, accuse; blame. 4, ask as a price; hold liable for payment. 5, defer payment for. 6, attack by rushing violently against. —v.i. make an onset. —n. 1, a load; a burden; a filling. 2, a command or instruction. 3, a duty, responsibility, or encumbrance. 4, an accusation. 5, a price, cost, or fee. 6, a violent onslaught.

char·gé' d'af·faires' (shär-zhā'dä-fâr') a diplomatic officer who is temporarily in charge of an embassy or legation.

charg'er (chär'jər) n. 1, a warhorse. 2, a large platter or tray.

char'i·ot (char'ē-ət) n. 1, an ancient two-wheeled horse-drawn vehicle. 2, a carriage. —**char''i·ot·eer'** (-tir') n. the driver of a chariot.

char'i·ty (char'ə-tē) n. 1, the quality of sympathetic understanding; philanthropy; tolerance. 2, alms. 3, an organization devoted to the relief of the unfortunate. —**char'i·ta·ble,** adj.

char'la·tan (shär'lə-tən) *n.* a pretender; quack; mountebank.

char'ley horse (chär'lē) a cramp in a muscle of arm or leg.

charm (chärm) *n.* 1, personal attractiveness; irresistible power to please or attract. 2, a symbol of occult power, as an amulet. —*v.t.* & *i.* fascinate; enchant; captivate. —**charm'ing,** *adj.* highly attractive.

char'nel (chär'nəl) *n.* a place where dead bodies are deposited.

chart (chärt) *n.* 1, a map; a drawn or written guide. 2, a systematic record of development or change. —*v.t.* make a map of; record.

char'ter (chär'tər) *n.* 1, a written instrument giving a right or privilege. 2, a fundamental statement of purpose and scope; a constitution. —*v.t.* 1, authorize; empower. 2, lease or hire.

char·treuse' (shär-trūz') *n.* 1, a liqueur. 2, a greenish yellow color.

char'y (chär'ē) *adj.* very cautious; suspicious. —**char'i·ness,** *n.*

chase (chās) *v.t.* 1, follow after in order to overtake, capture, or kill; pursue; hunt. 2, drive away. 3, decorate (metal) by tooling. —*v.i.* move briskly. —*n.* 1, the act of chasing. 2, what is chased; quarry. 3, the sport of hunting. 4, a frame in which type is locked for printing.

chas'er (chā'sər) *n.* 1, a milder drink taken after liquor. 2, (*Colloq.*) a roué.

chasm (kaz'əm) *n.* 1, a deep gulf or fissure. 2, a wide divergency.

chas'sis (shas'ē) *n.* [*pl.* -**sis**] 1, a supporting framework. 2, the frame, wheels, and engine of an automobile, without the body; a radio receiving apparatus without a cabinet.

chaste (chāst) *adj.* 1, abstaining from carnal love. 2, pure; not ornate or fanciful in design.

chas'ten (chā'sən) *v.t.* 1, punish; reprimand. 2, make chaste.

chas·tise' (chas-tīz') *v.t.* punish, esp. corporally. —**chas·tise'ment,** *n.*

chas'ti·ty (chas'tə-tē) *n.* quality or state of being chaste.

chat *v.i.* [**chat'ted, -ting**] converse desultorily; make talk. —**chat'ty,** *adj.*

cha·teau' (shà-tō') *n.* [*pl.* -**teaux'** (-tōz')] a French castle; an elaborate country house.

chat'tel (chat'əl) *n.* a movable piece of personal property.

chat'ter (chat'ər) *v.i.* 1, make rapid clacking sounds having little or no meaning. 2, talk rapidly but aimlessly. 3, vibrate noisily. —*n.* 1,

chattering sounds as made by monkeys, birds, etc. 2, idle or senseless talk; gossip. —**chat'ter·box",** *n.* (*Slang*) one who talks incessantly.

chauf'feur (shō'fər) *n.* one hired to drive an automobile.

chau·tau'qua (shə-tä'kwə) *n.* a community assembly for educational or recreational purposes.

chau'vin·ism (shō'və-niz-əm) *n.* excessive and blindly prejudiced patriotism. —**chau'vin·ist,** *n.* —**chau"vin·is'tic,** *adj.* —**chau"vin·is'·ti·cal·ly,** *adv.*

cheap (chēp) *adj.* 1, available at a low price. 2, of little value. 3, miserly; mean; petty. 4, unfair; dishonorable. —**cheap'en,** *v.t.* & *i.* lessen in price. —**cheap'ness,** *n.*

cheap'skate" *n.* a stingy person.

cheat (chēt) *v.t.* 1, mislead; defraud; swindle. 2, escape from; elude. —*v.i.* 1, practice deception or trickery. 2, be unfaithful. —*n.* 1, a swindler, esp. a card sharper. 2, an impostor. 3, an act of fraud.

check (chek) *n.* 1, an obstruction, hindrance, or stop; a device for stopping. 2, a stoppage or rebuff. 3, a test of operation; verification of accounts; investigation or examination (often **check-up**). 4, a mark (√) signifying disposition or approval. 5, a written order to a bank to pay money. 6, a piece of paper used as a receipt, token, etc. 7, one of a pattern of squares alternating in color. 8, in chess, jeopardy of the king. 9, a counter; a poker chip. —*v.t.* 1, impede; stop. 2, test; verify; investigate. 3, make a check mark (√) upon. 4, put or accept in temporary custody. 5, send (baggage) under privilege of a passenger ticket. 6, in chess, threaten to capture (the king). —*v.i.* 1, make a test or investigation. 2, prove to be right or accurate. 3, pause; stop. 4, in poker, stay in without betting. —*interj.* (*Colloq.*) Correct! All right!

check'er (chek'ər) *n.* 1, one who checks; a record-keeper. 2, one of the pieces for checkers. —**check'-ered** (-ərd) *adj.* marked with a pattern of squares of alternating color.

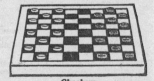

Checkers

check'ers (chek'ərz) *n.sing.* a game for two played on a checkered board (*checkerboard*).

check'mate" *n.* 1, (*Chess*) a position in which one's king is attacked and cannot escape capture. 2, defeat; frustration. —*v.t.* put in checkmate; overthrow.

check'off" (chek'âf") *n.* the withholding of union dues from a payroll on behalf of the union.

cheek (chēk) *n.* 1, the side of the face below the eye-line. 2, impudence; overweening self-assurance. —**cheek'y**, *adj.* impudent.

cheep (chēp) *n.* the high cry of a young bird; chirp. —*v.t.* & *i.* chirp.

cheer (chir) *n.* 1, state of mind. 2, gaiety; animation. 3, a shout of joy; applause. —*v.t.* & *i.* 1, encourage. 2, applaud with shouts.

cheer'ful (-fəl) *adj.* full of cheer; blithe. —**cheer'ful·ness**, *n.*

cheer'y (-ē) *adj.* in good spirits; gay. —**cheer'i·ness**, *n.*

cheese (chēz) *n.* a food made of aged milk solids.

cheese'cloth" *n.* a coarse cotton cloth of open texture.

chees'y (chē'zē) *adj.* (*Colloq.*) unsubstantial; shoddy.

chee'tah (chē'tə) *n.* a leopardlike animal of Asia and Africa.

chef (shef) *n.* a head cook.

chem'i·cal (kem'i-kəl) *adj.* pert. to chemistry. —*n.* a substance produced by or used in a chemical process.

che·mise' (shə-mēz') *n.* a loose-fitting undergarment.

chem'is·try (kem'is-trē) *n.* the general science of the composition, properties, and phenomena of elementary substances. —**chem'ist**, *n.*

che·nille' (shə-nēl') *n.* 1, a fluffy yarn of cotton, silk, etc. 2, a fabric woven with such yarn.

cheque (chek) *n.* (*Brit.*) check.

cher'ish *v.t.* hold dear; treat with affection; nurse.

che·root' (shə-root') *n.* a cigar with square, open ends.

cher'ry (cher'ē) *n.* 1, a tree bearing small, red, pitted fruit; its wood; its fruit. 2, a bright red color.

cher'ub (cher'əb) *n.* 1, [*pl.* cher'u·bim] an angel represented as a child with wings. 2, a child with a round, plump face; a beautiful or innocent person. —**che·ru'bic** (che-roo'bik) *adj.* —**che·ru'bi·cal·ly**, *adv.*

chess (ches) *n.* a game for two played on a board of 64 checkered squares.

chest *n.* 1, a box, esp. a strong one for holding valuables. 2, the human body between the neck and belly; the thorax.

ches'ter·field" (ches'tər-fēld") *n.* 1, a single-breasted overcoat. 2, a kind of sofa.

chest'nut (ches'nut) *n.* 1, a tree of the beech family; its wood; its edible nut. 2, a reddish brown color. 3, (*Slang*) a hackneyed joke. —*adj.* reddish brown.

chest'y (ches'tē) *adj.* (*Slang*) conceited.

chev"a·lier' (shev'ə-lir') *n.* 1, knight; a gallant man. 2, a rank of membership in an honorable order.

chev'i·ot (shev'ē-ət) *n.* a worsted fabric of twill weave.

chev'ron (shev'rən) *n.* a striped badge denoting military rank.

chew (choo) *v.t.* 1, bite and grind with the teeth. 2, meditate on; discuss. —*n.* a portion chewed, as of tobacco. —**chew the rag** (*Slang*) converse at length.

chi (kī) *n.* the twenty-second letter of the Greek alphabet (X, x).

chi·a"ro·scu'ro (kē-är"ə-skūr'ō) *n.* 1, the distribution of light and shade in a picture. 2, a drawing in black and white.

chic (shēk) *adj.* stylish; fashionable.

chi·can'er·y (shi-kā'nə-rē) *n.* adroit but dishonest maneuvering or scheming.

chick (chik) *n.* 1, a young chicken or other bird. 2, (*Slang*) a young girl.

chick'a·dee" (chik'ə-dē") *n.* a small No. Amer. bird of the titmouse family.

chick'en (chik'ən) *n.* 1, a young domestic fowl. 2, (*Slang*) a girl; a young woman. —**chick"en·heart'ed**, *adj.* timid. —**chicken** pox, a mild, contagious, eruptive disease.

chic'le (chik'əl) *n.* a gum from certain trees, the basis of chewing gum.

chic'o·ry (chik'ə-rē) *n.* 1, a plant whose root is used as a substitute or adulterant for coffee. 2, a salad herb.

chide (chīd) *v.t.* & *i.* reprove mildly.

chief (chēf) *n.* 1, the head man; commander; leader. 2, the most important part or aspect. —*adj.* highest in rank or importance.

chief'tain (-tən) *n.* the leader of a tribe, clan, or band.

chif·fon' (shi-fon') *n.* a thin, gauzelike fabric.

chif"fo·nier' (shif'ə-nir') *n.* a chest of drawers; a bureau.

chig'ger (chig'ər) *n.* 1, the larva of certain mites whose bite causes severe itching. 2, a flea: the *chigoe*.

chi'gnon (shēn'yon) *n.* a coil of hair, worn at the back of the head by women.

chi·hua'hua (chē-wä'wä) *n.* a breed of tiny dog.

chil'blain" (chil'blān") *n.* a sore, esp. on the foot, resulting from exposure to cold.

child (chīld) *n.* [*pl.* **chil'dren** (chil'drən)] a young human offspring; an infant, boy or girl. —**with child,** pregnant. —**child's play,** a very easy task.

child'birth" *n.* the giving birth to a child; parturition.

child'hood" *n.* the state or time of being a child.

child'ish *adj.* unseemingly immature. —**child'ish·ness,** *n.*

chil'dren (chil'drən) *n.* pl. of *child.*

chil'i (chil'ē) *n.* a hot seasoning made of dried pods of red pepper.

chill (chil) *n.* **1,** an acute sensation of cold, often with shivering. **2,** a degree of cold. —*v.t.* **1,** make cold. **2,** dispirit; discourage. —*v.i.* be fearful. —**chill'y,** *adj.*

chime (chīm) *n.* **1,** a bell or tube producing a bell-like tone; a set of such bells. **2,** harmonious sound or relation; concord. —*v.i.* **1,** produce harmonious sounds. **2,** harmonize; agree. **3,** (with *in*) add one's word; agree. —*v.t.* give forth (a sound).

chi·me'ra (ki-mir'ə) *n.* **1,** a mythical monster, part lion, goat, and serpent. **2,** a fantastic or vain hope. —**chi·mer'i·cal** (ki-mer'i-kəl) *adj.*

chim'ney (chim'nē) *n.* a tube, duct, or flue to carry off smoke.

chim"pan·zee' (chim"pan-zē') *n.* a large anthropoid ape of W. Africa.

chin *n.* the point of the jaw. —*v.i.* [chinned, chin'ning] (*Slang*) chat; talk. —**chin oneself,** pull one's body upward toward an elevated horizontal bar, for exercise.

chi'na (chī'nə) *n.* a porcelain ware; dishes; crockery.

chin·chil'la (chin-chil'ə) *n.* a small, fur-bearing rodent of South America; its fur.

Chinchilla

Chi·nese' (chī-nēz') *adj.* pert. to China. —*n.* **1,** the language of China. **2,** one descended from the people of China.

chink *n.* a small rift, fissure, or cleft. —*v.i.* **1,** crack. **2,** make a sharp metallic sound. —*v.t.* **1,** split. **2,** fill up cracks; calk.

chintz (chints) *n.* a printed cotton fabric, usually glazed.

chip *n.* **1,** a small fragment, as of wood or stone. **2,** a small disk used as a counter or token; poker chip. —*v.t.* [chipped, chip'ping] cut or knock off fragments from. —*v.i.* **1,**

break off in small pieces. **2,** (often with *in*) contribute a chip or money.

chip'munk *n.* a small squirrel-like rodent.

chip'per (chip'ər) *v.i.* chirp; twitter. —*adj.* (*Colloq.*) lively; gay.

chi·ro- *pref.* hand.

chi·rog'ra·phy (kī-rog'rə-fē) *n.* handwriting.

chi·rop'o·dy (kī-rop'ə-dē) *n.* the treatment of foot ailments. —**chi·rop'o·dist,** *n.*

chi"ro·prac'tic (kī"rō-prak'tik) *n.* the treatment of ailments by manipulating the bones. —**chi·ro·prac"-tor,** *n.*

chirp (chērp) *n.* a short, shrill sound made by birds or insects. —*v.i.* utter with a chirp.

chir'rup (chir'əp) *n.* & *v.* chirp.

chis'el (chiz'əl) *n.* a bladed tool for cutting wood or metal. —*v.t.* & *i.* **1,** cut or trim with a chisel. **2,** (*Slang*) seek an undue advantage.

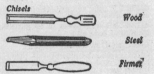

Chisels — Wood, Steel, Firmer

chit *n.* **1,** a pert young person (esp. a girl) or animal. **2,** a memorandum of indebtedness for a minor purchase.

chit'chat" *n.* idle talk.

chiv'al·ry (shiv'əl-rē) *n.* **1,** the institution of medieval knighthood. **2,** gallantry; honor. —**chiv'al·rous,** *adj.*

chive (chīv) *n.* (usually *pl.*) an onionlike herb used for seasoning.

chlo'ral (klôr'əl) *n.* a hypnotic preparation from chlorine. —**chloral hydrate,** a solution of this substance.

chlo'ride (klôr'īd) *n.* a compound of chlorine and one other element.

chlo'rine (klôr'ēn) *n.* a gaseous chemical element, no. 17, symbol Cl.

chlo'ro·form" (klôr'ə-fôrm") *n.* a volatile, colorless liquid used as an anesthetic.

chlo'ro·phyll (klôr'ə-fil) *n.* the green coloring principle in plants.

chock (chok) *n.* a block of wood or stone used as a stop to prevent rolling. —**chock-"full,** *adj.* full.

choc'o·late (chok'ə-lit) *n.* **1,** a food or flavoring made from the cacao bean. **2,** a beverage or candy flavored with it. **3,** a dark brown color.

fat, fāte, fär, fâre, fåll, åsk; met, hē, hêr, maybē; pin, pīne; not, nōte, ôr, tool

choice (chois) *n.* **1,** the act of choosing. **2,** opportunity or right to choose; option. **3,** what is chosen; preference; alternative. **4,** the best part. —*adj.* superior; select; excellent. —**choice'ness,** *n.*

choir (kwīr) *n.* **1,** a chorus in a church; a group of angels singing. **2,** the choir's section in a church.

choke (chōk) *v.t.* **1,** stop the breath of by stopping the windpipe; strangle. **2,** stop by filling; obstruct; stifle. —*v.i.* **1,** suffer constriction of the windpipe. **2,** be crammed full or overcrowded. —*n.* **1,** a constriction or blockage in a passage. **2,** an instrument for shutting off air from the carburetor of a gas engine.

chol'er (kol'ər) *n.* anger; ill-temper; irascibility. —**chol'er·ic,** *adj.*

chol'er·a (kol'ər-ə) *n.* **1,** an infectious disease, often fatal; the plague. **2,** a less serious disorder of the digestive organs.

choose (chooz) *v.t.* [**chose** (chōz), **cho'sen**] select from two or more; give preference to; decide upon. —*v.i.* make a choice. —**choos'y,** *adj.* (*Colloq.*) hard to please.

chop *v.t.* [**chopped, chop'ping**] **1,** cut with a quick blow; hew. **2,** cut into pieces; mince. —*v.i.* **1,** make heavy strokes, as with an ax. **2,** turn or shift suddenly. —*n.* **1,** a cutting stroke; a hard blow. **2,** a slice of meat cut from the loin, containing the rib. **3,** a brisk, irregular motion of waves. —**chop'per,** *n.* —**chop suey** (soo'ē) a stew served in Chinese restaurants.

chop'py (-ē) *adj.* rough; jerky.

cho'ral (kôr'əl) *adj.* pert. to a chorus or choir.

cho·rale' (kə-rál') *n.* a simple sacred tune.

chord (kôrd) *n.* **1,** a cord; a string of a musical instrument; an anatomical cord. **2,** a group of three or more tones sounding simultaneously. **3,** a straight line intersecting a curve at two points. **4,** a connecting member, as of a bridge truss.

chore (chōr) *n.* a minor job; (*pl.*) routine household duties.

cho"re·og'ra·phy (kôr"ē·og'rə-fē) *n.* the art of dancing; composition of exhibition dances. —**cho"re·og'ra·pher,** *n.* a designer of dances.

cho'rus (kôr'əs) *n.* **1,** a group of persons singing together. **2,** any group acting together in support of a soloist or principal. **3,** a composition for a chorus; a refrain; the principal melody of a popular song. —*v.t.* utter in concert.

chor'is·ter (kôr'is-tər) *n.* a member of a chorus.

chose (chōz) *v.* pret. of *choose.*

cho'sen (chō'zən) *v.* p.p. of *choose.*

chow *n.* **1,** a Chinese breed of dog. **2,** (*Colloq.*) food; meals. —**chow'-chow",** *n.* a mixed, highly-seasoned dish; a pickle preserve. —**chow**

mein (mān) a Chinese dish of meat, vegetables, and fried noodles.

chow'der (-dər) *n.* a thick soup, usually of sea food, as clams.

Christ (krīst) *n.* the Messiah; Jesus, as fulfilling his prophesied coming.

chris'ten (kris'ən) *v.t.* **1,** baptize and receive into the Christian church. **2,** give a name to.

Chris'tian (kris'chən) *n.* one who professes the religious principles of Jesus Christ. —*adj.* pert. to these religious principles or any church based on them. —**Chris"ti·an'i·ty,** *n.* —**Christian name,** given name; first name.

Christ'mas (kris'məs) *n.* the festival celebrating the birth of Christ; Dec. 25.

chro·mat'ic (krō-mat'ik) *adj.* **1,** pert. to color. **2,** (*Music*) involving tones foreign to the diatonic scale. —**chro·mat'i·cal·ly,** *adv.*

chrome (krōm) *n.* chromium, esp. in alloy or as a source of pigments.

chro'mi·um (krō'mē-əm) *n.* a metallic chemical element, no. 24, symbol Cr.

chro·mo- *pref.* **1,** color. **2,** chromium.

chro'mo·some" (krō'mə-sōm") *n.* a threadlike body in a germ cell, a carrier of hereditary characters.

chron- *pref.* of time. Also, **chron·o-.**

chron'ic (kron'ik) *adj.* of long standing; inveterate; continual. —**chron'i·cal·ly,** *adv.*

chron'i·cle (kron'i-kəl) *n.* an account of events in order of time; a history. —*v.t.* record or narrate in order of time.

chron"o·log'i·cal (kron"ə-loj'i-kəl) *adj.* arranged in order of time.

chro·nol'o·gy (krə-nol'ə-jē) *n.* **1,** the science of determining the dates or historical order of past events. **2,** a statement of the order in time of particular events.

chro·nom'e·ter (krə-nom'ə-tər) *n.* a clock of great accuracy.

chrys'a·lis (kris'ə-lis) *n.* the pupa of certain insects, as the moth.

chrys·an'the·mum (kri-san'thə-məm) *n.* a large flower.

chrys'o·lite" (kris'ə-līt") *n.* a semi-precious stone, green or yellow.

chub'by (chub'ē) *adj.* plump.

chuck (chuk) *n.* **1,** a device to grip work in a turning machine. **2,** a cut of beef. —*v.t.* **1,** pat, usually on the chin. **2,** toss (often with *out*).

chuck'le (chuk'əl) *v.i.* laugh in a suppressed manner.

chuck-'luck" (chuk'luk") *n.* a game of betting on casts of three dice.

chug *n.* a short explosive sound. —*v.i.* [chugged, chug'ging] make such sounds

chuk'ker (chuk'ər) *n.* one of the periods of play in polo

chum *n.* an intimate; a close companion. —chum'my, *adj*

chump *n.* 1, (*Colloq.*) a blockhead. 2, a block of wood.

chunk *n.* 1, an irregular solid piece, as of coal; a lump. 2, a considerable amount. —chunk'y, *adj.* stocky; thickset.

church (chẽrch) *n.* 1, an edifice for religious worship; the chief services held there. 2, a body or organization of Christian believers; a denomination —church'man (-mən) *n.* 1, a clergyman. 2, an active member of a church.

churl (chẽrl) *n.* a surly or coarse person. —churl'ish, *adj.* rude; surly.

churn (chẽrn) *n.* 1, a device for agitating milk, to separate the butter fats from it. 2, a similar agitating device. —*v.t.* agitate (milk) to make butter. —*v.i.* 1, operate a churn. 2, be nervously excited or agitated.

chute (shoot) *n.* 1, an inclined trough, channel, or duct, esp. for the conveyance of fluid solids, as sand, by gravity. 2, any channel providing a steep descent. —'chute, *n.* a parachute.

ci-ca'da (si-kā'də) *n.* an insect that makes a shrill sound by vibrating certain membranes, as esp. the locust

cic'a-trix (sik'ə-triks) *n.* [*pl.* -tri'ces (-tri'sēz)] the new tissue that forms a scar. Also, cic'a-trice (-tris).

-cide *suf.* denoting a killer (of), or the act of killing. — -cid'al, *suf.* forming adjectives.

ci'der (si'dər) *n.* expressed apple juice, fresh or slightly fermented.

ci-gar' (si-gär') *n.* a cylindrical roll of tobacco leaves, for smoking

cig"a-rette' (sig"ə-ret') *n.* shredded or granular tobacco contained within a paper tube, for smoking. Also, cig"a-ret'.

cil'i-a (sil'i-ə) *n. pl.* [*sing.* -um] the eyelashes; similar short hairs or hairlike processes.

cinch (sinch) *n.* 1, a saddle-girth. 2, (*Colloq.*) anything easy or sure of accomplishment. —*v.t.* 1, tighten as a surrounding band. 2, assure

cin-cho'na (sin-kō'nə) *n.* a tropical tree, or its bark, yielding quinine.

cinc'ture (sink'chər) *n.* a girdle; a belt. —*v.t.* engirdle; encircle.

cin'der (sin'dər) *n.* a sandlike globular particle of burned matter; (*pl.*) ashes.

cin'e-ma (sin'ə-mə) *n.* a motion picture; a motion picture theater. —cin"e-mat'ic, *adj*.

cin'na-bar" (sin'ə-bär") *n.* red mercuric sulfide: an ore of mercury.

cin'na-mon (sin'ə-mən) *n.* the dried bark of a certain tree used as a spice. —*adj.* light brown.

ci'pher (si'fər) *n.* 1, the digit zero (0). 2, any Arabic numeral. 3, a secret code; the message written in it; the key to it. —*v.t.* calculate numerically.

cir'cle (sẽr'kəl) *n.* 1, a closed curve, the locus of all points equidistant from a fixed point, or center, within. 2, a ring. 3, a cycle; a series culminating in a return to the starting point. —*v.t.* travel around the outside of. —*v.i.* move in a circle.

cir'clet (sẽr'klit) *n.* a ring.

cir'cuit (sẽr'kit) *n.* 1, a closed path providing continuous passage of fluids or electricity. 2, a route regularly followed; an itinerary.

cir-cu'i-tous (sẽr-kū'i-təs) *adj.* not direct; roundabout. —cir-cu'i-tous-ness, *n.*

cir'cu-lar (sẽr'kyə-lər) *adj.* 1, in the shape of a circle. 2, roundabout; wandering. —*n.* a letter or brochure for general circulation.

cir'cu-late" (sẽr'kū-lāt") *v.i.* move through a circuit; (of persons), move about among other people. —*v.t.* disseminate; spread. —cir'cu-la-to"ry, *adj.*

cir"cu-la'tion (sẽr'kū-lā'shən) *n.* 1, the act of diffusion or dissemination. 2, continuous passage through a closed system, as the blood.

cir-cum- *pref.* going around.

cir"cum-ci'sion (sẽr'kəm-sizh'ən) *n.* removal of the foreskin of males, esp. as a religious rite. —cir'cum-cise" (-sīz") *v.t.*

cir-cum'fer-ence (sẽr-kum'fər-əns) *n.* the distance around a circle, sphere, or other closed curved figure or object.

cir'cum-flex" (sẽr'kəm-fleks") *n.* a diacritical mark (^), as ê.

cir"cum-lo-cu'tion (sẽr'kəm-lō-kū'shən) *n.* studied indirectness of speech; evasion of a point.

cir"cum-scribe' (sẽr'kəm-skrīb') *v.t.* limit; bound; restrain within fixed bounds. —cir"cum-scrip'tion (-skrip'shən) *n.*

cir"cum-spect" (sẽr'kəm-spekt") *adj.* careful of one's behavior; discreet. —cir"cum-spec'tion, *n.*

---

cir'cum·stance" (sẽr'kəm-stans") n. 1, a concomitant condition or situation; one of the factors influencing a decision. 2, (pl.) existing conditions; economic status. 3, (Archaic) ceremonious display.

cir"cum·stan'tial (-stan'shəl) adj. 1, pert. to circumstances. 2, based on incidental details; presumptive.

cir"cum·stan'ti·ate" (sẽr"kəm-stan'shē-āt") v.t. support with evidence; prove to be true; document. —cir"cum·stan·ti·a'tion, n.

cir"cum·vent' (sẽr"kəm-vent') v.t. evade (an impediment) by going around it; outwit. —cir"cum·ven'tion, n.

cir'cus (sẽr'kəs) n. 1, a traveling show, including acrobats, clowns, wild animal displays, etc.; the company of performers in such show. 2, any entertaining display likened to a circus; a good time. 3, a circular area, as an arena or (Brit.) an open space where several streets converge.

cir·rho'sis (si-rō'sis) n. a disease, esp. of the liver, characterized by hardening of tissues.

cir'ro- pref. cirrus.

cir'rus (sir'əs) n. [pl. -ri (-rī)] a cloud formation notably long, stratified, and of filamentous structure.

cis- pref. on this side of, as cisalpine, on this (the Roman) side of the Alps.

cis'tern (sis'tərn) n. an underground tank to hold a supply of fresh water.

cit'a·del (sit'ə-dəl) n. a fortress, usually at the edge of a town.

ci·ta'tion (si-tā'shən) n. 1, act or result of citing; a citing; quotation. 2, a commendatory mention.

cite (sīt) v.t. mention in specific connection; quote; refer to in support.

cit'i·fied' (sit'i-fīd") adj. having the habits of a city dweller.

cit'i·zen (sit'ə-zən) n. 1, an enfranchised member of a state or nation. 2, civilian. —cit'i·zen·ry (-rē) n. citizens collectively. —cit'i·zen·ship, n.

cit'ric acid (sit'rik) an acid found in lemons and similar fruit.

cit'ron (sit'rən) n. a fruit resembling the lemon; a candied preserve made of its rind.

cit'ron·el'la (sit"rə-nel'ə) n. an oil used in perfumes and soaps, and to repel insects.

cit'rus (sit'rəs) n. a species of tree, including the lime, lemon, etc. —adj. [also, cit'rous] containing citric acid.

cit'y (sit'ē) n. a large or important town.

civ'et (siv'it) n. 1, a glandular secretion of the civet cat, used in perfumery. 2, the civet cat, a feline of Asia and Africa.

civ'ic (siv'ik) adj. pert. to the affairs of a city or community, or to citizenship.

civ'ics (siv'iks) n.sing. the study of the processes of government and duties of citizenship.

civ'il (siv'əl) adj. 1, pert. to the state, its laws, administration, etc. 2, pert. to a private citizen; not military, ecclesiastic, etc. 3, courteous; polite. 4, within a nation, as a civil war. —civil engineering, the engineering of public-works construction, as bridges. —civil service, nonelected, permanent government employees collectively.

ci·vil'ian (si-vil'yən) n. one engaged in civil, not military, pursuits. —adj. not military.

ci·vil'i·ty (si-vil'ə-tē) n. politeness.

civ"i·li·za'tion (siv"i-lə-zā'shən) n. 1, civilized peoples, states and facilities collectively. 2, act of civilizing.

civ'i·lize' (siv'ə-līz") v.t. educate in the usages of organized society.

clab'ber (klab'ər) n. soured, coagulated milk, not fully separated into curds and whey. —v.i. coagulate.

clack (klak) n. a quick, sharp, repeated sound. —v.t. & i. 1, make a sharp, repeated sound; let the tongue vibrate. 2, prattle.

clad (klad) v. clothed; dressed.

claim (klām) v.t. 1, assert a right to; demand. 2, (Colloq.) assert as fact; contend. —n. a demand for something due; the thing demanded. —claim'ant, n. —claim'ing race, a horse race among horses offered for sale at the same price.

clair·voy'ance (klār-voi'əns) n. extrasensory sight or perception. —clair·voy'ant, n. & adj.

clam (klam) n. 1, any of several varieties of bivalve mollusks. 2, an uncommunicative person.

clam'ber (klam'bər) v.i. ascend by climbing, often with difficulty.

clam'my (klam'ē) adj. cold and damp. —clam'mi·ness, n.

clam'or (klam'ər) n. noise; noisy ado; a vociferous demand or complaint. —v.i. make an outcry; demand loudly. Also, clam'our. —clam'or·ous, adj.

clamp (klamp) n. a device for holding objects, or fastening them together temporarily. —v.t. fasten with or as with a clamp. —v.i. (with down) become strict.

clan (klan) n. 1, a family or tribe, esp. Scottish. 2, any social set; clique. —clan'nish, adj. —clans'man (klanz'mən) n. a kinsman.

clan·des'tine (klan-des'tin) adj. secret; covert; furtive.

clang (klang) n. the sound of a gong or hammer; the ring of metal when struck. —v.i. & t. make such a sound.

clan'gor (klang'gər) n. 1, a clanging sound. 2, clamor.

clank (klank) n. a sharp, metallic sound. —v.t. strike (an object) to produce such a sound. —v.i. give out such a sound.

clap (klap) v.t. [clapped, clap'ping] 1, strike together (as the hands) producing a sharp sound. 2, place or dispose of hastily. —v.i. strike with the hands together, for applause, attention, etc. —n. 1, the sound of clapping hands; applause. 2, a blow with the flat of the hand.

clap'board (klab'ərd) n. a wood siding for houses, in which the boards overlap.

clap'per (klap'ər) n. the tongue of a bell.

clap'trap" (klap'trap") n. insincere and diversionary talk; nonsense.

claque (klak) n. a group of persons hired to applaud a performer.

clar'et (klar'ət) n. a red wine from Bordeaux; its color.

clar'i·fy" (klar'ə-fī") v.t. & i. 1, make clear to the sight or understanding. 2, free from turbidity; become clear. —clar'i·fi·ca'tion, n.

Clarinet

clar"i·net' (klar'ə-net') n. a singly-reeded woodwind musical instrument.

clar'i·on (klar'ē-ən) adj. obtrusively clear and high-pitched, as a trumpet's sound.

clar'i·ty (klar'ə-tē) n. clearness.

clash (klash) v.i. collide so as to make a loud, harsh noise; meet in conflict. —v.t. strike together violently and noisily. —n. a collision of physical objects, opinions, etc.; conflict.

clasp (klåsp) n. 1, a small latch for holding two things together. 2, a joining of the hands; an embrace. —v.t. fasten together; embrace; grasp.

class (klås) n. 1, order or rank, esp. of persons; caste. 2, a category. 3, a group of persons with a common interest, esp. such a group in student session. 4, (Colloq.) smartness; beauty; modishness. —v.t. arrange according to class; classify.

clas'sic (klas'ik) n. 1, a creation of enduring value or esteem, as a musical or literary composition. 2, a standard; a perfect specimen. —adj. characterized by enduring value. —clas'si·cal, adj.

clas"si·fi·ca'tion (klas"i-fi-kā'-shən) n. 1, act of classifying. 2, a class or category.

clas'si·fied" (klas'i-fīd") adj. 1, arranged by topic, group, etc. 2, (Mil.) secret, confidential, or restricted.

clas'si·fy" (klas'ə-fī") v.t. 1, sort into groups having common characteristics. 2, assign a place in a group.

class'y (klas'ē) adj. (Slang) high-grade; modish.

clat'ter (klat'ər) n. a rattling or clashing sound, as of dishes roughly handled. —v.i. make such a sound.

clause (klåz) n. 1, a sentence element containing at least a subject and verb. 2, a stipulation, modification, or condition of a document; a paragraph. —claus'al, adj.

claus"tro·pho'bi·a (klås"trə-fō'bē-ə) n. a morbid fear of being shut in or confined.

clav'i·chord" (klav'ə-kôrd") n. an ancient musical instrument, precursor of the piano.

clav'i·cle (klav'ə-kəl) n. the collarbone.

Claw Hammer   *Bird's claw*

claw (klå) n. 1, a hook or talon on a limb, esp. the foot, of a living creature. 2, a tool or device for grasping. —v.t. & i. scratch; tear or rend.

clay (klå) n. 1, plastic earth in the form of thick mud, used in making brick, for modeling, etc. 2, the human body. 3, one easily influenced.

clean (klēn) adj. 1, free from dirt or irrelevant substances; pure; unadulterated. 2, free from error or sin. 3, fastidious. —v.t. remove foreign or superfluous material from; wash. —clean'ness, n. —clean up (Colloq.) make much money.

clean-'cut" adj. shapely and clean-looking.

clean'er n. 1, one who cleans. 2, a washing agent.

clean'ly (klen'lē) adj. clean. —clean'li·ness, n.

cleanse (klenz) v.t. clean; dry-clean. —cleans'er (klen'zər) n.

clear (klir) adj. 1, easily understood or perceived; not turbid or cloudy; unobstructed; transparent. 2, untroubled, innocent. —v.t. 1, remove burdens or obstructions from; clarify; free from debt, encumbrance or accusation. 2, make a net profit of. 3, jump over. 4, (with up) explain lucidly; solve. 5, (often with away or off) remove; sweep away. —v.i. 1, (often with up) become bright or unclouded. **2.** (of a check) be paid. **3.** (often with *out*) depart hastily; go. —**clear′ness**, *n.*

clear′ance (-əns) *n.* **1.** act of clearing. **2.** the space between two objects; room to pass.

clear′cut″ *adj.* distinct; obvious.

clear′ing (klir′ing) *n.* a tract of land cleared of trees. —**clearing house**, a coöperative institution through which banks settle their mutual accounts.

cleat (klēt) *n.* a crosspiece serving to join and strengthen a number of longitudinal strips; a similar crosspiece attached to increase traction.

cleave (klēv) *v.i.* adhere; stick; cling. —*v.t.* split; rend asunder; force apart. —*v.i.* come apart; divide; split. —**cleav′age** (-ij) *n.*

cleav′er (klē′vər) *n.* a heavy knife for chopping through bone.

clef (klef) *n.* (*Music*) a character placed at the beginning of a staff to indicate the location of the governing tonality.

cleft (kleft) *n.* a crack; crevice; split. —*v.t.* p.p. of *cleave*.

clem′a·tis (klem′ə-tis) *n.* a climbing vine bearing small white flowers.

clem′en·cy (klem′ən-sē) *n.* mildness; leniency; mercy.

clem′ent (klem′ənt) *adj.* **1.** merciful; lenient. **2.** mild; agreeable.

clench (klench) *v.t.* close tightly, as the fist or teeth.

cler′gy (klěr′jē) *n.* priests, ministers, or ecclesiastical officials collectively. —**cler′gy·man** (-mən) *n.* any member of the clergy.

cler′ic (kler′ik) *n.* a clergyman.

cler′i·cal (kler′ə-kəl) *adj.* **1.** pert. to the clergy or to affairs of the church. **2.** pert. to written records, copies, or to office work.

clerk (klěrk) *n.* **1.** a salesperson in a shop. **2.** an assistant in an office. **3.** an official of a branch of government who keeps records. **4.** (*Archaic*) a lay officer of the church; any literate person. —*v.i.* serve as a clerk. —**clerk′ship**, *n.*

clev′er (klev′ər) *adj.* **1.** shrewd; quick to learn; skillful; quick-witted. **2.** ingenious. —**clev′er·ness**, *n.*

clew (kloo) *n.* a hint, indication or tangible guide to the solution of a mystery or problem. Also, **clue.**

cli·ché′ (klē-shā′) *n.* (*Fr.*) an outworn expression; a stale or trite remark; literally, a stereotype.

click (klik) *n.* a small, sharp snap. —*v.i.* make such a sound. **2.** (*Colloq.*) be successful.

cli′ent (klī′ənt) *n.* a customer, esp. the recipient of professional, esp. legal, services.

cli′en·tele′ (klē′ən-tel′; klī′-) *n.* a body of clients of a lawyer, doctor, etc.

cliff (klif) *n.* an abrupt wall of rock; precipice.

cli·mac′ter·ic (klī-mak′tər-ik) *n.* a critical period, esp. the menopause. —*adj.* pert. to a critical time.

cli·mac′tic (klī-mak′tik) *adj.* pert. to a climax. —**cli·mac′ti·cal·ly,** *adv.*

cli′mate (klī′mit) *n.* the customary pattern of the weather for any specific locality. —**cli·mat′ic,** *adj.* —**cli·mat′i·cal·ly,** *adv.*

cli′max (klī′maks) *n.* **1.** the culmination of one or more events. **2.** the highest point of action, stress, motion, etc. **3.** the most effective point of a narrative, drama, or argument. —*v.t.* bring to the highest or most effective point.

climb (klīm) *v.t. & i.* **1.** ascend with effort; toil upward. **2.** rise slowly. **3.** (with *down*) descend. —*n.* an ascent.

clime (klīm) *n.* (*Poetic*) a place or region of the earth.

clinch (klinch) *v.t.* **1.** secure tightly; fasten by bending the point (of a nail, etc.) sideways after driving it through; clench. **2.** make certain of; consolidate. —*v.i.* (*Colloq.*) embrace; in boxing, grasp the opponent with the arms. —*n.* the result of clinching. —**clinch′er,** *n.* that which clinches, esp. a decisive argument.

cling (kling) *v.i.* [**clung, cling′ing**] adhere; be fastened to; hold tenaciously to.

clin′ic (klin′ik) *n.* a place for medical examination and treatment, often free, for experimental or instructive purposes. —**clin′i·cal,** *adj.* pert. to or used in medical practice.

clink (klink) *n.* **1.** a high-pitched, fine sound, as of struck glass. **2.** (*Slang*) a jail.

clink′er (kling′kər) *n.* a vitreous residue of various fuels; a piece of slag.

clip (klip) *n.* **1.** a mechanical clasping device, as a *paper clip, cartridge clip.* **2.** a fast gait. —*v.t.* [**clipped** (klipt), **clip′ping**] **1.** fasten together by a spring-actuated device. **2.** cut, as with shears; truncate. **3.** cuff with a glancing blow.

clip′per (klip′ər) *n.* **1.** any of various tools that cut by shearing. **2.** something that travels swiftly. esp. a square-rigged, speedy sailing ship, or an airliner.

clip′ping *n.* a piece clipped or cut out.

clique (klēk) *n.* a small exclusive social coterie. —**cli′quish** (-kish) *adj.*

cloak (klōk) *n.* **1.** a loose-fitting, sleeveless outer garment. **2.** a disguise; pretext; cover. —*v.t.* cover; conceal.

cloche (klōsh) *n.* 1, a bell-shaped woman's hat. 2, a bell-shaped or deep concave glass cover.

clock (klok) *n.* 1, a stationary timepiece. 2, a vertical ornament on the ankle of a sock. —*v.t.* (*Colloq.*) measure the speed of; time.

Clockwise

Counterclockwise

Clockface

clock'wise" (klok'wīz") *adj.* in the direction of travel of a clock's hands: from left to right around a circle.

clock'work" *n.* the mechanism of a clock, or one similarly exact and inexorable.

clod (klod) *n.* 1, a compacted chunk of earth. 2, a stupid, stolid person. —**clod'dish,** *adj.*

clod'hop"per *n.* 1, a rustic; boor. 2, (*pl.*) heavy work shoes.

clog (klog) *n.* 1, a block or encumbrance; any impediment or hindrance. 2, a type of thick-soled shoe. 3, a dance in which heavy shoes tap the rhythm: *clog dance.* —*v.t.* [**clogged, clog'ging**] encumber; hinder; impede. —*v.i.* 1, become clogged. 2, dance a clog dance.

cloi"son-né' (kloi"zə-nā') *n.* decorative work of enamel sections in a pattern of metal strips.

clois'ter (klois'tər) *n.* 1, an arched walk surrounding a courtyard; an arcade or colonnade. 2, a place of religious retirement. —**clois'tered** (-tərd) *adj.* 1, secluded. 2, having a cloister. —**clois'tral** (-trol) *adj.*

close (klōz) *v.t.* 1, stop up; shut. 2, join; fill, as a gap. 3, finish; conclude. —*v.i.* 1, unite; come together. 2, (with *in*) approach; draw near. 3, come to an end; terminate. 4, consummate a sale or agreement. 5, fight in bodily contact; grapple. —*n.* 1, conclusion; termination. 2, (klōs) an enclosed yard; court. —*adj.* (klōs) 1, near to; in contact with. 2, restricted in space; wanting fresh air; stuffy. 3, compact; dense. 4, secretive; reticent. 5, (*Colloq.*) penurious; miserly. —*adv.* (klōs) 1, near. 2, in a closed manner. —**closed car,** an automobile having windows and a hard top. —**closed shop,** a shop employing union members only. —**close'ness,** *n.*

clos'et (kloz'it) *n.* a small room for retirement or storage. —**clos'et-ed,** *adj.* shut up in a private room.

close-'up" (klōs'-) *n.* a near view; a picture taken at close range.

clo'sure (klō'zhər) *n.* 1, act of closing; state of being closed. 2, that which closes, as a bottle cap.

clot (klot) *n.* soft or fluid matter, as blood or cream, coagulated into a mass. —*v.t. & i.* [**clot'ted, -ting**] form a clot. —**clot'ty,** *adj.*

cloth (klâth) *n.* 1, fabric woven from filaments of wool, cotton, etc. 2, (*pl.* klâthz) a specific piece of such material for a designated purpose. 3, the professional dress of a clergyman. —*adj.* made of cloth.

clothe (klōth) *v.t.* [**clothed** or **clad, cloth'ing**] attire; cover with, or as with, clothing.

clothes (klōz) *n.pl.* 1, wearing apparel. 2, cloth coverings, esp. for beds. —**clothes'pin",** *n.* a small clip for fastening clothes on a line.

cloth'ier (klōth'yər) *n.* a manufacturer or retailer of clothes.

cloth'ing (klō'thing) *n.* wearing apparel; cloth coverings in general.

clo'ture (klō'chər) *n.* a stopping of a debate by parliamentary rule.

cloud (klowd) *n.* 1, white or gray masses of suspended water or ice particles at varying heights above the earth. 2, anything resembling a cloud, as dust. 3, anything that darkens, threatens, or obscures. —*v.t.* 1, obscure; darken. 2, place under suspicion; sully. —*v.i.* grow cloudy; become obscured. —**cloud'y,** *adj.*

cloud'burst" *n.* a heavy rainfall.

clout (klowt) *v.t.* strike with the hand; cuff. —*n.* a blow.

clove (klōv) *n.* 1, one of the small bulbs from the mother-bulb, as a clove of garlic. 2, a spice, the dried flower buds of the clove tree.

clo'ven (klō'vən) *adj.* parted; divided; split.

clo'ver (klō'vər) *n.* a common garden plant, useful as forage.

clo'ver-leaf" *n.* an arrangement of road intersections to avoid direct crossings.

clown (klown) *n.* 1, a comedian, esp. in a circus; a buffoon. 2, (*Archaic*) a rustic; an uncouth person. —*v.i.* act the buffoon; parody. —**clown'ish,** *adj.* rude or comical.

cloy (kloi) *v.t. & i.* surfeit; seem excessive (to).

club (klub) *n.* 1, a stick to be used as a weapon; a cudgel; a bat or stick as used in various games. 2, any playing card designated by the trefoil (♣). 3, a group of persons joined by a common interest; its quarters. —*v.t.* [**clubbed, club'bing**] 1, strike or beat with a club. 2, use as a weapon. 3, pool; unite. —*v.i.* (with *together*) unite; act jointly.

club'foot" *n.* a deformed foot.

cluck (kluk) n. 1, the sound made by suddenly separating the tongue from the hard palate. 2, the sound of a hen calling her chicks. —v.i. utter such sounds.

clue (kloo) n. clew.

clump (klump) n. 1, a shapeless mass of solid material. 2, a cluster of trees or shrubs. —v.i. walk heavily and clumsily. —clump′y, adj.

clum′sy (klum′zē) adj. awkward; blundering; ill-adapted. —clum′siness, n.

clung (klung) v. pret. & p.p. of cling.

clus′ter (klus′tər) n. a closely grouped number of things, as fruits or persons; a bunch. —v.i. & t. bunch together.

clutch (kluch) v.t. 1, grasp with the hands. 2, (with at) try to grasp. —v.i. try to seize something. —n. 1, (often pl.) a strong grip; powerful control. 2, a device to engage a driven member with the driving force. 3, a brood of eggs or chickens.

clut′ter (klut′ər) n. a disorderly state or litter. —v.t. (often with up) strew in confusion.

co- pref. as one of two or more; jointly.

coach (kōch) n. 1, carriage; passenger vehicle. 2, a tutor or instructor. —v.t. instruct; train.

co·ad′ju·tor (kō-aj′ə-tər) n. an assistant, as of a bishop or prelate.

co·ag′u·late″ (kō-ag′yə-lāt″) v.i. become clotted or congealed. —v.t. curdle; congeal. —co·ag″u·la′tion, n.

coal (kōl) n. 1, a blackish carbonaceous mineral used as fuel. 2, a lump of coal; (pl.) any burning lumps.

co″a·lesce′ (kō″ə-les′) v.i. grow together; unite. —co″a·les′cence, n.

co″a·li′tion (kō″ə-lish′ən) n. 1, a temporary alliance. 2, fusion into one mass.

coarse (kōrs) adj. 1, of rough finish or texture. 2, crude; unrefined. —coars′en (kōr′sən) v.t. make coarse. —coarse′ness, n.

coast (kōst) n. the shore line; land by the sea. —v.i. proceed without power, by gravity or inertia. —coast′al, adj. —Coast Guard, a U. S. armed service.

coast′er (-ər) n. 1, a vehicle that will coast, as a sled. 2, a small table mat. 3, a serving tray on wheels.

coat (kōt) n. 1, an outer garment with sleeves. 2, anything that covers the entire surface, as paint, an animal′s fur, etc. —v.t. cover with a bonded or close-fitting layer of anything. —coat′ing, n. a layer of some substance, as paint. —coat of arms, a shield distinctively emblazoned.

coax (kōks) v.t. & t. beg by fondling or flattery; wheedle; cajole.

co·ax′i·al (kō-ak′sē-əl) adj. having a common axis; but (of a cable) capable of transmitting different and distinguishable impulses.

cob (kob) n. 1, the spike upon which grains of corn grow: corncob. 2, a small, strong horse. 3, the male swan.

co′balt (kō′bålt) n. a hard metallic element, no. 27, symbol Co. —adj. deep blue.

cob′ble (kob′əl) v.t. & t. make or repair shoes; mend or patch, esp. clumsily.

cob′bler (kob′lər) n. 1, a shoemaker. 2, a dessert or drink made with fruit.

cob′ble·stone″ n. a paving stone with convex upper surface.

co′bra (kō′brə) n. a poisonous snake of Asia and India.

cob′web″ (kob′web″) n. 1, the net spun by the spider. 2, any similar flimsy structure.

co′ca (kō′kə) n. the dried leaf of a So. Amer. shrub, used medicinally as a tonic or mild stimulant.

co·caine′ (kō-kān′) n. an alkaloid of coca, used as an anesthetic and narcotic.

coch″i·neal′ (koch″ə-nēl′) n. a scarlet dye made from dried Central Amer. insects.

cock (kok) n. 1, the male of various birds, esp. of domestic fowl; a rooster. 2, a leader. 3, a conical pile of hay. 4, an upward tilt, as of a head, hat, etc. 5, a faucet or valve. —v.t. 1, turn up on one side. 2, draw back the hammer of (a gun).

cock·ade′ (-ād′) n. a rosette worn on the hat as a badge.

cock″a·too′ (-ə-too′) n. a crested Australian parrot.

cock′a·trice (kok′ə-tris) n. a fabulous deadly serpent.

cock′crow″ n. dawn.

cock′er (-ər) n. a small long-haired hunting dog: cocker spaniel.

cock′er·el (-ər-əl) n. a young cock.

cock′eyed″ (-īd″) adj. 1, crosseyed. 2, (Slang) twisted; absurd. 3, (Slang) drunk.

cock′le (kok′əl) n. 1, a weed. 2, an edible mollusk with two fluted shells. 3, a shallow boat. —cockles of the heart, inmost depths of feeling.

cock′ney (kok′nē) n. a native of the East End of London; the dialect of this region.

cock'pit" *n.* **1,** the space for pilots in an airplane. **2,** a recess in the after deck of a yacht, etc. **3,** a place for cockfighting.

cock'roach" *n.* an insect infesting houses.

cocks'comb" (koks'kŏm") *n.* a crimson-flowered plant: the *celosia.*

cock'sure" *adj.* overconfident.

cock'tail" *n.* a mixed drink, or dish of fruit, shellfish, etc. served before a meal.

cock'y (kok'ē) *adj.* conceited. —**cock'i·ness,** *n.*

co'coa (kō'kō) *n.* **1,** a powder made from cacao seed; a hot drink made from this powder and milk. **2,** a brown color.

co'co·nut" (kō'kə-nut") *n.* the large, hard fruit of a tropical tree (coconut palm).

co·coon' (kō-koon') *n.* a silky case in which certain larvae develop.

cod (kod) *n.* a No. Atlantic food fish. Also, **cod'fish".**

cod'dle (kod'əl) *v.t.* **1,** humor; pamper. **2,** cook in hot but not boiling water.

code (kōd) *n.* **1,** a systematized collection of laws. **2,** any set of rules. **3,** a system of signals for telegraphic or secret communication.

co'deine (kō'dēn) *n.* a narcotic derivative of opium.

codg'er (koj'ər) *n.* (*Colloq.*) an old person.

cod'i·cil (kod'ə-səl) *n.* a [supplement to a will.

cod'i·fy" (kod'i-fī") *v.t.* arrange systematically; reduce to a code. —**cod"i·fi·ca'tion,** *n.*

co'ed" (kō'ed") *n.* (*Slang*) a female student in a coeducational college.

co"ed·u·ca'tion (kō"ed-yə-kā'shən) *n.* education of students of both sexes together. —**co"ed·u·ca'tion·al,** *adj.*

co"ef·fi'cient (kō"ə-fish'ənt) *n.* a multiplier.

co·erce' (kō-ērs') *v.t.* compel by force. —**co·er'cion** (-shən) *n.*

co·e'val (kō-ē'vəl) *adj.* of the same age; contemporary.

cof'fee (kâf'ē) *n.* **1,** a drink made from the seeds of a tropical shrub; the shrub or seeds (coffee beans). **2,** a brown color.

cof'fer (kâf'ər) *n.* a chest, esp. one for valuables.

cof'fin (kâf'in) *n.* a box in which a corpse is buried.

cog (kog) *n.* a tooth on a gear wheel (*cogwheel*).

co'gent (kō'jənt) *adj.* convincing; forcible. —**co'gen·cy,** *n.*

cog'i·tate" (koj'ə-tāt") *v.i.* & *t;* ponder; plan. —**cog"i·ta'tion,** *n.*

co'gnac (kōn'yak) *n.* a Fr. brandy:

cog'nate (kog'nāt) *adj.* related: —**cog·na'tion,** *n.*

cog·ni'tion (kog-nish'ən) *n.* the process of acquiring a mental image; perception; cognizance.

cog'ni·zance (kog'ni-zəns) *n.* **1,** awareness; notice. **2,** range of observation. —**cog'ni·zant,** *adj.*

cog·no'men (kog-nō'mən) *n.* **1,** a surname. **2,** among Romans, the third or family name. **3,** a nickname.

co·hab'it (kō-hab'it) *v.i.* live together, esp. as husband and wife. —**co·hab"i·ta'tion,** *n.*

co·here' (kō-hir') *v.i.* **1,** stick together. **2,** be logically consistent or connected. —**co·her'ence,** *n.* —**co·her'ent,** *adj.*

co·he'sion (kō-hē'zhən) *n.* a sticking together of like particles. —**co·he'sive** (-siv) *adj.*

co'hort (kō'hôrt) *n.* a band, esp. of warriors.

coif (koif) *n.* **1,** a close-fitting peasant cap. **2,** a nun's hood-shaped cap.

coif·feur' (kwä-fēr') *n.* a hairdresser.

coif·fure' (kwä-fyûr') *n.* a manner of arranging the hair; a headdress.

Coils

Induction Coil   *Rope Coil*

coil (koil) *v.t.* & *i.* twist into spiral shape. —*n.* a length of coiled rope, wire, pipe, etc.

coin (koin) *n.* a piece of metal authorized for use as money. —*v.t.* **1,** make (metal) into money. **2,** make (money) by minting metal. **3,** invent, as a word. **4,** (*Colloq.*) gain (money) rapidly. —**coin'er,** *n.* a counterfeiter.

coin'age (koin'ij) *n.* **1,** the act or process of coining; money coined. **2,** currency. **3,** a thing invented.

co"in·cide' (kō"in-sīd') *v.i.* **1,** occupy the same space or time. **2,** correspond exactly. **3,** concur; agree.

co·in'ci·dence (kō-in'si-dəns) *n.* **1,** exact correspondence in space or time. **2,** a notable occurrence of events apparently accidental. —**co·in'ci·dent, co·in"ci·den'tal,** *adj.*

co·i'tion (kō-ish'ən) *n.* sexual intercourse.

coke (kōk) *n.* **1,** a fuel, the solid residue of coal baked but not burned. **2,** (*Slang*) cocaine. **3,** (*T.N.*) a soft drink: *Coca-Cola.*

col·an·der (kol'ən-dər) *n.* a strainer used in cooking.

cold (kōld) *adj.* **1,** below the temperature comfortable to the body; chilling. **2,** lacking bodily heat. **3,** not heated. **4,** unresponsive; indifferent; lacking in enthusiasm. —*n.* **1,** a condition of low temperature. **2,** a sensation produced by lack of heat. **3,** an ailment affecting the mucous membranes of the nose and throat. —**cold'ness,** *n.*

cold'blood'ed (-blud"id) *adj.* **1,** deliberate; unsympathetic; cruel. **2,** pert. to fishes and reptiles. —**cold'blood'ed·ness,** *n.*

cold shoulder a rebuff; deliberate disregard.

cold war a period of bitterly unfriendly diplomatic relations.

cole (kōl) *n.* a plant of the cabbage family; rape.

cole'slaw" (kōl'slâ") *n.* finely sliced cabbage.

col'ic (kol'ik) *n.* severe griping abdominal pains. —**col'ick·y,** *adj.*

col'i·se'um (kol'ə-sē'əm) *n.* a large public amphitheater.

co·li'tis (kō-lī'tis) *n.* inflammation of the colon.

col·lab'o·rate' (kə-lab'ə-rāt') *v.i.* **1,** work with another, esp. in writing. **2,** in wartime, work with the enemy. —**col·lab'o·ra'tion,** *n.* —**col·lab'o·ra'tion·ist,** *n.* one who works with the enemy. —**col·lab'o·ra"tor,** *n.* a joint author.

col·lapse' (kə-laps') *v.i. & t.* **1,** break, fall in, or give way. **2,** fail. **3,** break down physically. **4,** fold up intentionally, as an umbrella. —*n.* a sudden failure or falling in. —**col·laps'i·ble,** *adj.*

col'lar (kol'ər) *n.* a band or harness worn around the neck. —*v.t.* **1,** put a collar on. **2,** grasp by the collar. **3,** (*Slang*) seize; apprehend.

col'lar·bone" *n.* a bone connecting the breastbone with the shoulder blade; the clavicle.

col'lard (kol'ərd) *n.* a kind of kale.

col·late' (kə-lāt') *v.t.* **1,** compare in detail. **2,** put (pages, etc.) in proper order.

col·lat'er·al (kə-lat'ər-əl) *adj.* **1,** attendant on, but subordinate to, the main issue. **2,** side by side; parallel. **3,** descended from the same ancestor, but in a different line. —*n.* something given as additional security for a loan.

col·la'tion (ko-lā'shən) *n.* **1,** act of collating. **2,** a light meal.

col'league (kol'ēg) *n.* a professional associate.

col·lect' (kə-lekt') *v.t.* **1,** gather together. **2,** receive payment of. **3,** get (contributions, etc.) from others. **4,** acquire as a hobby. **5,** regain command of (oneself). —*v.i.* assemble; accumulate. —*n.* (kol'ekt) a short prayer. —**col·lec'tion,** *n.* —**col·lec'tor,** *n.*

col·lec'tive (kə-lek'tiv) *adj.* **1,** combined. **2,** belonging to, or exercised by, an aggregate of persons. **3,** treating a number of objects as one unit, as *a collective noun.* —**col·lec'tiv·ism,** *n.* the socialistic principle of state ownership.

col·leen' (ko-lēn') *n.* (*Irish*) girl.

col'lege (kol'ij) *n.* **1,** an institution of higher learning. **2,** one of the separate schools of a university. **3,** a body of men having certain powers and rights.

col·le'gi·an (kə-lē'jē-ən) *n.* a college student.

col·le'gi·ate (kə-lē'jē-ət) *adj.* **1,** pert. to a college or college customs. **2,** pert. to a church allied with others.

col·lide' (kə-līd') *v.i.* come into violent contact; conflict.

col'lie (kol'ē) *n.* a Scot. sheep dog.

col'lier (kol'yər) *n.* **1,** a coal miner. **2,** a vessel for shipping coal. —**col'lier·y,** *n.* a coal mine.

col·lin'e·ar (kə-lin'ē-ər) *adj.* lying in the same straight line.

Collie

col·li'sion (kə-lizh'ən) *n.* act or result of colliding; clash.

col·lo'di·on (kə-lō'dē-ən) *n.* a cellulose solution used as a protective coating.

col·lo'qui·al (kə-lō'kwē-əl) *adj.* belonging to ordinary, everyday speech. —**col·lo'qui·al·ism,** *n.*

col'lo·quy (kol'ə-kwē) *n.* **1,** a conversation. **2,** a discussion; conference.

col·lu'sion (kə-loo'zhən) *n.* a secret agreement for a fraudulent purpose. —**col·lu'sive** (-siv) *adj.*

co·logne' (kə-lōn') *n.* a fragrant toilet water.

co'lon (kō'lən) *n.* **1,** the large intestine. **2,** a mark (:) of punctuation, introducing an example or conclusion.

colo'nel (kẽr'nəl) *n.* a military officer ranking next below a brigadier general. —**colo'nel·cy,** *n.*

co·lo'ni·al (kə-lō'nē-əl) *adj.* being

or pert. to a colony. —n. a native of a colony.

col'on·nade" (kol'ə-nād") *n.* a series of columns.

col'o·ny (kol'ə-nē) *n.* 1, a body of people who settle in a new country but remain subject to the mother country; the place of settlement. 2, people of one nationality or occupation living close together. —col'o·nist, *n.* —col'o·nize" (-nīz") *v.t. & i.*

col'or (kul'ər) *n.* 1, any of the hues of the rainbow; also, any tint or shade made by mixing these hues. 2, complexion. 3, a pigment. 4, outward appearance; general characteristics. 5, (*pl.*) a flag. 6, (*pl.*) a symbolic colored ribbon or ornament; the clothes of a jockey. —*v.t.* 1, dye. 2, misrepresent. —*v.i.* blush. Also, col'our. —col'or·a'tion, *n.*

col'o·ra·tu'ra (kul'ə-rə-tyūr'ə) *n.* a soprano of high range.

col'or-blind" *adj.* unable to distinguish different colors normally.

col'ored (-ərd) *adj.* 1, having color. 2, belonging to a nonwhite race, esp. the Negro race. 3, biased; deceptive.

col'or·ful (-fəl) *adj.* 1, full of color. 2, picturesque; dramatic.

col'or·ing *n.* 1, complexion; hue. 2, dye.

col'or·less *adj.* 1, without color. 2, lacking interest.

co·los'sal (kə-los'əl) *adj.* huge; gigantic.

co·los'sus (kə-los'əs) *n.* a gigantic statue; any great thing or person.

co·los'trum (kə-los'trəm) *n.* milk secreted for several days before and after childbirth.

colt (kōlt) *n.* 1, a young male horse. 2, (*cap.*) (*T.N.*) a type of revolver.

col'um·bine" (kol'əm-bīn") *n.* a plant having spurred flowers.

co·lum'bi·um (kə-lum'bē-əm) *n.* a steel-gray metallic element, no. 41, symbol Cb; also called niobium.

col'umn (kol'əm) *n.* 1, an upright pillar supporting some part of a building. 2, anything resembling a pillar in use, position, or appearance. 3, a vertical row of figures or type. 4, a regular department in a newspaper. 5, a formation or line of soldiers or ships. —co·lum'nar (kə-lum'nər) *adj.*

col'um·nist (kol'əm-ist) *n.* the writer of a regular newspaper feature.

com- *pref.* with; jointly; entirely.

co'ma (kō'mə) *n.* a state of prolonged stupor, caused by injury, disease, or poison.

com'a·tose" (kom'ə-tōs") *adj.* 1, in a coma. 2, lethargic.

comb (kōm) *n.* 1, a toothed instrument for arranging the hair, currying horses, carding wool or fibers, etc. 2, a rooster's crest. 3, reticulated cells, as a honeycomb. —*v.t.* 1, dress (hair); card (wool, etc.). 2, search thoroughly.

com'bat (kom'bat) *n.* a fight; a battle. —*v.t. & i.* (kəm-bat') fight against; oppose. —com'bat·ant (-bə-tənt) *n. & adj.* —com·bat'ive, *adj.*

com"bi·na'tion (kom"bə-nā'shən) *n.* 1, a coming together so as to form a group, sum, product, etc.; the group, etc. so formed. 2, a one-piece undergarment. 3, the series of numbers which when dialed will open a keyless lock.

com·bine' (kəm-bīn') *v.t. & i.* join; unite. —*n.* (kom'bīn") 1, a harvesting machine. 2, (*Colloq.*) a union of important persons, parties, or corporations.

com·bus'tion (kəm-bus'chən) *n.* the act or process of burning. —com·bus'ti·ble, *adj. & n.*

come (kum) *v.i.* [**came** (kām), **come**, **com'ing**] 1, move toward; approach. 2, arrive, in space, time, or sequence. 3, appear as the result of something; be derived from. 4, become. 5, happen; occur. 6, extend to a given point. 7, be attained or acquired. —come across, 1, meet. 2, deliver. —come around, 1, recover. 2, submit. —come off, succeed; occur. —come over, happen to. —come through, 1, survive. 2, produce as expected. —come to, 1, regain consciousness.

come'back" *n.* (*Colloq.*) 1, a recovery of lost position. 2, a retort.

co·me'di·an (kə-mē'dē·ən) *n.* an actor or writer of comedy. —co·me'di·enne' (-en') *n. fem.*

come'down" *n.* a humiliating experience.

com'e·dy (kom'ə-dē) *n.* 1, a light, amusing drama ending happily. 2, the comic element in anything. 3, any comic incident.

come'ly (kum'lē) *adj.* good-looking. —come'li·ness, *n.*

come-'on" *n.* a lure; gimmick.

com'er (kum'ər) *n.* (*Colloq.*) one likely to be successful.

co·mes'ti·ble (kə-mes'tə-bəl) *n. & adj.* edible.

com'et (kom'et) *n.* a moving celestial body with a luminous tail.

com'fit (kum'fit) *n.* a bonbon.

com'fort (kum'fərt) *v.t.* console. —*n.* 1, solace; consolation. 2, one who brings solace. 3, the feeling of consolation. 4, a state or feeling of well-being and content. 5, (*pl.*) things that contribute to such a state. 6, a bed covering.

com'fort·a·ble (kum'fərt·ə-bəl) *adj.* 1, affording ease. 2, free from pain or distress. 3, (*Colloq.*) sufficient.

com'fort·er *n.* 1, a bedcovering. 2, a scarf. 3, one who comforts.

com'ic (kom'ik) *adj.* **1**, pert. to comedy. **2**, comical; funny. —*n.* **1**, a comedian. **2**, (*pl.*) comic pictures, esp. in a newspaper; funny papers. **3**, a magazine presenting stories in cartoon style. —**com'i·cal**, *adj.* droll; funny; exciting mirth. —**comic strip**, a series of drawings in cartoon style, developing a narrative.

com'i·ty (kom'ə-tē) *n.* courtesy, esp. between nations.

com'ma (kom'ə) *n.* a punctuation mark (,) indicating a brief or minor pause.

com·mand' (kə-mảnd') *v.t.* & *i.* **1**, order or require with authority. **2**, exercise supreme power (over). **3**, overlook, as from a height. —*n.* **1**, an order. **2**, authority to order. **3**, power to control; mastery; complete knowledge or skill. **4**, a naval or military force under the control of a certain officer. —**command performance**, a theatrical performance before a king, etc.

com"man·dant' (kom"ən-dänt') *n.* the officer in command of a military installation, fortress, etc.

com"man·deer' (kom"ən-dir') *v.t.* **1**, seize for military purposes. **2**, seize arbitrarily.

com·mand'er (kə-man'dər) *n.* **1**, a leader; chief officer. **2**, in the U.S. Navy, the rank next below captain.

com·mand'ment (kə-mand'mənt) *n.* **1**, a command; a charge. **2**, one of the Ten Commandments.

com·man'do (kə-man'dō) *n.* [*pl.* -dos] a member of a body of picked troops for raiding enemy territory.

com·mem'o·rate (kə-mem'ə-rāt") *v.t.* **1**, honor the memory of in a formal manner. **2**, serve as a memento of. —**com·mem'o·ra'tion**, *n.* —**com·mem'o·ra'tive**, *adj.*

com·mence' (kə-mens') *v.t.* & *i.* begin.

com·mence'ment (-mənt) *n.* **1**, a beginning. **2**, the graduation exercises of a school or college.

com·mend' (kə-mend') *v.t.* **1**, praise. **2**, recommend. **3**, entrust or give in charge. —**com·mend'a·ble**, *adj.*

com"men·da'tion (kom"ən-dā'shən) *n.* a citation of praise.

com·men'su·ra·ble (kə-men'shə-rə-bəl) *adj.* comparable in measure; proportionate.

com·men'su·rate (kə-men'shə-rət) *adj.* **1**, of equal size. **2**, corresponding in amount, degree, or size; comparable. **3**, adequate.

com'ment (kom'ent) *n.* **1**, a remark or observation, esp. a note explaining or criticizing a book. **2**, talk; gossip. —*v.i.* make remarks.

com'men·tar"y (kom'ən-tār"ē) *n.* an explanatory discourse.

com'men·ta"tor (kom'ən-tā"tər) *n.* one who reports and comments on current events.

com'merce (kom'ẽrs) *n.* trade on a large scale, esp. between countries; business.

com·mer'cial (kə-mẽr'shəl) *adj.* pert. to, or engaged in, or accruing from, trade. —*n.* the advertising material on a radio or television program. —**com·mer'cial·ize"** (-īz") *v.t.* exploit; turn to account.

com·min'gle (kə-ming'gəl) *v.t.* & *i.* mingle together; blend.

com·mis'er·ate" (kə-miz'ə-rāt") *v.t.* pity; condole with. —**com·mis'er·a'tion**, *n.*

com"mis·sar' (kom"ə-sär') *n.* the head of a government department in the U.S.S.R. —**com"mis·sar'i·at** (-sär'ē-ət) *n.* a department of a military or (in the U. S. S. R.) government organization.

com'mis·sar"y (kom'ə-sär"ē) *n.* **1**, a store supplying food and supplies, as in a camp. **2**, a deputy.

com·mis'sion (kə-mish'ən) *n.* **1**, the act of doing or perpetrating. **2**, a warrant to inquire and report. **3**, a body of persons entrusted with special duties. **4**, a matter entrusted to another; assignment. **5**, authority to act as agent; also, the fee paid. **6**, a document conferring naval or military rank. —*v.t.* **1**, delegate; appoint. **2**, confer rank or authority on. **3**, equip (a ship) for active service.

com·mis'sion·er *n.* **1**, the head of a commission or of one of certain governmental departments. **2**, an agent.

com·mit' (kə-mit') *v.t.* [com-mit'ted, -ting] **1**, entrust to another's care. **2**, consign to custody. **3**, perpetrate (a sin, crime, etc.). **4**, refer to a committee, as a bill. **5**, involve in risk. **6**, bind (oneself); pledge.

com·mit'ment (-mənt) *n.* **1**, act of committing. **2**, a pledge; something undertaken.

com·mit'tee (kə-mit'ē) *n.* a body of persons appointed for specific duties.

com·mode' (kə-mōd') *n.* a small bedside cupboard.

com·mo'di·ous (kə-mō'dē-əs) *adj.* roomy and spacious. —**com·mo'dious·ness**, *n.*

com·mod'i·ty (kə-mod'ə-tē) *n.* **1**, an article of commerce. **2**, a useful thing.

com'mo·dore" (kom'ə-dôr") *n.* the senior or commanding officer of more than one ship or yacht; in the U. S. Navy, a rank next above captain.

com'mon (kom'ən) *adj.* **1,** shared by, or equally true of, two or more; joint; united. **2,** public; general. **3,** familiar; usual. **4,** not notable; ordinary. **5,** vulgar; coarse. —*n.* **1,** a tract of public land; a park. **2,** (*pl.*) a college dining hall; its food. **3,** (*pl.*) (*cap.*) the elective house of Parliament. —**common law,** the system of law based on custom and court decisions, not statutes. —**common noun,** a noun designating any of a class. —**common sense,** good judgment in simple matters. —**common stock,** shares of ownership of a company, having voting rights but no fixed dividend.

com'mon·al·ty (kom'ən-əl-tē) *n.* **1,** the common people. **2,** the members of a corporation.

com'mon·er (kom'ən-ər) *n.* a person without noble rank.

com'mon·place' *adj.* ordinary; not unusual or original.

com'mon·wealth' *n.* a state or union of states.

com·mo'tion (kə-mō'shən) *n.* **1,** violent agitation. **2,** disorder; public unrest.

com·mu'nal (kom'yoo-nəl) *adj.* pert. to, or owned by, a community; public.

com·mune' (kə-mūn') *v.t.* interchange thoughts and feelings; converse. —*n.* (kom'ūn) a community.

com·mu'ni·cant (-kənt) *n.* one who communicates; one who takes communion.

com·mu'ni·cate' (kə-mū'ni-kāt') *v.t.* convey, impart. —*v.i.* **1,** converse; get in touch by letter, etc. **2,** be connected, as rooms. —**com·mu'ni·ca·ble,** *adj.*

com·mu'ni·ca'tion (-kā'shən) *n.* **1,** act of communicating. **2,** a message. **3,** a means or way of communicating; passage.

com·mu'ni·ca·tive (-kə-tiv) *adj.* informative; talkative.

com·mun'ion (kə-mūn'yən) *n.* **1,** a sharing; fellowship. **2,** (*cap.*) celebration of the Lord's Supper.

com·mu''ni·qué' (kə-mū''nə-kā') *n.* an official communication or bulletin.

com'mu·nism (kom'yə-niz-əm) *n.* a social theory that the common people should own all property and means of production.

com'mu·nist (kom'yə-nist) *adj.* pert. to a political party or government advocating communism, esp. (*cap.*) in the U.S.S.R. —*n.* an advocate of such theory, or member of such government or such party.

com·mu'ni·ty (kə-mū'nə-tē) *n.* **1,** all persons living in a particular locality. **2,** a group having interests or religion in common. **3,** joint sharing.

com·mute' (kə-mūt') *v.t.* substitute another thing for, esp. to reduce the severity of a penalty, obligation, etc. —*v.i.* travel daily between a city and suburb. —**com''mu·ta'tion,** *n.* —**com·mut'er,** *n.*

com·pact' (kəm-pakt') *adj.* **1,** closely packed together; solid; dense. **2,** concise. —*v.t.* —*n.* (kom'pakt) **1,** a small case containing powder and rouge. **2,** an agreement; treaty.

com·pan'ion (kəm-pan'yən) *n.* **1,** an associate; comrade. **2,** a paid attendant. **3,** a mate; one of a pair of matched objects. —**com·pan'ion·a·ble,** *adj.* agreeable; friendly.

com·pan'ion·ship *n.* friendship.

com·pan'ion·way' *n.* a stair from deck to cabins on a ship.

com'pa·ny (kum'pə-nē) *n.* **1,** a group of persons assembled, working, or associating together. **2,** someone to talk or commune with. **3,** guests. **4,** a business firm. **5,** a military unit; a ship's crew.

com'pa·ra·ble (kom'pə-rə-bəl) *adj.* capable of being, or worthy to be, compared.

com·par'a·tive (kəm-par'ə-tiv) *adj.* **1,** relative; based on comparison. **2,** (*Gram.*) expressing a higher degree, as when modified by *more.* —*n.* (*Gram.*) a comparative form.

com·pare' (kəm-pâr') *v.t.* **1,** represent as similar. **2,** note the resemblance and differences of. **3,** (*Gram.*) give the degrees of comparison of. —*v.i.* admit of comparison. —*n.* comparison.

com·par'i·son (kəm-par'i-sən) *n.* **1,** act of comparing. **2,** an illustration; simile. **3,** a comparable state or condition. **4,** (*Gram.*) the inflection of an adjective or adverb to show difference in degree.

com·part'ment (kəm-pärt'mənt) *n.* a chamber, cell, or space partitioned off. —*v.t.* divide into compartments.

Compass card   *Bow compass*

com'pass (kum'pəs) *n.* **1,** extent within limits; boundary; range. **2,** an instrument showing the magnetic North. **3,** (often *pl.*) a pivoted instrument for describing circles, etc. —*v.t.* 1, encompass; encircle. 2, accomplish.

com·pas'sion (kəm-pash'ən) *n.* sympathy, esp. pity. —**com·pas'sion·ate,** *adj.* sympathetic; merciful.

com·pat'i·ble (kəm-pat'ə-bəl) *adj.* 1, consistent. 2, congenial; harmonious. —**com·pat"i·bil'i·ty,** *n.*

com·pa'tri·ot (kəm-pā'trē-ət) *n.* a fellow countryman. —*adj.* of the same country.

com'peer (kom'pir) *n.* an associate, equal, or fellow.

com·pel' (kəm-pel') *v.t.* [-**pelled'**, -**pel'ling**] coerce; oblige.

com·pen'di·um (kəm-pen'dē-əm) *n.* a summary. —**com·pen'di·ous,** *adj.* concise.

com'pen·sate" (kom'pən-sāt") *v.t. & i.* 1, make up (for); offset. 2, pay (for); recompense. —**com·pen'sa·to·ry,** *adj.*

com"pen·sa'tion (kom"pən-sā'shən) *n.* 1, act or result of compensating; offset; pay. 2, regular payments, in lieu of wages, to a worker injured on the job: *workmen's compensation.*

com·pete' (kəm-pēt') *v.i.* contend with another; vie.

com'pe·tence (kom'pə-təns) *n.* 1, fitness; adequacy. 2, sufficient means for living comfortably.

com'pe·tent (-tənt) *adj.* 1, capable; adequate. 2, permissible.

com"pe·ti'tion (kom"pə-tish'ən) *n.* 1, rivalry; the struggle for trade, preëminence, etc. 2, a match between contestants. —**com·pet'i·tive** (kəm-pet'ə-tiv) *adj.*

com·pet'i·tor (kəm-pet'i-tər) *n.* 1, one who competes. 2, opponent; rival.

com·pile' (kəm-pīl') *v.t.* collect from various sources, esp. literary material for a book. —**com"pi·la'tion,** *n.* —**com·pil'er,** *n.*

com·pla'cen·cy (kəm-plā'sən-sē) *n.* self-satisfaction. Also, **com·pla'cence.** —**com·pla'cent,** *adj.*

com·plain' (kəm-plān') *v.i.* 1, express pain, resentment, etc.; find fault. 2, make a formal charge. —**com·plain'ant,** *n.*

com·plaint' (kəm-plānt') *n.* 1, an expression of discontent, pain, etc. 2, a bodily ailment. 3, (*Law*) a statement of the cause of action in a civil suit.

com·plai'sant (kəm-plā'zənt) *adj.* agreeable; compliant. —**com·plai'sance,** *n.*

com'ple·ment (kom'plə-mənt) *n.* 1, that which fills up or completes. 2, one of two parts needed to form a whole. —*v.t.* (-ment') fill out; complete. —**com"ple·men'ta·ry,** *adj.*

com·plete' (kəm-plēt') *adj.* 1, having all its parts; whole. 2, absolute; thorough. 3, concluded. —*v.t.* 1, supply what is lacking to. 2, finish. —**com·ple'tion** (-plē'shən) *n.*

com·plex' (kəm-pleks') *adj.* 1, composed of many parts. 2, involved; complicated; perplexing. —*n.* (kom'pleks) 1, a complex condition or situation. 2, (*Psych.*) a group of emotional experiences, often having an unsuspected effect. 3, (*Colloq.*) an obsession.

com·plex'ion (kəm-plek'shən) *n.* 1, the hue or texture of the skin, esp. of the face. 2, general appearance; aspect.

com·plex'i·ty (kom-plek'sə-tē) *n.* intricacy.

com·pli'ant (kəm-plī'ənt) *adj.* complying; yielding to the wishes of others. —**com·pli'ance,** *n.*

com'pli·cate" (kom'plə-kāt") *v.t.* render intricate or involved. —**com"pli·ca'tion,** *n.*

com'pli·cat"ed *adj.* complex; (*Colloq.*) confusing.

com·plic'i·ty (kəm-plis'ə-tē) *n.* the state of being an accomplice.

com'pli·ment (kom'plə-mənt) *n.* 1, an expression of praise or admiration. 2, (*pl.*) formal greetings.

com"pli·men'ta·ry (kom"plə-men'tə-rē) *adj.* 1, conveying, or given as, a compliment. 2, given free.

com·ply' (kəm-plī') *v.i.* acquiesce in another's wish, command, etc.

com·po'nent (kəm-pō'nənt) *adj.* forming a part of. —*n.* a constituent part.

com·port' (kəm-pôrt') *v.t.* behave (oneself). —*v.i.* (with *with*) accord; fit, suit. —**com·port'ment,** *n.* behavior.

com·pose' (kəm-pōz') *v.t.* 1, form by putting parts together. 2, be the parts of. 3, construct in some creative way, esp. original music. 4, calm; quiet. 5, settle (differences); adjust. 6, set (type). —*v.i.* write music. —**com·posed',** *adj.* calm; serene. —**com·pos'er,** *n.* one who composes music.

com·pos'ite (kəm-poz'it) *adj. & n.* 1, made up of distinct parts. 2, (*Bot.*) having small flowers arranged compactly.

com"po·si'tion (kom"pə-zish'ən) *n.* act or result of composing; a piece of music, essay, etc.; a compound; structure.

com·pos'i·tor (kəm-poz'ə-tər) *n.* one who sets type.

com'post (kom'pōst) *n.* a mixture of decaying leaves, etc., used as fertilizer.

com·po'sure (kəm-pō'zhər) *n.* serenity; calmness.

com'pote (kom'pōt) n. 1, stewed fruit. 2, a small dish.

com·pound' (kom-pownd') v.t. 1, combine (two or more ingredients). 2, form by mixing or joining. 3, fail to prosecute (a criminal) for a consideration. —adj. (kom'pownd) composed of two or more elements. —n. 1, something compound. 2, an enclosure for houses. —**compound fracture**, an open wound as well as a broken bone. —**compound interest**, interest paid on accrued interest.

com"pre·hend' (kom"prē-hend') v.t. 1, include within a certain extent of time or space. 2, understand.

com"pre·hen·si·ble (kom"prē-hen'sə-bəl) adj. understandable; intelligible. —**com"pre·hen'si·bil'i·ty**, n.

com"pre·hen'sion (kom"prē-hen'shən) n. 1, act or result of comprehending; power to comprehend. 2, inclusion; perception.

com"pre·hen'sive (kom"prē-hen'siv) adj. of large scope; inclusive. —**com"pre·hen'sive·ness**, n.

com·press' (kəm-pres') v.t. reduce the bulk of by applied pressure; pack tightly together; condense. —n. (kom'pres) a soft pad used to apply moisture, pressure, etc. —**com·pres'sion** (-presh'ən) n. —**com·pres'sor** (-pres'ər) n. a device for compressing, esp. gas or air.

com·prise' (kəm-prīz') v.t. 1, include. 2, consist of.

com'pro·mise (kom'prə-mīz") n. 1, the settlement of differences by mutual concessions. 2, a middle course; something intermediate. —v.t. 1, adjust by compromise. 2, expose to suspicion or scandal. —v.i. make a compromise.

comp·tom'e·ter (komp-tom'ə-tər) n. (T.N.) a high-speed calculating machine.

comp·trol'ler (kən-trōl'ər) n. a chief accounting officer. Also, controller. —**comp·trol'ler·ship**, n.

com·pul'sion (kəm-pul'shən) n. 1, the act of compelling; coercion; impulse.

com·pul'sive (-siv) adj. (Psych.) pert. to or compelled by a force of which the subject is not conscious.

com·pul'so·ry (-sə-rē) adj. 1, compelling. 2, obligatory.

com·punc'tion (kəm-punk'shən) n. a slight regret or prick of conscience.

com·pute' (kəm-pūt') v.t. & i. calculate; reckon. —**com"pu·ta'tion**, n.

com'rade (kom'rəd) n. a close friend. —**com'rade·ship**, n.

con (kon) v.t. [conned, con'ning] 1, pore over; learn. 2, (Slang) swindle. 3, direct the course (of a ship). —adv. against. —**conning tower**, the pilot house of a warship.

con- pref. a form of com-.

con·cat'e·nate" (kon-kat'ə-nāt") v.t. link together. —**con·cat"e·na'tion**, n.

con·cave' (kon-kāv') adj. with an outline or surface curved like the inside of a ball; curved inward. —**con·cav'i·ty** (kən-kav'ə-tē) n.

con·ceal' (kən-sēl') v.t. keep secret or hidden; secrete; hide. —**con·ceal'ment**, n.

con·cede' (kən-sēd') v.t. 1, grant, as a right or privilege. 2, admit as true.

con·ceit' (kən-sēt') n. 1, an exaggerated opinion of one's own ability, etc. 2, a quaint or humorous fancy. —**con·ceit'ed**, adj. vain.

con·ceive' (kən-sēv') v.t. & i. 1, form in the mind; 2, believe; have a feeling. 3, become pregnant (with young). —**con·ceiv'a·ble**, adj. believable.

con'cen·trate" (kon'sən-trāt") v.t. 1, bring together at one point; focus. 2, increase the strength of by removing foreign elements. —v.i. 1, meet at a common center. 2, employ all one's power or attention.

con"cen·tra'tion (kon"sən-trā'shən) n. 1, act or result of concentrating; assembly; intensification. 2, close attention or application, as in study. —**concentration camp**, a camp in which prisoners or refugees are confined.

con·cen'tric (kən-sen'trik) adj. having a common center. —**con·cen'tri·cal·ly**, adv.

con'cept (kon'sept) n. a mentally conceived image. —**con·cep'tu·al**, adj.

con·cep'tion (kən-sep'shən) n. act or effect of conceiving; an idea; notion.

con·cern' (kən-sērn') v.t. 1, relate to. 2, (with in or with) interest or occupy. 3, disturb; trouble. —n. 1, a matter of interest. 2, solicitude; anxiety. 3, a business firm. —**con·cern'ing**, prep. relating to; about.

con'cert (kon'sērt) n. 1, agreement in a plan or design. 2, a musical performance. 3, musical harmony; unison. —**con·cert'ed**, adj. in unison; harmonious.

con"cer'ti·na (kon"sər-tē'nə) n. a small accordion, hexagonal in shape.

Concertina

con·cer'to (kən-cher'tō) n. [pl. -tos (-tōz)] a musical composition, usually for a solo instrument with accompaniment.

con·ces'sion (kən-sesh'ən) *n.* 1, the act or effect of conceding; the thing or point conceded. 2, a grant or lease by an authority to a business. —**con·ces'sion·aire'** (-ə-nâr') *n.* the recipient of such a grant or lease.

conch (konch) *n.* a large, spiral sea shell.

con"ci·erge' (kon"sē-erzh') *n.* (*Fr.*) a doorkeeper or janitor.

con·cil'i·ate" (kən-sil'ē-āt") *v.t.* overcome the hostility of; pacify. —**con·cil'i·a'tion,** *n.* —**con·cil'i·a·to·ry** (-ə-tôr-ē) *adj.*

con·cise' (kən-sīs') *adj.* brief and compact; terse. —**con·cise'ness,** *n.*

con'clave (kon'klāv) *n.* 1, a private assembly. 2, the meeting of the cardinals for election of a Pope.

con·clude' (kən-klood') *v.t.* 1, bring to an end; finish; decide finally; determine. 2, deduce; infer. —*v.i.* 1, come to an end. 2, decide.

con·clu'sion (kən-kloo'zhən) *n.* 1, the end. 2, the final part or stage. 3, a result; outcome. 4, a proposition inferred logically from premises. —**con·clu'sive** (-siv) *adj.* decisive.

con·coct' (kən-kokt') *v.t.* 1, combine and prepare, as in cooking. 2, devise; contrive, as a plot. —**con·coc'tion,** *n.*

con·com'i·tant (kon-kom'ə-tənt) *adj.* attending; going together. —*n.* an accompanying thing or circumstance.

con'cord (kon'kôrd) *n.* 1, harmony; unanimity. 2, peace. 3, an agreement; a treaty.

con·cord'ance (kon-kôr'dəns) *n.* 1, agreement. 2, an index of words, as of those in the Bible.

con·cor'dat (kon-kôr'dat) *n.* a treaty.

con'course (kon'kôrs) *n.* 1, a throng; crowd. 2, an open place, as a public square.

con'crete (kon'krēt) *adj.* 1, existing in material form; real, not abstract. 2, specific, not general. 3, consisting of concrete. —*n.* a building material made of sand, cement, etc. —**con·crete'ness,** *n.* —**con·cre'tion,** *n.*

con'cu·bine' (kon'kū-bīn') *n.* a woman cohabiting with a man but not married to him. —**con·cu'bi·nage** (-bə-nij) *n.*

con·cu'pis·cence (kon-kū'pə-səns) *n.* sensual appetite or desire. —**con·cu'pis·cent,** *adj.*

con·cur' (kən-kér') *v.i.* [-**curred'**, -**cur'ring**] 1, happen together; coincide; exist side by side. 2, agree in opinion. —**con·cur'rence,** *n.* —**con·cur'rent,** *adj.*

con·cus'sion (kən-kush'ən) *n.* the shock occasioned by a collision or blow.

con·demn' (kən-dem') *v.t.* 1, express disapprobation of; censure. 2, find guilty; sentence to punishment. 3, pronounce unfit for use. 4, claim for public use. —**con"dem·na'tion,** *n.*

con·dense' (kən-dens') *v.t. & i.* 1, make more compact. 2, express in fewer words. 3, compress; reduce (gas, vapor) to a liquid or solid. —**con"den·sa'tion,** *n.*

con·dens'er (-sər) *n.* a device for liquefying vapors, concentrating light rays or electric current, etc.

con"de·scend' (kon"di-send') *v.i.* 1, deal as an equal with one of inferior rank. 2, waive ceremony or dignity; deign (to do something). 3, deal patronizingly, as though conscious of superior rank. —**con"de·scen'sion,** *n.*

con·dign' (kən-dīn') *adj.* fitting; deserved.

con'di·ment (kon'də-mənt) *n.* something to give relish to food, as pepper.

con·di'tion (kən-dish'ən) *n.* 1, a mode or state of being of a person or thing. 2, social rank. 3, state of health. 4, a stipulation or provision; a prerequisite. —*v.t.* 1, limit by, or subject to, a condition. 2, put into a certain condition. —**con·di'tion·al,** *adj.* provisional.

con·dole' (kən-dōl') *v.i.* express sympathy for grief or misfortune. —**con·do'lence,** *n.*

con·done' (kən-dōn') *v.t.* forgive, overlook, extenuate, or justify (another's offense). —**con·done'ment,** **con"do·na'tion** (kon"də-nā'shən) *n.*

con'dor (kon'dər) *n.* a large So. Amer. vulture.

con·duce' (kən-doos') *v.i.* (with *to*) contribute to a result. —**con·du'cive** (-siv) *adj.*

con·duct' (kən-dukt') *v.t.* 1, act as leader of; guide; escort. 2, manage; carry on. 3, behave (oneself). 4, transmit; convey. —*v.i.* act as musical director. —*n.* (kon'dukt) 1, management. 2, deportment. 3, escort. —**con·duc'tion,** *n.* —**con·duc'tive,** *adj.*

con"duc·tiv'i·ty (kon"duk-tiv'ə-tē) *n.* power of transmitting heat, electricity, etc.

con·duc'tor (kən-duk'tər) *n.* 1, one who conducts, esp. an orchestra; leader. 2, the person in charge of a train, trolley car, etc. 3, a substance that transmits heat, electricity, etc.

con'duit (kon'dit) *n.* a channel or tube that conducts fluids, electric wires, etc.

cone (kōn) *n.* **1,** a solid generated by a line passing through a fixed point and a given plane curve. **2,** anything resembling this figure.

Cones
Right   *Oblique*

con·fab'u·late" (kən-fab'yə-lāt") *v.i.* converse. —**con'fab,** *n.* & *v.i.* (*Colloq.*).

con·fec'tion (kən-fek'shən) *n.* **1,** a sweet preparation, esp. candy. **2,** a frilly dress. —**con·fec'tion·er,** *n.* one who sells candy. —**con·fec'tion·er·y** (-ner-ē) *n.* his shop.

con·fed·er·a·cy (kən-fed'ə-rə-sē) *n.* **1,** a league; alliance. **2,** (*cap.* with *the*) the eleven southern states that seceded from the U. S. in 1860-61.

con·fed·er·ate (kən-fed'ər-ət) *adj.* **1,** united in a league; party to a confederation. **2,** (*cap.*) pert. to the Confederacy. —*n.* **1,** a member of a confederation. **2,** an accomplice. —*v.t.* & *i.* (-rāt") unite in a league. —**con·fed'er·a'tion,** *n.* a league.

con·fer' (kən-fēr') *v.t.* [-ferred', -fer'ring] (with *on*) bestow. —*v.i.* consult together.

con'fer·ence (kon'fər-əns) *n.* **1,** a meeting for consultation. **2,** a league, as of churches, athletic teams, etc.

con·fess' (kən-fes') *v.t.* **1,** admit (having done something discreditable); acknowledge (guilt or belief). **2,** (of a priest) hear the confession of. —*v.i.* admit a crime, fault, etc.

con·fes'sion (kən-fesh'ən) *n.* the act or a statement of confessing. —**con·fes'sion·al** (-əl) *n.* a booth where a priest hears confessions.

con·fes'sor (kən-fes'ər) *n.* a priest who hears confessions.

con·fet'ti (kən-fet'ē) *n.* bits of colored paper thrown as a joyous gesture.

con"fi·dant' (kon"fi-dänt') *n.* one trusted with secrets. —**con"fi·dante',** *n. fem.*

con·fide' (kən-fīd') *v.t.* **1,** entrust. **2,** reveal privately. —*v.i.* (with *in*) **1,** have trust. **2,** entrust a secret.

con'fi·dence (kon'fi-dəns) *n.* **1,** firm trust; reliance. **2,** self-assurance; boldness. **3,** an assured state of mind. **4,** a state of trust and intimacy. **5,** a secret confided. —**confidence man,** a swindler.

con'fi·dent (kon'fi-dənt) *adj.* **1,** fully assured. **2,** bold; self-assured.

con"fi·den'tial (kon"fi-den'shəl) *adj.* **1,** secret; private. **2,** entrusted with private affairs. **3,** intimate.

con·fig"u·ra'tion (kən-fig"yə-rā'shən) *n.* **1,** form. **2,** placement.

con·fine' (kən-fīn') *v.t.* **1,** restrict within bounds; imprison. **2,** keep indoors, as by sickness, esp. by childbirth. —**con·fine'ment,** *n.*

con'fines (kon'fīnz) *n.pl.* boundaries.

con·firm' (kən-fērm') *v.t.* **1,** establish more firmly; strengthen. **2,** put past doubt; verify. **3,** make valid. **4,** admit to church membership. —**con"fir·ma'tion,** *n.* —**con·firm'a·to"ry,** *adj.*

con·firmed' (kən-fērmd') *adj.* **1,** settled. **2,** inveterate; chronic.

con'fis·cate" (kon'fis-kāt") *v.t.* **1,** appropriate, by way of penalty, to public use. **2,** take away by, or as if by, authority. —**con"fis·ca'tion,** *n.*

con"fla·gra'tion (kon"flə-grā'shən) *n.* a large-scale fire.

con·flict' (kən-flikt') *v.i.* clash; be contrary. —*n.* (kon'flikt) **1,** a combat. **2,** discord; antagonism.

con'flu·ence (kon'flū-əns) *n.* **1,** a flowing together of streams; their place of meeting. **2,** the coming together of people; a crowd. —**con'flu·ent,** *adj.*

con·form' (kən-fôrm') *v.t.* bring into harmony; adapt. —*v.i.* be in accord; comply.

con"for·ma'tion (kon"fər-mā'shən) *n.* **1,** structure. **2,** adaptation.

con·form'ist *n.* one who conforms, esp. to the usages of the Church of England.

con·form'i·ty (-ə-tē) *n.* accordance; agreement.

con·found' (kon-fownd') *v.t.* **1,** throw into confusion; perplex; astound. **2,** mistake for another.

con·found'ed *adj.* (*Colloq.*) damnable.

con·frere' (kon'frār) *n.* a colleague.

con·front' (kən-frunt') *v.t.* **1,** stand facing; meet. **2,** meet in hostility. **3,** bring face to face (with).

con·fuse' (kən-fūz') *v.t.* **1,** throw into disorder. **2,** perplex; disconcert. **3,** mistake for another. —**con·fu'sion,** *n.*

con·fute' (kən-fūt') *v.t.* prove false; disprove. —**con"fu·ta'tion,** *n.*

con·geal' (kən-jēl') *v.t.* & *i.* freeze; stiffen; harden, esp. as an effect of cold.

con·gen'ial (kən-jēn'yəl) *adj.* **1,** kindred; like; sympathetic. **2,** agreeable; pleasing. —**con·ge"ni·al'i·ty,** *n.*

con·gen'i·tal (kən-jen'ə-təl) *adj.* existing at birth.

con'ger (kong'gər) *n.* a large marine eel.

con·gest' (kən-jest') *v.t.* **1,** overcrowd. **2,** overfill with blood. —**con·ges'tion,** *n.*

con·glom'er·ate (kən-glom'ər-ət) *adj.* collected or clustered together. —*n.* a mass of varied and incongruous materials. —*v.t.* & *i.* (-rāt') collect into a mass. —**con·glom'er·a'tion,** *n.*

con·grat'u·late'' (kən-grach'ə-lāt') *v.t.* express pleasure at the happiness or triumph of (a person); felicitate. —**con·grat'u·la'tion,** *n.*

con''gre·gate'' (kon'gri-gāt'') *v.t.* & *i.* gather together; assemble.

con''gre·ga'tion (kon''gri-gā'shən) *n.* **1,** act of congregating. **2,** a gathering, esp. of persons for religious worship.

con''gre·ga'tion·al *adj.* **1,** pert. to a congregation. **2,** (*cap.*) pert. to a certain Protestant denomination.

con'gress (kon'gris) *n.* **1,** a formal meeting of delegates for discussion; a conference. **2,** (*cap.*) the legislative body of the U.S. **3,** intercourse. —**con·gres'sion·al** (kən-gresh'ən-əl) *adj.* —**con'gress·man,** *n.* (often *cap.*) a member of the U.S. Congress. —**con'gress·wom''an,** *n.fem.*

con'gru·ent (kong'groo-ənt) *adj.* **1,** agreeing; harmonious. **2,** (*Geom.*) superposable. —**con'gru·ence,** *n.*

con·gru'i·ty (kong-groo'ə-tē) *n.* congruousness.

con'gru·ous (kong'groo-əs) *adj.* well adapted; appropriate; consistent. —**con'gru·ous·ness,** *n.*

con'ic (kon'ik) *adj.* (also, **con'i·cal**) having the shape of or like a cone. —*n.* (*Geom.*) an ellipse, parabola, or hyperbola.

co'ni·fer (kon'i-fər) *n.* a cone-bearing plant. —**co·nif'er·ous** (kō-nif'ər-əs) *adj.*

con·jec'ture (kən-jek'chər) *n.* an opinion not founded on sufficient evidence; a guess; a surmise. —*v.t.* & *i.* guess. —**con·jec'tur·al,** *adj.*

con·join' (kən-join') *v.t.* & *i.* join; associate. —**con·joint',** *adj.*

con'ju·gal (kon'jə-gəl) *adj.* pert. to marriage; connubial.

con'ju·gate'' (kon'jə-gāt'') *v.t.* give in order the forms of (a verb). —*adj.* formed in a pair; coupled. —**con''ju·ga'tion,** *n.* **1,** inflection of verbs. **2,** conjunction.

con·junct' (kən-junkt') *adj.* joined together; united. —**con·junc'tive,** *adj.*

con·junc'tion (kən-junk'shən) *n.* **1,** act of joining. **2,** union; connection. **3,** a word that joins sentences, clauses, phrases, or words, as *and.*

con·junc''ti·vi'tis (kən-junk''tə-vi'tis) *n.* inflammation of the mucous membrane of the eyelids.

con·junc'ture (kən-junk'chər) *n.* **1,** a combination of circumstances. **2,** a crisis.

con·jure (kon'jər) *v.t.* & *i.* **1,** call up or bring about by, or as if by, magic; practice magic. **2,** (kən-jūr') entreat solemnly. —**con'ju·ra'tion,** *n.*

con'jur·er (kon'jər-ər) *n.* a magician. Also, **con'jur·or.**

conk (konk) (*Slang*) *v.t.* thump. —*v.i.* (with *out*) fail; stop running.

con·nect' (kə-nekt') *v.t.* & *i.* **1,** associate mentally. **2,** join; associate closely. **3,** (with *with*) establish communication or juncture. —**con·nec'tive,** *adj.* & *n.*

con·nec'tion (kə-nek'shən) *n.* **1,** the state of being connected; union; a connecting part. **2,** family relationship; a distant relative. **3,** (*pl.*) associates. **4,** continuity of words or ideas. **5,** a bond; tie. **6,** (often *pl.*) a meeting of trains, etc., for transfer of passengers.

con·nip'tion (kə-nip'shən) *n.* (*Colloq.*) hysterical excitement.

con·nive' (kə-nīv') *v.i.* secretly abet or permit a wrong. —**con·niv'ance,** *n.*

con''nois·seur' (kon''ə-sēr') *n.* a discriminating critic.

con·note' (kə-nōt') *v.t.* imply; suggest; denote secondarily. —**con''no·ta'tion,** *n.*

con·nu'bi·al (kə-nū'bē-əl) *adj.* pert. to marriage.

con'quer (kong'kər) *v.t.* **1,** subdue by force. **2,** overcome; surmount. —**con'quer·or,** *n.*

con'quest (kon'kwest) *n.* **1,** subjugation by force; victory. **2,** that which is subdued or won.

con''san·guin'i·ty (kon''sang-gwin'ə-tē) *n.* relationship by blood.

con'science (kon'shəns) *n.* one's moral sense of right and wrong.

con''sci·en'tious (kon''shē-en'shəs) *adj.* **1,** scrupulous. **2,** done according to conscience.

con'scion·a·ble (kon'shən-ə-bəl) *adj.* conforming to one's conscience; just.

con'scious (kon'shəs) *adj.* **1,** aware of one's existence, feelings, and thoughts. **2,** in a waking, not comatose, state. **3,** aware. **4,** intentional. —**con'scious·ness,** *n.*

con'script (kon'skript) *n.* one pressed into military or naval service. —*v.t.* (kən-skript') draft. —**con·scrip'tion,** *n.*

con'se·crate'' (kon'si-krāt'') *v.t.* dedicate to a sacred purpose or service. —**con''se·cra'tion,** *n.*

con·sec'u·tive (kən-sek'ū-tiv) *adj.* succeeding one another in regular order.

con·sen'sus (kən-sen'səs) n. 1, agreement in opinion, feeling, etc. 2, general agreement, as of opinion.

con·sent' (kən-sent') v.i. agree; yield; accede. —n. voluntary compliance; permission.

con'se·quence (kon'sə-kwens) n. 1, that which follows as the result of some preceding act, cause, etc. 2, significance. 3, distinction; importance in rank, etc.

con'se·quent (kon'sə-kwent) adj. 1, resulting. 2, following logically. —con'se·quent·ly, adv. in consequence of; therefore.

con'se·quen'tial (kon"si-kwen'shəl) adj. 1, important; 2, consequent.

con'ser·va'tion (kon"sər-vā'shən) n. preservation, esp. of natural resources.

con·serv'a·tive (kən-sûr'və-tiv) adj. 1, opposed to change. 2, moderate; not extreme. 3, protecting from loss, waste, or injury. —n. a conservative person. —con·serv'a·tism, n.

con·serv'a·to·ry (-tôr'ē) n. 1, a greenhouse. 2, a school, esp. of music.

con·serve' (kən-sûrv') v.t. preserve from loss, waste, etc. —n. (kon'sûrv) a fruit preserve.

con·sid'er (kən-sid'ər) v.i. 1, ponder; study. 2, make allowance for. 3, hold in esteem. 4, believe; judge.

con·sid'er·a·ble adj. 1, notable; important. 2, not small. —n. (Colloq.) much.

con·sid'er·ate (-ət) adj. thoughtful of others.

con·sid'er·a'tion n. 1, careful reflection. 2, thoughtfulness of others. 3, something to be reckoned with. 4, motive; reason. 5, a fee; compensation.

con·sid'ered (-ərd) adj. '1, taken into account. 2, deliberate; intentional.

con·sid'er·ing prep. taking into account; in view of.

con·sign' (kən-sīn') v.t. 1, hand over; commit formally. 2, assign. 3, send or address (goods) to, for sale or custody. —con·sign'or, n.

con·sign'ment (-mənt) n. 1, act of consigning; something consigned; a shipment. 2, the condition that goods received will not be paid for unless they are sold.

con·sist' (kən-sist') v.i. (with of) be composed; (with in) exist.

con·sist'en·cy (-ən-sē) n. 1, solidity; degree of density, esp. of liquids. 2, harmony; correspondence. 3, state of being consistent.

con·sist'ent (-ənt) adj. 1, congruous; in accord. 2, conforming

regularly to the same pattern, habits, principles, etc.

con·sis'to·ry (kən-sis'tə-rē) n. an ecclesiastical council or meeting.

con'so·la'tion (kon"sə-lā'shən) n. act or effect of consoling; solace.

con·sole' (kən-sōl') v.t. comfort in time of sorrow; solace.

con'sole (kon'sōl) 1, the cabinet containing the keyboard, etc. of an organ. 2, a floor cabinet, as for a radio. 3, a supporting bracket.

con·sol'i·date' (kən-sol'ə-dāt') v.t. 1, make solid or firm; strengthen. 2, unite firmly in one body; combine. —con·sol'i·da'tion, n.

con'som·mé' (kon"sə-mā') n. a strong, clear meat soup.

con'so·nant (kon'sə-nənt) adj. 1, agreeing in sound. 2, consistent. 3, relating to consonants. —n. an alphabetical element other than a vowel. —con'so·nance, n.

con'sort (kon'sôrt) n. 1, a husband or wife. 2, a vessel sailing with another. —v.i. (kən-sôrt') (with with) associate; agree.

con·spic'u·ous (kən-spik'ū-əs) adj. 1, easily seen. 2, attracting attention. —con·spic'u·ous·ness, n.

con·spir'a·cy (kən-spir'ə-sē) n. a combination of persons for an evil purpose; a plot. —con·spir'a·tor, n. one who joins in a conspiracy.

con·spire' (kən-spīr') v.i. 1, combine for an unlawful purpose; plot secretly. 2, concur to one end.

con'sta·ble (kon'stə-bəl) n. an officer of the peace; a policeman.

con·stab'u·lar·y (kən-stab'ye-lər-ē) n. a body of constables; police. —adj. [also, con·stab'u·lar (-lər)] pert. to police work.

con'stan·cy (kon'stən-sē) n. state of being constant; fidelity.

con'stant (kon'stənt) adj. 1, regularly recurring. 2, ceaseless. 3, steadfast; resolute. 4, unvarying.

Constellation

con'stel·la'tion (kon"stə-lā'shən) n. a group of fixed stars.

con″ster·na′tion (kon″stər-nā′-shən) n. terrified amazement; dismay.

con″sti·pa′tion (kon″sti-pā′shən) n. difficulty in moving the bowels. —con′sti·pate″ (-pāt″) v.t.

con·stit′u·en·cy (kən-stich′oo-ən-sē) n. a body of voters.

con·stit′u·ent (kən-stich′oo-ənt) n. 1, a necessary part. 2, a voter or resident in a legislative district. —adj. being one necessary part.

con′sti·tute″ (kon′sti-tūt″) v.t. 1, make up; form as a necessary part. 2, establish by lawful authority. 3, appoint.

con″sti·tu′tion (kon″sti-too′shən) n. 1, natural composition, qualities, structure, etc. 2, a code of principles or laws forming the basis of a government or organization; the document of such a code.

con″sti·tu′tion·al (-əl) adj. 1, inherent; basic; essential. 2, beneficial to health. —con″sti·tu″tion·al′i·ty (-al′ə-tē) n.

con·strain′ (kən-strān′) v.t. 1, compel; oblige. 2, bind; confine. 3, repress; restrain. —con·straint′, n.

con·strict′ (kən-strikt′) v.t. cause to shrink; cramp; crush. —con·stric′tion, n. —con·stric′tor, n.

con·struct′ (kən-strukt′) v.t. 1, build; make. 2, frame in the mind. —con·struc′tor, n.

con·struc′tion (kən-struk′shən) n. 1, the act or method of building or constructing; a structure; an interpretation. 2, (Gram.) arrangement and connection of words in a sentence. 3, act of construing.

con·struc′tive (-tiv) adj. 1, building; beneficial to progress. 2, inferential.

con·strue′ (kən-stroo′) v.t. 1, analyze grammatically. 2, translate. 3, interpret.

con′sul (kon′səl) n. 1, a diplomatic officer chiefly concerned with trade. 2, (Hist.) a chief magistrate. —con′su·lar, adj. —con′su·late (sə-lət) n.

con·sult′ (kən-sult′) v.t. 1, ask the advice of; refer to. 2, consider; have regard for. —v.i. confer. —con·sult′ant, n.

con″sul·ta′tion (kon″səl-tā′shən) n. act of consulting; conference. —con·sul′ta·tive (kən-sul′tə-tiv) adj. advisory.

con·sume′ (kən-soom′) v.t. 1, devour; eat; destroy. 2, use up; spend, as time. —con·sum′er, n. the ultimate user of a commodity.

con′sum·mate″ (kon′sə-māt″) v.t. raise to the highest degree; perfect. —adj. (kən-sum′it) complete; perfect. —con″sum·ma′tion, n.

con·sump′tion (kən-sump′shən) n. 1, the act or effect of consuming; the amount consumed. 2, tuberculosis of the lungs.

con·sump′tive (-tiv) adj. wasteful. —n. & adj. (one) affected with tuberculosis.

con′tact (kon′takt) n. 1, a meeting or touching of two things or (Colloq.) persons. 2, a business or social acquaintance or introduction. —v.t. & i. (Colloq.) get in touch (with). —contact man, a go-between.

con·ta′gion (kən-tā′jən) n. 1, the communication of a disease by contact; the disease; plague. 2, rapid spread of disease, feelings, etc.

con·ta′gious (kən-tā′jəs) adj. 1, communicable; spreading. 2, (Colloq.) hard to resist. —con·ta′gious·ness, n.

con·tain′ (kən-tān′) v.t. 1, keep within bounds; restrain; enclose. 2, comprise; have a capacity of; hold. —con·tain′er, n. a vessel, can, box, bottle, etc.

con·tam′i·nate (kən-tam′i-nāt″) v.t. make impure by mixture; taint; pollute. —con·tam′i·na′tion, n.

con·temn′ (kən-tem′) v.t. scorn.

con′tem·plate″ (kon′təm-plāt″) v.t. 1, view or reflect upon attentively. 2, intend; expect. —v.i. meditate. —con″tem·pla′tion, n. —con″tem·pla′tive, adj.

con″tem″po·ra′ne·ous (kən-tem″pə-rā′nē-əs) adj. contemporary.

con·tem′po·rar′y (kən-tem′pə-rer′ē) adj. 1, living or occurring at the same time. 2, of the same age. —n. a person contemporary with the subject.

con·tempt′ (kən-tempt′) n. 1, the act of despising. 2, a feeling of disdain. 3, (Law) defiance of a court, etc.

con·tempt′i·ble (kən-temp′tə-bəl) adj. meriting scorn; despicable. —con·tempt′i·bil′i·ty, n.

con·temp′tu·ous (kən-temp′-choo-əs) adj. expressing disdain; scornful. —con·temp′tu·ous·ness, n.

con·tend′ (kən-tend′) v.i. 1, compete; struggle in opposition. 2, assert in argument.

con·tent′ (kon′tent) n. 1, (pl.) all that is contained in a receptacle. 2, (pl.) subject matter, as of a book. 3, the gist or substance, as of a sermon, etc. 4, capacity.

con·tent′ (kən-tent′) adj. satisfied; easy in mind. —v.t. satisfy. —content′ed, adj. satisfied; placidly happy. —con·tent′ment, n.

con·ten′tion (kən-ten′shən) n. 1, act of contending; a struggle, debate, etc. 2, rivalry; strife.

con·ten′tious (kən-ten′shəs) adj. argumentative. —con·ten′tious·ness, n.

con'test (kon'test) *n.* 1, a struggle; fight; controversy. 2, a competitive game. —*v.t.* (kən-test') 1, compete or vie for. 2, challenge; dispute. —**con·test'ant**, *n.* one who competes.

con'text (kon'tekst) *n.* related or adjoining passages of a book, etc. —**con·tex'tu·al**, *adj.*

con·tig'u·ous (kən-tig'ū-əs) *adj.* touching at the border; adjoining. —**con''ti·gu'i·ty**, *n.*

con'ti·nence (kon'tə-nəns) *n.* self-restraint.

con'ti·nent (kon'ti-nənt) *n.* 1, one of the six principal land masses of the globe. 2, (*cap.* with *the*) the mainland of Europe. —*adj.* exercising continence; chaste. —**con''ti·nen'tal**, *adj.* pert. to a continent, esp. (*cap.*) the mainland of Europe.

con·tin'gen·cy (kən-tin'jən-sē) *n.* 1, a circumstance; what may happen. 2, dependence.

con·tin'gent (kən-tin'jənt) *adj.* 1, depending on something not certain; conditional. 2, accidental. —*n.* a quota; a delegation.

con·tin'u·al (kən-tin'ū-əl) *adj.* constant; often repeated.

con·tin'u·ance (-əns) *n.* 1, a keeping on; duration. 2, uninterrupted succession. 3, (*Law*) postponement.

con·tin''u·a'tion (-ā'shən) *n.* 1, act of continuing; state of being continued. 2, an extension or prolongation.

con·tin'ue (kən-tin'ū) *v.t.* 1, prolong; extend. 2, keep on with; not cease from. 3, resume the course of. 4, retain, as in office. —*v.i.* 1, persist; keep on. 2, resume after interruption. 3, abide or stay. 4, last; endure.

con''ti·nu'i·ty (kon''ti-nū'ə-tē) *n.* 1, unbroken connection or sequence. 2, a script for a motion picture, radio show, etc.

con·tin'u·ous (kən-tin'ū-əs) *adj.* without cessation or interruption.

con·tort' (kən-tôrt') *v.t.* twist out of shape.

con·tor'tion (kən-tôr'shən) *n.* a twisting out of shape. —**con·tor'tion·ist**, *n.* a performer who contorts his body.

con'tour (kon'tŭr) *n. & adj.* the outline, as of a figure, coast, etc. —contour farming, prevention of erosion by tilling land according to its shape.

con·tra- *pref.* against; opposite.

con''tra·band' (kon''trə-band'') *adj.* prohibited by law from being imported or exported. —*n.* 1, smuggling. 2, smuggled goods.

con''tra·cep'tion (kon''trə-sep'-shən) *n.* birth control. —**con''tra·cep'tive**, *n. & adj.*

con'tract (kon'trakt) *n.* 1, a legal or business agreement. 2, in certain games, the highest bid. —*v.t.* (kən-trakt') 1, make smaller; condense; abridge. 2, acquire (a habit, disease, etc.); incur; enter into. —*v.i.* 1, enter into an agreement. 2, shrink.

con·trac'tile (kən-trak'til) *adj.* having the function or power of contracting, as a muscle.

con·trac'tion (-shən) *n.* 1, a shrinking; shrinkage. 2, a shortened form of a word or phrase.

con·trac'tor (-tər) *n.* one who agrees to undertake a project, esp. in construction.

con·trac'tu·al (kən-trak'choo-əl) *adj.* pert. to a contract.

con''tra·dict' (kon''trə-dikt') *v.t.* 1, assert the contrary of. 2, deny the words of. 3, be contrary to. —**con''tra·dic'tion**, *n.* —**con''tra·dic'to·ry**, *adj. & n.*

con·tral'to (kən-tral'tō) *n.* [*pl.* -tos] the lowest female voice.

con·trap'tion (kən-trap'shən) *n.* (*Colloq.*) a contrivance or gadget.

con''tra·pun'tal (kon''trə-punt'əl) *adj.* pert. to counterpoint.

con'tra·ry (kon'trer-ē) *adj.* 1, diametrically opposed; opposite. 2, conflicting. 3, perverse. —*n.* the opposite in sense or meaning. —**con·tra'ri·ness**, *n.*

con·trast' (kən-tràst') *v.t. & i.* compare by showing differences. —*n.* (kon'trast) 1, the act of contrasting. 2, a striking difference.

con''tra·vene' (kon''trə-vēn') *v.t.* 1, conflict with. 2, violate. —**con''tra·ven'tion**, *n.*

con''tre·temps'' (kon''trə-toǹ'') *n.* [*pl.* -con·tre·temps''] an embarrassing occurrence.

con·trib'ute (kən-trib'yət) *v.t.* 1, give with others, as to a charity. 2, write for a magazine, etc. —*v.i.* have a share; be of use. —**con''tri·bu'tion** (-bū'shən) *n.* —**con·trib'u·tor**, *n.* —**con·trib'u·to·ry**, *adj.* helping toward a result.

con·trite' (kən-trīt') *adj.* humbly penitent. —**con·tri'tion** (-trish'ən) *n.*

con·triv'ance (kən-trī'vəns) *n.* 1, a mechanical device. 2, a means of doing.

con·trive' (kən-trīv') *v.t.* devise or bring about by clever planning. —*v.i.* 1, scheme. 2, (with *to*) manage to.

con·trol' (kən-trōl') *v.t.* [-trolled', -trol'ling] 1, exercise power over; restrain; govern; dominate. 2, regulate. 3, verify by comparison. —*n.* 1, restraint. 2, authority to govern, regulate, or manage. 3, the apparatus for operating a machine. —**con·trol'ler**, *n.* comptroller.

con''tro·ver'sial (kon''trə-vēr'-shəl) *adj.* being or causing a controversy.

con'tro·ver"sy (kon'trə-vėr"sē) *n.* contention; an argument or debate.

con"tro·vert' (kon"trə-vėrt') *v.t.* 1, argue against; dispute or deny. 2, discuss; debate. —**con"tro·vert'i·ble,** *adj.*

con·tu·ma·cy (kon'tyū-mə-sē) *n.* contempt of lawful authority. —**con'tu·ma'cious** (-mā'shəs) *adj.*

con·tu·me·ly (kon'tyū-mə-lē) *n.* contemptuous abuse. —**con"tu·me'li·ous** (-mē'lē-əs) *adj.*

con·tu'sion (kən-too'zhən) *n.* a bruise.

co·nun'drum (kə-nun'drəm) *n.* a riddle; a hard question.

con"va·lesce' (kon"və-les') *v.i.* recover gradually after sickness. —**con"va·les'cence,** *n.* —**con"va·les'cent,** *adj. & n.*

con·vene' (kən-vēn') *v.t. & i.* assemble for some public purpose.

con·ven'ience (kən-vēn'yəns) *n.* 1, suitability; accessibility; opportuneness. 2, (often *pl.*) that which adds to comfort. —**con·ven'ient,** *adj.*

con'vent (kon'vənt) *n.* a home of nuns; nunnery.

con·ven'tion (kən-ven'shən) *n.* 1, an assembly; a formal meeting. 2, an agreement, esp. international. 3, a fixed custom or usage. —**con·ven'tion·al,** *adj.* conforming to custom. —**con·ven"tion·al'i·ty,** *n.*

con·verge' (kən-vėrj') *v.i.* 1, incline toward each other, as lines; tend to meet. 2, approach. —**con·ver'gence,** *n.* —**con·ver'gent,** *adj.*

con·ver'sant (kon'vər-sənt) *adj.* acquainted; well-informed.

con"ver·sa'tion (kon"vər-sā'shən) *n.* informal, familiar talk. —**con"ver·sa'tion·al,** *adj.*

con·verse' (kən-vėrs') *v.i.* talk informally. —*n.* (kon'vėrs) informal talk; conversation.

con'verse (kon'vėrs) *adj.* transposed; reversed. —*n.* the reverse; opposite.

con·ver'sion (kən-vėr'shən) *n.* act or effect of converting; change.

con·vert' (kən-vėrt') *v.t.* 1, change into another form; exchange. 2, persuade to change in policy, religion, etc. 3, (*Law*) appropriate illegally. —*n.* (kon'vėrt) a converted person, esp. as to religion. —**con·vert'er, con·ver'tor,** *n.*

con·vert'i·ble *adj.* 1, capable of being converted. 2, of an automobile, having a folding top. —*n.* a convertible automobile. —**con·vert"i·bil'i·ty,** *n.*

con·vex' (kon-veks') *adj.* curved like the outside surface of a sphere. —**con·vex'i·ty,** *n.*

con·vey' (kən-vā') *v.t.* 1, carry from one place to another; transport. 2, transmit. 3, communicate; impart. 3, (*Law*) transfer title of.

con·vey'ance *n.* 1, act or result of conveying. 2, a vehicle.

con·vey'or *n.* a contrivance for conveying, as a moving belt.

con·vict' (kən-vikt') *v.t.* prove or find guilty. —*n.* (kon'vikt) a convicted prisoner.

con·vic'tion (kən-vik'shən) *n.* 1, act or effect of convicting or convincing. 2, a firm belief.

con·vince' (kən-vins') *v.t.* cause (a person) to believe. —**con·vinc'ing,** *adj.* assuring by proof; persuasive.

con·viv'i·al (kən-viv'ē-əl) *adj.* 1, fond of feasting; gay; jovial. 2, festive. —**con·viv"i·al'i·ty,** *n.*

con"vo·ca'tion (kon"vō-kā'shən) *n.* 1, act or result of convoking. 2, an assembly.

con·voke' (kən-vōk') *v.t.* summon to assemble.

con"vo·lute" (kon'və-loot") *adj.* rolled up; coiled. —**con"vo·lu'tion,** *n.*

con·voy' (kən-voi') *v.t.* escort for protection. —*n.* (kon'voi) a protecting force or ship; a fleet or group under escort.

con·vulse' (kən-vuls') *v.t.* 1, contract spasmodically. 2, disturb violently. 3, cause to laugh uncontrollably. —**con·vul'sion,** *n.* —**con·vul'sive** (-siv) *adj.*

co'ny (kō'nē) *n.* rabbit fur dyed to imitate sealskin.

coo (koo) *v.i.* murmur like a pigeon or dove; talk fondly.

cook (kûk) *v.t.* 1, prepare (food) by heating; apply heat to. 2, (with *up*) concoct. —*v.i.* 1, undergo cooking. 2, work as a cook. —*n.* one who cooks food. —**cook'er·y** (-ə-rē) *n.*

cook'ie (kûk'ē) *n.* a small, flat cake. Also, **cook'y.**

cool (kool) *adj.* 1, neither warm nor very cold. 2, calm; not excited. 3, lacking cordiality. 4, (of colors) green, blue, or violet. 5, (*Colloq.*) not overstated. —*v.t. & i.* make or become cool or cooler. —**cool'ness,** *n.*

cool'er *n.* 1, a cold room or space. 2, (*Slang*) jail.

coo'lie (koo'lē) *n.* a Chinese unskilled laborer.

coon (koon) *n.* raccoon. —**coon's age** (*Slang*) a long time.

coop (koop) *n.* 1, a small crate or pen, as for poultry. 2, any small place. —*v.t.* (with *up*) confine.

coop'er (koo'pər) *n.* one who

makes barrels and casks. —coop'er·age (-ij) n.

co·öp'er·ate (kō-op'e-rāt″) v.i. work together toward a common goal. —co·öp″er·a'tion, n.

co·öp'er·a·tive (-tiv) adj. willing to coöperate. —n. [also (Slang) co'-öp″] a business owned by those it serves or buys from.

co·ör'di·nate (kō-ôr'də-nāt″) v.t. bring into harmony or proper relation. —adj. (-nət) of the same rank or degree. —co·ör″di·na'tion, n.

coot (koot) n. 1, a swimming and diving bird. 2, (Colloq.) a fool.

coot'ie (koo'tē) n. (Slang) a louse.

cop (kop) n. (Slang) a policeman. —v.t. [copped, cop'ping] 1, steal. 2, catch.

cope (kōp) n. a mantle worn by priests. —v.i. contend or struggle successfully.

cop'ing (kō'ping) n. the uppermost stones or bricks in a wall.

co'pi·ous (kō'pē-əs) adj. abundant; plentiful. —co'pi·ous·ness, n.

cop'per (kop'ər) n. 1, a tough, ductile metallic element, no. 29, symbol Cu. 2, its color, reddish brown. 3, a penny. 4, (Slang) a policeman. —cop'per·y, adj.

cop'per·head″ n. a venomous Amer. snake.

cop'ra (kop'rə) n. the dried meat of the coconut, yielding oil.

copse (kops) n. a thicket.

cop'u·la (kop'yə-lə) n. 1, a link or coupling. 2, (Gram.) the verb to be.

cop'u·late (-lāt″) v.i. unite. —cop″-u·la'tion, n. —cop'u·la″tive (-lā″tiv) adj.

cop'y (kop'ē) n. 1, an imitation; a reproduction. 2, one of a number of duplicates, as a book, magazine, etc. 3, matter to be set in type. —v.t. 1, make a copy of. 2, imitate. —cop'y·ist, n.

cop'y·hold″er n. an assistant to a proofreader.

cop'y·read″er n. one who edits copy.

cop'y·right″ n. the sole right to reproduce a literary or artistic work. —v.t. secure such right on.

co·quette' (kō-ket') n. a flirt.

cor'al (kôr'əl) n. 1, a hard, horny skeleton of tiny marine animals. 2, a yellowish-red color.

cord (kôrd) n. 1, string or small rope. 2, any ropelike structure; a tendon. 3, a cubic measure, 8 x 4 x 4 ft., used esp. for firewood. 3, a rib or ridge in a textile. —cord'age, n. cords, ropes, etc.

cor'dial (kôr'jəl) adj. friendly; hearty. —n. a sweet, aromatic liquor. —cor·dial'i·ty (-jal'ə-tē) n.

cor·dil'le·ra (kôr-dil'ə-rə) n. an extensive chain of mountains.

cord'ite (kôr'dīt) n. a smokeless explosive powder.

cor'don (kôr'dən) n. 1, a series or line, as of forts. 2, an ornamental braid.

cor'du·roy″ (kôr'də-roi″) n. a heavy, ribbed fabric; (pl.) trousers of this fabric.

core (kōr) n. 1, the innermost or essential part; pith. 2, the center of an apple, pear, etc.

co″re·op'sis (kôr'ē-op'sis) n. a plant with a bright-yellow flower.

co-″re·spond'ent (kō″rə-spon'dənt) n. a joint defendant in a divorce suit.

co″ri·an'der (kôr'ē-an'dər) n. an herb; its seeds, used in cookery.

cork (kôrk) n. 1, the light, elastic outer bark of a species of oak. 2, a piece of cork used as a stopper for a bottle. —v.t. seal; stop up.

cork'age (-ij) n. a restaurant's charge for serving a patron's liquor.

cork'er (-ər) n. (Slang) a good fellow, thing, joke, etc.

cork'ing adj. (Slang) very good.

cork'screw″ n. a metal spiral used for drawing out cork stoppers. —adj. twisted; tortuous. —v.i. follow a tortuous course.

corm (kôrm) n. a fleshy underground stem resembling a bulb.

cor'mo·rant (kôr'mə-rənt) n. a large fish-eating sea bird. —adj. greedy.

corn (kôrn) n. 1, a single seed of a cereal plant. 2, grain: in the U. S., maize; in England, wheat; in Scotland, oats. 3, a callus, esp. on a toe. 4, (Slang) triteness; mawkishness. —v.t. preserve (beef) in brine.

corn'cob″ n. the hard core of an ear of corn.

cor'ne·a (kôr'nē-ə) n. the firm transparent covering of the eye.

cor'ne·ous (kôr'nē-əs) adj. horny.

cor'ner (kôr'nər) n. 1, the intersection of, or the space between, two converging lines or surfaces; a point where streets meet; an angle. 2, a nook. 3, a region; a remote place. 4, an awkward position. 5, a monopoly. —v.t. 1, force into a difficult position. 2, monopolize.

cor'ner·stone" n. a stone, often inscribed, at a corner of a building; hence, a basis.

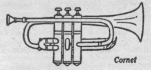

Cornet

cor·net' (kôr-net') n. a brass musical instrument of the trumpet class.

corn'flow"er n. any of several blue or white flowers.

cor'nice (kôr'nis) n. an ornamental molding at the top edge of a wall.

corn pone (pōn) a hard cake made of corn meal.

corn'starch" n. starch obtained from corn, used in puddings, etc.

cor·nu·co·pi·a (kôr"nū-kō'pė·ə) n. a horn overflowing with fruit, symbolizing abundance.

corn'y (kôr'nė) adj. (Slang) trite.

co·rol'la (kə-rol'ə) n. the petals of a flower collectively.

cor'ol·lar"y (kor'ə-ler"ė) n. a natural sequence or concomitant result.

co·ro'na (kə-rō'nə) n. 1, the luminous circle on the rim of the sun; a similar luminous effect. 2, a halo; crown. —**co·ro'nal**, adj.

cor'o·nar"y (kor'ə-ner"ė) adj. 1, like a crown. 2, pert. to arteries around the heart.

cor"o·na'tion (kor"ə-nā'shən) n. the crowning of a king or queen.

cor'o·ner (kor'ə-nər) n. the presiding officer at an inquest into a cause of death.

cor'o·net (kor'ə-net) n. 1, a crown indicating noble rank. 2, an ornamental headdress.

cor'po·ral (kôr'pə-rəl) n. the lowest noncommissioned army officer. —adj. pert. to the body. —**corporal punishment**, punishment inflicted on the body, as flogging.

cor'po·rate (kôr'pə-rət) adj. 1, being or pert. to a corporation. 2, pert. to a body.

cor"po·ra'tion (kôr"pə·rā'shən) n. 1, a company or association chartered to act as an individual. 2, (Slang) a fat belly.

cor·po're·al (kôr-pôr'ė·əl) adj. bodily; material; not spiritual.

corps (kôr) n. [pl. corps (kôrz)] 1, persons associated in some way, considered as a group. 2, (Mil.) a unit of two or more divisions; the officers of any unit; a special detail.

corpse (kôrps) n. a dead body.

cor'pu·lence (kôr'pyə-ləns) n. fatness; obesity. —**cor'pu·lent**, adj.

cor'pus (kôr'pəs) n. 1, the body of a human or animal. 2, a body of writings, as laws.

cor'pus·cle (kôr'pəs-əl) n. 1, a minute body or cell in the blood. 2, a minute particle.

cor·ral' (kə-ral') n. an enclosure for horses or cattle. —v.t. [-ralled', -ral'ling] 1, pen up. 2, seize; collect.

cor·rect' (kə-rekt') v.t. 1, note or mark errors in. 2, rectify. 3, discipline. —adj. 1, true; accurate. 2, conforming to good taste, etc. —**cor·rec'tive**, adj. —**cor·rect'ness**, n.

cor·rec'tion (kə-rek'shən) n. 1, act of correcting. 2, an emendation; rectification; adjustment; rebuke.

cor're·late" (kor'ə-lāt") v.t. show or find to be related or connected. —**cor"re·la'tion**, n.

cor·rel'a·tive (kə-rel'ə-tiv) adj. 1, having a mutual relation. 2, (Gram.) complementary, as neither and nor.

cor"re·spond' (kor"ə-spond') v.i. 1, be similar or analogous. 2, conform; match; fit. 3, communicate by letter. —**cor"re·spond'ence**, n.

cor"re·spond'ent (-ənt) n. 1, a writer of letters. 2, a reporter or agent in a distant place.

cor'ri·dor (kor'i-dər) n. a narrow passageway.

cor·rob'o·rate' (kə-rob'ə-rāt') v.t. confirm (another's report). —**cor·rob"o·ra'tion**, n. —**cor·rob'o·ra·tive**, adj.

cor·rode' (kə-rōd') v.t. & i. wear or eat away gradually, esp. by chemical action.

cor·ro'sion (kə-rō'zhən) n. act or effect of corroding; a gradual eating or wearing away. —**cor·ro'sive** (-siv) adj. & n.

Corrugated paper   *Corrugated iron*

cor'ru·gate" (kor'ə-gāt") v.t. & i. make wrinkles or folds (in). —**cor"ru·ga'tion**, n.

cor·rupt' (kə-rupt') adj. 1, dishonest; open to bribery. 2, debased; evil. 3, tainted. —v.t. 1, influence for evil; bribe; pervert. 2, make impure; taint; injure. —**cor·rupt'i·ble**, adj. —**cor·rupt'ness**, n.

cor·rup'tion (kə-rup'shən) *n.* act or effect of corrupting; dishonesty; perversion.

cor·sage' (kôr-säzh') *n.* a small bouquet of flowers to be worn.

cor'sair (kôr'sâr) *n.* a pirate.

cor'set (kôr'sit) *n.* a stiffened girdle worn to shape the figure.

cor·tege' (kôr-tāzh') *n.* 1, a procession. 2, a retinue.

cor'tex (kôr'teks) *n.* 1, bark, as of a tree. 2, the layer of gray matter covering the brain. —**cor'ti·cal,** *adj.*

cor'ti·sone (kôr'ti-sōn) *n.* a hormone used in treating various diseases.

co·run'dum (kə-run'dəm) *n.* a very hard mineral used as an abrasive and, in some forms, a gem (ruby, sapphire, etc.).

cor'us·cate' (kôr'ə-skāt') *v.i.* emit vivid flashes of light. —**cor'us·ca'tion,** *n.*

cor·vette' (kôr-vet') *n.* a small warship used as an escort.

cor'vine (kôr'vin) *adj.* pert. to the crow.

cor'y·phée' (kôr'ə-fā') *n.* a ballet dancer.

cos·met'ic (koz-met'ik) *n.* a preparation for beautifying the skin.

cos'mic (kos'mik) *adj.* 1, pert. to the universe; vast. 2, orderly. — **cos'mi·cal·ly,** *adv.* —**cosmic rays,** certain rays or streams of particles, present in space, of which the exact nature is not known.

cos'mo·pol'i·tan (koz'mə-pol'ə-tən) *adj.* 1, familiar with all the world; at home anywhere. 2, peopled from all the world, as a city. —*n.* [also, **cos·mop'o·lite'**] a cosmopolitan person.

cos'mos (koz'məs) *n.* 1, the universe as an ordered whole. 2, a tall annual plant with daisylike flowers.

Cos'sack (kos'ak) *n.* one of a Russian tribe famous as cavalrymen.

cost (kåst) *n.* 1, the price paid, or to be paid, for a thing or service; expense; outlay. 2, loss of any kind; suffering. —*v.i.* [*pret. & p.p.* **cost**] 1, have as a price. 2, cause the loss of. —*v.t.* cause expenditure or loss.

cost'ly (-lē) *adj.* expensive. — **cost'li·ness,** *n.*

cost-'plus' *n.* a fixed surcharge.

cos'tume (kos'tūm) *n.* 1, dress in general; a particular style of dress. 2, fancy dress; dress for stage wear.

co'sy (kō'zē) *adj.* cozy. —**co'si·ness,** *n.*

cot (kot) *n.* a small, light bed.

cote (kōt) *n.* a pen or coop.

co'te·rie (kō'tə-rē) *n.* a social group; set; clique.

co·til'lion (kō-til'yən) *n.* 1, a fancy square dance. 2, a ball.

cot'tage (kot'ij) *n.* a small house. —**cottage cheese,** a soft cheese made from sour milk curds.

cot'ter (kot'ər) *n.* 1, a Scottish peasant. 2, a split pin or bolt: *cotter pin.*

cot'ton (kot'ən) *n.* a soft white fibrous mass from a plant (cotton plant); thread spun, cloth woven, etc. from cotton. —**cot'ton·y,** *adj.*

cot'ton·seed" *n. & adj.* the seeds of cotton, which yield an oil.

cot'ton·tail" *n.* a white-tailed rabbit.

cot'ton·wood" (kot'ən-wůd") *n.* an Amer. tree of the poplar family; the abele.

cot'y·le'don (kot'ə-lē'dən) *n.* (*Bot.*) the primary leaf of a plant.

couch (kowch) *n.* a lounge; a small bed. —*v.t.* 1, express (meaning) in words. 2, set; lay.

cou'gar (koo'gər) *n.* a large tawny Amer. cat; the puma.

cough (kåf) *v.i.* 1, expel air from the lungs with effort and noise. 2, (with *up*) expel by coughing, as phlegm; (*Slang*) surrender; pay out. —*n.* an act of coughing; a disease that causes coughing.

could (kůd) *v.* pret. of *can.*

cou'lee (koo'lē) *n.* a deep ravine.

coun'cil (kown'səl) *n.* a deliberative assembly. —**coun'cil·or,** *n.*

coun'sel (kown'səl) *n.* 1, an interchange of opinions; consultation. 2, advice. 3, a lawyer; legal representatives. —*v.t. & i.* advise; recommend. —**coun'se·lor,** *n.*

count (kownt) *v.t.* 1, enumerate one by one; reckon. 2, consider; deem. —*v.i.* 1, name numbers in order. 2, be of value. 3, (with *on*) depend; rely. —*n.* 1, the act of reckoning. 2, the result obtained. 3, (*Law*) a charge in an indictment. 4, a rank and title of nobility. —**count'down",** *n.* a process of counting the seconds remaining before an event, esp. the launching of a spacecraft, is to occur.

coun'te·nance (kown'tə-nəns) *n.* 1, the face. 2, expression of the face. 3, favor; approval. —*v.t.* aid; encourage; show approval of.

count'er (kown'tər) *n.* 1, a device for keeping count; a token. 2, a bench or case over which goods are sold. 3, the opposite or contrary. —*adj.* contrary; opposite. —*adv.* contrary. —*v.t. & i.* 1, oppose; contradict. 2, retaliate; strike back.

coun'ter- *pref.* denoting: 1, opposition. 2, oppositeness. 3, a complement.

coun"ter·act' *v.t.* offset; neutralize.

coun"ter·clock'wise *adj. & adv.* in reverse of clockwise.

coun'ter·feit (kown'tər-fit) *adj.* forged; spurious. —*n.* an imitation, esp. of a coin or banknote. —*v.t. & i.* imitate (money, etc.) fraudulently. —coun'ter·feit·er, *n.*

coun'ter·mand" (kown'tər-mànd") *v.t.* revoke; overrule.

coun'ter·pane" *n.* a bedspread.

coun'ter·part" *n.* a duplicate; facsimile.

coun'ter·point" (kown'tər-point") *n.* (*Music*) the combining of different melodies.

coun'ter·poise" *n.* a balancing weight; equilibrium.

coun'ter·sign" *v.t.* add an authenticating signature to. —*n.* a password.

coun'ter·sink" *v.t.* sink (the head of a screw) into a hole.

coun'ter·weight" *n.* a weight used to balance another.

count'ess (kown'tis) *n.fem.* the wife of a count or earl.

count'less (-ləs) *adj.* so numerous as to be uncountable.

coun'try (kun'trė) *n.* 1, land in general; a region; a particular kind of region. 2, a nation, its territory or people. 3, any rural region. —*adj.* pert. to, or characteristic of, rural regions. —country club, a club with a golf course.

coun'try·side" *n.* the surrounding (rural) scene.

coun'ty (kown'tė) *n.* a political division of a state; its inhabitants.

coup (koo) *n.* a sudden strategic move; a blow; stroke.

cou·pé' (koo-pā') *n.* 1, a two-doored closed automobile. 2, a closed carriage for two.

cou'ple (kup'əl) *n.* 1, two of a kind. 2, a man and woman associated together. —*v.t.* connect; link; pair.

coup'let (kup'lət) *n.* two successive rhyming lines.

coup'ling (kup'ling) *n.* a device for connecting things, as railroad cars, etc.

cou'pon (koo'pon) *n.* a slip to be detached from a bond, advertisement, etc. and exchanged for something.

cour'age (kẽr'ij) *n.* lack of fear; bravery; valor.

cou·ra'geous (kə-rā'jəs) *adj.* intrepid; brave.

cour'i·er (kẽr'ė-ər) *n.* 1, a messenger. 2, a paid escort of travelers.

course (kōrs) *n.* 1, a moving forward; passage. 2, the line of motion. 3, the path or ground covered; a place for playing golf; a race track. 4, progressive phases, as in a disease. 5, a series, as of lectures, studies, etc. 6, method of procedure. 7, a succession of acts, practices, etc. 8, any part of a meal served at one time. —*v.t.* run, hunt, or chase after. —*v.i.* move swiftly.

cours'er (kôr'sər) *n.* 1, a plover-like bird. 2, (*Poetic*) a swift horse.

court (kōrt) *n.* 1, a space enclosed by buildings: *courtyard.* 2, a level area for certain games, as tennis. 3, a sovereign's household; a general reception by him. 4, a sovereign's authority. 5, a hall of justice; a session there; the judge or judges presiding. —*v.t.* 1, seek the favor of. 2, woo. 3, aspire to; invite. —*v.i.* woo.

cour'te·ous (kẽr'tė-əs) *adj.* showing courtesy; polite.

cour'te·san (kōr'tə-zən) *n.* a harlot.

cour'te·sy (kẽr'tə-sė) *n.* 1, kind and thoughtful behavior toward another; politeness; gracious attention. 2, a favor or indulgence.

court'house" *n.* a building for law courts and governmental offices.

cour'ti·er (kôr'tė-ər) *n.* a person in attendance at a royal court.

court-"mar'tial *n.* [*pl.* courts-"-mar'tial] a military or naval court. —*v.t.* try by court-martial.

court'ship" *n.* a wooing, esp. of a woman.

court'yard" *n.* an enclosed yard in or near a building.

cous'in (kuz'ən) *n.* a child of one's uncle, aunt, or cousin.

cou·tu·rier' (koo-tûr-yā') *n.* a male dressmaker and designer. —cou·tu·rière' (-yär') *n.fem.*

cove (kōv) *n.* 1, a sheltered inlet. 2, (*Brit. Slang*) fellow; man.

cov'e·nant (kuv'ə-nənt) *n.* a solemn agreement. —*v.t. & i.* promise.

cov'er (kuv'ər) *v.t.* 1, put something over or upon; lie upon; close the opening of; shield; protect; coat; clothe. 2, extend over the entire surface of; hide; screen. 3, travel or pass over. 4, include; comprise. 5, aim at directly, as with a gun. 6, insure for some specified risk. 7, (*Colloq.*) report the news of (an event, place, etc.) —*v.i.* 1, be spread or lie over an entire thing or surface. 2, replace a hat. —*n.* 1, something laid or lying over a thing to close, conceal, or protect it. 2, a screen; disguise. 3, shelter. 4, table fittings for one person. —cover charge, a restaurant's extra charge for a floor show.

cov'er·age (-ij) *n.* protection by insurance or funds in reserve.

cov'er·alls" (-âlz) *n.pl.* protective work garments.

cov'er·let *n.* a bedspread.

cov'ert (kuv'ərt) *adj.* 1, secret; hidden. 2, sheltered. —*n.* a thicket; hiding place, esp. for game.

cov'et (kuv'it) *v.t.* long for; desire enviously. —**cov'et·ous,** *adj.*

cov'ey (kuv'ė) *n.* a small flock of birds, esp. quail.

cow (kou) *n.* the female of various large animals, esp. of domestic cattle.

cow'ard (kou'ərd) *n.* one who shrinks from pain or danger. —**cow'ard·ice** (-is) *n.* —**cow'ard·ly,** *adj.*

cow'boy *n.* a worker on a cattle ranch. Also, **cow'hand, cow'punch"er.**

cow'catch"er *n.* the guarding front frame of a locomotive.

cow'er (kow'ər) *v.i.* bend down or crouch in fear, shame, etc.

cow'hide *n.* leather from the skin of cattle.

cowl (kowl) *n.* 1, a monk's hooded garment; its hood. 2, the front of an automobile's body.

cow'lick *n.* an unruly tuft of hair.

cowl'ing *n.* a metal cover or housing.

cow'pox (kow'poks") *n.* an eruptive disease of cows, caused by a virus used in smallpox vaccination.

cow'rie (kow'rė) *n.* a small marine shell, used by various peoples for money.

cow'slip (kow'slip) *n.* the marsh marigold.

cox'comb" (koks'kōm") *n.* a vain, conceited fellow.

cox'swain (kok'sən) *n.* a helmsman of a rowed boat.

coy (koi) *adj.* exhibiting pretended shyness. —**coy'ness,** *n.*

coy·o'te (kī-ō'tė) *n.* a small tawny wolf of western No. Amer.

coy'pu (koi'poo) *n.* a So. Amer. rodent.

coz'en (kuz'ən) *v.t. & i.* cheat; defraud. —**coz'en·age,** *n.*

co'zy (kō'zė) *adj.* warm and snug. —**co'zi·ness,** *n.*

crab (krab) *n.* 1, an edible crustacean. 2, (*Colloq.*) a cross, surly person. 3, a tree, the crab apple; its fruit. 4, (*cap.*) a northern constellation; a sign of the Zodiac: Cancer. —*v.i.* [**crabbed, crab'bing**] (*Colloq.*) find fault.

crab'ap"ple *n.* a variety of small, sour apple.

crab'bed (krab'id) *adj.* 1, peevish; cross. 2, cramped; illegible.

crack (krak) *v.i. & t.* 1, snap with a sudden sharp sound. 2, split without separating. 3, of a voice, break. 4, (*Colloq.*) lose effectiveness or courage. 5, (*Colloq.*) tell (a joke). 6, distill (petroleum) under

pressure. —*n.* 1, a sharp snapping sound or report. 2, a narrow fissure; slight break. 3, a resounding blow. 4, (*Slang*) an attempt. 5, (*Slang*) a gibe. —*adj.* (*Colloq.*) excellent.

cracked (krakt) *adj.* 1, broken. 2, (*Colloq.*) crazy.

crack'er *n.* 1, a thin, crisp biscuit. 2, a poor white farmer of Ga. and Fla.

crack'er·jack" *adj.* [also, **crack'ing**] (*Colloq.*) excellent; first-class. —*n.* a popcorn confection.

crack'le (krak'əl) *v.i.* give out repeated, sharp, snapping noises.

crack'ling *n.* the crisp browned skin of roast pork.

crack'pot" *n.* (*Slang*) an eccentric person.

cracks'man (-mən) *n.* [*pl.* **-men**] a burglar.

crack-'up *n.* a crash; breakdown.

cra'dle (krā'dəl) *n.* a baby's crib, usually on rockers; hence, birthplace; origin; infancy. —*v.t.* place in, or hold as in, a cradle.

craft (kråft) *n.* 1, [*pl.* **craft**] a vessel; boat; ship, etc. 2, a trade requiring manual skill; a guild. 3, skill; dexterity. 4, cunning; guile.

crafts'man (-mən) *n.* [*pl.* **-men**] an artisan. —**crafts'man·ship,** *n.*

craft'y (-ė) *adj.* guileful. —**craft'i·ness,** *n.*

crag (krag) *n.* a steep, rugged rock. —**crag'gy,** *adj.*

cram (kram) *v.t.* [**crammed, cram'ming**] 1, fill overfull; pack or stuff in. 2, eat greedily. —*v.i.* 1, stuff oneself. 2, study intensely for an examination.

cramp (kramp) *n.* 1, a sudden, painful contraction of a muscle. 2, (*pl.*) griping pain in the abdomen. —*v.t.* hinder from free action; hamper; confine narrowly. —**cramped,** *adj.* too small or close.

cran'ber"ry (kran'ber'ė) *n.* the tart red berry of a bog plant; the plant.

crane (krān) *n.* 1, a large, long-legged wading bird. 2, a machine for lifting and moving heavy weights; derrick. —*v.i. & t.* stretch out (the neck).

cra'ni·um (krā'nė-əm) *n.* the part of the skull containing the brain. —**cra'ni·al,** *adj.*

crank (krank) *n.* 1, a device, as a bent axle, for imparting or converting rotary motion.

Crane

2, an eccentric person. —*v.t. & i.* operate by a crank.

crank'shaft" *n.* the cranking shaft of an (esp. automobile) engine.

crank'y (krang'kė) *adj.* irritable; hard to please. —**crank'i·ness,** *n.*

cran'ny (kran'ė) *n.* crevice; crack.

crape (krāp) *n.* crêpe.

craps (kraps) *n.* a gambling dice game.

crash (krash) *n.* 1, a loud harsh sound of things breaking. 2, a collision. 3, financial failure or ruin. 4, a coarse, rough fabric of linen or cotton. —*v.t. & i.* 1, smash; shatter. 2, (*Slang*) intrude.

crass (kras) *adj.* gross; obtuse. —**crass'ness,** *n.*

crate (krāt) *n.* a box made of wooden slats. —*v.t.* put into a crate or protecting frame.

cra'ter (krā'tər) *n.* 1, the mouth of a volcano. 2, the pit made by an exploding bomb or shell.

cra·vat' (krə-vat') *n.* a necktie.

crave (krāv) *v.t.* 1, long for. 2, beg for.

cra'ven (krā'vən) *n.* a cowardly, abject person. —*adj.* cowardly.

crav'ing (krā'ving) *n.* extreme desire.

craw (krâ) *n.* the crop of a bird.

craw'fish" (krâ'fish") *n.* a crustacean resembling a lobster. Also, **cray'fish** (krā'-).

crawl (krâl) *v.i.* 1, move on hands and knees or by drawing the body along the ground. 2, advance slowly or feebly. 3, be or feel overrun by creeping things. —*n.* 1, a creeping progress. 2, a fast swimming stroke.

cray'on (krā'ən) *n.* a stick of chalk, wax, etc. for drawing or writing.

craze (krāz) *v.t. & i.* make or become insane. —*n.* a fad.

cra'zy (krā'zė) *adj.* insane; wildly excited. —**cra'zi·ness,** *n.* —**crazy bone,** the point of the elbow.—**crazy quilt,** a patchwork quilt.

creak (krēk) *v.t.* make a squeaking noise. —**creak'y,** *adj.*

cream (krēm) *n.* 1, the rich, oily part of milk. 2, something smooth like cream, as a sauce, paste, etc. 3, the choice part of anything. 4, a yellowish-white color. —*v.t.* beat to a smooth consistency. —**cream'y,** *adj.* —**cold cream,** a cosmetic ointment.

cream'er *n.* a cream pitcher.

cream'er·y (-ər-ė) *n.* a factory where butter and cheese are made.

crease (krēs) *n.* a long thin mark made by folding; a wrinkle. —*v.t. & i.* make or become wrinkled.

cre·ate' (krė-āt') *v.t.* 1, bring into being; cause to exist. 2, invest with rank. 3, give rise to; originate.

cre·a'tion (krė-ā'shən) *n.* 1, act or result of creating; invention; an original product. 2, the world or universe.

cre·a'tive (-tiv) *adj.* inventive; originating. —**cre·a'tive·ness,** *n.*

cre·a'tor (-tər) *n.* 1, one who creates. 2, (*cap.*) God.

crea'ture (krē'chər) *n.* 1, a living animal or human. 2, one created or controlled by another.

cre'dence (krē'dəns) *n.* belief.

cre·den'tials (kri-den'shəls) *n. pl.* attesting documents.

cred'i·ble (kred'ə-bəl) *adj.* worthy of belief; believable. —**cred'i·bil'i·ty,** *n.*

cred'it (kred'it) *n.* 1, faith; belief. 2, credibility. 3, an acknowledgment of worth or accomplishment. 4, good reputation, esp. in financial affairs; borrowing power. 5, a sum in a person's favor in an account. —*v.t.* 1, believe; have faith in. 2, acknowledge the worth of; record a payment received, etc.

cred'it·a·ble *adj.* deserving of esteem or praise.

cred'i·tor (kred'i-tər) *n.* one to whom money is owed.

cre'do (krē'dō) *n.* [*pl.* -**dos** (-dōz)] a statement of beliefs; a creed.

cre·du'li·ty (kre-dū'lə-tė) *n.* willingness to believe; gullibility.

cred'u·lous (krej'ə-ləs) *adj.* too willing to believe; gullible.

creed (krēd) *n.* 1, a brief statement of belief, esp. religious. 2, a sect; denomination; belief.

creek (krēk) *n.* a small river.

creel (krēl) *n.* a wickerwork basket for carrying fish.

creep (krēp) *v.i.* [*pret. & p.p.* **crept** (krept)] 1, move with the body close to the ground. 2, move slowly, feebly, or stealthily. 3, crawl. 4, grow along the ground.

creep'er *n.* 1, a vine. 2, (*pl.*) a garment worn by infants.

creeps *n.pl.* a sensation of horror.

creep'y *adj.* creeping; causing horror. —**creep'i·ness,** *n.*

cre'mate (krē'māt) *v.t.* reduce to ashes, as a corpse. —**cre·ma'tion,** *n.*

cre'ma·to·ry (krē'mə-tôr-ė) *n.* a furnace for cremation. Also, **cre'ma·to'ri·um** (-tôr'ė-əm).

crème de menthe (krĕm də-mint′) (*Fr.*) a mint-flavored liqueur.

Cre′ole (krē′ōl) *n.* 1, an American of Fr. or Sp. ancestry. 2, (*Colloq.*) erroneously, a person part Negro. —*adj.* in the style (as of cooking), dialect, etc. of Creoles.

cre′o·sote (krē′ə-sōt′) *n.* an oily liquid from wood tar, an antiseptic and preservative.

crepe (krāp) *n.* a crinkled fabric, usually of silk, often worn in black as a sign of mourning. Also, crape. —**crêpe de Chine** (də-shēn′) a very thin silk crêpe. —**crêpes Suzette** (krāp′ soo-zet′) Fr. pancakes cooked in burning liqueurs.

crep′i·tate (krep′ə-tāt′) *v.i.* crackle. —**crep′i·tant**, *adj.* —**crep″i·ta′tion**, *n.*

crept (krept) *v.* pret. & p.p. of *creep.*

cre·scen′do (krə-shen′dō) *adj.* & *adv.* (*Music*) gradually increasing in force or loudness.

cres′cent (kres′ənt) *adj.* 1, growing; increasing. 2, shaped like the new moon. Also, crape. —*n.* something in this shape.

Crescent

cress (kres) *n.* a plant of the mustard family with crisp, pungent leaves.

crest (krest) *n.* 1, a comb or tuft on a bird's head. 2, the top of a helmet; the figure above an escutcheon. 3, the top; peak, as of a hill, wave, etc.

crest′fall″en *adj.* dejected; abashed.

cre′tin (krē′tin) *n.* an idiot due to thyroid deficiency. —**cre′tin·ism**, *n.*

cre·tonne′ (kri-ton′) *n.* an unglazed printed cotton fabric.

cre·vasse′ (krə-vas′) *n.* a crack, as in a glacier or levee.

crev′ice (krev′is) *n.* a crack; fissure.

crew (kroo) *n.* a working force of men, esp. of a ship or train. —*v.* pret. of *crow.*

crib (krib) *n.* 1, a high-sided bed for a child. 2, a slatted bin for storage of grain. —*v.t.* [cribbed, crib′bing] 1, confine. 2, (*Colloq.*) plagiarize; prepare (a language lesson) from a translation. —**crib′ber**, *n.*

crib′bage (krib′ij) *n.* a card game.

crick′et (krik′it) *n.* 1, a jumping insect. 2, a Brit. ball game similar to baseball.

cri′er (krī′ər) *n.* one who cries, as a hawker or public announcer.

crime (krīm) *n.* an offense punishable by law.

crim′i·nal (krim′i-nəl) *adj.* pert. to or constituting crime. —*n.* a person guilty of a crime. —**crim″i·nal′i·ty**, *n.*

crim″i·nol′o·gy (krim″ə-nol′ə-jē) *n.* the study of crime or crime-detection. —**crim″i·nol′o·gist**, *n.*

crimp (krimp) *v.t.* pinch into folds or flutings; give a wavy appearance to. —*n.* a fluting; a wave, as in hair.

crim′son (krim′zən) *n.* & *adj.* a deep-red color.

cringe (krinj) *v.i.* wince; shrink, esp. with fear or servility.

crin′kle (kring′kəl) *v.t.* & *i.* make wrinkles or ripples (in); twist. —**crink′ly**, *adj.*

crin′o·line (krin′ə-lin) *n.* 1, a stiff cotton fabric. 2, a hoop skirt.

crip′ple (krip′əl) *n.* a physically disabled person. —*v.t.* lame; disable.

cri′sis (krī′sis) *n.* [*pl.* **-ses** (-sēz)] a decisive point or condition; a turning point; a climax.

crisp (krisp) *adj.* 1, brittle; crumbly; short, as pastry; not limp. 2, fresh. 3, pithy; terse. 4, crinkled; tightly curled. —**crisp′ness**, *n.*

criss′cross″ (kris′krôs″) *v.t.* formed in or marked by crossing lines. —*adv.* crosswise. —*n.* a crisscross mark or pattern.

cri·te′ri·on (krī-tir′ē-ən) *n.* [*pl.* **-a** (-ə)] a standard for comparison or judgment.

crit′ic (krit′ik) *n.* 1, one who appraises the merit of others' works, esp. artistic or literary. 2, one who censures.

crit′i·cal (krit′i-kəl) *adj.* 1, censorious. 2, pert. to criticism. 3, pert. to a crisis.

crit′i·cism (krit′i-siz-əm) *n.* the act or judgment of a critic.

crit′i·cize (krit′i-sīz″) *v.t.* & *i.* judge as a critic, esp. adversely.

cri·tique′ (kri-tēk′) *n.* a critical review.

croak (krōk) *n.* a hoarse, guttural sound, as of a frog. —*v.i.* 1, utter a croak. 2, (*Slang*) die.

croak′er (krō′kər) *n.* 1, a frog or croaking fish. 2, (*Slang*) a doctor.

cro·chet′ (krō-shā′) *n.* a kind of knitting done with one hooked needle. —*v.t.* & *i.* make such work.

crock (krok) *n.* an earthenware vessel or jar.

crock′er·y (-ə-rē) *n.* earthenware dishes.

croc'o·dile" (krok'ə-dīl") *n.* a large horny-skinned aquatic reptile. —**crocodile tears**, insincere grief.

Crocodile

cro'cus (krō'kəs) *n.* a dwarf bulb flowering in earliest spring.

crone (krōn) *n.* an old woman.

cro'ny (krō'nē) *n.* a chum.

crook (krŭk) *n.* **1,** a bend; curve; hook. **2,** a bent or curved staff, part, tool, etc. **3,** a dishonest person.

crook'ed (krŭk'id) *adj.* **1,** not straight; winding. **2,** dishonest. —**crook'ed·ness,** *n.*

croon (kroon) *v.t. & i.* sing softly and plaintively.

crop (krop) *n.* **1,** plants grown and harvested; the useful yield of a particular plant, field, or season. **2,** a riding whip. **3,** a pouch in a bird's gullet. **4,** hair cut close to the head. —*v.t.* [cropped, crop'ping] **1,** cut or bite off the tips of. **2,** cut short, as a tail, hair, etc. —*v.i.* (with *up*) appear unexpectedly.

crop'per (krop'ər) *n.* a fall from horseback; hence, a failure.

cro·quet' (krō-kā') *n.* a lawn game of driving balls through wickets.

cro·quette' (krō-ket') *n.* a ball of finely minced meat, rice, etc.

Crosses
1—Latin   2—Greek   3—Maltese
4—St. Andrew

cross (krås) *n.* **1,** two intersecting stakes, bars, or lines; (*cap.*) the cross on which Christ died; a replica of this as a religious symbol. **2,** hence, a burden; misfortune. **3,** an intermixture of breeds. —*adj.* **1,** transverse; intersecting. **2,** contrary; opposed. **3,** peevish; fretful. **4,** hybrid. —*v.t.* **1,** draw (a line) or place (a thing) across another. **2,** (with *out*) cancel. **3,** go across. **4,** make the sign of the cross on or over. **5,** meet and pass. **6,** thwart; oppose. **7,** mix the breed of. —*v.i.* **1,** intersect. **2,** pass from one side to the other. **3,** meet and pass. **4,** interbreed.

—**cross fire,** shooting from different positions so the lines cross. —**cross purposes,** conflicting purposes or tactics. —**cross reference,** a note directing attention to another part of the same document. —**cross section,** a cut through a solid; hence, a view of all parts or aspects.

cross- *pref.* **1,** across; transverse. **2,** opposing; antagonistic; counter.

cross'bar" *n.* a transverse bar.

cross'bones" *n.* crossed bones, a symbol of piracy.

cross'bow" (-bō") *n.* a bow mounted on a catapulting device.

cross'breed" *v.t.* [pret. & p.p. -bred"] mix (breeds).

cross-"ex·am'ine *v.t.* question a hostile witness or person. Also, **cross-"ques'tion.**

cross'eyed" (-īd") *adj.* having one or both eyes directed abnormally.

cross'ing *n.* **1,** an intersection of roads. **2,** a place suitable for crossing a road, river, etc. **3,** act of opposing.

cross'patch" *n.* (*Colloq.*) a cross person.

cross'roads" *n.* an intersection of roads.

cross'town" *adj.* across the width of a town.

cross'wise" *adv.* across. Also, **cross'ways".**

cross'word" puzzle a game of fitting defined words to squares in a diagram.

crotch (kroch) *n.* the angle where two branches, legs, etc. divide.

crotch'et·y (kroch'it-ē) *adj.* given to odd or eccentric fancies; cranky.

cro'ton oil (krō'tən) a powerful purgative oil.

crouch (krowch) *v.i.* stoop low.

croup (kroop) *n.* a disease of young children marked by difficult breathing. —**croup'y,** *adj.*

crou'pi·er (kroo'pē-ər) *n.* (*Fr.*) an employee of a gambling casino.

crou'ton (kroo'ton) *n.* a small piece of toast put in soup, etc.

crow (krō) *v.i.* **1,** [pret. also **crew**] utter the cry of a rooster. **2,** brag; gloat. —*n.* **1,** a rooster's cry. **2,** a large, glossy black bird; raven.

crow'bar" (krō'bär") *n.* a heavy iron bar used for prying.

crowd (krowd) *n.* **1,** a multitude; throng. **2,** the populace. **3,** (*Colloq.*) a clique; coterie. —*v.t.* **1,** squeeze; cram. **2,** fill to excess. —*v.i.* come in numbers; swarm.

tub, cūte, pŭll; label; oil, owl; go, chip, she, thin, *then*, sing, ink; *see p. 6*

crow'foot *n.* [*pl.* -foots"] a plant with leaves divided like a bird's foot.

crown (krown) *n.* **1,** a monarch's jeweled headdress; hence, the sovereign; royal authority. **2,** a wreath for the head. **3,** the highest part of anything. **4,** the exposed part of a tooth. **5,** an English silver coin, 5 shillings. —*v.t.* **1,** put a crown on. **2,** confer honor or sovereignty upon. **3,** put the finishing touch to. **4,** (*Colloq.*) hit on the head. —**crown prince,** the heir apparent to a throne.

Crowns

1—Crown of Henry V of England
2—Crown of Prince of Wales
3—Crown of man's felt hat

crow's-'foot *n.* [*pl.* -feet] a wrinkle shaped like a bird's foot.

crow's-'nest *n.* a lookout's perch.

cro'zier (krō'zhər) *n.* the pastoral staff of a bishop or abbot. Also, **cro'sier.**

cru'cial (kroo'shəl) *adj.* decisive; critical.

cru'ci·ble (kroo'sə-bəl) *n.* a caldron for melting ores, metals, etc.

cru''ci·fix (kroo'si-fiks") *n.* a representation of Christ on the cross.

cru''ci·fix'ion (kroo'sə-fik'shən) *n.* **1,** the act of crucifying. **2,** (*cap.*) the death of Christ on the cross.

cru'ci·form (kroo'sə-fôrm") *adj.* cross-shaped.

cru'ci·fy'' (kroo'si-fī") *v.t.* put to death by nailing to a cross.

crude (krood) *adj.* **1,** in a raw or unprepared state. **2,** unrefined; unpolished. —**crude'ness, cru'di·ty,** *n.*

cru'el (kroo'əl) *adj.* deliberately causing suffering to others; pitiless. —**cru'el·ty** (-tē) *n.*

cru'et (kroo'it) *n.* a glass vial, as for oil or vinegar.

cruise (krooz) *v.i.* drive or sail about with no definite destination. —*n.* an ocean trip for pleasure.

cruis'er (kroo'zər) *n.* **1,** a warship somewhat smaller than a battleship. **2,** a small yacht.

crul'ler (krul'ər) *n.* a ring or twist of deep-fried cake; a doughnut.

crumb (krum) *n.* **1,** a small fragment, esp. of bread. **2,** (*Slang*) an insignificant person. —**crumb'y,** *adj.*

crum'ble (krum'bəl) *v.t. & i.* break into small bits; disintegrate. —**crum'bly** (-blē) *adj.*

crum'pet (krum'pət) *n.* an unsweetened muffin, usually toasted before served.

crum'ple (krum'pəl) *v.t. & i.* rumple; wrinkle.

crunch (krunch) *v.t. & i.* chew, grind, or trample noisily.

cru·sade' (kroo-sād') *n.* a zealous campaign, often ill-fated, to defend a cause. —*v.i.* participate in a crusade. —**cru·sad'er,** *n.* one engaged in a crusade, esp. (*cap.*) in the "holy wars" of the Middle Ages.

crush (krush) *v.t.* **1,** squeeze out of shape; mash; rumple. **2,** grind into bits. **3,** conquer. —*n.* **1,** sudden, violent pressure. **2,** a crowd. **3,** (*Slang*) an infatuation; the object of it.

crust (krust) *n.* **1,** a hard outer layer or coating; the outside of bread, a pie, etc. **2,** an end (heel) of a loaf of bread. **3,** either of the two casings of a pie. **4,** (*Slang*) nerve. —**crust'y,** *adj.* surly; curt.

crus·ta'cean (krus-tā'shən) *n.* a hard-shelled, usually aquatic, animal, as a crab, lobster, etc.

crutch (kruch) *n.* **1,** a support to fit under the arm, used by the lame. **2,** any means of support.

crux (kruks) *n.* a critical and puzzling point or phase.

cry (krī) *v.i.* **1,** call loudly. **2,** weep. **3,** utter a characteristic sound, as an animal. —*v.t.* **1,** proclaim. **2,** offer (wares) by shouting. —*n.* **1,** any vehement outcry. **2,** a shout to attract attention. **3,** a fit of weeping.

cry'ba''by *n.* (*Colloq.*) a chronic complainer.

crypt (kript) *n.* **1,** an underground vault. **2,** a secret code or cipher.

cryp'tic (krip'tik) *adj.* hidden; secret; occult. —**cryp'ti·cal·ly,** *adv.*

cryp'to·graph (krip'tə-grăf) *n.* **1,** a device for putting text into cipher. **2,** [also, **cryp'to·gram**] a message in secret code or cipher. —**cryp·tog'ra·pher** (-tog'rə-fər) *n.* —**cryp·tog'ra·phy,** *n.*

crys'tal (kris'təl) *n.* **1,** transparent quartz. **2,** a glass of unusual brilliance. **3,** the transparent disk over a watch face. **4,** a characteristically faceted body or particle. —*adj.* clear. —**crys'tal·line** (-lin) *adj.*

crys'tal·lize'' (-līz") *v.i. & t.* take, or cause to take, definite form or shape, esp. in crystals. —**crys''tal·li·za'tion,** *n.*

cub (kub) *n.* **1,** the young of the fox, bear, wolf, lion, and tiger. **2,** a child.

fat, fāte, fär, fāre, fâll, ásk; met, hē, hêr, maybê; pin, pīne; not, nōte, ôr, tool

3, a prospective Boy Scout. **4,** a tyro. —*adj.* untrained.

cub'by·hole" (kub'ē-) *n.* a small compartment or room.

cube (kūb) *n.* **1,** a solid with six square faces. **2,** the square of a number again multiplied by the number. —*v.t.* **1,** raise to the third power. **2,** cut into cubes. —**cu'bic,** *adj.*

cu'bi·cle (kū'bə-kəl) *n.* a small room or compartment.

cub'ism (kū'biz-əm) *n.* a form of modern art characterized by the use of geometrical forms. —**cub'ist,** *n. & adj.*

cu'bit (kū'bit) *n.* an ancient measure of length, about 18 inches.

cuck'old (kuk'əld) *n.* the husband of an unfaithful wife.

cuck'oo (koo'koo) *n.* a Europ. bird uttering a sound like "cuckoo." —*adj.* (*Colloq.*) crazy. —**cuckoo clock,** a clock from which a puppet cuckoo pops out to call the hour.

Cuckoo

cu'cum·ber (kū'kum-bər) *n.* a trailing plant; its long, green, edible fruit.

cud (kud) *n.* **1,** swallowed food brought up for rechewing by a ruminant. **2,** (*Slang*) a wad for chewing.

cud'dle (kud'əl) *v.t.* hug; embrace; fondle. —*v.i.* lie close and snug.

cudg'el (kuj'əl) *n.* a short thick club. —*v.t.* beat with a club.

cue (kū) *n.* **1,** a guiding suggestion; hint. **2,** in a play, the spoken words that signal the next speech or action. **3,** a tapering rod used to strike a billiard ball. **4,** a pigtail. **5,** a queue; line. —*v.t.* remind or signal to (an actor).

cuff (kuf) *n.* **1,** an ornamental band or fold, as on a sleeve. **2,** a slap. —*v.t.* slap. —**on the cuff** (*Slang*) on credit.

cui·sine' (kwi-zēn') *n.* kitchen; mode of cooking.

-cule (kūl) *suf.* small; diminutive.

cu'li·nar"y (kū'lə-ner"ē) *adj.* pert. to cooking or to the kitchen.

cull (kul) *v.t.* select and gather. —*n.* a rejected item.

cul'mi·nate" (kul'mə-nāt") *v.i.* reach the highest point. —**cul"mi·na'tion,** *n.*

cul'pa·ble (kul'pə-bəl) *adj.* deserving censure; blameworthy. —**cul"pa·bil'i·ty,** *n.*

cul'prit (kul'prit) *n.* an offender; the guilty one.

cult (kult) *n.* the persons and rites associated with an object of worship or veneration.

cul'ti·vate" (kul'tə-vāt") *v.t.* **1,** prepare or condition (land) for crops. **2,** promote the growth of; foster; develop; refine. **3,** seek the society of. —**cul'ti·vat"ed,** *adj.* —**cul"ti·va'tion,** *n.* —**cul'ti·va"tor,** *n.* a plowing machine.

cul'ture (kul'chər) *n.* **1,** a state of civilization; customs; esp., a high level of development. **2,** the growing of bacteria for scientific use; the product of such culture. **3,** tillage. **4,** improvement; refinement. —**cul'tur·al,** *adj.* —**cul'tured,** *adj.*

cul'vert (kul'vərt) *n.* a conduit under a road, railroad, etc.

cum'ber (kum'bər) *v.t.* overload; hamper; impede. —**cum'ber·some, cum'brous,** *adj.* unwieldy; burdensome.

cum'mer·bund" (kum'ər-bund") *n.* a sash.

cu'mu·la"tive (kū'myə-lā"tiv) *adj.* increasing by accumulation.

cu'mu·lus (kū'myə-ləs) *n.* [*pl.* **-li** (-lī)] a cloud in the form of heaped-up white masses.

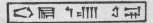

Cuneiform Writing

cu·ne'i·form" (kū-nē'ə-fôrm") *adj.* wedge-shaped, as the characters in ancient Persian, etc. inscriptions.

cun'ning (kun'ing) *adj.* ingenious; sly; (*Colloq.*) cute.

cup (kup) *n.* a bowl-shaped vessel, usually with a handle, to drink from; its contents or capacity; anything of similar concavity. —**cup'ful** (-fûl) *n.* —**cupped,** *adj.* held to form a hollow, as the hands.

cup'board (kub'ərd) *n.* a cabinet or closet fitted with shelves.

cu·pid'i·ty (kū-pid'ə-tē) *n.* immoderate greed.

cu'po·la (kū'pə-lə) *n.* a small dome rising above a roof.

cur (kėr) *n.* **1,** a snappish dog. **2,** a surly, ill-bred fellow.

cu·ra're (kyû-rä'rē) *n.* a poisonous substance obtained from a South American plant.

cu'rate (kyûr'it) *n.* an assistant to a rector or vicar. —**cu'ra·cy** (-ə-sē) *n.*

cur'a·tive (kyûr'ə-tiv) *adj.* curing. —*n.* a remedy.

cu·ra'tor (kyū-rā'tər) n. the custodian of a museum, art gallery, etc. —cu·ra'tor·ship, n.

curb (kẽrb) v.t. hold in check; control. —n. 1, a check; restraint. 2, [also, curb'stone"] the raised edge of a street. 3, a minor securities market.

curd (kẽrd) n. coagulated milk solids.

cur'dle (kẽr'dəl) v.t. & i. congeal, as into curd.

cure (kyûr) n. 1, restoration to health. 2, a method of treatment. 3, a remedy. —v.t. 1, heal; make well. 2, remedy (an evil). 3, preserve by drying or salting.

cur'few (kẽr'fū) n. a time or signal (as a bell) after which all, or certain, persons must be indoors.

cu'ri·o (kyūr'è-ō) n. an object of art, esp. if rare or unusual.

cu'ri·os'i·ty (kyûr"è-os'ə-tè) n. 1, state of being curious. 2, a rare or unusual thing.

cu'ri·ous (kyûr'è-əs) adj. 1, eager to learn; inquisitive; prying. 2, (Colloq.) strange; odd; rare.

curl (kẽrl) n. 1, a ringlet of hair. 2, something spiral-shaped. —v.t. & i. form into, or take the form of, a curl; coil. —curl'y, adj.

cur'lew (kẽr'loo) n. a wading bird with a long, slender bill.

curl'i·cue (kẽr'li-kū") n. a fancy twist or curl. Also, curl'y·cue".

curl'ing (kẽr'ling) n. a Scot. game, like hockey, played on ice.

cur'rant (kẽr'ənt) n. 1, a shrub bearing red acid berries; the berry. 2, a small seedless raisin.

cur'ren·cy (kẽr'ən-sè) n. 1, the state of being current; circulation. 2, money in actual use.

cur'rent (kẽr'ənt) adj. 1, widely circulated; prevalent. 2, belonging to the immediate present. —n. 1, a moving stream of water, air, electricity, etc. 2, general course, as of events, opinions, etc.

cur·ric'u·lum (kə-rik'yə-ləm) n. 1, a regular course of study. 2, an accepted schedule; routine. —cur·ric'u·lar, adj.

cur'ry (kẽr'è) v.t. 1, rub down (a horse) with a comb. 2, dress (leather). —n. a spice, sauce flavored with it, or food served with such a sauce, from India.

curse (kẽrs) n. 1, the invoking of evil on a person; the evil inflicted. 2, an invocation of evil; oath; profanity. 3, an affliction; bane. —v.t. 1, call down evil upon; swear at profanely. 2, blaspheme. 3, harm;

afflict. —v.i. swear profanely. —curs'ed (-sid) adj.

cur'sive (kẽr'siv) adj. in script.

cur'so·ry (kẽr'sə-rè) adj. hasty and superficial, as an examination, a glance, etc.

curt (kẽrt) adj. short; abrupt. —curt'ness, n.

cur·tail' (kər-tāl') v.t. cut short; deprive of. —cur·tail'ment, n.

cur'tain (kẽr'tən) n. fabric hung to adorn or conceal, as at windows, before a stage, etc. —v.t. conceal. —curtain call, a reappearance of an actor, to receive applause. —curtain raiser, an act before the main show.

curt'sy (kẽrt'sè) n. a woman's deep bow with genuflection. Also, curt'sey.

cur'va·ture (kẽr'və-chûr) n. a curving or degree of curve.

curve (kẽrv) n. a continuous bent line without angles. —v.t. & i. bend from a straight line.

cush'ion (kûsh'ən) n. 1, a pillow or soft pad. 2, something elastic to absorb shock. 3, the padded rim of a billiard table. —v.t. 1, hold or place in a soft base. 2, absorb the impact or shock of.

cusp (kusp) n. a point, as on the crown of a tooth or a crescent.

cus'pid (kus'pid) n. a pointed tooth; canine.

cus'pi·dor" (kus'pə-dôr") n. a spittoon.

cuss (kus) (Colloq.) v.i. & t. swear (at); curse. —n. a fellow.

cus'tard (kus'tərd) n. a cooked dessert of eggs and milk.

cus·to'di·an (kus-tō'dè-ən) n. a caretaker; guardian.

cus'to·dy (kus'tə-dè) n. 1, guardianship; care, esp. in trust. 2, imprisonment; arrest. —cus·to'di·al (kəs-tō'dè-əl) adj.

cus'tom (kus'təm) n. 1, usual practice or habit; convention. 2, patronage. 3, (pl.) duties levied on imported goods. —adj. made or making to order. —custom house, a government office for collecting customs duties. —cus'tom-made" adj. made to order for an individual customer.

cus'tom·ar"y (kus'tə-mer"è) adj. 1, usual. 2, established by custom.

cus'tom·er (kus'tə-mər) n. one who buys goods from another; a patron.

cut (kut) v.t. [cut, cut'ting] 1, penetrate or sever with a sharp edge; gash; reap; trim. 2, intersect; divide into parts. 3, cause pain to; injure; insult. 4, hit; strike (at).

5, shape, as a garment. **6,** abridge; reduce. **7,** absent oneself from. **8,** refuse to recognize. —*v.i.* **1,** make a slit or gash. **2,** admit of being cut. **3,** go by a shorter route. —*n.* **1,** the act or result of cutting. **2,** an engraved block for printing a picture; a picture so printed. —*cut´-and-dried´, adj.* by rote; invariable. —cut out (*for* or *to be*), apt; suited. —cut up, act foolish or frivolous.

cu·ta´ne·ous (kū-tā´nė-əs) *adj.* pert. to the skin.

cut´a·way´ *n.* a long tailcoat.

cute (kūt) *adj.* **1,** winning; attractive. **2,** coy. —**cute´ness,** *n.*

cu´ti·cle (kū´tə-kəl) *n.* **1,** the outer layer of skin. **2,** the skin at the base of a fingernail.

cut´lass (kut´ləs) *n.* a short sword with a wide curved blade.

cut´ler·y (kut´lə-rē) *n.* edged or cutting tools collectively.

cut´let (kut´lit) *n.* **1,** a thin slice of meat. **2,** a croquette.

cut´off´ *n.* **1,** a shorter way. **2,** a valve.

cut´ter *n.* **1,** one who or that which cuts. **2,** a swift ship; launch. **3,** a sleigh.

cut´throat´ *n.* a thug. —*adj.* relentless.

cut´tle·fish´ (kut´əl-fish´) *n.* a marine mollusk.

cy·an´ic (sī-an´ik) *adj.* blue.

cy´a·nide´ (sī´ə-nīd´) *n.* potassium cyanide, a deadly poison.

cy·an´o·gen (sī-an´ə-jən) *n.* a colorless, poisonous gas.

cyc´la·men (sik´lə-mən) *n.* a plant of the primrose family.

cy´cle (sī´kəl) *n.* **1,** a period of years in which certain phenomena recur; any long period; an age. **2,** a series or round. —*v.i.* ride on a bicycle. —**cy´clic,** *adj.* —**cy´cli·cal·ly,** *adv.*

cy´clist (sī´klist) *n.* a bicycle rider.

cy´clone (sī´klōn) *n.* a storm caused by rotating winds; hurricane. —**cy·clon´ic** (sī-klon´ik) *adj.*

cy´clo·pe´dic (sī´klə-pē´dik) *adj.* pert. to a cyclopedia (encyclopedia); hence, of great range. —**cy´clo·pe´di·cal·ly,** *adv.*

cy´clo·tron´ (sī´klə-tron´) *n.* an apparatus for bombarding the nuclei of atoms with other atomic particles.

cyg´net (sig´nit) *n.* a young swan.

cyl·in·der (sil´in-dər) *n.* **1,** a solid generated by the revolution of a rectangle on one of its sides. **2,** any body or space having this shape; the piston chamber of an engine, etc. —**cy·lin´dri·cal** (sə-lin´dri-kəl) *adj.*

cym´bal (sim´bəl) *n.* (*Music*) one of a pair of metal concave plates that ring when struck together. —**cym´bal·ist,** *n.*

cyn´ic (sin´ik) *n.* a sneering fault-finder. —**cyn´i·cism** (-siz-əm) *n.*

cyn´i·cal (sin´i-kəl) *adj.* incredulous of man's goodness; sarcastic.

cy´no·sure´ (sī´nə-shŭr´) *n.* a center of attention.

cy´press (sī´prəs) *n.* a cone-bearing evergreen tree.

cyst (sist) *n.* (*Pathol.*) a diseased sac in the body. —**cys´tic,** *adj.*

cys·ti´tis (sis-tī´tis) *n.* inflammation of the urinary bladder.

cy·tol´o·gy (sī-tol´ə-jė) *n.* the science treating of cells.

czar (zär) *n.* **1,** the title of the former emperors of Russia. **2,** a despot. Also, **tsar.** —**cza·ri´na** (zä-rē´nə) *n.fem.*

Czech (chek) *n. & adj.* of the Slavic people of Bohemia in Czechoslovakia, their language, etc.

D

D, d (dē) *n.* the fourth letter of the English alphabet.

dab *v.t. & i.* [**dabbed, dab´bing**] touch lightly; pat; moisten in spots. —*n.* **1,** a gentle blow. **2,** a small amount; bit. **3,** a flat fish.

dab´ble (dab´əl) *v.i.* **1,** splash or play in water. **2,** do anything in a superficial manner. —**dab´bler,** *n.*

dace (dās) *n.* a small river fish.

dachs´hund´ (däks´hŭnd´) *n.* a small dog with very short legs.

Da´cron (dā´krən) *n.* a yarn or fabric made of a certain plastic.

dac´tyl (dak´təl) *n.* a metrical foot: one syllable stressed then two unstressed, as ten´der-ly. —**dac·tyl´ic,** *adj.*

dac´´ty·lol´o·gy (dak´´tə-lol´ə-jė) *n.* conversing by means of the fingers; language of the deaf and dumb.

dad *n.* (*Colloq.*) father. Also, **dad´dy** (-ė).

da´da (dä´də) *n.* a style in art producing meaningless or apparently irrational expressions.

da´do (dā´dō) *n.* **1,** the part of a pedestal between the base and the cornice. **2,** a decorative covering for the lower part of a wall.

daf´fo·dil (daf´ə-dil) *n.* an early spring flower, yellow in color, of the narcissus family.

daff´y (daf´ė) *adj.* (*Colloq.*) crazy; silly. —**daf´fi·ness,** *n.*

daft (däft) *adj.* foolish; silly; insane.

dag´ger (dag´ər) *n.* **1,** a pointed short straight weapon for stabbing. **2,** a reference mark (†) in printing.

da·guerre´o·type´ (də-ger´ə-tīp´) *n.* **1,** an early process in photography. **2**, a picture produced by such process.

dahl′ia (dăl′yà) *n.* a plant bearing large, brilliantly colored flowers.

dai′ly (dā′lè) *adj. & adv.* happening every day; diurnal. —*n.* a newspaper published every day.

dain′ty (dān′tè) *adj.* of delicate beauty or exquisite taste; neat; fastidious. —*n.* a delicacy; tidbit. —**dain′ti·ness**, *n.*

dai′qui·ri (dī′kə-rè) *n.* a cocktail of rum, lemon or lime juice, and sugar.

dair′y (dâr′è) *n.* **1**, a milk farm. **2**, a building where milk is made into butter and cheese. **3**, a company or shop that makes or sells dairy products. —**dair′y·maid** (-mād) *n.* —**dair′y·man** (-mən) *n.*

da′is (dā′ìs) *n.* a raised platform.

dai′sy (dā′zè) *n.* **1**, a common spring wildflower. **2**, (*Slang*) something considered highly.

dale (dāl) *n.* a small valley; a space between two hills.

dal′ly (dal′è) *v.i.* **1**, play without seriousness; trifle, esp. with another's affections. **2**, idle; delay. —**dal′li·ance** (dal′yəns) *n.*

Dal·ma′tian (dal-mā′shən) *n.* a breed of dog.

dam *n.* **1**, a wall to confine a flow of water, as a river, and raise its level; a floodgate. **2**, any barrier or obstruction that stops a flow. **3**, the female parent of a quadruped. —*v.t.* [**dammed, dam′ming**] **1**, build a dam across (a stream, etc.). **2**, confine; shut up.

Dalmatian

dam′age (dam′ij) *n.* **1**, hurt; harm; injury; loss. **2**, (*pl.*) (*Law*) money awarded for a loss sustained. —*v.t.* hurt; injure.

dam′ask (dam′əsk) *n. & adj.* **1**, linen or silk woven into patterns, esp. for table linen. **2**, a rose color.

dame (dām) *n.* **1**, a woman. **2**, (*cap.*) a British title of honor given to women, equivalent to Sir.

damn (dam) *v.t. & i.* **1**, condemn to hell. **2**, curse; swear. **3**, pronounce bad; censure. —*n.* an oath. —**damned**, *adj.* consigned to perdition; detestable.

dam′na·ble (dam′nə-bəl) *adj.* worthy of condemnation.

dam·na′tion (dam-nā′shən) *n.* **1**, condemnation. **2**, eternal punishment.

damp *adj.* moderately wet; moist.

—*n.* **1**, a condition of extreme humidity; moisture. **2**, a poisonous vapor in coal mines. —*v.t.* **1**, moisten; wet. **2**, dispirit; deaden. **3**, extinguish; smother. —**damp′en** (-ən) *v.t. & i.* make or become damp. —**damp′ness**, *n.*

damp′er (dam′pər) *n.* **1**, something that checks or discourages. **2**, a metal plate in a flue to regulate draft. **3**, (*Music*) a device in a piano to check vibration of the strings.

dam′sel (dam′zəl) *n.* a maiden; girl.

dam′son (dam′zən) *n.* a black plum.

dance (dàns) *v.i.* **1**, move the body and feet rhythmically to music. **2**, move quiveringly from emotion. **3**, bound up and down. —*v.t.* cause to move up and down. —*n.* **1**, a succession of ordered steps and movements to music. **2**, a tune to which people dance. **3**, a party for dancing; ball. —**danc′er**, *n.*

dan·de·li′on (dan′də-lī′ən) *n.* a common herb with a large, bright yellow flower.

dan′der (dan′dər) *n.* (*Colloq.*) temper; anger.

dan′dle (dan′dəl) *v.t.* move (an infant) up and down in the arms or on the knee; fondle.

dan′druff (dan′drəf) *n.* a crust that forms on the scalp and comes off in small scales or dust.

dan′dy (dan′dè) *n.* **1**, a dude; fop. **2**, (*Slang*) something especially acceptable or excellent. —*adj.* very good; quite suitable.

dan′ger (dān′jər) *n.* exposure to injury, loss, pain, or other evil. —**dan′ger·ous**, *adj.* **1**, not safe; hazardous. **2**, causing danger.

dan′gle (dang′gəl) *v.i. & t.* hang loosely; be pending or suspended.

dank *adj.* unpleasantly damp; humid; moist. —**dank′ness**, *n.*

dan·seuse′ (dàn-sûz′) *n.* a female professional dancer.

dap′per (dap′ər) *adj.* **1**, carefully dressed and groomed (of a man); neat; trim. **2**, little and active.

dap′ple (dap′əl) *v.t.* mark with different-colored spots.

dare (dâr) *v.t.* **1**, challenge; defy. **2**, face boldly. —*v.i.* [*pret.* **dared** or **durst** (dêrst)] have courage; venture. —*n.* a challenge. —**dar′ing**, *n.* boldness; recklessness; intrepidity.

dare′dev″il (dâr′dev″əl) *n.* a reckless person. —*adj.* rash; venturesome; reckless. —**dare′dev″il·try**, *n.*

dark (därk) *adj.* **1**, without illumination; unlighted. **2**, not light in color, as skin or a shade. **3**, shaded;

obscure; concealed. **4,** gloomy; dreary; morose; glowering. **5,** wicked; sinister. —*n.* **1,** absence of light; nightfall. **2,** secrecy. **3,** ignorance. **4,** a color or shade not light. —**dark′ness,** *n.*

dark′en (där′kən) *v.t. & i.* make or become dark or darker.

dark horse an unexpected contestant or winner.

dark′room″ *n.* a darkened room, used for handling and developing photographic film.

dark′y (där′kē) *n. (Offensive)* a Negro.

dar′ling (där′ling) *n. & adj.* favorite; dear; beloved.

darn (därn) *v.t.* **1,** mend by interweaving stitches of yarn or thread. **2,** *(Colloq.)* damn (a mild form). —*adj.* [also, **darned**] damned. —*n.* **1,** a torn spot so mended. **2,** a mild oath.

dar′nel (där′nəl) *n.* a common field weed.

dart (därt) *n.* **1,** a pointed missile, usually thrown by the hand as a weapon or in a game. **2,** *(pl.)* a game of target shooting with darts. **3,** a sudden, swift progressive movement; a dash. —*v.t. & i.* **1,** throw or thrust suddenly. **2,** suddenly spring or start forward.

dash *v.t.* **1,** strike or thrust suddenly and violently, so as to shatter. **2,** sprinkle; spatter. **3,** (with *off*) sketch or write, in a hasty manner. **4,** cast down; frustrate. —*v.i.* rush violently, esp. for a brief distance. —*n.* **1,** a sudden and violent blow or thrust. **2,** a splashing of a liquid; a small amount of a fluid added to a concoction, as for flavoring. **3,** a vigorous, energetic manner; striking appearance or behavior. **4,** a horizontal stroke (—) used in punctuation to signify a sudden change of thought. **5,** a long signal in telegraphic code, transcribed as —•. **6,** a swift rush, esp. a short race.

dash′board″ (dash′bôrd″) *n.* a panel facing the driver of a vehicle.

dash′er (dash′ər) *n.* **1,** that which dashes. **2,** a plunging arm in a machine.

dash′ing *adj.* high-spirited; gay; romantic.

das′tard (das′tərd) *n.* a coward. —**das′tard·ly,** *adj.* cowardly; mean; reprehensible.

da′ta (dā′tə) *n. pl.* [*sing.* **da′tum**] facts or truths given or admitted and used as a basis for conclusions.

date (dāt) *n.* **1,** the time or period of an event, usually stated by year and often month and day. **2,** a time of execution, as marked on a document, etc. **3,** *(Colloq.)* an appointment; engagement. **4,** a tree, the date palm, or its edible fruit. —*v.t.* **1,** mark with a time. **2,** note or set

the time of. **3,** *(Colloq.)* make an appointment with, in courtship. —*v.i.* exist from a point in time. —**dat′ed,** *adj.* **1,** marked with a date; classified by date. **2,** old-fashioned.

da′tive (dā′tiv) *n. & adj.* a grammatical case signifying the indirect object.

da·tu′ra (də-tyū′rə) *n.* a poisonous plant with a disagreeable odor and narcotic properties.

daub (dâb) *v.t. & i.* **1,** smear or cover roughly. **2,** spread or pat (a substance) on something. **3,** paint badly or coarsely. —*n.* **1,** a spot of paint, etc.; a smear. **2,** an inartistic painting. —**daub′er,** *n.* an inept painter.

daugh′ter (dâ′tər) *n.* **1,** a girl or woman considered with reference to her parents. **2,** a female descendant of any degree. —**daugh′ter-in-law″,** *n.* a son's wife.

daugh′ter·ly (-lē) *adj.* like or befitting a daughter.

daunt (dânt) *v.t.* intimidate; discourage. —**daunt′less,** *adj.* fearless; intrepid.

dau′phin (dâ′fin) *n.* title of the heir apparent to the crown of France (1349-1830).

dav′en·port (dav′ən-pôrt″) *n.* a sofa, often one convertible to a bed.

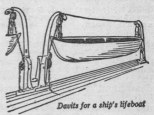

Davits for a ship's lifeboat

dav′it (dav′it) *n.* an apparatus for suspending, lowering, or hoisting a boat or anchor.

daw′dle (dâ′dəl) *v.i. & t. (Colloq.)* idle; loiter; trifle; waste time.

dawn (dân) *n.* **1,** the break of day. **2,** the beginning of anything. —*v.i.* **1,** begin to grow light. **2,** begin to open or expand. **3,** begin to be evident.

day (dā) *n.* **1,** the period between the rising and setting of the sun. **2,** the time of one revolution of the earth on its axis, 24 hours. **3,** (often *pl.*) an epoch; era. **4,** a definite period of glory, influence, activity, etc. —**day bed,** a couch that may be used as a bed.

day′break″ *n.* dawn; sunrise.

day′dream″ *n.* a train of fanciful thoughts while awake.

day letter a telegram sent by day but at a reduced rate for deferred delivery.

day'light" *n.* direct, not reflected, light from the sun. —**daylight saving time,** a reckoning of time, used in summer, that sets timepieces ahead by one hour in order to afford an extra period of daylight.

day'time" *n.* the hours between sunrise and sunset.

daze (dāz) *n.* a sensation of confusion or bewilderment. —*v.t.* stun; bewilder; astound.

daz'zle (daz'əl) *v.t.* overpower with an excess of light, brilliance, or magnificence.

de- (dē) *pref.* 1, down, as in *degrade.* 2, off; away; not; as in *detach, deformed.* 3, same as *dis-*.

dea'con (dē'kən) *n.* a cleric or layman who assists a minister. —**dea'con·ess,** *n.fem.*

dead (ded) *adj.* 1, not living; not existing; deceased. 2, void; useless; forgotten. 3, complete, as *a dead stop;* exact. 4, lacking feeling; lacking the power to rebound; dull. 5, lacking interest, appeal, or flavor. —*adv.* completely; exactly. —*n.* 1, that or those which no longer exist. 2, an extreme or culminating point.

dead'beat" *n.* (*Slang*) one who avoids paying.

dead'en (ded'ən) *v.t.* 1, deprive of sensation; make less acute; dull; weaken; retard; lessen. 2, make soundproof.

dead end a point at which a street or other passageway stops abruptly.

dead'eye" *n.* 1, a device used by seamen to extend the shrouds and stays. 2, (*Slang*) an expert rifleman.

dead'head" *n.* one who obtains any privilege without paying for it.

dead heat a race in which two or more contestants finish exactly even.

dead letter a letter that is unclaimed or cannot be delivered.

dead'line" *n.* a time on or before which a task must be completed.

dead'lock" *n.* an impasse.

dead'ly (ded'lē) *adj.* 1, able to kill; lethal. 2, relentless; malignant. 3, suggestive of death or deadness. 4, (*Colloq.*)exceedingly dull. —**dead'li·ness,** *n.*

dead'pan" (*Slang*) *adj.* lacking expression of any feeling, as the face. —*n.* a face that has no expression.

dead reckoning the calculation of a ship's place at sea from the log and compass.

deaf (def) *adj.* 1, unable to hear. 2, refusing to listen; unpersuaded. —**deaf'ness,** *n.*

deaf'en (-ən) *v.t.* 1, make deaf. 2, seem too loud to (someone). —**deaf'en·ing,** *adj.* unpleasantly loud.

deaf'mute" *n.* one who is both deaf and dumb.

deal (dēl) *v.t.* [*pret. & p.p.* dealt (delt)] 1, apportion; distribute. 2, deliver, as a blow. —*v.i.* 1, (with *out*) dispose (of); be concerned; negotiate. 2, (with *in*) trade; do business. 3, distribute playing cards in a game. —*n.* 1, a transaction; a business arrangement; an agreement. 2, a portion; a large quantity. 3, the distribution of cards, the cards as distributed, and the play of them.

deal'er (dē'lər) *n.* 1, a merchant; one who buys and resells the product of another. 2, one who deals (cards). —**deal'er·ship",** *n.* the right to sell a manufacturer's product in a specific territory.

deal'ing (dē'ling) *n.* 1, behavior; conduct. 2, (usually *pl.*) business transactions.

dean (dēn) *n.* 1, an ecclesiastical title. 2, the faculty head of a university or college. 3, the senior member of any group. —**dean'er·y** (-ə-rē) *n.* the residence of a dean.

dear (dir) *adj.* 1, beloved. 2, valuable. 3, costly. 4, a perfunctory salutation in letters, as *Dear Sirs.* —*n.* a term of endearment; darling. —**dear'ness,** *n.*

dearth (dėrth) *n.* scarcity; lack.

death (deth) *n.* 1, the act of dying; cessation, esp. of life. 2, (*cap.*) the personification of the inevitability of death. 3, lack of existence; the state of being dead. 4, a plague; a fatal disease. —**death'bed"** *n.* the bed in which a person dies. —**death'ly,** *adv.* suggestive of death.

de·ba'cle (dā-bä'kəl) *n.* 1, an utter failure; a sudden inglorious end. 2, a stampede; panic.

de·bar' (di-bär') *v.t.* [**de·barred', -bar'ring**] shut out; exclude; preclude. —**de·bar'ment,** *n.*

de·bark' (di-bärk') *v.t. & i.* leave a ship to go ashore; disembark; land from a vessel. —**de"bar·ka'tion,** *n.*

de·base' (di-bās') *v.t.* degrade; adulterate. —**de·base'ment,** *n.*

de·bat'a·ble (di-bāt'ə-bəl) *adj.* subject to question or doubt; moot.

de·bate' (di-bāt') *v.i. & t.* 1, discuss; engage in an argument for and against; dispute; contend. 2, reflect; consider. —*n.* 1, a controversy; a contest by argument. 2, a quarrel.

de·bauch' (di-bäch') *v.t.* corrupt; ruin. —*v.i.* engage in wild and dissipated living. —*n.* an intemperate party; carousal.

de·bauch'er·y (-ə-rĕ) *n.* immoral and excessive indulgence.

de·ben'ture (di-ben'chər) *n.* **1**, a writ acknowledging a debt. **2**, an unsecured interest-bearing bond.

de·bil'i·tate" (di-bil'ə-tāt") *v.t.* weaken; enfeeble. —**de·bil"i·ta'tion,** *n.*

de·bil'i·ty (di-bil'ə-tĕ) *n.* feebleness.

deb'it *n.* **1**, a recorded item of money owed; a charge. **2**, an entry on the left-hand side of the ledger, which carries all items charged to an account. —*v.t.* charge with or as a debt.

deb"o·nair' (deb'ə-nâr') *adj.* gay; lighthearted; affable; courteous.

de·bouch' (di-boosh') *v.i.* come out; emerge, as from a narrow passage into the open. —**de·bouch'ment,** *n.*

de·bris' (də-brē') *n.* fragments of a former whole; rubbish; ruins.

debt (det) *n.* **1**, that which is owed. **2**, an obligation to make payment in money or kind. —**debt'or,** *n.* one who owes something.

de·bunk' (dê-bunk') *v.t.* (*Colloq.*) strip of sham; show the truth of.

de·but' (di-bū') *n.* a first public appearance.

deb'u·tante" (deb'yû-tänt") *n.* a young woman during her first season in society.

dec·a- (dek'ə) *pref.* ten; tenfold.

dec'ade (dek'ād) *n.* **1**, a period of ten consecutive years. **2**, a set of ten.

de·ca'dence (di-kā'dəns) *n.* a process or state of decay or deterioration. —**de·ca'dent,** *adj.*

dec'a·gon" (dek'ə-gon") *n.* a ten-sided plane figure.

dec"a·he'dron (dek'ə-hē'drən) *n.* a solid figure having 10 faces.

de·cal"co·ma'ni·a (di-kal'kə-mā'nê-ə) *n.* a picture or design that can be transferred to wood, glass, china, or other smooth surfaces. Also (*Colloq.*) **de·cal'.**

Dec'a·logue" (dek'ə-lâg") *n.* the Ten Commandments.

de·camp' (di-kamp') *v.i.* **1**, march off; break camp. **2**, depart unceremoniously; run away.

de·cant' (di-kant') *v.t.* **1**, pour gently, as liquor from its sediment. **2**, transfer (a liquor) from one container to a smaller one. —**de·cant'er,** *n.* a fancy bottle from which liquor is served.

Decanter

de·cap'i·tate" (di-kap'i-tāt") *v.t.* cut off the head of; behead. —**de·cap"i·ta'tion,** *n.*

de·cath'lon (di-kath'lon) *n.* an athletic contest consisting of ten separate track or field events.

de·cay' (di-kā') *v.i. & t.* become dead matter; rot; decompose; deteriorate. —*n.* **1**, loss of soundness, health, substance, etc.; deterioration. **2**, dead or decomposed matter.

de·cease' (di-sēs') *n.* death; demise. —*v.i.* die.

de·ce'dent (di-sē'dənt) *n.* (*Law*) one who is dead.

de·ceit' (di-sēt') *n.* **1**, the act of deceiving; fraud; cheating; artifice. **2**, something that tricks or deceives. —**de·ceit'ful,** *adj.* tending to deceive.

de·ceive' (di-sēv') *v.t.* give a false impression to; mislead; delude; cheat; trick. —*v.i.* be untruthful; lie; misrepresent.

de·cel'er·ate" (dê-sel'ə-rāt") *v.t. & i.* lessen the speed of; slow down. —**de·cel"er·a'tion,** *n.*

De·cem'ber (di-sem'bər) *n.* the twelfth month of the year.

de'cen·cy (dē'sən-sê) *n.* state or quality of being decent.

de·cen'ni·al (di-sen'ê-əl) *adj.* occurring once in 10 years; marking the end of a ten-year period. —*n.* observance of a tenth anniversary.

de'cent (dē'sənt) *adj.* **1**, respectable; ethical; moral. **2**, in good taste; becoming; suitable; proper. **3**, virtuous; modest. **4**, fair; good enough.

de·cep'tion (di-sep'shən) *n.* **1**, the act of misleading. **2**, a misrepresentation; artifice; fraud. —**de·cep'tive,** *adj.* intended to or tending to deceive.

dec'i- (des'ə) *pref.* one-tenth; divided by ten.

dec'i·bel" (des'ə-bel") *n.* a unit for measuring the loudness of sounds.

de·cide' (di-sīd') *v.t.* **1**, make up one's mind; settle or determine a question. **2**, choose; exercise an option. —*v.i.* **1**, determine; settle. **2**, arbitrate. —**de·cid'ed,** *adj.* **1**, unmistakable. **2**, determined.

de·cid'u·ous (di-sij'oo-əs) *adj.* **1**, shedding the leaves annually, as trees. **2**, falling off, as leaves; transitory.

dec'i·mal (des'ə-məl) *adj.* pert. to 10 or tenths. —*n.* a fraction with a power of ten for its denominator. —**decimal point,** a dot to show that the number following is a decimal.

dec'i·mate" (des'ə-māt") *v.t.* destroy a great number of, literally one tenth. —**dec"i·ma'tion,** *n.*

de·ci'pher (di-sī'fər) *v.t.* 1, translate from cipher to clear language; decode. 2, find the meaning of. —**de·ci'pher·ment**, *n.*

de·ci'sion (di-sizh'ən) *n.* 1, the act of making up one's mind. 2, determination; resolution. 3, a judgment, as of a court of law.

de·ci'sive (di-sī'siv) *adj.* final; conclusive; resolute. —**de·ci'sive·ness**, *n.*

deck (dek) *n.* 1, the floor of a ship. 2, a package, as of playing cards. —*v.t.* (often with *out*) adorn; array.

deck'le (dek'əl) *n.* 1, a device used in paper-making. 2, the ragged edge characteristic of handmade paper. —**deck'le-edged'**, *adj.*

de·claim' (di-klām') *v.t. & i.* 1, speak or write in an oratorical or pompous style. 2, make a formal speech.

dec''la·ma'tion (dek''lə-mā'shən) *n.* act or result of declaiming. —**de·clam'a·to·ry** (di-klam'ə-tôr-ē) *adj.*

dec''la·ra'tion (dek''lə-rā'shən) *n.* 1, act of declaring. 2, statement; assertion. 3, (*Cards*) the high bid.

de·clar'a·tive (di-klar'ə-tiv) *adj.* positive; constituting a statement.

de·clare' (di-klâr') *v.t. & i.* 1, assert explicitly; state; say. 2, announce; proclaim formally. 3, bid.

dé·clas·sé' (de-klà-sā') (*Fr.*) *adj.* having lost social standing.

de·clen'sion (di-klen'shən) *n.* 1, descent. 2, deterioration. 3, (*Gram.*) inflection of nouns, etc.

de·cline' (di-klīn') *v.t.* 1, bend or slant down; droop. 2, approach termination; deteriorate. 3, refuse. 4, (*Gram.*) inflect, as a noun or adjective. —*v.t.* 1, depress; bend down. 2, refuse; reject. —*n.* 1, a falling off; decay. 2, a gradual diminishing. —**dec''li·na'tion** (dek''li-nā'shən) *n.*

de·cliv'i·ty (di-kliv'ə-tē) *n.* a downward slope.

de·coct' (di-kokt') *v.t.* extract by boiling. —**de·coc'tion**, *n.*

de·code' (dē-kōd') *v.t.* translate a message from code.

dé·col·le·tage' (dā-kol'ə-täzh'') *n.* (*Fr.*) a low-necked gown, or the wearing of it.

dé''col·le·té' (dā''kol-tā') *adj.* low-necked, as an evening gown.

de''com·pose' (dē''kəm-pōz') *v.t. & i.* 1, resolve into its original parts. 2, decay. —**de''com·po·si'tion**, *n.*

dé·cor' (dā-kôr') *n.* (*Fr.*) a plan or theme of decorative arrangement, esp. of a room.

dec'o·rate'' (dek'ə-rāt'') *v.t.* 1, embellish; ornament. 2, reward or distinguish, as with a medal. 3, paint; refinish. 4, design and outfit (a room, show window, etc.). —**dec'o·ra''tor**, *n.*

dec''o·ra'tion (dek''ə-rā'shən) *n.* 1, act of decorating. 2, an ornament, medal, ribbon, etc. —**dec'o·ra·tive**, *adj.* adding beauty; ornamental.

dec'o·rous (dek'ə-rəs) *adj.* well-behaved; proper; seemly.

de·co'rum (di-kôr'əm) *n.* propriety.

de·coy' (di-koi') *n.* 1, a live or imitation bird used as a lure to attract wild fowl. 2, a stratagem. 3, one who allures, as into a trap. —*v.t. & t.* lure; entice.

de·crease' (di-krēs') *v.t. & t.* become or make less; diminish; reduce. —*n.* (dē'krēs) a reduction; diminution; falling off.

de·cree' (di-krē') *n.* an edict; a law; a judgment, esp. of a court of equity. —*v.t. & i.* order; promulgate.

de·crep'it (di-krep'it) *adj.* weakened, esp. by age; infirm. —**de·crep'i·tude** (-tood') *n.*

de·crep'i·tate' (di-krep'ə-tāt') *v.t. & t.* crackle, esp. in roasting. —**de·crep''i·ta'tion**, *n.*

de·cry' (di-krī') *v.t.* blame; deplore; disparage; censure.

dec'u·ple (dek'yû-pəl) *adj.* tenfold. —*n.* a number repeated 10 times.

de·cus'sate (di-kus'āt) *v.t. & t.* intersect, like an X. —*adj.* intersecting. —**de''cus·sa'tion**, *n.*

ded'i·cate'' (ded'i-kāt'') *v.t.* 1, set aside or mark for a specific purpose, esp. testimonial; consecrate; devote. 2, inscribe or address (a book, etc.) to someone. —**ded''i·ca'tion**, *n.* —**ded'i·ca·to·ry** (di-kə-tôr-ē) *adj.*

de·duce' (di-doos') *v.t.* derive or conclude by reasoning. —**de·duc'i·ble**, *adj.*

de·duct' (di-dukt') *v.t.* take away; subtract. —**de·duct'i·ble**, *adj.* capable of being subtracted.

de·duc'tion (di-duk'shən) *n.* 1, act or result of deducting or deducing. 2, reasoning from the general to the particular. —**de·duc'tive**, *adj.*

deed (dēd) *n.* 1, a thing done; an act. 2, an exploit. 3, a legal document for conveying real estate. —*v.t.* transfer by deed.

deem (dēm) *v.t.* hold as an opinion; think; judge.

deep (dēp) *adj.* 1, extending far downward, backward, or within. 2, studiously engaged; absorbed. 3, implicated; involved. 4, profound; abstruse. 5, wise; penetrating. 6, low in pitch. 7, dark and rich in color; intense. 8, heartfelt. —*n.* 1, the sea. 2, the culminating point. —**deep'en**, *v.t. & i.* increase in depth. —**deep'ness**, *n.*

Deep'freeze" n. (T.N.) a cabinet in which food can be frozen and stored.

deep'laid" adj. secret and crafty, as a scheme.

deep'seat"ed adj. firmly imbedded.

deer (dir) n. [pl. deer] a ruminant mammal, the male of which bears deciduous horns or antlers.

Deer

de·face' (di-fās') v.t. mar the face or surface of; disfigure. —de·face'ment, n.

de·fal'cate (di-fal'kāt) v.i. misappropriate money, etc.; embezzle. —de'fal·ca'tion (dē"fal-kā'shən) n. act of defalcating; the amount so taken.

def"a·ma'tion (def"ə-mā'shən) n. act or effect of defaming; slander or libel.

de·fam'a·to·ry (di-fam'ə-tôr-ē) adj. slanderous.

de·fame' (di-fām') v.t. dishonor by injurious reports; slander.

de·fault' (di-fâlt') v.i. & t. 1, fail in fulfilling an obligation or duty, esp. legal or financial. 2, (Sports) lose (a match) by failure to appear. —n. a deficiency; failure of duty.

de·feat' (di-fēt') v.t. 1, conquer or overcome, in a battle or contest. 2, thwart; baffle. —n. a setback; the act of defeating or being defeated; a loss. —de·feat'ism, n. the will to surrender without fighting. —de·feat'ist, n.

def'e·cate" (def'ə-kāt") v.t. & i. clear of impurities. —def"e·ca'tion, n.

de·fect' (di-fekt') n. 1, a fault; an imperfection. 2, a deficiency.

de·fec'tion (di-fek'shən) n. desertion.

de·fec'tive (di-fek'tiv) adj. 1, imperfect. 2, subnormal (in intelligence). —n. a subnormal person. —de·fec'tive·ness, n.

de·fend' (di-fend') v.t. & i. 1, guard against danger; shield. 2, vindicate; uphold. 3, contest (in court).

de·fend'ant (di-fen'dənt) n. (Law) one who is sued.

de·fend'er (di-fen'dər) n. 1, one who guards. 2, one who resists attack.

de·fense' (di-fens') n. 1, resistance against assault. 2, a fortification; a safeguard. 3, a speech in vindication. 4, (Law) the argument and evidence of the defendant; the defendant and his counsel. Also, defence. —de·fense'less, adj. helpless; vulnerable. —de·fen'si·ble, adj. capable of being defended.

de·fen'sive (di-fen'siv) adj. 1, pert. to defense or to that which defends. 2, defending; fearing or expecting attack. —n. 1, resistance to attack. 2, a defending party or side. —de·fen'sive·ness, n.

de·fer' (di-fėr') v.i. & t. [-ferred', -fer'ring] 1, yield to another's opinion. 2, delay; postpone. —de·fer'ment, n. postponement.

def'er·ence (def'ə-rəns) n. submission to the judgment of another; respect. —def"er·en'tial (-ren'shəl) adj. respectful.

de·fi'ance (di-fī'əns) n. 1, a challenge to fight. 2, contempt of authority or an opposing force. —de·fi'ant, adj. full of antagonism; challenging.

de·fi'cient (di-fish'ənt) adj. inadequate; imperfect. —de·fi'cien·cy, n.

def'i·cit (def'ə-sit) n. a shortage, esp. in money.

de·file' (di-fīl') v.t. soil; befoul; desecrate; sully. —v.t. march off in a line. —n. a narrow mountain passage. —de·file'ment, n. corruption; desecration.

de·fine' (di-fīn') v.t. 1, set the limits of; prescribe. 2, state the meaning of; describe; explain.

def'i·nite (def'ə-nit) adj. 1, having fixed or clear limits; exact; certain. 2, positive; unequivocal. —definite article (Gram.) in English, the. —def'i·nite·ness, n.

def"i·ni'tion (def"ə-nish'ən) n. act or effect of defining; a statement of the meaning of a word.

de·fin'i·tive (di-fin'ə-tiv) adj. conclusive; fixed; final. —de·fin'i·tive·ness, n.

de·flate' (di-flāt') v.t. 1, remove the air or gas from; reduce in size or importance. 2, lower, as prices.

de·fla'tion (di-flā'shən) n. 1, act of deflating. 2, a decrease in volume, and circulation of money.

de·flect' (di-flekt') v.i. & t. turn aside; bend away. —de·flec'tion, n. —de·flec'tive, adj.

def"lo·ra'tion (def"lə-rā'shən) n. act or result of deflowering.

de·flow'er (di-flow'ər) v.t. 1, strip of flowers. 2, despoil of beauty. 3, ravish.

de·fo'li·ate" (di-fō'lē-āt") v.t. & i. strip (a tree) of leaves. —de·fo'li·a'tion, n.

de·form' (di-fôrm') v.t. 1, mar the natural shape of; disfigure. 2, render ugly; spoil. —de"for·ma'tion (dē"fôr-mā'shən) n. —de·formed', adj. misshapen.

de·form'i·ty (di-fôr'mə-tè) *n.* physical malformation; defect in shape or structure.

de·fraud' (di-frâd') *v.t.* deprive of, by misrepresenting; cheat; dupe.

de·fray' (di-frā') *v.t.* pay for. —**de·fray'al,** *n.*

de"frost' (dē"frôst') *v.t.* remove frost or ice from.

deft *adj.* dextrous; skillful. —**deft'ness,** *n.*

de·funct' (di-funkt') *adj.* dead.

de·fy' (di-fi') *v.t.* 1, challenge; dare. 2, brave; show contempt for.

de·gen'er·a·cy (di-jen'ə-rə-sè) *n.* state of being degenerate; corruptness.

de·gen'er·ate" (di-jen'ə-rāt") *v.i.* pass from a better to an inferior state; deteriorate. —*adj.* (-ət) degraded; worthless. —*n.* (-ət) one of low morals. —**de·gen"er·a'tion,** *n.*

de·grade' (di-grād') *v.t.* 1, reduce in rank or degree. 2, demean; debase. —**deg"ra·da'tion** (deg"rə-dā'shən *n.*

de·gree' (di-grē') *n.* 1, a step in a series. 2, a stage of progress. 3, grade; rank; station. 4, (*Gram.*) a stage in the comparison of an adjective or adverb. 5, a title indicating academic rank or achievement. 6, a unit of temperature. 7, intensive quantity; extent; measure. 8, (*Geom.*, etc.) the 360th part of the circumference of a circle. 9, (*Law*) a distinction in culpability.

de·his'cence (di-his'əns) *n.* (*Bot.*) the opening of the capsules of plants to discharge seeds or pollen. —**de·his'cent,** *adj.*

de·hy'drate (dè-hī'drāt) *v.t.* & *i.* deprive of, or lose, water. —**de"hy·dra'tion,** *n.*

de'ice' (dē'īs') *v.t.* remove ice from. —**de"ic'ers,** *n.pl.* attachments on airplane wings, that vibrate to shake off ice.

de'i·fy' (dē'ə-fī') *v.t.* make a god of; worship; exalt. —**de"i·fi·ca'tion** (-fi-kā'shən) *n.*

deign (dān) *v.i.* condescend; stoop (to an act). —*v.t.* grant.

de'ism (dē'iz-əm) *n.* belief in God. —**de'ist,** *n.*

de'i·ty (dē'ə-tè) *n.* 1, divine nature. 2, a god or goddess.

de·ject' (di-jekt') *v.t.* cast down; dishearten. —**de·ject'ed,** *adj.* sad; depressed. —**de·jec'tion,** *n.* sadness; gloom; discouragement.

de·late' (di-lāt') *v.t.* spread abroad; make public. —**de·la'tion,** *n.*

de·lay' (di-lā') *v.i.* & *t.* 1, procrastinate; wait; put off; defer;

postpone. 2, retard; detain. —*n.* a putting off; a postponement; a stay.

de'le (dē'lè) *v.t.* take out; delete.

de·lec'ta·ble (di-lek'tə-bəl) *adj.* delightful; very pleasing. —**de·lec"ta·bil'i·ty,** **de"lec·ta'tion** (dē"lek-tā'shən) *n.*

del'e·gate (del'i-gət) *n.* one who acts for or represents another or a group; an emissary. —*v.t.* (-gāt') 1, entrust; empower. 2, send as a representative with power to transact business; depute.

del"e·ga'tion (del"i-gā'shən) *n.* 1, act of delegating; what is delegated. 2, a group of delegates.

de·lete' (di-lēt') *v.t.* take out; expunge; erase. —**de·le'tion,** *n.*

del"e·te'ri·ous (del"ə-tir'è-əs) *adj.* injurious. —**del"e·te'ri·ous·ness,** *n.*

delft *n.* a kind of glazed pottery.

de·lib'er·ate" (di-lib'ər-āt") *v.i.* & *t.* reflect carefully; consider. —*adj.* (-ət) 1, careful; unhurried. 2, intentional.

de·lib"er·a'tion (di-lib"ə-rā'shən) *n.* 1, act of deliberating; careful thought. 2, (*pl.*) conference or discussion among a deliberative body.

de·lib'er·a'tive (di-lib'ə-rā'tiv) *adj.* reflecting and weighing carefully. —**deliberative body,** a legislature, committee, etc.

del'i·ca·cy (del'i-kə-sè) *n.* the state or act of being delicate; a delicate thing, esp. a choice food.

del'i·cate (del'i-kət) *adj.* 1, minutely perfect; exquisite. 2, requiring tact or skill. 3, fragile; of a weak constitution. 4, considerate; tactful; sensitive. 5, choice, as food.

del"i·ca·tes'sen (del"ə-kə-tes'ən) *n. pl.* prepared foods, as salads, cooked meats. —*n. sing.* a store where these are sold.

de·li'cious (di-lish'əs) *adj.* highly pleasing to the taste or smell; delightful. —**de·li'cious·ness,** *n.*

de·light' (di-līt') *n.* a high degree of pleasure or satisfaction, or that which affords it. —*v.t.* & *i.* thrill with pleasure. —**de·light'ful,** *adj.* very enjoyable; very attractive.

de·lin'e·ate" (di-lin'è-āt") *v.t.* mark the outline of; describe; depict; sketch. —**de·lin"e·a'tion,** *n.*

de·lin'quent (di-ling'kwənt) *n.* one who fails to perform a duty or to fill an obligation; an offender; a culprit. —**de·lin'quen·cy,** *n.*

del"i·quesce' (del"ə-kwes') *v.i.* melt; become liquid from absorbing moisture. —**del"i·ques'cence,** *n.* —**del"i·ques'cent,** *adj.*

de·lir'i·um (di-lir'è-əm) *n.* 1, a temporary disordered mental state, marked by delusions. **2**, violent excitement; mad rapture. **—de·lir'i·ous**, *adj.*

de·liv'er (di-liv'ər) *v.t.* **1**, set free; liberate; release. **2**, give or hand over; transport to a consignee. **3**, surrender; yield. **4**, give birth to. **5**, cast, as a blow; throw, as a ball. **6**, utter; enunciate.

de·liv'er·ance (-əns) *n.* **1**, delivery, esp. from restraint; rescue. **2**, an expressed thought; a pronouncement.

de·liv'er·y (-ē) *n.* **1**, act of delivering; transport of goods, letters, etc. **2**, a handing over. **3**, release; rescue. **4**, the giving of birth. **5**, manner of delivering. **6**, something delivered.

dell (del) *n.* a small shady valley; a glen.

del·phin'i·um (del-fin'ē-əm) *n.* a handsome garden plant; the larkspur.

del'ta (del'tə) *n.* **1**, the fourth letter of the Greek alphabet ($\triangle$, δ). **2**, a triangular deposit at the mouth of a river split into branches.

Delphinium

del'toid *adj.* triangular. **—n.** the shoulder muscle.

de·lude' (di-lood') *v.t.* convince that something false is true; deceive; cheat.

del'uge (del'ūj) *n.* a heavy downpour of rain; a flood. **—v.t. 1**, overflow. **2**, overwhelm.

de·lu'sion (di-loo'zhən) *n.* **1**, a false belief. **2**, a persistent and false mental conception of facts as they relate to oneself.

de·lu'sive (di-loo'siv) *adj.* **1**, being a delusion. **2**, deluding.

de·lu'so·ry (di-loo'sə-rē) *adj.* tending to delude; delusive.

de luxe (də luks') (*Fr.*) of highest quality; luxurious.

delve (delv) *v.i.* **1**, dig. **2**, carry on laborious and continued research.

dem'a·gogue" (dem'ə-gâg") *n.* **1**, an unprincipled popular orator or leader. **2**, a rabble rouser. **—dem'a·gog"uer·y** (-ə-rē) *n.* **—dem"a·gog'ic** (-goj'ik) *adj.* **—dem"a·gog'i·cal·ly**, *adv.*

de·mand' (di-mànd') *v.t.* **1**, claim by right. **2**, ask insistently. **3**, require; need; call for. **—n. 1**, an authoritative claim. **2**, an urgent request. **3**, that which is demanded. **4**, the state of being sought after. **5**, (*Econ.*) the desire to purchase goods coupled with the power to do so. **—de·mand'ing**, *adj.* **1**, arduous; difficult. **2**, hard to please.

de"mar·ca'tion (dē"mär-kā'shən) *n.* a marking of bounds.

dé·marche' (dē-märsh') *n.* (*Fr.*) a way of procedure; a move or step, esp. one involving a change of policy.

de·mean' (di-mēn') *v.t.* debase; lower.

de·mean'or (di-mēn'ər) *n.* behavior; bearing. Also, **de·mean'our.**

de·ment'ed (di-men'ted) *adj.* insane.

de·men'tia (di-men'shə) *n.* impairment of the mental powers; insanity.

de·mer'it (dē-mer'it) *n.* **1**, a fault. **2**, a mark given for bad conduct or deficiency.

dem·i- (dem-ē; -i) *pref.* half.

dem'i·god" *n.* **1**, an inferior or minor deity. **2**, a being half god and half human.

dem'i·john" (dem'i-jon") *n.* a large jug, usually incased in wicker.

de·mil'i·ta·rize" (dē-mil'i-tə-rīz") *v.t.* **1**, remove troops, fortifications, etc. from. **2**, transfer from military to civil control. **—de·mil'i·ta·ri·za'tion**, *n.*

dem'i·monde" (dem'i-mond") *n.* women of poor reputation; the world in which they move. **—dem'i·mon·daine"** (-dān") *n.* a member of the demimonde.

Demijohn

de·mise' (di-mīz') *n.* **1**, death. **2**, transfer of an estate by death. **—v.t. & i.** transfer, as an estate.

de·mit' (di-mit') *v.t.* [**-mit'ted, -ting**] resign.

dem'i·tasse" (dem'i-tàs") *n.* a small cup of, or for, black coffee.

de·mo'bi·lize" (dē-mō'bə-līz") *v.t.* disband, as troops. **—de·mo'bi·li·za'tion** (-li-zā'shən) *n.*

de·moc'ra·cy (di-mok'rə-sē) *n.* **1**, government by the people. **2**, political and social equality in general; belief in this.

dem'o·crat" (dem'ə-krat") *n.* **1**, a believer in democracy. **2**, one who treats all others as his equals. **3**, (*cap.*) a member of the Democratic political party in the U.S. **—dem'o·crat'ic**, *adj.* **—dem'o·crat'i·cal·ly**, *adv.*

de·mod'ed (di-mō'did) *adj.* out of fashion.

de·mol'ish (di-mol'ish) *v.t.* throw or pull down; destroy. —**dem″o·li'tion** (dem″ə-lish'ən) *n.*

de'mon (dē'mən) *n.* **1**, an evil spirit; a devil. **2**, a wicked or cruel person. **3**, (*Colloq.*) an energetic person. —**de·mo'ni·ac** (di-mō'nĭ-ak), **de″mo·ni'a·cal** (dē″mō-nī'ə-kəl) *adj.*

de·mon'e·tize″ (dē-mon'ə-tīz″) *v.t.* withdraw from use as money. —**de·mon″e·ti·za'tion**, *n.*

de·mon'stra·ble (di-mon'strə-bəl) *adj.* capable of proof by demonstration. —**de·mon″stra·bil'i·ty,** *n.*

dem'on·strate″ (dem'ən-strāt″) *v.t. & i.* **1**, describe or explain by use of examples. **2**, establish the truth of by reasoning; prove. **3**, exhibit and put to test publicly. **4**, point out; make evident. **5**, make a show of force; assemble to show approval or protest.

dem″on·stra'tion (-strā'shən) *n.* **1**, act of demonstrating; exhibition; display. **2**, manifestation of feelings; a show of force, protest, etc.

de·mon'stra·tive (di-mon'strə-tiv) *adj.* **1**, strongly exhibiting one's feelings. **2**, conclusive, as proof. **3**, (*Gram.*) pointing out an object, as *this, that.* —**de·mon'stra·tive·ness,** *n.*

dem'on·stra″tor (dem'ən-strā'tər) *n.* one who or that which demonstrates, esp. an automobile so used.

de·mor'al·ize″ (di-môr'ə-līz″) *v.t.* **1**, corrupt. **2**, deprive of spirit or energy; dishearten. **3**, throw into confusion or disorder. —**de·mor″al·i·za'tion** (-ə-zā'shən) *n.*

de·mote' (di-mōt') *v.t.* reduce in rank or class. —**de·mo'tion,** *n.*

de·mul'cent (di-mul'sənt) *adj.* softening; mollifying; soothing.

de·mur' (di-mēr') *v.i.* [-**murred'**, -**mur'ring**] take exception; object. —*n.* objection. —**de·mur'ral,** *n.*

de·mure' (di-myûr') *adj.* **1**, affectedly modest; prim. **2**, sedate. —**de·mure'ness,** *n.*

de·mur'rage (di-mēr'ij) *n.* detention of a vessel or freight car beyond the time stipulated; the charge for such delay.

de·mur'rer (di-mēr'ər) *n.* (*Law*) a plea that the case be dismissed though the facts alleged are conceded.

den *n.* **1**, a cave for a wild beast. **2**, a haunt; squalid resort. **3**, a small, snug private room.

de·na'ture (dē-nā'chər) *v.t.* change the nature of, esp. of alcohol, to render it unfit to drink.

-den'dron *suf.* tree.

den'gue (deng'gā) *n.* a tropical disease: *dandy-fever.*

de·ni'al (di-nī'əl) *n.* **1**, the act of contradiction; negation. **2**, refusal to grant a request. **3**, a refusal to accept or acknowledge. **4**, restraint of personal desires; poverty.

de·nier' (də-nir') *n.* the measure of weight or fineness of a yarn.

den'im (den'əm) *n.* a coarse twilled cotton cloth.

den'i·zen (den'ə-zən) *n.* a dweller; an inhabitant.

de·nom'i·nate″ (di-nom'ə-nāt″) *v.t.* give a specific name to; designate.

de·nom″i·na'tion (di-nom″i-nā'-shən) *n.* **1**, act of naming; a name. **2**, a religious sect. **3**, a unit in a series, as of quantity, value, etc.

de·nom'i·na″tor (di-nom′i-nā″tər) *n.* (*Math.*) the part of a fraction that represents the divisor: in ½, 2 is the denominator.

de·note' (di-nōt') *v.t.* **1**, point out and identify; designate. **2**, be a sign or symptom of; indicate. —**de″no·ta'tion** (dē″nō-tā'shən) *n.*

dé″noue·ment' (dā″noo-män') *n.* the solution of a plot, as in a play.

de·nounce' (di-nowns') *v.t.* **1**, blame or brand publicly; stigmatize. **2**, inform against; condemn. **3**, announce the intention of abrogating a treaty. —**de·nounce'ment,** *n.*

dense (dens) *adj.* **1**, having great closeness of parts; thick; compact. **2**, stupid. —**dense'ness, den'si·ty** (-sə-tē) *n.*

dent *n.* a small hollow or depression made by a blow. —*v.t. & i.* make a dent (in).

den'tal (den'təl) *adj.* pert. to the teeth.

den'ti·frice (den'tə-fris) *n.* a preparation for cleaning the teeth.

den'tin *n.* the hard tissue of a tooth, under the enamel. Also, **den'tine.**

den'tist *n.* a doctor for the teeth. —**den'tist·ry** (-rē) *n.* the science of treating the teeth; dental surgery.

den'ture (den'chər) *n.* a set of false teeth.

de·nude' (di-nūd') *v.t.* strip or divest of all covering.

de·nun″ci·a'tion (di-nun″sē·ā'-shən) *n.* act or result of denouncing. —**de·nun'ci·a·to·ry** (-ə-tôr-ē) *adj.*

de·ny' (di-nī') *v.t.* **1**, refuse to admit the truth of; contradict. **2**, refuse to give or grant. **3**, refuse to accept or admit. **4**, renounce; disown.

de'o·dar″ (dē'ə-där″) *n.* an E. Indian evergreen tree.

de·o'dor·ant (dē-ō'də-rənt) *n.* a preparation that destroys unpleasant odor. —*adj.* deodorizing.

de·o'dor·ize" (dē-ō'də-rīz") v.t. remove odor from. —**de·o'dor·i·za'tion,** n.

de·part' (di-pärt') v.i. 1, go or move away; leave (often with from). 2, deviate; abandon. 3, die. —**de·par'ture** (di-pär'chər) n.

de·part'ment (di-pärt'mənt) n. a separate part or division of a complex system; a branch of a business, government, etc. —**de·part·men'tal** (di-pärt"men'təl) adj. pert. to a department; organized into departments. —**department store,** a retail store dealing in many different kinds of merchandise.

de·pend' (di-pend') v.i. 1, be contingent upon something; hang. 2, (with on or upon) repose confidence; rely. 3, (with on) rely upon for maintenance. —**de·pend'a·ble,** adj. reliable; trustworthy. —**de·pen'dence,** n.

de·pen'den·cy (di-pen'dən-sē) n. 1, dependence. 2, an appurtenance. 3, a territory that is dependent upon, but not a part of, a nation.

de·pen'dent (di-pen'dənt) adj. 1, depending (on) or subject (to). 2, conditional. 3, hanging down. —n. [also, de·pen'dant] one who is supported by another.

de·pict' (di-pikt') v.t. portray by a picture or words. —**de·pic'tion,** n.

dep'i·late" (dep'ə-lāt") v.t. remove the hair from. —**dep"i·la'tion,** n.

de·pil'a·to·ry (di-pil'ə-tôr-ē) n. a preparation for removing unwanted hair.

de·plete' (di-plēt') v.t. exhaust by drawing away, as resources, strength, vital powers. —**de·ple'tion,** n.

de·plore' (di-plôr') v.t. regret; lament. —**de·plor'a·ble,** adj. lamentable; calamitous.

de·ploy' (di-ploi') v.t. & i. (Mil.) spread out on a more extended front. —**de·ploy'ment,** n.

de·po'nent (di-pō'nənt) n. one who gives sworn testimony in writing.

de·pop'u·late" (dē-pop'yə-lāt") v.t. deprive of inhabitants, as by killing or expelling them. —**de·pop"u·la'tion,** n.

de·port' (di-pôrt') v.t. 1, transport forcibly; exile. 2, behave (oneself). —**de"por·ta'tion** (dē"pôr-tā'shən) n.

de·port'ment (-mənt) n. behavior; conduct.

de·pose' (di-pōz') v.t. 1, remove from a high office. 2, testify.

de·pos'it (di-poz'it) v.t. 1, lay down; put; precipitate. 2, place in safekeeping, esp. money in a bank. —n. 1, anything entrusted, as money in a bank. 2, a pledge; a part payment. 3, that which is laid, thrown

down, or settled, as sand from a body of water. 4, a natural accumulation of a mineral in the earth.

dep"o·si'tion (dep'ə-zish'ən) n. 1, act or effect of deposing. 2, sworn testimony.

de·pos'i·tor (di-poz'ə-tər) n. one who deposits, esp. money in a bank.

de·pos'i·to·ry (di-poz'ə-tôr-ē) n. a place where something is deposited; a bank.

de'pot (dē'pō) n. 1, a warehouse; a railroad station. 2, (Mil.) a redistribution point for supplies.

de·prave' (di-prāv') v.t. pervert; corrupt. —**de·prav'i·ty** (di-prav'ə-tē) n.

dep're·cate" (dep'rə-kāt") v.t. plead against; express disapproval of. —**dep"re·ca'tion,** n. —**dep're·ca·to·ry** (-kə-tôr-ē) adj.

de·pre'ci·ate" (di-prē'shē-āt") v.t. & i. 1, become worth less; lessen the value of. 2, belittle. —**de·pre'ci·a'tion,** n. a decrease in value; the amount of the decrease.

dep're·date" (dep'rə-dāt") v.t. & i. lay waste; plunder. —**dep"re·da'tion,** n.

de·press' (di-pres') v.t. 1, press or move downward. 2, weaken. 3, sadden. —**de·pres'sive** (-iv) adj. —**de·pres'sor,** n.

de·pres'sant (di-pres'ent) n. & adj. a sedative.

de·pres'sion (di-presh'ən) n. 1, act of depressing, or state of being depressed. 2, a hollow. 3, an unwarranted and prolonged condition of emotional dejection. 4, a period of decline in business activity.

dep'ri·va'tion (dep'ri-vā'shən) n. 1, act of depriving. 2, poverty; want.

de·prive' (di-prīv') v.t. 1, divest; strip. 2, withhold; prevent from possessing.

depth n. 1, deepness; distance measured downward, inward, or backward. 2, intensity. 3, profundity. —**depth charge,** a mine set to explode at a certain depth.

dep"u·ta'tion (dep'yū-tā'shən) n. 1, appointment to act for another. 2, a group of deputies.

de·pute' (di-pūt') v.t. 1, appoint as an agent. 2, assign to an agent.

dep'u·tize" (dep'yū-tīz") v.t. appoint as agent.

dep'u·ty (dep'yə-tē) n. a representative, assistant, or agent, esp. of a public officer; one deputed.

de·rail' (dē-rāl') v.t. & i. run (a train) off the track. —**de·rail'ment,** n.

de·range' (di-rānj') v.t. 1, disarrange. **2,** disorder the mind of. —de•range'ment, *n.*

der'by (dĕr'bē) *n.* **1,** a man's hat with a stiff rounded crown and narrow brim. **2,** (*cap.*) any of several horse races.

der'e•lict (der'ə-likt) *adj.* **1,** abandoned. **2,** unfaithful. —*n.* **1,** anything abandoned, esp. a ship. **2,** an outcast. **3,** one guilty of neglect. —der'e•lic'tion, *n.*

de•ride' (di-rīd') *v.t.* laugh at contemptuously; mock.

de•ri'sion (di-rizh'ən) *n.* **1,** act of deriding; ridicule. **2,** an object of ridicule or mockery. —de•ri'sive (di-rī'siv) *adj.*

der"i•va'tion (der"i-vā'shən) *n.* **1,** act of deriving. **2,** source.

de•riv'a•tive (di-riv'ə-tiv) *n.* & *adj.* what is derived.

de•rive' (di-rīv') *v.t.* **1,** draw or receive from a source or origin. **2,** deduce; infer. **3,** trace the development of (a word).

derm-, -derm *pref.* & *suf.* skin.

der"ma•tol'o•gy (dĕr"mə-tol'ə-jē) *n.* the science of the skin and its diseases. —der"ma•tol'o•gist, *n.* a practitioner in this science.

der'o•gate' (der'ə-gāt') *v.t.* & *i.* detract from; disparage; depreciate. —der"o•ga'tion, *n.* —de•rog'a•to•ry (di-rog'ə-tôr-ē), de•rog'a•tive, *adj.*

der'rick (der'ik) *n.* **1,** an apparatus for hoisting; a crane. **2,** the framework over an oil well.

Derricks

der'rin•ger (der'in-jər) *n.* an antique short-barreled pistol.

der'vish (dĕr'vish) *n.* a member of a Mohammedan religious cult.

des'cant (des'kant) *n.* **1,** a melody. **2,** a variation; varied discourse. —*v.i.* (des-kant') **1,** sing. **2,** enlarge upon a topic.

de•scend' (di-send') *v.i.* **1,** move downward. **2,** slope downward. **3,** proceed from an original; be derived. **4,** lower oneself morally or socially. —*v.t.* go down upon or along. —de•scend'ent, *adj.*

de•scend'ant (di-sen'dənt) *n.* one descended from an ancestor.

de•scent' (di-sent') *n.* **1,** act or process of descending. **2,** a downward passage or slope. **3,** ancestral lineage.

de•scribe' (di-skrīb') *v.t.* **1,** portray in words. **2,** trace out; outline.

de•scrip'tion (di-skrip'shən) *n.* **1,** the act of representing a thing by words or pictures or signs; such a

representation. **2,** a category. —de•scrip'tive, *adj.* serving to describe.

de•scry' (di-skrī') *v.t.* catch sight of; detect.

des'e•crate' (des'ə-krāt') *v.t.* treat with sacrilege; profane. —des'e•cra'tion, *n.*

des'ert (dez'ərt) *n.* **1,** a dry sandy wasteland. **2,** a wilderness.

de•sert' (di-zĕrt') *v.t.* & *i.* **1,** abandon; forsake. **2,** leave (the army, etc.) without leave and not intending to return. —*n.* (often *pl.*) something deserved. —de•sert'er, *n.* one who deserts, esp. from military service. —de•ser'tion, *n.*

de•serve' (di-zĕrv') *v.t.* & *i.* be entitled to receive, as reward or punishment; be worthy of. —de•serv'ing, *adj.* meritorious; worthy.

des'ic•cate' (des'ə-kāt') *v.t.* & *t.* **1,** dry up; wither. **2,** preserve (food) by drying. —des'ic•ca'tion, *n.*

de•sid'er•a'tum (di-sid"ə-rā'təm) *n.* [*pl.* -ta (-tə)] something desired or needed.

de•sign' (di-zīn') *v.t.* **1,** draw a plan or outline of; sketch. **2,** plan a detailed pattern. **3,** plan; contrive. **4,** intend; purpose. —*v.i.* do original artwork; make an original plan. —*n.* **1,** a preliminary drawing; a plan. **2,** the arrangement of details in a piece of art. **3,** a scheme, esp. a hostile scheme. —de•sign'er, *n.*

des'ig•nate' (dez'ig-nāt') *v.t.* **1,** mark; point out; specify. **2,** name. **3,** appoint. —des'ig•na'tion, *n.*

de•sign'ing *adj.* craftily planning; artful. —*n.* the art of design.

de•sire' (di-zīr') *v.t.* **1,** wish or long for; crave. **2,** ask for; solicit. —*n.* **1,** a wish; craving; longing. **2,** sensual feeling. **3,** a request. **4,** an object wished for. —de•sir'a•ble, *adj.* worth desiring. —de•sir'ous, *adj.* feeling desire.

de•sist' (di-zist') *v.i.* stop; forbear.

desk *n.* **1,** a table for writing, reading, or study. **2,** an official position, esp. in journalism. —desk'work", *n.* clerical work.

des'o•late (des'ə-lət) *adj.* **1,** solitary; lonely; miserable. **2,** uninhabited; abandoned. **3,** barren; ravaged. —*v.t.* (-lāt') make desolate. —des'o•la'tion, *n.*

de•spair' (di-spâr') *v.i.* give up all hope. —*n.* utter lack of hope.

des•patch' (di-spach') *v.t.* & *n.* dispatch.

des'per•a'do (des"pə-rā'dō) *n.* a reckless outlaw.

des'per•ate (des'pər-ət) *adj.* **1,** driven by despair; frantic; reckless. **2,** beyond hope. **3,** extremely dangerous. —des"per•a'tion, *n.*

des'pi·ca·ble (des'pi-kə-bəl) *adj.* to be despised; contemptible.

de·spise' (di-spīz') *v.t.* look down upon; scorn.

de·spite' (di-spīt') *prep.* notwithstanding; in spite of.

de·spoil' (di-spoil') *v.t.* pillage; plunder. —de·spoil'ment, *n.*

de·spond'ent (di-spon'dənt) *adj.* depressed; melancholy. —de·spond'en·cy, *n.*

des'pot (des'pət) *n.* an absolute ruler; a tyrant. —des·pot'ic (-pot'ik) *adj.* —des·pot'i·cal·ly, *adv.* —des'pot·ism, *n.*

des·sert' (di-zėrt') *n.* a sweet served as the last course of a meal.

des'ti·na'tion (des'tə-nā'shən) *n.* 1, the predetermined end of a journey. 2, the purpose for which anything is intended.

des'tine (des'tin) *v.t.* 1, set apart; appoint for a special purpose. 2, predetermine unalterably, as by divine decree.

des'ti·ny (des'tə-nē) *n.* 1, fate; fortune. 2, the inevitable.

des'ti·tute" (des'tə-toot") *adj.* 1, (with *of*) wholly lacking something needed. 2, indigent; extremely poor. —des'ti·tu'tion, *n.*

de·stroy' (di-stroi') *v.t.* 1, totally demolish; ruin; spoil. 2, annihilate; slay. —de·stroy'er, *n.* 1, one who destroys. 2, a type of naval vessel.

de·struc'tion (di-struk'shən) *n.* 1, the act of destroying; a scene of ruin. 2, a force that destroys. —de·struc'tive, *adj.* 1, destroying. 2, causing damage; hurtful.

des'ue·tude" (des'wə-tūd") *n.* disuse.

des'ul·to·ry (des'əl-tôr-ē) *adj.* aimless; disconnected; unmethodical.

de·tach' (di-tach') *v.t.* 1, unfasten; disunite; separate. 2, (*Mil.*) dispatch on a distinct mission. —de·tached', *adj.* 1, separate; independent. 2, impartial in judgment. 3, preoccupied; aloof.

de·tach'ment (di-tach'mənt) *n.* 1, (*Mil.*) troops or ships detached for a special task. 2, aloofness.

de·tail' (di-tāl') *v.t.* 1, express by particulars; enumerate. 2, (*Mil.*) appoint to a special duty. —*n.* 1, an individual part; a particular. 2, (*Mil.*) selection of an individual or a body of troops for a special service; those selected. —de·tailed', *adj.* complete in all particulars.

de·tain' (di-tān') *v.t.* 1, hold back; prevent from proceeding; delay. 2, (*Law*) hold in custody. —de·ten'tion, *n.*

de·tect' (di-tekt') *v.t.* find out; discover (what is hidden or obscure). —de·tec'tion, *n.*

de·tec'tive (di-tek'tiv) *n.* a person whose occupation is investigating crimes.

de·tec'tor (-tər) *n.* an instrument for detecting something.

de·ter' (di-tėr') *v.t.* [-terred', -ter'ring] discourage and stop, esp. by inciting fear or doubt. —de·ter'ment, *n.*

de·ter'gent (di-tėr'jənt) *n.* a cleansing substance. —*adj.* cleansing.

de·te'ri·o·rate" (di-tir'ē-ə-rāt") *v.t. & i.* grow worse; reduce in worth; impair. —de·te'ri·o·ra'tion, *n.*

de·ter'mi·nate (di-tėr'mi-nət) *adj.* definite; fixed.

de·ter'mi·na'tion (di-tėr'mi-nā'shən) *n.* 1, act of determining. 2, a definite decision. 3, firmness. 4, exact measurement.

de·ter'mine (di-tėr'min) *v.t.* 1, resolve; decide. 2, find out; ascertain. 3, bring to a conclusion; end. 4, give direction to. 5, restrict. 6, decree; ordain. —*v.i.* come to a decision. —de·ter'mined, *adj.* resolute; firm.

de·ter'rent (di-tėr'ənt) *adj.* deterring. —*n.* that which deters.

de·test' (di-test') *v.t.* dislike intensely; abhor. —de·test'a·ble, *adj.* hateful. —de"tes·ta'tion (dē"tes-tā'shən) *n.*

de·throne' (dē-thrōn') *v.t.* remove from a reigning or controlling position; depose. —de·throne'ment, *n.*

det'o·nate" (det'ə-nāt") *v.i. & t.* explode or cause to explode; explode loudly. —det'o·na'tion, *n.* —det'o·na"tor, *n.* a substance that causes explosion, as of a bomb.

de'tour" (dē'tůr) *n.* a roundabout way used when the main road is temporarily closed. —*v.i. & t.* go around.

de·tract' (di-trakt') *v.t. & i.* (with *from*) disparage; reduce; take away a part, esp. from reputation. —de·trac'tion, *n.* —de·trac'tive, *adj.* —de·trac'tor, *n.*

det'ri·ment (det'rə-mənt) *n.* an injury or loss, or that which causes it. —det'ri·men'tal (-men'təl) *adj.*

de·tri'tus (di-trī'təs) *n.* (*Geol.*) loose particles eroded from solid rock by water or ice.

deuce (doos) *n.* 1, (*Playing Cards or Dice*) two. 2, (*Tennis*) a tied score in a game. —the deuce! an exclamation of annoyance.

deu·te'ri·um (dū-tir'ē-əm) *n.* a heavy isotope of hydrogen.

de·val'u·ate" (dē-val'yū-āt") *v.t.* lower the value of, esp. of currency. —de·val'u·a'tion, *n.*

dev'as·tate" (dev'ə-stāt") *v.t.* lay waste; pillage. —**dev'as·ta'tion,** *n.*

de·vel'op (di-vel'əp) *v.i. & t.* **1,** advance or expand to a more complex or complete form; train; improve. **2,** unfold gradually; disclose; become apparent. **3,** process a photographic film, causing the image to become visible.

de·vel'op·ment (-mənt) *n.* **1,** act of developing or being developed. **2,** what is developed; a new or newly discovered event or fact.

de'vi·ate" (dē'vē-āt") *v.i. & t.* turn aside from a course; digress from a line of reasoning. —**de'vi·a'tion,** *n.*

de·vice' (di-vīs') *n.* **1,** a contrivance; a gadget. **2,** a scheme; trick. **3,** a heraldic design, as on a coat of arms. **4,** (*pl.*) will; inclination; pleasure.

dev'il (dev'əl) *n.* **1,** (*cap.*) the supreme evil spirit; Satan. **2,** any evil spirit; a demon. **3,** a cruel, fiendish person. **4,** a reckless person, as a *daredevil.* **5,** an expletive: *the devil.* **6,** a printer's errand boy. —*v.t.* **1,** (*Colloq.*) bother; torment. **2,** in cooking, season highly. —**dev'il·ish,** *adj.* **1,** fiendish. **2,** roguish. —**dev'il·ment,** dev'il·try (-trē) *n.* mischief; roguishness.

dev'il·fish" *n.* a large marine animal, esp. an octopus.

Devilfish

de'vi·ous (dē'vē-əs) *adj.* out of the direct or common way; circuitous. —**de'vi·ous·ness,** *n.*

de·vise' (di-vīz') *v.t. & i.* **1,** think out; concoct; scheme. **2,** transmit (property) by will; bequeath. —*n.* a will; the act of transmitting by will. —**di·vis'er,** di·vi'sor, *n.* —**de·vi'see"** (-zē") *n.*

de·void' (di-void') *adj.* (with *of*) empty; destitute or lacking.

de·volve' (di-volv') *v.t. & i.* transmit or delegate to another; (with *upon*) pass to. —**dev"o·lu'tion** (dev-ə-loo'shən) *n.*

de·vote' (di-vōt') *v.t.* **1,** give or apply, as time to a hobby. **2,** consecrate or dedicate. —**de·vot'ed,** *adj.* ardently attached; dedicated.

dev"o·tee' (dev"ə-tē') *n.* one ardently devoted, as to religion; a zealot.

de·vo'tion (de-vō'shən) *n.* **1,** act of devoting; dedication; consecration. **2,** piety; godliness. **3,** affection; love; zeal. **4,** (*pl.*) prayers; religious worship.

de·vour' (di-vowr') *v.t.* **1,** swallow up; eat ravenously. **2,** consume; destroy. **3,** absorb; take in, as a book.

de·vout' (di-vowt') *adj.* devoted to religion or religious worship. —**de·vout'ness,** *n.*

dew (dū) *n.* small drops of moisture condensed from the atmosphere at night.

dew'ber"ry (doo'ber'ē) *n.* a trailing plant or its fruit, similar to blackberry.

dew'claw" *n.* a useless inner claw in the foot of some dogs.

dew'-drop" *n.* a globule of dew.

dew'lap" (doo'lap") *n.* the pendulous skin under the throat of some animals.

dew'y (dū'ē) *adj.* **1,** moist with or like dew. **2,** fresh; young. —**dew'i·ness,** *n.*

dex·ter'i·ty (deks-ter'ə-tē) *n.* manual or mental adroitness; skill. —**dex'ter·ous** (deks'tər-əs) *adj.*

dex'tro- *pref.* right; turning to the right.

dex'trose (deks'trōs) *n.* a form of sugar, obtained commercially from starch.

dex'trous (deks'trəs) *adj.* dexterous.

dhole (dōl) *n.* a wild Asiatic dog.

dhow (dow) *n.* a light Arab sailing vessel.

di- *pref.* two; twofold; double.

di"a·be'tes (dī'ə-bē'tis) *n.* a disease commonly due to the inability of the body to use sugar. —**di"a·bet'ic** (dī'ə-bet'ik) *adj. & n.*

di"a·bol'ic (dī'ə-bol'ik) *adj.* devilish; infernal. Also, **di"a·bol'i·cal.**

di"a·crit'i·cal (dī'ə-krit'ə-kəl) *adj.* serving to distinguish. —**diacritical mark,** a mark that indicates the exact pronunciation of a letter; accent mark.

di'a·dem" (dī'ə-dem") *n.* **1,** a crown. **2,** a jeweled headband.

di'ag·nose' (dī'əg-nōs') *v.t.* ascertain; analyze; determine the nature of, esp. of a disease.

di'ag·no'sis (dī'ig-nō'sis) *n.* [*pl.* -ses (-sēz)] analysis of present condition, esp. of a disease. —**di"ag·nos'tic** (-nos'tik) *adj.* —**di"ag·nos'ti·cal·ly,** *adv.*

di'ag·nos·ti'cian (dī'əg-nos-tish'ən) *n.* a doctor skilled in making diagnoses.

di·ag'o·nal (dī-ag'ə-nəl) *adj.* **1,** extending, as a line, from one angle to another not adjacent, within a polygon. **2,** oblique; slanting; marked by oblique lines. —*n.* a diagonal line or direction.

di'a·gram" (dī'ə-gram") *n.* a chart or plan, esp. a drawing made for demonstrating or graphic analysis.

—*v.t.* chart; plan in detail. —**di'a-gram-mat'ic** (-grə-mat'ik) *adj.* — **di'a-gram-mat'i-cal-ly,** *adv.*

di'al (dī'əl) *n.* **1,** the face on which time is indicated, as on a clock or *sundial.* **2,** any face on which a pointer indicates something, as pressure. **3,** the round index disk on a telephone, used to signal for connections. —*v.t.* measure or signal for, with a dial. —**dial tone,** a buzzing signal indicating that a telephone's dial may be used.

di'a-lect' (dī'ə-lekt') *n.* the special idiom of a locality or class. —**di'a-lec'tal,** *adj.*

di'a-lec'tic (dī'ə-lek'tik) *adj.* **1,** relating to the art of reasoning or discussion. **2,** pert. to dialect. —*n.* **1,** the art of debating, or of logical discussion. **2,** (*pl.*) logic. —**di'a-lec'-ti-cal-ly,** *adv.*

di'a-logue' (dī'ə-lâg') *n.* conversation between two or more persons. Also, **di'a-log'.**

di-am'e-ter (dī-am'ə-tər) *n.* a line dividing a circle into halves.

di'a-met'ri-cal (dī'ə-met'ri-kəl) *adj.* **1,** pert. to a diameter. **2,** absolute; complete.

dia'mond (dī'mənd) *n.* **1,** a form of pure carbon, extremely hard and brilliant; a precious stone. **2,** a quadrilateral, esp. a rhombus, viewed with an angle uppermost (◇). **3,** a playing card so marked. **4,** a baseball field, esp. the infield.

dia'mond-back' (dī'mənd-bak') *n.* **1,** a kind of rattlesnake. **2,** a kind of terrapin.

di'a-net'ics (dī'ə-net'iks) *n. sing.* a proposed therapy for mental disorders, esp. neuroses.

di'a-pa'son (dī'ə-pā'zən) *n.* **1,** the entire range of a voice or an instrument. **2,** correct tune or pitch.

di'a-per (dī'ə-pər) *n.* **1,** an infant's breech cloth. **2,** a white unbleached linen or cotton fabric with a woven pattern.

di-aph'a-nous (dī-af'ə-nəs) *adj.* transparent or translucent.

di'a-phragm'' (dī'ə-fram'') *n.* **1,** the muscular partition that separates the thorax from the abdomen; the midriff. **2,** any thin piece of metal that serves as a partition, as the vibrating disk of a telephone. —**di'a-phrag-mat'ic** (-frag-mat'ik) *adj.* —**di'a-phrag-mat'i-cal-ly,** *adv.*

di''ar-rhe'a (dī'ə-rē'ə) *n.* abnormally frequent evacuation of the bowels. —**di''ar-rhet'ic** (-ret'ik) *adj.*

di'a-ry (dī'ə-rē) *n.* a daily record; journal.

di-as'to-le (dī-as'tə-lē) *n.* the rhythmical dilation of the heart.

di'a-ther''my (dī'ə-thėr''mē) *n.* (*Pathol.*) treatment with radiant heat. —**di'a-ther'mic,** *adj.*

di'a-tom (dī'ə-təm) *n.* any of a large family of microscopic, one-celled sea and freshwater plants.

di''a-ton'ic (dī'ə-ton'ik) *adj.* (*Music*) pert. to a normal scale—major or minor—of eight tones to the octave. —**di'a-ton'i-cal-ly,** *adv.*

di'a-tribe'' (dī'ə-trīb'') *n.* a bitter and abusive denunciation.

dib'ble (dib'əl) *n.* a gardening tool for making holes in the ground.

dice (dīs) *n.* (*pl.* of **die**) small cubes, esp. those having each face stamped with a different number of spots, used in gambling. —*v.t.* cut into small cubes, as food.

Die

di-chot'o-my (di-kot'ə-mē) *n.* a subdivision into two parts.

dick (dik) *n.* (*Slang*) a detective.

dick'er (dik'ər) *v.i.* (*Colloq.*) bargain; barter; haggle. —*n.* a haggling deal.

dick'ey (dik'ē) *n.* **1,** a child's bib. **2,** a separate or false shirt front. **3,** a seat at the back of a vehicle. **4,** a small bird.

Dick test a test to determine susceptibility to scarlet fever.

Dic'ta-phone'' (dik'tə-fōn'') *n.* a recording machine used for dictating; a trade name.

dic'tate (dik'tāt) *v.t. & i.* **1,** express orally for another to write down. **2,** prescribe with authority; command. —*n.* **1,** an order; a command. **2,** a guiding principle; a maxim. —**dic-ta'tion,** *n.*

dic'ta-tor (dik'tā-tər) *n.* **1,** a person exercising unlimited powers of government; an absolute ruler. **2,** one who dictates. —**dic''ta-to'ri-al** (dik''tə-tôr'ē-əl) *adj.* —**dic'ta-tor-ship,** *n.*

dic'tion (dik'shən) *n.* **1,** manner of expression or choice of words in speaking or writing. **2,** enunciation.

dic'tion-ar-y (dik'shə-ner-ē) *n.* a book defining and listing in alphabetical order the principal words of a language, or a particular class of words.

Dic'to-graph'' (dik'tə-graf'') *n.* (*T.N.*) a recording instrument used chiefly for obtaining evidence.

dic'tum (dik'təm) *n.* [*pl.* -ta] a positive or authoritative statement.

did *v.* pret. of **do.**

di-dac'tic (dī-dak'tik) *adj.* instructive; expository. —**di-dac'ti-cal-ly,** *adv.*

did'dle (did'əl) *v.i. & t.* (*Colloq.*) **1,** waste time; dawdle. **2,** swindle.

die (dī) *v.i.* [died, dy'ing] 1, cease to live; expire. 2, come to an end. 3, (with *away* or *out*) fade away. 4, (*Colloq.*) desire keenly. —*n.* 1, an engraved stamp used for impressing a design. 2, any of various mechanical devices, as a tool for cutting the threads of screws. 3, sing. of *dice.* —**die'hard'**, *n.* & *adj.* one who resists to the end; conservative.

di'e·lec'tric (dī'ə-lek'trik) *n.* a nonconducting substance. —*adj.* nonconducting.

di·er·e·sis (dī-er'ə-sis) *n.* [*pl.* -ses (-sēz)] 1, the separate pronunciation of two adjacent vowels. 2, a mark (··) indicating such pronunciation.

die'sel (dē'zəl) *n.* an internal-combustion engine employing the heat of compression to ignite fuel oil.

di'et (dī'ət) *n.* 1, food and drink regularly consumed. 2, a prescribed course of food. 3, regimen. —*v.t.* eat according to a diet. —**di'e·tar·y** (-ter-ē) *adj.*

di'e·tet'ics (dī'ə-tet'iks) *n.* the science of regulating the diet.

di'e·ti'tian (dī'ə-tish'ən) *n.* one trained to plan meals.

dif'fer (dif'ər) *v.i.* 1, be unlike or distinct (with *from*). 2, (with *with*) disagree, in opinion.

dif'fer·ence (dif'ər-əns) *n.* 1, a dissimilarity; a distinction. 2, a controversy; a dispute. 3, discrimination. 4, (*Math.*) the remainder after a number has been subtracted.

dif'fer·ent (dif'ər-ənt) *adj.* unlike; not the same.

dif"fer·en'tial (dif'ə-ren'shəl) *n.* 1, (*Math.*) an infinitesimal difference between two values of a variable quantity. 2, in automobiles, a gear arrangement that allows the outer driving wheel to turn faster on a curve. —*adj.* making, showing, or having a difference.

dif"fer·en'ti·ate' (dif'ə-ren'shē-āt') *v.t.* & *i.* make, constitute, or observe a difference (between). —**dif"fer·en'ti·a'tion**, *n.*

dif'fi·cult' (dif'ə-kult') *adj.* 1, presenting an obstacle or perplexing problem; not easy; hard to do or understand; arduous. 2, hard to please or persuade; not compliant; troublesome.

dif'fi·cul·ty (dif'i-kul-tē) *n.* 1, that which is hard to understand or to overcome. 2, a troublesome or embarrassing situation; (*pl.*) want of money. 3, an objection; reluctance.

dif'fi·dence (dif'ə-dəns) *n.* want of self-confidence; shyness. —**dif'fi·dent**, *adj.*

dif·frac'tion (di-frak'shən) *n.* 1, in optics, the modification of light or deflection of its rays. 2, a modifi-

cation of sound waves passing by a large building, etc.

dif·fuse' (di-fūz') *v.t.* & *i.* pour out and spread; send out in all directions; scatter. —*adj.* (di-fūs') 1, widely spread. 2, verbose. —**dif·fu'sion** (-zhən) *n.* —**dif·fu'sive** (-siv) *adj.*

dig *v.t.* & *i.* (dug, dig'ging) 1, turn up, or scoop out, as earth, with a trowel or spade; excavate. 2, work hard; find out by effort or research. 3, (with *in*) make a hole or trench for military protection. —*n.* 1, a thrust; a poke. 2, (*Colloq.*) a sarcastic remark. —**dig'ger**, *n.*

di·gest' (di-jest') *v.t.* 1, convert food in the body for assimilation. 2, assimilate mentally; think over. —*n.* (dī'jest) a condensed collection or summary. —**di·gest'i·ble**, *adj.*

di·ges'tion (di-jes'chən) *n.* act or process of assimilating food. —**di·ges'tive**, *adj.*

dig'gings (dig'ingz) *n.* 1, an excavation or mine. 2, (*Colloq.*) living quarters.

dig'it (dij'it) *n.* 1, a finger or toe; 2, any number under ten.

dig'i·tal·is (dij'ə-tal'is) *n.* 1, a genus of plants, esp. the foxglove. 2, a drug obtained from its leaves used as a heart stimulant.

dig'ni·fy' (dig'nə-fī') *v.t.* 1, confer honor upon; ennoble. 2, give an undeservedly important name to. —**dig'ni·fied**, *adj.* marked by dignity; noble; stately.

dig'ni·tar·y (dig'ni-ter-ē) *n.* one who holds an exalted rank or office.

dig'ni·ty (dig'nə-tē) *n.* 1, worthiness; high rank. 2, self-respecting or noble mien or deportment; importance.

di·gress' (di-gres') *v.i.* turn away from the main subject; deviate; wander. —**di·gres'sion** (-gresh'ən) *n.*

di·he'dral (dī-hē'drəl) *adj.* 1, having two plane faces, as a crystal. 2, forming an angle, as between the walls of a room.

dike (dīk) *n.* an embankment built to prevent flooding by a river or the ocean.

di·lap'i·date" (di-lap'ə-dāt") *v.t.* & *i.* ruin, or fall into partial or total ruin. —**di·lap'i·dat'ed**, *adj.* —**di·lap'i·da'tion**, *n.*

di·late' (di-lāt') *v.t.* & *i.* 1, expand; make larger; distend. 2, expatiate (upon). —**di·la'tion**. **dil'a·ta'tion** (dil'ə-tā'shən) *n.* —**di·la'tor**, *n.*

dil'a·to·ry (dil'ə-tôr-ē) *adj.* given to delay; procrastinating.

di·lem'ma (di-lem'ə) *n.* a choice between alternatives equally undesirable.

dil′′et·tan′te (dil′ə-tän′tē) *n.* one who pursues art or literature for amusement; a dabbler.

dil′i·gence (dil′ə-jəns) *n.* constant and persistent attention to one's work; industry. —**dil′i·gent**, *adj.*

dill (dil) *n.* an aromatic herb.

dil′ly·dal′ly (dil′ē-dal′ē) *v.i.* (*Colloq.*) loiter; waste time; vacillate.

dil′u·ent (dil′ū-ənt) *n.* a fluid used to dilute another.

di·lute′ (di-loot′) *v.t.* weaken by an admixture of water or other liquid; reduce in strength. —**di·lu′tion,** *n.*

di·lu′vi·al (di-loo′vē-əl) *adj.* 1, pert. to a flood or deluge. 2, pert. to any debris deposited by a flood.

dim *adj.* [**dim′mer, -mest**] 1, not bright or clear; not well lighted. 2, obscure; vague; not understood. 3, not comprehending clearly. —*v.i.* & *t.* [**dimmed, dim′ming**] make dim or dimmer. —**dim′ness,** *n.*

dime (dim) *n.* a U. S. silver coin worth ten cents.

di·men′sion (di-men′shən) *n.* measure in one direction; length, breadth, or thickness. —**di·men′sion·al,** *adj.*

di·min′ish *v.t.* & *i.* make less or smaller by any means; lessen. —**dim′i·nu′tion** (dim′i-nū′shən) *n.*

di·min·u·en′do (di-min′ū-en′-dō) *n.* (*Music*) a gradual lessening of the volume of sound.

di·min′u·tive (di-min′ū-tiv) *adj.* very small; tiny. —*n.* 1, a small thing or person. 2, a word form denoting smallness, affection, etc.

dim′i·ty (dim′ə-tē) *n.* a thin cotton fabric with woven corded stripes.

dim′mer (dim′ər) *n.* 1, a device that reduces the intensity of a light. 2, (*pl.*) dim lights. —*adj.* more dim.

dim-′out′ *n.* a partial reduction in lighting in a city, to conserve electricity or escape attacking aircraft.

dim′ple (dim′pəl) *n.* a natural hollow in some soft part of the body, as in the cheek. —*v.i.* show a dimple, as by smiling.

din *n.* a continued clattering or ringing noise; a clamor.

dine (din) *v.i.* eat the chief meal of the day. —*v.t.* give a dinner to or for.

din′er (di′nər) *n.* 1, one taking dinner. 2, a railroad car, or similar structure, where meals are served.

di·nette′ (di-net′) *n.* a small room or alcove to eat in.

ding *n.* [also, **ding-′dong′′**] the sound of a bell.

din′ghy (ding′gē) *n.* a small boat, usually for rowing.

din′gy (din′jē) *adj.* dirty; not fresh; tarnished. —**din′gi·ness,** *n.*

dink′y (dink′ē) *adj.* small; tiny. —*n.* [also **dink′ey**] a little locomotive.

din′ner (din′ər) *n.* 1, the principal meal. 2, an entertainment; banquet.

di′no·saur′′ (di′nə-sôr′′) *n.* an extinct gigantic reptile. —**di′no·sau′-ri·an** (-rē-ən) *adj.*

dint *n.* 1, a dent. 2, power; force.

di′o·cese′′ (di′ə-sēs′′) *n.* the district under the care of a bishop. —**di·oc′e·san** (di-os′i-sən) *adj.*

di′ode (di′ōd) *n.* in electronics, a vacuum tube used as a rectifier.

di′o·ram′a (di′ə-ram′ə) *n.* a continuous painting exhibited in a dark room with spectacular lighting effects. —**di′o·ram′ic,** *adj.*

di·ox′ide (di-ok′sid) *n.* (*Chem.*) an oxide having two oxygen atoms per molecule.

dip *v.t.* [**dipped, dip′ping**] 1, immerse temporarily in a liquid. 2, lower and raise, as a bird's wings. 3, scoop up. —*v.i.* 1, plunge into temporarily. 2, (with *into*) investigate; be interested. 3, incline downward. 4, sink. —*n.* 1, the act or result of dipping; a short swim. 2, a sloping downward. 3, a liquid to dip something in, as for tinting or disinfection.

diph·the′ri·a (dif-thir′ē-ə) *n.* an infectious disease in which a membrane forms over the air passage.

diph′thong (dif′thäng) *n.* two adjacent vowels pronounced in one syllable.

di·plo′ma (di-plō′mə) *n.* a certificate given by a school or college showing graduation.

di·plo′ma·cy (di-plō′mə-sē) *n.* 1, the art of negotiation between nations. 2, tact.

dip′lo·mat′ (dip′lə-mat′) *n.* one skilled in diplomacy. Also, **di·plo′-ma·tist** (di-plō′mə-tist).

dip′lo·mat′ic (-ik) *adj.* 1, pert. to the work of a diplomat. 2, tactful. —**dip′lo·mat′i·cal·ly,** *adv.*

dip′per (dip′ər) *n.* 1, a utensil for ladling or scooping out something. 2, (*cap.*) either of two constellations: *Big Dipper; Little Dipper.*

dip′so·ma′ni·a (dip′sə-mā′nē-ə) *n.* an irresistible craving for intoxicants. —**dip′so·ma′ni·ac,** *n.*

dire (dir) *adj.* dreadful; fearful; disastrous. —**dire′ful,** *adj.* —**dire′-ness,** *n.*

di·rect′ (di-rekt′) *v.t.* 1, aim or point toward an object. 2, point out a course to. **3**, regulate; guide or lead. **4**, order; command. **5**, address (a letter); address (words) to a person. **6**, conduct an orchestra or choir. —*adj.* **1**, straightforward; open; sincere. **2**, personal; firsthand. —di·rect'ness, *n.*

di·rect' cur'rent electric current that flows always in the same direction.

di·rec'tion (də-rek'shən) *n.* **1**, relative position, as along a line or to a place. **2**, act of directing; administration; management. **3**, the act of aiming or pointing out a course. **4**, an order; a regulation; instruction. —di·rec'tion·al, *adj.*

di·rec'tive (də-rek'tiv) *n.* an instruction; a statement of policy.

di·rec'tor (də-rek'tər) *n.* one who directs, esp. a company or theatrical production. —di·rec'to·rate (-ət) *n.* a body of directors. —di·rec'tor·ship, *n.*

di·rec'to·ry (də-rek'tə-rē) *n.* **1**, a book listing names and addresses. **2**, (*cap.*) a French government, 1795–99, during the French Revolution.

dirge (dẽrj) *n.* music or poetry expressing grief.

Dirigible

dir'i·gi·ble (dir'i-jə-bəl) *n.* a large cigar-shaped rigid airship, capable of being steered. —*adj.* capable of being directed or steered.

dirk (dẽrk) *n.* a dagger.

dirn'dl (dẽrn'dəl) *n.* a colorful peasant dress.

dirt (dẽrt) *n.* **1**, any filthy substance, as dust, mud, etc. **2**, earth or soil. **3**, anything mean or worthless; gossip. —*adj.* granular; unpaved, as a road.

dirt'y (dẽr'tē) *adj.* **1**, soiling. **2**, unclean; sullied. **3**, base; low; contemptible. **4**, rainy (of the weather). —*v.t.* sully. —dirt'i·ness, *n.*

dis- *pref.* **1**, separate; not joined. **2**, not; negation in an active sense (thus: something *unproved* may never have been tried, something *disproved* has been tried and found false). [In addition to words defined in the text, the following words may be defined by assuming active lack or negation of the root word, which see in each case.]

dis″ac·cord'
dis″af·firm'
dis″al·low'
dis″ap·pro·ba'- tion
dis″ar·range'
dis″as·sem'ble
dis″as·so'ci·ate'
dis″be·lieve'
dis·bur'den
dis″con·nect'
dis·coun'te- nance
dis″em·bark'
dis″em·bar'rass
dis″em·bod'y
dis″em·bow'el
dis″en·chant'
dis″en·cum'ber
dis″en·gage'
dis″en·tan'gle
dis″en·twine'
dis″es·tab'lish
dis·fa'vor
dis·fran'chise
dis·har'mo·ny
dis·hon'est
dis″il·lu'sion
dis″in·cli·na'tion
dis″in·fec'tion
dis″in·gen'u·ous
dis·join'
dis·junc'tion
dis·loy'al
dis″o·blige'
dis·pir'it
dis″pro·por'tion
dis·rel'ish
dis″re·mem'ber
dis″re·spect'
dis·robe'
dis·rup'ture
dis·ser'vice
dis·sim'i·lar
dis″si·mil'i·tude
dis″sym'me·try
dis·trust'
dis·un'ion
dis″u·nite'
dis·use'

dis·a'ble (dis-ā'bəl) *v.t.* deprive of physical, mental, or legal power; incapacitate. —dis″a·bil'i·ty, *n.*

dis″a·buse' (dis″ə-būz') *v.t.* set right; undeceive.

dis″ad·van'tage (dis″ad-van'tij) *n.* **1**, that which prevents success or makes it difficult. **2**, a loss to profit, reputation, etc.; a drawback. —dis″ad″van·ta'geous, *adj.*

dis″af·fect' (dis″ə-fekt') *v.t.* make unfriendly or discontented. —dis″af·fec'tion, *n.* ill will.

dis″a·gree' (dis″ə-grē') *v.i.* **1**, (with *with*) differ. **2**, quarrel. **3**, be incompatible or unsuitable. —dis″a·gree'a·ble, *adj.* bad-tempered; distasteful.

dis″a·gree'ment (-mənt) *n.* **1**, act of disagreeing. **2**, a quarrel; controversy. **3**, discrepancy; difference.

dis″ap·pear' (dis″ə-pir') *v.i.* pass out of sight or existence; vanish. —dis″ap·pear'ance, *n.*

dis″ap·point' (dis″ə-point') *v.t. & i.* fail to fulfill the expectations of (someone). —dis″ap·point'ment, *n.*

dis″ap·prove' (dis″ə-proov') *v.t. & i.* **1**, condemn. **2**, decline to sanction. —*v.i.* feel or express disfavor (with *of*). —dis″ap·prov'al, *n.*

dis·arm' (dis-ärm') *v.t.* **1**, deprive of weapons. **2**, deprive of resentment; make friendly. —*v.i.* reduce or curtail military power. —dis·ar'ma·ment, *n.* —dis·arm'ing, *adj.* inducing friendliness.

dis″ar·ray' (dis″ə-rā') *v.t.* **1**, divest; disrobe. **2**, throw into disorder; rout. —*n.* **1**, confusion. **2**, disorderly dress.

dis·as'ter (di-zas'tər) *n.* a great misfortune; a catastrophe. —dis·as'trous, *adj.*

dis″a·vow' (dis″ə-vow') *v.t.* disown; deny; repudiate. —**dis"a·vow'-al**, n.

dis·band' v.i. & t. dissolve, as a band or group; dismiss, as troops from an army. —**dis·band'ment**, n.

dis·bar' (dis-bär') v.t. [-barred', -bar'ring] withdraw the right (of a lawyer) to practice law. —**dis·bar'ment**, n.

dis·burse' (dis-bėrs') v.t. pay out; expend. —**dis·burse'ment**, n.

disc (disk) n. disk.

dis·card' (dis-kärd') v.t. cast off; reject; throw away as useless. —n. (dis'kärd') 1, something cast off. 2, a place of disposal.

dis·cern' (di-zėrn') v.t. & t. distinguish by the eye or the intellect; perceive; discriminate. —**dis·cern'i·ble**, adj. —**dis·cern'ing**, adj. discriminating; keen. —**dis·cern'ment**, n.

dis·charge' (dis-chärj') n. 1, the act of unloading. 2, the act of firing a missile or a weapon. 3, removal by taking away, settlement, or payment. 4, a flowing out; emission. 5, freeing, as of a prisoner; release, as of a soldier (also, a certificate of such release); dismissal, as of an employee. 6, that which is emitted. 7, performance; execution. —v.t. 1, unload. 2, emit (as water). 3, set free; dismiss; absolve. 4, fulfill (a duty); execute. 5, fire, as a gun.

dis·ci'ple (di-sī'pəl) n. one who adheres to the doctrines of another; a follower, esp. (often cap.) an Apostle.

dis"ci·pli·nar'i·an (dis'ə-pli-när'ē-ən) n. an exacting master.

dis'ci·pli·nar"y (dis'ə-pli-ner'ē) adj. pert. to or promoting discipline.

dis'ci·pline (dis'ə-plin) n. 1, mental and moral training. 2, obedience to rules. 3, correction; chastisement. —v.t. 1, train. 2, chastise.

dis·claim' (dis-klām') v.t. renounce; deny; disown. —**dis·claim'er**, n. a statement of disavowal.

dis·close' (dis-klōz') v.t. bring to light; uncover; make known. —**dis·clo'sure** (-klō'zhər) n.

dis·col'or (dis-kul'ər) v.t. & i. 1, alter the natural hue of. 2, stain. —**dis·col'or·a'tion**, n.

dis·com'fit (dis-kum'fit) v.t. embarrass; frustrate. —**dis·com'fi·ture** (-fi-chər) n.

dis·com'fort (dis-kum'fėrt) n. uneasiness; pain.

dis"com·mode' (dis"kə-mōd') v.t. put to inconvenience; trouble.

dis"com·pose' (dis"kum-pōz') v.t. unsettle; agitate; disturb. —**dis"com·po'sure** (-pō'zhər) n. embarrassment.

dis"con·cert' (dis"kən-sėrt') v.t. 1, perturb; confuse. 2, throw into disorder.

dis·con'so·late (dis-kon'sə-lət) adj. without consolation; sorrowful.

dis·con·tent' (dis"kən-tent') n. want of satisfaction; uneasiness of mind. —v.t. make unhappy. —**dis"con·tent'ed**, adj. not contented; restive; unhappy.

dis·con·tin'u·ance (dis-kən-tin'u-əns) n. lack of continued connection.

dis·con·tin'ue (dis-kən-tin'ū) v.t. cease; break off; interrupt. —v.i. come to a stop or end. —**dis"con·tin'u·a'tion**, n.

dis"con"ti·nu'i·ty (dis-con'ti-nū'ə-tē) n. a gap; lack of cohesion.

dis'cord (dis'kôrd) n. 1, want of agreement; contention; strife. 2, (Music) want of harmony; a dissonance. 3, any confused noise. —**dis·cord'ant**, adj.

dis'count (dis'kownt) v.t. 1, deduct from the settlement of, as of a bill or charge account. 2, disregard; make allowance for exaggeration. 3, lessen effectiveness of by anticipating the outcome. 4, (Com.) buy or sell for less than face value, as a promissory note before maturity. —n. a deduction.

dis·cour'age (dis-kėr'ij) v.t. 1, cause to lose spirit or hope. 2, obstruct by opposition. 3, dissuade (with from). —**dis·cour'age·ment**, n.

dis'course (dis'kôrs) n. 1, expression of ideas by words; a conversation. 2, a formal discussion or written treatment of a subject. —v.i. (dis-kôrs') converse; talk.

dis·cour'te·ous (dis-kėr'tē-əs) adj. uncivil; rude.

dis·cour'te·sy (dis-kėr'tə-sē) n. 1, incivility; ill manners; rudeness. 2, an impolite act.

dis·cov'er (dis-kuv'ər) v.t. gain first sight or knowledge of something hitherto unknown. —**dis·cov'er·er**, n.

dis·cov'er·y (-ē) n. 1, act of discovering. 2, something discovered.

dis·cred'it (dis-kred'it) v.t. 1, not to believe. 2, injure the reputation of; destroy confidence in. —n. 1, a loss of reputation or honor. 2, doubt; disbelief. —**dis·cred'it·a·ble**, adj. blameworthy.

dis·creet' (dis-krēt') adj. careful of appearances; tactful. —**dis·creet'ness**, n.

dis·crep'an·cy (dis-krep'ən-sē) n. an unexplained difference; inconsistency.

dis·cre'tion (dis-kresh'ən) n. 1, act or state of being discreet. 2, judgment; power to decide. —dis·cre'tion·a·ry (-er-ē) adj.

dis·crim'i·nate" (dis-krim'ə-nāt') v.i. & t. judge (respective merits). —dis·crim'i·nat'ing, adj. showing good taste. —dis·crim'i·na'tion, n.

dis·cur'sive (dis-kẽr'siv) adj. rambling from topic to topic; digressive. —dis·cur'sive·ness, n.

dis'cus (dis'kəs) n. a heavy disk used in weight-throwing contests.

Discus Thrower

dis·cuss' (dis-kus') v.t. talk about; debate. —dis·cus'sion (dis-kush'ən) n.

dis·dain' (dis-dān') v.t. & i. 1, look down upon; scorn; despise. 2, not deign or stoop. —n. scorn. —dis·dain'ful, adj.

dis·ease' (di-zēz') n. a condition of ill health; malady. —v.t. infect with disease.

dis·fig'ure (dis-fig'yər) v.t. mar; deface. —dis·fig'ure·ment, n.

dis·gorge' (dis-gôrj') v.t.& i. throw out or emit, esp. violently; vomit. —dis·gorge'ment, n.

dis·grace' (dis-grās') n. acute shame; ignominy; loss of reputation. —v.t. shame; discredit. —dis·grace'ful, adj. shameful.

dis·grun'tled (dis-grun'təld) adj. not contented; cross. —dis·grun'tle, v.t. —dis·grun'tle·ment, n.

dis·guise' (dis-gīz') v.t. conceal the identity or real nature of; give a misleading appearance to. —n. a covering that masks or misleads.

dis·gust' n. extreme repugnance; loathing. —v.t. cause to feel loathing; offend.

dish n. 1, a receptacle or vessel, esp. for food. 2, a particular prepared food. 3, (Slang) something very welcome. —v.t. (often with out or up) serve, as food.

dis"ha·bille' (dis'ə-bēl') n. 1, the state of being carelessly dressed; undress. 2, a loose morning dress.

dish'cloth" n. a cloth with which dishes are washed.

dis·heart'en (dis-här'tən) v.t. cause to lose spirit or courage.

di·shev'el (di-shev'əl) v.t. muss, esp. the clothing or hair; tousle. —di·shev'el·ment, n.

dis·hon'or (di-son'ər) v.t. 1, bring shame upon. 2, fail to meet (an obligation). —n. disgrace. —dis·hon'or·a·ble, adj.

dish'pan" n. a pan in which dishes are washed.

dish'wa"ter n. water in which dishes will be or have been washed.

dis"in·fect' (dis'in-fekt') v.t. remove infection or a source of infection from. —dis"in·fect'ant, n. a preparation for disinfecting.

dis"in·her'it (dis'in-her'it) v.t. cut off (an heir) from an inheritance. —dis"in·her'i·tance, n.

dis·in'te·grate" (dis-in'tə-grāt')v.t. & i. separate into parts; go to pieces. —dis·in'te·gra'tion, n.

dis"in·ter' (dis'in-tẽr') v.t.[-terred', -ter'ring] dig up something buried; unearth. —dis"in·ter'ment, n.

dis·in'ter·est·ed (dis-in'tə-res-tid) adj. unbiased; unselfish.

dis·joint'ed adj. not coherent; not properly connected.

disk n. 1, any flat circular plate or surface. 2, (Colloq.) a phonograph record. Also, disc. —disk jockey, a radio announcer who plays phonograph records.

dis·like' (dis-līk') n. fixed aversion or distaste. —v.t. feel aversion toward. —dis·lik'a·ble, adj.

dis'lo·cate" (dis'lō-kāt') v.t. 1, displace; put out of joint or position. 2, interrupt the continuity or order of. —dis'lo·ca'tion, n.

dis·lodge' (dis-loj') v.t. remove or drive from a habitation or a position occupied. —dis·lodg'ment, n.

dis'mal (diz'məl) adj. gloomy; dreary; cheerless; doleful. —dis'mal·ness, n.

dis·man'tle (dis-man'təl) v.t. 1, strip of equipment or defenses. 2, take to pieces. —dis·man'tle·ment, n.

dis·may' (dis-mā') v.t. utterly dishearten. —n. complete loss of courage; fright.

dis·mem'ber (dis-mem'bər) v.t. 1, tear limb from limb. 2, separate into parts. —dis·mem'ber·ment, n.

dis·miss' (dis-mis') v.t. 1, send away; order or give permission to depart. 2, discard; discharge from employment. 3, put out of mind, as a subject. —dis·miss'al, n.

dis·mount' (dis-mownt') v.i. get off, as from a horse or bicycle. —v.t. 1, unhorse. 2, remove from a frame or setting, as a jewel. 3, take apart, as a machine.

dis"o·be'di·ence (dis"ə-bē'dē·əns) n. refusal to obey. —dis"o·be'di·ent, adj.

dis"o·bey' (dis'ə-bā') v.t. & i. neglect or refuse to obey.

dis·or'der (dis-ôr'dər) n. 1, lack of order; confusion. 2, tumult; dis-

fat, fāte, fär, fâre, fâll, ásk; met, hē, hẽr, maybē; pin, pīne; not, nōte, ôr, tool turbance of the peace. **3,** disturbance of the body or mind; a diseased state. —*v.t.* **1,** put in improper arrangement. **2,** unsettle the normal conditions of body or mind.

dis·or'dered *adj.* **1,** confused. **2,** mentally ill.

dis·or'der·ly *adj.* **1,** untidy. **2,** unruly; immoral. —**dis·or'der·li·ness,** *n.*

dis·or'gan·ize' (dis-ôr'gə-nīz") *v.t.* destroy the system or arrangement of. —**dis·or"gan·i·za'tion** (-i-zā'shən) *n.* a breaking down or absence of system.

dis·own' (dis-ōn') *v.t.* refuse to admit ownership or responsibility.

dis·par'age (dis-par'ij) *v.t.* speak slightingly of; discredit. —**dis·par'age·ment,** *n.*

dis'pa·rate (dis'pə-rət) *adj.* essentially different; unequal. —**dis·par'i·ty** (dis-par'ə-tē) *n.*

dis·pas'sion (dis-pash'ən) *n.* freedom from passion or emotion; impartiality. —**dis·pas'sion·ate,** *adj.*

dis·patch' (dis-pach') *v.t.* **1,** send off or away. **2,** transact speedily. **3,** kill. —*n.* **1,** a sending off or away. **2,** dismissal. **3,** speed; haste. **4,** a written message. Also, **despatch.**

dis·pel' (dis-pel') *v.t.* [-**pelled'**, -**pel'ling**] drive off or away.

dis·pen'sa·ry (dis-pen'sə-rē) *n.* a place where medicines are given out.

dis"pen·sa'tion (dis"pən-sā'shən) *n.* **1,** act of dispensing. **2,** that which is dispensed by God to man. **3,** a relaxation of a law, esp. ecclesiastical.

dis·pen'sa·to·ry (dis-pen'sə-tôr-ē) *adj.* pert. to the dispensing of medicines.

dis·pense' (dis-pens') *v.t.* **1,** deal out; distribute. **2,** administer, as laws. **3,** excuse; exempt. —*v.i.* **1,** (with *with*) permit the omission of: do without. **2,** compound (drugs, prescriptions).

dis·perse' (dis-pêrs') *v.t.* **1,** scatter; diffuse. **2,** dissipate; cause to vanish. —*v.i.* separate. —**dis·per'sal** (-səl), **dis·per'sion** (-shən) *n.*

dis·place' (dis-plās') *v.t.* **1,** put out of the usual or proper place; remove from office. **2,** replace. —**displaced person,** one driven from his home by war.

dis·place'ment (dis-plās'mənt) *n.* **1,** act of displacing. **2,** the weight or volume of water displaced by a submerged body. **3,** the volume swept out by a piston.

dis·play' (dis-plā') *v.t. & i.* show; exhibit. —*n.* an exhibition.

dis·please' (dis-plēz') *v.t. & i.* offend; be disagreeable (to). —**dis·pleas'ure** (-plezh'ər) *n.* vexation.

dis·port' (dis-pôrt') *v.i.* make merry; play.

dis·pose' (dis-pōz') *v.t.* **1,** place in a particular order; arrange. **2,** regulate; adjust. **3,** incline the mind or heart of. —*v.i.* **1,** (with *of*) part with. **2,** control. —**dis·pos'al,** *n.*

dis"po·si'tion (dis"pə-zish'ən) *n.* **1,** an arrangement of parts. **2,** definite settlement; ultimate destination. **3,** innate temper; natural tendency of the mind.

dis·pos·sess' (dis"pə-zes') *v.t.* deprive of actual occupancy; dislodge. —**dis"pos·ses'sion,** *n.*

dis·proof' *n.* proof to the contrary; refutation.

dis·prove' (dis-proov') *v.t.* prove to be false or erroneous.

dis"pu·ta'tion (dis"pū-tā'shən) *n.* a controversy; debate. —**dis"pu·ta'tious,** *adj.*

dis·pute' (dis-pūt') *v.i.* argue; debate; wrangle. —*v.t.* argue about or against. —*n.* a controversy; a quarrel. —**dis·put'a·ble,** *adj.* —**dis·put'ant,** *n.*

dis·qual'i·fy' (dis-kwol'ə-fī") *v.t.* make unfit or ineligible. —**dis·qual'i·fi·ca'tion** (-fi-kā'shən) *n.*

dis·qui'et (dis-kwī'ət) *v.t.* deprive of peace; make uneasy or restless. —*n.* an uneasy feeling or state; unrest. —**dis·qui'e·tude** (-ə-tood) *n.*

dis"qui·si'tion (dis"kwi-zish'ən)*n.* a dissertation; treatise.

dis"re·gard' (dis"ri-gärd') *v.t.* ignore. —*n.* failure to observe; neglect.

dis"re·pair' (dis"ri-pâr') *n.* the state of being in bad condition.

dis"re·pute' (dis"ri-pūt') *n.* loss or want of good reputation. —**dis·rep'u·ta·ble** (dis-rep'yə-tə-bəl) *adj.* of low character.

dis·rupt' *v.t. & i.* break asunder; separate forcibly. —**dis·rup'tion,** *n.* —**dis·rup'tive,** *adj.*

dis·sat'is·fy" (dis-sat'is-fī") *v.t.* fail to satisfy or please; render discontented. —**dis·sat"is·fac'tion,** *n.*

dis·sect' (di-sekt') *v.t.* **1,** cut in pieces; separate the parts of. **2,** examine point by point; analyze. —**dis·sec'tion,** *n.*

dis·sem'ble (di-sem'bəl) *v.t. & i.* give a false impression about; conceal one's real motives. —**dis·sem'blance** (-blans) *n.*

dis·sem'i·nate" (di-sem'ə-nāt") *v.t.* scatter abroad; sow. —**dis·sem"i·na'tion,** *n.*

dis·sen'sion (di-sen'shən) *n.* violent disagreement; strife; discord.

dis·sent' (di-sent') *v.i.* feel or express a negative opinion. —*n.* difference of opinion. —**dis·sent'er,** *n.* one who disagrees, esp. with the doctrines of the Church of England.

dis·sen'tient (di-sen'shənt) *adj.* dissenting. —*n.* one who dissents. —dis·sen'tious (-shəs) *adj.*

dis"ser·ta'tion (dis"ər-tā'shən) *n.* a formal discourse or essay.

dis'si·dence (dis'ə-dəns) *n.* difference in opinion; disagreement. —dis'si·dent, *adj. & n.*

dis·sim'u·late' (di-sim'yə-lāt') *v.t. & i.* disguise; make pretense; feign. —dis·sim"u·la'tion, *n.*

dis'si·pate" (dis'i-pāt") *v.t.* 1, scatter; dispel. 2, expend wastefully. —*v.i.* 1, come to an end or vanish. 2, act dissolutely. —dis'si·pat"ed, *adj.* 1, dissolute. 2, dispersed. —dis"si·pa'tion, *n.*

dis·so'ci·ate' (di-sō'shē-āt') *v.t.* sever the connection of; separate. —dis·so"ci·a'tion, *n.*

dis'so·lute (dis'ə-loot') *adj.* loose in behavior and morals; wanton. —dis'so·lute·ness, *n.*

dis"so·lu'tion (dis"ə-loo'shən) *n.* act of dissolving or being dissolved.

dis·solve' (di-zolv') *v.t.* 1, liquefy by means of heat or absorption. 2, disunite; separate into parts; break up. 3, solve; explain, as a mystery. —*v.i.* 1, become fluid. 2, come to an end; crumble or waste away. 3, disappear gradually; fade from sight.

dis'so·nance (dis'ə-nəns) *n.* 1, an inharmonious combination of sounds. 2, disagreement; discord. —dis'so·nant, *adj.*

dis·suade' (di-swād') *v.t.* change from a purpose by advice, persuasion, or argument. —dis·sua'sion (-zhən) *n.*

dis'taff (dis'tåf) *n.* 1, a cleft stick for holding wool, flax, etc. in spinning. 2, woman, her activities or work.

dis'tance (dis'təns) *n.* 1, measure of interval in space or time. 2, remoteness.

dis'tant (dis'tənt) *adj.* 1, situated at a different point in space or time. 2, remote; far off. 3, haughty; cool; reserved.

dis·taste' (dis-tāst') *n.* aversion; dislike. —dis·taste'ful, *adj.* displeasing; offensive.

dis·tem'per (dis-tem'pər) *n.* 1, a serious disease of animals, esp. dogs. 2, bad humor. 3, mural paint or painting using eggs as sizing.

dis·tend' *v.t.* dilate; expand. —*v.i.* swell. —dis·ten'tion, *n.*

dis·till' (dis-til') *v.i.* fall in drops. —*v.t.* 1, let fall in drops. 2, purify. 3, extract by process of distillation.

dis"til·la'tion (dis"tə-lā'shən) *n.* 1, the vaporization and subsequent condensation of a liquid. 2, a distilled liquid.

dis·till'er·y (dis-til'ə-rē) *n.* a place where alcoholic liquors other than ale or beer are made.

dis·tinct' (dis-tinkt') *adj.* 1, separate; different. 2, well-defined; not blurred; very plain; unmistakable; clear. —dis·tinct'ness, *n.*

dis·tinc'tion (dis-tink'shən) *n.* 1, act of distinguishing. 2, a distinguishing quality or characteristic; difference in general. 3, an honor; eminence; superiority.

dis·tinc'tive (dis-tink'tiv) *adj.* 1, different; marking a difference. 2, characteristic. —dis·tinc'tive·ness, *n.*

dis·tin'guish (dis-ting'gwish) *v.t.* 1, mark, recognize, or see as distinct or different. 2, separate by classification. 3, discern critically; judge. 4, treat with honor. —*v.i.* make a distinction (between). —dis·tin'guish·a·ble, *adj.* capable of being perceived and recognized. —dis·tin'guished, *adj.* eminent; celebrated.

dis·tort' (dis-tört') *v.t.* twist out of shape; pervert; misrepresent. —dis·tor'tion, *n.*

dis·tract' (dis-trakt') *v.t.* 1, divert the attention of. 2, confuse; bewilder. 3, derange. —dis·tract'ed, *adj.* 1, diverted. 2, bewildered.

dis·trac'tion (dis-trak'shən) *n.* 1, act of distracting or being distracted. 2, what distracts; a diversion. 3, frenzy; (*Colloq.*) madness.

dis·traint' (dis-trānt') *n.* (*Law*) a seizing of property, as for debt.

dis·trait' (dis-trā') *adj.* abstracted; absent-minded; inattentive.

dis·traught' (dis-trât') *adj.* bewildered; perplexed; deranged.

dis·tress' (dis-tres') *n.* 1, pain or suffering of body or mind. 2, calamity; adversity. 3, the state of needing help; danger. —*v.t.* make miserable. —dis·tress'ful, *adj.* distressing.

dis·trib'ute (dis-trib'ūt) *v.t.* 1, parcel out; apportion. 2, classify. 3, spread out. —dis"tri·bu'tion (dis"tri-bū'shən) *n.*

dis·trib'u·tor (dis-trib'yə-tər) *n.* 1, one who distributes; esp., a wholesale dealer. 2, a device for distributing, esp. electricity to the spark plugs of an engine.

dis'trict (dis'trikt) *n.* a section of a city or state; a region in general. —district attorney, the public prosecutor for a city or county.

dis·turb' (dis-tėrb') v.t. 1, agitate; disquiet; molest. 2, interfere with; interrupt.

dis·turb'ance (-əns) n. 1, something that disturbs; a feeling of disquiet; a disease. 2, an illegally noisy commotion.

ditch (dich) n. a trench or channel dug in the earth. —v.t. 1, drain by or surround with a ditch. 2, throw or run into a ditch. 3, (Slang) cast off; escape from.

dith'er (dith'ər) n: 1, a nervous, excited state. 2, commotion.

dit'to (dit'ō) n. [pl. -tos] the same thing: expressed by two small marks (").

dit'ty (dit'ē) n. a little song:

di'u·ret'ic (dī'yū-ret'ik) adj. promoting urination. —di'u·re'sis (-rē'sis) n.

di·ur'nal (dī-ėr'nəl) adj. pert: to day; daily.

di'va (dē'vä) n. a prima donna.

div'a·gate' (div'ə-gāt') v.i. stray; digress. —div'a·ga'tion, n: digression.

di'van (dī'van) n. 1, a kind of sofa. 2, (di-van') a council of state in Turkey.

dive (dīv) v.i. 1, plunge head first downward or forward, esp. into water. 2, submerge. 3, engage deeply in anything. —n. 1, a headfirst plunge, esp. into water. 2, (Colloq.) a seamy place. —dive bomber, a bombing plane that aims its bombs by diving toward its target. —div'er, n.

di·verge' (di-vėrj') v.i. 1, branch off in different directions. 2, take different courses or ways (of thought; of life). 3, differ from a typical form. —di·ver'gence, di·ver'gen·cy, n: —di·ver'gent, adj.

di·verse' (di-vėrs') adj. essentially different; varied. Also, **di'vers** (dī'vėrz). —di·verse'ness, n.

di·ver'si·fy' (di-vėr'si-fī') v.t. give variety to. —di·ver'si·fi·ca'tion (-fi-kā'shən) n.

di·ver'sion (di-vėr'zhən) n. 1, act of diverting. 2, a turning aside; a detour. 3, recreation; amusement; a pastime.

di·ver'si·ty (di-vėr'sə-tē) n: 1, essential difference. 2, variety.

di·vert' (di-vėrt') v.t. 1, turn aside or away from a course or an aim. 2, amuse; entertain.

di·vest' v.t. 1, strip of clothes, arms, or equipment; despoil. 2, deprive of rights, privileges, or authority. —di·ves'ti·ture (-ti-chər), di·vest'ment, n:

di·vide' (di-vīd') v.t. 1, separate into parts or pieces. 2, disjoin;

sever the union of. 3, make or keep distinct. 4, distribute; share. 5, (Math.) perform the process of division. —v.i. go apart. —n. a watershed. —di·vid'ers, n. compasses.

div'i·dend' (div'ə-dend') n. 1, a sum to be divided and distributed, as to shareholders; the share of each. 2, (Math.) a number or quantity to be divided by another.

div'i·na'tion (div'ə-nā'shən) n. the foretelling of the future or discovering of that which is hidden.

di·vine' (di-vīn') adj. 1, of the nature of, proceeding from, or pert. to God; sacred. 2, heavenly; excellent. —n. a clergyman. —v.t. learn by divination. —v.i. surmise.

di·vin'er (di-vī'nər) n. 1, one who divines. 2, a rod supposed to locate subterranean water: divining rod.

di·vin'i·ty (di-vin'ə-tē) n. 1, the character of being godly or divine. 2, (cap.) God. 3, a confection.

di·vis'i·ble (di-viz'ə-bəl) adj. capable of being divided, esp. (Math.) without a remainder. —di·vis'i·bil'i·ty, n.

di·vi'sion (di-vizh'ən) n. 1, separation. 2, a partition. 3, a definite part; a self-sufficient unit of an army. 4, disunion; discord. 5, (Math.) the process of finding how many times a number (divisor) or quantity is contained in another (dividend).

di·vi'sion·al (-əl) adj. pert. to a division. —n. (pl.) examinations of candidates for academic degrees.

di·vi'sor (di-vī'zer) n. a number by which another is divided.

di·vorce' (di-vôrs') n. 1, a legal dissolution of the marriage bond. 2, complete separation. —v.t. obtain a divorce (from). —di·vor'cée' (-sā') n. a divorced woman. —di·vorce'ment, n.

div'ot (div'ət) n. a piece of turf cut out by a golfer's club.

di·vulge' (di-vulj') v.t. tell or make known; reveal. —di·vul'gence, n.

Dix'ie (dik'sē) n. the southern states of the U.S. —Dix'ie·crat' (-krat') n. a Democrat who places sectional before party interests.

diz'zy (diz'ē) adj. 1, having a whirling sensation in the head; giddy. 2, causing dizziness. 3, (Slang) silly; foolish. —diz'zi·ness, n.

do (doo) v.t. [did, done (dun), do'ing] 1, perform; carry out. 2, perform the action or work required by the nature of the case, as do one's hair. 3, cause; render. 4, complete; finish. 5, put forth; exert. 6, (Slang) cheat; swindle. —v.i. 1, work. 2, act or behave. 3, fare; prosper. 4, serve the purpose. —aux. v. forming an emphatic pres. or past indicative with an infinitive, as I did go. —do away with, destroy. —do for destroy; kill. —do in, 1, kill. 2, swindle. —do up, 1, wrap. 2, dress.

do (dō) n. (*Music*) the first tone of a scale.

dob'bin (dob'in) n. a common name for a work horse.

Do'ber·man pin'scher (dō'bər·man pin'shər) a breed of slender, smooth-coated dog.

doc'ile (dos'əl) adj. amenable; easily managed. —do·cil'i·ty (do-sil'ə-tē) n.

dock (dok) n. 1, an enclosed water space in which a ship floats while being loaded or unloaded; a slip or pier; a wharf. 2, the place where a prisoner stands in court. 3, a coarse herb or weed. 4, the stump of an animal's tail. —v.t. 1, cut off; clip, as a dog's tail. 2, deduct from, as wages. 3, bring or draw (a vessel) into a dock. —v.i. arrive at a wharf or dock.

dock'et (dok'it) n. 1, (*Law*) a list of cases for trial; any such agenda. 2, (*Law*) a register of judgments.

dock'yard'' n. a place where ships are built or repaired.

doc'tor (dok'tər) n. 1, a physician. 2, a person holding the highest degree a university can confer in his or her special field. —v.t. (*Colloq.*) 1, treat medicinally. 2, repair; patch up. 3, adulterate; tamper with. —doc'tor·ate (-ət) n.

doc'trine (dok'trin) n. a principle or body of principles; a tenet; a dogma. —doc'tri·nal, adj.

doc'u·ment (dok'yə-mənt) n. a written or printed paper containing a record or statement. —v.t. (-ment'') cite or provide documents for authority. —doc''u·men'tal, adj. —doc''u·men·ta'tion, n.

doc''u·men'ta·ry (dok''yə-men'tə-rē) adj. of or pert. to documents. —n. an educational motion picture consisting of factual sequences.

dod'der (dod'ər) v.i. tremble; shake; totter.

dodge (doj) v.i. & t. suddenly jump or step aside; evade. —n. an act of evasion; a trick, stratagem, or clever device.

do'do (dō'dō) n. an extinct flightless bird.

doe (dō) n. the female of the deer, most antelopes, the hare, and rabbit. —doe'skin'' n. 1, a fine leather. 2, a finely twilled woolen cloth.

do'er (doo'ər) n. 1, one who does (something). 2, one who accomplishes a great deal.

does (duz) v. 3rd pers. sing., pres. ind., of do.

doff (dof) v.t. take off (any article of dress).

dog (dâg; dog) n. 1, a domesticated quadruped descended from different wild species of the genus *Canis*, as the wolf, fox, or jackal. 2, a mechanical device for holding. 3, a mean worthless fellow. —v.t. [dogged, dog'ging] hound; keep at the heels of; worry. —dog it, give up, through fear. —dog tag, a dog's license plate; (*Slang*) a soldier's identification disk.

doge (dōj) n. title of the former rulers of Venice and Genoa.

dog'ear'' n. 1, a dog's ear. 2, a frayed corner. —v.t. turn down the corner of a page. —v.i. fray.

dog'fight'' n. combat between war planes at close quarters.

dog'fish'' n. any of a variety of small sharks.

dog'ged (dog'id) adj. obstinate; persistent. —dog'ged·ness, n.

dog'ger·el (dâg'ər-əl) n. light, inept verse.

dog'house'' n. a hut for a dog. —in the doghouse (*Slang*) in disfavor.

do'gie (dō'gē) n. a stray calf.

dog'ma (dâg'mə) n. a rigidly held principle or doctrine, esp. in a religion; precept. —dog'ma·tism, n.

dog·mat'ic (dâg-mat'ik) adj. 1, pert. to a dogma. 2, positive; adhering rigidly to a tenet. —dog·mat'i·cal·ly, adv.

dog'tooth'' n. [pl. -teeth''] 1, eyetooth. 2, an ornamental molding. —dogtooth violet, an early spring wild flower.

dog'wood'' n. a shrub or tree bearing clusters of flowers.

doi'ly (doi'lē) n. a small ornamental mat for use on a table.

dol'drums (dol'drəmz) n. pl. 1, low spirits; the dumps. 2, zones of calm in the ocean near the Equator.

dole (dōl) n. 1, alms. 2, (*Brit.*) money granted to the unemployed. —v.t. hand out sparingly.

dole'ful (dōl'fəl) adj. showing sorrow; sad. —dole'ful·ness, n.

doll (dol) n. 1, a toy baby for children; a puppet. 2, (*Slang*) a girl. —v.t. & t. (with *up*) put on one's best clothes.

dol'lar (dol'ər) n. 1, the basis of decimal coinage. 2, a coin or treasury certificate of one dollar value, in the U.S. worth 100 cents. —dollar diplomacy, use (by the U. S.) of money to implement foreign policy.

Dodo

dol'ly (dol'ĕ) n. 1, diminutive of *doll*. 2, any of several mechanical devices, esp. a low platform on rollers for moving heavy loads.

do'lor (dō'lər) n. sorrow.

dol'or·ous (dol'ər-əs) adj. sad; mournful. —**dol'or·ous·ness**, n.

dol'phin (dol'fin) n. a sea mammal of the whale family.

dolt (dōlt) n. a dull, stupid person.

-dom (-dəm) suf. the estate, condition or rank of, as *kingdom*.

do·main' (dō-mān') n. 1, territory owned or governed. 2, sphere of action or knowledge.

dome (dōm) n. 1, a hemispherical roof; a large cupola. 2, (*Slang*) head.

do·mes'tic (də-mes'tik) adj. 1, relating to the household. 2, pert. to one's own country; not foreign. 3, tame, as an animal. —n. a household servant. —**do·mes'ti·cal·ly**, adv.

do·mes'ti·cate' (də-mes'ti-kāt') v.t. convert to home life; tame. —**do·mes'ti·ca'tion**, n.

do"mes·tic'i·ty (dō"mes·tis'ə·tē) n. the state of liking home life.

dom'i·cile (dom'ə-səl) n. a place of residence.

dom'i·nant (dom'ə-nənt) adj. 1, exercising rule or authority. 2, most conspicuous; overshadowing. —**dom'i·nance**, n.

dom'i·nate' (dom'ə-nāt') v.t. & i. govern; control; hold control; be most conspicuous. —**dom'i·na'tion**, n.

dom'i·neer' (dom'ə-nir') v.i. & t. rule in an overbearing or arrogant manner; swagger; tyrannize. —**dom'i·neer'ing**, adj. overbearing.

Do·min'i·can (də-min'ə-kən) n. & adj. one of a Rom. Cath. religious order founded by St. Dominic in the early 13th century.

dom'i·nie (dom'ə-nē) n. a clergyman; priest.

do·min'ion (də-min'yən) n. 1, supreme authority; control. 2, a territory under a sovereign, now esp. one having strong powers of self-government.

dom'i·no" (dom'ə-nō") n. 1, a small tile of wood or bone, marked with dots; (*pl.*) a game played with such tiles. 2, a masquerade costume, esp. a cloak; a half-mask.

don v.t. [**donned**, **don'ning**] put on. —n. 1, (*cap.*) a Spanish nobleman; his title: Sir, Mr. 2, a fellow or tutor in an English university. —**do'ña** (dō'nyä) n.fem.

do'nate (dō'nāt) v.t. & i. bestow as a gift; contribute. —**do·na'tion**, n.

done (dun) v. p.p. of *do*.

don'key (dong'kē) n. 1, the ass. 2, a stupid person.

do'nor (dō'nər) n. one who gives.

doo'dle (doo'dəl) v.i. 1, (*Slang*) draw or scribble aimlessly. 2, play a bagpipe.

doom n. 1, destiny, esp. when unhappy or destructive; fate. 2, a judgment; a sentence. 3, the last judgment: *doomsday*. —v.t. condemn to ruin.

door (dôr) n. 1, a barrier that swings on hinges or slides for opening or closing a passageway. 2, any means of access, entrance, or exit.

door'keep"er n. one who guards an entrance.

door'man (-mən) n. [*pl.* -men] an attendant at the door of a hotel, club, etc.

door'step" n. threshold.

door'way" n. the opening in which a door is mounted.

dope (dōp) n. (*Colloq.*) 1, a narcotic drug; such drugs collectively. 2, information; a private hint. 3, (*Slang*) a stupid person. —v.t. 1, (*Colloq.*) drug. 2, (*Slang*) (with *out*) solve, as a mystery.

dor'mant (dôr'mənt) adj. in a state of rest or inactivity. —**dor'man·cy**, n.

dor'mer (dôr'mər) n. a window in a projection under a gable.

dor'mi·to·ry (dôr'mə·tôr·ē) n. a building or large room in which many persons sleep.

dor'mouse (dôr'mows) n. [*pl.* -mice] (-mīs")] a squirrel-like hibernating rodent.

dor'sal (dôr'səl) adj. pert. to, on, or situated near, the back.

do'ry (dôr'ē) n. 1, a small, flat-bottomed boat. 2, an edible sea fish.

dose (dōs) n. 1, a prescribed quantity of medicine to be taken at one time. 2, anything disagreeable to take. —v.t. give a dose to. —**dos'age**, n.

dos'si·er (dos'ē·ā") n. a complete file of information on a person or affair.

dot n. 1, a minute, round spot; a speck. 2, a dowry. —v.t. & i. [**dot'ted**, **-ting**] mark with a dot or dots.

dot'age (dō'tij) n. 1, senility. 2, excessive fondness.

do'tard (dō'tərd) n. an old, foolish man.

dote (dōt) v.i. 1, be weak-minded from age. 2, (with *on*) lavish extravagant fondness.

dou'ble (dub'əl) adj. 1, being a pair; duplicated. 2, twofold; twice as much, as large, as thick, etc. 3, folded once. —n. 1, a twofold quantity or size. 2, a duplicate; a counterpart. **3**, a fold. **4**, an understudy. **5**, esp. in bridge, an increase in scoring values. **6**, in baseball, a two-base hit. **7**, (*pl.*) esp. in tennis, play with two on a side. —*v.t.* **1**, make double. **2**, contain twice as much or as many. **3**, fold once, as a blanket. **4**, repeat; duplicate. —*v.i.* **1**, increase or grow to twofold. **2**, turn in the opposite direction. —**double dealing**, treachery.—**double meaning**, intentional ambiguity. —**double take** (*Slang*) sudden, delayed understanding.

double bass (*Music*) the largest and deepest-toned viol; bass viol.

dou''ble-cross' *v.t.* (*Slang*) betray the confidence of. —*n.* betrayal.

dou'ble-head'er (dub'əl-hed'ər) *n.* **1**, two separate baseball games played consecutively by the same teams on the same day. **2**, a train drawn by two engines.

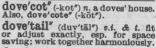

Double Bass

dou'blet (dub'lət) *n.* **1**, a pair of like things. **2**, one of such a pair. **3**, a close-fitting jacket formerly worn by men.

dou'ble-talk'' *n.* rapid talk mingling real words with nonsense; gibberish.

dou.bloon' (dub-loon') *n.* a former Spanish gold coin, worth about five dollars.

doubt (dowt) *n.* **1**, an unsettled state of opinion; indecision. **2**, a matter of uncertainty. **3**, an objection. —*v.i.* feel doubt. —*v.t.* question the accuracy or honesty of. —**doubt'ful**, *adj.* **1**, feeling doubt; hesitant. **2**, unlikely. —**doubt'less**, *adj.* certainly.

douche (doosh) *n.* a liquid spray of water to clean or heal some organ of the body, or the instrument or syringe used. —*v.i.* & *t.* so spray.

dough (dō) *n.* **1**, the paste for bread or pastry ready to be baked. **2**, (*Slang*) money.

dough'boy'' a U.S. soldier in World War I.

dough'nut'' *n.* a ring-shaped cake fried in deep fat.

dough'ty (dow'tē) *adj.* fearless; strong. —**dough'ti.ness**, *n.*

dour (dūr) *adj.* hard; inflexible. sour in mien. —**dour'ness**, *n.*

douse (dows) *v.t.* **1**, immerse in or splash with water. **2**, extinguish.

dove (duv) *n.* **1**, a pigeon or related bird. **2**, an emblem of innocence and affection.

dove'cot'' (-kot'') *n.* a doves' house. Also, **dove'cote''** (-kōt'').

dove'tail'' (duv'tāl'') *v.i.* & *t.* fit or adjust exactly, esp. for space saving; work together harmoniously.

dow'a.ger (dow'ə-jər) *n.* **1**, a widow endowed with property from her husband. **2**, (*Colloq.*) a dignified-looking elderly woman.

dow'dy (dow'dē) *adj.* slovenly; ill-dressed. —**dow'di.ness**, *n.*

dow'el (dow'əl) *n.* a pin or tenon used for fastening together two pieces of wood, stone, etc.

dow'er (dow'ər) *n.* **1**, the property that a woman brings to her husband at marriage; dowry. **2**, real estate granted by law to a widow for her lifetime. **3**, one's portion of natural gifts. —*v.t.* supply with a dowry.

down *adv.* **1**, [also, **down'ward** (-wərd)] in a descending direction; from higher to lower; from earlier to later times; from a greater to a less or lower rate. **2**, on the ground; at the bottom or lowest point; into disrepute. **3**, in writing; on paper. **4**, firmly; closely. —*adj.* **1**, downward. **2**, behind, in a score. **3**, dejected; ill-disposed. —*prep.* in a descending direction upon or along. —*n.* **1**, downward movement. **2**, a unit of play or progress in football. **3**, the soft feathers, as on a young bird; under-plumage. **4**, any soft hairy growth. **5**, a hill; a dune. —*v.i.* & *t.* go or cause to go down.

down'cast'' *adj.* dejected.

down'fall'' *n.* defeat; ruin.

down'grade'' *n.* **1**, a downward slope or course. **2**, deterioration.

down''heart'ed *adj.* discouraged.

down'hill'' *adj.* & *adv.* in a descending direction down a slope.

down'pour'' *n.* heavy rainfall.

down'right'' *adj.* **1**, direct; plain; blunt. **2**, complete; utter; absolute. —*adv.* thoroughly; completely. —**down'right'ness**, *n.*

down'stairs'' *adv.* & *adj.* toward or on a lower floor.

down'town'' *adv.* & *adj.* at, to or of the business section of a city.

down'trod''den (-dən) *adj.* oppressed.

down'ward (-wərd) *adv.* [also, **down'wards**] **1**, from a higher to a lower place, state, degree, etc. **2**, away from a source. —*adj.* descending.

down'y (dow'nē) *adj.* **1**, covered with down. **2**, like down; soft and fluffy. —**down'i.ness**, *n.*

dow'ry (dow'rē) *n.* the estate that a bride brings to her husband.

dox·ol·o·gy (doks-ol'ə-jē) *n.* a hymn or psalm of praise of God.

doze (dōz) *n.* a light sleep. —*v.t.* nap.

doz·en (duz'ən) *n.* twelve units.

drab *adj.* [drab'ber, -best] 1, of a yellowish-gray tint. 2, monotonous; dull. —**drab'ness,** *n.*

draft (dråft) *n.* 1, the act of drawing, dragging, or hauling. 2, a drink. 3, a heavy demand. 4, conscription. 5, the depth a loaded ship sinks in water. 6, a written order for payment, as a check. 7, a current of air; a device to produce or control the air flow. 8, a first sketch; an outline. —*v.t.* make a draft of, upon, or from. Also, **draught.**

drafts'man (dråfts'mən) *n.* [*pl.* -men] one who draws plans, sketches, or designs.

draft'y (dråf'tē) *adj.* causing or exposed to currents of air. —**draft'i-ness,** *n.*

drag *v.t. & i.* [dragged, drag'ging] 1, pull; haul. 2, (often with *along*) draw, move, or proceed slowly, heavily, or tiresomely. 3, draw a grapnel through a body of water in search of something; dredge. 4, harrow. —*n.* 1, something designed to be dragged or hauled; a brake; an impediment; hindrance. 2, the act of dragging. 3, (*Slang*) influence. 4, (*Slang*) a street; district.

drag'net" *n.* 1, a net for fishing. 2, (*Colloq.*) a canvass, esp. by the police.

drag'on (drag'-ən) *n.* a fabulous fire-breathing serpentine animal of great size and fierceness.

Dragon

drag'on·fly" (drag'ən-flī") *n.* a large insect with two pairs of wings: the *devil's darning needle.*

dra·goon' (drə-goon') *n.* an armed cavalry soldier. —*v.t.* persecute or oppress by armed force.

drain (drān) *v.t. & i.* 1, draw off or flow off gradually. 2, empty or exhaust gradually. —*n.* 1, the act of draining. 2, a passage or pipe used for draining.

drain'age (drā'nij) *n.* 1, a gradual flowing off; that which flows off. 2, a system of sewers for draining. 3, area drained.

drake (drāk) *n.* the male duck.

dram *n.* 1, a unit of weight, one-sixteenth ounce in avoirdupois weight. 2, a small drink, esp. of spirits.

dra·ma (drä'mə) *n.* 1, a literary composition written for the stage; a play. 2, that branch of literature dealing with the writing and production of plays; all plays, classic and modern. 3, a human course of events.

dra·mat'ic (drə-mat'ik) *adj.* 1, pert. to drama. 2, intensely interesting; eventful. —**dra·mat'i·cal·ly,** *adv.*

dram'a·tist (dram'ə-tist) *n.* a playwright.

dram'a·tize" (-tīz") *v.t.* express dramatically. —**dram"a·ti·za'tion** (-ti-zā'shən) *n.*

drank *v.* p.t. of *drink.*

drape (drāp) *v.t.* 1, cover with or adorn with cloth or hangings. 2, arrange or adjust in folds. —*n.* 1, a heavy curtain. —**drap'er,** *n.* a dealer in cloths.

dra'per·y (drā'pə-rē) *n.* textile fabrics used for draping. (*pl.*) curtains.

dras'tic (dras'tik) *adj.* having extreme and immediate effect; radical; harsh. —**dras'ti·cal·ly,** *adv.*

draught (dråft) 1, draft. 2, (*pl.*) checkers.

draw (drà) *v.t.* [drew (droo), drawn, draw'ing] 1, pull; drag. 2, take out, as money from a bank. 3, derive; obtain from some source. 4, induce; attract, as a crowd. 5, deduce; infer. 6, inhale; suck in. 7, drain. 8, tie (a game). 9, (with *out*) extract the essence of; encourage to talk. 10, (often with *out*) stretch; lengthen; prolong. 11, obtain as due, as salary. 12, sketch in lines or words; make a picture or draft of. —*v.i.* 1, move (toward or away). 2, attract attendance. 3, sketch. 4, make a draft or a demand (upon). 5, be susceptible to a draft, as a pipe. 6, take a weapon out of its holder. 7, tie (a score). —*n.* 1, the act of drawing; that which is drawn. 2, a tie score. 3, movable part of a drawbridge.

draw'back" *n.* a disadvantage; a hindrance.

draw'bridge" *n.* a bridge that can be raised or turned to permit vessels to pass through.

draw'er (dròr) *n.* 1, a sliding box-shaped compartment in a piece of furniture. 2, (drä'ər) one who draws, esp. a check or draft. 3, (*pl.*) (dròrz) an undergarment worn on the lower part of the body.

draw'ing (drä'ing) *n.* 1, the art of sketching, esp. pictures; a picture or illustration; a plan. 2, the selection of the winners in a lottery.

draw'ing-room" *n.* a room used for the reception of company.

drawl (dràl) *v.t. & i.* speak in a slow, dragged-out tone. —*n.* this manner of speech.

drawn (drån) v. p.p. of *draw.* —*adj.* 1, disemboweled, as a fowl prepared for cooking. 2, strained from weariness or grief.

dray (drā) n. a low horse-drawn cart for heavy loads. —**dray'horse**, n. —**dray'man** (-mən) n.

dread (dred) v.t. & i. fear greatly; be in great fear. —n. 1, great fear. 2, awe. —*adj.* fearsome.

dread'ful (-fəl) *adj.* 1, causing great fear or awe. 2, frightful; shocking; horrible. —**dread'fulness**, n.

dread'nought' (dred'nåt') n. a powerful battleship.

dream (drēm) n. 1, images or ideas occurring in the mind during sleep. 2, a vision of the fancy. 3, (*Colloq.*) something delightful. —v.i. & t. 1, imagine during sleep. 2, think idly; indulge in reverie. 3, plan vaguely; be unduly hopeful (of). —**dream'er**, n. a visionary.

dream'land (-lənd) n. sleep; the realm of fancy.

dream'y (drē'mē) *adj.* 1, vague; fanciful. 2, peaceful. 3, delightful. —**dream'i·ness**, n.

drear'y (drir'ē) *adj.* dismal; gloomy; tedious. Also, **drear.** —**drear'i·ness**, n.

dredge (drej) n. a scooping machine or instrument for clearing a channel, as in a river. —v.t. & i. 1, clear out by use of a dredge. 2, sprinkle flour upon, as in roasting meat.

dregs (dregz) n.pl. worthless residue, as the sediment of liquors.

drench v.t. wet thoroughly.

dress (dres) v.t. 1, put clothes on; attire. 2, bandage, as a wound. 3, prepare; make ready. 4, put in orderly arrangement, as the hair; adorn. —v.i. 1, clothe oneself. 2, come into proper alignment. —n. 1, clothing; attire. 2, a woman's frock.

dress'er (-ər) n. 1, one who dresses another, esp. in the theater; one who adjusts, trims, etc. 2, a bedroom chest of drawers with a mirror; a bureau.

dress'ing (-ing) n. 1, the act of one who dresses. 2, bandages applied to a wound. 3, sauce or stuffing for food. 4 a sizing, as starch, for fabrics. —**dressing gown**, a bathrobe; lounging robe.

dress'mak'er n. a seamstress.

dress'y (-ē) *adj.* (of clothes) stylish or formal. —**dress'i·ness**, n.

drew (droo) v. pret. of *draw.*

drib'ble (drib'əl) v.i. 1, fall in drops. 2, slaver. —v.t. 1, let fall in drops. 2, in some games, kick, or bounce the ball forward. —n. a dripping of water.

drib'let (drib'lit) n. a tiny amount.

dri'er (drī'ər) n. 1, a substance that accelerates drying. 2, an apparatus for removing moisture.

drift n. 1, the direction in which something is driven; the thing driven; the impelling force. 2, a heap of any matter driven together, as by wind. 3, a current, as of water; general current or intention; trend. —v.i. float or be carried at random by the force of wind or tide; hence, fig., be carried involuntarily into a course of action.

drift'wood' n. wood and debris cast ashore by drift or tide.

drill (dril) n. 1, a tool for boring holes. 2, military training, esp. in parade exercises. 3, teaching by repeated exercises; a test; quiz. 4, an agricultural machine for planting seeds. 5, a heavy cotton fabric. —v.t. 1, pierce with a drill. 2, exercise; train; quiz. 3, sow in rows, as wheat. —**drill'mas'ter**, n. a teacher, esp. of soldiers.

drink v.t. [**drank**, **drunk**, **drink'ing**] 1, swallow (a liquid) 2, take in (a liquid) in any way; imbibe; absorb. 3, (often with *in*) take in through the senses. —v.i. 1, swallow water or other fluid; habitually imbibe alcoholic liquors. 2, (with *to*) salute in drinking. —n. 1, any liquid taken into the stomach. 2, alcoholic liquor. 3, a potion; a draught. —**drink'er**, n. one who habitually drinks liquor.

drip v.i. & t. [**dripped**, **drip'ping**] fall or let fall in drops. —n. 1, a falling in drops. 2, a receptacle for catching the overflow. 3, (*Slang*) an unattractive person.

drive (drīv) v.t. [**drove** (drōv), **driv'en** (driv'ən), **driv'ing**] 1, force to move, esp. forward; impel; hammer in. 2, set or direct in motion, as an automobile; carry forward. 3, chase (game); hunt. 4, incite to a course of action or a state of mind; urge; press. —v.i. 1, be impelled. 2, move forcibly. 3, be conveyed, as in an automobile. 4, aim; tend. 5, in golf, hit the ball off the tee. 6, work energetically. —n. 1, a trip in an automobile. 2, a private road; driveway. 3, the urging together of animals, as for roundup. 4, a campaign to collect something, as money, members, sales. 5, extreme haste or strong action. 6, the power to drive; energy; ambition.

drive-'in' n. a restaurant or theater serving people who remain in automobiles.

driv'el (driv'əl) v.i. 1, drool; slaver. 2, talk foolishly. —n. act or result of driveling.

driv'er (drī'vər) n. 1, one who, or

that which drives; a chauffeur. **2**, a form of golf club (No. 1 wood).

drive'way" n. a private lane.

driz'zle (driz'əl) v.i. rain in small drops. —n. a light rain.

droll (drōl) adj. facetious; comical; amusing. —droll'er·y, n.

drom'e·dar·y (drom'ə-der-ē) n. the Arabian one-humped camel.

drone (drōn) v.i. & t. utter a dull, unvaried sound, as a bee; hence, speak in a monotonous tone. —n. **1**, a monotonous, continued sound. **2**, the male honeybee. **3**, an idler.

drool v.i. drivel; slaver, esp. with greed or anticipated pleasure.

droop v.i. **1**, sink or hang down, as from weakness or exhaustion. **2**, languish; decline. —v.t. let sink or hang down. —n. **1**, the act of drooping; a drooping state. **2**, (Slang) a killjoy. —droop'y, adj.

drop n. **1**, a small free-falling globule of liquid, as of rain; anything that resembles it. **2**, a small quantity. **3**, a sudden fall or descent; the distance covered by such. **4**, a hanging; a curtain. **5**, a chute; a trapdoor. —v.i. & t. [dropped, drop'ping] **1**, fall or let fall in globules. **2**, drip. **3**, fall; descend. **4**, sink or let sink to a lower position, level, state, or condition. **5**, fall dead. **6**, let go; dismiss. **7**, utter or write in an offhand manner. —drop kick (Football) a kick given to a dropped ball on the rebound. —drop shipment, shipment by a manufacturer direct to his dealer's customer.

drop'sy (drop'sē) n. an abnormal accumulation of serous fluid in the body. —drop'si·cal (-kəl) adj.

drosh'ky (drosh'kē) n. a Russian horsedrawn passenger vehicle, as a cab.

dross (drâs) n. **1**, the waste matter thrown off from molten metal. **2**, any refuse.

drought (drowt) n. long-continued dry weather. Also, drouth (drowth).

drove (drōv) v. pret. of drive. —n. a number of cattle, sheep, etc. driven in a herd. —drov'er, n. a driver of or dealer in such animals.

drown v.t. & i. **1**, suffocate or be suffocated by immersion in water or other liquid. **2**, flood; submerge; overwhelm.

drowse (drowz) v.i. be half asleep; be heavy or dull. —n. a half-sleep.

drow'sy (drow'zē) adj. sleepy. —drow'si·ness, n.

drub v.t. [drubbed, drub'bing] beat; cudgel. —drub'bing, n. a bad beating or defeat.

drudge (druj) v.i. labor at hard, uninteresting tasks. —n. an overworked person. —drudg'er·y (-ə-rē) n.

drug n. **1**, any substance used in the composition or preparation of medicines. **2**, a narcotic. **3**, a commodity unsalable because of overproduction. —v.t. [drugged, drug'ging] **1**, mix or dose with drugs. **2**, surfeit.

drug'gist (-ist) n. a pharmacist.

drug'store" n. a store that deals in drugs and, usually, other merchandise.

dru'id (droo'id) n. a priest of the ancient Celts.

drum n. **1**, a musical instrument consisting of a hollow frame covered on the top by a tightly stretched membrane which is beaten with sticks in playing. **2**, anything drumshaped. **3**, a fish. **4**, a membrane in the ear. —v.i. [drummed, drum'ming] **1**, play a drum. **2**, tap on something with the fingers. **3**, sound like a drum; resound. —v.t. **1**, (Mil.) expel formally. **2**, impress, as an idea into someone. **3**, (with up) attract or solicit, as trade.

drum'mer (-ər) n. **1**, a traveling salesman. **2**, one who plays a drum.

drum'stick" n. **1**, a stick with which a drum is beaten. **2**, the leg of a fowl.

drunk v. p.p. of drink. —adj. intoxicated by liquor. —n. **1**, a spree. **2**, an inebriated person. —drunk'en (-ən) adj. intoxicated. —drunk'en·ness, n.

drunk'ard (-ərd) n. a person given to excessive drinking of liquor.

drupe (droop) n. a stone fruit, as the plum, cherry, or peach. —drupe'let, n. a small drupe, as a section of a berry, containing a hard seed.

dry (drī) adj. **1**, without moisture; not wet. **2**, not giving milk, as a dry cow; empty, as a dry well. **3**, thirsty. **4**, barren; uninteresting. **5**, grave in manner but humorous or sarcastic. **6**, free from sweetness, as certain wines. **7**, (Colloq.) of or pert. to prohibition of alcoholic beverages. —v.t. & i. free from or lose moisture. —n. (Colloq.) prohibitionist. —dry'ness, n.

dry'ad (drī'ad) n. a wood nymph.

dry cell a sealed storage battery.

dry-'clean" v.t. wash (clothes, etc.) in benzene, gasoline, etc.

dry dock a structure for holding a ship out of water, for repairs, etc.

dry goods textile fabrics, etc.

dry ice frozen carbon dioxide.

du'al (doo'əl) adj. relating to or consisting of two parts; twofold.

du·al·i·ty (doo-al'ə-tē) n. the state of being twofold.

dub v.t. [dubbed, dub'bing] **1**, confer a new dignity or name upon.

2, rub or dress so as to make smooth. **3,** record from or on a previous sound track.

du·bi·e·ty (doo-bī'ə-tē) *n.* doubtfulness.

du·bi·ous (doo'bē-əs) *adj.* **1,** of questionable value. **2,** doubtful; hesitating. —**du'bi·ous·ness,** *n.*

du'cal (doo'kəl) *adj.* of or pert. to a duke.

duc'at (duk'ət) *n.* **1,** a former Europ. gold coin. **2,** (*pl.*) (*Slang*) money.

duch'ess (duch'əs) *n.* the wife of a duke.

duch'y (duch'ē) *n.* the territory of a duke or duchess; a dukedom.

duck (duk) **1,** any of many species of broad-, flat-billed water birds. **2,** (*Colloq.*) a likable person. **3,** a strong cotton or linen fabric; (*pl.*) clothes made of it. **4,** a diving inclination of the head. **5,** a brief dip or plunge in water. —*v.t.* & *i.* **1,** plunge briefly into water. **2,** bob or bow the head suddenly. **3,** dodge by bending down or aside suddenly. **4,** evade.

duck'bill' *n.* the platypus.

duck'ling *n.* a young duck.

duck'pin' *n.* a small bowling pin; (*pl.*) a bowling game.

duck'y (duk'ē) (*Colloq.*) *adj.* excellent.

duct (dukt) *n.* any tube or canal by which a fluid is conducted or conveyed. —**ductless gland,** any of certain glands, as the thyroid, giving off their secretions directly into the blood stream.

duc'tile (duk'təl) *adj.* **1,** capable of being drawn out into wire or threads. **2,** complying; easily led. —**duc·til'i·ty** (-til'ə-tē) *n.*

dud *n.* **1,** (*pl.*) (*Colloq.*) old clothes. **2,** a bomb, shell or firecracker that fails to explode. **3,** a failure.

dude (dood) *n.* **1,** an overdressed man; a fop. **2,** a city person; a tenderfoot. —**dude ranch,** a resort modeled on a cattle ranch.

dudg'eon (duj'ən) *n.* resentment; sullen anger.

due (doo) *adj.* **1,** owed; payable. **2,** suitable. **3,** expected or looked for. **4,** attributable. —*n.* **1,** that which is owed or required; a debt; an obligation. **2,** (*pl.*) a toll; a fee. —**due'bill',** *n.* a written acknowledgment of a debt, made payable in goods or services.

du'el (doo'əl) *n.* **1,** a premeditated combat between two persons with deadly weapons. **2,** any two-sided contest. —**du'el·ist,** *n.*

du·en'na (dū-en'ə) *n.* a chaperon.

du·et' (doo-et') *n.* (*Music*) a composition for two performers; the performance or performers.

duf'fel (duf'əl) *n.* **1,** a coarse woolen thick-napped cloth. **2,** a sportsman's or camper's outfit. —**duffel bag,** a large cloth carrying bag.

duf'fer (duf'ər) *n.* **1,** a peddler. **2,** (*Slang*) a stupid or inefficient person; a poor player at a game.

dug *v.* pret. & p.p. of **dig.**

dug'out' *n.* **1,** a boat hollowed out from a log. **2,** a shelter in the ground, esp. in trench warfare.

duke (dook) *n.* **1,** a hereditary title of nobility equivalent to or next below a prince. **2,** the ruler of a duchy. —**duke'dom** (-dəm) *n.*

dul'cet (dul'sit) *adj.* sweet; harmonious; agreeable.

dul'ci·mer (dul'sə-mər) *n.* a precursor of the pianoforte.

dull (dul) **1,** not understanding readily; stupid. **2,** tedious; boring; uninteresting. **3,** not quick or keen in perception. **4,** dismal; cheerless. **5,** not bright or clear; dim. **6,** not sharp; blunt. —*v.t.* & *i.* make or become dull. —**dull'ness,** *n.*

dull'ard (-ərd) *n.* a stupid person; a blockhead.

du'ly (doo'lē) *adv.* in a due manner; properly.

Du'ma (doo'mä) *n.* the former Russian lower house of parliament.

dumb (dum) *adj.* **1,** not having the power of speech. **2,** mute; silent. **3,** (*Colloq.*) stupid. —**dumb'ness,** *n.*

dumb'bell' *n.* **1,** a weight for gymnastic exercise. **2,** (*Slang*) a dolt.

Dumbbell

dumb'wait'er *n.* an elevator to convey food or small articles.

dum·found' (dum-fownd') *v.t.* strike dumb; confuse; confound.

dum'my (dum'ē) *n.* **1,** one who is dumb; a mute. **2,** a figurehead, model, effigy, etc. **3,** the high bidder's partner or his cards, exposed on the table, in bridge and other card games. **4,** (*Colloq.*) a stupid person; a dolt. —*adj.* sham; set up for appearances only.

dump *v.t.* **1,** throw down or let slide down a mass or body of something; unload. **2,** sell (quantities of stocks, merchandise, etc.) regardless of price. —*n.* **1,** a place for dumping loads, esp. rubbish. **2,** (*Mil.*) temporary storage place for supplies. **3,** (*pl.*) a state of depression; the doldrums.

dump'ish *adj.* morose; depressed in spirits. —**dump'ish·ness,** *n.*

dump'ling *n.* a lump of dough boiled in soup, stew, etc.

dump'y (-ê) *adj.* short and thick; squat. —**dump'i·ness,** *n.*

dun *v.t. & i.* [dunned, dun'ning] urge to pay a debt. —*n.* a demand for payment. —*adj.* of a dull gray-ish-brown color.

dunce (duns) *n.* a dull-witted stupid person; an ignoramus. —**dunce cap,** a cone of paper worn as a cap to mark a stupid student.

dune (doon) *n.* a hill of sand heaped up by the wind.

dung *n.* animal excrement; manure.

dun'ga·ree' (dung″gə-rē′) *n.* **1,** a coarse cotton material, generally blue. **2,** (*pl.*) work clothes made from this material.

dun'geon (dun'jən) *n.* a deep, dark place of confinement.

dung'hill' *n.* **1,** a heap of manure. **2,** anything mean, vile, or low.

dunk *v.t.* dip, esp. bread into coffee before eating it.

Dunk'ard (-ərd) *n.* one of a certain religious sect. Also, **Dunk'er.**

dun'nage (dun'ij) *n.* **1,** loose wood used to pack a ship's cargo. **2,** baggage.

du'o (doo′ō) *n.* a couple; pair.

du·o- *pref.* two.

du'o·dec'i·mal (dū″ə-des′ə-məl) *adj.* reckoning by twelves and the powers of twelve.

du'o·de'num (dū″ə-dē′nəm) *n.* the first portion of the small intestine, immediately connected with the stomach. —**du'o·de'nal,** *adj.*

dupe (doop) *v.t.* deceive; trick; mislead. —*n.* a person easily deceived. —**dup'er·y,** *n.*

du'plex (doo′pleks) *adj.* double; twofold. —*n.* **1,** an apartment of two floors. **2,** a two-family house.

du'pli·cate (doo′plə-kit) *adj.* **1,** double; twofold. **2,** exactly like something done before. —*n.* an exact copy; a facsimile. —*v.t.* (-kāt″) make a copy or copies of. —**du″pli·ca'tion,** *n.* —**du'pli·ca″tor,** *n.*

du·plic'i·ty (doo-plis′ə-tē) *n.* bad faith; dissimulation; hypocrisy; double dealing.

du'ra·ble (dyûr′ə-bəl) *adj.* lasting; long-wearing; not perishable or changeable. —**du″ra·bil'i·ty,** *n.*

du·ral'u·min (dyū-ral′yə-min) (*T.N.*) a strong and light alloy of aluminum.

dur'ance (dyûr′əns) *n.* imprisonment; involuntary confinement of any kind.

du·ra'tion (dyû-rā′shən) *n.* the length of time during which anything continues or lasts.

dur'bar (dėr′bär) *n.* in India, a prince's audience room, or an official audience or reception.

du'ress (dyûr′is) *n.* **1,** restraint of personal liberty; imprisonment. **2,** coercion.

dur'ing (dûr′ing) *prep.* in the time or course of; throughout the continuance of.

dusk *n.* **1,** the state between light and darkness, esp. at twilight. **2,** partial darkness; shadow. **3,** swarthi-ness.

dusk'y (dus′kē) *adj.* dark, as at dusk. —**dusk'i·ness,** *n.*

dust *n.* **1,** fine, dry particles of earth or other matter. **2,** a dead body; remains. **3,** the ground; a low condition. **4,** a small quantity of any powdered substance sprinkled over something. —*v.t.* **1,** free from dust or sweep away dust from. **2,** sprinkle with a powder.

dust bowl an area where the dry topsoil is blown about by the wind.

dust'er (dus′tər) *n.* **1,** a cloth or implement for removing dust. **2,** a light overcoat.

dust'y (dus′tē) *adj.* being covered with or charged with dust. —**dust'i·ness,** *n.*

Dutch (duch) *adj.* pert. to the Netherlands, its people or language. —**in Dutch,** in trouble. —**Dutch oven,** a kettle for baking. —**Dutch treat,** a party in which each pays his share. —**Dutch uncle,** a severe but well-wishing critic. —**Dutch wife,** a bolster used as a sleeping companion.

du'te·ous (doo′tē-əs) *adj.* performing the duties required; obedient. —**du'te·ous·ness,** *n.*

du'ti·a·ble (doo′tē-ə-bəl) *adj.* subject to customs duty.

du'ti·ful (doo′tē-fəl) *adj.* **1,** duteous. **2,** loyal; diligent. —**du'ti·ful·ness,** *n.*

du'ty (doo′tē) *n.* **1,** good behavior owed to one's parents or superiors. **2,** service requisite to one's position. **3,** any moral obligation. **4,** a tax; excise or customs dues.

dwarf (dwôrf) *n.* a person, animal or plant much below ordinary size. —*adj.* below average size. —*v.t.* **1,** hinder from growing; stunt. **2,** cause to seem small by comparison. —*v.i.* become less. —**dwarf'ish,** *adj.*

dwell (dwel) *v.i.* [*pret. & p.p.* dwelt or dwelled] **1,** stay; remain. **2,** abide as a permanent resident; reside. **3,** (usually with *on*) dilate upon, as a topic. —**dwell'er,** *n.* a resident. —**dwell'ing,** *n.* a house for human occupation.

dwin'dle (dwin'dəl) *v.i.* diminish; become less; shrink; waste away.

dy'ad (dī'ad) *n.* 1, two units treated as one. 2, an element with a valence of two, as oxygen in H_2O. 3, (*Biol.*) a secondary unit of organization; one of a pair of chromosomes.

dye (dī) *n.* 1, a liquid or other matter used to change the color of something else. 2, a particular color; tint. —*v.t.* [dyed, dye'ing] change the color of, with a dye. —dy'er, *n.* —dye'stuff", *n.* a substance used for making dye.

dy·nam'ic (dī-nam'ik) *adj.* 1, full of force and energy; active; potent. 2, pert. to dynamics. —dy·nam'i·cal·ly, *adv.*

dy·nam'ics (dī-nam'iks) *n.* 1, a branch of mechanics treating of motion. 2, (construed as *pl.*) the principles of active operation in any field.

dy'na·mite" (dī'nə-mīt") *n.* an explosive, nitroglycerin mixed with sand. —*v.t.* blow up with dynamite.

dy'na·mo" (dī'nə-mō") *n.* [*pl.* -mos"] a machine that converts mechanical energy into electrical energy.

dy"na·mom'e·ter (dī"nə-mom'i-tər) *n.* an instrument for measuring force or power.

dy'nas·ty (dī'nəs-tē) *n.* 1, a succession of rulers or monarchs of the same line or family. 2, the period during which a dynasty rules. —dy'nast, *n.* a ruler. —dy·nas'tic, *adj.*

dyne (dīn) *n.* (*Physics*) the unit of force in the centimeter-gram-second system.

dys- (dis) *pref.* with difficulty; difficultly.

dys'en·ter"y (dis'ən-ter'ē) *n.* a disease of the large intestine characterized by diarrhetic discharge of blood and mucus from the bowels.

dys·pep'sia (dis-pep'shə) *n.* impaired power of digestion.

dys·pep'tic (dis-pep'tik) *adj. & n.* (a person) afflicted with dyspepsia, hence gloomy or irritable. —dys·pep'ti·cal·ly, *adv.*

dys·pro'si·um (dis-prō'sē-əm) *n.* a metallic element, no. 66, symbol Dy, one of the rare earths.

E

E, e (ē) the fifth letter of the English alphabet.

each (ēch) *adj.* every (unit) (of a group or series considered one by one). —*pron.* every one individually. —*adv.* apiece.

ea'ger (ē'gər) *adj.* having keen desire or longing; being impatient, intent or earnest. —ea'ger·ness, *n.*

ea'gle (ē'gəl) *n.* 1, a large bird of prey. 2, a conventional representation of an eagle. 3, a U. S. ten-dollar gold piece. 4, in golf, two below par on a hole. —ea'glet, *n.* a young eagle.

Eagle

ear (ir) *n.* 1, the organ of hearing in mammals; the external part alone. 2, the sense of hearing; ability to discriminate among sounds. 3, attention; heed. 4, something likened to an ear. 5, the part of a cereal plant that contains the grains.

ear'drum" *n.* the tympanum.

earl (ērl) *n.* a British nobleman ranking above a viscount and below a marquis. —earl'dom, *n.*

ear'ly (ēr'lē) *adv. & adj.* 1, occurring near the beginning. 2, of ancient date. 3, before an appointed time. 4, in the near future. —ear'li·ness, *n.*

ear'mark" *n.* a mark of identification. —*v.t.* 1, mark for identification. 2, set aside for a specific purpose.

earn (ērn) *v.t.* 1, gain in return for labor or service, or as profit. 2, deserve; merit.

ear'nest (ēr'nəst) *adj.* 1, serious in purpose or effort; sincere. 2, diligent; zealous. 3, important; grave. 4, showing sincerity. —*n.* a pledge. —earnest money, money given to bind a contract. —ear'nest·ness, *n.*

earn'ings (ēr'ningz) *n.pl.* wages; profits.

ear'ring" *n.* an ornament worn on the ear.

ear'shot *n.* range of hearing.

earth (ērth) *n.* 1, the globe or planet we inhabit. 2, the solid matter of the globe. 3, the loose material of the globe's surface; sand, soil, etc. 4, the inhabitants of the globe; the world.

earth'en (ēr'thən) *adj.* made of earth, clay, etc. —earth'en·ware", *n.* vessels of baked clay.

earth'ly (-lē) *adj.* worldly; material. —earth'li·ness, *n.*

earth'nut" *n.* an edible nut or plant part that grows underground; a tuber.

earth'quake" *n.* a trembling or shaking of the earth's surface.

earth'work" *n.* a structure of earth, as a rampart.

earth'worm" *n.* any of various burrowing worms.

earth'y (ẽr'thē) *adj.* **1,** of or like earth. **2,** worldly or coarse. —**earth'i-ness,** *n.*

ear'wig" *n.* a small harmless insect.

ease (ēz) *n.* **1,** physical comfort. **2,** mental tranquillity. **3,** freedom from difficulty; facility. **4,** unaffectedness. —*v.t.* **1,** put in a state of ease; rid of pain, anxiety, etc. **2,** lessen; mitigate. **3,** make less difficult. —*v.i.* become less painful, severe, difficult, etc.

ea'sel (ē'zəl) *n.* a stand for supporting a picture, blackboard, etc.

ease'ment (ēz'mənt) *n.* **1,** the act of easing. **2,** (*Law*) a right to use land owned by another person.

east (ēst) *n.* **1,** one of the four cardinal points of the compass, 90 degrees clockwise from north. **2,** (usually *cap.*) a region lying in this direction, as the Orient. —*adj.* in, toward or from the east.

East'er (ēs'tər) *n.* the festival commemorating the resurrection of Jesus Christ, observed on the first Sunday after the first full moon that occurs on or after March 21.

east'er·ly (-ər-lē) *adj. & adv.* toward or from the east.

east'ern (-ərn) *adj.* in or pert. to the east. —**east'ern·er,** *n.*

east'ward (-wərd) *adj. & adv.* toward the east.

eas'y (ē'zē) *adj.* **1,** not difficult. **2,** comfortable; tranquil. **3,** not oppressive. —**eas'i·ness,** *n.*

eas'y·go'ing *adj.* calm and unhurried in manner or pace.

eat (ēt) *v.t.* **1,** take into the mouth and swallow for nourishment (esp. of nonliquid food). **2,** consume by corrosion, rust, etc. —*v.i.* dine; consume food. —*n.* (*pl.*) (*Colloq.*) food. —**eat'a·bles,** *n.pl.* articles of food.

eaves (ēvz) *n.pl.* the edge of a roof overhanging the walls.

eaves'drop" *v.i.* listen secretly.

ebb (eb) *v.i.* flow back, as tidal water; recede; fall away. —*n.* **1,** a receding or ebbing. **2,** a decline.

eb'on·y (eb'ən-ē) *n.* a hard, durable wood from various trees. —*adj.* **1,** of ebony. **2,** black.

e·bul'li·ent (i-bul'yənt) *adj.* greatly excited or demonstrative; boiling. —**e·bul'li·ence,** *n.*

eb''ul·li'tion (eb'ə-lish'ən) *n.* **1,** an outburst of feeling, passion, etc. **2,** a boiling up or overflow of liquid.

ec·cen'tric (ek-sen'trik) *adj.* **1,** off center; not having the same center. **2,** elliptical, not circular. **3,** deviating from usual or recognized form; queer. —*n.* **1,** a queer or erratic person. **2,** a contrivance for transforming rotary to linear motion.

—**ec·cen'tri·cal·ly,** *adv.* —**ec"cen·tric'i·ty** (ek"sən-tris'ə-tē) *n.*

ec·cle"si·as'tic (e-klē"zē-as'tik) *n.* a clergyman. —**ec·cle"si·as'ti·cal,** *adj.* pert. to the church or clergy.

ech'e·lon" (esh'ə-lon") *n.* **1,** a level of command. **2,** a steplike deployment of military or naval units.

ech'o (ek'ō) *n.* **1,** repetition of a sound by reflection of the sound waves. **2,** sympathetic response; one who so responds. —*v.i.* produce an echo. —*v.t.* repeat or imitate.

é·clair' (ā-klār') *n.* a frosted, filled cake.

é·clat' (ā-klä') *n.* brilliant effect; splendor.

ec·lec'tic (ek-lek'tik) *adj.* selective; not following any one school of thought. —**ec·lec'ti·cal·ly,** *adv.*

e·clipse' (i-klips') *n.* **1,** obscuration of the light of the sun by intervention of the moon (*solar eclipse*), or of the moon by intervention of the earth (*lunar eclipse*). **2,** any obscuration or diminution of light, brilliance, glory, etc. —*v.t.* **1,** cast a shadow upon. **2,** surpass.

e·clip'tic (i-klip'tik) *n. & adj.* the great circle which is the apparent annual path of the sun.

ec'logue (ek'log) *n.* a short pastoral poem.

e"co·nom'ic (ē"kə-nom'ik; ek"ə-) *adj.* **1,** utilitarian. **2,** pert. to economics. —**e"co·nom'i·cal,** *adj.* thrifty.

e"co·nom'ics (ē"kə-nom'iks; ek"-ə-) *n.* the science of the production and distribution of goods and services.

e·con'o·mist (i-kon'ə-mist) *n.* a scientist in the field of economics.

e·con'o·mize" (i-kon'ə-mīz") *v.i.* manage frugally.

e·con'o·my (i-kon'ə-mē) *n.* **1,** avoidance of or freedom from waste in expenditure or management; thrift. **2,** a system of management of resources, esp. pecuniary.

ec'ru (ek'roo) *adj. & n.* light tan.

ec'sta·sy (ek'stə-sē) *n.* overpowering emotion or exaltation; rapture. —**ec·stat'ic** (ek-stat'ik), *adj.* —**ec·stat'i·cal·ly,** *adv.*

ec·to- *pref.* (ek'tō) external; outer.

ec'to·plasm" (ek'tə-plaz-əm) *n.* a visible exudation, in spiritualism.

ec"u·men'i·cal (ek"yū-men'i-kəl) *adj.* **1,** general; universal. **2,** belonging to the whole Christian church.

ec'ze·ma (eg'zə-mə) *n.* an inflammation of the skin, often attended by exudation of lymph.

-ed *suf.* **1,** possessed of: forming adjectives from nouns, as *moneyed.* **2,** forming past tenses of verbs.

ed'dy (ed'ĕ) n. a rotary motion in a stream of liquid or gas; a small whirl or vortex. —v.i. whirl; spin.

e'del·weiss (ā'dəl-wīs") n. a flowering herb of alpine regions.

e·de'ma (ĕ-dē'mə) n. a disease in which body liquids collect in the tissues, causing swelling; dropsy. —e·dem'ic (ĕ-dem'ĭk) adj.

edge (ej) n. 1, the extreme border or margin of anything; verge; brink; rim. 2, the line of junction of two faces of a solid object; the sharpened side of a blade. 3, sharpness; keenness; acuteness. 4, (Colloq.) advantage. —v.t. 1, put an edge or border on. 2, sharpen. —v.i. move sidewise; advance gradually. —edg'y (ej'ĕ) adj. irritable; nervous.

ed'i·ble (ed'ə-bəl) adj. fit to be eaten as food. —n. something eatable. —ed'i·bil'i·ty, n.

e'dict (ē'dikt) n. a decree or proclamation issued by an authority.

ed'i·fice (ed'ə-fis) n. a building, esp. one that is large and imposing.

ed'i·fy (ed'i-fī") v.t. build up faith, belief, or knowledge in (a person); persuade; instruct. —ed·i·fi·ca'tion (-fi-kā'shən) n.

ed'it v.t. 1, prepare (a manuscript) for publication by revising, correcting, etc. 2, supervise (a publication) by collecting and preparing materials.

e·di'tion (i-dish'ən) n. the whole number of copies of a work printed at one time.

ed'i·tor (ed'i-tər) n. 1, one who edits; one who corrects, compiles, etc. 2, one who selects the contents of a publication.

ed'i·to'ri·al (ed'i-tôr'ē-əl) n. an article presenting the opinion of an editor. —adj. pert. to editing or an editor. —ed'i·to'ri·al·ize (-īz") v.i. express an opinion, esp. in reporting news.

ed'u·cate' (ed'yə-kāt") v.t. 1, impart knowledge and training to; develop mentally and morally by instruction. 2, send to school; provide schooling for.

ed'u·ca'tion (ed'yə-kā'shən) n. 1, act or process of educating; instruction. 2, the science of teaching; pedagogy. —ed'u·ca'tion·al, adj.

ed'u·ca'tor (ed'yə-kā'tər) n. a teacher.

e·duce' (ĕ-dūs") v.t. draw out; elicit; develop. —e·duc'tion, n.

-ee (ē) suf. the object or recipient of, as draftee, one who is drafted.

eel (ēl) n. an elongated fish without ventral fins, resembling a snake.

ee'rie (ir'ĕ) adj. inspiring fear; strange; weird. —ee'ri·ness, n.

ef·face' (e-fās") v.t. 1, rub out; erase; obliterate. 2, make inconspicuous. —ef·face'ment, n.

ef·fect' (e-fekt') n. 1, what is produced by a cause; something that follows as a consequence; a result. 2, power to produce results; force; validity. 3, the state of being operative, in force, or active. 4, (pl.) property, esp. personal. —v.t. produce as a result; be the cause or agent of; make happen; achieve.

ef·fec'tive (e-fek'tiv) adj. 1, productive; efficient. 2, having a desired effect; successful. —ef·fec'tive·ness, n.

ef·fec'tu·al (e-fek'choo-əl) adj. producing a desired effect. —ef·fec'tu·al'i·ty, n.

ef·fec'tu·ate' (e-fek'choo-āt") v.t. make happen; cause. —ef·fec'tu·a'tion, n.

ef·fem'i·na·cy (e-fem'i-nə-sĕ) n. quality of being like a woman.

ef·fem'i·nate (e-fem'ə-nət) adj. having the qualities of the female sex; womanish (applied to men).

ef"fer·vesce' (ef"ər-ves') v.i. 1, bubble and hiss, like a boiling liquid. 2, exhibit excitement or liveliness. —ef"fer·ves'cence, n. —ef"fer·ves'cent, adj.

ef·fete' (ə-fēt') adj. worn out by age; staled by usage; exhausted.

ef"fi·ca'cious (ef"i-kā'shəs) adj. having power adequate to an intended purpose; effective; effectual. —ef'fi·ca·cy (-kə-sĕ) n.

ef·fi'cient (i-fish'ənt) adj. 1, adequate in performance or operation; capable; competent. 2, (of a machine) giving a relatively high output of work. 3, acting as a cause; producing an effect; causative. —ef·fi'cien·cy, n.

ef'fi·gy (ef'ə-jĕ) n. a life-sized sculptured likeness or dummy of a person.

ef"flo·resce' (ef"lō-res') v.i. 1, burst into bloom; blossom. 2, (Chem.) decompose into powdery substance. —ef"flo·res'cence, n. —ef"flo·res'cent, adj.

ef·flu'vi·um (i-floo'vē-əm) n. [pl. -a (-ə)] an unpleasant vapor or emanation from something.

ef'fort (ef'ərt) n. 1, voluntary exertion to perform an action. 2, a strenuous attempt. 3, a work; an achievement.

ef·fron'ter·y (i-frun'tə-rĕ) n. barefaced impropriety; shamelessness; impudence.

ef·ful'gent (i-ful'jənt) adj. radiantly bright. —ef·ful'gence, n.

ef·fuse' (e-fūz') v.t. pour out; shed. —v.i. seep out; exude. —adj. (e-fūs') loosely spread out. —ef·fu'sion (i-fū'zhən) n. —ef·fu'sive (-siv) adj. gushing.

egg (eg) *n.* **1,** the reproductive cell and its envelopes, as formed in a female animal. **2,** this cell and its nourishment enclosed in a hard rounded shell, such as produced by birds. **3,** anything resembling a hen's egg.

egg'nog" (eg'nog") *n.* a drink made of beaten eggs, sugar, and milk, often with an alcoholic beverage.

egg'plant' *n.* a plant having edible egg-shaped fruit, sometimes yellow.

Eggplant

e'gis (ē'jis) *n.* protection; sponsorship. Also, **ae'-gis.**

eg'lan·tine" (eg'lən-tīn") *n.* any of several brier plants.

e'go (ē'gō) *n.* [*pl.* -gos] the "I"; that which feels, acts, and thinks; the self.

e'go·ism (ē'gō-iz-əm) *n.* **1,** the doctrine that self-interest is the basis of all behavior. **2,** conceit. —**e'go·ist,** *n.*

e'go·tism (ē'gə-tiz-əm) *n.* the habit of talking too much about oneself; conceit. —**e'go·tist,** *n.* —**e'go·tis'tic** (-tis'tik) *adj.* —**e'go·tis'ti·cal·ly,** *adv.*

e·gre'gious (i-grē'jəs) *adj.* extraordinarily flagrant. —**e·gre'gious·ness,** *n.*

e'gress (ē'gres) *n.* **1,** the act of going out; departure. **2,** a way for going out; an exit. —**e·gres'sion** (i-gresh'ən) *n.*

e'gret (ē'gret) *n.* **1,** any of various herons. **2,** a plume from an egret.

E·gyp'tian (i-jip'shən) *adj.* pert. to Egypt, its people, customs, etc. —*n.* a native of Egypt.

eh (ā) *interj.* what?

ei'der (ī'dər) *n.* a large sea duck, whose breast feathers are prized for stuffing pillows, etc.

eight (āt) *n. & adj.* the cardinal number between seven and nine, expressed by 8. —**eighth** (ātth) *adj.* the ordinal of this number, also written 8th. —*n.* one of 8 equal parts.

eigh"teen' (ā"tēn') *n. & adj.* eight plus ten, 18. —**eigh"teenth'** (-tēnth') *adj. & n.*

eight'y (ā'tē) *n. & adj.* eight ti .es ten, 80. —**eight'i·eth** (-əth) *adj. & n.*

ei'ther (ē'thər; ī'-) *adj.* one or the other of two. **2,** each of two. —*pron.* one or the other. —*adv.* also; further, esp. in emphatic denial. —*conj.* precedes the first of two coördinate alternatives, the second being preceded by *or*.

e·jac'u·late" (i-jak'yə-lāt") *v.t.* **1,** utter suddenly and briefly; exclaim. **2,** emit forcibly; discharge. —**e·jac'u·la'tion,** *n.*

e·ject' (i-jekt') *v.t.* throw out; drive away; expel; evict. —**e·jec'tion,** *n.* —**e·jec'tor,** *n.*

eke (ēk) *v.t.* (with *out*) **1,** obtain with difficulty. **2,** supplement.

e·lab'o·rate (i-lab'ə-rət) *adj.* **1,** worked out with great care or exactness. **2,** intricate; involved. —*v.t. & i.* (-rāt') work out with precision, in full detail; add details. —**e·lab'o·rate·ness,** *n.* —**e·lab'o·ra'tion,** *n.*

e'land (ē'lənd) *n.* a large Afr. antelope.

e·lapse' (i-laps') *v.i.* (of time) pass away.

e·las'tic (i-las'tik) *adj.* **1,** tending to revert to an original shape after distortion (of a solid); tending to expand (as a gas). **2,** highly flexible. **3,** recovering original form or condition readily; buoyant. —*n.* an elastic cord or band. —**e·las'ti·cal·ly,** *adv.* —**e"las·tic'i·ty** (ē"las-tis'ə-tē) *n.*

e·late' (i-lāt') *v.t.* make proud or exultant; gratify. —**e·la'tion,** *n.* great joy.

el'bow (el'bō) *n.* **1,** the joint connecting the long bones of the arm. **2,** an angle or bend. —*v.t. & i.* push with the elbows; jostle. —**el'bow·room",** *n.* enough space for comfort.

eld'er (el'dər) *adj.* older; senior. —*n.* **1,** a senior in age. **2,** a leader or legislator in a tribe, community, or church. **3,** a shrub or small tree, bearing a reddish fruit.

eld'er·ber"ry *n.* the small dark berry of the elder plant, used in wine, medicine, etc.

eld'er·ly (-lē) *adj.* rather old. —**eld'er·li·ness,** *n.*

eld'est (el'dəst) *adj.* oldest.

e·lect' (i-lekt') *v.t.* **1,** select for office by vote. **2,** choose; prefer; determine in favor of. —*adj.* **1,** voted into office but not yet inducted. **2,** chosen. **3,** superior; select; choice. —*n.* a person or persons chosen or worthy to be chosen.

e·lec'tion (i-lek'shən) *n.* act of electing; balloting. —**e·lec'tion·eer'** (-ir') *v.t.* solicit votes.

e·lec'tive (i-lek'tiv) *adj.* **1,** chosen by election. **2,** having the duty or power to elect. **3,** optional. —*n.* an optional academic course.

e·lec'tor (i-lek'tər) *n.* one qualified to vote. —**e·lec'to·rate** (-tər-ət) *n.* body of voters.

e·lec'tor·al (i-lek'tər-əl) *adj.* pert. to election or electors. —**electoral college,** the body of persons chosen by popular vote to elect the president and vice-president of the U.S.

e·lec′tric (i-lek′trik) *adj.* **1,** of or pert. to electricity. **2,** operated by the power of electricity. **3,** startling; exciting. Also, **e·lec′tri·cal** (-tri-kəl). —**electric chair,** a chairlike device used for electrocution.

e·lec″tri′cian (i-lek″trish′ən) *n.* a craftsman skilled in making, repairing or operating electric equipment.

e·lec″tric′i·ty (i-lek″tris′ə-tē) *n.* **1,** a force, manifest in magnetism, lightning, etc., utilized by man for power, light, etc. **2,** a flow of electric current.

e·lec′tri·fy″ (i-lek′tri-fī″) *v.t.* **1,** charge with electricity. **2,** equip for operation by electricity. **3,** startle greatly; thrill. —**e·lec″tri·fi·ca′tion** (-fi-kā′shən) *n.*

e·lec·tro- *pref.* pert. to or employing electricity.

CHEMICAL ELEMENTS

actinium	mercury
aluminum	molybdenum
americium	neodymium
antimony	neon
argon	neptunium
arsenic	nickel
astatine	niobium
athenium	nitrogen
barium	osmium
berkelium	oxygen
beryllium	palladium
bismuth	phosphorus
boron	platinum
bromine	plutonium
cadmium	polonium
calcium	potassium
californium	praseodymium
carbon	promethium
centurium	protactinium
cerium	radium
cesium	radon
chlorine	rhenium
chromium	rhodium
cobalt	rubidium
copper	ruthenium
curium	samarium
dysprosium	scandium
erbium	selenium
europium	silicon
fluorine	silver
francium	sodium
gadolinium	strontium
gallium	sulfur
germanium	tantalum
gold	technetium
hafnium	tellurium
helium	terbium
holmium	thallium
hydrogen	thorium
indium	thulium
iodine	tin
iridium	titanium
iron	tungsten
krypton	uranium
lanthanum	vanadium
lead	xenon
lithium	ytterbium
lutetium	yttrium
magnesium	zinc
manganese	zirconium

---

e·lec′tro·cute″ (i-lek′trə-kūt″) *v.t.* kill by electric shock. —**e·lec″tro·cu′tion,** *n.* —**e·lec″tro·cu′tion·ist,** *n.*

e·lec′trode (i-lek′trōd) *n.* a conductor of electricity, esp. the terminal of such a conductor.

e·lec·trol′y·sis (i-lek″trol′ə-sis) *n.* the decomposition of a chemical compound by an electric current. —**e·lec″tro·lyt′ic** (-lit′ik) *adj.*

e·lec′tro·lyte″ (i-lek′trə-līt″) *n.* a liquid or solid that conducts electricity by flow of ions.

e·lec″tro·mo′tive (i-lek″trə-mō′tiv) *adj.* pert. to, or producing, electric current.

e·lec′tron (i-lek′tron) *n.* one of the fundamental particles of matter, believed to be the unit of negative electricity. —**e·lec·tron′ic,** *adj.* —**e·lec·tron′i·cal·ly,** *adv.* —**e·lec·tron′ics,** *n.,* the science dealing with the action of electrons.

e·lec″tro·type″ (i-lek′trə-tīp″) *n.* a printing plate made by an electrolytic process.

el″ee·mos′y·nar·y (el″ə-mos′ə-ner-ē) *adj.* charitable.

el′e·gant (el′i-gənt) *adj.* having or exhibiting good taste; luxurious. —**el′e·gance,** *n.*

el·e′gi·ac (e-lē′jē-ak) *adj.* expressing sorrow.

el′e·gy (el′ə-jē) *n.* a mournful poem or song, esp. in lament for the dead. —**el′e·gize″** (-jīz″) *v.t. & i.*

el′e·ment (el′i-mənt) *n.* **1,** that of which anything is in part composed; component; constituent. **2,** (*Chem.*) one of the substances of which all matter is composed, believed to be formed by particles or forces common to all. **3,** (*pl.*) rudimentary principles of an art or science. **4,** that in which something exists; proper or natural environment. **5,** (*pl.*) atmospheric forces. —**el′e·men′tal,** *adj.* basic; primal. —**el″e·men′ta·ry,** *adj.* simple; pert. to elements or first principles.

el′e·phant (el′ə-fənt) *n.* a large mammal of Afr. and India having a long prehensile proboscis or trunk and long ivory tusks. —**white elephant,** a burdensome or embarrassing possession.—**el′e·phan′tine** (-fan′tin) *adj.* huge.

Elephant

el″e·phan·ti′a·sis (el″ə-fən-tī′ə-sis) *n.* a disease causing enlargement of bodily parts.

el′e·vate″ (el′i-vāt″) *v.t.* **1,** move to a higher level or station; raise; lift up. **2,** cheer.

el″e·va′tion (el″i-vā′shən) *n.* **1,** act of elevating. **2,** a high place;

eminence. **3,** a drawing or plan of a vertical surface of a structure. **4,** altitude above the ground.

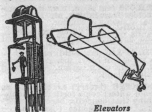

Elevators

el'e·va"tor (el'ĭ-vā"tər) *n.* **1,** a platform or small room capable of being raised or lowered to carry passengers or freight. **2,** a building for storage of grain, etc. **3,** a type of rudder on an airplane.

e·lev'en (ĭ-lev'ən) *n. & adj.* the cardinal number between ten and twelve, expressed by 11. —**e·lev'enth** (-ənth) *adj.* the ordinal of this number, also written 11th. —*n.* one of 11 equal parts.

elf *n.* [*pl.* **elves** (elvz)] an imaginary tiny being of mischievous character; sprite; fairy. —**elf'in,** *adj.*

e·lic'it (ĭ-lis'ĭt) *v.t.* draw out; bring forth; evoke. —**e·lic"i·ta'tion,** *n.*

e·lide' (ĭ-līd') *v.t.* omit or slur over, as in speech.

el'i·gi·ble (el'ĭ-jə-bəl) *adj.* **1,** fit to be chosen; worthy or deserving of choice. **2,** available and desirable as a husband. **3,** legally qualified. —**el"i·gi·bil'i·ty,** *n.*

e·lim'i·nate" (ĭ-lim'ĭ-nāt") *v.t.* **1,** get rid of; remove. **2,** omit; ignore. **3,** expel; secrete. —**e·lim"i·na'tion,** *n.*

e·li'sion (ĭ-lizh'ən) *n.* act or result of eliding; omission.

e·lite' (ā-lēt') *n.* a superior or choice part, esp. of a human society.

e·lix'ir (ĭ-lik'sər) *n.* **1,** a supposed substance sought by alchemists to transmute baser metals into gold and to prolong life. **2,** a palatable medicine; any invigorating drink.

elk *n.* **1,** a large deer. **2,** the wapiti.

ell (el) *n.* **1,** an addition to a building at right angles to the main part. **2,** a measure of length, 45 inches.

el·lipse' (ĭ-lips') *n.* the curve traced by a moving point, the sum of whose distances from two fixed points (the *foci*) remains constant; a closed curve, somewhat oval-shaped. —**el·lip'ti·cal** (ĭ-lip'tĭ-kəl) *adj.*

Ellipse

el·lip'sis (ĭ-lip'sĭs) *n.* [*pl.* **-ses** (-sēz)] the omission of words from a sentence, sometimes indicated by (. . .).

elm *n.* a tree with wide-spreading branches; its wood.

el"o·cu'tion (el"ə-kū'shən) *n.* the study and practice of effective public speaking. —**el"o·cu'tion·ar·y,** *adj.* —**el"o·cu'tion·ist,** *n.*

e·lon'gate (ĭ-lông'gāt) *v.t.* make longer; extend. —*v.i.* become long or longer. —**e"lon·ga'tion** (ē"lông-gā'shən) *n.*

e·lope' (ĭ-lōp') *v.i.* **1,** run away with a lover. **2,** break loose from ties; escape. —**e·lope'ment,** *n.*

el'o·quent (el'ə-kwənt) *adj.* **1,** having the power to speak vividly and appropriately. **2,** stirring; persuasive. —**el'o·quence,** *n.*

else (els) *adv.* otherwise; differently; instead. —*adj.* besides; in addition.

else'where" (els'hwãr") *adv.* in or to another place.

e·lu'ci·date" (ĭ-loo'sĭ-dāt") *v.t.* make clear; explain. —**e·lu"ci·da'tion,** *n.*

e·lude' (ĭ-lood') *v.t.* avoid or escape by stratagem or deceit; evade.

e·lu'sion (ĭ-loo'zhən) *n.* act of eluding; evasion.

e·lu'sive (ĭ-loo'sĭv) *adj.* hard to grasp or catch; slippery. —**e·lu'sive·ness,** *n.*

e·lu'so·ry (ĭ-loo'sə-rē) *adj.* tending to slip away; evasive.

elves (elvz) *n.* pl. of **elf.**

em *n.* a square space, in printing type: usually the pica, 12 points.

em- (em *or* im) *pref.* same as **en-.**

e·ma'ci·ate" (ĭ-mā'shē-āt") *v.t.* make lean by gradual wasting away of flesh. —**e·ma"ci·a'tion,** *n.*

em'a·nate" (em'ə-nāt") *v.i.* flow out or issue; proceed from a source. —**em"a·na'tion,** *n.*

e·man'ci·pate" (ĭ-man'sĭ-pāt") *v.t.* set free from a restraint; liberate. —**e·man"ci·pa'tion,** *n.* —**e·man'ci·pa"tor,** *n.*

e·mas'cu·late" (ĭ-mas'kyə-lāt") *v.t.* deprive of manhood, strength, or vigor. —**e·mas"cu·la'tion,** *n.*

em·balm' (em-bäm') *v.t.* treat (a dead body) with balm, drugs, etc. to preserve it. —**em·balm'ment,** *n.*

em·bank' (em-bank') *v.t.* enclose or confine with a ridge, as of earth. —**em·bank'ment,** *n.* a protecting bank or wall.

em·bar'go (em-bär'gō) *n.* a restraint, hindrance or prohibition, esp. of commerce or shipping by government order.

em·bark' (em-bärk') *v.i.* **1,** go aboard a ship. **2,** set out; make a start. —*v.t.* put or receive aboard a ship. —em'bar·ka'tion, *n.*

em·bar'rass (em-bar'əs) *v.t.* 1, make self-conscious or ashamed; disconcert. 2, perplex; hamper; impede. —em·bar'rass·ment, *n.*

em'bas·sy (em'bə-sē) *n.* 1, an ambassador and his staff. 2, the headquarters of this body.

em·bat'tled (em-bat'əld) *adj.* prepared for or involved in battle.

em·bed' *v.t.* [-bed'ded, -ding] place in a bed; fix firmly in a surrounding substance.

em·bel'lish (em-bel'ish) *v.t.* 1, beautify with ornamentation; adorn. 2, add fictitious detail to (a tale). —em·bel'lish·ment, *n.*

em'ber (em'bər) *n.* a smoldering coal; (*pl.*) dying remains.

em·bez'zle (em-bez'əl) *v.t.* take (property in trust) for one's own use. —em·bez'zle·ment, *n.*

em·bit'ter (em-bit'ər) *v.t.* make resentful. —em·bit'ter·ment, *n.*

em·bla'zon (em-blā'zən) *v.t.* 1, depict on a heraldic shield. 2, decorate; illuminate. 3, celebrate; proclaim. —em·bla'zon·ment, *n.* —bla'zon·ry (-rē) *n.* heraldic decoration.

em'blem (em'bləm) *n.* an object or a design symbolizing an idea, quality, or the like; a flag; a badge. —em'blem·at'ic (-mat'ik) *adj.* —em'blem·at'i·cal·ly, *adv.*

em·bod'y (em-bod'ē) *v.t.* 1, invest with a body; make concrete; express in concrete form. 2, collect into a body; organize. 3, comprise; include. —em·bod'i·ment, *n.*

em·bo·lism (em'bə-liz-əm) *n.* obstruction by a blood clot.

em·boss' (em-bâs') *v.t.* represent in raised designs or relief. —em·boss'ment, *n.*

em·brace' (em-brās') *v.t.* 1, clasp in the arms; hug. 2, enclose; contain; include. 3, take or receive willingly; adopt. —*n.* a hug; grasp.

em·bra'sure (em-brā'zhər) *n.* a flared opening for a window or door, having a larger aperture on one side of the wall than on the other.

em·broi'der (em-broi'dər) *v.t.* 1, decorate with ornamental needlework. 2, embellish; elaborate. —em·broi'der·y, *n.*

em·broil' *v.t.* involve in contention or strife. —em·broil'ment, *n.*

em'bry·o' (em'brē-ō') *n.* 1, an organism in its earliest stages of development after fertilization of the germ cell. 2, the rudimentary or formative stage of anything. —*adj.* undeveloped. —em'bry·on'ic (-on'ik) *adj.* undeveloped; rudimentary. —em'bry·oh'i·cal·ly, *adv.*

em'bry·ol'o·gy (em'brē-ol'ə-jē) *n.* the science of the origin and development of the embryo. —em'bry·ol'o·gist (-jist) *n.*

em·cee' (em'sē) *n.* master of ceremonies (from initials, M. C.).

e·mend' (ē-mend') *v.t.* remove faults or errors from; revise; correct. —e'men·da'tion, *n.*

em'er·ald (em'ər-əld) *n. & adj.* 1, a variety of beryl, prized as a gem. 2, of its color, green. —Emerald Isle, Ireland.

e·merge' (i-mērj') *v.i.* rise out, as from water; come forth from something that conceals; become apparent. —e·mer'gence (-jəns) *n.* —e·mer'gent, *adj.*

e·mer'gen·cy (i-mēr'jən-sē) *n.* a sudden and urgent occasion for action; pressing necessity.

e·mer'i·tus (i-mer'i-təs) *adj.* retired from active duty but retaining honorary title.

e·mer'sion (i-mēr'shən) *n.* the act of emerging.

em'er·y (em'ə-rē) *n.* a mixture of pulverized minerals used as an abrasive.

e·met'ic (i-met'ik) *n.* a medicine to induce vomiting.

em'i·grant (em'i-grənt) *n.* one who emigrates. —*adj.* emigrating.

em'i·grate' (em'i-grāt') *v.i.* leave a country or region to settle elsewhere. —em'i·gra'tion, *n.*

em'i·nence (em'i-nəns) *n.* 1, high repute. 2, a hill. 3, (*cap.*) title of honor of a cardinal.

em'i·nent (em'i-nənt) *adj.* 1, high in rank, office, worth, etc. 2, conspicuous; noteworthy. —eminent domain, the right of a government to buy property for public use.

e·mir' *n.* a Mohammedan prince.

em'is·sar·y (em'i-ser-ē) *n.* a person sent out on a mission; an agent.

e·mis'sion (i-mish'ən) *n.* 1, the act of emitting or issuing. 2, something issued; emanation.

e·mit' (i-mit') *v.t.* [-mit'ted, -ting] 1, send forth; give out; utter. 2, issue.

e·mol'lient (i-mol'yənt) *n.* a substance that softens or soothes.

e·mol'u·ment (e-mol'ū-mənt) *n.* salary or fees for services; gain.

e·mo'tion (i-mō'shən) *n.* 1, a state of mind in which feeling, sentiment, or attitude is predominant (over cognition and volition). 2, a specific feeling, as love, joy, etc. —e·mo'tion·al, *adj.* 1, pert. to or affecting the emotions. 2, easily stirred.

em'per·or (em'pər-ər) *n.* the ruler of an empire.

em·pha·sis (em'fə-sis) *n.* [*pl.* -ses (-sēz')] stress laid upon anything; vigor or force in expression. —**em·phat'ic** (em-fat'ik) *adj.* —**em·phat'i·cal·ly,** *adv.*

em·pha·size (em'fə-sīz") *v.t.* place emphasis on; stress.

em·pire (em'pīr) *n.* **1,** a group of countries or peoples with a single government or emperor. **2,** supreme power. **3,** area of influence; domain.

em·pir·ic (em-pir'ik) *n.* **1,** one who follows an empirical method. **2,** a quack or charlatan. —**em·pir'i·cism** (-siz-əm) *n.*

em·pir'i·cal (em-pir'ə-kəl) *adj.* **1,** derived from experience. **2,** derived from observation without reliance on theory.

em·ploy' (em-ploi') *v.t.* **1,** use. **2,** give occupation to. —**em·ploy·ee** (-ē") *n.* —**em·ploy'er,** *n.* —**em·ploy'·ment,** *n.*

em·po'ri·um (em-pôr'ē-əm) *n.* [*pl.* -a (-ə)] a shop that sells a variety of articles; department store.

em·pow'er (em-pow'ər) *v.t.* authorize; commission; license. —**em·pow'er·ment,** *n.*

em'press (em'prəs) *n.* the wife of an emperor, or a woman ruler of an empire.

emp·ty (emp'tē) *adj.* **1,** containing nothing. **2,** lacking in effect, value, etc.; meaningless. **3,** (*Colloq.*) hungry. —*v.t.* remove the contents of. —*v.i.* unload; discharge; become empty. —**emp'ti·ness,** *n.*

em·py·re'an (em"pə-rē'ən) *n.* the highest heaven, once supposed to be pure fire. —*adj.* celestial. — **em"py·re'al,** *adj.*

e'mu (ē'mū) *n.* a large flightless Australian bird.

em'u·late (em'·ū·lāt') *v.t.* strive to equal or excel; vie with. —**em"·u·la'tion,** *n.* —**em'u·lous,** *adj.*

e·mul·si·fy (i-mul'si-fī")*v.t.* make into an emulsion. —**e·mul'si·fi·ca'tion,** *n.*

e·mul'sion (i-mul'shən) *n.* a mixture of liquids, minute globules of one being suspended in a second that does not dissolve the first.

Emu

em *n.* (*Print.*) one-half em.

en- (en *or* in) *pref.* **1,** in; into. **2,** used to indicate a transitive verb.

-en (ən) *suf.* forming: **1,** verbs from nouns and adjectives, as *lengthen.* **2,** diminutive nouns, as *maiden.* **3,** adjectives meaning made of, as *golden.*

en·a'ble (en-ā'bəl) *v.t.* make able; furnish with power, ability, or means.

en·act' (en-akt') *v.t.* **1,** make into a law; decree; accomplish. **2,** act the part of (in a play). —**en·act'ment,** *n.*

e·nam'el (i-nam'əl) *n.* **1,** a glassy substance applied to pottery, metalware, etc. **2,** a paint that dries in a hard, glossy surface. **3,** the outermost and hardest part of a tooth. —*v.t.* apply enamel to; coat.

en·am'or (in-am'ər) *v.t.* inflame with love; charm; captivate. Also, **en·am'our.**

en·camp' (en-kamp') *v.i.* form or lodge in a camp. —**en·camp'ment,** *n.* **1,** act of camping. **2,** a camp.

en·case' (en-kās') *v.t.* enclose in or as in a case. —**en·case'ment,** *n.*

-ence (əns) *suf.* forming nouns denoting act, state or quality. Also, **-en·cy** (ən-sē).

en·ceph"a·li'tis (en-sef"ə-li'tis) *n.* inflammation of the brain.

en·chant' (en-chänt') *v.t.* **1,** put a magical spell on. **2,** delight to a high degree; charm; fascinate. —**en·chant'ment,** *n.* —**en·chant'ress** (-rəs) *n.fem.*

en·cir'cle (en-sēr'kəl) *v.t.* **1,** form a circle around; enclose. **2,** move around; make a circle of. —**en·cir'cle·ment,** *n.*

en'clave (en'klāv) *n.* a country wholly surrounded by a foreign country.

en·close' (en-klōz') *v.t.* **1,** surround; shut in; confine. **2,** insert in the same envelope. Also, **in·close'.**

en·clo'sure (en-klō'zhər) *n.* **1,** act of enclosing. **2,** something enclosed. **3,** that which encloses, as a fence. Also, **in·clo'sure.**

en·co'mi·um (en-kō'mē-əm) *n.* extravagant praise.

en·com'pass (en-kum'pəs) *v.t.* **1,** surround; encircle. **2,** contain. —**en·com'pass·ment,** *n.*

en'core (än"kôr) *n.* a repeated performance, or additional act.

en·coun'ter (en-kown'tər) *v.t. & i.* **1,** meet, esp. by chance. **2,** meet in strife or contention. —*n.* a meeting or conflict.

en·cour'age (en-kėr'ij) *v.t.* **1,** inspire with courage or confidence; lead on; incite. **2,** support. —**en·cour'ag·ing,** *adj.* promoting optimism. —**en·cour'age·ment,** *n.*

en·croach' (en-krōch') *v.i.* enter upon the domain of another; trespass; make inroads. —**en·croach'·ment,** *n.*

en·cum'ber (en-kum'bər) *v.t.* hinder, as with a load; burden with obligations or difficulties. —**en·cum'ber·ment,** *n.*

en·cum'brance (en-kum'brəns) *n.* 1, a burden or hindrance. 2, a legal obligation.

en·cyc'li·cal (en-sīk'li-kəl) *n.* a general letter from the Pope.

en·cy'clo·pe'di·a (en-sī"klə-pē'dē-ə) *n.* a work treating of various branches of knowledge, or various topics. —**en·cy'clo·pe'dic**, *adj.* wide in scope; comprehensive. —**en·cy'clo·pe'di·cal·ly**, *adv.*

end *n.* 1, one of the terminal points or parts of something that is longer than it is wide. 2, an outermost boundary. 3, the terminal moment in time; finish; cessation; the concluding part. 4, death; extinction. 5, purpose; aim. 6, outcome; result. 7, the position of a player in football and other games. —*v.t.* bring to an end; stop; halt. —*v.i.* 1, come to an end; cease; finish. 2, result.

en·dan'ger (en-dān'jər) *v.t.* put into danger; expose to loss or injury. —**en·dan'ger·ment**, *n.*

en·dear' (en-dir') *v.t.* make dear or beloved. —**en·dear'ment**, *n.*

en·deav'or (en-dev'ər) *v.i.* exert oneself to do something; strive. —*n.* effort. Also, **en·deav'our.**

en·dem'ic (en-dem'ik) *adj.* peculiar to a locality or a people (esp. of disease). —**en·dem'i·cal·ly**, *adv.*

end'ing *n.* 1, act of coming or bringing to a close; termination. 2, the final stage or part.

en'dive (en'dīv) *n.* a plant whose leaves are used in salad.

end'less (-ləs) *adj.* 1, extending without end in space or time; infinite. 2, having the ends joined to form a ring. —**end'less·ness**, *n.*

en·do- *pref.* within.

en'do·crine" (en'dō-krīn") *adj.* secreting internally. —**endocrine glands,** various glands that directly affect certain organs of the body.

en·dorse' (en-dôrs') *v.t.* 1, approve; ratify; sustain. 2, write one's name or initials upon, as a mark of approval, payment received, obligation, etc. —**en·dorse'ment**, *n.*

en·dow' *v.t.* 1, provide with a permanent source of income. 2, bestow upon; give; furnish or equip. —**en·dow'ment**, *n.*

en·due' (en-dū') *v.t.* endow with some quality, ability, etc.

en·dure' (en-dyûr') *v.t.* 1, undergo; sustain. 2, sustain without impairment or yielding. 3, bear with patience; put up with. —*v.i.* continue to exist. —**en·dur'ance**, *n.*

end'ways' (-wāz") *adv.* 1, with the end upward or forward. 2, toward the ends; lengthwise. 3, on end; end to end. Also, **end'wise"** (-wīz").

en'e·ma (en'ə-mə) *n.* an injection of a liquid into the rectum.

en'e·my (en'ə-mē) *n.* 1, one who opposes or seeks to inflict injury on another. 2, an opposing military force; a hostile foreign country, or a national of such a country. 3, anything injurious or antagonistic.

en"er·get'ic (en"ər-jet'ik) *adj.* manifesting energy; vigorous in action; powerful in force or effect. —**en"er·get'i·cal·ly**, *adv.*

en'er·gy (en'ər-jē) *n.* 1, vigor in the exertion of power; strength in action; forcefulness of expression. 2, action; activity; operation. 3, (*Physics*) capacity to produce motion or heat. —**en'er·gize"** (-jīz") *v.t.*

en'er·vate" (en'ər-vāt") *v.t.* deprive of nerve or strength; weaken. —**en"er·va'tion**, *n.*

en·force' (en-fôrs') *v.t.* 1, put or keep in force; compel obedience to. 2, impose by force. —**en·force'a·ble**, *adj.* —**en·force'ment**, *n.*

en·fran'chise (en-fran'chīz) *v.t.* 1, grant a franchise to. 2, give the right to vote. —**en·fran'chise·ment**, *n.*

en·gage' (en-gāj') *v.t.* 1, obtain the services or use of; employ; hire. 2, betroth. 3, bind by pledge or promise. 4, gain the attention of; attract. 5, meet in conflict with. 6, interlock. —**en·gag'ing**, *adj.* attractive; pleasing.

en·gage'ment (-mənt) *n.* 1, act or effect of engaging; state of being engaged. 2, betrothal.

en·gen'der (en-jen'dər) *v.t.* give rise to; bring forth; cause; excite.

en'gine (en'jən) *n.* 1, any machine that converts energy into work. 2, any mechanical contrivance.

en"gi·neer' (en"jə-nir') *n.* 1, one who operates an engine. 2, one versed in the principles and practice of any department of engineering. —*v.t.* 1, plan or direct, as an engineer. 2, contrive.

en"gi·neer'ing *n.* 1, the work or profession of an engineer. 2, the science of making practical application of knowledge in any field. 3, skillful management or contrivance.

Eng'lish (ing'glish) *adj.* pert. to England, its people, customs, etc. —*n.* the English language.

en·grave' (en-grāv') *v.t.* 1, cut in; produce by incision of a surface, as wood, metal, stone; carve in sunken patterns. 2, produce by etching with acid, as in photoengraving. 3, impress deeply.

en·grav'ing (en-grā'ving) *n.* 1, the art of making designs by cutting or etching plates. 2, an engraved plate. 3, a print or impression from such a plate.

en·gross' (en-grōs') *v.t.* 1, occupy wholly (as the attention of a person). 2, write out in a document, in a special style of handwriting. **3,** monopolize the supply of. —**en·gross'ment,** n.

en·gulf' v.t. swallow; submerge.

en·hance' (en-hâns') v.t. raise to a higher degree; intensify; make more important or effective. —**en·hance'ment,** n.

e·nig·ma (i-nig'mə) n. a riddle; anything puzzling. —**en'ig·mat'ic** (en'ig-mat'ik; ē'nig-) adj. —**en'ig·mat'i·cal·ly,** adv.

en·join' v.t. **1,** command (a person) to do something; prescribe (a course of conduct). **2,** (Law) prohibit or restrain by injunction.

en·joy' (en-joi') v.t. **1,** feel joy in doing or perceiving; find pleasure in. **2,** have possession or use of. —**en·joy'ment,** n.

en·large' (en-lärj') v.t. **1,** make larger; extend; augment. **2,** increase in capacity or scope; expand. —v.i. **1,** become larger; expand. **2,** be diffuse in speaking or writing; expatiate. —**en·large'ment,** n. act or result of enlarging; esp., a photograph extended in size.

en·light'en (en-lī'tən) v.t. give intellectual or spiritual light to; impart knowledge to; instruct. —**en·light'en·ment,** n.

en·list' v.t. & i. **1,** enter, as a name on a list; enroll. **2,** engage in a service or cause, as a military service. —**en·list'ment,** n.

en·liv·en (en-lī'vən) v.t. give life or activity to; animate; make vigorous, or gay. —**en·liv'en·ment,** n.

en·mi·ty (en'mə-tē) n. hostility; hatred; ill will; antagonism.

en·no'ble (e-nō'bəl) v.t. elevate in rank, dignity, or worth. —**en·no'ble·ment,** n.

en·nui (än'wē) n. weariness or discontent arising from satiety or lack of interest; boredom.

e·nor'mi·ty (i-nôr'mə-tē) n. **1,** something outrageously offensive or heinous. **2,** atrociousness.

e·nor'mous (i-nôr'məs) adj. **1,** greatly exceeding the usual size; huge; immense. **2,** extremely wicked; atrocious. —**e·nor'mous·ness,** n.

e·nough' (i-nuf') adj. answering the purpose; adequate; sufficient; satisfactory. —adv. **1,** in sufficient quantity or degree. **2,** to a notable extent; fully.

en·rage' (en-rāj') v.t. excite rage in; provoke anger or fury in.

en·rap·ture (en-rap'chər) v.t. put in rapture; delight extremely.

en·rich' v.t. **1,** make rich; supply with abundant property. **2,** supply with anything (as knowledge) in abundance. **3,** make better in quality. —**en·rich'ment,** n.

en·roll' (en-rōl') v.i. & t. enlist. —**en·roll'ment,** n. **en·rol'ment,** n.

en·sconce' (en-skons') v.t. **1,** settle firmly or snugly. **2,** cover; hide.

en·sem'ble (än-säm'bəl) n. **1,** the whole; all parts taken together. **2,** the costume of a person, esp. when all parts are in harmony.

en·shrine' (en-shrīn') v.t. **1,** enclose in or as in a shrine. **2,** preserve with care; cherish. —**en·shrine'ment,** n.

en·shroud' (en-shrowd') v.t. wrap in or as in a shroud; conceal.

en'sign (en'sīn) n. **1,** the identifying flag of a company of soldiers, army, nation, vessel, etc. **2,** a badge of rank or office; an emblem or token. **3,** (-sin) the lowest commissioned rank in the U. S. Navy.

en'si·lage (en'sə-lij) n. fodder preserved in a silo or pit.

en·slave' (en-slāv') v.t. make a slave of; put in bondage. —**en·slave'ment,** n.

en·snare' (en-snār') v.t. trap. —**en·snare'ment,** n.

en·sue' (en-soo') v.i. **1,** follow in order; come after. **2,** follow as a consequence.

en·sure' (en-shûr') v.t. **1,** make sure or certain to occur, come, or be. **2,** make safe or secure. **3,** insure.

-ent (ənt) suf. forming adjectives or nouns denoting doing or doer.

en·tail' (en-tāl') v.t. **1,** bring about; cause to ensue; involve as a consequence. **2,** impose as a burden. **3,** limit the inheritance of (property) to a specified line of heirs. —**en·tail'ment,** n.

en·tan'gle (en-tang'gəl) v.t. **1,** involve in difficulties; perplex. **2,** make complicated. —**en·tan'gle·ment,** n.

en·tente' (än-tänt') n. an understanding, esp. among nations friendly to one another.

en'ter (en'tər) v.t. **1,** come into; go into; penetrate. **2,** put in; insert. **3,** become a member of; join; admit to membership. **4,** take the first step in; begin upon; become involved in. **5,** make a record of; register. —v.i. **1,** come or go in. **2,** make a beginning. **3,** take an interest or part in an enterprise.

en·ter'ic (en-ter'ik) adj. intestinal. —n. typhoid fever.

en'ter·prise' (en'tər-prīz") n. **1,** something undertaken; a project, mission, business, etc., esp. one requiring boldness or perseverance. **2,** boldness in undertakings. —**en'ter·pris"ing,** adj. ready and energetic in carrying out projects.

en"ter·tain' (en"tər-tān') v.t. **1,** afford amusement or diversion. **2,** accommodate as a guest. **3,** admit into the mind; give heed to; harbor.

—*v.i.* exercise hospitality; receive guests.

en"ter·tain'ment (-mənt) *n.* **1,** act or result of entertaining; state of being entertained. **2,** a show, party, etc.

en·thrall' (en-thrâl') *v.t.* **1,** captivate; charm. **2,** put or hold in bondage. —**en·thrall'ment,** *n.*

en·throne' (en-thrōn') *v.t.* place on a throne; invest with authority. —**en·throne'ment,** *n.*

en·thu'si·asm (en-thoo'zē-az-əm) *n.* **1,** absorbing possession of the mind by an interest, study, or pursuit; ardent interest. **2,** (*Archaic*) extravagant religious fervor. —**en·thu'si·ast,** *n.* —**en·thu'si·as'tic,** *adj.* —**en·thu'si·as'ti·cal·ly,** *adv.*

en·tice' (en-tīs') *v.t.* draw on by exciting hope or desire; allure; attract. —**en·tice'ment,** *n.*

en·tire' (en-tīr') *adj.* whole; complete; not broken or diminished; intact. —**en·tire'ness,** *n.*

en·tire'ty (-tē) *n.* **1,** the whole of something. **2,** completeness.

en·ti'tle (en-tī'təl) *v.t.* **1,** give a right to; furnish with grounds for a claim. **2,** give a title or name to.

en·ti·ty (en'tə-tē) *n.* **1,** something that has real existence; a thing. **2,** existence; being.

en·tomb' (en-toom') *v.t.* place in a tomb; bury. —**en·tomb'ment,** *n.*

en·to·mo- *pref.* meaning "insect."

en"to·mol'o·gy (en'tə-mol'ə-jē) *n.* the study of insects. —**en"to·mo·log'i·cal,** *adj.* —**en"to·mol'o·gist,** *n.*

en"tou·rage' (än"tû-räzh') *n.* the attendants or followers of a person.

en'trails (en'trəlz) *n. pl.* **1,** the intestines or bowels. **2,** the internal parts or contents of anything.

en'trance (en'trəns) *n.* **1,** the act of entering. **2,** a means or place of access; an opening or passage for entering.

en·trance' (en-tràns') *v.t.* **1,** fill with delight or wonder; enrapture. **2,** put in a trance.

en'trant (en'trənt) *n.* one who enters, as into a club, college, competition, etc.

en·trap' *v.t.* [-**trapped'**, -**trap'ping**] catch in a trap; snare. —**en·trap'ment,** *n.*

en·treat' (en-trēt') *v.t.* ask earnestly; implore; beseech.

en·treat'y (en-trē'tē) *n.* **1,** act of entreating. **2,** a prayer; petition.

en'tree (än'trā) *n.* **1,** (U. S.) the main dish of a dinner, other than a roast. **2,** a dish served between chief courses of a dinner. **3,** the right or privilege of entering.

en·trench' *v.t.* **1,** fortify by digging trenches around, or putting in a trench. **2,** establish in a position of security. —*v.i.* encroach; trespass. —**en·trench'ment,** *n.*

en"tre·pre·neur' (än"trə-prə-nêr') *n.* **1,** an employer of workmen. **2,** one who undertakes an enterprise.

en·trust' *v.t.* **1,** (with *to*) transfer or commit, with confidence. **2,** (with *with*) charge with a trust or responsibility.

en'try (en'trē) *n.* **1,** the act of entering; entrance. **2,** an opening or passage for entering; a vestibule. **3,** an item entered in a register, account book, etc.

en·twine' (en-twīn') *v.t. & i.* curl about or together. —**en·twine'ment,** *n.*

e·nu'mer·ate (i-nū'mə-rāt') *v.t.* **1,** name one by one; mention separately. **2,** count; ascertain the number of. —**e·nu"mer·a'tion,** *n.*

e·nun'ci·ate (i-nun'sē-āt') *v.t. & i.* utter or pronounce, as words or syllables, esp. with reference to manner. —*v.t.* proclaim; announce distinctly. —**e·nun"ci·a'tion,** *n.*

en·vel'op (en-vel'əp) *v.t.* surround entirely; form a covering about; wrap up. —**en·vel'op·ment,** *n.*

en've·lope (en'və-lōp) *n.* **1,** any covering or wrapping. **2,** a cover for a letter.

en'vi·a·ble (en'vē-ə-bəl) *adj.* of an excellence to invite envy. —**en'vi·a·ble·ness,** *n.*

en'vi·ous (en'vē-əs) *adj.* feeling or showing envy. —**en'vi·ous·ness,** *n.*

en·vi'ron·ment (en-vī'rən-mənt) *n.* the aggregate of surrounding things or conditions; the totality of external influences on an organism. —**en·vi'ron·men'tal,** *adj.*

en·vi'rons (en-vī'rənz) *n. pl.* the region surrounding a place; outskirts or suburbs.

en'voy (en'voi) *n.* **1,** an agent sent on a mission, esp. diplomatic. **2,** a postscript to a composition.

en'vy (en'vē) *n.* a feeling of mortification or discontent excited by seeing the superiority or prosperity of another person; desire for the possessions or advantages of another; ill will combined with jealousy. —*v.t.* regard with envy.

en'zyme (en'zīm) *n.* a substance that acts as a catalyst in metabolism.

e·o- (ē-ō-) *pref.* early; primeval.

e'on (ē'ən) *n.* **1,** an indefinitely long period of time. **2,** the longest division of geologic time.

ep'au·let" (ep'ə-let") *n.* an ornamental badge on the shoulder.

Epaulet

é·pée' (e-pā') *n.* a thin, pointed sword used in fencing.

e·phed'rine (i-fed'rin) *n.* a drug used to relieve nasal congestion.

e·phem'er·al (i-fem'ər-əl) *adj.* lasting only one day or a very short time; transitory.

epi- *pref.* to; against.

ep'ic (ep'ik) *adj.* 1, pert. to a poem or poetry narrating in lofty style the achievements and adventures of a hero. 2, of heroic character or style; imposing. —*n.* an epic poem or story. —**ep'i·cal·ly,** *adv.*

ep'i·cene" (ep'i-sēn") *adj.* both masculine and feminine.

ep'i·cure" (ep'ə-kyûr") *n.* 1, one of refined taste in eating and drinking. 2, one given to sensual pleasure. —**ep'i·cu·re'an** (-rē'ən) *adj.*

ep'i·dem'ic (ep'ə-dem'ik) *adj.* (of a disease) appearing in a large number of cases at the same time in a locality. —*n.* a temporary prevalence of a disease in a community. —**ep'i·dem'i·cal·ly,** *adv.*

ep'i·der'mis (ep'ə-dêr'mis) *n.* the outermost skin, membrane, integument, or layer of an organic body.

ep'i·glot'tis (ep'i-glot'is) *n.* the flap of cartilage that covers the glottis during swallowing.

ep'i·gram" (ep'ə-gram") *n.* a terse, witty saying, usually satirical. —**ep'i·gram·mat'ic**(-grə-mat'ik) *adj.* —**ep'i·gram·mat'i·cal·ly,** *adv.*

ep'i·lep'sy (ep'ə-lep'sē) *n.* a nervous disease characterized by loss of consciousness and muscular spasm.

ep'i·lep'tic (ep'ə-lep'tik) *adj.* pert. to epilepsy. —*n.* a person afflicted with epilepsy.

ep'i·logue" (ep'ə-lâg") *n.* the concluding part of a discourse; a section added at the end.

E·piph'a·ny (i-pif'ə-nē) *n.* a Christian festival, Jan. 6.

e·pis'co·pa·cy (i-pis'kə-pə-sē) *n.* 1, a form of church government in which the chief ministers are bishops. 2, the office of a bishop.

e·pis'co·pal (i-pis'kə-pəl) *adj.* 1, pert. to a bishop. 2, (*cap.*) designating a Protestant sect governed by bishops. —**E·pis"co·pa'lian** (-pāl'yən) *n.* a member of this sect.

ep'i·sode" (ep'ə-sōd") *n.* 1, an incident in a series of events or a narrative; one happening. 2, (*Music*) a digressive passage, as in a fugue. —**ep'i·sod'ic** (-sod'ik) *adj.* —**ep'i·sod'i·cal·ly,** *adv.*

e·pis'tle (i-pis'əl) *n.* a written communication; a letter, esp. a formal discourse, as (*cap.*) any of the apostolic letters in the New Testament. —**e·pis'to·lar·y** (-tə-ler-ē) *adj.*

ep'i·taph" (ep'ə-tâf") *n.* 1, a memorial inscription on a monument. 2, any similar commemorative writing.

ep'i·thet" (ep'ə-thet") *n.* a name or phrase used to characterize a person or thing. —**ep'i·thet'ic, ep'i·thet'i·cal,** *adj.*

e·pit'o·me (i-pit'ə-mē) *n.* a brief summary of a subject or writing; an abridgment or abstract. —**e·pit'o·mize"** (-mīz") *v.t.*

ep'och (ep'ək) *n.* 1, a period of time marked by distinctive events; a division of a geologic period. 2, a point of time distinguished by some remarkable event. —**ep'och·al,** *adj.*

ep'si·lon" (ep'sə-lon") *n.* the fifth letter of the Greek alphabet (E, ε).

eq'ua·ble (ek'wə-bəl) *adj.* uniform in action, intensity, or state; even; steady; tranquil. —**eq"ua·bil'i·ty,** *n.*

e'qual (ē'kwəl) *adj.* 1, having one measure; the same in magnitude, quantity, degree, worth, etc. 2, evenly balanced; level; uniform in operation. —*v.t.* be or become equal to; make or do something equal to. —**e·qual'i·ty** (i-kwol'ə-tē) *n.*

e'qual·ize" (ē'kwə-līz") *v.t.* make equal or uniform. —**e"qual·i·za'tion,** *n.*

e"qua·nim'i·ty (ē'kwə-nim'ə-tē) *n.* evenness of mind or temper; calmness under stress.

e·quate' (i-kwāt') *v.t.* state the equality of; put in an equation.

e·qua'tion (i-kwā'shən) *n.* (*Math.*) a statement of relation between two quantities, indicated by an equals sign (=) or other symbol.

e·qua'tor (i-kwā'tər) *n.* a circle dividing the surface of a sphere into two equal parts. —**e"qua·tor'i·al** (ē'kwə-tôr'ē-əl) *adj.*

eq'uer·ry (ek'wə-rē) *n.* 1, an attendant in a royal household. 2, an officer in charge of horses.

e·ques'tri·an (i-kwes'trē-ən) *adj.* 1, pert. to horsemen or horsemanship. 2, mounted on horseback. —*n.* one who rides a horse. —**e·ques"tri·enne'** (-en') *n.fem.*

e·qui- *pref.* equal.

e"qui·dis'tant (ē"kwə-dis'tənt) *adj.* equally distant.

e"qui·lat'er·al (ē"kwə-lat'ər-əl) *adj.* having all sides of equal length.

e"qui·li'brate (ē"kwə-lī'brāt) *v.t. & i.* be or put in equal balance. —**e"qui·li·bra'tion,** *n.*

e"qui·lib'ri·um (ē"kwə-lib'rē-əm) *n.* 1, a state of rest or balance through equality of counteracting forces. 2, mental stability.

e'qui·nox" (ē'kwi-noks") *n.* either of the two annual occasions, about Mar. 21 and Sept. 22, when night and day are of equal length. —**e"qui·noc'tial** (-nok'shəl) *adj.*

e·quip' (ĭ-kwĭp') *v.t.* [-quipped', -quip'ping] fit out with what is needed to execute an undertaking; rig for service.

eq'ui·page (ĕk'wə-pĭj) *n.* a carriage.

e·quip'ment (ĭ-kwĭp'mənt) *n.* **1,** act of equipping; state of being equipped. **2,** that which equips; supplies; gear.

e'qui·poise' (ē'kwə-poiz") *n.* **1,** equal distribution of weight. **2,** a counterbalance.

eq'ui·ta·ble (ĕk'wi-tə-bəl) *adj.* fair. —**eq'ui·ta·ble·ness,** *n.*

eq'ui·ty (ĕk'wi-tē) *n.* **1,** impartial justice; fairness. **2,** (*Law*) the application of common principles of fair-dealing, to supplement statute law. **3,** a net financial interest in a property.

e·quiv'a·lent (i-kwĭv'ə-lənt) *adj.* **1,** the same in magnitude, meaning, effect, etc. **2,** corresponding in position or function. —*n.* substantially the same thing. —**e·quiv'a·lence,** *n.*

e·quiv'o·cal (i-kwĭv'ə-kəl) *adj.* **1,** of uncertain meaning; ambiguous. **2,** of doubtful origin; dubious.

e·quiv'o·cate" (i-kwĭv'ə-kāt") *v.i.* use ambiguous expressions; be evasive. —**e·quiv"o·ca'tion,** *n.*

er (ĕr) *interj.* an expression of hesitancy.

-er (-ər) *suf.* **1,** added to verbs to denote a person or implement performing the act; added to nouns to denote a performer, follower, or resident of. **2,** forming the comparative degree of adjectives and adverbs.

e'ra (ir'ə) *n.* a period of time of distinctive historical character.

e·rad'i·cate" (ĭ-rad'ĭ-kāt") *v.t.* pull up by the roots; destroy utterly. —**e·rad"i·ca'tion,** *n.* —**e·rad'i·ca'tor,** *n.*

e·rase' (ĭ-rās') *v.t.* rub or scratch out; clear (of writing, transcribed sound, etc.) —**e·ras'er,** *n.* a utensil, device or substance (as rubber) for erasing.

e·ras'ure (ĭ-rā'shər) *n.* **1,** act of erasing. **2,** a place where something has been erased.

er'bi·um (ĕr'bē-əm) *n.* a chemical element of the rare-earth group, no. 68, symbol Er.

ere (âr) *prep.* before (in time). —*conj.* before; sooner or rather than.

e·rect' (ĭ-rekt') *v.t.* **1,** build; construct. **2,** set up; establish; found. **3,** raise to an upright position. —*adj.* upright. —**e·rec'tion,** *n.*

er'e·mite" (er'ə-mīt") *n.* a hermit, esp. religious.

erg (ĕrg) *n.* a unit of work. Also, **er'gon.**

er'go (ĕr'gō) *conj.* (*Lat.*) therefore.

er·gos'ter·ol" (ər-gos'tə-rōl") *n.* a food supplement taken for its Vitamin D content.

er'got (ĕr'gət) *n.* a fungus, in rye and other cereals, yielding a medicine used to check hemorrhage.

er'mine (ĕr'min) *n.* **1,** a white-furred weasel; its fur. **2,** the office or dignity of a judge.

Ermine

e·rode' (ĭ-rōd') *v.t. & i.* wear away slowly.

e·ro'sion (i-rō'zhən) *n.* a washing or wearing away of the earth's surface.

e·rot'ic (i-rot'ik) *adj.* pert. to love. —**e·rot'i·cal·ly,** *adv.*

err (ĕr) *v.i.* **1,** go astray; be mistaken; blunder. **2,** sin.

er'rand (er'ənd) *n.* **1,** a special business entrusted to a messenger; a commission. **2,** a short trip to execute a commission.

er'rant (er'ənt) *adj.* **1,** wandering; roving. **2,** deviating; erring.

er·rat'ic (i-rat'ik) *adj.* **1,** wandering; off course. **2,** tending to err. **3,** eccentric. —**er·rat'i·cal·ly,** *adv.*

er·ra'tum (i-rā'təm) *n.* [*pl.* -ta (-tə)] an error in a book; misprint.

er·ro'ne·ous (i-rō'nē-əs) *adj.* incorrect. —**er·ro'ne·ous·ness,** *n.*

er'ror (er'ər) *n.* **1,** a deviation from truth; a mistake; an inaccuracy. **2,** moral wrongdoing; an offense. **3,** difference from a true value or standard.

er·satz' (er-zätz') *adj. & n.* (*Ger.*) substitute.

Erse (ĕrs) *n.* Gaelic.

erst'while" (ĕrst'hwīl") *adj.* former.

e·ruct' (i-rukt') *v.t. & i.* emit or issue violently, esp. wind from the stomach; belch. —**e·ruc'tate** (-tāt) *v.t. & i.* —**e·ruc"ta'tion,** *n.*

er·u·di'tion (er'ū-dish'ən) *n.* knowledge gained by study; learning. —**er'u·dite'** (-dīt") *adj.*

e·rupt' (i-rupt') *v.i. & t.* burst forth suddenly and violently, like a volcano. —**e·rup'tive,** *adj.*

e·rup'tion (i-rup'shən) *n.* **1,** a bursting forth. **2,** a rash.

er'y·sip'e·las (er'ə-sip'ə-ləs) *n.* an acute, infectious skin disease.

es'ca·la"tor (es'kə-lā"tər) *n.* a moving stairway for transporting passengers from one level to another. —**escalator clause,** a provision in labor contracts permitting periodic adjustment of wage scales.

es·cal'lop (es-kol'əp) *v.t.* **1,** bake (food) in a sauce, with crumbs on top. **2,** scallop. —*n.* scallop.

es'ca·pade" (es'kə-pād') *n.* a wild prank; a foolish adventure.

es·cape' (es-kāp') *v.i.* **1**, get away or flee, as from capture or confinement; evade or avoid threatened harm. **2**, leak out, as a liquid. —*v.t.* slip away from; elude. —*n.* act of escaping.

es·cape'ment (es-kāp'mənt) *n.* a contrivance for alternately releasing and stopping a moving part, as in a clock.

es·cap'ism (es-kāp'iz-əm) *n.* diversion of thought from unpleasant reality. —**es·cap'ist,** *n.*

es'ca·role" (es'kə-rōl') *n.* a variety of endive.

es·chew' (es-choo') *v.t.* shun.

es·cort' (es-kôrt') *v.t.* accompany on a trip as a companion or protector; convoy. —*n.* (es'kôrt) one who escorts; a body of attendants.

es'crow (es'krō) *n.* a conditional contract of which the consideration is deposited in trust.

es·cu'do (es-koo'dō) *n.* [*pl.* -dos] a coin or monetary unit of various Spanish- and Portuguese-speaking countries.

es'cu·lent (es'kū-lənt) *adj.* fit to be used for food; edible.

es·cutch'eon (es-kuch'ən) *n.* the shield on which armorial bearings are emblazoned.

Escutcheon

-ese (ēs or ēz) *suf.* denoting the language or inhabitants of a place.

Es'ki·mo" (es'ki-mō') *n.* [*pl.* -mos"] **1**, one of the race idigenous to arctic North America. **2**, a malemute or husky.

e·soph'a·gus (ē-sof'ə-gəs) *n.* [*pl.* -gi (-jī)] the food canal of an animal, from mouth to stomach; the gullet.

es"o·ter'ic (es"ə-ter'ik) *adj.* understood by, or intended for, only a select few; secret; mysterious. —**es"o·ter'i·cal·ly,** *adv.*

es·pe'cial (es-pesh'əl) *adj.* **1**, special; distinguished from others of the same kind. **2**, exceptional.

Es"pe·ran'to (es"pə-rän'tō) *n.* a proposed universal language.

es"pi·o·nage (es'pē-ə-nij) *n.* the practice of spying.

es"pla·nade' (es"plə-nād') *n.* a public ground for walking or riding; a level, open area.

es·pouse' (es-powz') *v.t.* **1**, take as a spouse; wed. **2**, adopt or advocate, as a cause. —**es·pous'al,** *n.*

es·py' (es-pī') *v.t.* catch sight of.

es·quire' (es-kwīr') *n.* **1**, a title of politeness, added after a man's last name in addressing him by letter: usually *Esq.* **2**, (*Hist.*) an attendant on a knight.

-ess (əs or is) *suf.* forming feminine nouns, as *seeress.*

es'say (es'ā) *n.* **1**, a literary composition on a particular subject. **2**, an effort or attempt. —*v.t.* (e-sā') endeavor; try. —**es'say'ist,** *n.*

es'sence (es'əns) *n.* **1**, the distinctive characteristic of something. **2**, the inward nature or true substance of something. **3**, a liquid containing a substance in concentrated form, as a perfume.

es·sen'tial (ə-sen'shəl) *adj.* **1**, absolutely necessary; indispensable. **2**, relating to inmost nature; basic; fundamental. **3**, pert. to or yielding a liquid essence. —*n.* a basic part or aspect; an element.

es·tab'lish (es-tab'lish) *v.t.* **1**, set up on a firm basis; found; fix. **2**, install, as in a position. **3**, show to be valid; prove.

es·tab'lish·ment (-mənt) *n.* **1**, act of establishing; state of being established. **2**, something established, as a household, business, institution.

es·tate' (es-tāt') *n.* **1**, a piece of landed property. **2**, a person's entire property and possessions. **3**, a person's worldly condition or circumstances; status; rank. **4**, a political or social class.

es·teem' (es-tēm') *v.t.* **1**, set a high value on; regard favorably. **2**, estimate; rate. —*n.* **1**, favorable opinion; respect. **2**, judgment of worth.

es'ter (es'tər) *n.* a chemical compound, analogous to a salt and often fragrant.

es'thete (es'thēt) *n.* one who cultivates appreciation of the beautiful.

es·thet'ic (es-thet'ik) *adj.* pert. to beauty. Also, **aes·thet'ic.** —**es·thet'i·cal·ly,** *adv.*

es·thet'ics (-iks) *n.* the philosophy of beauty and good taste.

es'ti·ma·ble (es'tə-mə-bəl) *adj.* **1**, worthy of esteem. **2**, capable of being estimated or valued.

es'ti·mate" (es'tə-māt') *v.t.* form an opinion of, as to value, value, etc. —*n.* (es'tə-mət) an opinion, judgment, or approximate calculation; a tentative price or charge. —*n.* **1**, the act of estimating; opinion. **2**, esteem.

es'ti·val (es'tə-vəl) *adj.* pert. to summer.

es·top' *v.t.* [-topped', -top'ping] prevent, bar, or stop. —**es·top'pel** (-əl) *n.*

es·trange' (es-trānj') *v.t.* cause to be hostile; alienate the affections of. —**es·trange'ment,** *n.*

es·tro·gen (es'trə-jən) *n.* a substance that stimulates production of certain sex hormones.

es·tu·ar·y (es'choo-er-ē) *n.* the mouth of a river, subject to tides.

-et *suf.* diminutive, as *owlet.*

e'ta (ā'tə) the seventh letter of the Greek alphabet (H, η).

et cet'er·a (et set'ər-ə) (*Lat.*) and others; and so on: usually, etc., *abbr.*

etch (ech) *v.t.* 1, cut (the surface of a metal plate, etc.) with acid, in order to form a design. 2, engrave with a stylus. —**etch'ing,** *n.* a printed impression from an etched plate.

e·ter'nal (i-tėr'nəl) *adj.* 1, existing throughout all time; without beginning or end. 2, incessant. 3, (*cap.*) God.

e·ter'ni·ty (i-tėr'nə-tē) *n.* 1, time without beginning or end; infinite duration. 2, a seemingly endless period of time.

-eth *suf.* 1, forming ordinal numbers, as twentieth. 2, (*Archaic*) forming the third person singular of verbs, as *he readeth,* now *reads.*

eth'ane (eth'ān) *n.* a colorless, combustible gas.

e'ther (ē'thər) *n.* 1, a compound of sulfuric acid and alcohol, used as a solvent and anesthetic. 2, the sky.

e·the're·al (i-thir'ē-əl) *adj.* 1, airy; light; intangible. 2, heavenly.

eth'i·cal (eth'i-kəl) *adj.* in accordance with accepted principles of conduct.

eth'ics (eth'iks) *n. pl.* 1, the principles of honor and morality. 2, accepted rules of conduct. 3, the moral principles of an individual. —**eth'ic,** *adj.* pert. to morals.

E·thi·o'pi·an (ē'thē-ō'pē-ən) *adj.* pert. to Ethiopia. —*n.* 1, a native of Ethiopia. 2, (*incorrectly*) a Negro.

eth'nic (eth'nik) *adj.* 1, pert. to a people distinguished by race, language, culture, etc. 2, heathen; pagan. —**eth'ni·cal,** *adj.*

eth·nol'o·gy (eth-nol'ə-jē) *n.* the science of the origin, history, customs, etc. of peoples. —**eth'no·log'i·cal,** *adj.* —**eth·nol'o·gist,** *n.*

eth'yl (eth'əl) *n.* (*Chem.*) a radical of alcohol. —**ethyl fluid,** tetraethyl lead, added to gasoline to reduce engine knock.

e"ti·ol'o·gy (ē"tē-ol'ə-jē) *n.* the study of causes. —**e"ti·o·log'i·cal,** *adj.* —**e"ti·ol'o·gist,** *n.*

et'i·quette" (et'i-ket') *n.* the conventional requirements of polite behavior; proprieties of conduct; good manners.

-ette *suf.* 1, little, small, as *kitchenette.* 2, feminine, as *suffragette.* 3, imitation, as *leatherette.*

é·tude' (ā-tūd') *n.* a musical composition intended as an exercise in technique, but often of esthetic value.

e·tui' (ā-twē') *n.* a small box, as for notions.

et"y·mol'o·gy (et'i-mol'ə-jē) *n.* 1, the study of the structure and history of words. 2, the derivation or history of a given word. —**et"y·mo·log'i·cal,** *adj.* —**et"y·mol'o·gist,** *n.*

eu·ca·lyp'tus (ū'kə-lip'təs) *n.* a tree of the myrtle family; its wood or aromatic oil.

Eucalyptus

Eu'cha·rist (ū'kə-rist) *n.* the sacrament of the Lord's Supper; Holy Communion.

eu'chre (ū'kər) *n.* a card game. —*v.t.* swindle; outsmart.

Eu'clid (ū'klid) *n.* 1, the system of geometry of Euclid (c. 300 B.C.). 2, geometry. —**Eu·clid'i·an** (ū-klid'ē-ən) *adj.*

eu·gen'ics (ū-jen'iks) *n.* the science of improving the human race through the regulation of parenthood. —**eu·gen'ic,** *adj.* —**eu·gen'i·cal·ly,** *adv.*

eu'lo·gy (ū'lə-jē) *n.* high praise; a speech or writing that lauds a person, esp. one deceased, or a thing. —**eu"lo·gis'tic** (-jis'tik) *adj.* —**eu"lo·gis'ti·cal·ly,** *adv.* —**eu'lo·gize"** (-jīz") *v.t.* deliver a eulogy about.

eu'nuch (ū'nək) *n.* a castrated man.

eu·pep'si·a (ū-pep'shə) *n.* good digestion. —**eu·pep'tic** (-tik) *adj.*

eu'phe·mism (ū'fə-miz-əm) *n.* 1, the use of a mild word in place of a plainer but possibly offensive one. 2, a word or expression thus substituted. —**eu"phe·mis'tic** (-mis'tik) *adj.* —**eu"phe·mis'ti·cal·ly,** *adv.*

eu·pho'ni·ous (ū-fō'nē-əs) *adj.* pleasing in sound. —**eu·pho'ni·ous·ness,** *n.*

eu'pho·ny (ū'fə-nē) *n.* harmonious arrangement of sounds, esp. of words. —**eu·phon'ic,** *adj.* —**eu·phon'i·cal·ly,** *adv.*

eu·pho'ri·a (ū-fōr'ē-ə) *n.* a feeling or state of well-being.

eu·phu·ism (ū'fū-iz-əm) *n.* an excessively ornate style in writing. —**eu"phu·is'tic**, *adj.* —**eu"phu·is'ti·cal·ly**, *adv.*

Eur·a'sian (yū-rā'zhən) *n.* a person of mixed Europ. and Asiatic blood.

eu·re'ka (yū-rē'kə) *interj.* I have found it!

Eu"ro·pe'an (yūr"ə-pē'ən) *adj.* pert. to Europe. —*n.* a native of Europe. —European plan, in hotelkeeping, rental of room only, with meals not included.

eu·ro'pi·um (yū-rō'pē·əm) *n.* a rare-earth chemical element, no. 63, symbol Eu.

Eu·sta'chi·an tube (ū-stā'kē·ən) the canal between the eardrum and pharynx.

eu"tha·na'sia (ū"thə·nā'zhə) *n.* **1,** painless death. **2,** mercy-killing.

e·vac'u·ate' (i-vak'ū-āt") *v.t.* **1,** make empty; free from something contained. **2,** vacate; withdraw from. **3,** excrete. —**e·vac"u·a'tion,** *n.*

e·vac"u·ee' (-ē") *n.* a person removed from a place of danger.

e·vade' (i-vād') *v.t.* **1,** escape from; avoid capture by; elude. **2,** circumvent by trickery. **3,** baffle.

e·val'u·ate' (i-val'ū-āt") *v.t.* ascertain the value or amount of. —**e·val"u·a'tion,** *n.*

ev"a·nesce' (ev"ə-nes') *v.t.* fade away; disappear gradually; vanish. —**ev"a·nes'cence,** *n.* —**ev"a·nes'cent,** *adj.*

e·van'gel (i-van'jəl) *n.* the Christian gospel.

e"van·gel'i·cal (ē"van-jel'ə-kəl) *adj.* **1,** pert. to the Gospels or to evangelism. **2,** (of churches) adhering strictly to Protestant theology, esp. in interpretation of the Gospels.

e·van'ge·list (i-van'jə-list) *n.* **1,** one of the apostles Matthew, Mark, Luke, John. **2,** a preacher of the gospel, esp. a revivalist. —**e·van'ge·lism,** *n.*

e·van'ge·lize' (-līz") *v.t. & i.* preach the gospel (to); convert to Christianity.

e·vap'o·rate' (i-vap'ə-rāt") *v.i.* **1,** pass off as vapor. **2,** disappear; be dissipated. —**e·vap"o·ra'tion,** *n.*

e·va'sion (i-vā'zhən) *n.* **1,** the act of evading. **2,** a trick or subterfuge; an equivocation.

e·va'sive (i-vā'siv) *adj.* **1,** using artifice to escape or avoid. **2,** escaping observation or understanding; elusive. —**e·va'sive·ness,** *n.*

eve (ēv) *n.* **1,** the night or the day before (a date, festival, etc.). **2,** the time just preceding an event. **3,** evening.

e'ven (ē'vən) *adj.* **1,** level; plane; smooth. **2,** uniform in action or character; unvarying. **3,** equal; on the same line or level. **4,** divisible by **2.** **5,** whole; having no fractional part. **6,** not easily excited; placid. —*adv.* **1,** uniformly; equally; wholly; evenly. **2,** just; exactly; moreover; likewise; fully (used to emphasize or strengthen an assertion). —*v.t.* make even. —**e'ven·ness,** *n.*

eve'ning (ēv'ning) *n.* **1,** the latter part of the day; the time from sunset to darkness, or from first darkness to bedtime. **2,** the latter part or decline of any term of existence.

e·vent' (i-vent') *n.* **1,** something that happens; an occurrence. **2,** an incident of special interest. **3,** an outcome, issue, or consequence. **4,** one item of a series.

e·vent'ful (-fəl) *adj.* **1,** full of striking events, as a period of time. **2,** having important results or outcome. —**e·vent'ful·ness,** *n.*

e'ven·tide" *n.* evening.

e·ven'tu·al (i-ven'choo-əl) *adj.* **1,** happening or to happen finally; ultimate. **2,** contingent.

e·ven"tu·al'i·ty (i-ven"choo-al'ə-tē) *n.* an event that may come to pass.

e·ven'tu·ate" (i-ven'choo-āt") *v.i.* happen as an outcome; result. —**e·ven"tu·a'tion,** *n.*

ev'er (ev'ər) *adv.* **1,** at all times; always; continually. **2,** at any time. **3,** in any degree; at all.

ev'er·glade" *n.* a tract of low, swampy ground.

ev'er·green" *n.* a plant or tree that has green leaves throughout the entire year. —*adj.* always fresh.

ev"er·last'ing *adj.* **1,** perpetual; eternal. **2,** (*cap.*) God.

ev"er·more' *adv.* forever after.

e·vert' (i-vērt') *v.t.* turn outward or inside out. —**e·ver'sion,** *n.*

ev'er·y (ev'rē) *adj.* **1,** each without exception; all (of an aggregate taken one by one). **2,** the greatest possible, in extent or degree.

ev'er·y·bod"y *n.* every person.

ev'er·y·day" *adj.* commonplace; usual.

ev'er·y·one" *n.* every person.

ev'er·y·thing" *n.* all things.

ev'er·y·where" *adv.* **1,** in all places. **2,** wherever.

e·vict' (i-vikt') *v.t.* expel, esp. by judicial order; dispossess. —**e·vic'tion,** *n.*

ev'i·dence (ev'i·dəns) *n.* **1,** the means of proving or disproving an alleged fact; testimony, exhibits, etc. offered as proof; an indication of proof. **2,** the state of being clear or certain. —*v.t.* show clearly; prove.

ev'i·dent (ev'i-dənt) *adj.* plainly seen or perceived; manifest; obvious. —**ev'i·dent·ly**, *adv.* apparently.

e'vil (ē'vəl) *adj.* 1, immoral; wicked. 2, harmful; disastrous. 3, bad; ill-reputed. —*n.* 1, violation of moral principles; improper conduct. 2, injury; misfortune. 3, a cause of injury or mischief. —**e·vil'do·er**, *n.* one who sins. —**e'vil·ness**, *n.*

e·vince' (i-vins') *v.t.* show clearly; —**e·vince'ment**, *n.*

e·vis'cer·ate' (i-vis'ə-rāt') *v.t.* 1, remove the viscera from; disembowel. 2, deprive of essential parts. exhibit; manifest. —**e·vis'cer·a'tion**, *n.*

e·voke' (i-vōk') *v.t.* bring into the mind; cause to appear; call forth. —**ev'o·ca'tion**, *n.*

ev'o·lu'tion (ev'ə-loo'shən) *n.* 1, the act of evolving; formation, growth, or development. 2, (*Biol.*) the continuous modification of organic species; the steps in adaptation to environment. 3, something evolved. —**ev'o·lu'tion·a·ry**, *adj.*

e·volve' (i-volv') *v.t.* 1, form gradually, as though by unfolding; develop. 2, emit. —*v.i.* come into being, or change, gradually.

ewe (ū) *n.* a female sheep.

ew'er (ū'ər) *n.* a water pitcher with a wide mouth.

ex- *pref.* 1, out; out of. 2, (hyphenated) formerly, as *ex-president.*

ex·ac'er·bate' (eg-zas'ər-bāt') *v.t.* embitter; make more bitter, angry or violent; irritate; aggravate. —**ex·ac'er·ba'tion**, *n.*

Ewer

ex·act' (eg-zakt') *v.t.* compel to be paid or yielded; require. —*adj.* 1, strictly accurate or correct. 2, admitting of no deviation; strict. —**ex·act'ing**, *adj.* holding to strict standards. —**ex·act'ness**, *n.*

ex·ac'tion (eg-zak'shən) *n.* something exacted; extortion.

ex·ac'ti·tude (eg-zak'ti-tood) *n.* preciseness; strictness.

ex·ag'ger·ate' (eg-zaj'ə-rāt') *v.t.* 1, represent as large, important, etc. beyond the truth; magnify falsely. 2, enlarge or increase abnormally. —*v.i.* overstate. —**ex·ag'ger·at'ed**, *adj.* unduly enlarged. —**ex·ag'ger·a'tion**, *n.*

ex·alt' (eg-zält') *v.t.* 1, elevate in rank, honor, power, etc. 2, praise; extol. 3, inspire; elate. —**ex'al·ta'tion**, *n.*

ex·am' (ig-zam') *n.* (*Colloq.*) a test,

in school, requiring a written answer.

ex·am'i·na'tion (eg-zam'i-nā'shən) *n.* 1, act or process of examining or being examined. 2, a series of questions asked as a test.

ex·am'ine (eg-zam'in) *v.t.* 1, look at carefully; inspect; scrutinize. 2, inquire into; investigate. 3, test; interrogate.

ex·am'ple (ig-zam'pəl) *n.* 1, one of a number of things that shows the character of all; a sample. 2, a specimen or instance serving to illustrate or explain. 3, a model.

ex·as'per·ate' (eg-zas'pə-rāt') *v.t.* irritate extremely; annoy; make angry. —**ex·as'per·a'tion**, *n.*

ex'ca·vate' (eks'kə-vāt') *v.t.* 1, make a cavity or hollow in; dig into. 2, form by scooping out material. 3, unearth. —**ex'ca·va'tion**, *n.* —**ex'ca·va'tor**, *n.*

ex·ceed' (ek-sēd') *v.t.* 1, go beyond in quantity, degree, etc. 2, be superior to; surpass. —*v.i.* be greater than others; excel. —**ex·ceed'ing·ly**, *adv.* extremely; (*Colloq.*) very.

ex·cel' (ek-sel') *v.t. & i.* [-celled', -cel'ling] be superior (to); surpass; outdo.

ex'cel·lence (ek'sə-ləns) *n.* great merit or efficiency.

ex'cel·len·cy (ek'sə-lən-sē) *n.* (usually *cap.*) a title of address to certain high officials.

ex'cel·lent (ek'sə-lənt) *adj.* remarkably good; of superior merit.

ex·cel'si·or (ek-sel'sē-ər) *n.* wood shavings, used for packing.

ex·cept' (ik-sept') *prep.* leaving out; excluding; but for. —*conj.* 1, with this exception; otherwise than. 2, (*Archaic*) unless. —*v.t.* leave out; exclude. —*v.i.* make objection.

ex·cep'tion (ik-sep'shən) *n.* 1, exclusion. 2, something excepted; an instance not conforming to a general rule. 3, an objection. 4, slight anger or resentment. —**ex·cep'tion·a·ble**, *adj.* subject to objection. —**ex·cep'tion·al**, *adj.* unusual.

ex'cerpt (ek'sĕrpt) *n.* an extract from something written or printed. —*v.t.* (ek-sĕrpt') cite or cull (such an extract).

ex·cess' (ek-ses'; ek'ses) *n.* 1, the state of being more or too much. 2, a surplus or remainder. 3, immoderate indulgence of the appetites. —*adj.* more than enough; extra.

ex·ces'sive (-siv) *adj.* 1, superfluous. 2, unduly great; extreme. —**ex·ces'sive·ness**, *n.*

ex·change' (eks-chānj') *v.t.* give in return for something else; give and receive reciprocally. —*v.i.* 1, trade. 2, be taken or received in exchanging. —n. 1, the act of exchanging; mutual substitution. 2, something given or received in exchanging; checks, drafts, etc. 3, the rate at which one currency may be converted to another. 4, a percentage or fee charged for exchanging. 5, a place of exchange, as of stocks, drafts, etc.; a central telephone switchboard.

ex·cheq'uer (eks-chek'ər) n. 1, a treasury, esp. a government treasury. 2, (*Colloq.*) funds.

ex·cise' (ek'sīz') n. a tax imposed on commodities, occupations, etc. within a country. —v.t. 1, impose an excise tax upon. 2, cut off or out; delete. —ex·ci'sion (ek-sizh'ən) n.

ex·cite' (ek-sīt') v.t. 1, arouse the emotions of; stimulate. 2, stir; agitate. —ex·cit'a·ble, adj. easy to excite.— ex·cit'ed, adj. 1, emotionally aroused. 2, enthusiastic. —ex·cit'ing, adj. 1, tending to stir up. 2, causing enthusiasm; appealing.

ex·cite'ment (ik-sīt'mənt) n. 1, the state of being excited. 2, commotion; ado.

ex·claim' (eks-klām') v.i. cry out in astonishment, alarm, etc.; speak with vehemence. —v.i. say loudly and vehemently.

ex"cla·ma'tion (eks-klə-mā'shən) n. the act of exclaiming; what is exclaimed. —**exclamation point**, the symbol (!) used in punctuation for vehement expression.

ex·clam'a·to·ry (eks-klam'ə-tôr-ē) adj. 1, spoken vehemently. 2, marked with an exclamation point.

ex·clude' (ek-sklood') v.t. 1, shut out; omit. 2, thrust out; eject; expel.

ex·clu'sion (ik-skloo'zhən) n. act of excluding; state of being excluded.

ex·clu'sive (ik-skloo'siv) adj. 1, shutting out all others or all else from admission or consideration. 2, incompatible with something else. 3, (often with *of*) with the exception of. 4, select; snobbish. —ex·clu'sive·ness, n.

ex"com·mu'ni·cate" (eks"kə-mū'ni-kāt') v.t. cut off from communion or membership, esp. in respect to a church by ecclesiastical sentence. —ex"com·mu'ni·ca'tion, n.

ex·co'ri·ate" (ek-skôr'ē-āt') v.t. 1, denounce or censure violently. 2, remove the skin or outer covering from. —ex·co'ri·a'tion, n.

ex·cre·ment (eks'krə-mənt) n. waste matter eliminated from the living body, esp. the feces.

ex·cres'cence (ik-skres'əns) n. 1, an abnormal outgrowth on a body, as a wart. 2, a normal outgrowth, as hair. —ex·cres'cent, adj. superfluous.

ex·crete' (ek-skrēt') v.t. discharge from an organic body, as waste matter. —ex·cre'tion, n. act of excreting; something excreted.

ex·cru'ci·at"ing (ik-skroo'shē-ā'-ting) adj. extremely painful.

ex·cul'pate" (eks'kul-pāt') v.t. clear from a charge of fault or guilt; exonerate. —ex"cul·pa'tion, n. —ex·cul'pa·to·ry (eks-kulp'ə-tôr-ē) adj.

ex·cur'sion (ik-skėr'zhən) n. 1, a journey, usually for a specific purpose, and return to the starting point; a jaunt. 2, a train or boat ride at a reduced fare. 3, a digression or deviation. —ex·cur'sion·ist, n.

ex·cuse' (ek-skūz') v.t. 1, pardon; forgive; overlook. 2, apologize for; justify. 3, release from an obligation or duty. 4, refrain from exacting; remit. —n. (ek-skūs') 1, a plea offered or reason given for excusing. 2, a pretext or subterfuge. —ex·cus'a·ble (iks-kūz'ə-bəl) adj.

ex'e·cra·ble (ek'si-krə-bəl) adj. detestable. —ex'e·cra·ble·ness, n.

ex'e·crate" (ek'sə-krāt') v.t. 1, detest utterly; abhor. 2, denounce as abominable; curse. —ex"e·cra'tion, n. 1, the act of execrating. 2, a curse; denunciation.

ex"e·cute" (ek'sə-kūt') v.t. 1, do; perform; carry out. 2, enact. 3, put to death according to law.

ex"e·cu'tion (ek'si-kū'shən) n. 1, act of executing. 2, style or effectiveness of performance. 3, capital punishment. —ex"e·cu'tion·er, n. the officer who inflicts capital punishment.

ex·ec'u·tive (ig-zek'ū-tiv) adj. 1, concerned with doing, performing, or carrying into effect. 2, pert. to management or administration. —n. a person or body having executive duties or abilities. —**Chief Executive**, the president of the U.S.

ex·ec'u·tor (ig-zek'yə-tər) n. one designated to perform specified duties, esp. the provisions of a will. —ex·ec'u·trix (-triks) n.fem.

ex"e·ge'sis (ek'sə-jē'sis) n. interpretation, esp. of the Scriptures. —ex"e·gete" (-jēt') n. an expert at exegesis. —ex"e·get'ic (-jet'ik) adj.

ex·em'plar (ig-zem'plar) n. an example, esp. an ideal one; a model.

ex·em'pla·ry (ig-zem'plə-rē) adj. 1, worthy of imitation. 2, serving as a model or example.

ex·em'pli·fy" (eg-zem'pli-fī') v.t. 1, explain or illustrate by an example. 2, be an example of. —ex"em'pli·fi·ca'tion (-fi-kā'shən) n.

ex·empt' (eg-zempt') v.t. free from an obligation; except. —adj. excepted or released. —ex·emp'tion, n.

ex'er·cise" (ek'sər-sīz') n. 1, exertion of mind or body for development or training. **2,** active performance or use. **3,** a composition, drill, device, etc., designed for practice. **4,** (usually *pl.*) ceremonies; rites. —*v.t.* **1,** employ actively; perform; use. **2,** give practice or training to. **3,** make uneasy; disturb. —*v.t.* take bodily exercise.

ex·ert' (eg-zûrt') *v.t.* **1,** put to use, as strength, ability, power, etc. **2,** bestir (oneself) vigorously.

ex·er'tion (eg-zûr'shən) *n.* **1,** act of exerting. **2,** a great effort.

ex''ha·la'tion (eks''ə-lā'shən) *n.* **1,** act of exhaling. **2,** what is exhaled.

ex·hale' (eks-hāl') *v.t.* breathe out. —*v.t.* give off as a vapor.

ex·haust' (eg-zâst') *v.t.* **1,** draw out the entire contents of; make empty or useless. **2,** tire out; fatigue. —*n.* the exhalation of waste gases, as from an engine. —**ex·haust'i·ble,** *adj.*

ex·haus'tion (eg-zâs'chən) *n.* **1,** act of exhausting; state of being exhausted. **2,** complete expenditure; utter fatigue. —**ex·haus'tive,** *adj.* thorough.

ex·hib'it (eg-zib'it) *v.t.* **1,** offer to view; place on show. **2,** manifest, as a quality of character. —*v.t.* hold an exhibition. —*n.* **1,** exhibition. **2,** something exhibited; a concrete thing offered in evidence.

ex''hi·bi'tion (ek''sə-bish'ən) *n.* **1,** the act of exhibiting. **2,** a public display, as of works of art, goods, etc.

ex''hi·bi'tion·ist *n.* one who feels a compulsive urge to be noticed. —**ex''hi·bi'tion·ism,** *n.*

ex·hib'i·tor (eg-zib'i-tər) *n.* one who displays; the operator of a theater.

ex·hil'a·rate'' (eg-zil'ə-rāt') *v.t.* make cheerful or joyous. —**ex·hil'a·ra'tion,** *n.*

ex·hort' (eg-zôrt') *v.t.* urge to a course of action; incite; admonish. —**ex''hor·ta'tion** (ek''sər-tā'shən) *n.*

ex·hume' (eks-hūm') *v.t.* dig up (something buried, esp. a body). —**ex''hu·ma'tion** (ek''sū-mā'shən) *n.*

ex·i'gen·cy (ek'si-jən-sē) *n.* **1,** a state of affairs requiring prompt action; an emergency. **2,** pressing necessity. —**ex'i·gent,** *adj.*

ex·ig'u·ous (ig-zig'ū-əs) *adj.* scanty; sparse. —**ex·ig'u·ous·ness,** *n.*

ex·ile' (eg'zīl) *n.* **1,** expulsion from one's country; banishment. **2,** prolonged absence from home or country. **3,** one exiled. —*v.t.* banish.

ex·ist' (eg-zist') *v.t.* have actual being; be; live.

ex·ist'ence (-əns) *n.* **1,** state of existing; life. **2,** reality. —**ex·ist'ent,** *n.*

ex·it (ek'sit) *n.* **1,** a way of departure; a passage out. **2,** a departure. —*v.t.* go out or away.

ex·o- *pref.* outside of.

ex'o·dus (ek'sə-dəs) *n.* a mass departure.

ex·on'er·ate'' (eg-zon'ə-rāt') *v.t.* relieve of blame or accusation; exculpate; clear. —**ex·on''er·a'tion,** *n.*

ex·or'bi·tant (ig-zôr'bə-tənt) *adj.* going beyond usual or proper bounds; excessive; inordinate.

ex'or·cise'' (ek'sôr-sīz') *v.t.* **1,** expel (evil spirits) by magical or religious rites. **2,** rid of evil spirits, etc. by rites. —**ex'or·cism** (-siz-əm) *n.*

ex''o·ter'ic (ek''sə-ter'ik) *adj.* readily understood; commonplace.

ex·ot'ic (ig-zot'ik) *adj.* **1,** of foreign origin or character; strange. **2,** (*Colloq.*) striking in appearance. —**ex·ot'i·cal·ly,** *adv.*

ex·pand' (ek-spand') *v.t.* **1,** increase in extent, bulk, amount, etc. **2,** spread or stretch out; unfold.

ex·panse' (ik-spans') *n.* an uninterrupted stretch or area.

ex·pan'sion (ek-span'shən) *n.* **1,** act of expanding; state of being expanded. **2,** an enlargement, increase, etc.

ex·pan'sive (ek-span'siv) *adj.* **1,** wide; extensive; comprehensive. **2,** gregarious; sociable; friendly. —**ex·pan'sive·ness,** *n.*

ex·pa'ti·ate'' (ek-spā'shē-āt') *v.t.* deal with copiously, as in writing. —**ex·pa'ti·a'tion,** *n.*

ex·pa'tri·ate (eks-pā'trē-ət) *n.* one living, as though permanently, away from his country. —*v.t.* (-āt') banish. —**ex·pa'tri·a'tion,** *n.*

ex·pect' (ek-spekt') *v.t.* **1,** look forward to; anticipate; await as likely to happen or appear. **2,** (*Colloq.*) suppose; conclude.

ex·pec'tan·cy (ek-spek'tən-sē) *n.* **1,** act of expecting; expectation. **2,** that which is expected. **3,** contingency.

ex·pec'tant (-tənt) *adj.* expecting; eagerly awaiting.

ex''pec·ta'tion (ek''spek-tā'shən) *n.* **1,** act of expecting; expectancy. **2,** something expected or awaited, as a legacy.

ex·pec'to·rate'' (ek-spek'tə-rāt') *v.t. & t.* spit out from the mouth. —**ex·pec''to·ra'tion,** *n.*

ex·pe'di·ent (ik-spē'dē-ənt) *adj.* **1,** serving to promote a desired object; advisable. **2,** conducive to present advantage or self-interest. —*n.* **1,** a means to an end. **2,** a makeshift. —**ex·pe'di·en·cy, ex·pe'di·ence,** *n.*

ex·pe·dite' (eks'pə-dīt") *v.t.* 1, quicken the progress of. 2, dispatch. —**ex"pe·dit'er,** *n.* one who directs the course of a project through a series of government or business departments.

ex"pe·di'tion (eks"pə-dish'ən) *n.* 1, an excursion made by a company of persons for a specific purpose. 2, the state of being expedited; promptness or speed. —**ex"pe·di'tion·ar·y** (-er-ê) *adj.* making a journey.

ex"pe·di'tious (eks"pə-dish'əs) *adj.* quick. —**ex"pe·di'tious·ness,** *n.*

ex·pel' (ek-spel') *v.t.* [-pelled', -pel'ling] drive out or away; eject; emit. —**ex·pel'lant,** *adj. & n.*

ex·pend' (ek-spend') *v.t.* 1, use up. 2, pay out; spend. —**ex·pend'a·ble,** *adj.* dispensable; not too valuable to spare.

ex·pend'i·ture (ek-spen'di-chər) *n.* 1, consumption; disbursement. 2, something expended; outlay.

ex·pense' (ik-spens') *n.* 1, cost; charge; an expenditure. 2, (*pl.*) charges, incurred for another; to be reimbursed. 3, damage or loss.

ex·pen'sive (ik-spen'siv) *adj.* high in price or cost. —**ex·pen'sive·ness,** *n.*

ex·pe'ri·ence (ik-spir'ê-əns) *n.* 1, the process or fact of learning by personally observing, encountering, testing, or undergoing something. 2, knowledge or skill gained by this process. 3, a particular instance of observing, encountering, etc.; an event in which one is involved. —*v.t.* meet, undergo, or feel. —**ex·pe'ri·enced,** *adj.* adept or knowing through experience; expert.

ex·per'i·ment (ik-sper'ə-mənt) *n.* 1, a trial or test. 2, the process of learning by observation. —*v.t.* make a trial or test. —**ex·per'i·men'tal** (-men'təl) *adj.* 1, done as a trial. 2, based on observation, not theory. —**ex·per'i·men·ta'tion,** *n.*

ex'pert (eks'pərt) *adj.* having great knowledge or skill; learned; dexterous. —*n.* one especially skilled or learned; an authority. —**ex·pert'ness,** *n.*

ex'pi·a·ble (eks'pê-ə-bəl) *adj.* capable of being atoned for; pardonable.

ex'pi·ate" (eks'pê-āt") *v.t.* atone for; make amends for. —**ex"pi·a'tion,** *n.*

ex"pi·ra'tion (ek"spə-rā'shən) *n.* 1, the end; termination. 2, a breathing out.

ex·pir'a·to·ry (ek-spī'rə-tôr-ê) *adj.* pert. to emission of air from the lungs.

ex·pire' (ek-spīr') *v.i.* 1, come to an end; die; close. 2, breathe out; exhale. —*v.t.* breathe out; emit.

ex·plain' (ek-splān') *v.t.* 1, make plain or clear to the mind. 2, describe; interpret; analyze. 3, show the cause or reason of; account for. —*v.i.* give an explanation.

ex"pla·na'tion (ek"splə-nā'shən) *n.* 1, the act of explaining; the facts or assertions that explain something. 2, a clarification; solution; apology; excuse.

ex·plan'a·to·ry (ek-splan'ə-tôr-ê) *adj.* serving to explain.

ex'ple·tive (eks'plə-tiv) *adj.* added merely to fill out or to give emphasis (of a word or phrase). —*n.* an interjection; an oath or imprecation.

ex'pli·ca·ble (eks'pli-kə-bəl) *adj.* capable of being explained.

ex·plic'it (ik-splis'it) *adj.* 1, (of words, ideas) fully or clearly expressed, not merely implied; definite. 2, (of persons) outspoken. —**ex·plic'it·ness,** *n.*

ex·plode' (ek-splōd') *v.i.* 1, burst suddenly; fly to pieces with noise and violence. 2, break into action, speech, etc. suddenly and vehemently. —*v.t.* 1, cause to explode. 2, disprove; discredit.

ex'ploit (eks'ploit) *n.* a notable achievement; conspicuous act or deed. —*v.t.* (ek-sploit') 1, make complete use of. 2, turn to one's own advantage; utilize selfishly. —**ex"ploi·ta'tion,** *n.*

ex"plo·ra'tion (eks"plôr-ā'shən) *n.* 1, the act of exploring. 2, adventurous penetration of unknown territory. —**ex·plor'a·to·ry** (ik-splôr'ə-tôr-ê) *adj.*

ex·plore' (ek-splôr') *v.t.* 1, travel over or through (a region) for purpose of observation and discovery. 2, inquire into; examine; investigate. —*v.i.* engage in exploring.

ex·plor'er (ik-splôr'ər) *n.* one who explores unknown territories.

ex·plo'sion (eks-plō'zhən) *n.* the act of exploding; the loud noise attending such act.

ex·plo'sive (eks-plō'siv) *adj.* tending to explode. —*n.* that which explodes or causes explosion, as dynamite.

ex·po'nent (ik-spō'nənt) *n.* 1, one who expounds or explains. 2, representative, advocate, or symbol of something. 3, (*Math.*) a superscript written after a quantity to indicate the power to which it is to be raised, as the ^{2} in 3^2 ($= 3 \times 3$).

ex·port' (ek-spôrt') *v.t.* send (a commodity) to another place or country for sale. —*n.* (eks'pôrt) 1, something exported. 2, the act or business of exporting. —*adj.* pert.

to or suitable for exporting. —ex'por·ta'tion, *n.* —ex·port'er, *n.* one whose business is exporting merchandise.

ex·pose' (ek-spōz') *v.t.* 1, lay open to view; uncover; reveal. 2, show the secret intentions or motives of. 3, leave unprotected. —ex·pos'al, *n.*

ex"po·sé' (ek"spō-zā') *n.* an exposure, esp. of something discreditable.

ex"po·si'tion (eks"pə-zish'ən) *n.* 1, an exhibit or show, as of products of art or manufacture. 2, the act of exposing or explaining. 3, a detailed explanation.

ex·pos'i·to·ry (ek-spoz'ə-tôr-ē) *adj.* serving to explain.

ex·pos'tu·late (ek-spos'chə-lāt') *v.i.* reason earnestly; remonstrate. —ex·pos'tu·la'tion, *n.*

ex·po'sure (ik-spō'zhər) *n.* 1, the act of exposing; the state of being exposed. 2, in photography, the admission of light to a sensitized plate or film; the duration of such action. 3, the compass direction confronted.

ex·pound' (ek-spownd') *v.t.* set forth the principles of; explain.

ex·press' (ek-spres') *v.t.* 1, put (thought, ideas) into tangible or communicable form, as words, pictures, etc. 2, manifest; reveal; make explicit. 3, press or squeeze out. 4, send as express. —*adj.* 1, made known clearly or explicitly; directly stated or represented; precise. 2, special; specially direct and fast. —*n.* 1, a specially direct and fast train or other carrier. 2, a system of rapid transportation of packages and money; goods transported by this system. —ex·press'i·ble, *adj.*

ex·pres'sion (ik-spresh'ən) *n.* 1, the act of expressing. 2, the word or phrase, picture, etc. that makes something known. 3, the style in which something is expressed. 4, outward manifestation; appearance of face; intonation of voice.

ex·pres'sive (ik-spres'iv) *adj.* 1, pert. to expression. 2, revealing; readily understood. —ex·pres'sive·ness, *n.*

ex·pro'pri·ate" (eks-prō'prē-āt') *v.t.* 1, take for public use by right of eminent domain. 2, dispossess. —ex·pro"pri·a'tion, *n.* —ex·pro'pri·a'tor, *n.*

ex·pul'sion (ik-spul'shən) *n.* the act of expelling or being expelled.

ex·punge' (ek-spunj') *v.t.* blot or wipe out; erase; destroy.

ex'pur·gate" (eks'pər-gāt") *v.t.* purge or cleanse, esp. by deletion. —ex"pur·ga'tion, *n.* —ex'pur·ga'tor, *n.*

ex'qui·site (eks'kwi-zit) *adj.* 1, exceedingly beautiful, fine, dainty, elegant, etc. 2, giving pleasure or pain in the highest degree; intense; keen. 3, very accurate; delicate in action or function. —ex'qui·site·ness, *n.*

ex'tant (eks'tant) *adj.* in existence.

ex·tem"po·ra'ne·ous (ik-stem"-pə-rā'nē-əs) *adj.* made, spoken, or performed without previous preparation; improvised at the moment. —ex·tem"po·ra'ne·ous·ness, *n.*

ex·tem'po·re (ek-stem'pə-rē) *adj. & adv.* impromptu.

ex·tem'po·rize" (ek-stem'pə-rīz") *v.t. & i.* speak extemporaneously; improvise.

ex·tend' (ek-stend') *v.t.* 1, stretch out in space; carry forward; enlarge. 2, continue in time; prolong; postpone. 3, put forth; offer; bestow; impart. —*v.i.* 1, be stretched or laid out. 2, (with *to*) reach; include or cover. 3, increase in length, duration, scope, etc. —ex·tend'ed, *adj.* stretched out; prolonged; extensive.

ex·ten'si·ble (ek-sten'sə-bəl) *adj.* capable of being extended.

ex·ten'sion (ek-sten'shən) *n.* 1, the act of extending; state of being extended. 2, an addition or prolongation. 3, scope; range; extent.

ex·ten'sive (ek-sten'siv) *adj.* great in scope; thorough. —ex·ten'sive·ness, *n.*

ex·tent' (ik-stent') *n.* the space or degree to which something extends; length; bulk; size; limit.

ex·ten'u·ate" (ek-sten'ū-āt") *v.t.* make smaller in degree or appearance; make (a fault, crime, etc.) less blamable. —ex·ten'u·at'ed, *adj.* shrunken; thin. —ex·ten'u·a'tion, *n.*

ex·te'ri·or (ik-stir'ē-ər) *adj.* being outside; pert. to the outer surface, side, or part; outward; outlying. —*n.* the outer surface or part.

ex·ter'mi·nate" (ek-stēr'mi-nāt") *v.t.* destroy utterly; extirpate. —ex·ter'mi·na'tion, *n.*

ex·ter'nal (ik-stēr'nəl) *adj.* 1, exterior. 2, located outside and apart; separate. 3, pert. to the outside of the body. 4, outside the mind; having material existence. 5, pert. to outward manifestation.

ex·tinct' (ik-stinkt') *adj.* 1, extinguished, as a fire. 2, having ceased; out of existence; no longer living. —ex·tinc'tion, *n.*

ex·tin'guish (ek-sting'gwish) *v.t.* 1, put out, as a fire; quench. 2, put an end to; destroy; suppress. —ex·tin'guish·er, *n.* a device for putting out a fire. —ex·tin'guish·ment, *n.*

ex'tir·pate" (ek'stər-pāt") *v.t.* pull

up by the roots; eradicate; destroy totally. —**ex'tir·pa'tion**, *n.*

ex·tol' (ek-stŏl') *v.t.* [-tolled', -tol'- ling] speak in laudatory terms of; praise highly.

ex·tort' (ek-stôrt') *v.t.* obtain by force or compulsion; wrest from another by intimidation.

ex·tor'tion (ik-stôr'shən) *n.* ex- action of payment by threat; black- mail. —**ex·tor'tion·ate** (-ət) *adj.* ex- orbitant in price; demanding too much.

ex'tra (eks'trə) *adj.* more than what is usual; due, or expected; additional; supplementary. —*adv.* beyond the ordinary standard, amount, or degree; unusually. —*n.* 1, some- thing additional or superior. 2, a special edition of a newspaper. 3, an added worker, as an actor hired by the day.

ex·tra- *pref.* outside; beyond.

ex·tract' (ek-strakt') *v.t.* 1, remove forcibly from a fixed position; pull out. 2, separate, as a constituent part from the whole. 3, derive from a particular source; deduce; select. —*n.* (eks'trakt) 1, something ex- tracted. 2, a substance or prepa- ration obtained by distillation or other chemical means. 3, a passage from a book, etc.; excerpt; quota- tion. —**ex·trac'tion**, *n.* —**ex·trac'- tor**, *n.*

ex'tra·cur·ric'u·lar (ek'strə-kə- rik'yə-lər) *adj.* pert. to school activi- ties outside the regular courses of study.

ex'tra·dite' (eks'trə-dīt') *v.t.* 1, deliver up (a prisoner or fugitive) to another nation or jurisdiction. 2, secure custody of a person by extradition. —**ex'tra·di'tion** (-dish'- ən) *n.*

ex'tra·mu'ral (eks'trə-myūr'əl) *adj.* outside the walls, as of a college; not confined to one's own base or group.

ex·tra'ne·ous (ek-strā'nē-əs) *adj.* not belonging or proper to a thing; not intrinsic or essential; foreign. —**ex·tra'ne·ous·ness**, *n.*

ex'tra·or'di·nar'y (ek-strôr'də- ner'ē) *adj.* 1, not of the usual or regular kind. 2, exceeding the com- mon degree; remarkable; wonderful.

ex'tra·sen'so·ry (eks'trə-sen'sə- rē) *adj.* beyond the perception of the recognized senses.

ex'tra·ter'ri·to'ri·al (eks'trə- ter''i-tôr'ē-əl) *adj.* not subject to the jurisdiction of local authorities.

ex·trav'a·gant (ik-strav'ə-gant) *adj.* 1, wasteful of money; inclined to spend unnecessarily. 2, high in price. 3, profuse; irregular; fantastic. —**ex·trav'a·gance**, *n.*

ex·trav'a·gan'za (ik-strav'ə- gan'zə) *n.* a dramatic or musical show of elaborate or fantastic na- ture.

ex·treme' (ik-strēm') *adj.* 1, ut- most in degree, as largest, smallest, etc.; greatest in degree. 2, farthest from the center. 3, last; final. 4, very immoderate in action, opinion, etc. —*n.* 1, the utmost or greatest degree. 2, something immoderate or fantastic. 3, the first or last. —**ex- treme'ly**, *adv.* exceedingly; very. —**ex·treme'ness**, *n.*

ex·trem'ist (ek-strē'mist) *n.* one who goes to extremes in opinions or actions.

ex·trem'i·ty (ik-strem'ə-tē) *n.* 1, the outer or terminal point; the limit or boundary. 2, an end part; a hand, foot, etc. 3, the utmost de- gree. 4, (often *pl.*) a condition of great peril, distress, or want. 5, (*pl.*) the last moments before death.

ex'tri·cate' (eks'trə-kāt') *v.t.* dis- entangle; set free; liberate. —**ex'- tri·ca·ble**, *adj.* —**ex'tri·ca'tion**, *n.*

ex·trin'sic (eks-trin'sik) *adj.* 1, being outside and separate; coming from without. 2, not inherent or essential; extraneous. —**ex·trin'si- cal·ly**, *adv.*

ex'tro·vert' (eks'trə-vĕrt') *n. & adj.* (*Psychol.*) a person concerned chiefly with what is outside his own mind. —**ex'tro·ver'sion** (-zhən) *n.*

ex·trude' (ek-strood') *v.t.* 1, thrust out; expel. 2, form (a plastic prod- uct) by ejection through a shaped opening. —*v.i.* project outward; protrude. —**ex·tru'sion** (-zhən) *n.*

ex·u'ber·ant (eg-zoo'bər-ənt) *adj.* 1, effusive in feeling or expression; lavish. 2, copious to excess; over- flowing. —**ex·u'ber·ance**, *n.*

ex·ude' (eg-zood') *v.i.* ooze out, like sweat through the pores. —*v.t.* emit or discharge slowly. —**ex'u- da'tion** (eks'ū-dā'shən) *n.*

ex·ult' (eg-zult') *v.i.* show or feel self-congratulatory joy; rejoice in triumph. —**ex·ult'ant**, *adj.* rejoicing. —**ex'ul·ta'tion** (eks'əl-tā'shən) *n.*

ex·u'vi·ate' (eg-zoo'vē-āt') *v.t.* shed or cast off, as skin or shell; molt. —**ex·u'vi·a'tion**, *n.*

eye (ī) *n.* 1, the organ of vision in man and the high- er animals. 2, vi- sion; the field of sight; observa- tion; watchful at- tention. 3, mental view; opinion; estimation. 4, something resembling an eye; a colored spot; a bud or shoot. 5, a hole in an instrument or tool; a loop of rope or wire; a hook or catch. 6, the center of a hurricane. —*v.t.* ogle; observe; watch.

Eyeglasses

eye'ball' (ī'bal') *n.* the ball-like mass of the eye.

eye'brow' (ī'brow') *n.* the ridge above the eye.

eye'glass' (ī'glàs') *n.* 1, (*pl.*) one of a pair of lenses worn before the eye to correct faulty vision. 2, the eyepiece of an optical instrument.

eye'lash" (ī'lash") n. one of the hairs growing at the edge of the eyelid.

eye'let (ī'lət) n. a small round hole, as in paper, leather, fabric, etc., bound around the rim.

eye'lid" (ī'lid") n. the skin that moves over the eyeball.

eye opener 1, a surprising occurrence. 2, a drink of liquor early in the day.

eye'piece" (ī'pēs") n. the lens of an optical instrument to which the eye is applied.

eye'sight" (ī'sīt") n. the faculty of seeing; vision.

eye'sore" (ī'sōr") n. an object of offensive appearance.

Eyespot of a peacock feather

eye'spot" n. a visual organ of lower animals; any eyelike spot of color.

eye'strain" n. excessive or incorrect use of the eyes.

eye'tooth" (ī'tooth") n. either of the two canine teeth of the upper jaw.

eye'wit"ness n. one who testifies concerning an occurrence which he has seen.

ey'rie (ār'ē; ī'rē) n. aerie.

F

F, f (ef) the sixth letter in the English alphabet.

fa (fä) n. (*Music*) the fourth tone of a diatonic scale.

fa'ble (fā'bəl) n. 1, a fictitious tale conveying a moral. 2, a myth; legend. 3, a lie. —**fa'bled**, adj. legendary; fictitious.

fab'ric (fab'rik) n. 1, frame; structure; composition. 2, a woven or knitted material; cloth.

fab'ri·cate" (fab'rə-kāt") v.t. 1, build or manufacture. 2, construct by assembling parts. 3, concoct falsely. —**fab'ri·ca'tion**, n.

fab'u·lous (fab'yə-ləs) adj. 1, mythical; not actual. 2, incredible;

hence, immense or great. —**fba'u·lous·ness**, n.

fa·cade' (fə-säd') n. the chief exterior face of a building.

face (fās) n. 1, the front of the head; countenance. 2, expression; a look. 3, outward aspect. 4, prestige; reputation. 5, effrontery. 6, the principal surface of anything. —v.t. 1, have the face or front toward. 2, meet boldly. 3, cover the surface of, with anything. —v.i. front in any given direction. —**face card**, king, queen or jack, in playing cards. —**face'-lift"ing**, n. removal of wrinkles by plastic surgery. —**face value**, par or promised value.

fac'et (fas'it) n. one of the small surfaces of a cut gem.

Facets

fa·ce'tious (fə-sē'shəs) adj. humorous; joking. —**fa·ce'tious·ness**, n.

fa'cial (fā'shəl) adj. of the face. —n. a facial massage.

fac'ile (fas'il) adj. 1, ready; quick; skillful. 2, affable.

fa·cil'i·tate" (fə-sil'ə-tāt") v.t. make easier. —**fa·cil'i·ta'tion**, n.

fa·cil'i·ty (fə-sil'ə-tē) n. 1, ease. 2, talent; dexterity. 3, (*pl.*) conveniences.

fac'ing (fās'ing) n. 1, an outer covering, as of different stone on a wall. 2, a different material on the edge of a garment.

fac·sim'i·le (fak-sim'ə-lē) n. an exact copy.

fact (fakt) n. 1, something known to have occurred or to be true. 2, the quality of being actual. 3, the statement of something done or known to be true.

fac'tion (fak'shən) n. a group or clique in a party, state, etc., seeking to promote partisan interests.

fac'tious (fak'shəs) adj. opposing; contentious. —**fac'tious·ness**, n.

fac·ti'tious (fak-tish'əs) adj. artificial; sham; made-up. —**fac·ti'tious·ness**, n.

fac'tor (fak'tər) n. 1, an agent, distributor, or private banker. 2, any contributing cause or element. 3, (*Math*.) one of the numbers which when multiplied together produce a given result. —v.t. 1, handle as agent; lend money on accounts receivable. 2, (*Math*.) produce from given factors; separate into factors.

fac·to'ri·al (fak-tôr'ē-əl) adj. 1, pert. to a factor. 2, (*Math*.) the product of consecutive integers from an integer to 1, written (!), as, 3! (= 3 × 2 × 1).

fac'to·ry (fak'tə·rē) *n.* a building for manufacturing.

fac·to'tum (fak·tō'təm) *n.* a person hired to do all kinds of work.

fac'tu·al (fak'choo-əl) *adj.* 1, pert. to facts. 2, true; real; actual.

fac'ul·ta"tive (fak'əl-tā"tiv) *adj.* 1, conferring or comprising a power. 2, optional.

fac'ul·ty (fak'əl-tē) *n.* 1, a physical or mental power. 2, a special aptitude; ability; knack. 3, the teaching body collectively of a school.

fad *n.* a passing style or interest. —fad'dist, *n.* one who follows fads.

fade (fād) *v.i.* 1, lose color, freshness, or vigor. 2, grow dim; die gradually. —*v.t.* 1, cause to fade. 2, (*Slang*) accept a bet, in craps.

fag *v.t. & i.* [fagged, fag'ging] weary; exhaust. —*n.* (*Slang*) a cigarette.

fag'ot (fag'ət) *n.* a bundle of sticks used for fuel. Also, fag'got.

Fahr'en·heit" (far'ən·hīt") *n.* a thermometric scale on which +32° is the freezing and +212° the boiling point of water.

fail (fāl) *v.i.* 1, fall short; be deficient. 2, become weaker. 3, prove to be lacking in what is expected or desired. 4, go bankrupt. —*v.t.* 1, not fulfill the expectations of; disappoint. 2, assign a grade insufficient for passing. —fail'ing, *n.* a fault.

faille (fāl; fil) *n.* a ribbed silk or rayon fabric.

fail'ure (fāl'yər) *n.* 1, the act of failing; a falling short; nonperformance; deterioration; bankruptcy. 2, an unsuccessful person or thing.

fain (fān) *adv.* (*Archaic*) willingly; gladly.

faint (fānt) *adj.* 1, not easily seen or heard; weak in tone, color, sound, etc.; indistinct; pale. 2, feeble; weak; about to swoon. —*v.i.* swoon. —faint"heart'ed, *adj.* diffident; timid. —faint'ness, *n.*

fair (fār) *adj.* 1, good to look upon; beautiful. 2, blond; light-colored. 3, spotless; pure. 4, legal; within bounds, as a hit ball in baseball. 5, just; unbiased. 6, passably good. 7, clear; unclouded; bright; not stormy. 8, womanly; feminine. —*adv.* 1, according to rule. 2, favorably; passably well. 3, squarely. —*n.* 1, a competitive exhibition of farm products, handwork, etc. 2, a sale or bazaar, as for charity. 3, a regular meeting, at a stated time and place, of buyers and sellers. —fair'ness, *n.*

fair'haired" (-hārd') *adj.* 1, having blond hair. 2, unduly favored.

fair"spo'ken *adj.* polite in speech.

fair'way" (fār'wā") *n.* 1, in golf, the mowed strip between tee and putting green. 2, the navigable part of a river or harbor.

fair'y (fār'ē) *n.* a tiny spirit capable of assuming various forms and of interfering in human affairs. —fair'y·land", *n.* the land where fairies live; any enchanting place. —fairy tale, 1, a story about fairies, for children. 2, a preposterous tale; a lie.

faith (fāth) *n.* 1, belief without proof, esp. in God; confidence; reliance. 2, loyalty; fidelity to an agreement or promise. 3, a religious creed.

faith'ful (-fəl) *adj.* 1, loyal. 2, conscientious. 3, exact; true. —faith'-ful·ness, *n.*

faith'less (-ləs) *adj.* false to a promise or obligation. —faith'less-ness, *n.*

fake (fāk) *v.t. & i.* (*Colloq.*) imitate fraudulently; pretend; feign. —*adj.* not genuine. —*n.* 1, a counterfeit; a fraudulent imitation. 2, a false pretender; an impostor. —fak'er, *n.* 1, one who fakes. 2, a swindler.

fa·kir' (fə·kir') *n.* a religious mendicant, esp. Moslem or Hindu.

fal'con (fál'kən) *n.* a small, swift hawk, esp. one trained to hunt.

fal'con·ry (-rē) *n.* the sport of hunting with falcons.

Falcon

fall (fál) *v.i.* [fell, fall'en, fall'ing] 1, drop or sink from a higher to a lower level; descend rapidly; decline. 2, (sometimes with *down*) tumble to the ground, esp. after stumbling. 3, die. 4, come by chance. 5, occur. 6, pass from one condition to another. 7, (with *away*) decline; (with *for*) be deceived by; (with *in*) take one's place in line; hence, agree; (with *out*) quarrel; (with *through*) not come to exist; miscarry. —*n.* the season from Sept. 22 to Dec. 21; autumn.

fal'la·cy (fal'ə·sē) *n.* 1, an error or flaw, esp. in reasoning. 2, a false idea. —fal·la'cious (fə·lā'shəs) *adj.*

fal'li·ble (fal'ə·bəl) *adj.* apt to be mistaken; capable of committing error. —fal"li·bil'i·ty, *n.*

fal'low (fal'ō) *adj.* 1, plowed but not sowed. 2, not in use; idle. 3, a pale, yellowish color.

false (fáls) *adj.* 1, not according to fact; untrue; erroneous; wrong. 2, not truthful. 3, treacherous; deceitful; disloyal. **4,** sham; artificial. —**false'ness,** *n.*

false'hood" *n.* a lie.

fal·set'to (fål-set'ō) *n.* [*pl.* **-tos**] a voice, esp. a man's voice, that is artificially high.

fal'sies (fål'sĕz) *n.pl.* forms worn by women to fill out their bosoms.

fal'si·fy" (fål'si-fī") *v.t.* **1,** misrepresent; deceive. **2,** alter fraudulently. —**fal"si·fi·ca'tion** (-fi-kā'shən) *n.*

fal'si·ty (fål'sə-tē) *n.* **1,** the quality of being false. **2,** a lie.

fal'ter (fål'tər) *v.i.* **1,** be unsteady; stumble. **2,** be hesitant in speech; stammer. **3,** waver, in action or purpose.

fame (fām) *n.* renown; widespread reputation; rumor. —**famed,** *adj.*

fa·mil'iar (fə-mil'yər) *adj.* **1,** closely intimate. **2,** well versed or acquainted. **3,** well known and remembered; common. **4,** overfree; presuming. —*n.* an intimate associate. —**fa·mil"i·ar'i·ty** (fə-mil"yar'ə-tē) *n.* —**fa·mil'iar·ize"** (-īz") *v.t.* make well acquainted or well known.

fam'i·ly (fam'ə-lē) *n.* **1,** a household. **2,** kindred, esp. one's own spouse, parents, and children. **3,** descendants of a common ancestor; a tribe. **4,** lineage. **5,** a group of things with some common feature. —**family tree,** a genealogical chart.

fam'ine (fam'in) *n.* extreme scarcity of food; starvation.

fam'ish *v.t. & i.* starve; suffer extreme hunger. —**fam'ish·ment,** *n.*

fa'mous (fā'məs) *adj.* widely known; renowned; noted or notorious.

fan *n.* **1,** a device for stirring the air, either mechanical or manual. **2,** (*Slang*) a devotee of a sport, hobby, etc. —*v.t. & i.* [**fanned, fan'ning**] **1,** drive air upon; wave a fan. **2,** rouse; excite. **3,** spread out like a fan. **4,** in baseball, strike out.

fa·nat'ic (fə-nat'ik) *n.* a zealot, esp. in religion. —*adj.* extreme; excessive. —**fa·nat'i·cal,** *adj.* —**fa·nat'i·cism,** *n.*

fan'ci·er (fan'sē-ər) *n.* one with a special interest, as in dogs or plants. —*adj.* comp. of *fancy.*

fan'ci·ful (fan'si-fəl) *adj.* **1,** whimsical; unreal. **2,** curiously designed.

fan'cy (fan'sē) *n.* **1,** the capacity for imaginative vision; an idea or notion of something unreal or fantastic but pleasing; a delusion. **2,** a whim. **3,** fondness; liking. —*adj.* **1,** chiefly imagined or imaginative; whimsical. **2,** not plain. **3,** of best quality; superfine. **4,** extravagant. **5,** done with skill. —*v.t.* **1,** imagine.

2, suppose; assume. **3,** like; wish for; prefer. —**fan'cied,** *adj.* imaginary. —**fan'ci·ness,** *n.*

fan·dan'go (fan-dang'gō) *n.* [*pl.* **-gos**] a lively Spanish dance; the music for it.

fan'fare (fan'fâr) *n.* a flourish of trumpets; ceremony; ostentation.

fang *n.* a sharp tooth, esp. of an animal or poisonous snake.

fan'light" *n.* a fan-shaped window above a door.

fan'tail" (fan'tāl") *n.* a pigeon with a fan-shaped tail.

fan'tan" *n.* **1,** a card game. **2,** a Chinese gambling game.

fan·ta·si·a (fan-tā'zhē-ə) *n.* an unconventional musical piece.

fan·tas'tic (fan-tas'tik) *adj.* **1,** imagined or unreal and hardly possible. **2,** grotesque. —**fan·tas'ti·cal·ly,** *adv.*

fan'ta·sy (fan'tə-sē) *n.* **1,** unrestrained imagination. **2,** an illusory mental image; a visionary idea. Also, **phan'ta·sy.**

far (fär) *adj.* [**far'ther** (-*th*ər),**-thest**] **1,** remote in time or space. **2,** more distant of the two. —*adv.* **1,** widely. **2,** by a great deal. **3,** to a definite distance, point, or degree.

farce (färs) *n.* **1,** a comedy of exaggerated humor. **2,** a mockery; a fiasco. —**far'ci·cal** (fär'si-kəl) *adj.*

fare (fâr) *v.i.* **1,** proceed; go; travel. **2,** have good or bad health, fortune, or treatment. **3,** eat and drink. —*n.* **1,** the amount charged for passage; any charge or rate. **2,** a paying passenger. **3,** food served.

fare"well' (fâr"wel') *interj.* goodbye. —*n.* a leave-taking.

far"fetched' (fär'fecht') *adj.* too complex or unnatural to be readily grasped or believed.

far"flung' (fär"flung') *adj.* **1,** widely dispersed. **2,** extensive.

fa·ri'na (fə-rē'nə) *n.* meal or flour made from cereal grains.

farm (färm) *n.* a tract of land on which crops, animals, etc. are raised. —*v.t. & i.* **1,** use (land) as a farm. **2,** develop by cultivation.

farm'er (fär'mər) *n.* **1,** one who farms professionally. **2,** a rustic.

farm'ing *n.* agriculture.

farm'yard" *n.* the ground around buildings on a farm.

far'o (fâr'ō) *n.* a card game.

far·ra'go (fə-rä'gō) *n.* a confused mixture.

far'ri·er (far'ē-ər) *n.* one who shoes horses.

far'row (far'ō) *n.* a litter of pigs. —*v.t. & i.* give birth to (pigs).

---

fat, fāte, fär, fâre, fåll, åsk; met, hē, hĕr, maybė; pin, pīne; not, nōte, ôr, tool

far'sight'ed (fär'sī"tid) *adj.* **1,** able to perceive distant sights. **2,** having foresight. —**far'sight'ed-ness,** *n.*

far'ther (fär'thər) more remote or extended: comp. of *far.*

far'thing (fär'thing) *n.*; a Brit. coin formerly worth ¼ U.S. cent.

far'thin·gale' (fär'thing-gāl') *n.* a kind of hoop skirt.

fas'ces (fas'ēz) *n. pl.* [*sing.* -cis] a bundle of rods bound as a staff for an ax blade.

fas'ci·nate' (fas'ə-nāt") *v.t.* attract irresistibly; bewitch; enchant. —**fas'ci·na'tion,** *n.* —**fas'ci·na·tor,** *n.* a woman's lace scarf.

fas'cism (fash'iz-əm) *n.* a strongly nationalistic regime characterized by regimentation, rigid censorship, and suppression of opposition.

Fasces

fas'cist (fash'ist) *n.* a supporter of fascism or a believer in its policies. —*adj.* reactionary; intolerant. —**fas·cis'tic** (fə-shis'tik) *adj.* —**fas·cis'ti·cal·ly,** *adv.*

fash'ion (fash'ən) *n.* **1,** prevailing mode, esp. of dress; present custom. **2,** people of polite society collectively. **3,** external shape; form. **4,** manner or way (of doing something). —*v.t.* make; fabricate; give a particular shape or form to. —**fashion plate,** a stylishly dressed person.

fash'ion·a·ble (-ə-bəl) *adj.* **1,** stylish. **2,** favored by polite society. —**fash'ion·a·ble·ness,** *n.*

fast (fàst) *adj.* **1,** moving at a rapid pace; swift; quick. **2,** without delay. **3,** conducive to rapidity, as a *fast track.* **4,** of a clock, showing too advanced time; of time (*Colloq.*) daylight saving. **5,** loose in morals; dissipated. **6,** firmly fixed; tight; steadfast. **7,** not subject to fading; lasting. —*adv.* rapidly; firmly; soundly. —*n.* voluntary abstinence from food. —*v.i.* abstain from eating.

fas'ten (fàs'ən) *v.t. & i.* **1,** attach firmly; fix firmly in position; make secure. **2,** direct (the eyes, etc.) steadily. —**fas'ten·ing,** *n.* a clasp, lock, hook, etc.

fas·tid'i·ous (fas-tid'ē-əs) *adj.* hard to please; overnice. —**fas·tid'i·ous·ness,** *n.*

fast'ness (fàst'nəs) *n.* **1,** state of being fast; speed. **2,** an impregnable place.

fat *adj.* [**fat'ter, -test**] **1,** bulging with much, or too much, flesh; corpulent; plump. **2,** consisting of fat; greasy. **3,** rich in some desirable element. **4,** fertile; fruitful; profitable. —*n.* **1,** the oily solid substance in animal tissue, yellowish white in color; suet. **2,** the best part of anything. —**fat'ness,** *n.*

fa'tal (fā'təl) *adj.* **1,** causing death or ruin. **2,** fateful. —**fa'tal·ness,** *n.*

fa'tal·ism (fā'tə-liz-əm) *n.* the belief that all events are predetermined and hence inevitable. —**fa'tal·ist,** *n.* —**fa'tal·is'tic,** *adj.*

fa·tal'i·ty (fā-tal'ə-tē) *n.* a fatal disaster; a death in a disaster.

fate (fāt) *n.* **1,** a power that supposedly predetermines what is to happen. **2,** destiny; lot. **3,** ultimate outcome.

fat'ed (fā'tid) *adj.* **1,** predetermined by fate. **2,** doomed.

fate'ful (-fəl) *adj.* **1,** momentous. **2,** controlled by destiny. **3,** prophetic. **4,** disastrous. —**fate'ful·ness,** *n.*

fat'head" *n.* (*Colloq.*) a stupid person; a dolt.

fa'ther (fä'thər) *n.* **1,** a male parent. **2,** (*cap.*) God. **3,** any ancestor. **4,** one who originates, makes possible, or inspires, something. **5,** the title given to certain priests. **6,** one of the leading citizens. —**fa'ther·hood,** *n.* —**fa'ther-in-law",** *n.* the father of one's husband or wife.

fa'ther·land" *n.* one's native country.

fa'ther·ly (-lē) *adj.* paternal; like a father. —**fa'ther·li·ness,** *n.*

fath'om (fath'əm) *n.* a nautical measure of length, 6 feet. —*v.t.* **1,** measure in fathoms; reach the bottom of. **2,** understand thoroughly. —**fath'om·less** (-ləs) *adj.* too deep to fathom.

fa·tigue' (fə-tēg') *n.* weariness from physical or mental exertion. —*v.t.* weary with labor.

fat'ted (fat'id) *adj.* fattened.

fat'ten (fat'ən) *v.t.* **1,** feed so as to make fat. **2,** enrich; increase. —*v.i.* become fatter.

fat'ty (fat'ē) *adj.* of or like fat.

fa·tu'i·ty (fə-too'ə-tē) *n.* **1,** fatuousness. **2,** a foolish act or thing.

fat'u·ous (fach'oo-əs) *adj.* complacently silly; inane. —**fat'u·ous·ness,** *n.*

fau'cet (fà'sit) *n.* a device for controlling the flow of a liquid from a pipe or container; a tap.

fault (fàlt) *n.* **1,** whatever is not perfect or not satisfactory; a defect; flaw; imperfection; failing; error; mistake. **2,** a cause for blame. **3,** a break in continuity, esp. in rock formation. **4,** in tennis, etc., an improper service. —**fault'find'ing,** *adj.* given to carping. —**fault'less,** *adj.* perfect; irreproachable. —**fault'y,** *adj.* having some defects; erroneous; erratic.

tub, cūte, pŭll; label; oil, owl; go, chip, she, thin, then, sing, ink; *see p. 6*

faun (fän) *n.* a Roman rural deity, part goat and part man.

fau'na (fâ'nə) *n.* the animals of a region or period.

fa'vor (fā'vər) *n.* 1, a spirit of approval, good will, or liking; partiality. 2, an act of kindness, not of self-seeking. 3, a small gift, esp. to a guest at a party; a token. 4, in business idiom, a letter. —*v.t.* 1, prefer. 2, advocate; support. 3, (*Colloq.*) resemble in facial aspect. Also, **fa'vour.** —**fa'vored,** *adj.* 1, blessed. 2, appearing.

Faun (Rubens)

fa'vor·a·ble (-ə-bəl) *adj.* 1, inclined to approve; affirmative. 2, advantageous. —**fa'vor·a·ble·ness,** *n.*

fa'vor·ite (fā'vər-it) *adj.* preferred. —*n.* 1, a person or thing preferred or popular. 2, a contestant deemed most likely to win. —**fa'vor·it·ism,** *n.* partiality.

fawn (fân) *v.i.* show affection as a dog, by hand-licking, etc.; hence, cringe and flatter. —*n.* 1, a young deer. 2, a very light tan color.

fay (fā) *n.* an elf; fairy.

faze (fāz) *v.t.* (*Colloq.*) ruffle; daunt.

fe'al·ty (fē'əl-tē) *n.* fidelity, esp. to a lord.

fear (fir) *n.* 1, anticipation of misfortune or pain; the state of being afraid. 2, something dreaded. 3, anxiety. 4, reverent awe, as of God. —*v.t. & i.* feel fear (of).

fear'ful (-fəl) *adj.* 1, timid; apprehensive. 2, fearsome. —**fear'ful·ness,** *n.*

fear'less (-ləs) *adj.* feeling no fear. —**fear'less·ness,** *n.*

fear'some (-səm) *adj.* causing fear; terrible. —**fear'some·ness,** *n.*

fea'si·ble (fē'zə-bəl) *adj.* 1, possible of realization. 2, suitable. —**fea'si·bil'i·ty,** *n.*

feast (fēst) *n.* 1, a sumptuous meal. 2, festival, esp. religious. —*v.t.* 1, entertain with a feast. 2, gratify; delight. —*v.i.* 1, have a feast. 2, dwell with delight.

feat (fēt) *n.* an act of remarkable skill or valor.

feath'er (feth'ər) *n.* 1, one of the light outgrowths from a bird's skin. 2, (*pl.*) plumage; hence, attire. 3, something light. —*v.t. & i.* 1, grow, or provide with, feathers. 2, turn (an oar) almost to a horizontal position. —**feath'er·y,** *adj.*

feath'er·weight" *n.* a boxer of 118 to 126 pounds.

fea'ture (fē'chər) *n.* 1, any part of the face; (*pl.*) facial appearance. 2, a distinctive or prominent characteristic. 3, an item of unusual interest or attraction; an article in a magazine, newspaper, etc. 4, a motion picture of full length; the main motion picture shown in a theater. —*v.t.* give prominence to.

feb'ri·fuge" (feb'ri-fūj") *n.* a medicine to combat fever.

fe'brile (fē'brəl) *adj.* feverish.

Feb'ru·ar·y (feb'roo-er-ē) *n.* the second month of the year.

fe'cal (fē'kəl) *adj.* pert. to feces.

fe'ces (fē'sēz) *n.pl.* excrement.

fec'u·lent (fek'yə-lənt) *adj.* muddy; foul. —**fec'u·lence,** *n.*

fe'cund (fē'kund) *adj.* prolific; fertile. —**fe·cund'i·ty** (fi-kun'də-tē) *n.*

fed *v.* pret. & p.p. of *feed.*

fed'er·al (fed'ər-əl) *adj.* pert. to a nation formed by the union of several sovereign states, esp. to the government of the U. S.

fed'er·al·ism (fed'ər-ə-liz-əm) *n.* the doctrine or practice of federal government; advocacy of a strong federal government. —**fed'er·al·ist,** *n.*

fed'er·ate" (fed'ə-rāt") *v.t. & i.* join (states, clubs, etc.) in a union.

fed'er·a'tion (fed"ə-rā'shən) *n.* 1, act of uniting or being united. 2, league; confederacy. —**fed'er·a"tive** *adj.*

fe·do'ra (fə-dôr'ə) *n.* a man's soft felt hat.

fee (fē) *n.* 1, a charge for services, privileges, etc. 2, a tip. 3, land held under a feudal overlord. —*v.t.* give a fee to. —**fee simple,** absolute ownership.

fee'ble (fē'bəl) *adj.* 1, lacking energy or power; very weak; infirm. 2, showing weakness; halfhearted; ineffective. —**fee'ble·ness,** *n.*

feed (fēd) *v.t. & i.* [*pret. & p.p.* fed] 1, give food to. 2, supply what is needed for the growth, operation, or maintenance of. 3, satisfy; gratify. —*v.i.* take food; eat. —*n.* 1, food, esp. for cattle, etc.; fodder. 2, (*Colloq.*) a meal. 3, a feeding mechanism. —**feed'bag",** *n.* a bag from which a horse feeds.

feel (fēl) *v.t.* [*pret. & p.p.* felt] 1, perceive by the sense of touch; examine by touching. 2, have a sensation of; be conscious of being, as warm, happy, etc. 3, know intuitively; infer. 4, suffer the consequences of. 5, explore by touch; find (one's way) cautiously by any means. —*v.i.* 1, have a sensation of any kind; perceive oneself to be (in a certain condition, as ill). 2, touch something to feel it; grope. 3, be capable of, or experience, emotion. 4, seem to the touch.

feel'er (fē'lər) *n.* **1,** the organ of touch of certain insects and animals. **2,** a remark advanced to find out the views of others.

feel'ing (fē'ling) *n.* **1,** the sense of touch. **2,** sensation of any kind. **3,** emotion; the capacity to feel emotion. **4,** an unreasoned conviction. —**feel'ing·ly,** *adv.* **1,** emotionally. **2,** sympathetically.

feet (fēt) *n.* pl. of *foot*.

feign (fān) *v.i. & t.* pretend.

feint (fānt) *n.* an apparent aiming at one point when another is the real object of attack.

feld'spar' (feld'spär") *n.* a mineral found in many common rocks, used in making porcelain.

fe·lic'i·tate' (fi-lis'ə-tāt") *v.t.* express happy sympathy with; congratulate. —**fe·lic'i·ta'tion,** *n.*

fe·lic'i·tous (fi-lis'ə-təs) *adj.* well-chosen; apt. —**fe·lic'i·tous·ness,** *n.*

fe·lic'i·ty (fi-lis'ə-tē) *n.* **1,** happiness; a source of happiness. **2,** aptness; grace.

fe'line (fē'līn) *n.* an animal of the cat family. —*adj.* of the cat family; catlike; sly.

fell (fel) *v.t.* strike down by a blow or cut. —*adj.* ruthless; terrible. —*v.i.* pret. of *fall.*

fel'loe (fel'ō) *n.* the rim of a wheel when extended by spokes from a hub. Also, **fel'ly** (-ē).

fel'low (fel'ō) *n.* **1,** a comrade. **2,** one of a pair; a mate; an equal. **3,** (*Colloq.*) a person, esp. male. **4,** a member of a learned society. **5,** a graduate student on a fellowship. —*adj.* in the same class, occupation, or condition.

fel'low·ship (fel'ə-ship) *n.* **1,** a body of fellows or associates. **2,** companionship; community of interests. **3,** a grant of money for further study.

fel'on (fel'ən) *n.* **1,** a person convicted of a felony; a criminal. **2,** an acute inflammation near the fingernail or toenail.

fel'o·ny (fel'ə-nē) *n.* a major crime. —**fe·lo'ni·ous** (fə-lō'nē-əs) *adj.*

felt *n.* a pressed fabric made of wool, hair, or fur. —*v.* pret. & p.p. of *feel.*

fe'male (fē'māl) *adj.* **1,** of the sex bearing young or yielding offspring. **2,** feminine. **3,** (*Mech.*) concave for the reception of a fitting part. —*n.* a female person, animal, or thing.

fem'i·nine (fem'ə-nin) *adj.* **1,** relating to, or like, woman. **2,** (*Gram.*) of the gender to which words applying to women belong. —**fem'i·nin'i·ty** (-ə-tē) *n.* **1,** womanliness. **2,** females collectively.

fem'i·nism (fem'ə-niz-əm) *n.* advocacy of increased political activity or rights for women. —**fem'i·nist,** *n.*

fe'mur (fē'mər) *n.* the thigh bone. —**fem'o·ral** (fem'ə-rəl) *adj.*

fen *n.* low, marshy ground.

fence (fens) *n.* **1,** an enclosing barrier. **2,** (*Slang*) a receiver of stolen goods. —*v.t.* (usually with *in*) surround with a fence. —*v.i.* **1,** use a sword or foil for sport or in self-defense. **2,** parry; evade. —**fenc'er,** *n.* one skilled in swordplay. —**fenc'ing,** *n.* **1,** swordplay, esp. for sport. **2,** fences collectively.

fend *v.t.* ward off. —*v.i.* make shift: *fend for oneself.*

fend'er (fen'dər) *n.* a protective guard, as on an automobile or before a fireplace.

fe·nes'tra (fi-nes'trə) *n.* a window-like opening.

fen"es·tra'tion (fen'ə-strā'shən) *n.* windows, their number and location.

fen'nel (fen'əl) *n.* an aromatic herb, used in cookery.

fe'ral (fir'əl) *adj.* wild; untamed; hence, savage.

fer-de-lance' (fer-də-läns') *n.* a venomous snake.

fer'ment (fér'ment) *n.* **1,** a substance that causes fermentation. **2,** commotion. —*v.t. & i.* (fər-ment') **1,** cause or undergo fermentation (in). **2,** excite; arouse; seethe.

fer"men·ta'tion (fér"mən-tā'-shən) *n.* **1,** the chemical change produced in a substance by the action of organisms, as when milk sours. **2,** unrest; agitation.

fern (férn) *n.* any of a large group of flowerless plants that propagate from spores.

fe·ro'cious (fə-rō'shəs) *adj.* very fierce; savage.

fe·roc'i·ty (fə-ros'ə-tē) *n.* cruel fierceness.

fer'ret (fer'it) *n.* a slim, lithe animal used to hunt rabbits and rats. —*v.t.* drive out of a hiding place; search out, as a criminal or a secret.

Ferret

fer'ri-, fer'ro- *pref.* iron.

Fer'ris wheel (fer'is) an amusement-park attraction, a large upright rotating wheel with seats for passengers.

fer'rous (fer'əs) *adj.* containing or derived from iron.

fer'rule (fer'ool) *n.* a metal ring or cap for strengthening a tool handle, end of a cane, etc.

fer'ry (fer'ē) n. 1, provision for conveying passengers or goods across water. 2, the boat or raft so used: ferryboat. —v.t. transport on a ferry.

fer'tile (fėr'təl) adj. 1, producing crops, offspring, etc. abundantly; fruitful; prolific. 2, capable of reproducing or developing. —fer.til'i.ty (fėr-til'ə-tē) n.

fer'ti.lize (fėr'tə-līz") v.t. make productive, as by impregnating (an egg, etc.) or enriching (the soil). —fer"ti.li.za'tion (-li-zā'shən) n. —fer'ti.liz"er, n. a substance that enriches the soil, as manure.

fer'ule (fer'əl) n. 1, a ruler for punishing children. 2, (-ool) ferrule.

fer'vent (fėr'vənt) adj. 1, earnest; ardent. 2, hot; glowing. —fer'ven.cy, n.

fer'vid (fėr'vid) adj. glowing with enthusiasm; vehement. —fer'vid.ness, n.

fer'vor (fėr'vər) n. 1, ardent feeling; zeal. 2, intense heat. Also, fer'vour.

fes'cue (fes'kū) n. a grass much used for pasture or lawns.

fes'tal (fes'təl) adj. pert. to a feast; gala.

fes'ter (fes'tər) v.t. 1, become filled with pus; suppurate. 2, rankle.

fes'ti.val (fes'tə-vəl) n. 1, a feast or celebration, religious or anniversary. 2, a gathering for entertainment or rejoicing.

fes'tive (fes'tiv) adj. pert. to a feast or festival; joyous; gay. —fes'tive.ness, n.

fes.tiv'i.ty (fes-tiv'ə-tē) n. 1, gaiety; rejoicing. 2, (pl.) festive observances or activities.

fes.toon' n. a rope of flowers, ribbons, etc., hung in a loop. —v.t. hang with festoons; decorate.

fe'tal (fē'təl) adj. pert. to a fetus.

fetch (fech) v.t. & i. 1, go after and bring back. 2, sell for. —fetch'ing, adj. (Colloq.) alluring; attractive.

fete (fāt) n. a festival. —v.t. entertain in honor of.

fet'id adj. having an offensive stench. —fet'id.ness, n.

fet'ish n. 1, an object supposed to embody a spirit. 2, an object of abnormal love or passion. —fet'ish.ism, n. —fet'ish.ist, n.

fet'lock (fet'lok) n. a projection above and behind a horse's hoof; a tuft of hair at this point.

fet'ter (fet'ər) n. 1, a shackle. 2, a check; restraint. —v.t. confine in fetters; restrain.

fet'ter.bush" (fet'ər-bûsh") n. an evergreen shrub.

fet'tle (fet'əl) n. state of health or spirits; condition.

fe'tus (fē'təs) n. the unborn young of an animal.

feud (fūd) n. a long-standing strife between clans or families; a quarrel. —v.i. quarrel. —feud'ist, n.

feu'dal (fū'dəl) adj. 1, pert. to the system whereby a vassal held land in fief from a lord to whom he owed allegiance and certain services. 2, pert. to the period of the feudal system, the Middle Ages. —feu'dal.ism, n. practice or advocacy of the feudal system or a similar modern system.

fe'ver (fē'vər) n. 1, a body temperature higher than normal; in humans, more than 98.6° F. 2, a disease marked by weakness and high temperature. 3, intense agitation.

fe'ver.few" (fē'vər-fū") n. a perennial garden herb.

fe'ver.ish (fē'vər-ish) adj. 1, having a fever. 2, impatient; excited. —fe'ver.ish.ness, n.

few (fū) adj. not many.

fez n. a tasseled red cap formerly worn by Turks.

fi"an.cé' (fē"än-sā') n. a man engaged to be married. —fi"an.cée', n.fem.

fi.as'co (fē-as'kō) n. [pl. -cos] an ignominious failure.

fi'at (fī'ət) n. a decree or sanction.

fib n. a trivial lie. —v.i. [fibbed, fib'bing] tell a fib.

fi'ber (fī'bər) n. 1, one of the fine threadlike parts forming plant and animal tissue. 2, a substance made of these parts, esp. when capable of being spun or woven. 3, quality; character. Also, fi'bre. —fi'brous, adj. —fi'ber.board", n. a building material of compressed wood fiber.

fib'u.la (fib'ū-lə) n. the thinner of the two bones of the lower leg.

fich'u (fish'oo) n. a triangular scarf of lace, muslin, etc.

fick'le (fik'əl) adj. inconstant; changeable. —fick'le.ness, n.

fic'tion (fik'shən) n. 1, literature in which the plot and the characters are imaginary. 2, a statement contrary to fact. —fic'tion.al, adj.

fic.ti'tious (fik-tish'əs) adj. 1. imaginary. 2, feigned. 3, false. —ficti'tious.ness, n.

fid'dle (fid'əl) n. a violin. —v.i. 1, (Colloq.) play on the violin. 2, move the hands and fingers idly; trifle. —fid'dler, n. —fiddler crab, a small crab, one of whose claws is disproportionately large.

fid'dle.sticks" (fid'əl-stiks") interj. nonsense!

fid'dling (fid'ling) *adj.* (*Colloq.*) trivial; ineffectual.

fi·del'i·ty (fi-del'ə-tē) *n.* 1, faithfulness; loyalty. 2, accuracy; exactness.

fidg'et (fij'it) *v.i.* 1, make restless or uneasy movements; squirm. —*n.* (*pl.*) a restless mood. —**fidg'et·y,** *adj.*

fi·du'ci·ar·y (fi-doo'shē-er-ē) *adj.* pert. to a trust. —*n.* a trustee.

fie (fī) *interj.* for shame!

fief (fēf) *n.* an estate held under feudal law.

field (fēld) *n.* 1, a tract of cleared land for cultivation, pasture, etc.; an area considered in relation to a specific use, as sports, hunting. 2, a wide expanse; an unimpeded course. 3, a sphere of activity; a class of enterprise, interest, study, etc.; a business. 4, a battlefield; a battle; warfare. 5, a background, as of a photograph; a visible area; scope. 6, a group considered as one for betting purposes; several unfavored horses in a race; several improbable numbers at dice; etc. —*v.t.* 1, put a team into competition. 2, catch and return (a ball). —**field day,** an outing, esp. one devoted to athletic games. —**field glass,** binoculars. —**field marshal,** a high- or the highest-ranking military officer. —**field of honor,** the scene of a duel or battle. —**field rank** (*Mil.*) the rank of major to colonel (**field officer**).

field'er (-ər) *n.* (*Baseball*) 1, a player whose side is not at bat. 2, an outfielder.

field'piece" *n.* a cannon.

fiend (fēnd) *n.* 1, a devil; a demon; a diabolically cruel person. 2, (*Colloq.*) an addict of some practice, sport, etc. —**fiend'ish,** *adj.* cruel.

fierce (fīrs) *adj.* 1, eager to kill or injure; savage; ferocious. 2, violent; raging; intense. —**fierce'ness,** *n.*

fi'er·y (fīr'ē) *adj.* 1, glowing, etc., like fire; burning; hot. 2, passionate; spirited. —**fi'er·i·ness,** *n.*

fi·es'ta (fē-es'tə) *n.* (*Span.*) a holiday or festival, esp. religious.

fife (fīf) *n.* a shrill musical instrument like a flute.

fif"teen' (fif'tēn') *n. & adj.* the cardinal number between fourteen and sixteen, expressed by 15. —**fif"teenth'** (-tēnth') *n. & adj.* the ordinal of this number; 15th. —*n.* one of 15 equal parts.

fifth *n. & adj.* the ordinal of five, also written 5th. —*n.* 1, one of 5 equal parts. 2, a measure of liquor, one-fifth gallon. —**fifth column,** a body of citizens who serve enemy interests. —**take the fifth,** refuse to testify or to answer a question, by invoking the Fifth Amendment, under which one cannot be required to testify against himself.

fif'ty (fif'tē) *n. & adj.* the cardinal number between forty-nine and fifty-one, expressed by 50. —**fif'tieth,** *n. & adj.* the ordinal of this number; also written 50th. —*n.* one of 50 equal parts.

fig *n.* a tropical tree; its pulpy, pear-shaped fruit.

fight (fīt) *v.i.* [*pret. & p.p.* **fought** (fât)] 1, engage in combat. 2, strive; contend. —*v.t.* 1, war against. 2, contend with. —*n.* 1, a battle or contest. 2, willingness to fight.

fight'er (-ər) *n.* 1, one who fights. 2, a warplane designed to fight enemy planes.

fig'ment (fig'mənt) *n.* something feigned or imagined; a pure invention.

fig'ur·a·tive (fig'yər-ə-tiv) *adj.* 1, symbolical; not literal. 2, full of figures of speech; flowery. —**fig'ur·a·tive·ness,** *n.*

fig'ure (fig'yər) *n.* 1, form; shape; outline. 2, a likeness of a form, as in art. 3, the bodily form. 4, an outline traced by a skater; a movement of a dance; the pattern of a fabric; a design, esp. an ornate one. 5, a rhetorical symbol: a *figure of speech.* 6, a personage. 7, a numerical symbol; (*pl.*) mathematics; computation. 8, price. —*v.t.* 1, (often with *out*) calculate; indicate by numbers. 2, form; shape; portray, esp. in sculpture; see in imagination. 3, ornament with a design. —*v.i.* 1, take prominent part. 2, (*Colloq.*) calculate; deduce.

fig'ure·head" (fig'yər-hed") *n.* 1, an ornamental figure on a ship's bow. 2, a person of nominal but no real authority.

fil'a·ment (fil'ə-mənt) *n.* 1, a fine threadlike fiber, as of a cobweb, wire, etc. 2, the slender stalk bearing an anther in a flower.

fi'lar (fī'lər) *adj.* threadlike.

fil'bert (fil'bərt) *n.* the edible nut of the hazel; a hazelnut.

filch *v.t.* steal; pilfer.

file (fīl) *n.* 1, a folder, case, or device for keeping papers in order; the papers so kept. 2, a row of persons, esp. soldiers, one behind the other. 3, a metal tool with a ridged surface for smoothing or cutting metal, wood, etc. —*v.t.* 1, put (papers) in a file; record officially. 2, smooth or cut with a file. —*v.i.* march in file.

fi·let' mi"gnon' (fi-lā' mē"nyon') (*Fr.*) a tenderloin of beefsteak.

fil'i·al (fil'ē-əl) *adj.* pert. to or appropriate to a son or daughter.

fil'i·bus"ter (fil'ə-bus"tər) *n.* 1, the tactics, in the U.S. Senate, of prolonged speaking to prevent or delay legislation. 2, a freebooter. —*v.i.* 1, speak in a filibuster. 2, act like or be a freebooter.

---

tub, cūte, pûll; label; oil, owl; go, chip, she, thin, *then,* sing, ink; *see p. 6*

fil'i·gree (fĭl'ə-grē") *n. & adj.* ornamental openwork of fine wire.

fil'ing (fī'lĭng) *n.* (usually *pl.*) a scrap filed off a larger piece. —**fil'ing cabinet**, a set of drawers for holding filed papers.

Filigree

fill (fĭl) *v.t.* **1**, occupy the entire capacity of. **2**, make full; be perceptible throughout; pervade. **3**, occupy (a position); perform the duties of. **4**, secure an occupant or incumbent for (a job, etc.). **5**, put an appropriate substance into (a cavity, hole, crack, etc.); stop up. **6**, feed to satiation. **7**, carry out (an order). —*v.i.* take in a filling quantity. —*n.* **1**, enough to satisfy. **2**, a filling. —**fill'er**, *n.* material used for filling, esp. the inside tobacco of a cigar, a base paint to fill cracks, etc. —**fill'ing**, *n.* that which is used to fill, esp. to fill a cavity in a tooth, or the crust of a pie.

fil'let (fĭl'et) **1**, a narrow band for the hair. **2**, a thin, narrow strip, as a molding. **3**, [also, **fi·let'** (fĭ-lā')] a boneless piece of meat or fish.

fil'lip (fĭl'əp) *n.* **1**, a snap of the fingers. **2**, a stimulus; incentive.

fil'ly (fĭl'ė) *n.* a young mare.

film *n.* **1**, a very thin layer, as of oil, coating the surface of something. **2**, a cellulose sheet, coated for photography; the developed negative of a picture. **3**, a mist; haze. **4**, a thin membrane. **5**, a motion picture. —*v.t.* photograph. —**film'y**, *adj.*

fil'ter (fĭl'tər) *n.* **1**, any porous material for trapping solids from a fluid. **2**, any similar device, as for separating light rays. —*v.t. & i.* pass through a filter.

filth *n.* **1**, foul matter; a dirty condition. **2**, corruption; obscene matter. —**filth'i·ness**, *n.* —**filth'y**, *adj.*

fil'trate (fĭl'trāt) *v.t. & i.* filter. —*n.* filtered liquid. —**fil·tra'tion**, *n.*

fin *n.* a membranous winglike projection from the body of a fish; anything resembling it. —**finned**, *adj.* **fin'ny**, *adj.*

fi·na'gle (fĭ-nā'gəl) *v.t. & i.* obtain or contrive unscrupulously.

fi'nal (fī'nəl) *adj.* **1**, last; ultimate. **2**, decisive. —*n.* (*pl.*) **1**, a deciding contest. **2**, the last college examinations. —**fi'nal·ist**, *n.* one competing in the deciding match.

fi·na'le (fĭ-nä'lė) *n.* a closing scene, esp. of a musical performance.

fi·nance' (fĭ-nans'; fī'-) *n.* **1**, management of monetary affairs, esp.

in banking and government. **2**, bankers, capitalists, and investors collectively. **3**, (*pl.*) monetary resources or revenue. —*v.t.* supply with money. —**fi·nan'cial** (-shəl) *adj.*

fin"an·cier' (fĭn"ən-sir') *n.* a capitalist or banker.

finch *n.* any of various small songbirds, as the sparrow.

find (fīnd) *v.t.* [*pret. & p.p.* **found**] **1**, locate by searching; come across by chance; discover. **2**, arrive at (a result, etc.); conclude; (*Law*) declare. —*n.* a valuable discovery. —**find'er**, *n.* one who or that which finds, esp. a device for locating a view for photographing. —**find'ing**, *n.* **1**, a decision or verdict. **2**, (*pl.*) small accessories or materials.

fine (fīn) *adj.* **1**, pure, as unalloyed gold; superior in quality, texture, etc. **2**, delicate, not coarse; of small diameter; ground into very small particles; very thin or keen, as a blade. **3**, discriminating. **4**, elegant; handsome. —*n.* a money penalty for a breach of law. —*v.t.* punish by a fine. —**fine arts**, painting, engraving, architecture, and sculpture. —**fine'ness**, *n.* the degree of purity, thinness, etc.

fin'er·y (fī'nə-rė) *n.* showy clothes and jewelry.

fi·nesse' (fĭ-nes') *n.* **1**, delicate skill. **2**, cunning; artful management. **3**, in card games, a play to trap an opponent's card.

fin'ger (fĭng'gər) *n.* **1**, one of the five terminal members of the hand, esp. one other than the thumb. **2**, anything like or operating like a finger. —*v.t.* touch; handle. —**fin'ger·ing**, *n.* (*Music*) the action or use of the fingers in playing.

fin'ger·ling (fĭng'gər-lĭng) *n.* a finger-length fish.

fin'ger·nail" *n.* the horny cap at the end of the finger.

fin'ger·print" *n.* an impression of the lines on the tips of the fingers, used for identification.

fin'i·al (fĭn'ė-əl) *n.* the ornamental tip of a spire, cap on a shaft, etc.

fin'i·cal (fĭn'ə-kəl) *adj.* unduly particular or fussy. Also, **fin'ick·ing**, **fin'ick·y**.

fi'nis (fĭ'nĭs) *n.* the end.

fin'ish *v.t.* **1**, bring to an end; terminate. **2**, use up. **3**, complete; perfect. **4**, paint; polish. —*n.* **1**, the end. **2**, the final work done upon an object. **3**, the way in which something is finished, as furniture. **4**, social polish; poise. —**fin'ished**, *adj.* **1**, completed; perfected; polished. **2**, highly accomplished. —**finishing school**, a private secondary school for girls.

fi'nite (fī'nīt) *adj.* having limits; restricted. —**fi'nite·ness**, *n.*

fink *n.* (*Slang*) a strikebreaker.

fin'nan had'die (fin'ən had'ē) *n.* smoked haddock.

fiord (fyôrd) *n.* a narrow arm of the sea between high cliffs. Also, **fjord**.

fir (fėr) *n.* an evergreen, cone-bearing tree or its wood.

fire (fīr) *n.* 1, the heat and light caused by burning. 2, a burning of fuel; a conflagration, as of a building, forest, etc. 3, a discharge of firearms. 4, ardor; zeal; brilliancy. —*v.t.* 1, set ablaze. 2, subject to great heat. 3, animate; inspire. 4, discharge, as a gun. 5, (*Colloq.*) dismiss from a job.

Fir

fire'arm" *n.* a weapon that propels a missile by an explosive.

fire'box" *n.* the fuel chamber of a furnace or locomotive.

fire'brand" *n.* 1, a piece of burning wood. 2, one who stirs up strife.

fire'bug" *n.* one who intentionally starts destructive fires.

fire'crack"er *n.* a small explosive-filled tube, set off to make a noise.

fire'damp" *n.* a combustible gas occurring in coal mines.

fire'dog" *n.* an andiron.

fire engine a motor vehicle equipped to combat fires.

fire'fly" *n.* a small beetle that emits light.

fire'man (-mən) *n.* [*pl.* -men] 1 one employed to prevent or extinguish fires. 2, one who tends a fire as in a boiler; a stoker.

fire'place" *n.* a recess lined with bricks or stones in which a fire is built for cooking or warmth.

fire'proof" *adj.* made of fire-resisting material.

fire'side" *n.* the hearth; home.

fire'trap" *n.* a building likely to be dangerous in case of fire.

fire'wa"ter *n.* (*Colloq.*) strong liquor.

fire'works" *n.pl.* explosives set off to produce noise or display.

fir'kin (fėr'kin) *n.* a small cask.

firm (fėrm) *adj.* 1, not easy to shake, move, press in, puncture, etc.; steady; rigid; compact; solid; tough. 2, stanch; loyal. 3, positive; unalterable. —*n.* a business partnership; a company. —**firm'ness,** *n.*

fir'ma·ment (fėr'mə-mənt) *n.* the visible sky; the heavens.

first (fėrst) *adj.* 1, foremost in time, place, importance, etc. 2, the ordinal of one. —*adv.* before all others in place, time, rank, etc. —*n.* a person or thing that is first. —**first aid,** emergency treatment of the injured. —**first lieutenant,** an army officer ranking below a captain and above a second lieutenant. —**first person** (*Gram.*) the relation between a verb and its subject, so called when the subject is the speaker.

first'class" *adj.* of best quality.

first'hand" *adj.* direct, not by hearsay.

first'rate" *adj.* of best quality; excellent. —*adv.* (*Colloq.*) very well.

firth (fėrth) *n.* an arm of the sea.

fis'cal (fis'kəl) *adj.* pert. to financial matters, esp. governmental.

fish *n.* [*pl.* **fishes** or **fish**] 1, a completely aquatic vertebrate, usually with scales and fins. 2, (*Slang*) a dupe. —*v.i. & t.* 1, try to catch fish. 2, search for anything hidden. 3, seek to get indirectly; draw out.

fish'er·man (-ėr-mən) *n.* [*pl.* **-men**] a person or vessel engaged in fishing.

fish'er·y (-ə-rē) *n.* 1, the business of fishing. 2, a fishing ground.

fish'hook" *n.* a hook used in catching fish.

fish'wife" *n.* a scurrilous woman.

fish'y (-ē) *adj.* 1, like fish in appearance, smell, etc. 2, improbable; questionable. 3, expressionless. —**fish'i·ness,** *n.*

fis'sion (fish'ən) *n.* a splitting into parts. —**fis'sion·a·ble,** *adj.* (of a chemical element) composed of atoms that will split.

fis'sure (fish'ər) *n.* a crack or cleft.

fist *n.* the hand clenched. —**fist'-fight",** *n.* a fight with the fists.

fist'ic (-ik) *adj.* pert. to boxing.

fist'i·cuffs" (-i-kufs") *n.pl.* a fight with the fists.

fis'tu·la (fis'chu-lə) *n.* an ulcerous passage from an abscess or an internal organ to the surface.

fit *adj.* [**fit'ter,** **-test**] 1, proper; suitable. 2, ready; prepared; in top condition. —*v.t.* [**fit'ted,** **-ting**] 1, adapt. 2, equip; supply. —*v.i.* 1, be meet or proper. 2, be of the right shape, size, etc. —*n.* 1, something that is suitable. 2, a convulsion; a sudden attack, as of epilepsy. 3, an outburst, as of emotion, energy, etc. —**fit'ness,** *n.*

fit'ful (fit'fəl) *adj.* capricious; intermittent. —**fit'ful·ness,** *n.*

fit'ter (-ər) *n.* one who fits clothes on others.

fit'ting (-ing) *adj.* suitable; proper. —*n.* 1, act of fitting. 2, (*pl.*) furnishings.

five (fīv) *n. & adj.* the cardinal number between four and six, expressed by 5.

fix (fiks) *v.t.* 1, fasten firmly. 2, settle definitely; establish (a time or place). 3, make fast or permanent, as dye. 4, arrange; repair. 5, (*Slang*) bribe. —*n.* (*Colloq.*) a predicament. —**fix'ings,** *n.pl.* (*Colloq.*) trimmings.

fix·a'tion (fik-sā'shən) *n.* 1, the state of being fixed. 2, an obsession. 3, a premature cessation of emotional development.

fix'ture (fiks'chər) *n.* 1, an article of furniture attached to the room. 2, a person or thing that cannot be removed.

fizz (fiz) *v.i.* make a hissing sound; effervesce. —*n.* such a sound.

fiz'zle (fiz'əl) *v.i.* 1, make a hissing sound. 2, (*Colloq.*) peter out; fail. —*n.* act or effect of fizzling.

fjord (fyôrd) *n.* fiord.

flab'ber·gast (flab'ər-gast') *v.t.* (*Colloq.*) confound; astonish.

flab'by (flab'ē) *adj.* 1, lacking firmness; jellylike. 2, feeble. —**flab'-bi·ness,** *n.*

flac'cid (flak'sid) *adj.* soft; flabby. —**flac·cid'i·ty** (-sid'ə-tē), **flac'cid-ness,** *n.*

fla·con' (flȧ-kän') *n.* a small flask.

flag *n.* 1, a piece of cloth bearing a design for display as a signal, standard, etc. 2, an iris. —*v.t.* [flagged, flag'ging] 1, signal to with or as with a flag. 2, pave with flagstones. —*v.i.* droop; grow languid. —**flag officer,** a naval officer of rank of commodore or higher.

flag'el·late (flaj'ə-lāt') *v.t.* whip. **flag'el·lant,** *n.* —**flag''el·la'tion,** *n.*

flag'eo·let' (flaj'ə-let') *n.* a woodwind instrument.

fla·gi'tious (flə-jish'əs) *adj.* grossly wicked. —**fla·gi'tious·ness,** *n.*

flag'on (flag'ən) *n.* a covered pitcher for liquors.

flag'pole'' *n.* a pole on which a flag is hung.

fla'grant (flā'grənt) *adj.* overtly outrageous. —**fla'gran·cy,** *n.*

flag'ship'' *n.* the ship of the officer commanding a fleet.

flag'staff'' *n.* a staff by which a flag is hung or supported.

flag'stone'' *n.* a flat paving stone.

flail (flāl) *n.* a hand tool for threshing grain. —*v.t. & i.* 1, use a flail (on). 2, whip; beat.

flair (flâr) *n.* 1, discriminating taste. 2, a liking; bent.

flak *n.* antiaircraft fire.

flake (flāk) *n.* a small flat, scale-like particle. —*v.t. & i.* break or separate into flakes. —**flak'y,** *adj.*

flam'beau (flam'bō) *n.* 1, a flaming torch. 2, a large candlestick.

flam·boy'ant (flam-boi'ənt) *adj.* showy; ornate; gorgeous; florid. —**flam·boy'ance,** *n.*

flame (flām) *n.* 1, burning gas or vapor; the luminous, quivering tongue it makes; (*pl.*) a state of combustion. 2, burning zeal; ardor. 3, (*Slang*) a sweetheart. —*v.i.* 1, burn; shine. 2, break out like flame, in anger or passion. —**flam'ing,** *adj.* 1, fiery. 2, passionate; violent.

fla·min'go (flə-ming'gō) *n.* [*pl.* -gos] a long-legged tropical bird with scarlet plumage.

flange (flanj) *n.* a projecting rim.

flank *n.* 1, an animal's side between ribs and hip. 2, the side of anything. 3, (*Mil.*) the extreme right or left of an army or fleet. —*v.t.* 1, stand at the flank. 2, go around, or turn, the flank of.

Flamingo

flan'nel (flan'əl) *n.* 1, a soft woolen fabric. 2, (*pl.*) men's trousers made of flannel. 3, (*pl.*) woolen undergarments. —**flannel cake,** a pancake.

flan''nel·et' (flan'ə-let') *n.* a cotton fabric, used for wearing apparel. Also, **flan''nel·ette'.**

flap *n.* 1, anything broad, flat, and usually flexible, hanging loose. 2, the motion or noise of a swinging flap or wing. 3, a slap. —*v.t.* [flapped, flap'ping] swing as a flap; beat (wings, etc.) up and down. —*v.i.* swing to and fro; flap wings.

flap'jack'' *n.* a large pancake.

flap'per (-ər) *n.* 1, a flap. 2, a young duck or bird. 3, (*Colloq.*) a brash teen-age girl.

flare (flâr) *n.* 1, a glaring, wavering light. 2, a blazing light used as a signal. 3, an outburst, as of temper. 4, a spreading outward, as of a skirt. —*v.i.* be or form a flare. —**flare-'up'',** *n.* a burst of anger or flame.

flash *n.* 1, a sudden transitory burst of light or flame; an instantaneous outburst or sensation, as of wit, understanding, etc. 2, a glimpse. 3, an instant; a moment. 4, (*Colloq.*) ostentation. 5, a brief bulletin by telegraph. —*v.i.* blaze momentarily. be temporarily visible, brilliant, notable, etc. —*v.t.* send forth suddenly, esp. a signal or bulletin;

flash'back" *n.* a scene or event from the past, in a novel or motion picture.

flash'ing *n.* pieces of metal for waterproofing roofing joints.

flash'light" *n.* **1,** a small portable electric torch. **2,** a brilliant instantaneous light for taking pictures; a picture so taken.

flash'y (-ē) *adj.* showy; gaudy; momentarily brilliant.—**flash'i·ness,** *n.*

flask (flåsk) *n.* a narrow-necked glass or metal container.

flat *adj.* [**flat'ter, -test**] **1,** horizontally level and relatively smooth. **2,** spread out, lying, or fallen on a level surface; lying down. **3,** without qualification; positive; exact. **4,** defeated; (*Slang*) penniless. **5,** dull; stale; insipid. **6,** (*Music*) below the true pitch.—*adv.* in a flat manner.—*n.* **1,** a plain; a shoal. **2,** the flat part of anything. **3,** (*Slang*) a deflated tire. **4,** (*Music*) a note, marked (♭), lowered a half tone in pitch. **5,** an apartment.—*v.t.* & *i.* [**flat'ted, -ting**] lower (the pitch).—**flat'ness,** *n.*

flat'boat" *n.* a large flat-bottomed boat for transporting goods.

flat'car" *n.* a roofless, sideless freight car.

flat'fish" *n.* a broad, flat fish with both eyes on the upper side.

flat'foot" *n.* [*pl.* **-feet"**] **1,** a deformity of the foot due to fallen arches. **2,** (*Slang*) a policeman.—**flat'foot"ed,** *adj.*

flat'i"ron *n.* an iron for pressing clothes.

flat'ten (-ən) *v.t.* **1,** make flat. **2,** knock down.—*v.i.* become flat or level.

flat'ter (flat'ər) *v.t.* **1,** seek to gratify by undue praise. **2,** portray too favorably.—**flat'ter·y,** *n.* adulation.

flat'top" *n.* an aircraft carrier.

flat'u·lent (flach'ə-lənt) *adj.* **1,** producing or having gas in the stomach. **2,** pretentious.—**flat'u·lence,** *n.*

flat'ware" *n.* **1,** table dishes that are flat, as plates. **2,** silver table utensils.

flaunt (flånt) *v.t.* & *i.* parade impudently; make a gaudy display (of).

fla'vor (flā'vər) *n.* **1,** that quality which affects the taste; usually, the quality of appealing to the taste. **2,** a substance that imparts a distinctive taste. **3,** an interesting or distinctive quality in anything.—*v.t.* give flavor to. Also, **fla'vour.**—**fla'vor·ing,** *n.* a substance that flavors.

flaw (flå) *n.* a defect; imperfection.—**flaw'less,** *adj.* without a flaw; perfect.

flax (flaks) *n.* a blue-flowered plant grown for its fiber, used for making linen, and its seeds, for linseed oil.—**flax'seed",** *n.*

flax'en (flak'sən) *adj.* **1,** made of flax. **2,** of a light yellow color, as hair.

flay (flā) *v.t.* **1,** strip the skin from; **2,** censure severely.

flea (flē) *n.* a small, leaping, blood-sucking insect.—**flea'bite",** *n.* an inconsequential injury.

fleck (flek) *n.* a speck or small spot.—*v.t.* mark with spots.

fled *v.* pret. & p.p. of **flee**.

fledg'ling" (flej'ling) *n.* **1,** a young bird just able to fly. **2,** a young, inexperienced person.

flee (flē) *v.i.* & *t.* [*pret.* & *p.p.* **fled**] take flight (from); escape.

fleece (flēs) *n.* the woolly coat of a sheep.—*v.t.* swindle.—**fleec'y,** *adj.* soft and woolly; resembling fleece, as clouds.

fleet (flēt) *adj.* able to run fast; rapid; swift.—*n.* an organized group of ships or vehicles.—**Fleet Admiral,** highest rank in the U.S. Navy.—**fleet'ing,** *adj.* swiftly passing; transitory.—**fleet'ness,** *n.*

flesh *n.* **1,** the mass of muscular tissue, containing some fat, that constitutes the soft substance of the animal body. **2,** a similar substance, as of fruit. **3,** meat. **4,** kindred. **5,** bodily appetites or sensibilities.—*adj.* of the color of the skin.—**flesh'y,** *adj.* plump.

fletch'er (flech'ər) *n.* a maker of arrows.

fleur-"de-lis' (flēr"də-lē') *n.* **1,** (*Hist.*) the royal emblem of France. **2,** the iris.

flew (floo) *v.* pret. of fly.

flex (fleks) *v.t.* bend, as a part of the body.—**flex'ion** (flek'shən) *n.*

flex·i·ble (flek'sə-bəl) *adj.* **1,** easily bent. **2,** adaptable.—**flex'i·bil'i·ty,** *n.*

flick (flik) *n.* a light, sharp blow, as with the finger or a whip.—*v.t.* so strike.

flick'er (flik'ər) *v.i.* **1,** vibrate; quiver. **2,** burn fitfully.—*n.* **1,** a wavering light. **2,** a large woodpecker. **3,** (often *pl.*) (*Slang*) a motion picture.

Fleur-de-lis

fli'er (flī'ər) *n.* 1, one who or that which flies; an aviator. 2, a handbill. 3, a risk; a speculative or incidental financial venture. Also, **fly'er.**

flight (flīt) *n.* 1, the act, mode, or power of flying. 2, swift motion caused by any propelling force. 3, the distance or course a bird, missile, aircraft, etc., flies. 4, a number of creatures or things flying together. 5, (*fig.*) an imaginative or extravagant excursion or soaring. 6, hasty departure. 7, the stairs from one landing or story to the next.

flight'y (flī'tē) *adj.* given to whims, disordered fancies, etc.; capricious. —**flight'i-ness,** *n.*

flim'flam" *n.* & *v.t.* humbug.

flim'sy (flim'zē) *adj.* 1, loosely constructed or woven; unsubstantial. 2, weak; ineffectual. —**flim'si-ness,** *n.*

flinch *v.i.* shrink from anything painful or unpleasant.

fling *v.t.* & *i.* [*pret.* & *p.p.* **flung**] throw with violence; cast; hurl. —*n.* 1, the act of flinging. 2, a brief time of unrestrained pleasure. 3, a lively dance. 4, (*Colloq.*) a try.

flint *n.* a very hard, dark gray quartz that will strike sparks from steel. —**flint'lock",** *n.* an old type of musket. —**flint'y,** *adj.* obdurate.

flip *n.* 1, a flick; snap. 2, a sweet drink, usually containing wine or liquor. —*v.t.* [**flipped, flip'ping**] toss lightly. —*adj.* [**flip'per, -pest**] (*Colloq.*) pert.

flip'pant (flip'ənt) *adj.* disrespectful; treating serious things lightly. —**flip'pan-cy,** *n.*

flip'per (flip'ər) *n.* a limb used for swimming, as of a seal.

flirt (flėrt) *v.i.* 1, play at being in love, not seriously. 2, trifle (with an idea). —*n.* a coquette.

flir-ta'tion (flėr-tā'shən) *n.* a transient, not serious, love affair.

flir-ta'tious (flėr-tā'shəs) *adj.* given to flirting. —**flir-ta'tious-ness,** *n.*

flit *v.i.* [**flit'ted, -ting**] move lightly and swiftly.

flit'ter (-ər) *v.i.* flutter.

fliv'ver (fliv'ər) *n.* (*Slang*) a small, cheap automobile.

float (flōt) *v.i.* 1, be buoyed up by water or air. 2, drift idly and gently. —*v.t.* 1, cause to rest on, or rise to, the surface of a liquid. 2, start; launch, as a company, rumor, etc. —*n.* 1, something that floats, as an anchored raft, a buoy, etc. 2, a decorated vehicle in a parade. —**float'er,** *n.* 1, (*Colloq.*) one who moves from place to place, esp. a laborer. 2, an insurance policy that covers unspecified items. —**float'ing,** *adj.* 1, not attached. 2, not fixed or settled.

floc'cu-lent (flok'ū-lənt) *adj.* like tufts of wool; fleecy; flaky. —**floc'cu-lence,** *n.*

flock (flok) *n.* 1, a number of animals or birds of one kind keeping together; a congregation, esp. of a church. 2, a tuft of wool, cotton, etc. 3, powdered fibers of wool, cotton, etc. —*v.i.* congregate; go in crowds.

floe (flō) *n.* a mass of floating ice.

flog *v.t.* [**flogged, flog'ging**] thrash.

flood (flud) *n.* 1, a great volume of water overflowing land; a deluge. 2, a great outpouring, as of work, light, etc.; a superfluity. 3, inflow of the tide. —*v.t.* & *i.* 1, overflow. 2, issue or rise in great quantity.

flood'light" *n.* a bright light illuminating a large area.

floor (flōr) *n.* 1, the bottom surface of a room, cave, the ocean, etc. 2, a story of a building. 3, the right to address a meeting. —*v.t.* 1, furnish with a floor. 2, (*Colloq.*) knock down; confound. —**floor'ing,** *n.* material of which a floor is made. —**floor show,** a show in a cabaret. —**floor'walk"er,** *n.* a supervisor of sales in a store.

flop *v.i.* [**flopped, flop'ping**] 1, thrash about; flap. 2, fall down clumsily. 3, (*Slang*) fail. —*n.* (*Slang*) a failure. —**flop'py,** *adj.* lacking rigidity.

flop'house" (flop'hows") *n.* (*Slang*) a very cheap hotel.

flo'ra (flôr'ə) *n.* plant life peculiar to a region or era.

flo'ral (flôr'əl) *adj.* of or pert. to flowers.

flor'id (flôr'id) *adj.* 1, ruddy, as the complexion. 2, highly ornate.

flor'in (flôr'in) *n.* 1, the gulden. 2, an Eng. two-shilling coin.

flo'rist (flôr'ist) *n.* one who raises or sells flowers as a business.

floss (flâs) *n.* 1, the silky substance in certain plant pods. 2, silk filaments used in embroidery, etc. —**floss'y,** *adj.* 1, like floss. 2, (*Slang*) fancy.

flo-ta'tion (flō-tā'shən) *n.* 1, act or state of floating. 2, arrangement to receive a loan.

flo-til'la (flō-til'ə) *n.* a small fleet; a fleet of small vessels.

flot'sam (flot'səm) *n.* wreckage of a ship or its cargo, found floating.

flounce (flowns) *n.* 1, a deep ruffle sewed at its upper edge, on a skirt. 2, a petulant jerk of one's body. —*v.i.* move with a flounce.

floun'der (flown'dər) *v.i.* struggle awkwardly or helplessly. —*n.* a flatfish.

flour (flowr) *n.* the finely ground meal of grain, esp. of wheat; hence, any fine, soft powder. —**flour'y,** *adj.*

flour'ish (flĕr'ish) *v.i.* 1, thrive; prosper; be active. 2, wave about; hence, flaunt. —*n.* anything done by way of display, as a fanciful pen stroke, a fanfare, etc.

flout (flowt) *v.t. & i.* scoff (at).

flow (flō) *v.i.* 1, both progress and move internally, as the stream of a liquid; circulate. 2, issue from a source. 3, proceed smoothly or evenly. 4, rise, as the tide. —*n.* 1, the act of flowing; the amount that flows. 2, issuance; rise.

flow'er (flow'ər) *n.* 1, the seed-producing part of a plant, esp. when colorful and fragrant; a blossom. 2, a plant grown for its flowers. 3, the state of efflorescence. 4, the best part or finest example. 5, youthful vigor. —*v.i.* blossom.

flow'er·pot' *n.* a pot to hold earth in which a flower grows.

flow'er·y (-ē) *adj.* 1, of flowers. 2, florid; full of ornate phrases. —**flow'er·i·ness,** *n.*

flown (flōn) *v.* p.p. of *fly.*

flu (floo) *n.* influenza.

fluc'tu·ate' (fluk'choo-āt') *v.i.* change continually; vary irregularly; rise and fall, like waves. —**fluc'tu·a'tion,** *n.*

flue (floo) *n.* a passageway for smoke, etc., as in a chimney.

flu'ent (floo'ənt) *adj.* facile in speech; voluble; smoothly flowing. —**flu'en·cy,** *n.*

fluff (fluf) *n.* 1, a light puff of dust or nap; a downy mass, as hair. 2, (*Slang*) a mistake. —*v.t.* puff up in a light mass. —**fluff'y,** *adj.* soft and light.

flu'id (floo'id) *adj.* 1, capable of flowing; esp. liquid or gaseous. 2, not rigid or fixed. —*n.* a liquid or a gas. —**flu·id'i·ty** (-ə-tē) *n.* —**fluid ounce,** a measure of capacity, one sixteenth of a pint.

fluke (flook) *n.* 1, that part of an anchor which catches and holds. 2, the head of an arrow or harpoon; a lobe of a whale's tail. 3, (*Slang*) an accidental stroke; a lucky chance. —**fluk'y,** *adj.* unpredictable.

flume (floom) *n.* a natural or artificial channel for conveying water.

flum'mer·y (flum'ə-rē) *n.* 1, agreeable nonsense. 2, a porridge.

flum'mox (flum'əks) *v.t.* (*Slang*) confuse.

flung *v.* pret. & p.p. of *fling.*

flunk *v.t. & i.* (*Colloq.*) fail to award, or get, a passing grade.

flunk'y (flung'kē) *n.* 1, a liveried manservant. 2, a toady. Also, **flunk'ey.**

flu'o·res'cence (floo'ə-res'əns) *n.* the property of becoming self-luminous, or emitting radiation, when exposed to the direct action of light-rays; also, the emitted radiation. —**flu'o·res'cent,** *adj.* —**fluorescent light,** a mercury vapor lamp.

flu'o·rine' (floo'ə-rēn') *n.* a corrosive, pungent, gaseous element, no. 9, symbol F.

fluor'o·scope' (flūr'ə-skōp') *n.* a device for exposing objects to radiation, as x-ray, and viewing them on a screen.

flur'ry (flĕr'ē) *n.* 1, a sudden gust of wind. 2, temporary ado or commotion. —*v.t.* fluster.

flush *v.i.* 1, blush; glow. 2, be startled from cover. —*v.t.* 1, suffuse with color. 2, elate; thrill. 3, wash out with a copious flow of water. 4, startle (a bird) from cover. —*n.* 1, a blush; any warm coloring. 2, a rush of water, as for cleansing. 3, a rush of emotion; thrill. 4, glow; vigor. 5, a hand of cards all of the same suit. —*adj.* 1, full; well filled. 2, prosperous; well supplied with money. 3, in the same plane or line; level or even.

flus'ter (flus'tər) *v.t.* embarrass and confuse.

Flute

flute (floot) *n.* 1, a tubular woodwind musical instrument. 2, a groove or furrow, as in a pillar, or in a ruffle. —**flut'ed,** *adj.* grooved. —**flut'ist,** *n.*

flut'ter (flut'ər) *v.i. & t.* 1, flap the wings rapidly, as a bird; hover. 2, move or beat irregularly, as the heart. 3, be agitated. 4, wave, as a flag. —*n.* 1, quick irregular motion; rapid vibration. 2, agitation; stir. —**flut'ter·y,** *adj.* habitually fluttering.

flu'vi·al (floo'vē-əl) *adj.* pert. to rivers.

flux (fluks) *n.* 1, a flowing, as of a liquid. 2, continual change. 3, a substance used to promote fusing of metals, prevent oxidation, etc.

fly (flī) *v.i.* [flew (floo), flown (flōn); fly'ing] 1, move more or less horizontally through the air, not touching ground; be airborne. 2, pass swiftly. 3, flee. 4, wave in the air, as a flag. 5, go by airplane. 6, [*pret.* flied (flīd)] hit a baseball that is caught in the air. —*v.t.* 1, cause to be airborne. 2, operate, or travel over in, aircraft. 3, flee from. —*n.* 1, any of several two-winged insects, esp. the housefly. 2, a fish-hook disguised as a fly. 3, a strip of cloth on a garment to hide a fastening. 4, an extra roof for a tent. 5, a baseball batted high in the air. —**flying fish,** a fish with winglike fins, capable of brief flights out of the water. —**flying saucer**, a saucer-shaped, illuminated object often reportedly seen in the skies.

fly'blown' *adj.* maggoty.

fly-'by-night' *adj.* unreliable.—*n.* an unreliable person.

fly'catch'er *n.* a small insectivorous bird.

fly'leaf' *n.* a blank leaf at the beginning or end of a book.

fly'pa"per *n.* sticky paper for catching flies.

fly'speck' *n.* a fly's egg; a tiny spot.

fly'swat"ter (-swot"ter) *n.* a mat with a handle, for killing flies.

fly'weight' *n.* a boxer weighing 112 lbs. or less.

fly'wheel' *n.* a heavy wheel that tends to stabilize the speed of a machine.

foal (fōl) *n.* a young horse, ass, etc. —*v.t. & t.* bring forth (a foal).

foam (fōm) *n. & v.t.* froth.— **foam'y,** *adj.*

fob *n.* 1, a short watch chain; 2, a small pocket for a watch.

fo'cus (fō'kəs) *n.* [*pl.* -cus-es or -ci (-sī)] 1, the point at which rays, as of light, heat, etc. meet after reflection or refraction. 2, focal length. 3, an adjustment of eyes, camera, etc. for clear vision. 4, a center, as of interest, activity, etc. —*v.t.* 1, adjust the focus of. 2, bring into focus. —**fo'cal,** *adj.*

fod'der (fod'ər) *n.* dried food, as hay, straw, etc., for livestock.

foe (fō) *n.* an enemy; an opponent. —**foe'man** (-mən) *n.* [*pl.* -men] an enemy in war.

fog *n.* 1, a heavy mist at or near the earth's surface. 2, mental confusion. —*v.t. & t.* [fogged, fog'ging] make or become obscure or cloudy. —**fog'gy,** *adj.* thick with mist; obscure.

fog'horn' *n.* a horn for warning of an approach through fog.

fo'gy (fō'gē) *n.* one who is averse to change or to new ideas.

foi'ble (foi'bəl) *n.* a whimsy; a weakness.

foil *n.* 1, a very thin sheet of metal. 2, anything that sets off something by contrast. 3, a blunted fencing sword. —*v.t.* baffle; frustrate.

foist *v.t.* palm off as genuine.

fold (fōld) *v.t.* 1, bend double, as cloth, paper, etc.; restore to original shape by folding once or more. 2, clasp together, as arms; bring toward the body; embrace. 3, wrap (something) by folding paper over it. —*v.t.* 1, double together. 2, (*Slang*) close down as a play. —*n.* 1, a pleat. 2, a pen for sheep.

-fold *suf.* 1, multiplied by. 2, divided by.

fold'er (fōl'dər) *n.* 1, printed matter, as a map, circular, etc., folded into a booklet. 2, a stiff folded holder for loose papers.

fo'li-age (fō'lē-ij) *n.* the leaves of plants.

fo'li-o' (fō'lē-ō") *n.* 1, a sheet of paper folded once. 2, a book of sheets folded once; a book of largest size. 3, a page number.

folk (fōk) *n.* 1, people in general. 2, (*pl.*) one's relatives; people of a certain class. —*adj.* originating or widely used among the common people, as *folk song.*

folk'lore' *n.* the old traditions, beliefs, and superstitions of a people.

folk'sy (-sē) *adj.* sociable.

folk'ways' *n.pl.* traditional customs.

fol'li-cle (fol'ə-kəl) *n.* 1, a minute cavity or gland. 2, a dry one-celled seed vessel.

fol'low (fol'ō) *v.t.* 1, come after in place or order of time; succeed. 2, pursue. 3, understand. 4, emulate; accept as a guide or leader. 5, result from. —*v.t.* 1, go or come after another. 2, arise as a natural consequence or inference; result. —**fol'low-er,** *n.* an adherent; disciple.

fol'low-ing *n.* a body of supporters or patrons. —*adj.* coming next in order or time.

fol'low-through' *n.* 1, completion of a stroke, as in golf or tennis. 2, exploitation of an advantage.

fol'low-up' *n.* an act, letter, circular, call, etc. to sustain the effectiveness of a previous one.

fol'ly (fol'ē) *n.* 1, lack of good sense; foolishness. 2, a foolish act or undertaking.

fo-ment' (fō-ment') *v.t.* stir up; incite. —**fo"men-ta'tion,** *n.*

fond *adj.* 1, loving. 2, foolishly tender or trusting; doting. 3, inclined toward. —**fond'ness,** *n.*

fon'dle (fon'dəl) *v.t.* caress.

fon'due (fon'doo) *n.* a baked dish of cheese, butter, and eggs.

font *n.* 1, a receptacle for baptismal water. 2, a full assortment of one size and style of printing type.

food *n.* 1, an edible substance, usually solid, for the nourishment of the body. 2, anything that sustains or nourishes.

food'stuff' *n.* a grocery item.

fool *n.* 1, a silly or stupid person; 2, a court jester. —*v.t.* dupe; mislead. —*v.t.* 1, play the fool. 2, spend time idly. 3, (with *with*) play or tamper (with).

fool'har"dy *adj.* foolishly rash. — **fool'har"di-ness,** *n.*

fool'ish *adj.* silly; unwise. —**fool'-ish·ness,** *n.*

fool'proof' *adj.* surely effective, even if mismanaged.

fools'cap' (foolz'kap″) *n.* a size of paper, about 13 × 17 inches.

foot (fut) *n.* [*pl.* **feet** (fēt)] 1, the terminal part of the leg of a man or animal. 2, anything that resembles a foot in shape, function, or position; the bottom or lowest point. 3, a measure of length, 12 inches. 4, tread; step. 5, infantry. 6, a group of syllables forming a metrical unit in a verse. —*v.t.* 1, add up as numbers in a column. 2, (*Colloq.*) pay, as a bill.

foot'age (-ij) *n.* length in feet.

foot'ball″ *n.* a field game played with an inflated leather ball; the ball used.

Football

foot'hill″ *n.* one of the lower hills at the base of a mountain range.

foot'hold″ *n.* a secure position.

foot'ing *n.* 1, a foothold. 2, an assured position. 3, a foundation. 4, basis; relative standing.

foot'lights″ *n.pl.* the row of lights at floor level in front of a stage.

foot'loose″ *adj.* not tied down; free to travel.

foot'man (-mən) *n.* [*pl.* **-men**] a manservant for carriage, door, and table.

foot'note″ *n.* an explanatory note at the foot of a page.

foot'pad″ *n.* a highwayman.

foot-'pound' *n.* the energy required to raise one pound one foot.

foot'print″ *n.* the mark made by a foot.

foot'step″ *n.* 1, a tread of a foot or the sound it makes. 2, (*pl.*) the example set by a predecessor.

foot'stool″ *n.* a low stool on which to rest one's feet while sitting.

foot'work″ *n.* 1, agility on foot. 2, laborious walking.

foo'zle (foo'zəl) *v.t. & i.* bungle.

fop *n.* a man too concerned with dressing stylishly. —**fop'per·y** (-ə-rē) *n.* —**fop'pish,** *adj.*

for (fôr) *prep.* 1, in order to obtain. 2, to be used by, or given to; adapted to; appropriate to. 3, in favor of. 4, in place of; instead of; in consideration of. 5, in honor of. 6, because of; for want of. 7, over the space of; during. 8, toward. 9, with regard to. —*conj.* because.

for'age (fôr'ij) *n.* 1, food for live-stock, esp. pasturage. 2, a search for food. —*v.i. & t.* raid for food.

fo·ra'men (fō-rā'mən) *n.* a hole or passage, esp. in a bone.

for'ay (fôr'ā) *n.* a raid for plunder.

for·bear' (fôr-bâr′) *v.t.* [-bore′, -borne′, -bear'ing] refrain or abstain from. —*v.i.* hold back; be patient or lenient; —**for·bear'ance,** *n.*

for·bid' (fər-bid′) *v.t.* [-bade′, -bid-den, -ding] 1, order (something) not to be done; refuse to permit; prohibit. 2, order (someone) not to do something. —**for·bid'ding,** *adj.* repelling approach; disagreeable.

force (fôrs) *n.* 1, the capacity for exerting strength; power; might. 2, the power to coerce, persuade, convince, etc. 3, meaning; import. 4, military strength. 5, a body of men prepared for action. 6, (*pl.*) an army; physical resources. 7, (*Physics*) the cause of motion, or a change in the motion, of a body. —*v.t.* 1, compel by physical, mental, or moral means. 2, extort by violence. 3, effect by effort. 4, compel the acceptance of. 5, hasten the growth of. —**forced,** *adj.* 1, compulsory. 2, strained; unnatural. 3, caused by an emergency. —**force'ful,** *adj.* powerful; effective.

for'ceps (fôr'səps) *n.* an instrument for grasping or extracting; pincers.

for'ci·ble (fôr'sə-bəl) *adj.* effective; convincing.

ford (fôrd) *n.* a shallow place where a river can be crossed by wading. —*v.t.* pass across by a ford.

fore (fôr) *n.* the front. —*adv.* in or toward the bow of a ship. —*adj.* at or near the front; ahead in time, rank, etc. —*interj.* in golf, a warning to look out.

fore- (fôr) *pref.* 1, front. 2, previous; ahead of time. 3, ahead in rank; superior.

fore'arm″ *n.* the arm between elbow and wrist.

fore'bear″ *n.* an ancestor.

fore·bode' *v.t. & i.* 1, presage. 2, have a premonition of. —**fore-bod'ing,** *n.* a feeling that evil is impending.

fore'cast″ *n.* a prediction. —*v.t.* (fôr-kăst′) 1, foresee. 2, predict.

fore'cas·tle (fōk'səl) *n.* 1, the forward part of the upper deck of a vessel. 2, in merchant ships, the seamen's quarters.

fore·close' (fôr-klōz′) *v.t. & i.* (*Law*) take away the right to redeem (a mortgage). —**fore·clo'sure** (-zhər) *n.*

fore'fa″ther *n.* an ancestor.

fore'fin″ger *n.* the finger next to the thumb.

fore'front" n. the foremost place or part.

fore'gone" adj. 1, past. 2, settled in advance.

fore'ground" n. the part of a picture, etc. represented as being nearest the observer.

fore'hand" adj. 1, made on the right side of the body (of a right-handed player), as a tennis stroke. 2, done beforehand. —**fore'hand"ed,** adj. 1, ahead of time. 2, prudent; thrifty.

fore'head (fŏr'id) n. the front of the head or face above the eyes and below the hairline.

for'eign (for'in) adj. 1, situated outside one's own land. 2, relating to, or dealing with, other countries. 3, alien; not native. 4, not pertinent. —**for'eign-er,** n. a resident or native of another country.

fore"know' v.t. [pret. & p.p. -knew'] know beforehand. —**fore-knowl'edge,** n.

fore'leg" n. one of the front legs of an animal having four or more legs.

fore'man (-mən) n. [pl. -men] 1, a superintendent of workers. 2, the spokesman of a jury.

fore'mast" n. the mast nearest the bow of a ship.

fore'most" adj. & adv. first; chief.

fore'noon" n. morning.

fo·ren'sic (fə-ren'sik) adj. pert. to courts of law or to debate. —**foren'si·cal·ly,** adv.

fore"or·di·na'tion (fŏr"ŏr-də-nā'shən) n. predestination.

fore'quar"ter n. one of the front quarters in cutting a carcass for meat.

fore'run"ner n. a predecessor; a precursor.

fore·see' v.t. [-saw', -seen'] predict; anticipate.

fore·shad'ow v.t. give notice or indication of in advance.

fore'sight" n. 1, the power of foreseeing. 2, prudent care for the future.

fore'skin" n. the loose skin at the tip of the penis.

for'est (for'ist) n. a large area covered with a dense growth of trees. —**for'est·er,** n. one who works in a forest.

fore·stall' v.t. thwart by action in advance.

for'est·ry (-rė) n. the science of caring for forests.

fore·tell' v.t. & i. [pret. & p.p. -told'] prophesy.

fore'thought" n. anticipatory care.

for·ev'er (fŏr-ev'ər) adv. 1, eternally. 2, continually.

fore"warn' v.t. warn of a coming event.

fore'word" n. a preface in a book.

for'feit (fŏr'fit) n. 1, a deposit, hostage, or agreed penalty surrendered through neglect, default, a crime, error, etc. 2, a fine; a penalty. —v.i. & t. surrender (a forfeit). —**for'fei·ture** (-fi-chər) n.

for·gath'er (fŏr-gath'ər) v.i. assemble; associate.

forge (fŏrj) v.t. 1, hammer into shape while malleable through heat. 2, shape out in any way; fashion. 3, imitate fraudulently (a signature). —v.i. move ahead slowly but surely. —n. a smithy.

for'ger·y (fŏr'jə-rē) n. fraudulent imitation of a signature, document, etc.; the false signature or document.

for·get' (fər-get') v.t. [for·got', -got'ten or -got', -get'ting] 1, be unable, or fail, to remember. 2, omit or neglect (to act), unintentionally or willfully. 3, (with oneself) act or speak improperly. —**for·get'ful,** adj. apt to forget; thoughtless. —**for·get'ful·ness,** n.

Forget-Me-Not

for·get-'me-not' n. a tiny blue flower.

for·give' (fər-giv') v.t. [for·gave', -giv'en, -giv'ing] 1, grant pardon for (something) or to (someone). 2, remit (a debt). 3, cease to resent. —**for·give'ness,** n. willingness to forgive. —**for·giv'ing,** adj. ready to forgive.

for·go' (fŏr-gō') v.t. [for·went', -gone', -go'ing] give up; let pass.

fork (fŏrk) n. 1, a pronged tool for digging, lifting, etc., or for handling food at table. 2, a division or branch, as of a road, stream, etc.; the place of such division. —v.t. 1, use a fork on. 2, (with over) (Colloq.) surrender. —v.i. separate into branches.

for·lorn' (fŏr-lôrn') adj. 1, abandoned; forsaken. 2, wretched. 3, hopeless. —**for·lorn'ness,** n.

form (fôrm) n. 1, external shape; structure; style. 2, the human body. 3, something that determines shape; a mold or pattern. 4, a particular kind or condition. 5, type in a frame ready for printing. 6, a prescribed practice, as for conduct, ritual, etc.; a ceremony. 7, manner of doing something. 8, physical fitness. 9, a document with blanks to be filled in. 10, (Gram.) a change in a word, as by spelling, inflection, etc. —v.t. 1, make; shape. 2, train; mold, as character. **3**, be an element of; constitute. **4**, organize. **5**, develop. —*v.i.* take a definite shape or arrangement; develop.

for'mal (fôr'məl) *adj.* **1**, adhering to established form or mode; conventional; ceremonious; precise. **2**, not familiar or friendly in manner; stiff. **3**, perfunctory. —*n.* (*Colloq.*) **1**, a formal occasion. **2**, an evening dress.

form·al·de·hyde" (fôr-mal'də-hīd") *n.* a gas, used in solution, as a preservative and disinfectant.

for·mal'i·ty (fôr-mal'ə-tē) *n.* **1**, rigid conformity to conventions. **2**, ceremony; a rule of procedure; a perfunctory act.

for'mat (fôr'mat) *n.* the general style of a book or periodical.

for·ma'tion (fôr-mā'shən) *n.* **1**, the process of shaping. **2**, that which is shaped. **3**, formal structure or arrangement, esp. of troops.

form'a·tive (fôr'mə-tiv) *adj.* **1**, forming; shaping. **2**, pert. to development.

for'mer (fôr'mər) *adj.* **1**, preceding in time. **2**, the earlier or first mentioned of two. —**for'mer·ly**, *adv.* in time past.

for'mi·da·ble (fôr'mi-də-bəl) *adj.* **1**, exciting fear. **2**, hard to accomplish; alarmingly difficult. —**for'mi·da·bil'i·ty, for'mi·da·ble·ness**, *n.*

for'mu·la (fôr'mū-lə) *n.* **1**, a fixed rule or form for saying or doing something. **2**, expression by symbols of the constituents of a chemical compound, or of a mathematical rule or principle. **3**, a recipe.

for'mu·late" (fôr'mū-lāt") *v.t.* express as a formula; put into definite words. —**for'mu·la'tion**, *n.*

for'ni·cate" (fôr'ni-kāt") *v.i.* consummate a love affair when not married. —**for'ni·ca'tion**, *n.*

for·sake' (fôr-sāk') *v.t.* [**for·sook'** (-sůk'), **-sak'en** (-sā'kən), **-sak'ing**] renounce; abandon.

for·sooth' (fôr-sooth') *adv.* (*Archaic*) in truth; indeed.

for·swear' (fôr-swâr') *v.t.* [**for·swore', -sworn', -swear'ing**] deny or renounce upon oath; abjure. —*v.i.* commit perjury. —**for·sworn'**, *adj.* perjured.

for·syth'i·a (fôr-sith'ē-ə) *n.* a shrub bearing yellow flowers.

fort (fôrt) *n.* a strongly fortified place.

forte (fôrt) *n.* a strong point; one's special talent. —*adj. & adv.* (fôr'tē) (*Music*) loud; loudly.

forth (fôrth) *adv.* **1**, onward or forward in time or place. **2**, into view; from under cover. **3**, away.

forth'com"ing *adj.* **1**, approaching in time. **2**, available when needed.

forth'right" *adj.* outspoken; direct. —*adv.* **1**, directly. **2**, immediately. —**forth'right"ness**, *n.*

forth"with' *adv.* at once.

for'ti·eth (fôr'tē-əth) *adj. & n.* **1**, the ordinal of forty, also written 40th. **2**, one of 40 equal parts.

for"ti·fi·ca'tion (fôr"ti-fi-kā'shən) *n.* **1**, the act of strengthening. **2**, a fortified position.

for'ti·fy" (fôr'ti-fī") *v.t.* **1**, provide with military defenses. **2**, strengthen, against wear, etc. **3**, strengthen mentally, morally, or physically.

for·tis'si·mo" (fôr-tis'i-mō") *adj. & adv.* (*Music*) very loud.

for'ti·tude" (fôr'tə-tūd") *n.* the power to endure pain, hardship, etc.

fort'night" (fôrt'nīt") *n.* two weeks. —**fort'night"ly**, *adj. & adv.* (occurring) once each fortnight.

for'tress (fôr'tres) *n.* **1**, a fortified place; a group of forts. **2**, any stronghold.

for·tu'i·tous (fôr-tū'ə-təs) *adj.* coming by chance; accidental. —**for·tu'i·tous·ness, for·tu'i·ty**, *n.*

for'tu·nate (fôr'chə-nət) *adj.* **1**, having good fortune; lucky. **2**, resulting favorably.

for'tune (fôr'chən) *n.* **1**, success or failure as controlled or influenced by chance. **2**, wealth, esp. great wealth; good luck. **3**, chance; luck; destiny.

for'ty (fôr'tē) *n. & adj.* the cardinal number between thirty-nine and forty-one, expressed by 40.

for'ty·nin'er (fôr"tē-nī'nər) *n.* one who participated in the California gold rush of 1849.

fo'rum (fôr'əm) *n.* a public meeting; any medium for public discussion; a tribunal.

for'ward (fôr'wərd) *adj.* **1**, near or toward the front. **2**, well-advanced. **3**, eager; ready. **4**, presumptuous; bold. —*adv.* **1**, onward; ahead; toward the front. **2**, forth; into view. —**for'ward·ness**, *n.*

fos'sil (fos'əl) *n.* **1**, remains or traces of a prehistoric plant or animal found in earth, rocks, etc. **2**, an outdated person or thing. —**fos'sil·ize"** (-īz") *v.t. & i.*

fos'ter (fäs'tər) *v.t.* **1**, nourish; bring up. **2**, cherish. **3**, promote the growth or development of. —*adj.* equivalent to parent or child though not so related by blood. —**foster mother**, a woman who takes the place of a mother in caring for a child.

fought (fôt) v. pret. & p.p. of *fight*.

foul (fowl) adj. **1**, disgusting to the senses by reason of decay, turpitude, filthiness, etc.; noisome; hateful. **2**, clogged, as a chimney; choked; entangled, as a rope. **3**, against the rules; out of legal bounds; unfair. **4**, base; vicious; scurrilous. —n. **1**, a violation of the rules. **2**, a collision. —v.t. **1**, defile. **2**, clog; entangle. **3**, collide with. —v.i. become foul; commit a foul, n. —**foul'ness**, n.

fou·lard' (foo-lärd') n. a soft silk with a satin finish.

found (fownd) v.t. **1**, lay the basis or foundation of, as a building. **2**, establish, as a business or a dynasty. **3**, (with on) base. **4**, cast (metal) in a mold. **5**, pret. & p.p. of *find*. —n. food and lodging. —**found'er**, n.

foun·da'tion (fown-dā'shən) n. **1**, the base on which a building rests; hence, basis; underlying principle. **2**, an endowment, as for research, a charity, etc.

foun'der (fown'dər) v.i. **1**, fill and sink, as a ship. **2**, go lame, as a horse. **3**, fail utterly.

found'ling (fownd'ling) n. a deserted infant of unknown parentage.

found'ry (fown'drē) n. a place where metal is cast.

fount (fownt) n. a fountain; a source.

foun'tain (fown'tən) n. **1**, a natural spring; a source of water. **2**, an artificial jet of water; a basin to receive it. —**foun'tain-head'**, n. **1**, the head or source of a stream. **2**, a primary source, as of learning. —**fountain pen**, a pen containing a reservoir for ink.

four (fôr) n. & adj. the cardinal number between three and five, expressed by 4.

four'flush"er (fôr'flush"er) n. (Slang) a pretender.

four-'in-hand' n. **1**, a long necktie tied in a slip knot. **2**, a team of four horses driven by one person.

four'square' adj. steady; frank.

four"teen' (fôr"tēn') n. & adj. the cardinal number between thirteen and fifteen, expressed by 14. —**fourteenth'**, n. & adj. **1**, the ordinal of this number, also written 14th. **2**, one of fourteen equal parts.

fourth (fôrth) adj. & n. the ordinal of four; 4th. —n. one of four equal parts. —**fourth dimension**, time or duration, considered as a dimension in the space-time theory of relativity. —**fourth estate**, the press; journalists collectively. —**the Fourth**, July 4, Independence Day.

fowl n. **1**, a domestic hen or cock; its flesh as food. **2**, birds in general, esp. those used for food. —**fowl'er**, n. one who hunts wild birds. —**fowl'ing**, n. the hunting of birds. —**fowling piece**, a shotgun.

fox (foks) n. **1**, a wild animal of the wolf family, noted for its cunning. **2**, a crafty person. —v.t. (Slang) outwit.

Fox

fox'glove" (foks'gluv") n. a flowering plant, the source of digitalis.

fox'hole" (foks'hōl") n. a hastily dug pit for shelter from enemy fire.

fox trot a type of ballroom dance.

fox'y (fok'sē) adj. clever; sly. —**fox'i·ness**, n.

foy'er (foi'ər) n. a lobby, as of a hotel, theater, etc.

fra'cas (frā'kəs) n. a noisy fight.

frac'tion (frak'shən) n. **1**, a part of a unit, or of a whole. **2**, a scrap; a fragment. —**frac'tion·al**, adj.

frac'tious (frak'shəs) adj. **1**, cross; peevish. **2**, unruly. —**frac'tious·ness**, n.

frac'ture (frak'chər) n. a breaking, esp. of a bone. —v.t. & i. break.

frag'ile (fraj'əl) adj. easily broken; delicate; brittle. —**fra·gil'i·ty** (-jil'ə-tē) n.

frag'ment (frag'mənt) n. **1**, a part broken off. **2**, an unfinished part, as of a poem. —**frag'men·ta"ry**, adj. incomplete.

fra'grant (frā'grənt) adj. sweetscented; pleasant. —**fra'grance**, n.

frail (frāl) adj. **1**, fragile. **2**, morally or physically weak. —**frail'ty** (-tē) n.

frame (frām) v.t. **1**, construct; fit together. **2**, compose or devise, as a law or a poem; utter or express. **3**, surround with a frame, as a picture. **4**, (Slang) incriminate (a person) on false evidence. —n. **1**, something made of parts fitted and joined. **2**, any kind of structure for enclosing, supporting, or holding something. **3**, bodily structure. **4**, a state of mind; mood.

frame'up" n. (Slang) something fraudulently prearranged.

frame'work" n. the structure for supporting anything; an outline or basic plan.

franc (frank) n. the monetary unit of France, Belgium, and Switzerland; once worth, at par, about 20 U. S. cents.

fran'chise (fran'chīz) n. **1**, the right to vote. **2**, a special right granted, esp. by a government.

fran'gi·ble (fran'jə-bəl) *adj.* breakable. —**fran'gi·bil'i·ty,** *n.*

frank *adj.* unreserved in expressing one's sentiments; candid; undisguised. —*n.* the privilege of mailing letters free of postage. —*v.t.* mark for free mailing. —**frank'ness,** *n.*

Frank'en·stein" (frank'ən-stīn") *n.* a fictional character who created a creature (Frankenstein's monster) that destroyed him.

frank'furt"er (-fûr'tər) *n.* a reddish sausage of beef and pork.

frank'in·cense" (frank'in-sens") *n.* a gum resin burned as incense.

fran'tic (fran'tik) *adj.* frenzied; wild with excitement, pain, or fear. —**fran'ti·cal·ly,** *adv.*

frap·pé' (fra-pā') *n.* a mixed cold drink.

fra·ter'nal (frə-tûr'nəl) *adj.* 1, brotherly. 2, pert. to a fraternity.

fra·ter'ni·ty (frə-tûr'nə-tē) *n.* 1, brotherliness. 2, a society, or group, of men with common interests or tastes. 3, a college society or club.

frat'er·nize" (frat'ər-nīz") *v.t.* associate in a friendly manner. —**frat'er·ni·za'tion,** *n.*

frat'ri·cide" (frat'rə-sīd") *n.* 1, the killing of a brother. 2, one who commits this crime.

Frau (frow) *n.* (*Ger.*) a wife; Mrs. —**Fräu'lein"** (froi'līn") *n.* (*Ger.*) an unmarried woman; Miss.

fraud (frâd) *n.* 1, deceit; a trick. 2, (*Law*) dishonest practice; breach of confidence. 3, (*Colloq.*) a cheat.

fraud'u·lent (frâ'dyə-lent) *adj.* dishonest; based on or obtained by, fraud. —**fraud'u·lence,** *n.*

fraught (frât) *adj.* filled (with).

fray (frā) *n.* a battle; skirmish. —*v.t.* & *i.* ravel; wear thin, as cloth.

fraz'zle (fraz'əl) *v.i.* & *i.* (*Colloq.*) 1, fray. 2, exhaust; weary. —*n.* a ragged end; an exhausted state.

freak (frēk) *n.* 1, an abnormal person, plant, or thing. 2, a whim; vagary. —**freak'ish,** *adj.*

freck'le (frek'əl) *n.* a light-brown spot on the skin, caused by sunlight. —*v.t.* & *i.* cause or acquire freckles.

free (frē) *adj.* 1, enjoying personal liberty; not enslaved. 2, enjoying civil or political liberty; self-governing. 3, existing under civil liberty, as a country. 4, unrestricted in opinion, choice, or action; independent. 5, exempt, as from tax or restriction. 6, obtained without cost; given without charge. 7, lavish; profuse. 8, not bound or restricted by force. 9, unrestrained; unceremonious; not bound by fixed rules. 10, not literal or exact. 11, open to all. —*adv.* without charge. —*v.t.* unfetter; release; exempt; rid (with *of*). —**free'lance,** a self-employed writer who may sell to whom he pleases. —**free'verse,** verse without rhyme or regular meter.

-free (frē) *suf.* free of; lacking.

free'boot"er (frē'boo"tər) *n.* a pirate.

free'dom (-dəm) *n.* the state of being free; personal liberty or national independence. —**freedom of the press,** the right to publish fact and opinion without censorship.

free'-for-all" *n.* (*Colloq.*) a contest or fight open to all.

free'hand" *adj.* roughly drawn by hand. —**free'hand"ed,** *adj.* generous.

free hold" *n.* land owned outright.

Free'ma"son *n.* a member of the Free and Accepted Masons, a Christian secret order. —**free'ma"son·ry,** *n.* sympathetic fellowship.

free'si·a (frē'zhē-ə) *n.* a flowering plant.

free'stone" (frē'stōn") *adj.* of a fruit, one whose pulp does not cling to the stone.

free'think"er *n.* a person of independent religious opinions.

free'will" *adj.* voluntary.

freeze (frēz) *v.t.* [**froze** (frōz), **fro'zen, freez'ing**] 1, cause to congeal; change from a liquid to a solid state by loss of heat. 2, form ice on or in; injure or kill by cold. 3, fix at the present place, condition, price, etc. —*v.i.* 1, be turned into, or covered with, ice. 2, be injured or killed by intense cold. 3, suffer from, or as from, cold. —*n.* a freezing condition, as of weather. —**freez'er,** *n.* 1, a machine for freezing ice cream, etc. 2, a cold-storage cabinet.

freight (frāt) *n.* 1, transportation of goods by a common carrier. 2, goods so transported; cargo; shipment. 3, the charge for handling. 4, a train carrying freight. —*v.t.* 1, load with, or as with, cargo. 2, ship (goods) by freight. —**freight'er,** *n.* a ship used to transport goods.

French *adj.* pert. to France, its people, etc. —*n.* the language of France. —**French'man,** *n.*

French cuffs folding cuffs.

French doors a pair of doors opening in the middle. Also, **French window.**

French dressing a salad dressing of oil, vinegar, salt and spices.

French horn a brass wind instrument having a coiled tube ending in a flaring mouth.

French leave abrupt departure.

French toast bread, dipped in egg and milk and sautéed.

French Horn

fre·net'ic (fre-net'ik) *adj.* frenzied. —**fre·net'i·cal·ly**, *adv.*

fren'zy (fren'zē) *n.* **1**, violent mental agitation. **2**, delirious excitement. —**fren'zied**, *adj.*

fre'quen·cy (frē'kwən-sē) *n.* **1**, repeated occurrence. **2**, the rate of recurrence of a given event in a given time. —**frequency modulation**, in radio, alteration of wave length frequency to avoid distortion.

fre'quent (frē'kwənt) *adj.* **1**, happening often; occurring at short intervals. **2**, habitual; regular. —*v.t.* (*also*, frē-kwent') go often or habitually to.

fres'co (fres'kō) *n.* a mural painting on damp plaster.

fresh *adj.* **1**, having its original qualities; not faded, worn, or stale. **2**, novel; new; recent. **3**, cool; refreshing; of wind, brisk. **4**, of water, not salt; of food, not canned, preserved, or salted; recently grown, picked, slaughtered, etc. **5**, rested; not tired; invigorated; healthy. **6**, of a cow, recently having calved. **7**, inexperienced. **8**, (*Slang*) impudent. —**fresh'ness**, *n.*

fresh'en (-ən) *v.t.* make fresh.

fresh'et (fresh'it) *n.* a sudden seasonal rise in the level of a stream.

fresh'man (-mən) *n.* [*pl.* -men] a student in his first year in high school or college.

fresh'wa"ter *adj.* **1**, living in or accustomed to inland waters, not the sea. **2**, inexperienced, insignificant, or rustic.

fret *v.t.* [**fret'ted, -ting**] **1**, be continuously perturbed by worry, anxiety, annoyance, or resentment. **2**, become worn or corroded. —*v.t.* **1**, vex; irritate. **2**, chafe; rub. —*n.* **1**, irritation. **2**, a carved ornamental pattern; *fretwork*. **3**, a small ridge across the fingerboard of a stringed instrument. —**fret'ful**, *adj.* fretting; restless; peevish.

Freud'i·an (froi'dē-ən) *adj.* pert. to the theories of Sigmund Freud relating to neurotic and psychopathic conditions.

fri'a·ble (frī'ə-bəl) *adj.* easily crumbled. —**fri"a·bil'i·ty**, *n.*

fri'ar (frī'ər) *n.* a member of certain Rom. Cath. religious orders.

fric"as·see' (frik"ə-sē') *n.* a dish of meat or fowl cut in pieces and cooked in gravy. —*v.t.* so cook.

fric'tion (frik'shən) *n.* **1**, the rubbing of two surfaces together; opposition; conflict. **2**, the resistance to relative motion between two surfaces in contact. —**fric'tion·al**, *adj.*

Fri'day (frī'dē) *n.* the sixth day of the week.

fried (frīd) *v.* pret. & p.p. of fry. —*adj.* boiled in fat.

friend (frend) *n.* **1**, a person on intimate and affectionate terms with another. **2**, a supporter; well-wisher. **3**, (*cap.*) a member of the Religious Society of Friends; a Quaker. —**friend'ly**, *adj.* amicable; not hostile; favorable. —**friend'liness**, *n.* —**friend'ship**, *n.* the state of being friendly toward or intimate with another.

frieze (frēz) *n.* **1**, an ornamental or sculptured band around a wall. **2**, a heavy woolen cloth.

frig'ate (frig'it) *n.* **1**, (*Hist.*) a sailing warship, relatively equivalent to the cruiser. **2**, a modern light warship.

fright (frīt) *n.* **1**, sudden fear or terror. **2**, (*Colloq.*) a grotesque person or thing.

fright'en (-ən) *v.t.* terrify.

fright'ful (-fəl) *adj.* **1**, terrible. **2**, (*Colloq.*) unpleasant. —**fright'fulness**, *n.*

frig'id (frij'id) *adj.* **1**, icy; wintry. **2**, chilly in manner; formal. **3**, emotionally unresponsive. —**fri·gid'i·ty** (-jid'ə-tē) *n.*

frill (fril) *n.* **1**, a gathered or pleated ruffle; a trimming. **2**, (*Colloq.*) (*pl.*) affectations. **3**, a fancy detail or accessory. —**frill'y**, *adj.*

fringe (frinj) *n.* a raveled edge on a fabric; a fancy edging of tassels or twisted threads.

frip'per·y (frip'ə-rē) *n.* worthless finery; ostentation.

fri·sé' (fri-zā') *n.* an upholstery fabric, made of uncut loops.

frisk *v.i.* leap about; gambol. —*v.t.* (*Slang*) search (a person) for concealed weapons. —**frisk'y**, *adj.* playful.

frit'ter (frit'ər) *v.t.* waste on trifles, as time, energy, etc. —*n.* a small fried battercake.

fri·vol'i·ty (fri-vol'ə-tē) *n.* **1**, a frivolous act. **2**, merrymaking.

friv'o·lous (friv'ə-ləs) *adj.* **1**, not seriously intended; lacking in dignity; slight; trivial. **2**, silly; giddy. —**friv'o·lous·ness**, *n.*

friz'zle (friz'əl) *v.t.* **1**, curl crisply, as hair. **2**, cook with sizzling noise. —**friz'zly, friz'zy**, *adj.*

fro (frō) *adv.* back. —**to and fro**, back and forth.

frock (frok) *n.* **1**, a dress. **2**, a coarse outer garment worn by a monk, etc. —**frock coat**, a man's long-skirted coat.

frog (frâg) *n.* **1**, a small, tailless amphibian with great leaping and swimming ability. **2**, a lump of mucus in the throat. **3**, a fastening

frolic 193 fulfill

made of a button and a loop. **4**, a device that permits the intersection of two railway tracks.

frol'ic (frol'ik) *v.i.* [-icked, -icking] play merrily. —*n.* merrymaking; fun. —**frol'ic·some,** *adj.*

from *prep.* away; out of (a certain starting point); denoting removal, separation, distinction, etc.

frond *n.* a leaf of a fern, etc.

front (frunt) *n.* **1**, the foremost part or face of anything. **2**, manner of facing anything. **3**, position directly before a person or thing. **4**, land along the edge of a river, bay, etc. **5**, in war, the scene of actual fighting. **6**, bearing or demeanor. **7**, (*Colloq.*) an outward manifestation of wealth or importance. —*adj.* pert. to, or situated at, the front. —*v.t.* confront; have the front toward; face. —*v.i.* face in a certain direction. —**front foot,** a foot of frontage.

front'age (frun'tij) *n.* the distance a lot extends along a street, body of water, etc.

fron'tal (frun'təl) *adj.* **1**, at or of the front. **2**, pert. to the bone of the forehead.

fron·tier' (frun-tir') *n.* **1**, that part of a country that borders another country or an unsettled region. **2**, undeveloped spheres of knowledge, etc.

fron'tis·piece (frun'tis-pēs') *n.* an illustration facing the title page of a book.

frost (frâst) *n.* **1**, frozen dew or vapor. **2**, freezing weather. **3**, a frozen state of the ground. **4**, (*Slang*) a failure. **5**, (*Colloq.*) a coolness between persons. —*v.t.* **1**, cover with frost. **2**, injure by freezing. **3**, ice (a cake). —**frost'ed,** *adj.* iced. —**frost'ing,** *n.* **1**, a sugar coating for cake. **2**, a finish on metal or glass. —**frost'y,** *adj.* **1**, cold. **2**, gray, as hair.

frost'bite *n.* injury to body tissues, caused by exposure to intense cold.

froth (frâth) *n.* **1**, mass of fine bubbles on the surface of a liquid, at the mouth of a hard-ridden horse, etc.; foam. **2**, anything light and trivial. —*v.t. & i.* foam. —**froth'y,** *adj.* **1**, foaming. **2**, light; insubstantial.

fro'ward (frō'wərd) *adj.* willful; perverse. —**fro'ward·ness,** *n.*

frown *n.* a wrinkling of the brows, as in anger, perplexity, etc. —*v.i.* **1**, so wrinkle the brow. **2**, (with *upon*) disapprove.

frowz'y (frow'zē) *adj.* slovenly; unkempt. —**frowz'i·ness,** *n.*

froze (frōz) *v.* pret. of *freeze*.

fro'zen (frō'zən) *adj.* **1**, congealed by cold. **2**, frigid. **3**, lacking emo-

tion. **4**, refrigerated. **5**, not liquid, as assets. —*v.* p.p. of *freeze*.

fruc'ti·fy (fruk'tə-fī') *v.t.* make productive. —*v.i.* bear fruit. —**fruc'-ti·fi·ca'tion** (-fi-kā'shən) *n.*

fru'gal (froo'gəl) *adj.* economical; not wasteful; not lavish; sparing. —**fru·gal'i·ty** (froo-gal'ə-tē) *n.*

fruit (froot) *n.* **1**, any natural, useful yield of a plant. **2**, the seed of a plant and its enveloping tissues. **3**, the sweet fruit of certain trees and vines, as peach, pear, grape, etc. **4**, a result; consequence. —**fruit'ful,** *adj.* productive; profitable. —**fruit'less,** *adj.* unprofitable; barren.

fru·i'tion (froo-ish'ən) *n.* **1**, state of bearing fruit. **2**, realization; attainment, as of one's hopes.

frump *n.* a dowdy woman. —**frump'ish,** *adj.*

frus'trate (frus'trāt) *v.t.* prevent from fulfilling plans, hopes, etc.; balk; thwart; nullify.

frus·tra'tion (frus-trā'shən) *n.* **1**, act of frustrating; state of being frustrated. **2**, extreme disappointment.

frus'tum (frus'təm) *n.* the remainder of a truncated cone or pyramid.

fry (frī) *v.t. & i.* cook in hot fat. —*n.* **1**, a young fish. **2**, a swarm or brood of young; young children.

fuch'sia (fū'shə) *n.* a shrub or plant with drooping reddish tubular flowers.

fudge (fuj) *n.* **1**, nonsense. **2**, a creamy beaten chocolate candy.

fu'el (fū'əl) *n.* **1**, combustible material burned to supply heat or power. **2**, a means of increasing passion, etc. —*v.t. & i.* furnish with, or take on, fuel.

fu'gi·tive (fū'jə-tiv) *adj.* **1**, fleeing; having run away. **2**, evanescent; fleeting. **3**, of literature, of passing interest; transitory. —*n.* one who flees from pursuit, duty, etc.

fugue (fūg) *n.* a musical composition in which the theme is reintroduced by various parts.

Füh'rer (fyü'rər) *n.* (*Ger.*) leader; applied esp. to Adolf Hitler.

-ful (fəl) *suf.* **1**, full of; filled. **2**, characterized by. **3**, tending to, as *harmful.*

ful'crum (ful'krəm) *n.* the support on which a lever rests or turns.

Fulcrum & Lever

ful·fill' (ful-fil') *v.t.* **1**, carry into effect, as a promise. **2**, perform, as a duty. **3**, satisfy, as a desire. Also, **ful·fil'.** —**ful·fill'ment,** *n.*

tub, cūte, pūll; label; oil, owl; go, chip, she, thin, then, sing, ink; see p. 6

ful'gent (ful'jənt) *adj.* shining brightly. —**ful'gent·ness**, *n.*

fu·lig'i·nous (fū-lij'ə-nəs) *adj.* sooty; smoky. —**fu·lig'i·nous·ness**, *n.*

full (ful) *adj.* **1**, filled to capacity; holding all that can be held. **2**, complete according to standard; whole. **3**, rounded out; plump; ample. **4**, engrossed. **5**, abundantly supplied. **6**, at the peak of, as quality, force, volume, etc. —*adv.* **1**, entirely. **2**, exactly. —*n.* utmost extent. —**full'ness**, *n.* —**full stop**, a period.

full·blood'ed *adj.* **1**, of unmixed ancestry. **2**, virile.

full·blown' *adj.* fully developed.

full'er (ful'ər) *n.* **1**, one who treats cloth to thicken it. **2**, a hammer with a cylindrical striking surface. —**fuller's earth**, a claylike substance used as a filter and blotting material.

ful'mar (ful'mər) *n.* an Arctic sea bird related to the petrel.

ful'mi·nate'' (ful'mi·nāt'') *v.t.* & *i.* **1**, explode; detonate. **2**, (with *against*) issue denunciations. —**ful'-mi·na'tion**, *n.*

ful'some (ful'səm) *adj.* cloying; offensively excessive. —**ful'some·ness**, *n.*

fum'ble (fum'bəl) *v.i.* & *t.* **1**, grope about awkwardly; handle clumsily. **2**, in sports, fail to hold (the ball). —*n.* a slip; misplay.

fume (fūm) *n.* (usually *pl.*) smoke, gas, vapor, esp. if noxious. —*v.i.* **1**, emit fumes. **2**, be vexed; fret. —**fumed**, *adj.* colored by fumes, as woodwork.

fu'mi·gate'' (fū'mi·gāt'') *v.t.* treat with fumes to disinfect or to destroy pests. —**fu''mi·ga'tion**, *n.* —**fu'mi·ga'tor**, *n.*

fun *n.* anything that induces enjoyment, esp. mirthful; amusement; sport; joking.

func'tion (funk'shən) *n.* **1**, proper action by which any person, organ, office, structure, etc. fulfills its purpose or duty. **2**, a public ceremony or occasion.

func'tion·al (-əl) *adj.* **1**, pert. to a function. **2**, designed to perform some function; useful. —**functional disease**, a disease characterized by a morbid change in the function, but not in the tissues, of an organ. —**func'tion·al·ism**, *n.* the doctrine that functional utility should determine design (of furniture, etc.).

func'tion·ar·y (-er-ē) *n.* an official.

fund *n.* **1**, a stock or supply, esp. of money, set apart for a purpose. **2**, a store of anything, as knowledge. **3**, (*pl.*) available cash. —*v.t.* convert (a temporary debt) into a permanent debt bearing interest.

fun''da·men'tal (fun''də·men'təl) *adj.* serving as, or being an essential part of, a foundation; basic; primary; elementary. —*n.* a basic principle. —**fun''da·men'tal·ist**, *n.* one who accepts the Bible as literally true. —**fun''da·men'tal·ism**, *n.*

fu'ner·al (fū'nər·əl) *n.* the ceremony of burying a dead person.

fu·ne're·al (fū-nir'ē·əl) *adj.* **1**, dark; gloomy; sad. **2**, pert. to a funeral.

fun'gi·cide (fun'ji·sīd) *n.* an agent for destroying fungous growths, as athlete's foot.

fun'gus (fung'gəs) *n.* any of a group of non-green plants, including the molds, toadstools, rusts, etc. —**fun'gous**, *adj.*

fu·nic'u·lar (fū-nik'ū-lər) *adj.* pert. to, or worked by, a rope or cable. —*n.* a mountain cable railway.

funk *n.* (*Colloq.*) cowering fear.

fun'nel (fun'əl) *n.* **1**, a cone-shaped device for guiding something into a small opening. **2**, a smoke-stack. **3**, a shaft for ventilation.

fun'ny (fun'ē) *adj.* **1**, amusing; comical. **2**, (*Colloq.*) strange; odd. **3**, (*pl.*) (*Colloq.*) the comic strips; funny papers. —**fun'ni·ness**, *n.*

Funnels

fun'ny·bone'' *n.* **1**, a nerve in the elbow. **2**, sense of humor.

fur (fėr) *n.* the soft, fine hair of certain animals; their dressed skins, used for clothing. —**furred**, *adj.*

fur·be·low'' (fėr'bə·lō'') *n.* **1**, a plaited dress trimming; a flounce. **2**, any bit of finery.

fur'bish (fėr'bish) *v.t.* polish; burnish; renovate.

fu'ri·ous (fyûr'ē·əs) *adj.* **1**, raging; full of fury. **2**, violent, as a wind. **3**, energetic. —**fu'ri·ous·ness**, *n.*

furl (fėrl) *v.t.* roll up and fasten (a flag or sail).

fur'long (fėr'lâng) *n.* a measure of length, 220 yards.

fur'lough (fėr'lō) *n.* leave of absence for a soldier.

fur'nace (fėr'nis) *n.* a structure in which fuel is burned to make heat.

fur'nish (fėr'nish) *v.t.* supply with what is needed, esp. furniture; provide. —**fur'nish·ings**, *n.pl.* fittings of any kind.

fur·ni·ture (fẽr'nə-chər) *n.* **1,** movable articles, as chairs, desks, etc. for equipping a house, office, etc. **2,** any necessary apparatus.

fu'ror (fyur'ôr) *n.* **1,** great excitement. **2,** a prevailing craze.

fur'ri·er (fẽr'ē-ər) *n.* a maker of or dealer in fur garments.

fur'ring (fẽr'ing) *n.* **1,** fur for a garment. **2,** in building, thin boards providing a basis for laths, plaster, etc.

fur'row (fẽr'ō) *n.* **1,** a trench in the earth, esp. that made by a plow. **2,** a wrinkle. —*v.t.* make furrows in

fur'ry (fẽr'ē) *adj.* **1,** covered with fur. **2,** made of or like fur. —**fur'ri·ness,** *n.*

fur'ther (fẽr'thər) *adj.* [*superl.* **fur'thest**] **1,** more remote or extended; comp. of *far.* **2,** additional. —*adv.* **1,** to a greater distance or extent. **2,** also. —*v.t.* promote or advance, as a cause. —**fur'ther·ance,** *n.* advancement.

fur'ther·more" *adv.* besides; also.

fur'tive (fẽr'tiv) *adj.* sly; stealthy; done by stealth. —**fur'tive·ness,** *n.*

fu'ry (fyur'ē) *n.* **1,** violent passion; great anger. **2,** fierceness; violence.

furze (fẽrz) *n.* a shrub common on waste lands in Europe.

fuse (fūz) *n.* **1,** a casing filled with combustible material for exploding a shell, blast, etc. **2,** a protective strip of fusible metal inserted in an electric circuit. —*v.t. & i.* **1,** melt with extreme heat. **2,** blend, as if melted together; weld. —**fus'i·ble,** *adj.* —**fus"i·bil'i·ty,** *n.*

fu'se·lage (fū'zə-lij) *n.* the body of an airplane.

fu'sel oil (fū'zəl) a poisonous liquid, a by-product of distilleries, used in solvents.

fu'si·form" (fū'zə-fôrm") *adj.* spindle-shaped.

fu"sil·lade" (fū"zə-lād') *n.* simultaneous fire from many firearms.

fu'sion (fū'zhən) *n.* **1,** union by fusing. **2,** union of two or more political parties. **3,** in nuclear physics, union of parts of two atoms.

fuss (fus) *n.* **1,** much ado over trifles; bustle; confusion. **2,** (*Colloq.*) a petty quarrel. —*v.i.* worry, or be busy, over trifles. —*v.t.* confuse. —**fuss'y,** *adj.* unduly particular.

fus'tian (fus'chən) *n.* **1,** a coarse cotton fabric. **2,** high-flown speech; bombast.

fus'ty (fus'tē) *adj.* **1,** musty; stuffy. **2,** old-fashioned. —**fus'ti·ness,** *n.*

fu'tile (fū'təl) *adj.* **1,** ineffectual. **2,** idle; trifling. —**fu·til'i·ty** (-til'ə-tē) *n.*

fu'ture (fū'chər) *adj.* **1,** yet to come or happen. **2,** relating to later time. —*n.* **1,** times to come. **2,** prospects.

fu"tur·is'tic (fū"chər-is'tik) *adj.* anticipating the supposed art forms of the future. —**fu"tur·is'ti·cal·ly,** *adv.*

fu·tu'ri·ty (fū-tyur'ə-tē) *n.* the future; the state of being yet to come.

fuzz (fuz) *n.* fine, fluffy particles of wool, cotton, etc.; down. —**fuzz'y,** *adj.* —**fuzz'i·ness,** *n.*

-fy (-fī) *suf.* forming verbs meaning: **1,** make, as *simplify,* make simple. **2,** become, as *solidify,* become solid.

G

G, g (jē) the seventh letter of the English alphabet.

gab *v.i.* [**gabbed, gab'bing**] (*Colloq.*) talk idly; chatter. —*n.* idle talk. —**gab'by,** *adj.* very talkative.

gab'ar·dine" (gab'ər-dēn") *n.* cloth of wool or cotton, similar to serge.

gab'ble (gab'əl) *v.i.* **1,** cackle, as geese. **2,** talk volubly; jabber. —*n.* act or result of gabbling.

ga'ble (gā'bəl) *n.* the triangular expanse of wall between opposite edges of a sloping roof.

gad *n.* a pointed rod; a goad. —*v.i.* [**gad'ded, -ding**] ramble about idly. —*interj.* a euphemism for God. —**gad'der, gad'a·bout",** *n.* one who travels about aimlessly.

gad'fly" (gad'flī") *n.* a stinging insect annoying to cattle.

gadg'et (gaj'it) *n.* any small device, esp. mechanical. —**gadg"e·teer'** (-tir') *n.* one who makes or collects many gadgets.

Gael'ic (gā'lik) *adj.* pert. to the Celtic peoples, esp. Irish. —*n.* a language spoken by these peoples.

Gaff

gaff (gaf) *n.* **1,** a stick with an iron hook, for landing fish. **2,** a spar to extend a sail. **3,** (*Slang*) persistent teasing; expense.

gaf'fer (-ər) *n.* **1,** an old man. **2,** a gang boss, esp. in a carnival.

gag *n.* **1,** a thing thrust into the mouth to prevent outcry; hence, restraint of free speech. **2**, (*Slang*) a joke. —*v.t.* [gagged, gag'ging] put a gag on; silence. —*v.t.* retch.

gage (gāj) *n.* **1**, gauge. **2**, anything, as a glove, symbolizing a challenge.

gai·e·ty (gā'ə-tē) *n.* gayness; merrymaking; brightness.

gai'ly (gā'lē) *adv.* **1**, merrily. **2**, showily.

gain (gān) *v.t.* **1**, obtain (something valued or desired). **2**, acquire by accretion, as added weight. **3**, earn by effort. **4**, reach; arrive at. —*v.i.* **1**, benefit. **2**, make progress. **3**, put on weight. —*n.* **1**, profit. **2**, an increase.—**gain'ful**, *adj.* advantageous.

gain'say' (gān'sā') *v.t.* [-said', -say'ing] contradict; dispute.

gait (gāt) *n.* manner of running or walking. —**gait'ed**, *adj.* (of a horse) trained to various gaits.

gai'ter (gā'tər) *n.* a cloth or leather covering for the leg or ankle; a spat.

ga'la (gā'lə) *n.* a festival. —*adj.* festive.

gal'ax·y (gal'ək-sē) *n.* **1**, a luminous band of stars: **2**, (*cap.*) the Milky Way. **3**, an assemblage of splendid persons or things.

gale (gāl) *n.* **1**, a stiff wind. **2**, an outburst, as of laughter.

ga·le'na (gə-lē'nə) *n.* a mineral, an important ore of lead and silver.

gall (gâl) *n.* **1**, a bitter secretion of the liver; bile. **2**, rancor. **3**, (*Slang*) impudence. **4**, a sore made by chafing. **5**, a lump made by insects on trees, esp. oaks. —*v.t.* & *v.i.* **1**, make sore by rubbing. **2**, vex; annoy. —**gall bladder**, a sac in which the bile is stored.

gal'lant (gal'ənt) *adj.* **1**, brave; chivalrous. **2**, honorable; noble. **3**, (gə-länt') courtly; attentive to women. —*n.* (gə-länt') **1**, a dashing man of fashion. **2**, a ladies' man. —**gal'lant·ry** (-rē) *n.*

gal'le·on (gal'ē-ən) *n.* a former Span. sailing vessel.

gal'ler·y (gal'ə-rē) *n.* **1**, a long narrow passage often open at one side; a veranda. **2**, a room or building for the exhibition of works of art. **3**, a balcony, as in a theater.

gal'ley (gal'ē) *n.* **1**, an ancient seagoing vessel propelled by oars and sails. **2**, a rowboat larger than a gig. **3**, the kitchen of a ship. **4**, an oblong, shallow tray to hold set-up type; a proof printed from this type.

Gal'lic (gal'ik) *adj.* pert. to the Gauls; French.

gal'li·um (gal'ē-əm) *n.* a rare metallic element, no. 31, symbol Ga.

gal'li·vant (gal'i-vant) *v.i.* seek pleasure frivolously; gad about.

gal'lon (gal'ən) *n.* a measure of capacity; four quarts.

gal'lop (gal'əp) *n.* a rapid, springing gait, esp. of a horse. —*v.t.* cause to gallop. —*v.i.* run or ride at a gallop.

gal'lows (gal'ōz) *n.* a structure ("tree") with two upright posts and a crossbar at the top, for hanging criminals.

gall'stone" (gâl'stōn") *n.* a stony mass formed in the gall bladder.

gal'lus·es (gal'ə-siz) *n.pl.* suspenders.

gal'op (gal'əp) *n.* **1**, a lively dance: **2**, the music for it.

ga·lore' (gə-lôr') *adj.* & *adv.* in plenty; in abundance.

ga·losh' (gə-losh') *n.* a high overshoe.

gal·van'ic (gal-van'ik) *adj.* **1**, pert: to a current of electricity. **2**, stimulating; electric; spasmodic. —**galvan'i·cal·ly**, *adv.*

gal'va·nism (gal'və-niz-əm) *n.* production of electricity by chemical action.

gal'va·nize" (gal'və-nīz") *v.t.* **1**, shock or stimulate, as by electricity. **2**, plate or coat with metal by means of electricity. —**galvanized iron**, iron sheeting plated with zinc.

gam'bit *n.* in chess, an opening that loses a pawn but gains positional advantage.

gam'ble (gam'bəl) *v.i.* **1**, risk money on a game of chance. **2**, hazard something of value on an uncertain event. —*v.t.* risk; (with *away*) lose by gambling. —*n.* a risk. —**gam'bler**, *n.* —**gam'bling**, *n.*

gam·boge' (gam-bōj') *n.* a resin used as a yellow pigment or medicine.

gam'bol (gam'bəl) *v.i.* leap or skip about in frolic. —*n.* frolic.

gam'brel (gam'brəl) *n.* a joint in the hind leg of a horse.

game (gām) *n.* **1**, play; amusement. **2**, a contest played according to rules; a division of a contest; a winning score. **3**, a plan, scheme, or enterprise. **4**, wild animals, birds, or fish hunted for food or sport. —*adj.* (*Slang*) **1**, plucky. **2**, willing. **3**, lame. —**game'ness**, *n.*

game'cock" *n.* a cock bred to fight in exhibitions.

gam'ete (gam'ēt) *n.* (*Biol.*) a cell that unites with another for reproduction.

gam'in *n.* a neglected child; street urchin.

gam'ing (gā'ming) *n.* the playing of a game for money.

gam'ma (gam'ə) *n.* the third letter of the Greek alphabet (Γ, γ).

gamma glob'u·lin (glob'yə-lin) a drug formerly used against infantile paralysis, often called G. G.

gamma rays rays similar to x-rays, emitted by radioactive elements.

gam'mon (gam'ən) *n.* 1, a smoked ham. 2, trickery. 3, nonsense. 4, in backgammon, a won game of double value.

gam'ut (gam'ət) *n.* 1, the whole range of accepted musical tones. 2, range; scope.

gan'der (gan'dər) *n.* 1, the male goose. 2, (*Slang*) a careful look.

gang *n.* a company of persons acting or going about together.

gan'gling (gang'gling) *adj.* awkwardly tall and thin.

gan'gli·on (gang'glē-ən) *n.* 1, a knot on a nerve from which nerve fibers radiate. 2, a mass of gray matter in the central nervous system.

gang'plank″ *n.* a movable ramp to a ship.

gan'grene (gang'grēn) *n.* the rotting away of body tissue, due to stoppage of nourishment. —**gan'gre·nous,** *adj.*

gang'ster (gang'stər) *n.* a member of a lawless gang; a racketeer.

gang'way″ (gang'wā″) *n.* a passageway into or out of an enclosed space. —*interj.* stand aside! make way!

gan'net (gan'et) *n.* a large sea bird.

gant'let (gànt'lət) *n.* 1, a form of punishment or hazing in which the victim runs between two lanes of men who strike him as he passes. 2, a series of unpleasant things or events. 3, gauntlet.

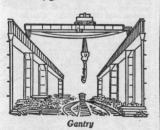

Gantry

gan'try (gan'trè) *n.* a supporting structure, as a framework or bridge.

gaol (jāl) *n. & v.t.* (*Brit.*) jail.

gap *n.* 1, an opening; a vacant space. 2, a notch in a mountain ridge. 3, a break in continuity.

gape (gāp) *v.i.* 1, open the mouth wide; yawn. 2, be wide open. 3, look amazed. —*n.* breach; gap.

gar (gär) *n.* a fish with a long, sharp snout.

ga·rage' (gə-räzh') *n.* a building where automobiles are stored or repaired.

Gar'and rifle (gar'ənd) a kind of automatic repeating rifle.

garb (gärb) *n.* clothes, esp. of a distinctive calling or period; attire. —*v.t.* clothe.

gar'bage (gär'bij) *n.* 1, waste matter from a kitchen; refuse. 2, a worthless assortment; nonsense.

gar'ble (gär'bəl) *v.t.* twist, in order to misrepresent; distort; misquote.

gar'den (gär'dən) *n.* 1, a plot of ground where flowers, fruits, or vegetables are grown. 2, a delightful spot. —*v.i.* lay out or work in a garden. —**gar'den·er,** *n.* one who tends a garden, esp. one employed to do so.

gar·de'ni·a (gär-dē'nyə) *n.* the white or yellow flower of a tropical shrub.

Gar·gan'tu·an (gär-gan'tū-ən) *adj.* enormous; gigantic.

gar'gle (gär'gəl) *v.i.* rinse the throat with medicinal liquid. —*n.* a liquid for rinsing the throat.

gar'goyle (gär'goil) *n.* (*Archit.*) a grotesque stone image.

gar'ish (gär'ish) *adj.* showy; over-decorated. —**gar'ish·ness,** *n.*

gar'land (gär'lənd) *n.* a wreath of flowers or leaves.

Gargoyle

gar'lic (gär'lik) *n.* a bulb with a strong onionlike flavor. —**gar'lick·y,** *adj.*

gar'ment (gär'mənt) *n.* any article of clothing.

gar'ner (gär'nər) *v.t.* reap, gather, and store, as in a granary; collect.

gar'net (gär'nit) *n.* a clear deep-red stone, used as a gem.

gar'nish (gär'nish) *n.* a decoration, esp. for food. —*v.t.* 1, adorn. 2, garnishee. —**gar'nish·ment,** *n.*

gar″nish·ee' (gär″ni-shē') *v.t.* [-eed'(-ēd'), -ee'ing] (*Law*) attach a defendant's property which is in the possession of a third party, esp. wages.

gar'ni·ture (gär'ni-chər) *n.* decoration; trimming.

gar'ret (gar'ət) *n.* an attic.

gar'ri·son (gar'ə-sən) *n.* troops stationed in a fort or fortified town.

gar·rote' (gə-rōt') *v.t.* kill by strangulation.

gar·ru'li·ty (gə-roo'lə-tē) *n.* quality of being garrulous.

gar'ru·lous (gar'yə-ləs) *adj.* given to talking too much. —**gar'ru·lous·ness,** *n.*

gar'ter (gär'tər) *n.* a band or other device to keep up a stocking.

gas *n.* **1,** any elastic, airlike fluid capable of indefinite expansion. **2,** such fluids used as anesthetic, fuel, etc. **3,** noxious fumes. **4,** (*Colloq.*) gasoline. —*v.i.* (gassed, gas'sing) (*Slang*) converse idly but at length. —*v.t.* poison with gas.

gas chamber a room in which a person is executed with gas.

gas'con·ade' (gas'kə-nād') *n.* boastful talk.

gas'e·ous (-ē-əs) *adj.* of or like gas.

gash *n.* a deep slash or cut. —*v.t.* cut deeply.

gas'ket (gas'kit) *n.* a strip of material used to seal a joint; a washer.

gas mask a mask worn for protection against poison gas.

gas'o·line" (gas'ə-lēn") *n.* an inflammable liquid distilled from petroleum, used esp. as a motor fuel. Also, **gas'o·lene".**

gasp (gàsp) *n.* a convulsive catching of the breath. —*v.i.* labor for breath painfully. —*v.t.* utter with quick, short breaths.

gas'tric (gas'trik) *adj.* pert. to the stomach. —**gas·tri'tis** (-trī'tis) *n.* inflammation of the stomach.

gas·tron'o·my (gas·tron'ə-mē) *n.* the art of preparing good food. —**gas"tro·nom'ic** (-trə-nom'ik) *adj.* —**gas"tro·nom'i·cal·ly,** *adv.*

gat *n.* (*Slang*) a pistol.

gate (gāt) *n.* **1,** an opening, esp. in a fence, hedge, or wall, for entrance and exit; a movable barrier at such an opening. **2,** (*Slang*) the money received from sale of admission tickets. **3,** (*Slang*) dismissal.

gate'way" *n.* a means of access.

gath'er (gath'ər) *v.t.* **1,** bring together; assemble. **2,** cull; pick. **3,** acquire; gain; amass. **4,** recover; marshal. **5,** infer. **6,** draw (cloth) into folds; pleat. —*v.i.* **1,** congregate. **2,** increase. **3,** come to a head, as a boil. —*n.* a fold or pleat in cloth. —**gath'er·ing,** *n.* an assemblage.

gauche (gōsh) *adj.* socially awkward. —**gau'che·rie** (gō'shə-rē) *n.*

Gau'cho (gow'chō) *n.* a cowboy of South America.

gaud'y (gâ'dē) *adj.* **1,** gay; bright. **2,** showy without taste. —**gaud'i·ness,** *n.*

gauge (gāj) *n.* **1,** a standard of measurement. **2,** a graduated instrument for measuring. —*v.t.* **1,** measure. **2,** estimate. Also, **gage.**

gaunt (gânt) *adj.* thin; haggard. —**gaunt'ness,** *n.*

gaunt'let (gânt'lət) *n.* **1,** a glove with a long, wide cuff. **2,** a challenge. **3,** a course beset by punishing or afflicting agencies. Also, **gant'let.**

gauze (gâz) *n.* a very thin, porous fabric of silk, cotton, wire, etc.

gave (gāv) *v.* pret. of *give.*

gav'el (gav'əl) *n.* a small mallet, used by a chairman or auctioneer.

ga·votte' (gə-vot') *n.* a dance similar to the minuet, but livelier.

gawk (gâk) *n.* an awkward fellow. —*v.i.* stare stupidly. —**gawk'y,** *adj.* clownish; clumsy.

gay (gā) *adj.* **1,** high-spirited; merry. **2,** bright; colorful; showy. —**gay'e·ty** (-ə-tē) *n.* —**gay'ness,** *n.*

gaze (gāz) *n.* a fixed, intent look. —*v.i.* look at intently.

ga·zelle' (gə-zel') *n.* a small, graceful antelope.

ga·zette' (gə-zet') *n.* **1,** a newspaper. **2,** an official government journal. —*v.t.* publish in such a journal.

gaz"et·teer' (gaz"ə-tir') *n.* a dictionary of geographical names.

Gazelle

gear (gir) *n.* **1,** equipment; apparatus; tools. **2,** a harness, as for horses, and its appurtenances. **3,** a wheel or part that engages another part of a machine, as by meshing teeth; a working unit of a machine, as steering gear. **4,** the adjustment of parts of a machine, with respect to speed or efficiency, as in *high gear, in gear.* —*v.t.* equip; harness. **2,** adjust the operation or speed of, with gears. —**gear'shift",** *n.* a mechanism for power transmission, as in an automobile.

gee (jē) *v.t., v.i. & interj.* turn or move to the right. —*v.i.* (*Colloq.*) suit; fit. —*interj.* (*Vulgar*) an expletive of mild feeling.

geese (gēs) *n.* pl. of *goose.*

Ge·hen'na (gi-hen'ə) *n.* a fiery place; hell.

Gei'ger counter (gī'gər) a device for detecting radioactivity.

gei'sha (gā'shə) *n.* a Japanese dancing girl.

gel'a·tin (jel'ə-tin) *n.* a granular transparent substance that congeals when cold; jelly. —**ge·lat'i·nous** (jə-lat'i-nəs) *adj.*

geld *v.t.* castrate. —**geld'ing,** *n.* a castrated animal, esp. a horse.

gel'id (jel'id) *adj.* very cold; icy. —**ge·lid'i·ty, gel'id·ness,** *n.*

gem (jem) *n.* 1, a precious stone. 2, an object of great beauty or worth.

gem'i·nate (jem'ə-nət) *adj.* in pairs, coupled. —*v.t. & i.* (-nāt") double. —**gem"i·na'tion,** *n.*

Gem'i·ni" (jem'ə-nī") *n.* a constellation, the Twins (see *zodiac*).

gen'darme (zhän'därm) *n.* (*Fr.*) a policeman.

gen'der (jen'dər) *n.* in grammar, the classification as masculine, feminine, or neuter.

gene (jēn) *n.* (*Biol.*) an element in the germ cell, concerned with the transmission of hereditary characteristics.

ge"ne·al'o·gy (jē"nē·al'ə-jē) *n.* record of descent from an ancestor; pedigree. —**ge"ne·a·log'i·cal,** *adj.* —**ge"ne·al'o·gist,** *n.* one whose vocation is tracing pedigrees.

gen'er·a (jen'ə-rə) *n.* pl. of *genus.*

gen'er·al (jen'ər-əl) *adj.* 1, pert. or applicable to all or most of an entire class or category; universal; not limited in scope. 2, widespread. 3, not specific or detailed; vague; indefinite. 4, usual; ordinary. 5, chief; highest-ranking. —*n.* 1, the highest-ranking army officer. 2, any officer ranking above a colonel. 3, the masses; the populace. —**gen'er·al·ship,** *n.*

gen"er·al·is'si·mo" (jen"ər-ə-lis'i-mō") *n.* a supreme military commander.

gen"er·al'i·ty (jen"ər-al'ə-tē) *n.* 1, the majority. 2, a statement that is essentially true but not specific.

gen'er·al·ize" (jen"ər-ə-līz") *v.t.* draw conclusions from varied evidence. —*v.t.* consider as or arrange by classes. —**gen"er·al·i·za'tion,** *n.*

gen'er·ate" (jen'ə-rāt") *v.t.* 1, bring into life. 2, produce; form. —**gen"er·a"tive,** *adj.*

gen"er·a'tion (jen"ə-rā'shən) *n.* 1, production by natural or artificial means. 2, the average difference in age between parent and child, usually counted as 30 years; each ancestor in a line of descent. 3, all persons living at the same time. 4, (*pl.*) descendants.

gen"er·a"tor (jen'ə-rā"tər) *n.* an apparatus for producing gas, steam or electricity.

ge·ner'ic (ji-ner'ik) *adj.* 1, pert. to a genus or class. 2, general, not specific. —**ge·ner'i·cal·ly,** *adv.*

gen"er·os'i·ty (jen'ə-ros'ə-tē) *n.* quality of being generous; liberality.

gen'er·ous (jen'ər-əs) *adj.* 1, free in giving; liberal. 2, abundant. 3, not mean or prejudiced.

gen'e·sis (jen'ə-sis) *n.* [*pl.* -ses" (-sēz")] 1, the origin of anything. 2, (*cap.*) the first book of the Old Testament.

ge·net'ics (ji-net'iks) *n. pl.* the study of the evolution of species and of heredity. —**ge·net'ic,** *adj.* —**ge·net'i·cal·ly,** *adv.*

gen'ial (jēn'yəl) *adj.* 1, friendly and kindly in manner; cordial; jovial. 2, favorable to growth or comfort. —**ge"ni·al'i·ty** (jē"nē·al'ə-tē) *n.*

ge'nie (jē'nē) *n.* a mythical spirit having power to perform miraculous deeds.

gen'i·tal (jen'ə-təl) *adj.* pert. to reproduction of animals. —*n.* (*pl.*) the organs of reproduction.

gen'i·tive (jen'ə-tiv) *n.* the grammatical case expressing possession or source; the possessive.

gen'ius (jēn'yəs) *n.* 1, the guiding spirit of a person or place. 2, natural fitness; aptitude; talent; bent. 3, exceptional mental and creative power. 4, a person with such power.

gen'o·cide" (jen'ə-sīd") *n.* deliberate extermination of an entire people.

gen're (zhän'rə) *n.* in painting, portrayal of scenes from everyday life.

gen·teel' (jen-tēl') *adj.* affectedly refined. —**gen·teel'ness,** *n.*

gen'tian (jen'shən) *n.* an herb bearing a blue flower.

gen'tile (jen'tīl) *n.* 1, (*Bible*) a person not a Jew. 2, in respect to any religious group, an outsider.

gen·til'i·ty (jen-til'ə-tē) *n.* 1, the state of being well-born or well-bred; all persons of good or noble birth. 2, gentleness; softness.

gen'tle (jen'təl) *adj.* 1, mild in manner or disposition; tender; peaceful; tame. 2, not rough or harsh; kind. 3, of good birth; belonging to the gentry. —**gen'tle·ness,** *n.* —**gentle sex,** women.

gen'tle·folk" *n.pl.* persons of good breeding.

gen'tle·man (jen'təl-mən) *n.* [*pl.* -men (-men)] 1, a man of good birth. 2, an honorable man of fine feelings. 3, (*pl.*) men; sirs. —**gen'tle·man·ly,** *adj.* refined; well-behaved. —**gen'tle·wom"an,** *n.fem.*

gen'try (jen'trĕ) *n.* **1,** people of good breeding and, usually, wealth. **2,** people of a particular class or group.

gen'u·flect" (jen'ū-flekt") *v.i.* bend the knee, esp. in worship. —**gen"u·flec'tion**, **gen"u·flex'ion,** *n.*

gen'u·ine (jen'yū-in) *adj.* **1,** not counterfeit; authentic. **2,** real; sincere. —**gen'u·ine·ness,** *n.*

ge'nus (jē'nəs) *n.* [*pl.* **gen'er·a** (jen'ə-rə)] (*Biol.*) a group of animals or plants having close relationship.

ge·o- *pref.* signifying earth.

ge·od'e·sy (jē-od'ə-sĕ) *n.* the science of measuring the shape and area of the earth. —**ge"o·det'ic** (jē"ō-det'ik) *adj.*

ge·og'ra·phy (jē-og'rə-fĕ) *n.* the science that deals with the earth, its plants and animals, climate, population, industries, etc. —**ge·og'ra·pher,** *n.* —**ge"o·graph'ic** (jē"ō-graf'ik), **ge"o·graph'i·cal,** *adj.*

ge·ol'o·gy (jē-ol'ə-jē) *n.* the science that deals with the history of the earth and its changes, esp. as recorded in its rocks. —**ge·o·log'i·cal,** *adj.* —**ge·ol'o·gist,** *n.*

ge·om'e·try (jē-om'ə-trĕ) *n.* that branch of mathematics dealing with the relations and measurements of lines, angles, surfaces, and solids. —**ge"o·met'ric** (jē"ə-met'rik), **ge"o·met'ri·cal,** *adj.* —**ge·om"e·tri'cian** (-trish'ən) *n.*

ge"o·pol'i·tics (jē"ō-pol'ə-tiks) *n.* the study or application of political science in the light of geographical influences and objectives.

Geor'gian (jôr'jən) *adj.* pert. to the period (1714–1830) of the reigns of George I to George IV of England.

ge·ra'ni·um (jə-rā'nē-əm) *n.* **1,** a wild flower with pinkish-blue blossoms. **2,** a cultivated plant with large heads of white, pink, or red flowers.

ger"i·at'rics (jer'ē-at'riks) *n.* the study and treatment of diseases attendant on old age.

germ (jẽrm) *n.* **1,** a microbe. **2,** the earliest stage of an organism. **3,** source; origin.

Ger'man (jẽr'mən) *adj.* pert. to Germany, its people, or language. —*n.* a native, or the language, of Germany. —**Ger·man'ic** (-man'ik) *adj.*

ger·mane' (jər-mān') *adj.* closely allied; relevant.

ger·ma'ni·um (jər-mā'nē-əm) *n.* a rare metallic element, no. 32, symbol Ge.

ger'mi·cide" (jẽr'mi-sīd") *n.* a substance to destroy germs. —**ger'mi·ci'dal,** *adj.*

ger'mi·nal (jẽr'mə-nəl) *adj.* sprouting; budding.

ger'mi·nate" (jẽr'mə-nāt") *v.i.* begin to grow; sprout. —**ger"mi·na'tion,** *n.*

ger'ry·man"der (ger'ē-man"dər) *v.t.* change the boundaries of election districts to give one political party an unfair advantage.

ger'und (jer'ənd) *n.* a noun formed from a verb and ending in -*ing.*

Ge·sta'po (gə-stä'pō) *n.* the state police of Nazi Germany.

ges'tate (jes'tāt) *v.t.* carry in the womb during pregnancy. —**ges·ta'tion,** *n.* pregnancy.

ges·tic'u·late" (jes-tik'yə-lāt") *v.i.* make gestures to convey meaning. —**ges·tic"u·la'tion,** *n.*

ges'ture (jes'chər) *n.* **1,** a movement of head or limbs to convey feeling or to emphasize or illustrate. **2,** something said or done for effect only. —*v.i.* make gestures.

get *v.t.* [**got, got** or **got'ten, get'ting**] **1,** acquire possession of, esp. by one's own efforts; obtain; receive. **2,** fetch. **3,** grasp; understand. **4,** cause to do or be done; cause to be; induce. **5,** produce; beget. —*v.i.* **1,** cause oneself to be or become; become. **2,** arrive. —*n.* offspring; a litter. —**get·a·way',** *n.* (*Slang*) escape. —**get away** (with), **1,** escape (the consequences of). —**get off, 1,** depart. **2,** escape punishment. —**get on, 1,** progress; proceed; succeed. **2,** grow older. —**get through** (to), reach; establish communication with, esp. by telephone. —**get up, 1,** arise. **2,** assemble. —**get-'up,** *n.* (*Colloq.*) costume; manner of dress.

gew'gaw" (gū'gâ") *n.* a piece of minor jewelry; bauble; plaything.

gey'ser (gī'zər) *n.* a hot spring that periodically spouts hot water and steam.

ghast'ly (gàst'lĕ) *adj.* **1,** very pale; haggard. **2,** morally shocking. —**ghast'li·ness,** *n.*

gher'kin (gẽr'kin) *n.* a small cucumber used for pickles.

ghet'to (get'ō) *n.* [*pl.* **-tos**] the Jewish quarter in a city.

ghost (gōst) *n.* **1,** a disembodied human spirit, esp. such a spirit thought of as returning to haunt the living; a specter. **2,** a mere shadow; a glimmering. —**ghost'ly,** *adj.* like a ghost. —**ghost writer,** an actual author for whose work another receives credit.

ghoul (gool) *n.* **1,** an imaginary spirit who preys on the dead. **2,** a grave robber. —**ghoul'ish,** *adj.*

G.I. *abbr.* Government Issue; (*Slang*) a soldier in the U.S. Army.

gi'ant (jī'ənt) *n.* **1,** an imaginary being of superhuman size. **2,** a person, animal, plant, or thing of great size. —*adj.* huge. —**gi′ant·ess**, *n.fem.*

gib′ber (jib′ər) *v.t.* talk nonsense; babble.

gib′ber·ish (jib′ər-ish) *n.* inarticulate talk; nonsense.

gib′bet (jib′ət) *n.* a gallows. —*v.t.* execute by hanging.

gib′bon (gib′ən) *n.* a small ape.

gib′bous (gib′əs) *adj.* convex, as the moon when more than half and less than full.

gibe (jīb) *v.t.* & *i.* mock; jeer; taunt. —*n.* a taunt.

Gibbon

gib′lets (jib′ləts) *n.pl.* the gizzard, liver and heart of poultry.

gid′dy (gid′ē) *adj.* 1, dizzy. 2, causing dizziness. 3, frivolous. —**gid′di·ness**, *n.*

gift *n.* 1, something given; a donation; a present. 2, the right or power to give. 3, a natural talent. —**gift′ed**, *adj.* endowed with unusual talent.

gig *n.* 1, a light, two-wheeled carriage. 2, a ship's boat.

gi·gan′tic (ji-gan′tik) *adj.* huge; enormous. —**gi·gan′ti·cal·ly**, *adv.*

gig′gle (gig′əl) *n.* a silly, half-suppressed laugh. —*v.i.* so laugh.

gig′o·lo (jig′ə-lō′) *n.* [*pl.* -los′] a man who, for pay, acts as an escort.

gig′ot (jig′ət) *n.* a puffed sleeve.

Gi′la monster (hē′lə) a large poisonous lizard of the American Southwest.

gild *v.t.* 1, overlay or coat with gold. 2, give a bright but misleading appearance to. —**gild′ing**, *n.* 1, superficial gold or simulated gold. 2, material for gilding, as gold leaf.

gill (gil) *n.* 1, the breathing organ of fish. 2, (jil) a liquid measure, one-fourth of a pint.

gil′ly·flow″er (jil′ē-flow″ər) *n.* 1, a cultivated flower-bearing plant. 2, a kind of apple.

gilt *n.* 1, gilding, esp. with an imitation of gold. 2, a young sow. —*adj.* gilded; imitative of gold.

gim′bals (jim′bəlz) *n.pl.* rings used for suspending anything, as a mariner's compass, so that it will remain level at all times.

gim′crack″ (jim′krak″) *n.* an intricate but useless device or ornament; a gewgaw.

gim′let (gim′lit) *n.* a hand tool for boring small holes.

gim′mick (gim′ik) *n.* 1, any small, concealed device used for trickery,

as by a magician. 2, any means of tricking the unwary, as a joker in a contract. 3, an inducement, as a premium, offered to make a sale.

gimp *n.* a braid used for trimming.

gin (jin) *n.* 1, an uncolored alcoholic liquor, distilled from grain. 2, a machine for separating the seeds from cotton. 3, a snare; trap. 4, [*also,* gin rummy] a card game for two. —*v.t.* put (cotton) through a gin.

gin′ger (jin′jər) *n.* 1, a tropical herb with a hot, spicy root, used in cooking and in medicine. 2, (*Colloq.*) vigor; vivacity.

gin′ger·bread″ (jin′jər-bred″) *n.* 1, a cake flavored with ginger. 2, excessively fancy decoration, in architecture.

gin′ger·ly (jin′jər-lē) *adv.* with extreme caution. —*adj.* slow and timid. —**gin′ger·li·ness**, *n.*

gin·gi·vi′tis (jin-jə-vī′tis) *n.* inflammation of the gums.

ging′ham (ging′əm) *n.* a cotton dress fabric woven in checks, plaids, or stripes.

gink′go (ging′kō) *n.* a tree with fan-shaped leaves, native to Japan and China.

gin′seng (jin′seng) *n.* a herb or shrub whose aromatic root is used in medicine.

gip′sy (jip′sē) *n.* gypsy.

gi·raffe′ (jə-raf′) *n.* an Afr. ruminant animal with extremely long neck and legs.

gird (gērd) *v.t.* [*pret.* & *p.p.* girt or gird′ed] 1, confine with a belt; make fast by binding. 2, encircle. 3, prepare for action; equip.

gird′er (gēr′dər) *n.* a main supporting beam, esp. of steel.

gir′dle (gēr′dəl) *n.* 1, a sash or belt for the waist. 2, an elastic undergarment to support the abdomen and shape the body. 3, a ring around a tree trunk. —*v.t.* bind; encircle.

girl (gērl) *n.* 1, a young woman or female child. 2, a maidservant. 3, (*Colloq.*) sweetheart. —**girl′hood**, *n.* —**girl′ish**, *adj.*

Girl Scout a member of the Girl Scouts, an association of girls 8 to about 18 years old.

girth (gērth) *n.* 1, a band around an animal's body to secure a saddle or load. 2, the distance around anything cylindrical; circumference.

gist (jist) *n.* the essence or substance of a matter; pith.

give (giv) *v.t.* [gave (gāv), giv′en, giv′ing] 1, bestow; make a present of; donate. 2, spend or pay, as money; exchange. 3, supply; deliver; convey. 4, (with *up*) yield;

concede. **5**, utter; impart. —*v.t.* **1**, bestow alms. **2**, (usually with *in* or *up*) yield; surrender. **3**, afford an opening. —*n.* lack of resistance; elasticity

give·a·way" (giv'ə-wā") *n.* **1**, an unintentional betrayal; a revelation. **2**, something free; a premium; a bargain. —*adj.* being a giveaway.

giv'en (giv'ən) *adj.* **1**, addicted; inclined. **2**, granted; agreed. **3**, (of a name) first, not the surname.

giz'zard (giz'ərd) *n.* the second stomach of a bird.

gla·cé' (glȧ-sā') *adj.* **1**, glossy; smooth. **2**, covered with a hard, shiny sugar coating.

gla'cial (glā'shəl) *adj.* pert. to ice or glaciers.

gla'cier (glā'shər) *n.* a slowly flowing mass or river of ice.

glad *adj.* [glad'der, -dest] **1**, joyful; bright; cheerful. **2**, joyous. —**glad'den** (-ən) *v.t. & t.* cause to be, or become, glad. —**glad'ness**, *n.*

glade (glād) *n.* a clear space in a forest.

glad'i·a"tor (glad'ē-ā"tər) *n.* in ancient Rome, a man who fought in the arena with men or wild beasts.

glad'i·o'lus (glad'ē-ō'ləs) *n.* a bulbous plant with a tall spike of large flowers. Also, **glad'i·o'la** (-lə).

glad'stone" bag a suitcase that opens into two equal compartments.

glair (glâr) *n.* the white of egg, used for sizing.

glam'our (glam'ər) *n.* alluring charm. Also, **glam'or.** —**glam'orous**, *adj.*

glance (glȧns) *n.* a brief, cursory look. —*v.i.* **1**, flash; gleam. **2**, take a hasty look. **3**, strike and be deflected.

gland *n.* an organ that secretes a substance to be used in the body. —**glan'du·lar** (glan'dyə-lər) *adj.*

glan'ders (glan'dərz) *n.* a contagious disease of horses.

glare (glâr) *n.* **1**, a dazzling light. **2**, a fierce look. **3**, a slippery surface, as of ice. —*v.i.* **1**, shine dazzlingly. **2**, stare fiercely.

glar'ing *adj.* **1**, shining dazzlingly. **2**, obvious; notorious.

glass (glȧs) *n.* **1**, a hard, brittle substance, usually transparent, made of silicates fused at high heat. **2**, an article, as a mirror, tumbler, etc., made of this substance; a telescope or binocular: *spyglass.* **3**, a tumblerful; the amount of liquid in a tumbler. **4**, (*pl.*) spectacles. —**glass'ful**, *n.*

glass·ine' (gla-sēn') *n.* a thin transparent paper.

glass'y (glȧs'ē) *adj.* **1**, like glass, esp. in smoothness. **2**, staring; expressionless. —**glass'i·ness**, *n.*

glau·co'ma (glȧ-kō'mə) *n.* a disease of the eye, a hardening of the eyeball.

glaze (glāz) *v.t.* **1**, furnish with glass, as a window sash. **2**, overlay (pottery, cloth, paper) with a glossy, hard surface. —*v.i.* become glassy. —*n.* a glassy appearance or sheen.

gla'zier (glā'zhər) *n.* one who works with glass.

gleam (glēm) *n.* **1**, a brief flash of light. **2**, luster. —*v.i.* emit dim rays of light.

glean (glēn) *v.t. & t.* gather (grain) after the reapers; pick up leavings.

glee (glē) *n.* **1**, mirth; delight. **2**, a musical piece for three or more voices. —**glee'ful**, *adj.* exultantly happy.

glen *n.* a narrow valley; dale.

glib *adj.* [glib'ber, -best] fluent but insincere. —**glib'ness**, *n.*

glide (glīd) *v.i.* move smoothly and easily. —*n.* **1**, a smooth, easy motion. **2**, the downward flight, without engine power, of an airplane.

glid'er (glī'dər) *n.* a motorless aircraft resembling an airplane.

glim'mer (glim'ər) *n.* a faint and wavering light. —*v.i.* shine faintly.

glim'mer·ing *n.* a faint trace, of light or anything.

glimpse (glimps) *n.* **1**, a momentary view. **2**, an inkling.—*v.t.* get a hasty view of.

glint *n.* a streaked reflection of light; a flash. —*v.i.* flash; sparkle.

glis·sade' (gli-säd') *n.* **1**, a sliding down a snow slope in a standing position. **2**, a glide in dancing.

glis·san'do (gli-sän'dō) *n.* (*Music*) the effect of sliding the finger across the keys or strings of an instrument.

glis'ten (glis'ən) *v.i.* shine with sparkling light; gleam.

glit'ter (glit'ər) *v.i.* **1**, send off shoots of light, as a gem; sparkle. **2**, be brilliant or showy. —*n.* **1**, sparkling light. **2**, splendor; allure.

gloam'ing (glō'ming) *n.* twilight.

gloat (glōt) *v.i.* **1**, gaze or ponder with spite, lust, or greed. **2**, show joy at another's misfortune.

glob'al (glō'bəl) *adj.* worldwide.

globe (glōb) *n.* **1**, a sphere; a ballshaped body. **2**, the earth. **3**, a sphere bearing a map of the earth. **4**, something of near-spherical shape, as an incandescent lamp, a bowl, etc.

globe'trot"ter *n.* one who travels all over the world.

glob′u·lar (glob′yə-lər) *adj.* spherical. – **glob′u·lar′i·ty,** *n.*

glob′ule (glob′ūl) *n.* a tiny, round particle

glock′en·spiel″ (glok′ən-spēl″) *n.* a musical instrument consisting of tuned bells or tubes played upon with hammers.

Glockenspiel

gloom *n.* **1,** dim shade; obscurity; cloudiness. **2,** melancholy; pessimism. **—gloom′y,** *adj.*

glo′ri·fy″ (glôr′i-fī″) *v.t.* **1,** worship. **2,** confer honor on. **3,** invest with beauty. **—glo′ri·fi·ca′tion,** *n.*

glo′ri·ous (glôr′ē-əs) *adj.* **1,** pert. to glory; blessed. **2,** illustrious; splendid. – **glo′ri·ous·ness,** *n.*

glo′ry (glôr′ē) *n.* **1,** exalted honor. **2,** splendor; radiance. **3,** celestial bliss. **4,** a source of pride. **5,** height of prosperity or renown. **6,** a halo. **—v.i.** exult; rejoice.

gloss (glâs) *n.* **1,** a smooth, mirror-like finish; luster. **2,** a deceptive exterior. **3,** an explanation or annotation to clarify a word or phrase.

glos′sa·ry (glos′ə-rē) *n.* an explanatory list of terms used in a text.

gloss′y (-ē) *adj.* having a gloss or sheen; lustrous. **—gloss′i·ness,** *n.*

-glot *suf.* denoting mastery of (a specified number of) languages.

glot′tis (glot′is) *n.* the opening at the top of the windpipe and between the vocal cords.

glove (gluv) *n.* **1,** a covering for the hand, with compartments for the thumb and fingers. **2,** a padded covering for the hand, used in certain sports. **—glov′er,** *n.* a maker of gloves.

glow (glō) *v.i.* **1,** throw out heat and light without flame; display dull light. **2,** be flushed with heat or emotion; redden, as from exertion. **3,** shine brightly. **—n. 1,** luminosity. **2,** brightness of color. **3,** ardor. **4,** bodily warmth.

glow′er (glow′ər) *v.i.* look menacing or angry; scowl; frown.

glow′worm″ (glō′wẽrm″) *n.* an insect or its larva that glows in the dark.

glu′cose (gloo′kōs) *n.* a light-colored syrup obtained from starch, cane sugar, etc., by the action of acids.

glue (gloo) *n.* a sticky, soluble substance that dries to a resinous hardness, used as an adhesive and sizing. **—glue′y,** *adj.*

glum *adj.* [**glum′mer, -mest**] disheartened; sullen. **—glum′ness,** *n.*

glut *v.t.* [**glut′ted, -ting**] fill to overflowing; satiate; overstock. **—n. 1,** a surfeit. **2,** supply exceeding demand.

glu′ten (gloo′tən) *n.* a sticky substance, highly nutritious, found in flour.

glu′ti·nous (gloo′tə-nəs) *adj.* sticky.

glut′ton (glut′ən) *n.* an excessive eater; a greedy person. **—glut′ton·ous,** *adj.* **—glut′ton·y,** *n.* greed.

glyc′er·in (glis′ər-in) *n.* a colorless syrupy liquid used in cosmetics, drugs, explosives, etc.

gly′co·gen (glī′kə-jən) *n.* the sugar formed in the body from carbohydrates.

glyp′tic (glip′tik) *adj.* pert. to carving and engraving.

G-′man″ (jē′man″) *n.* (*Slang*) an agent of the FBI.

gnarl (närl) *n.* a knot on a tree. **—v.t.** twist; knot. **—gnarled,** *adj.* full of knots; twisted.

gnash (nash) *v.t.* grate or grind (the teeth) together.

gnat (nat) *n.* any of several small biting insects.

gnaw (nâ) *v.t. & i.* **1,** bite or wear away with the front teeth. **2,** consume; torture as if by continual biting. **—gnaw′ing,** *n.* a continuous feeling of discomfort, as from hunger or remorse.

gneiss (nīs) *n.* rock composed of layers of quartz, mica, etc.

gnome (nōm) *n.* a dwarf, esp. an imaginary one living in the earth and guarding its treasures.

gno′mon (nō′mon) *n.* the arm on a sundial which by its shadow shows the time of day.

gnos′tic (nos′tik) *adj.* **1,** possessing mystic knowledge. **2,** (*cap.*) a believer in Gnosticism, a mystic, quasi-religious philosophy.

gnu (noo) *n.* an Afr. antelope resembling an ox.

go (gō) *v.i.* [**went, gone, go′ing**] **1,** move away (from where the speaker is); depart. **2,** be in motion; proceed; travel; be transported. **3,** succeed; fit; be suited. **4,** pass; elapse; cease to exist. **5,** extend; continue. **6,** operate; be in working order. **7,** be sold; be disposed of; be transferred. **8,** be a part of; belong. **—n.** (*Colloq.*) **1,** ambition; energy. **2,** a success. **3,** an agreement. **4,** an attempt; a try.

go′a (gō′ə) *n.* an antelope of Tibet.

goad (gōd) *n.* **1,** a sharp stick for driving cattle. **2,** any incentive.

—v.t. spur on, with or as with a goad; urge.

goal (gōl) *n.* **1,** the point that limits a race. **2,** the place, in some games, that players must reach to score; the score for reaching such a place. **3,** any object of ambition or desire. **—goal'ie,** *n.* goalkeeper. **—goal'keep"er,** *n.* (*Hockey*) the player who guards the goal.

goat (gōt) *n.* **1,** an agile, horned ruminant animal about the size of a sheep, valued for its milk and hair. **2,** (*Colloq.*) the victim of a joke; an innocent sufferer.

goat-ee' (gō-tē') *n.* a pointed beard.

goat'herd" *n.* one who tends goats.

goat'skin" *n.* leather made from the hide of a goat.

gob *n.* **1,** a mass or lump; a mouthful. **2,** (*Colloq.*) a sailor.

gob'ble (gob'əl) *v.t.* **1,** swallow hastily. **2,** (*Slang*) (often with *up*) seize greedily. **—v.i.** make a rattling noise in the throat, as a male turkey. **—n.** the cry of a male turkey. **—gob'bler,** *n.* a male turkey.

go-'be.tween" *n.* an intermediary.

gob'let (gob'lit) *n.* a drinking glass with a stem and base.

gob'lin *n.* a surly, malicious sprite.

god *n.* **1,** (*cap.*) the Supreme Being, creator and master of all. **2,** any being considered as divine. **3,** an idol. **4,** a person or thing made the object of supreme devotion. **—god'dess (-əs)** *n.fem.*

god'child" *n.* a child one sponsors at baptism. **—god'daugh"ter, god'fa"ther, god'moth"er, god'son",** *n.*

God'head" *n.* the state of being divine.

god'less (-ləs) *adj.* impious; wicked. **—god'less·ness,** *n.*

god'ly (-lē) *adj.* pious. **—god'li·ness,** *n.*

god'send" *n.* an unlooked-for acquisition or piece of good fortune.

god'wit *n.* a water bird akin to the snipe.

go-"get'ter *n.* (*Slang*) one who succeeds by vigorous pursuit of his object.

gog'gle (gog'əl) *v.i.* roll the eyes; blink. **—gog'gles,** *n. pl.* spectacles to protect against glare, dust, etc.

goi'ter (goi'tər) *n.* morbid swelling of the thyroid gland.

gold (gōld) *n.* **1,** a precious metallic element, no. 79, symbol Au, used in coinage and jewelry. **2,** money; wealth. **3,** a bright yellow color.

gold brick 1, anything sold as valuable that proves to be valueless. **2,** (*Slang*) in the U. S. Army, a soldier who cleverly evades onerous duty.

gold digger (*Slang*) a woman whose interest in men is mainly mercenary.

gold'en (gōl'dən) *adj.* **1,** made of gold. **2,** yellow. **3,** most auspicious. **4,** very precious; excellent. **5,** most flourishing. **6,** glamorous.

gold'en.rod" *n.* a wildflower with yellow flower-heads.

golden rule a rule of conduct: do unto others as you would have them do unto you.

gold-'filled" *adj.* heavily gold-plated.

gold'fish" *n.* a small yellow fish of the carp family.

gold leaf gold beaten into thin leaves.

gold'smith" *n.* a worker in gold.

gold standard a standard of value for a monetary system based on gold.

golf *n.* a game played on an extensive course, in which the object is to drive a ball into a series of holes in the fewest number of strokes.

gol'ly (gol'ē) *interj.* an exclamation of delight or surprise.

gon'ad *n.* in biology, a sex gland.

gon'do·la (gon'də-lə) *n.* **1,** a narrow, one-oared boat used on the canals of Venice. **2,** an open railroad freight car. **3,** the control car of an airship. **—gon"do·lier'** (-lir') *n.* the oarsman of a gondola.

Gondola

gone (gân) *v.* p.p. of go. **—adj.** **1,** ruined; failing. **2,** (*Colloq.*) (with *on*) in love; entranced. **—gon'er,** *n.* (*Slang*) a person or thing lost or past recovery.

gon'fa.lon (gon'fə-lən) *n.* a flag; standard.

gong (gâng) *n.* a metal disk giving a resonant tone when struck.

gon"or·rhe'a (gon"ə-rē'ə) *n.* a contagious disease of the genitals.

goo *n.* (*Slang*) a sticky substance.

goo'ber (goo'bər) *n.* the peanut.

good (gud) *adj.* [bet'ter, best] **1,** worthy of respect or commendation, by being beneficial, honest, noble, etc. **2,** useful; suited to the purpose; skillful or competent. **3,** virtuous; pure; well-behaved. **4,** thorough; complete; considerable. **5,** valid;

genuine; worthy of being believed or trusted. **6**, pleasant; agreeable. —*n.* **1**, what is right, just, or desirable. **2**, virtuous persons. **3**, (*pl.*) merchandise, esp. textiles; possessions. —*interj.* expressing agreement, approval, or congratulation.

good"bye' (gŭd"bī') *interj. & n.* **1**, a word spoken when parting from another; farewell. **2**, a parting, dismissal, or abandonment. Also, **good-"by'** [*pl.* **-bys'**], **good-"bye'**.

good'ies (gŭd'ēz) *n.pl.* candy.

good-"look'ing *adj.* handsome; comely.

good'ly (gŭd'lē) *adj.* adequate in quality, amount, etc.

good-na"tured *adj.* having a pleasant disposition; friendly and cheerful.

good'ness (gŭd'nəs) *n.* **1**, the state, quality or degree of being good. **2**, heaven; providence. —*interj.* a mild exclamation.

good will *n.* **1**, kindly feeling; cheerful readiness. **2**, the value to a business of its established position and patronage.

good'y (gŭd'ē) *interj.* expressing delight. —**good'y-good'y**, *adj.* priggish.

goof *n.* (*Slang*) a silly person. —*v.i.* make a mistake.

goon *n.* (*Slang*) a hired thug.

goop *n.* (*Slang*) an uncouth person.

goose (goos) *n.* [*pl.* **geese** (gēs)] **1**, a large web-footed bird, esp. the female, similar to a duck; its flesh. **2**, a silly person. **3**, [*pl.* **goos'es**] a tailor's iron.

Goose

goose'ber"ry (goos'ber"ē) *n.* a tart, greenish-brown berry, used in preserves.

goose flesh a roughened condition of the skin caused by cold or fear. Also, **goose pimples**.

goose'neck" (goos'nek") *n.* anything curved like a goose's neck, esp. an iron or rubber coupling.

goose step a stiff-kneed marching step, as used by German soldiers.

go'pher (gō'fər) *n.* **1**, a ground squirrel of the prairies. **2**, a burrowing rodent with large cheek pouches.

gore (gōr) *n.* **1**, a wedge-shaped piece of cloth used to vary width, as of a garment or sail. **2**, blood. —*v.t.* pierce, as with a horn.

gorge (gôrj) *n.* **1**, a narrow ravine. **2**, the gluttonous eating of a big

meal; a feast. **3**, food consumed; what has been swallowed. —*v.t. & i.* eat greedily; stuff.

gor'geous (gôr'jəs) *adj.* showy; magnificent. —**gor'geous·nes**—*n.*

go·ril'la (gə-ril'ə) *n.* **1**, the largest known manlike ape. **2**, a powerful, brutal man.

gor'mand·ize (gôr'mən-dīz") *v.i.* eat voraciously.

gorse (gôrs) *n.* a common Europ. weed; furze.

gor'y (gôr'ē) *adj.* **1**, like or covered with blood. **2**, involving bloodshed. —**gor'i·ness**, *n.*

gosh *interj.* a mild curse.

gos'ling (goz'ling) *n.* a young goose.

gos'pel (gos'pəl) *n.* **1**, the record of Christ's life and teachings. **2**, (*cap.*) any one of the first four books of the New Testament. **3**, any principle one believes in or preaches. **4**, absolute truth.

gos'sa·mer (gos'ə-mər) *n.* **1**, a cobweb. **2**, any thin, filmy material. —*adj.* cobweblike; unsubstantial.

gos'sip (gos'ip) *n.* **1**, trifling talk, esp. about other persons. **2**, [also, **gos'sip·er**] an idle talker. —*v.i.* discuss other persons' affairs.

got *v.* pret. & p.p. of **get**.

Goth'ic (goth'ik) *adj.* designating a type of architecture with pointed arches and high, steep roofs. —*n.* a style of printing type without serifs.

got'ten (got'ən) *v.* p.p. of **get**.

gouache (gwäsh) *n.* a way of painting with water colors; a painting so made.

gouge (gowj) *v.t.* **1**, scoop or tear out. **2**, (*Colloq.*) **1**, overcharge. **2**, cheat. —*n.* a chisel.

gou'lash (goo'läsh) *n.* **1**, a highly seasoned stew. **2**, a jumble.

gourd (gôrd) *n.* **1**, the fleshy fruit of a vine related to the squash and cucumber. **2**, the dried shell of this fruit, used as a dipper or vessel.

gour'mand (gûr'mənd) *n.* **1**, a glutton. **2**, a lover of good food.

gour'met (gûr'mā) *n.* a lover of good eating; an epicure.

gout (gowt) *n.* a painful inflammation of the joints, esp. of the big toe. —**gout'y**, *adj.* —**gout'i·ness**, *n.*

gov'ern (guv'ərn) *v.t. & i.* **1**, rule with authority. **2**, guide; control.

gov'er·ness (guv'ər-nəs) *n.* a woman tutor for children.

gov'ern·ment (guv'ərn-mənt) *n.* **1**, regulation; management. **2**, a state's established form of political rule. **3**, the body of persons authorized to govern; the administration. —**gov″ern·men′tal** (-men′təl) *adj.*

gov′er·nor (guv′ər-nər) *n.* **1**, one who governs; esp. the head of a state of the U. S. **2**, a device for regulating the speed of an engine.

gown *n.* **1**, a woman's dress. **2**, a loose robe worn officially by judges, clergymen, etc.; fig., the academic world. —*v.t.* put a gown on; dress.

grab *v.t.* [**grabbed, grab′bing**] **1**, seize violently or suddenly; snatch. **2**, obtain by violent or illegal means. —*n.* seizure. —**grab′ber,** *n.*

grace (grās) *n.* **1**, ease and elegance of manner or movement; charm. **2**, (often *pl.*) liking; favor; good will. **3**, virtue; kindness; politeness. **4**, postponement, as of a penalty or obligation; clemency. **5**, a prayer for blessing at a meal. **6**, divine favor. —*v.t.* **1**, adorn. **2**, honor; favor. —**grace′ful,** *adj.* beautiful and elegant in form, manner, and esp. movement. —**grace note** (*Music*) a note not essentialbut or namental.

gra′cious (grā′shəs) *adj.* **1**, kindly; courteous. **2**, charming; attractive. —*interj.* a mild expression of surprise. —**gra′cious·ness,** *n.*

grack′le (grak′əl) *n.* a blackbird.

gra·da′tion (grā-dā′shən) *n.* **1**, the act or process of classifying by grade, or becoming different in grade. **2**, a grade differing only slightly from near grades.

grade (grād) *n.* **1**, a step in any series, as of quality, etc.; degree. **2**, relative position in any scale; rank; standing or a mark of standing. **3**, one of the divisions of a school course; also, the pupils in any of these divisions. **4**, the rate of ascent and descent of a highway or railroad; also, a slope. —*v.t.* **1**, classify, as by relative quality; sort. **2**, make (a slope) level. —**grade crossing,** two roads or tracks crossing at the same level. —**grade school,** a primary school, below high school.

gra′di·ent (grā′dē-ənt) *n.* the amount or angle of slope.

ᵣrad′u·al (gra′joo-əl) *adj.* changing by degrees; not sudden or abrupt.

grad′u·ate (gra′joo-ət) *n.* **1**, one who has received an academic degree. **2**, a measuring glass. —*v.t.* (-āt) **1**, confer an academic degree upon. **2**, mark with degrees; calibrate. —*v.i.* (-āt) **1**, receive a degree or diploma. **2**, pass gradually. —**grad·u·a′tion,** *n.*

graft (gráft) *v.t.* **1**, unite or mix living tissue or plant shoots, for joint growth or reproduction; cross-breed. **2**, dishonestly accept (bribes, perquisites). —*n.* **1**, the act of grafting; a part grafted. **2**, dishonest use of office to get money or perquisites; anything so acquired.

gra′ham flour (grā′əm) whole-wheat flour.

grail (grāl) *n.* a cup. —**Holy Grail,** in legend, the cup used by Jesus at the Last Supper.

grain (grān) *n.* **1**, cereal grasses, or their seeds. **2**, a tiny, hard particle. **3**, the smallest unit of weight; an infinitesimal amount. **4**, the direction in which fibers run; texture, as of wood, stone, etc. **5**, the hair side of leather. —*v.t.* paint or emboss in the pattern of the grain of wood, leather, etc.

gram *n.* the unit of weight in the metric system, .0353 avoirdupois ounce.

-gram *suf.* denoting a writing, as *telegram.*

gram′mar (gram′ər) *n.* **1**, the science of word-endings and inflectional forms. **2**, mode of speaking and writing according to the principles of grammar. **3**, a book on grammar. —**gram·mar′i·an** (grə-mãr′ē-ən) *n.* a student of grammar. —**grammar school** (*U.S.*) an elementary school, grades 1 to 8.

gram·mat′i·cal (grə-mat′i-kəl) *adj.* **1**, pert. to grammar. **2**, correct in grammar.

gram′o·phone″ (gram′ə-fōn″) *n.* (*T.N.*) a phonograph.

gram′pus (gram′pəs) *n.* a large sea mammal related to the dolphin.

gran′a·ry (gran′ə-rē) *n.* a storage place for grain.

grand *adj.* **1**, imposing in size or effect; majestic; splendid. **2**, dignified; lofty; eminent. **3**, belonging to high society; elegant. **4**, main; comprehensive; all-embracing. **5**, designating the second generation in ascent or descent, as *grandfather, grandson.* —**grand′ness,** *n.*

grand duke 1, a royal prince, esp. in czarist Russia. **2**, the ruler of a grand duchy, a principality ranking next below a kingdom.

gran·dee′ (gran-dē′) *n.* a great nobleman; a man of comparable rank or pretensions.

gran′deur (gran′jūr) *n.* **1**, grandness; illustriousness. **2**, conspicuous splendor.

gran·dil′o·quent (gran-dil′ə-kwənt) *adj.* pompous, esp. in speech; bombastic. —**gran·dil′o·quence,** *n.*

gran′di·ose (gran′dē-ōs″) *adj.* **1**, ostentatiously imposing. **2**, bombastic; showy. —**gran″di·os′i·ty,** *n.*

grand jury a jury that indicts.

grand larceny the crime of stealing something of great value.

grand opera a play in which all dialogue is sung.

grand piano a piano with a horizontal, harp-shaped cabinet.

grand'stand n. the main structure for seating spectators at outdoor sporting events. —**grandstand play** (*Slang*) a competitor's feat intended solely to impress an audience.

grange (grānj) n. 1, (*Archaic*) a farm. 2, (*cap.*) a national society of farmers; one of its branches.

gran'ite (gran'it) n. a hard, durable rock.

gra·niv'o·rous (gra-niv'ə-rəs)adj. feeding on grain.

gran'ny (gran'ē) n. 1, grandmother; an old woman. 2, an incorrectly tied square knot.

grant (gránt) v.t. 1, convey by deed. 2, give; bestow. 3, concede to be true. —n. the act of granting; also, the thing (land, money, etc.) given. —**gran·tee'** (-tē') n. the recipient of a grant. —**grant'or**, n.

gran'u·late (gran'yə-lāt) v.t. 1, grind or form into granules. 2, roughen the surface of. —**gran'u·la'tion**, n.

gran'ule (gran'ūl) n. a fine grain or particle. —**gran'u·lar**, adj. composed of or formed in grains.

grape (grāp) n. 1, a juicy berry growing in clusters on a vine. 2, wine. 3, grape-sized cannon shot: *grapeshot*.

grape'fruit" n. a large citrus fruit.

grape'vine" n. 1, the vine that bears grapes. 2, (*Colloq.*) word-of-mouth transmission of secret information.

graph (gráf) n. a diagram showing the successive values of a changing quantity. —v.t. mark such values on cross-ruled paper.

-graph (gráf) suf. a writing or picturing, as in *telegraph, photograph*.

graph'ic (graf'ik) adj. 1, pert. to the arts of drawing, printing, engraving, etc. 2, vivid; lifelike. —**graph'i·cal·ly**, adv.

graph'ite (graf'īt) n. a soft, greasy, natural carbon used in lead pencils and as a lubricant.

-gra·phy (grə-fē) suf. writing or picturing, as in *photography, geography*.

grap'nel (grap'nəl) n. a hook with several prongs, for grappling.

grap'ple (grap'əl) v.t. lay fast hold of. —v.i. seize; come to close quarters with. —n. 1, a grapnel. 2, a clinch, as in wrestling.

grasp (grásp) v.t. 1, seize and hold. 2, understand. —n. 1, a grip; clasp. 2, possession. 3, comprehension. —**grasp'ing**, adj. covetous; miserly.

grass (grás) n. 1, green herbage sending up spikelike shoots or blades. 2, any of a large family of plants with hollow stems and grainlike seed. 3, a lawn; pasture.

grass'hop"per (grás'hop"ər) n. a large jumping insect destructive to crops.

grass'roots' adj. (*Colloq.*) emanating from the mass of people, as a cause, political movement, etc.

grass widow (*Colloq.*) a woman separated from her husband.

grass'y (-ē) adj. 1, covered with grass. 2, like grass.

grate (grāt) v.t. 1, reduce to particles by rubbing on a rough surface. 2, rub together with harsh sound. —v.i. 1, make a rasping noise. 2, cause irritation. —n. 1, a frame of iron bars, as in a door or window. 2, a box or frame of iron bars for holding burning fuel; a fireplace. —**grat'er**, n. a device for shredding or grating.

grate'ful (grāt'fəl) adj. 1, thankful. 2, soothing; pleasant.

grat'i·fy (grat'i-fī') v.t. please; satisfy; indulge. —**grat'i·fi·ca'tion**, n.

grat'ing (grā'ting) n. a latticework of wood or metal.

gra'tis (grā'tis) adv. without charge.

grat'i·tude" (grat'i-tood") n. thankfulness.

gra·tu'i·tous (grə-tū'i-təs) adj. 1, freely given. 2, uncalled for. —**gra·tu'i·tous·ness**, n.

gra·tu'i·ty (grə-tū'i-tē) n. an extra payment, not owed; a tip.

grave (grāv) adj. 1, earnest; sedate; dignified. 2, momentous; presenting a crisis. 3, somber; not gay. —n. an excavation for the burial of a body; a tomb; hence, death. —**grave'ness**, n. seriousness.

grav'el (grav'əl) n. fragments of rock larger than sand.

grav'en (grā'vən) adj. deeply carved or impressed; engraved.

grave'stone" n. a marker placed where a person is buried; a tombstone.

grave'yard" n. a cemetery.

grav'i·tate" (grav'i-tāt") v.i. 1, yield to the force that draws bodies together. 2, be attracted. —**grav'i·ta'tion**, n. —**grav'i·ta'tion·al**, adj. pert. to gravity or gravitation.

grav'i·ty (grav'ə-tē) *n.* 1, the force that draws all objects toward the center of the earth. 2, graveness.

gra·vure' (grə-vyûr') *n.* an intaglio printing process whereby liquid inks are deposited on paper from an engraved plate; such a plate; a print made by this process.

gra'vy (grā'vē) *n.* 1, the juice that escapes from meat in cooking; also, a sauce made from this juice. 2, (*Slang*) unearned profit.

gray (grā) *n.* a shade between, or mixture of, black and white. —*adj.* 1, of this shade. 2, cloudy; dismal. 3, aged; (of hair) whitened by age. Also, **grey. —gray'ish,** *adj.* —**gray matter** (*Colloq.*) brains; hence, intelligence.

gray'beard" *n.* an old man.

graze (grāz) *v.t.* 1, put (cattle) to pasture. 2, brush lightly in passing. —*v.i.* 1, feed on grass, etc., as cattle. 2, (often with *against*) barely touch. —*n.* a grazing touch; abrasion.

grease (grēs) *n.* 1, animal fat; any oily matter. 2, an oily lubricant much more viscous than liquid oil. —*v.t.* (grēz) 1, lubricate, esp. with grease. 2, (*Slang*) flatter; bribe. —**grease paint,** theatrical make-up.

greas'y (grē'zē) *adj.* 1, oily in feel or appearance. 2, slippery. —**greas'i·ness,** *n.*

great (grāt) *adj.* 1, conspicuously large or important; vast; numerous. 2, extreme. 3, long-continued. 4, notable; renowned; magnificent. 5, (*Colloq.*) most enjoyable. 6, one step more remote in relationship, as *great-grandfather*, the father of a grandfather. —**great-'aunt",** *n.* the aunt of a parent; grandaunt. —**great-'un"cle,** *n.* —**great circle,** any circle on a sphere having the same diameter as the sphere. —**Great Dane,** a breed of very large dog. —**great'ness,** *n.*

grebe (grēb) *n.* any of several diving birds allied to the loons.

Gre'cian (grē'shən) *adj.* pert. to Greece, esp. to the ancient Greeks and their culture; Greek.

greed (grēd) *n.* undue desire; avarice. —**greed'y,** *adj.* —**greed'i·ness,** *n.*

Greek (grēk) *adj.* pert. to Greece, its people and language. —*n.* a native or the language of Greece.

green (grēn) *adj.* 1, of the color of growing grass; a mixture of blue and yellow. 2, unripe; immature; not dried, seasoned, etc. 3, untrained; inexperienced. 4, new; recent. 5, pale; wan. —*n.* 1, the color of growing grass. 2, a common; a grassplot, esp. that around a hole on a golf course. 3, (*pl.*) cut foliage, esp. evergreens, for decoration. 4, (*pl.*) a cooked dish of leafy vegetables. —**green'ish,** *adj.* somewhat green. —**green'ness,** *n.*

green'back" *n.* a piece of U. S. paper money.

green'er·y (grē'nə-rē) *n.* a mass of green plants.

green'eyed" (grēn'īd") *adj.* (*Colloq.*) jealous.

green'gage" (grēn'gāj") *n.* a fine-flavored plum.

green'horn" *n.* (*Colloq.*) an inexperienced person; ignoramus.

green'house" *n.* a glass house in which plants are grown.

green light (*Colloq.*) permission to proceed.

green'sward" (-swôrd") *n.* grassy land; a lawn.

greet (grēt) *v.t.* 1, speak courteously to. 2, welcome; receive.

greet'ing *n.* 1, a spoken or written expression of salutation or good wishes. 2, (*pl.*) a friendly message. —**greeting card,** a printed message of congratulation, good will, etc.

gre·gar'i·ous (gri-gâr'ē-əs) *adj.* tending to live, associate, or congregate with others of the same kind; fond of company; sociable. —**gre·gar'i·ous·ness,** *n.*

Gre·gor'i·an calendar (gri-gôr'ē-ən) the calendar now in use, introduced by Pope Gregory XIII in 1582.

Gregorian chant a song used in the ritual of the Roman Catholic Church.

grem'lin *n.* a mischievous imp.

gre·nade' (gri-nād') *n.* a small bomb.

gren"a·dier (gren'ə-dir') *n.* 1, a soldier. 2, a No. Atlantic fish.

gren"a·dine' (gren'ə-dēn') *n.* 1, a flavoring syrup made from pomegranate juice. 2, a dress fabric.

grew (groo) *v.* pret. of *grow.*

grey (grā) *adj.* & *n.* gray.

grey'hound" (grā'hownd") *n.* a breed of tall, very slender, fleet dog.

grid *n.* 1, a grate or network of bars; gridiron. 2, a rigid lead plate for conducting current in a storage battery. 3, a grating between the electrodes of a vacuum tube.

grid'dle (grid'əl) *n.* a flat metal plate, heated from beneath, for cooking.

grid'i·ron (grid'ī"ərn) *n.* 1, a metal cooking utensil of separated bars on which food is broiled. 2, a football field.

grief (grēf) *n.* 1, deep sorrow; also

the cause of sorrow. **2,** disaster; failure.

griev'ance (grē'vəns) *n.* a real or fancied cause of complaint.

grieve (grēv) *v.t.* cause to suffer sorrow. —*v.i.* feel grief; mourn.

griev'ous (grē'vəs) *adj.* **1,** causing mental or physical pain. **2,** atrocious. —**griev'ous·ness,** *n.*

grif'fin (grif'in) *n.* a fabulous creature with an eagle's head and wings and a lion's body.

Griffin

grift *n.* (*Slang*) gambling pursuits generally. —**grift'er,** *n.* a confidence man or dishonest professional gambler.

grill (gril) *n.* **1,** a gridiron. **2,** a hotel bar or restaurant. **3,** a dish of various broiled meats. —*v.t.* **1,** broil (food) on a grill. **2,** subject to persistent questioning.

grille (gril) *n.* a metal grating.

grim *adj.* [**grim'mer, -mest**] **1,** forbidding. **2,** uncompromising; unyielding. **3,** frightful; cruel. —**grim'ness,** *n.*

gri·mace' (gri-mās') *n.* a twisting of the face, expressive of pain, disgust, etc. —*v.i.* make a grimace.

grime (grīm) *n.* deeply ingrained dirt. —**grim'y,** *adj.* dirty.

grin *n.* a broad smile that shows the teeth. —*v.i.* [**grinned, grin'ning**] make a grin; smile broadly.

grind (grīnd) *v.t.* [**ground, grind'ing**] **1,** subject to friction between two abrasive surfaces, or against one surface, so as to reduce to particles, wear away, etc.; pulverize; grate; sharpen; smooth; machine; shape. **2,** operate (a grinding machine or wheel), as by pedaling or turning a handle. **3,** oppress. —*v.i.* **1,** work at grinding. **2,** (*Slang*) work very hard. —*n.* **1,** a tedious routine. **2,** (*Slang*) a student who does nothing but study. —**grind'er,** *n.* a device for grinding.

grind'stone" *n.* a rotating abrasive wheel.

grin'go (gring'gō) *n.* in Latin Amer., an Anglo-Saxon person.

grip *v.t. & i.* [**gripped, grip'ping**] grasp firmly. —*n.* **1,** a firm grasp; the power or firmness of a grasp or hold. **2,** a ritual manner of clasping hands. **3,** a handle or hilt; a device for grasping or attaching. **4,** power; control. **5,** (*Colloq.*) a valise. **6,** (*Slang*) a stagehand.

gripe (grīp) *v.t.* squeeze painfully; distress, esp. cause colic in. —*v.i.* **1,**

have pain in the bowels. **2,** (*Slang*) complain. —*n.* **1,** a pang of colic. **2,** (*Slang*) a complaint. —**grip'er,** *n.* (*Slang*) a chronic grumbler.

grippe (grip) *n.* influenza.

gris'ly (griz'lē) *adj.* **1,** somewhat gray. **2,** gruesome; frightful. —**gris'li·ness,** *n.*

grist *n.* grain to be ground.

gris'tle (gris'əl) *n.* cartilage. —**gris'tly** (-lē) *adj.* composed of, or like, cartilage; tough.

grit *n.* **1,** tiny, rough particles; sand. **2,** a rough sandstone. **3,** pluck. **4,** (*pl.,* used as *sing.*) coarsely ground hominy. —*v.t. & i.* [**grit'ted, -ting**] grate; grind. —**grit'ty,** *adj.* **1,** sandy. **2,** plucky.

griz'zled (griz'əld) *adj.* mixed with gray, as hair.

griz'zly (griz'lē) *adj.* streaked with gray. —**grizzly bear,** a large savage bear of western No. America.

groan (grōn) *n.* a low, mournful sound uttered in pain or grief. —*v.t. & i.* utter such a sound.

groats (grōts) *n. pl.* crushed or coarsely ground grain.

gro'cer (grō'sər) *n.* a dealer in food supplies. —**gro'cer·ies** (-ēz) *n. pl.* food supplies. —**gro'cer·y,** *n.* a grocer's shop.

grog *n.* rum and water. —**grog'gy,** *adj.* confused and unsteady.

groin *n.* the depression between the abdomen and the thigh.

grom'met (grom'it) *n.* a ring or eyelet of metal.

groom *n.* **1,** a servant in charge of horses. **2,** a bridegroom. **3,** an attendant in a royal household. —*v.t.* **1,** tend (a horse). **2,** make neat and tidy. **3,** prepare (for a duty); coach; train. —**groom'ing,** *n.* personal appearance.

groove (groov) *n.* **1,** a channel cut by a tool; rut; furrow. **2,** an unprogressive routine; habit. —*v.t.* cut a groove in.

grope (grōp) *v.i.* feel about with the hands, as in the dark; seek aimlessly.

gros'grain" (grō'grān') *n.* a heavy corded silk fabric.

gross (grōs) *adj.* **1,** whole, without deductions; total. **2,** thick; fat; coarse; hence, vulgar, indelicate. **3,** dull; dense. **4,** flagrant. —*n.* twelve dozen; 144. —*v.t.* make a profit of, before deductions for expense or taxes. —**gross'ness,** *n.* vulgarity; indecency; obesity.

gro·tesque' (grō-tesk') *adj.* contorted; fantastic. —**gro·tesque'ness,** *n.*

grot'to (grot'ō) *n.* a cavern, esp. an artificial one; a bower.

grouch (growch) *n.* (*Colloq.*) 1, a fit of ill temper. 2, a surly person. —*v.i.* complain. —**grouch'y**, *adj.*

ground (grownd) *n.* 1, that part of the earth's surface that is not water; dry land; the composition of such surface; earth; soil. 2, a specific region; area. 3, a distance traversed. 4, a foundation; subject matter; a basis; a reason. 5, (*pl.*) a tract of land, esp. one attached to a dwelling. 6, (*pl.*) waste matter in ground form, as *coffee grounds.* 7, a conveyance of electrical current to the earth or a conductor of equivalent effect. —*adj.* 1, prepared by grinding. 2, at the level of the ground. —*v.t.* 1, set on the ground. 2, (*Aviation*) forbid to fly. 3, connect electrical current with the earth, etc. 4, run (a ship) aground. 5, teach fundamentals to. 6, pret. & p.p. of *grind.* —*v.i.* come to rest on the ground.

ground'er (grown'dər) *n.* (*Baseball*) a ball hit along the ground.

ground'less (-ləs) *adj.* with no adequate reason.

ground'ling (grownd'ling) *n.* 1, an animal or plant bound to or living close to the ground. 2, a materialistic person.

ground'nut" *n.* (*Brit.*) the peanut.

ground'work" *n.* preparatory work; foundation; basis.

group (groop) *n.* a number of persons or things gathered or classified together, usually because of likeness or common purpose. —*v.t.* & *i.* combine in a unit.

grouse (grows) *n.* [*pl.* grouse] any of several game birds. —*v.i.* (*Slang*) grumble.

grout (growt) *n.* a thin mortar mixed with gravel.

grove (grōv) *n.* a small wood; also, a group of cultivated fruit trees.

Grouse

grov'el (gruv'əl) *v.i.* crawl or be prone upon the earth; hence, humble oneself.

grow (grō) *v.i.* [grew (groo), grown (grōn), grow'ing] 1, increase in size, power, etc. 2, arise naturally. 3, become. —*v.t.* cause or permit to grow; plant and cultivate. —**grow up**, become adult; mature.

growl *n.* 1, a deep snarling noise. 2, a grumbling noise; complaint. —*v.t.* & *i.* make such a sound.

grown (grōn) *v.* p.p. of *grow.* —**grown'-up,** *n.* an adult.

growth (grōth) *n.* 1, act, process or result of growing. 2, a mass of morbid tissue, as a tumor.

grub *v.t.* [grubbed, grub'bing] 1, dig up by the roots. 2, remove roots, etc. from (land). —*v.i.* dig in the ground; hence, toil. —*n.* 1, the larva of an insect. 2, (*Slang*) food. —**grub'by,** *adj.* dirty.

grub'stake" *n.* the necessities for subsistence, supplied as an investment.

grudge (gruj) *n.* a feeling of resentment; a cause of hostility.

gru'el (groo'əl) *n.* thin porridge.

gru'el·ing (groo'əl-ing) *adj.* arduous; exhausting.

grue'some (groo'səm) *adj.* horribly repulsive. —**grue'some·ness,** *n.*

gruff (gruf) *adj.* rough; surly. —**gruff'ness,** *n.*

grum'ble (grum'bəl) *n.* a growl; a discontented mutter. —*v.i.* complain in a mutter; growl.

grump'y (grum'pē) *adj.* surly; glum. —**grump'i·ness,** *n.*

grunt *n.* a deep guttural sound, as that made by a hog. —*v.t.* & *i.* utter a grunt.

G-string" *n.* 1, on a musical instrument, a string tuned to G. 2, a string used as a belt to hold up a breechcloth.

gua'no (gwä'nō) *n.* [*pl.* -nos] a fertilizer made from the droppings of sea birds.

guar"an·tee" (gar"ən-tē') *n.* 1, a statement that a thing is as represented; warranty. 2, (*Law*) a promise to be responsible for another's debt or failure; property pledged as security for this promise. —*v.t.* 1, insure; promise. 2, (*Law*) be responsible for. Also, **guar'an·ty".** —**guar'an·tor"** (-tôr") *n.*

guard (gärd) *v.t.* protect; keep safe. —*v.i.* be cautious. —*n.* 1, a means of defense. 2, a watchful state. 3, a person or group of persons who guard; a sentry. 4, a device to prevent injury. —**guard'ed,** *adj.* wary; reticent. — **guard'house",** *n.* a military prison.

guard'i·an (gär'dē·ən) *n.* 1, a warden. 2, (*Law*) one entrusted with the person or property of another. —*adj.* guarding.

gua'va (gwä'və) *n.* the pulpy fruit of a tropical tree.

gu"ber·na·to'ri·al (gū"bər·nə·tôr'ē·əl) *adj.* pert. to a governor.

gudg'eon (guj'ən) *n.* a small fish used as bait.

guer'don (gêr'dən) *n.* a reward.

Guern'sey (gĕrn'zė) *n.* one of a breed of dairy cattle.

guer·ril'la (gə-ril'ə) *n.* a person engaged in irregular warfare.

guess (ges) *n.* an opinion reached at random or without reason; a conjecture. —*v.t.* **1**, form such an opinion; surmise. **2**, surmise correctly. —*v.i.* hazard an opinion. —**guess'work**″, *n.* the act of guessing; procedure based on guessing.

guest (gest) *n.* **1**, a person entertained at the home of another. **2**, a patron of a hotel, etc.

guf·faw' (gu-fä') *n.* a boisterous laugh. —*v.i.* laugh coarsely.

guid'ance (gī'dəns) *n.* the act of guiding; direction; management.

guide (gīd) *v.t.* **1**, show the way to; escort. **2**, direct; manage. —*n.* **1**, a person or thing that directs. **2**, a controlling device, as on a machine.

guided missile a rocket-driven explosive missile carrying radio apparatus by which its course may be corrected from the ground.

guide'post″ *n.* a post bearing a sign to direct travelers.

guild (gild) *n.* an association of persons in a common trade.

guil'der (gil'dər) *n.* gulden.

guile (gīl) *n.* craft; cunning. —**guile'less**, *adj.* naive.

guil'lo·tine″ (gil'ə-tēn″) *n.* a machine for decapitating a person.

guilt (gilt) *n.* the fact of having violated law or right. —**guilt'y**, *adj.*

guimpe (gamp) *n.* a woman's outer garment for the neck and shoulders.

guin'ea (gin'ė) *n.* a Brit. monetary unit, 21 shillings.

Guimpe

guinea hen a fowl domesticated for its meat and eggs.

guinea pig a small, short-tailed rodent, much used in medical research; hence, a person used as subject for experimentation.

guise (gīz) *n.* **1**, garb; dress; hence, semblance. **2**, cloak; cover.

gui·tar' (gi-tär') *n.* a six-stringed musical instrument plucked with the fingers. —**gui·tar'ist**, *n.*

gulch *n.* a gorge; ravine.

gul'den (gŭl'dən) *n.* the monetary unit of the Netherlands, worth about 40 cents.

gulf *n.* **1**, an arm of the sea extending into the land. **2**, an abyss.

gull (gul) *n.* **1**, a web-footed sea bird. **2**, a dupe.

gul'let (gul'it) *n.* the throat.

gul'li·ble (gul'ə-bəl) *adj.* easily deceived. —**gul'li·bil'i·ty**, *n.*

gul'ly (gul'ė) *n.* a narrow ravine.

gulp *v.t.* swallow hastily. —*v.i.* gasp; choke. —*n.* the act of gulping; a quantity gulped.

gum *n.* **1**, the firm flesh in which the teeth are set. **2**, a sticky substance. **3**, a tree yielding a viscid resin. —*v.t.* [**gummed**, **gum'ming**] stick together with gum. —*v.i.* become sticky. —**gum up**, spoil. —**gum'my**, *adj.* —**gum'mi·ness**, *n.*

gum arabic a gum derived from the acacia, used in medicines, etc.

gum'bo (gum'bō) *n.* [*pl.* **-bos** (-bōz)] **1**, a soup or dish made with okra. **2**, (*Colloq.*) sticky mud.

gum'drop″ *n.* a small candy made of gum arabic or gelatin.

gump'tion (gump'shən) *n.* (*Colloq.*) **1**, initiative; self-reliance. **2**, common sense.

gum'shoe″ *n.* **1**, (*Colloq.*) an overshoe. **2**, (*Slang*) a detective.

gun *n.* **1**, any of various portable firearms. **2**, a cannon. **3**, in airplanes, the throttle. —*v.t.* [**gunned**, **gun'ning**] **1**, hurt with a gun. **2**, (with *for*) pursue. **3**, accelerate.

gun'boat″ *n.* a small warship carrying mounted guns.

gun'cot''ton *n.* cotton treated with nitric acid, used in explosives; cellulose nitrate.

gun'man (-mən) *n.* [*pl.* **-men**] a hired ruffian.

gun'ner (gun'ər) *n.* the operator of a gun or cannon.

gun'ner·y (-ė) *n.* **1**, the making or operation of guns. **2**, artillery.

gun'ny (gun'ė) *n.* a coarse fabric made of jute or hemp fiber.

gun'pow''der *n.* an explosive powder for use in guns, blasting, etc.

gun'smith″ *n.* one who makes or repairs guns.

gun'wale (gun'əl) *n.* the upper edge of a ship's side.

gup'py (gup'ė) *n.* a very small fish.

gur'gle (gĕr'gəl) *v.i.* make a bubbling sound, as water flowing from a bottle. —*n.* this sound.

gush *v.i.* **1**, issue copiously and violently; flow out freely. **2**, (*Colloq.*) display sentiment effusively. —*v.t.* emit copiously. —*n.* a spouting forth.

gush'er (gush'ər) *n.* **1**, one given

to sentimental display. **2**, an oil well with a copious natural flow.

gush'y (gush'ē) *adj.* (*Colloq.*) overdemonstrative. —**gush'i·ness**, *n.*

gus'set (gus'et) *n.* a triangular piece of cloth inserted in a garment.

gust *n.* **1**, a sudden squall of wind. **2**, an outburst.

gus'ta·to·ry (gus'tə-tôr-ē) *adj.* pert. to the sense of taste.

gus'to (gus'tō) *n.* zest; enjoyment.

gust'y (gus'tē) *adj.* coming in gusts or squalls; windy. —**gust'i·ness**, *n.*

gut *n.* **1**, an intestine; (*pl.*) the bowels. **2**, animal intestines used as a string: *catgut*. **3**, a narrow defile; a channel. **4**, (*pl.*) (*Slang*) stamina courage. —*v.t.* [**gut'ted, gut'ting**] **1**, disembowel. **2**, plunder of contents; destroy the insides of.

gut'ta-per'cha (gut'ə-pẽr-chə) *n.* the dried juice of certain trees, which forms a whitish puttylike material.

gut'ter (gut'ər) *n.* **1**, a channel for carrying off water, as at the eaves of a roof or at a roadside. **2**, a debased state of living or thinking.

gut'ter-snipe" (gut'ər-snīp") *n.* a person, esp. a child, of lowly origin; a gamin.

gut'tur·al (gut'ər-əl) *adj.* pert. to or formed in, the throat; hoarse.

guy (gī) *n.* **1**, a rope, chain or wire used to steady something. **2**, (*Slang*) a fellow. —*v.t.* (*Colloq.*) tease.

guz'zle (guz'əl) *v.t. & i.* drink too much or too rapidly.

gym·na'si·um (jim-nā'zē-əm) *n.* building or room for athletic exercises. Also (*Colloq.*) **gym** (jim).

gym'nast (jim'nast) *n.* one skilled in acrobatic and similar physical exercises. —**gym·nas'tics**, *n.pl.* such exercises. —**gym·nas'tic**, *adj.* —**gym·nas'ti·cal·ly**, *adv.*

gy"ne·col'o·gy (jī'nə-kol'ə-jē) *n.* in medicine, the science of diseases of woman. —**gy"ne·col'o·gist**, *n.*

gy"no- (jī'-) *pref.* female; woman.

gyp (jip) *n.* (*Slang*) a cheat; swindler. —*v.t.* [**gypped, gyp'ping**] cheat.

gyp'sum (jip'səm) *n.* a soft mineral, from which plaster of Paris is made.

gyp'sy (jip'sē) *n.* a member of a vagabond, dark-skinned race; the language of this race. Also, **gip'sy**.

gy'rate (jī'rāt) *v.i.* move spirally; rotate. —**gy·ra'tion**, *n.*

gy·rene' (jī-rēn') *n.* (*Slang*) a U. S. Marine.

gy'ro- (jī'-) denoting a ring or circle.

gy'ro·scope" (jīrə-skōp") *n.* an instrument employing a rotating wheel to stabilize ships, etc.

gyve (jīv) *n.* (usually *pl.*) a fetter for the leg; shackle. —*v.t.* fetter.

H

H, h (āch) the eighth letter of the English alphabet.

ha (hä) *interj.* expressing triumph, or interrogation.

ha'be·as cor'pus (hā'bē-əs kôr'pəs) (*Law*) a writ demanding that a prisoner be given an immediate hearing or else be released.

hab'er·dash"er (hab'ər-dash"ər) *n.* a dealer in accessory articles of men's wear. —**hab'er·dash"er·y**, *n.* the shop of such a dealer.

ha·bil'i·ment (hə-bil'ə-mənt) *n.* (usually *pl.*) clothing; garments.

hab'it *n.* **1**, a tendency or disposition to act in a certain way, acquired by repetition of such acts. **2**, a usual mode of action; a custom or usage. **3**, a characteristic trait. **4**, (often *pl.*) a costume appropriate to a vocation or occasion. —*v.t.* clothe. —**hab'it·a·ble**, *adj.* capable of being lived in.

hab'i·tat" (hab'ə-tat") *n.* the natural home of an animal or plant; the characteristics, as climate, etc., of such a region.

hab"i·ta'tion (hab"ə-tā'shən) *n.* **1**, a place of abode; a dwelling. **2**, the act of inhabiting.

ha·bit'u·al (hə-bich'oo-əl) *adj.* customary; by habit.

ha·bit'u·ate" (hə-bich'oo-āt") *v.t.* **1**, accustom. **2**, frequent. —**ha·bit"u·a'tion**, *n.*

ha·bit'u·é" (hə-bich'û-ā") *n.* one who frequents a place.

ha·chure' (ha-shûr') *n.* shading of a drawing or map with lines; hatching.

ha"ci·en'da (hä'sē-en'də) (*Sp.*) *n.* a landed estate or the house on it.

hack (hak) *n.* **1**, a cut, gash, or notch. **2**, a tool for hacking, as an ax or hoe. **3**, a cough; an impediment in speech. **4**, a hackney; a taxicab. **5**, an overworked or jaded horse or person. **6**, a person hired to write according to demand. —*adj.* **1**, hired. **2**, hackneyed; trite. —*v.t.* **1**, notch or chop irregularly; strike. **2**, (with *out*) produce without enjoyment. **3**, hackney. —*v.i.* **1**, make cuts or notches. **2**, cough repeatedly; stutter. **3**, drive a hackney or taxicab. **4**, write for hire.

hack'le (hak'əl) *n.* **1**, the neck feathers of a fowl. **2**, a comb for dressing hemp, etc. —*v.t.* **1**, comb. **2**, hack roughly.

hack'ney (hak'nē) *n.* a horse or carriage kept for hire. —*adj.* hired out. —*v.t.* make stale or trite by overuse. —**hack'neyed**, *adj.*

hack'saw" (hak'sâ") *n.* a saw for cutting metal.

had *v.* pret. & p.p. of *have*.

had'dock (had'ək) *n.* a No. Atlantic food fish similar to the cod.

Ha'des (hā'dēz) *n.* the abode of the dead; hell.

haf'ni·um (haf'nē-əm) *n.* a metallic element, no. 72, symbol, Hf.

haft (håft) *n.* the handle of a cutting or thrusting instrument.

hag *n.* **1,** a repulsive or malicious old woman. **2,** a witch or sorceress. **3,** a fish related to the lamprey.

hag'gard (hag'ərd) *adj.* wildlooking, as from terror, suffering, or fatigue. —**hag'gard·ness,** *n.*

hag'gle (hag'əl) *v.i.* bargain in a petty manner; cavil. —*v.t.* cavil at. —*n.* dispute, esp. about price.

hag'i·o- (haj'ē-ō-) *pref.* saint.

ha'ha' (hä'hä') *n.* a laugh.

hail (hāl) *v.t.* **1,** salute; welcome; cheer. **2,** cry out to. **3,** pour down like hail. —*v.i.* pour down hail. —*n.* **1,** a cry or call to attract attention. **2,** a salutation or greeting. **3,** pellets of ice falling in showers: *hailstones.* —**Hail Mary!,** a prayer, the Ave Maria.

hair (hãr) *n.* **1,** one or the aggregate of the numerous fine filaments growing from the skin of most animals. **2,** any fine filament. **3,** a very small distance or degree.

hair'cloth'' *n.* an upholstery or lining fabric made of horsehair.

hair'cut'' *n.* a cutting or clipping of the hair.

hair'do'' (-doo'') *n.* any particular style of arranging a woman's hair.

hair'dress''er *n.* one who cuts and arranges women's hair.

hair'line'' *n.* a very thin line.

hair'pin'' *n.* a bent piece of wire, used to hold the hair in place. —*adj.* bent in form of a U.

hair'rais''ing *adj.* frightening.

hair'split''ting *n.* & *adj.* the practice of making excessively fine distinctions.

hair'spring'' *n.* a fine spiral spring in a timepiece.

hair'y (-ē) *adj.* having much hair. —**hair'i·ness,** *n.*

hake (hāk) *n.* a sea fish.

hal'berd (hal'bərd) *n.* a medieval weapon, comprising a blade and spiked points on a long shaft.

hal'cy·on (hal'sē-ən) *n.* a marine bird, the kingfisher. —*adj.* calm; quiet; undisturbed.

hale (hāl) *v.t.* drag forcibly; haul; pull. —*adj.* in good health; robust.

half (håf) *n.* [*pl.* **halves** (håvz)] **1,** one of two equal parts into which

something is divided. **2,** a tie score. **3,** 50 cents. —*adj.* **1,** being one half. **2,** partial; incomplete. —*adv.* **1,** to the extent or degree of a half. **2,** partly; somewhat. —**half brother** or **sister,** a brother or sister by one parent but not the other. —**better half** (*Slang*) wife.

half-'and-half'' *n.* a mixture of equal portions, esp. coffee and cream, or ale and beer.

half'back'' *n.* (*Football*) a player stationed behind the line.

half'breed'' *n.* an offspring of parents of different races.

half-'caste'' *n.* a person whose parents were of different castes.

half-cocked'' *adj.* & *adv.* insufficiently prepared; superficial(ly).

half'heart''ed *adj.* showing little eagerness, enthusiasm, or generosity. —**half'heart''ed·ness,** *n.*

half-'mast'' *n.* (of a flag) about halfway down its pole, as a mark of mourning or distress.

half'pen·ny (hā'pə-nē) *n.* a British bronze coin. Also, **half'pence''.**

half'tone'' *n.* a printing plate for reproducing a photograph.

half'track'' *n.* a motor truck having treads instead of rear wheels.

half'way'' *adv.* & *adj.* **1,** to or at half the distance or middle point. **2,** partial.

half'wit'' *n.* a feeble-minded person. —**half'wit''ted,** *adj.*

hal'i·but (hal'ə-bət) *n.* any of several large flatfishes.

hal'i·to'sis (hal'ə-tō'sis) *n.* foulodored breath.

hall (hål) *n.* **1,** a building or a large room devoted to some public or common use. **2,** an antechamber or corridor giving entrance to other rooms. **3,** a main house.

hal''le·lu'jah (hal''ə-loo'yə) *interj.* Praise ye the Lord!

hall'mark'' (hål'märk'') *n.* a mark, stamp or attestation of quality.

hal·loo' (ha-loo') *interj.* to attract attention. —*v.i.* & *t.* shout; call.

hal'low (hal'ō) *v.t.* set apart as holy; regard as sacred; consecrate. —**hal'lowed** (hal'ōd, hal'ō-id) *adj.*

Hal''low·een' (hal''ə-wēn') *n.* the evening of October 31, the eve of All Saints' Day.

hal·lu''ci·na'tion (hə-loo''sə-nā'shən) *n.* **1,** an apparent perception of something not actually perceptible. **2,** a false belief; illusion.

hall'way'' *n.* a vestibule; hall.

ha'lo (hā'lō) *n.* a circle of light around the head, as of a saint.

hal'o·gen (hal'ə-jən) *n.* any of the elements fluorine, chlorine, iodine, and bromine.

halt (hält) *v.i.* **1,** cease advancing; stop. **2,** waver; hesitate. —*v.t.* cause to halt. —*n.* a stop or pause. —*adj.* (*Archaic*) lame. —**halt'ing,** *adj.* hesitant.

hal'ter (hål'tər) *n.* **1,** a rope or strap having a noose, for leading or confining an animal. **2,** a woman's waist held in place by bands tied around the back and neck.

halve (håv) *v.t.* **1,** divide into two equal parts. **2,** reduce to a half. **3,** make equal scores in (a contest).

hal'yard (hal'yərd) *n.* a rope for raising and lowering a yard, sail, flag, etc.

ham *n.* **1,** the buttock of a hog; the meat from this quarter. **2,** the back of the knee; (*pl.*) the thighs. **3,** (*Slang*) an actor who overacts **4,** (*Slang*) an amateur, esp. in radio. —*v.i.* [hammed, ham'ming] (*Slang*) overact.

ham'burg"er (ham'bẽr"gər) *n.* **1,** chopped beef: *hamburg steak*. **2,** a sandwich of such meat in a bun.

ham'let (ham'lit) *n.* a small village.

ham'mer (ham'ər) *n.* **1,** an instrument for driving nails, beating metal etc., comprising a heavy solid head set on a handle. **2,** any of various instruments for pounding or striking. **3,** a metal ball with a flexible handle, used in throwing contests. —*v.t.* & *i.* beat, drive etc., with or as with a hammer.

ham'mer-head' (-hed") *n.* a kind of shark.

ham'mock (ham'ək) *n.* a heavy cloth suspended by cords, used as a bed.

ham'per (ham'pər) *v.t.* impede in motion or progress; hinder. —*n.* a large covered basket.

ham'ster (ham'stər) *n.* a small burrowing rodent.

ham'string" *n.* a tendon at the back of the knee. —*v.t.* [*pret.* & *p.p.* ham'strung"] cripple; disable.

Hamster

hand *n.* **1,** the end of the human arm, from wrist outward, comprising the palm and fingers; a corresponding part of certain animals. **2,** something resembling a hand, as a pointer on a clock. **3,** style of handwriting; a person's signature. **4,** a unit of linear measure, 4 inches. **5,** a manual laborer; an employee. **6,** help; aid; agency; participation. **7,** (often *pl.*) custody; possession or control. **8,** the cards dealt to a player in a game; a player; the period from one deal to the next. —*adj.* **1,** of the hand; to be carried by or worn on the hand. **2,** operated or made by hand. —*v.t.* **1,** deliver by hand. **2,** help; conduct.

hand'bag" *n.* a woman's purse.

hand'ball" *n.* an athletic game.

hand'bill" *n.* a printed notice.

hand'book" *n.* **1,** a compact treatise; a guidebook. **2,** the business of a bookmaker.

hand'car" *n.* a small hand-propelled railroad car.

hand'cuff" *n.* (usually *pl.*) a shackle fitting on the wrist. —*v.t.* put handcuffs on.

Handcuffs

-hand'ed (han'-did) *suf.* supplied with or done by a specified number of hands.

hand'ful" (-fůl") *n.* **1,** what the hand can hold; a small quantity or number. **2,** (*Colloq.*) a difficult task.

hand'i-cap" (han'di-kap") *n.* **1,** an extra burden placed upon a superior competitor in a contest. **2,** any encumbrance or disadvantage. **3,** a contest in which some of the entrants are handicapped. —*v.t.* [-capped", -cap"ping] **1,** place a handicap upon; rate. **2,** encumber; hinder. —**hand'i-cap"per,** *n.*

hand'i-craft" (han'di-kråft") *n.* **1,** skilled labor with the hands. **2,** a manual art. *Also,* **hand'craft".**

hand'i-work" (han'di-wẽrk") *n.* **1,** work done or something made by hand. **2,** the result of an action.

hand'ker-chief (hang'kər-chif) *n.* a small cloth carried for wiping the face or nose, etc.

han'dle (han'dəl) *v.t.* **1,** touch; manipulate, manage, or control with the hands. **2,** deal with; treat of. **3,** make use of; deal in; buy and sell. —*n.* **1,** the part of an implement, instrument, tool or weapon made to be gripped by the hand. **2,** a title, as *Mr.* —**han'dler,** *n.*

han'dle-bar" *n.* (usually *pl.*) one of the two bars with which a bicycle or motorcycle is steered.

hand'made" *adj.* not made by machinery.

hand'maid" *n.* a female servant.

hand-'me-down" *n.* a garment or other thing previously used by someone else. —*adj.* second-hand.

hand organ a hurdy-gurdy.

hand'out" *n.* (*Slang*) something given to a beggar.

hand'sel (han'səl) *n.* **1,** a gift; token.

hand'some (hand'səm) *adj.* **1,** agreeable to the eye. **2,** large; generous. —**hand'some-ness,** *n.*

hand'writ"ing (hand'rī"ting) *n.* **1,** writing by hand. **2,** a style of such writing.

hand'y (han'dē) *adj.* **1,** ready at hand; accessible. **2,** well-suited to use; easy to handle; convenient. **3,** skillful in using the hands; dexterous. —**hand'i·ness,** *n.*

han'dy·man" *n.* [*pl.* -**men"**] a man employed to do odd jobs.

hang [*pret. & p.p.* **hung**] *v.t.* **1,** support from above and not from below; suspend. **2,** [*pret. & p.p.* **hanged**] suspend by the neck until dead. **3,** let dangle; let bend or droop downward. **4,** attach, as wallpaper. —*v.i.* **1,** be suspended; dangle; swing freely. **2,** [*pret. & p.p.* **hanged**] be executed by hanging. **3,** be contingent or dependent. **4,** hold fast; cling. **5,** (with *around* or *out*) linger; loiter. **6,** impend. **7,** come to a standstill.

hang'ar (hang'ər) *n.* a shed for housing aircraft.

hang'dog" *adj.* mean-looking.

hang'er *n.* a device for hanging something, as clothes.

hang'ing *n.* **1,** capital punishment on the gallows. **2,** a drapery, hung tapestry, etc.

hang'man (-mən) *n.* [*pl.* -**men**] an executioner.

hang'nail" *n.* a tear in a fingernail or cuticle.

hang'out" *n.* (*Slang*) a place one frequents.

hang'o"ver *n.* (*Colloq.*) a belated effect of a previous act or condition; esp., illness induced by excessive drinking of liquor.

hank *n.* a skein as of thread or yarn; a coil or knot.

han'ker (hang'kər) *v.i.* have an uneasy craving; yearn keenly. —**han'ker·ing,** *n.*

han'ky-pan'ky (hang'kē-pang'-kē) *n.* trickery; legerdemain.

Hansom

han'som (han'səm) *n.* a two-passenger carriage with an elevated rear seat for the driver.

hap"haz'ard (hap"haz'ərd) *adj.* determined by chance; accidental; random. —*adv.* at random.

hap'less (hap'les) *adj.* unlucky; unfortunate. —**hap'less·ness,** *n.*

hap'pen (hap'ən) *v.i.* **1,** come to pass; take place; occur. **2,** occur by chance. —**hap'pen·ing,** *n.* an occurrence; event.

hap'py (hap'ē) *adj.* **1,** glad; joyous; satisfied; pleased. **2,** giving pleasure; agreeable. **3,** lucky; fortunate. **4,** very fitting; apt; felicitous. —**hap'pi·ness,** *n.* —**hap'py-go-luck'y,** *adj.* unworried; irresponsible.

ha'ra-ki'ri (hä'rə-kir'ē) *n.* (*Jap.*) suicide by ripping open the abdomen with a knife.

ha·rangue' (hə-rang') *n.* a long vehement speech; a tirade. —*v.t. & i.* address in a harangue; declaim.

har'ass (har'əs) *v.t.* annoy by repeated attacks; disturb or torment persistently. —**har'ass·ment,** *n.*

har'bin·ger (här'bin-jər) *n.* a forerunner that gives notice of the coming of another.

har'bor (här'bər) *n.* **1,** a bay, cove, etc. that affords shelter or anchorage for ships. **2,** a refuge. —*v.t.* **1,** give shelter to; protect; conceal. **2,** have in the mind, as suspicious feelings. Also, **har'bour.** —**har'bor·age,** *n.* shelter.

hard (härd) *adj.* **1,** solid in substance or texture; resistant to penetration or cutting; unyielding. **2,** enduring; resistant; tough. **3,** firmly formed; tight. **4,** difficult; not easy to do, understand, etc. **5,** requiring or displaying great energy or exertion. **6,** harsh; severe; violent. **7,** shrewd; unsentimental; unfriendly. —*adv.* **1,** vigorously; earnestly; intently. **2,** roughly; harshly. **3,** fully; closely. —**hard'ness,** *n.* —**hard liquor,** spirituous liquor of high alcoholic content. —**hard money, 1,** coins. **2,** cash. —**hard up,** short of funds. —**hard water,** water that contains mineral salts resistant to dissolving soap.

hard'bit"ten *adj.* obstinate; tough.

hard"boiled' (-boild') *adj.* **1,** boiled until hard. **2,** (*Colloq.*) unpitying; disillusioned; sophisticated.

hard'en (här'dən) *v.t. & i.* make or become harder.

hard'fist"ed (-fis"tid) *adj.* stingy.

hard'head"ed *adj.* **1,** realistic; practical. **2,** obstinate.

har'di·hood" (här'dē-hûd") *n.* boldness; venturesome spirit.

hard'ly (-lē) *adv.* **1,** barely; not quite. **2,** not probable. **3,** harshly.

hard'pan" *n.* a layer of hard clay, etc. underlying soft soil.

hard'ship *n.* something that exacts endurance, as suffering, want, adversity.

hard'tack *n.* hard, dry biscuits.

hard'ware *n.* wares made of metal, as tools, cutlery, etc.

har'dy (här'dė) *adj.* capable of resisting hardship; strong; enduring. —har'di·ness, *n.*

hare (här) *n.* a rodent quadruped similar to the rabbit.

hare'brained' (här'brānd') *adj.* reckless; giddy. —hare'brained'-ness, *n.*

hare'lip' (här'lip') *n.* a congenital deformation of the upper lip by a vertical cleft or fissure.

har'em (här'əm) *n.* 1, the women in an Oriental residence; their quarters. 2, (*Humorous*) a train of feminine admirers.

hark (härk) *v.i.* listen. —*interj.* Listen! Give attention! —hark back, retrace one's steps; revert.

hark'en (-ən) *v.i.* give heed.

har'le·quin (här'lə·kwin) *n.* a clown; a jester.

har'lot (här'lət) *n.* a prostitute.

harm (härm) *n.* physical or moral injury; damage; detriment; wrong; mischief. —*v.t.* injure; hurt; be detrimental to. —harm'ful, *adj.* injurious. —harm'ful·ness, *n.* —harm'less, *adj.* unable to harm. —harm'less·ness, *n.*

har·mon'ic (här·mon'ik) *adj.* 1, pert. to harmony. 2, in harmony; concordant. —har·mon'i·cal·ly, *adv.*

har·mon'i·ca (här·mon'ə·kə) *n.* a small musical instrument played by blowing; a mouth organ.

har·mon'ics (här·mon'iks) *n.* the science of musical sounds.

har·mo'ni·ous (här·mō'nė·əs) *adj.* 1, pleasing to the ear or eye. 2, agreeable; friendly. —har·mo'ni·ous·ness, *n.*

har·mo'ni·um (här·mō'nė·əm) *n.* a reed organ.

har'mo·nize' (här'mə·nīz') *v.t.* bring to accord or agreement. —*v.i.* sing in harmony. —har'mo·ni·za'tion, *n.*

har'mo·ny (här'mə·nė) *n.* 1, (*Music*) the sound of two or more simultaneous tones; the structure and relationship of chords. 2, a pleasing arrangement or combination of parts; congruity. 3, agreement, as in sentiments or interests; accord; peace and friendship.

har'ness (här'nəs) *n.* the straps and other gear put on a horse or other draft animal; any similar arrangement of straps. —*v.t.* 1, put a harness on. 2, link up for use;

make useful application of. —in harness, employed; active; at work.

harp (härp) *n.* 1, a musical instrument with strings played by plucking. 2, (*Slang*) (sometimes offensive) an Irishman. —*v.i.* (*Colloq.*) (with *on*) speak or write of repetitiously. —harp'ist, *n.*

Harp

har·poon' (här·poon') *n.* a barbed spear attached to a rope, used in capturing large fish or whales. —*v.t.* strike with a harpoon.

harp'si·chord' (härp'si·kôrd') *n.* a keyboard musical instrument.

har'py (här'pė) *n.* a repulsively greedy and unfeeling person, esp. a woman.

har'ri·dan (har'ə·dən) *n.* an odious old woman; a hag.

har'ri·er (har'ė·ər) *n.* 1, a breed of hunting dog. 2, a cross-country runner. 3, a hawk.

har'row (har'ō) *n.* an agricultural implement, as a heavy frame set with iron teeth, used to break up clods. —*v.t.* 1, draw a harrow over. 2, affect the feelings of; distress. —har'row·ing, *adj.* distressing.

har'ry (har'ė) *v.t.* harass; ravage.

harsh (härsh) *adj.* 1, rough to the senses; sharp, sour, discordant, irritating, etc. 2, severe in character or effect; hard. —harsh'ness, *n.*

hart (härt) *n.* a male of the deer.

har'um-scar'um (här'əm-skär'əm) *adj.* giddy; rash.

har'vest (här'vəst) *n.* 1, the gathering of crops. 2, the season for gathering crops; autumn. 3, a crop gathered, as grain. 4, a supply of anything gathered and stored; the product of any labor. —*v.t. & i.* gather or reap, as grain.

har'vest·er (här'vəs·tər) *n.* a machine that harvests grain.

has (haz) *v.* 3rd person singular of *have.*

has-'been' *n.* (*Colloq.*) a person formerly but no longer notable.

hash *n.* 1, a dish of chopped meat and potatoes. 2, any mixture, or muddle. —*v.t.* make hash of.

hash'ish (hash'ēsh) *n.* a narcotic preparation made from Indian hemp.

hasp (hàsp) *n.* a clasp for a door, etc.; a wire loop or hook.

has'sock (has'ək) *n.* 1, a thick hard cushion used as a footstool. 2, a clump or tuft of coarse grass.

haste (hāst) n. 1, swiftness; promptness. 2, undue or rash quickness. —v.i. hasten.

has'ten (hā'sən) v.i. go, move, or act quickly; hurry. —v.t. cause to go fast or faster; accelerate.

hast'y (hās'tē) adj. 1, unduly hurried or accelerated. 2, thoughtless. —hast'i·ness, n.

hat n. a covering for the head, esp. one worn outdoors, having a crown and brim. —pass the hat, take a collection; ask for contributions.

hatch (hach) v.t. 1, bring forth young from (an egg). 2, contrive or produce (a plan, a result). 3, mark lines for shading (a drawing). —v.i. 1, emerge from a shell. 2, be contrived or produced. —n. 1, what is hatched; a brood. 2, a fine line, as in engraving. 3, an opening or door: hatchway. 4, a cover for such an opening. —hatch'er·y (-ə-rē) n. a place for hatching eggs.

hatch'et (hach'it) n. a short-handled ax for use by one hand. —bury the hatchet, make peace.

hatch'et·man n. [pl. -men"] a paid assassin; a gunman.

hate (hāt) v.t. 1, regard with strong aversion or ill will; detest. 2, find unpalatable or unappealing. —v.i. feel hatred. —n. 1, passionate dislike or ill will. 2, something hated.

hate'ful (hāt'fəl) adj. 1, detestable; abhorrent. 2, malicious; malevolent. —hate'ful·ness, n.

hat'rack n. a rail or stand fitted with pegs to hold hats.

ha'tred (hā'trəd) n. passionate dislike; detestation.

hat'ter (hat'ər) n. one who makes or sells hats.

hau'berk (hâ'bərk) n. a coat of mail extending below the knees.

haugh'ty (hâ'tē) adj. disdainfully proud. —haugh'ti·ness, n.

haul (hâl) v.t. 1, pull or draw with force; move by pulling; drag. 2, (with up) call to account; arraign. —v.i. 1, pull; tug. 2, change direction; shift; veer. 3, (with off) withdraw; pull back the arm preparatory to a blow. —n. 1, a pulling with force. 2, the distance through which something is hauled. 3, a quantity gathered; (Colloq.) a valuable acquisition. —haul'age, n. the process of, or a fee for, hauling. —haul'er, n. one who hauls, esp. a truckman.

haunch (hânch) n. the fleshy part of the body above the thigh; hip.

haunt (hânt) v.t. 1, reappear to frequently after dying, as a ghost. 2, visit frequently. —v.i. reappear, as a specter. —n. 1, (often pl.) a place frequently visited. 2, (hant) (Dial.) a ghost, or his visiting ground.

hau·teur' (hō-tēr') n. haughtiness.

have (hav) v.t. [present indicative: I have; you have (Archaic, thou hast); he has (Archaic, hath); we, you, they have; pret. & p.p. had; hav'ing] 1, possess; own; hold. 2, acquire; obtain; receive. 3, contain; comprise; be in part. 4, hold in custody; control. 5, hold in the mind; entertain; maintain. 6, exhibit in action; exercise; show. 7, possess knowledge of; be affected with; experience. 8, procure to be done; permit; allow. 9, (with on) wear. 10, (Slang) outwit. —aux. v. used with a past participle to form a perfect tense, as I have done it, he had gone.

ha'ven (hā'vən) n. a harbor; a place of shelter or asylum.

hav'er·sack" (hav'ər-sak") n. a bag for provisions; knapsack.

hav'oc (hav'ək) n. general destruction; devastation.

haw (hâ) interj. 1, a command to turn left. 2, an expression marking indecision in speech. 3, ha; a guffaw.

hawk (hâk) n. 1, any of numerous birds of prey. 2, a hard cough; a noisy effort to clear the throat. —v.t. offer for sale; peddle. —v.i. 1, hunt with hawks. 2, try to cough. 3, peddle. —hawk'er, n. one who cries wares; peddler.

hawk'-eyed" (hâk'īd") adj. having keen vision.

Hawk

haw'ser (hâ'zər) n. a rope or cable used on a ship for mooring, etc.

haw'thorn" (hâ'thôrn") n. a thorny shrub or small tree, much used in hedges.

hay (hā) n. grass cut and dried for use as fodder.

hay'cock" (hā'kok") n. a conical pile of hay in a field.

hay fever an allergic reaction to pollen with symptoms like those of a cold.

hay'mak"er n. (Slang) a decisive blow; knockout punch.

hay'seed" n. (Colloq.) a rustic; a naive person.

hay'stack" n. a pile of hay.

hay'wire" adj. (Slang) crazy; hopelessly confused.

haz'ard (haz'ərd) n. 1, exposure to danger; risk; peril. 2, a fortuitous event; chance; accident. 3, something dangerous or obstructive; an obstacle. 4, something risked. 5, a dice game. —v.t. 1, put up as a stake; expose to danger or loss. 2, run the risk of incurring or bringing to pass. **3,** do or say tentatively. —**haz'ard·ous,** *adj.* dangerous.

haze (hāz) *n.* **1,** a thin mist or fog. **2,** obscurity; vagueness, as of thought. —*v.t.* play mischievous tricks on (a candidate for membership). —**ha'zy,** *adj.* foggy; vague.

ha'zel (hā'zəl) *n.* **1,** any of several shrubs or small trees. **2,** a pale brown color. —**ha'zel·nut",** *n.*

H-'bomb" *n.* hydrogen bomb.

he (hē) *pron.* [*poss.* **his;** *obj.* **him**] **1,** the third person, sing. masc.; a male, other than the speaker and the person addressed. **2,** any male. —*adj.* (*Colloq.*) male.

head (hed) *n.* **1,** the uppermost part of the human body, above the neck; the skull with its contents and integuments; the corresponding part of any animal. **2,** the head regarded as the seat of intelligence; understanding; will; inclination. **3,** the position or person of a leader or chief. **4,** the highest or foremost part; the top or summit; the obverse of a coin. **5,** the source, as of a stream. **6,** culmination; crisis; force; pressure. **7,** something like a head in position, form, or function; a rounded protuberance; the compact inflorescence of a plant, as cabbage; the membrane of a drum. **8,** an individual, taken as one of a number. **9,** a subject or topic; a title or subtitle; heading; headline. —*adj.* **1,** being at the head; foremost; principal. **2,** coming from in front. —*v.t.* **1,** be the chief of. **2,** go to the front of; lead; precede. **3,** turn or direct in advancing. **4,** oppose; check; restrain. —*v.i.* **1,** go in a direction. **2,** originate.

head'ache" *n.* a pain in the head.

-head'ed (hed'id) *suf.* **1,** having a specified kind of head or number of heads. **2,** having a specified mind or temperament, as *levelheaded.*

head'gear" *n.* a helmet; any covering for the head.

head'ing (hed'ing) *n.* **1,** a title or caption. **2,** something that forms a head or front.

head'land (hed'lənd) *n.* a point of land projecting into the sea; a cape.

head'light" *n.* a lamp to illuminate the road ahead.

head'line" *n.* a title in large type, as in a newspaper. —*v.t.* give prominent billing to; advertise.

head'long" *adv. & adj.* **1,** hastily; rashly. **2,** with head foremost.

head'mas"ter *n.* the principal of a boys' school.

head'quar"ters *n.pl.* or *sing.* **1,** a principal office or residence. **2,** a seat of command.

heads'man (hedz'mən) *n.* [*pl.* **-men**] an executioner.

head'stone" *n.* a stone placed at the head of a grave.

head'strong" *adj.* obstinate; willful.

head'wa"ters *n.pl.* the source and earliest tributaries of a river.

head'way" *n.* **1,** motion or impetus forward. **2,** clear space in height, as under a bridge.

head'y (hed'ē) *adj.* exhilarating; intoxicating. —**head'i·ness,** *n.*

heal (hēl) *v.t.* **1,** make whole or sound; restore to health. **2,** cleanse; purify; remedy; repair. —*v.t.* grow whole or sound; get well. —**heal'er,** *n.* one who heals, not a physician.

health (helth) *n.* **1,** freedom from disease; good condition; normal and efficient functioning. **2,** bodily condition. **3,** a toast. —**health'ful,** *adj.* conducive to health. —**health'y,** *adj.* sound; in good condition.

heap (hēp) *n.* **1,** a collection of things laid together, esp. in a raised pile. **2,** (*Colloq.*) a large number or quantity. **3,** (*Slang*) an automobile. —*v.t.* **1,** put together; pile; amass. **2,** bestow bountifully. —**heap'ing,** *adj.* filled above the level of a retaining wall.

hear (hir) *v.t.* **1,** perceive by ear. **2,** listen to; give attention to. **3,** be informed of. —*v.i.* **1,** possess the sense of hearing. **2,** be told; learn by report. —**hear'er,** *n.* one of an audience.

hear'ing *n.* **1,** ability to perceive by ear. **2,** an opportunity to be heard. **3,** an examination in a court of law. **4,** earshot.

hear'say" *n.* information communicated by another; gossip; rumor.

hearse (hėrs) *n.* a vehicle for bearing a corpse to a burial ground.

heart (härt) *n.* **1,** the principal organ that causes blood to circulate in the body. **2,** this organ regarded as the seat of vitality, intellect, emotion, etc. **3,** love; kindness; pity. **4,** courage; determination; enthusiasm. **5,** the inner, central, or essential part of anything. **6,** the symbol (♡); a playing card so marked.

heart'ache" *n.* mental anguish; sorrow or grief.

heart'break" *n.* overwhelming sorrow or grief. —**heart'bro"ken,** *adj.*

heart'burn" *n.* a burning sensation due to stomach acidity.

-heart'ed (här'tid) *suf.* having a specified kind of heart or sentiment.

heart'en (här'tən) *v.t.* incite with courage or good cheer; encourage.

heart'felt" *adj.* felt deeply; sincere.

hearth (härth) *n.* **1,** a place where a fire is built; a section of floor in front of an open fire. **2,** the home or domestic circle; the fireside.

fat, fāte, fär, fāre, fâll; àsk; met, hē, hėr, maybè; pin, pīne; not, nōte, ôr, tool

hearth'stone" n. a stone or one of the stones forming a fireplace.

heart'less adj. unfeeling; cruel. —**heart'less-ness,** n.

heart'sick' adj. unhappy; grieving. Also, **heart'sore".** —**heart'sick'ness, heart'sore"ness,** n.

heart'strings" n.pl. the deepest feelings.

heart'throb" n. a deep emotion or something that arouses it.

heart-'to-heart' adj. confidential; unreservedly revealing, as a talk.

heart'y (här'tė) adj. 1, friendly; cordial; affectionate. 2, vigorous; enthusiastic; zealous. 3, large; substantial. —n. a robust or brave person. —**heart'i-ness,** n.

heat (hēt) n. 1, the condition, caused by friction, expenditure of energy, etc., that induces the sensation one feels when exposed to fire and causes substances to expand; the sensation, effect, etc., of being hot. 2, high temperature; a hot condition, as of the atmosphere. 3, passionate feeling; rage, vehemence, excitement, etc. 4, the mating period of a female animal. 5, one division of an athletic contest; one heating of metal in a furnace, etc. —v.t. 1, make hot, hotter, or less cold. 2, inflame with feeling. —v.i. 1, become warmer. 2, become excited. —**heat'ed,** adj. excited; angry.

heath (hēth) n. 1, a tract of uncultivated waste land. 2, any of several evergreen shrubs.

hea'then (hē'thən) n. 1, an irreligious person. 2, a pagan.

heath'er (heth'ər) n. a variety of heath common in Scotland.

heave (hēv) v.t. 1, lift with marked effort; raise with exertion. 2, throw upward and outward; toss; hurl. 3, utter laboriously or painfully. —v.i. 1, be raised, thrown, or forced up; swell up; bulge out. 2, rise and fall, as the ocean. 3, breathe laboriously; pant. 4, vomit. —n. 1, the act of heaving; an upward thrust or movement. 2, the surface displacement of a geological fault. 3, (pl.) a respiratory disease of horses.

heav'en (hev'ən) n. 1, the abode of God; the place or state of existence of the blessed, after death. 2, (cap.) God; Providence. 3, a state of bliss; supreme happiness or exaltation. 4, (usually pl.) the visible sky; the firmament.

heav'en-ly (-lē) adj. 1, blissful; sublime. 2, pert. to heaven; in the heavens.

heav'en-ward (-wərd) adv. & adj. toward heaven; upward; aloft.

heav'y (hev'ė) adj. 1, having much weight; hard to lift or move. 2, of high specific gravity; dense. 3, of great volume, force, intensity, etc.; thick, coarse, broad, deep, loud, etc. 4, serious; intense; somber; dull; ponderous; sluggish. 5, hard to bear; hard to do. 6, pregnant. —n. a villainous character in a play. —**heav'i-ness,** n.

heav'y-hand'ed adj. 1, oppressive. 2, clumsy.

heav'y-heart'ed adj. sad; mournful; dejected.

heavy water water in which the hydrogen has been replaced by its heavier isotope deuterium.

heav'y-weight" n. a boxer weighing more than 175 lbs.

heb-dom'a-dal (heb-dom'ə-dəl) adj. weekly.

he-bet'ic (hi-bet'ik) adj. pert. to or occurring during puberty; immature.

He-bra'ic (hē-brā'ik) adj. 1, of or like the Hebrews; Jewish. 2, in or pert. to Hebrew.

He'brew (hē'broo) n. 1, a Semitic language; the official language of Israel. 2, a Jew.

hec'a-tomb" (hek'ə-tōm") n. a great slaughter; a mass sacrifice.

heck'le (hek'əl) v.t. harass with questions, objections, jibes, etc.

hec'tare (hek'tār) n. a measure of land, 10,000 square meters or about 2½ acres.

hec'tic (hek'tik) adj. 1, turbulent; excited; impassioned. 2, feverish; consumptive.

hect-o- pref. hundred.

hec'to-graph" (hek'tə-gráf") n. the process of copying writings by offset from a gelatin base.

hec'tor (hek'tər) v.t. bully; tease; harass.

hedge (hej) n. a barrier or fence formed by bushes or small trees growing close together. —v.t. 1, enclose by a hedge. 2, surround; hem in; obstruct. 3, protect (a bet) by betting on both sides. —v.i. 1, avoid a decisive course; veer aside; hesitate. 2, provide a means of retreat or escape; protect a risk by some offsetting transaction.

hedge'hog" n. 1, a small insectivorous mammal. 2, the porcupine.

hedge'hop" v.i. [-hopped", -hop"ping] fly an airplane dangerously near the ground.

he'don-ism (hē'də-niz-əm) n. the doctrine that pleasure or happiness is the highest good. —**he'don-ist,** n; —**he'don-is'tic,** adj. —**he'don-is'ti-cal-ly,** adv.

-he'dron (hē'drən) suf. denoting a solid figure with several faces.

heed (hēd) *v.t.* & *i.* give attention; observe; consider. —*n.* careful notice or consideration. —**heed′ful,** *adj.* —**heed′less,** *adj.* neglectful; unwary.

hee′haw″ (hē′hā″) *n.* the bray of an ass.

heel (hēl) *n.* 1, the back part of the foot. 2, the part of a stocking covering the heel; the rear support of a shoe. 3, the rear, concluding, or final part of something. 4, a tipping motion; a canted position. 5, (*Slang*) a low character; a cad. —*v.t.* 1, furnish with a heel. 2, follow on the heels of; pursue. 3, (*Colloq.*) arm; equip. 4, cause to tilt. —*v.i.* 1, tip to one side. 2, run; dance.

heft *v.t.* heave; try the weight of by lifting. —*n.* weight.

heft′y (hef′tē) *adj.* 1, heavy. 2, muscular; strong. —**heft′i·ness,** *n.*

he·gem′o·ny (hi-jem′ə-nē) *n.* leadership or predominance, esp. by one member of a confederation of states.

He·gi′ra (he-jī′rə) *n.* the flight of Mohammed from Mecca, A.D. 622.

heif′er (hef′ər) *n.* a female cow that has not produced a calf.

heigh (hā) *interj.* a cry for attention.

height (hīt) *n.* 1, vertical distance above the ground or base; altitude; elevation. 2, distance upward; stature. 3, elevation of degree or condition; eminence. 4, the state of being high; loftiness. 5, the highest part; top; apex. 6, the highest degree; the culminating point.

height′en (hī′tən) *v.t.* 1, increase the height of. 2, intensify. —*v.i.* 1, become higher. 2, become more intense.

hei′nous (hā′nəs) *adj.* wicked; reprehensible. —**hei′nous·ness,** *n.*

heir (âr) *n.* 1, one who inherits property from another; one who will inherit. 2, successor; beneficiary. —**heir apparent,** one who must inherit, if he survives. —**heir′ess,** *n.fem.* —**heir presumptive,** one who will inherit unless a more eligible candidate is born.

heir′loom″ (âr′loom″) *n.* a personal possession handed down from generation to generation in a family.

held *v.* pret. & p.p. of **hold.**

hel′i·cal (hel′i-kəl) *adj.* spiral.

hel′i·cop″ter (hel′ə-kop″tər) *n.* an aircraft that is given vertical lift as well as propulsion by a horizontal propeller.

he·li·o- (hē-lē-ō) *pref.* sun.

he′li·o·graph″ (hē′lē-ə-gráf″) *n.* a device for signaling by reflecting the rays of the sun.

he′li·o·trope″ (hē′lē-ə-trōp″) *n.* 1, a flower-bearing plant that turns

toward the sun. 2, a pale or pinkish purple color.

he′li·um (hē′lē-əm) *n.* an inert gaseous chemical element, no. 2, symbol He.

he′lix (hē′liks) *n.* 1, a spiral; a spiral part. 2, a coil; the typical curve of a screw thread.

hell (hel) *n.* 1, the abode or state of the wicked after death. 2, any place or state of great suffering or misery. 3, a place of low repute.

Heliotrope

hell′cat″ *n.* a violent woman.

Hel·len′ic (he-len′ik) *adj.* 1, Greek. 2, pert. to Amer. college fraternities and sororities.

hell′er (-ər) *n.* a wild or dissipated person.

hell′fire″ *n.* 1, the fire of hell. 2, punishment; retribution.

hell′hound″ *n.* a fiend.

hell′ion (hel′yən) *n.* a troublemaking, uncontrollable person.

hell′ish (-ish) *adj.* vile; unbearable. —**hell′ish·ness,** *n.*

hel·lo′ (he-lō′) *interj.* 1, a greeting; a conventional salutation in telephoning. 2, an exclamation of surprise.

helm *n.* 1, the tiller or wheel controlling the rudder of a ship. 2, the place or post of control.

hel′met (hel′mit) *n.* a protective covering for the head; any of various types of metal hats.

helms′man (helmz′mən) *n.* [*pl.* -men] a pilot.

hel′ot (hel′ət) *n.* a serf or slave.

help *v.t.* 1, give aid to; assist in doing or attaining. 2, bring relief to; succor; save. 3, mitigate; relieve. 4, repair; remedy. 5, serve or distribute food (to). —*v.i.* give aid; be of service. —*n.* 1, the act of helping; aid; relief; remedy. 2, someone or something that helps; an assistant; servants, esp. domestic; a remedy. —**help′er,** *n.* an assistant. —**help′ful,** *adj.* useful. —**help′less,** *adj.* entirely ineffective or dependent; unable to move or perform.

help′mate″ *n.* a spouse, esp. a wife. Also, **help′meet″.**

hel′ter-skel′ter (hel′tər-skel′tər) *adj.* & *adv.* with confused haste or commotion; in a disorderly hurry. —*n.* confused action; bustle.

helve (helv) *n.* the handle of an ax:

fat, fāte, fär, fâre, fäll, ásk; met, hē, hêr, maybē; pin, pīne; not, nōte, ôr, tool

hem *n.* **1,** a fold on the edge of a cloth, sewed down to prevent raveling. **2,** an edge, rim, or border. —*v.t.* [hemmed, hem'ming] **1,** form a hem on. **2,** (often with *in*) enclose; limit. —*interj.* a clearing of the throat; a mild exclamation to attract attention.

hem·i- *pref.* half.

hem'i·sphere" (hem'ə-sfir") *n.* half of a sphere, esp. of the terrestrial globe or celestial sphere: the No. and So. hemispheres are regarded as divided by the equator, the W. and E. hemispheres by the Atlantic and Pacific Oceans. —**hem'i·spher'i·cal** (-sfer'ə-kəl) *adj.*

hem'lock (hem'lok) *n.* **1,** an herb from which is obtained a powerful sedative. **2,** an evergreen tree of the spruce family.

he·mo- (hē-mə) *pref.* blood.

Hemlock (1)

he"mo·glo'bin (hē"mə-glō'bin) *n.* the coloring matter of the red blood corpuscles.

he"mo·phil'i·a (hē"mə-fil'ē-ə) *n.* an affliction in which the blood does not coagulate readily. —**he"mo·phil'i·ac,** *n.* one so afflicted.

hem'or·rhage (hem'ə-rij) *n.* a discharge of blood from a ruptured blood vessel.

hem'or·rhoid" (hem'ə-roid") *n.* a swelling of a vein in the rectum; a pile.

hemp *n.* any of various fibrous shrubs, used for cordage, fabrics, and narcotic drugs. —**hemp'en,** *adj.*

hem'stitch" *n.* a hem joined where threads have been pulled to make a decorative pattern.

hen *n.* **1,** a female fowl, esp. a chicken. **2,** a censorious married woman.

hence (hens) *adv.* **1,** as a consequence; for this reason; therefore. **2,** from this time; in the future. **3,** from this place. **4,** from this source or origin.

hence"forth' *adv.* from this time onward.

hench'man (hench'mən) *n.* [*pl.* -men] an attendant or follower.

hen'na (hen'ə) *n.* an Asiatic shrub; a reddish-brown dye made from it. —*v.t.* dye (esp. hair) with henna.

hen'ner·y (-ə-rē) *n.* a hen house.

hen'peck" (hen'pek") *v.t.* domineer over (said of a wife who thus rules her husband).

hep *adj.* (*Slang*) well-informed; being one of the elect. —**hep'cat",** *n.* (*Slang*) one thoroughly conversant with jazz.

he·pat'ic (hi-pat'ik) *adj.* pert. to the liver.

hep·ta- *pref.* seven.

her (hēr) *pron.* obj. and poss. case of *she.*

her'ald (her'əld) *n.* **1,** an announcer; crier; publisher. **2,** one who proclaims in advance; forerunner; harbinger. **3,** a messenger. **4,** one who regulates the use of armorial bearings. —*v.t.* give tidings of; announce. —**he·ral'dic** (he-ral'dik) *adj.* —**her'ald·ry** (-rē) *n.* the art and science of armorial bearings.

herb (ērb, hērb) *n.* an annual plant whose stem does not become woody, often used for medicine, flavoring, etc. —**her·ba'ceous** (hēr-bā'shəs) *adj.* —**herb'age,** *n.* herbs collectively or growing together.

her·biv'o·rous (hēr-biv'ə-rəs) *adj.* feeding on plants only.

her·cu'le·an (hēr-kū'lē-ən) *adj.* having or requiring prodigious strength, endurance, etc.

herd (hērd) *n.* **1,** a number of animals together. **2,** a mob; rabble. **3,** [also, herd'er] one who tends a herd. —*v.t.* drive together; tend or lead. —*v.i.* go together; unite.

herds'man (hērds'mən) *n.* [*pl.* -men] one who tends a herd of animals.

here (hir) *adv.* **1,** in or toward this place. **2,** at this time or juncture. —*interj.* **1,** I am present. **2,** come here!

here'a·bout" *adv.* about or near this place. Also, **here'a·bouts".**

here·af'ter *adv.* **1,** in the future. **2,** beyond this place or juncture. —*n.* future time, esp. after death.

here'by" *adv.* by this means or agency; as a result of this.

he·red'i·tar·y (hi-red'ə-tār-ē) *adj.* **1,** passing naturally from parent to offspring; descending by inheritance. **2,** pert. to heredity.

he·red'i·ty (hə-red'ə-tē) *n.* the transmission of qualities or characteristics from parents to offspring.

here·in' *adv.* **1,** in this place. **2,** in view of this.

here·of' *adv.* of or concerning this.

her'e·sy (her'ə-sē) *n.* an unorthodox doctrine or opinion, esp. in religion.

her'e·tic (her'ə-tik) *n.* one who holds an unorthodox opinion. —*adj.* of such opinion. —**he·ret'i·cal** (hə-ret'i-kəl) *adj.*

here·to' *adv.* to this.

here"to·fore' *adv.* before this time.

here'up·on" *adv.* at or immediately following this time or event.

her'it·a·ble (her'ə-tə-bəl) *adj.* capable of being inherited. —**her"it·a·bil'i·ty,** *n.*

her'it·age (her'ə-tij) *n.* **1,** something inherited. **2,** a condition, lot or portion acquired by being born.

her·maph'ro·dite" (hẽr-maf'rə-dīt") *n.* an animal or plant having both male and female organs of generation. —**her·maph'ro·dit'ic** (-dit'ik) *adj.*

her·met'ic (hẽr-met'ik) *adj.* made airtight by sealing, as a container. —**her·met'i·cal·ly,** *adv.*

her'mit (hẽr'mit) *n.* one who lives alone and avoids the society of others; a recluse. —**her'mit·age,** *n.* the dwelling of a hermit.

her'ni·a (hẽr'nē-ə) *n.* the protrusion of a bodily organ or tissue through its surrounding walls, esp. abdominal; a rupture.

he'ro (hir'ō) *n.* **1,** a man admired for his courage, fortitude, prowess, nobility, etc. **2,** the principal male character in a play, story, or poem.

he·ro'ic (hi-rō'ik) *adj.* **1,** pert. to or like a hero. **2,** having recourse to extreme measures; daring; drastic. **3,** larger than life-size (in art). —**he·ro'i·cal·ly,** *adv.*

he·ro'ics (hi-ro'iks) *n.* bombastic language; mawkish sentiment.

her'o·in (her'ō-in) *n.* a habit-forming drug, derivative of morphine.

her'o·ine (her'ō-in) *n.* a female hero.

her'o·ism (her'ō-iz-əm) *n.* heroic qualities or conduct.

her'on (her'ən) *n.* a wading bird with long legs, neck, and bill.

her"pe·tol'o·gy (hẽr"pə-tol'ə-jē) *n.* the branch of zoölogy dealing with reptiles and amphibians. —**her"pe·tol'o·gist,** *n.*

her'ring (her'ing) *n.* any of numerous small food fishes.

her'ring·bone" (her'ing-bōn") *n.* & *adj.* a pattern of oblique parallel lines in tiers alternating in direction.

hers (hẽrz) *pron.* poss. case of *she* used predicatively.

her·self' (hẽr-self') *pron.* emphatic and reflexive form of *her.*

hes'i·tan·cy (hez'i-tən-sē) *n.* hesitation.

hes'i·tant (hez'i-tənt) *adj.* hesitating or prone to hesitate; irresolute.

hes'i·tate" (hez'i-tāt") *v.i.* **1,** hold back in doubt or indecision. **2,** falter in speech; stammer. **3,** pause. —**hes"i·ta'tion,** *n.*

Hes'sian (hesh'ən) *n.* a person of Hesse (in Germany), esp. a soldier who fought against the U.S. in the Revolutionary War.

het·er·o- *pref.* different; other.

het'er·o·dox" (het'ər-ə-doks") *adj.* not orthodox; heretical. —**het'er·o·dox"y,** *n.*

het"er·o·ge'ne·ous (het"ər-ə-jē'nē-əs) *adj.* **1,** different in kind; widely dissimilar. **2,** composed of parts of different kinds; not homogeneous. —**het"er·o·ge'ne·ous·ness,** *n.*

hew (hū) *v.t. & i.* [*p.p.* **hewed** or **hewn**] **1,** cut with an ax, sword, etc.; chop. **2,** carve.

hex (heks) *v.t.* (*Dial.*) practice witchcraft on. —*n.* a spell.

hex·a- *pref.* six; sixfold.

hex'a·gon" (heks'ə-gon") *n.* a plane figure having six sides. —**hex·ag'o·nal** (-ag'ə-nəl) *adj.*

hex"yl·res·or'cin·ol" (hek"sil-rə-zôr'sə-nōl") *n.* an antiseptic compound.

hey (hā) *interj.* to draw attention.

hey'day" (hā'dā") *n.* highest vigor; full strength; acme.

hi·a'tus (hi-ā'təs) *n.* a space where something is missing; a gap; break.

hi·ber'nal (hī-bẽr'nəl) *adj.* pert. to winter.

hi'ber·nate" (hī'bər-nāt") *v.i.* pass the winter in seclusion and in a torpid condition, as do some animals. —**hi"ber·na'tion,** *n.*

Hi·ber'ni·an (hī-bẽr'nē-ən) *adj.* Irish. —*n.* a native of Ireland.

hi·bis'cus (hī-bis'kəs) *n.* a shrub having large, showy flowers.

hic'cup (hik'up) *n.* **1,** a spasmodic, involuntary, audible cutting-off of indrawn breath. **2,** (*pl.*) such spasms. —*v.i.* have the hiccups. Also, **hic'cough** (hik'up).

hick (hik) *n.* a person unfamiliar with city ways. —*adj.* countrified.

hick'o·ry (hik'ə-rē) *n.* a No. Amer. tree or its tough, springy wood.

hide (hīd) *v.t.* [**hid** (hid), **hid'den** (hid'ən) or **hid, hid'ing**] prevent from being discovered; secrete. —*v.i.* keep out of view. —*n.* **1,** the skin of an animal, raw or dressed. **2,** (*Slang*) the human skin.

hide'bound" (hīd'bownd") *adj.* narrow and stubborn in opinion.

hid'e·ous (hid'ē-əs) *adj.* frightful in appearance or character. —**hid'e·ous·ness,** *n.*

hide-'out" *n.* a secret lodging; retreat.

hid'ing (hīd'ing) *n.* **1,** the state of being hidden. **2,** (*Colloq.*) a thrashing.

hie (hī) *v.t.* go in haste.

hi'er·arch (hī'ər-ärk) *n.* one of authority in sacred matters. —**hi'er·ar'chal,** *adj.*

hi'er·ar"chy (hī'ə-rär"kè) *n.* **1,** a body of persons organized by rank, in church or government. **2,** a series of terms of different rank. —**hi'er·ar'chic, hi"er·ar'chi·cal,** *adj.*

hi"er·o·glyph'ic (hī"ər-ə-glif"ik)*adj.* **1,** pert. to a system of writing by conventionalized pictures, esp. ancient Egyptian. **2,** hard to decipher. —*n.* a hieroglyphic symbol.

Hieroglyphics

high (hī) *adj.* **1,** rising far above, or situated above, the ground or a base. **2,** elevated in rank, etc. **3,** expensive. **4,** intensified; large in measure or amount. **5,** (of meat) slightly tainted. **6,** in the upper range of sounds; shrill. **7,** (*Colloq.*) tipsy. —*adv.* at a high place or level; to a high degree. —*n.* **1,** something that is high or highest. **2,** the automobile gear giving greatest forward speed. **3,** an area of high atmospheric pressure. —**high school,** the ninth or tenth to twelfth grades. —**high sea,** the open ocean. —**high time** (*Colloq.*) almost too late.

high'ball" *n.* **1,** a drink of whiskey diluted with water, seltzer, etc. **2,** a railroad signal used to show a clear track. —*v.i.* (*Colloq.*) go ahead rapidly.

high'bind"er (-bīn'dər) *n.* a paid criminal, esp. Chinese.

high'boy" *n.* a tall chest of drawers.

high'brow" *n.* (*Colloq.*) a person of intellectual tastes. —*adj.* intellectual; abstruse.

high"fa·lu'tin (hī"fə-loo'tən) *adj.* (*Colloq.*) pretentious.

high'flown" *adj.* over-ambitious; (esp. of language) fancy.

high'fly"er *n.* one extravagant in aims or pretensions.

high-'hand'ed *adj.* overbearing; arbitrary. —**high-'hand'ed·ness,** *n.*

high-'hat' *adj.* (*Slang*) snobbish. —*v.t.* treat condescendingly.

high'land (-lənd) *n.* (often *pl.*) & *adj.* a mountainous region.

high'light" *n.* **1,** the point of most intense light. **2,** a conspicuous part or event. —*v.t.* emphasize.

high'ness (-nəs) *n.* **1,** the state of being high. **2,** (*cap.*) a title of address to royal persons.

high'road" *n.* **1,** a main road. **2,** any public route. **3,** an easy course.

high'strung" *adj.* nervous; tense.

high'toned" (-tōnd") *adj.* **1,** high in pitch. **2,** (*Colloq.*) stylish.

high'way" *n.* **1,** a main road. **2,** any public route, on land or water.

high'way·man (-mən) *n.* [*pl.* -men] a robber.

hi'jack" (hī'jak") *v.t.* (*Slang*) steal (contraband in transit).

hike (hīk) *v.i.* **1,** walk afield, for pleasure or training. **2,** (*Colloq.*) leave; walk away. **3,** raise with a jerk. —*n.* a walking trip; a march.

hi·lar'i·ous (hi-lâr'è-əs) *adj.* **1,** gay; exhilarated. **2,** causing great mirth. —**hi·lar'i·ty** (hi-lar'ə-tè), *n.*

hill (hil) *n.* **1,** a natural elevation of land. **2,** an artificial mound. —*v.t.* form into hills, as corn.

hill'bill"y *n.* a backwoods mountaineer. —*adj.* (esp. of music) in the style of mountain folksong.

hill'ock (hil'ək) *n.* a small hill.

hill'side" *n.* the side of a hill; sloping ground.

hill'y (-è) *adj.* **1,** abounding in hills. **2,** steep. —**hill'i·ness,** *n.*

hilt *n.* the handle of a weapon, esp. of a sword or dagger.

him *pron.* objective case of *he.*

him·self' *pron.* emphatic form of *him;* reflexive form of *he.*

hind (hīnd) *adj.* [*superl.* **hind'most"** or **hind'er·most"**] situated at the back; posterior. —*n.* a female deer.

hin'der (hin'dər) *v.t.* & *i.* prevent from acting or proceeding; impede.

hin'drance (hin'drəns) *n.* **1,** act of hindering; a stopping or checking. **2,** an obstacle.

hind'sight" *n.* judgment of what should have been done, after the result is known.

Hin'du (hin'doo) *n.* & *adj.* East Indian, in language and religion (Brahman). —**Hin'du·ism,** *n.*

hinge (hinj) *n.* **1,** a joint that permits movement, as for a door. **2,** a similar anatomical joint, as the knee. **3,** that on which something turns or depends; a controlling principle. —*v.t.* **1,** turn or depend on. **2,** attach by a hinge.

hint *n.* a covert suggestion or implication; an indirect allusion. —*v.t.* & *i.* intimate; imply.

hin'ter·land" (hin'tər-land") *n.* **1,** territory lying back of a coastal region. **2,** a remote region.

hip *n.* **1,** the projecting, fleshy part of the body around the pelvis; the haunch. **2,** the hip joint. —*interj.* a sound used in cheering.

---

tub, cūte, pûll; label; oil, owl; go, chip, she, thin, *then*, sing, ink; *see* p. 6

hipped (hipt) *adj.* (*Slang*) having an obsession.

Hip"po·crat'ic oath (hip'ə-krat'-ik) an oath embodying the obligations of a physician.

hip"po·drome" (hip'ə-drōm") *n.* an arena for spectacular exhibitions.

hip"po·pot'a·mus (hip'ə-pot'ə-məs) *n.* a large Afr. pachydermatous mammal that frequents rivers and lakes.

hir'cine (hėr'-sīn) *adj.* goatlike, esp. in odor.

hire (hīr) *v.t.* **1**, engage the services or use of, for pay; employ; rent. **2**, (sometimes with *out*) grant the services or use of, for pay. —*v.i.* (with *out*) lend one's services for pay. —*n.* **1**, wages; rental. **2**, the act of hiring or being hired. —**hire'ling**, *n.* one serving only for pay.

Hippopotamus

hir·sute' (hėr-soot') *adj.* hairy. —**hir·sute'ness**, *n.*

his (hiz) *pron.* poss. form of *he.*

His·pan'ic (his-pan'ik) *adj.* Spanish.

hiss (his) *v.t. & i.* **1**, make a sound like that of the letter *s* prolonged. **2**, express disapproval by making this sound. —*n.* such a sound.

hist *interj.* **1**, listen! **2**, silence!

his'ta·mine" (his'tə-mēn") *n.* an organic ammonia compound released by the body tissues in certain reactions, as of the common cold.

his·tol'o·gy (his-tol'ə-jē) *n.* the science that treats of organic tissues. —**his"to·log'i·cal**, *adj.*

his·to'ri·an (his-tôr'ē-ən) *n.* a writer of, or an authority on, history.

his·tor'ic (his-tor'ik) *adj.* **1**, in or pert. to history. **2**, important in history. Also, **his·tor'i·cal.**

his"to·ric'i·ty (his"tə-ris'ə-tē) *n.* historical authenticity.

his'to·ry (his'tə-rē) *n.* **1**, the branch of knowledge concerned with ascertaining and recording past events. **2**, an oral or written narrative of past events. **3**, a systematic description of natural phenomena.

his"tri·on'ic (his"trē-on'ik) *adj.* **1**, pert. to actors or acting. **2**, pretended; artificial; affected. —**his"-tri·on'i·cal·ly**, *adv.*

his"tri·on'ics (-iks) *n.pl.* **1**, theatricals. **2**, artificial speech or manner.

hit *v.t. & i.* [hit, hit'ting] **1**, deal a blow to; strike; collide with. **2**, reach, as with a missile. **3**, move by a stroke. **4**, assail in speech. **5**, meet with; find; (with *on*) discover. **6**, agree with; suit. —*n.* **1**, a blow, impact, or collision. **2**, (*Baseball*) a safely batted ball. **3**, (*Colloq.*) a successful performance or enterprise. —**hit-'and-run'**, *adj.* guilty of causing an automobile accident and not stopping to identify oneself. —**hit'ter**, *n.*

hitch (hich) *v.t.* **1**, fasten as with a rope, esp. temporarily; tether. **2**, pull up; raise by jerks. —*v.i.* **1**, be fastened, entangled. **2**, move jerkily. **3**, (*Colloq.*) work smoothly together; agree. —*n.* **1**, a joining or making fast. **2**, a knot. **3**, a temporary stoppage or obstruction. **4**, a jerk; a limping gait. **5**, (*Colloq.*) a task; working period; prison sentence.

hitch'hike" (hich'hīk") *v.i.* (*Colloq.*) travel by begging rides in strangers' automobiles.

hith'er (hith'ər) *adv.* to this place. —*adj.* on the nearer side. —**hith"er·to'**, *adv.* up to this time.

hive (hīv) *n.* **1**, a swarm of bees; any shelter they inhabit. **2**, a roomful of busy people. —*v.i.* enter a hive.

hives (hīvz) *n.* an eruptive skin disease.

ho (hō) *interj.* to call attention, express surprise, amusement, etc.

hoar (hôr) *adj.* **1**, white or gray, as frost. **2**, gray-haired with age. —**hoar'frost"**, *n.* frozen dew. —**hoar'y**, *adj.*

hoard (hôrd) *n.* a stock or store laid by for preservation or future use. —*v.t. & i.* amass; save.

hoarse (hôrs) *adj.* **1**, deep and harsh to the ear; raucous. **2**, having a husky voice. —**hoarse'ness**, *n.*

hoax (hōks) *n.* a mischievous deception; a practical joke. —*v.t.* deceive.

hob *n.* **1**, a shelf or projection in a fireplace. **2**, a stick used as a target. **3**, (*Colloq.*) mischief.

hob'ble (hob'əl) *v.i.* limp; proceed haltingly. —*v.t.* **1**, fetter by tying the legs together. **2**, impede in any way. —*n.* **1**, a limping gait. **2**, a rope used to tie the legs of an animal. —**hob'bling**, *adj.* limping.

hob'by (hob'ē) *n.* **1**, an occupation pursued for recreation. **2**, a stick or rocking vehicle with a horse's head, for children: *hobbyhorse.*

hob'gob"lin *n.* **1**, a mischievous imp. **2**, something that arouses fear.

hob'nail" *n.* a large-headed nail protecting the sole of a heavy shoe.

hob'nob" *v.i.* [-nobbed", -nob"-bing] associate constantly.

ho'bo (hō'bō) *n.* [*pl.* **-boes**] **1,** a tramp; vagrant. **2,** a migrant worker.

hock (hok) *n.* **1,** a protruding joint in the hind leg of a horse. **2,** a white Rhine wine. —*v.t.* **1,** hamstring. **2,** (*Colloq.*) pawn.

hock'ey (hok'ē) *n.* a game played with a puck and crooked sticks, either on the ground or on ice.

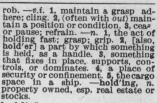

Hod   Hoe

hock'shop" *n.* (*Colloq.*) pawnshop.

ho'cus (hō'kəs) *v.t.* deceive by trickery.

ho'cus-po'cus (hō'kəs-pō'kəs) *n.* **1,** a jocular incantation uttered by a conjurer. **2,** a conjurer's trick; deception. —*v.t. & i.* deceive.

hod *n.* **1,** a trough fixed on a long handle, for carrying bricks or mortar. **2,** a coal scuttle.

hodge'podge" (hoj'poj") *n.* an indiscriminate mixture; a jumble.

hoe (hō) *n.* a blade fixed on a long handle, for cultivating earth, cutting weeds, etc. —*v.t. & i.* use a hoe (on).

hoe'cake" *n.* a baked cornmeal cake.

hog *n.* **1,** a pig, sow, or boar; a swine. **2,** a domesticated swine fattened for market. **3,** (*Colloq.*) a greedy or filthy person. —*v.t.* [**hogged, hog'ging**] (*Slang*) take more than one's share of. —**hog'gish,** *adj.*

hogs'head" (hogz'hed") *n.* **1,** a large barrel or cask. **2,** a unit of capacity.

hog'wash" *n.* **1,** swill given to hogs. **2,** (*Colloq.*) trash; nonsense.

hoi pol·loi' (hoi' pə-loi') (*Gk.*) the common people.

hoist *v.t.* raise or lift, esp. by machinery. —*n.* **1,** a contrivance for lifting, as an elevator. **2,** a lift or boost.

hoi'ty-toi'ty (hoi'tē-toi'tē) *adj.* **1,** giddy. **2,** haughty.

ho'kum (hō'kəm) *n.* (*Slang*) **1,** nonsense; buncombe. **2,** stereotyped humor.

hold (hōld) *v.t.* [*pret. & p.p.* **held**] **1,** keep fast, as in grasp of the hand; retain; cling to. **2,** keep back; withhold; restrain. **3,** have in possession; own; occupy. **4,** engage in; pursue; sustain. **5,** contain; have the capacity of. **6,** entertain in the mind; maintain. **7,** rule legally. **8,** (*with up*)

rob. —*v.i.* **1,** maintain a grasp adhere; cling. **2,** (often *with out*) maintain a position or condition. **3,** cease or pause; refrain. —*n.* **1,** the act of holding fast; grasp; grip. **2,** [also, hold'er] a part by which something is held, as a handle. **3,** something that fixes in place, supports, controls, or dominates. **4,** a place of security or confinement. **5,** the cargo space in a ship. —**hold'ing,** *n.* property owned, esp. real estate or stocks.

hold'o"ver *n.* a thing or condition retained from a previous time.

hold'up" (hōld'up') *n.* (*Colloq.*) a robbery under threat of bodily injury.

hole (hōl) *n.* **1,** an opening; aperture; perforation. **2,** a hollow place; cavity; excavation. **3,** any place that is dark, secluded, or dingy; a hiding-place; a dungeon. **4,** (*Golf*) the course from one tee to the corresponding hole. **5,** (*Colloq.*) an embarrassing predicament. **6,** (*Colloq.*) a flaw. —*v.t.* put into a hole. —*v.i.* (with *up*) go into seclusion or hiding; hibernate. —**hole'y,** *adj.* perforated.

hol'i·day" (hol'ə-dā") *n.* **1,** a commemorative day, fixed by law or custom, on which business is suspended. **2,** a vacation. —*adj.* festive; pert. to a holiday.

hol'ler (hol'ər) *v.t. & i. & n.* yell.

hol'low (hol'ō) *adj.* **1,** empty within; not solid. **2,** having a hole, cavity, or concavity; sunken, as cheeks. **3,** (of sound) low-pitched. **4,** of little worth; fruitless. **5,** insincere; false. **6,** hungry. —*n.* **1,** an empty space, hole, or cavity. **2,** a valley. —*v.t.* (with *out*) make hollow. —**hol'low·ness,** *n.*

hol'ly (hol'ē) *n.* a shrub with glossy leaves and red berries much used for Christmas decoration.

hol'ly·hock" (hol'ē-hok") *n.* a tall plant bearing large flowers.

holo- *pref.* whole, entire.

hol'o·caust" (hol'ə-kâst") *n.* great destruction of life, esp. by fire.

hol'o·graph (hol'ə-graf) *n. & adj.* (a document) written in the hand of its author. —**hol"o·graph'ic,** *adj.*

hol'ster (hōl'stər) *n.* a leather case for carrying a pistol.

ho'ly (hō'lē) *adj.* **1,** sacred; declared sacred by church authority. **2,** devoted to the service of God or the church; religious. **3,** pious; devout; saintly. —**hol'i·ness,** *n.*

hom'age (hom'ij) *n.* respect or reverence; tribute.

hom'burg (hom'bêrg) *n.* a style of man's felt hat.

home (hōm) *n.* **1,** the house, etc. where one resides; one's native land. **2,** the burrow or retreat of an animal. **3,** the region in which something is common or native. **4,** an institution for sheltering orphans, the aged, etc. **5,** in games, the goal or principal base. —*adj.* **1,** domestic. **2,** to the point. —*adv.* **1,** at, to, or toward home. **2,** to the point; effectively; all the way.

home'ly (hōm'lė) *adj.* **1,** unpretentious; comfortable. **2,** not handsome; plain. **3,** rude; not elegant. —**home'li·ness,** *n.*

home'made' *adj.* made at home, not in a factory.

homeo- *pref.* similar.

ho"me·op'a·thy (hō"mė·op'ə·thė) *n.* treatment of disease with drugs that produce symptoms similar to those of the disease. —**ho'me·o·path",** *n.* —**ho"me·o·path'ic,** *adj.* —**ho"me·o·path'i·cal·ly,** *adv.*

hom'er *n.* **1,** (*Baseball*) a home run. **2,** a homing pigeon.

home'sick' *adj.* depressed by longing for home. —**home'sick"ness,** *n.*

home'spun' *adj.* **1,** spun or woven at home, as cloth. **2,** plain; unpretentious.

home'stead' *n.* land and dwelling occupied by their owner. —**home'stead"er,** *n.* one who establishes a homestead in unsettled territory.

home'work' *n.* any work, esp. schoolwork, assigned to be done at home.

hom'i·cide" (hom'ə·sīd") *n.* the killing of one human being by another. —**hom'i·cid'al,** *adj.*

hom"i·let'ic (hom"ə·let'ik) *adj.* being or like a sermon. —**hom"i·let'i·cal·ly,** *adv.*

hom"i·let'ics (-iks) *n.* the composition or preaching of sermons.

hom'i·ly (hom'ə·lė) *n.* a moralizing discourse; a sermon.

hom'i·ny (hom'ə·nė) *n.* corn, ground or in hulled kernels, boiled in water or milk.

homo- *pref.* the same.

ho"mo·ge'ne·ous (hō"mə·jē'nė·əs) *adj.* **1,** composed of parts of the same kind; not heterogeneous. **2,** alike in kind. —**ho"mo·ge·ne'i·ty** (-jə·nē'ə·tė) *n.*

ho·mog'e·nize" (hō·moj'ə·nīz") *v.t.* make homogeneous; mix thoroughly, as milk and cream. —**ho·mog"e·ni·za'tion,** *n.*

ho·mol'o·gous (hō·mol'ə·gəs) *adj.* having the same relative position, proportion, value or structure. —**ho·mol'o·gy** (-jė) *n.*

hom'o·nym (hom'ə·nim) *n.* a word like another in sound but different in meaning, as *feet* and *feat.*

hom'o·phone" (hom'ə·fōn") *n.* a word pronounced like another but different in meaning, and often in spelling, as *too* and *two*; a homonym. —**hom"o·phon'ic** (-fon'ik) *adj.*

ho·moph'o·ny (hō·mof'ə·nė) *n.* **1,** sameness of sound. **2,** music having a principal melody or leading voice: monody.

ho"mo·sex'u·al (hō"mə·sek'shoo·əl) *adj.* feeling romantic love for persons of the same sex. —*n.* a homosexual person, esp. male. —**ho"mo·sex"u·al'i·ty,** *n.*

hone (hōn) *n.* a stone for sharpening razors, etc. —*v.t.* sharpen with a hone; whet. —*v.i.* (*Dial.*) yearn.

hon'est (on'ist) *adj.* **1,** having a sense of honor; upright and fair in dealing. **2,** sincere; truthful. **3,** genuine; unadulterated; virtuous. —**hon'es·ty,** *n.*

hon'ey (hun'ė) *n.* **1,** a sweet fluid produced by bees from the nectar of flowers. **2,** something sweet or delightful. **3,** a term of endearment. —**hon'eyed,** *adj.* sweet; fawning.

Queen   Drone

Worker

Honeybees

hon'ey·bee" *n.* a bee that gathers honey.

hon'ey·comb" *n.* **1,** a wax structure formed by bees for storing honey. **2,** any structure having many cells. —**hon'ey·combed",** *adj.*

hon'ey·dew" *n.* a sweet plant substance. —**honeydew melon,** a white-fleshed variety of muskmelon.

hon'ey·moon" *n.* **1,** a trip taken alone by a newly married couple. **2,** a brief period of amity.

hon'ey·suck"le *n.* a sweet-scented shrub or vine.

honk *n.* **1,** the cry of a wild goose. **2,** a similar sound, esp. of a warning horn. —*v.i.* utter such a sound.

hon'or (on'ər) *n.* **1,** high esteem; deferential admiration. **2,** high reputation; credit for honesty, etc. **3,** fidelity to principles or obligations; fairness in dealing; conformance with high standards of behavior. **4,** high rank, achievement, or distinction. **5,** a title, decoration, diploma, etc. **6,** (preceded by *his* or *your*) a title of address to a mayor or judge. **7,** chastity in a woman. —*v.t.* **1,** hold in honor; respect. **2,**

confer a mark of honor upon. **3**, treat with due respect; accept; credit; fulfill. Also, **hon'our.**

hon·or·a·ble (-ə-bəl) *adj.* **1**, worthy of respect. **2**, noble; upright. —**hon'or·a·ble·ness,** *n.*

hon"o·rar'i·um (on"ə-rār'ē-əm) *n.* [*pl.* -**a** (-ə)] a fee, as for professional services.

hon'or·ar·y (on'er-er-ē) *adj.* **1**, conferring honor, without usual requirements, duties, etc. **2**, done or given in token of honor. **3**, dependent on honor for fulfillment.

hooch *n.* (*Slang*) alcoholic liquor.

hood (hůd) *n.* **1**, a covering for the head, often attached to a cloak, etc. **2**, any hood-shaped covering, as over an automobile engine. **3**, (*Slang*) a hoodlum.

-hood (hůd) *suf.* the state or condition of being what is expressed by the foregoing word, as *likelihood*, the state of being likely.

hood'lum (hood'ləm) *n.* a rowdy; a ruffian.

hoo'doo *n.* **1**, voodoo. **2**, (*Colloq.*) bad luck; someone or something supposed to bring bad luck. —*v.t.* bring bad luck to.

hood'wink" *v.t.* deceive; impose upon.

hoo'ey (hoo'ē) *n. & interj.* (*Slang*) nonsense.

hoof (hůf) *n.* the horny casing that sheathes the foot of many quadrupeds; the entire foot. —*v.i.* (*Colloq.*) walk; dance. —**hoof'er,** *n.* (*Slang*) a professional dancer.

hook (hůk) *n.* **1**, a curved or angular piece of metal or the like, used to catch, hold, or sustain something. **2**, anything so bent or curved, as a spit of land. **3**, a curved course, as of a ball hit or thrown; a swinging blow in boxing. —*v.t.* **1**, use or make a hook. **2**, catch by artifice; trap. **3**, (*Slang*) pilfer. **4**, (with *up*) connect. —*v.i.* **1**, become attached. **2**, bend or curve. —**by hook or crook,** by any means. —**hook and eye,** a fastening device used on clothes.

hook'up" *n.* **1**, a diagram, as of radio apparatus. **2**, a system of radio stations.

hook'worm" *n.* a parasitic bloodsucking worm infesting the intestine.

hoo'li·gan (hoo'lə-gən) *n.* (*Slang*) a hoodlum.

hoop *n.* a circular band or ring, such as used on a barrel. —**hoop skirt,** a skirt stretched to bell-shape over a framework.

hoose'gow (hoos'gow) *n.* (*Slang*) a jail.

Hoo'sier (hoo'zhər) *n.* (*Slang*) a native of Indiana. —*adj.* of Indiana.

hoot *n.* **1**, the cry of an owl; any similar sound. **2**, a cry or noise of derision. —*v.i. & t.* utter this cry.

hop *v.i.* **1**, leap; move by short leaps. **2**, leap on one foot. **3**, (*Colloq.*) dance. **4**, (with *off*) begin a flight or journey. —*v.t.* [**hopped, hop'ping**] **1**, leap across. **2**, jump upon. —*n.* **1**, a short leap, esp. on one foot. **2**, a flight or journey. **3**, (*Colloq.*) a dance. **4**, (*Slang*) opium. **5**, a twining plant whose flowers (**hops**) are used in brewing.

hope (hōp) *v.t. & i.* expect or look forward to, with desire and confidence. —*n.* **1**, confidence in a future event; expectation of something desired. **2**, what is hoped for. **3**, something that arouses or justifies hope. —**hope'ful,** *adj.* —**hope'less,** *adj.* **1**, without hope. **2**, beyond repair, correction, or salvation.

hop'per (hop'ər) *n.* **1**, one who or that which hops, as certain insects. **2**, a trough or chute in a storage tank through which grain, coal, etc. is discharged.

hop'scotch" *n.* a children's game, played by hopping from square to square.

ho'ral (hôr'əl) *adj.* hourly; relating to hours.

horde (hôrd) *n.* a large troop or flock; a multitude.

hore'hound" (hôr'hownd") *n.* a perennial herb, used in making medicine and candy.

ho·ri'zon (hə-rī'zən) *n.* **1**, the apparent boundary between earth and sky. **2**, the limit of visual or intellectual perception.

hor·i·zon'tal (hor-i-zon'təl) *adj. & n.* parallel to the earth's surface; at right angles to a vertical line.

hor'mone (hôr'mōn) *n.* any of various substances normally secreted by glands.

horn (hôrn) *n.* **1**, a hard, spikelike growth on the head, as of cattle; the substance of which it is composed. **2**, something shaped like, or made of, or suggesting a horn, as a cusp of the moon. **3**, any of a variety of musical wind instruments, usually made of brass; any of various noise-producing instruments. —*adj.* made of horn. —**horn in,** intrude, as in a conversation. —**horn'y,** *adj.*

horn'bill" (hôrn'bil") *n.* a large bird.

hor'net (hôr'nit) *n.* a large insect of the wasp family.

horn'pipe" (hôrn'pīp") *n.* a lively solo dance popular among sailors.

horn'swog"gle (hôrn'swog'əl) *v.t.* (*Slang*) swindle; hoax.

ho·rol'o·gy (hō-rol'ə-jē) *n.* the art of making timepieces. —**hor"o·log'ic** (-loj'ik) *adj.* —**ho·rol'o·gist,** *n.*

hor'o·scope″ (hor'ə-skōp″) n. a plan of the positions of the planets, used by astrologers.

hor·ren'dous (hə-ren'dəs) adj. horrible; frightful.

hor'ri·ble (hor'ə-bəl) adj. exciting horror; dreadful; deplorable. —**hor'ri·ble·ness**, n.

hor'rid (hor'id) adj. unpleasant; disagreeable. —**hor'rid·ness**, n.

hor'ri·fy″ (hor'i-fī″) v.t. arouse horror.

hor'ror (hor'ər) n. 1, a painful emotion of fear or abhorrence; an intense aversion. 2, that which excites such a feeling.

hors d'oeuvres (ôr-dĕrvr') n. pl. (Fr.) assorted appetizers.

horse (hôrs) n. 1, a large, solid-hoofed domesticated quadruped, a draft or riding animal. 2, a male horse; a stallion. 3, a troop of horses; cavalry. 4, a supporting frame on legs. —v.t. provide with a horse; put on horseback. —v.i. (Slang) be playful or boisterous.

horse'back″ n. the part of a horse's back on which a rider sits.

horse'car″ n. a car drawn by a horse.

horse chestnut a flowering tree as the Ohio buckeye.

horse'hair″ n. & adj. the mane and tail hair of a horse; a fabric woven from it.

horse'laugh″ n. a derisive laugh.

horseless carriage automobile.

horse'man (-mən) n. [pl. -men] the rider or trainer of a horse.

horse'play″ n. boisterous behavior.

horse'pow″er n. a unit for measuring rate of work.

horse'rad″ish n. a cultivated plant; its root, ground and used as a condiment.

horse sense (Colloq.) good sense.

horse'shoe″ n. 1, the U-shaped iron plate nailed to a horse's hoof; anything so shaped. 2, (pl.) a game of quoits played with horseshoes.

Horseshoe

horse'whip″ n. a whip for urging a horse. —v.t. [-whipped″, -whip″ping] beat with a whip.

hors'y (hôr'sē) adj. 1, like a horse; gross. 2, interested in horses or horse racing. —**hors'i·ness**, n.

hor'ta·to·ry (hôr'tə-tôr-ē) adj. exhorting.

hor'ti·cul'ture (hôr'ti-kul″chər) n. the science and art of growing plants. —**hor'ti·cul'tur·al**, adj.

ho·san'na (hō-zan'ə) interj. & n. an exclamation in praise of God.

hose (hōz) n. 1, a flexible tube for conveying water. 2, [pl.] stockings or socks. —v.t. apply water through a hose.

ho'sier·y (hō'zhə-rē) n. stockings.

hos'pi·ta·ble (hos'pi-tə-bəl) adj. happy to welcome and entertain guests. —**hos'pi·ta·ble·ness**, etc.

hos'pi·tal (hos'pi-təl) n. an institution for the care and treatment of the sick and injured; any similar establishment, as for repairs.

hos'pi·tal'i·ty (hos'pə-tal'ə-tē) n. the reception of guests in a liberal and kindly way.

hos'pi·tal·i·za'tion (hos'pi-təl-i-zā'shən) n. insurance covering expenses incurred in a hospital.

host (hōst) n. 1, one who entertains another, esp. in his own house. 2, the proprietor of an inn or restaurant. 3, a great number of persons or things. 4, (cap.) the bread consecrated in the Eucharist.

hos'tage (hos'tij) n. a person or thing held as a pledge or security for the performance of an action.

hos'tel (hos'təl) n. a lodging house or inn. Also, **hos'tel·ry** (-rē).

host'ess (hōs'tis) n. 1, a female host. 2, a woman who greets patrons in a restaurant, etc.

hos'tile (hos'təl) adj. 1, opposed in feeling or action; antagonistic. 2, relating to an enemy.

hos·til'i·ty (hos-til'ə-tē) n. 1, antagonism. 2, (pl.) warfare.

hos'tler (hos'lər) n. a servant who tends horses at an inn.

hot adj. [hot'ter, -test] 1, having or giving the sensation of heat; of high temperature. 2, pungent to the taste; biting. 3, ardent in feeling; vehement; passionate. 4, fresh; keen; brisk. 5, (Slang) exciting; (of music) heightened by rhapsodic improvisation. 6, (Slang) wanted by the police. —**hot'ness**, n.

hot air (Slang) empty talk.

hot'bed″ n. 1, a glass-covered bed of soil. 2, a place where growth is rapid.

hot'blood″ed adj. excitable; impetuous. —**hot'blood'ed·ness**, n.

hot dog (Slang) a frankfurter on a roll.

ho·tel' (hō-tel') n. a public house that furnishes lodging, food, etc. to travelers or other guests.

hot'head"ed adj. of fiery temper; rash. —**hot'head"ed·ness**, n.

hot'house" n. a glass-covered area for raising plants.

hot rod (Slang) an automobile altered for greater speed.

hound (hownd) n. 1, any of various hunting dogs. 2, any dog. 3, (Slang) a mean, contemptible fellow. 4, (Slang) an addict. —v.t. harass.

hour (owr) n. 1, measure of time equal to 60 minutes or one twenty-fourth of a solar day. 2, a time of day. 3, an indefinite period of time; a particular or appointed time.

hour'glass" n. a device for measuring time by the flow of sand.

hou'ri (hū'rē) n. a beautiful maiden in the Mohammedan paradise.

hour'ly (-lē) adj. & adv. occurring each hour; continual or often.

Hourglass

house (hows) n. [pl. hous'es (how'ziz)] 1, a building for human use or occupation, esp. a dwelling. 2, any place of abode. 3, something that contains or houses; a cell or compartment. 4, a household. 5, a family including ancestors and descendants. 6, a body of persons; a legislature; a commercial establishment; an audience in a theater. 7, the management of a gaming house. —v.t. (howz) shelter.

house'hold" n. all the permanent residents of a dwelling house.

house'keep"ing n. the maintenance and management of a house, including the serving of meals. —**house'keep"er**, n.

house'maid" n. a female domestic servant. —**housemaid's knee**, inflammation of the bursa of the kneecap.

house'warm"ing n. a party to celebrate occupancy of a new house.

house'wife" n. a woman in charge of a household.

house'work" n. cooking, cleaning, etc.

hous'ing (how'zing) n. 1, houses collectively. 2, the act of putting in a house; the business of providing houses. 3, a cover, hood, or shield.

hove (hōv) v. pret. & p.p. of heave.

hov'el (huv'əl) n. a small, wretched house.

hov'er (huv'ər) v.i. 1, remain over one place while fluttering in the air.

2, linger about. 3, continue in an undecided state.

how adv. 1, in what way or manner; by what means. 2, to what extent; in what amount. 3, in what state or condition. 4, for what reason.

how·ev'er (how-ev'ər) conj. nevertheless; despite which. —adv. in whatever manner; to whatever extent or degree.

how'itz·er (how'it-sər) n. a rifled cannon for high-angle shots.

howl v.i. & t. 1, utter a loud, prolonged, and mournful cry, as a wolf. 2, cry out in pain, rage, etc. 3, make a wailing sound, as the wind. 4, laugh loudly. —n. such a cry.

howl'er (how'lər) n. 1, one who or that which howls. 2, a So. Amer. monkey. 3, (Colloq.) an amusing blunder.

how"so·ev'er adv. 1, in whatever manner. 2, to whatever degree.

hoy'den (hoi'dən) n. a rowdy girl; a tomboy.

hub n. 1, a block in the center of a wheel to which the spokes are joined. 2, a center of intellectual, commercial, or other activity.

hub'bub (hub'ub) n. a noise as of many voices or sounds; uproar.

huck'le·ber"ry (huk'əl-ber"ē) n. a low shrub or its dark-blue edible berry.

huck'ster (huk'stər) n. a street peddler, esp. of fruit and vegetables. —v.t. peddle.

hud'dle (hud'əl) v.t. draw closely together. —v.i. 1, crowd together. 2, (Colloq.) confer privately. —n. 1, a confused mass; a crowd. 2, (Colloq.) a secret conference.

hue (hū) n. 1, a color; color in general. 2, intensity of color; a tint. 3, clamor, esp. in hue and cry.

huff (huf) n. a sudden swell of anger or resentment. —v.i. 1, take offense. 2, puff or blow; pant.

hug v.t. & i. [hugged, hug'ging] 1, clasp tightly in the arms; embrace. 2, cling to mentally. 3, keep close to. —n. a close embrace.

huge (hūj) adj. very large. —**huge'ness**, n.

hu·la-hu'la (hoo'lə-hoo'lə) n. a Hawaiian dance.

hulk n. 1, the hull of a ship, esp. one that is dismantled or wrecked. 2, a bulky or unwieldy person or mass. —v.i. loom. —**hulk'ing**, adj.

hull (hul) n. 1, the body of a ship, exclusive of masts and other superstructure. 2, the fuselage of a seaplane. 3, the shell, husk, etc. of a nut, fruit, or grain. —v.t. remove the hull of.

tub, cūte, pŭll; label; oil, owl; go, chip, she, thin, then, sing, ink; see p. 6

hul'la·ba·loo" (hul'ə-bə-loo") n. noisy confusion.

hum v.t. & i. [hummed, hum'ming] 1, make a droning sound. 2, sing with closed lips. 3, make indistinct sounds; murmur. —n. a buzzing or droning sound. —interj. of hesitation, doubt, etc. —hum'ming, adj. 1, buzzing, etc. 2, intensely active.

hu'man (hū'mən) adj. pert. to man or mankind; being a man; having the nature of man.

hu·mane' (hū-mān') adj. 1, inclined to treat others, and animals, with kindness; benevolent; compassionate. 2, (of a branch of knowledge) tending to refine. —hu·mane'ness, n.

hu'man·ism (hū'mə-niz-əm) n. 1, a system of thought predominantly centered on human interests. 2, study of the humanities; literary culture. —hu'man·ist, n.

hu·man"i·tar'i·an (hū-man"ə-târ'ē-ən) adj. & n. concerned with the interests of all mankind; philanthropic.

hu·man'i·ty (hū-man'ə-tē) n. 1, the human race; mankind. 2, the quality of being human; human nature. 3, humaneness. 4, (usually pl.) any of the branches of learning embraced by philosophy, literature, languages, art, etc., excluding theology, natural and social sciences.

hu'man·ize" (hū'mə-nīz") v.t. make human or humane. —hu"man·i·za'tion (-i-zā'shən) n.

hu'man·kind" n. the human race; mankind.

hum'ble (hum'bəl) adj. 1, low in station; unimportant; lowly. 2, meek or modest in manner. —v.t. abase; humiliate. —hum'ble·ness, n.

hum'bug n. 1, a fraudulent trick; a hoax; sham. 2, an impostor. —v.t. [-bugged, -bug·ging] delude.

hum·ding'er (hum-ding'ər) n. (Slang) a remarkable person or thing.

hum'drum" adj. monotonous.

hu'mer·us (hū'mər-əs) n. [pl. -i (-ī)] the bone of the upper arm.

hu'mid (hū'mid) adj. moist; damp.

hu·mid'i·fy" (hū-mid'ə-fī") v.t. make damper. —hu·mid"i·fi·ca'tion, n.

hu·mid'i·ty (hū-mid'ə-tē) n. dampness; moisture in the air.

hu'mi·dor" (hū'mə-dôr") n. a container fitted to keep its contents moist, as for tobacco.

hu·mil'i·ate" (hū-mil'ē-āt") v.t. subject to shame or disgrace; abase in estimation; mortify. —hu·mil'i·a'tion, n.

hu·mil'i·ty (hū-mil'ə-tē) n. modesty in self-estimation; humbleness.

hum'ming·bird" (hum'ing-bėrd") n. a tiny bird whose wings hum from rapid vibration.

hum'mock (hum'ək) n. a knoll.

hu'mor (hū'mər) n. 1, the quality of inciting laughter, or of perceiving what is comical; drollery; facetiousness. 2, mental state; mood. 3, caprice; whim. 4, droll literature. —v.t. indulge; cater to the whims of. Also, **hu'mour.** —hu'mor·ist, n. a writer of humor. —hu'mor·ous, adj. funny; droll.

hump n. a protuberance or swelling, esp. a natural or morbid curvature of the back. —v.t. & i. 1, form or rise in a hump. 2, (Slang) exert oneself.

hump'back" n. 1, a hump on the back. 2, one who has a humpback.

humph (humf) interj. of contempt, doubt, dissatisfaction, etc.

hu'mus (hū'məs) n. decayed vegetable matter, important to the fertility of soil.

hunch n. 1, hump. 2, (Colloq.) a premonition or suspicion. —v.t. thrust out or up in a hump. —v.i. sidle or lunge forward. —hunch'back", n. humpback.

hun'dred (hun'drid) n. & adj. the cardinal number represented by 100, equal to ten times ten. —hun'dredth, n. & adj. the ordinal of this number, also written 100th.

hun'dred·fold" adv. & adj. a hundred times.

hun'dred·weight" n. 100 pounds in U.S., 110 pounds in England.

hung v. pret. & p.p. of hang.

hun'ger (hung'gər) n. 1, craving for food. 2, any strong desire. —v.i. feel hunger. —hun'gry (-grē) adj.

hunk n. (Colloq.) a large piece, lump, or chunk. —hunk'y [also, hunk'y-do'ry (-dôr'ē)] adj. (Slang) satisfactory; all right.

hunt v.t. & i. 1, chase (animals) for the purpose of catching or killing. 2, pursue; harry. 3, look for; search. —n. 1, the act or sport of chasing wild animals. 2, a pack of hunting dogs; a group of hunters. 3, any pursuit, search, or quest. —hunt'er, hunts'man, n.

hur'dle (hėr'dəl) n. 1, a barrier (as on a racetrack); a frame of crossed sticks, bars, etc. to be leaped over. 2, an obstacle or difficulty. —v.t. 1, leap over. 2, circumvent or overcome by any means. —hur'dler, n.

hur'dy-gur'dy (hėr'dē-gėr'dē) n. a musical instrument played by turning a crank; a barrel organ.

hurl (hėrl) v.t. & i. 1, throw; fling. 2, utter vehemently.

hurl'ing *n.* an Irish variant of hockey.

Hurling

hur"ly-bur'ly (hẽr"lḗ-bẽr'lḗ) *n.* & *adj.* tumult; confusion.

hur·rah' (hə-rä') *interj.* of applause, approval, or elation.

hur'ri·cane" (hẽr'ə-kān") *n.* a windstorm of intense severity; a tropical cyclone.

hur'ry (hẽr'ė) *v.i.* move or act with haste. —*v.t.* urge onward; impel to greater rapidity; hasten. —*n.* haste.

hurt (hẽrt) *v.t.* & *t.* **1,** cause bodily pain to. **2,** do harm or mischief to; injure; damage. **3,** grieve; distress. —*n.* **1,** an impairment; a wound. bruise, injury, etc. **2,** a cause of distress; an insult. —**hurt'ful,** *adj.* injurious.

hur'tle (hẽr'təl) *v.i.* rush violently and noisily.

hus'band (huz'bənd) *n.* a married man, in relation to his wife. —*v.t.* manage prudently; economize. —**hus'band·man,** *n.* a farmer.

hus'band·ry (-rė) *n.* **1,** farming; agriculture. **2,** thrifty management; frugality.

hush *interj.* to command silence. —*v.i.* become quiet or silent. —*v.t.* **1,** silence. **2,** calm; soothe; allay. —*n.* silence or quiet, esp. after noise. —**hush money,** a bribe to buy silence.

husk *n.* **1,** the outer covering of certain fruits and seeds, esp. corn. **2,** any similar dry covering. —*v.t.* remove the husk from.

hus'ky (hus'kė) *adj.* **1,** strong; burly. **2,** dry in the throat; hoarse. —*n.* a large Eskimo dog. —**hus'ki·ness,** *n.*

hus·sar' (hů-zär') *n.* a light-cavalryman.

hus'sy (huz'ė) *n.* a willful girl; a mean or worthless woman.

hus'tle (hus'əl) *v.i.* & *t.* **1,** move or act energetically; make haste. **2,** move by pushing or crowding.

hus'tler (hus'lər) *n.* **1,** an energetic worker. **2,** (*Slang*) a minor swindler.

hut *n.* a small, rude dwelling; a cabin.

hutch (huch) *n.* **1,** a box or coop for confining a small animal. **2,** a hut; a fisherman's shanty.

huz·za' (hə-zä') *interj.* hurrah.

hy'a·cinth (hī'ə-sinth) *n.* **1,** a bulbous plant having spikes of bell-shaped flowers. **2,** a semiprecious stone.

hy'brid (hī'brid) *n.* **1,** the offspring of animals or plants of different varieties, species, or genera; a crossbreed or mongrel. **2,** any product or mixture of two heterogeneous things. —*adj.* crossbred; diverse.

hy·dran'gea (hī-drān'jə) *n.* a shrub having showy clusters of flowers.

hy'drant (hī'drənt) *n.* a pipe for drawing water from a main pipe.

hy'drate (hī'drāt) *n.* any compound containing water in chemical combination. —**hy·dra'tion,** *n.*

hy·drau'lic (hī-drä'lik) *adj.* operated by water or other liquid. —**hy·drau'li·cal·ly,** *adv.*

hy·drau'lics (-liks) *n.* the science and engineering application of the motion of liquids.

hy·dro- *pref.* **1,** water. **2,** hydrogen.

hy'dro·e·lec'tric (hī'drō-ə-lek'trik) *adj.* pert. to the generation of electricity by water power.

hy'dro·gen (hī'drə-jən) *n.* a gas, the lightest of the chemical elements, no. 1, symbol H.

hydrogen bomb an atomic bomb based on fusion of an isotope of hydrogen.

hy·drom'e·ter (hī-drom'i-tər) *n.* an instrument for measuring the specific gravity of liquids.

hy"dro·pho'bi·a (hī"drə-fō'bē-ə) *n.* **1,** rabies. **2,** morbid fear of water.

hy'dro·plane" (hī'drə-plān") *n.* **1,** a type of seaplane. **2,** a high-powered speedboat. **3,** a horizontal rudder on a submersible boat.

hy'drous (hī'drəs) *adj.* containing water.

hy·e'na (hī-ē'nə) *n.* a carnivorous mammal of Afr. and Asia, whose cry resembles a laugh.

hy'giene (hī'jēn) *n.* the science that deals with the preservation of health.

hy"gi·en'ic (hī"jė-en'ik) *adj.* **1,** sanitary. **2,** pert. to hygiene. —**hy"gi·en'i·cal·ly,** *adv.*

hy·grom'e·ter (hī-grom'ə-tər) *n.* an instrument for measuring the humidity of the atmosphere.

hy"me·ne'al (hī"mə-nē'əl) *adj.* pert. to marriage.

hymn (him) *n.* **1,** a song in worship of God. **2,** any song or ode of praise.

hym′nal (him′nəl) *n.* a book of hymns. —*adj.* pert. to hymns.

hy·per- *pref.* over; in excess; exaggerated.

hy·per′bo·la (hī-pĕr′bə-lə) *n.* a curve, one of the conic sections.

Hyperbola

hy·per′bo·le (hī-pĕr′bə-lē) *n.* obvious exaggeration; an extravagant statement.

hy″per·bol′ic (hī″pər-bol′ik) *adj.* 1, pert. to or being a hyperbola. 2, of or being hyperbole.

hy·per′tro·phy (hī-pĕr′trə-fē) *n.* excessive development of an organ of the body.

hy′phen (hī′fən) *n.* the symbol (-) used to join the parts of compound words, indicate syllabication, etc. —**hy′phen·ate″** (-āt″) *v.t.*

hyp·no′sis (hip-nō′sis) *n.* a condition similar to sleep, but usually induced artificially; a trance.

hyp·not′ic (hip-not′ik) *adj.* 1, pert. to hypnosis; susceptible to hypnotism. 2, inducing sleep. —**hyp·not′i·cal·ly,** *adv.*

hyp′no·tize″ (hip′nə-tīz″) *v.t.* put to sleep by persuasion or mental ascendancy. —**hyp′no·tism,** *n.* —**hyp′no·tist,** *n.*

hy′po (hī′pō) *n.* 1, a photographic fixing agent. 2, hypodermic.

hy·po- *pref.* under.

hy″po·chon′dri·ac″ (hī″pə-kon′dri-ak″) *n. & adj.* one who is morbidly anxious about his health or suffers imagined ills. —**hy″po·chon′dri·a** (-ə) *n.*

hy·poc′ri·sy (hi-pok′rə-sē) *n.* false pretension to personal qualities or principles not actually possessed.

hyp′o·crite (hip′ə-krit) *n.* one who pretends to beliefs, sentiments, etc. he does not actually feel. —**hyp″o·crit′i·cal,** *adj.*

hy″po·der′mic (hī″pə-der′mik) *adj.* under the skin. —*n.* 1, a remedy applied under the skin. 2, a syringe for hypodermic injection. —**hy″po·der′mi·cal·ly,** *adv.*

hy·pot′e·nuse″ (hī-pot′ə-nūs″) *n.* the longest side of a right triangle.

hy·poth′e·cate″ (hī-poth′ə-kāt″) *v.t.* pledge to a creditor as security. —**hy·poth″e·ca′tion,** *n.*

hy·poth′e·sis (hī-poth′ə-sis) *n.* [*pl.* **-ses** (-sēz)] a tentative assertion about natural phenomena, assumed but not positively known; a postulate. —**hy·poth′e·size″** (-sīz″) *v.t. & i.*

hy″po·thet′i·cal (hī″pə-thet′i-kəl) *adj.* 1, taken as a hypothesis. 2, conjectural; supposed.

hys′sop (his′əp) *n.* an aromatic flowering herb.

hys·ter·ec′to·my (his-tə-rek′tə-mē) *n.* surgical removal of the uterus.

hys·te′ri·a (his-tir′ē-ə) *n.* a disorder marked by violent emotional outbreaks.

hys·ter′ic (his-ter′ik) *n.* 1, one subject to hysteria. 2, (*pl.*) a fit of hysteria. —**hys·ter′i·cal,** *adj.*

I

I, i (ī) 1, the ninth letter of the English alphabet. 2, the personal pronoun, first person.

i·am′bic (ī-am′bik) *n.* an iamb or iambus, a foot in poetry constituting an unstressed then a stressed syllable. —*adj.* (of verse) in iambics.

I·ber′i·an (ī-bir′ē-ən) *adj.* pert. to the region of Spain and Portugal.

i′bex (ī′beks) *n.* a Europ. wild goat with long, curved horns.

i′bis (ī′bis) *n.* a wading bird related to the heron and stork.

-i·ble *suf.* same as **-able.**

-ic (ik) *suf.* forming adjectives: 1, like. 2, pert. to. 3, composed of. Also, **-i·cal** (ī-kəl).

ice (īs) *n.* 1, the solid form of water, produced by freezing. 2, any frozen liquid. 3, a confection of frozen fruit juice. 4, ice cream. 5, icing. 6, reserve; formality. 7, (*Slang*) diamonds. 8, (*Slang*) graft; bribes paid for freedom from arrest. —*v.t.* 1, cool with ice. 2, change into ice; freeze. 3, cover with icing. —*v.i.* freeze. —*adj.* iced; icy. —**ice box,** a refrigerator. —**ice cream,** a frozen confection. —**ice water,** very cold water.

ice′berg″ (īs′bērg″) *n.* 1, a mass of ice floating at sea. 2, (*Colloq.*) a cold, unemotional person.

ice′man″ *n.* [*pl.* **-men**] one who sells ice.

ich′thy·o- (ik′thē-ō) *pref.* fish.

ich″thy·ol′o·gy (ik″thē-ol′ə-jē) *n.* the study of fishes. —**ich″thy·o·log′i·cal,** *adj.* —**ich″thy·ol′o·gist,** *n.*

i′ci·cle (ī′si-kəl) *n.* a spike of ice formed when dripping water freezes.

ic′ing (ī′sing) *n.* a preparation of sugar used for covering cakes, etc. frosting.

i′con (ī′kon) *n.* a sacred image.

i·con′o·clast″ (ī-kon′ə-klast″) *n.* one who challenges cherished beliefs.

—i·con′o·clas′tic, *adj.* **—i·con′o·clas′ti·cal·ly,** *adv.*

i′cy (ī′sē) *adj.* **1,** made of or abounding with ice. **2,** like ice; cold. **—i′ci·ly,** *adv.* **—i′ci·ness,** *n.*

id *n.* (*Psychoanal.*) a person's urge to pleasure and the exercise of the libido.

i·de′a (ī-dē′ə) *n.* **1,** something existing in the mind; conception; thought. **2,** an attitude of mind; opinion; belief; impression. **3,** a notion, vagary, or fantasy. **4,** a plan of action; purpose; intention.

i·de′al (ī-dē′əl) *n.* something imagined in a state of perfection; a goal; a model. **—adj. 1,** perfect, highly desirable, worthy of emulation, etc. **2,** existing only in idea. **3,** not real; impractical; visionary.

i·de′al·ism (ī-dē′ə-liz-əm) *n.* **1,** a tendency to wish or believe things to be ideal, or better than they are. **2,** a constant effort to achieve perfection. **—i·de′al·ist,** *n.* **—i·de′al·is′tic,** *adj.* **—i·de′al·is′ti·cal·ly,** *adv.*

i·de′al·ize″ (ī-dē′ə-līz″) *v.t.* regard as ideal, usually in disregard of fact. **—i·de′al·i·za′tion,** *n.*

i·den′ti·cal (ī-den′ti-kəl) *adj.* **1,** being the same. **2,** exactly or much alike.

i·den″ti·fi·ca′tion (ī-den′tə-fi-kā′-shən) *n.* **1,** act of identifying. **2,** a mark or means of identifying.

i·den′ti·fy″ (ī-den′ti-fī″) *v.t.* **1,** recognize or establish as being a particular kind, individual, etc. **2,** show to be identical.

i·den′ti·ty (ī-den′tə-tē) *n.* **1,** what a thing or person is; a name, classification, etc. **2,** recognizable individuality. **3,** sameness. **4,** exact or close likeness.

i″de·ol′o·gy (ī″dē-ol′ə-jē) *n.* **1,** the aggregate of ideas, beliefs, doctrines, etc. of a large group of persons; popularly, a system of government. **2,** the science of ideas. **—i″de·o·log′i·cal,** *adj.*

ides (īdz) *n.pl.* in ancient Rome, the 15th day of March, May, July, October; the 13th of other months.

id′i·o·cy (id′ē-ə-sē) *n.* the condition of an idiot.

id′i·om (id′ē-əm) *n.* **1,** a form of expression peculiar to a language. **2,** a dialect. **3,** the peculiar character of a language. **4,** a distinct style, as in music, art, etc.

id″i·o·mat′ic (id″ē-ə-mat′ik) *adj.* **1,** conforming to idiom. **2,** colloquial. **—id″i·o·mat′i·cal·ly,** *adv.*

id″i·o·syn′cra·sy (id″ē-ə-sin′krə-sē) *n.* a peculiarity, as of behavior.

id′i·ot (id′ē-ət) *n.* a person born mentally deficient, incapable of developing beyond a four-year

mental level. **—id·i·ot′ic** (-ot′ik) *adj.* **—id·i·ot′i·cal·ly,** *adv.*

i′dle (ī′dəl) *adj.* **1,** doing nothing; inactive; unemployed. **2,** not in use or operation. **3,** lazy; slothful. **4,** useless; ineffective; futile. **5,** trivial; pointless; groundless. **—v.i. 1,** pass the time in idleness. **2,** move slowly; saunter; loiter. **3,** (of a machine) run while not connected to do work. **—i′dle·ness,** *n.* **—i′dler,** *n.* **1,** a gear or device that idles. **2,** a loafer.

i′dol (ī′dəl) *n.* **1,** an image of a deity, used as an object of worship. **2,** a person or thing adored or revered. **3,** a phantom; a false idea. **—i′dol·ize″,** *v.t.*

i″dol′a·ter (ī′dol′ə-tər) *n.* an idol worshiper.

i·dol′a·try (ī-dol′ə-trē) *n.* the worship of idols. **—i·dol′a·trous,** *adj.*

i′dyl (ī′dəl) *n.* **1,** a descriptive or narrative poem, esp. pastoral. **2,** a simple, appealing episode or scene. **—i·dyl′lic** (ī-dil′ik) *adj.* simple.

-ier (ir) *suf.* same as **-er** or **-eer.**

if *conj.* **1,** in case that; supposing that; on condition that. **2,** whether. **3,** even though. **—n.** a condition; a supposition. **—if′fy,** *adj.* (*Colloq.*) uncertain; contingent.

ig′loo *n.* a domed Eskimo hut, made of blocks of snow and ice.

ig′ne·ous (ig′nē-əs) *adj.* **1,** produced by intense heat, as rock of volcanic origin. **2,** pert. to fire.

Igloo

ig·nite′ (ig-nīt′) *v.t.* & *i.* set on fire; begin to burn; kindle.

ig·ni′tion (ig-nish′ən) *n.* **1,** act of igniting; state of being ignited. **2,** a means, device, or process for igniting, esp. the electrical system of an internal combustion engine.

ig·no′ble (ig-nō′bəl) *adj.* **1,** low in character; base; dishonorable. **2,** low in birth or station. **—ig·no′ble·ness,** *n.*

ig″no·min′i·ous (ig″nə-min′ē-əs) *adj.* causing or deserving humiliation, disgrace, or public contempt.

ig′no·min·y (ig′nə-min-ē) *n.* public disgrace.

ig″no·ra′mus (ig″nə-rā′məs) *n.* an ignorant person.

ig′no·rant (ig′nə-rənt) *adj.* **1,** having little or no knowledge; unlearned. **2,** unaware; uninformed. **—ig′no·rance,** *n.*

ig·nore′ (ig-nôr′) *v.t.* pass by without notice; pay no heed to.

i·gua′na (i-gwä′nə) *n.* a large lizard of tropical America.

il- *pref.* same as **in-,** but used before an *l.*

il'i·ac" (il'ē-ak") adj. pert. to the ilium, the large anterior bone of the pelvis.

ilk n. sort, kind, family, class, etc.

ill (il) adj. 1, impaired in health; unwell; sick. 2, wicked; bad. 3, causing evil; deleterious; malevolent. 4, unfriendly; cross; crabbed. 5, unfavorable; adverse. 6, unskillful; bungling. —adv. 1, wickedly. 2, unfortunately; unfavorably; in a hostile manner. 3, with difficulty or hardship; faultily. —n. 1, a bodily ailment; disease. 2, injury; harm; misfortune; trouble. —ill will, hostility. —ill'ness, n.

ill-'bred" adj. uncouth; impolite.

il·le'gal (i-lē'gal) adj. contrary to law. —il"le·gal'i·ty (il"li-gal'ə-tē) n.

il·leg'i·ble (i-lej'ə-bəl) adj. impossible or hard to read. —il·leg"i·bil'i·ty, n.

il"le·git'i·mate (il"i-jit'ə-mət) adj. 1, unlawful; invalid. 2, born out of wedlock. —il"le·git'i·ma·cy, n.

ill-'fa"vored adj. ugly; unpleasant.

ill-"got'ten adj. obtained by illegal or dishonest means.

il·lic'it (i-lis'it) adj. 1, unlawful; unlicensed. 2, clandestine. —il·lic'it·ness, n.

il·lim'it·a·ble (i-lim'i-tə-bəl) adj. infinite; too great to measure.

il·lit'er·ate (i-lit'ər-ət) adj. unable to read and write. —n. an illiterate person. —il·lit'er·a·cy, n.

il·log'i·cal (i-loj'i-kəl) adj. contravening or disregarding the rules of logic. —il·log"i·cal'i·ty (-kal'ə-tē) n.

ill-'starred" adj. unfortunate.

il·lu'mi·nate (i-loo'mə-nāt") v.t. 1, furnish with a light; light up; enlighten. 2, make clear; explain; elucidate. 3, decorate in color by hand. —il·lu"mi·na'tion, n. —il·lu'mi·na"tor, n.

il·lu'sion (i-loo'zhən) n. something that deceives the eye or mind; a mistaken perception or belief. —il·lu'sive (-siv), il·lu'so·ry (-sə-rē) adj.

il'lus·trate" (il'ə-strāt") v.t. 1, furnish with pictures, diagrams, etc. to adorn or elucidate. 2, make clear or intelligible, as with examples. —il·lus'tra·tive (i-lus'trə-tiv), adj.

il"lus·tra'tion (il"ə-strā'shən) n. 1, something that illustrates, as a picture. 2, act of illustrating.

il'lus·tra"tor (il'ə-strā"tər) n. an artist who makes illustrations for books or periodicals.

il·lus'tri·ous (i-lus'trē-əs) adj. very distinguished; conspicuous; eminent. —il·lus'tri·ous·ness, n.

im- pref. same as in-, but used before b, m, or p. [In addition to words defined in the text, the following words formed by prefixing im- (not) have merely the negative sense of the positive term. For pronunciation of such words, listed below or defined in the text, refer to the vocabulary for the pronunciation of the positive term.]

im·bal'ance	im·per'ma·nent
im·meas'ur·a·ble	im·per'me·a·ble
	im·per'son·al
im·mov'a·ble	im"per·turb'a·ble
im·mu'ta·ble	
im·pal'pa·ble	im·plau'si·ble
im·par'i·ty	im·pol'i·tic
im·pen'e·tra·ble	im·prac'ti·cal
im·pen'i·tent	im·prob'a·ble
im"per·cep'ti·ble	im·pro'bi·ty
im·per'ish·a·ble	im·prov'i·dent

im'age (im'ij) n. 1, a representation of the form and features of a person or thing, in a picture, statue, etc. 2, a reflection in a mirror. 3, a mental picture; a written description; a figure of speech. 4, any counterpart or copy; a likeness or similitude. 5, symbol. —v.t. 1, picture in the mind; imagine. 2, make an image of.

im'age·ry (-rē) n. 1, imaginative thought or expression. 2, images collectively.

i·mag'i·nar·y (i-maj'ə-ner-ē) adj. existing only in the imagination or fancy; not real.

i·mag"i·na'tion (i-maj"ə-nā'shən) n. 1, the act or faculty of forming mental images of objects. 2, the faculty of forming ideas and ideals. 3, fancy, ideal, concept, etc.

im·ag'i·na·tive (i-maj'ə-nā-tiv) adj. having lively imagination.

im·ag'ine (i-maj'in) v.t. 1, form a mental image of. 2, think; believe; suppose; conjecture; guess, etc. —v.i. 1, exercise the imagination. 2, think; fancy. —im·ag'i·na·ble, adj.

i·mam' (i-mäm') n. a Moslem priest.

im'be·cile (im'bə-sil) n. a person of defective mentality, but above the level of an idiot. —im"be·cil'ic, adj. —im"be·cil'i·ty, n.

im·bed' v.t. [-bed'ded, -ding] bury; set (in something).

im·bibe' (im-bīb') v.t. 1, drink. 2, absorb; take in.

im·bro'glio (im-brōl'yō) n. an intricate, confused, or perplexing state of affairs.

im·bue' (im-bū') v.t. saturate; dye; impregnate, as with sentiments, opinions, etc. —im·bue'ment, n.

im'i·tate (im'ə-tāt') *v.t.* **1,** copy in manner or action; follow as a model; mimic; simulate. **2,** make a copy of. —**im'i·ta·ble,** *adj.* —**im'i·ta"tive,** *adj.* —**im'i·ta·tor,** *n.*

im"i·ta'tion (im'ə-tā'shən) *n.* the act or a product of imitating; a copy, likeness, or counterfeit. —*adj.* made to imitate a genuine, and usually superior, article.

im·mac'u·la·cy (i-mak'yə-lə-sē) *n.* condition of being immaculate.

im·mac'u·late (i-mak'yə-lit) *adj.* **1,** perfectly clean; spotless. **2,** free from moral blemish; pure. —**im·mac'u·late·ness,** *n.*

im'ma·nent (im'ə-nənt) *adj.* remaining within; intrinsic. —**im'ma·nence,** *n.*

im"ma·te'ri·al (im'ə-tir'ē-əl) *adj.* of little or no significance; irrelevant. —**im"ma·te'ri·al·ness,** *n.*

im"ma·ture' (im'ə-tyũr') *adj.* not ripe or fully developed; youthful. —**im"ma·tur'i·ty,** *n.*

im·me'di·a·cy (i-mē'dē-ə-sē) *n.* urgency, due to lack of intervening time.

im·me'di·ate (i-mē'dē-ət) *adj.* **1,** without any time intervening; instant. **2,** of the present moment. **3,** not separated; next; nearest. **4,** direct. —**im·me'di·ate·ness,** *n.*

im"me·mo'ri·al (im'ə-môr'ē-əl) *adj.* of a time beyond memory, record, or knowledge.

im·mense' (i-mens') *adj.* **1,** very large; huge; vast. **2,** boundless. **3,** (*Slang*) excellent. —**im·mense'ness,** *n.*

im·men'si·ty (i-men'sə-tē) immenseness.

im·merse' (i-mẽrs') *v.t.* **1,** plunge into, esp. deeply. **2,** involve or interest deeply. —**im·mer'sion** (-shən) *n.*

im'mi·grant (im'i-grənt) *n.* one who immigrates.

im'mi·grate" (im'ə-grāt") *v.t.* come to settle in a new habitat or country. —**im'mi·gra'tion,** *n.*

im'mi·nent (im'ə-nənt) *adj.* likely to occur soon; impending. —**im'mi·nence,** *n.*

im·mo'bile (i-mō'bil) *adj.* not movable or moving. —**im·mo·bil'i·ty,** *n.*

im·mo'bi·lize" (i-mō'bə-līz") *v.t.* render incapable of moving. —**im·mo"bi·li·za'tion,** *n.*

im·mod'er·ate (i-mod'ər-ət) *adj.* not confined to just or reasonable limits; intemperate. —**im·mod'er·a'tion,** *n.*

im·mod'est (i-mod'ist) *adj.* **1,** not proper; indecent; **2,** boastful. —**im·mod'es·ty,** *n.*

im'mo·late" (im'ə-lāt") *v.t.* kill as a sacrificial victim. —**im"mo·la'tion,** *n.*

im·mor'al (i-môr'əl) *adj.* not conforming to moral law. —**im"mo·ral'i·ty** (im'ə-ral'ə-tē) *n.* wickedness; vice.

im·mor'tal (i-môr'təl) *adj.* not subject to death, cessation, or oblivion. —*n.* one who is immortal. —**im"mor·tal'i·ty** (im'ər-tal'ə-tē) *n.*

im·mor'tal·ize" (-īz") *v.t.* make immortal or forever famous. —**im·mor"tal·i·za'tion,** *n.*

im"mor·telle' (im'ôr-tel') *n.* a plant or flower that retains form and color when it dies.

im·mune' (i-mūn') *adj.* not liable; exempt, as from a disease. —**im·mu'ni·ty** (i-mū'nə-tē) *n.*

im'mu·nize" (im'yə-nīz") *v.t.* protect, as from disease by inoculation. —**im"mu·ni·za'tion,** *n.*

im·mure' (i-myũr') *v.t.* surround with walls; confine. —**im·mure'ment,** *n.*

imp *n.* a small prankish sprite or child. —**imp'ish,** *adj.* mischievous.

Imp

im'pact (im'pakt) *n.* **1,** the striking of one body against another; collision. **2,** the force of a collision. —*v.t.* press closely; pack in. —**im·pact'ed,** *adj.* tightly packed; wedged in. —**im·pac'tion,** *n.*

im·pair' (im-pār') *v.t.* & *i.* make or become worse; damage; weaken. —**im·pair'ment,** *n.*

im·pale' (im-pāl') *v.t.* **1,** thrust a sharpened stake through; transfix. **2,** fence in. —**im·pale'ment,** *n.*

im·pan'el (im-pan'əl) *v.t.* enroll or summon (a jury). —**im·pan'el·ment,** *n.*

im·part' (im-pärt') *v.t.* **1,** make known; tell. **2,** give; bestow; share. —**im"par·ta'tion,** *n.*

im·par'tial (im-pär'shəl) *adj.* not biased; equitable; just. —**im·par"ti·al'i·ty** (-shē-al'ə-tē) *n.*

im·passe' (im-pas') *n.* a condition in which progress or escape is blocked; a deadlock.

im·pas'sion (im-pash'ən) *v.t.* move or affect with passion. —**im·pas'sioned,** *adj.* filled with emotion; ardent.

im·pas'sive (im-pas'iv) *adj.* **1,** free of emotion; unmoved; apathetic. **2,** serene; calm. —**im·pas'sive·ness,** **im"pas·siv'i·ty** (im'pə-siv'ə-tē) *n.*

im·pa'tient (im-pā'shənt) *adj.* not

tranquil; restive; eager. —**im·pa′-tience,** *n.*

im·peach′ (im-pēch′) *v.t.* **1,** accuse (a public official) of misconduct; discredit; disparage. —**im·peach′-ment,** *n.*

im·pec′ca·ble (im-pek′ə-bəl) *adj.* without fault or blemish; irre-proachable. —**im·pec″ca·bil′i·ty,** *n.*

im″pe·cu′ni·ous (im″pə-kū′nē-əs) *adj.* without money; poor. —**im″pe-cu′ni·ous·ness,** *n.*

im·pede′ (im-pēd′) *v.t.* check or retard the progress of; hinder; ob-struct.

im·ped′i·ment (im-ped′ə-mənt) *n.* a load; hindrance.

im·pel′ *v.t.* [-**pelled′, pel′ling**] **1,** incite or constrain to an action; urge. **2,** drive onward.

im·pend′ *v.i.* be on the point of occurring; be imminent.

im·per′a·tive (im-per′ə-tiv) *adj.* **1,** expressing command; peremptory. **2,** not to be evaded; obligatory. **3,** (*Gram.*) of verbs, the mood ex-pressing command. —**im·per′a·tive-ness,** *n.*

im·per′fect (im-pėr′fikt) *adj.* **1,** faulty; defective; incomplete. **2,** (*Gram.*) of verbs, expressing past but not completed action; past pro-gressive, as, *he was singing.* —**im″-per·fec′tion,** *n.*

im·per′fo·rate (im-pėr′fə-rit) *adj.* not pierced. —*n.* a postage stamp not perforated for separation.

im·pe′ri·al (im-pir′ē-əl) *adj.* **1,** pert. to an empire or emperor. **2,** august; commanding. **3,** grand; superior in size or quality. —*n.* **1,** a short narrow beard under the lower lip. **2,** a former Russian gold coin.

im·pe′ri·al·ism (-iz-əm) *n.* the policy of expanding national terri-tory. —**im·pe′ri·al·ist,** *n.* —**im·pe′-ri·al·is′tic,** *adj.* —**im·pe′ri·al·is′ti-cal·ly,** *adv.*

im·per′il (im-per′əl) *v.t.* put in peril; endanger. —**im·per′il·ment,** *n.*

im·pe′ri·ous (im-pir′ē-əs) *adj.* **1,** domineering. **2,** imperative; urgent. —**im·pe′ri·ous·ness,** *n.*

im·per′son·ate″ (im-pėr′sə-nāt″) *v.t.* pretend to be; assume the char-acter of; play the rôle of. —**im·per′-son·a′tion,** *n.* —**im·per′son·a·tor,** *n.*

im·per′ti·nent (im-pėr′tə-nənt) *adj.* **1,** unmannerly in conduct; forward; insolent. **2,** not pertinent; irrelevant. —**im·per′ti·nence,** *n.*

im·per′vi·ous (im-pėr′vē-əs) *adj.* **1,** not permeable. **2,** resistant to persuasion. —**im·per′vi·ous·ness,** *n.*

im″pe·ti′go (im″pə-tī′gō) *n.* a contagious skin disease, esp. of children.

im·pet′u·ous (im-pech′oo-əs) *adj.* sudden and vehement in action. —**im·pet″u·os′i·ty** (-os′ə-tē), **im·pet′-u·ous·ness,** *n.*

im′pe·tus (im′pə-təs) *n.* **1,** energy of motion; the power with which a moving body tends to maintain its velocity. **2,** impulse; incentive.

im·pi′e·ty (im-pī′ə-tē) *n.* lack of reverence; wickedness.

im·pinge′ (im-pinj′) *v.i.* (with *on, against,* etc.) **1,** collide. **2,** encroach. —**im·pinge′ment,** *n.*

im′pi·ous (im′pē-əs) *adj.* lacking reverence for God; profane. —**im′-pi·ous·ness,** *n.*

im·pla′ca·ble (im-plā′kə-bəl) *adj.* not to be placated or appeased; in-exorable. —**im·pla′ca·ble·ness, im-pla′ca·bil′i·ty,** *n.*

im·plant′ (im-plant′) *v.t.* **1,** plant in the mind; inculcate; instill. **2,** set in a place; imbed. —**im″plan·ta′-tion,** *n.*

im′ple·ment (im′plə-mənt) *n.* **1,** an instrument, tool, or utensil. **2,** a means of doing or enacting; an agent. —*v.t.* (-ment″) **1,** enact; exe-cute. **2,** provide with implements or means. —**im″ple·men·ta′tion,** *n.*

im′pli·cate″ (im′pli-kāt″) *v.t.* show to be involved or concerned with; entangle.

im″pli·ca′tion (im″pli-kā′shən) *n.* **1,** something implied; the act of im-plying. **2,** the condition of being implicated or involved.

im·plic′it (im-plis′it) *adj.* **1,** to be assumed, though not directly ex-pressed; implied. **2,** unquestioning, as of faith. —**im·plic′it·ness,** *n.*

im·plore′ (im-plôr′) *v.t.* **1,** be-seech; entreat. **2,** request urgently.

im·plo′sion (im-plō′zhən) *n.* a bursting inward. —**im·plo′sive,** *adj.*

im·ply′ (im-plī′) *v.t.* **1,** suggest or indicate without expressing directly. **2,** necessarily involve; entail.

im″po·lite′ (im″pə-līt′) *adj.* dis-courteous. —**im″po·lite′ness,** *n.*

im·pon′der·a·ble (im-pon′dər-ə-bəl) *adj.* not to be weighed or evalu-ated; too vague to meditate upon. —**im·pon″der·a·bil′i·ty,** *n.*

im·port′ (im-pôrt′) *v.t.* **1,** bring in, as wares from a foreign country. **2,** denote; signify. **3,** have a bearing on. —*v.i.* be of importance. —*n.* (im′pôrt) **1,** something imported from abroad; the act or business of importing. **2,** meaning; implication. **3,** importance; consequence. —**im″-por·ta′tion** (im″pər-tā′shən) *n.*

im·por′tance (im-pôr′təns) *n.* state of being important.

im·por′tant (im-pôr′tənt) *adj.* **1,** of great weight in meaning, significance, or consequence. **2**, urgent. **3**, eminent; prominent; influential. **4**, pompous.

im"por·tune' (im"pôr-tūn') *v.t.* & *i.* **1**, beset with entreaties. **2**, ask for persistently; beg. —**im·por'tu·nate**, *adj.* —**im"por·tu'ni·ty**, *n.*

im·pose' (im-pōz') *v.t.* **1**, lay as a burden; levy, inflict, or enforce. **2**, palm off. **3**, obtrude (oneself) upon others. **4**, lay on; put; lay out (printing type) in proper order. —**im·pos'ing**, *adj.* stately; impressive.

im"po·si'tion (im"pə-zish'ən) *n.* **1**, act or manner of imposing. **2**, a burden placed on another's good will.

im·pos'si·ble (im-pos'ə-bəl) *adj.* **1**, nonexistent or false; sure not to happen. **2**, that cannot be done; utterly impracticable. **3**, (*Colloq.*) very unattractive. —**im·pos"si·bil'i·ty**, *n.*

im'post (im'pōst) *n.* a tax or tribute, esp. a customs duty.

im·pos'tor (im-pos'tər) *n.* one who deceitfully assumes a false name or character.

im·pos'ture (im-pos'chər) *n.* false assumption of another's name, etc.

im'po·tent (im'pə-tənt) *adj.* lacking strength, power, or virility. —**im'po·tence, im'po·ten·cy**, *n.*

im·pound' (im-pownd') *v.t.* **1**, shut in a pen; restrain within bounds. **2**, seize and keep in custody. —**im·pound'age, im·pound'ment**, *n.*

im·pov'er·ish (im-pov'ər-ish) *v.t.* **1**, make indigent. **2**, cause to deteriorate. —**im·pov'er·ish·ment**, *n.*

im'pre·cate' (im'prə-kāt') *v.t.* invoke a curse or evil upon. —**im"pre·ca'tion**, *n.*

im·preg'na·ble (im-preg'nə-bəl) *adj.* **1**, not to be taken or overcome by force; invincible. **2**, capable of being impregnated. —**im·preg"na·bil'i·ty**, *n.*

im·preg'nate (im-preg'nāt) *v.t.* **1**, make pregnant; fertilize. **2**, permeate or saturate. —**im"preg·na'tion**, *n.*

im"pre·sa'ri·o' (im"prə-sär'ē-ō') *n.* a theatrical producer or manager, esp. of an opera company.

im·press' (im-pres') *v.t.* **1**, affect deeply as to mind or feelings. **2**, fix firmly in the mind. **3**, press; stamp; imprint. **4**, seize for public use; force into service. —*n.* (im'pres) **1**, a product of stamping or printing. **2**, distinctive appearance or character. —**im·press'i·ble**, *adj.*

im·pres'sion (im-presh'ən) *n.* **1**, effect produced, as by perception or sensation; an idea, image, etc., esp. if vague. **2**, the act of impressing; a mark, mold, copy, etc. made by pressing, stamping, or printing. **3**, an edition. —**im·pres'sion·a·ble**, *adj.* easily impressed; susceptible.

—**im·pres'sion·ism**, *n.* a style of nonobjective expression in art. —**im·pres'sion·ist**, *n.*

im·pres'sive (-siv) *adj.* tending to excite admiration. —**im·pres'sive·ness**, *n.*

im·press'ment (-mənt) *n.* a forcing into service.

im"pri·ma'tur (im"pri-mā'tər) *n.* an official license to publish.

im·print' *v.t.* produce or fix by, or as by, pressure; print; stamp. —*n.* (im'print) **1**, a distinctive mark; a maker's or seller's name, esp. a publisher's. **2**, effect produced; impression.

im·pris'on (im-priz'ən) *v.t.* put in prison; confine. —**im·pris'on·ment**, *n.*

im·promp'tu (im-promp'tū) *adj.* **1**, done without previous preparation. **2**, hastily prepared; improvised. —*adv.* extemporaneously.

im·prop'er (im-prop'ər) *adj.* not proper; not moral; incorrect; indecorous. —**im·prop'er·ness**, *n.*

im"pro·pri'e·ty (im"prə-prī'ə-tē) *n.* improper action; an error; a breach of propriety.

im·prove' (im-proov') *v.t.* **1**, make better. **2**, make (land) more valuable, esp. by erecting buildings. —*v.i.* become better; increase in value or utility.

im·prove'ment (-mənt) *n.* **1**, act or result of improving. **2**, construction, or a structure, that improves real property.

im'pro·vise" (im'prə-vīz") *v.t.* make or do hastily or without previous preparation; extemporize, esp. in music. —**im"pro·vi·sa'tion**, *n.*

im·pru'dent (im-proo'dənt) *adj.* indiscreet; rash. —**im·pru'dence**, *n.*

im'pu·dent (im'pyə-dənt) *adj.* offensively forward in behavior; insolent; saucy. —**im'pu·dence**, *n.*

im·pugn' (im-pūn') *v.t.* challenge as false. —**im·pugn'ment**, *n.*

im'pulse (im'puls) *n.* **1**, force acting suddenly; a thrust or push. **2**, a stimulation of the mind to action; a sudden inclination. **3**, the intensity or momentum of a force; induced motion; impetus. —**im·pul'sive**, *adj.* impetuous.

im·pu'ni·ty (im-pū'nə-tē) *n.* exemption from punishment.

im·pure' (im-pyûr') *adj.* **1**, not simple or homogeneous; mixed with extraneous matter; tainted. **2**, obscene. —**im·pure'ness**, *n.*

im·pu'ri·ty (im-pyûr'ə-tē) *n.* **1**, something not pure; a flaw. **2**, impureness.

im·pute' (im-pūt') *v.t.* charge, ascribe, or attribute, esp. something discreditable. —**im"pu·ta'tion**, *n.*

in *prep.* denoting presence, existence, situation, inclusion, action etc. within limits, as of place, time, condition, circumstances, etc. —*adv.* 1, at, to, or toward (a place, condition, relation, etc.) 2, inward; on the inside; at home; in occupancy. 3, having the turn to play in a game. 4, accepted; elected.

in- *pref.* 1, in, as in *income.* 2, used to form or intensify verbs, as *intrust;* often replaced by en-. 3, not: used to impart a negative sense, as in *inactive.* (See also un-.) [In addition to words defined in the text, the following words formed by prefixing in-(-not) have merely the negative sense of the positive term. For pronunciation of such words, refer to the vocabulary for the pronunciation of the positive term.]

in″a·bil′i·ty
in″ac·ces′si·ble
in·ac′cu·rate
in·ac′tive
in·ad′e·quate
in″ad·mis′si·ble
in″ad·vis′a·ble
in·al′ien·a·ble
in·ap′pli·ca·ble
in″ap·pre′ci·a·ble
in″ap·pro′pri·ate
in·ar′tis′tic
in·au′di·ble
in·aus·pi′cious
in·cal′cu·la·ble
in·ca′pa·ble
in·ci·vil′i·ty
in·cog′ni·zant
in″com·bus′ti·ble
in″com·men′su·rate
in″com·mu′ni·ca·ble
in″com·plete′
in″com·pre·hen′·si·ble
in″com·press′ible
in″con·ceiv′a·ble
in″con·clu′sive
in″con·sid′er·ate
in″con·sist′ent
in″con·sol′a·ble
in″con·test′a·ble
in″con·tro·vert′·i·ble
in″cor·po′re·al
in″cor·rect′
in″cor·rupt′i·ble
in·cur′a·ble
in·cu′ri·ous
in·dec′o·rous

in″de·fen′si·ble
in″de·fin′a·ble
in″de·scrib′a·ble
in″de·struct′i·ble
in·di·rect′
in″dis·cern′i·ble
in″dis·pen′sa·ble
in″dis·put′a·ble
in″dis·sol′u·ble
in″dis·tinct′
in″dis·tin′guish·a·ble
in″di·vis′i·ble
in·ed′i·ble
in″ef·fec′tive
in″ef·fec′tu·al
in″ef·fi·ca·cy
in″ef·fi′cient
in″e·las′tic
in·el′e·gant
in·el′i·gi·ble
in·el′o·quent
in″e·qual′i·ty
in″e·rad′i·ca·ble
in″es·cap′a·ble
in″ex·act′
in″ex·cus′a·ble
in″ex·haust′i·ble
in″ex·pe′di·ent
in″ex·pen′sive
in″ex′pert
in·ex′pi·a·ble
in″ex·plic′a·ble
in″ex·press′i·ble
in″ex·tin′guish·a·ble
in″ex·tri·ca·ble
in·fer′tile
in·fre′quent
in″har·mo′ni·ous
in·hos′pi·ta·ble
in·im′i·ta·ble
in″ju·di′cious
in·jus′tice

in·nu′mer·a·ble
in·op′er·a·ble
in·op′er·a·tive
in·op·por·tune′
in″or·gan′ic
in·sa′ti·a·ble
in·sen′sate
in·sen′si·tive
in″sep′a·ra·ble
in″so·bri′e·ty
in·sol′u·ble

in″sub·stan′tial
in″suf′fer·a·ble
in″suf·fi′cient
in″sup·port′a·ble
in″sur·mount′a·ble
in·trac′ta·ble
in·var′i·a·ble
in·ver′te·brate
in·vis′i·ble
in·vul′ner·a·ble

in·ad·vert′ent (in″əd-vėr′tənt) *adj.* 1, unintentional; accidental. 2, not attentive; negligent. —**in″·ad·vert′ence,** *n.*

in·am″o·ra′ta (in-am″ə-rä′tə) *n.:* a woman with whom one is in love.

in·ane′ (in-ān′) *adj.* void of sense or intelligence; silly. —**in·an′i·ty** (in-an′ə-tē) *n.*

in·an′i·mate (in-an′i-mət) *adj.* not alive; quiescent.

in·ar·tic′u·late (in″är-tik′yə-lət) *adj.* 1, not articulate. 2, lacking facility in speech or expression. —**in″ar·tic′u·late·ness,** *n.*

in″as·much′ as (in″iz-much′) *adv.* 1, in view of the fact; considering that. 2, in so far as; to the degree of.

in·at·ten′tion (in″ə-ten′shən) *n.* failure to be attentive or thoughtful. —**in″at·ten′tive** (-tiv) *adj.*

in·au·gu·ral (in-â′gyū-rəl) *adj.* inaugurating; pert. to an inauguration.

in·au′gu·rate″ (in-â′gyə-rāt″) *v.t.* 1, make a formal beginning of; initiate. 2, install in office. —**in·aug″u·ra′tion,** *n.*

in′born″ (in′bôrn″) *adj.* implanted by nature; innate.

in′bred″ *adj.* 1, produced by inbreeding. 2, innate.

in′breed″ing (in′brē′ding) *n.* the mating of closely-related individuals.

In′ca (ing′kə) *n.* 1, a member of an American Indian people of ancient Peru. 2, a king of this people.

in″can·des′cent (in″kən-des′ənt) *adj.* 1, rendered luminous by heat. 2, white-hot; glowing; brilliant. —**in″can·des′cence,** *n.*

in″can·ta′tion (in″kan-tā′shən) *n.* the uttering of magical words.

in″ca·pac′i·tate″ (in″kə-pas′ə-tāt″) *v.t.* render unfit; disqualify: —**in″ca·pac′i·ta′tion,** *n.*

in″ca·pac′i·ty (-ə-tē) *n.* inability to perform; incompetence.

in·car′cer·ate″ (in-kär′sə-rāt″) *v.t.* put or hold in prison. —**in·car′cer·a′tion,** *n.*

in·car′nate (in-kär′nət) *adj.* embodied in flesh. —*v.t.* (-nāt) 1, em-

fat, fāte, fär, fåre, fåll, åsk; met, hē, hėr, maybē; pin, pīne; not, nōte, ôr, tool body in flesh. **2**, typify. —**in″car·na′tion**, *n*. existence in bodily form.

in·cau′tious (in-kâ′shəs) *adj*. not cautious; done or uttered with insufficient thought or discretion. —**in·cau′tious·ness**, *n*.

in·cen′di·ar·y (in-sen′dê-er-ê) *adj*. **1**, pert. to arson. **2**, used in starting a fire. **3**, tending to excite violence; inflammatory. —*n*. **1**, one who or that which starts destructive fires. **2**, an agitator. —**in·cen′di·ar·ism** (-ə-riz-əm) *n*.

in′cense (in′sens) *n*. **1**, an aromatic material or the perfume it produces when burned. **2**, any agreeable odor.

in·cense′ (in-sens′) *v.t.* excite to anger or resentment; enrage. —**in·cense′ment**, *n*.

in·cen′tive (in-sen′tiv) *n*. something that incites to action; motive; spur. —*adj*. stimulating.

in·cep′tion (in-sep′shən) *n*. a beginning; initiation. —**in·cep′tive**, *adj*.

in·ces′sant (in-ses′ənt) *adj*. unceasing; continuing without interruption. —**in·ces′san·cy**, *n*.

in′cest (in′sest) *n*. illicit intercourse between closely related persons. —**in·ces′tu·ous** (in-ses′choo-əs) *adj*.

inch *n*. a unit of length, one twelfth of a foot. —*v.t. & i.* move by small degrees.

in·cho′ate (in-kō′it) *adj*. just begun; rudimentary. —**in·cho′ate·ness**, *n*.

in·ci·dence (in′si-dəns) *n*. **1**, frequency or range of occurrence; extent of effects. **2**, manner or direction of a fall; course. **3**, partial coincidence.

in·ci·dent (in′si-dənt) *n*. **1**, an occurrence or event; a casual happening. **2**, an episode. **3**, a result or casual feature of something else. —*adj*. **1**, dependent; pertaining. **2**, falling or striking on something.

in″ci·den′tal (in″si-den′təl) *adj*. **1**, pert. to or constituting an incident. **2**, casual; minor.

in·cin′er·ate′ (in-sin′ə-rāt′) *v.t.* burn to ashes. —**in·cin′er·a′tion**, *n*. —**in·cin′er·a′tor**, *n*. a furnace for burning waste.

in·cip′i·ent (in-sip′ê-ənt) *adj*. beginning to exist or appear. —**in·cip′i·ence, in·cip′i·en·cy**, *n*.

in·cise′ (in-sīz′) *v.t.* cut into; engrave.

in·ci′sion (in-sizh′ən) *n*. **1**, act of cutting into. **2**, a cut or gash.

in·ci′sive (in-sī′siv) *adj*. **1**, sharply expressive; penetrating; trenchant. **2**, adapted for cutting. —**in·ci′sive·ness**, *n*.

in·ci′sor (in-sī′zər) *n*. a tooth adapted for cutting.

in·cite′ (in-sīt′) *v.t.* **1**, move (a person) to action; urge or stimulate. **2**, stir up (an action); instigate. —**in·cite′ment**, *n*.

in·clem′ent (in-klem′ənt) *adj*. (of weather) harsh; tempestuous. —**in·clem′en·cy**, *n*.

in″cli·na′tion (in″klə-nā′shən) *n*. **1**, a preference or liking; disposition; bent. **2**, the act of inclining; the state of being inclined. **3**, a slanted position; the angle of a slant.

in·cline′ (in-klīn′) *v.i.* **1**, have a tendency or preference. **2**, be slanted or oblique. **3**, approximate. —*v.t.* **1**, give a tendency to. **2**, bend; bow; slant. —*n*. (in′klīn) a slope.

in·close′ (in-klōz′) *v.t.* enclose.

in·clude′ (in-klood′) *v.t.* **1**, contain as a part; take in; embrace or cover. **2**, be composed of; comprise. —**in·clu′sion** (-zhən) *n*.

in·clu′sive (in-kloo′siv) *adj*. **1**, including the stated limits. **2**, wide in extent; comprehensive. —**in·clu′sive·ness**, *n*.

in·cog′ni·to″ (in-kog′ni-tō″) *adj. & adv.* with real name or identity concealed.

in″co·her′ent (in″kō-hir′ənt) *adj*. **1**, without apparent unity or connection; incongruous. **2**, not logical or coördinated in expression; confused; chaotic. **3**, lacking physical cohesion. —**in″co·her′ence**, *n*.

in′come (in′kum) *n*. **1**, money received as wages, interest, etc. **2**, profit.

in″com·mode′ (in″kə-mōd′) *v.t.* subject to inconvenience.

in″com·mu′ni·ca·do (in″kə-mū″nê-kä′dō) *adj*. shut off from any communication with others.

in·com′pa·ra·ble (in-kom′pə-rə-bəl) *adj*. **1**, without a rival; unequaled; matchless. **2**, not comparable. —**in·com′pa·ra·bil′i·ty**, *n*.

in″com·pat′i·ble (in″kəm-pat′ə-bəl) *adj*. not compatible; esp. of persons, unable to live together in harmony. —**in″com·pat·i·bil′i·ty**, *n*.

in·com′pe·tent (in-kom′pə-tənt) *adj*. not fit or capable. —*n*. one inadequate to a task, esp. mentally. —**in·com′pe·tence**, *n*.

in·con′gru·ous (in-kong′groo-əs) *adj*. **1**, out of place; unsuitable; inappropriate; inconsistent. **2**, comprised of inharmonious parts; disjointed. —**in″con·gru·i′ty** (in″kən-groo′ə-tê), **in·con′gru·ous·ness**, *n*.

in″con·se·quen′tial (in″kon-sə-kwen′shəl) *adj*. **1**, of no importance or effect; trivial. **2**, not consequent.

in·con·sid′er·a·ble (in″kən-sid′-ər-ə-bəl) *adj*. too few or small to matter; unimportant. —**in″con·sid′er·a·ble·ness**, *n*.

in″con·spic′u·ous (in″kən-spik′-yoo-əs) *adj.* too small or retiring to notice; not readily perceived. —**in″con·spic′u·ous·ness**, *n.*

in·con′stant (in-kon′stənt) *adj.* not loyal; not faithful. —**in·con′stan·cy**, *n.*

in·con′ti·nent (in-kon′tə-nənt) *adj.* not holding or held in; unrestrained; intemperate. —**in·con′ti·nence**, *n.*

in″con·ven′ience (in″kən-vēn′-yəns) *n.* discomfort; trouble. —*v.t.* put to trouble. —**in″con·ven′ient**, *adj.* causing difficulty.

in·cor′po·rate″ (in-kôr′pə-rāt″) *v.t.* 1, organize into a corporation; unite in a society, etc. 2, combine; introduce as an integral part. —*v.i.* unite in a corporation, society, etc., or a body, mass, etc. —**in·cor″po·ra′tion**, *n.*

in·cor′ri·gi·ble (in-kor′i-jə-bəl) *adj.* resistant to correction or reform; beyond reform. —**in·cor″ri·gi·bil′i·ty**, *n.*

in·crease′ (in-krēs′) *v.t.* make greater; extend in bulk, size, number, degree, etc.; enlarge; augment; enhance. —*v.i.* 1, become greater. 2, multiply. —*n.* (in′krēs) 1, the act of increasing. 2, the amount, result, or product of increase.

in·cred′i·ble (in-kred′ə-bəl) *adj.* 1, not believable. 2, (*Colloq.*) extraordinary. —**in·cred′i·bil′i·ty**, *n.*

in″cre·du′li·ty (in″krə-dū′lə-tē) *n.* disbelief; skepticism. —**in·cred′u·lous** (in-krej′ə-ləs) *adj.*

in′cre·ment (in′krə-mənt) *n.* something added; augmentation; growth.

in·crim′i·nate″ (in-krim′ə-nāt″) *v.t.* show to be involved in a crime; charge; accuse. —**in·crim″i·na′tion**, *n.*

in·crust′ (in-krust′) *v.t.* form into a crust; cover or line with a hard coating. —**in″crus·ta′tion**, *n.*

in′cu·bate″ (in′kyə-bāt″) *v.t.* 1, hatch (eggs). 2, maintain at a temperature favorable to growth. 3, produce as though by hatching. —*v.i.* sit on eggs; brood. —**in″cu·ba′tion**, *n.* —**in′cu·ba″tor**, *n.* a heated apparatus for hatching eggs, nurturing babies, etc.

Incubator

in′cu·bus (in′kyə-bəs) *n.* a male demon imagined to disturb sleep; hence, a nightmare.

in·cul′cate (in-kul′kāt) *v.t.* impress on the mind, as by admonition. —**in″cul·ca′tion**, *n.*

in·cul′pate (in-kul′pāt) *v.t.* accuse of wrongdoing. —**in″cul·pa′tion**, *n.*

in·cum′bent (in-kum′bənt) *adj.* 1, resting on one as a duty or obligation. 2, leaning on something. —*n.* an office-holder. —**in·cum′ben·cy**, *n.*

in·cur′ (in-kẽr′) *v.t.* [**in·curred′**, **-cur′ring**] 1, encounter as an experience. 2, bring on oneself. —**in·cur′rence**, *n.*

in·cur′sion (in-kẽr′zhən) *n.* a sudden running in; an inroad or invasion. —**in·cur′sive** (-siv) *adj.*

in·debt′ed (in-det′id) *adj.* owing; under obligation. —**in·debt′ed·ness**, *n.* fact of owing; amount owed.

in·de′cent (in-dē′sənt) *adj.* 1, not fit to be done, seen, or heard in polite company; indelicate. 2, immodest. —**in·de′cen·cy**, *n.*

in″de·ci′sion (in″di-sizh′ən) *n.* vacillation; irresolution.

in″de·ci′sive (-sī′-siv) *adj.* 1, inconclusive. 2, unable to decide. —**in″de·ci′sive·ness**, *n.*

in·deed′ (in-dēd′) *adv.* in fact; in reality; in truth. —*interj.* expressing doubt, surprise or agreement.

in″de·fat′i·ga·ble (in″di-fat′ə-gə-bəl) *adj.* not easily fatigued; not yielding to fatigue. —**in″de·fat″i·ga·bil′i·ty**, *n.*

in·def′i·nite (in-def′ə-nit) *adj.* 1, having no fixed or specified limit; infinite. 2, vague. 3, indeterminate. —**indefinite article**, a or an. —**in·def′i·nite·ness**, *n.*

in·del′i·ble (in-del′ə-bəl) *adj.* not capable of being deleted or obliterated. —**in·del″i·bil′i·ty**, *n.*

in·del′i·cate (in-del′i-kət) *adj.* coarse; gross; immodest; unrefined. —**in·del′i·ca·cy** (-kə-sē) *n.*

in·dem′ni·fy″ (in-dem′nə-fī″) *v.t.* compensate for or guarantee against damage, loss, or expenses incurred. —**in·dem″ni·fi·ca′tion**, *n.*

in·dem′ni·ty (in-dem′nə-tē) *n.* 1, what is paid as compensation or reimbursement. 2, security given against damage or loss. 3, exemption from liability.

in·dent′ (in-dent′) *v.t.* make a dent, notch, or recess in; begin (a line of writing) to the right of the left margin. —**in″den·ta′tion** (in″den-tā′shən) *n.*

in·den′ture (in-den′chər) *n.* 1, a contract binding a person to service, esp. an apprentice. 2, a sealed deed, contract, etc. —*v.t.* so bind.

in″de·pen′dence (in″di-pen′dəns) *n.* condition of being independent;

freedom from control or influence. —**Independence Day,** July 4, on which the United States declared themselves sovereign.

in″de·pen′dent (in″di-pen′dent) *adj.* **1,** not contingent on something else for existence, operation, etc. **2,** not influenced by others in opinion, conduct, etc. **3,** not affiliated; sovereign in authority. **4,** having ample income without working. —*n.* someone or something independent.

in″de·ter′min·a·ble (in″di-tēr′mə-nə-bəl) *adj.* incapable of being determined, limited, established, etc.

in″de·ter′mi·nate (in″di-tēr′mə-nət) *adj.* **1,** not fixed or established; not precise or clear. **2,** not determinable. —**in″de·ter′mi·nate·ness,** *n.*

in′dex (in′deks) *n.* [*pl.* **in′dex·es,** in′di·ces″ (in′də-sēz″)] **1,** an alphabetized list of items and their locations. **2,** a pointer; the symbol (☞). **3,** a quality, trait, etc. **4,** the forefinger. **5,** (*Math.*) an operative symbol, as an exponent. **6,** (*cap.*) a list of books forbidden to Roman Catholics. —*v.t.* **1,** furnish with or enter in an index. **2,** point out.

India ink a black drawing ink.

In′di·an (in′dē-ən) *adj. & n.* **1,** pert. to the aboriginal inhabitants of North and South America. **2,** pert. to the inhabitants of India or the East Indies. —**Indian club,** a wooden club swung for exercise. —**Indian giver,** a person who takes back a gift he made. —**Indian summer,** warm days late in the fall.

in′di·cate (in′di-kāt″) *v.t.* **1,** point out; direct attention to. **2,** imply. —**in″di·ca′tion,** *n.*

in·dic′a·tive (in-dik′ə-tiv) *adj.* **1,** pointing out; betokening. **2,** (*Gram.*) expressing a statement or question.

in′di·ca″tor (in″di-kā′tər) *n.* an instrument or part that indicates.

in·dict′ (in-dīt′) *v.t.* charge with an offense, esp. a criminal one. —**in·dict′ment,** *n.*

in·dif′fer·ent (in-dif′ər-ənt) *adj.* **1,** feeling no interest or anxiety; apathetic. **2,** unbiased; impartial. **3,** not making a difference. **4,** mediocre; moderate in amount or degree. —**in·dif′fer·ence,** *n.*

in·dig′e·nous (in-dij′ə-nəs) *adj.* originating in a particular region; native. —**in·dig′e·nous·ness,** *n.*

in′di·gent (in′di-jənt) *adj.* destitute; poor; needy. —**in′di·gence,** *n.*

in″di·gest′i·ble (in″di-jes′tə-bəl) *adj.* hard to digest or assimilate. —**in″di·gest′i·bil′i·ty,** *n.*

in″di·ges′tion (in″di-jes′chən) *n.* pain caused by inability to digest food properly.

in·dig′nant (in-dig′nənt) *adj.* feeling or showing anger, esp. righteous anger; resentful.

in″dig·na′tion (in″dig-nā′shən) *n.* righteous anger over injustice, etc.

in·dig′ni·ty (in-dig′nə-tē) *n.* an injury or affront to one's dignity; a slight; humiliation.

in′di·go″ (in′di-gō″) *n.* **1,** a dark blue dye. **2,** a violet-blue color.

in·dis·creet′ (in-dis-krēt′) *adj.* not prudent. —**in·dis·creet′ness,** *n.*

in·dis·cre′tion (-kresh′ən) *n.* act of being indiscreet; error of judgment.

in″dis·crim′i·nate (in″dis-krim′ə-nit) *adj.* not carefully selected; heterogeneous. —**in″dis·crim′i·na′tion,** *n.* —**in″dis·crim′i·nate·ness,** *n.*

in″dis·posed′ (in″dis-pōzd′) *adj.* **1,** somewhat sick or ill. **2,** not inclined; unwilling. —**in″dis·po·si′tion** (-pə-zish′ən) *n.*

in·dite′ (in-dīt′) *v.t.* put into verbal form; write or compose. —**in·dite′ment,** *n.*

in″di·vid′u·al (in″di-vij′oo-əl) *adj.* **1,** relating to one person or thing. **2,** not divisible without loss of identity. **3,** single; particular. **4,** having peculiar characteristics. —*n.* a single person, animal, or thing.

in·di·vid′u·al·ism (-iz-əm) *n.* independence in personal behavior. —**in·di·vid′u·al·ist,** *n.* —**in·di·vid′u·al·is′tic,** *adj.*

in·di·vid′u·al′i·ty (-al′ə-tē) *n.* the state of being distinct and unlike others; peculiar character.

in·doc′tri·nate″ (in-dok′tri-nāt″) *v.t.* imbue with a particular belief or principle. —**in·doc″tri·na′tion,** *n.*

In′do-Eu″ro·pe′an (in′dō-) *adj.* pert. to a family of languages spoken chiefly in Europe.

in′do·lent (in′də-lənt) *adj.* lazy; sluggish. —**in′do·lence,** *n.*

in·dom′i·ta·ble (in-dom′i-tə-bəl) *adj.* that cannot be subdued or repressed. —**in·dom″i·ta·bil′i·ty,** *n.*

in′door′ (in′dôr′) *adj.* in a building; not in open air. —**in′doors′,** *adv.*

in·dorse′ (in-dôrs′) *v.t.* endorse.

in·du′bi·ta·ble (in-doo′bi-tə-bəl) *adj.* not to be doubted; sure. —**in·du′bi·ta·ble·ness,** *n.*

in·duce′ (in-dūs′) *v.t.* **1,** lead by persuasion or influence; prevail upon; incite. **2,** produce or cause. **3,** produce by induction. **4,** infer.

in·duce′ment (-mənt) *n.* **1,** act or result of inducing. **2,** incentive.

in·duct′ (in-dukt′) *v.t.* install in office; initiate.

in·duc′tion (in-duk′shən) *n.* **1,** installation of a person into office. **2,** the excitation of an electromagnetic field by a neighboring body, without direct contact. **3,** the process of drawing a general conclusion from particular facts. **4**, the act of inducing. —**in-duc′tive**, *adj.*

in-due′ (in-dū′) *v.t.* endow; supply.

in-dulge′ (in-dulj′) *v.t.* yield to or comply with (an inclination or person); humor. —*v.i.* yield to one's own inclination. —**in-dul′gent**, *adj.*

in-dul′gence (in-dul′jəns) *n.* **1**, gratification of desire. **2**, an extension of time. **3**, (*Rom. Cath.*) remission of punishment; relaxation of law.

in-dus′tri-al (in-dus′trē-əl) *adj.* pert. to large-scale manufacturing. —**in-dus′tri-al-ist**, *n.*

in-dus′tri-ous (in-dus′trē-əs) *adj.* hard-working; diligent; assiduous. —**in-dus′tri-ous-ness**, *n.*

in′dus-try (in′dəs-trē) *n.* **1**, a manufacturing trade. **2**, manufacturing and business generally. **3**, diligence; application to tasks.

in-e′bri-ate′ (in-ē′brē-āt′) *v.t.* make drunk; intoxicate. —**in-e′bri-a′tion**, *n.*

in′e-bri′e-ty (in′i-brī′ə-tē) *n.* drunkenness.

in-ef′fa-ble (in-ef′ə-bəl) *adj.* inexpressible; too sacred to speak of. —**in-ef′fa-bil′i-ty**, *n.*

in′e-luc′ta-ble (in′i-luk′tə-bəl) *adj.* not to be eluded or overcome.

in-ept′ *adj.* **1**, not apt, fit, or suited. **2**, inefficient. —**in-ept′ness**, **in-ept′i-tude**, *n.*

in-eq′ui-ta-ble (in-ek′wi-tə-bəl) *adj.* unfair; unjust.

in-eq′ui-ty (in-ek′wə-tē) *n.* injustice; something that is unfair.

in-ert′ (in-ĕrt′) *adj.* **1**, having no inherent power to move or act. **2**, lacking active properties. **3**, sluggish. —**in-ert′ness**, *n.*

in-er′tia (in-ĕr′shə) *n.* **1**, the property of matter whereby a body remains at rest or in uniform rectilinear motion unless acted upon by an external force. **2**, inertness; inactivity.

in-es′ti-ma-ble (in-es′tə-mə-bəl) *adj.* not to be estimated; beyond measure. —**in-es′ti-ma-bil′i-ty**, *n.*

in-ev′i-ta-ble (in-ev′i-tə-bəl) *adj.* **1**, unavoidable. **2**, sure to come or happen. —**in-ev′i-ta-bil′i-ty**, *n.*

in-ex′o-ra-ble (in-ek′sə-rə-bəl) *adj.* not to be persuaded or moved; unrelenting. —**in-ex′o-ra-ble-ness**, *n.*

in′ex-pe′ri-ence (in′ik-spir′ē-əns) *n.* lack of knowledge or skill gained from experience.

in-fal′li-ble (in-fal′ə-bəl) *adj.* **1**, free from fallacy; not liable to error. **2**, unfailingly certain; trustworthy; sure. —**in-fal′li-bil′i-ty**, *n.*

in′fa-mous (in′fə-məs) *adj.* no-

toriously evil; shamefully bad; wicked. —**in′fa-my** (in′fə-mē) *n.*

in′fan-cy (in′fən-sē) *n.* condition or period of being an infant.

in′fant (in′fənt) *n.* **1**, a baby or young child. **2**, (*Law*) anyone under legal age. —*adj.* **1**, being an infant, legally a minor. **2**, incipient.

in′fan-tile″ (in′fən-tīl″) *adj.* being or like a baby. —**infantile paralysis**, poliomyelitis.

in′fan-try (in′fən-trē) *n.* soldiers that serve on foot: a branch of military forces. —**in′fan-try-man**, *n.*

in-fat′u-ate′ (in-fach′oo-āt′) *v.t.* inspire with foolish passion, esp. of love. —**in-fat′u-a′tion**, *n.*

in-fect′ (in-fekt′) *v.t.* **1**, impregnate with germs; affect with disease. **2**, imbue; taint. —**in-fec′tion**, *n.*

in-fec′tious (-shəs) *adj.* **1**, communicable by transmission of germs. **2**, spreading rapidly; hard to resist. —**in-fec′tious-ness**, *n.*

in-fer′ (in-fĕr′) *v.t. & i.* [**in-ferred′**, **in-fer′ring**] conclude by reasoning; opine; derive from evidence.

in′fer-ence (in′fə-rəns) *n.* **1**, act of inferring. **2**, a conclusion or presumption. —**in″fer-en′tial** (-ren′shəl) *adj.*

in-fe′ri-or (in-fir′ē-ər) *adj.* **1**, lower in rank, grade, etc. **2**, markedly poor in quality. **3**, lower in place or position. —*n.* someone or something inferior. —**in-fe′ri-or′i-ty** (-or′ē-tē) *n.*

in-fer′nal (in-fĕr′nəl) *adj.* **1**, pert. to mythical lower regions. **2**, hellish; diabolical.

in-fer′no (in-fĕr′nō) *n.* [*pl.* **-nos**] hell; the nether regions.

in-fest′ *v.t.* **1**, invade and swarm over, like vermin. **2**, pervade noxiously. —**in″fes-ta′tion**, *n.*

in′fi-del (in′fə-dəl) *adj.* **1**, having no religious faith. **2**, not of a particular religion. —*n.* an unbeliever.

in″fi-del′i-ty (in″fə-del′ə-tē) *n.* **1**, unfaithfulness; disloyalty. **2**, lack of faith.

in′field″ (in′fēld″) *n.* the baseball diamond; the four players (*infielders*) stationed there.

in-fil′trate (in-fil′trāt) *v.t.* filter into or through; permeate. —**in″fil-tra′tion** (in″fəl-trā′shən) *n.*

in′fi-nite (in′fə-nit) *adj.* **1**, great beyond measurement or counting; without limit; interminable. **2**, absolute. —*n.* **1**, something limitless; boundless space. **2**, (*cap.*) God. —**in′fi-nite-ness**, *n.*

in″fin-i-tes′i-mal (in″fin-i-tes′ə-məl) *adj.* immeasurably small.

in-fin′i-tive (in-fin′ə-tiv) *n.* the form of a verb merely expressing its sense: used after *to*, as *to go*.

in·fin'i·ty (in-fin'ə-tē) *n.* **1,** boundless extension; unlimited quantity or number. **2,** the condition of being infinite.

in·firm' (in-fẽrm') *adj.* not in good health; weak; faltering.

in·fir'ma·ry (in-fẽr'mə-rē) *n.* a place for the care of the sick or injured.

in·fir'mi·ty (in-fẽr'mə-tē) *n.* illness; weakness.

in·flame' (in-flām') *v.t.* **1,** excite highly; make more violent; aggravate. **2,** affect with bodily inflammation. **3,** set on fire.

in·flam'ma·ble (in-flam'ə-bəl) *adj.* capable of burning; combustible. —**in·flam''ma·bil'i·ty,** *n.*

in''flam·ma'tion (in''flə-ma'shən) *n.* a morbid condition of the body characterized by heat, swelling, redness, etc.

in·flam'ma·to·ry (in-flam'ə-tôr-ē) *adj.* serving to inflame.

in·flate' (in-flāt') *v.t. & t.* **1,** fill with air or other gas; distend; swell. **2,** elate. **3,** (of currency, prices, etc.) raise or expand.

in·fla'tion *n.* a condition in which the money in circulation is excessive for the commodities on sale or being sold. —**in·fla'tion·ar·y,** *adj.*

in·flect' (in-flekt') *v.t.* **1,** turn from a direct course; bend. **2,** modulate (the voice); vary (a word) by inflection.

in·flec'tion (in-flek'shən) *n.* **1,** change of pitch or tone in speaking; modulation. **2,** variation of a word to show plurality, person, part of speech, etc. **3,** a bend or angle; a change of curvature. —**in·flec'tion·al,** in-flec'tive, *adj.*

in·flex'i·ble (in-flek'sə-bəl) *adj.* **1,** not to be bent; rigid. **2,** stubborn. —**in·flex''i·bil'i·ty,** *n.*

in·flict' (in-flikt') *v.t.* impose (something undesired); cause to be suffered or borne. —**in·flic'tion,** *n.*

in''flo·res'cence (in''flō-res'əns) *n.* **1,** the flowering part of a plant; flowers collectively; a flower. **2,** the fact or stage of blossoming. —**in''flo·res'cent,** *adj.*

in·flu·ence (in'floo-əns) *n.* **1,** power to control or affect others by authority, persuasion, example, etc. **2,** a person or thing that exerts such power. —*v.t.* exercise influence on.

in''flu·en'tial (-en'shəl) *adj.* **1,** able to exert much influence. **2,** influencing.

in''flu·en'za (in''floo-en'zə) *n.* a highly contagious disease characterized by nasal catarrh, bronchial inflammation, and prostration.

in'flux'' (in'fluks'') *n.* **1,** a flowing in. **2,** the place where something flows in.

in·form' (in-fôrm') *v.t.* **1,** communicate facts to; make known to; tell. **2,** instruct. —*v.i.* give information, esp. about a criminal.

in·for'mal (in-fôr'məl) *adj.* unconventional; familiar in manner; irregular. —*n.* a party at which formal dress is not required. —**in''for·mal'i·ty** (in''fər-mal'ə-tē) *n.*

in·form'ant (in-fôr'mənt) *n.* one who communicates facts.

in''for·ma'tion (in''fər-mā'shən) *n.* **1,** act or result of informing; news. **2,** an official criminal charge.

in·form'a·tive (in-fôr'mə-tiv) *adj.* imparting news or knowledge.

in·form'er (in-fôr'mər) *n.* **1,** one who exposes a wrongdoer to official punishment. **2,** informant.

in·fra- *pref.* below; beneath.

in·frac'tion (in-frak'shən) *n.* breach; violation.

in''fra·red' (in''frə-red') *n. & adj.* radiation outside the visible spectrum, at the red end.

in·fringe' (in-frinj') *v.t.* violate; transgress. —*v.i.* encroach; trespass. —**in·fringe'ment,** *n.*

in·fu'ri·ate' (in-fyûr'ē-āt') *v.t.* make furious; enrage.

in·fuse' (in-fūz') *v.t.* **1,** cause to penetrate. **2,** permeate like a liquid; imbue. **3,** soak. —**in·fu'sion,** *n.*

in·gen'ious (in-jēn'yəs) *adj.* showing cleverness in contrivance or construction. —**in·gen'ious·ness,** *n.*

in·gé·nue' (an-zhə-nū') *n.* an ingenuous young woman, in a play.

in''ge·nu'i·ty (in''jə-nū'ə-tē) *n.* cleverness; inventiveness.

in·gen'u·ous (in-jen'ū-əs) *adj.* free from guile; candid. —**in·gen'·u·ous·ness,** *n.*

in·glo'ri·ous (in-glôr'ē-əs) *adj.* dishonorable; shameful. —**in·glo'ri·ous·ness,** *n.*

in'got (ing'gət) *n.* a mass of metal roughly shaped by casting or rolling.

in·grain' (in-grān') *v.t.* fix firmly, as in the mind.

in'grate (in'grāt) *n.* one who is ungrateful.

in·gra'ti·ate'' (in-grā'shē-āt'') *v.t.* establish (oneself) in the favor of another. —**in·gra''ti·a'tion,** *n.*

in·grat'i·tude (in-grat'i-tood) *n.* ungratefulness.

in·gre'di·ent (in-grē'dē-ənt) *n.* an essential part of a compound or mixture; constituent; element.

in'gress (in'gres) *n.* entrance.

in'grown'' (in'grōn'') *adj.* grown into the flesh, as, an *ingrown* toenail.

in·gur'gi·tate" (in-gĕr'jə-tāt") *v.t.* swallow; gulp. —**in·gur"gi·ta'tion,** *n.*

in·hab'it *v.t.* live or dwell in.

in·hab'it·ant (-tənt) *n.* a resident.

in·hal'ant (in-hā'lənt) *n.* medicinal vapor; an apparatus for dispensing it.

in·hale' (in-hāl') *v.t.* draw in by or as by breathing. —*v.i.* breathe in. —**in"ha·la'tion** (in"hə-lā'shən) *n.*

in·her'ent (in-hir'ənt) *adj.* belonging intrinsically; innate. —**in·her'ence, in·her·en·cy,** *n.*

in·her'it *v.t. & i.* 1, receive (property, etc.) as an heir; acquire by gift or succession. 2, receive (qualities, etc.) from progenitors; possess intrinsically. —**in·her'it·ance,** *n.* —**in·her'i·tor,** *n.*

in·hib'it *v.t.* 1, check or repress, as an impulse. 2, forbid; prohibit. —**in·hib'i·tive,** *adj.*

in"hi·bi'tion (in"ə-bish'ən) *n.* the checking, restraining, or blocking of a mental process, physiological reaction, etc.

in·hu'man (in-hū'mən) *adj.* 1, cruel; bestial. 2, supernatural. —**in"hu·man'i·ty,** *n.*

in·im'i·cal (in-im'i-kəl) *adj.* 1, harmful. 2, like an enemy; hostile.

in·iq'ui·tous (i-nik'wə-təs) *adj.* 1, lacking equity; grossly unjust. 2, wicked; sinful. —**in·iq'ui·ty** (-tē) *n.*

in·i'tial (i-nish'əl) *adj.* 1, placed at the beginning. 2, pert. to the beginning or first stage. —*n.* the first letter of a word. —*v.t.* mark with the initials of one's name.

in·i'ti·ate" (i-nish'ē-āt") *v.t.* 1, set going; begin; originate. 2, give instruction to. 3, induct to membership in a club, etc. —**in·i"ti·a'tion,** *n.*

in·i'ti·a·tive (i-nish'ē-ə-tiv) *n.* 1, readiness and ability to initiate, take the lead, contrive, etc. 2, the first step; leading movement.

in·ject' (in-jekt') *v.t.* 1, put in by driving force, as liquid into a cavity. 2, insert; interject.

in·jec'tion (in-jek'shən) *n.* 1, act or result of injecting; an enema, hypodermic, etc. 2, a substance or thing injected.

in·junc'tion (in-junk'shən) *n.* 1, a command; order; admonition. 2, the act of enjoining. —**in·junc'tive,** *adj.*

in·jure (in'jər) *v.t.* do harm to; hurt; damage; impair.

in·ju'ri·ous (in-jūr'ē-əs) *adj.* damaging; hurtful. —**in·ju'ri·ous·ness,** *n.*

in'ju·ry (in'jə-rē) *n.* act or result of injuring; hurt; damage.

ink *n.* a fluid used for writing or printing.

ink'ling *n.* a vague idea or notion; a hint or intimation.

ink'well" *n.* a cup for holding ink.

ink'y (-ē) *adj.* like ink; black.

in'land (in'lənd) *adj.* 1, away from the coast or border. 2, domestic to a country. —*adv.* toward the interior.

in·lay' (in-lā') *v.t.* [**in·laid', in·lay'ing**] 1, decorate with pieces set on the surface. 2, apply to a surface, in a decorative pattern. 3, graft (a shoot) upon a plant. —*n.* (in'lā") 1, something inlaid or for inlaying. 2, a filling for a tooth.

in'let *n.* an arm of a sea or lake extending into the land.

in'mate" (in'māt") *n.* an inhabitant or lodger; one confined in an institution.

in'most" (in'mōst") *adj.* farthest within; deepest.

inn (in) *n.* a hotel, esp. a small one.

in·nate' (i-nāt') *adj.* existing in one from birth; inborn. —**in·nate'ness,** *n.*

in'ner (in'ər) *adj.* [*superl.* **in'ner·most"**] 1, situated in or farther within. 2, mental or spiritual; not outward. 3, private; concealed.

in'ning (in'ing) *n.* 1, (*Baseball*) a period in which each side has a turn at bat. 2, (often *pl.*) a time of power.

in'no·cent (in'ə-sənt) *adj.* 1, not guilty; upright; harmless. 2, naïve; artless. 3, devoid. —**in'no·cence,** *n.*

in·noc'u·ous (i-nok'ū-əs) *adj.* harmless. —**in·noc'u·ous·ness,** *n.*

in'no·vate" (in'ə-vāt") *v.t. & i.* introduce something new. —**in"no·va'tion,** *n.* —**in'no·va"tor,** *n.*

in"nu·en'do (in"ū-en'dō) *n.* an insinuation; unfriendly hint.

in·oc'u·late" (i-nok'yə-lāt") *v.t.* 1, inject an immunizing agent into. 2, imbue. —**in·oc"u·la'tion,** *n.*

in"of·fen'sive (in"ə-fen'siv) *adj.* harmless; not annoying. —**in"of·fen'sive·ness,** *n.*

in·or'di·nate (in-ôr'də-nət) *adj.* beyond proper limits; excessive.

in"pa"tient (in'pā"shənt) *n.* a hospital patient who is lodged there.

in'quest (in'kwest) *n.* a legal inquiry, esp. as to the cause of death, before a jury.

in·quire' (in-kwīr') *v.t. & i.* ask (about); seek knowledge (of).

in·quir'y (in-kwīr'ē; in'kwə-rē) *n.* 1, search for information or knowledge; interrogation; investigation. 2, a question.

in"qui·si'tion (in"kwə-zish'ən) *n.* 1, examination; a formal inquiry.

2, (*cap.*) (*Hist.*) a court for the suppression of heresy.

in·quis'i·tive (in-kwiz'ə-tiv) *adj.* unduly curious; prying. —**in·quis'i·tive·ness,** *n.*

in·quis'i·tor (in-kwiz'i-tər) *n.* one who conducts an inquisition.

in'road" (in'rōd") *n.* a forcible or insidious encroachment; a raid.

in·sane' (in-sān') *adj.* crazy; not legally responsible for one's actions. —**in·san'i·ty** (in-san'ə-tē) *n.*

in·scribe' (in-skrīb') *v.t.* **1,** write or engrave; mark with letters or signs. **2,** write or draw inside of.

in·scrip'tion (in-skrip'shən) *n.* something inscribed, as on a monument or coin.

in·scru'ta·ble (in-skroo'tə-bəl) *adj.* not to be read by scrutiny or investigation. —**in·scru'ta·bil'i·ty,** *n.*

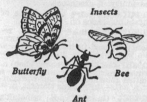

Insects

Butterfly   *Bee*

Ant

in'sect (in'sekt) *n.* **1,** any member of a class of tiny winged invertebrates. **2,** a contemptible person.

in·sec'ti·cide (in-sek'ti-sīd') *n.* a substance to kill insects.

in"sec·tiv'o·rous (in"sek-tiv'ə-rəs) *adj.* feeding on insects.

in"se·cure' (in"si-kyûr') *adj.* **1,** feeling unsafe. **2,** not tightly fastened; not safe. —**in"se·cu'ri·ty,** *n.*

in·sen'si·ble (in-sen'sə-bəl) *adj.* **1,** deprived of sensation; unconscious; unfeeling. **2,** imperceptible. —**in·sen'si·bil'i·ty,** *n.*

in·sert' (in-sėrt') *v.t.* put in; place inside of or among. —*n.* (in'sėrt) something inserted. —**in·ser'tion,** *n.* **1,** the act of inserting. **2,** an insert.

in'set" *n.* something set in; an insert, esp. in a book, illustration, etc. —*v.t.* insert.

in·side' (in-sīd') *prep. & adv.* in or into; within a body or limit (of space or time). —*n.* **1,** the inner part; interior region; inner surface. **2,** the contents; (*pl.*) the alimentary tract; mental feelings. —*adj.* **1,** interior; internal. **2,** indoor. **3,** specially privileged. —**in"sid'er,** *n.* (*Colloq.*) one who has special access to secrets or privileges.

in·sid'i·ous (in-sid'ē-əs) *adj.* **1,** operating stealthily with evil effect.

2, deceitful; treacherous. —**in·sid'i·ous·ness,** *n.*

in·sight" (in'sīt") *n.* **1,** penetrating discernment; intuition. **2,** a sudden awareness.

in·sig'ni·a (in-sig'nē-ə) *n. sing. & pl.* [*sing.* also, **in·sig'ne**] a badge of office or honor; an emblem.

in"sig·nif'i·cant (in"sig-nif'ə-kənt) *adj.* without importance; trivial. —**in"sig·nif'i·cance,** *n.*

in"sin·cere' (in"sin-sir') *adj.* not sincere; hypocritical. —**in"sin·cer'i·ty** (-ser'ə-tē) *n.*

in·sin'u·ate" (in-sin'yū-āt") *v.t.* **1,** hint or suggest indirectly; imply slyly. **2,** introduce by devious means or by slow degrees. —**in·sin"u·a'tion,** *n.*

in·sip'id *adj.* **1,** lacking flavor or savor. **2,** uninteresting; dull. —**in"si·pid'i·ty** (in"si-pid'ə-tē) *n.*

in·sist' *v.t.* **1,** (with *on*) enforce by command; assert or argue emphatically. **2,** persevere in action. —**in·sist'ence,** *n.* —**in·sist'ent,** *adj.*

in'sole" (in'sōl) *n.* the inner sole of a shoe.

in'so·lent (in'sə-lənt) *adj.* contemptuously rude, disrespectful, or insulting. —**in'so·lence,** *n.*

in·sol'vent (in-sol'vənt) *adj.* having greater liabilities than assets; bankrupt. —**in·sol'ven·cy,** *n.*

in·som'ni·a (in-som'nē-ə) *n.* inability to sleep, esp. when chronic.

in·som'ni·ac (-ak) *n.* one who suffers insomnia.

in"so·much' *adv.* inasmuch (as).

in·sou'ci·ant (in-soo'sē-ənt) *adj.* carefree; unconcerned. —**in·sou'ci·ance,** *n.*

in·spect' (in-spekt') *v.t.* look at closely; examine critically. —**in·spec'tion,** *n.* —**in·spec'tor,** *n.* one who inspects; a title of various executive or supervisory officers.

in"spi·ra'tion (in"spə-rā'shən) *n.* **1,** any influence, esp. supernatural or intuitive, that inspires thought or action; thought so suggested. **2,** the act of inspiring; the state of being inspired. —**in"spi·ra'tion·al,** *adj.*

in·spire' (in-spīr') *v.t.* **1,** stimulate to activity; animate; instigate; impel. **2,** breathe in; inhale. —**in·spir'a·to·ry** (-ə-tôr-ē) *adj.*

in"sta·bil'i·ty (in"stə-bil'ə-tē) *n.* unsteadiness; lack of firmness; changeability.

in·stall' (in-stâl') *v.t.* **1,** place in position for service or use. **2,** induct into office; seat.

in"stal·la'tion (in"stə-lā'shən) *n.* **1,** act or result of installing. **2,** something installed, as a fixed machine.

in·stall'ment (in-stäl'mənt) n. one part of anything divided for periodical receipt or issuance, as a debt, a serial story, etc. Also, **in·stal'ment.**

in'stance (in'stəns) n. 1, an event that is one of many; a case; an example. 2, instigation; suggestion.

in'stant (in'stənt) n. 1, a small or infinitesimal interval of time; a moment. 2, the present time or moment. —adj. 1, immediate. 2, of present time, esp. of the present month. —**in·stan·ta'ne·ous** (-tā'nē-əs) adj. done in an instant.

in·stead' (in-sted') adv. in place (of another).

in'step' n. the arched upper surface of the human foot.

in'sti·gate" (in'sti-gāt") v.t. goad on, urge, or stimulate (a person); foment (an action). —**in"sti·ga'tion,** n. —**in'sti·ga"tor,** n.

in·still' (in-stil') v.t. 1, infuse slowly into the mind or feelings. 2, pour in by drops. —**in"stil·la'tion** (in"stə-lā'shən) n.

in'stinct (in'stinkt) n. 1, an inborn tendency to act or respond in a particular way. 2, aptitude. —**in·stinc'tive,** adj.

in'sti·tute" (in'sti-toot") v.t. set up; establish; appoint. —n. a corporate group, school, etc., devoted to scientific work, etc.

in"sti·tu'tion (in"sti-too'shən) n. 1, an organization for the promotion of a particular object; the building it occupies. 2, an established custom. 3, act or result of instituting. —**in"sti·tu'tion·al,** adj.

in·struct' (in-strukt') v.t. 1, give directions to; order; command. 2, train. 3, apprise.

in·struc'tion (in-struk'shən) n. 1, act or result of instructing; teaching. 2, an order; direction.

in·struc'tive (-tiv) adj. serving to teach. —**in·struc'tive·ness,** n.

in·struc'tor (-tər) n. a teacher; in colleges, one below professorial rank.

in'stru·ment (in'strə-mənt) n. 1, any mechanical device or contrivance; a tool, implement, or apparatus. 2, a contrivance for producing musical sounds. 3, a formal legal document. 4, an agent, agency, or means. —**in"stru·men'tal,** adj. —**in"stru·men·tal'i·ty,** n. agency. —**in"stru·men·ta'tion,** n. orchestration.

in"sub·or'di·nate (in"sə-bôr'də-nət) adj. disobedient; defiant. —**in"sub·or"di·na'tion,** n.

in'su·lar (in'sū-lər) adj. 1, pert. to an island; detached; hemmed in. 2, provincial; narrow-minded. —**in"su·lar'i·ty** (-lar'ə-tē) n.

in'su·late" (in'sə-lāt") v.t. 1, shield with material that isolates from heat, sound, electricity, etc. 2, isolate. —**in"su·la'tion,** n. —**in'su·la"tor,** n. that which insulates, esp. a nonconductor of electricity.

in'su·lin (in'sə-lin) n. a preparation from the pancreas of animals, used in treating diabetes.

in·sult' v.t. cause to take offense; affront. —n. (in'sult) an affront to self-respect.

in·su'per·a·ble (in-soo'pər-ə-bəl) adj. incapable of being surmounted or overcome. —**in·su"per·a·bil'i·ty,** n.

in·sur'a·ble (in-shûr'ə-bəl) adj. acceptable to an underwriter. —**in·sur'a·bil'i·ty,** n.

in·sur'ance (in-shûr'əns) n. 1, a contract whereby one party agrees to compensate another for loss through fire, death, etc. 2, the business of insuring or underwriting. 3, indemnity. 4, assurance.

in·sure' (in-shûr') v.t. 1, issue or obtain insurance on. 2, assure.

in·sur'gent (in-sēr'jənt) adj. revolting against established government; engaged in insurrection. —n. one who revolts. —**in·sur'gence,** n.

in"sur·rec'tion (in"sə-rek'shən) n. armed resistance to authority; a limited rebellion. —**in"sur·rec'tion·ar·y,** adj. —**in"sur·rec'tion·ist,** n.

in·tact' (in-takt') adj. remaining uninjured, unimpaired, whole, or complete. —**in·tact'ness,** n.

in·tagl'io (in-tāl'yō) n. 1, incised engraving. 2, the process of printing from engraved plates.

in·take" n. a taking or drawing in; consumption.

in·tan'gi·ble (in-tan'jə-bəl) adj. not able to be touched or grasped; vague. —**in·tan"gi·bil'i·ty,** n.

in'te·ger (in'tə-jər) n. a whole number, not fractional.

in'te·gral (in'tə-grəl) adj. 1, being an essential part of a whole; component; intrinsic. 2, being an integer; involving integers. 3, entire.

in'te·grate" (in'tə-grāt") v.t. form into a whole; bring together.

in·te·gra'tion (-grā'shən) n. act or effect of integrating; mixing of white persons and Negroes, as in schools.

in·teg'ri·ty (in-teg'rə-tē) n. 1, fidelity to moral principles; honesty. 2, soundness; completeness.

in·teg'u·ment (in-teg'yə-mənt) n. a natural covering, as skin, shell, rind, etc.

in'tel·lect' (in'tə-lekt") n. 1, the mind in its aspect of knowing and understanding (but not of feeling or willing). 2, mental capacity.

in"tel·lec'tu·al (in"tə-lek'choo-əl) adj. pert. to, perceived by, or appealing to the intellect. —n. an intelligent and informed person.

in·tel'li·gence (in-tel'i-jəns) n. 1, the power of knowing and understanding; mental capacity. 2, news; information, esp. secret information. 3, a staff of persons engaged in obtaining information. —**intelligence quotient**, a number representing a score made in an intelligence test.

in·tel'li·gent (in-tel'i-jənt) adj. 1, quick to understand. 2, marked by or indicating intelligence.

in·tel'li·gent'si·a (in-tel'i-jen'sē-ə) n. pl. the highly educated classes; the intellectuals.

in·tel'li·gi·ble (in-tel'ə-jə-bəl) adj. capable of being understood; comprehensible. —**in·tel'li·gi·bil'i·ty**, n.

in·tem'per·ate (in-tem'pər-ət) adj. 1, excessive; unrestrained; severe. —**in·tem'per·ance**, **in·tem'per·ate·ness**, n.

in·tend' v.t. have in mind as a purpose; plan to do, use, give, etc. —**in·tend'ed**, n. (Colloq.) fiancé.

in·tense' (in-tens') adj. 1, existing in high degree; strong; acute. 2, vehement; earnest; ardent. —**in·tense'ness**, n.

in·ten'si·fy'' (in-ten'si-fī'') v.t. & i. make or become intense or more intense. —**in·ten'si·fi·ca'tion**, n.

in·ten'si·ty (-sə-tē) n. condition or degree of intenseness.

in·ten'sive (-siv) adj. extreme; very acute. —n. (Gram.) something that emphasizes, as self in himself. —**in·ten'sive·ness**, n.

in·tent' n. intention; aim; plan. —adj. 1, firmly fixed or directed upon an object. 2, earnest; sedulous.

in·ten'tion (-shən) n. 1, the act of intending; something intended; purpose; aim. 2, (pl.) (Colloq.) design with respect to proposing marriage. —**in·ten'tion·al**, adj. done purposely.

in·ter' (in-tĕr') v.t. [in·terred', in·ter'ring] place in a grave or tomb; bury. —**in·ter'ment**, n.

in·ter- pref. between; among; together; mutually or reciprocally. [In addition to words defined in the text, the following words have the same sense as their root words, extended by the prefix to indicate interaction.]

in"ter·col·le'gi·ate	in"ter·o'ce·an'ic
in"ter·co·lo'ni·al	in"ter·play'
in"ter·com·mu'·ni·cate"	in"ter·plead'
	in"ter·ra'cial
in"ter·de·nom'i·na'tion·al	in"ter·scho·las'·tic
in"ter·de·pend'·ent	in"ter·trib'al
	in"ter·twine'
in"ter·mix'	in"ter·twist'
	in"ter·wo'ven

in"ter·act' (in"tər-akt') v.i. act on each other or one another. —**in"·ter·ac'tion**, n.

in"ter·cede' (in"tər-sēd') v.i. mediate between two contending parties.

in"ter·cept' (in"tər-sept') v.t. 1, interpose between. 2, seize in passage; cut off. —**in"ter·cep'tion**, n.

in"ter·ces'sion (in"tər-sesh'ən) n. 1, act of interceding. 2, a prayer for mercy. —**in"ter·ces"sor** (-ses"ər) n.

in"ter·change' (in"tər-chānj') v.t. 1, put each (of two things) in the place of the other. 2, transpose; exchange. 3, alternate; vary. —v.i. change reciprocally. —n. mutual exchange; alternate succession. —**in"ter·change'a·ble** (-ə-bəl) adj.

in"ter·com'' (in'tər-kom") n. a device for talking between rooms or offices of the same house or suite.

in"ter·course'' (in'tər-kôrs") n. communication between persons; exchange of ideas; conversation.

in"ter·dict'' (in'tər-dikt") v.t. forbid peremptorily; restrain by injunction; debar. —n. 1, a prohibitory order or decree. 2, (Rom. Cath.) denial of certain sacraments. —**in"·ter·dic'tion**, n.

in"ter·est (in'tər-ist) n. 1, a feeling of concern, curiosity, etc.; the object that arouses such feeling. 2, connection, esp. through investment, with a business. 3, benefit; advantage; profit. 4, (pl.) a group of persons or companies allied in business. 5, selfish consideration. 6, payment for the use of money: the rate or amount. —v.t. engage or excite the attention or curiosity of. —**in"ter·est·ing**, adj. attracting attention.

in"ter·fere' (in"tər-fir') v.i. 1, thrust oneself into the affairs of others; meddle. 2, collide; be obstructive. —**in"ter'fer'ence**, n.

in'ter·im (in'tər-im) n. an intervening time; the meantime. —adj. provisional; temporary.

in·te'ri·or (in-tir'ē-ər) adj. 1, being inside something; internal. 2, inland; domestic; indoor; mental. —n. the internal part; the inside, as of a room, country, etc.

in"ter·ject'' (in"tər-jekt") v.t. thrust between other things; insert; interpolate. —**in"ter·jec'tion**, n. 1, the act of interjecting. 2, an exclamatory utterance.

in"ter·lace'' (in"tər-lās") v.t. weave together; intersperse.

in"ter·lard'' (in"tər-lärd") v.t. mix or insert among other things; diversify.

in"ter·line'' (in"tər-līn") v.t. 1, insert between lines of writing. 2, furnish (a garment) with an extra lining. —**in"ter·lin'e·ar** (-lin'ē-ər) *adj.* between lines. —**in"ter·lin'ing**, *n.* an extra, inside lining.

in"ter·lock' (in"tər-lok') *v.t. & i.* fasten or become fastened together.

in"ter·lo·cu'tion (in"tər-lō-kū'shən) *n.* conversation; dialogue.

in"ter·loc'u·tor (in"tər-lok'yū-tər) *n.* one with whom one is conversing.

in"ter·loc'u·to·ry (in"tər-lok'yū-tôr-ē) **1**, of speech or conversation. **2**, interpolated. **3**, (of a legal ruling) not final.

in"ter·lope' (in"tər-lōp') *v.t.* intrude, as in a business, without right.

in'ter·lude" (in'tər-lood") *n.* **1**, an intervening time, period, or stage; an episode of such time. **2**, a short performance between acts.

in"ter·mar'ry (in"tər-mar'ē) *v.i.* marry within the limits of a family or group. —**in"ter·mar'riage**, *n.*

in"ter·me'di·ar·y (in"tər-mē'dē-er-ē) *adj.* **1**, intermediate. **2**, serving as an intermediary. —*n.* a mediator; messenger; go-between.

in"ter·me'di·ate (in"tər-mē'dē-ət) *adj.* situated between two extremes; coming between, in position or degree; intervening.

in"ter·mez'zo (in"tər-met'sō) *n.* [*pl.* -**zos** or -**zi** (-sē)] a musical composition played between the acts; an independent piece in similar style.

in·ter'mi·na·ble (in-tėr'mə-nə-bəl) *adj.* never ending; long drawn-out.

in"ter·min'gle (in"tər-ming'gəl) *v.t.* mix together; combine.

in"ter·mis'sion (in"tər-mish'ən) *n.* a period of temporary cessation; a pause or recess.

in"ter·mit'tent (in"tər-mit'ənt) *adj.* ceasing and recurring at intervals. —**in"ter·mit'tence**, *n.*

in·tern' (in-tėrn') *v.t.* confine within prescribed limits, esp. hold aliens, ships, etc. during a war. —**in·tern'ment**, *n.*

in·ter'nal (in-tėr'nəl) *adj.* **1**, situated within something; enclosed; inside. **2**, pert. to an inner part; domestic; subjective. **3**, (of a medicine, etc.) to be taken into the body. —**internal combustion**, power generated by an explosion inside a chamber, as in the cylinder of a gasoline engine.

in"ter·na'tion·al (in"tər-nash'ən-əl) *adj.* **1**, pert. to the relations between nations. **2**, involving more than one nation. —*n.* (*cap.*) any of several international federations of socialist or communistic groups.

in'terne" (in'tėrn") *n.* a doctor residing in a hospital for training.

in"ter·ne'cine (in"tər-nē'sin) *adj.* accompanied by mutual slaughter; extremely destructive.

in·tern'ist (in-tėrn'ist) *n.* a physician, internal medicine specialist.

in·ter'po·late" (in-tėr'pə-lāt") *v.t.* insert between other things; introduce (something new or extraneous). —**in·ter'po·la'tion**, *n.*

in"ter·pose' (in"tər-pōz') *v.t.* place between or among; interrupt with. —*v.i.* come between things or persons, as an obstacle or mediator. —**in"ter·po·si'tion** (-pə-zish'ən) *n.*

in·ter'pret (in-tėr'prit) *v.t.* **1**, show the meaning of; explain; elucidate; translate. **2**, construe in a particular way, as a part in a play. —**in·ter'pre·ta'tion**, *n.* —**in·ter'pre·ta'tive**, **in·ter'pre·tive**, *adj.*

in"ter·reg'num (in"tər-reg'nəm) *n.* an interval between one reign and the next; a breach of continuity.

in·ter'ro·gate" (in-ter'ə-gāt") *v.t. & i.* ask a question or questions (of). —**in·ter'ro·ga'tor**, *n.*

in·ter"ro·ga'tion (-gā'shən) *n.* **1**, a question or questioning. **2**, the symbol (?).

in"ter·rog'a·tive (in"tə-rog'ə-tiv) *adj.* asking a question. Also, **in"ter·rog'a·to·ry** (-tôr-ē).

in"ter·rupt' (in"tə-rupt') *v.t.* **1**, make a gap in; bring to a pause or stop. **2**, intrude upon the action or speech of. —**in"ter·rup'tion**, *n.*

in"ter·sect' (in"tər-sekt') *v.t. & i.* cut or divide; cross (one another).

in"ter·sec'tion (-sek'shən) *n.* **1**, the act of intersecting. **2**, a point where lines or roads meet.

in"ter·sperse" (in"tər-spėrs') *v.t.* **1**, scatter among other things. **2**, diversify by placing various things here and there.

in"ter·state" (in"tər-stāt') *adj.* between different states; in the U.S. concerning two or more states and so within Federal jurisdiction.

in·ter'stice (in-tėr'stis) *n.* [*pl.* **in·ter'sti·ces** (-siz)] an intervening space; a small narrow opening.

in"ter·ur'ban (in"tər-ėr'bən) *adj.* between cities. —*n.* a trolley car running between cities.

in'ter·val (in'tər-vəl) *n.* **1**, the time between two events. **2**, an intermission. **3**, the distance between two objects; a difference in degree, etc. **4**, an empty space; a gap.

in"ter·vene' (in"tər-vēn') *v.i.* **1**, happen between things, persons, or events. **2**, intercede; interfere. —**in"ter·ven'tion** (-ven'shən) *n.*

in"ter·view" (in'tər-vū') *n.* **1**, a meeting of persons face to face. **2**, a questioning; examination. —*v.t.* meet to question.

in·tes'tate (in-tes'tāt) *adj.* 1, having made no will. 2, not bequeathed. —*n.* one who dies without having made a will. —**in·tes'ta·cy,** *n.*

in·tes'tine (in-tes'tin) *n.* the lower part of the alimentary tract; the bowel. —**in·tes'tin·al,** *adj.*

in'ti·ma·cy (in'ti-mə-sē) *n.* 1, condition of being intimate. 2, an act evidencing close familiarity with a person.

in'ti·mate (in'tə-mət) *adj.* 1, close in personal relations; familiar; closely allied. 2, personal; private. 3, pert. to the inmost parts or essential nature. —*n.* a close friend. —*v.t.* (-māt") suggest; hint; imply. —**in"-ti·ma'tion,** *n.* suggestion; a hint.

in·tim'i·date" (in-tim'ə-dāt") *v.t.* make timid or fearful; overawe. —**in·tim"i·da'tion,** *n.*

in'to (in'too) *prep.* 1, to and in, implying motion. 2, (*Math.*) as a division of.

in·tol'er·a·ble (in-tol'ər-ə-bəl) *adj.* unbearable. —**in·tol"er·a·bil'i·ty, in·tol'er·a·ble·ness,** *n.*

in·tol'er·ant (in-tol'ər-ənt) *adj.* 1, angered by contrary opinions or beliefs. 2, unable to accept or bear. —**in·tol'er·ance,** *n.*

in"to·na'tion (in"tə-nā'shən) *n.* 1, a particular modulation of the voice. 2, the act of intoning.

in·tone' (in-tōn') *v.t. & i.* 1, utter in a singing voice; chant. 2, utter in a particular tone, esp. a monotone.

in·tox'i·cant (in-tok'si-kənt) *n.* that which intoxicates, esp. an alcoholic beverage.

in·tox'i·cate" (in-tok'si-kāt") *v.t.* 1, make drunk with liquor. 2, excite to elation, enthusiasm, etc. 3, poison. —*v.i.* cause intoxication. —**in·tox"i·ca'tion,** *n.*

in·tra- *pref.* within.

in"tra·mu'ral (in"trə-myûr'əl)*adj.* confined to, or within the walls or limits of, a school, city, etc.

in·tran'si·gent (in-tran'sə-jənt) *adj.* refusing to agree or compromise. —*n.* one who is uncompromising. —**in·tran'si·gence,** *n.*

in·tran'si·tive (in-tran'sə-tiv) *adj.* (*Gram.*) of a verb, not acting directly on an object, as *I laugh.*

in"tra·ve'nous (in"trə-vē'nəs) *adj.* within or into a vein.

in·trench' *v.t.* establish in a trench or similarly secure position. —**in·trench'ment,** *n.*

in·trep'id *adj.* undaunted; fearless. —**in"tre·pid'i·ty** (in"trə-pid'ə-tē) *n.*

in'tri·cate (in'tri-kət) *adj.* perplexingly tangled; complex. —**in'-tri·ca·cy** (-kə-sē) *n.*

in·trigue' (in-trēg') *v.t.* excite to interest or curiosity. —*v.i.* engage in underhand plotting. —*n.* a clandestine plot or love affair; plotting.

in·trin'sic (in-trin'zik) *adj.* being an innate or essential part; inherent. —**in·trin'si·cal·ly,** *adv.*

in"tro·duce' (in"trə-dūs') *v.t.* 1, bring into notice, use, or practice. 2, begin; provide with a preface. 3, present (a person) to another or to society. 4, lead (a person) to a particular experience. 5, put in; insert.

in"tro·duc'tion (in"trə-duk'shən) *n.* 1, act or result of introducing. 2, that which introduces, as a preface. —**in"tro·duc'to·ry** (-tə-rē) *adj.*

in"tro·spec'tion (in"trə-spek'-shən) *n.* observation of one's own mental state.

in"tro·spec'tive (-tiv) *adj.* observing or tending to think about one's thoughts, feelings, etc.

in"tro·vert" (in'trə-vērt") *n.* a person chiefly concerned with his own thoughts. —*v.t.* turn inward. —**in"tro·ver'sion** (-zhən) *n.*

in·trude' (in-trood') *v.t.* thrust in forcibly. —*v.i.* thrust oneself in, esp. without warrant or welcome.

in·tru'sion (in-troo'zhən) *n.* 1, act or result of intruding. 2, an unwelcome visit or entrance.

in·tru'sive (in-troo'siv) *adj.* intruding; being an intrusion. —**in·tru'sive·ness,** *n.*

in·trust' *v.t.* entrust.

in"tu·i'tion (in"too-ish'ən) *n.* comprehension without effort of reasoning; instinctive knowledge. —**in·tu'i·tive** (in-too'ə-tiv) *adj.*

in"un·date' (in'un-dāte") *v.t.* flood; deluge. —**in"un·da'tion,** *n.*

in·ure' (in-yûr') *v.t.* deaden the sensibility of. —*v.i.* (*Law*) pass (to); serve. —**in·ure'ment,** *n.*

in·vade' (in-vād') *v.t.* 1, enter as an enemy; penetrate; raid. 2, intrude upon; encroach upon.

in'va·lid (in'və-lid) *n.* a sick or disabled person. —*adj.* infirm; sickly.

in·val'id *adj.* not valid; without force.

in·val'i·date" (in-val'i-dāt") *v.t.* remove validity from; annul. —**in·val"i·da'tion,** *n.*

in·val'u·a·ble (in-val'ū-ə-bəl) *adj.* of immeasurably great value. —**in·val'u·a·ble·ness,** *n.*

in·va'sion (in-vā'zhən) *n.* act or result of invading.

in·vec'tive (in-vek'tiv) *n.* vehement denunciation or vituperation. —*adj.* censorious; abusive.

in·veigh' (in-vā') *v.i.* make a verbal attack.

in·vei'gle (in-vā'gəl) *v.t.* lead astray artfully; entice. —**in·vei'gle·ment**, *n.*

in·vent' *v.t.* 1, be first to devise; originate. 2, fabricate, as a story. —*v.i.* create something new. —**in·ven'tor**, *n.*

in·ven'tion (in-ven'shən) *n.* 1, act of inventing. 2, something invented; an original creation. 3, a lie.

in·ven'tive (in-ven'tiv) *adj.* apt at inventing; creative. —**in·ven'tive·ness**, *n.*

in'ven·to·ry (in'vən-tôr-ē) *n.* 1, a descriptive list of articles; a catalog of contents, stock, etc. 2, the value of a stock of goods. —*v.t.* list; catalog.

in·verse' (in-vèrs') *adj.* 1, opposite or contrary in meaning, sense, application, etc. 2, reversed in position or direction; inverted. —*n.* that which is inverse.

in·ver'sion (in-vèr'zhən) *n.* 1, reversal; transposition. 2, alteration of the natural order of words.

in·vert' (in-vèrt') *v.t.* reverse in position or condition; turn over; transpose; reverse in meaning, application, tendency, etc. —*n.* (in'vert) the opposite or contrary thing.

in·vest' *v.t.* 1, put (money) to profitable use. 2, install; endow. 3, dress. 4, hem in; besiege. —*v.i.* invest money.

in·ves'ti·gate" (in-ves'ti-gāt") *v.t. & i.* examine in detail; inquire into. —**in·ves"ti·ga'tion**, *n.* —**in·ves'ti·ga"tor**, *n.*

in·ves'ti·ture (in-ves'ti-chər) *n.* 1, act or effect of installing in office. 2, a robe or token of office.

in·vest'ment (-mənt) *n.* act or result of investing; money invested.

in·vet'er·ate (in-vet'ər-ət) *adj.* firmly established or addicted by habit, custom, or usage. —**in·vet'er·a·cy**, *n.*

in·vid'i·ous (in-vid'ē-əs) *adj.* 1, prompted by envy or ill will. 2, unfair; odious. —**in·vid'i·ous·ness**, *n.*

in·vig'or·ate" (in-vig'ə-rāt") *v.t.* strengthen; animate. —**in·vig"or·a'tion**, *n.*

in·vin'ci·ble (in-vin'sə-bəl) *adj.* unconquerable. —**in·vin"ci·bil'i·ty**, **in·vin'ci·ble·ness**, *n.*

in·vi'o·la·ble (in-vī'ə-lə-bəl) *adj.* not to be violated; invulnerable. —**in·vi"o·la·bil'i·ty**, *n.*

in·vi'o·late (in-vī'ə-lət) *adj.* 1, not desecrated, infringed, or impaired. 2, not to be violated.

in"vi·ta'tion (in"vi-tā'shən) *n.* 1, act of inviting. 2, a request to be present; an allurement.

in·vite' (in-vīt') *v.t.* 1, ask (a person) to come; request the presence of. 2, solicit, allure, tempt, etc. 3, lay oneself open to. —*n.* (in'vīt) (*Slang*) an invitation.

in"vo·ca'tion (in"vō-kā'shən) *n.* 1, act of invoking. 2, a prayer.

in'voice (in'vois) *n.* a list of items shipped; a bill for them. —*v.t.* list and bill for.

in·voke' (in-vōk') *v.t.* 1, call on for aid or protection, esp. as addressing a deity. 2, call for; utilize, as a law.

in·vol'un·tar"y (in-vol'ən-ter"ē) *adj.* 1, not willed or intentional. 2, done unwillingly. —**in·vol'un·tar"i·ness**, *n.*

in'vo·lute" (in'və-loot") *adj.* rolled inward; involved; intricate. —**in"vo·lu'tion**, *n.* something involute.

in·volve' (in-volv') *v.t.* 1, contain or include; entail; imply. 2, affect or be affected by. 3, combine inextricably; implicate. 4, make intricate or complex. —**in·volve'ment**, *n.*

in'ward (in'wərd) *adv.* [also, in'wards] toward the inside or center; in the mind or soul. —*adj.* 1, being within; directed toward the inside or center. 2, pert. to inner parts; in the mind. —**in'ward·ness**, *n.*

i'o·dine" (ī'ə-dīn") *n.* 1, a nonmetallic chemical element, used medicinally, no. 53, symbol I. 2, an antiseptic solution: *tincture of iodine.*

i'on (ī'ən) *n.* an atom or molecule bearing an electric charge.

i·o'ni·um (ī-ō'nē-əm) *n.* a radioactive chemical element, no. 90, symbol Io.

i·on'o·sphere" (ī-on'ə-sfīr") *n.* the outer regions of the earth's atmosphere, from about 60 miles outward.

i·o'ta (ī-ō'tə) *n.* 1, the ninth letter of the Greek alphabet (I, ι). 2, a small quantity.

I O U *n.* a written acknowledgment of a debt (= I owe you).

ip'e·cac" (ip'ə-kak") *n.* a So. Amer. shrub; an emetic drug made from it.

I.Q. (ī'kū') *n.* intelligence quotient.

ir- *pref.* not (the equivalent of in-, used before an initial r). [In addition to words defined in the text, the following words formed by prefixing ir- (= not) have merely the negative sense of the positive term.]

ir·ra'tion·al	ir"re·duc'i·ble
ir"re·claim'a·ble	ir·ref'u·ta·ble
ir·rec'on·cil'a·ble	ir·rel'e·vant
ir"re·cov'er·a·ble	ir"re·me'di·a·ble
ir"re·deem'a·ble	ir"re·mov'a·ble
	ir·rep'a·ra·ble
	ir"re·place'a·ble
	ir"re·press'i·ble

ir"re·proach'a·   ir"re·triev'a·ble
ble   ir"re·ver'ent
ir"re·sist'i·ble   ir"re·vers'i·ble
ir·res'o·lute"   ir"re·vo·ca·ble

i·ras'ci·ble (i-ras'ə-bəl) *adj.* easily provoked to anger; hot-tempered. —i·ras"ci·bil'i·ty, *n.*

i'rate (ī'rāt) *adj.* angry; incensed.

ire (īr) *n.* anger; resentment.

i·ren'ic (ī-ren'ik) *adj.* tending to promote peace. —i·ren'i·cal·ly, *adv.*

ir"i·des'cent (ir"ə-des'ənt) *adj.* glittering with changeable colors, like a rainbow. —ir"i·des'cence, *n.*

i·rid'i·um (i-rid'ē-əm) *n.* a metallic chemical element, similar to platinum, no. 77, symbol Ir.

i'ris (ī'ris) *n.* 1, the colored diaphragm of the eye surrounding the pupil. 2, any of various flowering plants. 3, the rainbow, or a similar iridescence.

I'rish (ī'rish) *adj.* pert. to Ireland, its people, customs, etc. —*n.* the Gaelic language; Erse. — I'rish·man, *n.*

irk (ėrk) *v.t.* annoy; bore. —irk'some, *adj.* boring; annoying. —irk'some·ness, *n.*

Iris

i'ron (ī'ərn) *n.* 1, a metallic chemical element, no. 26, symbol Fe; this metal, widely fabricated. 2, a tool; implement, utensil, weapon, etc. of this metal; a harpoon; (*Slang*) a gun; (*pl.*) shackles; an implement for pressing clothes; a type of golf club. 3, something hard, unyielding, etc. 4, a tonic containing iron. —*adj.* 1, made of iron. 2, like iron; hard; enduring, steadfast, etc. —*v.t. & i.* press (clothes, etc.) —iron lung, a chamber in which a paralyzed person is placed to enable him to breathe.

i'ron·clad" *adj.* 1, armored, as a warship. 2, unassailable; unbreakable, as an agreement.

i·ron'ic (ī-ron'ik) *adj.* 1, being irony; sarcastic. 2, frustrating. Also, i·ron'i·cal.

i'ro·ny (ī'rə·nē) *n.* 1, a figure of speech: emphasis by stating the opposite; covert sarcasm. 2, the frustration of hopes.

ir·ra'di·ate (i-rā'dē-āt") *v.t.* 1, throw rays of light upon. 2, make clear. —*v.i.* emit rays or radiant energy. —ir·ra'di·a'tion, *n.*

ir·reg'u·lar (i-reg'yə-lər) *adj.* 1, not regular. 2, against the rules. —ir·reg"u·lar'i·ty (-lar'ə-tē) *n.*

ir"re·li'gious (ir"i-lij'əs) *adj.* 1, not devout; 2, profane. —ir"re·li'gious·ness, *n.*

ir"re·spec'tive (ir"i-spek'tiv) *adj.* regardless of; independent of.

ir"re·spon'si·ble (ir"i-spon'sə-bəl) *adj.* 1, having no sense of responsibility; not trustworthy. 2, not accountable, as for one's own actions. —ir"re·spon"si·bil'i·ty, *n.*

ir'ri·gate" (ir'ə-gāt") *v.t.* 1, supply (land) with water through artificial channels. 2, wash with a flow of liquid, as a wound. —ir"ri·ga'tion, *n.*

ir'ri·ta·ble (ir'ə-tə-bəl) *adj.* irascible. —ir"ri·ta·bil'i·ty, *n.*

ir'ri·tant (ir'ə-tənt) *n. & adj.* something that irritates.

ir'ri·tate" (ir'ə-tāt") *v.t.* 1, excite to resentment or anger; vex; annoy. 2, make sore or painful; chafe. —ir"ri·ta'tion, *n.*

ir·rup'tion (i-rup'shən) *n.* a bursting in; a sudden invasion. —ir·rup'tive, *adj.*

is (iz) *v.* 3rd. pers. sing. pres. indicative of *be.*

-ise *suf.* same as -ize.

-ish *suf.* having some characteristics of.

i'sin·glass" (ī'zing-glås") *n.* 1, a form of translucent gelatin. 2, mica.

Is'lam (is'ləm) *n.* the Mohammedan religion; its followers and realm.

is'land (ī'lənd) *n.* 1, a body of land entirely surrounded by water. 2, something isolated or surrounded.

isle (īl) *n.* a small island. Also, is'let (ī'lət).

-ism (iz-əm) *suf.* of nouns implying practice, system, doctrine, theory, or principle.

i'so- (ī'sō) *pref.* 1, equal. 2, (*Chem.*) isomeric.

i'so·bar" (ī'sə-bär") *n.* a line connecting, on a map, all places where the barometric pressure is the same.

i'so·late" (ī'sə-lāt") *v.t.* 1, place apart; make separate. 2, single out; rid of extraneous matter.

i"so·la'tion (ī'sə-lā'shən) *n.* 1, the act of isolating; the state of being isolated. 2, a national policy of nonparticipation in international affairs. —i"so·la'tion·ism, *n.* pursuit or support of this policy. —i"so·la'tion·ist, *n.*

i'so·mer (ī'sə-mər) *n.* a chemical compound of the same composition (as another) but in different arrangement. —i"so·mer'ic (-mer'ik) *adj.*

i"so·met'ric (ī"sə-met'rik) *adj.* of equal measure; regularly spaced.

i·sos'ce·les" (ī-sos'ə-lēz") *adj.* (of a triangle) having two equal sides.

i'so·therm" (ī'sə-thėrm") *n.* a line connecting all places that have the same mean temperature. —i"so·ther'mal, *adj.*

i'so·tope" (ī'sə-tōp") n. a chemical element, nearly identical (with another or others) but differing in atomic weight.

Is·ra'el·i (iz·rā'ə·lē) adj. & n. pert. to the modern country of Israel.

is'sue (ish'oo) n. 1, the act of sending out; publication; emission. 2, what is sent out, esp. a quantity issued at one time. 3, an outflow; product, result, outcome, etc.; offspring or progeny. 4, a point in question or dispute; a principal question. —v.t. 1, send out; publish; promulgate; distribute. 2, emit; discharge. —v.i. 1, go or come out; flow out; emerge. 2, arise as a result or yield. —**is'su·ance,** n.

-ist suf. of nouns denoting a supporter or adherent (of a doctrine, etc.), as capitalist; a practitioner or expert, as strategist; a performer on a named instrument, as violinist.

isth'mus (is'məs) n. a narrow strip of land connecting two larger bodies.

it pron. [poss. **its**] 1, a personal pron., third person sing., neuter gender. 2, a pron. of indefinite sense, as in What is it? 3, a particle used for grammatical completeness in certain idiomatic constructions, as It is ten o'clock. Let us call it a day. —n. (Colloq.) 1, a person who is the center of attention, or (esp. in children's games) solely given an onerous duty. 2, (Slang) attractiveness to the opposite sex. —**it's** (its) contraction it is.

I·tal'ian (i·tal'yən) adj. & n. pert. to Italy or its inhabitants or language.

i·tal'ic (i·tal'ik) n. & adj. a style of type with sloped letters, thus: italic. —**i·tal'i·cize"** (-sīz") v.t.

itch (ich) v.i. 1, feel or produce an inclination to scratch an affected part. 2, desire eagerly. —n. 1, tingling sensation in the skin. 2, an itching skin disease; scabies. 3, a persistent desire. —**itch'y,** adj.

-ite (-īt) suf. 1, denoting a supporter, follower, associate, or inhabitant. 2, denoting certain kinds of minerals, chemical compounds, etc.

i'tem (ī'təm) n. 1, one article of a collection, list, enumeration, etc. 2, a separate article, particular, or piece, as in a newspaper.

i'tem·ize" (ī'tə·mīz") v.t. make a particularized list of.

it'er·ate" (it'ə·rāt") v.t. utter or say again or repeatedly. —**it"er·a'tion,** n. —**it'er·a·tive,** adj.

i·tin'er·ant (ī·tin'ə·rənt) adj. traveling from place to place. —n. a traveler. —**i·tin'er·an·cy,** n.

i·tin'er·ar·y (ī·tin'ə·rər·ē) n. a plan of travel, esp. a proposed route.

it·self' pron. reflexive or emphatic form of it.

i'vo·ry (ī'və·rē) n. 1, the bony substance of a tusk, esp. of an elephant. 2, (Slang) a tooth; (pl.) piano keys; (pl.) dice. 3, the color of ivory, creamy white. —**ivory tower,** a dream world.

i'vy (ī'vē) n. any of several climbing or trailing plants.

-ize (īz) suf. forming verbs denoting application of the action denoted by the root, as emphasize, make emphatic.

iz'zard (iz'ərd) n. (Colloq.) z.

J

J, j (jā) the tenth letter of the English alphabet.

jab v.t. & i. [jabbed, jab'bing] strike suddenly and sharply; prod; poke. —n. a sharp thrust.

jab'ber (jab'ər) v.t. & t. talk rapidly in an incoherent way.

ja·bot' (zha·bō') n. a frill or ruffle in a bosom of a shirt.

jack (jak) n. 1, a mechanical contrivance for lifting. 2, one of the face cards in a pack of playing cards; knave. 3, a small flag. 4, jackass; jackrabbit; jackdaw; any of several fishes, as the pike. 5, a fellow. 6, (Slang) money. —v.t. (usually with up) hoist; raise.

jack'al (jak'âl) n. a wild dog of Asia and Africa.

jack'ass" (-as") n. 1, a male donkey. 2, a stupid or foolish person.

jack'daw" (-dâ") n. 1, a Europ. crow. 2, an Amer. grackle.

Jackal

jack'et (jak'it) n. 1, a tailless coat. 2, any outer covering, as a protective wrapper on a book.

jack'knife" (jak'nīf") n. a large folding pocket knife.

jack pine a tree found in northern U. S. and Canada.

jack'pot" n. an unusually large prize.

jack'rab"bit n. a large hare.

Jac"o·be'an (jak"ə·bē'ən) adj. pert. to or contemporary with James I of England.

Jac'o·bite (jak'ə·bīt) n. supporter of James II of England or the Stuart dynasty.

jade (jād) n. 1, a green mineral prized for jewelry. 2, a shade of green. 3, a dissolute woman. 4, an inferior or worn-out horse. —*v.t.* & *i.* make or become exhausted by overwork.

jae′ger (yā′gər) *n.* 1, a predatory bird, the skua. 2, a hunter. 3, (*pl.*) (jā′gərz) long underwear.

jag *n.* 1, a sharp notch or tooth. 2, (*Slang*) alcoholic intoxication.

jag′ged (jag′id) *adj.* having sharp projections; irregular.

jag′uar (jag′wär) *n.* a large, ferocious cat of Central and So. Amer.

jai a·lai′ (hī ä-lī′) a game resembling squash but played with basketlike rackets.

jail (jāl) *n.* a place of detention for convicted criminals or persons awaiting trial. —*v.t.* put in a jail. —jail′er, *n.* an officer of a jail.

ja·lop′y (jə-lop′ē) *n.* (*Colloq.*) a decrepit automobile.

jam *v.t.* [jammed, jam′ming] 1, thrust or squeeze in so as to stick fast; crowd so as to hinder motion or extrication. 2, interfere with a radio broadcast) by another on the same frequency. —*v.i.* 1, become wedged in place. 2, (*Slang*) enliven music or dancing by improvisations. —*n.* 1, an obstruction. 2, a fruit preserve. 3, (*Slang*) a predicament.

jamb (jam) *n.* a vertical side member in the frame of a door or window.

jam″bo·ree′ (jam″bə-rē′) *n.* (*Slang*) a festive gathering.

jan′gle (jang′gəl) *v.i.* & *t.* make a harsh or metallic sound.

jan′i·tor (jan′ə-tər) *n.* the caretaker of a building. —jan′i·tress, *n.*

Jan′u·ar′y (jan′yū-er′ē) *n.* the first month of the year.

ja·pan′ (jə-pan′) *n.* a varnish that gives a hard, glossy finish.

Jap′a·nese′ (jap′ə-nēz′) *adj.* pert. to Japan. —*n.* 1, the language of Japan. 2, (-nēs′) one descended from the people of Japan.

ja·pon′i·ca (jə-pon′ə-kə) *n.* a shrub with scarlet flowers and yellow fruit; the Japanese quince.

jar (jär) *v.t.* & *i.* [jarred, jar′ring] 1, jolt suddenly; rattle; make a harsh sound. 2, affect unpleasantly; annoy or disconcert. —*n.* 1, a harsh impact; a shock. 2, a wide-mouthed vessel.

jar′di·nière′ (jär′də-nir′) *n.* an ornamental flowerpot.

jar′gon (jär′gən) *n.* 1, confused or meaningless talk. 2, language peculiar to a group or profession; cant.

jas′mine (jas′min) *n.* any of several shrubs bearing fragrant yellow or red flowers.

jas′per (jas′pər) *n.* a variety of quartz used for making ornaments.

jaun′dice (jân′dis) *n.* a disease that causes a yellowish tinge in the skin. —jaun′diced (-dist) *adj.* adversely biased.

jaunt (jânt) *n.* a short trip, made for pleasure.

jaun′ty (jân′tē) *adj.* 1, sprightly. 2, smart in appearance. —jaun′ti·ness, *n.*

jave′lin (jav′lin) *n.* a spear made to be thrown by hand.

jaw (jâ) *n.* 1, either of the two bony structures that form the mouth. 2, anything likened to a jaw, for holding or seizing. —*v.i.* (*Slang*) talk; chatter; scold.

jaw′break″er (jâ′brā″kər) *n.* (*Colloq.*) 1, any word hard to pronounce. 2, a hard candy.

jay (jā) *n.* any of several common birds, as *blue jay*.

jay′walk″ (jā′wâk″) *v.i.* (*Colloq.*) cross a street against a traffic light, or between regular crossings.

jazz (jaz) *n.* dance music in a certain syncopated style. —*v.t.* (*Slang*) (usually with *up*) enliven.

jeal′ous (jel′əs) *adj.* 1, feeling or actuated by envy or resentment, as of a more successful rival. 2, proceeding from distrust. 3, intolerant of rivalry. —jeal′ous·y, *n.*

jean (jēn) *n.* 1, a twilled cotton fabric. 2, (*pl.*) trousers or overalls of jean.

jeep (jēp) *n.* a small all-purpose military automobile.

jeer (jir) *v.i.* & *t.* scoff at; deride; mock. —*n.* gibe; taunt.

Je·ho′vah (jē-hō′və) *n.* the name of God in the Old Testament.

je′hu (jē′hū) *n.* a reckless driver of a cart or car.

je·june′ (ji-joon′) *adj.* deficient in sense, substance, or taste.

jell (jel) *v.i.* 1, coagulate; become jelly. 2, achieve a planned stage or form.

jel′ly (jel′ē) *n.* 1, a semisolid food made by congealing fruit syrup or meat juice. 2, any preparation of a soft, gelatinous consistency.

jel′ly·fish″ (jel′ē-fish″) *n.* a marine invertebrate with a soft umbrella-shaped body, often with long tentacles.

jen′ny (jen′ē) *n.* 1, a type of spinning machine. 2, the female of some species, as the ass. 3, an airplane used for training fliers.

jeop′ard·y (jep′ər-dē) *n.* risk; danger. —jeop′ard·ize″, *v.t.* imperil.

jer″e·mi′ad (jer″ə-mī′ad) n. discourse of a lugubrious or complaining character.

jerk (jėrk) v.i. & t. pull suddenly; tug or twist. —n. 1, a sudden start or thrust. 2, (Slang) an inexpert or unsophisticated person.

jer′kin (jėr′kin) n. a sleeveless jacket.

jerk′wa″ter (jėrk′wä″tėr) adj. (Colloq.) located away from a main line; provincial.

jerk′y (jėr′kē) adj. tending to jerk; spasmodic. —jerk′i·ness, n.

jer′sey (jėr′zē) n. 1, a close-knitted fabric. 2, a knitted shirt or jacket. 3, (cap.) a breed of dairy cattle.

jest (jest) v.t. speak facetiously, playfully, or derisively. —n. a joke. —jest′er, n. a person retained to amuse a king; fool.

Jes′u·it (jezh′ū-it) n. a member of the Society of Jesus, a Roman Catholic religious order.

jet n. 1, a gush of fluid from a spout. 2, a spout. 3, a black coal used in making ornaments. 4, glossy black. —v.i. & t. [jet′ted, -ting] spurt; emit. —adj. black. —jet propulsion, propelling force exerted (on aircraft or rockets) by exhaust of gases from burning.

jet′sam (jet′səm) n. goods thrown overboard to lighten a ship.

jet′ti·son (jet′ə-sən) v.t. throw goods overboard, to lighten a ship.

jet′ty (jet′ē) n. 1, a pier built in water to deflect currents or shelter an anchorage. 2, a landing wharf.

Jew (joo) n. a descendant of the Hebrew people or follower of their religion; an Israelite. —Jew′ish, adj.

jew′el (joo′əl) n. 1, a gem; a precious stone, cut and polished, for adornment or for uses requiring great durability, as in the bearings of a watch. 2, anything valuable. —jew′el·er, n. a seller of jewelry.

jew′el·ry (-rē) n. gems and precious metals made into ornaments.

Jew′ry (joo′rē) n. 1, Jews collectively. 2, a ghetto.

jew′s-′harp″ (jooz′härp″) n. a metal reed in a round frame that is plucked and caused to sound different tones by movements of the mouth.

Jew's-harp

jib n. 1, a triangular sail set foreward of a mast. 2, a projecting arm, as in a gibbet or derrick.

jibe (jīb) v.i. 1, shift abruptly from one side to the other, as the boom of a sail. 2, (Colloq.) agree with; be in harmony with. —n. gibe.

jif′fy (jif′ē) n. (Colloq.) a moment.

jig n. 1, a tool for holding or guiding, as on a drill or lathe. 2, a lively dance in triple time. —v.i. & t. [jigged, jig′ging] dance or play a jig; jump about.

jig′ger (jig′ėr) n. 1, a mast or sail near the stern, as on a yawl. 2, a mechanical device that operates with a jerky motion, as a tripper. 3, a 1½-oz. measure.

jig′gle (jig′əl) v.i. & t. move to and fro in quick, jerky motion. —n. act of jiggling; a jiggling motion.

jig′saw″ n. a saw designed to cut designs in wood. —jigsaw puzzle, a picture cut into many pieces to be fitted together.

jilt v.t. dismiss (a sweetheart).

Jim Crow segregation of Negroes.

jim′my (jim′ē) n. a small prying tool used by burglars. —v.t. pry open.

jim′son weed (jim′sən) a noxious weed with white flowers; datura.

jin′gle (jing′gəl) v.i. & t. make tinkling sounds. —n. 1, a metallic clinking sound. 2, verse constructed more for sound than sense.

jin′go (jing′gō) n. one who favors lavish armament or a bellicose foreign policy. —jin′go·ism, n.

jinks n. pl. (Colloq.) pranks; lively merrymaking; usually high jinks.

Jinrikisha

jin·rik′i·sha (jin-rik′shä) n. a two-wheeled vehicle pulled by a man.

jinx (jinks) n. (Colloq.) a supposed influence for bad luck.

jit′ney (jit′nē) n. (Colloq.) 1, a public cab. 2, (Slang) a U. S. nickel.

jit′ter (jit′ėr) v.i. show nervousness or apprehension. —n. nervousness. —jit′ter·y, adj. very nervous.

jit′ter·bug″ v.i. [-bugged″, -bug″ging] dance to swing music with violent convulsive movements. —n. one who so dances.

jive (jīv) n. a patois of certain U.S. Negroes, used by jazz musicians.

job n. **1,** one's profession, trade or employment. **2,** a specific task or stint of work. **3,** (*Colloq.*) matter; state of affairs. —v.t. [jobbed, job'bing] do work by the piece. —v.t. **1,** portion out work. **2,** buy or sell in large or odd quantities, for resale to retailers. —job'ber, n. a wholesaler. —job'ber·y, n. corruption in a position of trust.

jock'ey (jok'ē) v.t. & i. **1,** bring about by skillful maneuvering. **2,** obtain advantage by trickery. —n. a professional rider of race horses. —disk jockey, a radio announcer on a program of recorded music.

jock'strap' (jok'strap') n. a supporter worn by male athletes.

jo·cose' (jō-kōs') adj. facetious; humorous. —jo·cos'i·ty (-kos'ə-tē) n.

joc'u·lar (jok'yə-lər) adj. playful; joking. —joc'u·lar'i·ty (-lar'ə-tē) n.

joc'und (jok'ənd) adj. cheerful; merry. —jo·cun'di·ty (jō-kun'də-tē) n.

jodh'purs (jod'pərz) n.pl. riding breeches, close-fitting below the knee.

Joe (jō) n. (*Colloq.*) a fellow.

jog v.t. [jogged, jog'ging] push slightly; nudge. —v.t. **1,** move with a jolting motion. **2,** (with *on* or *along*) proceed steadily or unevenfully. —n. **1,** a poke; nudge. **2,** a projection; an irregularity of surface. **3,** a notch.

jog'gle (jog'əl) v.i. & t. move joltingly; jiggle.

John Doe (*Law*) a defendant or prisoner whose name is not known.

join v.t. & i. **1,** put together; combine. **2,** unite with; become a member of. **3,** connect.

join'er (-ər) n. **1,** one who joins. **2,** woodworker; carpenter.

joint n. **1,** a place where two things come together and are united; a seam; a hinge. **2,** a large cut of meat. **3,** (*Slang*) a disreputable place. —adj. **1,** joined in relation or interest, as *joint* owners. **2,** shared by different individuals.

join'ture (join'chər) n. (*Law*) an estate settled before marriage.

joist n. one of the horizontal timbers to which are fastened the boards of a floor or laths of a ceiling.

joke (jōk) n. something said or done to excite laughter; a jest. —v.t. say or do something playful; jest.

jok'er (jō'kər) n. **1,** one who jokes. **2,** an extra card in a pack of playing cards. **3,** a clause in a document that weakens its intended effect.

jol'ly (jol'ē) adj. gaily cheerful; full of merriment. —jol'li·ty (-ə-tē) n.

jolt (jōlt) v.t. & i. shake with sudden jerks; move with a jerking motion. —n. a sudden jerk.

Jo'nah (jō'nə) n. one reputed to bring bad luck.

jon'quil (jong'kwil) n. a plant with pale yellow flowers.

jo'rum (jôr'əm) n. a large bowl for mixing liquors.

josh v.t. & i. (*Slang*) tease or chaff good-naturedly.

jos'tle (jos'əl) v.t. push against; bump so as to render unsteady. —v.i. shove and be shoved about, as in a crowd.

jot n. a very small quantity. —v.t. [jot'ted, -ting] (usually with *down*) make a written memorandum of.

joule (jowl) n. a unit of work, equal to 10,000,000 ergs.

jounce (jowns) v.i. & t. shake up and down violently; bounce.

jour'nal (jẽr'nal) n. **1,** a record of daily transactions or events. **2,** a book for keeping such records. **3,** a newspaper or magazine.

jour'nal·ism (jẽr'nə-liz-əm) n. newspaper or magazine writing. —jour'nal·ist, n. —jour'nal·is'tic, adj. —jour'nal·is'ti·cal·ly, adv.

jour'ney (jẽr'nē) n. a trip from one place to another. —v.i. travel.

jour'ney·man (-mən) n. [pl. -men] a trained worker at a skilled trade.

joust (jowst) n. a combat between armored knights with lances.

Jove (jōv) n. Jupiter, supreme god of the Romans. —Jo'vi·an, adj.

jo'vi·al (jō'vē-əl) adj. cheerful; gay; jolly. —jo'vi·al'i·ty (-al'ə-tē) n.

jowl (jowl) n. **1,** the cheek. **2,** a fold of flesh hanging from the jaw.

joy (joi) n. an emotion of sudden pleasure; exultant satisfaction; keen delight. —joy'ful, joy'ous, adj.

joy stick the lever that controls the directions of an airplane's flight.

ju'bi·lant (joo'bə-lənt) adj. triumphantly glad; exultant.

ju'bi·la'tion (joo'bə-lā'shən) n. rejoicing; glee.

ju'bi·lee' (joo'bə-lē') n. **1,** a special occasion or manifestation of joyousness. **2,** fiftieth anniversary.

Ju'da·ism (joo'də-iz-əm) n. the religion of Jews, or adherence to it.

judge (juj) v.t. **1,** hear and determine authoritatively, as a controversy. **2,** hold as an opinion; deem; consider. —v.i. **1,** pass judgment on a cause. **2,** make a critical determination; estimate the value or magnitude of anything. —n. **1,** a public officer empowered to administer justice; a magistrate. **2,** an arbiter; one qualified to judge.

tub, cūte, pull; label; oil, owl; go, chip, she, thin, *t*hen, sing, ink; *see p. 6*

judg'ment (juj'mənt) *n.* **1,** the act of judging. **2,** the ability to make accurate determinations; discernment. **3,** a decision, award, or sentence, as of a court of law.

ju'di·ca·ture (joo'də-kə-chər) *n.* **1,** the administration of justice. **2,** the whole body of judges and courts. **3,** the jurisdiction of a court.

ju·di'cial (joo-dish'əl) *adj.* pert. to a judge, to a court of law, or to the administration of justice.

ju·di'ci·a·ry (joo-dish'ē-er-ē) *n.* judges collectively. —*adj.* pert. to court judges.

ju·di'cious (joo-dish'əs) *adj.* having or exercising sound judgment; prudent. —ju·di'cious·ness, *n.*

ju'do (joo'dō) *n.* a system of exercise and personal defense.

jug *n.* **1,** a vessel for holding liquids; pitcher. **2,** (*Slang*) a jail.

ju'gal (joo'gəl) *adj.* pert. to the cheekbone.

jug'ger·naut" (jug'ər-nât") *n.* an irresistible force.

jug'gle (jug'əl) *v.i.* **1,** perform feats of dexterity or legerdemain. **2,** practice artifice or imposture. —*v.t.* manipulate by trickery.

jug'gler (jug'lər) *n.* a performer of tricks of dexterity, as tossing and keeping balls in the air. —jug'gler·y, *n.*

jug'u·lar (jug'yə-lər) *adj.* pert. to the neck, or to one of the large veins in the neck.

juice (joos) *n.* **1,** the watery part of vegetables, esp. of fruits. **2,** the fluid part of an animal body or substance. **3,** (*Slang*) motor fuel. **4,** (*Slang*) electric current.

juic'y (joo'sē) *adj.* **1,** full of juice. **2,** interesting; pithy. —juic'i·ness, *n.*

ju·jit'su (joo-jit'soo) *n.* a Japanese method of wrestling.

juke box (jook) (*Slang*) a coin-activated phonograph.

ju'lep (joo'lip) *n.* a sweet drink. —mint julep, iced bourbon whiskey flavored with mint leaves.

Ju·ly' (jû-lī') *n.* the seventh month of the year.

jum'ble (jum'bəl) *v.t.* mix in a confused mass; put together without order. —*v.i.* become mixed. —*n.* **1,** a confused mass or collection. **2,** a state of disorder.

jum'bo (jum'bō) *n.* [*pl.* -bos] a very large individual of its kind. —*adj.* very large.

jump *v.i.* **1,** spring from the ground or from any support; leap. **2,** move with a leap; jolt; throb.

3, rise abruptly in amount, intensity, etc. —*v.t.* **1,** spring or leap over. **2,** cause to leap or jolt. **3,** give no heed to; disregard. —*n.* **1,** the act of jumping; a leap. **2,** a sudden rise; a jolt. **3,** an omission; an abrupt transition.

jump'er (-ər) *n.* **1,** one who jumps. **2,** any mechanical device that operates with a jumping motion. **3,** a loose outer garment; (*pl.*) overalls.

jump'y (-ē) *adj.* nervous. —jump'i·ness, *n.*

junc'tion (junk'shən) *n.* **1,** act of joining or uniting; coalition. **2,** place of meeting or joining.

junc'ture (junk'chər) *n.* **1,** a point of time. **2,** a seam.

June (joon) *n.* the sixth month of the year.

jun'gle (jung'gəl) *n.* **1,** a dense growth of rank and tangled vegetation; a wilderness. **2,** (*Slang*) a camping-ground of tramps.

jun'ior (joon'yər) *n.* **1,** one younger than another. **2,** one of less experience or inferior standing in his profession than another. **3,** a student in the next-to-last year of the high school or college course. —*adj.* **1,** younger. **2,** pert. to juniors. —junior high, a school teaching grades 7, 8, and 9. —junior college, a school teaching two years of a college course.

ju'ni·per (joo'nə-pər) *n.* a coniferous evergreen shrub, used in making gin and certain medicines.

junk *n.* **1,** worn-out or discarded material; trash. **2,** a Chinese sailing vessel. **3,** (*Slang*) narcotic drugs. —*v.t.* (*Colloq.*) throw away; discard.

Jun'ker (yûng'kər) *n.* a member of the German aristocratic class.

jun'ket (jung'kit) *n.* **1,** a custard, milk sweetened and flavored, curdled with rennet. **2,** a picnic; an excursion. —*v.i. & t.* feast; regale; go on a pleasure trip.

jun'ta (jun'tə) *n.* a consultative or legislative assembly, esp. Spanish.

jun'to (jun'tō) *n.* [*pl.* -tos] a secret political combine.

Ju'pi·ter (joo'pi-tər) *n.* **1,** the chief god in Roman mythology. **2,** the largest planet in the solar system.

ju·rid'i·cal (jû-rid'ə-kəl) *adj.* relating to administrative law.

ju"ris·dic'tion (jûr"is-dik'shən) *n.* **1,** the right of making and enforcing laws. **2,** the domain over which a given authority extends.

ju"ris·pru'dence (jûr"is-proo'dəns) *n.* **1,** the science of law. **2,** the body of laws existing in a given state or nation.

ju′rist (jŭr′ist) *n.* one who professes the science of law.

ju′ror (jŭr′ər) *n.* a member of a jury. Also, **ju′ry·man.**

ju′ry (jŭr′ĕ) *n.* a group of persons appointed to hear evidence and decide facts. —*adj.* (*Naut.*) rigged in an emergency; makeshift.

just *adj.* 1, right in law or ethics. 2, fair-minded; good in intention; impartial. 3, based on right; legitimate. 4, in correct accordance with a standard. —*adv.* 1, precisely. 2, very nearly. 3, barely; by a narrow margin. 4, (*Colloq.*) wholly; positively. —**just′ness,** *n.* fairness.

jus′tice (jus′tis) *n.* 1, conformity to moral principles or law; just conduct. 2, merited reward or punishment. 3, the administration of law; authority; jurisdiction. 4, a judicial officer; a judge. —**justice of the peace,** a minor local judge.

jus′ti·fy (jus′tə-fī″) *v.t. & i.* 1, prove or show to be just or conformable to justice, reason, law, etc. 2, declare innocent or blameless. 3, make precise; adjust; (*Printing*) make successive lines of type of equal length. —**jus″ti·fi′a·ble,** *adj.* defensible. —**jus″ti·fi·ca′tion,** *n.*

jut *v.i.* (jut′ted, -ting) (usually with *out*) extend beyond the main body or line. —*n.* a projection.

jute (joot) *n.* 1, a plant that grows in warm, moist climate; its fiber. 2, a coarse fabric made from jute.

ju′ve·nile (joo′və-nəl) *adj.* 1, young; youthful. 2, pert. to or suited for young persons. —*n.* a young person. —**ju″ve·nil′i·ty,** *n.*

ju″ve·nil′i·a (joo″və-nil′ē-ə) *n.* works produced in youth.

jux″ta·pose′ (juks″tə-pōz′) *v.t.* place side by side or close together. —**jux″ta·po·si′tion** (-pə-zish′ən) *n.*

K

K, k (kā) the eleventh letter of the English alphabet.

Kai′ser (kī′zər) *n.* (*Ger.*) Emperor; esp. Wilhelm II, German emperor during World War I.

ka″ka·po′ (kä″kä-pō′) *n.* [*pl.* -pos] a large nocturnal parrot of New Zealand.

kale (kāl) *n.* 1, a variety of cabbage with curled or wrinkled leaves. 2, (*Slang*) money.

ka·lei′do·scope″ (kə-lī′də-skōp″) *n.* an optical instrument for creating, by reflection, colorful symmetrical patterns. —**ka·lei′do·scop′ic**

(-skop′ik) *adj.* —**ka·lei′do·scop′i·cal·ly,** *adv.*

kal′so·mine″ (kal′sə-mīn″) *v.t. & n.* whitewash.

ka″mi·ka′ze (kä″mi-kä′zĕ) *adj. & n. pl.* (*Jap.*) (aircraft pilots) sworn to make suicidal attacks.

Ka·nak′a (kə-nak′ə) *n.* a Hawaiian.

kan″ga·roo′ (kang″gə-roo′) *n.* a marsupial of Australia having powerful hind legs developed for leaping. —**kangaroo court,** an unofficial group that acts as a court of law.

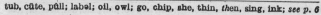

Kangaroo

ka′o·lin (kā′ə-lin) *n.* a white clay used in making porcelain.

ka′pok (kā′pok) *n.* a tropical tree whose seeds yield a silky wool used for stuffing cushions, etc.

kap′pa (kap′ə) *n.* the tenth letter of the Greek alphabet (K κ).

ka·put′ (kä-pŭt′) *adj.* (*Slang*) ruined; done for.

kar′a·kul (kar′ə-kəl) *n.* an Asiatic breed of sheep; its fur.

ka′ty·did (kā′tĕ-did) *n.* a large Amer. grasshopper.

kay′ak (kī′ak) *n.* a light Eskimo boat made of sealskins.

kay′o (kā′ō) *v.t.* (*Slang*) knock out, in pugilism.

kedge (kej) *v.t. & i.* pull or warp (a ship) by the rope of an anchor. —*n.* a small anchor.

keel (kēl) *n.* 1, a central longitudinal member from which a frame is built upwards, as on a ship. 2, any central main stem, as on a leaf. —**keel over,** turn upside-down.

keen (kēn) *adj.* 1, having a sharp edge or point. 2, acutely harsh or painful; biting. 3, having sharp perception of senses or mind. 4, intense in feeling; ardent. —**keen′ness,** *n.*

keep (kēp) *v.t.* [*pret. & p.p.* kept] 1, maintain possession or custody of; retain. 2, continue or maintain in action or conduct. 3, carry out; perform; observe; fulfill. 4, preserve; protect; care for; support. 5, hold; detain; restrain. —*v.i.* 1, continue (action, state, etc.). 2, endure; last. —*n.* 1, board and lodging; subsistence; maintenance. 2, the stronghold of a castle. —**keep′er,** *n.* a guardian, guard, or warden. —**keep′ing,** *n.* congruity; appropriateness.

keep′sake″ (kēp′sāk″) *n.* a souvenir or memento.

keg *n.* a small barrel.

kelp *n.* a large brown seaweed.

ken *n.* range of sight or knowledge.

ken'nel (ken'əl) *n.* a house for a dog or (also *pl.*) dogs. —*v.t.* & *i.* lodge in a kennel.

ke'no (kē'nō) *n.* a lottery game, precursor of bingo.

kep'i (kep'ē) *n.* a French military cap.

kept *v.* pret. & p.p. of *keep.*

kerb (kėrb) *n.* (*Brit.*) street curb.

ker'chief (kėr'chif) *n.* 1, a cloth worn as a headdress, esp. by women. 2, handkerchief.

kerf (kėrf) *n.* a cut, as made by a saw.

ker'nel (kėr'nəl) *n.* 1, the substance, often edible, inside a nut or fruit stone. 2, a grain or seed, as of corn. 3, gist; nucleus.

ker'o·sene (ker'ə-sēn") *n.* an oil, distilled from coal or petroleum, used for heat and illumination.

ketch (kech) *n.* a small sailing vessel.

ketch'up (kech'əp) *n.* catchup.

ket'tle (ket'əl) *n.* a covered vessel for the heating of liquids or for cooking.

ket'tle·drum" *n.* a drumhead on a metal hemisphere, capable of being tuned.

kew'pie (kū'pē) *n.* a caricatural picture or doll of a cherub.

key (kē) *n.* 1, an instrument for opening and closing a lock, valve, circuit, etc. 2, a control lever operated by the fingers, as on a telegraph, typewriter, piano, horn. 3, something explanatory; a translation of cipher, symbols, problems, perplexities, etc. 4, (*Music*) the tonic note or name of a scale; a key signature; the tonality implied by a sequence of chords. 5, pitch; degree of intensity; tone or mood. —*v.t.* provide with a key or reference system. —keyed up, tense.

key'board" *n.* the row of keys for controlling a piano, typewriter, etc.

key'hole" *n.* the opening through which a key is inserted in a lock.

key'note" *n.* main theme or principle.

Keystone

key'stone" *n.* the central stone bearing the pressure of other stones in an arch; hence, any essential member.

khak'i (kak'ē) *n.* an olive-drab or yellowish-brown color or cloth.

khan (kän) *n.* an Asiatic title of respect.

khe·dive' (kə-dēv') *n.* formerly, title of the Turkish viceroy of Egypt.

kib'itz·er (kib'it-sər) *n.* an onlooker who gives unwanted advice, esp. at a card game. —kib'itz, *v.i.* & *i.*

ki'bosh (kī'bosh) *n.* (*Slang*) 1, nonsense. 2, a ruinous curse or spell.

kick (kik) *v.t.* 1, strike with the foot. 2, strike in recoiling. —*v.i.* 1, thrust the foot forward or outward. 2, recoil, as a firearm. 3, (*Slang*) complain; resist. —*n.* 1, a blow with the foot. 2, a recoil. 3, (*Slang*) a complaint or objection. 4, (*Colloq.*) vigor; excitement or thrill; the stimulating quality of liquor.

kick'back *n.* 1, a violent reaction. 2, the return of a portion of a worker's pay to an employer.

kid *n.* 1, a young goat. 2, leather made from the skin of a young goat. 3, (*Colloq.*) a child; youngster. —*v.t.* & *i.* [kid'ded, -ding] (*Slang*) tease.

kid'nap (kid'nap) *v.t.* abduct, or carry off forcibly (a human being).

kid'ney (kid'nē) *n.* either of two bean-shaped organs that excrete urine. —*adj.* kidney-shaped.

kill (kil) *v.t.* 1, put to death; slay. 2, destroy; extinguish; nullify; cancel; veto; neutralize. —*n.* 1, the act of killing. 2, the culmination of a hunt or quest; an animal killed.

kill'ing (kil'ing) *n.* 1, the act of killing. 2, (*Colloq.*) a highly successful stroke of business. —*adj.* 1, deadly; exhausting. 2, (*Colloq.*) funny.

kill'joy" *n.* one who spoils the enjoyment of others.

kiln (kil) *n.* an oven for drying or baking, as bricks. —*v.t.* bake.

kil·o- *pref.* thousand; 1,000 times.

kil'o·cy"cle (kil'ə-sī"kəl) *n.* 1,000 cycles per second.

kil'o·gram" (kil'ə-gram") *n.* 1,000 grams, equal to 2.2 pounds.

kil'o·me'ter (kil'ə-mē'tər) *n.* 1,000 meters, about .62 mile.

kil'o·watt" (kil'ə-wot") *n.* 1,000 watts. —kilowatt hour, consumption of 1,000 watts throughout one hour.

kilt *n.* a short plaid skirt, esp. as worn by Scotsmen.

kil'ter (kil'tər) *n.* (*Colloq.*) good working condition.

ki·mo'no (kə-mō'nə) *n.* [pl. -nos] 1, a gownlike Japanese outer garment. 2, a dressing gown; bathrobe.

kin *n.* 1, one's relatives collectively. 2, relationship of those having common descent. —*adj.* 1, related by blood; of the same family or clan. 2, of the same kind or nature. —kin'ship, *n.*

kind (kīnd) *n.* **1,** natural constitution or character. **2,** a class of persons or things of the same character; a category. **3,** an individual representative (of a class). —*adj.* of a sympathetic nature; benevolent.

kin'der·gar'ten (kin'dər-gär″tən) *n.* a school or class for children of pre-school age.

kin'dle (kin'dəl) *v.t.* **1,** set on fire. **2,** inspire; stir up. —*v.i.* **1,** catch fire. **2,** become animated.

kin'dling (kin'dling) *n.* small pieces of material for starting fires.

kind'ly (-lē) *adj.* agreeable; considerate. —*adv.* **1,** in a kind way. **2,** if you please. —**kind'li·ness,** *n.*

kind'ness (-nəs) *n.* sympathetic nature; benevolence.

kin'dred *n.* & *adj.* kin.

kin'e·scope″ (kin'ə-skōp″) *n.* (*T.N.*) **1,** the tube and screen used in a television receiver. **2,** a film record of a television broadcast.

ki·net'ic (ki-net'ik) *adj.* caused by or pert. to motion. —**ki·net'i·cal·ly,** *adv.*

kin'folk″ *n.pl.* relatives.

king *n.* **1,** a male sovereign; a monarch. **2,** a person or thing of preëminent rank in a class. **3,** a playing card bearing the picture of a king; the chief piece in chess; in checkers, a piece that has been crowned. —**king'ly,** *adj.* majestic. —**king'ship,** *n.*

king'dom (-dəm) *n.* **1,** the realm of a king. **2,** any society or classification. **3,** one of the classes (animal, vegetable, mineral) of matter.

king'fish″er (-ər) *n.* a kind of diving bird.

Kingfisher

king'pin″ *n.* **1,** one of the bolts on which the steering axle of a vehicle pivots. **2,** (*Slang*) chief; boss.

king-'size″ *adj.* extra-large.

kink *n.* **1,** a knotlike curl, as in a wire. **2,** a muscular cramp. **3,** a mental twist; obstinate notion; crotchet. —*v.i.* & *t.* twist; curl. —**kink'y** (-ē) *adj.*

kin'ka·jou″ (king'kə-joo″) *n.* an animal with a long, prehensile tail.

kins'man (kinz'mən) *n.* [*pl.* -**men**] a male relative.

ki·osk' (kē-osk') *n.* a small building, as a newsstand or booth.

kip'per (kip'ər) *v.t.* prepare (fish) by salting and smoking. —*n.* a fish so prepared, esp. a herring.

kis'met (kiz'met) *n.* fate; destiny.

kiss (kis) *v.t.* & *i.* **1,** touch (esp. the lips of another) with the lips, as a caress or salutation. **2,** touch gently in any way. —*n.* **1,** the act of kissing. **2,** a gentle touch or contact. **3,** a kind of candy.

kit *n.* **1,** an assemblage of tools, materials, supplies, etc. **2,** a case for containing such an outfit.

kitch'en (kich'ən) *n.* a room in which food is cooked. —**kitch'en·ette'** (-ə-net') *n.* a very small kitchen.

kite (kīt) *n.* **1,** a light contrivance, held captive by a long cord, designed to be supported in air by the wind. **2,** a variety of hawk. **3,** a fictitious commercial bill or check. —*v.t.* (*Slang*) cash (a check) against funds not yet deposited.

kith *n.* one's friends collectively (now used only in *kith and kin*).

kit'ten (kit'ən) *n.* a young cat. —**kit'ten·ish,** *adj.* playful.

kit'ty (kit'ē) *n.* **1,** a pool formed by card players to defray expenses, etc. **2,** in a card game, the widow. **3,** pet name for a cat.

ki'wi (kē'wē) *n.* **1,** a flightless bird of New Zealand. **2,** (*Colloq.*) a non-flying aviation officer.

Klans'man (klanz'mən) *n.* [*pl.* -**men**] a member of the Ku Klux Klan.

klep″to·ma'ni·a (klep″tə-mā'nē-ə) *n.* morbid addiction to stealing without regard to personal needs. —**klep″to·ma'ni·ac,** *n.*

Klieg light (klēg) a very bright electric light for motion-picture photography, etc.

knack (nak) *n.* aptitude; talent.

knap'sack″ (nap'sak″) *n.* a bag strapped to the shoulders.

knave (nāv) *n.* **1,** rascal. **2,** in playing cards, a jack. —**knav'er·y** (nā'və-rē) *n.* dishonesty. —**knav'ish,** *adj.* dishonest.

knead (nēd) *v.t.* manipulate (dough, plastic material, the body in massaging, etc.) by squeezing, pressing, and thumping.

knee (nē) *n.* **1,** the joint between the two main parts of the leg. **2,** a hinge; a sharp bend or crook. —*v.t.* strike with the knee.

knee'cap″ *n.* the bone at the front of the knee joint.

kneel (nēl) *v.i.* [*pret.* & *p.p.* **knelt**] rest on one or both bended knees.

knell (nel) *n.* the sound of a bell, esp. when rung at a death or funeral.

knick'ers (nik'ərz) *n. pl.* short breeches gathered at the knee. Also, **knick'er·bock″ers** (-bok″ərz).

knick'knack″ (nik'nak″) *n.* an

---

tub, cūte, půll; label; oil, owl; go, chip, she, thin, *then*, sing, ink; *see p. 6* unsubstantial article of food, furniture, or dress.

knife (nīf) *n.* [*pl.* **knives** (nīvz)] a cutting tool; a sharp-edged blade with attached handle. —*v.t.* cut or stab with a knife.

knight (nīt) *n.* 1, medieval mounted soldier of noble birth. 2, a title (marked in the Brit. Empire by the title Sir) conferred on men in recognition of merit. 3, a chivalrous person. 4, a chess piece. —**knight′hood**, *n.* —**knight′ly**, *adj.*

knit (nīt) *v.t.* & *i.* [**knit′ted**, -**ting**] 1, make (fabric) by interlooping a single strand of yarn on needles. 2, join closely. 3, contract (one's brows). 4, grow together, as bones.

knob (nob) *n.* 1, a rounded projection. 2, a hill. —**knob′by** (-ē) *adj.*

knock (nok) *v.t.* 1, hit; strike; rap. 2, (*Slang*) criticize harshly. —*v.i.* 1, strike a blow. 2, collide. 3, make a noise, as repeated blows or collisions; (of a motor) detonate. —*n.* 1, the act of knocking. 2, the sound of a knock. 3, (*Slang*) a deprecating criticism or comment. —**knock down**, 1, sell finally, at auction. 2, strike (an opponent) so that he falls, in pugilism. —**knocked down**, disassembled (as machinery) for shipment, storage, or repair. —**knock off**, 1, stop working. 2, complete successfully.

knock′er (-ər) *n.* 1, one who knocks. 2, a device for rapping at a door: *doorknocker.*

knock′kneed′ (-nēd′) *adj.* having legs that bend inward.

knock′out *n.* 1, victory won by knocking out an opponent. 2,(*Slang*) a very prepossessing or beautiful thing or person. —**knock out**, eliminate or defeat finally; in pugilism, knock down (an opponent) so that he cannot rise and continue. —**knockout drops**, chloral hydrate, when criminally used to drug someone.

knoll (nōl) *n.* a small rounded hill.

knot (not) *n.* 1, an interlacement of loops in a cord, rope, or ribbon, drawn tight into a bunch, made for fastening or ornament. 2, any bunch, cluster, lump, knob, or protuberance. 3, a bond of association; a tie. 4, a puzzle, problem, or perplexity. 5, a unit of speed, one nautical mile per hour. 6, the embedded end of a tree branch. —*v.t.* [**knot′ted**, -**ting**] 1, fasten with a knot; form a knot in. 2, form lumps. —*v.i.* become knotted, snarled, or lumpy. —**knot′hole′**, *n.* a hole left by the removal of a knot from wood. —**knot′ty** (-ē) *adj.*

knout (nowt) *n.* a whip or scourge.

know (nō) *v.t.* [**knew** (noo), **known** (nōn), **know′ing**] 1, perceive as fact or truth. 2, have information of; be acquainted with. 3, recognize or distinguish in comparison. —*v.i.* 1, have

knowledge or information. 2, have insight or perception.

know-′how″ *n.* (*Slang*) expertness.

know′ing *adj.* aware; shrewd.

knowl′edge (nol′ij) *n.* 1, awareness of facts, truths, or principles; cognizance. 2, erudition. 3, what is known; a body of accumulated facts. —**knowl′edge-a-ble**, *adj.* wise.

known (nōn) *v.*, p.p. of *know.*

knuck′le (nuk′əl) *n.* 1, a joint of the finger. 2, a cut of meat, esp. from the knee. 3, a protuberance of a hinge. —*v.i.* 1, (with *down*) apply oneself earnestly to a task. 2, (with *under*) submit; yield.

knurl (nērl) *n.* one of a series of ridges, as on a thumbscrew, to afford a grip. —*v.t.* roughen.

ko-a′la (kō-ä′lə) *n.* a small Australian marsupial resembling a bear.

kohl′ra″bi (kōl′rä″bē) *n.* a plant cultivated for its edible stem.

ko-lin′sky (kə-lin′skē) *n.* a Siberian mink, and its golden-brown fur.

ko′peck (kō′pek) *n.* a former Russian coin, worth about ½ cent.

Ko-ran′ (kō-rän′) *n.* the sacred book of the Mohammedans.

ko′sher (kō′shər) *adj.* 1, conformant to Jewish dietary law. 2, (*Slang*) approved; genuine.

kow″tow′ *v.i.* 1, touch the forehead to the ground. 2, fawn; cringe. —*n.* a low bow.

kraal (kräl) *n.* 1, a South African village. 2, a cattle pen.

kraft (kräft) *n.* a heavy brown wrapping paper.

krem′lin *n.* 1, a Russian castle. 2, (*cap.*) former headquarters of the Soviet government, in Moscow.

kro′na (krō′nə) *n.* a Swedish coin.

kro′ne (krō′nə) *n.* any of various coins, Danish, Norwegian, or Austrian.

kryp′ton (krip′ton) *n.* an inert gaseous chemical element, no. 36, symbol Kr.

ku′dos (kū′dos) *n.* glory; praise.

Ku Klux Klan (koo′kluks′klan′) a secret terroristic society in the U.S., opposed to Negroes, Jews, and Roman Catholics.

ku-lak′ (koo-läk′) *n.* formerly, a freeholding peasant, in Russia.

ku′miss (koo′mis) *n.* 1, a beverage made from fermented milk.

kum′quat (kum′kwot) *n.* a subtropical shrub with a pulpy citrus fruit, used chiefly for preserves.

Kuo′min′tang′ (kwō′min′tang′) *n.* a political party of China.

Kyr′i-e″ e-le′i-son″ (kir′ē-ē″ə-lā′-ə-son″) (*Gk.*) a chant of prayer: Lord, have mercy.

L

L, l (el) the twelfth letter of the English alphabet.

la (lä) *n.* the sixth note of the diatonic scale. —*interj.* of surprise.

la'bel (lā'bel) *n.* **1**, a slip of paper bearing a name, price, destination, or other particulars, to be fixed on an article or parcel. **2**, a mark or title of identification. **3**, any small strip or flap of paper, ribbon, etc. —*v.t.* attach or assign a label to.

la'bi·al (lā'bė-əl) *adj.* **1**, pert. to the lips or a liplike part. **2**, pert. to sounds produced by the lips, as *p*.

la'bile (lā'bil) *adj.* apt to lapse or err; unstable. —**la·bil'i·ty,** *n.*

la'bor (lā'bər) *n.* **1**, bodily toil for the earning of a livelihood. **2**, the class of persons engaged in such toil. **3**, hard work. **4**, a task. **5**, the pangs of childbirth; travail. —*v.i.* **1**, work; toil. **2**, be burdened or oppressed. **3**, be in travail. —*v.t.* work at persistently. Also, **la'bour.**

lab'o·ra·to·ry (lab'rə-tôr-ė) *n.* a room or building equipped for scientific research.

Labor Day the first Monday in September, a holiday for members of labor unions.

la'bored (lā'bərd) *adj.* done laboriously.

la·bo'ri·ous (lə-bôr'ė-əs) *adj.* **1**, not easy. **2**, diligent; assiduous. —**la·bo'ri·ous·ness,** *n.*

la·bur'num (lə-bẽr'nəm) *n.* a small leguminous tree.

lab'y·rinth (lab'ə-rinth) *n.* **1**, an intricate combination of passages difficult to find a way through or out of; a maze. **2**, any thing or condition confusingly intricate. **3**, the canals in the human inner ear. —**lab'y·rin'thine** (-thin) *adj.*

lac (lak) *n.* **1**, a resinous substance used in making varnishes. **2**, shellac. **3**, (*Pharm.*) milk.

lace (lās) *n.* **1**, an ornamental fabric or net of fine threads. **2**, a cord used for drawing together edges of cloth or leather. **3**, ornamental cord or braid. —*v.t.* **1**, bind with a lace. **2**, intertwine. **3**, add spirits to, as coffee. **4**, (*Colloq.*) beat; thrash.

lac'er·ate (las'ə-rāt) *v.t.* **1**, tear roughly; mangle. **2**, afflict. —**lac'er·a'tion,** *n.*

lach'ry·mal (lak'rə-məl) *adj.* pert. to weeping or tears.

lach'ry·mose (-mōs) *adj.* tending to shed or induce tears.

lac'ing (lā'sing) *n.* **1**, a cord fastening. **2**, a beating.

lack (lak) *n.* **1**, deficiency or absence of something needed, desired, or usual. **2**, what is lacking. —*v.t. & i.* be without; be deficient (in).

lack'a·dai'si·cal (lak'ə-dā'zi-kəl) *adj.* languid; listless.

lack'ey (lak'ė) *n.* **1**, a manservant; a liveried attendant. **2**, a servile follower.

lack'lus"ter *adj.* dull.

la·con'ic (lə-kon'ik) *adj.* expressing much in few words; pithy. —**la·con'i·cal·ly,** *adv.*

lac'quer (lak'ər) *n.* **1**, a varnish made with natural or synthetic resins. **2**, decorative work covered with lacquer and polished. —*v.t.* coat with lacquer.

la·crosse' (lə-krâs') *n.* an athletic field game played with a small ball and long-handled rackets (*crosses*).

lac·ta'tion (lak-tā'shən) *n.* **1**, the formation or secretion of milk. **2**, the period of suckling.

lac'te·al (lak'tė-əl) *adj.* pert. to milk; resembling milk.

lac'tic (lak'tik) *adj.* pert. to or derived from milk. —**lactic acid,** an acid found in sour milk, etc.

lac'tose" (lak'tōs") *n.* milk sugar.

la·cu'na (lə-kū'nə) *n.* a gap.

lac'y (lā'sė) *adj.* netlike. —**lac'i·ness,** *n.*

lad *n.* a boy or youth.

lad'der (lad'ər) *n.* **1**, an apparatus for ascending, comprising a series of horizontal bars fixed to one or two vertical posts. **2**, a blemish in a fabric, caused by the breaking of a warp thread. **3**, any means or way of ascent.

lad'die (lâd'ė) *n.* lad.

lade (lād) *v.t.* [*p.p.* **lad'en**] **1**, load; burden. **2**, bail out with a ladle.

lad'ing (lā'ding) *n.* a cargo.

la'dle (lā'dəl) *n.* a spoon for dipping; a dipper. —*v.t.* dip out or convey with a ladle.

la'dy (lā'dė) *n.* **1**, a woman of good breeding or social position. **2**, (*cap.*) a title in Brit. peerage. **3**, a wife; the mistress of a household. —*adj.* female.

la'dy·bug" *n.* a small flying beetle. Also, **la'dy·bird".**

la'dy·fin"ger *n.* a sponge cake shaped like a finger.

la'dy·kill"er *n.* (*Slang*) a man fascinating to women.

la'dy·like" *adj.* befitting a lady, as in behavior.

la'dy·love" *n.* sweetheart.

la'dy·ship" *n.* title or rank of a lord's wife.

lag v.i. [lagged, lag'ging] 1, move slowly; fall behind in progress; hang back. 2, in games, drive a ball toward a line. —n. 1, a falling behind; the amount of retardation. 2, a hoop around a cylinder.

la'ger (lä'gər) n. aged beer.

lag'gard (lag'ərd) n. one who lags. —adj. lagging.

la·gniappe' (lan-yap') n. a tip; largess.

la·goon' (lə-goon') n. a shallow lake or channel.

la'ic (lā'ik) adj. pert. to the laity; secular.

laid (lād) v. pret. & p.p. of lay.

lain (lān) v. p.p. of lie.

lair (lār) n. the den of a wild animal; a resting place.

laird (lārd) n. (Scot.) lord.

la'i·ty (lā'ə-tē) n. laymen; all those outside the clergy or a particular profession.

lake (lāk) n. a large body of water surrounded by land.

lam v.t. [lammed, lam'ming] (Slang) thrash; beat. —v.i. (Slang) run away.

la'ma (lä'mə) n. a priest or monk of the religion of Tibet.

la'ma·ser'y (lä'mə-ser"ē) n. a monastery of lamas.

lamb (lam) n. 1, a young sheep; its meat. 2, one who is gentle, meek, or gullible.

lam·baste' (lam-bāst') v.t. whack; pound.

lamb'da (lam'də) n. the eleventh letter of the Greek alphabet (Λ, λ).

lam'bent (lam'bənt) adj. 1, moving lightly; licking. 2, softly bright; gleaming. —lam'ben·cy (-sē) n.

lamb'kin n. a little lamb.

lame (lām) adj. 1, physically disabled; limping. 2, ineffectual; halting. —v.t. make lame. —lame duck (Colloq.) an officeholder soon to be succeeded. —lame'ness, n.

la·mé' (la-mā') n. a fabric made of metallic threads interwoven with silk, wool, or cotton.

la·ment' (lə-ment') v.i. & t. express sorrow (for); mourn; bewail. —n. an expression of grief; an elegy. —lam'en·ta·ble (lam'ən-tə-bəl) adj. regrettable. —lam"en·ta'tion, n.

lam'i·na (lam'ə-nə) n. 1, a thin layer or scale. 2, layers.

lam'i·nate" (lam'ə-nāt') v.t. press (layers) together. —adj. in layers. —lam"i·na'tion, n.

lamp n. 1, a vessel for burning an illuminant; any device, chemical or electrical, for providing light. 2, (pl.) (Slang) the eyes.

lamp'black" n. soot used as a black pigment.

Lantern

Lamp

lam·poon' n. a satire aimed at a person. —v.t. assail in a lampoon.

lam'prey (lam'prē) n. a snake-like fish.

lance (läns) n. a weapon comprising a sharp-pointed head on a long shaft. —v.t. prick or cut open.

lan'cet (län'sit) n. a surgical knife.

land n. 1, the surface of the earth, esp. the dry parts. 2, a particular tract; a region or country. 3, a tract as property; real estate. —v.t. 1, discharge (passengers or freight); transfer to land. 2, catch or capture. —v.i. 1, disembark. 2, arrive at a place or condition.

land'fall" n. the land first sighted from the sea.

land'hold"er n. an owner of land. Also, land'own"er.

land'ing n. 1, a place where persons or goods are landed. 2, a platform in a staircase. —landing gear, the wheels, pontoons, etc. on which an aircraft rests on land or water.

land'la'dy n. a woman landlord.

land'locked" (-lokt") adj. (of water) sheltered or enclosed by land.

land'lord" n. 1, an owner of rented land, buildings, etc. 2, the proprietor of a hotel, etc.

land'lub"ber (-lub"ər) n. one unaccustomed to being on a ship at sea.

land'mark" n. 1, a conspicuous object serving to bound or identify a place. 2, a memorable event.

land'scape" n. a view or picture of rural scenery. —v.t. beautify (land).

land'slide" n. 1, the falling of a large mass of earth down a steep slope. 2, an overwhelming victory.

lane (lān) n. 1, a narrow passage; a rural road or path. 2, a fixed route, as across an ocean.

lan'guage (lang'gwij) n. 1, the aggregate of words comprising a system of communication between persons in speech or writing. 2, such a system peculiar to a country, race, etc. 3, expression of thought in any way. 4, linguistics. 5, diction.

lan'guid (lang'gwid) adj. 1, sluggish from weakness, fatigue, or lack of energy. 2, spiritless; listless. —lan'guid·ness, n.

lan'guish (lang'gwish) v.i. be languid; droop, as from grief or longing. —lan'guish·ment, *n.*

lan'guor (lang'gər) *n.* lack of spirit or vigor; dreaminess. —lan'guor·ous, *adj.*

lank *adj.* meagerly thin; gaunt. —lank'y, *adj.* slim and tall.

lan'o·lin (lan'ə-lin) *n.* a fat from sheep's wool, used in cosmetics, etc.

lan'tern (lan'tərn) *n.* 1, a portable lamp. 2, the lamp chamber of a lighthouse.—lan'tern·jawed' (-jăd') *adj.* thin-faced, with bulging jaws.

lan'yard (lan'yərd) *n.* a short length of cord used in rigging, etc.

lap *n.* 1, the platform formed by the thighs when one sits. 2, support or shelter, like the mother's lap to the child. 3, the part of one body that lies on another; overlap. 4, the distance or material required to go around something once. 5, a rotating wheel for cutting or polishing gems. 6, the act or sound of lapping liquid. —*v.t.* [lapped, lap'ping] 1, fold; wrap. 2, cover partly. 3, get ahead of (a competitor) by one circuit of the racecourse. 4, cut or polish with a lap wheel. 5, lick up (a liquid) with the tongue. 6, wash against; lick. —*v.i.* 1, be folded. 2, overlap. 3, ripple, as waves. —lap dog, a small pet dog.

la·pel' (lə-pel') *n.* a fold in the front of a coat below the collar.

lap'i·dar·y (lap'ə-der-ē) *n.* 1, a skilled worker on gems. 2, an engraver of monuments.

lap'in *n.* a rabbit; rabbit fur.

lap'is laz'u·li'' (lap'is laz'yŭ-lī'') *n.* a semiprecious stone; its color, sky-blue.

Lap'land''er (lap'lan''dər) *n.* Lapp.

Lapp (lap) *n.* one of a people of Mongolian descent, inhabiting Lapland.

lap'pet (lap'it) *n.* a loosely-hanging part, as a flap; the wattle of a fowl.

lapse (laps) *n.* 1, the passing by or away, as of time; termination or cessation, as of a privilege. 2, a careless mistake; failure; error. —*v.i.* 1, pass by or away gradually; end. 2, deteriorate. 3, err.

lar'board (lär'bərd) *adj.* (*Naut.*) left; port; opposite of *starboard.*

lar'ce·ny (lär'sə-nē) *n.* the wrongful taking of another's goods; theft. —lar'ce·nous, *adj.*

larch (lärch) *n.* a coniferous tree; its wood.

lard (lärd) *n.* a grease for cooking, prepared from hogs' fat. —*v.t.* 1, grease. 2, garnish or ornament.

lard'er (lär'dər) *n.* a pantry; a stock of food.

large (lärj) *adj.* great in size, amount, number, degree, range,

scale, etc. —at large, 1, not caught or confined. 2, at length; fully. 3, (*Politics*) representing no specified district. —large'ly, *adv.* in great part. —large'ness, *n.*

lar'gess (lär'jes) *n.* a liberal gift; generous bestowal of gifts.

lar'go (lär'gō) *adj.* (*Music*) slow.

lar'i·at (lar'ē-ət) *n.* 1, a lasso. 2, a rope used to picket a horse.

lark (lärk) *n.* 1, any of numerous songbirds. 2, a merry adventure; jovial frolic. —*v.i.* play pranks.

lark'spur'' (lärk'spër'') *n.* a flowering plant; delphinium.

lar'rup (lar'əp) *v.t.* (*Colloq.*) flog; beat.

lar'va (lär'və) *n.* [*pl.* -vae (-vē)] the young of any animal that undergoes metamorphosis. —lar'val, *adj.*

lar''yn·gi'tis (lar''in-jī'tis) *n.* inflammation of the larynx.

lar'ynx (lar'inks) *n.* the part of the windpipe containing the vocal cords. —la·ryn'ge·al (lə-rin'jē·əl) *adj.*

las·civ'i·ous (lə-siv'ē-əs) *adj.* 1, inciting to lust. 2, wanton; lewd. —las·civ'i·ous·ness, *n.*

lash *n.* 1, the flexible part of a whip. 2, a blow with a whip; a sweeping movement. 3, a stroke of sarcasm or censure; eyelash.—*v.t.* 1, flog. 2, beat or dash against. 3, assail violently with words. 4, fasten with cord. —*v.i.* (with *out*) burst into violent action or speech.

lass (las) *n.* girl. Also, las'sie (-ē).

las'si·tude (las'i-tūd) *n.* weariness; languor.

las'so (las'ō) *n.* a rope with a noose used to catch animals. —*v.t.* catch in the noose of a lasso.

last (lást) *v.i.* 1, continue to exist or progress; endure. 2, continue unexhausted. —*n.* 1, that which is after all others. 2, end; conclusion. 3, a model of the human foot, on which shoes are formed. —*adj.* 1, being after all others in time, place, order, etc. 2, being all that remains; final. 3, most recent; latest. —*adv.* 1, after all others. 2, finally. 3, on the most recent occasion. —last'ing, *adj.* enduring; permanent.

latch (lach) *n.* a device for holding shut a door or gate. —*v.t.* lock.

latch'et (lach'ət) *n.* shoestring.

late (lát) *adj.* 1, coming after the usual or proper time. 2, protracted in time. 3, coming near the end. 4, recent. 5, recently changed, ended, or deceased. —*adv.* 1, after the usual or proper time. 2, not long since. —of late, recently. —lat'er, *adv.* after some passage of time. —late'ly, *adv.* recently. — late'ness, *n.*

la'tent (lā'tənt) *adj.* hidden; dormant; undeveloped. —**la'ten·cy**, *n.*

lat'er·al (lat'ər-əl) *adj.* pert. to the side.

la'tex (lā'teks) *n.* a milky liquid occurring in many plants, as rubber.

lath (làth) *n.* a narrow strip of wood; such strips collectively.

lathe (lāth) *n.* a machine that rotates wood or metal while it is shaped by a tool.

lath'er (lath'ər) *n.* **1**, froth produced by soap and water. **2**, froth produced by profuse sweating.

Lat'in *n.* **1**, the language spoken by the ancient inhabitants of Rome. **2**, a member of any Latin race. —*adj.* **1**, pert. to the Latin language. **2**, pert. to any people speaking a language derived from Latin. —**Latin American**, pert. to the Spanish- and Portuguese-speaking American countries. —**Latin Quarter**, a community of artists or section where they live.

lat'i·tude" (lat'i-tūd″) *n.* **1**, freedom from narrow restriction. **2**, the distance of a point on the earth's surface from the equator. —**lat'i·tu'di·nal**, *adj.*

la·trine' (lə-trēn') *n.* a privy.

lat'ter (lat'ər) *adj.* **1**, being the second of two mentioned. **2**, more recent. —**Latter-day Saints**, the Mormons. —**lat'ter·ly**, *adv.* **1**, recently. **2**, toward the end.

Lattice

lat'tice (lat'is) *n.* an open network of laths, rods, etc.

laud (lâd) *v.t.* praise highly; extol. —**laud'a·ble**, *adj.* worthy of praise.

lau'da·num (lâ'də-nəm) *n.* a medicinal tincture of opium.

laud'a·to·ry (lâd'ə-tôr'ē) *adj.* praising.

laugh (làf) *v.i.* **1**, make a convulsive or chuckling noise excited by merriment or pleasure. **2**, (with *at*) be amused by; deride. —*n.* an expression of mirth or joy by an explosive noise. —**laugh'a·ble**, *adj.* funny. —**laughing gas**, nitrous oxide, used as an anesthetic.

laugh'ing·stock" *n.* a person or thing ridiculed.

laugh'ter (-tər) *n.* the act or sound of laughing.

launch (lânch) *v.t.* **1**, set or slide (a boat) into the water. **2**, give initial impulse to; set going. **3**, send forth; hurl. —*v.i.* begin action or speech. —*n.* a large open boat.

laun'der (lân'dər) *v.t. & i.* wash and iron (clothes). —**laun'der·er**, *n.* —**laun'dress**, *n.fem.*

laun'dry (lân'drē) *n.* **1**, an establishment for laundering. **2**, what is laundered.

lau're·ate (lâ'rē-ət) *adj.* crowned with laurel, as a mark of honor. —*n.* one honored, esp. a poet.

lau'rel (lor'əl) *n.* **1**, a small evergreen tree; the bay tree. **2**, any of several trees and shrubs having similar leaves. **3**, a wreath of laurel leaves, as an emblem of honor. **4**, (*pl.*) honor for achievement.

la'va (lä'və) *n.* molten rock thrown out by a volcano.

lav"a·liere' (làv'ə-lir') *n.* an ornament pendant from a chain.

lav'a·to·ry (lav'ə-tôr'ē) *n.* **1**, a small room for personal washing. **2**, a wash basin.

lave (lāv) *v.i. & t.* wash; bathe.

lav'en·der (lav'ən-dər) *n.* **1**, an aromatic shrub used in perfumery. **2**, a pale blue-purple color.

lav'ish *adj.* extravagant; generous; abundant; profuse. —*v.t.* expend or bestow in generous amount. —**lav'ish·ness**, *n.*

law (lâ) *n.* **1**, a rule of action prescribed by an authority. **2**, a collection or system of such rules. **3**, jurisprudence; the profession dealing with legal procedure; the bar. **4**, a proposition asserting a natural truth. **5**, litigation. **6**, (*Colloq.*) a law-enforcement officer. **7**, (often *cap.*) the first five books of the Old Testament. —**law'-a·bid"ing**, *adj.* obedient to the law.

law'ful (-fəl) *adj.* allowed or sanctioned by law. —**law'ful·ness**, *n.*

law'less (-ləs) *adj.* **1**, contrary to or defiant of law. **2**, not regulated by laws. —**law'less·ness**, *n.*

law'mak"er *n.* a legislator.

lawn (lân) *n.* **1**, a tract of ground covered by mowed grass. **2**, a thin linen or cotton fabric.

law'suit" *n.* an action to seek justice in a civil court.

law'yer (loi'yər) *n.* a legal counselor.

lax (laks) *adj.* **1**, lacking in strictness; careless; remiss. **2**, not tense or firm; relaxed. **3**, vague. —**lax'i·ty** (-ə-tē), **lax'ness**, *n.*

lax'a·tive (lak'sə-tiv) *n. & adj.* a mild purgative.

lay (lā) *v.t.* [*pret. & p.p.* laid (lād)] **1**, cause to lie; put in a position, situation, or condition (with *up, down, by, away*, etc.); arrange. **2**, overthrow; allay. **3**, contrive. **4**, wager. **5**, bring forth (eggs). **6**, impute; ascribe. —*v.t.* bring forth eggs. —*v.* *pret.* of lie. —*n.* **1**, relative position or arrangement. **2**, a lyric poem or song. —*adj.* pert. to the laity.

lay′er (lā′ər) *n.* **1**, a thickness of some material lying on another. **2**, that which lays.

lay·ette′ (lā-et′) *n.* an outfit of clothing, bedding, etc. for a new-born baby.

lay′man (-mən) *n.* [*pl.* -men] any member of the laity.

lay′off′ (lā′âf′) *n.* temporary suspension of employment.

lay′out′ (lā′owt′) *n.* **1**, a sketch, plan, or design. **2**, an arrangement, as of furniture; a set of materials or tools; equipment.

laze (lāz) *v.i. & t.* lounge.

la′zy (lā′zē) *adj.* **1**, disinclined to exertion; indolent. **2**, slow; sluggish; languid. —**la′zi·ness**, *n.*

lea (lē) *n.* a meadow.

leach (lēch) *v.t. & i.* wash or drain by percolation of liquid.

lead (led) *n.* **1**, a heavy, soft metal, chemical element no. 82, symbol Pb. **2**, something made of lead; a weight, bullet, etc. **3**, graphite; *black lead.* —*v.t.* **1**, treat, weight, etc., with lead. **2**, (*Printing*) space between lines.

lead (lēd) *v.t.* [*pret. & p.p.* led] **1**, go before as a guide; conduct; influence; induce. **2**, direct; control. **3**, go or be first in. **4**, play as the first card. —*v.i.* **1**, act as a guide. **2**, provide passage or access; be conducive. **3**, go first; be in advance; be in command. **4**, make the first play. —*n.* **1**, guidance; direction. **2**, the condition of being first; precedence. **3**, a clue. **4**, the opening words of a story. **5**, the principal rôle. **6**, a wire for conducting electric current.

lead′en (led′ən) *adj.* **1**, made of lead. **2**, sluggish; gloomy. **3**, of a dull gray color.

lead′er (lē′dər) *n.* **1**, one who or that which leads; a chief, director, etc. **2**, (*Brit.*) an editorial. —**lead′er·ship**, *n.*

leaf (lēf) *n.* [*pl.* leaves (lēvz)] **1**, a flat green blade growing from a stem of a plant. **2**, petal. **3**, a sheet of paper; a page. **4**, a sheet of wood, metal, etc. —**leaf′y**, *adj.*

leaf′age (lē′fij) *n.* foliage.

leaf′let (-lət) *n.* a pamphlet or circular.

league (lēg) *n.* **1**, a confederation of states, parties, etc.; alliance; association. **2**, a measure of distance, about 3 miles. —*v.t. & i.* combine.

leak (lēk) *n.* **1**, an unintended aperture allowing the escape of a fluid; any avenue of unintended entrance or escape, as of information. **2**, the act of leaking. —*v.t.* enter, escape, or allow to escape through an unintended crack, etc.

leak′age (lē′kij) *n.* act of leaking; the amount that leaks.

leak′y (lē′kē) *adj.* not perfectly sealed. —**leak′i·ness**, *n.*

lean (lēn) *v.i.* **1**, deviate from an upright position; tilt; bend. **2**, incline in feeling, opinion, etc. **3**, rest against or rely on something. —*v.t.* cause to rest against something. —*n.* **1**, a slant. **2**, meat without fat. —*adj.* **1**, not fat or plump; thin; spare. **2**, containing no fat. **3**, scanty; meager. —**lean′ness**, *n.*

lean′ing *n.* a tendency; desire.

lean′to′ *n.* a rude shelter slanting from the ground to supporting posts.

leap (lēp) *v.i.* **1**, spring through the air; jump; bound. **2**, start eagerly. —*v.i.* jump over or across; vault. —*n.* **1**, a jump or bound. **2**, a sudden rise or start. —**leap year**, a year containing an extra day (Feb. 29).

leap′frog′ *n.* a gymnastic game.

learn (lėrn) *v.t. & i.* **1**, acquire knowledge or skill (in). **2**, become informed of or acquainted (with). **3**, memorize. —**learn′ed** (lėr′nəd) *adj.* erudite. —**learn′er**, *n.* a student. —**learn′ing**, *n.* systematic knowledge.

lease (lēs) *v.t.* grant or obtain the use of (land, buildings, etc.) at a fixed rental. —*n.* a written instrument granting such use.

lease′hold′ *n.* property held under lease.

leash (lēsh) *n.* a cord or thong, esp. for restraining an animal. —*v.t.* hold in check.

least (lēst) *adj.* [*superl.* of less] little beyond all others.

leath′er (leth′ər) *n.* animal skin prepared for use by tanning, etc. —*v.t.* make, cover, or furnish with leather. —**leath′ern**, *adj.* made of leather. —**leath′er·y**, *adj.* tough, like leather.

leath′er·neck″ *n.* (*Slang*) a U. S. marine.

leave (lēv) *v.t.* [*pret. & p.p.* left] **1**, go away from; quit. **2**, let remain. **3**, omit; postpone. **4**, (with *off*) stop doing; desist from. **5**, have remaining; bequeath. —*v.i.* go away; depart. —*n.* **1**, permission. **2**, a period of absence by permission. **3**, departure. **4**, (*pl.*) pl. of *leaf*.

leav′en (lev′ən) *n.* **1**, a batch of fermenting dough. **2**, an influence that effects a gradual change. —*v.t.* add leavening to; change.

leav′en·ing *n.* that which causes a leaven; yeast.

leave-′tak″ing *n.* farewell.

leav′ings *n.pl.* residue.

lech'er (lech'ər) *n.* a lewd man. —**lech'er·ous**, *adj.* —**lech'er·y**, *n.*

lec'tern (lek'tərn) *n.* a reading stand.

lec'tor (lek'tər) *n.* a reader.

lec'ture (lek'chər) *n.* **1**, a discourse to an audience; an address. **2**, a long, tedious reprimand. —*v.t.* address; rebuke. —**lec'tur·er**, *n.* one who delivers addresses.

led *v.* pret. & p.p. of *lead.*

ledge (lej) *n.* a flat projecting part; a rim; a shelf.

ledg'er (lej'ər) *n.* a book for recording debits and credits.

lee (lē) *n.* shelter; the side of a ship away from the wind. —**lee'ward** (-wərd) *adj.*

leech (lēch) *n.* **1**, a blood-sucking worm. **2**, an instrument for drawing out blood. **3**, a parasitic person.

leek (lēk) *n.* a bulbous plant allied to the onion.

leer (lir) *v.i.* cast a suggestive or malicious look. —*n.* an oblique glance. —**leer'y**, *adj. (Slang)* wary.

lees (lēz) *n.pl.* dregs.

lee'way" *n.* room for movement, expansion, discretion, etc.

left *adj.* pert. to the side or direction that is westward as one faces north. —*n.* **1**, the left side. **2**, (often *cap.*) radical political parties. —*v.* pret. of *leave.*

left'hand"ed *adj.* [also, left'-hand"] **1**, preferring the use of the left hand. **2**, toward the left. **3**, *(Colloq.)* insincere. —*adv.* for or with the left hand.

left'ist *n.* a radical.

left'o"ver *n.* a bit of food saved from a meal.

left"wing' *adj.* pert. to the parties or doctrines of the left.

leg *n.* **1**, one of the limbs that support and move the human or animal body; any vertical supporting member. **2**, the part of a garment covering the leg. **3**, a straight segment. **4**, one contest of a series. —**leg it**, walk; run fast.

leg'a·cy (leg'ə-sē) *n.* property left by will; a bequest.

le'gal (lē'gəl) *adj.* **1**, permitted or established by law; lawful. **2**, pert. to the practice or administration of law. —**le·gal'i·ty** (li-gal'ə-tē) *n.* lawfulness. —**le'gal·ize** (-īz") *v.t.* make legal. —**legal tender**, currency that must be accepted by a creditor.

leg'ate (leg'ət) *n.* an envoy.

leg"a·tee' (-ə-tē') *n.* one who receives a legacy.

le·ga'tion (li-gā'shən) *n.* **1**, the staff and headquarters of a diplomatic officer.

le·ga'to (li-gä'tō) *adj. (Music)* without breaks between the successive tones.

leg'end (lej'ənd) *n.* **1**, a widely-accepted but unverified story. **2**, an inscription; a caption; a written key. —**leg'end·ar·y**, *adj.*

leg"er·de·main' (lej"ər-də-mān') *n.* sleight of hand; conjuring.

-legged (legd or leg'gid) *suf.* having a specified leg or number of legs.

leg'gings (leg'ingz) *n.pl.* outer coverings for the legs.

leg'gy (leg'ē) *adj.* having long legs.

leg'horn" *n.* **1**, a small domestic fowl. **2**, a hat made of straw from Livorno (Leghorn), Italy.

leg'i·ble (lej'ə-bəl) *adj.* that may be read; written plainly. —**leg"i·bil'i·ty**, *n.*

le'gion (lē'jən) *n.* **1**, a large body of armed men. **2**, any multitude of persons or things. —**le'gion·ar·y**, *adj.*

le"gion·naire' (lē"jə-nãr') *n.* a member of a legion.

leg'is·late" (lej'is-lāt") *v.i.* prepare and enact laws. —*v.t.* effect by legislation. —**leg'is·la"tor**, *n.*

leg"is·la'tion (lej"is-lā'shən) *n.* the enactment of laws; the laws. —**leg'is·la"tive**, *adj.*

leg'is·la"ture (lej'is-lā"chər) *n.* a body that prepares and enacts laws.

le·git'i·ma·cy (lə-jit'i-mə-sē) *n.* state of being legitimate; lawfulness.

le·git'i·mate (lə-jit'i-mət) *adj.* **1**, conforming to law; proper. **2**, born of parents legally married. **3**, logically correct; valid. **4**, regular; genuine. —*v.t.* (-māt") make or declare to be legitimate. —**le·git'i·mize'** (-mīz"), **le·git'i·ma·tize"** (-mə-tīz") *v.t.* —**le·git"i·mi·za'tion**, *n.*

leg'ume (leg'ūm) *n.* a plant having pods that divide into halves, as peas and beans; the pods. —**le·gu'mi·nous** (lə-gū'mi-nəs) *adj.*

le'i (lā'ē) *n. (Hawaiian)* a wreath of flowers around the neck.

lei'sure (lē'zhər) *n.* **1**, freedom from necessary occupation; spare time. **2**, convenience. —*adj.* unoccupied; idle. —**lei'sure·ly** (-lē) *adj. & adv.* without haste.

lem'ming (lem'ing) *n.* a mouselike rodent of northern regions.

Lemming

lem'on (lem'ən) *n.* **1**, a subtropical tree; its citrus fruit. **2**, a pale yellow color. 3, (*Colloq.*) something inferior; a failure. —*adj.* light yellow.

lem″on·ade′ (-ād′) *n.* a beverage of sweetened lemon juice and water.

le′mur (lē′mer) *n.* a small arboreal mammal related to the monkey.

lend *v.t.* [*pret. & p.p.* lent] 1, give temporary custody and use of. 2, give use of (money), usually for a consideration. 3, impart; furnish; accommodate (oneself) to. —*v.i.* make a loan (of or to).

length *n.* 1, distance along a line; linear measure. 2, the longest dimension of a body. 3, duration in time. 4, a piece, stretch, period, etc.

length′en (leng′then) *v.t. & i.* make or become longer.

length′wise′ *adv.* in the direction of the longest axis. Also, **length′ways′**.

length′y (leng′thē) *adj.* very long. —**length′i·ness,** *n.*

le′ni·ent (lē′nē-ent) *adj.* disposed to act without severity; merciful; gentle. —**le′ni·en·cy** (-sē), **len′i·ty** (len′ə-tē) *n.*

lens (lenz) *n.* 1, transparent glass, etc., having one or two curved surfaces, for altering the direction of light rays. 2, a similar structure in the eye: *crystalline lens.*

Lent *n.* an annual period of fasting or penitence in Christian ritual. —**Lent′en,** *adj.*

len′til *n.* a leguminous plant.

len′to (len′tō) *adj. & adv.* (*Music*) slow; slowly.

Le′o (lē′ō) *n.* a constellation, the Lion (see *zodiac*).

le′o·nine′ (lē′ə-nīn′) *adj.* like a lion; pert. to a lion.

leop′ard (lep′-ərd) *n.* a large, ferocious animal of the cat family.

Leopard

lep′er (lep′ər) *n.* one afflicted with leprosy.

lep′re·chaun′ (lep′ri-kân′) *n.* a helpful sprite, in Irish folklore.

lep′ro·sy (lep′rə-sē) *n.* a chronic bacillic disease of the skin and nerves. —**lep′rous** (-rəs) *adj.*

Les′bi·an (lez′bē-ən) *n.* 1, a resident of the island of Lesbos. 2, a homosexual female.

lese maj′es·ty (lēz′) an offense against, or indignity to, a sovereign or state's sovereignty.

le′sion (lē′zhən) *n.* an injury or wound.

less (les) *adv.* to a smaller extent or degree. —*adj.* [less′er, least] not so much, so large, or so important; smaller in extent. —*prep.* minus.

-less (-ləs or -les) *suf.* without; lacking.

les·see′ (le-sē′) *n.* one to whom a lease is granted.

less′en (-ən) *v.t. & i.* make or become less.

les′son (les′ən) *n.* 1, anything learned by study or experience. 2, a session of instruction. 3, a reproof or punishment.

les′sor (les′ôr) *n.* one who grants a lease.

lest *conj.* for fear that; to avoid.

let *v.t.* [let, let′ting] 1, allow; permit. 2, lease; rent out; assign. 3, propose, cause, or do (as in *Let us go*). —*v.i.* be leased or rented. —let on, divulge.

-let *suf.* little.

let′down″ *n.* 1, a decrease in force or tension. 2, disappointment.

le′thal (lē′thəl) *adj.* causing death.

leth′ar·gy (leth′ər-jē) *n.* disinclination to move; sluggishness. —**le·thar′gic** (lə-thär′jik) *adj.* —**le·thar′gi·cal·ly,** *adv.*

let′ter (let′ər) *n.* 1, a sign representing a voiced sound; one of the characters in writing or printing. 2, a written communication. 3, (*pl.*) literature. 4, literal wording. —*v.t.* mark with letters. —letter of credit, a draft on one bank by another, usually given to a traveler. —letter of marque (märk) (*Hist.*) a state's license to a shipowner to confiscate foreign shipping.

let′tered (-ərd) *adj.* 1, in separate letters, not script. 2, learned.

let′ter·head″ *n.* a printed heading on letter paper.

let′ter·ing *n.* the letters (usually hand-drawn) in an inscription, etc.

let′ter-per′fect *adj.* exactly correct.

let′ter·press″ *n. & adj.* printing by direct impression of inked type on paper.

let′tuce (let′əs) *n.* a plant with large green leaves, used in salad.

let′up″ *n.* a pause for rest.

leu′co·cyte″ (loo′kə-sīt″) *n.* a white blood corpuscle.

leu·ke′mi·a (loo-kē′mē-ə) *n.* excessive production of white blood corpuscles.

lev′ee (lev′ē) *n.* 1, an embankment confining a river; a dike. 2, a social reception, esp. for a large group.

lev′el (lev′əl) *adj.* 1, being in a horizontal plane. 2, having a smooth, even surface. 3, (of two or more things) rising to the same elevation; equal in degree, etc. 4, uniform; unbroken; even. —*n.* 1, an imaginary line or plane parallel to the surface of water at rest. 2, any instrument for determining such a line or plane. **3,** degree of elevation. **4,** a level surface. —*v.t.* **1,** make level. **2,** raze. **3,** aim. —*v.i.* **1,** seek or achieve a level condition. **2,** take aim; direct a purpose. **3,** (*Colloq.*) be honest or candid. —**lev'el·ness,** *n.*

lev'el·head''ed *adj.* calm and sound in judgment.

lev'er (lev'ər; lē'vər) *n.* **1,** a bar resting on and tending to rotate about a fixed point, the fulcrum, when force is applied at one end.

lev'er·age (-ij) *n.* **1,** the action of a lever; the mechanical advantage it provides. **2,** force; coercion.

le·vi'a·than (li-vī'ə-thən) *n.* something of huge size, esp. a sea animal or ship.

lev'i·tate'' (lev'ə-tāt'') *v.i.* & *t.* float or cause to float in air. —**lev'i·ta'tion,** *n.*

lev'i·ty (lev'ə-tē) *n.* **1,** lack of seriousness; frivolity. **2,** lightness in weight.

lev'y (lev'ē) *v.t.* **1,** assess or collect (taxes). **2,** raise or gather (troops). **3,** stir up; set in motion. —*n.* an assessing or assessment.

lewd (lood) *adj.* lascivious; indecent; obscene. —**lewd'ness,** *n.*

lew'is·ite'' (loo'i-sīt'') *n.* a poison gas designed for warfare.

lex''i·cog'ra·phy (lek''si-kog'rə-fē) *n.* the writing of dictionaries. —**lex''i·cog'ra·pher** (-kog'rə-fər) *n.* —**lex''i·co·graph'ic** (-kō-graf'ik) *adj.*

lex'i·con (lek'si-kən) *n.* **1,** a dictionary. **2,** a special vocabulary.

li''a·bil'i·ty (lī''ə-bil'ə-tē) *n.* **1,** the state of being liable. **2,** a debt; a debit.

li'a·ble (lī'ə-bəl) *adj.* **1,** under legal obligation; responsible; answerable. **2,** affected by a present or future influence, esp. injurious. **3,** (*Colloq.*) apt; likely; probable.

li'ai''son'' (lē'ā''zon'') *n.* **1,** contact maintained between independent forces. **2,** (*Colloq.*) an illicit affair.

li·a'na (lē-ä'nə) *n.* a tropical climbing or twining plant.

li'ar (lī'ər) *n.* one who tells a lie.

li·ba'tion (lī-bā'shən) *n.* **1,** a ceremonial pouring out of wine. **2,** (*Colloq.*) a drink; tippling.

li'bel (lī'bəl) *n.* defamation of a person in writing or printing. —**li'bel·ous,** *adj.*

lib'er·al (lib'ər-əl) *adj.* **1,** favoring progress and reform in social institutions, and the fullest practicable liberty of individual action. **2,** (*cap.*) (*Brit.*) of a certain political party. **3,** tolerant. **4,** not strict. **5,** bountiful; generous. —**lib'er·al·ism,** *n.* —**lib'er·al·ness,** *n.*

lib''er·al'i·ty (lib''ə-ral'ə-tē) *n.* tolerance; generosity.

lib'er·al·ize'' (-īz'') *v.t.* give broader range or greater tolerance to. —**lib''er·al·i·za'tion,** *n.*

lib'er·ate'' (lib'ə-rāt'') *v.t.* set free. —**lib''er·a'tion** (-ā'shən) *n.*

lib'er·tine'' (lib'ər-tēn'') *n.* & *adj.* a dissolute or licentious man.

lib'er·ty (lib'ər-tē) *n.* **1,** freedom from bondage, captivity, restraint, etc. **2,** permission granted. **3,** a presumptuous act. —**at liberty,** not engaged; not employed.

li·bid'i·nous (li-bid'ə-nəs) *adj.* lewd; lustful.

li·bi'do (li-bē'dō) *n.* the will to live; all one's energies and desires.

Li'bra (lī'brə) *n.* a constellation, the Balance (see *zodiac*).

li·brar'i·an (lī-brâr'ē-ən) *n.* a skilled worker in a library.

li'brar''y (lī'brer''ē) *n,* **1,** a collection of books, manuscripts, etc. **2,** a room or building where such a collection is available.

li·bret'to (li-bret'ō) *n.* the text or words of a musical composition, esp. an opera. —**li·bret'tist,** *n.* the writer of a libretto.

lice (līs) *n.* pl. of *louse.*

li'cense (lī'səns) *n.* **1,** permission to do something, esp. a formal authorization; an official permit. **2,** intentional unconventionality, in art. **3,** undue freedom of action or speech. —*v.t.* grant permission for; issue a license to; authorize. —**li''cen·see'** (-sē') *n.* one to whom a license is granted. —**li'cens·er, li'cen·sor,** *n.*

li·cen'tious (lī-sen'shəs) *adj.* lewd; dissolute; immoral. —**li·cen'tious·ness,** *n.*

li'chen (lī'kən) *n.* any of a variety of mosslike fungoid plants.

lick (lik) *v.t.* **1,** pass the tongue over. **2,** stroke lightly. **3,** (*Colloq.*) thrash; whip; defeat. —*n.* **1,** a stroke with or as with the tongue. **2,** (*Colloq.*) a hard blow; a vigorous effort. **3,** a natural deposit of salt which animals lick. **4,** (*Colloq.*) gait.

lic'o·rice (lik'ə-ris) *n.* a leguminous plant; its roots, used as flavoring.

lid *n.* **1,** a movable cover. **2,** eyelid. **3,** (*Colloq.*) a hat.

lie (lī) *v.i.* [**lay** (lā), **lain** (lān), **ly'ing**] **1,** rest in a recumbent or prostrate position; stretch out horizontally. **2,** be at rest; be buried; remain inactive. **3,** (with *down*) rest, press, weigh, or depend. **4,** be in a specified place, direction, or position; be found or occur. **5,** consist; comprise. **6,** (with *in*) be confined in childbirth. **7,** (with *to*) head into the wind so as to be as stationary as possible (of a ship). **8,** [*pret. & p.p.* **lied**] speak falsely; have a deceitful appearance. —*n.* **1,** relative position, direction, etc. **2,** a falsehood; a false appearance. —**give the lie to,** accuse of lying.

lief (lēf) *adv.* willingly; gladly.

liege (lēj) *n.* in feudal custom, a lord or vassal. —*adj.* loyal.

lien (lēn) *n.* the right to hold another's property while pressing a claim against him.

lieu (loo) *n.* place; stead.

lieu·ten·ant (loo-ten'ənt) *n.* **1,** an officer next below the rank of captain (Army) or lieutenant commander (Navy). **2,** assistant; deputy. —**lieu·ten·an·cy** (-ən-sē) *n.* —**lieutenant colonel, commander, general,** officers of the grade next lower than colonel, commander, general, respectively. —**lieutenant governor,** the office in a U. S. state corresponding to vice-president in the U. S. government.

life (līf) *n.* **1,** the aggregate of the powers of metabolism, reproduction, mobility, etc. **2,** animals and plants collectively. **3,** duration of existence. **4,** a condition or course of living; career; station. **5,** a biography. **6,** animation; vivacity; vigor.

life'boat *n.* a boat in which to escape from a sinking ship.

life buoy a buoyant ring used to keep one afloat in the water.

life insurance insurance whose proceeds are payable when the insured person dies.

life'less (-ləs) *adj.* **1,** without life; dead. **2,** without spirit; dull; listless. —**life'less·ness,** *n.*

life'line" *n.* **1,** a cable by which a person can be hauled out of the water. **2,** a vital line of transportation or communication.

life'long" *adj.* enduring throughout (one's) life.

Life preserver

life preserver a buoyant belt to be worn when in the water.

lif'er (lī'fər) *n.* (*Slang*) one sentenced to prison until his death.

life span the longest period of expectancy of life.

life'time" *n.* **1,** the duration of one's life. **2,** (*Colloq.*) a relatively long time. —*adj.* throughout one's life.

life'work" *n.* the calling or occupation one adopts permanently.

lift *v.t.* **1,** move upward in space; raise; elevate. **2,** exalt. **3,** display; sing loudly with (the voice). **4,** (*Colloq.*) steal. —*v.i.* **1,** exert lifting force. **2,** rise. —*n.* **1,** the act of raising or rising; the distance, force applied, or weight lifted. **2,** a helping upward or onward; a ride. **3,** an elevator. **4,** exaltation of feeling.

lig'a·ment (lig'ə-mənt) *n.* a band of tissue connecting bodily parts.

lig'a·ture" (lig'ə-chūr") *n.* **1,** the act of tying up or binding; the band, bandage, etc. used. **2,** a stroke connecting letters, notes in music, etc.; the joint character, as ff, ffl.

light (līt) *n.* **1,** that which makes things visible; illumination. **2,** the state of being visible. **3,** electromagnetic radiation, esp. that to which the eye is sensitive. **4,** a source of illumination, as a lamp; a luminous body. **5,** daytime. **6,** a window or window pane. **7,** a means of igniting, as a match. **8,** clarification. **9,** (*pl.*) point of view; principles of conduct. **10,** that which is light. —*adj.* **1,** illuminated, not dark. **2,** pale or whitish in color. **3,** of little weight; not heavy; not heavy enough. **4,** of little density or specific gravity. **5,** moderate. **6,** not burdensome or oppressive; easy. **7,** not serious or profound. —*v.t.* [*pret. & p.p.* light'ed— or lit] **1,** illuminate. **2,** ignite. **3,** (with *up*) make bright. —*v.i.* **1,** catch fire; (often with *up*) become bright. **2,** dismount; alight. **3,** come to rest; land. **4,** (with *on*) come or meet by chance. **5,** (*Colloq.*) (with *into*) attack. —**light'ness,** *n.*

light'en (-ən) *v.t. & i.* make or become light or lighter.

light'er (-ər) *n.* **1,** a device for igniting. **2,** a barge or boat for freight.

light-'fin"gered *adj.* addicted to stealing.

light-'foot"ed *adj.* nimble in footwork.

light'head"ed *adj.* **1,** dizzy. **2,** frivolous.

light'heart"ed *adj.* carefree.

light heavyweight a boxer weighing 160 to 175 pounds.

light'house" *n.* a tower displaying a warning or guiding light.

light'ing *n.* a method or effect of illumination.

light'ning (līt'ning) *n.* a sudden flash of light by the discharge of atmospheric electricity. —**lightning bug**, firefly. —**lightning rod**, a metal rod designed to ground the charge from a stroke of lightning.

light'weight" n. a boxer weighing 127 to 135 pounds.

light year the distance a ray of light travels in a year, about 5,880 billion miles.

lig'ne·ous (lig'nė-əs) adj. of or like wood.

lig'nin n. a tissue found in wood.

lig'nite (lig'nīt) n. imperfectly formed coal, resembling wood.

like (līk) v.t. regard with favor; be pleased with; feel affection toward; enjoy. —v.i. feel inclined; wish; choose. —adj. 1, having resemblance; similar; analogous; corresponding. 2, characteristic of. —n. something equivalent or similar. —adv. (Colloq.) likely; probably. —prep. similar to; in the manner of. —conj. (Colloq.) as: as though. —**lik'a·ble,** adj.

-like suf. resembling.

like'li·hood" (-lė-hůd") n. probability; expectancy.

like'ly (-lė) adj. 1, probably destined to happen or be. 2, credible. 3, suitable; preferred.

lik'en (lī'kən) v.t. represent as similar; compare.

like'ness (-nəs) n. 1, a picture, etc., esp. a faithful one. 2, resemblance.

like'wise" adv. 1, also; moreover. 2, in like manner.

lik'ing (lī'king) n. a feeling of preference, favor, or enjoyment.

li'lac (lī'lək) n. 1, a shrub having large clusters of fragrant flowers. 2, a pale purple color.

Lil'li·pu'tian (lil"i-pū'shən) adj. & n. of minute size; tiny.

lilt n. gay, lively rhythm or tone.

lil'y (lil'ė) n. any of various bulbous plants with showy bell- or horn-shaped flowers. —adj. 1, pert. to the lily. 2, white; pale; fair. 3, pure; unsullied. —**lily pad**, the floating leaf of the water lily.

Li'ma bean (lī'mə) a bean with a flat, oval seed.

limb (lim) n. 1, a member of an animal body apart from the head and trunk: a leg, arm, wing, etc. 2, a large branch of a tree. 3, a projecting part; an outgrowth, offshoot, etc. —**out on a limb** (Colloq.) in a precarious situation.

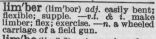

Lily

lim'ber (lim'bər) adj. easily bent; flexible; supple. —v.t. & i. make limber; flex; exercise. —n. a wheeled carriage of a field gun.

lim'bo (lim'bō) n. 1, a region where certain souls of the dead reside. 2, fig., a place of oblivion or discard.

Lim'burg"er (lim'bėr"gər) n. a kind of strong cheese.

lime (līm) n. 1, a tropical tree allied to the lemon; its greenish-yellow citrus fruit. 2, oxide of calcium, prepared from limestone (quicklime or unslaked lime) used in cement and mortar. 3, a sticky substance: birdlime. —**lim'y,** adj.

lime'light" n. a strong light thrown on a stage; hence, publicity.

lim'er·ick (lim'ər-ik) n. a five-line stanza used in humorous verse.

lime'stone" (līm'stōn") n. rock composed chiefly of calcium carbonate.

lim'ey (lī'mė) n. (Colloq.; often offensive) a British sailor or ship.

lim'it n. 1, an extreme point or line; boundary; terminal. 2, a bound of any kind. —v.t. restrict; confine. —**lim"i·ta'tion,** n.

lim'it·ed n. an express train. —**limited company,** a corporation.

limn (lim) v.t. draw; portray.

lim'ou·sine" (lim'ə-zēn") n. an enclosed automobile carrying seven.

limp v.i. 1, walk with a jerky or lame step. 2, proceed in a halting, faulty manner. —n. a lame walk or gait. —adj. lacking rigidity or stiffness; flexible; flaccid. —**limp'ness,** n.

lim'pet (lim'pət) n. a sea mollusk.

lim'pid adj. transparent; clear; lucid. —**lim·pid'i·ty, lim'pid·ness,** n.

lin'den (lin'dən) n. a tree with wide heart-shaped leaves.

line (līn) n. 1, a straight mark of little breadth; a band, stripe, furrow, wrinkle, etc. 2, a string, cord, or rope. 3, a row or rank. 4, a row of written or printed letters; a verse of poetry; a short written message. 5, a connected series. 6, a boundary or limit. 7, a connecting wire, pipe, etc. 8, a railroad, steamship, or other transport service. 9, a direction; a bearing. 10, business or occupation. 11, (Slang) flirtatious banter. 12, (pl.) plan of construction or action; words to be spoken in a play. —v.t. 1, bring into line; put in a row; mark with lines; delineate. 2, provide with a lining. —v.i. (often with up) form in a row; become aligned.

lin'e·age (lin'ė-ij) n. line of descent; family.

lin'e·al (lin'ė-əl) adj. in direct line of descent.

lin'e·a·ment (lin'ē-ə-mənt) *n.* a feature, esp. facial.

lin'e·ar (lin'ē-ər) *adj.* 1, involving measurement in only one dimension. 2, composed of or involving lines.

line'man (-mən) *n.* [*pl.* -men] one who works on, or with, a line of wire, etc., as of long distance telephone. Also, **lines'man**.

lin'en (lin'ən) *n. & adj.* thread, yarn, or cloth made from flax.

lin'er (li'nər) *n.* 1, a ship, airplane, etc. of a transport line. 2, any instrument for drawing lines. 3, a material for lining.

lines'man (līnz'mən) *n.* [*pl.* -men] 1, in sports, an official who watches boundaries or lines of a playing field. 2, a lineman.

line'up'' *n.* an array or combination of persons or things.

-ling *suf.* 1, denoting connection with, as *hireling.* 2, diminutive, as *duckling.*

lin'ger (ling'gər) *v.i.* 1, remain beyond a usual or appointed time. 2, dawdle; delay.

lin''ge·rie' (lan''zhə-rē') *n.* women's underclothing.

lin'go (ling'gō) *n.* (*Colloq.*) argot.

lin'gual (ling'gwəl) *adj.* 1, pert. to language. 2, pert. to the tongue.

lin'guist (ling'gwist) *n.* one who knows languages; a polyglot.

lin·guis'tics (ling-gwis'tiks) *n.* the science of language. — **lin·guis'tic**, *adj.* — **lin·guis'ti·cal·ly**, *adv.*

lin'i·ment (lin'ə-mənt) *n.* a soothing liquid medicine for the skin.

lin'ing (li'ning) *n.* an interior coating or layer.

link *n.* 1, one of the pieces comprising a chain. 2, something that connects. 3, a loop. 4, a surveyor's unit of measure, 7.92 inches. 5, (*pl.*) a golf course. — **link'age**, *n.*

lin'net (lin'it) *n.* a small Europ. songbird.

li·no'le·um (li-nō'lē-əm) *n.* a floor covering of heavily coated fabric.

lin'o·type'' (li'nə-tīp'') *n.* (*T.N.*) a typesetting machine, which casts each line as a unit.

lin'seed'' (lin'sēd'') *n.* seed of flax.

lint *n.* small bits of fiber or thread.

lin'tel (lin'təl) *n.* a horizontal beam over a doorway, etc.

li'on (li'ən) *n.* 1, a large, ferocious cat of Afr. and Asia. 2, a strong, courageous man. 3, a sought-after person; a celebrity. — **li'on·ess**, *n. fem.*

li'on·heart''ed *adj.* courageous.

li'on·ize'' (-īz'') *v.t.* treat as a celebrity.

lip *n.* 1, either of the two fleshy parts forming the opening of the mouth. 2, (*pl.*) speech; utterance. 3, (*Slang*) impudent talk. 4, a lip-like organ or part; rim; edge. — **lip reading**, the reading of the movements of another's lips, as by a deaf person. — **lip service**, insincere praise or agreement.

lip'stick'' *n.* a stick of cosmetic used to redden the lips.

liq'ue·fy'' (lik'wi-fī'') *v.t. & i.* make or become liquid. — **liq''ue·fac'tion**, *n.*

li·queur' (li-kŏr') *n.* a sweet, flavored alcoholic liquor.

liq'uid (lik'wid) *n.* any fluid substance neither solid nor gaseous. — *adj.* 1, being or pert. to a liquid. 2, like a liquid; clear, transparent, flowing, etc. 3, in cash or readily convertible to cash. — **li·quid'i·ty** (-ə-tē) *n.*

liq'ui·date'' (lik'wi-dāt'') *v.t. & i.* 1, pay or settle (debts, etc.); convert to cash. 2, finally close (business affairs, etc.). 3, (*Slang*) kill. — **liq''ui·da'tion**, *n.*

liq'uor (lik'ər) *n.* 1, a distilled alcoholic beverage. 2, any liquid.

li'ra (lē'rä) *n.* [*pl.* li're] the monetary unit of Italy, worth about ½ U. S. cent.

lisle (līl) *adj.* knitted of fine, strong cotton or linen yarn.

lisp *n.* the pronouncing of *s* and *z* like *th.* — *v.t. & i.* so pronounce.

lis'some (lis'əm) *adj.* supple.

list *n.* 1, a record of a number of items; an enumeration. 2, a leaning to one side, as of a ship. 3, selvage. 4, a ridge or furrow. 5, (*pl.*) an arena for jousts. — *v.t.* make a record of; enter or arrange in a list. — *v.i.* 1, tilt; careen. 2, (*Archaic*) like; wish. 3, listen.

lis'ten (lis'ən) *v.i.* 1, try to hear. 2, give heed; be compliant.

list'er (lis'tər) *n.* a plow for cutting furrows.

list'less (list'ləs) *adj.* indifferent; languid. — **list'less·ness**, *n.*

lit *v.* pret. & p.p. of *light.* — *adj.* (*Slang*) drunk.

lit'a·ny (lit'ə-nē) *n.* a ceremonial prayer with responses.

li'tchi (lē'chē) *n.* a Chinese tree; its sweet nut.

li'ter (lē'tər) *n.* a liquid measure, about 1.0567 U.S. quarts. Also, **li'tre**.

lit'er·a·cy (lit'ə-rə-sē) *n.* ability to read and write.

lit'er·al (lit'ər-əl) *adj.* 1, in accordance with the strict meanings of words; not figurative or metaphorical. **2,** (of persons) strict in interpretation; unimaginative; prosaic. **3,** true to fact. **4,** pert. to letters of the alphabet. —**lit′er·al·ism,** n.

lit′er·ar·y (lit′ə-rer-ē) adj. **1,** pert. to literature. **2,** engaged in writing; learned in literature.

lit′er·ate (lit′ər-ət) adj. able to read and write. —n. one who is literate.

lit″e·ra′ti (lit″ə-rä′tē) n.pl. learned persons.

lit′er·a·ture (lit′ər-ə-chûr) n. **1,** artistic writings. **2,** the aggregate of all writings of a people, period, topic, etc. **3,** literary work. **4,** (Colloq.) printed matter, esp. advertising pamphlets.

lith- pref. stone.

-lith suf. stone.

lithe (lith) adj. easily bent; pliant; flexible; supple. —**lithe′ness,** n.

lith′i·at″ed (lith′ē-ā″tid) adj. treated with lithium, which imparts a citrous flavor. —**lithia water,** lithiated water.

lith′i·um (lith′ē-əm) n. a metallic chemical element, no. 3, symbol Li.

lith′o·graph″ (lith′ə-grȧf″) n. a print produced by lithography. —**lith″o·graph′ic,** adj. —**lith″o·graph′i·cal·ly,** adv.

li·thog′ra·phy (li-thog′rə-fē) n. printing, now usually by offset, from a stone or equivalent surface on which certain parts are chemically treated to reject ink. —**li·thog′ra·pher,** n.

lith′o·sphere″ (lith′ə-sfir″) n. the earth's crust.

lit′i·gant (lit′i-gənt) n. a disputant at law.

lit′i·gate″ (lit′i-gāt″) v.i. & t. contest in court. —**lit″i·ga′tion,** n.

li·ti′gious (li-tij′əs) adj. quick to litigate. —**li·ti′gious·ness,** n.

lit′mus paper (lit′məs) a paper that changes color to blue in alkaline, to red in acid solutions.

lit′ter (lit′ər) n. **1,** a number of young brought forth at one birth. **2,** a portable bed. **3,** loose straw, etc. for bedding. **4,** rubbish; disorder. —v.t. scatter (things) about.

lit′tle (lit′əl) adj. [less or less′er, least; or lit′tler, -tlest] **1,** small in size, amount, number, degree, or duration; not large or much. **2,** unimportant; low in station. **3,** petty; mean. —adv. **1,** in small degree; not much. **2,** not at all. —**lit′tle·ness,** n.

lit′tle·neck″ n. a small edible clam.

lit′to·ral (lit′ə-rəl) adj. & n. shore.

lit′ur·gy (lit′ər-jē) n. a ritual of public worship. —**li·tur′gi·cal** (li-tȇr′ji-kəl) adj.

liv′a·ble (liv′ə-bəl) adj. habitable; endurable.

live (liv) v.i. **1,** have life, as an animal or plant. **2,** remain alive; survive. **3,** continue in existence, operation, etc. **4,** dwell; reside. **5,** have experience. —v.t. pass (a kind of life); experience. —adj. (līv) **1,** having life; alive; energetic. **2,** burning; carrying electric current; unexploded (of a shell).

-lived (-līvd) suf. aged.

live′li·hood″ (līv′lē-hŏŏd″) n. an occupation that furnishes means of support.

live′long″ (liv′-) adj. entire.

live′ly (līv′lē) adj. **1,** full of life. **2,** vivid; bright. **3,** buoyant; elastic. —**live′li·ness,** n.

liv′en (lī′vən) v.t. & i. make or become lively.

liv′er (liv′ər) n. **1,** the vital organ that secretes bile, etc. **2,** an animal liver as meat.

liv′er·ied (liv′ər-ēd) adj. uniformed.

liv′er·ish (liv′ər-ish) adj. **1,** having a disorder of the liver. **2,** disagreeable in manner.

liv′er·wurst″ (liv′ər-wȇrst″) n. liver sausage.

liv′er·y (liv′ə-rē) n. **1,** a uniform, esp. one worn by a domestic servant. **2,** the keeping and letting of horses for hire.

live′stock″ (līv′-) n. useful domestic animals, esp. cattle.

live wire (līv) **1,** a wire carrying electric current. **2,** (Slang) a go-getter.

liv′id adj. dull bluish in color, as a bruise. —**liv′id·ness,** n.

liv′ing (liv′-) n. **1,** livelihood; (Brit.) a rector's post. —**living room,** a parlor.

liz′ard (liz′ərd) n. a small four-legged reptile with a long scaly body.

lla′ma (lä′mə) n. a large ruminant of So. Amer.; its fine, soft hair.

lla′no (lä′nō) n. [pl. -nos] a plain.

Llama

load (lōd) n. **1,** that which is carried in a conveyance; the amount that can be carried or contained at one time. **2,** a burden. **3,** (Slang) too much liquor imbibed. —v.t. **1,** put a load on or into; fill; charge. **2,** weigh down; burden; encumber; oppress. —*v.i.* take on a load.

load'stone" *n.* lodestone.

loaf (lōf) *n.* [*pl.* **loaves** (lōvz)] a formed mass of bread, cake, or other food. —*v.t.* & *i.* lounge; idle away time.

loaf'er (-ər) *n.* **1,** an idler. **2,** a lounging shoe or slipper.

loam (lōm) *n.* **1,** soil rich in organic matter. **2,** a mixture of sand, sawdust, etc. used to make molds.

loan (lōn) *n.* something lent; the act of lending. —*v.t.* & *i.* (*Colloq.*) lend. —**loan shark,** a usurer.

loath (lōth) *adj.* reluctant.

loathe (lōth) *v.t.* hate; detest. —**loath'ing,** *n.* aversion, disgust, or hatred. —**loath'some,** *adj.* hateful.

lob *v.t.* & *i.* [**lobbed, lob'bing**] strike or toss a ball so that it moves slowly in a high arc.

lob'by (lob'ė) *n.* **1,** a vestibule or anteroom. **2,** persons who seek to influence legislators. —*v.t.* solicit the support of legislators. —**lob'by-ist,** *n.*

lobe (lōb) *n.* a globular or rounded part, esp. of the ear.

lob'ster (lob'stər) *n.* an edible marine crustacean having two large claws. —**lobster shift,** the working hours from midnight to 8 a.m.

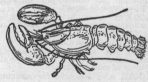

Lobster

lo'cal (lō'kəl) *adj.* **1,** pert. to situation in space; occurring in or particular to a specified place. **2,** (of a train) stopping at many or all stations.

lo-cale' (-kal') *n.* the scene of specified events.

lo-cal'i-ty (-kal'ə-tē) *n.* a place; community; section.

lo'cal-ize (-īz') *v.t.* restrict to a particular place. —**lo"cal-i-za'tion,** *n.*

lo'cate (lō'kāt) *v.t.* **1,** discover or describe the place or locality of. **2,** establish in a particular place; settle. —**lo-ca'tion,** *n.*

lock (lok) *n.* **1,** a device that fastens and prevents the opening, detachment, movement, etc. of a door, part, etc.; a catch or brake. **2,** a boxlike enclosure in a water-

course, with gates at each end, for moving boats from one level to another. **3,** any of various wrestling holds. **4,** a tress of hair; (*pl.*) hair of the head. —*v.t.* **1,** fasten, secure, or arrest. **2,** close (a lock). **3,** (with *up* or *in*) shut in; confine; isolate. **4,** (with *out*) exclude forcibly. **5,** fix or unite firmly. —*v.i.* become locked.

lock'er (-ər) *n.* a cabinet that can be locked.

lock'et (-it) *n.* a hinged case worn on a necklace.

lock'jaw" *n.* tetanus.

lock'out" *n.* refusal to employ union labor formerly employed.

lock'smith" *n.* a skilled worker on locks.

lock'up" *n.* (*Colloq.*) a jail.

lo'co (lō'kō) *adj.* (*Slang*) crazy, as from eating locoweed, an intoxicating plant.

lo"co-mo'tion (lō"kə-mō'shən) *n.* the act or power of moving from place to place.

Locomotives

lo"co-mo'tive (-tiv) *adj.* pert. to or having the power of locomotion. —*n.* the self-propelled vehicle that pulls a railroad train.

lo"co-mo'tor (-tər) *adj.* pert. to locomotion. —**locomotor ataxia** (ə-tak'sē-ə) a form of paralysis.

lo'cus (lō'kəs) *n.* [*pl.* **lo'ci** (lō'sī)] a place; locality.

lo'cust (lō'kəst) *n.* **1,** a variety of voracious grasshoppers or cicadas. **2,** a thorny, white-flowered tree.

lo-cu'tion (lō-kū'shən) *n.* style of speech; a phrase or expression.

lode (lōd) *n.* a mineral deposit or vein, esp. of metal ore.

lode'star" (lōd'stär") *n.* a star that serves to guide, esp. Polaris.

lode'stone" *n.* a mineral having magnetic attraction for iron.

lodge (loj) *n.* **1,** a temporary habitation. **2,** a fraternal society; its place. —*v.t.* **1,** provide lodging for; shelter; harbor. **2,** put in a place; deposit. —*v.i.* **1,** live in hired quarters. **2,** come to rest in a place. —**lodg'er,** *n.* one living in hired quarters. —**lodg'ing,** *n.* (often *pl.*) quarters hired for residence.

loft (lâft) *n.* **1,** the space directly under the roof of a building. **2,** a large room used for light manufacturing. **3,** a lifting stroke or impetus. —*v.t.* & *i.* send upward; rise.

loft'y (lȧf'tē) *adj.* high; elevated; exalted. —**loft'i·ness,** *n.*

log (lȧg) *n.* **1,** a bulky piece of timber; a section of the trunk or a large branch of a tree. **2,** a device for measuring the speed and progress of a ship; a record of this: logbook. **3,** a record or register. **4,** a stolid or stupid person. **5,** logarithm. —*v.t.* [logged, log'ging] **1,** cut into logs. **2,** record. —*v.i.* cut down trees; gather timber. —**log'ger,** *n.* one who cuts trees for lumber.

lo'gan·ber'ry (lō'gən-ber'ē) *n.* a berry similar to a blackberry.

log'a·rithm (log'ə-rith-əm) *n.* the exponent that must be applied to a fixed number (base) to produce a given number. —**log"a·rith'mic** (-mik) *adj.*

loge (lōzh) *n.* a box or area of special seats in a theater.

log'ger·head" (lȧg'ər-hed") *n.* a stupid person. —**at loggerheads,** engaged in dispute.

log'gia (loj'ə) *n.* a gallery or partly open room.

log'ic (loj'ik) *n.* the science of correct reasoning. —**lo·gi'cian** (lō-jish'ən) *n.*

log'i·cal (loj'i-kəl) *adj.* reasonable; persuasive; to be expected.

lo·gis'tics (lō-jis'tiks) *n.* (*Mil.*) the science of transport and supply. —**lo·gis'tic,** *adj.* —**lo·gis'ti·cal·ly,** *adv.*

log'roll"ing *n.* **1,** the rolling of floating logs with the feet. **2,** (*Colloq.*) the trading of favors among politicians.

lo'gy (lō'gē) *adj.* sluggish; dull.

loin *n.* the part of a body between the lower ribs and hipbone; meat from this part of an animal. —**loin'cloth",** *n.* a cloth worn around the hips.

loi'ter (loi'tər) *v.i.* **1,** linger idly. **2,** waste time; delay; lag.

loll (lol) *v.i.* lean or lie in a languid, indolent manner.

lol'li·pop" (lol'ē-pop") *n.* a kind of hard candy on the end of a stick.

lone (lōn) *adj.* **1,** being alone; solitary; isolated. **2,** unmarried.

lone'ly (-lē) *adj.* **1,** remote from other habitations. **2,** [also, lone'some] dejected from being alone. —**lone'li·ness, lone'some·ness,** *n.*

long (lȧng) *adj.* **1,** having great extent in time or space. **2,** having a specified length or duration. **3,** far away; distant in time. **4,** tall; great

in amount, number, or ratio. —*adv.* **1,** to a protracted extent, esp. in time. **2,** to a specified extent. —*n.* **1,** a long time. **2,** something long. —*v.i.* feel a strong desire; yearn; hanker.

long distance telephone service between different cities.

long'drawn" *adj.* prolonged.

lon·gev'i·ty (lȧn-jev'ə-tē) *n.* duration of life; long life.

long green (*Slang*) paper money.

long'hand" *n.* ordinary handwriting.

long'horn" *n.* a kind of cattle.

long'ing *n.* prolonged desire.

lon'gi·tude" (lon'jə-tūd") *n.* distance on the earth's surface east or west of a given meridian, esp. that of Greenwich. —**lon"gi·tu'di·nal,** *adj.*

long'shore'man (-mən) *n.* [*pl.* -**men**] one who loads or unloads ships.

long ton 2,240 pounds.

long'wind"ed *adj.* tediously long (of a speech, etc.). —**long'wind"ed·ness,** *n.*

look (lŏk) *v.i.* **1,** use the eyes; exercise the power of vision. **2,** afford a view or outlook. **3,** keep watch; take heed. **4,** expect or hope (for). **5,** appear. —*v.t.* **1,** (usually with *up*) try to find. **2,** suggest by a look or appearance. —*n.* **1,** a visual examination or search. **2,** the act of looking. **3,** (often *pl.*) outward appearance or aspect.

look'er *n.* **1,** a watcher. **2,** a handsome person. —**look"er-on',** *n.* a spectator.

look'ing glass a mirror.

look'out" *n.* **1,** a watch kept; a watchman; his post. **2,** (*Colloq.*) an object of care or concern.

loom *n.* a machine for weaving cloth from yarn or thread. —*v.i.* **1,** come into view indistinctly. **2,** seem large or portentous.

loon *n.* a fish-eating diving bird.

loon'y *adj.* & *n.* (*Colloq.*) crazy.

loop *n.* **1,** a portion of rope, ribbon, etc. doubled back on itself to form an open eye. **2,** something of similar shape. —*v.t.* make a loop in; make into a loop; encircle with a loop. —*v.i.* move in a loop.

loop'hole" *n.* any means of escape or evasion.

loose (loos) *adj.* **1,** free from fetters or restraint; joined slackly or not at all; not tight or close; not bundled. **2,** open or porous. **3,** slack; diffuse; not concise. **4,** wanton; dissolute. —*v.t.* **1,** make loose; set free; release; untie. **2,** relax; —**loose'ness,** *n.*

loos'en (loo'sən) *v.t.* & *i.* make or become loose or looser.

loot *n.* booty seized in war; plunder; spoils; something stolen. —*v.t.* pillage; rob. —**loot′er,** *n.*

lop *v.t.* [**lopped, lop′ping**] **1,** cut off; trim by cutting off superfluous parts. **2,** let droop. —*v.i.* droop.

lope (lōp) *v.i.* move with a long, easy stride; canter. —*n.* this gait.

lop′sid″ed (lop′sī″dĭd) *adj.* heavier on, or leaning to, one side. —**lop′sid″ed·ness,** *n.*

lo·qua′cious (lō-kwā′shəs) *adj.* talkative. —**lo·quac′i·ty** (-kwas′ə-tē) *n.*

lo′ran (lôr′ən) *n.* an electronic device by which a navigator can determine his position from radio signals.

lord (lôrd) *n.* **1,** a master; a nobleman: a title of rank. **2,** (*cap.*) God; Jesus Christ.

lord′ly (-lē) *adj.* **1,** imperious; insolent. **2,** befitting a lord; magnificent. —**lord′li·ness,** *n.*

lore (lôr) *n.* the store of knowledge about a particular subject.

lor·gnette′ (lôr-nyet′) *n.* eyeglasses mounted on a handle.

lorn (lôrn) *adj.* forsaken; desolate (*obs.* except in compounds, as *lovelorn*).

lor′ry (lor′ē) *n.* a truck, esp. (*Brit.*) a motor truck.

lo′ry (lôr′ē) *n.* a small Pacific parrot.

lose (looz) *v.t.* [*pret.* & *p.p.* **lost**] **1,** miss and not know where to find. **2,** be deprived of; be parted from. **3,** cease to have. **4,** cause or suffer defeat in (a game). —*v.i.* suffer loss; be defeated. —**los′er,** *n.*

loss (lâs) *n.* **1,** failure to hold, keep, or preserve. **2,** that which is lost. **3,** wastage. **4,** defeat; ruin. —**at a loss,** bewildered; uncertain.

lost (lâst) *adj.* **1,** no longer possessed. **2,** wasted. **3,** unable to find one's way. —*v.* pret. & p.p. of *lose.*

lot *n.* **1,** a station or condition determined by chance or destiny. **2,** a means of deciding something by chance. **3,** a distinct portion or parcel, esp. of land. **4,** (*Colloq.*) a great many; a great deal.

lo′tion (lō′shən) *n.* a liquid medicine for the skin.

lot′ter·y (lot′ə-rē) *n.* a method of selling numbered tickets and awarding prizes to the holders of certain numbers drawn by lot.

lot′to (lot′ō) *n.* a kind of lottery game; bingo.

lo′tus (lō′təs) *n.* **1,** a plant of Greek legend, possibly a jujube shrub or nettle tree. **2,** any of a variety of water lilies. **3,** a genus of leguminous plants.

loud (lowd) *adj.* **1,** strongly audible. **2,** vehement; noisy. **3,** stormy; turbulent. **4,** urgent; emphatic. **5,** excessively showy; overdone. **6,** vulgar in manners or taste. —**loud′ness,** *n.*

loud′mouthed″ (-mowthd″) *adj.* arrogantly talkative.

loud′speak″er *n.* a device for amplifying sound to make it widely audible.

lounge (lownj) *v.i.* **1,** move or recline listlessly; loll. **2,** pass the time idly. —*n.* **1,** a public waiting room. **2,** a kind of long sofa. **3,** an indolent gait or stooping posture.

louse (lows) *n.* [*pl.* **lice** (līs)] **1,** a small blood-sucking insect; any of various other parasitic insects. **2,** (*Slang*) a contemptible person.

lous′y (low′zē) *adj.* **1,** infested with lice. **2,** (*Slang*) mean or contemptible. **3,** (*Slang*) abundantly supplied. —**lous′i·ness,** *n.*

lout (lowt) *n.* an awkward, uncouth or boorish fellow. —**lout′ish,** *adj.*

lou′ver (loo′vər) *n.* a slit, esp. one of a number serving as air vents.

love (luv) *n.* **1,** affection for another person, esp. of the opposite sex. **2,** an object of affection; a sweetheart. **3,** any strong liking or affection. **4,** (in games) a score of zero. —*v.t.* & *i.* have love, affection, or liking for. —**lov′a·ble,** *adj.*

love′lorn″ *adj.* forsaken by a loved one.

love′ly (-lē) *adj.* beautiful; delightful. —**love′li·ness,** *n.*

lov′er (luv′ər) *n.* one who loves, esp. a man who loves a woman.

love seat a settee for two.

love′sick″ *adj.* disconsolate because of unrequited love.

lov′ing *adj.* very affectionate. —**loving cup,** a large cup from which many can drink; such a cup used as a trophy.

low (lō) *adj.* **1,** situated not far above the ground or base; not high; below a usual or standard level. **2,** deep. **3,** prostrate or dead. **4,** not high in scale, quality, or degree; moderate; simple. **5,** inferior. **6,** base; mean; coarse. **7,** not many in number. **8,** not loud; soft; feeble. **9,** dejected; depressed. —*adv.* **1,** in a low position, degree, etc. **2,** cheaply. **3,** in low tone or pitch; quietly. —*n.* **1,** that which is low. **2,** the lowest gear ratio for forward progress in an automobile transmission. **3,** the sound uttered by cattle. —*v.i.* & *t.* sound or utter as cattle do; moo.

low′boy″ *n.* a chest of drawers on short legs.

low′brow″ *n.* & *adj.* (*Slang*) one of low intellectual tastes.

low'down" (*Slang*) *adj.* contemptible. —*n.* inside information.

low'er (lō'ər) *v.t.* **1,** cause to descend; take down. **2,** reduce; degrade; humble; humiliate. —*v.i.* **1,** decrease. **2,** descend; sink. —**low'er-case'**, *adj.* in letters not capitals.

low'er (low'ər) *v.i.* **1,** scowl; frown. **2,** appear dark and threatening.

low'land (lō'lənd) *n.* territory low in elevation.

low'ly (lō'lē) *adj.* humble. —**low'-li-ness,** *n.*

loy'al (loi'əl) *adj.* **1,** faithful; constant in devotion or regard. **2,** manifesting fidelity. —**loy'al-ist,** *n.* one who remains loyal to a government during a rebellion.

loy'al-ty (-tē) *n.* state of being loyal; fidelity.

loz'enge (loz'ənj) *n.* **1,** a sweet pill. **2,** a diamond-shaped figure.

lub'ber (lub'ər) *n.* a clumsy or stupid fellow; an unskillful sailor. —**lub'ber-ly,** *adj.*

lu'bri-cant (loo'bri-kənt) *n.* a material for lubricating, as grease.

lu'bri-cate" (loo'bri-kāt") *v.t.* **1,** apply oil or grease to. **2,** make smooth. —**lu"bri-ca'tion,** *n.*

lu-cerne' (loo-sērn') *n.* alfalfa.

lu'cid (loo'sid) *adj.* **1,** clear; easily understood; distinct. **2,** sane; rational. **3,** shining. —**lu-cid'i-ty,** *n.*

lu'cite (loo'sit) *n.* (*T.N.*) a plastic having unusual transparency and properties of light transmission.

luck (luk) *n.* **1,** a trend of chance events. **2,** good fortune.

luck'y (-ē) *adj.* **1,** bringing good fortune; favorable. **2,** fortunate. **3,** chance; fortuitous. —**luck'i-ness,** *n.*

lu'cra-tive (loo'krə-tiv) *adj.* yielding gain; profitable.

lu'cre (loo'kər) *n.* money; profit (usually contemptuous).

lu'cu-brate" (loo'kyū-brāt") *v.i.* work or study laboriously, esp. at night. —**lu"cu-bra'tion,** *n.*

lu'di-crous (loo'di-krəs) *adj.* absurd; ridiculous. —**lu'di-crous-ness,** *n.*

luff (luf) *v.i.* turn the bow of a ship toward the wind. —*n.* the foreward edge of a fore-and-aft sail.

lug *v.t. & i.* [lugged, lug'ging] carry or drag with effort. —*n.* **1,** a yank, tug, or haul. **2,** a projecting earlike part; a tab, flange, or cam. **3,** a sluggish fellow.

lug'gage (lug'ij) *n.* trunks, valises, etc.; baggage.

lug'ger (lug'ər) *n.* a vessel rigged with lugsails. —**lug'sail",** *n.* a quadrilateral sail.

lu-gu'bri-ous (loo-gū'brē-əs) *adj.* mournful; doleful; dejected. —**lu-gu'bri-ous-ness,** *n.*

luke'warm" (look'wôrm") *adj.* **1,** tepid; unenthusastic. —**luke'warm'-ness,** *n.*

lull (lul) *v.t.* soothe; assuage; calm. —*v.i.* become quiet; subside. —*n.* a period of temporary quiet or rest.

lull'a-by" (lul'ə-bī") *n.* a song to lull a child to sleep.

lum-ba'go (lum-bā'gō) *n.* rheumatic pain in muscles of the back.

lum'bar (lum'bər) *adj.* pert. to the loins.

lum'ber (lum'bər) *n.* timber sawed or split for use. —*v.i.* walk clumsily. —**lum'ber-ing,** *adj.* clumsy in gait.

lum'ber-jack" *n.* one who cuts lumber.

lu'mi-nar-y (loo'mə-ner-ē) *n.* **1,** a celestial body, as the sun; a light. **2,** one who enlightens mankind.

lu"mi-nes'cence (loo"mə-nes'əns) *n.* emission of light without heat. —**lu"mi-nes'cent,** *adj.*

lu'mi-nous (loo'mə-nəs) *adj.* **1,** giving out light. **2,** bright; resplendent. **3,** clear; lucid. **4,** intellectually brilliant. —**lu-mi-nos'i-ty** (-nos'ə-tē) *n.*

lum'mox (lum'əks) *n.* (*Colloq.*) a clumsy or stupid person.

lump *n.* **1,** a mass of solid matter with no particular shape. **2,** a protuberance, knob, or swelling. **3,** a dull, stolid person. **4,** in the form of a lump. —*v.t.* work into a mass; deal with as a whole. —*v.i.* **1,** form a lump. **2,** move heavily. —**lump'y, lump'ish,** *adj.* —**lump it,** endure something disagreeable.

lu'na-cy (loo'nə-sē) *n.* insanity.

lu'nar (loo'nər) *adj.* pert. to the moon.

lu'na-tic (loo'nə-tik) *n.* a crazy person. —*adj.* crazy.

lunch *n.* **1,** a midday meal. **2,** any light meal. —*v.i.* eat a lunch.

lunch'eon (lun'chən) *n.* lunch.

lune (loon) *n.* a figure bounded by two arcs of circles; a crescent. —**lu'nate** (-nāt) *adj.* —**lu-nette'** (-net') *n.* something crescent-shaped.

lung *n.* one of the two large spongy organs of breathing in man and the higher vertebrates. —**iron lung,** a chamber to assist respiration by alternations of air pressure.

lunge (lunj) *n.* a sudden forward movement. —*v.i.* so move.

lu'pine (loo'pin) *adj.* pert. to a wolf.

lurch (lērch) *v.i.* sway suddenly to one side; list; stagger. —*n.* **1,** an act of lurching. **2,** an untenable situation; bad defeat in a game.

lure (lūr) *n.* something used to allure, entice, or trap; a bait or decoy. —*v.t.* entice.

lu'rid (lūr'id) *adj.* **1,** lighted up with a fiery glare. **2,** sensational; exaggerated. —**lur'id·ness,** *n.*

lurk (lĕrk) *v.i.* **1,** lie in concealment; exist unperceived or unsuspected. **2,** skulk; slink.

lus'cious (lush'əs) *adj.* very pleasing to taste or smell; delightful. —**lus'cious·ness,** *n.*

lush *adj.* **1,** fresh and juicy. **2,** luxuriant. —*n.* (*Slang*) a drunkard. —**lush'ness,** *n.*

lust *n.* intense longing for possession or enjoyment; passionate or lewd desire. —*v.i.* feel lust. —**lust'ful,** *adj.*

lus'ter (lus'tər) *n.* **1,** the quality of shining with light emitted or reflected; radiance; glitter. **2,** a glossy finish. **3,** distinction; brilliancy. Also, **lus'tre.** —**lus'trous,** *adj.*

lust'y (lus'tē) *adj.* vigorous; robust; healthy; lively. —**lust'i·ness,** *n.*

Lute

lute (loot) *n.* a medieval musical instrument similar to a mandolin.

Lu'ther·an (loo'thə-rən) *adj.* & *n.* pert. to the Protestant Church founded by Martin Luther.

lux·u'ri·ant (lug-zhūr'ē-ənt) *adj.* **1,** growing or producing in abundance; plentiful; profuse. **2,** florid; superabundant. —**lux·u'ri·ance,** *n.*

lux·u'ri·ate (lug-zhūr'ē-āt) *v.i.* enjoy luxury or abundance. —**lux·u'ri·a'tion,** *n.*

lux·u'ri·ous (lug-zhūr'ē-əs) *adj.* characterized by luxury.

lux'u·ry (luk'shə-rē) *n.* **1,** abundant means of self-indulgence. **2,** something enjoyable but not necessary; a delicacy.

-ly (-lē) *suf.* **1,** in a specified manner: forming adverbs, as *blindly*, in a blind manner. **2,** like: forming adjectives, as *saintly*, like a saint.

ly'can·thrope' (lī'kən-thrōp') *n.* a werewolf; an insane person who imagines himself to be a wolf. —**ly·can'thro·py** (lī-kan'thrə-pē) *n.*

ly·ce'um (lī-sē'əm) *n.* **1,** a literary association. **2,** a lecture hall.

lye (lī) *n.* a caustic solution of any alkaline salt, used in making soap.

ly"ing-in' *adj.* confinement in childbirth.

lymph (limf) *n.* a yellowish alkaline fluid in animal bodies.

lym·phat'ic (lim-fat'ik) *adj.* **1,** pert. to lymph. **2,** sluggish.

lynch (linch) *v.t.* execute (a person) without authority or process of law.

lynx (links) *n.* a wildcat.

lyre (līr) *n.* a stringed musical instrument of ancient Greece.

lyr'ic (lir'ik) *adj.* **1,** pert. to singing; songlike. **2,** concerned with thoughts and feelings; romantic. **3,** (of a voice) delicate in quality and without great range. —*n.* **1,** a lyric poem or song. **2,** (*Colloq.*) the words of a song. —**lyr'i·cal,** *adj.* —**lyr'i·cist,** *n.*

M

M, m (em) the thirteenth letter of the English alphabet.

ma (mä) *n.* (*Colloq.*) mother.

ma'am (mȧm; məm) *n.* (*Colloq.*) a term of address to women; madam.

ma·ca'bre (mə-kä'brə) *adj.* gruesome, as suggestive of the dance of death (*danse macabre*).

mac·ad'am (mə-kad'əm) *n.* a road of crushed stone, usually with an asphalt surface. —*adj.* made of such materials. —**mac·ad'am·ize'** (-īz') *v.t.*

ma·caque' (mə-käk') *n.* a short-tailed monkey of Asia.

mac'a·ro'ni (mak"ə-rō'nē) *n.* thin tubes of dried wheat paste, as food.

mac"a·roon' (mak"ə-roon') *n.* a small sweet cake.

ma·caw' (mə-kä') *n.* a long-tailed parrot of tropical America.

mace (mās) *n.* **1,** a clublike weapon. **2,** a spice resembling nutmeg.

mac'er·ate" (mas'ə-rāt") *v.t.* **1,** separate or soften by digestion or soaking. **2,** make thin. —*v.i.* grow thin; waste away. —**mac"er·a'tion,** *n.*

Macaw

Mach (mäk) *adv.* in relation to the speed of sound at a given altitude, as *Mach 2* = twice the speed of sound (2 being the **Mach number**).

ma·che'te (mä-chā'tā, mə-shet') *n.* a heavy knife.

Mach"i·a·vel'li·an (mak"ē·ə-vel'ē-ən) *adj.* pert. to Niccolo di Bernardo Machiavelli, Italian statesman, or to his political philosophy of ruthlessness and unscrupulousness.

mach'i·nate (mak'ə-nāt) v.t. & i. plan or plot, esp. with evil intent. —**mach"i·na'tion**, n.

ma·chine' (mə-shēn') n. 1, any device that transfers or converts energy from one form to another, esp. for manufacturing. 2, an automobile. 3, a sewing machine. 4, persons acting together for a common purpose, as a *political machine*. —v.t. grind to a smooth finish with a machine. —**machine gun**, a mounted rifle that fires automatically and continuously.

ma·chin'e·ry (mə-shē'nə-rē) n. 1, machines or parts of machines, collectively. 2, a system, not mechanical, designed to keep anything going.

ma·chin'ist (mə-shē'nist) n. a skilled operator of precision machinery; a toolmaker.

mack'er·el (mak'ər-əl) n. a food fish of the No. Atlantic.

mack'i·naw" (mak'ə-nâ') n. a short, woolen outer coat.

mack'in·tosh" (mak'in-tosh') n. a raincoat of rubber-coated cloth.

mac·ro- *pref.* large; great.

mac'ro·cosm (mak'rə-koz-əm) n. the great world; the universe.

ma'cron (mā'kron) n. the diacritical mark indicating a long vowel, as on ā.

mac"ro·scop'ic (mak"rə-skop'ik) adj. visible to the naked eye. —**mac"ro·scop'i·cal·ly**, adv.

mad adj. [**mad'der, -dest**] 1, mentally deranged; irresponsible; irrational. 2, of a dog, rabid. 3, disorderly; ill-advised. 4, infatuated; in love. 5, (*Colloq.*) angry. —**mad'ness,** n.

mad'am (mad'əm) n. a polite term of address to a woman. Also (*Fr.*) **ma·dame'** (mà-dàm') [*pl.* **mes·dames'** (mā-dàm')].

mad'cap" (mad'kap') adj. wild; flighty. —n. an unrestrained, adventurous person.

mad'den (mad'ən) v.t. 1, make mad. 2, infuriate.

mad'der (mad'ər) n. a herb; a dye, usually red, made from its root.

made (mād) v. pret. & p.p. of *make*. —adj. (*Colloq.*) 1, artificially produced. 2, assured of success.

mad"e·moi·selle' (mad"mwə-zel') n. [*pl.* **mes"de·moi·selles"** (mād"-)] (*Fr.*) an unmarried woman; miss.

made-'up' (mād'up') adj. 1, invented; fictional. 2, adorned with cosmetics, as a face. 3, put together; assembled.

mad'house" n. 1, a lunatic asylum. 2, a place in a state of confusion.

mad'man" n. [*pl.* -men**"**] an insane person. —**mad'wom"an,** n.*fem.*

Ma·don'na (mə-don'ə) n. a picture or statue of the Virgin Mary.

mad'ras (mad'rəs) n. a cotton fabric, usually with a bright-colored design.

mad'ri·gal (mad'ri-gəl) n. a medieval poem or song.

mael'strom (māl'strəm) n. a whirlpool; great and destructive agitation.

maes'tro (mīs'trō) n. [*pl.* -tros] a master, esp. an eminent musical composer or conductor.

Ma'fi·a" (mä'fē-ä") n. a Sicilian criminal organization, the Black Hand, active also in other countries.

mag"a·zine' (mag'ə-zēn') n. 1, a periodical publication, issued not oftener than weekly. 2, a depository for ammunition. 3, a storehouse. 4, a supply chamber, as in a weapon.

ma·gen'ta (mə-jen'tə) n. & adj. a color or dye, reddish purple.

mag'got (mag'ət) n. the larva of an insect; a worm. —**mag'got·y,** adj.

Ma'gi (mā'jī) n. pl. 1, priests, in ancient Persia. 2, the "Three Wise Men," Matt. 2:1–12.

mag'ic (maj'ik) n. 1, the pretended art of controlling the supernatural; sorcery. 2, legerdemain. 3, charm; enchantment. —adj. [also **mag'i·cal**] 1, as by supernatural agency. 2, delightful. —**mag'i·cal·ly,** adv.

ma·gi'cian (mə-jish'ən) n. a conjurer.

mag"is·te'ri·al (maj"is-tir'ē-əl) adj. 1, pert. to a magistrate. 2, authoritative; imperious.

mag'is·trate" (maj'is-trāt') n. a minor judge or judicial officer. —**mag'is·tra·cy** (-trə-sē) n.

mag·nan'i·mous (mag-nan'ə-məs) adj. generous; high-minded; noble. —**mag"na·nim'i·ty** (-nə-nim'i-tē) n.

mag'nate (mag'nāt) n. a person of importance, esp. in industry.

mag·ne'sia (mag-nē'zhə) n. an oxide of magnesium, used medicinally.

mag·ne'si·um (mag-nē'zhē-əm) n. a metallic chemical element, no. 12, symbol Mg.

mag'net (mag'nit) n. 1, a body that attracts iron or steel; a lodestone. 2, anything that draws persons toward it; an attraction. —**mag·net'ic** (-net'ik) adj. —**mag·net'i·cal·ly,** adv.

---

fat, fāte, fär, fâre, fâll, åsk; met, hē, hêr, maybè; pin, pīne; not, nōte, ôr, tool

mag'net·ism (mag'nə-tiz-əm) n. 1, the properties of attraction. 2, charm. 3, act or result of magnetizing.

mag'ne·tite" (mag'nə-tīt") n. an iron ore, often with magnetic properties; lodestone.

mag'net·ize" (mag'nə-tīz") v.t. make a magnet of, esp. by electricity.

mag·ne'to (mag-nē'tō) n. [pl. -tos] a generator of electricity by use of magnets.

mag·ni- pref. large; great.

mag·nif'i·cent (mag-nif'ə-sent) adj. 1, great in size or extent. 2, splendid; brilliant. 3, noble; sublime. —mag·nif'i·cence, n.

mag'ni·fy" (mag'nə-fī") v.t. 1, make greater. 2, make to appear greater. 3, glorify; extol. —mag'ni·fi·ca'tion, n. — mag'ni·fi"er, n.

mag·nil'o·quent (mag-nil'ə-kwənt) adj. affectedly lofty. —mag·nil'o·quence, n.

mag'ni·tude" (mag'nə-tūd") n. 1, physical greatness; relative size. 2, importance; moral greatness. 3, the measure of brightness of a star.

mag·no'li·a (mag-nō'lē-ə) n. an evergreen tree with large, fragrant blossoms.

mag'num (mag'nəm) n. 1, a two-quart wine bottle. 2, [pl. -na (-nə)] a wrist bone.

mag'pie" (mag'pī") n. 1, a noisy bird. 2, a chattering person.

Mag'yar (mä'dyər) n. a member of the basic Hungarian race; the language of Hungary.

ma"ha·ra'jah (mä"hə-rä'jə) n. a ruling prince in India. Also, ma"ha·ra'ja. —ma"ha·ra'nee (-nē) n.fem.

ma·hat'ma (mə-hät'mə) n. a sage or saint in Brahmanism.

mah'jongg" (mä'jäng") n. a Chinese game, played with domino-like tiles.

mahl'stick" (mäl'stik") n. a stick held by a painter as support for his brush.

ma·hog'a·ny (mə-hog'ə-nē) n. a tropical Amer. tree or its hard, reddish-brown wood.

Ma·hom'et·an (mə-hom'ə-tən) n. & adj. Mohammedan.

ma·hout' (mə-howt') n. the keeper and driver of an elephant.

maid (mād) n. 1, a girl; an unmarried woman. 2, a female servant. —maid of honor, the chief unmarried attendant on a bride.

maid'en (mā'dən) n. 1, an unmarried girl or woman. 2, a new, untried animal or thing; a horse that has not won a race. —adj. unmarried; unused; first or earliest. —maid'en·hood, n. —maid'en·ly, adj.

maid'en·hair" (mā'dən-bâr") n. a delicate, feathery fern.

mail (māl) n. 1, letters or packages sent by post. 2, the postal system. 3, flexible armor of metal rings, interlinked. —v.t. send by mail. —mailed, adj. armored.

mail'man" n. [pl. -men"] one employed to deliver mail.

maim (mām) v.t. 1, disable, by wounding or mutilation. 2, impair.

main (mān) adj. 1, chief; principal. 2, sheer; utmost; as, by main strength. —n. 1, a principal pipe or duct. 2, the open ocean. 3, strength; force. —main'ly, adv. chiefly.

main'land (-lənd) n. a principal mass of land; a continent.

main'spring" n. 1, the principal spring in a watch. 2, chief source or motive.

main'stay" n. a chief support.

main·tain' (mān-tān') v.t. 1, preserve; keep in condition. 2, support; provide for. 3, defend in argument. 4, assert to be true. —main'te·nance (mān'tə-nəns) n.

mai"tre d'hô·tel' (me"tr-dō-tel') n. 1, a butler; headwaiter. 2, the owner or manager of a hotel.

maize (māz) n. 1, a cereal plant; Indian corn, in the U. S. called corn. 2, a yellow color.

ma·jes'tic (mə-jes'tik) adj. possessing majesty; grand; sublime. —ma·jes'ti·cal·ly, adv.

maj'es·ty (maj'is-tē) n. 1, stateliness; grandeur. 2, sovereignty. 3, a royal personage.

ma·jol'i·ca (mə-jol'ə-kə) n. a glazed pottery.

ma'jor (mā'jər) adj. 1, greater in importance, quantity, or extent. 2, senior. 3, of legal age. 4, (Music) pert. to a certain scale or larger interval. —n. 1, an army officer ranking next above captain. 2, a principal field of study. —v.t. (with in) adopt as a principal field of study. —major general, the fourth-highest-ranking army officer. —major league, one of the highest-ranking leagues of professional baseball teams.

ma"jor·do'mo (-dō'mō) n. [pl. -mos] the manager of a large household or estate.

ma·jor'i·ty (mə-jor'ə-tē) n. 1, the greater part or number; the excess of the greater over the smaller. 2, full legal age. 3, the military rank of a major.

---

tub, cūte, pŭll; label; oil, owl; go, chip, she, thin, then, sing, ink; see p. 6

make (māk) *v.t.* [*pret. & p.p.* made (mād)] **1**, bring into being. **2**, form; put in condition. **3**, compel. **4**, appoint. **5**, constitute; compose. **6**, judge; infer; estimate. **7**, arrive at; reach; achieve. **8**, earn; acquire. **9**, (with *out*) discern; understand; (*Colloq.*) assert. **10**, (with *up*) fabricate, as a story; adorn with cosmetics, as one's face; arrange, as type for printing. **11**, (with *up to*) ingratiate oneself with. —*v.i.* **1**, cause to be as specified. **2**, be of effect; operate. **3**, go (toward or away from). **4**, (with *out*) fare. **5**, (with *up*) become reconciled; prepare one's face with cosmetics. —*n.* **1**, construction; nature; brand. **2**, the process of manufacture. —**make out**, **1**, write out (a form). **2**, see. **3**, get along; manage. —**make over**, **1**, alter; remodel. **2**, transfer title to; hand over. —**make up**, **1**, become reconciled. **2**, invent. **3**, prepare; apply cosmetics (to).

make-'be·lieve' *adj.* pretended. —*n.* pretense, as children's play.

make-'read'y *n.* adjustment to produce even printing.

make'shift *n. & adj.* a temporary expedient.

make-'up' *n.* **1**, composition: character or nature. **2**, the arrangement of type, etc. for printing. **3**, cosmetics; the use of cosmetics or costume.

mal- *pref.* bad; imperfect.

mal'ad·just'ed (mal'-jus'tid) *adj.* **1**, badly adjusted. **2**, (*Psych.*) not fully adapted to social living. —**mal'ad·just'ment**, *n.*

mal'a·droit' (mal'-droit') *adj.* inexpert; awkward.

mal'a·dy (mal'-dē) *n.* **1**, a disease. **2**, any disordered state or condition.

ma·laise' (ma-lāz') *n.* **1**, (*Fr.*) an indefinite feeling of uneasiness or discomfort.

mal'a·prop·ism (mal'-prop-iz-m) *n.* a blunder in speech, through ignorance of a word or meaning.

mal'ap·ro·pos' (mal'ap-r-pō') *adj. & adv.* inappropriate.

ma'lar (mā'lr) *n.* the cheek bone.

ma·lar'i·a (m-lār'ē-) *n.* an intermittent or remittent fever. —**ma·lar'i·al, ma·lar'i·ous**, *adj.*

Ma·lay' (m-lā') *n.* one of the race of brown men inhabiting the Malay Peninsula. —**Ma·lay'an**, *adj.*

mal'con·tent' (mal'kn-tent') *adj.* discontented. —*n.* a discontented person.

male (māl) *adj.* **1**, pertaining to the sex that begets young. **2**, characteristic of this sex; masculine. **3**, (*Mech.*) shaped to be inserted into a socket. —*n.* **1**, a man. **2**, a male animal.

mal'e·dic'tion (mal'-dik'shn) *n.* **1**, evil speaking. **2**, a curse.

mal'e·fac"tor (mal'-fak"tr) *n.* **1**, a law-breaker. **2**, one who does evil. —**mal'e·fac'tion**, *n.*

ma·lef'i·cent (m-lef'-snt) *adj.* having an evil effect or intent. —**ma·lef'i·cence**, *n.*

ma'le·mute" (mä'l-mūt") *n.* an Eskimo working dog.

ma·lev'o·lent (m-lev'-lnt) *adj.* wishing evil to others; hostile. —**ma·lev'o·lence**, *n.*

mal·fea'sance (mal-fē'zns) *n.* performance of a wrongful act. —**mal·fea'sant**, *adj.*

mal"for·ma'tion (mal"fr-mā'shn) *n.* a faulty construction, as of a part of the body. —**mal·formed'**, *adj.*

mal'ic (mal'ik) *adj.* pert. to apples.

mal'ice (mal'is) *n.* **1**, a disposition to inflict injury; ill will. **2**, a hostile act.

ma·li'cious (m-lish's) *adj.* bearing malice; intending harm.

ma·lign' (m-līn') *v.t.* speak ill of; defame. —*adj.* pernicious; malicious.

ma·lig'nant (m-lig'nnt) *adj.* **1**, threatening danger. **2**, deadly or growing worse, as a cancerous tumor. —**ma·lig'nan·cy, ma·lig'ni·ty**, *n.*

ma·lin'ger (m-ling'gr) *v.i.* feign illness. —**ma·ling'er·er**, *n.*

mall (mål) *n.* **1**, a heavy mallet. **2**, a shaded public walk.

mal'lard (mal'rd) *n.* the common wild duck.

mal'le·a·ble (mal'ē-·bl) *adj.* **1**, capable of being extended by beating or rolling. **2**, adaptable. —**mal'le·a·bil'i·ty**, *n.*

mal'let (mal'it) *n.* **1**, a small wooden hammer. **2**, a long-handled club, as used in croquet or polo.

mal'low (mal'ō) *n.* a shrub or tree bearing pink or white flowers.

malm'sey (mäm'zē) *n.* a variety of grape.

mal"nu·tri'tion (mal"noo-trish'-n) *n.* imperfect, or lack of, nutrition.

mal·o'dor·ous (mal-ō'dr-s) *adj.* having an offensive odor. —**mal·o'dor·ous·ness**, *n.*

mal·prac'tice (mal-prak'tis) *n.* improper conduct, esp. by a physician.

malt (målt) *n.* **1**, partially germinated grain, used in brewing. **2**, ale.

Mal·tese' (mål-tēz') *adj.* pert. to the island of Malta.

malt'ose (mål'tōs) *n.* grape sugar.

mal·treat' (mal-trēt') *v.t.* treat badly; abuse. —**mal·treat'ment**, *n.*

ma'ma (mä'm) *n.* mamma;

mam'ba (măm'bə) n. a poisonous African snake.

mam'bo" (mom'bō") n. a lively ballroom dance.

mam'ma (mä'mə or mä-mä') n. 1, [also, ma'ma] mother. 2, (mam'ə) [pl. -mae (-mē)] a gland secreting milk.

mam'mal (mam'əl) n. an animal whose young feed upon milk from the breast. —mam·ma'li·an (ma-mā'lē-ən) adj.

mam'ma·ry (mam'ə-rē) adj. pert. to the mammae or breasts.

mam'mon (mam'ən) n. 1, material wealth. 2, (cap.) the apotheosis of riches and avarice.

mam'moth (mam'əth) n. an extinct species of elephant, very large. —adj. gigantic; immense.

mam'my (mam'ē) n. 1, mother. 2, a colored female nurse.

man n. [pl. men] 1, a mammal of the genus Homo. 2, a person; a human being. 3, the human race; mankind. 4, an adult human male. 5, (Colloq.) a husband. 6, a strong, virile, brave or accomplished man. 7, a piece in a game, as chess. —v.t. [manned, man'ning] supply with men, as for service or defense.

-man (mən) suf. [pl. -men] in compounds, denoting a man who does, acts, has, etc. as indicated by the root word.

man'a·cle (man'ə-kəl) n. (usually pl.) a shackle; handcuff. —v.t. fetter; restrain.

man'age (man'ij) v.t. 1, control physically, as a horse. 2, control by direction or persuasion. 3, contrive; bring about. —v.i. direct or control affairs. —man'age·a·ble, adj.

man'age·ment (-mənt) n. 1, act of managing. 2, owners and executives as distinguished from labor.

man'ag·er (man'ij-ər) n. one who directs any operations. —man"a·ger'i·al (-ə-jir'ē-əl) adj.

man"a·tee' (man'ə-tē') n. a seacow; a large sea mammal.

Man·chu' (man-choo') n. a member of a tribe from Manchuria, long the rulers of China; their language.

man·da'mus (man-dā'mes) n. (Law) a writ directing an inferior court, person, etc., to perform a specific act.

man'da·rin (man'də-rin) n. 1, a Chinese official. 2, a Chinese dialect. 3, an Asiatic citrus fruit.

man'date (man'dāt) n. 1, a command. 2, an order or injunction, as from a superior court to an inferior one. 3, a commission, as to one nation to manage the affairs of another.

man'da·to·ry (man'də-tôr-ē) adj. compulsory; officially required.

man'di·ble (man'də-bəl) n. a bone of the lower jaw. —man·dib'u·lar (-dib'yə-lər) adj.

man'do·lin" (man'də-lin") n. a musical instrument of the lute class, having metal strings in pairs.

Mandolin

man'drake (man'drāk) n. a poisonous herb of Europe.

man'drel (man'drəl) n. a cylindrical bar used to support work being turned on a lathe.

man'drill (man'dril) n. a large, ferocious Afr. baboon.

mane (mān) n. the long hair on the neck of some animals, as the horse or the lion. —maned (mānd) adj.

ma·neu'ver (mə-noo'vər) n. 1, a planned and regulated strategic movement, particularly of troops or warships. 2, an adroit move. —v.t. & i. manipulate; move skillfully. Also, ma·nœu'vre.

man'ful (-fəl) adj. brave. —man'ful·ness, n.

man'ga·nese" (mang'gə-nēs") n. a metallic chemical element, no. 25, symbol Mn. —man·gan'ic (man-gan'ik) adj.

mange (mānj) n. a skin disease of animals, which causes loss of hair and eruptions.

man'gel-wur'zel (mang'gəl-wër'zəl) n. a beetlike root used as fodder.

man'ger (mān'jər) n. a trough or box for feeding animals.

man'gle (mang'gəl) v.t. 1, cut or slash; disfigure. 2, mar. —n. a machine for ironing cloth.

man'go (mang'gō) n. the luscious, slightly acid fruit of a tropical tree.

man'grove (man'grōv) n. a tropical tree, a source of tannic acid.

man'gy (mān'jē) adj. 1, infected with mange. 2, shabby; mean; petty. —man'gi·ness, n.

man'han"dle v.t. 1, handle roughly. 2, move by man power.

man'hole" n. a hole for entering a sewer, steam boiler, etc.

man'hood" (-hûd") n. 1, the state or condition of being a man. 2, courage; virility.

ma'ni·a (mā'nē-ə) n. 1, a form of insanity, marked by great excitement. 2, a great desire or enthusiasm.

-ma·ni·a (mā'nē-ə) suf. denoting love or enthusiasm for.

ma'ni·ac (mā'nē-ak) n. a madman. —ma·ni'a·cal (mə-nī'ə-kəl) adj.

man'ic (man'ik) *adj.* pert. to or affected with mania. —**manic depressive**, having a mental disorder marked by recurrent cycles of excitation and depression.

man'i·cure" (man'ə-kyûr") *n.* care of the hands and fingernails. —*v.t.* trim; polish. —**man'i·cur"ist**, *n.*

man'i·fest" (man'ə-fest") *adj.* readily perceived; obvious. —*v.t.* demonstrate; give evidence of. —*n.* a list of a shipment. —**man"i·fes·ta'tion**, *n.* a demonstration; display.

man"i·fes'to (man"ə-fes'tō) *n.* a public declaration; a proclamation.

man'i·fold" (man'ə-fōld") *adj.* 1, of many kinds; varied. 2, having many parts, features, or activities. 3, numerous. —*n.* 1, a carbon or duplicated copy; facsimile. 2, thin paper for making many carbon copies. 3, a pipe with several connections.

man'i·kin (man'ə-kin) *n.* 1, a little man. 2, a mannequin.

ma·nil'a (mə-nil'ə) *n.* 1, a Philippine fiber used for cordage, heavy wrapping paper, etc. 2, a cigar.

ma·nip'u·late" (mə-nip'yə-lāt") *v.t.* 1, handle with skill. 2, influence; manage. 3, adapt or change. —**ma·nip"u·la'tion**, *n.*

man'kind" *n.* the human race.

man'ly (-lè) *adj.* having the ideal qualities of a man. —**man'li·ness**, *n.*

man'na (man'ə) *n.* spiritual food.

man'ne·quin (man'ə-kin) *n.* 1, a person who models clothes for sale. 2, a dummy used by artists and tailors.

man'ner (man'ər) *n.* 1, a mode of action; method. 2, customary way of doing; habit; style. 3, personal bearing and behavior. 4, kind; sort. 5, (*pl.*) polite, courteous deportment. —**man'nered**, **man'ner·ly**, *adj.* —**man'ner·less**, *adj.*

man'ner·ism (man'ə-riz-əm) *n.* a habitual peculiarity of deportment or speech; idiosyncrasy.

man'nish (-ish) *adj.* unbecomingly masculine. —**man'nish·ness**, *n.*

ma·noeu'vre (mə-noo'vər) *v.* maneuver.

man-"of-war' *n.* [*pl.* **men-"**] a warship.

ma·nom'e·ter (mə-nom'ə-tər) *n.* an instrument for measuring the pressure of gases or liquids. —**man"o·met'ric** (man"ə-met'rik) *adj.*

man'or (man'ər) *n.* in England, a landed estate, vested with certain rights. —**ma·no'ri·al** (mə-nôr'è-əl) *adj.*

man'sard (man'särd) *n.* a roof having two slopes, one steeper than the other.

manse (mans) *n.* a parsonage.

man'sion (man'shən) *n.* a large and stately residence.

man'slaugh"ter (man'slä"tər) *n.* (*Law*) the unlawful killing of another without malice aforethought.

man'tel (man'təl) *n.* the facing above and around a fireplace. —**man'tel·piece"**, *n.* the shelf of a mantel.

man·til'la (man-til'ə) *n.* 1, a lace head-covering. 2, a light cloak.

man'tis *n.* [*pl.* -**tes** (-tèz)] a carnivorous insect: *praying mantis.*

man'tle (man'təl), *n.* 1, a loose cloak. 2, any covering. 3, an incandescent hood for a gas jet. —*v.t. & i.* cover or be covered.

man'u·al (man'ū-əl) *adj.* pert. to or done by the hands. —*n.* 1, a book of instructions. 2, a routine.

man"u·fac'ture (man"yə-fak'chər) *n.* the making of goods, by hand or machinery. —*v.i.* engage in such a business. —*v.t.* 1, make (goods); fabricate. 2, produce artificially; invent. —**man"u·fac'tur·er**, *n.*

man"u·mis'sion (man"yə-mish'ən) *n.* liberation from slavery. —**man'u·mit'**, *v.t.* liberate.

ma·nure' (mə-nyûr') *n.* any substance, chiefly animal feces, used to fertilize land.

man'u·script" (man'yə-skript") *n.* 1, a book or document written by hand. 2, an original copy, not set in type. —*adj.* handwritten.

Manx (manks) *adj.* pert. to the Isle of Man.—**Manx cat**, a tailless cat.

Manx Cat

man'y (men'è) *n.* a large number. —*adj.* [**more, most**] numerous.

map *n.* a drawing of all or a part of the earth's surface, or the heavens; a chart. —*v.t.* [**mapped, map'ping**] 1, draw a map. 2, plan.

ma'ple (mā'pəl) *n.* a shade tree, valued for its hard wood and for the sugar-producing sap of some species.

Ma·quis' (ma-kē') *n.sing. & pl.* the French underground in World War II. —**ma·quis·ard'** (ma-kè-zär') *n.* a member of the Maquis.

mar (mär) *v.t.* [**marred, mar'ring**] 1, disfigure; scratch. 2, impair in quality.

mar'a·bou" (mar'ə-boo") *n.* 1, a large stork. 2, a marabou's plume or feathers, used for trimming.

mar"a·schi'no (mar"ə-skē'nō) *n.* a cordial distilled from wild cherries.

mar'a·thon" (mar'ə-thon") *n.* 1, a foot-race of about 26 miles. 2, any test of endurance.

ma·raud′ (mə-râd′) *v.i.* rove in search of plunder. —**ma·raud′er**, *n.*

mar′ble (mär′bəl) *n.* 1, hard crystalline limestone, used in sculpture and architecture. 2, a small ball of glass, agate, etc., used in a child's game. 3, (*pl.*) the game played with such balls. —*adj.* made of, or like, marble.

mar′bling (mär′bling) *n.* an imitation of, or appearance like, variegated marble. —**mar′bled**, *adj.*

mar·ca·site″ (mär′kə-sīt″) *n.* a yellowish crystalline mineral, used in ornaments.

mar·cel′ (mär-sel′) *n.* a method of putting waves in hair.

march (märch) *v.i.* 1, proceed on foot. 2, walk with regular, concerted steps, as soldiers. —*v.t.* cause to march. —*n.* 1, the act of marching; progress from one place to another. 2, the distance of a single marching. 3, a musical composition, to whose rhythm persons march. 4, border land; a frontier.

March *n.* the third month of the year.

mar′chion·ess″ (mär′shə-nes″) *n.* the wife or widow of a marquess.

Mar′di gras′ (mär′dè-grä′) the celebration of Shrove Tuesday.

mare (mâr) *n.* a female horse.

mare′s-′nest″ (mârz′nest″) *n.* a nonexistent discovery; a hoax.

mar′ga·rine″ (mär′jə-rēn″) *n.* a vegetable or animal fat product similar to butter.

mar′gin (mär′jin) *n.* 1, a bordering space, as along a river, or on a letter or page. 2, allowance for error or security, as in a business transaction. 3, the difference between selling price and cost. —**mar′gin·al**, *adj.* 1, on the edge. 2, making little or no provision for error.

mar′gue·rite″ (mär′gə-rēt′) *n.* a daisylike flower.

mar′i·gold″ (mar′i-gōld″) *n.* a flower, usually yellow or orange.

ma″ri·jua′na (mä″rə-hwä′nə) *n.* a hemplike plant whose leaves, smoked in cigarettes, are exhilarating, but toxic.

ma·rim′ba (mə-rim′bə) *n.* a musical instrument, having strips of wood that produce bell-like tones when struck with hammers.

mar″i·nade′ (mar″ə-nād′) *n.* 1, a sauce used in marinating. 2, a pickle preserve.

mar′i·nate″ (mar′ə-nāt″) *v.t.* preserve by salting or pickling: steep in dressing. —**mar″i·na′tion**, *n.*

ma·rine′ (mə-rēn′) *adj.* pert. to the sea, or navigation; nautical. —*n.* 1,

shipping in general. 2, a soldier serving on a ship; in U. S. (*cap.*) a member of the Marine Corps.

mar′i·ner (mar′ə-nər) *n.* a seaman.

mar″i·o·nette′ (mar″ē-ə-net′) *n.* a puppet moved by strings.

mar′i·tal (mar′i-təl) *adj.* pert. to marriage or the married condition.

mar′i·time″ (mar′i-tīm″) *adj.* pert. to or bordering on the sea.

mar′jo·ram (mär′jə-rəm) *n.* an aromatic herb used as a flavoring.

mark (märk) *n.* 1, a visible impression, as a line, stain, etc. 2, a distinguishing symbol or peculiarity. 3, a significant indication. 4, a symbol denoting ownership or origin, as a *trade mark.* 5, a rating or grade, as in school. 6, a target; a goal or aim. 7, a Ger. monetary unit. 8, a standard. —*v.t.* make a mark on. —**mark time,** 1, (*Mil.*) move the feet as in marching but without advancing. 2, suspend progress; pause and wait.

marked (märkt) *adj.* branded; conspicuous; doomed.

mark′er (mär′kər) *n.* 1, anything used as a mark; a counter, tombstone, etc. 2, (*Slang*) a memorandum; an I O U.

mar′ket (mär′kit) *n.* 1, an assemblage of people, or a place, for buying and selling; a store. 2, trade; rate of sale; demand. —*v.t.* offer for sale; sell. —**mar′ket·a·ble**, *adj.* —**market place**, an open space in a town where markets are held.

marks′man (märks′mən) *n.* one skilled in shooting. —**marks′man·ship**, *n.*

mark′up″ *n.* the amount added to a cost price, for profit.

mar′lin (mär′lin) *n.* a large game fish.

mar′line·spike″ (mär′lin-spīk″) *n.* (*Naut.*) an iron spike used in twisting or splicing rope.

mar′ma·lade″ (mär′mə-lād″) *n.* a preserve containing pieces of fruit.

mar·mo′re·al (mar-môr′ē-əl) *adj.* of marble.

mar′mo·set″ (mär′mə-zet″) *n.* a small Central Amer. monkey.

mar′mot (mär′mət) *n.* any of various rodents, as the woodchuck.

ma·roon′ (mə-roon′) *v.t.* abandon on a desolate island; isolate. —*adj.* & *n.* dark red.

mar·quee′ (mär-kē′) *n.* a projecting roof above a door or sidewalk.

mar′que·try (mär′kə-trē) *n.* inlaid work on furniture.

mar′quis (mär′kwis) *n.* a nobleman, ranking between a count or earl and a duke. Also (*Brit.*) **mar'-quess**. —**mar·quise'** (mär-kēz') *n.* *fem.* wife of a marquis.

mar"qui·sette' (mär"kwi-zet') *n.* a light, gauzelike fabric.

mar'riage (mar'ij) *n.* **1**, the legal union of a man and a woman; a wedding. **2**, the state of being married or united. —**mar'riage·a·ble**, *adj.* eligible to be married.

mar'ron (mar'ən) *n.* a chestnut, esp. candied.

mar'row (mar'ō) *n.* **1**, a soft tissue in the interior of the bones. **2**, the essence; the real meaning. **3**, vitality.

mar'ry (mar'ē) *v.t.* **1**, unite in wedlock. **2**, take for husband or wife. —*v.i.* wed.

Mars (märz) *n.* **1**, the planet fourth from the sun, and nearest the earth. **2**, the Roman god of war.

Mar"seil·laise' (mär"sə-lāz') *n.* the French national song.

marsh (märsh) *n.* low, wet land; a swamp. —**marsh'y**, *adj.*

mar'shal (mär'shəl) *n.* **1**, a high military officer. **2**, a judicial, or police, officer. **3**, a person in charge of ceremonies, etc. —*v.t.* arrange in order; gather.

marsh'mal"low (märsh'mal"ō) *n.* a confection of gelatin and sugar.

mar·su'pi·al (mär-soo'pē-əl) *n.* a mammal having a *marsupium*, or external pouch, for its young, as the kangaroo.

Marsupial Pouch

mart (märt) *n.* a market.

mar'ten (mär'tən) *n.* an Amer. fur-bearing animal; its fur.

mar'tial (mär'shəl) *adj.* warlike; military; soldierly. —**martial law**, rule by military, not civil, authority.

mar'tin (mär'tən) *n.* a swallow-like bird.

mar"ti·net' (mär"tə-net') *n.* a rigid disciplinarian.

mar'tin·gale' (mär'tən-gāl") *n.* **1**, in a horse's harness, a strap between the girth and the bit. **2**, (*Naut.*) a short spar under the bowsprit.

mar·ti'ni (mär-tē'nē) *n.* a cocktail of gin and dry vermouth.

mar'tyr (mär'tər) *n.* one who suffers in defense of a belief or cause. —**mar'tyr·dom**, *n.* —**mar'tyr·ize"** (-īz") *v.t.*

mar'vel (mär'vəl) *n.* a wonderful or extraordinary thing. —*v.t.* & *i.* wonder at; be moved by wonder. —**mar'vel·ous**, *adj.* extraordinary.

Marx'ism (märk'siz-əm) *n.* the socialistic theory originated by the German economist, Karl Marx. —**Marx'i·an**, *adj.* —**Marx'ist**, *n.*

mar'zi·pan" (mär'zə-pan") *n.* an almond confection.

mas·car'a (mas-kar'ə) *n.* a cosmetic used on the eyelashes.

mas'cot (mas'kət) *n.* an animal or person supposed to bring good luck.

mas'cu·line (mas'kyə-lin) *adj.* male; manly; (of a woman) mannish. —**mas"cu·lin'i·ty**, *n.*

mash *n.* a pulpy mixture, esp. of grain, etc., for feed, distilling, etc. —*v.t.* crush; make into a mash.

mash'ie (mash'ē) *n.* a golf club used in making lofting shots, No. 5 iron.

mask (mȧsk) *n.* **1**, a covering for the face, worn for disguise, protection, etc. **2**, anything that conceals; a pretense. **3**, a masquerade. **4**, a likeness of a face, cast in plaster. —*v.t.* & *i.* disguise or conceal.

mas'o·chism (mas'ə-kiz-əm) *n.* pleasure derived from self-suffering or humiliation. —**mas'o·chist**, *n.* —**mas"o·chis'tic**, *adj.*

ma'son (mā'sən) *n.* **1**, one who builds with brick, stone, etc. **2**, (*cap.*) a Freemason. —**Ma·son'ic** (-sön'ik) *adj.* —**Mason jar**, a glass jar with an airtight closure.

Mason-Dixon line a surveyor's line, the boundary between Pennsylvania and Maryland, once considered as separating slave from free territory.

ma'son·ite" (mā'sə-nīt") *n.* sheets of pressed wood fiber, used for partitions and as insulation.

ma'son·ry (mā'sən-rē) *n.* **1**, stonework. **2**, (*cap.*) Freemasonry.

masque (mȧsk) *n.* **1**, a dramatic entertainment. **2**, a masquerade.

mas"quer·ade' (mas"kə-rād') *n.* **1**, a gathering where masks are worn. **2**, a disguise; concealment; false pretense. —*v.i.* go about under false pretenses.

mass (mas) *n.* **1**, a body of matter; a lump. **2**, an assemblage of particles or things, as troops. **3**, (*pl.*) the proletariat. **4**, the bulk; the greater part. **5**, bulk; magnitude. **6**, (*cap.*) a church service. —*v.t.* collect into a mass. —*v.i.* assemble. —**mass meeting**, a large or general assembly.

mas'sa·cre (mas'ə-kər) *n.* the indiscriminate, wholesale killing of humans. —*v.t.* kill; defeat decisively.

mas·sage' (mə-säzh') *n.* treatment of the muscles by rubbing, kneading, etc. —*v.t.* so treat.

mas·seur' (ma-sēr') *n.* one who massages therapeutically. —**masseuse'** (ma-sūz') *n.fem.*

mas'sive (mas'iv) *adj.* **1,** bulky; heavy. **2,** substantial; imposing. —**mas'sive·ness,** *n.*

mast (mȧst) *n.* **1,** a vertical support for yards, sails, etc., on a ship. **2,** any tall pole.

mas'ter (mȧs'tər) *n.* **1,** one who has chief authority or control. **2,** one eminently skilled in an occupation, art, or science. —*adj.* **1,** chief or principal; predominant. **2,** eminently skilled. —*v.t.* become master of; subdue. —**master hand,** an expert. —**master key,** a key opening many locks. —**master of ceremonies,** a person who introduces the speakers, performers, etc., as at a show.

mas'ter·ful (-fəl) *adj.* **1,** authoritative; domineering. **2,** masterly. —**mas'ter·ful·ness,** *n.*

mas'ter·ly (-lē) *adj.* skilled. —**mas'ter·li·ness,** *n.*

mas'ter·piece" *n.* a work of surpassing excellence.

mas'ter·y (mȧs'tə·rē) *n.* power of control; command.

mast'head" *n.* **1,** the top of a ship's mast. **2,** a statement of ownership, etc., in a newspaper.

mas'tic (mas'tik) *n.* **1,** a resin. **2,** a cement used in masonry or plastering.

mas'ti·cate" (mas'tə·kāt") *v.t. & i.* **1,** chew. **2,** crush or knead into pulp. —**mas'ti·ca'tion,** *n.*

mas'tiff (mȧs'tif) *n.* a large dog.

mas·ti'tis (mas·tī'tis) *n.* inflammation of the breast.

mas'to·don" (mas'tə·don") *n.* an extinct, elephantlike mammal.

Mastiff

mas'toid *n.* a bony prominence below and behind the ear. —*adj.* **1,** pert. to the mastoid. **2,** shaped like a nipple. —**mas"toid·i'tis,** inflammation of the mastoid.

mas"tur·ba'tion (mas"tər·bā'shən) *n.* sexual self-gratification. —**mas'tur·bate",** *v.t.*

mat *n.* **1,** a piece of fabric, woven of straw, etc., used on the floor, on a table, etc. **2,** a thick mass, as of weeds or hair. **3,** a lusterless surface. **4,** a matrix, in printing. —*v.t.* [**mat'ted, -ting**] **1,** cover with, or form into, a mat. **2,** finish with a dull surface. —*v.i.* become entangled. —*adj.* dull in surface.

mat'a·dor" (mat'ə·dôr") *n.* in a bullfight, the one who kills the bull.

match (mach) *n.* **1,** an equal; a peer. **2,** a pair; a mating. **3,** a contest, as in golf. **4,** a chemically-tipped piece of wood, etc., that ignites on friction. —*v.t.* mate; bring into agreement; equal. —*v.i.* contend; correspond; suit; harmonize. —**match'less,** *adj.* having no equal.

match'mak"er *n.* one who arranges matrimonial matches, or athletic contests.

mate (māt) *n.* **1,** a husband or wife. **2,** one of a pair; a counterpart. **3,** an habitual associate. **4,** an officer on a merchant ship. **5,** checkmate. —*v.t.* join as a mate; marry; pair. —*v.i.* take a mate; marry.

ma·te'ri·al (mə·tir'ē·əl) *n.* **1,** a constituent principle or element; substance; raw matter to be developed. **2,** a textile fabric. —*adj.* **1,** physical; corporeal; not spiritual. **2,** important; essential.

ma·te'ri·al·ism (-iz·əm) *n.* devotion to material, rather than spiritual, needs or interests; self-interest. —**ma·te'ri·al·ist,** *n.* —**ma·te"ri·al·is'tic,** *adj.* —**ma·te"ri·al·is'ti·cal·ly,** *adv.*

ma·te'ri·al·ize" (-īz") *v.t. & i.* give to, or assume, material form or perceptible existence. —**ma·te"ri·al·i·za'tion,** *n.*

ma·te'ri·al·ly (-ə·lē) *adv.* to an important extent.

ma·té·ri·el' (mə·tir·ē·el') *n.* equipment and supplies, esp. military.

ma·ter'nal (mə·tẽr'nəl) *adj.* pert. to, befitting, or related to, a mother.

ma·ter'ni·ty (mə·tẽr'nə·tē) *n.* state of being a mother.

math"e·mat'i·cal (math"ə·mat'i·kəl) *adj.* **1,** pert. to mathematics. **2,** exact; precise.

math"e·mat'ics (math"ə·mat'iks) *n.* the science of numbers in all their relations and applications. —**math"e·ma·ti'cian** (-mə·tish'ən) *n.*

mat'in·al (mat'ə·nəl) *adj.* pert. to matins or morning.

mat"i·nee' (mat"ə·nā') *n.* a daytime dramatic performance.

mat'ins (mat'inz) *n.pl.* morning church services.

ma'tri- *pref.* mother.

ma'tri·arch (mā'trē·ärk) *n.* a woman having chief authority in a household. —**ma"tri·ar'chal,** *adj.*

ma'tri·ar'chy (mā'trē·är"kē) *n.* a social system ruled by mothers or women.

ma·tric'u·late" (mə·trik'yə·lāt") *v.t. & i.* enroll, or be enrolled, in a college. —**ma·tric"u·la'tion,** *n.*

mat"ri·mo'ny (mat"rə·mō'nē) *n.* the ceremony or sacrament of marriage. —**mat"ri·mo'ni·al,** *adj.*

ma'trix (mā'triks) *n.* [*pl.* **-tri·ces** (-tri·sēz)] **1,** that which forms or determines. **2,** a mold.

ma'tron (mā'trən) *n.* **1**, a married woman. **2**, a woman in charge, as in an institution. —**ma'tron·ly**, *adj.* like a matron in manner or appearance; staid.

matte (mat) *n.* an impure product of the smelting of certain ores.

mat'ted (mat'id) *adj.* covered with, or formed into, a mat or tangled mass.

mat'ter (mat'ər) *n.* **1**, the substance of which physical objects consist. **2**, any particular kind of substance, as *printed matter.* **3**, pus. **4**, the substance, as of a book. **5**, a thing of consequence; affair; business. —*v.i.* **1**, be of consequence. **2**, form or excrete pus.

mat'ter-of-course' *adj.* in the natural course of things.

mat'ter-of-fact' *adj.* **1**, commonplace. **2**, unimaginative.

mat'ting (mat'ing) *n.* matted fabric; material for making mats.

mat'tock (mat'ək) *n.* a tool like a pickax, but with one end broad.

mat'tress (mat'ris) *n.* a cloth case filled with padding, used as or on a bed.

ma·ture' (mə-tyûr') *adj.* complete in natural growth; ripe; fully developed. —*v.t.* & *i.* age; become mature. —**ma·tu'ri·ty**, *n.*

ma·tu'ti·nal (mə-tū'tə-nəl) *adj.* in the morning.

mat'zoth (mät'zōth) *n.pl.* [*sing.* mat'zo (-zə)] unleavened bread.

maud'lin (mâd'lin) *adj.* tearfully, or drunkenly, sentimental.

maul (mâl) *n.* a heavy hammer. —*v.t.* handle roughly.

maun'der (mân'dər) *v.i.* talk or move about in a rambling way.

mau"so·le'um (mâ"sə-lē'əm) *n.* a grand and stately tomb.

mauve (mōv) *n.* & *adj.* a color or dye, pale bluish purple.

mav'er·ick (mav'ər-ik) *n.* **1**, an unbranded cow or calf. **2**, a dissenter.

ma'vis (mā'vis) *n.* the Europ. song-thrush.

ma·vour'neen (mə-vûr'nēn) *n.* (*Irish*) my darling.

maw (mâ) *n.* the throat; gullet.

mawk'ish (mâ'kish) *adj.* nauseating; sickeningly sentimental. —**mawk'ish·ness**, *n.*

max·il'la (mak-sil'ə) *n.* [*pl.* -lae (-ē)] the upper jawbone. —**max'il·lar·y** (mak'sə-ler-ē) *adj.*

max'im (mak'sim) *n.* a pithy expression of a general truth, or a rule of conduct.

max'i·mum (mak'sə-məm) *n.* [*pl.* -ma or -mums] & *adj.* the greatest quantity or amount possible. —**max'i·mal** (-məl) *adj.*

may (mā) *aux. v.* [*pret.* might] expressing possibility, permission, wish, or contingency.

May *n.* the fifth month of the year.

Ma'ya (mä'yə) *n.* a member of a race formerly inhabiting Central America; their language. —**Ma'yan**, *adj.* & *n.*

may'be (mā'bē) *adv.* perhaps.

May Day May 1, often celebrated with a spring festival, and also by organized labor.

may'flow"er (mā'flow"ər) *n.* a spring-flowering plant, esp. the trailing arbutus.

may'hem (mā'hem) *n.* the infliction of serious bodily injury.

may"on·naise' (mā"ə-nāz') *n.* a thick salad dressing.

may'or (mā'ər) *n.* the principal officer of a municipality. —**may'or·al·ty**, *n.* —**may'or·ess**, *n.fem.*

May'pole' *n.* a pole around which persons dance on May Day, holding streamers from its top.

maze (māz) *n.* **1**, a labyrinth; a deception. **2**, bewilderment.

ma·zu'ma (mə-zoo'mə) *n.* (*Slang*) money.

ma·zur'ka (mə-zêr'kə) *n.* a lively Polish dance.

me (mē) *pron.* obj. of *I.*

mead (mēd) *n.* a fermented liquor of honey and yeast.

mead'ow (med'ō) *n.* a piece of land for raising hay or for pasture.

mea'ger (mē'gər) *adj.* lean; thin; without richness or fullness; scanty. —**mea'ger·ness**, *n.*

meal (mēl) *n.* **1**, a regular repast; sufficient food to satisfy the appetite. **2**, edible grain ground to a powder. **3**, any coarsely ground substance.

meal'y (mē'lē) *adj.* **1**, resembling, or covered with, meal. **2**, pale, as the complexion. —**meal'i·ness**, *n.*

meal'y-mouthed" (mē'lē-mow*th*d") *adj.* inclined to speak evasively; insincere.

mean (mēn) *v.t.* [*pret.* & *p.p.* meant (ment)] **1**, intend; purpose; have in mind for a particular use. **2**, signify; denote; express. —*v.i.* have intentions of some kind. —*adj.* **1**, inferior in quality; low in station; of small importance. **2**, miserly; stingy. **3**, (*Colloq.*) nasty; vicious; in poor health. —*n.* **1**, something midway between two extremes. **2**, (*pl.*) what implements a plan; resources, esp. pecuniary. —**mean'ness**, *n.*

me·an'der (mĕ·an'dẽr) *v.i.* wander aimlessly; pursue a winding course.

mean'ing (mē'ning) *n.* that which is expressed; significance; import. —*adj.* significant.

mean'time" (mēn'tīm") *n.* the intervening time. —*adv.* in the interval, Also, **mean'while"**.

mea'sles (mē'zəlz) *n.* an infectious, eruptive disease, chiefly in children.

mea'sly (mē'zlē) *adj.* **1**, infected with measles. **2**, poor; inadequate. —**mea'sli·ness**, *n.*

meas'ure (mezh'ẽr) *n.* **1**, a unit or standard for determining extent, volume, quantity, etc. by comparison. **2**, any standard of comparison, estimation, or judgment. **3**, the instrument, act or system of measurement. **4**, any definite quantity measured. **5**, a legislative bill. **6**, a rhythmical unit or movement, in poetry, music, or dance. —*v.t.* ascertain the extent of; estimate; appraise. —**meas'ured**, *adj.* **1**, ascertained or regulated by measure. **2**, regular; deliberate. —**meas'ure·less**, *adj.* unlimited.

meas'ure·ment (-mənt) *n.* **1**, act of measuring. **2**, the dimension, etc. ascertained.

meat (mēt) *n.* **1**, the flesh of animals, used for food. **2**, the edible part of anything; the material part; gist. —**meat'y**, *adj.* **1**, like meat. **2**, pithy.

Mec'ca (mek'ə) *n.* the holy city of Islam, goal of Moslem pilgrims; hence, a goal.

me·chan'ic (mə·kan'ik) *n.* a skilled worker with tools.

me·chan'i·cal (mə·kan'ə·kəl) *adj.* **1**, pert. to, operated by, or produced by, a mechanism or machine. **2**, artificial; not spontaneous; lacking in life or spirit. **3**, effected by physical forces; materialistic.

me·chan'ics (mə·kan'iks) *n.* **1**, the science of mechanical forces and motion. **2**, the science of machinery and mechanical appliances.

mech'an·ism (mek'ə·niz-əm) *n.* **1**, machinery. **2**, the agency by which an effect is produced or a purpose accomplished. **3**, mechanical execution.

mech'a·nize" (mek'ə-nīz") *v.t.* **1**, make mechanical. **2**, (*Mil.*) equip with armored motor vehicles. —**mech"a·ni·za'tion**, *n.*

med'al (med'əl) *n.* a coinlike piece of metal inscribed to commemorate an event. —**med'al·ist**, *n.* one who has won a medal.

me·dal'lion (mə·dal'yən) *n.* a large carved medal.

med'dle (med'əl) *v.i.* interfere unjustifiedly. —**med'dler**, *n.* —**med'dle·some**, *adj.* disposed to meddle.

me'di·al (mē'dĕ·əl) *adj.* intermediate; average; ordinary.

me'di·an (mē'dĕ·ən) *adj.* being the dividing line or plane between two parts; middle.

me'di·ate" (mē'dĕ·āt") *v.t.* & *i.* reconcile (opposing forces); settle (a dispute); effect an agreement between others. —**me"di·a'tion**, *n.* —**me'di·a"tor**, *n.*

med'ic (med'ik) *n.* (*Slang*) **1**, a doctor. **2**, a member of a medical corps.

med'i·cal (med'i-kəl) *adj.* **1**, pert. to the science or practice of medicine. **2**, curative.

me·dic'a·ment (mə·dik'ə-mənt) *n.* any substance for healing wounds or curing disease.

med'i·cate" (med'i-kāt") *v.t.* treat with medicine. —**med"i·ca'tion**, *n.* **1**, the use of medicine. **2**, a remedy.

med'i·cine (med'ə-sən) *n.* **1**, the science of treating disease or preserving health. **2**, a substance for treating disease; a remedy. —**medic'i·nal** (mə-dis'ə-nəl) *adj.* —**medicine ball**, a heavy ball, thrown for exercise. —**medicine man**, among primitive peoples, a healer by magic.

med'i·co" (med'i-kō") *n.* [*pl.* -**cos**] (*Slang*) a doctor.

me"di·e'val (mē"dĕ·ē'vəl) *adj.* pert. to, or characteristic of, the Middle Ages. Also, **me"di·ae'val**.

me"di·o'cre (mē"dĕ·ō"kẽr) *adj.* of moderate quality; ordinary. —**me"di·oc'ri·ty** (-ok'rə-tĕ) *n.*

med'i·tate" (med'i-tāt") *v.t.* intend; plan. —*v.i.* brood. —**med"i·ta'tion**, *n.* —**med'i·ta"tive**, *adj.*

me'di·um (mē'dĕ·əm) *n.* **1**, something intermediate; a mean. **2**, an intervening substance, person, agency, or instrumentality, through which something exists or an effect is produced; in spiritualism, a person through whom the dead speak. **3**, [usually *pl.*] **me'di·a**] a publication, etc. used by an advertiser. —*adj.* intermediate.

med'lar (med'lẽr) *n.* a small tree, or its apple-like fruit.

med'ley (med'lĕ) *n.* a mixture; a combination, as of songs.

me·dul'la (mi-dul'ə) *n.* (*Anatomy*) the marrow or center of an organ, etc. —**medulla ob"lon·ga'ta** (ob"-long-gä'tə) the part of the brain adjoining the spinal cord.

meek (mēk) *adj.* submissive; humble. —**meek'ness**, *n.*

meer'schaum (mir'shəm) *n.* a silicate used for the bowls of tobacco pipes.

meet (mēt) v.t. [pret. & p.p. met]
1, come together, or into contact,
with. 2, encounter; welcome. 3,
conform to; answer; refute. —v.i.
1, come together; combine; agree.
2, come into contact. —n. a meeting, as of huntsmen. —adj. suitable.

meet'ing n. 1, a coming together;
a junction. 2, an encounter, sometimes hostile, as a duel. 3, an assembly or gathering: —**meeting
house,** a church.

meg·a- pref. 1, great. 2, a million
times.

meg'a·cy"cle (meg'ə-sī"kəl) n. a
million cycles: applied to wave
lengths.

meg·al·o- pref. very
large.

meg"a·lo·ma'ni·a
(meg"ə-lə-mā'nē-ə) n. a
mania or delusion of
greatness or wealth.
—**meg"a·lo·ma'ni·ac,** n.

meg'a·phone" (meg'-
ə-fōn") n. an instrument
for magnifying sound.

mel'an·cho'li·a
(mel'ən-kō'lē-ə) n. a
mental disease marked
by great depression of
spirits.

Megaphone

mel'an·chol"y (mel'ən-kol'ē) n. a
gloomy state of mind; depression.
—adj. sad. —**mel"an·chol'ic,** adj.
—**mel'an·chol'i·cal·ly,** adv.

Mel"a·ne'sian (mel'ə-nē'zhən)adj.
pert. to one of the principal regions
of island groups in the So. Pacific.

mé·lange' (me-länzh') n. a mixture; a medley.

mel'a·nin (mel'ə-nin) n. the dark
pigment in the hair, skin, etc.

mel·a·no- pref. black.

meld n. a scoring combination of
cards. —v.t. & i. announce or exhibit such cards.

me·lée (mā'lā) n. a general hand-
to-hand fight.

mel'io·rate" (mēl'yə-rāt") v.t. & i.
make or become better. —**mel"io-
ra'tion,** n.

mel·lif'lu·ous (mə-lif'loo-əs) adj.
smoothly and sweetly flowing; flowing with honey. Also, **mel·lif'lu·ent.**
—**mel·lif'lu·ous·ness,** n.

mel'low (mel'ō) adj. 1, soft, esp.
from ripeness. 2, softened; matured;
good-humored. —v.t. & i. make or
become mellow. —**mel'low·ness,** n.

me·lo'de·on (mə-lō'dē-ən) n. a
small organ.

me·lod'ic (mə-lod'ik) adj. tuneful;
pert. to melody. —**me·lod'i·cal·ly,**
adv.

me·lo'di·ous (mə-lō'dē-əs) adj.
musical; tuneful. —**me·lo'di·ous·
ness,** n.

mel"o·dra"ma (mel'ə-drà"mə) n.
a play with a sensational plot and
exaggerated sentiment.

mel"o·dra·mat'ic (-drə-mat'ik)
adj. affecting undue sentiment.
—**mel"o·dra·mat'i·cal·ly,** adv.

mel'o·dy (mel'ə-dē) n. a tune; the
air of a musical composition; a
succession of musical tones.

mel'on (mel'ən) n. a large fruit
with a juicy flesh inside a rind.

melt v.t. & i. 1, make or become
liquid through heat. 2, dissolve. 3,
dwindle; blend. 4, be softened to
tenderness, sympathy, etc. —**melting pot,** a country or city that assim-
ilates and unites immigrants of various national origins.

mem'ber (mem'bər) n. 1, a part
of any aggregate or whole. 2, a part
of the body; a vital organ; a limb.
3, each of the persons composing a
society, party, or legislative body.
—**mem'ber·ship,** n. the state of
being a member, as of a party; the
total number of such members.

mem'brane (mem'brān) n. a
sheet of thin tissue, lining an organ,
connecting parts, etc. —**mem'bra-
nous** (-brə-nəs) adj.

me·men'to (mə-men'tō) n. [pl.
-tos] a reminder; a souvenir.

mem'o (mem'ō) n. [pl. -os] a
memorandum.

mem'oir (mem'wär) n. 1, a record
of facts. 2, (pl.) a narrative of facts
and events, esp. of one's own life.

mem"o·ra·ble (mem'ə-rə-bəl) adj.
worthy to be remembered.

mem"o·ran'dum (mem"ə-ran'-
dəm) n. [pl. -dums or -da] 1, a record. 2, a note to help the memory.

me·mo'ri·al (mə-môr'ē-əl) n. 1,
a commemorative monument, etc.
2, a petition. —adj. commemorating.
—**me·mo'ri·al·ize"** (-īz") v.t.

mem"o·rize" (mem'ə-rīz") v.t. commit to memory.

mem'o·ry (mem'ə-rē) n. 1, the
mental capacity of retaining and
reviving impressions; remembrance;
recollection. 2, the state of being
remembered. 3, that which is remembered.

men n. pl. of *man.*

men'ace (men'is) n. a threat or
threatening. —v.t. threaten.

mé·nage' (mā-näzh') n. a household.

me·nag'er·ie (mə-naj'ə-rē) n. a
collection or exhibition of wild
animals.

mend v.t. repair; make whole; correct; improve. —v.i. improve in
health; become whole. —n. 1, a
mended place. 2, recovery from
sickness.

men·da'cious (men-dā'shəs) *adj.* 1, untrue. 2, untruthful. —**men·dac'i·ty** (-das'ə-tē) *n.*

men'di·cant (men'di-kənt) *n.* a beggar. —*adj.* begging. —**men'di·can·cy,** *n.*

me'ni·al (mē'nē-əl) *n.* 1, a domestic servant. 2, a servile person. —*adj.* lowly; servile.

men·in·gi'tis (men"in-jī'tis) *n.* inflammation of the membranes of the brain and spinal cord.

Men'no·nite'' (men'ə-nīt'') *n.* a member of a certain fundamentalist Protestant sect.

men'o·pause'' (men'ə-pâz'') *n.* the final cessation of the menses; change of life.

men'ses (men'sēz) *n.pl.* the monthly discharge from the uterus.

men'stru·ate'' (men'stroo-āt'') *v.i.* discharge the menses. —**men'stru·al,** *adj.* —**men'stru·a'tion,** *n.*

men'sur·a·ble (men'shər-ə-bəl) *adj.* measurable. —**men'su·ra'tion,** *n.* the process of measuring.

-ment (mənt) *suf.* the act, fact or result of doing (the root word).

men'tal (men'təl) *adj.* pert. to, or performed by, the mind or intellect.

men·tal'i·ty (men-tal'ə-tē) *n.* 1, mental capacity. 2, the mind.

men'thol (men'thol) *n.* a crystalline substance derived from oil of peppermint, useful in treating nasal disorders. —**men'tho·lat''ed,** *adj.* treated with or containing menthol.

men'tion (men'shən) *v.t.* refer to briefly or incidentally. —*n.* a brief reference.

men'tor (men'tôr) *n.* a wise adviser; a trusted teacher and counselor.

men'u (men'ū) *n.* a bill of fare.

me·ow' (mē-ow') *n.* the whining sound made by a cat. —*v.i.* so cry.

me·phi'tis (mi-fī'tis) *n.* a noxious or poisonous exhalation; a stench. —**me·phit'ic** (-fit'ik) *adj.*

mer'can·tile (mėr'kən-til) *adj.* pert. to merchants or trading; commercial.

mer'ce·nar'y (mėr'sə-ner'ē) *adj.* serving only for gain; avaricious. —*n.* a hired soldier; a hireling.

mer'cer (mėr'sər) *n.* a dealer in cloth.

mer'cer·ize'' (mėr'sə-rīz'') *v.t.* treat cotton fabric with caustic alkali, to increase its luster and strength.

mer'chan·dise'' (mėr'chən-dīz'') *n.* commodities bought and sold. —*v.t. & i.* market.

mer'chant (mėr'chənt) *n.* one who buys and sells commodities.

— **merchant marine,** ships used in commerce; their crews.

mer'chant·man (mėr'chənt-mən) *n.* [*pl.* -men] a trading vessel.

mer·ci' (mer-sē') *interj.* (Fr.) thank you.

mer'ci·ful (mėr'si-fəl) *adj.* compassionate; lenient.

mer'ci·less (-ləs) *adj.* pitiless. —**mer'ci·less·ness,** *n.*

mer·cu'ri·al (mər-kyûr'ē-əl) *adj.* 1, [also, **mer·cu'ric**] pert. to mercury. 2, sprightly; changeable.

mer·cu'ro·chrome'' (mər-kyûr'ə-krōm'') *n.* an antiseptic or germicide.

mer'cu·ry (mėr'kyə-rē) *n.* a fluid metallic element, no. 80, symbol Hg.

mer'cy (mėr'sē) *n.* 1, compassionate leniency toward an enemy or wrongdoer. 2, discretionary power to punish or spare.

mere (mir) *adj.* simple; only. —**mere'ly** (-lē) *adv.* simply; solely.

mer''e·tri'cious (mer''ə-trish'əs) *adj.* deceitfully alluring; tawdry. —**mer''e·tri'cious·ness,** *n.*

mer·gan'ser (mər-gan'sər) *n.* a fish-eating duck.

merge (mėrj) *v.i.* 1, be absorbed; lose identity. 2, unite. —*v.t.* cause to be absorbed or unite.

merg'er (mėr'jər) *n.* a uniting of two or more businesses.

me·rid'i·an (mə-rid'ē-ən) *n.* 1, a great circle, of the earth or the heavens, passing through the poles; half of this circle. 2, the zenith; midday. —**me·rid'i·o·nal,** *adj.*

me·ringue' (mə-rang') *n.* a white-of-egg and sugar coating for pastry.

me·ri'no (mə-rē'nō) *n.* [*pl.* -nos] a sheep prized for its fine wool.

mer'it *n.* 1, a commendable quality; worthiness. 2, (*pl.*) the qualities by which something is evaluated. —*v.t.* deserve.

mer''i·to'ri·ous (mer''i-tôr'ē-əs) *adj.* deserving of praise or reward.

merle (mėrl) *n.* the Europ. blackbird.

mer'lin (mėr'lin) *n.* a small hawk.

mer'maid (mėr'mād'') *n.* an imaginary marine woman, with the tail of a fish, *n.masc.*

Mermaid

mer'ry (mer'ē) *adj.* 1, festive. 2, mirthful. —**mer'ri·ment,** *n.*

mer"ry-an'drew (mer'ė-an'droo) n. a clown; buffoon.

mer'ry-go-round" (mer'ė-gō-rownd") n. a revolving platform fitted with hobbyhorses, etc.

mer'ry-mak"er (-mā'kər) n. a reveler. —**mer'ry-mak"ing**, n.

me'sa (mā'sə) n. a tableland.

més-al'li-ance (mā-zal'ė-əns) n. a marriage with a social inferior.

més-cal' (mes-kal') n. 1, a cactus. 2, an intoxicating beverage.

mesh n. an open space of a net; a network. —v.t. 1, entangle; enmesh. 2, engage, as gear teeth. —v.i. become engaged; work efficiently (with another).

mes'mer-ism (mes'mə-riz-əm) n. hypnotism. —**mes-mer'ic** (-mer'ik) adj. —**mes'mer-ist**, n. —**mes'mer-ize"**, v.t.

mes-o- pref. middle.

mes'o-tron" (mes'ə-tron") n. a particle of 200 times the mass of an electron.

Mes"o-zo'ic (mes"ə-zō'ik) adj. pert. to a geological era, the age of reptiles.

mes-quite' (mes-kēt') n. a shrub of the Southwest U. S., on which grazing cattle feed.

mess (mes) n. 1, an untidy condition or mass. 2, a confused situation. 3, a group taking meals together; such a meal. —v.t. make untidy; muddle. —v.i. 1, eat in company. 2, act or work haphazardly.

mes'sage (mes'ij) n. a verbal or written communication.

mes'sen-ger (mes'ən-jər) n. one who bears a message or goes on an errand.

Mes-si'ah (mə-sī'ə) n. 1, the prophesied deliverer of the Jews; a savior. 2, to Christians, Jesus Christ.

mess'mate" n. an associate in a ship's mess.

mess'y (-ė) adj. untidy. —**mess'i-ness**, n.

mes-ti'zo (mes-tē'zō) n. a person of mixed blood, as Spanish and Amer. Indian. —**mes-ti'za**, n. fem.

met v. pret. & p.p. of meet.

met-a- pref. along with; after; over; also denoting change or transformation.

me-tab'o-lism (mə-tab'ə-liz-əm) n. the chemical process of absorbing food. —**met"a-bol'ic** (met"ə-bol'ik) adj.

met'al (met'əl) n. an elementary substance possessing opacity, conductivity, plasticity, and a peculiar luster, as gold, silver, etc.; an alloy of such substances. —**me-tal'lic** (mə-tal'ik) adj. —**me-tal'li-cal-ly**, adv.

met'al-loid" (met'ə-loid") n. an element having some but not all of the properties of a metal.

met'al-lur"gy (met'ə-lēr"jė) n. the science of separating metals from their ores, treating metals, and compounding alloys. —**met"al-lur'gic**, adj. —**met'al-lur'gist**, n.

met"a-mor'pho-sis (met"ə-môr'fə-sis) n. a complete change of form, structure, or appearance. —**met"a-mor'phic**, adj.

met'a-phor (met'ə-fər) n. a figure of speech, based on some resemblance of a literal to an implied subject. —**met"a-phor'i-cal** (-fôr'i-kəl), **met"a-phor'ic**, adj.

met"a-phys'ics (met"ə-fiz'iks) n. philosophy in general; particularly the science of essential principles, or the more abstruse or abstract principles. —**met"a-phys'i-cal**, adj. concerned with the abstract. —**met"a-phy-si'cian**, n.

met'a-plasm (met'ə-plaz-əm) n. the lifeless matter included with protoplasm in a cell.

me-tas'ta-sis (mə-tas'tə-sis) n. 1, a change of substance. 2, transference of a disease to another part of the body. 3, a sudden rhetorical transition. —**met"a-stat'ic**, adj.

met"a-tar'sus (met"ə-tär'sus) n. [pl. -si (-sī)] the foot bone between the ankle and toes. —**met"a-tar'sal**, adj.

Met"a-zo'a (met"ə-zō'ə) n. all those animals which are above the Protozoa, and have two or more cells. —**Met"a-zo'an**, adj. & n.

mete (mēt) v.t. apportion by measure.

me-temp"sy-cho'sis (mə-temp"sə-kō'sis) n. [pl. -ses (-sēz)] the passing of the soul after death into another body; reincarnation.

me'te-or (mē'tė-ər) n. a shooting star.

me"te-or'ic (-or'ik) adj. 1, pert. to a meteor. 2, transiently brilliant. —**me"te-or'i-cal-ly**, adv.

me'te-or-ite" (-īt") n. a mass of stone or metal that reaches the earth from outer space.

me"te-or-ol'o-gy (mē"tė-ə-rol'ə-jė) n. the scientific study of the atmosphere, the weather, etc. —**me"te-or-o-log'i-cal**, adj.

me'ter (mē'tər) n. 1, the metric unit of length, 39.37 inches. 2, poetic or musical rhythm or measure. 3, an instrument that measures, as gas, water, etc. Also, **me'tre**.

meth'ane (meth'ān) n. an inflammable natural gas.

meth'od (meth'əd) *n.* systematic procedure; a plan or system of conduct or action. —**me·thod'i·cal**, *adj.* following a method; orderly.

Meth'od·ist (meth'ə-dist) *n.* a member of the Methodist Episcopal Church, a principal Protestant sect. — **Meth'od·ism**, *n.*

meth'yl (meth'il) *n.* a derivative of methane. —**methyl alcohol**, wood alcohol.

me·tic'u·lous (mə-tik'yə-ləs) *adj.* finically careful. —**me·tic'u·lous·ness**, *n.*

mé·tier' (me-tyā') *n.* 1, profession; trade. 2, appropriate field or surroundings.

met'ra·zol" (met'rə-zōl") *n.* (*T.N.*) a drug, a heart and lung stimulant.

met'ric (met'rik) *adj.* 1, pert. to the meter (measure of length). 2, pert. to measurement. —**metric system**, a decimal system of weights and measures.

met'ri·cal (met'ri-kəl) *adj.* composed in meter, as verse.

met'ro·nome" (met'rə-nōm") *n.* a mechanical contrivance for signaling intervals of time.

me·trop'o·lis (mə-trop'ə-lis) *n.* the chief city of a country or region.

met"ro·pol'i·tan (met"rə-pol'ə-tən) *adj.* characteristic of a metropolis. —*n.* 1, an inhabitant of a metropolis. 2, (*cap.*) a title in the Orthodox Church, equivalent to archbishop.

-me·try *suf.* measurement.

met'tle (met'əl) *n.* natural temperament; courage. —**met'tle·some**, *adj.* spirited.

mew (mū) *n.* 1, an enclosure. 2, (*pl.*) a set of stables around a court. 3, meow. —*v.i.* meow.

Mex'i·can (mek'si-kən) *adj.* & *n.* pert. to Mexico, its language or inhabitants.

mez'za·nine" (mez'ə-nēn") *n.* a low story between two principal stories.

mez·zo- (met'sō-) *pref.* intermediate.

mez'zo-so·pran'o (met'sō-sə-prän'ō) *n.* a voice intermediate between soprano and contralto.

mez'zo·tint" (met'sō-tint") *n.* an engraving made by roughening a copper or other metallic surface.

mi (mē) *n.* the third tone in the diatonic scale.

mi·aou' (mė-ow') *n.* & *v.i.* meow.

mi·as'ma (mī-az'mə) *n.* noxious emanation.

mi'ca (mī'kə) *n.* a mineral, readily separable into thin sheets.

mice (mīs) *n. pl.* of *mouse.*

mi·cro- *pref.* very small. Also, before vowels, **mi'cr-.**

mi'crobe (mī'krōb) *n.* a germ; a bacterium. —**mi·cro'bic**, *adj.*

mi'cro·cosm (mī'krə-koz-əm) *n.* 1, a little world; a world in miniature. 2, fig., man.

mi'cro·film" (mī'krə-film") *n.* the film used in microphotography.

mi·crom'e·ter (mī-krom'ə-tər) *n.* a precision instrument for measuring distances in thousandths of an inch or less.

mi'cron (mī'kron) *n.* [*pl.* -**ora**, -**crons**] one millionth of a meter.

Mi"cro·ne'sian (mī"krə-nē'zhən) *adj.* pert. to a certain group of very small islands in the So. Pacific.

mi'cro·ôr'gan·ism (mī"krō-ôr'gə-niz-əm) *n.* an organism of microscopic side; a microbe, germ, etc.

mi'cro·phone" (mī-krə-fōn") *n.* an instrument that transforms sound waves into variations in an electric current; used esp. in telephonic and radio transmission.

mi"cro·pho'to·graph" (mī"krō-fō'tə-gràf") *n.* a minute film reproduction, esp. of printed or written matter, read by enlargement on a screen.

mi'cro·scope" (mī'krə-skōp") *n.* an instrument that magnifies objects not visible to the naked eye.

mi"cro·scop'ic (-skop'ik), *adj.* 1, pert. to a microscope. 2, extremely small. —**mi"cro·scop'i·cal·ly**, *adv.*

mi'cro·tome" (mī'krə-tōm") *n.* an instrument for cutting tissue, etc., into thin sections for examination under the microscope.

mid *adj.* middle. —*prep.* amid; among.

mid'day" (mid'dā") *n.* the middle of the day; noon.

mid'dle (mid'əl) *adj.* 1, equally distant from the extremes or limits. 2, intermediate; intervening. —*n.* 1, the center; a middle point or area. 2, the waist; the stomach. —**Middle Ages**, the period between classical antiquity and the Renaissance, roughly A.D. 500 to 1400. —**middle class**, an intermediate social or economic class. —**middle ear** (*Anat.*) the tympanum. —**Middle West**, the north central states of the U.S.

mid'dle-aged' (mid'əl-âjd') *adj.* intermediate in age; from about 45 to 60 years old.

mid'dle·man" (mid'əl-man") *n.* [*pl.* -**men**] an intermediary; esp. in business, a wholesaler or retailer.

mid'dle·weight" (mid'əl-wāt") *n.* a boxer weighing 148 to 160 lbs.

mid'dling (mid'ling) *adj.* 1, of medium quality or size. 2, (*Colloq.*) in moderate health.

mid'dy (mid'ė) *n.* **1,** a loose blouse with a sailor collar: *middy blouse.* **2,** a midshipman.

midge (mij) *n.* a small fly.

midg'et (mij'it) *n.* a very small person or thing.

mid'i'ron (mid'ī"ẽrn) *n.* a golf club used for long approach shots, no. 2 iron.

mid'land (mid'lənd) *adj.* in the interior of a country; inland.

mid'night" (mid'nīt") *n.* 12 o'clock at night. —*adj.* **1,** at midnight. **2,** intensely black.

mid'riff (mid'rif) *n.* the diaphragm.

mid'ship"man (mid'ship"mən). *n.* [*pl.* -men] one in training to be a naval officer; his rank.

midst *n.* an interior or central position; middle.

mid'stream" *n.* the middle of a stream, current of affairs, etc.

mid'way" (mid'wā") *adj.* half-way. —*n.* a place for side shows at a fair.

Mid'west' *n.* Middle West.

mid'wife" (mid'wīf") *n.* a woman who assists at childbirth. —**mid'-wife"ry,** *n.*

mien (mēn) *n.* a person's bearing, manner, appearance.

miff (mif) *v.t.* (*Colloq.*) offend.

might (mīt) *n.* effective power; ability. —*aux.* *v.* pret. of *may.*

might'y (mī'tė) *adj.* powerful; momentous. —*adv.* (*Colloq.*) very. —**might'i·ness,** *n.*

mi"gnon·ette' (min"yə-net') *n.* a fragrant garden plant.

mi'graine (mī'grān) *n.* a severe headache, sometimes accompanied by nausea.

mi'grant (mī'grənt) *n.* one who or that which migrates. —*adj.* migrating.

mi'grate (mī'grāt) *v.t.* **1,** go from one country or place of residence to settle in another. **2,** move periodically from one region or latitude to another, esp. birds. —**mi·gra'tion,** *n.* —**mi'gra·to·ry,** *adj.*

mi·ka'do (mi-kä'dō) *n.* the emperor of Japan.

mike (mīk) (*Slang*) *n.* a microphone. —*v.t.* measure with a micrometer.

mil *n.* a unit of length, .001 of an inch.

milch *adj.* giving milk, as a cow.

mild (mīld) *adj.* even-tempered; gentle; temperate; moderate in intensity or degree; not severe, as

weather; not sharp, as flavor. —**mild'ness,** *n.*

mil'dew (mil'doo) *n.* **1,** a fungus disease of plants. **2,** a white fungus coating on fabrics, leather, etc., from exposure to moisture. —*v.t. & i.* become covered with mildew.

mile (mīl) *n.* a Brit. and Amer. unit of distance, 5,280 ft. (*statute mile*) on land, 6,080 ft. (*nautical mile*) at sea.

mile'age (mī'lij) *n.* **1,** the miles traveled in a given time. **2,** a fixed charge per mile. **3,** a traveling allowance.

mil'er (mī'lẽr) *n.* a runner trained to race a mile.

mile'stone" (mīl'stōn") *n.* **1,** a stone distance-marker along a highway. **2,** an important event in life; a birthday.

mil'i·ar'i·a (mil"ė-âr'ė-ə) *n.* an inflammatory skin disease. —**mil'i·ar·y,** *adj.*

mi·lieu' (mė-lyû') *n.* surroundings; environment.

mil'i·tant (mil'ə-tənt) *adj.* **1,** aggressive. **2,** engaged in warfare. —*n.* one engaged in warfare. —**mil'i·tan·cy,** *n.*

mil'i·ta·rism (mil'ə-tə-riz-əm) *n.* extreme emphasis on military power in state policy. —**mil'i·ta·rist,** *n.* —**mil'i·ta·ris"tic,** *adj.*

mil'i·tar"y (mil'ə-ter"ė) *adj.* **1,** pert. to the army, a soldier, or affairs of war; soldierly. **2,** pert. to any arm or instrument of warfare. —*n.* the army.

mil'i·tate" (mil'ə-tāt") *v.i.* have weight or force, against or for.

mi·li'tia (mi-lish'ə) *n.* a body of citizen soldiers, called out only in emergencies. —**mi·li'tia·man,** *n.*

milk *n.* **1,** a whitish liquid secreted by the mammary glands of female mammals for feeding their young. **2,** any liquid resembling this. —*v.t.* **1,** extract milk from a cow, etc. **2,** extract; draw out; exploit. —**milk fever,** a fever coincident with lactation —**milk leg,** thrombosis and swelling of the large veins of the leg. —**milk tooth,** one of the temporary teeth of a young child or animal; baby tooth.

milk'maid" *n.* a girl who milks cows.

milk'man" *n.* [*pl.* -men] a man who delivers milk for a dairy.

milk shake an iced drink of milk, a flavoring syrup, and usually ice cream, shaken together.

milk'sop" *n.* a soft, effeminate man.

milk'weed" (milk'wēd") *n.* a plant having milky juice.

milk′wort′ (milk′wẽrt′) *n.* a flowering herb or shrub.

milk′y (mil′kẻ) *adj.* **1**, like milk. **2**, white. **—milk′i·ness,** *n.* **—Milky Way,** a luminous band in the heavens, composed of innumerable stars.

mill (mil) *n.* **1**, a manufacturing establishment; factory. **2**, a building equipped to grind grain into flour. **3**, any of various machines for grinding, or otherwise working materials into proper form. **4**, one tenth of a cent in U. S. money. **—v.i.** move in a circle, as cattle. **—v.t. 1**, grind, etc., in or with a mill. **2**, groove the edge of (a coin, etc.).

mil·len′ni·um (mi-len′ẻ-əm) *n.* **1**, a thousand years; a thousandth anniversary. **2**, any period of universal happiness.

mill′er (mil′ər) *n.* **1**, one who operates a grain mill. **2**, a small moth.

mil′let (mil′it) *n.* a cereal grass, grown for grain or fodder.

mil·li- (mil-ə) *pref.* thousand; in the metric system, one-thousandth. **—mil′li·gram′,** 1/1000th gram. — **mil′li·me′ter,** *n.* 1/1000th meter, .04 inch.

mil′liard (mil′yərd) *n.* (*Brit.*) one thousand million; billion.

mil′li·ner (mil′ə-nər) *n.* one who makes or sells women's hats. **—mil′li·ner′y,** *n.* women's hats.

mil′lion (mil′yən) *n.* one thousand times one thousand: 1,000,000.

mil′lion·aire′ (mil′yə-nâr′) *n.* a person worth a million dollars, pounds, etc.; a very rich person.

mil′lionth (mil′yənth) *adj.* & *n.* the ordinal of one million, also written 1,000,000th; one of one million equal parts.

mill′race′ (mil′rās′) *n.* the current of water that drives a mill, or the channel in which it flows.

mill′stone′ (mil′stōn′) *n.* **1**, one of two heavy circular stones between which grain is ground. **2**, a heavy burden.

milque′toast′ (milk′tōst′) *n.* (*Slang*) a timid person.

mil′reis′ (mil′rās′) *n.* the monetary unit of Brazil, worth about 5 U. S. cents.

mime (mīm) *n.* **1**, a mummer. **2**, in ancient drama, a farce.

mim′e·o·graph′ (mim′ẻ-ə-gràf′) *n.* (*T.N.*) a device for duplicating letters, etc. by means of stencils. **—v.t.** copy by mimeograph.

mim′ic (mim′ik) *v.t.* [**mim′icked,** **mim′ick·ing**] imitate, esp. derisively. **—n.** an imitator; one apt at mimicking. **—adj. 1**, imitative. **2**, simulated, esp. on a smaller scale.

mim′ic·ry (-rẻ) *n.* act or result of mimicking.

mi·mo′sa (mi-mō′sə) *n.* a tropical tree or shrub having globular flowers. **—mim′o·sa′ceous** (-sä′shəs) *adj.*

min″a·ret′ (min″ə-ret′) *n.* a slender tower attached to a mosque.

min′a·to′ry (min′ə-tôr′ẻ) *adj.* menacing.

mince (mins) *v.t.* **1**, cut into small pieces. **2**, speak of euphemistically; minimize; moderate. **—v.i.** walk daintily; act or speak with affected delicacy. **—minc′ing,** *adj.* affectedly elegant.

mince′meat′ (mins′-mēt′) *n.* **1**, a pie filling of minced suet, fruits, etc. **2**, anything chopped into small pieces.

Minaret

mind (mīnd) *n.* **1**, that with which a living being feels, wills, and thinks; the ego. **2**, the intellect, as distinguished from feeling and volition; intellectual ability. **3**, reason; sanity. **4**, opinion; inclination; disposition **5**, purpose; intention. **6**, memory. **—v.t.** & *i.* **1**, pay attention to; obey. **2**, take care of; attend to. **3**, care about; object to.

-mind′ed *suf.* **1**, inclined. **2**, having such a mind, as *high-minded*, *weak-minded*.

mind′ful (-fəl) *adj.* aware. **—mind′ful·ness,** *n.*

mine (mīn) *pron.* poss. of *I*; belonging to me. **—n. 1**, a deposit of mineral ores or coal, or the excavation made for removing them. **2**, an abounding source of anything. **3**, a charge of explosives submerged in the water or buried on land. **4**, an excavated passage for placing explosives under enemy fortifications. **—v.t.** & *i.* **1**, extract ores, etc. **2**, make subterranean passages. **3**, lay explosives mines. **—min′er,** *n.* **—min′ing,** *n.* —mine field, an area on land or water systematically covered with mines. **— mine layer,** a naval vessel specially equipped for placing mines. **—mine sweeper,** a naval vessel that clears away mines.

min′er·al (min′ər-əl) *n.* **1**, an inorganic substance occurring in nature, of a definite chemical composition and definite structure. **2**, anything inorganic. **—adj. 1**, of or pert. to minerals. **2**, containing minerals.

min″er·al′o·gy (min″ər-al′ə-jẻ) *n.* the science of minerals. **—min″er·al′o·gist,** *n.*

min″e·stro′ne (min″ə-strō′nẻ) *n.* an Ital. soup containing vegetables, herbs, etc.

min′gle (ming′gəl) *v.t.* & *i.* **1**, mix; blend; unite. **2**, associate.

min′i·a·ture (min′ẻ-ə-chər) *n.* **1**, anything represented on a greatly reduced scale. **2,** anything small, esp. a portrait. —*adj.* small.

min'im (min'əm) *n.* **1,** the smallest unit of liquid measure, about one drop. **2,** something very small. **3,** (*Music*) an eighth note.

min'i·mize" (min'ə-mīz") *v.t.* **1,** reduce to a minimum. **2,** belittle.

min'i·mum (min'ə-məm) *n.* the least possible, or lowest actual, degree, amount, etc. —**min'i·mal,** *adj.*

min'ion (min'yən) *n.* an obsequious favorite, as of a prince.

min'is·ter (min'is-tər) *n.* **1,** a clergyman; pastor. **2,** a diplomatic envoy. **3,** (esp. *Brit.*) a high state official, esp. head of a department. —*v.i.* (with *to*) attend; care for; contribute. —**min'is·trant** (-trənt) *n.* & *adj.*

min"is·te'ri·al (-tir'ē-əl) *adj.* pert. to a minister or ministry.

min"is·tra'tion (-trā'shən) *n.* the act of serving or helping; an act of service or aid. —**min"is·tra'tive,** *adj.*

min'is·try (min'is-trē) *n.* **1,** the office or function of a clergyman or minister of state. **2,** the clergy, or the ministers of state, collectively. **3,** (*Brit.*) an administrative department of the government.

mink *n.* a fur-bearing aquatic animal; its fur.

min'now (min'ō) *n.* a small fresh-water fish.

Mink

mi'nor (mī'nər) *adj.* **1,** lesser in importance, size, or extent. **2,** under legal age. **3,** (*Music*) pert. to a certain scale or smaller interval. —*n.* **1,** one not of legal age. **2,** a secondary field of study.

mi·nor'i·ty (mi-nor'ə-tē) *n.* **1,** the lesser part or number; less than half. **2,** a less numerous party or group, as political or racial, among a more numerous. **3,** the state of being below legal age.

min'ster (min'stər) *n.* a church or cathedral.

min'strel (min'strəl) *n.* **1,** originally, an itinerant musician or singer, esp. of ballads. **2,** a black-faced singer or comedian.

mint *n.* **1,** any of several aromatic herbs. **2,** a mint-flavored confection. **3,** a place where money is coined under governmental authority. **4,** a vast amount. —*adj.* unused (of a postage stamp). —*v.t.* coin (money). —mint julep, a drink made of whiskey, sugar, ice, and fresh mint.

mint'age (-ij) *n.* the process, result, or cost of minting.

min'u·end" (min'ū-end") *n.* a number from which another number is to be subtracted.

min"u·et' (min"ū-et') *n.* a slow and stately ballroom dance.

mi'nus (mī'nəs) *prep.* **1,** less (by a certain amount). **2,** lacking. —*adj.* **1,** less than nothing; negative. **2,** (*Math.*) denoting subtraction, as the minus sign (—).

mi·nus'cule (mi-nus'kūl) *adj.* small, esp. of letters; not capital.

min·ute (min'it) *n.* **1,** the sixtieth part of an hour; 60 seconds. **2,** a short space of time. **3,** a moment; a point of time. **4,** a summary; a rough draft. **5,** (*pl.*) a record of the proceedings at a meeting. **6,** the sixtieth part of a degree, as of longitude. —*adj.* quickly prepared.

mi·nute' (mī-nūt') *adj.* **1,** extremely small in size. **2,** very small in scope. —**mi·nute'ness,** *n.*

min'ute·man" (min'it-man") *n.* [*pl.* -men] an Amer. militiaman of Revolutionary times.

mi·nu'ti·ae (mi-nū'shē-ē) *n. pl.* [*sing.* -a (-ə)] trivial details.

minx (minks) *n.* a pert girl.

mir'a·cle (mir'ə-kəl) *n.* **1,** an act or happening attributed to supernatural power. **2,** a wonderful thing.

mi·rac'u·lous (mi-rak'yə-ləs) *adj.* being, or like, a miracle; wonderful.

mi·rage' (mi-räzh') *n.* an optical illusion by which images of distant objects can be seen.

mire (mīr) *n.* **1,** wet, slimy ground; deep mud. **2,** filth. —*v.t.* **1,** sink or fix in mire. **2,** soil with filth. **3,** involve in difficulties. —*v.i.* sink in mire. —**mir'y,** *adj.* muddy; filthy.

mir'ror (mir'ər) *n.* **1,** a surface that reflects clear images; a looking-glass. **2,** anything that gives a true picture or reflection. —*v.t.* reflect.

mirth (mērth) *n.* festive gaiety; amusement; laughter. —**mirth'ful,** *adj.* **1,** full of mirth. **2,** causing mirth. —**mirth'less,** *adj.* gloomy.

mis- *pref.* **1,** bad; wrong; erroneous. **2,** negative. **3,** hating.

mis"ad·ven'ture (mis"əd-ven'chər) *n.* a mishap; ill fortune.

mis"an·thrope" (mis'ən-thrōp") *n.* a hater of mankind. Also, **mis·an'thro·pist** (mis-an'thrə-pist).

mis·an'thro·py (mis-an'thrə-pē) *n.* dislike of, or distrust toward, mankind. —**mis"an·throp'ic** (mis"ən-throp'ik) *adj.* —**mis·an·throp'i·cal·ly,** *adv.*

mis"ap·pre·hend' (mis"ap-rē-hend')- *v.t.* misunderstand.—**mis"ap·pre·hen'sion** (-shən) *n.*

mis"ap·pro'pri·ate" (mis"ə-prō'prē-āt") *v.t.* put to a wrong or dishonest use, as funds. —**mis"ap·pro'pri·a'tion,** *n.*

mis"be·got'ten (mis"bĕ-got'ən) adj. illegitimate.

mis"be·have' (mis"bĕ-hāv') v.i. behave badly. —**mis"be·hav'ior,** n.

mis"be·lieve' (mis"bə-lēv') v.t. doubt.

mis·cal'cu·late" (mis-kal'kyə-lāt") v.t. & i. calculate incorrectly. —**mis"cal·cu·la'tion,** n.

mis·car'riage (mis-kar'ij) n. **1,** failure to arrive at a just result, as of justice. **2,** failure to arrive at destination, as a letter. **3,** untimely or premature delivery of young. —**mis·car'ry,** v.i.

mis"ce·ge·na'tion (mis"i-jə-nā'shən) n. interbreeding between races.

mis"cel·la'ne·ous (mis"ə-lā'nē-əs) adj. consisting of a mixture; diversified; varied.

mis"cel·la'ny (mis'ə-lā'nē) n. a collection of literary compositions on varied subjects.

mis·chance' (mis-chàns') n. a mishap; ill luck.

mis'chief (mis'chif) n. **1,** an injury; a petty annoyance; trouble. **2,** a cause or source of trouble.

mis'chie·vous (mis'chə-vəs) adj. **1,** injurious; annoying. **2,** fond of mischief; teasing. —**mis'chie·vous·ness,** n.

mis'ci·ble (mis'ə-bəl) adj. capable of being mixed. —**mis"ci·bil'i·ty,** n.

mis"con·ceive' (mis"kən-sēv') v.t. & i. misunderstand. —**mis"con·cep'tion,** n.

mis·con'duct (mis-kon'dukt) n. **1,** improper conduct. **2,** unlawful conduct, as by an official, lawyer, etc. —**mis"con·duct',** v.t. mismanage.

mis"con·strue' (mis"kən-stroo') v.t. misinterpret. —**mis"con·struc'tion,** n.

mis'cre·ant (mis'krē-ənt) n. a villain; a scoundrel. —adj. villainous. —**mis'cre·an·cy,** n.

mis·cue' (mis-kū') n. **1,** a slip of the cue (at billiards). **2,** a failure to take a hint, or to answer one's cue (in the theater). —v.i. make a miscue.

mis·deed' (mis-dēd') n. a wicked action.

mis"de·mean'or (mis"də-mē'nər) n. **1,** (Law) an offense less serious than a felony. **2,** misbehavior.

mis"di·rect' (mis"di-rekt') v.t. **1,** give erroneous information or instruction to. **2,** address incorrectly (a letter, etc.). —**mis"di·rec'tion,** n.

mi'ser (mī'zər) n. an avaricious, niggardly person; one who hoards money. —**mi'ser·ly,** adj. —**mi'ser·li·ness,** n.

mis'er·a·ble (miz'ər-ə-bəl) adj. **1,** wretched; unhappy; poor. **2,** mani-

festing, causing, or attended with, misery. **3,** mean; contemptible. **4,** (Colloq.) ailing.

mis'er·y (miz'ə-rē) n. **1,** physical or mental suffering; wretchedness; poverty. **2,** a cause of suffering. **3,** (Colloq.) a bodily ailment.

mis·fea'sance (mis-fē'zəns) n. the misuse of power; a wrongful exercise of lawful authority.

mis·fire' (mis-fīr') v.i. fail to explode or fire.

mis'fit n. **1,** something that does not fit, as a garment of the wrong size; state of being unsuitable. **2,** a person poorly adapted to his job, society, etc.

mis·for'tune (mis-fôr'chən) n. **1,** bad luck; adversity. **2,** a mishap; a calamity.

mis·giv'ing n. a feeling of doubt or apprehension.

mis·guide' (mis-gīd') v.t. advise badly; mislead.

mis'hap n. an unfortunate occurrence.

mish'mash" n. a jumble.

mis"in·form' (mis"in-fôrm') v.t. give false information to.

mis"in·ter'pret (mis"in-tẽr'prit) v.t. understand, or explain, incorrectly.

mis·judge' (mis-juj') v.t. & i. have an unjust or incorrect opinion (of). —**mis·judg'ment,** n.

mis·lay' (mis-lā') v.t. [pret. & p.p. mis·laid'] **1,** lay away and forget. **2,** place incorrectly.

mis·lead' (mis-lēd') v.t. lead astray; lead into error; delude.

mis·man'age (mis-man'ij) v.t. & i. manage badly. —**mis·man'age·ment,** n.

mis·no'mer (mis-nō'mər) n. a misapplied term, name, or designation; a misnaming.

mi·sog'y·ny (mi-soj'ə-nē) n. hatred of women. —**mi·sog'y·nist,** n.

mis·place' (mis-plās') v.t. **1,** put in a wrong place. **2,** bestow unwisely, as confidence.

mis'print' n. a typographical error. —**mis·print',** v.t. & i. print incorrectly.

mis"pro·nounce' (mis-prə-nowns') v.t. & i. pronounce incorrectly. —**mis"pro·nun'ci·a'tion,** n.

mis·quote' (mis-kwōt') v.t. & i. quote incorrectly. —**mis"quo·ta'tion,** n.

mis·read' (mis-rēd') v.t. misinterpret.

mis"rep·re·sent' (mis"rep-ri-zent') v.t. represent falsely or imperfectly. —**mis"rep·re·sen·ta'tion,** n.

mis·rule' (mis-rool') *v.t.* govern badly. —*n.* **1,** bad or unwise rule. **2,** disorder.

miss (mis) *v.t.* **1,** fail to reach or attain what is aimed at, expected, or desired. **2,** feel the want of, or absence of. **3,** avoid. **4,** overlook. —*v.i.* fail to attain; be unsuccessful. —*n.* **1,** a failure to accomplish, etc. **2,** a girl; an unmarried woman.

mis'sal (mis'əl) *n.* a prayer book.

mis·shap'en (mi-shā'pən) *adj.* deformed. —**mis·shap'en·ness,** *n.*

mis'sile (mis'əl) *n.* an object or weapon that can be hurled or shot.

miss'ing (mis'ing) *adj.* absent; lacking. —**missing link,** a hypothetical primate proposed as having linked ape and man, in evolution.

mis'sion (mish'ən) *n.* **1,** a sending; a charge to go and perform a specific service or duty. **2,** a delegation so sent. **3,** the service or duty for which one is sent. **4,** a self-imposed duty or function. **5,** (often *pl.*) an organized effort for the spread of religion in foreign lands.

mis'sion·ar'y (mish'ə-ner'ē) *n.* one sent to spread his religion in a foreign land.

mis'sive (mis'iv) *n.* a written message.

mis·spell' (mis-spel') *v.t.* spell incorrectly. —**mis·spelt',** *adj.*

mis·spent' *adj.* squandered. —**mis·spend',** *v.t.*

mis·state' (mis-stāt') *v.t.* state incorrectly or misleadingly. —**mis·state'ment,** *n.*

mis·step' (mis-step') *n.* **1,** a stumble. **2,** a mistake in conduct.

mist *n.* **1,** a cloud of minute globules of water, near the ground; a fog. **2,** a precipitation much finer than rain. **3,** a haze; something that veils or obscures. —*v.t. & i.* make or become misty.

mis·take' (mi-stāk') *v.t.* [**mistook'** ('-tŭk'), **mis·tak'en, -tak'ing**] choose erroneously; regard (something) as other than it is; misunderstand. —*v.i.* be in error. —*n.* an error in action, opinion, or judgment. —**mis·tak'en,** *adj.* **1,** erroneous. **2,** being in error.

mis'ter (mis'tər) *n.* a conventional title for a man, usually written Mr.

mis·time' (mis-tīm') *v.t.* say or do inopportunely.

mis'tle·toe" (mis'əl-tō") *n.* a parasitic plant, with white berries, used in Christmas decorations.

mis'tral (mis'trəl) *n.* a cold, dry northwest wind from the Mediterranean.

mis·treat' (mis-trēt') *v.t.* treat badly; abuse. —**mis·treat'ment,** *n.*

mis'tress (mis'tris) *n.* **1,** a woman who has authority or control, as of a house or servants. **2,** the female owner, as of a dog. **3,** a woman serving as wife without being married.

mis·tri'al (mis-trī'əl) *n.* (*Law*) a trial not concluded because of error, or because of disagreement of the jury.

mis·trust' *n.* lack of trust; suspicion. —*v.t. & i.* distrust. —**mis·trust'ful,** *adj.*

mist'y (mis'tē) *adj.* **1,** accompanied by, or resembling, mist. **2,** indistinct; obscure. —**mist'i·ness,** *n.*

mis"un·der·stand' (mis"un-dər-stand') *v.t. & i.* [*pret. & p.p.* **mis"un·der·stood'**] misinterpret; understand wrongly.

mis"un·der·stand'ing *n.* **1,** disagreement. **2,** a misconception.

mis"un·der·stood' *adj.* **1,** incorrectly interpreted. **2,** unappreciated.

mis·us'age (mis-ūs'ij) *n.* **1,** improper use, as of words. **2,** bad treatment.

mis·use' (mis-ūz') *v.t.* **1,** make a false or improper use of. **2,** maltreat. —*n.* (mis-ūs') improper use; abuse.

mite (mīt) *n.* **1,** a very small sum of money, or contribution. **2,** a very small person or thing. **3,** an insect that infests plants and foods.

Miter Joint

mi'ter (mī'tər) *n.* **1,** the official headdress of a bishop. **2,** a surface cut for a miter joint, a joining of two pieces beveled at equal angles. **3,** a jig or form for cutting such a surface. —*v.t.* cut so as to join in a miter joint. Also, **mi'tre.**

mit'i·gate" (mit'ə-gāt") *v.t. & i.* lessen or moderate in severity. —**mit'i·ga'tion,** *n.*

mitt (mit) *n.* **1,** a long glove without fingers. **2,** (*Baseball*) a thickly padded glove. **3,** a mitten. **4,** (*Slang*) a hand.

mit'ten (mit'ən) *n.* a glove that encloses the four fingers together and the thumb separately.

mix (miks) *v.t.* **1,** unite or blend into one mass. **2,** mingle indiscriminately; crossbreed. **3,** (with *up*) confuse. —*v.i.* **1,** become mixed. **2,** associate. —*n.* a mixture.

mixed (mikst) *adj.* **1,** blended by mixing. **2,** indiscriminate; assorted. **3,** (*Colloq.*) mentally confused.

mix'er (-ər) *n.* **1,** one who or that which mixes. **2,** a sociable person.

fat, fāte, fär, fāre, fäll, àsk; met, hē, hėr, maybē; pin, pīne; not, nōte, ôr, tool

mix′ture (miks′chər) *n.* the act, state, or result of mixing; a conglomeration; medley.

mix′up″ (miks′up″) *n.* a confused situation; a tangle.

miz′zen·mast (miz′ən-màst″) *n.* the after or third mast of a vessel.

mne·mon′ic (ni-mon′ik) *adj.* pert. to or assisting the memory. —mne-mon′i·cal·ly, *adv.*

mo′a (mō′ə) *n.* a large extinct bird of N. Z.

moan (mōn) *v.i.* **1,** utter a low inarticulate sound expressive of suffering. **2,** make a similar sound, as the wind. —*n.* such a sound.

moat (mōt) *n.* a deep, water-filled trench around a fortified place.

mob *n.* **1,** an incoherent, disorderly crowd of people. **2,** any assemblage of persons or things (used disparagingly). **3,** the common mass of people. —*v.t.* [mobbed, mob′bing] crowd around or attack. —mob·oc′ra·cy, *n.* rule by the mob.

mo′bile (mō′bəl) *adj.* **1,** easily moving or movable. **2,** changing easily; facile; responsive. —mo·bil′i·ty (mō-bil′ə-tē) *n.*

mo′bi·lize (mō′bə-līz″) *v.t. & i.* organize or put in readiness for service. —mo″bi·li·za′tion, *n.*

moc′ca·sin (mok′ə-sən) *n.* **1,** a shoe of soft leather. **2,** a venomous water snake.

mo′cha (mō′kə) *n.* **1,** a choice coffee. **2,** a flavor of chocolate and coffee. **3,** a fine glove leather.

mock (mok) *v.t.* **1,** ridicule; deride; mimic. **2,** defy; deceive. —*v.i.* scoff; jeer. —*adj.* being an imitation, as a *mock battle.*

mock′er·y (mok′ə-rē) *n.* **1,** ridicule; object of ridicule. **2,** an imitation; a travesty.

mock′ing·bird″ (mok′ing-bėrd″) *n.* an imitative song bird of the So. U. S.

mock orange a shrub, the common syringa.

mock-′up″ (mok′up″) *n.* a model, built to scale, as of a machine.

mode (mōd) *n.* **1,** a manner of acting or doing; method. **2,** the manner of existence or action of anything. **3,** the customary usage; the prevailing fashion. **4,** (*Music*) a form of scale. **5,** (*Gram.*) mood. —mod′al (mō′dəl) *adj.*

mod′el (mod′əl) *n.* **1,** a standard for imitation or comparison. **2,** a copy, usually in miniature. **3,** an image for later reproduction. **4,** a subject for an artist. **5,** one employed to wear and display clothes, pose for pictures, etc. —*adj.* **1,** serving as a model. **2,** exemplary.

—*v.t. & i.* **1,** form according to, or make, a model. **2,** act as a model.

mod′er·ate (mod′ər-it) *adj.* **1,** restrained; temperate; kept or keeping within reasonable limits. **2,** medium; mediocre. —*n.* one who avoids extreme opinions or actions. —*v.t. & i.* (mod′ə-rāt″) **1,** make or become less severe or intense. **2,** preside over a meeting. —mod·er·a′tion, *n.* temperance. — mod′er·a′tor, *n.* a presiding officer.

mod′ern (mod′ərn) *adj.* pert. to or characteristic of present or recent times. —*n.* a person of the present era, or of modern tastes.

mod′ern·ism (-iz-əm) *n.* practice or advocacy of radically new customs, design, etc. —mod′ern·ist, *n. & adj.* —mod′ern·is′tic, *adj.*

mod′ern·ize″ (-īz″) *v.t. & i.* make or become modern; renovate. —mod″ern·i·za′tion, *n.*

mod′est (mod′ist) *adj.* **1,** manifesting humility, propriety, and restraint. **2,** moderate. **3,** decent; decorous. —mod′es·ty, *n.*

mod′i·cum (mod′ə-kəm) *n.* a small or moderate quantity.

mod′i·fy″ (mod′ə-fī″) *v.t.* **1,** change the properties, form, or function of. **2,** moderate. **3,** (*Gram.*) qualify or describe (another word). —mod″i·fi·ca′tion, *n.* —mod′i·fi″er, *n.*

mod′ish (mō′dish) *adj.* fashionable —mod′ish·ness, *n.*

mo·diste′ (mō-dēst′) *n.* a maker or seller of women's hats, dresses, etc.

mod′u·late″ (moj′ə-lāt″) *v.t.* **1,** make softer in tone; regulate. **2,** vary or inflect the sound or utterance of. **3,** (*Radio*) vary the frequency of the transmitted wave. —mod″u·la′tion, *n.* —mod′u·la″tor, *n.*

mod′ule (moj′ool) *n.* a unit of measure, esp. of building materials.

mo′gul (mō′gəl) *n.* an important person; a member of the (orig. Mongolian) ruling class.

mo′hair″ (mō′hãr″) *n.* the fleece of an Angora goat; a fabric made of it.

Mo·ham′med·an (mō-ham′ə-dən) *n.* a follower of Mohammed or his religion. —*adj.* Moslem.

moi′e·ty (moi′ə-tē) *n.* **1,** a half part. **2,** a share.

moil *v.i.* work hard. —*n.* drudgery; —moil′er, *n.*

moire (mwär) *n.* a watered silk or wool fabric.

moi·ré′ (mwä-rā′) *adj.* watered; wavelike.

moist *adj.* damp; slightly wet; tearful (of the eyes). —moist′ness, *n.*

mois′ten (mois′ən) *v.t. & i.* make or become damp.

mois′ture (mois′chər) *n.* diffused wetness.

mo'lar (mō'lər) *n.* a grinding tooth.

mo·las'ses (mō-las'iz) *n.* a dark syrup produced in making sugar.

mold (mōld) *n.* 1, a shape or form, esp. for shaping molten or plastic material. 2, something shaped in or on a mold, or the shape imparted to it. 3, native character. 4, a furry fungus growth, esp. on food or decaying matter. 5, soft, rich earth. —*v.t.* shape, form, or fashion, esp. in or on a mold. —*v.t.* & *i.* make or become fungus mold. Also, **mould**. —**mold'y,** *adj.* covered with fungus mold.

mold'board" (mōld'bôrd") *n.* the curved surface of a plow blade.

mold'er (mōl'dər) *v.i.* & *t.* turn to mold or dust by natural decay. —*n.* one who molds.

mold'ing (mōl'ding) *n.* 1, (*Archit.*) a decorative border. 2, something molded.

mole(mōl) *n.* 1, a small dark permanent blemish on the human skin. 2, a small mammal, living chiefly underground. 3, a massive stone breakwater.

Mole

mol'e·cule" (mol'ə-kūl") *n.* 1, the smallest possible physical unit of an element or compound, composed of atoms. 2, a very small particle. —**mo·lec'u·lar** (mə-lek'yə-lər) *adj.*

mole'hill" *n.* 1, a small mound of earth raised by burrowing moles. 2, an unimportant obstacle.

mole'skin" (mōl'skin") *n.* 1, a stout cotton fabric. 2, the soft gray fur of the mole.

mo·lest' (mə-lest') *v.t.* trouble; interfere with injuriously. —**mo"les·ta'tion** (mō"les-tā'shən) *n.*

moll (mol) *n.* (*Slang*) the woman companion of a gangster.

mol'li·fy" (mol'ə-fī") *v.t.* 1, soften. 2, soothe; appease. —**mol"li·fi·ca'tion,** *n.* —**mol'li·fi"er,** *n.*

mol'lusk (mol'əsk) *n.* an invertebrate animal with a soft body and usually a hard shell, as a snail or oyster. Also, **mol'lusc.**

mol'ly·cod"dle (mol'ē-kod"əl) *n.* a pampered boy. —*v.t.* pamper.

molt (mōlt) *v.t.* & *i.* shed feathers (as a bird) or skin. Also, **moult.**

mol'ten (mōl'tən) *adj.* melted.

mo·lyb'de·num (mə-lib'də-nəm) *n.* an element used in alloys, no. 32, symbol Mo. —**mo·lyb'dic,** *adj.*

mom *n.* (*Colloq.*) mamma; mother.

mo'ment (mō'mənt) *n.* 1, an indefinitely small space of time; a minute. 2, the present time; instant. 3, importance; consequence.

mo'men·tar"y (mō'mən-ter"ē) *adj.* very brief. —**mo"men·tar'i·ly** (-tār'ə-lē) *adv.* for a moment; at any moment.

mo·men'tous (mō-men'təs) *adj.* of great consequence. —**mo·men'tous·ness,** *n.*

mo·men'tum (mō-men'təm) *n.* impetus; the quantity of motion of a body: the mass times the velocity.

mon'ad *n.* 1, (*Biol.*) a single-celled organism. 2, (*Chem.*) an element having a valence of one. 3, a unit. —**mo·nad'ic,** *adj.*

mon'arch (mon'ərk) *n.* a hereditary sovereign; king; ruler. —**mo·nar'chal,** (mə-när'kəl) *adj.*

mon'ar·chy (mon'ər-kē) *n.* a government headed by a monarch. —**mon'ar·chist** (-kist) *n.* one who favors such form of government.

mon'as·ter·y (mon'ə-ster-ē) *n.* the premises occupied by monks.

mo·nas'tic (mə-nas'tik) *adj.* pert. to austere life in seclusion, as of monks. —**mo·nas'ti·cism,** *n.*

Mon'day (mun'dē) *n.* the second day of the week.

Mo·nel' metal (mō-nel') (*T.N.*) a nonrusting alloy of nickel.

mon'e·tar·y (mon'ə-ter-ē) *adj.* of or pert. to money.

mon'e·tize" (mon'ə-tīz") *v.t.* legalize as, or coin into, money.

mon'ey (mun'ē) *n.* 1, coin; stamped metal or banknotes authorized as a medium of exchange. 2, available assets; wealth; credit. —**mon'eyed,** *adj.* wealthy. —**money order,** an order for payment of money, esp. one issued at a post office.

mon'ey·bag" (mun'ē-bag") *n.* (*Slang*) a rich man.

mon'ger (mung'gər) *n.* 1, a dealer, as a *fishmonger.* 2, one sordidly active, as a *scandalmonger.*

Mon·gol'i·an (mon-gō'lē-ən) *adj.* & *n.* pert. to Mongolia or to the yellow-skinned races of eastern Asia.

mon'goose (mong'goos) *n.* [*pl.* -gooses] a slender ferretlike animal of India.

mon'grel (mong'grəl) *n.* 1, a dog of mixed breed. 2, any plant, animal, or thing of mixed breed or elements. —*adj.* mixed; not pure.

mon'i·ker (mon'ə-kər) *n.* (*Slang*) a name or nickname.

mon'ism (mon'iz-əm) *n.* the metaphysical doctrine that mind and matter are not separate substances. —**mon'ist,** *n.*

mo·ni′tion (mō-nish′ən) *n.* a warning.

mon′i·tor (mon′ə-tər) *n.* 1, a pupil charged with overseeing other pupils. 2, one who admonishes; a warning. —*v.t. & i.* listen to radio broadcasts for checking purposes.

monk (munk) *n.* a man withdrawn from the world under religious vows.

mon′key (mung′kè) *n.* 1, any mammal of the order *Primates* except man, the lemur, and the apes. 2, a mischievous child or person. 3, any of various machines.—*v.t.* (*Colloq.*) trifle; fool. —**monkey jacket**, a sailor's jacket. —**mon′key-shine″**, *n.* (*Slang*) a mischievous prank. **monkey suit,** (*Slang*) a tailcoat. —**monkey wrench,** an adjustable wrench.

monks′hood (munks′hůd) *n.* a plant having a hooded flower.

mono- *pref.* single; alone.

mon′o·chrome″ (mon′ə-krōm″) *n.* a painting in different shades of a single color. —**mon′o·chro·mat′ic,** *adj.* pert. to one color or one wave length.

mon′o·cle (mon′ə-kəl) *n.* an eyeglass for one eye. —**mo·noc′u·lar,** *adj.* having, pert. to, or intended for, one eye.

mon′o·dy (mon′ə-dè) *n.* 1, a musical composition in which one voice-part predominates. 2, a mourner's lament, in a poem or ode. —**mo·nod′ic** (mə-nod′ik) *adj.*

mo·nog′a·my (mə-nog′ə-mè) *n.* the practice of marrying only once, or being married to only one person at a time. —**mo·nog′a·mist,** *n.* —**mo·nog′a·mous,** *adj.*

mon′o·gram″ (mon′ə-gram″) *n.* a design combining two or more letters, esp. initials.

mon′o·graph″ (mon′ə-gråf″) *n.* a treatise on a single subject. —**mon′-o·graph′ic,** *adj.*

mon′o·lith (mon′ə-lith) *n.* a single stone; a structure of a single stone, as an obelisk. —**mon′o·lith′ic,** *adj.*

mon′o·logue″ (mon′ə-låg″) *n.* a discourse, poem, or dramatic part, by a single speaker. —**mon′o·log″-ist,** *n.*

mon″o·ma′ni·a (mon″ə-mā′nè-ə) *n.* an exaggerated interest in one thing; a specific delusion. —**mon″o-ma′ni·ac,** *n.*

mon″,o·met′al·lism (mon″ə-met′ə-liz″əm) *n.* the use of one metal only as a monetary standard.

mo·nop′o·list (mə-nop′ə-list) *n.* one who establishes or advocates a monopoly. —**mo·nop′o·lis′ti·cal·ly,** *adv.*

mo·nop′o·lize″ (-līz″) *v.t.* have exclusive control or possession of.

mo·nop′o·ly (mə-nop′ə-lè) *n.* 1, exclusive control of a commodity. 2, an exclusive privilege to carry on a traffic or service. 3, the subject of, or a company having, a monopoly.

mon′o·syl″la·ble (mon′ə-sil″ə-bəl) *n.* a word of one syllable. —**mon″o·syl·lab′ic,** *adj.*

mon′o·the·ism (mon′ə-thē-iz-əm) *n.* the doctrine or belief that there is but one God. —**mon′o·the″ist,** *n. & adj.* —**mon′o·the·is′tic,** *adj.*

mon′o·tone″ (mon′ə-tōn″) *n.* 1, (*Music*) a single unvaried tone. 2, speaking or singing without inflection or variation in pitch. 3, sameness of style in writing.

mo·not′o·nous (mə-not′ə-nəs) *adj.* 1, continued in the same tone. 2, tiresome.

mo·not′o·ny (mə-not′ə-nè) *n.* boring lack of variety; sameness.

mon′o·type″ (mon′ə-tīp″) *n.* 1, (*T.N.*) a machine for setting type; type set by such a machine. 2, a print from a picture painted on a metal plate.

mon·sieur′ (mə-syû′) *n.* [*pl.* messieurs′ (mā-syû′; mes′ərz)] (*Fr.*) 1, mister. 2, sir.

Mon·si′gnor (mon-sēn′yər) *n.* a title given to certain dignitaries of the Rom. Cath. Church.

mon·soon′ *n.* the seasonal wind, or the rainy season, of So. Asia.

mon′ster (mon′stər) *n.* 1, a fabulous half-human animal. 2, an abnormal or malformed animal or plant. 3, a huge animal. 4, a morally deformed person. —*adj.* huge.

mon·stros′i·ty (mon-stros′ə-tè) *n.* state of being monstrous; anything monstrous.

mon′strous (mon′strəs) *adj.* 1, abnormal. 2, huge. 3, frightful; shocking. —**mon′strous·ness,** *n.*

mon·tage′ (mon-täzh′) *n.* the combination of elements of different pictures, esp. photographic.

month (munth) *n.* 1, one-twelfth of a solar year; about 30 days; four weeks. 2, any of the twelve parts of the calendar year, as January; etc.

month′ly (-lè) *adj.* once a month; every month; continuing for a month. —*n.* a periodical published once a month.

mon′u·ment (mon′yə-mənt) *n.* 1, a memorial structure or statue; a tomb or tombstone. 2, any enduring memorial. —**mon″u·men′tal,** *adj.* imposing; notable.

moo *n.* the sound a cow makes.

mooch (*Slang*) *v.i.* 1, skulk; hang about. 2, make love by petting. —*v.t.* get without payment; cadge.

mood n. 1, state of mind or feeling; disposition. 2, (pl.) fits of uncertainty or gloominess. 3, (Gram.) any of a series of verb inflections that denote whether a verb expresses fact, wish, questions, etc.

mood'y (moo'dè) adj. gloomy; sullen; pensive. —**mood'i·ness**, n.

moon n. 1, the heavenly body that revolves around the earth monthly and shines by the sun's reflected light. 2, a lunar month. 3, any planetary satellite. 4, anything resembling an orb or a crescent. —v.i. behave listlessly or idly. —**moon'y**, adj. listless.

moon'beam" n. a beam of light from the moon.

moon blindness a disease of horses.

moon'calf" (moon'kåf") n. an imbecile.

moon'flow"er (moon'flow'ər) n. a night-blooming plant.

moon'light" n. & adj. the light of the moon. —**moon'lit"**, adj.

moon'shine" (moon'shīn") n. 1, moonlight. 2, nonsensical talk. 3, (Colloq.) illicitly distilled liquor. —**moon'shin"er**, n. (Colloq.) an illicit distiller.

moon'stone" (moon'stōn") n. a variety of feldspar used as a gem.

moon-'struck" (moon'struk") adj. crazed or bemused.

moor (mûr) n. a tract of open waste land, often swampy; heath. —v.t. & i. secure (esp. a ship) in one place, by cables or anchors. —**moor'age**, n. a place for mooring.

Moor (mûr) n. any member of the dark-skinned No. African Moslem people who formerly occupied Spain.

moor'ing n. the cables for, or the place of, mooring.

Moor'ish (mûr'ish) adj. pert. to the Mohammedan Arabs of northwest Africa.

moose (moos) n. sing. & pl. a large antlered animal of the deer family.

moot adj. debatable.

mop n. 1, a bunch of yarn, etc. on a handle, for washing floors. 2, a thick mass (as of hair). —v.t. [mopped, mop'ping] clean with or as with a mop; wipe clean.

Moose

mop'board" (mop'bôrd") n. a baseboard.

mope (mōp) v.i. be listless, gloomy, or melancholy. —**mop'ish**, adj.

mop'pet (mop'it) n. a doll; a little girl; a child.

mo·quette' (mō-ket') n. a thick velvety carpet.

mo·raine' (mə-rān') n. the accumulation of boulders, gravel, etc. deposited by a glacier.

mor'al (mor'əl) adj. 1, pert. to the distinction between right and wrong, and the rules of right conduct. 2, conforming to these rules. 3, based on ethical, rather than legal rights. 4, ethically or virtually, but not literally, true, as a moral victory. —n. 1, the moral lesson in a fable, experience, etc. 2, moral conduct or character. —**mor'al·ist**, n. a moral person or a student of morality.

mo·rale' (mə-ral') n. moral or mental condition as regards courage, confidence, etc.

mor·al'i·ty (mə-ral'ə-tè) n. quality of being moral; virtue.

mor'al·ize" (-īz") v.i. & t. reflect on or explain in a moral sense.

mor'al·ly (-lè) adv. 1, virtuously. 2, virtually.

mo·rass' (mə-ras') n. a marsh; bog.

mor·a·to'ri·um (môr'ə-tôr'è-əm) n. an authorization to delay payment. —**mor'a·to·ry**, adj.

mo'ray (môr'ā) n. a savage eel.

mor'bid (môr'bid) adj. 1, diseased. 2, mentally unhealthy. —**mor·bid'i·ty**, **mor'bid·ness**, n.

mor'dant (môr'dənt) adj. 1, biting; sarcastic. 2, having the property to fix colors. —**mor'dan·cy**, n.

more (môr) adj. 1, [superl. most] in greater measure or number. 2, additional. —n. a greater or additional quantity or number. —adv. to a greater extent.

mo·reen' (mə-rēn') n. a heavy wool, or wool and cotton, fabric.

mo·rel' (mə-rel') n. an edible mushroom.

more·o'ver (môr-ō'vər) adv. further; besides.

mo'res (môr'ēz) n. pl. customs of behavior.

mor·ga·nat'ic (môr'gə-nat'ik) adj. denoting a marriage between a man of high rank and a woman who does not share his rank. —**mor'ga·nat'i·cal·ly**, adv.

morgue (môrg) n. 1, a place where the bodies of unknown dead persons are kept until identified. 2, the reference files of a newspaper.

mor'i·bund" (môr'ə-bund") adj. in a dying state.

Mor'mon (môr'mən) n. a member of the Church of Jesus Christ of Latter-Day Saints.

morn (môrn) n. morning.

morn'ing (môr'ning) *n.* **1,** the period between midnight and noon, or dawn and noon. **2,** the early part of anything. —Also, **morn.**

morn'ing-glo"ry (môr'ning-glōr'ē) *n.* a climbing plant with cone-shaped flowers.

mo-roc'co (mə-rok'ō) *n.* a fine goatskin leather.

mo'ron (môr'on) *n.* a person whose mentality does not develop beyond the 12-year-old level. —**mo-ron'ic,** *adj.*

mo-rose' (mə-rōs') *adj.* sullenly ill-humored. —**mo-rose'ness,** *n.*

morph-, mor-pho- *pref.* form; as a *suf.,* **-morph, -mor-phic, -mor-phous.**

mor'phine (môr'fēn) *n.* a habit-forming narcotic, used medicinally to dull pain.

mor-phol'o-gy (môr-fol'ə-jē) *n.* the science of form and structure, as of animals and plants. —**mor"pho-log'ic, mor"pho-log'i-cal,** *adj.* —**mor"phol'o-gist,** *n.*

mor'row (mor'ō) *n.* the next day after this.

Morse code (môrs) an alphabet of dots, dashes, and spaces, used in telegraphy and signaling.

MORSE CODES

	I	II		I	II
A	.-	.-	N	-.	-.
B	-...	-...	O	---	. .
C	-.-.	.. .	P	.--.	.....
D	-..	-..	Q	--.-	..-.
E	.	.	R	.-.	. ..
F	..-.	.-.	S	...	...
G	--.	--.	T	-	—
H	....	....	U	..-	..-
I	..	..	V	...-	...-
J	.---	-.-.	W	.--	.--
K	-.-	-.-	X	-..-	.-..
L	.-..	—	Y	-.--	.. ..
M	--	--	Z	--..	... .

I. International Morse Code
II. American Morse Code

mor'sel (môr'səl) *n.* a small piece or quantity, esp. of food.

mor'tal (môr'təl) *adj.* **1,** subject to death; hence, human. **2,** deadly; fatal. **3,** implacable. **4,** grievous. —*n.* a human being.

mor-tal'i-ty (môr-tal'ə-tē) *n.* **1,** the condition of being mortal. **2,** deaths; death rate.

mor'tar (môr'tər) *n.* **1,** a bowl or device in which substances are pounded and ground. **2,** a cannon, firing at high angles. **3,** a mixture of cement used in building.

mor'tar-board" (môr'tər-bôrd") *n.* **1,** a board for holding mortar. **2,** an academic cap with a flat, square top.

mort'gage (môr'gij) *n.* (*Law*) a conditional conveyance of property as security for a loan. —*v.t.* put a mortgage on. —**mort"ga-gor'** (-jôr') *n.* one who so pledges property. —**mort"ga-gee'** (-jē') *n.* one who grants such a loan.

mor-ti'cian (môr-tish'ən) *n.* an undertaker.

mor'ti-fy" (môr'tə-fī") *v.t. & i.* **1,** humiliate. **2,** subject (the body) to ascetic discipline. **3,** affect with gangrene. —**mor"ti-fi-ca'tion,** *n.*

mor'tise (môr'tis) *n.* a cavity or recess to receive an inserted part, *e.g.* a tenon in joining wood. —*v.t.* make, or fasten by, a mortise.

mor'tu-ar"y (môr'choo-er"ē) *n.* a place for temporary reception of the dead. —*adj.* pert. to burial or death.

mo-sa'ic (mō-zā'ik) *n.* a picture or decoration composed of small pieces of material, separate photographs, etc. —*adj.* **1,** pert. to a mosaic. **2,** composed of diverse elements. **3,** (*cap.*) pert. to Moses or his writings.

mo'sey (mō'zē) *v.i.* (*Slang*) stroll.

Mos'lem (mos'ləm) *adj.* pert. to the Mohammedan religion or civilization. —*n.* a Mohammedan.

mosque (mosk) *n.* a Mohammedan place of worship.

mos-qui'to (mə-skē'tō) *n.* an insect that bites animals and draws blood. —**mosquito boat,** a fast motorboat equipped with torpedoes.

moss (mâs) *n.* a plant growing in tufts or mats, usually green, on moist ground, rocks, etc. —**moss'y,** *adj.*

moss'back" *n.* a person of antiquated or conservative opinions.

most (mōst) *adj.* greatest in quantity or number. —*n.* **1,** the greatest quantity or number. **2,** the majority. —*adv.* to the greatest extent.

-most *suf.* a superlative: foremost.

most'ly (-lē) *adv.* chiefly; mainly.

mot (mō) *n.* a witticism.

mote (mōt) *n.* a speck, as of dust.

mo-tel' (mō-tel') *n.* motor court.

moth (mâth) *n.* **1,** a nocturnal insect resembling the butterfly. **2,** a larva that destroys woolen fabrics. —**moth ball,** a ball of naphthalene to repel clothes moths.

moth'eat"en (-ē'tən) *adj.* shabby.

moth'er (muth'ər) *n.* **1,** a female parent. **2,** an elderly woman. **3,** the superior of a convent, etc. **4,** one who exercises the authority or protective care of a mother; a matron. —*adj.* **1,** maternal. **2,** native; giving origin. —*v.t.* **1,** give origin to. **2,** protect tenderly or solicitously.

tub, cūte, pŭll; label; oil, owl; go, chip, she, thin, *then,* sing, ink; *see p. 6*

—**moth'er.hood,** n. —**mother hubbard** (hub'ərd) a full loose gown for women.

moth'er-in-law" n. the mother of one's wife or husband.

moth'er.land" n. the land of one's birth or ancestry.

moth'er.ly (-lĕ) adj. & adv. like or befitting a mother. —**moth'er.li-ness,** n.

moth'er-of-pearl' n. the iridescent lining of an oyster shell, etc.

mo.tif' (mō-tēf') n. a dominant theme; a short musical phrase.

mo'tile (mō'təl) adj. (Biol.) capable of moving spontaneously. —**mo.til'-i.ty,** n.

mo'tion (mō'shən) n. 1, the process, power, or manner, of moving. 2, a movement; gesture. 3, a proposal; suggestion; application. —v.t. & i. direct by a motion or gesture. —**motion picture,** consecutive pictures shown so as to give an illusion of motion.

mo'ti.vate" (mō'tə-vāt") v.t. provide with a motive; induce. —**mo'-ti.va'tion,** n.

mo'tive (mō'tiv) n. 1, a mental force that induces an act; a determining impulse. 2, intention; purpose; design. —adj. 1, causing, or pert. to, motion. 2, constituting a motive.

mot'ley (mot'lĕ) adj. 1, composed of discordant elements; heterogeneous. 2, consisting of, or wearing, a combination of different colors.

mo'tor (mō'tər) n. 1, a source of mechanical power. 2, a machine that transforms the energy of water, steam, electricity, etc. into mechanical energy; engine. 3, an automobile: motor car. —adj. 1, causing or imparting motion. 2, pert. to an automobile. —v.i. ride in an automobile.

mo'tor.boat" n. a boat propelled by a gas or electric engine.

mo'tor.cade" (-kād") n. a procession of automobiles.

mo'tor-car" n. automobile.

motor court, a group of cabins serving as an inn for motorists.

mo'tor.cy'cle (-sī'kəl) n. a bicycle driven by a motor.

mo'tor.ist n. one who travels in an automobile.

mo'tor.ize" (-īz") v.t. equip with motor-driven vehicles.

mo'tor-man (mō'tər-mən) n. [pl. -men] the operator of a trolley car.

mot'tle" (mot'əl) v.t. mark with different colored spots. —n. a diversifying spot or blotch; variegated coloring. —**mot'tled,** adj.

mot'to (mot'ō) n. a phrase, or word, expressive of one's guiding principle.

moue (moo) n. (Fr.) a pout.

mou.lage' (moo-läzh') n. a plaster mold of a footprint, etc. to be used as evidence.

mould (mōld) n. mold.

moult (mōlt) n. molt.

mound (mownd) n. 1, a natural or artificial elevation of earth. 2, a raised mass of anything, as hay. —v.t. heap up.

mount (mownt) v.t. 1, get up on; ascend. 2, place at an elevation; set in proper position. 3, equip with or place on a horse. 4, preserve and stuff (an animal skin). —v.i. 1, ascend. 2, rise in amount. —n. 1, the act of mounting. 2, a horse, etc., for riding. 3, a support; setting. 4, a mountain or hill.

moun'tain (mown'tən) n. 1, a considerable and abrupt elevation of land. 2, something resembling this in size. 3, something relatively very large. —**mountain lion,** cougar.

moun"tain.eer' (-ir') n. 1, one who lives in a mountainous region. 2, a mountain climber.

moun'tain.ous (-əs) adj. 1, abounding in mountains. 2, resembling a mountain; huge. —**moun'tain.ous-ness,** n.

moun'te.bank" (mown'tə-bank") n. a charlatan; an itinerant seller of quack medicines.

mount'ed (mown'tid) adj. 1, riding, or serving while riding, as police on horseback. 2, fixed on a support, etc.

moun'tie (mown'tē) n. a mounted policeman, esp. (cap.) of Canada.

mount'ing n. a support; setting.

mourn (mōrn) v.i. & t. 1, feel or express sorrow, esp. for the dead. 2, wear or display the customary tokens of sorrow. 3, regret the loss of; deplore.

mourn'er n. one who mourns, esp. (at a funeral) a relative. —**mourners' bench,** at a revival meeting, a seat for penitent sinners.

mourn'ful (-fəl) adj. 1, sorrowful. 2, gloomy; dreary. —**mourn'-ful-ness,** n.

mourn'ing n. the conventional tokens of sorrow, as black dress, etc.

mouse (mows) n. [pl. mice (mīs)] a small rodent.

mous'er (mow'zər) n. an animal, esp. a cat, that catches mice.

mousse (moos) n. a frozen dessert of whipped cream, eggs, etc.

mous'y (mow'sĕ) adj. resembling a mouse; drab; colorless; quiet. —**mous'i-ness,** n.

fat, fāte, fär, fāre, fâll, ásk; met, hē, hēr, maybē; pin, pīne; not, nōte, ôr, tool

mouth (mowth) *n.* [*pl.* mouths (mowthz)] 1, the opening through or in which an animal takes food, masticates, and gives vocal utterance; the oral cavity. 2, a similar opening, as of a cave, a vise, etc. 3, the end of a river. —*v.t.* (mowth) 1, utter pompously. 2, put into, or rub with, the mouth. —*v.i.* declaim pompously; make a grimace.

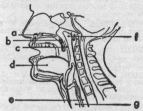

Mouth and Throat

a. Hard Palate
b. Soft Palate
c. Uvula
d. Tongue
e. Oesophagus
f. Pharynx
g. Trachea

mouth'ful *n.* 1, enough to fill the mouth. 2, (*Slang*) a sage remark.

mouth organ a harmonica.

mouth'piece" (mowth'pēs") *n.* 1, a part of an instrument, etc. forming a mouth, or to which the mouth is applied. 2, a person, newspaper, etc. acting as a spokesman for others. 3, (*Slang*) a lawyer.

mouth'y (mow'thė) *adj.* loud-mouthed. —**mouth'i·ness,** *n.*

mou'ton (moo'ton) *n.* sheep's wool used as fur in garments.

move (moov) *v.i.* & *t.* 1, change from one place to another; be or set in motion; advance. 2, have a regular motion; revolve. 3, be sold (as stock); circulate (as in society); take action. 4, make an application or proposal. 5, arouse (the emotions of); touch the feelings of. —*n.* 1, the act of moving; a change of residence; an action toward an end. 2, in a game, the right or turn to play. —**mov'a·ble,** *adj.* & *n.* a piece of furniture not fixed in place; an article of personal property.

move'ment (moov'mənt) *n.* 1, the act or manner of moving. 2, a change of positions, as troops or ships. 3, the progress of events; a tendency or trend. 4, the suggestion of action, as in a painting. 5, the works (of a watch, etc.) 6, (*Music*) a principal division of a composition.

mov'er (moo'vər) *n.* a truckman who moves household things.

mov'ie (moo'vė) *n.* (*Colloq.*) a motion picture.

mov'ing (moo'ving) *adj.* 1, having or creating motion. 2, actuating. 3, exciting the emotions. —**moving picture,** motion picture.

mow (mō) *v.t.* & *i.* [*p.p.* mowed or mown (mōn)] 1, cut down (grass, etc.) with a machine or scythe. 2, cut down men in battle. —*n.* (mow) a place in a barn for storing hay.

Mr. (mis'tər) *abbr.* [*pl.* Messrs.; see *monsieur*] mister.

Mrs. (miz'iz) *abbr.* [*pl.* Mmes.; see *madame*] mistress; a title before the surname of a married woman.

mu (mū) the 12th letter of the Greek alphabet (M, μ).

much *adj.* [more, most] in great quantity. —*n.* 1, a great quantity. 2, a great or important thing. —*adv.* 1, to a great extent. 2, approximately.

mu'ci·lage (mū'sə-lij) *n.* 1, an adhesive gum or glue. 2, a gummy secretion in plants. —**mu"ci·lag'i·nous** (-laj'ə-nəs) *adj.*

muck (muk) *n.* 1, filth; dirt. 2, manure. 3, highly organic soil. 4, useless rock. —**muck'y,** *adj.*

muck'rake" (muk'rāk") *v.t.* (*Colloq.*) expose political corruption.

mu'cous (mū'kəs) *adj.* pert. to, or secreting, mucus. —**mucous membrane,** the membrane lining an internal organ.

mu'cus (mū'kəs) *n.* a viscid fluid secreted in the mucous membrane.

mud *n.* wet, soft earth; mire.

mud'cat" (mud'kat") *n.* a large catfish.

mud dauber a wasp.

mud'dle (mud'əl) *v.t.* & *t.* 1, mix up; confuse. 2, confuse mentally; intoxicate. 3, make muddy or turbid. —*n.* 1, a mess. 2, intellectual confusion.

mud'dler (mud'lər) *n.* 1, a stick for mixing drinks. 2, one who acts confusedly or haphazardly.

mud'dy (mud'ė) *adj.* 1, covered with mud. 2, not clear; obscure. —*v.t.* make muddy.—**mud'di·ness,** *n.*

mud'guard" *n.* a fender, as on an automobile.

mud hen a marsh bird, esp. a coot.

mud'suck"er (mud'suk"ər) *n.* a Calif. fish.

mu·ez'zin (mū-ez'in) *n.* the crier who calls Mohammedans to prayer.

muff (muf) *n.* a cylindrical cover for warming both hands. —*v.t.* & *i.* (*Colloq.*) perform clumsily; bungle.

muf'fin (muf'in) *n.* a small round bread.

muf'fle (muf'əl) *v.t.* 1, wrap up, esp. in a cloak or scarf. 2, deaden (sound) by wrapping. —*v.i.* (with up) wrap oneself well.

muf'fler (muf'lər) *n.* 1, a scarf. 2, a device for deadening sound, as on an engine.

muf'ti (-tè) n. 1, civilian dress. 2, a Mohammedan religious officer.

mug n. 1, a cup with a handle. 2, (Slang) the mouth; the face; a wry expression. —v.t. & i. [mugged, mug'ging] (Slang) 1, photograph. 2, throttle from behind. 3, grimace.

mug'ger (mug'ər) n. 1, a crocodile. 2, one who mugs.

mug'gy (mug'è) adj. (of weather, etc.) humid and hot. —mug'gi·ness, n.

mu·lat'to (mū-lat'ō) n. the offspring of a white person and a Negro. —adj. light-brown in color.

mul'ber'ry (mul'ber'è) n. 1, a tree or its berrylike, collective fruit. 2, a dull reddish-purple color.

mulch n. a protective covering of straw, etc. around trees, etc.

mulct (mulkt) v.t. deprive of something by penalty or trickery. —n. a fine.

mule (mūl) n. 1, the offspring of a mare and a male donkey. 2, a stubborn person. 3, a machine for spinning cotton. 4, a slipper open at the heel. —mul'ish, adj. stubborn.

mu''le·teer' (mū''lə-tir') n. a driver of mules; mule skinner.

mu'ley (mū'lè) n. a cow. —adj. (of cattle) hornless.

mull (mul) v.i. ponder. —v.t. 1, make a failure of. 2, heat, sweeten, and spice, as wine or ale. 3, think over. —n. a kind of muslin.

mul'lein (mul'in) n. any of various flowering plants or weeds.

mul'let (mul'it) n. any of various marine or fresh-water fishes.

mul'li·gan (mul'ə-gən) n. (Slang) a meat and vegetable stew.

mul''li·ga·taw'ny (mul''è-gə-tâ'nè) n. a soup flavored with curry.

mul·ti- pref. many.

mul''ti·far'i·ous (mul''tì-fâr'ĕ-əs) adj. having many differing parts.

Mul'ti·graph'' (mul'tì-gràf'') n. (T.N.) a small printing press, for form letters, etc.

mul''ti·mil''lion·aire' (mul''tì-) n. one who owns property worth several millions of dollars.

mul''ti·par'tite (mul''tè-pär'tit) adj. 1, having many parts. 2, of or between three or more nations.

mul'ti·ple (mul'tì-pəl) adj. manifold; having many parts, individuals, etc. —n. (Math.) the product of multiplying a number by a whole number. —multiple sclerosis, a hardening of the tissues in various parts of the body, affecting the nervous system and causing defects in speech and sight, and weakness.

mul''ti·pli·cand' (mul''tə-pli-kand') n. a number to be multiplied by another.

mul''ti·pli·ca'tion (mul''tə-pli-kā'shən) n. act or process of multiplying.

mul''ti·plic'i·ty (mul''tə-plis'ə-tè) n. a great number.

mul'ti·ply'' (mul'tì-plī'') v.t. & i. 1, increase the number or quantity. 2, increase by propagation or procreation. 3, (Math.) add as many units of one number as there are units in a second number. —mul'ti·pli''er, n.

mul'ti·tude'' (mul'tì-tood'') n. a great number; a crowd of persons. —mul''ti·tu'di·nous, adj.

mum adj. [mum'mer, -mest] silent. —n. (Colloq.) 1, a chrysanthemum. 2, another.

mum'ble (mum'bəl) v.i. & i. 1, speak inarticulately or indistinctly. 2, chew with the gums. —n. an inarticulate sound.

mum'bo jum'bo (mum'bō jum'-bō) 1, an object of superstitious awe; a fetish. 2, senseless incantation.

mum'mer (mum'ər) n. one who wears a mask; a disguised reveler.

mum'mer·y (mum'ə-rè) n. 1, a performance of mummers; burlesque. 2, insincere ceremony.

mum'mi·fy'' (mum'ə-fī'') v.t. & i. make or become a mummy. —mum''mi·fi·ca'tion, n.

mum'my (mum'è) n. 1, a human body embalmed by the ancient Egyptians; any desiccated corpse. 2, a withered living being. 3, (Colloq.) mother.

mumps n. an inflammation and swelling of the salivary glands.

munch v.t. & i. chew continuously and noisily.

mun'dane (mun'dān) adj. pert. to the world or universe; worldly. —mun·dane'ness, n.

mu·nic'i·pal (mū-nis'ì-pəl) adj. pert. to the government of a city.

mu·nic''i·pal'i·ty (mū-nis''ì-pal'ə-tè) n. a city or town having corporate existence.

mu·nif'i·cent (mū-nif'ì-sənt) adj. generous; spending liberally. —munif'i·cence, n.

mu·ni'tion (mū-nish'ən) n. (usually pl.) materials for carrying on war, esp. ammunition.

mu'ral (myūr'əl) adj. pert. to, or placed on, a wall. —n. a painting directly on or covering a wall.

mur'der (mėr'dər) n. homicide with malice aforethought. —v.t. 1, kill with premeditated malice. 2, kill barbarously. 3, mar by poor execution. —mur'der·er, n. —mur'der·ess, n. fem.

mur'der.ous *adj.* pert. to, or capable of, murder; deadly. —**mur'der-ous-ness,** *n.*

murk (mẽrk) *n.* haze.

murk'y (mẽr'kẽ) *adj.* **1,** dark. **2,** obscured; hazy. —**murk'i-ness,** *n.*

mur'mur (mẽr'mər) *n.* **1,** a low, indistinct sound; a subdued hum, as of voices, a brook, the wind, etc. **2,** a muttered complaint. **3,** an abnormal sound in the body, esp. the heart. —*v.t.* & *i.* utter (such a sound). —**mur'mur-ous,** *adj.*

mur'rain (mur'ən) *n.* a disease of cattle, esp. anthrax.

mus'cat (mus'kət) *n.* a variety of grape.

mus'cle (mus'əl) *n.* **1,** a fixed bunch of fibers in an animal body which produces movement by contracting and dilating. **2,** muscular strength; brawn. —*v.i.* (with *in*) (*Colloq.*) force one's way in. —**mus'cle-bound',** *adj.* having inelastic muscles.

Mus'co-vite' (mus'kə-vīt') *adj.* & *n.* of or pert. to Muscovy (Russia), its people or language.

mus'cu-lar (mus'kyə-lər) *adj.* of or pert. to muscle; very strong. —**mus'cu-lar'i-ty,** *n.*

muse (mūz) *v.i.* & *t.* **1,** ponder; reflect. **2,** gaze meditatively. —*n.* **1,** a poet's inspiration or genius. **2,** (*cap.*) a goddess presiding over one of the arts. —**mus'ing,** *adj. & n.*

mu-sette' bag (mū-zet') an army officer's bag for personal belongings.

mu-se'um (mū-zē'əm) *n.* a building for an exhibit of art, science, etc.

mush *n.* **1,** anything soft and pulpy. **2,** a food, made of meal and water. **3,** (*Colloq.*) maudlin sentiment. **4,** a journey over snow with a dog team. —*v.i.* drive a dog team.

mush'room' *n.* any of various large fungi, esp. the edible varieties. —*v.i.* grow or spread rapidly.

mush'y (-ē) *adj.* **1,** pulpy. **2,** sentimental. —**mush'i-ness,** *n.*

mu'sic (mū'zik) *n.* **1,** the combining of sounds and tones as a form of artistic expression. **2,** a composition rendered by instruments or singing voices; a copy or copies of such a composition. **3,** any pleasing combination of sounds, as of the wind. —**mu'si-cal,** *adj.* pert. to, producing, or skilled in, music.

mu"si-cale' (mū"zi-kal') *n.* a program of music.

mu-si'cian (mū-zish'ən) *n.* one who composes or performs music.

musk *n.* an odoriferous animal secretion used in perfumery. —**musk'y,** *adj.*

mus'kel-lunge' (mus'kə-lunj') *n.* a large, fresh-water game fish.

mus'ket (mus'kit) *n.* a hand gun for soldiers.

mus"ket-eer' (mus"kə-tir') *n.* a soldier, orig. one who carried a musket.

mus'ket-ry (-rē) *n.* **1,** troops armed with muskets. **2,** firing practice.

musk'mel'on (musk'mel'ən) *n.* a small sweet variety of melon.

musk ox a ruminant mammal intermediate between the sheep and the ox.

musk'rat' *n.* a No. Amer. aquatic rodent; its fur.

mus'lin (muz'lin) *n.* a cotton fabric, esp. used for sheets.

muss (mus) *n.* an untidy or confused state. —*v.t.* disarrange. —**muss'y,** *adj.*

mus'sel (mus'əl) *n.* any bivalve mollusk, esp. the fresh-water clam.

must *v.i.* be obliged or compelled to. —*n.* (*Colloq.*) a necessary thing. —*adj.* (*Colloq.*) required.

mus'tache (mus'tash) *n.* the hair on a man's upper lip. Also, **mous-tache', mus-ta'chio** (mus-tä'-shō) *n.*

mus'tang *n.* an Amer. wild horse.

mus'tard (mus'tərd) *n.* a plant; its seed made into a paste, used as a condiment or medicinally. —**mustard gas,** a chemical liquid used in warfare. —**mustard plaster,** a poultice containing mustard, used as a counterirritant, as for chest colds.

Mustache

mus'ter (mus'tər) *v.t.* **1,** assemble, esp. troops. **2,** (with *in*) enlist; (with *out*) discharge. —*v.i.* assemble. —*n.* assembly; enrollment list.

mus'ty (mus'tē) *adj.* **1,** having a stale odor or taste. **2,** antiquated. —**mus'ti-ness,** *n.*

mu'tate (mū'tāt) *v.t.* & *i.* change; alter. —**mu'ta-ble,** *adj.* —**mu'tant,** *adj.* & *n.*

mu-ta'tion *n.* (*Biol.*) a sudden change in characteristics.

mute (mūt) *adj.* **1,** silent; not speaking. **2,** incapable of speech. —*n.* **1,** one incapable of speech. **2,** a device to deaden the resonance of a musical instrument. —*v.t.* deaden the resonance of. —**mute'ness,** *n.*

mu'ti-late' (mū'tə-lāt') *v.t.* maim or disfigure, esp. by depriving of a limb. —**mu"ti-la'tion,** *n.*

mu'ti-neer' (mū'tə-nir') *n.* one who commits mutiny.

mu'ti.nous (-nəs) *adj.* **1,** being or pert. to mutiny. **2,** rebellious.

mu'ti.ny (mū'tə-nė) *n.* a revolt, esp. by soldiers or seamen, against lawful authority. —*v.i.* revolt.

mutt (mut) *n.* (*Slang*) **1,** a stupid person. **2,** a mongrel dog.

mut'ter (mut'ər) *v.t. & i.* utter indistinctly in a low tone; grumble.

mut'ton (mut'ən) *n.* the flesh of a grown sheep, used as food.

mu'tu.al (mū'choo-əl) *adj.* **1,** preferred, exerted, or performed by, each of two with respect to the other; reciprocal. **2,** pert. alike to both or all sides; shared alike. **3,** denoting a company whose members share the expenses and the profits. —**mu'tu.al'i.ty,** *n.* reciprocity.

mu.zhik' (moo-zhik') *n.* a Russian peasant.

muz'zle (muz'əl) *n.* **1,** the mouth of a gun barrel. **2,** the jaws and nose of an animal. **3,** a device to prevent an animal from biting. —*v.t.* **1,** equip with a muzzle to prevent biting. **2,** restrain from speech.

muz'zy (muz'ė) *adj.* dazed.

my (mī) *pron.* poss. form of *I.* —*interj.* expressing surprise.

my.o'pi.a (mī-ō'pė-ə) *n.* nearsightedness. —**my.op'ic** (-op'ik) *adj.*

my.o'sis (mī-ō'sis) *n.* abnormal contraction of the pupil of the eye. —**my.ot'ic** (-ot'ik) *adj.*

my"o.so'tis (mī"ə-sō'tis) *n.* the forget-me-not.

myr'i.ad (mir'ė-əd) *n. & adj.* **1,** ten thousand. **2,** many.

myr'mi.don" (mẽr'mə-don") *n.* a follower who obeys without question or scruple.

myrrh (mẽr) *n.* an aromatic resin of certain plants, used for incense.

myr'tle (mẽr'təl) *n.* any of various evergreen plants.

my.self' (mī-self') *pron.* [*pl.* ourselves'] an emphatic form of I; reflexive form of *me.*

nys.te'ri.ous (mis-tir'ė-əs) *adj.* pert. to a mystery; obscure; puzzling. —**mys.te'ri.ous.ness,** *n.*

mys'ter.y (mis'tə-rė) *n.* **1,** a fact or phenomenon whose meaning or cause is unknown; an enigma or puzzle. **2,** a story or novel about crime, esp. murder. **3,** a religious sacrament; (*pl.*) ancient religious rites.

mys'tic (mis'tik) *adj.* **1,** known only to those of special comprehension or especially initiated; obscure. **2,** occult. **3,** pert. to mystery or mysticism. —*n.* one who believes in, or practices, mysticism. —**mys'ti.cal,** *adj.*

mys'ti.cism (mis'tə-siz-əm) *n.* a mode of thought founded on spiritual illumination or intuition.

mys'ti.fy" (mis'tə-fī") *v.t.* perplex; bewilder. —**mys"ti.fi.ca'tion,** *n.*

myth (mith) *n.* **1,** a legendary story; fable. **2,** a fictitious person, thing, or happening. —**myth'i.cal,** *adj.*

my.thol'o.gy (mi-thol'ə-jė) *n.* a body or system of myths concerning a particular person or race. —**myth"o.log'i.cal** (mith"ə-loj'i-kəl) *adj.*

N

N, n (en) the fourteenth letter of the English alphabet.

nab *v.t.* [**nabbed, nab'bing**] (*Colloq.*) **1,** seize suddenly. **2,** arrest.

na'bob (nā'bob) *n.* a very rich man.

na.celle' (nə-sel') *n.* a cabin or enclosed shelter on an aircraft.

na'cre (nā'kər) *n.* mother-of-pearl.

na'dir (nā'dər) *n.* **1,** that point of the heavens directly below the observer. **2,** the lowest point.

nag *v.t. & i.* [**nagged, nag'ging**] annoy by constant scolding or urging. —*n.* (*Colloq.*) a horse, esp. an inferior horse.

nai'ad (nī'ad) *n.* a water nymph of springs and streams.

nail (nāl) *n.* **1,** the horny covering at the end of a finger or toe. **2,** a slender pointed piece of metal, used to hold things together, esp. wood. —*v.t.* **1,** fasten with nails. **2,** (*Colloq.*) catch; secure. **3,** detect and expose.

nain'sook (nān'sûk) *n.* a fine, soft cotton fabric.

na.ive' (nä-ēv') *adj.* unsophisticated; artless. —**na.ive.té'** (-tā') *n.*

na'ked (nā'kid) *adj.* **1,** unclothed; nude. **2,** without the usual covering; bare; exposed. **3,** plain; undisguised. —**na'ked.ness,** *n.*

nam'by-pam'by (nam'bė-pam'bė) *adj.* insipid; inanely sentimental.

name (nām) *n.* **1,** a word by which a person, place, or thing is known. **2,** a descriptive word or title. **3,** reputation, good or bad. **4,** fame; great reputation. **5,** a family; clan. **6,** a famous person. —*v.t.* **1,** give a name to. **2,** mention; specify. **3,** appoint. **4,** identify.

name'less (-ləs) *adj.* **1,** obscure. **2,** anonymous. **3,** illegitimate. —**name'less.ness,** *n.*

name'ly (-lė) *adv.* that is to say.

name'sake" *n.* one who is named for another.

nan·keen′ (nan-kēn′) *n.* **1,** a yellow cotton cloth. **2,** a type of porcelain. Also, **nan·kin′**.

nan′ny (nan′ē) *n.* **1,** a child's word for nurse. **2,** a female goat.

nap *n.* **1,** the soft, fuzzy surface of some fabrics. **2,** a short sleep. —*v.t.* [**napped, nap′ping**] **1,** take a short sleep. **2,** be off guard.

na′palm (nā′päm) *n.* jellied gasoline, used in incendiary weapons.

nape (nāp) *n.* the back of the neck.

na′per·y (nā′pə-rē) *n.* table linens.

naph′tha (nap′thə) *n.* a volatile liquid distilled from petroleum, used for dry cleaning, etc.

naph′tha·lene″ (naf′thə-lēn″) *n.* a coal tar derivative, used for dyes or as a moth repellent.

nap′kin *n.* a small square of cloth or paper, esp. one used at table.

na·po′le·on (nə-pō′lē-ən) *n.* **1,** a former Fr. gold coin. **2,** a kind of layer cake. **3,** a high boot.

nar·cis′sism (när-sis′iz-əm) *n.* an abnormal tendency to admire one's own perfections. Also, **nar′cism.**

nar·cis′sus (när-sis′əs) *n.* a spring-flowering, bulbous plant, as the daffodil and jonquil.

nar·co′sis (när-kō′sis) *n.* stupor induced by drugs.

nar·cot′ic (när-kot′ik) *n. & adj.* a drug that dulls the senses, relieves pain, and produces sleep.

Narcissus

nar·es (nār′ēz) *n. pl.* [*sing.* **nar′is**] the nostrils. —**nar′i·al,** *adj.*

nar·rate″ (na′rāt″) *v.t. & i.* give an account of; relate. —**nar·ra′tion,** *n.* —**nar·ra′tor,** *n.*

nar′ra·tive (na′rə-tiv) *n.* a story. —*adj.* of or being a story.

nar′row (nar′ō) *adj.* **1,** of small width; not broad. **2,** limited in extent, resources, point of view, etc. **3,** with little margin; close. —*v.t. & i.* lessen; contract. —*n.* (*pl.*) the shallow part of a river; a strait. —**nar′row-gauge″,** *adj.* having (railroad) tracks less than the usual 56½ inches apart. —**nar′row-mind″ed,** *adj.* intolerant; bigoted. —**nar′row·ness,** *n.*

nar′whal (när′wəl) *n.* an arctic sea mammal, related to the whale, with a long, straight tusk.

na′sal (nā′zəl) *adj.* pert. to the nose; pronounced through the nose.

nas′cent (nās′ənt) *adj.* beginning to exist or to grow. —**nas′cen·cy,** *n.*

nas·tur′tium (na-stér′shəm) *n.* a plant bearing fragrant flowers.

nas′ty (nas′tē) *adj.* **1,** physically filthy; offensive. **2,** indecent; objectionable. **3,** stormy, as weather. **4,** troublesome. **5,** vicious. —**nas·ti·ness,** *n.*

na′tal (nā′təl) *adj.* pert. to one's birth.

na′tant (nā′tənt) *adj.* swimming; floating.

na′tion (nā′shən) *n.* **1,** a race of people having a common descent, language, and culture. **2,** a body of people constituting a political unit under one government.

na′tion·al (nash′ən-əl) *adj.* common to the whole nation; public; governmental. —*n.* a citizen. —**Na′tional Guard,** the militia of the U. S. states, each commanded by the governor except in wartime.

na′tion·al·ism (nash′ə-nə-liz-əm) *n.* advocacy of the utmost political advancement of one's nation or people. —**na′tion·al·ist,** *n.* —**na″tion·al·is′tic,** *adj.*

na″tion·al′i·ty (nash′ə-nal′ə-tē) *n.* **1,** membership in a particular nation. **2,** a race of people; a nation.

na′tion·al·ize″ (-īz″) *v.t.* place under government control or ownership. —**na″tion·al·i·za′tion,** *n.*

na′tive (hā′tiv) *adj.* **1,** pert. to one by birth or by the place of one's birth. **2,** not of foreign origin or production. **3,** natural; innate. —*n.* **1,** one born in a certain place or country. **2,** one of the original inhabitants.

na·tiv′i·ty (nā-tiv′ə-tē) *n.* **1,** birth; also, time, place, and manner of birth. **2,** (*cap.*) the birth of Christ.

NATO (nā′tō) *n. & adj.* North Atlantic Treaty Organization, a group of nations coöperating to oppose the spread of communism.

nat′ty (nat′ē) *adj.* (*Colloq.*) smartly spruce; trim. —**nat′ti·ness,** *n.*

nat′u·ral (nach′ə-rəl) *adj.* **1,** not artificial; formed by nature. **2,** pert. to, or in a state of, nature. **3,** proper; reasonable; not unusual. **4,** innate. **5,** easy; unaffected; kindly. **6,** (*Music*) neither sharp nor flat. **7,** (of children) illegitimate. —*n.* **1,** something that is natural. **2,** (*Colloq.*) a person or thing sure to succeed. **3,** an idiot. —**natural history,** the study of plant and animal life, behavior, etc. —**nat′u·ral·ness,** *n.*

nat′u·ral·ist (-ist) *n.* a scholar of plant and animal life.

nat′u·ral·ize″ (-īz″) *v.t.* admit (an alien) to citizenship. —**nat″u·ral·i·za′tion,** *n.*

na′ture (nā′chər) *n.* **1,** the material universe; the forces at work in the universe, independently of man or his acts. **2,** the essential character of a person or thing. **3,** kind; sort.

naught (nât) *n.* **1,** nothing. **2,** a zero; a cipher (0).

naugh′ty (nâ′tē) *adj.* **1,** disobedient. **2**, improper. **—naugh'ti·ness**, *n*.

nau'sea (nâ'sha) *n*. **1**, an inclination to vomit. **2**, a feeling of disgust.

nau'se·ate" (nâ'sè-āt") *v.t.* sicken.

nau'seous (nâ'shas) *adj.* causing nausea. **—nau'seous·ness**, *n*.

nau'ti·cal (nâ'ti-kəl) *adj.* pert. to ships, seamen, or navigation.

nau'ti·lus (nâ'ti-ləs) *n*. a mollusk with a spiral chambered shell.

na'val (nā'vəl) *adj.* pert. to a navy.

nave (nāv) *n*. the main body of a church from chancel to entrance.

na'vel (nā'vəl) *n*. the depression in the center of the abdomen.

nav'i·ga·ble (nav'i-gə-bəl) *adj.* **1**, affording passage to ships. **2**, capable of being steered, as a dirigible.

nav'i·gate" (nav'i-gāt") *v.t.* & *i*. **1**, travel by water; sail over or on. **2**, sail or steer a ship. **—nav'i·ga'tion**, *n*. **—nav'i·ga"tor**, *n*. one who plots the course of ships or aircraft.

na'vy (nā'vè) *n*. **1**, all the war vessels of a nation. **2**, (usually *cap.*) a nation's naval organization.

nay (nā) *n*. **1**, no; a refusal. **2**, a negative vote. **—adv.** not only so, but; indeed.

Naz"a·rene' (naz"ə-rēn') *n*. & *adj.* of or pert. to Nazareth. **—the Nazarene**, Jesus Christ.

Na'zi (not'sè) *n*. a member of the former National Socialist party, which controlled Germany 1933 to 1945. **—Na'zism** (not'siz-əm) *n*. the principles of this party, fascistic and anti-Semitic.

Ne·an'der·thal" (nè-an'dər-täl") *adj.* pert. to a species of man existing in the paleolithic period.

neap (nēp) *adj.* designating the lowest high tide in the lunar month.

near (nir) *adj.* **1**, not remote; close to; close. **2**, closely akin. **3**, intimate, as friends. **4**, on the left (opposed to *off*). **5**, (*Colloq.*) stingy. **—adv.** **1**, not far off. **2**, closely. **3**, nearly. **—prep.** close by or to. **—v.i.** & *t*. come close (to). **—near-"by'**, *adj.*, *adv.* & *prep.* close at hand. **—near'ly**, *adv.* **1**, closely. **2**, almost. **—near'ness**, *n*.

near'sight'ed *adj.* able to see clearly only at short distances. **—near'sight"ed·ness**, *n*.

neat (nēt) *adj.* **1**, tidy; orderly. **2**, adroit; effective. **3**, pure; undiluted. **—neat'ness**, *n*.

neb'u·la (neb'yə-lə) *n*. [*pl.* **-lae** (-lè), **-las**] a luminous patch in the sky made by distant star clusters or masses of gas. **—neb'u·lar**, *adj.*

neb'u·lous (neb'yə-ləs) *adj.* **1**, cloudy; hazy. **2**, indistinct; vague; confused. **—neb"u·los'i·ty**, **neb'u·lous·ness**, *n*.

nec'es·sar"y (nes'ə-ser"è) *adj.* **1**, inevitably resulting from the nature of things. **2**, required; essential; indispensable. **—n.** an essential thing.

ne·ces'si·tate" (nə-ses'ə-tāt") *v.t.* render unavoidable; compel.

ne·ces'si·tous (nə-ses'ə-təs) *adj.* very poor; needy.

ne·ces'si·ty (nə-ses'ə-tè) *n*. **1**, the state or fact of being inevitable or necessary. **2**, something essential, esp. to existence. **3**, poverty; great need. **4**, compulsion.

neck (nek) *n*. **1**, the slender part of the body between the head and shoulders. **2**, in a garment, the part closest to the neck. **3**, something resembling a neck; an isthmus. **—v.i.** (*Slang*) kiss and pet.

Necks

Human neck; neck of a bottle; neck of a musical instrument; clam neck; necks of land.

neck'er·chief (nek'ər-chif) *n*. a scarf worn around the neck.

neck'lace (nek'les) *n*. any flexible ornament worn around the neck.

neck'tie" (nek'tī") *n*. a decorative band worn around the neck.

neck'wear" *n*. neckties, etc.

nec·ro- *pref.* dead; death; corpse.

nec'ro·man"cy (nek'rə-man"sè) *n*. **1**, divination by conversing with the dead. **2**, magic in general.

ne·cro'sis (ne-krō'sis) *n*. death of bodily tissue; gangrene. **—ne·crot'ic** (-krot'ik) *adj.*

nec'tar (nek'tər) *n*. **1**, in mythology, the wine of the gods. **2**, any delicious drink. **3**, a sweet secretion.

nec"ta·rine' (nek"tə-rēn') *n*. a form of peach with a smooth skin.

née (nā) *adj.* born; whose maiden name was.

need (nēd) *n*. **1**, necessity or lack; urgent want. **2**, time of difficulty; emergency. **3**, poverty. **—v.t.** be in want of. **—v.i.** **1**, be obliged. **2**, be necessary.

nee'dle (nē'dəl) *n*. **1**, a slender pointed instrument with a hole for thread, used in sewing. **2**, any of various similar instruments, as for knitting, in a phonograph, on a hypodermic syringe, etc. **3**, a leaf of a pine tree. **4**, the pointer on the dial of an instrument, esp. the magnetized pointer in a compass. **5**, something resembling a needle, as an obelisk. —*v.t.* (*Colloq.*) vex or goad by repeated gibes.

nee'dle-point" *n.* **1**, lace made on a paper pattern. **2**, a kind of embroidery.

need'less (-ləs) *adj.* unnecessary. —**need'less-ness**, *n.*

nee'dle-work" *n.* sewing or embroidery.

need'y (nē'dè) *adj.* very poor. —**need'i-ness**, *n.*

ne'er (nãr) *contraction* never.

ne'er-'do-well" (nãr'doo-wel") *n.* an idle, worthless person.

ne-far'i-ous (ni-fãr'é-əs) *adj.* unspeakably wicked. —**ne-far'i-ous-ness**, *n.*

ne-gate' (ne-gāt') *v.t.* deny; nullify. —**ne-ga'tion**, *n.*

neg'a-tive (neg'ə-tiv) *adj.* **1**, expressing denial or refusal; not affirmative; not positive. **2**, lacking positive or distinguishing qualities. **3**, (*Math.*) denoting subtraction; minus. —*n.* **1**, a negative statement, reply, or word. **2**, in a debate, the side that denies or refutes. **3**, (*Photog.*) a plate or film from which a print is made; the image in reverse. —*v.t.* refuse assent.

neg-lect' (ni-glekt') *v.t.* **1**, disregard. **2**, be remiss about; leave uncared for. **3**, fail in duty or performance through carelessness. —*n.* **1**, lack of attention or care. **2**, negligence. —**neg-lect'ful**, *adj.* careless.

neg'li-gee' (neg'lə-zhã') *n.* a woman's loose, informal house gown.

neg'li-gent (neg'lə-jənt) *adj.* **1**, guilty of or characterized by neglect, esp. of duty. **2**, (*Law*) failing to exercise due care. —**neg'li-gence**, *n.*

neg'li-gi-ble (neg'li-jə-bəl) *adj.* of little importance. —**neg'li-gi-bil'i-ty**, *n.*

ne-go'ti-a-ble (ni-gō'shè-ə-bəl) *adj.* capable of being negotiated; transferable. —**ne-go'ti-a-bil'i-ty**, *n.*

ne-go'ti-ate' (ni-gō'shè-āt") *v.t.* discuss with others the terms of a diplomatic, political, or business matter. —*v.t.* **1**, bring about by mutual discussions. **2**, sell (notes, securities, etc.). —**ne-go'ti-a'tion**, *n.*

Ne-gri'to (ni-grē'tō) *n.* a member of one of the dwarfish Negroid peoples of Asia or Africa.

Ne'gro (nē'grō) *n.* a member of the darkest-skinned, or black, race. —*adj.* of, or pert. to, this race. —**Ne'gress**, *n. fem.*

neigh (nā) *n.* the prolonged cry of a horse; a whinny. —*v.i.* whinny.

neigh'bor (nā'bər) *n.* **1**, one who lives near another. **2**, a person or thing next or near another. **3**, a fellow being. —*v.t.* adjoin; be near to. Also, **neighbour**. —**neigh'bor-ing**, *adj.* nearby.

neigh'bor-hood" *n.* **1**, the vicinity; a district of a particular kind. **2**, the persons in a locality.

neigh'bor-ly (-lè) *adj.* appropriate to a neighbor; accommodating. —**neigh'bor-li-ness**, *n.*

nei'ther (nē'thər; nï'-) *adj., adv., conj. & pron.* not either.

nem'e-sis (nem'ə-sis) *n.* [*pl.* -ses" (-sēz")] an agent of vengeance.

neo- (nē-ō) *pref.* new; recent.

ne"o-lith'ic (nē"ō-lith'ik) *adj.* pert. to the later stone age.

ne-ol'o-gism (nè-ol'ə-jiz-əm) *n.* a new word, usage, or expression.

ne'on (nē'on) *n.* an inert gaseous element, no. 10, symbol Ne, much used in electric signs.

ne'o-phyte" (nē'ə-fīt") *n.* **1**, a beginner; a novice. **2**, a convert.

ne'o-plasm (nē'ə-plaz-əm) *n.* any morbid growth, as a tumor. —**ne"o-plas'tic**, *adj.*

ne'o-plas'ty (nē'ə-plas'tè) *n.* restoration by plastic surgery.

ne'o-prene" (nē'ə-prēn") *n.* a kind of synthetic rubber.

ne"o-ter'ic (nē'ə-ter'ik) *adj.* recent; modern. —*n.* a modern writer, etc.

ne-pen'the (ni-pen'thè) *n.* anything that induces forgetfulness of pain or care.

neph'ew (nef'ū) *n.* a son of one's sister or brother.

ne-phri'tis (ni-frī'tis) *n.* inflammation of the kidneys.

nep'o-tism (nep'ə-tiz-əm) *n.* undue favoritism to relatives. —**nep'ot'ic** (nə-pot'ik) *adj.* —**ne-pot'i-cal-ly**, *adv.*

nep-tu'ni-um (nep-tū'nè-əm) *n.* an artificially produced radioactive element, no. 93, symbol Np.

ne're-id (nir'è-id) *n.* a sea nymph.

nerve (nẽrv) *n.* **1**, a bundle of fibers, one of many conveying impulses of motion and sensation from the brain to all parts of the body. **2**, force; energy. **3**, courage. **4**, (*pl.*) acute nervousness. **5**, (*Slang*) audacity. —*v.t.* give strength or courage to.

nerve'less (-ləs) *adj.* **1**, lacking courage. **2**, listless; weak. —**nerve'less-ness**, *n.*

nerv'ous (nẽrv'əs) *adj.* **1**, made up of, or affecting, the nerves. **2**, high-strung; easily agitated. **3**, timid; uneasy. —**nerv'ous-ness**, *n.*

nerv'y (nẽr'vè) *adj.* brash; bold.

nes'cience (nesh'əns) *n.* ignorance.

-ness (nəs) *suf.* quality or state of being (the root word): added to adjectives to form nouns. (A terminal -y regularly changes to -i before -ness.)

nest *n.* **1,** a place used by or made by birds, insects, turtles, etc. for laying eggs and hatching young. **2,** any snug retreat. **3,** a graduated set of articles, as bowls, tables, etc. fitted one within the other. —*v.i.* sit on or build a nest. —**nest egg,** a fund of money saved for an emergency.

nes'tle (nes'əl) *v.i. & t.* **1,** lie close and snug. **2,** settle comfortably; snuggle.

nest'ling (nest'ling; nes'-) *n.* a young bird in the nest.

net *n.* **1,** a contrivance made of coarse string tied in mesnes, for catching fish, birds, etc. **2,** a snare; a trap. **3,** a fine fabric of open mesh for dresses, veils, etc. **4,** anything woven or tied in meshes. **5,** clear profit. —*adj.* **1,** remaining as profit after all necessary deductions (taxes, expenses, etc.) **2,** without discount. —*v.t.* [netted, -ting] **1,** capture, as with a net. **2,** spread a net over. **3,** earn as clear profit.

neth'er (neth'ər) *adj.* under; lower.

net'ting (net'ing) *n.* any meshed fabric of thread, rope, wire, etc.

net'tle (net'əl) *n.* a coarse herb with stinging hairs. —*v.t.* vex.

net'work *n.* **1,** anything of intersecting lines resembling a net. **2,** a chain of radio stations.

Nettle

neu'ral (nyûr'əl) *adj.* pert. to the nerves or the nervous system.

neu·ral'gia (nyû-ral'jə) *n.* an acute intermittent pain along the course of a nerve. —**neu·ral'gic,** *adj.* —**neu·ral'gi·cal·ly,** *adv.*

neu''ras·the'ni·a (nyûr''əs-thē'nē-ə) *n.* nervous exhaustion. —**neu''ras·then'ic** (-then'ik) *adj. & n.*

neu·ri'tis (nyû-rī'tis) *n.* inflammation or continued pain in a nerve.

neuro- *pref.* nerve.

neu·rol'o·gy (nyû-rol'ə-jē) *n.* the branch of science dealing with the nervous system and its diseases. —**neu''ro·log'i·cal,** *adj.* —**neu·rol'o·gist,** *n.*

neu'ron (nyûr'on) *n.* a nerve cell. Also, **neu'rone** (-ōn).

neu·ro'sis (nyû-rō'sis) *n.* [*pl.* -ses (sēz)] a functional nervous disease or emotional disorder. —**neu·rot'ic** (-rot'ik) *adj. & n.* —**neu·rot'i·cal·ly,** *adv.*

neu'ter (noo'tər) *adj.* (*Gram.*) neither masculine nor feminine.

neu'tral (noo'trəl) *adj.* **1,** taking neither side in a war, quarrel, or dispute. **2,** with no decided qualities or characteristics; indifferent. **3,** of a color, gray; subdued in tone. —*n.* a neutral power, one of its subjects or its vessels.

neu·tral'i·ty (noo-tral'ə-tē) *n.* state of being neutral.

neu'tral·ize (noo'trə-līz'') *v.t.* **1,** render neutral or inactive. **2,** counteract. —**neu''tral·i·za'tion,** *n.*

neu'tron (noo'tron) *n.* a minute uncharged particle of matter.

nev'er (nev'ər) *adv.* **1,** not ever. **2,** not at all.

nev''er·the·less (nev''ər-thə-les') *adv. & conj.* in spite of that; yet.

new (noo) *adj.* **1,** recently made, discovered, invented, etc. **2,** unfamiliar. **3,** not the same as before; different. **4,** not used before. **5,** starting afresh; unaccustomed. **6,** not previously well known. —*adv.* recently; freshly. —**New Deal,** the principles of the Democratic Party under Franklin D. Roosevelt. —**new'ness,** *n.*

new'born'' *adj.* born not more than a few hours ago.

new'com''er *n.* one recently arrived.

new'el (noo'əl) *n.* **1,** the center pillar of a flight of winding stairs. **2,** a post on a stairway.

new''fan'gled (-fang'gəld) *adj.* novel. —**new·fan'gled·ness,** *n.*

New'found·land (noo'fənd-lənd) *n.* a very large, shaggy dog.

news (nooz) *n.* **1,** tidings, esp. of recent public events **2,** the reports published in a newspaper. **3,** (*Colloq.*) a matter not previously known. —**news'boy'',** *n.* a boy who sells or delivers newspapers. —**news'cast'',** *n.* a radio broadcast of current news. —**news'pa''per,** *n.* a printed publication giving chiefly news. —**news'print'',** *n.* a cheap paper used in newspapers. —**news'reel'',** *n.* motion pictures of current events. —**news'stand'',** *n.* a stand where newspapers are sold.

news'y (noo'zē) *adj.* full of news; informative. —**news'i·ness,** *n.*

newt (noot) *n.* a small, semiaquatic salamander.

New Testament the books of the Holy Bible relating to Jesus Christ or Christianity.

New Year a year just beginning. —**New Year's Day,** Jan. 1. —**New Year's Eve,** Dec. 31.

next (nekst) *adj. & adv.* **1,** nearest. **2,** immediately following in time, place, order, etc. —*prep.* nearest to.

nex'us (nek'səs) *n.* [*pl.* nex'us] **1,** a tie; link. **2,** a connected series.

nib *n.* **1**, the point of anything, esp. of a pen. **2**, a bird's beak.

nib'ble (nib'əl) *v.i. & t.* bite off small pieces (of). —*n.* a small bite.

nib'lick (nib'lik) *n.* a golf club for high lofting shots; no. 9 iron.

nice (nīs) *adj.* **1**, requiring precision or tact. **2**, subtle, as a distinction. **3**, delicately sensitive; minutely accurate. **4**, fastidious; refined; discriminating. **5**, (*Colloq.*) pleasing or pleasant; attractive; kind. —**nice'ness**, *n.*

ni'ce·ty (nī'sə-tē) *n.* **1**, precision; accuracy. **2**, a minute distinction or detail. **3**, something choice.

niche (nich) *n.* **1**, a recess in a wall, as for a vase, statue, etc. **2**, a suitable place or position.

nick (nik) *n.* **1**, a notch. **2**, a slightly chipped place, as on a dish. **3**, the exact moment (of time). —*v.t.* make a notch in; chip.

nick'el (nik'əl) *n.* **1**, a hard silvery-white metallic element much used in alloys, no. 28, symbol Ni. **2**, a U. S. 5-cent piece.

nick'name (nik'nām") *n.* an additional or substitute name.

nic'o·tine (nik'ə-tēn") *n.* a poisonous colorless, oily liquid extracted from tobacco.

ni'dus (nī'dəs) *n.* [*pl.* **-di** (-dī)] **1**, a nest, esp. for insects' eggs. **2**, a place where disease germs may develop.

niece (nēs) *n.* a daughter of one's brother or sister.

nif'ty (nif'tē) (*Slang*) *adj.* smart; stylish. —*n.* a smart remark.

nig'gard·ly (nig'ərd-lē) *adj.* stingy; miserly. —**nig'gard·li·ness**, *n.*

nig'ger (nig'ər) *n.* (a word not in good taste) Negro.

nig'gle (nig'əl) *v.t.* trifle.

nigh (nī) *adj., adv. & prep.* near.

night (nīt) *n.* **1**, the time from sunset to sunrise. **2**, nightfall. **3**, darkness; also, a time of affliction or ignorance.

night'cap (nīt'kap") *n.* **1**, a cap worn at night in bed. **2**, a drink taken just before retiring.

night club a cabaret.

night'dress *n.* a garment worn in bed.

night'fall *n.* the coming of night.

night'gown *n.* a dress worn in bed.

night'hawk *n.* **1**, any of various nocturnal hawks. **2**, (*Colloq.*) night owl.

night'in·gale (nīt'ən-gāl") *n.* a European thrush famous for its song.

night letter, a telegram transmitted at a reduced price during the night.

night'mare *n.* **1**, any oppressive terrifying dream. **2**, any threatening, haunting thought or experience.

Nightingale

night owl a person accustomed to late hours.

night'shade *n.* any of several plants, as belladonna or henbane.

night'shirt *n.* a loose knee-length garment worn in bed by men.

night stick a billy.

night'time *n.* night.

ni'hil·ism (nī'ə-liz-əm) *n.* **1**, a doctrine that denies moral principles and social obligations. **2**, an extreme anarchistic movement. —**ni'hil·ist**, *n.* —**ni"hil·is'tic**, *adj.*

nil *n.* nothing.

nim'ble (nim'bəl) *adj.* **1**, lively; quick; agile. **2**, alert; acute. —**nim'ble·ness**, *n.*

nim'bus (nim'bəs) *n.* in art, a bright cloud or a halo around the head of a divine or saintly person.

nin'com·poop (nin'kəm-poop") *n.* a simpleton.

nine (nīn) *n. & adj.* the cardinal number between eight and ten, expressed by 9. —**ninth**, *adj. & n.* the ordinal of this number, also written 9th; one of nine equal parts.

nine'pins *n. sing.* a bowling game using nine pins.

nine'teen (nīn'tēn") *n. & adj.* nine plus ten: 19. —**nine'teenth**, *adj. & n.*

nine'ty (nīn'tē) *n. & adj.* ten times nine: 90. —**nine'ti·eth**, *adj. & n.*

nin'ny (nin'ē) *n.* a simpleton.

ni·o'bi·um (nī-ō'bē-əm) *n.* columbium.

nip *v. t.* [**nipped, nip'ping**] **1**, pinch; bite. **2**, pinch off. **3**, benumb; blast, as by cold. **4**, check in growth, as a plot. —*n.* **1**, a pinch; bite. **2**, chill or sting in the air. **3**, a small drink. —**nip and tuck**, (in a contest) almost exactly even; unpredictable in outcome.

nip'per (nip'ər) *n.* **1**, the large claw of a crab or lobster. **2**, (*pl.*) pincers.

nip'ple (nip'əl) *n.* **1**, the milk duct of the female breast. **2**, the mouthpiece of a nursing bottle. **3**, a short piece of pipe threaded at both ends.

tŭb, cūte, pŭll; label; oil, owl; go, chip, she, thin, then, sing, ink; see p. 6

Nip″pon·ese′ (nip″ə-nēz′) *n.* & *adj.* Japanese.

nip′py (nip′ē) *adj.* sharp; biting.

nir·va′na (nēr-vä′nə) *n.* a state of detachment and dispassion.

Ni′sei′ (nē′sā′) *n.* a native U. S. citizen of Japanese ancestry.

nit *n.* the egg or young of a parasitic insect, as the louse.

ni′ter (nī′tər) *n.* nitrate of potassium, a white salt used in gunpowder; saltpeter. Also, **ni′tre**.

ni′ton (nī′ton) *n.* radon.

ni′trate (nī′trāt) *n.* a chemical compound of nitric acid, used as a fertilizer.

nit′ric (nī′trik) *adj.* 1, containing nitrogen. 2, pert. to niter. —**nitric acid**, a corrosive compound of nitrogen, used in making dyes, explosives, plastics, etc.

ni″tro·cel′lu·lose (nī″trə-sel′yə-lōs) *n.* a plastic compound of nitrogen and cellulose.

ni′tro·gen (nī′trə-jən) *n.* a colorless, odorless gaseous element, no. 7, symbol N., forming four-fifths of the volume of air.

ni″tro·glyc′er·in (nī″trə-glis′ər-in) *n.* a highly explosive oil.

ni′trous oxide (nī′trəs) an anesthetic, laughing gas.

nit′wit *n.* (*Slang*) a stupid person.

nix (niks) *n.*, *adv.* & *interj.* (*Slang*) nothing; no.

no (nō) *adv.* a word of denial, refusal, or dissent; a negative. —*adj.* not any; not at all. —*n.* 1, a denial or refusal. 2, a negative vote.

nob *n.* (*Slang*) 1, a socially-prominent person. 2, the head.

No·bel′ Prize (nō-bel′) a prize in money (about $40,000) given for an achievement in science, literature, or the advancement of peace, endowed by Alfred Nobel, Swed. inventor.

no·bil′i·ty (nō-bil′ə-tē) *n.* state of being noble.

no′ble (nō′bəl) *adj.* 1, of high birth, rank, or title. 2, of lofty character. 3, stately; imposing. 4, admirably conceived or executed. 5, choice; excellent. —*n.* a peer: *nobleman.*

no′bod′y (nō′bod′ē) *n.* 1, no one. 2, a person of no social standing.

nock (nok) *n.* a notch in a bow or arrow.

noc·tur′nal (nok-tēr′nəl) *adj.* 1, pert. to, or occurring in, the night. 2, active at night, as certain animals.

noc′turne (nok′tərn) *n.* a dreamy, pensive musical piece.

nod *n.* a short, quick inclination of the head, as in a greeting; approval, command, etc. —*v.t.* & *i.* [nod′ded,

-ding] 1, incline the head in assent, etc. 2, drowse; become inattentive.

node (nōd) *n.* 1, a knot; knob. 2, a hard swelling. —**nod′al** (nō′dəl) *adj.*

nod′ule (nod′ūl) *n.* a little knot or lump. —**nod′u·lous**, *adj.*

No·el′ (nō-el′) *n.* Christmas.

nog′gin (nog′in) *n.* 1, a small mug. 2, a small amount of liquor; a gill. 3, (*Colloq.*) the head.

noil *n.* a short fiber, esp. of wool.

noise (noiz) *n.* 1, a sound of any kind, esp. when loud or disagreeable. 2, outcry; clamor. —*v.t.* spread the report of; make public. —**nois′y**, *adj.* full of, or making, loud sounds.

noi′some (noi′səm) *adj.* 1, ill-smelling; disgusting. 2, injurious.

no′mad (nō′mad) *n.* a member of a roving tribe; a wanderer. —**no·mad′ic**, *adj.* —**no·mad′i·cal·ly**, *adv.*

no man's land territory between entrenched enemy forces.

nom de plume (nom′də-ploom″) (*Fr.*) a pen name.

no′men·cla″ture (nō′mən-klā′-chər) *n.* a system of names.

nom·i·nal (nom′i-nəl) *adj.* 1, existing in name only; so-called. 2, so small as to be virtually nothing. 3, pert. to a name. —**nominal value**, the named or face value; par value.

nom′i·nate″ (nom′ə-nāt″) *v.t.* 1, propose for an elective office. 2, appoint to an office. —**nom″i·na′tion**, *n.*

nom′i·na·tive (nom′i-nā-tiv) *adj.* 1, requiring nomination. 2, (*Gram.*) designating the case of the subject of a verb. —*n.* this case.

nom′i·nee′ (nom′i-nē″) *n.* a person nominated for office.

non- *pref.* used freely before nouns, adjectives, and adverbs with the general meaning of *not*, being less emphatic than *un-* or *in-*.

non′age (non′ij) *n.* legal minority.

non″a·ge·nar′i·an (non″ə-jə-nār′-ē-ən) *n.* a person 90 years of age or older, but less than 100.

non′a·gon″ (non′ə-gon″) *n.* a polygon having nine sides and nine angles.

non′bel·lig′er·ent *n.* & *adj.* (being) a nation that is not at war but is openly assisting a nation at war.

nonce (nons) *n.* the time being; this one time.

non′cha·lance (non′shə-ləns) *n.* coolness; disinterested self-possession. —**non′cha·lant** (-lənt) *adj.*

non′com″ (non′kom″) *n.* (*Colloq.*) a noncommissioned officer.

non·com′bat·ant *n.* 1, a person in the armed forces whose duties do not include fighting. 2, a civilian in wartime.

---

fat, fāte, fär, fåre, fåll, åsk; met, hē, hêr, maybē; pin, pīne; not, nõte, õr, tool

non″com·mis′sioned *adj.* not having a commission, as an officer of the rank of corporal or sergeant.

non″com·mit′tal (-kə-mit′əl) *adj.* not committing oneself or itself to a positive view or course.

non″con·duc′tor *n.* a substance that does not readily conduct electricity, heat, etc.

non″con·form′i·ty *n.* refusal or failure to conform, esp. to some established church. **—non″con·form′ist,** *n.*

non·de·script″ (non-də-skript″) *adj.* not easily classified; of no particular kind or sort.

none (nun) *pron.* **1,** no one. **2,** not any. —*adv.* in no degree. —*adj.* not any. **—none′the·less′,** *adv.* no less; nevertheless.

non″ef·fec′tive *n.* a soldier or sailor not fit for duty.

non·en′ti·ty (non-en′tə-tē) *n.* **1,** a person or thing of no importance. **2,** something not exciting.

non″es·sen′tial *adj.* not essential or necessary.

none′such″ (nun′such″) *n.* a person or thing that has no equal.

non″ex·ist′ence *n.* condition of not existing; something that does not exist. **—non″ex·ist′ent,** *adj.*

non·fea′sance (non-fē′zəns) *n.* (*Law*) omission to do something that should have been done.

non·fic′tion *n.* literature dealing with real persons and events, as history or biography.

non″in·ter·ven′tion (non″in-tər-ven′shən) *n.* refusal to intervene, esp. in the affairs of other nations.

non″pa·reil′ (non″pə-rel′) *n.* & *adj.* (some one or thing) having no equal; peerless. *—n.* a brightly colored finch of the So. U. S.

non·plus′ *v.t.* perplex; confound.

non″prof′it *adj.* not intended to earn a profit, as an incorporated charity.

non·res′i·dent *adj.* exercising rights or performing duties (as of franchise, membership, position, etc.) while residing relatively far away. *—n.* one who lives elsewhere.

non″sec·tar′i·an (non″sek-tār′ē-ən)′ *adj.* favoring no particular religious sect, as a school, association, etc.

non′sense (non′sens) *n.* senseless or absurd words, ideas, or conduct. **—non·sen′si·cal,** *adj.*

non·stop′ *adj.* & *adv.* without a single stop, as a journey.

non″sup·port′ *n.* (*Law*) failure to provide maintenance by one who is obligated to do so.

non·un′ion *adj.* **1,** not conforming to trade-union requirements. **2,** not having membership in, or a contract with, a trade-union.

noo′dle (noo′dəl) *n.* **1,** dough rolled into thin, flat strips; a form of macaroni. **2,** (*Slang*) the head.

nook (nûk) *n.* a recess; an out-of-the-way corner or retreat.

noon *n.* **1,** twelve o'clock midday. **2,** (*Colloq.*) a recess for lunch. **—noon′day″,** *adj.* at noon. **—noon′-time″,** *n.* noon.

noose (noos) *n.* **1,** a loop with a sliding knot, as in a lasso. **2,** (with *the*) death by hanging.

nor (nôr) *conj.* and not; neither.

Nor′dic (nôr′dik) *adj.* pert. to or designating a Caucasian race characterized by blond hair, blue eyes, and tall stature, as the Scandinavians and Anglo-Saxons. *—n.* a person of Nordic ancestry.

norm (nôrm) *n.* **1,** a standard; pattern. **2,** a type.

nor′mal (nôr′məl) *adj.* **1,** conforming to a certain type or standard; regular; average. **2,** free from mental defect. *—n.* the standard; the average. **—nor′mal·cy, nor·mal′-i·ty,** *n.* state of being normal; a normal condition. **—normal school,** a college where teachers are trained.

Nor′man (nôr′mən) *n.* [*pl.* **-mans**] **1,** one of the French who conquered England in 1066. **2,** a native of Normandy. *—adj.* of the Normans or Normandy.

Norse (nôrs) *adj.* **1,** pert. to ancient Scandinavia. **2,** Norwegian.

north (nôrth) *n.* **1,** the point of the compass on the right hand of a person facing the setting sun; the direction toward that point. **2,** a region or country lying north of another; (*cap.,* with *the*) in the U. S., the region lying north of Maryland, the Ohio River, and Missouri. *—adj.* & *adv.* in, toward, or from the direction of north.**—north′ward,** *adv.*

north″east′ *n.* & *adj.* midway between north and east. **—north″east′-er,** *n.* a gale from the northeast. **—north″east′ern,** *adj.*

north′er (nôr′thər) *n.* a strong, cold wind from the north.

north′er·ly (nôr′thər-lē) *adj.* in or toward the north.

north′ern (nôr′thərn) *adj.* pert. to, living in, coming from, or going toward the north. **—north′ern·er,** *n.* a resident or native of the north. **—northern lights,** the aurora borealis. **—north′ern·most″,** *adj.* furthest north.

north′land (-land) *n.* **1,** a northern region, or the northern part of any country. **2,** (*cap.*) the Scandinavian Peninsula.

North Pole 1, the north end of the earth's axis of rotation. **2,** the zenith of this point.

tub, cūte, pûll; label; oil, owl; go, chip, she, thin, *then*, sing, ink; *see p. 6*

North Star Polaris, a bright star near the North Pole of the heavens.

north″**west**′ *n. & adj.* midway between north and west. —**north**″**west**′**er**, *n.* a gale from the northwest. —**north**″**west**′**ern**, *adj.*

Nor·we′**gian** (nôr-wē′jən) *adj. & n.* pert. to Norway, its language or inhabitants.

nor′**west**′**er** (nôr-wes′tər) *n.* a seaman's oilskin raincoat.

nose (nōz) *n.* 1, that feature of the face above the mouth, containing the nostrils or respiratory passage; the organ of smell. 2, sense of smell, as of a dog. 3, something likened to a nose in shape; the forward or projecting part of anything. —*v.t. & i.* 1, detect by smell. 2, rub with the nose. 3, push slowly forward, as a ship. 4, (with *out*) (*Colloq.*) defeat by a narrow margin. 5, pry curiously. —**nose**′**dive**, a headlong plunge of an airplane. —**nose**′**gay**″, *n.* a bouquet. —**nos**′**ey, nos**′**y,** *adj.* prying.

nos·tal′**gia** (nos-tal′jə) *n.* homesickness; sentimental recollection of the past. —**nos·tal**′**gic** (-jik) *adj.* —**nos·tal**′**gi·cal·ly,** *adv.*

nos′**tril** (nos′trəl) *n.* an external opening of the nose.

nos′**trum** (nos′trəm) *n.* a medicine, esp. a quack remedy.

not *adv.* a word expressing denial, refusal, or negation.

no′**ta·ble** (nō′tə-bəl) *adj.* worthy of note; remarkable; eminent. —*n.* a prominent or important person.

no′**ta·rize**″ (nō′tə-rīz″) *v.t.* attest to (a sworn statement).

no′**ta·ry** (nō′tə-rē) *n.* a person licensed to attest deeds, take affidavits, etc.; *notary public.* —**no·tar**′**i·al** (nō-târ′ē-əl) *adj.*

no·ta′**tion** (nō-tā′shən) *n.* 1, the act of taking notes; a note. 2, a system, or set of symbols, for representing numbers and quantities by symbols, in mathematics and music.

notch (noch) *n.* 1, a nick or slot in the edge of something. 2, a narrow defile between mountains.

1	2	3	4	5	6	7	8	9

Notes: 1, double whole note (brève). 2, whole note (semibrève). 3, half note (minim). 4, quarter note (crotchet). 5, eighth note (quaver). 6, sixteenth note (semiquaver). 7, thirty-second note (demisemiquaver). 8, sixty-fourth note (hemidemisemiquaver). 9, a group of thirty-second notes.

note (nōt) *n.* 1, a mark or record to assist the memory. 2, fame or distinction; importance or consequence. 3, notice; heed. 4, an annotation, as in a book. 5, a memorandum. 6, a short letter; also, a formal diplomatic communication. 7, (*pl.*) a brief record of facts, impressions, a speech, etc. 8, a written promise to pay. 9, a sound; cry; a musical tone or a symbol of it in musical notation. —*v.t.* 1, observe carefully. 2, make a record of. 3, make mention of. —**note**′**book**″, *n.* a book of blank pages for making notes. —**not**′**ed,** 1, famous; well known. 2, noticed. —**note**′**wor·thy,** *adj.* notable.

noth′**ing** (nuth′ing) *n.* 1, that which does not exist; absence of everything; not anything. 2, a trifle. 3, a zero. —*adv.* in no way. —**noth**′**ing·ness,** *n.* nonexistence.

no′**tice** (nō′tis) *n.* 1, observation; attention; cognizance. 2, any written statement giving an order, information, or warning. 3, a brief review, as of a book, play, etc. 4, public attention. —*v.t.* 1, perceive; observe. 2, remark upon; acknowledge. 3, heed. —**no**′**tice·a·ble,** *adj.*

no′**ti·fy**″ (nō′ti-fī″) *v.t.* give attention to; inform. —**no**′**ti·fi·ca**′**tion,** *n.*

no′**tion** (nō′shən) *n.* 1, a general idea; a somewhat vague belief. 2, a view; an opinion. 3, a whim; a fancy. 4, (*pl.*) various small wares.

no″**to·ri**′**e·ty** (nō″tə-rī′ə-tē) *n.* state or fact of being notorious.

no·to′**ri·ous** (nō-tôr′ē-əs) *adj.* widely but not favorably known.

not″**with·stand**′**ing** (not″with-stand′ing) *adv.* nevertheless. —*prep.* in spite of. —*conj.* although.

nou′**gat** (noo′gət) *n.* a glazed candy. —**nou**′**ga·tine,** *n.* a chocolate-covered nougat.

nought (nât) *adv.,adj. & n.* naught.

noun (nown) *n.* (*Gram.*) a word denoting a person, place, or thing.

nour′**ish** (nĕr′ish) *v.t.* 1, supply with substances that are assimilated and maintain life and growth; feed. 2, foster; maintain. —**nour**′**ish·ment,** *n.* 1, feeding. 2, food.

nov′**el** (nov′əl) *adj.* previously unknown; unusual; new and striking. —*n.* a long narrative portraying fictitious characters and events in a realistic manner. —**nov**′**el·ette,** *n.* a short novel. —**nov**′**el·ist,** *n.* a writer of novels.

nov′**el·ty** (nov′əl-tē) *n.* 1, the quality of being new and fresh. 2, a new experience or thing. 3, a new or unusual article of trade.

No·vem′**ber** (nō-vem′bər) *n.* the eleventh month of the year.

no·ve′**na** (no-vē′nə) *n.* a devotion consisting of nine days of prayer.

nov′**ice** (nov′is) *n.* 1, a beginner. 2, a monk or nun who has not yet taken vows.

no·vit′i·ate (nō-vish′ė-ət) *n.* a probationary period.

no′vo·caine″ (nō′və-kān″) *n.*(*T.N.*) a local anesthetic.

now *adj.* **1,** at the present time; at once. **2,** but lately. **3,** nowadays; under existing circumstances.—*conj.* since. —*n.* this very time. —**now′a-days″,** *adv.* at present; in this age.

no′where″ (nō′hwār″) *adv.* in, at, or to no place; not anywhere.

no′wise″ (nō′wīz″) *adv.* in no way.

nox′ious (nok′shəs) *adj.* injurious. —**nox′ious-ness,** *n.*

noz′zle (noz′əl) *n.* a terminal spout, as on a hose or pipe.

nth (enth) *adj.* **1,** (*Math.*) being the last term, or any at random, of a series. **2,** superlative.

nu (noo) *n.* the thirteenth letter of the Greek alphabet (N, ν).

nu·ance′ (noo-äns′) *n.* a delicate degree or shade of difference.

nub *n.* **1,** a knob. **2,** (*Colloq.*) the gist of a story.

nub′bin (nub′in) *n.* **1,** a small piece. **2,** an underdeveloped corn ear.

nu′bile (noo′bil) *adj.* marriageable. —**nu·bil′i·ty,** *n.*

nu′cle·ar (noo′klė-ər) *adj.* **1,** being or pert. to a nucleus. **2,** pert. to the study of atomic nuclei. —**nuclear fission,** the breakdown of the atomic nucleus of an element into two or more nuclei of lower atomic number, part of the mass being converted into energy.

nu′cle·us (noo′klė-əs) *n.* [*pl.* -i (-ī)] **1,** a central mass about which other matter collects; a starting point for growth or development. **2,** (*Biol.*) the kernel of a cell. **3,** (*Physics*) the center of an atom.

nude (nood) *adj.* naked; bare. —*n.* in art, an undraped figure. —**nude′ness,** *n.* —**nud′ism,** *n.* the practice of going naked. —**nud′ist,** *n.*

nudge (nuj) *v.t.* prod gently, as a hint or signal. —*n.* a gentle prod.

nu′di·ty (noo′də-tė) *n.* nudeness.

nu′ga·to″ry (noo′gə-tôr″ė) *adj.* **1,** worthless. **2,** ineffectual.

nug′get (nug′ət) *n.* a lump, esp. of native gold.

nui′sance (noo′səns) *n.* an annoying or obnoxious person or thing.

null (nul) *adj.* **1,** of no effect. **2,** nonexistent.

nul′li·fy″ (nul′i-fī″) *v.t.* **1,** render invalid. **2,** make ineffective. —**nul″-li·fi·ca′tion,** *n.*

nul′li·ty (nul′ə-tė) *n.* something invalid, null, without legal force, etc.

numb (num) *adj.* without sensation; powerless to feel or act. —*v.t.* make numb. —**numb′ness,** *n.*

num′ber (num′bər) *n.* **1,** the sum of an aggregation of persons or things. **2,** the symbol that stands for this sum. **3,** a particular numeral assigned to one of a series. **4,** (*Gram.*) inflection of nouns depending on quantity, as singular or plural. **5,** a large, but not precisely counted, aggregation. **6,** (*pl.*) a considerable aggregation; superiority. **7,** (*pl.*) a type of lottery. **8,** one issue of a periodical. **9,** a musical composition; a verse; a recitation; an act, as in vaudeville. —*v.t.* **1,** count. **2,** include in a class. **3,** assign a number to. **4,** limit in number. —**num′ber-less,** *adj.* too many to number; countless.

nu′mer·al (noo′mər-əl) *n.* & *adj.* a symbol or word denoting a number, as 9 or nine.

nu′mer·ate″ (noo′mə-rāt″) *v.t.* enumerate; count. —**nu″mer·a′tion,** *n.*

nu′mer·a″tor (noo′mə-rā′tər) *n.* in a fraction, the number above the line showing how many parts of a unit are taken.

nu·mer′i·cal (noo-mer′i-kəl) *adj.* pert. to, or expressed in, numbers.

nu″mer·ol′o·gy (noo″mə-rol′ə-jė) *n.* the study of the occult meaning of numbers. —**nu″mer·ol′o·gist,** *n.*

nu″mer·ous (noo′mər-əs) *adj.* a great many. —**nu′mer·ous-ness,** *n.*

nu″mis·mat′ics (noo″miz-mat′-iks) *n.* the science of coins and medals. —**nu·mis′ma·tist,** *n.*

num′skull″ (num′skul″) *n.* a dolt.

nun *n.* a woman living under religious vows in a convent. —**nun′-ner·y** (-ə-rė) *n.* a convent.

nun′ci·o″ (nun′shė-ō″) *n.* a diplomatic agent of the Pope.

nup′tial (nup′shəl) *adj.* pert. to marriage or a wedding ceremony. —*n.* (*pl.*) a wedding.

nurse (nėrs) *n.* **1,** a woman in charge of young children. **2,** one who cares for the sick. —*v.t.* **1,** take care of, as children or invalids. **2,** suckle; feed from the breast. **3,** foster; encourage. —**nurse′maid″,** *n.* a maid who takes care of children.

nurs′er·y (nėr′sə-rė) *n.* **1,** a room set apart for children. **2,** a place where young trees, shrubs and plants are grown for sale.

nur′ture (nėr′chər) *v.t.* **1,** give nourishment to; feed. **2,** rear; train.

nut *n.* **1,** the fruit of certain trees, consisting of a kernel in a hard shell; the kernel itself. **2,** a small perforated metal block internally threaded to fit a bolt. **3,** a difficult problem. **4,** (*Slang*) the head. **5,** (*Slang*) fixed expenses; overhead.

6, (*Slang*) a crazy person. —**nuts,** *interj.* of disgust or defiance.

nu·ta'tion (noo-tā'shen) *n.* **1,** a wedding. **2,** (*Pathol.*) an involuntary shaking of the head. —**nu'tant,** *adj.*

nut'crack"er (nut'krak"er) *n.* **1,** an instrument for cracking nuts. **2,** a Europ. bird that feeds on nuts.

nut'hatch" (nut'hach") *n.* a small bird that creeps on tree trunks.

nut'meg *n.* the seed of an East Indian tree, used as a spice.

nu'tri·a (noo'trē-ə) *n.* the coypu or its fur, resembling beaver.

nu'tri·ent (noo'trē ənt) *n. & adj.* (something) affording nutrition.

nu'tri·ment (noo'tri-mənt) *n.* nourishment.

nu·tri'tion (noo-trish'ən) *n.* **1,** the process by which food is converted into living tissue. **2,** the act of nourishing; food. —**nu·tri'tion·al,** *adj.* —**nu·tri'tious,** *adj.* nourishing. —**nu'tri·tive** (-trə-tiv) *adj.*

nut'shell" *n.* **1,** the shell of a nut. **2,** a pithy condensation; summary.

nut'ty (-ē) *adj.* **1,** like a nut, esp. in flavor. **2,** (*Slang*) crazy. —**nut'ti·ness,** *n.*

nuz'zle (nuz'əl) *v.t. & i.* **1,** dig, push, or rub with the nose. **2,** nestle; snuggle.

nyc"ta·lo'pi·a (nik"tə-lō'pē-ə) *n.* night blindness.

ny'lon (nī'lon) *n.* a synthetic thermoplastic product that can be spun into fibers of great toughness and elasticity, used in hosiery, clothing, bristles, cordage, etc.

nymph (nimf) *n.* **1,** (*Myth.*) a semidivine maiden inhabiting streams, forests, hills, etc. **2,** a beautiful young woman. **3,** the young of certain insects.

nym"pho·ma'ni·a (nim"fə-mā'nē-ə) *n.* uncontrollable amorous passion in women. —**nym"pho·ma'ni·ac,** *n.*

O

O, o (ō) **1,** the fifteenth letter of the English alphabet. **2,** (*cap.*) as a numeral, zero.

oaf (ōf) *n.* a simpleton; a lout.

oak (ōk) *n.* a valuable hardwood tree, whose fruit is the acorn. —**oak'en,** *adj.* —**Oak Leaf Cluster,** an insignia, traditionally in the shape of oak leaves, signifying that a medal previously awarded has been earned again.

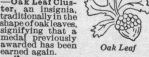

Oak Leaf

oa'kum (ō'kəm) *n.* loose rope fibers, used for calking ships.

oar (ôr) *n.* a shaft of wood, broad at one end, for rowing a boat. —**oar'lock",** *n.* a U-shaped oar rest on the side of a boat. —**oars'man** (orz'mən) *n.* a rower.

o·a'sis (o-ā'sis) *n.* [*pl.* **-ses** (-sēz)] a fertile spot in a desert; a watering place.

oat (ōt) *n.* a cereal plant or its seeds, used for food, esp. for horses. —**oat'en,** *adj.*

oat'meal" *n.* **1,** crushed and hulled oats. **2,** oat porridge.

oath (ōth) *n.* a solemn statement, with God as witness.

ob- *pref.* **1,** toward; facing. **2,** against. **3,** upon or over.

ob"bli·ga'to (ob"lə-gä'tō) *n.* [*pl.* **-tos, -ti** (-tē)] (*Music*) an accompaniment of independent importance.

ob'du·rate (ob'dyə-rət) *adj.* resisting entreaty; hardhearted. —**ob'du·ra·cy,** *n.*

o·be'di·ent (ō-bē'dē-ənt) *adj.* submissive to authority; willing to obey. —**o·be'di·ence,** *n.*

o·bei'sance (ō-bā'səns) *n.* a bow, as a mark of deference.

ob'e·lisk (ob'ə-lisk) *n.* a four-sided shaft of stone tapering to a pyramidal apex.

o·bese' (ō-bēs') *adj.* very fat. —**o·bes'i·ty,** *n.*

o·bey' (ō-bā') *v.t.* comply with the command of. —*v.i.* do as bidden.

ob·fus'cate (ob-fus'kāt) *v.t.* darken; obscure; bewilder. —**ob"fus·ca'tion,** *n.*

o·bit'u·ar"y (ō-bich'oo-er'ē) *n.* a notice, esp. in a newspaper, of a person's death, with a brief biography.

ob'ject (ob'jikt) *n.* **1,** a material thing. **2,** a person or thing to which action or feeling is directed. **3,** purpose; goal; aim. **4,** (*Gram.*) a word or clause toward which the action of the verb is directed.

ob·ject' (əb-jekt') *v.i.* offer opposition; disapprove.

ob·jec'tion (ob-jek'shən) *n.* **1,** an expression of opposition or disapproval. **2,** an adverse reason.

ob·jec'tion·a·ble (-ə-bəl) *adj.* undesirable; unpleasant.

ob·jec'tive (-tiv) *n.* a goal; aim. —*adj.* **1,** dealing with external facts and not with thoughts and feelings. **2,** free from personal prejudices; unbiased. —**objective case** (*Gram.*) the case of the direct object of a verb. —**ob"jec·tiv'i·ty** (ob"jek-tiv'ə-tē) *n.*

ob'jur·gate" (ob'jər-gāt") *v.t.* berate; rebuke. —**ob"jur·ga'tion,** *n.*

ob'late (ob'lāt) *adj.* flattened at the poles. —*n.* (*Rom. Cath.*) a person devoted to monastic work.

ob·la'tion (ob-lā'shən) *n.* a religious offering; sacrifice.

ob'li·gate" (ob'lə-gāt") *v.t.* bind by some legal or moral tie, sense of duty, etc.

ob"li·ga'tion (-gā'shən) *n.* **1,** the binding power of a promise, contract, sense of duty, etc. **2,** a debt. **3,** the state of being bound to do something.

ob·lig'a·to"ry (ob-lig'ə-tôr-ē) *adj.* compulsory; necessary.

o·blige' (ə-blīj') *v.t.* **1,** bind, constrain, or compel by any physical, moral, or legal force or influence. **2,** lay under obligation by some favor; render a favor to. —**o·blig'ing,** *adj.* accommodating.

ob·lique' (ə-blēk') *adj.* **1,** slanting. **2,** indirectly aimed or expressed. —**ob·liq'ui·ty** (ə-blīk'wə-tē) *n.*

ob·lit'er·ate" (ə-blit'ə-rāt") *v.t.* blot out; efface entirely. —**ob·lit"er·a'tion,** *n.*

ob·liv'i·on (ə-bliv'ē-ən) *n.* **1,** the state of being forgotten. **2,** forgetfulness. —**ob·liv'i·ous,** *adj.* forgetful; unmindful.

ob'long (ob'lâng) *adj.* **1,** longer than broad and with sides parallel. **2,** elongated. —*n.* a rectangle.

ob'lo·quy (ob'lə-kwē) *n.* **1,** abusive language; slander. **2,** disgrace.

ob·nox'ious (əb-nok'shəs) *adj.* odious; objectionable. —**ob·nox'ious·ness,** *n.*

o'boe (ō'bō) *n.* a wood-wind instrument with a penetrating tone. —**o'bo·ist,** *n.*

Oboe

ob·scene' (əb-sēn') *adj.* offensive to modest sensibilities (said of words, pictures, etc.); indecent; lewd. —**ob·scen'i·ty** (-sen'ə-tē) *n.*

ob·scure' (əb-skyûr') *adj.* **1,** vague; not clearly expressed. **2,** murky; dim. **3,** remote; hidden. **4,** humble; lowly. —**ob·scure'ness,** *n.*

ob·scu'ri·ty (əb-skûr'ə-tē) *n.* **1,** state of being obscure. **2,** lack of fame or recognition.

ob'se·quies (ob'sə-kwēz) *n. pl.* funeral rites.

ob·se'qui·ous (əb-sē'kwē-əs) *adj.* fawning; servile; deferential. —**ob·se'qui·ous·ness,** *n.*

ob·serv'ance (əb-zĕr'vəns) *n.* **1,** the act of complying with some law, custom, rule, etc. **2,** a customary rite or ceremony.

ob·serv'ant (əb-zĕr'vənt) *adj.* **1,** taking keen notice. **2,** apt at noticing details; attentive; mindful.

ob"ser·va'tion (ob"zər-vā'shən) *n.* **1,** the act of seeing and noting; notice. **2,** the observing of scientific phenomena; the record so obtained. **3,** a remark or comment. **4,** the faculty of observing.

ob·serv'a·to"ry (ob-zĕr'və-tôr'ē) *n.* **1,** a building equipped with instruments for studying natural phenomena. **2,** a high tower for affording an extensive view.

ob·serve' (əb-zĕrv') *v.t.* **1,** take note of; watch. **2,** remark; comment. **3,** comply with; obey. **4,** celebrate with due ceremony. —**ob·serv'er,** *n.* a spectator.

ob·sess' (əb-ses') *v.t.* dominate the mind.

ob·ses'sion (-sesh'ən) *n.* **1,** excessive preoccupation with an idea or delusion. **2,** the idea or delusion.

ob·sid'i·an (ob-sid'ē-ən) *n.* a dark volcanic rock resembling glass.

ob"so·les'cent (ob"sə-les'ənt) *adj.* becoming obsolete. —**ob"so·les'cence,** *n.*

ob'so·lete" (ob'sə-lēt") *adj.* gone out of use; out of date. —**ob'so·lete·ness,** *n.*

ob'sta·cle (ob'stə-kəl) *n.* an obstruction; hindrance.

ob·stet'rics (əb-stet'riks) *n.* the medical science of care during pregnancy and childbirth. —**ob·stet'ric, ob·stet'ri·cal,** *adj.* —**ob"ste·tri'cian** (ob"stə-trish'ən) *n.*

ob'sti·nate (ob'sti-nət) *adj.* stubbornly persistent. —**ob'sti·na·cy,** *n.*

ob·strep'er·ous (əb-strep'ər-əs) *adj.* noisy; unruly. —**ob·strep'er·ous·ness,** *n.*

ob·struct' (əb-strukt') *v.t.* **1,** block so as to prevent passing; interfere with. **2,** retard; delay. **3,** shut out from sight, as a view.

ob·struc'tion (-struk'shən) *n.* a barrier or hindrance. —**ob·struc'tive,** *adj.*

ob·tain' (əb-tān') *v.t.* get possession of, esp. by some effort; acquire. —*v.i.* be established or in vogue.

ob·trude' (əb-trood') *v.t.* **1,** thrust forward unasked. **2,** push out; form by forcing through an opening of proper shape. —*v.i.* intrude. —**ob·tru'sion** (-zhən) *n.* —**ob·tru'sive** (-siv) *adj.* given to intruding.

ob·tuse' (əb-toos') *adj.* **1,** not sensitive; stupid. **2,** blunt in form. **3,** of angles, larger than a right angle. —**ob·tuse'ness,** *n.*

ob·verse' (ob-vĕrs') *adj.* **1,** facing the observer; on the top or front side. **2,** (*Bot.*) narrower at the base

tub, cūte, pûll; label; oil, owl; go, chip, she, thin, *t*hen, sing, ink; *see p. 6* than at the top. —*n.* (ob'vĕrs) 1, the side of a coin bearing the head or main design. 2, a counterpart.

ob'vi·ate (ob'vē-āt") *v.t.* meet and clear away, as difficulties; make unnecessary. —**ob"vi·a'tion** (-ā'shən) *n.*

ob'vi·ous (ob'vē-əs) *adj.* plainly seen or understood; evident. —**ob'vi·ous·ness,** *n.*

oc"a·ri'na (ok"ə-rē'nə) *n.* an egg-shaped musical wind instrument.

oc·ca'sion (ə-kā'zhən) *n.* 1, a special event, ceremony, etc. 2, reason; motive; need. 3, opportunity; a favorable moment. 4, a cause; that which brings about an unexpected result. 5, a particular time; the time of a special happening.

oc·ca'sion·al (-əl) *adj.* 1, occurring now and then. 2, incidental.

oc'ci·dent (ok'si-dənt) *n.* the west; esp., Europe and the Western Hemisphere. —**oc"ci·den'tal,** *adj.*

oc'ci·put" (ok'si-put") *n.* the back part of the skull. —**oc·cip'i·tal** (ok-sip'ə-təl) *adj.*

oc·clude' (ə-klood') *v.t.* 1, shut in or out; also, close, as pores. 2, absorb. —**oc·clu'sion** (-zhən) *n.*

oc·cult' (o-kult') *adj.* 1, beyond ordinary understanding. 2, secret; known only to the initiated.

oc"cul·ta'tion (ok"ul-tā'shən) *n.* the disappearance from view, esp. of a star or planet.

oc'cu·pan·cy (ok'yə-pən-sē) act of occupying; state of being an occupant.

oc'cu·pant (ok'yə-pənt) *n.* one who resides in a place; a tenant.

oc'cu·pa'tion (ok"yə-pā'shən) *n.* 1, possession; occupancy. 2, the stationing of controlling forces in enemy territory. 3, means of filling one's time; regular employment; a job. —**oc"cu·pa'tion·al,** *adj.* pert. to an occupation, esp. a trade.

oc'cu·py" (ok'yə-pī") *v.t.* 1, become established in, as a building, enemy territory, etc. 2, hold, as an office. 3, take up or fill, as space, time, attention, etc. 4, engage the attention of; employ.

oc·cur' (ə-kẽr') *v.i.* [**oc·curred'**, **-cur'ring**] 1, take place; happen. 2, come to mind. 3, be found; exist. —**oc·cur'rence,** *n.* a happening.

o'cean (ō'shən) *n.* 1, the body of salt water covering three-fourths of the earth's surface; any of the five great divisions of this body. 2, a vast amount. —**o"ce·an'ic** (-shē-an'ik) *adj.*

o·cel'lus (ō-sel'əs) *n.* a eyelike spot of color, as in a peacock's tail.

o'ce·lot" (ō'sə-lot") *n.* an Amer. leopardlike cat.

o'cher (ō'kər) *n.* an earth containing iron, used as a yellow or orange pigment. Also, **o'chre.**

o'clock' (ə-klok') *adv.* on the clock; hours, etc. since noon or midnight.

oct- *pref.* eight.

oc'ta·gon" (ok'tə-gon") *n.* a polygon with eight sides and eight angles. —**oc·tag'o·nal** (ok-tag'ə-nəl) *adj.*

oc'tane (ok'tān) *n.* 1, an isomeric hydrocarbon found in petroleum. 2, the measure of the power-producing quality of gasoline.

oc'tant (ok'tant) *n.* 1, the eighth part of a circle, 45°. 2, a navigational instrument resembling a sextant.

oc'tave (ok'tiv) *n.* (*Music*) 1, a note eight diatonic degrees above or below another note. 2, an interval of eight degrees. 3, the whole series of notes within this interval.

oc·ta'vo (ok-tā'vō) *adj.* of a book, having pages about 6 x 9 inches, or somewhat less, written 8vo.

oc·tet' (ok-tet') *n.* a group of, or a composition for, eight voices or instruments.

Oc·to'ber (ok-tō'bər) *n.* the tenth month of the year.

oc"to·ge·nar'i·an (ok"tə-jə-nār'ē-ən) *n.* a person at least 80 but less than 90 years of age.

oc'to·pus (ok'tə-pəs) *n.* a sea mollusk having eight arms with sucking disks.

Octopus

oc"to·roon' (ok"tə-roon') *n.* a person having one-eighth Negro blood.

oc'u·lar (ok'yə-lər) *adj.* 1, pert. to the eye. 2, perceived by the eye; visual.

oc'u·list (ok'yə-list) *n.* a doctor who examines and treats the eye.

odd (od) *adj.* 1, eccentric; queer; strange. 2, casual; occasional; differing from the ordinary. 3, not paired; lacking a mate. 4, extra; left over after an even division; not exactly divisible by two. 5, a small surplus; a little more. —*adv.* more or less. —**odd'ness,** *n.*

odd'i·ty (-ə-tē) *n.* a strange person or thing.

odds (odz) *n. pl.* 1, excess in favor of one as compared with another; advantage; superiority. 2, balance of probability. 3, in sports, a handicap. 4, variance; disagreement. —**at odds,** in disagreement.

odds and ends miscellaneous articles.

ode (ōd) *n.* a lyric poem of exalted and dignified style. —**od'ic,** *adj.*

o'di·ous (ō'dē-əs) *adj.* deserving of hate; repugnant. —**o'di·ous·ness,** *n.*

o'di·um (ō'dē-əm) *n.* **1,** hatred. **2,** disgrace.

o·dom'e·ter (ō-dom'ə-tər) *n.* an instrument for measuring the distance traveled by a wheeled vehicle.

o'don·tol'o·gy (ō-don-tol'ə-jē) *n.* the science relating to the teeth.

o'dor (ō'dər) *n.* **1,** effect on the sense of smell, pleasant or unpleasant. **2,** repute. Also, **o'dour.**

o'dor·if'er·ous (ō'də-rif'ər-əs) *adj.* giving forth an odor. —**o·dor·if'er·ous·ness,** *n.*

o'dor·ous (ō'dər-əs) *adj.* having an odor, esp. a fragrant one.

of (uv) *prep.* **1,** indicating separation, derivation, source, or origin: from. **2,** concerning; about. **3,** indicating composition or substance. **4,** indicating possession: belonging to. **5,** containing.

off (âf) *adv.* **1,** away; at, or to, a distance. **2,** not on, touching, or attached. **3,** so as to stop or end entirely. **4,** away from work. —*prep.* **1,** away from. **2,** deviating from standard. **3,** to seaward of. **4,** less than. **5,** temporarily relieved of. **6,** (*Slang*) refraining from. —*adj.* **1,** on the right side of a vehicle or animal. **2,** disengaged, as an *off day.* **3,** below normal. **4,** disconnected; discontinued. **5,** provided for. **6,** (*Colloq.*) in error. —**off and on,** intermittently.

of'fal (âf'əl) *n.* refuse; garbage.

off-'chance *n. & adj.* a remote possibility.

off·col'or *adj.* **1,** of poor color; inferior, as a gem. **2,** (*Colloq.*) improper.

of·fend' (ə-fend') *v.t.* cause resentment in; displease. —*v.i.* **1,** sin. **2,** cause indignation, dislike, or resentment. —**of·fend'er,** *n.* **1,** one who offends; a culprit. **2,** an aggressor.

of·fense' (ə-fense') *n.* **1,** an attack; assault. **2,** a cause of displeasure; an affront. **3,** anger; annoyance. **4,** a sin. **5,** the attacking side. Also, **of·fence'.**

of·fen'sive (ə-fen'siv) *adj.* **1,** offending. **2,** attacking. —*n.* **1,** the state of being the attacker. **2,** an aggressive campaign; an attack. —**of·fen'sive·ness,** *n.*

of'fer (âf'ər) *v.t. & i.* **1,** present or put forward for acceptance. **2,** put forward, as a suggestion; propose; suggest. **3,** volunteer (to do something). **4,** present as an act of devotion to God. **5,** present for sale, tender **6,** as a bid. —*n.* the act of

offering; condition of being offered; a proposal; a bid. —**of'fer·ing,** *n.* something offered; a gift, esp. in an offertory.

of'fer·to'ry (of'ər-tôr'ē) *n.* the offering and collection of gifts at a religious service; the rites at that time.

off'hand' *adj.* **1,** impromptu. **2,** free and easy. —**off'hand''ed,** *adj.* casual.

of'fice (of'is) *n.* **1,** a position of trust, esp. in public service. **2,** the duties of such a position. **3,** official employment. **4,** a service or task. **5,** a prescribed form of worship. **6,** a room for transacting business. **7,** the quarters and staff of a governmental department.

of'fi·cer (of'ə-sər) *n.* **1,** a holder of public or civil office. **2,** a person of (usually, commissioned) rank in the army, navy, etc. **3,** a policeman. **4,** an executive in a society, corporation, etc.

of·fi'cial (ə-fish'əl) *n.* a person holding office. —*adj.* **1,** pert. to an office or to the discharge of the duties of an office. **2,** properly authorized. **3,** formal.

of·fi'ci·ate' (ə-fish-āt') *v.i.* **1,** act in an official capacity, esp. on some special occasion. **2,** conduct a religious service. —**of·fi'ci·a'tion,** *n.*

of·fi'cious (ə-fish'əs) *adj.* acting unduly important; meddling; obtrusive. —**of·fi'cious·ness,** *n.*

off'ing (âf'ing) *n.* a place or result to be reached in the future but at present remote. —**in the offing,** in the near future.

off'ish *adj.* (*Colloq.*) reserved or distant in manner. —**off'ish·ness,** *n.*

off'set' *v.t.* [-**set'**, -**set'ting**] **1,** place (one thing) over against another; balance. **2,** (of printing) blot. —*n.* **1,** something that balances or compensates. **2,** the start. **3,** a type of lithography.

off'shoot' (âf'shoot') *n.* **1,** a branch from a main stem. **2,** a lateral branch, as of a family.

off'shore' *adv.* **1,** a short distance out to sea. **2,** away from the shore.

off'spring' (âf'spring') *n.* a child or children; a descendant.

of'ten (âf'ən) *adv.* many times; in many cases. Also, **oft, of'ten·times''.**

o'gle (ō'gəl) *v.t. & t.* stare (at) covetously; leer.

o'gre (ō'gər) *n.* **1,** in fairy tales, a man-eating giant. **2,** a terrifying person.

oh (ō) *interj.* expressing surprise, pain, etc.

ohm (ōm) *n.* the unit of electrical resistance.

-oid *suf.* like; resembling.

oil *n.* **1,** any of various vegetable, animal, or mineral substances that tend to reduce the friction of surfaces rubbing against each other, inflammable and used for heat, lubrication, medicines, perfumes, etc. **2,** in art, a paint made of oil mixed with pigment; a picture painted in oils. —*v.t.* **1,** lubricate or treat with oil. **2,** *(Colloq.)* placate; flatter. —**oil′er,** *n.* a tankship for transporting oil.

oil′cloth″ *n.* cloth coated with a glossy, water-resistant substance.

oil′skin″ *n.* **1,** a cloth made waterproof with oil. **2,** *(pl.)* garments made of this cloth.

oil′y (oi′lē) *adj.* **1,** like oil. **2,** smooth in manner; unctuous; fawning. —**oil′i·ness,** *n.*

oint′ment (oint′mənt) *n.* a salve for healing or beautifying the skin.

O.K. (ō′kā′) *(Colloq.) adj. & adv.* satisfactory; all right. —*v.t.* approve. Also, **o′kay′.**

o·ka′pi (ō-kä′pē) *n.* an Afr. mammal related to the giraffe.

o′kie (ō′kē) *n. (Opprobious)* a migrant worker.

o′kra (ō′krə) *n.* a vegetable grown for its green mucilaginous pods.

·ol·a·try *suf.* worship of.

old (ōld) *adj.* **1,** advanced in years; having existed or lived long, or for most of its life span. **2,** of a (specified) age. **3,** of long standing. **4,** experienced. **5,** not new, fresh, or recent. **6,** not modern; antique. **7,** belonging to an earlier time, stage, etc. —**old′ness,** *n.*

old′en (ōl′dən) *adj.* ancient.

old-fash′ioned *adj.* **1,** holding to old ideas or customs. **2,** out of style.

Old Glory the flag of the U. S.; the Stars and Stripes.

old maid 1, an elderly woman who has never married. **2,** *(Colloq.)* a prim, fastidious person.

old-′style″ *adj.* according to the Julian calendar, several days earlier than the modern calendar.

Old Testament all the books of the Holy Bible written before the Christian era.

Old World Europe and Asia.

o″le·ag′i·nous (ō″lē-aj′ə-nəs) *adj.* oily; unctuous. —**o″le·ag′i·nous·ness,** *n.*

o′le·in (ō′lē-in) *n.* an oily substance found in most animal and vegetable fats and oils.

o″le·o·mar′ga·rine″ (ō″lē-ō-mär′jə-rēn″) *n.* an animal and vegetable fat used like butter. Also, **o′le·o″.**

ol·fac′to·ry (ol-fak′tə-rē) *adj.* pert. to the sense of smell.

ol′i·gar″chy (ol′ə-gär″kē) *n.* government in which power is in the hands of a few. —**ol″i·gar′chic,** *adj.*

o′li·o″ (ō′lē-ō″) *n.* **1,** a stew. **2,** a medley; miscellany.

ol′ive (ol′iv) *n.* **1,** an evergreen tree of warm climates grown for

Olive Tree

its fruit, wood, or oil; its small, oval, fruit, ripe or green. **2,** a yellowish-green color. —**olive branch,** a symbol of peace. —**olive oil,** oil pressed from olives, used in food and medicines.

O·lym′pic games (ō-lim′pik) **1,** athletic contests in ancient Greece. **2,** international athletic contests, held every four years in a different country.

o·me′ga (ō-mē′gə) *n.* the twenty-fourth and last letter of the Greek alphabet (Ω, ω).

om′e·let (om′lit) *n.* beaten eggs cooked as a pancake. Also, **om′e·lette.**

o′men (ō′mən) *n.* a sign or event prophetic of the future; an augury.

om′i·cron″ (om′i-kron″) *n.* the fifteenth letter of the Greek alphabet (O, ο).

om′i·nous (om′i-nəs) *adj.* foretelling disaster; threatening. —**om′i·nous·ness,** *n.*

o·mis′sion (ō-mish′ən) *n.* **1,** neglect or failure to do something. **2,** the act of leaving out; the thing left out.

o·mit′ (ō-mit′) *v.t.* [**o·mit′ted, -ting**] **1,** leave out. **2,** leave undone; neglect.

omni- *pref.* all.

om′ni·bus″ (om′nə-bus″) *n.* **1,** a large passenger motor vehicle. **2,** a volume of related literary works. —*adj.* comprising or providing for many objects or items.

om·nip′o·tent (om-nip′ə-tənt) *adj.* having infinite power. —**om·nip′o·tence,** *n.*

om″ni·pres′ent (om″nə-prez′ənt) *adj.* present everywhere at the same time. —**om″ni·pres′ence,** *n.*

om·nis′cient (om-nish′ənt) *adj.* all-knowing. —**om·nis′cience,** *n.*

om·niv′o·rous (om-niv′ə-rəs) *adj.* eating both animal and vegetable foods; devouring everything. —**om·niv′o·rous·ness,** *n.*

on *prep.* **1,** above and in contact with. **2,** dependent on; supported by. **3,** near or adjacent to. **4,** in regard to. **5,** at the time of. **6,** (*Colloq.*) at the expense of. —*adv.* **1,** in or into place or position. **2,** in progress. **3,** into action or use. **4,** forward.

on'a·ger (on'ə-jər) *n.* a wild ass of Central Asia.

once (wuns) *adv.* **1,** at one time; formerly. **2,** one time only. **3,** even for one time; ever. —**at once, 1,** simultaneously. **2,** immediately.

one (wun) *n.* **1,** the lowest whole number, expressed by **1.** **2,** a single person or thing; a unit —*adj.* **1,** a single. **2,** any. **3,** some. **4,** the same. **5,** united. —**one by one,** singly.

one-'horse' *adj.* (*Colloq.*) small and unimportant.

on'er·ous (on'ər-əs) *adj.* burdensome. —**on'er·ous·ness,** *n.*

one·self' *pron.* reflexive form of *one*. —**be oneself,** behave as usual.

one'sid'ed *adj.* **1,** unequal. **2,** unfair; partial. —**one'sid'ed·ness,** *n.*

one-'track' *adj.* **1,** having one track. **2,** (*Colloq.*) narrow.

one-'way' *adj.* permitting traffic in one direction only.

on'ion (un'yən) *n.* a plant with a pungent edible bulb.

on'ion·skin" (un'yən-skin") *n.* a very thin translucent paper.

on'look"er (-ər) *n.* spectator.

on'ly (ōn'lē) *adj.* **1,** single; sole. **2,** best. —*adv.* **1,** alone; solely. **2,** merely; no more than. —*conj.* but; excepting that.

on"o·mat'o·poe'ia (on"ə-mat"ə-pē'ə) *n.* imitation of natural sounds in word formation or rhetoric. —**on"o·mat"o·po·et'ic** (-pō'et'ik) *adj.*

on'rush" *n.* a rush forward.

on'set' *n.* **1,** an attack. **2,** a beginning; start.

on'slaught" (on'slät") *n.* a violent attack.

on'to (on'too) *prep.* to a place on; upon.

on·tol'o·gy (on-tol'ə-jē) *n.* the branch of metaphysics dealing with the nature of being. —**on"to·log'i·cal,** *adj.* —**on·tol'o·gist,** *n.*

o'nus (ō'nəs) *n.* a burden; a charge.

on'ward (on'wərd) *adv. & adj.* toward the front; forward. —**on'wards,** *adv.*

on'yx (on'iks) *n.* a quartz with parallel colored bands.

o·ö- *pref.* egg.

oo'dles (oo'dəlz) *n.pl.* (*Colloq.*) a large quantity.

oo'long (oo'lâng) *n.* a variety of tea from Formosa.

oomph (oomf) *n.* (*Colloq.*) sex appeal.

ooze (ooz) *n.* soft mud or slime, esp. on the bed of the ocean. —*v.i.* seep or leak slowly. —**oo'zy,** *adj.*

o·pac'i·ty (ō-pas'ə-tē) *n.* state of being opaque.

o'pal (ō'pəl) *n.* an iridescent mineral valued as a gem. —**o"pal·es'cent,** *adj.* —**o'pal·ine** (-in) *adj.*

o·paque' (ō-pāk') *adj.* **1,** not letting light through. **2,** dull. **3,** obscure.

o'pen (ō'pən) *adj.* **1,** permitting passage through; not shut or closed. **2,** without a cover; not protected. **3,** unfilled, as a position; unengaged, as time. **4,** free to use; public. **5,** unrestrained; unrestricted. **6,** undecided. **7,** without concealment; frank. **8,** spread out; unfolded. **9,** ready. —*v.i.* **1,** unfasten; raise the covering of; move aside. **2,** remove obstructions from. **3,** unfold; spread out. **4,** reveal; disclose. **5,** make accessible, esp. for trade, settlement, etc. **6,** start; initiate. **7,** make an opening in. —*v.i.* **1,** afford a view, entrance, or egress, etc. **2,** unfold; come apart; become open. **3,** become more visible. **4,** commence. —*n.* **1,** the outdoors; **2,** public view. —**o'pen·er,** *n.* —**o'pen·ness,** *n.*

o'pen-and-shut" *adj.* perfectly obvious.

open door in diplomacy, free and equal trade opportunities for all.

o'pen-hand"ed *adj.* generous.

o'pen·ing *n.* **1,** a beginning. **2,** an open space; a gap, breach, clearing, etc. **3,** a business opportunity; vacancy.

o'pen-mind"ed *adj.* unprejudiced. —**o'pen·mind"ed·ness,** *n.*

o'pen-mouthed" *adj.* gaping with astonishment.

open shop a shop open to non-union labor.

op'er·a (op'ər-ə) *n.* **1,** a drama wholly sung. **2,** pl. of *opus*. —**op"er·at'ic,** *adj.* —**op"er·at'i·cal·ly,** *adv.*

op'er·a·ble (op'ər-ə-bəl) *adj.* permitting surgical treatment.

opera glass a small binocular. Also, **opera glasses.**

op'er·ate" (op'ə-rāt") *v.i.* **1,** perform or be at work; act. **2,** be effective. **3,** perform a surgical operation. **4,** deal heavily in securities, etc. —*v.t.* direct the working of. —**op'er·a"tor,** *n.*

op"er·a'tion (op"ər-ā'shən) *n.* **1,** act or method of working; action; agency. **2,** (*Mil.*) a strategic project, movement, or campaign. **3,** surgical treatment. **4,** a business transaction. —**op"er·a'tion·al,** *adj.*

---

tub, cūte, pŭll; label; oil, owl; go, chip, she, thin, then, sing, ink; *see p. 6*

op'er·a·tive (op'ə-rā-tiv) *adj.* **1,** acting; effective. **2,** practical. **3,** pert. to surgical operations. —*n.* **1,** a workman. **2,** a private detective.

op"er·et'ta (op"ə-ret'ə) *n.* a drama set to gay music.

o·phid'i·an (ō-fid'ē-ən) *adj.* pert. to snakes.

oph·thal'mic (of-thal'mik) *adj.* pert. to the eye.

oph"thal·mol'o·gy (of"thəl-mol'ə-jē) *n.* the study of the eye and its diseases. —**oph"thal·mol'o·gist,** *n.*

o'pi·ate (ō'pē-ət) *n.* a narcotic drug, esp. one containing opium.

o·pine' (ō-pīn') *v.t. & t.* give an opinion; think.

o·pin'ion (ə-pin'yən) *n.* **1,** a conclusion; view. **2,** a view held by many at once; public opinion. **3,** estimation; judgment.

o·pin'ion·at"ed (ə-pin'yə-nā"tid) *adj.* obstinate in one's opinion.

o'pi·um (ō'pē-əm) *n.* a narcotic drug derived from the poppy.

o·pos'sum (ō-pos'əm) *n.* a marsupial of the So. U. S.

op·po'nent (ə-pō'nənt) *n.* an antagonist; adversary.

Opossum

op"por·tune' (op"ər-tūn') *adj.* timely; appropriate. —**op"por·tune'ness,** *n.*

op"por·tun'ism (op"ər-tū'niz-əm) *n.* quickness to grasp opportunities, often unscrupulously. —**op"por·tun'ist,** *n.*

op·por·tu'ni·ty (op"ər-tū'nə-tē) *n.* a favorable occasion or time.

op·pose' (ə-pōz') *v.t.* **1,** set against or opposite to (something else). **2,** be hostile to; object to; resist. **3,** contrast; offset.

op'po·site (op'ə-zit) *adj.* **1,** situated on the other side; facing. **2,** going the other way. **3,** radically different. —*n.* something opposed.

op"po·si'tion (op"ə-zish'ən) *n.* **1,** act of opposing; state of being opposite. **2,** resistance; antagonism. **3,** the political party opposed to the party in power.

op·press' (ə-pres') *v.t.* **1,** lie heavily on (the mind); weigh down. **2,** treat tyrannically. —**op·pres'sion** (-presh'ən) *n.* —**op·pres'sive** (-pres'iv) *adj.* —**op·pres'sor,** *n.* a tyrant.

op·pro'bri·ous (ə-prō'brē-əs) *adj.* abusive; insulting; vile. —**op·pro'bri·um,** *n.* infamy; reproach.

op'tic (op'tik) *adj.* pert. to vision or to the eye. —*n.* the eye. —**op'ti·cal,** *adj.*

op·ti'cian (op-tish'ən) *n.* one who makes and sells eyeglasses, etc.

op'tics *n.* the science that deals with vision and light.

op'ti·mism (op'tə-miz-əm) *n.* **1,** the belief that good will prevail. **2,** cheerful hopefulness. —**op'ti·mist,** *n.* —**op"ti·mis'tic,** *adj.* —**op"ti·mis'ti·cal·ly,** *adv.*

op'ti·mum (op'ti-məm) *n. & adj.* the best; the most favorable.

op'tion (op'shən) *n.* **1,** the right or power of choice. **2,** the thing that is or may be chosen. **3,** a purchased right to buy later. —**op'tion·al,** *adj.*

op·tom'e·try (op-tom'ə-trē) *n.* the measurement of vision and fitting of glasses. —**op·tom'e·trist,** *n.*

o'pus (ō'pəs) *n.* [*pl.* op'e·ra] a work, esp. of music.

or (ôr) *conj.* a connective between words, clauses, terms, etc., indicating an alternative or explanation.

or'a·cle (or'ə-kəl) *n.* **1,** a deity that utters answers to questions; hence, an authoritative voice. **2,** the answers given. —**o·rac'u·lar** (â-rak'yə-lər) *adj.*

o'ral (ôr'əl) *adj.* **1,** spoken; not written. **2,** pert. to the mouth.

or'ange (or'inj) *n.* **1,** the round, juicy, deep yellow citrus fruit of a tropical evergreen tree; the tree. **2,** a reddish-yellow color. —**orange pe'koe** (pē'kō) a black tea from Ceylon or India.

o·rang'u·tan' (ō-rang'ū-tan') *n.* an ape of Borneo and Sumatra.

o·rate' (ō-rāt') *v.i.* (*Humorous*) deliver an oration.

o·ra'tion (ō-rā'shən) *n.* a formal and dignified public speech.

or'a·tor (or'ə-tər) *n.* an eloquent public speaker.

or"a·to'ri·o (ôr"ə-tôr'ē-ō) *n.* a composition for choral singing, usually on a sacred theme.

or'a·to·ry (or'ə-tôr-ē) *n.* eloquent public speaking. —**or"a·tor'i·cal,** *adj.*

orb (ôrb) *n.* a sphere; globe; esp., a heavenly body.

or'bit (ôr'bit) *n.* **1,** a regular circuit or path, esp. of a planet around a star or a satellite around a planet. **2,** the eye socket. —**or'bit·al,** *adj.*

or'chard (ôr'chərd) *n.* a grove of fruit trees.

or'ches·tra (ôr'kis-trə) *n.* **1,** a group of players on various musical instruments. **2,** the main floor of a theater. —**or·ches'tral,** *adj.*

or'ches.tra'tion (ŏrk″əs-trā'shən) *n.* music arranged in separate parts for an orchestra. —**or'ches.trate'**, *v.t. & i.*

or'chid (ŏr'kid) *n.* **1,** any of a large order of tropical plants with brilliant flowers. **2,** a bluish purple.

Orchid

or.dain' (ŏr-dān') *v.t.* **1,** decree; enact. **2,** appoint. **3,** confer holy orders upon.

or.deal' (ŏr-dēl') *n.* a severe test; a trying experience.

or'der (ŏr'dər) *n.* **1,** an authoritative direction; a command. **2,** a direction to buy, sell, or furnish something. **3,** a sequence; systematic arrangement. **4,** class; kind; rank. **5,** a classification of plants and animals. **6,** a prescribed mode of procedure. **7,** (*pl.*) religious ordination; clerical rank. **8,** a society of persons, esp. monastic. **9,** an honorary society or institution. **10,** conformity to law or authority. —*v.t.* **1,** command; bid. **2,** direct; manage. **3,** give an order for. —*v.i.* give a command. —**in order to,** **for** the purpose of.

or'der.ly (ŏr'dər-lē) *adj.* **1,** arranged in order; neat; tidy. **2,** well managed. **3,** peaceable. —*n.* **1,** an officer's aide. **2,** a male hospital attendant. —**or'der.li.ness,** *n.*

or'di.nal (ŏr'də-nəl) *adj.* defining a thing's position in a series, as first, second, etc. —*n.* an ordinal number.

or'di.nance (ŏr'də-nəns) *n.* a law or decree; a regulation.

or'di.nar'y (ŏr'də-ner″ē) *adj.* **1,** usual; customary. **2,** mediocre.

or″di.na'tion (ŏr'də-nā'shən) *n.* act or effect of ordaining.

ord'nance (ŏrd'nəns) *n.* **1,** heavy artillery. **2,** weapons of all kinds, ammunition, etc.

ore (ŏr) *n.* a mineral or rock from which metal is extracted.

o.re'ga.no (ō-rā'gə-nō) *n.* an aromatic herb.

or'gan (ŏr'gən) *n.* **1,** a part of a plant or animal body which does some vital work. **2,** a medium of communication, esp. a sectarian or political newspaper. **3,** a large musical instrument played by releasing compressed air through pipes. —**organ grinder,** one who operates a hand organ in the streets and solicits money.

or'gan.dy (ŏr'gən-dē) *n.* a sheer, stiffened muslin.

or.gan'ic (ŏr-gan'ik) *adj.* **1,** pert. to an organ of the body. **2,** pert. to

or derived from plant and animal matter; containing carbon. **3,** systematized. **4,** structural. —**or.gan'i.cal.ly,** *adv.*

or'gan.ism (ŏr'gə-niz-əm) *n.* any living thing; any whole with interdependent parts.

or'gan.ist *n.* one who plays an organ.

or″gan.i.za'tion (-ə-zā'shən) *n.* **1,** the process of organizing. **2,** that which is organized, as a business, a club, etc.

or'gan.ize″ (ŏr'gə-nīz″) *v.t.* **1,** unite the separate elements of into a smoothly working unit. **2,** set going; start. —*v.i.* combine.

or'gasm (ŏr'gaz-əm) *n.* a crisis or consummation in love-making.

or'gy (ŏr'jē) *n.* **1,** a drunken carousal. **2,** excessive indulgence. —**or″gi.as'tic,** *adj.* —**or″gi.as'ti.cal.ly,** *adv.*

o'ri.ent (ŏr'ē-ənt) *n.* **1,** the east. **2,** (*cap.*) the Asiatic countries. —*v.t.* [also, **o'ri.en.tate″**] **1,** place so as to face the east. **2,** adjust with relation to circumstances, facts, etc. —**o″ri.en.ta'tion,** *n.*

o″ri.en'tal (ŏr″ē-en'təl) *adj.* **1,** eastern. **2,** (often *cap.*) of the Far East. —*n.* a person of a Far Eastern race.

or'i.fice (or'ə-fis) *n.* a mouthlike aperture.

or'i.gin (or'ə-jin) *n.* **1,** a source; a beginning. **2,** ancestry.

o.rig'i.nal (ə-rij'i-nəl) *adj.* **1,** occurring first. **2,** not copied or imitated. **3,** novel; fresh. **4,** creative; inventive. —*n.* a model, pattern, or first and authentic example. —**o.rig'i.nal'i.ty** (-nal'ə-tē) *n.*

o.rig'i.nate″ (ə-rij'i-nāt″) *v.t. & i.* begin; initiate. —**o.rig'i.na'tion,** *n.* —**o.rig'i.na'tor,** *n.*

o'ri.ole″ (ŏr'ē-ōl″) *n.* an Amer. bird with black and orange plumage.

O.ri'on (ō-rī'ən) *n.* a constellation near the Equator.

or'i.son (or'i-zən) *n.* a prayer.

or'lon (ŏr'lon) *n.* a synthetic fabric used for outer clothing.

or'mo.lu″ (ŏr'mə-loo″) *n.* **1,** gold prepared for gilding. **2,** imitation gold.

or'na.ment (ŏr'nə-mənt) *n.* **1,** anything that beautifies or adorns. **2,** a person who confers grace or honor to his position, society, etc. —*v.t.* adorn. —**or″na.men'tal** (-men'tal) *adj.* —**or″na.men.ta'tion,** *n.*

or.nate' (ŏr-nāt') *adj.* elaborately adorned. —**or.nate'ness,** *n.*

or″ni.thol'o.gy (ŏr″ni-thol'ə-jē) *n.* the study of birds. —**or″ni.tho.log'i.cal** (-thə-loj'i-kəl) *adj.* —**or″ni.thol'o.gist,** *n.*

o'ro·tund" (ōr'ə-tund") *adj.* 1, rich and full (of the voice). 2, pompous (of rhetoric or delivery).

or'phan (ôr'fən) *n.* a child bereft by death of its parents. —**or'phan·age,** *n.* a home for orphans.

or'ris (or'is) *n.* a kind of iris; its root, used for perfume.

or·tho- *pref.* straight; upright; correct.

or"tho·don'tia (ôr"thə-don'shə) *n.* the dental science of straightening the teeth. —**or"tho·don'tist,** *n.*

or'tho·dox" (ôr'thə-doks") *adj.* 1, holding sound, generally accepted views, esp. on religion. 2, approved; conventional. —**Orthodox Church,** a Christian church in eastern Europe. —**or'tho·dox"y** (-ē) *n.*

or·thog'o·nal (ôr-thog'ə-nəl) *adj.* of right angles; rectangular.

or·thog'ra·phy (ôr-thog'rə-fē) *n.* correct spelling. —**or'tho·graph'ic,** *adj.*

or"tho·pe'dic (ôr"thə-pē'dik) *adj.* (*Med.*) pert. to or employed in the correction of deformities. —**or"tho·pe'di·cal·ly,** *adv.* —**or"tho·pe'dist,** *n.*

or'to·lan (ôr'tə-lən) *n.* a Europ. bunting; the bobolink.

Os'car (os'kər) *n.* (*Colloq.*) the statuette signifying an Academy Award.

os'cil·late" (os'ə-lāt") *v.i.* 1, move to and fro, as a pendulum. 2, vacillate; fluctuate. —**os"cil·la'tion,** *n.* —**os'cil·la"tor,** *n.*

os'cu·late" (os'kyə-lāt") *v.t. & i.* kiss. —**os"cu·la'tion,** *n.*

o'sier (ō'zhər) *n.* a willow whose twigs are used for baskets, etc.

-o·sis (-ō-sis) *suf.* [*pl.* **-o·ses** (-sēz)] abnormal condition of.

os'mi·um (oz'mē-əm) *n.* a hard, heavy metallic element, no. 76, symbol Os, similar to platinum.

os·mo'sis (oz-mō'sis) *n.* the tendency of liquids to pass through porous partitions and become diffused.

os'prey (os'prē) *n.* a large fish-eating bird.

os'se·ous (os'ē-əs) *adj.* made of or like bone.

os'si·fy" (os'i-fī") *v.t. & i.* change into bone. —**os"si·fi·ca'tion,** *n.*

os·ten'si·ble (os-ten'sə-bəl) *adj.* appearing outwardly; professed.

os"ten·ta'tion (os"ten-tā'shən) *n.* a pretentious display. —**os"ten·ta'tious,** *adj.*

os"te·ol'o·gy (os"tē-ol'ə-jē) *n.* the science dealing with the bones.

os"te·op'a·thy (os"tē-op'ə-thē) *n.* a system of medicine which holds that disease is chiefly due to derangement of the bones. —**os'te·o·path"** (os'tē-ə-path") *n.*

os'tra·cize" (os'trə-sīz") *v.t.* banish from society, etc. —**os'tra·cism,** *n.*

os'trich *n.* a very large flightless bird of Africa, valued for its plumes.

oth'er (uth'ər) *adj.* 1, different from the one just mentioned. 2, the remaining one or ones. 3, additional. 4, different; not the same. —*adv.* otherwise. —*pron.* 1, the second of two. 2, a different person or thing.

oth'er·wise" *adv.* in a different way. —*conj.* else.

o·tol'o·gy (ō-tol'ə-je) *n.* the science of the ear and its diseases. —**o·tol'o·gist,** *n.*

ot'ter (ot'ər) *n.* an aquatic animal; its dark-brown fur.

ot'to·man (ot'ə-mən) *n.* a cushioned footstool or bench.

Otter

ouch (owch) *interj.* an exclamation of pain.

ought (ât) *aux. v.* be bound, or obliged, or sure (to): followed by an infinitive.

oui·ja (wē'jə) *n.* a board and pointer supposed mystically to spell out words.

ounce (owns) *n.* 1, a measure of weight, one-twelfth of a pound troy, one-sixteenth of a pound avoirdupois. 2, one-sixteenth of a pint; *fluid ounce.* 3, the snow leopard of Asia.

our (owr) *pron. & adj.* poss. form of *we.* —**ours,** *pron.* form of *our* used predicatively. —**our·selves',** *pron.*

oust (owst) *v.t.* drive out.

out (owt) *adv.* 1, away from or not in a place, position, state, etc. 2, into sight or existence; forth. 3, to exhaustion, extinction, or conclusion. 4, at variance; in error; minus. 5, not in vogue. 6, by reason of. 7, (*Baseball*) temporarily retired from action. —*n.* (*Colloq.*) 1, a means of escape or excuse. 2, (*pl.*) bad terms. 3, one who is out. —*v.i.* become known.

out- *pref.* away; beyond; outside; outer: used in many compounds.

out-'and-out' *adj.* absolute; complete.

out·bid' *v.t.* bid more than.

out'board" (owt'bôrd") *adj. & adv.* on or to the outside of a boat; away from the center.

out'bound" *adj.* going away.

out'break" (owt'brāk") *n.* 1, a sudden eruption; an outburst. 2, a riot or insurrection.

out'build"ing (owt'bil"ding) *n.* a small, detached building, subordinate to another.

out'burst" (owt'bĕrst") *n.* a sudden pouring forth; an outbreak of emotion.

out'cast" (owt'kåst") *n.* **1,** a person cast out, as from home. **2,** discarded matter.

out-class' (owt-klås') *v.t.* be ahead of; surpass.

out'come" (owt'kum") *n.* the result, consequence, or issue.

out'cry" (owt'krī") *n.* a loud cry, as of distress; clamor. —*v.t.* cry louder than.

out-dat'ed (owt-dāt'id) *adj.* obsolete; out-of-date; antiquated.

out-dis'tance *v.t.* go farther than.

out-do' *v.t.* do better than; surpass; excel.

out'door" (owt'dōr") *adj.* in open air, not in a building. —**out-doors'**, *adv. & n.*

out'er (ow'tẽr) *adj.* **1,** exterior. **2,** farther out. —**out'er-most"**, *adj.* farthest out.

out'field" (owt'fēld") *n.* the part of a baseball field outside the diamond; the three players (*outfielders*) stationed there.

out'fit" *n.* **1,** equipment for a special purpose, trade, etc.; fittings. **2,** a special group of persons, as a company, a military unit. —*v.t.* [-fit'ted, -ting] equip.

out-flank' *v.t.* go beyond the extent of (an army's) flank.

out'go" (owt'gō") *n.* **1,** expenditure. **2,** outflow. —**out'go"ing**, *adj.* going out; vacating; retiring.

out-grow' *v.t.* **1,** grow too large or able for. **2,** surpass in growing.

out'growth" *n.* a natural development or result; an offshoot.

out'house" *n.* a privy.

out'ing *n.* a pleasure trip.

out'land"er (owt'lan"dẽr) *n.* a foreigner; stranger.

out-land'ish (owt-lan'dish) *adj.* unfamiliar; bizarre; odd.

out-last' *v.t.* last longer than; outlive.

out'law" (owt'lå") *n.* a habitual criminal. —*v.t.* **1,** make illegal or legally unenforceable. **2,** deprive of the protection of the law. —**out'law"ry**, *n.*

out'lay" (owt'lā") *n.* expenditure, as of money, effort, etc.

out'let" (owt'let") *n.* **1,** a means of exit or escape. **2,** a market for goods. **3,** a letting out; discharge.

out'line" *n.* **1,** the line tracing the exterior shape of an object. **2,** a drawing showing only this shape. **3,** a rough draft, as of a speech, plan, etc. **4,** a summary; (*pl.*) the gist. —*v.t.* make an outline of; describe briefly.

out-live' *v.t.* live longer than.

out'look" *n.* **1,** a view or scene from a place. **2,** the prospect for the future. **3,** mental attitude.

out'ly"ing (owt'lī"ing) *adj.* remote from the center; outside a boundary.

out"mod'ed (-mō'did) *adj.* out of fashion.

out-num'ber *v.t.* be more numerous than.

out-'of-date" *adj.* no longer in style; antiquated; obsolete.

out-'of-door" *adj.* outside; outdoor. —**out-"of-doors'**, *adv. & n.*

out-"of-the-way" *adj.* secluded;

out'pa"tient (owt'pā"shent) *n.* a person treated at, but not staying in, a hospital.

out'post" (owt'pōst") *n.* a station distant from an army; troops stationed there as a guard.

out'put" (owt'pût") *n.* **1,** production of goods, crops, work, etc. **2,** the amount produced; yield.

out'rage" *n.* **1,** a shameful wrong. **2,** cruel or wanton violence. —*v.t.* **1,** assault. **2,** transgress shamefully. **3,** offend grossly.

out-ra'geous (-rāj'əs) *adj.* flagrantly contrary to law, order, or decency. —**out-ra'geous-ness**, *n.*

out-rank' *v.t.* rank higher than.

out'rid'er *n.* a horseback rider attending a carriage.

out'rig"ger *n.* a projection from the side of a ship or boat, to give stability, support oars, etc.

out'right" (owt'rīt") *adv.* **1,** all at once; entirely. **2,** openly. —*adj.* **1,** complete; total. **2,** unqualified.

out-run' *v.t.* run faster than.

out'set" (owt'set") *n.* the beginning.

out-shine' *v.t.* shine more brightly than; surpass in fame.

out'side' *n.* **1,** the region beyond an enclosure or boundary. **2,** the outer surface; external aspect. **3,** the utmost limit. —*adj.* **1,** external. **2,** coming from beyond a given place or group. **3,** apart from one's regular occupation. —*adv.* **1,** on or to the outer side. **2,** outdoors. —*prep.* **1,** outward from. **2,** beyond. —**out'sid'er**, *n.* one not belonging to a particular sect, etc.

out'size' *n.* a size not standard; esp., an unusually large size. —**out'-sized"**, *adj.*

out'skirts (owt'skẽrtz) *n.pl.* an outer part; a bordering district.

out"smart" *v.t.* (*Colloq.*) get the better of by cunning or cleverness.

out'spo"ken (owt'spō"kən) *adj.* frank; said without reserve.

out·stand'ing (owt-stan'ding) *adj.* 1, prominent; notable. 2, not paid or settled. 3, standing apart; detached; opposing.

out·strip' (owt-strip') *v.t.* get ahead of; surpass; outdo.

out'ward (-word) *adj.* 1, going away. 2, external; seen from the outside. 3, visible. —*adv.* [also, **out'wards**] toward the outside; out.

out·wear' (owt-wâr') *v.t.* 1, last longer than. 2, wear out; exhaust.

out·weigh' (owt-wā') *v.t.* exceed in weight, importance, or influence.

out·wit' (owt-wit') *v.t.* get the better of by superior cleverness.

out·worn' (owt-wôrn') *adj.* 1, obsolete; outgrown. 2, worn out, as clothes; exhausted.

o'val (ō'vəl) *adj.* elliptical.

o'va·ry (ō'və-rē) *n.* the organ in a female in which egg cells are formed. —**o·va'ri·an** (-vâr'ē-ən) *adj.*

o·vate' (ō-vāt') *adj.* egg-shaped.

o·va'tion (ō-vā'shən) *n.* enthusiastic public acclaim.

ov'en (uv'ən) *n.* a chamber, as in a stove, for baking or drying.

o'ver (ō'vər) *prep.* 1, higher than; above; covering. 2, above and across; to or on the other side of. 3, more than. 4, during. 5, about; concerning. 6, in preference to. —*adv.* 1, on the top. 2, across. 3, yonder; on the other side. 4, from one to another. 5, so as to show the other side. 6, above the rim or top. 7, from beginning to end. 8, in excess. 9, once more. 10, at one end. 11, (*Colloq.*) successfully. —*adj.* 1, higher up. 2, in excess; surplus. 3, finished; past.

o'ver- *pref.* over; beyond; extra.

o"ver·act' (ō"vər-akt') *v.i.* & *t.* be excessively dramatic; overplay.

o"ver·age' (ō"vər-āj') *adj.* beyond the proper age; too old.

o'ver·age (ō'vər-ij) *n.* excess of goods, money, etc.

o'ver·all (ō'vər-âl) *adj.* extending to both or all extremes; covering all parts. —*n.* (*pl.*) a one-piece outer garment worn to protect the clothes.

o"ver·bal'ance (ō'vər-bal'əns) *v.t.* 1, outweigh. 2, tip over.

o"ver·bear'ing (ō'vər-bâr'ing) *adj.* haughty; arrogant; dictatorial.

[The following words may be defined by assuming the prefix *over-* to mean "excessive" in the case of nouns; "too much, too far, too long," etc. in the case of verbs; "too" or "excessively" in the case of adjectives and adverbs.]

o"ver·a·bun'dance, *n.*
o"ver·ac'tive, *adj.*
o"ver·am·bi'tious, *adj.*
o"ver·anx'ious, *adj.*
o"ver·awe', *v.t.*
o"ver·bold', *adj.*
o"ver·bur'den, *v.t.*
o"ver·bus'y, *adj.*
o"ver·buy', *v.i.* & *t.*
o"ver·cap'i·tal·ize", *v.t.*
o"ver·care'ful, *adj.*
o"ver·cau'tious, *adj.*
o"ver·charge', *v.i.* & *t.*
o"ver·con'fi·dent, *adj.*
o"ver·con·serv'a·tive, *adj.*
o"ver·cook', *v.t.*
o"ver·crit'i·cal, *adj.*
o"ver·crowd', *v.t.*
o"ver·cu'ri·ous, *adj.*
o"ver·do', *v.i.* & *t.*
o"ver·done', *adj.*
o"ver·dose', *n.*
o"ver·ea'ger, *adj.*
o"ver·eat', *v.i.*
o"ver·e·mo'tion·al, *adj.*
o"ver·em'pha·size", *v.t.*
o"ver·en·thu'si·as'tic, *adj.*

o"ver·ex·cite', *v.t.*
o"ver·ex'er·cise", *v.i.* & *t.*
o"ver·ex·ert', *v.t.*
o"ver·ex·pan'sion, *n.*
o"ver·ex·pose', *v.t.*
o"ver·fa·mil'iar, *adj.*
o"ver·fa·tigue', *v.t.*
o"ver·feed', *v.t.*
o"ver·fill', *v.t.*
o"ver·fond', *adj.*
o"ver·has'ty, *adj.*
o"ver·heat', *v.t.* & *i.*
o"ver·in·dulge', *v.i.*
o"ver·load', *v.t.*
o"ver·long', *adv.* & *adj.*
o"ver·mod'est, *adj.*
o"ver·much', *adv.*
o"ver·pay', *v.t.* & *i.*
o"ver·pay'ment, *n.*
o"ver·plump', *adj.*
o"ver·pop'u·la'tion, *n.*
o"ver·praise', *v.t.*
o"ver·pro·duce', *v.t.* & *t.*
o"ver·pro·duc'tion, *n.*
o"ver·reach', *v.i.* & *t.*
o"ver·re·li'gious, *adj.*
o"ver·ripe', *adj.*
o"ver·rule', *v.t.*

o"ver·scru'pu·lous, *adj.*
o"ver·sell', *v.t.* & *i.*
o"ver·sen'si·tive, *adj.*
o"ver·set', *v.t.*
o"ver·sim"pli·fi·ca'tion, *n.*
o"ver·sim'pli·fy", *v.t.* & *i.*
o"ver·spread', *adj.* & *v.t.*
o"ver·stay', *v.i.*
o"ver·stim'u·late", *v.t.*
o"ver·stock', *v.t.*
o'ver·stock', *n.*
o"ver·strict", *adj.*
o"ver·stu'di·ous, *adj.*
o"ver·sub·scribe', *v.t.*
o"ver·sup·ply', *n.* & *v.*
o"ver·sus·pi'cious, *adj.*
o"ver·sweet', *adj.*
o"ver·talk'a·tive, *adj.*
o"ver·task', *v.t.*
o"ver·tax', *v.t.*
o"ver·tire', *v.t.* & *i.*
o"ver·trained', *adj.*
o"ver·val"u·a'tion, *n.*
o"ver·val'ue, *v.t.*
o"ver·ve'he·ment, *adj.*
o"ver·write', *v.i.* & *t.*
o"ver·zeal'ous, *adj.*

---

fat, fāte, fär, fâre, fâll, ȧsk; met, hē, hêr, maybē; pin, pīne; not, nōte, ôr, tool

o"ver·bid' (ō'vər-bid') *v.t.* bid higher than. —*v.i.* bid too much. —*n.* a higher bid.

o'ver·board" (ō'vər-bōrd') *adv.* 1, off a ship into the water. 2, (*Colloq.*) to a rash or extravagant extent.

o"ver·call" (o'vər-kâl") *v.t.* bid higher than, in a card game.

o"ver·cast" (o'vər-kâst") *adj.* 1, darkened, esp. by clouds. 2, sewn by long stitches over an edge, as to prevent raveling.

o'ver·clothes" (ō'vər-klōz") *n.pl.* outer garments, as for outdoor wear.

o"ver·cloud" (ō'vər-klowd') *v.t. & i.* overspread with clouds; make or become gloomy.

o"ver·coat" (ō'vər-kōt") *n.* a long outer coat, esp. for cold weather.

o"ver·come' *v.t.* 1, defeat; conquer. 2, successfully resist (an impulse, etc.). —*adj.* feeling great emotion.

o"ver·draft" (ō'vər-drâft") *n.* 1, a draft exceeding one's credit balance, esp. at a bank. 2, any excess draft or demand. 3, an air draft above a fire, or passing downward.

o"ver·draw" (ō'vər-drâ') *v.t. & i.* 1, draw out or back too much or too far. 2, exaggerate in depicting.

o"ver·dress" (ō'vər-dres') *v.i. & t.* dress too ostentatiously.

o"ver·drive' (ō'vər-drīv') *v.t.* drive or work too hard; push to excess. —*n.* (ō'vər-drīv") a gear arrangement whereby a wheel or propeller rotates faster than the driving shaft.

o"ver·due' (ō'vər-doo') *adj.* due at a previous time; past due.

o"ver·es'ti·mate" (ō'vər-es'tə-māt') *v.t. & i.* 1, rate too highly. 2, estimate to be more than the reality. —*n.* (-mat) an excessive estimate. —**o"ver·es'ti·ma'tion,** *n.*

o"ver·flow" (ō'vər-flō') *v.t. & i.* 1, flood. 2, run over the edge or boundary (of). —*n.* (ō'vər-flō") 1, a flowing over; that which flows over. 2, an outlet for excess fluid.

o"ver·grown" (ō'vər-grōn') *adj.* covered with a growth of vegetation, hair, etc.

o'ver·hand' (ō'vər-hand') *adj. & adv.* with the hand above or raised.

o"ver·hang' *v.t. & i.* [-hung, -hang'ing] 1, extend or project over. 2, impend; threaten. —*n.* (ō'vər-hang"), a projecting part; the extent of this projection.

o'ver·haul' (ō'vər-hâl") *v.t.* 1, examine or repair thoroughly. 2, overtake. —*n.* inspection.

o'ver·head' (ō'vər-hed') *adj.* 1, above one's head; in the sky. 2, applicable to all; average. —*n.* the fixed expenses of a business, as for

rent, etc. —*adv.* (ō'vər-hed') 1, aloft; on high. 2, so as to be completely submerged.

o"ver·hear' (ō'vər-hir') *v.t. & i.* hear without the speaker's knowledge or intention.

o"ver·joyed' (ō'vər-joid') *adj.* exceedingly glad; overcome with joy.

o'ver·land' (ō'vər-land') *adj. & adv.* across dry land; by land.

o"ver·lap' (ō'vər-lap') *v.t. & i.* cover partly and extend beyond. —*n.* (ō'vər-lap') the part lapping over.

o"ver·lay' (ō'vər-lā') *v.t.* 1, place on something else. 2, cover, esp. with a decorative layer. —*n.* (ō'vər-lā") something laid on something else.

o"ver·look' (ō'vər-lùk") *v.t.* 1, fail to notice. 2, ignore; condone. 3, afford a view of, from a higher position. 4, supervise.

o'ver·lord' (ō'vər-lôrd") *n.* a master; a chief lord.

o'ver·ly (ō'vər-lē) *adv.* excessively.

o'ver·night" (ō'vər-nīt") *adj.* 1, done during the night. 2, intended for one night's use. —*adv.* (ō'vər-nīt') during the night.

o"ver·pass" (ō'vər-pâs") *n.* a bridge over a road. —*v.t.* (ō'vər-pâs') *v.t.* go over or beyond; surmount.

o"ver·play' (ō'vər-plā') *v.t. & i.* act or make a play with more force than is proper; exaggerate.

o"ver·pleased' (ō'vər-plēzd') *adj.* too pleased (used chiefly in the negative, to express dissatisfaction).

o"ver·pow'er (ō'vər-pow'ər) *v.t.* 1, conquer or subdue by superior force. 2, overwhelm, as with emotion. 3, equip with too much power.

o"ver·rate' (o'vər-rāt') *v.t.* value too highly; overestimate.

o"ver·ride' (ō'vər-rīd') *v.t.* 1, prevail over; outweigh; overrule. 2, trample down. 3, extend over; overlap.

o"ver·run' (o'vər-run') *v.t.* 1, swarm over in great numbers. 2, roam over; spread throughout. 3, run beyond; exceed.

o"ver·seas" (ō'vər-sēz') *adj.* 1, situated beyond a sea; foreign. 2, pert. to sea travel. —*adv.* (ō'vər-sēz') beyond a sea; abroad.

o"ver·see' (ō'vər-sē') *v.t.* 1, supervise; direct. 2, observe; watch. —**o'ver·se'er,** *n.*

o"ver·shad'ow (ō'vər-shad'ō) *v.t.* 1, darken, as by casting a shadow on. 2, cause to seem less important.

o'ver·shoe" (ō'vər-shoo') *n.* a shoe

worn over another; a waterproof shoe, as a rubber or galosh.

o"ver·shoot' (ō"vər-shoot') *v.t.* & *i.* shoot or go beyond (a proper mark or limit).

o'ver·shot' *adj.* **1,** driven from above, as a water wheel. **2,** with the upper jaw overhanging the lower, as on a dog.

o'ver·sight" (ō'vər-sīt") *n.* **1,** an omission or error due to failure to notice. **2,** supervision; care.

o"ver·size' (ō"vər-sīz") *adj.* larger than is usual or proper. —*n.* an oversize article. Also, **o'ver·sized".**

o"ver·sleep' (ō"vər-slēp') *v.i.* sleep too late.

o"ver·state' (ō"vər-stāt') *v.t.* state too strongly; exaggerate. —**o"ver·state'ment,** *n.*

o"ver·step' (ō"vər-step') *v.t.* go beyond; transgress.

o'ver·stuffed" (ō'vər-stuft") *adj.* (of furniture) covered with thick stuffing and upholstery.

o'vert (ō'vĕrt) *adj.* plain to the view; open.

o"ver·take' (ō"vər-tāk') *v.t.* catch up with, as in pursuing.

o"ver·throw' (ō"vər-thrō') *v.t.* **1,** defeat; force out of power; put an end to. **2,** knock down; upset. —*n.* defeat; demolition.

o'ver·time' (ō'vər-tīm") *n.* **1,** time spent working after regular hours; pay for such work. **2,** an extra period beyond the usual, as in sports. —*adj.* & *adv.* requiring extra time. —*v.t.* (ō"vər-tīm') give too much time to, as in photographic processes.

o'ver·tone' (ō'vər-tōn') *n.* **1,** a higher, secondary tone of a basic musical tone. **2,** (*pl.*) additional meaning; connotation.

o"ver·trump' (ō"vər-trump") *v.t.* play a higher trump than.

o'ver·ture (ō'vər-chŭr) *n.* **1,** an orchestral prelude to an opera, play, etc. **2,** a proposal; a suggestion that negotiations begin.

o"ver·turn' (ō"vər-tĕrn') *v.t.* & *i.* **1,** overthrow. **2,** upset; capsize.

o"ver·ween'ing (ō"vər-wē'ning) *adj.* arrogant; presumptuous.

o"ver·weigh' (ō"vər-wā') *v.t.* **1,** exceed in weight. **2,** weigh down; oppress. —**o'ver·weight"** (-wāt") *adj.*

o"ver·whelm' (ō"vər-hwelm') *v.t.* **1,** cover, bury, load, or weigh upon overpoweringly; crush; oppress. **2,** overcome with emotion.

o"ver·work' (ō"vər-wĕrk') *v.i.* work too hard. —*v.t.* **1,** weary with too much work. **2,** excite excessively.

3, elaborate too much. —*n.* (ō'vər-wĕrk") extra work.

o"ver·wrought' (ō"vər-rāt') *adj.* **1,** weary or nervous, esp. from overwork or excitement. **2,** too elaborate.

o'vine (ō'vīn) *adj.* pert. to sheep.

o·vip'a·rous (ō-vip'ə-rəs) *adj.* producing eggs.

o'void (ō'void) *adj.* egg-shaped.

o'vule (ō'vūl) *n.* a rudimentary egg or seed.

o'vum (ō'vəm) *n.* [*pl.* **o'va** (-və)] the female reproductive cell.

owe (ō) *v.t.* **1,** be under obligation to pay, render, etc. **2,** be indebted to or for. —**ow'ing,** *adj.* owed; due. —**owing to,** because of.

owl *n.* **1,** a nocturnal bird of prey, with hooked beak and strong claws. **2,** a solemn person. **3,** a person of nocturnal habits. —**owl'et,** *n.* a young, or small, owl. —**owl·ish,** *adj.* affecting a solemn or wise manner.

Owl

own (ōn) *v.t.* **1,** possess by right. **2,** admit; concede. —*adj.* belonging to or concerning only oneself or itself. —**own'er,** *n.* —**own'er·ship",** *n.*

ox (oks) *n.* [*pl.* **ox'en** (-ən)] the emasculated adult male of the domestic cattle family.

ox'a·lis (ok'sə-lis) *n.* a plant with white or pink flowers.

ox'eye" (oks'ī") *n.* **1,** a daisylike plant. **2,** a small U. S. shore bird, as the sandpiper.

ox'ford (oks'fərd) *n.* **1,** a low shoe. **2,** a cotton or rayon fabric used as shirting. —**oxford gray,** a dark gray.

ox'ide (ok'sīd) *n.* a compound of oxygen with another element.

ox'i·dize" (ok'sə-dīz") *v.t.* & *i.* combine with oxygen. —**ox"i·da'tion,** *n.*

ox"y·a·cet'y·lene (ok"sē-ə-set'ə-lēn) *adj.* pert. to a gas that burns with a very hot flame, used for welding and cutting metal.

ox'y·gen (ok'sə-jən) *n.* a gaseous element, no. 8, symbol O, colorless, odorless, and essential to all life.

o'yez (ō'yes; -yez) *interj.* hear! attention!

oys'ter (ois'tər) *n.* an edible saltwater bivalve mollusk. —**oyster plant,** a vegetable, the salsify.

o'zone (ō'zōn) *n.* **1,** an ionized form of oxygen. **2,** (*Colloq.*) pure air.

For additional words beginning with "over-", see page 326.

fat, fāte, fär, fāre, fäll, ȧsk; met, hē, hēr, maybė; pin, pīne; not, nōte, ôr, tool

P

P, p (pē) the sixteenth letter of the English alphabet.

pa (pä) n. (Colloq.) papa;

pab'u.lum (pab'ye-ləm) n. food.

pace (pās) n. 1, a single step or its distance. 2, mode or rate of walking or progressing; gait; speed. 3, a gait of horses. 4, (pl.) gaits; accomplishments. —v.t. 1, set the rate for. 2, (usually with off) measure by counting steps. 3, walk back and forth across. —v.i. walk in even steps; go at a pace. —pac'er, n. a pacing horse. —pace'mak"er, n. the leader in a race.

pach'y.derm" (pak'i-dĕrm") n. a thick-skinned quadruped, esp. an elephant or rhinoceros. —pach'y.der'ma.tous, adj.

pa.cif'ic (pə-sif'ik) adj. peaceable; conciliatory; calm. —n. (cap.) the Pacific Ocean. —pa.cif'i.cal.ly, adv.

pac'i.fi"er (pas'i-fī"ər) n. a simulated nipple for a baby.

pac'i.fism (-fiz-əm) n. opposition to war for any reason. —pac'i.fist, n.

pac'i.fy" (-fī") v.t. appease; calm. —pac'i.fi.ca'tion, n.

pack (pak) n. 1, a bundle tied up; a packing; a package, esp. of cards or cigarettes. 2, a group of persons or animals; a gang. —v.t. 1, put in a bundle or a piece of baggage. 2, compress; cram; fill (a space). 3, carry, esp. on the back. 4, (with off) send away. —v.i. stow personal things for traveling. —adj. that carries things.

pack'age (-ij) n. a small wrapped bundle. —pack'ag.ing, n.

pack'er (-ər) n. one who packs; esp., a wholesale supplier of meat.

pack'et (-it) n. 1, a small, compact bundle or portion. 2, a small merchant ship.

pack'ing n. material for a protective wad.

pact (pakt) n. an agreement.

pad n. 1, a small wad of something soft; a cushion. 2, the soft sole of an animal's paw. 3, a leaf of a water lily. 3, a writing tablet. —v.t. [pad'ded, -ding] 1, fill out or cushion with pads. 2, add needless or fraudulent items to. —v.i. walk or trot steadily. —pad'ding, n.

pad'dle (pad'əl) n. a short oar; a similar broad-bladed implement. — v.t. & i. 1, propel (a canoe). 2, dabble (as the feet) in shallow water. 3, spank.

paddle wheel, a large wheel with boards around the rim for propelling a boat.

Paddle Boat

pad'dock (pad'ək) n. a small enclosed field near a stable.

pad'lock" (pad'lok") n. a portable lock with a hinged arm. —v.t. fasten with a padlock; close officially.

pa'dre (pä'drė) n. 1, a priest. 2, a chaplain.

pae'an (pē'ən) n. a song of joy.

pa'gan (pā'gən) n. an idolater.

page (pāj) n. 1, one side of a printed leaf of a book, etc. 2, a messenger boy, esp. one in an honorary position. —v.t. 1, number the pages of. 2, summon (a person) from a crowd by calling his name.

pag'eant (paj'ənt) n. a showy spectacle. —pag'eant.ry (-rė) n.

pa.go'da (pə-gō'də) n. in the Far East, a many-storied tower.

paid (pād) v. pret. & p.p. of pay.

pail (pāl) n. an open vessel for carrying liquids; a bucket.

pain (pān) n. 1, suffering of body or mind. 2, (pl.) great care. —v.t. cause suffering to. —pain'ful, adj.

pains'tak"ing (pānz'tāk"ing) adj. very careful.

paint (pānt) n. 1, a pigmented oil or liquid that forms a coloring or protective coating when dry. 2, rouge. —v.t. & i. 1, apply paint (to). 2, portray, esp. with oil paints on canvas; make paintings. — paint'er, n. one who paints (houses, etc., or paintings) professionally. —paint'ing, n. a painted picture.

pair (pâr) n. 1, a matched set of two things. 2, a married couple. 3, two cards of the same rank. —v.t. & i. 1, match (two things). 2, join or go off in couples.

pais'ley (pāz'lė) n. & adj. a thin, soft woolen fabric.

pa.jam'as (pə-jăm'əz) n.pl. loose coat and trousers for sleeping or lounging. Also, Brit., py.jam'as.

pal n. (Slang) friend; chum.

pal'ace (pal'is) n. 1, the residence of a sovereign. 2, a magnificent building.

pal'an·quin' (pal'ən-kēn') *n.* a litter borne by men.

pal'at·a·ble (pal'ə-tə-bəl) *adj.* tasty; acceptable. —**pal"at·a·bil'i·ty,** *n.*

pal'ate (pal'ĭt) *n.* **1,** the roof of the mouth. **2,** the sense of taste; liking. —**pal'a·tal,** *adj.*

pa·la'tial (pə-lā'shəl) *adj.* grand, like (or as in) a palace.

pa·lat'i·nate (pə-lat'ĭ-nāt") *n.* a palatine's state or domain.

pal'a·tine" (pal'ə-tīn") *adj.* having royal privileges. —*n.* a palatine nobleman.

pa·lav'er (pə-lav'ər) *n.* idle talk; cajolery. —*v.i.* chat.

pale (pāl) *adj.* **1,** wan; lacking color; in a light shade. **2,** faint; lacking brilliance. —*n.* **1,** a pointed stake; picket. **2,** a strictly bounded area. —*v.t. & i.* **1,** make wan; dim. —**pale'ness,** *n.*

pale'face" *n.* a white person (supposedly so called by Amer. Indians).

pa·le·o- *pref.* **1,** remote in the past. **2,** early; primitive.

pa"le·o·lith'ic (pā'lē-ə-lĭth'ĭk) *adj.* pert. to the Old Stone Age.

pa"le·on·tol'o·gy (pā'lē-ən-tol'ə-jē) *n.* the scientific study of life in past geologic periods. —**pa"le·on·to·log'i·cal,** *adj.* —**pa"le·on·tol'o·gist,** *n.*

pal'ette (pal'ĭt) *n.* the thin board on which an artist mixes his colors.

pal'frey (pal'frē) *n.* a saddle horse.

pal'in·drome" (pal'in·drōm") *n.* a word or sentence whose letters read the same backwards as forwards, as *level.*

pal'ing (pāl'ing) *n.* a row of pales; fencing.

pal'i·sade" (pal'ə·sād') *n.* **1,** a fence of pointed stakes. **2,** (*pl.*) a line of sheer cliffs.

pall (pâl) *n.* **1,** a cloth thrown over a coffin. **2,** the coffin. **3,** a gloomy, blanketing effect. —*v.i.* become boring.

pal·la'di·um (pə-lā'dē-əm) *n.* **1,** a rare metallic element of the platinum group, no. 46, symbol Pd. **2,** any safeguard, esp. of liberty or rights.

pall'bear"er *n.* a coffin-bearer at a funeral.

pal'let (pal'ĭt) *n.* a bed of straw or rags.

pal'li·ate" (pal'ē·āt") *v.t.* **1,** make excuses for, as a crime. **2,** relieve without curing, as a disease. —**pal"li·a'tion,** *n.* —**pal'li·a"tive,** *n. & adj.*

pal'lid (pal'ĭd) *adj.* pale; wan.

pal'lor (pal'ər) *n.* paleness.

palm (päm) *n.* **1,** that surface of the hand toward which the fingers bend. **2,** any of various tropical trees. **3,** a leaf of this tree as a symbol of victory. —*v.t.* **1,** conceal in the hand. **2,** (with *off*) get rid of unfairly.

palm'er (-ər) *n.* a pilgrim returning from the Holy Land.

pal·met'to (pal-met'ō) *n.* [*pl.* -tos] a palm tree with fan-shaped leaves.

palm'is·try (pä'mis-trē) *n.* fortune-telling from the markings of the palm. —**palm'ist,** *n.*

Palm Sunday the Sunday before Easter, commemorating Christ's entry into Jerusalem.

palm'y (pä'mē) *adj.* flourishing.

pal'o·mi'no (pal'ə-mē'nō) *n.* [*pl.* -nos] a gray or golden horse, usually with near-white mane and tail, bred in the southwest U. S.

pal'pa·ble (pal'pə-bəl) *adj.* readily perceived; obvious. —**pal'pa·ble·ness,** *n.*

pal'pi·tate" (pal'pə-tāt") *v.i.* pulsate; throb. —**pal"pi·ta'tion,** *n.*

pal'sy (pâl'zē) *n.* paralysis; commonly, uncontrolled shaking. —**pal'sied,** *adj.*

pal'ter (pâl'tər) *v.i.* play false; trifle.

pal'try (pâl'trē) *adj.* worthless; trifling. —**pal'tri·ness,** *n.*

pam'pas (pam'pəz) *n. pl.* in So. Amer., vast treeless plains.

pam'per (pam'pər) *v.t.* overindulge; humor.

pam'phlet (pam'flĭt) *n.* a small printed tract; a booklet. —**pam"phlet·eer'** (-flə-tir') *n.* a writer of polemical essays.

pan *n.* **1,** a hollow vessel for cooking. **2,** any similar shallow vessel. —*v.t. & i.* [**panned,** **pan'ning**] **1,** cook or wash in a pan. **2,** (*Slang*) criticize harshly. **3,** yield gold. **4,** (with *out*) succeed.

pan- *pref.* all; every; united.

pan"a·ce'a (pan'ə-sē'ə) *n.* a remedy for all ills.

pan"a·ma" (pan'ə-mä") *n.* a hat woven of fine leaf shoots or straws.

Pan-"A·mer'i·can *adj.* embracing all the sovereign countries of the Western Hemisphere; lit., all-American.

pan"a·tel'a (pan'ə-tel'ə) *n.* a shape of cigar.

pan'cake" (pan'kāk") *n.* **1,** a thin, fried battercake. **2,** in aviation, an abrupt, almost vertical landing. **3,** a flat facial paint.

---

fat, fāte, fär, fâre, fâll, ȧsk; met, hē, hêr, maybē; pin, pīne; not, nōte, ôr, tool

pan"chro·mat'ic (pan"krō-mat'-ik) *adj.* sensitive to light of all colors.

pan'cre·as (pan'krē-əs) *n.* a large gland secreting a digestive fluid; as meat, called *sweetbread.* —**pan"cre·at'ic,** *adj.*

pan'da (pan'də) *n.* 1, a raccoonlike animal of India. 2, [giant panda] a bearlike animal of Tibet.

Panda

pan"de·mo'ni·um (pan"də-mō'nē-əm) *n.* a wild, lawless uproar.

pan'der (pan'dər) *v.i.* (with *to*) minister to base desires.

pan'dit *n.* in India, a wise person; scholar.

pane (pān) *n.* a sheet of glass in a door or window.

pan"e·gyr'ic (pan"ə-jir'ik) *n.* an oration or writing of high praise.

pan'el (pan'əl) *n.* 1, a flat section, raised or sunken, in a wall, door, etc. 2, a strip inserted in a skirt. 3, a list of eligible jurors; a group of speakers. —**pan'eled,** *adj.* —**pan'el·ing,** *n.*

pan'el·ist (-ist) *n.* a member of a panel; one of several persons who discuss events, play games, etc. on a radio or television show.

pang *n.* a sudden sharp pain.

pan"han"dler (pan"han"dlər) *n.* (*Slang*) a street beggar who is not blind, crippled, etc.

Pan"hel·len'ic (pan"hə-len'ik) *adj.* 1, representing all fraternities and sororities in a college. 2, embracing all the states of ancient Greece.

pan'ic (pan'ik) *n.* 1, a sudden, extreme fright. 2, rapidly spreading alarm, esp. in financial circles. —**pan'ick·y** (-ik-ē) *adj.* —**pan'ic·strick'en, pan'ic·struck",** *adj.*

pan'nier (pan'yər) *n.* a basket, usually of wicker, esp. one of a pair.

pan'o·ply (pan'ə-plē) *n.* 1, a full set of armor. 2, splendid array.

pan"o·ram'a (pan"ə-ràm'ə) *n.* an unbroken or widely extended view. —**pan"o·ram'ic,** *adj.* —**pan"o·ram'i·cal·ly,** *adv.*

pan'sy (pan'zē) *n.* a plant of the violet family, with velvety, variously colored flowers.

pant *v.i.* 1, breathe deeply and rapidly; throb. 2, yearn.

pan"ta·lets' (pan"tə-letz') *n.pl.* a woman's long drawers.

pan"ta·loons' (pan"tə-loonz') *n.pl.* trousers.

pan'the·ism (pan'thē-iz-əm) *n.* the doctrine that the existing universe is God. —**pan'the·ist,** *n.* —**pan"the·is'tic,** *adj.* —**pan"the·is'ti·cal·ly,** *adv.*

pan'the·on" (pan'thē-on") *n.* 1, a dedicated building, as a temple or mausoleum. 2, (*cap.*) a temple of ancient Rome.

pan'ther (pan'thər) *n.* 1, a leopard. 2, the American puma or cougar.

pan'ties (pan'tēz) *n.pl.* (*Colloq.*) a woman's short drawers.

pan'to·graph" (pan'tə·gràf") *n.* 1, an instrument for copying a drawing to a given scale. 2, the extensible wire contact on an electric locomotive. —**pan"to·graph'ic,** *adj.* —**pan"to·graph'i·cal·ly,** *adv.*

pan'to·mime" (pan'tə-mīm") *n.* acting, or a play, done solely by gestures and facial expressions. —**pan"to·mim'ic** (-mim'ik) *adj.*

pan'try (pan'trē) *n.* a small room for storing food and dishes.

pants *n.pl.* (*Colloq.*) 1, trousers. 2, drawers.

pan'zer (pan'zər) *adj.* (*Ger.*) armored, as a division of troops.

pap *n.* a soft food for babies.

pa'pa (pä'pə) *n.* father.

pa'pa·cy (pā'pə-sē) *n.* the office, term, jurisdiction, or institution of the Pope. —**pa'pal,** *adj.*

pa·paw' (pä·pä') *n.* a tree of the southern U.S. or its edible fruit.

pa·pa'ya (pə-pä'yə) *n.* a tropical tree or its sweet, juicy fruit.

pa'per (pā'pər) *n.* 1, a thin, flexible material made in sheets of pressed fibers. 2, a newspaper. 3, an essay; article. 4, a document; (*pl.*) credentials. 5, bank notes; bills of exchange. —*adj.* of or on paper. —*v.t.* 1, cover with wallpaper. 2, fill (a theater) with an unpaying audience. —**pa'per·y,** *adj.*

paper hanger one who hangs wallpaper as a trade.

paper nautilus a variety of thin-shelled sea mollusk.

pa'per·weight" *n.* a weight to hold down loose papers.

pa"pier-ma·ché' (pä"pər-mə-shä') *n.* a plastic material of ground or compressed paper.

paper work the writing of records, reports, etc.

pa·pil'la (pə-pil'ə) *n.* [*pl.* -lae (-ē)] a small nipplelike projection. —**pap'il·lar·y** (pap'ə-ler-ē) *adj.*

pa'pist (pā'pist) *n.* one who favors Roman Catholicism or papal supremacy.

pa·poose' (pa-poos') *n.* a No. Amer. Indian baby.

pa'pri·ka (pä'pri-kä) *n.* a mild red pepper.

pa·py'rus (pə-pī'rəs) *n.* a paper made by the ancient Egyptians.

par (pär) *n.* **1,** full or nominal value of money, stocks, etc. **2,** equal footing. **3,** an accepted standard; (*Golf*) the score an expert should make.

pa'ra (pä'rä) *n.* the monetary unit of Turkey, worth about 10 U. S. cents.

pa·ra- *pref.* **1,** beside; beyond. **2,** (*Med.*) faulty; abnormal.

par'a·ble (par'ə-bəl) *n.* a fictitious story pointing a moral.

pa·rab'o·la (pə-rab'ə-lə) *n.* a curve formed by the intersection of a cone by a plane parallel to its side. —**par"a·bol'ic** (par'ə-bol'ik) *adj.*

Parabola

par'a·chute" (par'ə-shoot") *n.* an apparatus to retard the speed of a falling body. —*v.i.* descend by parachute. —**par"a·chut'ist,** *n.*

pa·rade' (pə-rād') *n.* **1,** a formal procession; troops assembled for review. **2,** a display; a passing in review. —*v.t. & i.* pass in review.

par'a·digm (par'ə-dim) *n.* (*Gram.*) a list of the inflected forms of a word.

par'a·dise" (par'ə-dīs") *n.* heaven.

par'a·dox" (par'ə-doks") *n.* **1,** a seemingly absurd but possibly true statement. **2,** something self-contradictory. —**par"a·dox'i·cal,** *adj.*

par'af·fin (par'ə-fin) *n.* an odorless, waxy substance used for candles, sealing, etc. Also, **par'af·fine.**

par'a·gon" (par'ə-gon") *n.* a model of perfection.

par'a·graph" (par'ə-graf") *n.* a separate section of a writing, usually having an indented first line, or marked with the sign (¶).

par'a·keet" (par'ə-kēt") *n.* a small, long-tailed parrot.

par·al'de·hyde" (pə-ral'də-hīd") *n.* a liquid used as a sedative and hypnotic.

par'al·lax" (par'ə-laks") *n.* the apparent shifting of an object when the observer's position changes.

par'al·lel" (par'ə-lel") *adj.* **1,** of lines or planes, never intersecting; equidistant at all points. **2,** similar; analogous. —*n.* **1,** something parallel or similar to another. **2,** comparison. **3,** one of the imaginary lines indicating degrees of latitude. —*v.t.* **1,** compare. **2,** run parallel to. **3,** correspond to. —**par'al·lel'ism,** *n.*

par"al·lel"e·pi·ped" (-ə-pī'pid") *n.* a solid figure with six sides, all parallelograms.

par"al·lel'o·gram" (-ə-gram") *n.* a quadrilateral whose opposite sides are parallel.

pa·ral'y·sis (pə-ral'ə-sis) *n.* complete or partial loss of power to feel or move.

par"a·lyt'ic (par'ə-lit'ik) *n. & adj.* one who is paralyzed.

par'a·lyze" (par'ə-līz") *v.t.* **1,** affect with paralysis. **2,** render helpless or ineffective.

pa·ram'e·ter (pə-ram'ə-tər) *n.* (*Math.*) a variable quantity whose values depend on the special case.

par'a·mount" (par'ə-mownt") *adj.* superior to all others.

par'a·mour" (par'ə-mûr") *n.* an illicit lover.

par"a·noi'a (par'ə-noi'ə) *n.* insanity marked by delusions of grandeur or persecution. —**par"a·noi'ac,** *n.*

par'a·pet" (par'ə-pit) *n.* **1,** (*Mil.*) a rampart; breastwork. **2,** a low wall at the edge of a balcony, bridge, etc.

par"a·pher·nal'ia (par'ə-fər·nāl'yə) *n. pl.* **1,** personal belongings. **2,** equipment; trappings.

par'a·phrase" (par'ə-frāz") *n.* an expression of the same meaning in other words. —*v.t. & i.* restate.

par"a·ple'gi·a (par'ə-plē'jē-ə) *n.* paralysis from the waist down. —**par"a·pleg'ic** (-plej'ik) *n. & adj.*

par'a·sang" (par'ə-sang") *n.* an ancient Persian measure, about 3½ miles.

par'a·site" (par'ə-sīt") *n.* an animal or plant that lives in or on or at the expense of another. —**par"a·sit'ic** (-sit'ik), **par"a·sit'i·cal,** *adj.*

par'a·sol" (par'ə-sâl") *n.* a light, dainty sunshade.

par"a·troop"er (par'ə-troo"pər) *n.* a soldier dropped by parachute in enemy territory.

par'a·vane" (par'ə-vān") *n.* a device to protect vessels against mines.

par'boil" (pär'boil") *v.t.* **1,** boil slightly. **2,** overheat.

par'cel (pär'səl) *n.* **1,** a package. **2,** a small piece, as of land. —*v.t.* separate and dole out. —**parcel post,** postal transmission of packages.

parch (pärch) *v.t. & i.* **1,** dry out by heat. **2,** shrivel; dry up.

parch'ment (-mənt) *n.* sheep- or goatskin prepared to take writing; paper resembling it.

pard (pärd) *n.* (*Slang*) partner.

par'don (pär'dən) *v.t.* excuse; forgive, as a person or offense; free (a person) from penalty. —*n.* a release from punishment.

pare (pār) *v.t.* 1, cut or shave off the skin or edge of. 2, reduce.

par"e·gor'ic (par'ə-gor'ik) *n.* a medicine for relieving pain.

par'ent (pār'ənt) *n.* 1, a father or mother; a progenitor. 2, a cause; source. —**par'ent·age** (-tij) *n.* —**pa·ren'tal** (pə-ren'təl) *adj.* —**par'ent·hood",** *n.*

pa·ren'the·sis (pə-ren'thə-sis) *n.* [*pl.* -ses (-sēz)] 1, an inserted explanatory word, clause, etc. 2, either of the curves ( ) enclosing insertions. —**par"en·thet'i·cal,** *adj.*

pa·re'sis (pə-rē'sis) *n.* partial paralysis. —**pa·ret'ic** (-ret'ik) *adj. & n.*

par·fait' (pär-fā') *n.* a frozen dessert of whipped cream, etc.

pa·ri'ah (pə-rī'ə) *n.* an outcast.

pa·ri'e·tal (pə-rī'ə-təl) *adj.* pert. to a wall-like structure, esp. the sides of the skull.

par'i·mu'tu·el (par'ē-mū'choo-əl) *n.* (usually *pl.*) a method of dividing the money bet on horse races, etc., among winning bettors.

par'ing (pār'ing) *n.* something pared off; slice; peel.

Paris green a poisonous green powder used as an insecticide.

par'ish *n.* 1, the district under a clergyman's care. 2, a county.

pa·rish'ion·er (pə-rish'ən-ər) *n.* a member of a church parish.

par'i·ty (par'ə-tē) *n.* equality; equality with or equivalence to a fixed value or standard.

park (pärk) *n.* ground set apart for public use, esp. for recreation or sports. —*v.t. & i.* leave (an automobile) temporarily on a street or in a lot.

par'ka (pär'kə) *n.* a shirtlike coat made of fur or fleece-lined woolen, usually hooded.

park'way" *n.* a wide, landscaped thoroughfare.

par'lance (pär'ləns) *n.* way of speaking; language.

par·lay' (pär-lā') *v.t. & i.* bet a previously won bet and its winnings.

par'ley (pär'lē) *n.* a conference, esp. between hostile parties. —*v.i.* confer; hold a parley.

par'lia·ment (pär'lə-mənt) *n.* a legislative assembly, esp. (*cap.*) of Great Britain.

par"lia·men'ta·ry (-men'tə-rē) *adj.* pert. to the rules of procedure of legislative bodies. —**par"lia·men-**

tar'i·an (-tār'ē-ən) *n.* one versed in such procedure.

par'lor (pär'lor) *n.* 1, a reception or lounging room. 2, a private meeting or dining room in a hotel, etc.; a shop. Also, par'lour. —**parlor car,** an extra-fare railroad car.

par'lor·maid" *n.* housemaid.

par'lous (pär'ləs) *adj.* dangerous.

Par·nas'sus (pär-nas'əs) *n.* a center of or inspiration for poetic or artistic works.

pa·ro'chi·al (pə-rō'kē-əl) *adj.* 1, pert. to a parish. 2, local; provincial. —**parochial school,** one maintained by a church parish, esp. Rom. Cath.

par'o·dy (par'ə-dē) *n.* a humorous imitation of an author's or artist's style; a burlesque. —**par'o·dist,** *n.*

pa·role' (pə-rōl') *n.* 1, a prisoner's promise not to escape. 2, a conditional release from prison. —*v.t.* release on parole.

par·ox'ysm (par'ək-siz-əm) *n.* a spasm; violent outburst.

par·quet' (pär-kā') *n.* 1, [also, **par'quet·ry** (-ket-rē)] inlaid flooring of different woods. 2, the main floor of a theater.

par'ri·cide" (par'ə-sīd") *n.* the killer or killing of one's parent.

Parquetry

par'rot (par'ət) *n.* 1, a tropical bird of brilliant plumage, capable of imitating speech. 2, one who echoes the words of another. —*v.t.* imitate.

par'ry (par'ē) *v.t.* turn aside; ward off. —*n.* a warding off.

parse (pärs) *v.t.* resolve (a sentence) into its grammatical parts.

par'sec" (pär'sek") *n.* a unit of distance, about 3.26 light years.

Par'see (pär'sē) *n.* a member of a Zoroastrian sect in India.

par'si·mo"ny (pär'sə-mō"nē) *n.* excessive frugality. —**par"si·mo'ni·ous,** *adj.* stingy.

pars'ley (pärs'lē) *n.* an herb with aromatic leaves used as a garnish and seasoning.

pars'nip (pärs'nip) *n.* a plant with a white, edible root.

par'son (pär'sən) *n.* a clergyman; preacher.

par'son·age (-ij) *n.* the residence of a clergyman.

part (pärt) *n.* 1, a piece of a whole; a section; an essential element, as of a machine. 2, a person's share or duty. 3, a rôle, as in a play. 4, in music, the melody assigned to any voice or instrument. 5, a side in a dispute. **6**, (*pl.*) abilities. **7**, a division in the hair. —*v.t.* **1**, divide into sections. **2**, separate; hold apart. —*v.i.* **1**, become separated or sundered. **2**, (with *with*) let go. —**part'i.ble**, *adj.* —**part'ing**, *n.* —part of speech, a classification of the form or function of a word, as noun, adjective, etc.

par.take' (pär-tāk') *v.i.* [-**took'**, -tak'en] have or take a share.

par.terre' (pär-tār') *n.* **1**, the rear of a theater's main floor. **2**, an ornamental pattern of flower beds.

par''the.no.gen'e.sis (pär''thə-nō-jen'ə-sis) *n.* reproduction from an unfertilized egg.

par'tial (pär'shəl) *adj.* **1**, affecting a part only; not total. **2**, (with *to*) having a liking for. **3**, biased. —**par''ti.al'i.ty** (-shē-al'ə-tē) *n.*

par.tic'i.pant (pär-tis'i-pənt) *n.* one who participates.

par.tic'i.pate'' (pär-tis'i-pāt'') *v.i.* have a share; take part in something. —**par.tic'i.pa'tion**, *n.*

par''ti.ci''ple (pär'tə-sip''əl) *n.* a part of a verb used as both verb and adjective. —**par''ti.cip'i.al**, *adj.*

par'ti.cle (pär'tə-kəl) *n.* **1**, a minute piece or amount. **2**, a minor part of speech, as an article (*the*), conjunction, etc.

par''ti.col''ored (pär'tē-kul''ərd) *adj.* variegated.

par.tic'u.lar (pər-tik'yə-lər) *adj.* **1**, belonging or relating to a single person, place, or thing; not general. **2**, apart from others; separate. **3**, unusual; notable. **4**, detailed; careful. **5**, nice; fastidious. —*n.* an item; detail. —**par.tic'u.lar'i.ty** (-lar'ə-tē) *n.* —**par.tic'u.lar.ly**, *adv.* especially; specifically.

par'ti.san (pär'tə-zən) *n.* **1**, an adherent, often biased, of a party or cause. **2**, a guerrilla. —*adj.* **1**, pert. or belonging to a political party. **2**, biased. —**par'ti.san.ship**, *n.*

par.ti''tion (pär-tish'ən) *n.* **1**, division; separation. **2**, that which separates, esp. a dividing wall. —*v.t.* divide by a partition.

part'ner (pärt'nər) *n.* one who is associated with another, as in business, dancing, marriage, etc.

part'ner.ship'' *n.* **1**, the state of being partners. **2**, a business firm of partners, not incorporated.

par'tridge (pär'trij) *n.* a game bird; the quail; ruffed grouse.

par''tu.ri''tion (pär''tyu̇-rish'ən)

Partridge

n. childbirth. —**par.tur'i.ent**, *adj.*

par'ty (pär'tē) *n.* **1**, a body of persons; a detachment of troops; an organization of persons acting together politically. **2**, a person concerned in some action, as a contract; (*Colloq.*) a person. **3**, a social gathering. —**party line**, **1**, a telephone line shared by different houses. **2**, the dogma of a political party. —**party wall**, a wall common to two houses.

par've.nu'' (pär've-nū'') *n.* an upstart; one newly rich.

pas'chal (pas'kəl) *adj.* pert. to Easter, or to the Passover.

pa.sha' (pə-shä') *n.* a Turkish title of authority. Also, **pa.cha'**.

pass (pås) *v.i.* **1**, move from one place or condition to another. **2**, vanish; (often with *away*) die. **3**, be enacted, as a law. **4**, undergo a test successfully. **5**, occur; happen. **6**, (with *on*) pronounce an opinion. **7**, go by unnoticed. **8**, be accepted at face value. **9**, take no action; decline to bid. —*v.t.* **1**, go by or over. **2**, spend, as time. **3**, undergo successfully. **4**, gain the approval of; give legal effect to. **5**, utter; pronounce. **6**, hand over; transfer. —*n.* **1**, an act of passing. **2**, a defile in the mountains. **3**, state of affairs, as a *sorry pass*. **4**, a free ticket; (*Mil.*) a written leave of absence. **5**, (*Slang*) a feinted blow. **6**, (*Slang*) an amorous advance. —**pass muster**, be found up to standard. —**pass the buck**, shift responsibility.

pass'a.ble *adj.* **1**, navigable; traversable. **2**, only fairly good.

pas'sage (pas'ij) *n.* **1**, a passing or moving. **2**, a means of passing, as a channel, alley, etc. **3**, a voyage; accommodations for it. **4**, an excerpt from a book, speech, etc. **5**, enactment, as of a law. **6**, an interchange, as of vows, blows, etc.

pas'sage.way'' *n.* passage (def. 2).

pass'book'' *n.* a bank book.

pas.sé' (pà-sā') *adj.* outmoded.

pas'sen.ger (pas'ən-jər) *n.* a traveler on some form of conveyance.

pass''er-by' *n.* [*pl.* **pass''ers-by'**] one who happens to go by.

pass'ing *n.* death. —*adj.* **1**, now happening; current. **2**, cursory. **3**, fleeting.

pas'sion (pash'ən) *n.* **1**, intense emotion: anger; rage; ardent love; zeal; enthusiasm. **2**, the object of admiration. **3**, (*cap.*) the sufferings of Christ in his last days. —**pas'sion.ate** (-ət) *adj.*

pas'sive (pas'iv) *adj.* **1**, unresisting; not opposing. **2**, not acting, but acted upon; (*Gram.*) naming that form of a transitive verb in which the subject is acted upon. —**pas'-sive·ness**, n.

pas·siv'i·ty (pə-siv'ə-tĕ) n. unresisting acceptance.

Pass'o"ver n. the feast of unleavened bread (Ex. 12).

pass'port" n. official permission to travel.

pass'word" n. a secret word to distinguish friend from foe.

past (pàst) adj. 1, gone by in time. 2, just gone by. 3, no longer in office. 4, (Gram.) indicating a time gone by. —n. 1, bygone time; events of that time. 2, a person's past history, esp. a discreditable one. —prep. beyond in time, position, or condition. —adv. by.

paste (pāst) n. 1, an adhesive substance, usually one containing starch. 2, dough for pastry or macaroni, etc. 3, a material ground to a creamy consistency. 4, a compound used for making artificial gems. —v.t. 1, cause to adhere with paste. 2, (Slang) wallop.

paste'board" n. 1, a board made from paper pasted or pressed together. 2, (Slang) a ticket or playing card.

pas·tel' (pas-tel') n. a pale and light shade of color; a drawing with pastel crayons.

pas'teur·ize" (pas'tə-rīz") v.t. partially sterilize a liquid, as milk, by heating it. —**pas'teur·i·za'tion**, n.

pas·tille' (pas-tēl') n. 1, a cone of incense. 2, a medicated lozenge.

pas'time" (pàs'tīm") n. an agreeable occupation; amusement.

pas'tor (pàs'tər) n. a minister in charge of a parish; a clergyman. —**pas'tor·ate** (-ət) n.

pas'tor·al (-əl) adj. 1, pert. to the duties of a pastor. 2, pert. to shepherds or country life.

pas'try (pās'trĕ) n. food with a shortened crust, as pies, patties, etc.

pas'ture (pàs'chər) n. grassland for grazing cattle. —v.t. put to graze. —**pas'tur·age** (-ij) n.

past'y (pās'tĕ) adj. 1, of or like paste. 2, pale. —n. a meat pie. —**past'i·ness**, n.

pat v.t. [**pat'ted, -ting**] tap or stroke gently with the hand. —n. 1, a light blow. 2, a small molded mass. —adj. [**pat'ter, -test**] apt. —adv. exactly.

patch (pach) n. 1, a piece of cloth, metal, etc., used to cover a hole or worn place. 2, a small piece, as a plot of ground. —v.t. 1, mend with a patch. 2, (with up) repair; reconcile.

patch'work" n. something made

up of fragments of different kinds, colors, or shapes.

pate (pāt) n. the top of the head.

pa·tel'la (pə-tel'ə) n. the kneecap.

pat'ent (pat'ənt; pā'-) n. an official document (letters patent) granting a privilege, esp. a temporary monopoly to an inventor. —adj. 1, open for all to read; plain; obvious. 2, patented. —v.t. obtain a patent for. —**patent leather**, a leather or coated fabric with a hard, glossy surface. —**patent medicine**, a packaged medicine with patented name.

pat'ent·ee' (pat'ən-tē') n. one to whom a patent is issued.

pa·ter'nal (pə-tĕr'nəl) adj. 1, fatherly. 2, inherited from, or related through, a father.

pa·ter'nal·ism (-iz-əm) n. excessive governmental regulation. —**pa·ter'nal·is'tic**, adj. —**pa·ter'nal·is'ti·cal·ly**, adv.

pa·ter'ni·ty (pə-tĕr'nə-tĕ) n. male parentage; fatherhood.

pa'ter·nos'ter (pā'tər-nos"tər) n. a prayer, esp. the Lord's Prayer.

path (pàth) n. 1, a footway; any road. 2, course; track. —**path'way"**, n.

pa·thet'ic (pə-thet'ik) adj. exciting pity. —**pa·thet'i·cal·ly**, adv.

-path·ic suf. disease.

path·o- pref. disease.

path"o·gen'ic (path"ə-jen'ik) adj. causing disease.

pa·thol'o·gy (pə-thol'ə-jĕ) n. the science of the nature and origin of disease. —**path"o·log'i·cal**, adj. —**pa·thol'o·gist**, n.

pa'thos (pā'thos) n. a quality that evokes pity or sadness.

-path·y suf. 1, feeling. 2, disease.

pa'tience (pā'shəns) n. 1, endurance of pain or provocation without complaint. 2, the power to wait calmly. 3, perseverance. 4, (Cards) solitaire.

pa'tient (pā'shənt) adj. having patience. —n. a person under medical care.

pat'i·na (pat'ə-nə) n. a film that forms on a surface, esp. of bronze; a mellowing due to age.

pa'ti·o" (pä'tĕ-ō") n. a courtyard.

pat'ois (pat'wä) n. a dialect.

pa'tri·arch" (pā'trĕ-ärk") n. 1, a father or ruler of a tribe. 2, a high church dignitary. 3, a venerable old man. —**pa"tri·ar'chal**, adj. —**pa'tri·ar"chy**, n. government by the father or fathers.

pa·tri'cian (pə-trish'ən) n. an aristocrat. —adj. of noble birth.

pat′ri·cide″ (pat′rə-sīd″) n. the killer or killing of one's father.

pat′ri·mon″y (pat′rə-mō″nè) n. an inheritance from any ancestor. —pat″ri·mo′ni·al, adj.

pa′tri·ot (pā′trè-ət) n. one who loves and defends his country. —pa″tri·ot′ic (-ot′ik) adj. —pa″tri·ot′i·cal·ly, adv. —pa′tri·ot·ism, n.

pa·trol′ (pə-trōl′) v.t. & i. [patrolled′, -trol′ling] traverse as a guard. —n. the act of patrolling; a person or troop that patrols. —pa·trol′man, n. a policeman.

pa′tron (pā′trən) n. 1, an influential supporter or donor. 2, a guardian saint. 3, a regular customer of a shop. —pa′tron·ess, n.fem.

pa′tron·age (-ij) n. 1, support; favor. 2, customers. 3, the power to appoint jobholders.

pa′tron·ize″ (-īz″) v.t. 1, give one's support or custom to. 2, treat with condescension.

pat′ro·nym′ic (pat′rə-nim′ik) n. a family name. —adj. being or pert. to a family name.

pat′ter (pat′ər) v.i. 1, make quick, short taps; run with short steps. 2, talk glibly. —v.t. repeat mechanically. —n. 1, a succession of light taps. 2, rapid, glib speech.

pat′tern (pat′ərn) n. 1, an example; ideal. 2, a model to be copied. 3, a decorative design. —v.t. make conform (to some pattern).

pat′ty (pat′è) n. a cup-shaped shell of pastry.

pau′ci·ty (pā′sə·tè) n. smallness of quantity.

paunch (pânch) n. the belly.

pau′per (pā′pər) n. a destitute person; a recipient of charity. —pau′per·ism, n. —pau′per·ize″ (-īz″) v.t. impoverish.

pause (pâz) n. an interval of silence or inaction. —v.i. stop, hesitate, linger, for a time.

pave (pāv) v.t. 1, cover with bricks, cement, etc. 2, facilitate. —pave′ment, pav′ing, n. a paved surface, as a sidewalk.

pa·vil′ion (pə-vil′yən) n. a light building or tent for recreation, etc.

paw (pâ) n. an animal's foot with nails or claws. —v.t. & i. 1, strike or scrape with the foot. 2, touch, stroke, or handle rudely.

pawl (pâl) n. a short pivoted bar acting as a brake in a machine.

pawn (pân) n. 1, the chess piece of least value; hence, a person used as a tool. 2, a pledge; something pawned. —v.t. deposit as security for a loan. —pawn′bro″ker, n. a

person licensed to lend money on pledged property. —pawn′shop″, n.

pay (pā) v.t. [paid (pād), pay′ing] 1, compensate (a person) for services rendered or goods supplied. 2, discharge, as a debt; hand over, as money. 3, render, as a compliment. 4, be profitable to. —v.i. 1, discharge a debt. 2, be advantageous. —n. 1, wages; salary. 2, employment for gain. —pay′a·ble, adj. due.

pay′day″ n. the day on which employees receive their pay.

pay·ee′ (pā-ē′) n. one who receives payment.

pay′load″ n. the weight a vehicle carries in freight or paying passengers.

pay′mas″ter n. the official who pays laborers, troops, etc.

pay′ment (-mənt) n. 1, act of paying. 2, that which is paid.

pay′off″ n. (Slang) a final reckoning.

pay′roll″ n. a list of persons to be paid (wages), or the wages paid.

pea (pē) n. the round, edible green seed of a leguminous vine; the vine. —pea jacket, a short outer coat.

peace (pēs) n. 1, freedom from war or civil disorder. 2, a contract to end war. 3, harmony in human relations. 4, tranquillity; quietness. —peace′a·ble, adj. not quarrelsome; loving peace.

peace′ful (-fəl) adj. 1, quiet; tranquil. 2, peaceable. —peace′ful·ness, n.

peace officer a policeman, constable, sheriff, etc.

peace′time″ n. a period of not being at war.

peach (pēch) n. 1, a round juicy fruit with a fuzzy, red-tinged skin; the tree bearing it. 2, a yellowish-red color. 3, (Slang) a person highly approved of. —v.i. (Slang) inform.

Peacock

pea′cock″ (pē′kok″) n. a male bird with long brilliant tail feathers. —pea′hen″, n.fem.

peak (pēk) *n.* 1, the pointed end of anything. 2, a steep mountain. 3, a visor. 4, the highest point.

peak'ed (pēk'id) *adj.* (*Colloq.*) thin; sickly.

peal (pēl) *n.* the loud ringing of a bell, or of thunder, laughter, etc. —*v.t. & i.* ring.

pea'nut" (pē'nut") *n.* a plant of the pea family whose pods ripen under ground; its edible nutlike seed.

pear (pâr) *n.* the juicy fruit of a tree related to the apple; the tree.

pearl (pêrl) *n.* 1, a hard lustrous body found in the shells of certain mollusks and valued as a gem. 2, a pale, bluish-gray color. —**pearl'y,** *adj.* like pearl; lustrous.

peas'ant (pez'ənt) *n.* a countryman; rustic. —**peas'ant·ry** (-rē) *n.*

peat (pēt) *n.* partly decomposed vegetable matter found in bogs, used, when dried, for fuel.

peb'ble (peb'əl) *n.* a small stone worn smooth by water. —*v.t.* grain, as leather. —**peb'bly,** *adj.*

pe·can' (pi-kän') *n.* a species of hickory tree or its thin-shelled nut.

pec"ca·dil'lo (pek"ə-dil'ō) *n.* a trifling offense.

pec'ca·ry (pek'ə-rē) *n.* a hoglike animal of tropical America.

peck (pek) *n.* 1, a unit of capacity: in dry measure, 8 quarts or one-fourth of a bushel. 2, a quick, sharp stroke, as with a bird's beak or a pointed tool. —*v.t. & i.* 1, strike or pick up, with, or as with, the beak. 2, nag. 3, eat in bits.

pec'tin (pek'tin) *n.* a substance that causes jelling. —**pec'tic,** *adj.*

pec'to·ral (pek'tə-rəl) *adj.* pert. to the chest.

pec'u·late" (pek'yə-lāt") *v.t. & i.* embezzle. —**pec"u·la'tion,** *n.*

pe·cul'iar (pi-kūl'yər) *adj.* 1, characteristic of or belonging exclusively to. 2, special. 3, odd; queer. —**pe·cu"li·ar'i·ty,** *n.*

pe·cu'ni·ar"y (pi-kū'nə-er"ē) *adj.* pert. to or consisting of money.

ped'a·gogue" (ped'ə-gog") *n.* a schoolteacher. Also, **ped'a·gog".** —**ped'a·go"gy** (-gō"jē) *n.* —**ped"a·gog'i·cal** (-goj'i-kəl) *adj.*

ped'al (ped'əl) *adj.* pert. to the foot. —*n.* a lever worked by the foot, as of a bicycle, organ, etc. —*v.t. & i.* work the pedals (of).

ped'ant (ped'ənt) *n.* one who parades or overvalues his learning. —**pe·dan'tic** (pə-dan'tik) *adj.* —**pe·dan'ti·cal·ly,** *adv.* —**ped'ant·ry** (-rē) *n.*

ped'dle (ped'əl) *v.t. & i.* sell from house to house. —**ped'dler,** *n.*

ped'es·tal (ped'is-təl) *n.* a supporting base, as of a column.

pe·des'tri·an (pə-des'trē-ən) *n.* one who walks. —*adj.* 1, walking. 2, prosaic; unimaginative.

pe"di·at'rics (pē"dē-at'riks) *n.* (*Med.*) the medical care and treatment of children. —**pe"di·a·tri'cian** (pē"dyə-trish'ən) *n.*

ped'i·cure" (ped'ə-kyūr") *n.* the care of the feet.

ped'i·gree" (ped'ə-grē") *n.* 1, lineage; descent. 2, a genealogical record. —**ped'i·greed",** *adj.* of known and pure breeding.

ped'i·ment (ped'ə-mənt) *n.* a triangular gable over the front of a building.

ped'lar (ped'lər) *n.* peddler.

pe·dom'e·ter (pi-dom'ə-tər) *n.* a watch-shaped instrument for recording steps taken in walking.

peek (pēk) *v.i.* peep slyly.

peel (pēl) *v.t.* strip the rind, skin, or bark from. —*v.i.* become stripped. —*n.* [also, **peel'ing**] the rind.

peen (pēn) *n.* the shaped top of a hammer's head.

peep (pēp) *v.i.* 1, begin to appear. 2, peer slyly or furtively. 3, chirp; cheep. —*n.* 1, a sly or furtive look. 2, a glimpse. 3, the cry of a young bird. 4, (*Slang*) a military automobile, larger than a jeep. —**peep'er,** *n.* a young frog. —**peep'hole"**, *n.*

peer (pir) *n.* 1, an equal; match. 2, a nobleman. —*v.i.* look sharply or curiously. —**peer'age,** *n.* the nobility. —**peer'ess,** *n.fem.* —**peer'less,** *adj.* matchless.

peeve (pēv) *v.t. & i.* make or become ill-tempered. —*n.* an annoyance.

pee'vish (pē'vish) *adj.* fretful; irritable. —**pee'vish·ness,** *n.*

peg *n.* 1, a tapering pin of wood or metal. 2, (*Brit.*) a drink of liquor. —*v.t.* [pegged, peg"ging] 1, fasten or mark with pegs. 2, set at a certain price. —take down a peg, humble.

peign·oir' (pān-wär') *n.* a woman's dressing gown.

pe·jo'ra·tive (pi-jôr'ə-tiv) *adj.* disparaging; depreciating. —*n.* a disparaging term.

Pe'king·ese'' (pē'kə-nēz'') *n.* a small Chinese dog.

pe'koe (pē'kō) *n.* a black India tea.

pe·lag'ic (pə-laj'ik) *adj.* marine; oceanic.

pelf *n.* booty; money.

pel'i·can (pel'ə-kən) *n.* a large water bird with a pouch under its bill.

pel·la'gra (pə-lā'grə) *n.* a skin disease affecting the nervous system, caused by deficient diet.

pel'let (pel'ət) *n.* a little ball of dough, lead, etc.; a pill.

pell-'mell' (pel'mel') *adv.* in confusion; headlong.

pel·lu'cid (pə-loo'sid) *adj.* 1, clear; limpid. 2, easily understood.

pelt *n.* 1, a hide, esp. with fur. —*v.t.* assail with missiles. —*v.i.* 1, beat violently. 2, move rapidly.

pel'vis *n.* [*pl.* -ves (-vēz)] the basin-shaped group of bones that support the spine. —**pel'vic** (-vik) *adj.*

pem'mi·can (pem'ə-kən) *n.* a dried meat paste, made into cakes.

pen *n.* 1, a small enclosure for animals. 2, an instrument for writing with ink. —*v.t.* [penned, pen'ning] 1, shut in; enclose. 2, write. —**pen name,** a pseudonym.

pe'nal (pē'nəl) *adj.* pert. to or inflicting punishment. —**pe'nal·ize''** (-īz'') *v.t.* inflict a penalty upon.

pen'al·ty (pen'əl-tē) *n.* a punitive forfeit; punishment.

pen'ance (pen'əns) *n.* self-inflicted punishment for sin.

pence (pens) *n. pl.* (*Brit.*) pennies.

pen'chant (pen'chənt) *n.* a strong nclination or liking.

pen'cil (pen'səl) *n.* a cylinder, as of wood, enclosing a soft solid substance for writing, marking, etc.

pend *v.i.* hang, as if balanced; await settlement.

pend'ant (pen'dənt) *n.* a hanging ornament.

pend'ent (pen'dənt) *adj.* 1, hanging. 2, pending.—**pen'den·cy,** *n.*

pen'du·lous (pen'jə-ləs) *adj.* hanging loosely. —**pen'du·lous·ness,** *n.*

pen'du·lum (pen'jə-ləm) *n.* a weight suspended on a swinging arm.

pen'e·trate'' (pen'i-trāt'') *v.t.* 1, pierce into or through. 2, enter and become part of; permeate. 3, see into; understand. —*v.t.* enter and make way. —**pen'e·tra·ble,** *adj.* —**pen'e·tra''tive,** *adj.* keen. —**pen''e·tra'tion,** *n.*

pen'guin (peng'gwin) *n.* a flightless aquatic bird.

pen''i·cil'lin (pen'ə-sil'ən) *n.* a powerful, bacteria-killing substance obtained from a green mold (*penicillium*).

pen·in'su·la (pə-nin'sə-lə) *n.* a body of land almost surrounded by water. —**pen·in'su·lar,** *adj.*

pe'nis (pē'nis) *n.* the male organ through which sperm and urine are discharged.

pen'i·tent (pen'ə-tənt) *adj.* repentant; contrite. —**pen'i·tence,** *n.* —**pen''i·ten'tial** (-ten'shəl) *adj.*

pen''i·ten'tia·ry (pen'ə-ten'shə-rē) *n.* a prison for criminals.

pen'knife'' *n.* a pocket knife.

pen'man (-mən) *n.* [*pl.* -men] one skilled in handwriting. —**pen'man·ship,** *n.* handwriting.

pen'nant (pen'ənt) *n.* a long, narrow flag, often one awarded to a victor.

pen'nate (pen'āt) *adj.* winged.

pen'ny (pen'ē) *n.* a copper coin worth one U. S. cent, or (*Brit.*) one-twelfth shilling. —**pen'ni·less,** *adj.* destitute.

pen'ny·weight'' *n.* a measure of weight, one-twentieth of a troy ounce.

pe·nol'o·gy (pē-nol'ə-jē) *n.* the science of prison management. —**pe''no·log'i·cal** (pē'nə-loj'i-kəl) *adj.* —**pe·nol'o·gist,** *n.*

pen'sion (pen'shən) *n.* 1, a regular payment for past services. 2, (pän-sē-än') (*Fr.*) a boarding house. —*v.t.* retire and pay a pension to. —**pen'sion·er,** *n.* one who is pensioned.

pen'sive (pen'siv) *adj.* reflective; thoughtful. —**pen'sive·ness,** *n.*

pent *adj.* (often with *up*) confined; shut up.

pen·ta- *pref.* five.

pen'ta·gon (pen'tə-gon) *n.* a five-sided figure. —**pen·tag'o·nal** (-tag'ə-nəl) *adj.*

Pen'ta·teuch'' (pen'tə-tūk'') *n.* the first five books of the Bible.

Pen'te·cost'' (pen'tə-kâst'') *n.* a Christian festival, Whitsunday.

pent'house'' (pent'hows'') *n.* an apartment or house on the roof of a building.

pe'nult (pē'nult) *n.* the next-to-last syllable.

pe·nul'ti·mate (pi-nul'ti-mət) *adj.* next to last.

pe·nur'i·ous (pə-nyūr'ē-əs) *adj.* stingy; miserly. —**pe·nur'i·ous·ness,** *n.*

pen'u·ry (pen'yə-rē) *n.* extreme poverty.

pe'on (pē'on) *n.* in Lat. Amer., a day-laborer. —**pe'on·age**, *n.* virtual slavery; serfdom.

pe'o·ny (pē'ə-nē) *n.* a plant bearing large, globular flowers.

peo'ple (pē'pəl) *n.* 1, the whole of a particular body or group of persons. 2, (*n.pl.*) the populace; the masses. 3, (*n.pl.*) (*Colloq.*) persons; relatives. —*v.t.* populate.

pep (*Slang*) *n.* energy; vigor. —*v.t.* [**pepped, pep'ping**] (with *up*) stimulate. —**pep'py**, *adj.*

pep'lum (pep'ləm) *n.* a short fitted overskirt.

pep'per (pep'ər) *n.* 1, a pungent spice. 2, a garden plant or its edible fruit. —*v.t.* 1, season with pepper. 2, sprinkle (on); pelt.

pep'per-and-salt' *adj.* mixed black and white.

pep'per·corn *n.* the berry of the pepper plant.

pep'per·mint (pep'ər-mint) *n.* a pungent herb, its oil, or candy flavored with it.

pep'per·y (-ē) *adj.* 1, hot; biting. 2, hot-tempered. —**pep'per·i·ness**, *n.*

pep'sin *n.* a digestive substance in the gastric juice. —**pep'tic**, *adj.* pert. to digestion.

per (pêr) *prep.* 1, by means of; through. 2, for or to each.

per"ad·ven'ture *adv.* perhaps.

per·am'bu·late" (pər-am'byə-lāt") *v.t.* walk about. —**per·am"bu·la'tion**, *n.* —**per·am'bu·la·to"ry**, *adj.*

per·am'bu·la"tor (-lā"tər) *n.* a baby carriage.

per an'num (an'əm) (*Lat.*) each year.

per·cale' (pər-kāl') *n.* a closely woven cotton fabric.

per cap'i·ta (kap'ə-tə) (*Lat.*) per person.

per·ceive' (pər-sēv') *v.t.* become aware of through the senses or the understanding. —**per·ceiv'a·ble**, *adj.*

per·cent' (pər-sent') *n.* parts per hundred.

per·cent'age (-ij) *n.* 1, rate or proportion per hundred; proportion; commission. 2, (*Colloq.*) profit; advantage.

per·cep'ti·ble (pər-sep'tə-bəl) *adj.* perceivable. —**per·cep"ti·bil'i·ty**, *n.*

per·cep'tion (pər-sep'shən) *n.* the act or faculty of perceiving.

per·cep'tive (-tive) *adj.* quick to perceive. —**per·cep'tive·ness**, *n.*

perch (pêrch) *n.* 1, any of various edible fishes. 2, any of several units of measure, as a rod, a sq. rod, etc. 3, a roost for birds. —*v.i.* roost.

per·chance' (pər-chåns) *adv.* perhaps.

Per'che·ron" (pêr'chə-ron") *n.* one of a breed of draft horses.

per·cip'i·ent (pər-sip'ē-ənt) *adj.* perceiving. —**per·cip'i·ence**, *n.*

per'co·late" (pêr'kə-lāt") *v.t.* pass (a liquid) through a porous substance. —*v.i.* seep; filter. —**per"co·la'tion**, *n.* —**per'co·la"tor**, *n.* a pot for cooking coffee.

per·cus'sion (pər-kush'ən) *n.* the forcible striking of one body against another. —**percussion cap**, a cap filled with powder on the end of a cartridge. —**percussion instrument**, a drum, cymbals, etc.

per di'em (pər dī'əm) a daily expense allowance (*Lat.*: by the day).

per·di'tion (pər-dish'ən) *n.* 1, utter ruin. 2, eternal damnation.

per"e·gri·na'tion (per"ə-grə-nā'shən) *n.* a wandering about from place to place.

per·emp'to·ry (pə-remp'tə-rē) *adj.* 1, admitting no refusal. 2, dogmatic; dictatorial.

per·en'ni·al (pə-ren'ē-əl) *adj.* 1, lasting several years, as a plant. 2, long-lasting; continuing. —*n.* a perennial plant.

per'fect (pêr'fikt) *adj.* 1, complete in every detail. 2, without defect; flawless. 3, of the highest type. 4, exact; precise. 5, thoroughly learned or skilled. 6, (*Colloq.*) utter; complete. 7, (*Gram.*) denoting the tense of a verb that expresses completed action. —*n.* the perfect tense. —*v.t.* (pər-fekt') 1, complete; finish. 2, make perfect. —**per·fec'tion** (pər-fek'shən), **per'fect·ness**, *n.*

per·fec'to (pər-fek'tō) *n.* a shape of cigar.

per'fi·dy (pêr'fə-dē) *n.* breach of faith; treachery. —**per·fid'i·ous**, *adj.*

per'fo·rate" (pêr'fə-rāt') *v.t.* bore through; make a series of holes in. —*adj.* perforated.

per"fo·ra'tion (pêr"fə-rā'shən) *n.* 1, act of perforating. 2, a hole or row of holes, as in paper.

per·force' (pər-fôrs') *adv.* of necessity.

per·form' (pər-fôrm') *v.t.* carry out; do. —*v.i.* 1, work; operate. 2, act, sing, or play in public. —**per·form'ance**, *n.*

per·fume' (pər-fūm') *v.t.* make fragrant. —*n.* 1, a pleasant scent; aroma. 2, a volatile sweet-smelling liquid.

per·fum'e·ry (pər-fūm'ə-rē) *n.* **1,** perfumes in general. **2,** a place where perfumes are made or sold.

per·func'to·ry(pər-funk'tə-rē)*adj.* done merely from a sense of duty; casual; superficial.

per'go·la (pĕr'gə-lə) *n.* a latticework over a walk; an arbor.

per·haps' (pər-haps') *adv.* possibly; it may be.

pe'ri (pē'rē) *n.* an elf; fairy.

per·i- *pref.* a-round; about.

Pergola

per'il (per'əl) *n.* danger; risk. —*v.t.* imperil. —**per'il·ous,** *adj.*

per·im'e·ter (pə-rim'i-tər) *n.* the outer boundary; circumference.

pe'ri·od (pir'ē-əd) *n.* **1,** an era; epoch. **2,** a specified division of time; a recurring event or its duration. **3,** the sign (.) marking the end of a declarative sentence. **4,** termination.

pe"ri·od'ic (pir'ē-od'ik) *adj.* recurring at regular intervals. —**pe"ri·o·dic'i·ty** (-ə-dis'ə-tē) *n.*

pe"ri·od'i·cal (pir"ē-od'ə-kəl) *adj.* **1,** periodic. **2,** published at regular intervals. —*n.* a periodical magazine.

per"i·pa·tet'ic (per"ə-pə-tet'ik) *adj.* walking about; itinerant.

pe·riph'e·ry (pə-rif'ə-rē) *n.* the outer boundary line. —**pe·riph'er·al,** *adj.*

per'i·scope (per'ə-skōp") *n.* an instrument for seeing above or around an obstacle.

per'ish *v.i.* waste away; disappear; die. —**per'ish·a·ble,** *adj.* & *n.* mortal; easily spoiled, as goods.

per"i·to·ne'um (per"ə-tə-nē'əm) *n.* the membrane lining the abdominal cavity.

per"i·to·ni'tis (per"ə-tə-ni'tis) *n.* inflammation of the peritoneum.

per'i·wig (per'i-wig) *n.* peruke.

per'i·win"kle (per'ə-wing"kəl) *n.* a trailing evergreen plant with blue flowers; myrtle.

per'jure (pĕr'jər) *v.t.* make (oneself) guilty of perjury. —**per'jured,** *adj.* constituting, or guilty of, perjury. —**per'jur·er,** *n.*

per'ju·ry (pĕr'jə-rē) *n.* the willful giving of false testimony under oath.

perk (pĕrk) *v.t.* & *i.* (with *up*) lift (one's head, ears) eagerly; be cheered.

per'ma·nent (pĕr'mə-nənt) *adj.* lasting; fixed; not temporary. —*n.* a long-lasting artificial wave for the hair. —**per'ma·nence,** *n.*

per'me·a·ble (pĕr'mē-ə-bəl) *adj.* porous. —**per"me·a·bil'i·ty,** *n.*

per'me·ate" (pĕr'mē-āt") *v.t.* & *i.* seep through the pores (of); penetrate; spread through. —**per"me·a'tion,** *n.*

per·mis'si·ble (pər-mis'ə-bəl) *adj.* allowable. —**per·mis"si·bil'i·ty,** *n.*

per·mis'sion (pĕr-mish'ən) *n.* act of permitting; consent; license.

per·mis'sive (pər-mis'iv) *adj.* **1,** permitted. **2,** permitting.

per'mit (pĕr'mit) *n.* a written license to do something. —*v.t.* (pər-mit') [**per·mit'ted,** **-ting**] **1,** allow. **2,** give formal consent to. —*v.i.* make possible..

per"mu·ta'tion (pĕr"mū-tā'shən) *n.* any possible arrangement of any units in a group.

per·mute' (pər-mūt') *v.t.* **1,** alter; **2,** make permutations of.

per·ni'cious(pər-nish'əs)*adj.* highly destructive; ruinous. —**per·ni'cious·ness,** *n.*

per·nick'et·y (pər-nik'ə-tē) *adj.* (*Colloq.*) excessively meticulous.

per"o·ra'tion (per"ə-rā'shən) *n.* an emphatic or summarizing conclusion of a speech.

per·ox'ide (pə-rok'sīd) *n.* **1,** a chemical compound with a high oxygen content. **2,** hydrogen peroxide, an antiseptic liquid.

per"pen·dic'u·lar (pĕr"pən-dik'yə-lər) *adj.* **1,** perfectly vertical. **2,** (*Geom.*) meeting a line or surface at right angles. —*n.* a vertical line. —**per"pen·dic"u·lar'i·ty,** *n.*

per'pe·trate" (pĕr'pə-trāt") *v.t.* commit (a crime); be guilty of. —**per"pe·tra'tion,** *n.* —**per'pe·tra"tor,** *n.*

per·pet'u·al (pər-pech'oo-əl) *adj.* **1,** everlasting. **2,** continuous.

per·pet'u·ate" (-āt") *v.t.* cause to continue indefinitely; preserve from oblivion. —**per·pet"u·a'tion,** *n.*

per"pe·tu'i·ty (pĕr"pə-tū'ə-tē) *n.* endless existence or duration.

per·plex' (pər-pleks') *v.t.* make confused or bewildered; puzzle. —**per·plex'i·ty,** *n.*

per'qui·site (pĕr'kwi-zit) *n.* extra payment received because of one's regular work, as a tip.

per'se·cute" (pĕr'si-kūt") *v.t.* **1,** make suffer for divergent principles; harass persistently. —**per"se·cu'tion,** *n.* —**per'se·cu"tor,** *n.*

per"se·vere' (pĕr"sə-vir') v.i. persist in something undertaken. —**per"se·ver'ance,** n.

Per'sian (pĕr'zhən) adj. & n. pert. to ancient Persia, or Iran, its people or language. —**Persian lamb,** a fur: caracul.

per'si·flage" (pĕr'si-fläzh") n. flippant, bantering talk.

per·sim'mon (pər-sim'ən) n. a tree or its pulpy, acid fruit.

per·sist' (pər-zist') v.i. 1, continue despite opposition. 2, endure; recur. —**per·sist'ence, per·sist'en·cy,** n. —**per·sist'ent,** adj.

per'son (pĕr'sən) n. 1, a human being. 2, the human body. 3, (Gram.) the distinction between the speaker (first person), person spoken to (second person), and person spoken of (third person).

per'son·a·ble (-ə-bəl) adj. attractive in manner and appearance.

per'son·age (-ij) n. an important person.

per'son·al (-əl) adj. 1, one's own; private. 2, done by oneself, not a representative or representation. 3, (of a remark) invidious. 4, (Gram.) denoting person. 5, of property, movable. —**per'son·al·ty** (-tē) n. personal property.

per·son·al'i·ty (-ə-tē) n. 1, distinctive character; individuality. 2, (pl.) gossip.

per·son'i·fy" (pər-son'ə-fī') v.t. 1, attribute human qualities to (an object, quality, etc.). 2, exemplify; typify. —**per·son"i·fi·ca'tion,** n.

per·son·nel' (pĕr"sə-nel') n. employees (of a particular employer).

per·spec'tive (pər-spek'tiv) n. 1, point of view. 2, the proper relative position of objects or phenomena one perceives.

per·spi·ca'cious (pĕr"spə-kā'shəs) adj. mentally acute. —**per"spi·cac'i·ty** (-kas'ə-tē) n.

per·spic'u·ous (pər-spik'ū-əs) adj. easily understood; lucid. —**per"spi·cu'i·ty** (-kū'ə-tē) n.

per·spire' (pər-spīr') v.i. & t. excrete waste fluids through the pores; sweat. —**per"spi·ra'tion,** n.

per·suade' (pər-swād') v.t. prevail upon by argument or entreaty; convince.

per·sua'sion (pər-swā'zhən) n. act or effect of persuading. —**per·sua'sive** (-siv) adj. serving to persuade.

pert (pĕrt) adj. saucy; impudent. —**pert'ness,** n.

per·tain' (pər-tān') v.i. (with to) 1, belong as a part. 2, have reference or relation; relate; bear upon; be connected with.

per"ti·na'cious (pĕr"ti·nā'shəs) adj. stubbornly holding to an opinion, purpose, etc. —**per"ti·nac'i·ty** (-nas'ə-tē) n.

per'ti·nent (pĕr'tə-nənt) adj. to the point; appropriate; relevant; pertaining. —**per'ti·nence,** n.

per·turb' (pər-tĕrb') v.t. agitate; disturb greatly. —**per"tur·ba'tion,** n.

per·tus'sis (pər-tus'əs) n. whooping cough.

pe·ruke' (pə-rook') n. a wig:

pe·ruse' (pə-rooz') v.t. read attentively. —**pe·rus'al,** n.

Pe·ru'vi·an (pə-roo'vē·ən) adj. of or pert. to Peru. —n. a native or citizen of Peru.

per·vade' (pər-vād') v.t. spread through every part of; permeate. —**per·va'sive,** adj.

per·verse' (pər-vĕrs') adj. selfwilled; contrary. —**per·verse'ness,** n. —**per·ver'si·ty,** n.

per·vert' (pər-vĕrt') v.t. 1, divert from its intended meaning, use, etc. 2, lead astray; corrupt. —n. (pĕr'vĕrt) a perverted person. —**per·ver'sion** (-zhən) n.

pe·se'ta (pə-sā'tə) n. the monetary unit of Spain, worth about 2½ U. S. cents.

pes'ky (pes'kē) adj. (Colloq.) troublesome. —**pes'ki·ness,** n.

pe'so (pā'sō) n. [pl. -sos] a coin of varying value used in Latin Amer.

pes'si·mism (pes'ə-miz-əm) n. a tendency to expect the worse. —**pes'si·mist,** n. —**pes'si·mis'tic,** adj. —**pes'si·mis'ti·cal·ly,** adv.

pest n. 1, a pestilence. 2, a person or thing that annoys; nuisance.

pes'ter (pes'tər) v.t. annoy.

pest'house" n. a hospital ward isolated because of infectious disease.

pes·tif'er·ous (pes-tif'ər-əs) adj. 1, bearing infection; noxious. 2, (Colloq.) annoying. —**pes·tif'er·ous·ness,** n.

pes'ti·lence (pes'tə-ləns) n. a devastating epidemic disease. —**pes"ti·len'tial** (-len'shəl) adj.

pes'ti·lent (pes'tə-lənt) adj. 1, poisonous. 2, injurious to morals. 3, troublesome.

pes'tle (pes'əl) n. a tool for pounding substances in a mortar.

pet n. 1, an animal or bird that is cherished. 2, a favorite. 3, a sulking mood. —*adj.* **1,** loved and fondled. **2,** favorite. **3,** expressing fondness. —*v.t.* & *i.* [**pet'ted, -ting**] fondle; engage in amorous caresses.

pet'al (pet'əl) *n.* a leaf of a flower.

pet'cock" *n.* a small faucet.

pe'ter (pē'tər) *v.i.* (*Colloq.*) (with *out*) become exhausted.

pe.tite' (pə-tēt') *n.* (*Fr.*) little. —**pe.tite'ness,** *n.*

pe.ti'tion (pə-tish'ən) *n.* **1,** an earnest entreaty; prayer. **2,** a formal written request. —*v.t.* address a petition to. —**pe.ti'tion.er,** *n.*

pet'rel (pet'rəl) *n.* a sea bird.

pet'ri.fy" (pet'rə-fī") *v.t.* & *i.* turn into stone. —**pet'ri.fac'tion,** *n.*

pet.ro- *pref.* stone.

pet'rol (pet'rəl) *n.* gasoline.

pet'ro.la'tum (pet"rə-lā'təm) *n.* an oil obtained from petroleum.

pe.tro'le.um (pə-trō'lē-əm) *n.* unrefined oil obtained from the earth.

pet'ti.coat" (pet'ē-kōt") *n.* a woman's underskirt.

pet'ti.fog"ger (pet'ē-fog"ər) *n.* a scheming lawyer. —**pet'ti.fog",** *v.i.*

pet'tish (pet'ish) *adj.* peevish. —**pet'tish.ness,** *n.*

pet'ty (pet'ē) *adj.* on a small scale; trivial; mean. —**pet'ti.ness,** *n.* —**petty officer,** a noncommissioned officer in the Navy.

pet'u.lant (pech'ə-lənt) *adj.* peevish; capricious. —**pet'u.lance,** *n.*

pe.tu'ni.a (pə-tū'nē-ə) *n.* a plant or its funnel-shaped flower.

pew (pū) *n.* a bench for worshipers in a church.

pew'ter (pū'tər) *n.* an alloy of tin and lead.

pha'e.ton (fā'ə-tən) *n.* **1,** a light four-wheeled carriage. **2,** a convertible sedan.

-phage *suf.* an eater of. — **-phagous,** *suf.* forming adjectives.

phag'o.cyte" (fag'ə-sīt") *n.* a white corpuscle in the blood, capable of destroying bacteria.

pha'lanx (fā'lanks) *n.* **1,** a body of troops in close formation; a solid group. **2,** [*pl.* **pha.lan'ges** (fə-lan'jēz)] any of the bones of the fingers or toes.

phal'lus (fal'əs) *n.* a symbol or image of the male reproductive organ. —**phal'lic,** *adj.*

phan'tasm (fan'taz-əm) *n.* **1,** a specter. **2,** fantasy; an illusion.

phan'ta.sy (fan'tə-sē) *n.* fantasy.

phan'tom (fan'təm) *n.* an apparition; specter; something unreal.

Phar'aoh (fâr'ō) *n.* a title of ancient Egyptian kings.

phar'i.see" (far'ə-sē") *n.* one who follows the letter, not the spirit, of the (religious) law. —**phar"i.sa'ic** (-sā'ik) *adj.* —**phar"i.sa'i.cal.ly,** *adv.*

phar"ma.ceu'tics (fär"mə-soo'tiks) *n.* pharmacy (def. 1). —**phar"ma.ceu'tic, phar"ma.ceu'ti.cal,** *adj.*

phar"ma.col'o.gy (fär"mə-col'ə-gē) *n.* the science of drugs. —**phar"ma.co.log'i.cal,** *adj.* —**phar"ma.col'o.gist,** *n.*

phar"ma.co.poe'ia (-kō-pē'yə) *n.* an official list of drugs and medicines.

phar'ma.cy (fär'mə-sē) *n.* **1,** the art of compounding drugs according to prescription. **2,** a drugstore. —**phar'ma.cist** (-sist) *n.*

phar'ynx (far'inks) *n.* [*pl.* **pha.ryn'ges** (fə-rin'jēz), phar'ynx.es**] the passage connecting the mouth with the esophagus. —**pha.ryn'ge.al** (fə-rin'jē-əl) *adj.*

phase (fāz) *n.* the aspect in which a thing appears; a stage.

pheas'ant (fez'ənt) *n.* a long-tailed game bird.

Pheasant

phe"no.bar'bi.tal" (fē"nō-bär'bi-tâl") *n.* a drug used as a hypnotic.

phe.nom'e.non" (fi-nom'ə-non") *n.* [*pl.* **-na** (-nə)] **1,** any observable fact in nature. **2,** an odd or notable thing. —**phe.nom'e.nal,** *adj.*

phi (fī) *n.* the twenty-first letter of the Greek alphabet (Φ, φ).

phi'al (fī'əl) *n.* vial.

phil- *pref.* loving; fond of.

phi.lan'der (fi-lan'dər) *v.i.* make trifling love to a woman; flirt.

phi.lan'thro.py (fi-lan'thrə-pē) *n.* **1,** love of mankind; altruism. **2,** a benevolent act, gift, etc. —**phil"an.throp'ic** (fil"ən-throp'ik) *adj.* —**phil"an.throp'i.cal.ly,** *adv.* —**phi.lan'thro.pist** (-thrə-pist) *n.*

phi.lat'e.ly (fi-lat'ə-lē) *n.* the collecting and study of stamps and related postal materials. —**phi.lat'e.list,** *n.*

phil"har.mon'ic (fil"här-mon'ik) *adj.* fond of or devoted to music.

Phil·ip·pine (fil'ə-pēn) *adj.* pert. to the Philippine Islands or Republic.

Phi·lis'tine (fi-lis'tin) *n.* an uncultured, materialistic person.

phi·lol'o·gy (fi-lol'ə-jē) *n.* the science of the origins, laws, etc. of languages. —**phil'o·log'i·cal**, *adj.* —**phi·lol'o·gist**, *n.*

phi·los'o·pher (fi-los'ə-fer) *n.* **1**, a student of philosophy. **2**, a philosophical person.

phil'o·soph'i·cal (fil'o-sof'ə-kəl) *adj.* **1**, pert. to philosophy. **2**, serene in adversity. Also, **phil'o·soph'ic**.

phi·los'o·phy (fi-los'ə-fē) *n.* **1**, the science dealing with the general causes and principles of things. **2**, personal attitude. —**phi·los'o·phize'** (-fīz") *v.i.*

phil'ter (fil'tər) *n.* a love potion. Also, **phil'tre**.

phle·bi'tis (fli-bī'tis) *n.* inflammation of a vein.

phlegm (flem) *n.* **1**, thick mucus secreted in throat and bronchi. **2**, sluggishness; apathy.

phleg·mat'ic (fleg-mat'ik) *adj.* **1**, apathetic; unexcitable. **2**, pert. to phlegm. —**phleg·mat'ic·al·ly**, *adv.*

phlox (floks) *n.* a tall, summer perennial bearing large flower heads.

-phobe (fōb) *suf.* one who fears or hates.

pho'bi·a (fō'bē-ə) *n.* an irrational fear or dread.

phoe'be (fē'bē) *n.* a bird, a small American flycatcher.

phoe'nix (fē'niks) *n.* a fabled bird that burned itself and rose from its own ashes.

Phlox

phon- *pref.* sound, voice, speech.

phone (fōn) *n.* (*Colloq.*) telephone.

pho·net'ic (fō-net'ik) *adj.* pert. to speech sounds; in spelling, using always the same symbol for each sound. —**pho·net'i·cal·ly**, *adv.* —**pho·net'ics**, *n.sing.*

pho'no·graph' (fō'nə-gråf") *n.* a machine for reproducing recorded sounds. —**pho'no·graph'ic**, *adj.*

pho'ny (fō'nē) *adj.* (*Slang*) fake; spurious. —*n.* a fake or faker.

phos'phate (fos'fāt) *n.* **1**, a compound of phosphorus used as a fertilizer. **2**, an effervescent drink.

phos"pho·res'cence (fos"fə-res'əns) *n.* the property of giving out luminous light without sensible heat. —**phos"pho·res'cent**, *adj.*

phos'pho·rus (fos'fə-rəs) *n.* a waxy, luminous nonmetallic element, no. 15, symbol P.

pho·to- (fō'tō) *pref.* **1**, light. **2**, photographic.

pho'to (fō'tō) *n.* photograph.

pho'to·e·lec'tric cell a device for controlling an electric circuit by light falling on it: *electric eye.*

pho"to·en·grav'ing *n.* a reproduction of pictures on letterpress printing plates by a photographic process.

photo finish (in a race) one so close that the winner must be determined from a photograph.

pho"to·gen'ic (-jen'ik) *adj.* easy to photograph effectively.

pho'to·graph" (fō'tə-gråf") *n.* a picture made by exposing a chemically treated surface to light. —**pho'to·graph'ic**, *adj.* —**pho'to·graph'i·cal·ly**, *adv.*

pho·tog'ra·phy (fə-tog'rə-fē) *n.* the taking of photographs. —**pho·tog'ra·pher**, *n.*

pho'ton (fō'ton) *n.* a particle of radiant energy moving with the velocity of light.

pho"to·off'set *n.* lithography from plates made photographically.

pho'to·play" *n.* a motion picture.

pho'to·sphere" *n.* the luminous envelope of the sun.

pho'to·stat" *n.* (*T.N.*) a facsimile or negative copy, photographed directly onto paper. —**pho'to·stat'ic**, *adj.*

pho'to·syn'the·sis *n.* the process by which plants make carbohydrates from light and air.

phrase (frāz) *n.* **1**, a group of words used as though one. **2**, a short, pithy expression. **3**, (*Music*) a group of notes played or sung connectedly. —*v.t.* express in words.

phra"se·ol'o·gy (frā"zē-ol'ə-jē) *n.* choice of words.

phre·net'ic (fri-net'ik) *adj.* **1**, insane; violent. **2**, fanatic; zealous. —**phre·net'i·cal·ly**, *adv.*

phre·nol'o·gy (fre-nol'ə-jē) *n.* character-reading from the form of the skull. —**phre·nol'o·gist**, *n.*

phthi'sis (thī'sis) *n.* **1**, tuberculosis of the lungs. **2**, bodily decay.

phy·lac'ter·y (fə-lak'tə-rē) *n.* **1**, a small leather box containing scriptures, worn by pious Jews. **2**, an amulet; talisman.

phy·lo- *pref.* tribe or race.

phy'lum (fī'ləm) *n.* [*pl.* **-la**] a primary division of the animal or vegetable kingdom.

phys'ic (fiz'ik) *n.* a medicine; specif., a cathartic.

phys'i·cal (fiz'i-kəl) *adj.* **1,** pert. to the body. **2,** pert. to nature or to the material. **3,** pert. to physics.

phy·si'cian (fə-zish'ən) *n.* a doctor of medicine.

phys'ics (fiz'iks) *n.* the science dealing with the properties of matter and energy. **—phys'i·cist** (-i-sist) *n.*

phys"i·og'no·my (fiz"ē-og'nə-mē) *n.* the face; external aspect.

phys"i·ol'o·gy (fiz"ē-ol'ə-jē) *n.* the science dealing with the processes of living. **—phys"i·o·log'i·cal,** *adj.* **—phys"i·ol'o·gist,** *n.*

phy·sique' (fi-zēk') *n.* the structure and development of the body.

pi (pī) *n.* **1,** the sixteenth letter of (the Greek alphabet (Π, π), also (π) denoting the ratio of the circumference of a circle to its diameter, about 3.1416. **2,** a jumbled mass of printing type. **—v.t.** [**pied, pie'ing**] jumble (type).

pi"a·nis'si·mo" (pē"ə-nis'i-mō") *adj. & adv.* very soft.

pi·an'ist (pē-an'ist; pē'ə-nist) *n.* one who plays on the piano.

pi·an'o (pē-an'ō) *n.* [*pl.* **-os**] a large stringed musical instrument with a keyboard. **—adj. & adv.** soft. **—pi·an'o·forte"** (-fôrt") *n.* a piano.

pi·as'ter (pē-as'tər) *n.* a coin, of varying value, of various countries, as Turkey and Egypt.

pi·az'za (pē-az'ə) *n.* **1,** a porch. **2,** (pē-ät'sə) a public square or walk.

pi'ca (pī'kə) *n.* (*Printing*) 12 points; a type of this depth.

pic·a·dor" (pik'ə-dôr") *n.* a mounted bull-fighter.

pic"a·resque' (pik"ə-resk') *adj.* (of fiction) dealing with rogues.

pic"a·yune' (pik"ə-ūn') *adj.* trifling; of little value.

pic'ca·lil'li (pik'ə-lil"ē) *n.* a pickle of chopped vegetables.

pic'co·lo" (pik'ə-lō") *n.* [*pl.* **-los"**] a small, high-pitched flute. **—pic'co·lo"ist,** *n.*

pick (pik) *n.* **1,** any of various pointed tools, large or small, as for loosening rock, chopping ice, etc.; a pickax. **2,** a hand-gathered crop. **3,** first choice; hence, the choicest. **—v.t. 1,** prick, pierce, clean, open,

etc., with a pointed tool. **2,** (often with *up*) acquire; gain; gather, as crops; take up; lift; pluck. **3,** (often with *out*) choose; select. **4,** rob; open (a lock) without a key. **5,** pull apart; shred. **6,** provoke (a quarrel); (with *on*) nag unfairly. **—v.i. 1,** use a pointed instrument. **2,** nibble at food. **3,** select. **4,** (with *up*) improve; recover. **—pick'er,** *n.* one who chooses wisely.

pick'a·back" *adv.* (riding) on a person's back and shoulders.

pick'a·nin'ny (pik'ə-nin"ē) *n.* (*Offensive*) a Negro child.

pick'ax" *n.* a heavy, wooden-handled digging tool.

Pickerel

pick'er·el (pik'ər-əl) *n.* an edible fish of the pike family.

pick'et (pik'et) *n.* **1,** a pointed stake. **2,** a small body of troops sent out to scout, guard, etc. **3,** a person, as a striking workman, stationed outside a place to protest its operations. **—v.t. & t. 1,** be or post a picket outside a place. **2,** tether.

pick'ings (-ingz) *n.pl.* (*Colloq.*) opportunity to glean or pilfer.

pick'le (pik'əl) *n.* a food preserved in brine or a vinegar solution. **—v.t.** preserve as a pickle. **—pick'led,** *adj.* (*Slang*) drunk.

pick-'me-up" *n.* a stimulating drink.

pick'pock"et *n.* one who steals from others' pockets.

pick-'up" *n.* **1,** an acquaintance met without an introduction. **2,** power of acceleration. **3,** a small open-body motor truck. **—adj.** made of odds and ends.

pic'nic (pik'nik) *n.* a short trip for an outdoor meal. **—v.i.** [**pic'nicked, -nick'ing**] go on a picnic. **—pic'nick·er,** *n.*

pi'cot (pē'kō) *n.* a small projecting loop on the edge of lace, fabric, etc.

pic·tor'i·al (pik-tôr'ē-əl) *adj.* expressed in, consisting of, or illustrated by pictures.

pic'ture (pik'chər) *n.* **1,** a painting, photograph, etc. depicting a person, object, or scene; an image; likeness. **2,** a description in words. **3,** (*pl.*) (*Colloq.*) a motion picture. **—v.t. 1,** portray, depict. **2,** imagine.

pic·tur·esque' (pik-chər-esk') *adj.* colorful; vivid. **—pic·tur·esque'·ness,** *n.*

pid'dling (pid'ling) *adj.* trifling; petty.

pidg'in (pij'ən) *n.* a dialect, *pidgin English*, used between oriental and English-speaking traders.

pie (pī) *n.* food baked in a pastry crust.

pie'bald" (pī'bâld") *adj.* having patches of color. —*n.* a piebald animal, esp. a horse.

piece (pēs) *n.* **1,** a fragment; a part or portion; a tract. **2,** a separate article, as of furniture, etc. **3,** an amount of work to be done. **4,** a definite quantity, as of cloth. **5,** one of the figures used in a game, as chess. **6,** a short literary or musical composition. —*v.t.* (often with *out*) extend or enlarge by adding material. —**piece goods,** dry goods. —**piece of eight,** an old Span. coin.

piece'meal" *adv.* bit by bit; gradually.

piece'work" *n.* work paid for by the piece.

pied (pīd) *adj.* of several colors.

pier (pir) *n.* **1,** a breakwater; a wharf projecting into the water. **2,** a support of a bridge span. **3,** solid masonry between windows, etc. —**pier glass,** a large high mirror.

pierce (pirs) *v.t.* **1,** make a hole in. **2,** stab; enter painfully. **3,** force a way into or through. **4,** wound or affect keenly. —**pierc'ing,** *adj.* (of sound) shrill.

pi'e·ty (pī'ə-tē) *n.* reverence for God; devoutness.

pif'fle (pif'əl) *n.* (*Slang*) nonsense.

pig *n.* **1,** a hog, esp. a young one. **2,** a greedy or dirty person. **3,** a mass of cast molten metal. —**pig iron,** crude iron cast into molds for further processing.

pi'geon (pij'ən) *n.* a dove or related bird.

Pigeon

pi'geon-heart"ed *adj.* easily frightened; meek.

pi'geon-hole" *n.* a small open compartment in a desk. —*v.t.* **1,** file in a pigeonhole; lay aside and ignore. **2,** classify.

pi'geon-toed" (-tōd") *adj.* having the toes turned in.

pig'gish (pig'ish) *adj.* like a pig; gluttonous or dirty. —**pig'gish·ness,** *n.*

pig'gy (-gē) *n.* a small pig.

pig'head"ed *adj.* stubborn.

pig'ment (pig'mənt) *n.* **1,** coloring matter. **2,** the natural coloring matter in the tissues of an animal or plant. —**pig"men·ta'tion,** *n.*

pig'skin" *n.* **1,** leather from pigs' skin. **2,** (*Colloq.*) a football.

pig'tail" *n.* a long hanging braid of hair.

pike (pīk) *n.* **1,** a steel-pointed weapon; a lance. **2,** an edible freshwater fish. **3,** a main road.

pik'er (pī'kər) *n.* (*Slang*) one who bets or spends in a small way.

pi·laf' (pi-läf') *n.* a dish of boiled rice and meat. Also, **pi·lau'** (-low').

pi·las'ter (pi-las'tər) *n.* a rectangular column built partly in a wall.

pile (pīl) *n.* **1,** soft hair; nap on cloth. **2,** a large supporting timber, etc., set in the ground. **3,** a massive edifice. **4,** a heap or mass. **5,** a pyre. **6,** (*Colloq.*) a large quantity; a fortune. —*v.t.* **1,** heap up. **2,** load. —*v.i.* (with *up*) form a heap; accumulate. —**pile driver,** a machine which drives piles by dropping a heavy weight (*drop hammer*) upon them.

pil'fer (pil'fər) *v.t.* & *i.* steal in small amounts. —**pil'fer·er,** *n.*

pil'grim *n.* **1,** one who travels, esp. to a holy place as an act of devotion. **2,** (*cap.*) one of the earliest English settlers in Massachusetts. —**pil'grim·age,** *n.* a journey.

pill (pil) *n.* **1,** a small tablet of medicine. **2,** (*Slang*) a disagreeable person.

pil'lage (pil'ij) *v.t.* & *i.* plunder, esp. in war; sack. —*n.* plunder.

pil'lar (pil'ər) *n.* a supporting or ornamental column; any mainstay.

pill'box" *n.* **1,** a small box for pills. **2,** (*Mil.*) a low, fortified machine-gun position.

pil'lion (pil'yən) *n.* an extra rear saddle or motorcycle seat.

pil'lo·ry (pil'ə-rē) *n.* a frame to hold an offender for exposure to public ridicule. —*v.t.* **1,** punish in the pillory. **2,** invoke scorn upon.

Pillory

pil'low (pil'ō) *n.* a soft cushion to rest the head upon. —*v.t.* lay on a pillow. —**pil'low·case",** **pil'low-slip",** *n.* a cover for a pillow.

pi'lot (pī'lət) *n.* **1,** one who steers or controls a ship or aircraft. **2,** a leader; guide. —*v.t.* direct the course of. —**pilot light,** a small flame from which to ignite a larger.

pi·men'to (pi-men'tō) *n.* [*pl.* -tos]

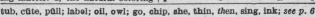

n. 1, the berry of a W. Indies tree; allspice; also, the tree. **2,** pimiento.

pi·mien'to (pi-myen'tō) *n.* [*pl.* -tos] a sweet red pepper.

pimp *n.* an agent or exploiter of prostitutes. —*v.i.* pander.

pim'ple (pim'pəl) *n.* a small eruption on the skin. —**pim'ply,** *adj.*

pin *n.* **1,** a pointed piece, esp. of thin wire, to join or attach things; a peg or bolt; a fastening device employing a pin. **2,** a piece of jewelry attached by a pin; a brooch. **3,** any of various pieces cut from a cylinder, as used in machines, bowling, etc. —*v.t.* [pinned, pin'ning] **1,** hold fast, esp. with a pin. **2,** (*Colloq.*) give a fraternity pin to (a girl) as a token of intention to become engaged.

Pins
Common
Cotter
Clothes
Hair

pin'a·fore" (pin'ə-fôr") *n.* a child's apron.

pin'ball" *n.* a bagatelle game in which the scores are electrically recorded.

pince-'nez" (pans'ne') *n.* (*Fr.*) eyeglasses held on the nose by a spring.

pin'cers (pin'sərz) *n. pl.* or *sing.* **1,** a gripping tool, two arms hinged off-center (see *pliers*). **2,** the gripping claws of lobsters, crabs, etc. **3,** (*Mil.*) simultaneous attacks from different directions.

pinch *v.t. & i.* **1,** nip or squeeze between two surfaces. **2,** cramp; afflict, as with cold, poverty, etc.; be frugal. **3,** (*Slang*) capture; arrest. **4,** (*Slang*) steal. —*n.* **1,** a squeeze; nip. **2,** a tiny amount. **3,** painful stress. **4,** a critical juncture; emergency. **5,** (*Slang*) a raid; arrest.

pinch-'hit" *v.i.* in baseball, go to bat for another; act as substitute, esp. in an emergency.

pin'cush"ion *n.* a small cushion in which to keep pins.

pine (pīn) *n.* a cone-bearing evergreen tree with needle-shaped leaves; its timber. —*v.i.* **1,** grieve; languish. **2,** long (for).

pine'ap"ple (pīn'ap"əl) *n.* **1,** a tropical plant or its sweet, juicy cone-shaped fruit. **2,** a small bomb in this shape.

pin'feath"ers *n.* feather stems just emerging.

ping *n.* the whistling sound of a projectile.

ping-'pong" *n.* (*T.N.*) table tennis.

pin'head" *n.* (*Colloq.*) **1,** a person with a very small head. **2,** a dolt.

pin'hole" *n.* a tiny hole or dent.

pin'ion (pin'yən) *n.* **1,** a small gear wheel. **2,** the end segment of a bird's wing; a feather; a wing. —*v.t.* restrain, as by cutting the wings or pinning the arms.

pink *n.* **1,** a garden plant or its spicy, fringed flower. **2,** a light-red color. **3,** a person mildly inclined to communism. **4,** the best degree. —*v.t.* **1,** pierce; prick. **2,** finish with a serrated edge.

pink'eye" *n.* a contagious disease of the eye; conjunctivitis.

pink'ie (-ē) *n.* the little finger.

pin money a small sum allowed for personal expenditures.

pin'nace (pin'is) *n.* a light, two-masted vessel; a small boat.

pin'na·cle (pin'ə-kəl) *n.* **1,** a sharp point or peak; a spire. **2,** the highest point; acme.

pin'nate (pin'āt) *adj.* shaped like a feather.

pi'noch"le (pē'nuk"əl) *n.* a card game.

pin'point" *n.* extreme exactitude; a pin's point or similar fineness. —*v.t.* locate exactly, as for precision bombing.

pint (pīnt) *n.* a measure of capacity, 16 liquid oz., one-half quart.

pin'tail" *n.* a wild duck with a pointed tail.

pin'to (pin'tō) *adj.* mottled. —*n.* a piebald horse or pony.

pin-'up girl an attractive young woman or her picture.

pin'wheel" *n.* **1,** a wheel that spins on a pin when blown upon. **2,** revolving fireworks.

pin'y (pī'nē) *adj.* of the pine.

pi"o·neer' (pī'ə-nir') *n.* one who goes ahead; an early settler. —*v.t. & i.* do or be first.

pi'ous (pī'əs) *adj.* **1,** godly; devout. **2,** pretending piety. —**pi'ous·ness,** *n.*

pip *n.* **1,** a disease of fowls. **2,** a small seed, as of an apple; something like it, as a spot on dice, a suit symbol on playing cards, etc. **3,** (*Slang*) something remarkable.

pipe (pīp) *n.* **1,** a long tube for conveying a fluid. **2,** a tube and its attached bowl, for smoking. **3,** one of the tubes of an organ. **4,** (*Archaic*) a musical wind instrument. **5,** a shrill voice; a bird's note. —*v.t.* **1,** supply with, or convey by, pipe. **2,** (*Naut.*) summon or salute with the sound of a whistle or pipe. **3,** utter in a shrill voice; whistle. —*v.i.* **1,** chirp; whistle. **2,** play on a pipe.

pipe dream a vain hope.

pipe line 1, a pipe for conveying oil or gas over long distances. 2, a means of obtaining secret information.

pipe organ a large musical instrument played by releasing compressed air through pipes.

pip'er n. a flutist or bagpiper.

pip'ing n. a trim of covered cord.

pip'pin (pip'in) n. 1, a variety of apple. 2, (Slang) something lovely.

pi'quant (pē'kənt) adj. agreeably pungent; attractive though racy. —pi'quan·cy, n.

pique (pēk) v.t. 1, wound the pride of; nettle. 2, arouse the interest of. —n. wounded pride; umbrage.

pi·qué' (pė-kā') n. a ribbed fabric.

pi·quet' (pi-ket') n. a card game for two.

pi'ra·cy (pī'rə-sē) n. act or crime of a pirate.

pi'rate (pī'rət) n. 1, a sea-robber; his ship. 2, one who steals a literary or artistic idea. —pi·rat'i·cal (pi-rat'i-kəl) adj.

pir"ou·ette' (pir'ə-wet') n. in ballet dancing, a spinning on the toes.

pis"ca·to'ri·al (pis"kə-tôr'ė-əl) adj. pert. to fishing or fishermen.

Pis'ces (pis'ēz) n. a constellation, the Fish (see zodiac).

pish interj. nonsense!

pis'mire (pis'mīr") n. an ant.

pis·ta'chi·o' (pis-tä'shė-ō") n. [pl. -os" (-ōz")] a tree bearing a greenish edible nut; the nut.

pis'til n. (Bot.) the seed-bearing organ of a flower.

pis'tol (pis'təl) n. a small firearm held and fired by one hand.

pis·tole' (pis-tōl') n. a former gold coin of various countries, esp. Spain.

pis'ton (pis'tən) n. a cylinder moving within a fitting bore to impart motion.

pit n. 1, a hole in the ground; an abyss; a mine, or shaft in a mine. 2, a depression; a small scar. 3, a small arena; (Brit.) the cheaper seats in a theater. 4, an area for trading in a stock or grain exchange, etc. 5, the stone of a fruit. —v.t. [pit'ted, -ting] 1, make scars in. 2, match (one person or force) against another. 3, remove the pits from, as fruit.

pitch (pich) v.t. 1, hurl; toss; throw. 2, set up, as a tent. 3, (Music) start (a tune) by sounding the key-note. —v.i. 1, toss something; specif., throw a ball to a batter. 2, encamp. 3, plunge headlong; also, incline; slope. 4, (with on or upon) decide. 5, rise and fall, as a ship at sea. —n. 1, a throw, toss. 2, a headlong fall. 3, the fore-and-aft plunging of a ship. 4, the extreme point or degree of height or depth. 5, slope; a declivity. 6, (Music) highness or lowness of tone. 7, a thick black substance; tar.

pitch'blende" (pich'blend") n. a lustrous black mineral, a source of radium and uranium.

pitch dark completely dark.

pitch'er (-ər) n. 1, a vessel with a handle for holding liquids. 2, the player in baseball who pitches.

pitch'fork" n. a tool for lifting hay.

pit'e·ous (pit'ė-əs) adj. sad; arousing pity. —pit'e·ous·ness, n.

pit'fall" n. a trap; a hidden danger.

pith n. 1, the spongy tissue in the stems of certain plants. 2, the essential part; gist. 3, vigor. —pith'y, adj.

pit'i·a·ble (pit'ė-ə-bəl) adj. deserving pity. —pit'i·a·ble·ness, n.

pit'i·ful (-fəl) adj. 1, deserving pity. 2, paltry. —pit'i·ful·ness, n.

pit'i·less (-ləs) adj. unmerciful. —pit'i·less·ness, n.

pit'tance (pit'əns) n. a very small quantity, esp. of money.

pi·tu'i·tar"y (pi-tū'ə-ter"ė) adj. pert. to a small endocrine gland.

pit'y (pit'ė) n. 1, a feeling of compassion for another's grief or suffering. 2, a cause of regret. —v.t. feel compassion for.

piv'ot (piv'ət) n. a pin on which an object turns; hence, a cardinal or critical point. —v.i. turn; hinge. —piv'ot·al, adj.

pix'i·lat"ed (pik'sə-lā'tid) adj. (Colloq.) mentally eccentric.

pix'y (pik'sė) n. a mischievous elf. Also, pix'ie.

plac'ard (plak'ərd) n. a notice posted in a public place; poster —v.t. place a poster on.

pla'cate (plā'kāt) v.t. pacify; conciliate. —pla'ca·to·ry, adj.

place (plās) n. 1, region; locality; spot; a particular spot or building. 2, room to stand or sit in. 3, the proper or allocated position for anything. 4, a job; situation. 5, social status; duty. 6, second in a horse race. —v.t. 1, put or set in a particular position; set in order; arrange. 2, find a home or job for. 3, put; repose. 4, locate; identify, as by association. —*v.i.* finish second. —**take place**, occur. —**place kick**, (*Football*) a kick of the ball held upright on the ground.

place'ment (-mənt) *n.* **1**, act or result of placing. **2**, employment. **3**, a place kick.

pla·cen·ta (plə-sen'tə) *n.* the organ in the womb to which the fetus is attached.

plac'er (plas'ər) *n.* in mining, a place where sand, gravel, etc., is washed for gold.

plac'id (plas'id) *adj.* serene; unruffled. —**pla·cid'i·ty**, *n.*

plack'et (plak'it) *n.* a slit in a skirt, coat tail, etc.

pla'gi·a·rism (plā'jə-riz-əm) *n.* the offering of another's artistic or literary work as one's own. —**pla'gi·a·rist**, *n.* —**pla'gi·a·rize**", *v.t. & i.*

plague (plāg) *n.* **1**, a pestilential epidemic disease. **2**, severe trouble; scourge. **3**, (*Colloq.*) a nuisance. —*v.t.* **1**, harass; annoy. **2**, afflict with the plague. —**pla'guy**, *adj.*

plaid (plad) *n.* a wool fabric with a tartan or similar pattern. —*adj.* having a crossbarred pattern.

plain (plān) *adj.* **1**, flat; level; unobstructed; open. **2**, easily understood. **3**, sheer; downright. **4**, without a figured pattern. **5**, not handsome or fancy; homely. **6**, simple; sincere; frank. —*n.* an extent of level country. —**plain'ness**, *n.*

plain'clothes"man (-mən) *n.* [*pl.* -men] a detective not in uniform.

plains'man (plānz'mən) *n.* [*pl.* -men] a dweller on an undeveloped plain.

plain'song" *n.* a liturgical chant.

plain-'spo'ken *adj.* frank. —**plain-'spo'ken·ness**, *n.*

plaint (plānt) *n.* **1**, a sad song; lamentation. **2**, a complaint.

plain'tiff (plān'tif) *n.* (*Law*) the person who brings suit.

plain'tive (plān'tiv) *adj.* mournful. —**plain'tive·ness**, *n.*

plait (plāt) *n.* **1**, a braid, as of hair. **2**, an overlapping fold; pleat. —*v.t.* braid (hair).

plan *n.* **1**, a diagram or drawing, esp. of an uncompleted structure. **2**, arrangement of parts in a certain design. **3**, a formulated scheme for getting something done. —*v.t.* [**planned, plan'ning**] **1**, make a design or diagram of. **2**, devise ways and means for. —*v.i.* decide on future acts. —**plan'ner**, *n.*

plane (plān) *adj.* level; flat. —*n.* **1**, a flat or level surface. **2**, a grade or

level, as of thought, etc. **3**, an airplane. **4**, a tool for smoothing wood. **5**, a type of tree, as the sycamore. —*v.t.* smooth with a plane.

plan'et (plan'it) *n.* a celestial body revolving around the sun. —**plan'e·tar·y**, *adj.*

plan"e·tar'i·um (plan"i-tār'ē-əm) *n.* [*pl.* -a] a device to represent the heavenly bodies and their movement.

plan'et·oid" *n.* a minor planet.

plank *n.* **1**, a long, thick board. **2**, an item of a political party's platform. —*v.t.* **1**, cover with planks. **2**, (with *down*) pay; deliver. **3**, cook and serve on a board.

plant (plant) *n.* **1**, a living organism, lacking voluntary motion, usually rooted in and growing from the soil. **2**, a seedling or cutting; anything planted. **3**, a factory; a business building and its equipment. —*v.t.* **1**, put in the ground to grow. **2**, set firmly in position. **3**, (*Slang*) secrete (something) to trick or incriminate someone.

plan'tain (plan'tin) *n.* **1**, a common weed with broad leaves. **2**, a tropical tree; its bananalike fruit.

plan·ta'tion (plan-tā'shən) *n.* a large estate on which cotton or sugar, etc. is cultivated.

plant'er *n.* a rich farmer; a plantation owner.

plaque (plak) *n.* an ornamental or commemorative tablet.

plas'ma (plaz'mə) *n.* the liquid part of blood, lymph, or milk.

plas'ter (plås'tər) *n.* **1**, a wet paste of lime, sand, water, etc. that dries to a hard smooth finish. **2**, a remedy spread on cloth and applied to the body. —*v.t.* **1**, apply plaster to. **2**, spread on. —**plas'tered**, *adj.* (*Slang*) drunk. —**plas'ter·ing**, *n.*

plaster cast **1**, a model (as of a statue) cast in plaster. **2**, (*Surgery*) a cast form to prevent movement.

plaster of Paris a white paste used in molding statuettes, panels, etc.

plas'tic (plas'tik) *adj.* capable of being molded, esp. by pressure; pliant. —*n.* a plastic substance, esp. one of a group of synthetic materials used as substitutes for wood, metal, etc. —**plas'ti·cal·ly**, *adv.* —**plastic surgery**, surgery to rectify deformities or mutilations.

plas·tic'i·ty (plas-tis'ə-tē) *n.* state of being plastic.

plate (plāt) *n.* **1**, a thin flat sheet of metal, glass, etc.; such a sheet used or prepared for any purpose, as printing, photography, etc. **2**, a shallow dish for food; its contents. **3**, gold and silver table dishes and utensils. **4**, a denture; a setting for false teeth. —*v.t.* apply a coating of metal to.

pla·teau' (pla-tō') *n.* an extent of elevated land; a tableland.

plat'en (plat'ən) *n.* **1**, the plate that presses paper against printing type. **2**, the roller of a typewriter.

plat'form (plat'fôrm) *n.* **1**, a raised flooring. **2**, a statement of political policies.

plat'i·num (plat'ə-nəm) *n.* a precious silver-white metallic element, no. 78, symbol Pt.

plat'i·tude" (plat'i-tood") *n.* a trite remark. —**plat"i·tu'di·nous,** *adj.*

pla·ton'ic (plə-ton'ik) *adj.* solely spiritual; not sensual. —**pla·ton'i·cal·ly,** *adv.*

pla·toon' (plə-toon') *n.* a body of troops, comprising several squads.

plat'ter (plat'ər) *n.* a broad shallow dish for serving food.

plat'y·pus (plat'ə-pəs) *n.* a small, egg-laying, aquatic mammal with a bill like a duck's.

Platypus

plau'dit (plä'dit) *n.* (usually *pl.*) applause.

plau'si·ble (plä'zə-bəl) *adj.* seemingly true or trustworthy. —**plau"si·bil'i·ty,** *n.*

play (plā) *v.i.* **1**, move lightly and quickly; flicker; dart. **2**, engage in a game; take recreation. **3**, act; behave. **4**, act on the stage; perform music. —*v.t.* **1**, engage in (a game); compete against; bet on. **2**, perform upon (a musical instrument). **3**, perform (a play, musical composition, trick, etc.); assume the rôle of. **4**, put in operation or motion. —*n.* **1**, brisk or free motion; freedom; scope. **2**, amusement; diversion; fun; jest. **3**, a dramatic work. **4**, in a game, one's turn to act; the move made or action taken.

play'bill" *n.* a theater program.

play'boy" *n.* (*Slang*) a rich, frivolous man.

play'er *n.* a performer in a game, play, etc.

play'ful *adj.* frolicsome; jocular. —**play'ful·ness,** *n.*

play'go"er *n.* one who regularly attends plays.

play'ground" *n.* a field for games, etc.

play'house" *n.* **1**, theater. **2**, a small house for children's play.

playing card one of the pasteboard cards, 2¼ or 2½ by 3½ inches, used in many games.

play'mate" *n.* a companion at play. Also, **play'fel"low.**

play'-off" *n.* a contest to decide a previous tie.

play'thing" *n.* a toy.

play'wright" *n.* a dramatist:

pla'za (plä'zə) *n.* an open square:

plea (plē) *n.* **1**, an entreaty. **2**, pretext; excuse. **3**, (*Law*) a defendant's answer to the charge against him.

plead (plēd) *v.i.* **1**, (with *with*) try to persuade; beg; implore. **2**, (*Law*) present a plea. —*v.t.* urge or allege as an excuse or defense. —**plead'ings,** *n. pl.* statements made in court.

pleas'ant (plez'ənt) *adj.* agreeable: —**pleas'ant·ness,** *n.*

pleas'ant·ry (plez'ən-trē) *n:* **1**, banter. **2**, a jest.

please (plēz) *v.t.* give satisfaction or delight to. —*v.i.* **1**, give satisfaction. **2**, choose; wish; think fit. —*adv.* if you so wish: a polite form in imperative construction, short for if [it] you please, as in *please do this.* —**pleas'ing,** *adj.* attractive; agreeable.

pleas'ure (plezh'ər) *n.* **1**, a feeling of enjoyment or delight. **2**, a cause or source of this feeling. **3**, desire; preference. —**pleas'ur·a·ble,** *adj.*

pleat (plēt) *n.* a fold, as of cloth: —*v.t.* lay in folds.

plebe (plēb) *n.* at Annapolis or West Point, a fourth-classman (freshman).

ple·be'ian (pli-bē'ən) *adj.* pert. to the common people; vulgar. —*n.* one of the common people.

pleb'i·scite" (pleb'ə-sīt") *n.* a vote by the whole people.

plec'trum (plek'trəm) *n.* a small disk for plucking the strings of a musical instrument.

pledge (plej) *n.* **1**, a thing given as security. **2**, a promise. —*v.t.* **1**, pawn. **2**, promise, esp. a donation.

ple'na·ry (plen'ə-rē) *adj.* full; unqualified.

plen"i·po·ten'ti·ar"y (plen'ē-pō-ten'shē-er'ē) *n.* an emissary, as an ambassador, with full powers. —*adj.* having full powers.

plen'i·tude" (plen'i-tood") *n:* abundance; fullness.

plen'te·ous (plen'tē-əs) *adj.* abundant. —**plen'te·ous·ness,** *n.*

plen'ti·ful (plen'ti-fəl) *adj.* **1**, ample. **2**, fruitful. —**plen'ti·ful·ness,** *n.*

plen'ty (plen'tē) *n.* an adequate supply; abundance.

pleth'o·ra (pleth'ə-rə) *n.* overfullness; superabundance.

pleu'ra (plūr'ə) *n.* the membrane lining of the chest.

pleu'ri·sy (plūr'ə-sē) *n.* inflammation of the pleura.

plex'i·glass" (plek'sə-glàs") (*T.N.*) a clear thermoplastic compound.

plex'us (plek'səs) *n.* a network, as of blood vessels and nerve fibers.

pli'a·ble (plī'ə-bəl) *adj.* 1, flexible. 2, compliant. —pli"a·bil'i·ty, *n.*

pli'ant (plī'ənt) *adj.* supple; pliable —pli'an·cy, *n.*

pli'ers (plī'ərz) *n. pl.* pincers with long, blunt jaws.

plight (plīt) *n.* 1, condition; predicament. —*v.t.* 1, pledge, as one's word, honor, etc. 2, betroth.

Pliers

Pincers

Plim'soll mark (plim'səl) a line showing a ship's safe load capacity.

plod *v.i.* [plod'ded, -ding] 1, trudge. 2, toil; drudge. —plod'der, *n.*

plop *n.* the sound of something falling into water without splashing. —*v.i. & t.* [plopped, plop'ping] fall, drop, or set with a plop.

plot *n.* 1, a small piece of ground. 2, a plan or map. 3, an intrigue; conspiracy. 4, the plan of a novel, play, etc. —*v.t.* [plot'ted, -ting] 1, chart; map; plan. 2, contrive. —*v.i.* conspire. —plot'ter, *n.*

plov'er (pluv'ər) *n.* a shore bird akin to the sandpiper.

plow *n.* an implement that furrows and turns over the soil. —*v.t. & i.* 1, till with a plow. 2, move, cleave, or push through. Also, plough. —plow'man (-mən) *n.*

Plow

plow'share" *n.* the cutting blade of a plow.

pluck (pluk) *v.t.* 1, pull off or up; pick. 2, strip (a fowl) of feathers. 3, jerk; twitch. 4, twang, as a banjo. —*n.* 1, a twitch; tug; twang. 2,

courage; spirit. —pluck'y, *adj.* courageous.

plug *n.* 1, a stopper. 2, a connection, as for a hose, an electrical wire, etc. 3, a cake of tobacco. 4, (*Colloq.*) a favorable remark. 5, (*Slang*) something unfit or worthless, esp. a horse. 6, an artificial lure in fishing. —*v.t.* [plugged, plug'ging] 1, stop up with a plug. 2, (*Colloq.*) shoot. 3, (*Colloq.*) publicize. —*v.i.* work steadily. —plug'ger, *n.* a dogged worker. —plug-ug"ly, *n.* (*Slang*) a rowdy; tough.

plum *n.* 1, the juicy, smooth-skinned fruit of a tree similar to the peach; the tree. 2, a raisin. 3, a prize; a good thing. 4, a bluish-red color.

plum'age (ploo'mij) *n.* feathers.

plumb (plum) *n.* 1, a ball of lead dropped on a line (plumb line) for testing perpendicularity, depth, etc. 2, the vertical. —*v.t.* test by a plumb line. —*adj.* vertical. —*adv.* 1, vertically. 2, exactly. 3, (*Colloq.*) utterly.

plum·ba'go (plum-bā'gō) *n.* graphite, used in lead pencils.

plumb'er (plum'ər) *n.* a worker on water pipes, bathroom fixtures, steam fitting, etc.

plumb'ing *n.* 1, the trade of a plumber. 2, piping and attached fixtures.

plume (ploom) *n.* a feather or bunch of feathers. —*v.t.* preen or adorn (oneself).

plum'met (plum'it) *n.* a plumb. —*v.i.* plunge straight down.

plump *v.i. & t.* 1, drop suddenly and heavily. 2, support (a candidate) vigorously. —*n.* a heavy fall. —*adj.* fat; well-rounded. —*adv.* heavily; flatly. —plump'ness, *n.*

plun'der (plun'dər) *v.t.* rob; take by force. —*n.* 1, robbery. 2, booty.

plunge (plunj) *v.t.* thrust suddenly (into a liquid, flesh, etc.) —*v.i.* 1, dive or leap. 2, rush headlong. 3, bet recklessly. —*n.* a sudden dive or leap. —plung'er, *n.*

plunk *v.i.* make a quick, hollow, metallic sound. —*v.t.* 1, twang. 2, drop or slap down. —*n.* the sound of plunking.

plu"per'fect (ploo"pər'fikt) *adj. & n.* (*Gram.*) past perfect, as *I had done it.*

plu'ral (plūr'əl) *adj.* designating more than one. —*n.* (*Gram.*) a plural form.

plu·ral'i·ty (plū-ral'ə-tē) *n.* the receipt of more votes than any other candidate; the amount of excess.

plus *adj.* **1,** indicating addition. **2,** additional. **3,** positive; more than zero. —*prep.* with the addition of. —*n.* **1,** the plus sign (+). **2,** something additional. —**plus fours,** long baggy knickerbockers.

plush *n.* a fabric like velvet, but with a longer pile.

plu·toc'ra·cy (ploo-tok'rə-sē) *n.* **1,** government by the rich. **2,** the influential rich.

plu'to·crat'' (ploo'tə-krat'') *n.* **1,** a very rich person. **2,** an adherent of plutocracy. —**plu''to·crat'ic,** *adj.* —**plu''to·crat'i·cal·ly,** *adv.*

plu·to'ni·um (ploo-tō'nē-əm) *n.* a radioactive chemical element, no. 94, symbol Pu.

plu'vi·ous (ploo'vē-əs) *adj.* pert. to rain; rainy. —**plu'vi·al,** *adj.*

ply (plī) *n.* a layer or strand. —*v.t.* **1,** wield diligently. **2,** work at steadily. —*v.i.* travel a course regularly.

ply'wood'' *n.* several layers of wood laminated together.

pneu·mat'ic (nū-mat'ik) *adj.* **1,** pert. to air. **2,** inflated with air. **3,** worked by compressed air. —**pneu·mat'i·cal·ly,** *adv.*

pneu·mo- *pref.* the lungs.

pneu·mo'ni·a (noo-mō'nyə) *n.* inflammation of the tissues of the lungs.

poach (pōch) *v.t. & i.* **1,** cook (egg) by breaking it into boiling water. **2,** trespass, esp. to hunt or fish. —**poach'er,** *n.* a trespasser.

pock (pok) *n.* a pus-filled eruption, as in smallpox. —**pock'mark'',** *n.*

pock'et (pok'it) *n.* **1,** a pouch inserted in a garment; its contents, esp. money. **2,** a cavity or hollow. —*adj.* of small size. —*v.t.* **1,** put in a pocket. **2,** appropriate; accept. **3,** suppress. —**pocket billiards,** a game of sinking balls in pockets on a billiard table. —**pocket veto,** the holding of a bill until it expires by law, in effect a veto.

pock'et·book'' *n.* a purse.

pock'et·knife'' *n.* a folding knife to be carried in the pocket.

pod *n.* the seed case of certain plants, as the pea or bean.

po·di'a·try (pō-dī'ə-trē) *n.* (*Med.*) the treatment of disorders of the feet. —**po·di'a·trist,** *n.*

po'di·um (pō'dē-əm) *n.* [*pl.* -a (-ə)] a speaker's or conductor's platform; dais.

po'em (pō'im) *n.* a composition in verse; lofty or imaginative writing or artistic expression.

po'et (pō'it) *n.* **1,** one who writes poems or is capable of lofty artistic expression. —**po'et·ess,** *n.fem.*

po'et·as''ter (pō'it-as''tər) *n.* a writer of poor verse.

po·et'ic (pō-et'ik) *adj.* **1,** of or pert. to poetry. **2,** befitting poetry. Also, **po·et'i·cal.** —**poetic license,** deviation from form to achieve a poetic effect.

poet laureate the official poet of a state or nation.

po'et·ry (-rē) *n.* **1,** expression in poems. **2,** poems collectively. Also, **po'e·sy** (-zē).

po'grom (pō'grəm) *n.* an organized massacre, esp. of Jews.

poign'ant (poin'yənt) *adj.* biting; painfully acute; affecting. —**poign'-an·cy,** *n.*

poin·set'ti·a (poin-set'ē-ə) *n.* a plant with large scarlet leaves.

point *n.* **1,** a sharp or tapering end. **2,** a telling or essential feature. **3,** precise degree. **4,** aim; purpose. **5,** an exact spot or time. **6,** a unit of counting, measuring, or scoring. **7,** a unit of measurement for type; about 1/72 of an inch. **8,** one of the divisions of a compass. **9,** the period, esp. as a decimal mark. —*v.t.* **1,** aim. **2,** (with *out*) indicate the direction or position of. —*v.i.* **1,** indicate direction with, or as with, the finger. **2,** tend; lead. **3,** face. —**point of view,** one's aspect of a subject or thing.

point'blank'' *adj.* direct; straightforward.

point'ed (-id) *adj.* sharp; pertinent; intended to affect a person. —**point'ed·ness,** *n.*

Pointer

point'er (-ər) *n.* **1,** a hand on a clock, etc. **2,** a tapering rod for pointing. **3,** a hunting dog. **4,** a bit of advice; a tip.

point'less (-ləs) *adj.* meaningless; purposeless. —**point'less·ness,** *n.*

poise (poiz) *n.* **1,** equilibrium. **2,** carriage; bearing; self-possession. —*v.t. & i.* balance.

poi'son (poi'zən) *n.* **1,** a substance that causes injury or death upon ingestion, contact, or injection. **2,** any baneful influence or doctrine. —*v.t.* give poison to; corrupt or spoil with poison. —**poi'son·ous,** *adj.* —**poison**

ivy, oak, sumac, plants that cause irritation of the skin.

poke (pōk) *v.t.* 1, thrust away, down, or through. 2, jab; prod, as with a stick. —*v.i.* 1, search; pry; grope. 2, make a thrust. 3, dawdle. —*n.* 1, a thrust; nudge. 2, a projecting brim on a bonnet. 3, a bag; sack. 4, a dawdler.

Poison Ivy

pok′er (pō′kər) *n.* 1, a steel bar for stirring a fire. 2, a card game.

pok′y (pō′kē) *adj.* 1, slow; boring. 2, of a room, small and shabby. —*n.* (*Colloq.*) a jail. Also, **pok′ey.** —**pok′i·ness,** *n.*

po′lar (pō′lər) *adj.* pert. to, or at. the poles of a sphere, esp. of the earth. —**polar bear,** a large, creamy-white bear of the Arctic.

Po·la′ris (pō-lār′is) *n.* the North Star.

po·lar′i·ty (pō-lār′ə-tē) *n.* the property whereby opposite magnetic poles, positive and negative, attract and repel respectively.

po″lar·i·za′tion (pō″lər-ə-zā′shən) *n.* a state in which light rays exhibit different qualities in different directions. —**po′lar·ize″,** (-īz″) *v.t.*

po′lar·oid″ *n.* (*T.N.*) an optical glass used to polarize light: to reduce glare, create the illusion of three-dimensional pictures, etc.

pole (pōl) *n.* 1, either end of the axis of a sphere; specif. either end (North Pole or South Pole) of the earth's axis. 2, either end of a magnet or terminal of an electric cell. 3, a long, slender, tapering piece of wood. 4, a measure of length, a rod, 5½ yds. 5, (*cap.*) a native of Poland. —*v.t.* 1, propel by a pole. 2, support by poles. —**pole vault,** an athletic contest of leaping, aided by a long pole.

pole′cat″ (pōl′kat″) *n.* 1, a small Europ. animal of the weasel family. 2, in the U. S., a skunk.

po·lem′ic (pō-lem′ik) *n.* argument about doctrines. —**po·lem′i·cal,** *adj.*

pole′star″ *n.* 1, the North Star. 2, a guide; lodestar.

po·lice′ (pə-lēs′) *n. sing. & pl.* 1, the civil department that maintains order and enforces the law. 2, (*Mil.*) the work of keeping a camp clean. —*v.t.* 1, guard and maintain order in. 2, clean up, as a camp. —**police dog,** a German shepherd dog.

po·lice′man (-mən) *n.* [*pl.* -**men**] a member of a police force. —**police′wom″an,** *n.fem.*

pol′i·cy (pol′ə-sē) *n.* 1, a course of conduct based on principle or advisability. 2, a contract of insurance. 3, a form of lottery.

pol″i·o·my″e·li′tis (pol″ē-ō-mī′ə-lī′tis) *n.* a spinal paralysis; infantile paralysis. Also, **pol′i·o.**

pol′ish *v.t.* 1, make smooth and glossy, as by rubbing. 2, give elegance or refinement to. —*n.* 1, a smooth, glossy finish. 2, a mixture for polishing. 3, refinement; elegance. —**polish off,** dispose of quickly.

Pol′ish (pō′lish) *adj. & n.* of or pert. to Poland, its people, language, etc.

Po·lit′bu″ro (pə-lit′byûr″ō) *n.* a policy-forming committee in the Communist Party of the U.S.S.R.

po·lite′ (pə-līt′) *adj.* 1, courteous; well-bred. 2, refined. —**po·lite′ness,** *n.*

pol′i·tic (pol′ə-tik) *adj.* 1, consisting of citizens. 2, wise; expedient.

po·lit′i·cal (pə-lit′i-kəl) *adj.* pert. to governmental affairs or to politics.

pol″i·ti′cian (pol″ə-tish′ən) *n.* one skilled or active in politics.

pol′i·tics (pol′ə-tiks) *n. sing.* 1, the science of government. 2, the activities of a political party. 3, (construed as *pl.*) political opinions.

pol′i·ty (pol′ə-tē) *n.* the system of a government.

pol′ka (pō′kə) *n.* a lively dance; the music for it.

polka dots a pattern of round spots on a fabric.

poll (pōl) *n.* 1, the voting at an election; the number of votes cast. 2, (*pl.*) a place of voting. 3, a survey of opinion. 4, the head. —*v.t.* 1, register the votes of; ask the opinions of. 2, receive as votes. 3, clip; shear; cut off. —**poll tax,** a tax on individuals who vote.

pol′len (pol′ən) *n.* the fertilizing element of a plant, a fine yellow powder.

pol′li·nate″ (pol′ə-nāt″) *v.t.* fertilize (a flower). —**pol′li·na′tion,** *n.*

pol′li·wog″ (pol′ē-wog″) *n.* a tadpole.

pol·lute′ (pə-loot′) *v.t.* make impure; soil; defile. —**pol·lu′tion,** *n.*

Pol″ly·an′na (pol″ē-an′ə) *n.* an over-optimistic person.

po′lo (pō′lō) *n.* a game similar to hockey but played on horseback.

pol'o·naise' (pŏl"ə-nāz') *n.* **1,** a stately Polish dance; the music for it. **2,** an outer dress for women.

po·lo'ni·um (pə-lō'nē-əm) *n.* a radioactive element, no. 84, symbol Po.

pol'ter·geist' (pōl'tər-gīst") *n.* a noisy ghost.

pol·troon' *n.* a coward. —**pol·troon'er·y,** *n.*

pol'y- (pŏl'ē) *pref.* many.

pol'y·an'dry (-an"drē) *n.* plural marriage by a woman. —**pol'y·an'drous,** *adj.*

pol'y·chrome" *adj.* having various colors. —*n.* a work of art done in several colors.

pol'y·clin'ic *adj.* treating various diseases.

pol'y·dac'tyl *adj.* having too many fingers or toes. —**pol'y·dac'tyl·ism,** *n.*

po·lyg'a·my (pə-lig'ə-mē) *n.* plural marriage by a man. —**po·lyg'a·mist,** *n.* —**po·lyg'a·mous,** *adj.*

pol'y·glot' *adj.* knowing or comprising several languages.

pol'y·gon' *n.* a closed plane figure with many sides and angles.

pol'y·he'dron (-hē'drən) *n.* [*pl.* -dra (-drə)] a many-sided solid.

pol'y·mer (-mər) *n.* a chemical compound with very complex and heavy molecules.

Pol"y·ne'sian (pŏl"i-nē'zhən) *adj. & n.* of or pert. to the peoples of the So. Pacific islands called Oceania.

pol'y·no'mi·al (-nō'mē-əl) *adj.* containing many names or terms. —**pol'y·no'mi·al·ism,** *n.*

pol'yp (pŏl'ip) *n.* **1,** an invertebrate marine animal. **2,** a small tumor.

pol'y·syl'la·ble *n.* a word having many (usually four or more) syllables. —**pol'y·syl·lab'ic** (-si-lab'ik) *adj.*

pol'y·tech'nic *adj.* teaching many sciences.

pol'y·the·ism *n.* belief in more than one god. —**pol'y·the·ist,** *n.* —**pol'y·the·is'tic,** **pol'y·the·is'ti·cal,** *adj.*

pom'ace (pum'is) *n.* a crushed pulpy residue.

po·made' (pō-mād') *n.* a scented ointment.

pome (pōm) *n.* the typical fruit of the apple family.

pome'gran"ate (pom'gran"it) *n.* a tropical tree; its pulpy fruit.

Pom"er·a'ni·an (pom"ə-rā'nē-ən) *n.* a small, long-haired dog.

pom'mel (pum'əl) *n.* a rounded knob on a saddle, etc. —*v.t.* pummel.

pomp *n.* splendor; showy display.

pom'pa·dour" (pom'pə-dôr") *n.* a hairdress, the hair straight back from the forehead.

pom'pa·no" (pom'pə-nō") *n.* a food fish of tropical seas.

pom'pom" *n.* a many-barreled anti-aircraft gun.

pom'pon *n.* **1,** a fluffy ball of feathers, wool, etc. **2,** a globelike flower, as a chrysanthemum.

pomp'ous (pom'pəs) *adj.* ostentatiously dignified or lofty. —**pom·pos'i·ty** (-pos'ə-tē), **pom'pous·ness,** *n.*

pon'cho (pon'chō) *n.* [*pl.* -chos] **1,** a rainproof cloak. **2,** a blanket used as a cloak, with a hole in it for the head.

pond *n.* a body of standing water smaller than a lake.

pon'der (pon'dər) *v.t. & i.* reflect (upon or over); consider deeply.

pon'der·ous (pon'dər-əs) *adj.* very heavy; hence, unwieldy; tedious.

pone (pōn) *n.* a cornmeal bread.

pon·gee' (pon-jē') *n.* a soft silk fabric.

pon'iard (pon'yərd) *n.* a dagger.

pon'tiff (pon'tif) *n.* a bishop; specif. the Pope. —**pon·tif'i·cal,** *adj.*

pon·tif'i·cate (pon-tif'i-kət) *n.* the office of a bishop. —*v.i.* (-kāt") assume an air of infallibility. —**pon·tif'i·ca'tion,** *n.*

pon·toon' *n.* **1,** a flat-bottomed boat. **2,** a floating support for a temporary bridge; a buoy. **3,** a float for a seaplane.

po'ny (pō'nē) *n.* **1,** a horse of a small, stocky, breed. **2,** (*Slang*) a trot; crib. **3,** a small liqueur glass.

pooch *n.* (*Slang*) dog.

poo'dle (poo'dəl) *n.* a breed of dog with wiry curled hair.

Poodles

pooh (poo) *interj.* of contempt.

pool *n.* **1,** a still, deep place in a river; a pond; puddle. **2,** an open tank of water for swimming. **3,** pocket billiards. **4,** the totality of bets made on a contingency; pot. **5**, a combination of business interests or investors. —*v.t.* put into a common fund.

poop *n.* a raised deck in a ship's stern. —*v.t.* (of a wave or a gust of wind) strike. —**pooped**, *adj.* (*Slang*) fatigued.

poor (pûr) *adj.* **1**, needy; not rich. **2**, lacking desirable qualities; inferior. **3**, spiritless. **4**, unfortunate; to be pitied. **5**, humble.

poor′house″ *n.* a home for paupers.

poor′ly (-lė) *adv.* & (*Colloq.*) *adj.* not well.

pop *n.* **1**, a short explosive sound. **2**, a soft drink. **3**, (*Colloq.*) papa. —*v.i.* [**popped**, **pop′ping**] **1**, make such a sound; burst. **2**, appear or disappear suddenly. —*v.t.* **1**, cause to burst or explode. **2**, put (in) quickly. —**pop the question** (*Colloq.*) propose marriage.

pop′corn″ *n.* a maize whose kernels burst when heated.

Pope (pōp) *n.* the bishop of Rome, leader of the Rom. Cath. Church. —**pop′ish**, *adj.* (*Offensive*) pert. to this church.

pop′gun″ *n.* a toy gun.

pop′in·jay″ (pop′in-jā″) *n.* **1**, a woodpecker. **2**, a vain person.

pop′lar (pop′lər) *n.* a tree with light soft wood; the wood.

pop′lin *n.* a ribbed fabric.

pop′o″ver *n.* a light muffin.

pop′pet (pop′it) *n.* a valve that opens by lifting from its seat.

pop′py (pop′ė) *n.* a flowering plant with a milky narcotic juice.

pop′py·cock″ (pop′ė-kok″) *n.* (*Colloq.*) nonsense; vain talk.

pop′u·lace (pop′yə-lis) *n.* the common people; the multitude.

pop′u·lar (pop′yə-lər) *adj.* **1**, pert. to, or intended for, the common people. **2**, generally liked. —**pop′u·lar′i·ty** (-lar′ə-tė) *n.* —**pop′u·lar·ize″** (-īz″) *v.t.*

pop′u·late″ (pop′yə-lāt″) *v.t.* supply with inhabitants.

pop′u·la′tion (pop′yə-lā′shən) *n.* **1**, total number of inhabitants of a place. **2**, the process of populating.

pop′u·lous (pop′yə-ləs) *adj.* thickly inhabited. —**pop′u·lous·ness**, *n.*

por′ce·lain (pôr′sə-lin) *n.* a fine, white, translucent china.

porch (pôrch) *n.* **1**, a covered approach to a doorway. **2**, a veranda.

por′cine (pôr′sīn) *adj.* pert. to swine.

por′cu·pine″ (pôr′kyə-pīn″) *n.* a small animal with sharp spines on its body and tail.

pore (pôr) *n.* a tiny opening, esp. in the skin. —*v.i.* (with *over*) meditate; ponder.

por′gy (pôr′jė) *n.* a small, edible sea fish.

pork (pôrk) *n.* the flesh of swine as food. —**pork barrel**, a government grant used for political patronage.

pork′er (-ər) *n.* a swine.

pork′pie″ *n.* a flat, low-crowned hat.

por·nog′ra·phy (pôr-nog′rə-fė) *n.* obscene art, writings, etc. —**por′no·graph′ic**, *adj.* —**por″no·graph′i·cal·ly**, *adv.*

por′ous (pôr′əs) *adj.* permeable by fluids. —**po·ros′i·ty** (pə-ros′ə-tė), **por′ous·ness**, *n.*

por′phy·ry (pôr′fə-rė) *n.* a hard rock embedded with crystals.

por′poise (pôr′pəs) *n.* a whale-like sea mammal, about 6 ft. long.

por′ridge (pôr′ij) *n.* a thin boiled cereal.

por′rin·ger (por′in-jər) *n.* a dish for cereal.

port (pôrt) *n.* **1**, a coast city where ships load and unload; a harbor; a haven. **2**, a porthole; an outlet. **3**, the left side of a ship. **4**, a sweet, dark-red wine. —*v.t.* **1**, turn (the helm) to the left. **2**, (*Mil.*) hold (a rifle) diagonally across the body.

port′a·ble (pôrt′ə-bəl) *adj.* capable of being carried; easily conveyed. —**port′a·bil′i·ty**, *n.*

por′tage (pôr′tij) *n.* **1**, the act or place of carrying boats overland from one stream to another. **2**, a fee for conveyance.

por′tal (pôr′təl) *n.* a doorway.

port·cul′lis (pôrt-kul′is) *n.* a gate that slides up and down, esp. as used in medieval castles.

por·tend′ (pôr-tend′) *v.t.* give a warning of; presage.

por′tent (pôr′tent) *n.* a dire or evil omen.

por·ten′tous (pôr-ten′təs) *adj.* **1**, foreshadowing evil. **2**, solemn. —**por·ten′tous·ness**, *n.*

por′ter (pôr′tər) *n.* **1**, one who carries baggage; a sleeping-car attendant. **2**, a doorkeeper or janitor. **3**, a heavy, dark beer.

por′ter·house″ (pôr′tər-hows″) *n.* a choice cut of beef; a T-bone steak.

port·fo'li·o (pôrt-fō'lē-ō) *n.* **1,** a flat case for carrying documents; a brief case. **2,** the office of a cabinet minister. **3,** an itemized account of securities, etc. held by an investor.

port'hole" (pôrt'hōl") *n.* a round window in a ship's side; an aperture in a wall.

por'ti·co" (pôr'ti-kō") *n.* a roof supported by columns, used as a porch or a detached shed.

por'tiere' (pôr'tyâr') *n.* a curtain hung in a doorway.

por'tion (pôr'shən) *n.* **1,** a part of a whole. **2,** a share. **3,** lot; destiny. **4,** a dowry. —*v.t.* **1,** allot in shares. **2,** dower.

port'ly (pôrt'lē) *adj.* **1,** fat; stout. **2,** stately; dignified.

port·man'teau (pôrt-man'tō) *n.* a traveling bag or suitcase.

por'trait (pôr'trit) *n.* a picture of a person, esp. one done in oils. —**por'trai·ture** (-trə-tyər) *n.*

por·tray' (pôr-trā') *v.t.* **1,** picture; describe vividly. **2,** enact. —**por·tray'al,** *n.*

Por'tu·guese (pôr'tyə-gēz) *adj.* & *n.* of or pert. to the people of Portugal, their language, etc.

pose (pōz) *v.t.* **1,** place (a model) suitably. **2,** propound, as a question. —*v.i.* **1,** act as a model. **2,** make a pretense. —*n.* **1,** attitude; position. **2,** an affectation.

pos'er (pō'zər) *n.* **1,** [also, po·seur' (-zėr')] an affected person; pretender. **2,** a puzzling question.

po·si'tion (pə-zish'ən) *n.* **1,** the place occupied by a person or thing; situation. **2,** bodily attitude or posture. **3,** point of view; opinion. **4,** rank; station, esp. high standing. **5,** a job; occupation. —**po·si'tion·al,** *adj.*

pos'i·tive (poz'ə-tiv) *adj.* **1,** stated explicitly; definite. **2,** confident; dogmatic; **3,** affirmative. **4,** real; actual; of numbers, greater than zero; plus. **5,** proving the presence of something in question. **6,** in photography, showing light and shade as in the original. **7,** noting the simple form of an adjective or adverb. **8,** of electricity, having a deficiency of electrons. —*n.* something positive. —**pos'i·tive·ness,** *n.*

pos'i·tron" (poz'ə-tron") *n.* a particle of positive electricity.

pos'se (pos'ē) *n.* a body of men helping a sheriff.

pos·sess' (pə-zes') *v.t.* **1,** have as one's property; own; have as a quality. **2,** obtain power over; dominate. —**pos·ses'sor,** *n.*

pos·sessed' (pə-zest') *adj.* **1,** in possession (of). **2,** afflicted by evil spirits.

pos·ses'sion (pə-zesh'ən) *n.* **1,** the state of having or controlling. **2,** something owned.

pos·ses'sive (-zes'iv) *adj.* **1,** pert. to ownership; jealous in ownership. **2,** (*Gram.*) denoting a possessor. —**po·ses'sive·ness,** *n.*

pos'si·ble (pos'ə-bəl) *adj.* **1,** capable of existing, occurring, or being done. **2,** that may do; worth consideration. —**pos"si·bil'i·ty,** *n.*

pos'si·bly (pos'ə-blē) *adv.* by any possibility; perhaps.

pos'sum (pos'əm) *n.* (*Colloq.*) an opossum.

post (pōst) *n.* **1,** an upright timber or stake. **2,** a station; assignment; job. **3,** a military station or its garrison; a trading station. **4,** a system or means of conveying letters, packages, etc.; the mail. —*v.t.* **1,** fasten (a notice) in a public place. **2,** mail (a letter). **3,** (*Colloq.*) supply with information. —*v.i.* **1,** travel in haste. **2,** move up and down in the saddle, when riding.

post- *pref.* after.

post'age (pōs'tij) *n.* the fee for conveying letters or packages; mailing charges. —**postage stamp,** an official stamp showing prepayment of postage.

post'al (pōs'təl) *adj.* pert. to the mail service. —**postal card,** postcard. —**postal note,** a check issued by the post office for transmission of money.

post'card" *n.* a card prepared for correspondence on one section or side, and address on the other.

post chaise a horsedrawn coach.

post'date" *v.t.* **1,** date (a contract, check, etc.) with a date later than the current one. **2,** be subsequent to in time.

post'er *n.* a posted notice; a placard.

pos·te'ri·or (pos-tir'ē-ər) *adj.* **1,** located in the back or rear. **2,** later. —*n.* the rump.

pos·ter'i·ty (pos-ter'ə-tē) *n.* **1,** descendants collectively. **2,** all future generations.

pos'tern (pos'tərn) *n.* a rear or secondary entrance.

post exchange (also *cap.*) a store or canteen for soldiers at an army post.

post·grad'u·ate (pōst-gra'joo-it) *adj.* pert. to study after graduation from a school or college. —*n.* a postgraduate student.

post'haste" (pōst'hāst") *adv.* by fastest means; speedily.

post'hu·mous (pos'tū-məs) *adj.* **1**, done by or awarded to a person now dead. **2**, born after the father's death.

pos·til'lion (pōs-til'yən) *n.* a rider on one of a team of two or four horses.

post'lude" (pōst'lood") *n.* (*Music*) an added or concluding piece.

post'man (-mən) *n.* [*pl.* -men] a mail carrier.

post'mark" *n.* an official mark canceling a postage stamp.

post'mas"ter *n.* a person in charge of a post office. —**post'mis"tress,** *n.fem.* —**Postmaster General,** a cabinet minister in charge of the post office.

post"me·rid'i·an (pōst"mə-rid'ē-ən) *adj.* after noon, usually *abbr.* P.M.

post-"mor'tem (pōst"môr'təm) *adj.* after death. —*n.* **1**, an autopsy. **2**, (*Slang*) discussion of card play after a game.

post office the government department that transmits mail, or one of its branch offices.

post'paid" *adj.* with postage prepaid.

post·pone' (pōst-pōn') *v.t.* defer until later; delay. —**post·pone'ment,** *n.*

post'script" (pōst'skript") *n.* a paragraph added to a letter finished and signed; any added part.

pos'tu·late" (pos'chə-lāt") *v.t. & i.* assert or assume as a basis for reasoning. —*n.* (-lət) **1,** an assumption; hypothesis. **2,** a prerequisite.

pos'ture (pos'chər) *n.* bodily position; carriage. —*v.i.* pose.

post'war" *adj.* after the (most recent) war.

po'sy (pō'zē) *n.* a flower.

pot *n.* **1,** a round deep vessel, as for cooking. **2,** an aggregate of stakes to be won; a prize. **3,** a wicker basket for catching fish, lobsters, etc. —*v.t.* [**pot'ted, -ting**] **1,** preserve in pots; plant in a pot. **2,** shoot (game) for food. —**go to pot** (*Colloq.*) go to pieces; be ruined. —**pot shot,** a random shot, or one at close range.

po'ta·ble (pō'tə-bəl) *adj.* drinkable. —*n.* (*pl.*) beverages.

pot'ash" *n.* a white chemical obtained by leaching wood ashes.

po·tas'si·um (pə-tas'ē-əm) *n.* a soft, silvery-white metallic element, no. 19, symbol K, used in drugs, fertilizers, etc. —**po·tas'sic,** *adj.*

po·ta'to (pə-tā'tō) *n.* a plant or its important edible tuber. —**potato chip,** a fried thin slice of potato.

pot'bel"ly *n.* (*Colloq.*) a fat or protruding belly.

pot'boil"er (pot'boi'lər) *n.* a work of art or literature produced solely for subsistence money.

po'ten·cy (pō'tən-sē) *n.* state or quality of being potent; power; ability.

po'tent (pō'tənt) *adj.* **1,** wielding power; strong; effective. **2,** capable of procreation.

po'ten·tate" (pō'tən-tāt") *n.* a ruler; monarch.

po·ten'tial (pə-ten'shəl) *adj.* **1,** possible. **2,** latent. —**po·ten'ti·al'i·ty** (-shē-al'ə-tē) *n.*

poth'er (poth'ər) *n.* confusion; bustle.

pot'hook" (pot'hůk") *n.* **1,** a hook used to lift or suspend pots. **2,** any S-shaped figure, as in writing; (*Humorous*) any stenographic symbol.

po'tion (pō'shən) *n.* a drink, as of medicine or poison.

pot'latch" (pot'lach) *n.* a ceremonious distribution of gifts.

pot'luck" (pot'luk") *n.* whatever food is on hand, without special buying.

pot·pour'ri (pot-pûr'ē; pō-poo-rē') *n.* a mixture or medley of spices, foods, musical or literary compositions, etc.

pot'tage (pot'ij) *n.* a stew.

pot'ter (pot'ər) *n.* one who makes pottery. —*v.i.* busy oneself over trifles; loiter; dawdle. —**potter's field,** a place for the burial of paupers or criminals. —**potter's wheel,** a rotating disk on which a potter shapes clay.

Potter's Wheel

pot'ter·y (-ē) *n.* dishes, vases, etc.; molded from clay and baked.

pouch (powch) *n.* **1,** a small bag or sack. **2,** a marsupium.

poul'tice (pōl'tis) *n.* a soft, warm mass applied to a sore spot.

poul'try (pōl'trē) *n.* domestic fowls collectively. —**poul'ter·er,** *n.* a dealer in poultry.

pounce (powns) *v.i.* (often with *on* or *upon*) swoop and seize suddenly. —*n.* a sudden spring.

pound (pownd) *n.* 1, a measure of weight, 16 avoirdupois or 12 troy ounces. 2, the Brit. monetary unit; its symbol (£). 3, an enclosure for stray animals. —*v.t.* 1, beat; pummel. 2, crush. —*v.i.* 1, hammer away steadily. 2, plod heavily. —**pound'-age,** *n.*

pound'al (pownd'dəl) *n.* the force which, acting for one second upon a mass of one pound, gives it a velocity of one foot per second.

pour (pôr) *v.t.* 1, cause to flow downward in a stream. 2, send forth copiously. —*v.i.* 1, flow. 2, rain hard. 3, issue in great numbers.

pout (powt) *v.i.* protrude the lips, as in sullenness. —*n.* a sulky mood.

pouter pigeon a pigeon with a puffed-out crop.

pov'er·ty (pov'ər·tē) *n.* 1, lack of money; need. 2, lack; scarcity. —**pov'er·ty-strick'en,** *adj.* impoverished.

pow'der (pow'dər) *n.* 1, a mixture of fine, dry particles, as pulverized talc used as a cosmetic; gunpowder; a dose of medicinal powder. 2, (*Slang*) sudden departure. —*v.t.* 1, sprinkle with or as with powder. 2, reduce to powder. —**pow'der·y,** *adj.*

powder puff 1, a pad for applying powder. 2, an effeminate man.

powder room a lavatory for women.

pow'er (pow'ər) *n.* 1, ability to do or act. 2, physical or mental strength or energy; influence; control. 3, an influential person; a nation considered as a military force. 4, the magnifying capacity of a lens. 5, any of the products obtained by multiplying a number by itself repeatedly; as, $2 \times 2 = 4$ (*2nd* power) $\times 2 = 8$ (*3rd* power) etc. —**power of attorney,** legal authority to act for another.

pow·er- *pref.* impelled by an engine.

pow'er·ful *adj.* strong; influential; mighty. —**pow'er·ful·ness,** *n.*

pow'er·house *n.* 1, a plant for generating electricity. 2, (*Colloq.*) something very strong.

pow'er·less *adj.* helpless; without authority. —**pow'er·less·ness,** *n.*

power politics diplomacy based on the threat of force.

pow'wow" *n.* 1, among N. Amer. Indians, a ceremony or conference. 2, (*Colloq.*) any conference. —*v.i.* confer.

pox (poks) *n.* a disease marked by eruptive pocks.

prac'ti·ca·ble (prak'ti-kə-bəl) *adj.* capable of being done or used. —**prac"ti·ca·bil'i·ty,** *n.*

prac'ti·cal (prak'ti-kəl) *adj.* 1, usable; useful. 2, taught by, or derived from, experience; advisable. 3, inclined to action rather than theory. 4, pert. to actual practice or action; not theoretical. —**prac"ti·cal'i·ty,** *n.* —**practical joke,** one that causes discomfort or embarrassment to someone.

prac'ti·cal·ly (-ē) *adv.* 1, in practice; actually. 2, (*Colloq.*) nearly; in effect.

prac'tice (prak'tis) *n.* 1, actual performance. 2, frequent performance; custom; usage. 3, the exercise of a profession, esp. medical. 4, repeated exercise, to gain skill —*v.t.* 1, carry out in action. 2, do repeatedly, esp. to gain skill. 3, follow as a profession. —*v.i.* 1, perform certain acts often. 2, engage in a profession. Also (*Brit.*) **prac'tise.**

prac·ti'tion·er (prak-tish'ən-ər) *n.* 1, one engaged in a profession. 2, in Christian Science, an authorized healer.

prag·mat'ic (prag-mat'ik) *adj.* 1, based on utility or effect; practical. 2, matter-of-fact. 3, dogmatic. —**prag·mat'i·cal·ly,** *adv.* —**prag'ma·tism,** *n.*

prai'rie (prâr'ē) *n.* a broad, level, treeless grassland. —**prairie dog,** a rodent of Amer. prairies. —**prairie schooner,** a covered wagon.

Prairie Dog

praise (prāz) *v.t.* 1, commend warmly. 2, glorify the attributes of (God). —*n.* compliments; applause.

praise'wor"thy *adj.* commendable. —**praise'wor"thi·ness,** *n.*

pram *n.* perambulator.

prance (prâns) *v.i.* 1, step proudly (of a horse's gait). 2, strut. —*n.* a prancing gait or stride.

pran'di·al (pran'dē·əl) *adj.* pert. to a meal, esp. dinner.

prank *n.* a playful or mischievous act. —**prank'ish,** *adj.*

prate (prāt) *v.t. & i.* chatter; babble; talk too much.

prat'tle (prat'əl) *v.i.* talk idly, like a child. —*n.* such talk.

prawn (prân) *n.* an edible shrimp-like crustacean.

pray (prā) *v.i.* ask God's grace. —*v.t.* **1,** beg; entreat. **2,** petition for. —*adv.* (*Archaic*) please.

prayer (prâr) *n.* **1,** a supplication to God; (*pl.*) a religious service. **2,** entreaty; petition. —**prayer book,** a book of forms for prayers.

prayer′ful (-fəl) *adj.* **1,** devout. **2,** entreating. —**prayer′ful-ness,** *n.*

pre- (prē) *pref.* before, in time, place, rank, sequence, etc.

preach (prēch) *v.t. & i.* **1,** deliver (a sermon). **2,** advocate earnestly; exhort. —**preach′ment,** *n.*

preach′er *n.* **1,** a clergyman. **2,** anyone who preaches.

pre′am″ble (prē′am″bəl) *n.* introductory remarks; a preface.

pre″ar·range (prē″ə-rānj′) *v.t.* arrange beforehand. —**pre″ar·range′-ment,** *n.*

pre·car′i·ous (pri-kâr′è-əs) *adj.* uncertain; insecure. —**pre·car′i-ous-ness,** *n.*

pre·cau′tion (pri-kâ′shən) *n.* **1,** an act done in advance to assure safety or benefit. **2,** prudent foresight. —**pre·cau′tion·ar·y,** *adj.*

pre·cede′ (prè-sēd′) *v.t. & i.* go before in place, time, rank, or importance. —**pre·ced′ing,** *adj.*

prec′e·dence (pres′i-dəns) *n.* **1,** the act of going before. **2,** the right of taking a more honored position.

prec′e·dent (pres′i-dənt) *n.* an identical or analogous previous example.

pre′cept (prē′sept) *n.* a rule for moral conduct; maxim. —**pre·cep′-tor,** *n.* a teacher.

pre′cinct (prē′sinkt) *n.* district.

pre″ci·os·i·ty (presh″è-os′ə-tè) *n.* overniceness; affectation.

pre′cious (presh′əs) *adj.* **1,** of great value. **2,** held in great esteem; dear. **3,** over-refined; affectedly clever or delicate. —**pre′cious-ness,** *n.*

prec′i·pice (pres′ə-pis) *n.* a very steep or overhanging cliff. —**pre·cip′i·tous** (pri-sip′i-təs) *adj.*

pre·cip′i·tant (pri-sip′ə-tənt) *adj.* rushing headlong; abrupt; hasty. —*n.* an agent that causes precipitation. —**pre·cip′i·tan·cy,** *n.*

pre·cip′i·tate″ (pri-sip′ə-tāt″) *v.t.* **1,** cast headlong. **2,** cause to happen suddenly or too soon. **3,** (*Chem.*) change from a state of solution to solid form. —*v.i.* (*Chem.*) separate from a solution, as a solid. —*adj.* **1,** headlong. **2,** acting hastily and unwisely. **3,** extremely sudden or abrupt.

pre·cip″i·ta′tion (pri-sip″i-tā′-shən) *n.* **1,** act of hurling down or falling headlong. **2,** impetuous ac-

tion. **3,** (*Chem.*) the process or effect of precipitating. **4,** rain, sleet, or snow; the quantity that falls.

pre·cip′i·tous (pri-sip′ə-təs) *adj.* **1,** overhasty; rash. **2,** steep.

pré·cis′ (prā-sē′) *n.* a concise summary.

pre·cise′ (pri-sīs′) *adj.* **1,** exactly defined; definite; accurate. **2,** punctilious; formal. **3,** exact; identical. —**pre·cise′ness,** *n.*

pre·ci′sion (pri-sizh′ən) *n.* preciseness; accuracy.

pre·clude′ (pri-klood′) *v.t.* impede; prevent.

pre·co′cious (pri-kō′shəs) *adj.* prematurely developed, esp. mentally. —**pre·co′cious-ness, pre·coc′i·ty** (pri-kos′ə-tè) *n.*

pre″con·ceive″ (prē″kən-sēv′) *v.t.* form an idea or opinion of in advance. —**pre″con·cep′tion** (-sep′-shən) *n.*

pre·cur′sor (pri-kēr′sər) *n.* a predecessor; a premonitory forerunner.

pred′a·to″ry (pred′ə-tôr′è) *adj.* **1,** plundering. **2,** preying upon others.

pred″e·ces′sor (pred″i-ses′ər) *n.* one who preceded another in the same position, etc.

pre·des″ti·na′tion (-ti-nā′shən) *n.* **1,** the belief that God has ordained all events to come. **2,** fate; destiny.

pre·des′tine (prè-des′tin) *v.t.* decide the course or fate of beforehand.

pre″de·ter′mine (prē″di-tēr′min) *v.t.* **1,** decide or ascertain beforehand. **2,** predestine.

pre·dic′a·ment (pri-dik′ə-mənt) *n.* a trying or dangerous situation; a dilemma.

pred′i·cate (pred′ə-kət) *n.* **1,** (*Gram.*) the part of a sentence that tells something about the subject. **2,** what is predicated. —*v.t.* (-kāt′) **1,** assert; declare. **2,** base.

pred′i·ca·tive (pred′i-kā-tiv) *adj.* of an adjective, being in the predicate and modifying the subject, as *clear in the sky is clear.*

pre·dict′ (pri-dikt′) *v.t. & i.* foretell; prophesy. —**pre·dic′tion,** *n.*

pre″di·lec′tion (prē″də-lek′shən) *n.* partiality; liking.

pre″dis·pose″ (prē″dis-pōz′) *v.t.* **1,** give a tendency or inclination to. **2,** dispose in advance. —**pre″dis·po·si′tion,** *n.* innate tendency.

pre·dom′i·nate″ (pri-dom′i-nāt″) *v.i. & t.* prevail (over); control; be the chief element. —**pre·dom′i-nance,** *n.* —**pre·dom′i·nant,** *adj.*

pre·ëm′i·nent (prè-em′i-nənt) *adj.* eminent above others. —**pre·ëm′i-nence,** *n.*

pre·ëmpt' (prē-empt') v.t. & i. occupy; seize; buy before another can. —pre·ëmp'tion, n. —pre·ëmp'tive, adj. —pre·ëmp'tor, n.

preen (prēn) v.t. 1, smooth (feathers) with the beak. 2, trim or adorn (oneself).

pre·fab'ri·cate' (prē-fab'ri-kāt') v.t. manufacture parts of, for later assembly, as houses. —pre·fab'ri·ca'tion, n.

pref'ace (pref'is) n. an introduction, as to a book or speech. —v.t. 1, give a preface to. 2, introduce; precede. —pref'a·to·ry, adj.

pre'fect (prē'fekt) n. 1, a chief magistrate; an administrative head. 2, a monitor in school. —pre'fec·ture, n.

pre·fer' (pri-fēr') v.t. [pre·ferred', -fer'ring] 1, choose, rather than another; like more. 2, advance; bring forward. —pref'er·a·ble (pref'ər-ə-bəl) adj. —preferred' stock, stock that receives a dividend before common stock.

pref'er·ence (pref'ə-rəns) n. 1, act of preferring; choice; favor. 2, preferred or superior position.

pref'er·en'tial (pref'ər-en'shəl) adj. favored; based on preference.

pre·fer'ment (pri-fēr'mənt) n. promotion.

pre'fix (prē'fiks) v.t. fix or place before. —n. in compound words, one or more letters or syllables that go before and qualify another word.

preg'na·ble (preg'nə-bəl) adj. capable of being taken by force.

preg'nant (preg'nənt) adj. 1, carrying unborn young. 2, fertile; inventive. 3, full of significance. —preg'nan·cy, n.

pre·hen'sile (pri-hen'sil) adj. fitted for grasping or holding, as claws.

pre'his·tor'ic (prē'his-tor'ik) adj. preceding recorded history. —pre'his·tor'i·cal·ly, adv.

pre·judge' (prē-juj') v.t. judge or condemn before proper inquiry.

prej'u·dice (prej'ə-dis) n. 1, an opinion, often unfavorable, formed without adequate reasons; bias. 2, disadvantageous effect. —v.t. 1, cause prejudice in. 2, damage. —prej'u·di'cial (-dish'əl) adj.

prel'ate (prel'ət) n. a high ecclesiastical dignitary. —prel'a·cy, n.

pre·lim'in·ar''y (pri-lim'i-ner'ē) adj. leading up to something more important. —n. (usually pl.) a preparatory act, feature, test, etc.

prel'ude (prel'ūd) n. 1, something preliminary or introductory. 2, (Music) an introductory movement.

pre'ma·ture'' (prē'mə-tyūr') adj. happening before maturity or too soon; overhasty.

pre''med'i·cal (prē''med'i-kəl) adj. preparing for the study of medicine.

pre·med'i·tate'' (prē-med'i-tāt') v.t. & i. consider or plan beforehand. —pre·med'i·ta'tion, n.

pre'mi·er (prē'mē-ər) adj. chief; foremost. —n. the chief minister of state; prime minister.

pre·mière' (pri-myär'; Colloq. pri-mir') n. a first performance; opening.

prem'ise (prem'is) n. 1, a previous statement from which something is inferred or concluded. 2, (pl.) real estate; a building and grounds.

pre'mi·um (prē'mē-əm) n. 1, a prize; reward; anything given as an inducement. 2, an amount to be paid for insurance. 3, an excess of value over cost.

pre'mo·ni'tion (prē''mə-nish'ən) n. a foreboding, as of impending danger.

pre·mon'i·to·ry (pri-mon'ə-tōr-ē) adj. forewarning.

pre·na'tal (prē''nā'təl) adj. occurring or existing before birth.

pre·oc'cu·py' (prē-ok'yə-pī') v.t. take the attention of, to the exclusion of other matters; engross; absorb. —pre·oc'cu·pied', adj. —pre·oc'cu·pa'tion, n.

pre'or·dain' (prē''ōr-dān') v.t. decree beforehand. —pre''or·di·na'tion, n.

prep adj. (Colloq.) preparatory; as, a prep school.

prep''a·ra'tion (prep''ə-rā'shən) n. the act, means, or result of preparing.

pre·par'a·to·ry (pri-par'ə-tōr-ē) adj. serving to make ready.

pre·pare' (pri-pär') v.t. 1, make ready for a particular purpose. 2, instruct. 3, provide; fit out. 4, make; manufacture; compound. —v.i. 1, put things in readiness. 2, make oneself ready.

pre·par'ed·ness n. the state of being prepared, esp. for war.

pre·pay' (prē-pā') v.t. pay or pay for in advance. —pre'paid'', adj.

pre·pon'der·ate'' (pri-pon'də-rāt') v.i. exceed in weight, influence, number, etc.; prevail. —pre·pon'der·ance, n. —pre·pon'der·ant, adj.

prep''o·si'tion (prep''ə-zish'ən) n. (Gram.) a part of speech serving to show the relation between a noun or pronoun and some other word. —prep''o·si'tion·al, adj.

pre''pos·sess' (prē''pə-zes') v.t.

1, impress favorably at the outset. 2, dominate, as a prejudice. —**pre′·pos·sess′ing**, adj. arousing favorable bias.

pre·pos′ter·ous (pri-pos′tər-əs) adj. contrary to common sense; glaringly absurd. —**pre·pos′ter·ous·ness**, n.

pre′puce (prē′pūs) n. the foreskin.

pre·req′ui·site (prē-rek′wə-zit) adj. necessary as an antecedent condition. —n. something needed in advance or at the outset.

pre·rog′a·tive (pri-rog′ə-tiv) n. a right or privilege inherent in one's office or position.

pres′age (pres′ij) n. an omen; foreboding. —v.t. (pri-sāj′) give a warning of; foretell.

pres′by·ter (prez′bi-tər) n. 1, a Presbyterian elder or minister. 2, a title of some clergymen.

Pres″by·te′ri·an (prez″bi-tir′ē-ən) adj. & n. pert. to a Prot. church governed by its ministers and elders.

pres′by·ter·y (-tər-ē) n. 1, a ruling council of a church; its jurisdiction. 2, a priest's residence.

pre′sci·ence (prē′shē-əns) n. foreknowledge; foresight.

pre·scribe′ (prē-skrīb′) v.t. 1, lay down beforehand as a rule. 2, advise the use of (a medicine).

pre′script (prē′skript) n. a rule.

pre·scrip′tion (pri-skrip′shən) n. 1, authoritative directions, esp. for a medicine. 2, the medicine.

pres′ence (prez′əns) n. 1, the fact of being present. 2, immediate vicinity. 3, a person's bearing, demeanor, etc. 4, a spirit. —presence of mind, alertness in emergencies.

pres′ent (prez′ənt) adj. 1, being at the place in question; here. 2, being or occurring at this time; not past or future. —n. 1, time now passing. 2, the present tense. 3, a gift.

pre·sent′ (pri-zent′) v.t. 1, make a gift to; offer as a gift. 2, introduce; exhibit; display. —**pre·sent′a·ble**, adj. in fit shape to be offered or seen.

pres″en·ta′tion (prez″ən-tā′shən) n. 1, act of presenting. 2, something presented; an exhibition, show, etc.

pre·sen′ti·ment (pri-zen′tə-mənt) n. a foreboding; premonition.

pres′ent·ly (-lē) adv. 1, soon. 2, at this time.

pre·sent′ment (-mənt) n. 1, presentation. 2, (Law) a statement or charge of an offense by a Grand Jury, based on its own knowledge.

pres″er·va′tion (prez″ər-vā′shən) n. act or effect of preserving.

pre·serv′a·tive (pri-zėrv′ə-tiv) adj. & n. serving to keep alive or sound.

pre·serve′ (pri-zėrv′) v.t. 1, keep safe or free from harm. 2, keep alive or permanent. 3, retain (a quality, condition). 4, keep (food) from decay by canning, etc. —n. 1, (usually pl.) fruit, jam, or jellies. 2, ground set aside for the protection of game.

pre·side′ (pri-zīd′) v.i. act as chairman of a meeting; act as head.

pres′i·den·cy (prez′i-dən-sē) n. 1, office, function, etc. of a president. 2, a territory governed by a president.

pres′i·dent (prez′i-dənt) n. 1, (often cap.) the highest executive officer of a republic, company, club, college, etc. 2, a chairman. —**pres″i·den′tial**, adj.

press (pres) v.t. 1, bear down upon; weigh heavily upon. 2, compress; squeeze out. 3, clasp in the arms. 4, smooth or flatten by pressure. 5, thrust upon others; push; thrust aside. 6, urge on; hurry. 7, conscript; draft. —v.i. 1, bear heavily. 2, crowd. 3, hurry. —n. 1, a crowding pressure; urgency. 3, a chest, as for clothes. 4, a machine that exerts pressure, as for printing. 5, the practice and industry of printing or publishing. 6, periodicals, newspapers, and their representatives, collectively. —**press agent**, one employed to solicit favorable publicity.

press′ing adj. urgent; persistent.

press′man (-mən) n. [pl. -men] operator of a printing press.

pres′sure (presh′ər) n. 1, a bearing down; squeezing. 2, the exertion of influence or authority. 3, trouble; burden. 4, demand on one's time or energy. —**pres′sur·ized**, adj. supplied with compressed air to increase the air pressure.

pres″ti·dig″i·ta′tion (pres″tə-dij″ə-tā′shən) n. sleight of hand. —**pres″ti·dig′i·ta′tor**, n.

pres·tige′ (pres-tēzh′) n. influence arising from reputation or esteem.

pres′to (pres′tō) adv. quickly.

pre·sume′ (pri-zoom′) v.t. 1, take for granted; assume. 2, take upon oneself; dare. —v.i. behave with undue familiarity. —**pre·sum′a·ble**, adj.

pre·sump′tion (pri-zump′shən) n. 1, the act of presuming. 2, something believed on inconclusive evidence.

pre·sump′tive (pri-zump′tiv) adj. justifying or based on presumption.

pre·sump′tu·ous (pri-zump′tyū̇-əs) *adj.* arrogant; overbold. —**pre-sump′tu·ous·ness,** *n.*

pre″sup·pose′ (prē″sə-pōz′) *v.t.* 1, assume in advance. 2, imply as an antecedent fact. —**pre″sup·po·si′tion,** *n.*

pre·tend′ (pri-tend′) *v.t.* 1, make believe; feign. 2, profess falsely. —*v.i.* 1, make pretense. 2, assert a claim, as to a throne, etc.

pre·tense′ (pri-tens′; prē′tens) *n.* 1, a sham; false profession; pretext. 2, a claim. Also, **pre·tence′.**

pre·ten′sion (pri-ten′shən) *n.* 1, a claim; allegation. 2, (often *pl.*) ostentation.

pre·ten′tious (pri-ten′shəs) *adj.* ostentatious; showy. —**pre·ten′-tious·ness,** *n.*

pre·ter- *pref.* beyond; more than.

pret′er·it (pret′ər-it) *adj.* (*Gram.*) expressing action or existence in the past. —*n.* the past tense.

pre′text (prē′tekst) *n.* an ostensible reason; excuse.

pret′ty (prit′ē) *adj.* pleasing, esp. to the eye; attractive. —*adv.* fairly; tolerably. —**pret′ti·ness,** *n.*

pret′zel (pret′səl) *n.* a hard dry biscuit crusted with salt, in form of a stick or knot.

pre·vail′ (pri-vāl′) *v.i.* 1, be victorious. 2, (with *on* or *upon*) persuade. 3, be prevalent.

prev′a·lent (prev′ə-lənt) *adj.* of wide use or occurrence; widespread. —**prev′a·lence,** *n.*

pre·var′i·cate (pri-var′ə-kāt″) *v.i.* be evasive; lie. —**pre·var′i·ca′tion,** *n.* —**pre·var′i·ca·tor,** *n.*

pre·vent′ (pri-vent′) *v.t.* hinder or keep from doing or happening; impede. —**pre·ven′tive,** *adj.*

pre·ven′ta·tive (pri-ven′tə-tive) *n.* that which prevents. —*adj.* preventing; precautionary.

pre·ven′tion (pri-ven′shən) *n.* act or effect of preventing.

pre″view″ (prē′vū″) *n.* 1, an advance showing, as of a motion picture before general release. 2, [also, **pre′vue″**] an excerpt from a motion picture shown to advertise it. —*v.t.* show or see in advance.

pre′vi·ous (prē′vē-əs) *adj.* earlier; prior; foregoing. —**pre′vi·ous·ness,** *n.*

pre·vi′sion (prē-vizh′ən) *n.* foreknowledge; premonition.

pre·war′ *adj.* before the (most recent) war.

prex′y (prek′sē) *n.* (*Slang*) president.

prey (prā) *n.* 1, an animal killed by another for food. 2, any victim. 3, predatory habits, as, *a bird of prey.* —*v.i.* (with *on* or *upon*) seize and devour an animal. 2, plunder.

price (prīs) *n.* 1, a consideration, esp. money, demanded in exchange for something. 2, cost or sacrifice. 3, the offer of a reward. 4, an acceptable bribe. —*v.t.* set or ask the price of. —**price′less,** *adj.* invaluable.

prick (prik) *n.* 1, a tiny hole or wound made by a pointed instrument. 2, a stinging sensation. —*v.t.* 1, make a tiny hole in. 2, cause sharp pain to. 3, (with *-up*) raise (ears) as does a dog or horse.

prick′le (prik′əl) *n.* a small thornlike projection. —*v.i.* tingle; sting. —**prick′ly,** *adj.* —**prickly heat,** an inflammation of the sweat glands.

pride (prīd) *n.* 1, a sense of one's own worth; self-respect. 2, undue self-esteem; haughtiness. 3, a feeling or object of delight. —*v.t.* be proud of (oneself). —**pride′ful,** *adj.*

priest (prēst) *n.* a person authorized to perform religious rites. —**priest′ess,** *n.fem.* —**priest′hood,** *n.* —**priest′ly,** *adj.*

prig *n.* one who makes a show of virtue. —**prig′gish,** *adj.*

prim *adj.* [**prim′mer, -mest**] stiffly formal; demure. —**prim′ness,** *n.*

pri′ma·cy (prī′mə-sē) *n.* state of being first in rank, importance, etc.

pri′ma don′na (prē′mə don′ə) the principal female singer in an opera.

pri′mal (prī′məl) *adj.* original; primeval.

pri′ma·ry (prī′mer-ē) *adj.* coming first; chief; principal; original; earliest; preliminary; elementary. —*n.* 1, the first. 2, an election to nominate candidates. —**primary colors,** in the spectrum, red, green, and blue; in pigments, red, yellow and blue.

pri′mate (prī′mit) *n.* 1, an archbishop. 2, one of an order of animals that includes man, the apes, etc.

prime (prīm) *adj.* 1, first in order of time, rank, degree. 2, of highest quality. 3, of a number, divisible only by itself and unity. —*n.* 1, the first part; earliest stage. 2, the part of highest quality. 3, the period of greatest vigor. —*v.t.* prepare; make ready; supply with priming. —**prime minister,** in some countries, the chief executive or cabinet officer.

prim′er *n.* 1, (prī′mər) that which primes; an instrument or charge to promote ignition. 2, (prim′ər) an elementary textbook, esp. a reader.

pri·me'val (prī-mē'vəl) *adj.* pert. to earliest times; primitive.

prim'ing (prī'ming) *n.* 1, powder, fuel, etc. used to ignite a charge, as in a firearm. 2, the adding of liquids to a pump, to start it. 3, a first coat of paint.

prim'i·tive (prim'ə-tiv) *adj.* 1, early in the history of the world or man; original. 2, simple; crude. 3, basic. —*n.* 1, an untrained artist. 2, a basic form of a word or equation.

pri"mo·gen'i·ture (prī"mə-jen'ə-chər) *n.* 1, the fact of being the first born. 2, the eldest son's right of inheritance or succession.

pri·mor'di·al (prī-môr'dē-əl) *adj.* original; earliest.

primp *v.t. & t.* dress (oneself) with elaborate care; prink.

prim'rose" (prim'rōz") *n.* a spring-flowering plant; its yellow flower.

prince (prins) *n.* 1, a ruler of a principality or small state. 2, a monarch. 3, the title of a son of a sovereign. 4, a title of high nobility. 5, a pre-eminent person. —**prin'cess**, *n. fem.*

Primrose

prince'ly *adj.* 1, royal. 2, lavish; magnificent. —**prince'li·ness**, *n.*

prin'ci·pal (prin'sə-pəl) *adj.* first in rank or importance; chief. —*n.* 1, one who takes a leading part. 2, the head of a school. 3, capital bearing interest. 4, the employer of an agent.

prin"ci·pal'i·ty (prin"sə-pal'ə-tē) *n.* the domain of a prince.

prin'ci·ple (prin'sə-pəl) *n.* 1, a fundamental truth or doctrine on which others are based. 2, (*pl.*) rules of conduct or ethical behavior.

prink *v.t. & i.* dress up; adorn.

print *n.* 1, a mark made by impression. 2, a seal or die. 3, anything printed; (of a book) publication. 4, cloth stamped with a design. —*v.t.* 1, impress; stamp. 2, produce (reading matter from type, a photograph from a film, etc.). 3, form (letters) in imitation of type.

print'er (-ər) *n.* 1, one whose business or trade is printing. 2, a device for copying (not applied to printing machinery).

print'ing *n.* 1, the process of producing the printed portion of books, etc. 2, the use of capital letters only, in handwriting. 3, something printed.

pri'or (prī'ər) *adj.* preceding in time, order, or importance. —*adv.* (with *to*) previous. —*n.* a superior in a religious order or house (*priory*). —**pri'or·ess**, *n. fem.*

pri·or'i·ty (prī-or'ə-tē) *n*: 1, the state of being prior. 2, a right of precedence.

prise (prīz) *v.t.* pry (def. 1).

prism (priz'əm) *n.* 1, a solid figure whose sides are parallelograms and whose ends are similar equal polygons and parallel. 2, a transparent body that separates light into its component colors. —**pris·mat'ic**, *adj.*

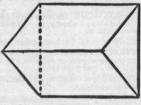
Prism

pris'on (priz'ən) *n.* a jail. —**pris'on·er**, one confined in or as in prison or forcibly restrained.

pris'sy (pris'ē) *adj.* (*Colloq.*) prim. —**pris'si·ness**, *n.*

pris'tine (pris'tēn) *adj.* original; primitive; unspoiled.

pri'va·cy (prī'və-sē) *n.* state of being private or alone.

pri'vate (prī'vit) *adj.* 1, personal; not public. 2, secret, confidential; being alone. 3, retired; secluded. —*n.* a soldier of lowest rank.

pri"va·teer' (prī"və-tir') *n.* a ship operating under a letter of marque; its commander.

pri·va'tion (prī-vā'shən) *n.* want; destitution.

priv'et (priv'it) *n.* an evergreen shrub, much used for hedges.

priv'i·lege (priv'ə-lij) *n.* a special advantage enjoyed by a person. —**priv'i·leged**, *adj.* exempt; favored.

priv'y (priv'ē) *adj.* 1, (with *to*) admitted to a secret. 2, private. —*n.* a small building used as a toilet. —**privy council**, a small advisory body.

prize (prīz) *n.* 1, a reward given as a symbol of superiority. 2, anything highly valued. 3, a ship seized from an enemy. —*v.t.* 1, value highly. 2, [also, **prise**], pry. —*adj.* 1, worthy of or given as a prize. 2, outstanding; superior. —**prize fight**, a professional boxing match. —**prize ring**, prize-fighting as a profession.

pro (prō) *n.* [*pl.* pros] 1, a proponent. 2, (*Colloq.*) a professional, esp. in sports. —*adv.* for the affirmative. —*prep.* for.

pro- *pref.* 1, in favor of. 2, on behalf of.

prob'a·bil'i·ty (prob″ə-bil'ə-tē) *n.* 1, likelihood. 2, that which appears true or likely. 3, (*pl.*) relative chances of occurrence; expectancy.

prob'a·ble (prob'ə-bəl) *adj.* to be expected; likely. —**prob'a·bly**, *adv.*

pro'bate (prō'bāt) *n.* (*Law*) official proof of a will. —*v.t.* submit for probate.

pro·ba'tion (prō-bā'shən) *n.* 1, a method or period of test or trial. 2, conditional release of a prisoner. —**pro·ba'tion·a·ry**, *adj.* —**pro·ba'tion·er**, *n.* one who is being tested.

probe (prōb) *n.* 1, a surgical instrument for exploring cavities, etc. 2, a searching investigation. —*v.t. & i.* search (into); explore.

pro'bi·ty (prō'bə-tē) *n.* integrity.

prob'lem (prob'ləm) *n.* 1, a difficult or perplexing matter; a troublesome person. 2, a proposition to be worked out. —**prob'lem·at'i·cal**, *adj.* questionable; doubtful.

pro·bos'cis (prō-bos'is) *n.* a long flexible nose or snout.

pro·ce'dure (prə-sē'jər) *n.* 1, a course or mode of action; a step taken. 2, customary process. —**pro·ce'dur·al**, *adj.*

pro·ceed' (prə-sēd') *v.i.* 1, go forward; continue or renew progress. 2, issue; come forth. 3, begin and carry on legal action.

pro·ceed'ing *n.* 1, a measure or step taken; a legal action. 2, (*pl.*) business done; a record of it.

pro'ceeds (prō'sēdz) *n.pl.* money taken in.

proc'ess (pros'es) *n.* 1, course; progress; lapse (of time). 2, a series of changes leading to some result. 3, a series of operations, as in manufacturing. 4, (*Anatomy*) an outgrowth; protuberance. 5, (*Law*) a summons. —*v.t.* subject to a special treatment.

pro·ces'sion (prə-sesh'ən) *n.* an array, formal march, or orderly series; those constituting it.

pro·ces'sion·al (-əl) *n.* a hymn to which clergy and choir enter.

pro·claim' (prō-klām') *v.t.* declare publicly; announce officially.

proc''la·ma'tion (prok″lə-mā'shən) *n.* act or result of proclaiming; announcement.

pro·cliv'i·ty (prō-kliv'ə-tē) *n.* inclination; tendency; predisposition.

pro·cras'ti·nate'' (prō-kras'tə-nāt″) *v.i.* delay action. —**pro·cras''ti·na'tion**, *n.* —**pro·cras'ti·na''tor**, *n.*

pro'cre·ate'' (prō'krē-āt″) *v.t.* engender; beget. —**pro''cre·a'tion**, *n.*

proc·tol'o·gy (prok-tol'ə-jē) *n.* (*Med.*) the study and treatment of rectal and anal diseases.

proc'tor (prok'tər) *n.* 1, a supervising official, esp. in a college. 2, a representative in a church court. —**proc·to'ri·al** (-tôr'ē-əl) *adj.*

proc'u·ra''tor (prok'yū-rā''tər) *n.* a colonial governor for ancient Rome.

pro·cure' (prə-kyūr') *v.t.* 1, contrive and effect. 2, obtain. —**pro·cure'ment**, *n.*

pro·cur'er (prō-kyūr'ər) *n.* a pimp. —**pro·cur'ess**, *n.fem.*

prod *n.* a goad. —*v.t.* [prod'ded, -ding] goad; poke.

prod'i·gal (prod'i-gəl) *adj.* 1, lavish; wasteful. 2, bountiful. —*n.* a spendthrift. —**prod''i·gal'i·ty**, *n.*

pro·di'gious (prə-dij'əs) *adj.* vast; huge; immense. —**pro·di'gious·ness**, *n.*

prod'i·gy (prod'ə-jē) *n.* something remarkable; a marvel.

pro·duce' (prə-dūs') *v.t.* 1, bring out; exhibit. 2, bear, yield. 3, bring about; effect. 4, make; manufacture. —*v.i.* yield. —*n.* (prod'ūs) yield; products, esp. agricultural.

prod'uct (prod'ukt) *n.* 1, that which is produced; an effect; result. 2, the number resulting from multiplication.

pro·duc'tion (prə-duk'shən) *n.* 1, act of bringing forward. 2, a product of physical or mental labor; esp., a theatrical presentation.

pro·duc'tive (prə-duk'tiv) *adj.* 1, creative; fertile. 2, profitable. —**pro·duc'tive·ness**, *n.*

pro·fane' (prə-fān') *adj.* 1, not sacred; irreverent; blasphemous. 2, vulgar. —*v.t.* pollute; debase. —**prof''a·na'tion** (prof″ə-nā'shən) *n.*

pro·fan'i·ty (prə-fan'ə-tē) *n.* blasphemy; swearing.

pro·fess' (prə-fes') *v.t.* 1, declare openly. 2, affirm faith in. 3, make a pretense of. —**pro·fessed'**, *adj.* avowed.

pro·fes'sion (prə-fesh'ən) *n.* 1, an avowal. 2, a vocation, esp. in a branch of science or learning; the body of persons engaged in such a vocation.

pro·fes'sion·al *adj.* pert. to or engaged in a profession, or in a sport for pay. —*n.* one working for pay, not an amateur. —pro·fes'-sion·al·ism, n.

pro·fes'sor (prə·fes'ər) n. a teacher of high rank. —pro·fes·sor·i·al (prŏf'ə·sôr'ē·əl) adj.

prof'fer (prof'ər) v.t. tender. —n. an offer.

pro·fi'cient (prə·fish'ənt) adj. skilled. —pro·fi'cien·cy, n.

pro'file (prō'fīl) n. 1, a side view of a face. 2, a contour. 3, (T.N.) a colorful biographical sketch.

prof'it n. 1, advantage; benefit. 2, monetary gain; excess of returns over costs; benefit. —prof'it·a·ble, adj. yielding a profit.

prof'it·eer' (prof'i·tir') n. one who profits unduly from the sale of necessities. —v.i. profit unduly.

prof'li·gate (prof'li·gət) adj. dissolute; recklessly extravagant. —n. a spendthrift. —prof'li·ga·cy, n.

pro·found' (prə·fownd') adj. 1, deep; thorough. 2, intense; deeply felt. —pro·found'ness, n.

pro·fun'di·ty (prə·fun'də·tē) n. profoundness; intellectual deepness.

pro·fuse' (prə·fūs') adj. liberal to excess; copious; abundant. —pro·fu'sion (-zhən) n.

pro·gen'i·tor (prō·jen'ə·tər) n. an ancestor in the direct line.

prog'e·ny (proj'ə·nē) n. offspring.

prog·no'sis (prog·nō'sis) n. a forecast. —prog·nos'tic (-nos'tik) adj. —prog·nos'ti·cal·ly, adv.

prog·nos'ti·cate' (prog·nos'tə·kāt') v.t. foretell; predict. —prog·nos'ti·ca'tion, n.

pro'gram (prō'gram) n. 1, a printed list of events, performers, etc., in any public entertainment. 2, a plan of procedure. —v.t. schedule. Also, pro'gramme.

prog'ress (prog'res) n. 1, a moving forward. 2, advance; development. —v.i. (prə·gres') 1, proceed; advance. 2, grow; develop.

pro·gres'sion (prə·gresh'ən) n. 1, a moving forward. 2, a sequence, as of events.

pro·gres'sive (prə·gres'iv) adj. 1, moving forward. 2, advocating new ideas, methods, etc. 3, (Gram.) indicating action going on at the time, as is going; was going. —n. one who is not conservative. —pro·gres'sive·ness, n.

pro·hib'it (prō·hib'it) v.t. 1, forbid. 2, prevent; hinder. —pro·hib'i·to·ry, adj.

pro"hi·bi'tion (prō"ə·bish'ən) n. act or effect of forbidding; esp. (U.S.) the period 1920–33 when the 18th Amendment was in effect. —pro"hi·bi'tion·ist, n. one favoring prohibition of alcoholic liquors.

pro·hib'i·tive (prə·hib'i·tiv) adj. tending to preclude or discourage, as a high price. —pro·hib'i·tive·ness, n.

proj'ect (proj'ekt) n. 1, a plan; scheme. 2, a piece of research; a problem undertaken in school. 3, a public works development, esp. in housing. —v.t. (prə·jekt') 1, cast forward; impose. 2, devise. 3, cause (light, shadow) to fall on a surface, as a screen. —v.i. jut out; protrude.

pro·jec'tile (prə·jek'til) n. a missile, as a bullet.

pro·jec'tion (prə·jek'shən) n. 1, act or effect of projecting. 2, a part that juts out.

pro·jec'tor (prə·jek'tər) n. an optical instrument that projects an image, as a motion picture.

pro'late (prō'lāt) adj. extended; elongated, as a spheroid.

pro'le·tar'i·at (prō'lə·târ'ē·ət) n. the laboring class. —pro'le·tar'i·an, adj. & n.

pro·lif'ic (prō·lif'ik) adj. 1, producing young, fruit, etc., abundantly. 2, producing much work, etc. —pro·lif'i·cal·ly, adv.

pro·lix' (prō·liks') adj. long and wordy; tedious. —pro·lix'i·ty, n.

pro'logue (prō'lâg) n. the introduction to a poem, play, etc.

pro·long' (prə·lâng') v.t. extend in time or length. —pro'lon·ga'tion, n.

prom'e·nade' (prom"ə·nād') n. 1, a stroll for pleasure; a place for strolling. 2, [also (Colloq.) prom] a dance; ball. —v.i. & t. take a stroll.

prom'i·nent (prom'ə·nənt) adj. 1, standing out; jutting. 2, conspicuous; distinguished. —prom'i·nence, n.

pro·mis'cu·ous (prə·mis'kū·əs) adj. 1, of all sorts and kinds; indiscriminate. 2, not discriminating in choice of companions. —prom'is·cu'i·ty (prom"is·kū'ə·tē) n.

prom'ise (prom'is) n. 1, one's pledge to another that one will or will not do something. 2, ground for hope. —v.t. 1, engage to do or give; give one's word to. 2, afford hope or expectation (of). —prom'is·ing, adj. encouraging; apparently due to succeed.

prom'is·so·ry (-sôr·ē) adj. stating an obligation to pay, as, a promissory note.

prom'on·to'ry (prom'ən·tôr'ē) n. high land jutting into the sea.

pro·mote' (prə·mōt') v.t. 1, encourage the growth or improvement of. 2, raise to a higher rank, class, or position. —pro·mot'er, n. one who helps to start an enterprise.

---

fat, fāte, fär, fāre, fäll, åsk; met, hē, hėr, maybē; pin, pīne; not, nōte, ôr, tool

pro·mo'tion (prə-mō'shən) *n.* **1,** act or effect of promoting. **2,** advancement in rank. **3,** an enterprise being promoted.

prompt *adj.* **1,** quick to act. **2,** given without delay. **3,** on time. —*v.t.* **1,** move or incite to action. **2,** remind (an actor, speaker) of his lines. —**promp'ti·tude** (-ti-tood) *n.* —**prompt'ness,** *n.*

pro·mul'gate (prō-mul'gāt) *v.t.* make known publicly; proclaim. —**pro"mul·ga'tion,** *n.*

prone (prōn) *adj.* **1,** lying face downward. **2,** having a natural tendency; inclined. —**prone'ness,** *n.*

prong *n.* a sharp point, as a tine.

pro'noun (prō'nown) *n.* a word (as *he, it*) used to represent a noun previously stated or understood. —**pro·nom'in·al,** *adj.*

pro·nounce' (prə-nowns') *v.t.* **1,** declare; utter. **2,** utter the recognized sound of (a word). —*v.i.* **1,** give as one's opinion. **2,** articulate words. —**pro·nounced',** *adj.* clearly so; decided. —**pro·nounce'ment,** *n.* a formal announcement.

pron'to (pron'tō) *adv.* (*Colloq.*) at once; immediately.

pro·nun"ci·a'tion (prə-nun'sē-ā'shən) *n.* the uttering of words, esp. with correct sounds and accents.

proof *n.* **1,** evidence that establishes a fact. **2,** a test; trial. **3,** an impression from composed type, taken for correction. —*adj.* **1,** (often as a *suf.*) able to withstand. **2,** of liquors, times ½ of 1% absolute alcohol, as, 90 proof is 45% alcohol.

proof'read' *v.t. & i.* [*pret. & p.p.* -read (-red)] read and correct.

prop *v.t.* [propped, prop'ping] support or keep from falling, as by placing something under or against. —*n.* **1,** a support. **2,** an airplane propeller. **3,** a part of a stage setting.

prop"a·gan'da (prop"ə-gan'də) *n.* ideas disseminated to support a doctrine. —**prop"a·gan'dist,** *n.* —**prop"a·gan'dize** (-dīz") *v.t. & i.*

prop'a·gate (prop'ə-gāt) *v.t.* **1,** cause to multiply by natural processes. **2,** spread; disseminate. —*v.i.* have offspring. —**prop"a·ga'tion,** *n.*

pro·pel' (prə-pel') *v.t.* [pro·pelled', -pel'ling] drive forward by force.

pro·pel'ler (prə-pel'ər) *n.* a device with revolving blades for driving forward a ship or airplane.

pro·pen'si·ty (prə-pen'sə-tē) *n.* a natural tendency; bent.

prop'er (prop'ər) *adj.* **1,** particularly suited; natural. **2,** fit; appropriate. **3,** taken in a strict sense.

4, accurate. **5,** decent; respectable. **6,** of a noun, naming one particular person, place, etc. —**prop'er·ness,** *n.*

prop'er·ty (prop'ər-tē) *n.* **1,** an essential attribute or quality. **2,** ownership. **3,** a thing owned, esp. real estate; a possession. **4,** (*pl.*) items in a stage setting.

proph'e·cy (prof'ə-sē) *n.* a prediction of the future.

proph'e·sy" (prof'ə-sī") *v.t. & i.* predict; foretell.

proph'et (prof'it) *n.* **1,** one who predicts. **2,** a spokesman, esp. one inspired by God.

pro·phet'ic (prə-fet'ik) *adj.* **1,** pert. to prophecy or a prophet. **2,** presaging. —**pro·phet'i·cal·ly,** *adv.*

pro"phy·lax'is (prō"fə-lak'sis) *n.* (*Med.*) preventive treatment. —**pro"phy·lac'tic,** *n. & adj.*

pro·pin'qui·ty (prō-ping'kwi-tē) *n.* nearness, in time, place, or blood.

pro·pi'ti·ate" (prō-pish'ē-āt") *v.t.* appease; conciliate. —**pro·pi"ti·a'tion,** *n.* —**pro·pi'ti·a·to·ry,** *adj.*

pro·pi'tious (prə-pish'əs) *adj.* **1,** kindly disposed. **2,** favorable. —**pro·pi'tious·ness,** *n.*

pro·po'nent (prə-pō'nənt) *n.* one who proposes or supports something.

pro·por'tion (prə-pôr'shən) *n.* **1,** the relation of one thing or part to another in respect to size, degree, or quantity. **2,** symmetrical arrangement; harmony. **3,** just or proper share. **4,** (*pl.*) dimensions. —**pro·por'tion·al,** *adj.* —**pro·por'tion·ate** (-ət) *adj.*

pro·pose' (prə-pōz') *v.t.* **1,** offer for consideration, acceptance, admission, or adoption. **2,** put forward as a plan; suggest. —*v.i.* **1,** intend. **2,** make an offer of marriage. —**pro·pos'al,** *n.*

prop"o·si'tion (prop"ə-zish'ən) *n.* **1,** a subject for study, discussion, etc.; a problem. **2,** (*Colloq.*) a project, undertaking, situation, etc. **3,** a proposal.

pro·pound' (prə-pownd') *v.t.* offer for consideration, as a question.

pro·pri'e·tar"y (prə-prī'ə-ter"ē) *adj.* **1,** pert. to an owner; holding property. **2,** privately owned.

pro·pri'e·tor *n.* an owner. —**pro·pri'e·tress,** *n.fem.* —**pro·pri'e·tor·ship,** *n.*

pro·pri'e·ty (prə-prī'ə-tē) *n.* **1,** fitness; rightness. **2,** correct behavior; decorum. **3,** (*pl.*) the standards of conduct approved by society.

pro·pul'sion (prə-pul'shən) *n.* **1,** a propelling forward. **2,** driving force.

pro·rate' (prō-rāt') *v.t.* divide proportionally. —**pro·ra'tion,** *n.*

pro·sa'ic (prō-zā'ik) *adj.* unromantic; commonplace. —**pro·sa'i·cal·ly,** *adv.*

pro·sce'ni·um (prō-sē'nē·əm) *n.* 1, a stage. 2, the front of the stage, before the curtain.

pro·scribe' (prō-skrīb') *v.t.* 1, prohibit. 2, banish. —**pro·scrip'tion,** *n.*

prose (prōz) *n.* ordinary language; not poetry. —**pros'y,** *adj.* dull.

pros'e·cute" (pros'ə-kūt") *v.t.* 1, institute legal proceedings against. 2, pursue (an object). —*v.i.* sue.

pros"e·cu'tion (-kū'shən) *n.* 1, act or result of prosecuting. 2, the side that prosecutes.

pros'e·cu"tor *n.* the state's attorney.

pros'e·lyte" (pros'ə-līt") *n.* a convert from one creed, sect, or party to another. —**pros'e·ly·tize"** (-lə-tīz") *v.t. & i.* attempt to convert.

pros'o·dy (pros'ə-dē) *n.* the science of metrical versification.

pros'pect (pros'pekt) *n.* 1, a view; scene. 2, what one hopes for; expectation. 3, a possible buyer, client, etc. —*v.t. & i.* explore (a district) for ores, oil, etc. —**pro·spec'tive,** *adj.* expected. —**pros'pec·tor,** *n.* one who seeks ores.

pros·pec'tus (prə-spek'təs) *n.* a descriptive pamphlet; catalog.

pros'per (pros'pər) *v.i.* succeed; thrive. —**pros'per·ous,** *adj.* prospering.

pros·per'i·ty (pros-per'ə-tē) *n.* 1, success. 2, a period of economic well-being.

pros'tate (pros'tāt) *n. & adj.* a gland in males. —**pros·tat'ic,** *adj.*

pros'ti·tute" (pros'tə-tūt") *v.t.* devote (one's honor, talents, person) to base purposes. —*n.* a harlot. —**pros'ti·tu'tion,** *n.*

pros'trate (pros'trāt) *adj.* 1, lying flat; laid low. 2, bowing low. —*v.t.* —**pros·tra'tion,** *n.*

pro·tag'o·nist (prō-tag'ə-nist) *n.* the leading figure, as in a play.

pro'te·an (prō'tē-ən) *adj.* readily assuming many shapes.

pro·tect' (prə-tekt') *v.t.* shield from harm, damage, etc. —**pro·tec'tor,** *n.*

pro·tec'tion *n.* 1, act or effect of protecting; that which keeps safe. 2, support of domestic prices by a tariff. 3, immunity from arrest, purchased by bribery.

pro·tec'tive *adj.* 1, serving to protect or supply protection. 2, wishing to protect. —**pro·tec'tive·ness,** *n.*

pro·tec'tor·ate (-ət) *n.* a state controlled and protected by a stronger state.

pro'té·gé" (prō'tə-zhā") *n.* a person protected or aided by another.

pro'te·in (prō'tē·in) *n.* an organic substance, an essential element of diet; formerly called *proteid.*

pro'test (prō'test) *v.i. & t.* 1, declare solemnly. 2, remonstrate; object to. 3, declare to be dishonored by nonpayment, as a check, etc. —*n.* a formal declaration of disapproval. —**prot"es·ta'tion,** *n.*

Prot'es·tant (prot'is·tənt) *adj.* pert. to a Christian church not Roman or Orthodox Catholic. —*n.* a member of such a church. —**Prot'es·tant·ism,** *n.*

pro'tha·la'mi·um (prō"thə·lā'mē·əm) *n.* a pre-wedding ode.

pro·to- *pref.* first in time; principal; chief.

pro'to·col" (prō'tə-kol") *n.* 1, a draft of a treaty or agreement. 2, the highly formal procedure in official society.

pro'ton (prō'ton) *n.* a particle of the atom, carrying a positive charge of electricity.

pro'to·plasm (prō'tə-plaz-əm) *n.* the substance of which all animal and plant cells are composed. —**pro'to·plas'mic,** *adj.*

pro'to·type" (prō'tə-tīp") *n.* the original form; pattern; model.

pro"to·zo'an (prō"tə-zō'ən) *n.* a microscopic one-celled animal.

pro·tract' (prō-trakt') *v.t.* 1, prolong. 2, draw to scale; chart. —**pro·trac'tion,** *n.*

pro·trac'tor (ər) *n.* 1, a muscle that extends a part of the body. 2, a device for measuring angles.

Protractor

pro·trude' (prō-trood') *v.i. & t.* stick out; project. —**pro·tru'sion,** *n.*

pro·tu'ber·ant (prō-tū'bər-ənt) *adj.* bulging out; prominent. —**pro·tu'ber·ance,** *n.*

proud (prowd) *adj.* 1, haughty; arrogant. 2, self-respectful. 3, being gratified or elated. 4, imposing; splendid. 3, spirited. —**proud'ness,** *n.*

prove (proov) *v.t.* 1, test the qualities of. 2, make certain, by adducing evidence. 3, probate. 4, make a proof of (type). —*v.i.* turn out (to be). —**prov′en,** *adj.* proved.

prov′en·der (prov′ən-dər) *n.* dry food for animals; fodder.

prov′erb (prov′ẽrb) *n.* a well-known truth expressed as a maxim. —**pro·ver′bi·al,** *adj.*

pro·vide′ (prə-vīd′) *v.t.* 1, procure beforehand. 2, (with *with*) furnish. —*v.i.* 1, furnish supplies; take precautions. 2, supply what is needed. 3, stipulate. —**pro·vid′ed,** *conj.* on the condition that.

prov′i·dence (prov′i-dəns) *n.* 1, thrift; economy. 2, (*Cap.*) God; divine care.

prov′i·dent (prov′i-dənt) *adj.* thrifty; foresighted.

prov′i·den′tial (prov′i-den′shəl) *adj.* 1, of or by divine guidance. 2, opportune.

prov′ince (prov′ins) *n.* 1, an administrative division of a country. 2, (*pl.*) rural regions. 3, a proper sphere of action.

pro·vin′cial (prə-vin′shəl) *adj.* 1, of a province. 2, rustic. 3, narrow; not cosmopolitan. —**pro·vin′cial·ism,** *n.*

pro·vi′sion (prə-vizh′ən) *n.* 1, preparation. 2, (*pl.*) stores; supplies, as of food. 3, a proviso; condition, as in a contract. —**pro·vi′sion·al,** *adj.* 1, conditional. 2, temporary.

pro·vi′so (prə-vī′zō) *n.* [*pl.* -sos (-zōz)] a condition, esp. in a contract.

prov″o·ca′tion (prov″ə-kā′shən) *n.* 1, act or effect of provoking. 2, a cause of anger or resentment. 3, stimulus; incitement.

pro·voc′a·tive (prə-vok′ə-tiv) *adj.* serving to provoke, arouse, or stimulate. —**pro·voc′a·tive·ness,** *n.*

pro·voke′ (prə-vōk′) *v.t.* 1, incense; irritate. 2, arouse; goad. 3, incite; stir up.

prov′ost (prov′əst) *n.* a supervisor or head. —**provost marshal,** a chief of military police.

prow *n.* the foremost surface of a ship; bow.

prow′ess (prow′is) *n.* 1, valor. 2, great skill or ability.

prowl *v.i.* & *t.* roam about stealthily. —*n.* act of prowling. —**prowl car,** a radio-equipped police automobile.

prox′i·mate (prok′si-mət) *adj.* next; immediate.

prox·im′i·ty (prok-sim′ə-tē) *n.* nearness. —**proximity fuse,** a device to explode a bomb when it approaches its object.

prox′y (prok′sē) *n.* authority to act for another.

prude (prood) *n.* an affectedly modest person. —**prud′er·y,** *n.* —**prud′ish,** *adj.*

pru′dence (proo′dəns) *n.* discretion; foresight; careful judgment. —**pru·den′tial** (-den′shəl) *adj.*

pru′dent (proo′dənt) *adj.* 1, judicious; wise. 2, discreet; circumspect.

prune (proon) *n.* a dried plum. —*v.t.* & *i.* trim off something superfluous, esp. branches.

pru′ri·ent (prûr′ē·ənt) *adj.* lewd in thought. —**pru′ri·ence,** *n.*

Prus′sian (prush′ən) *adj.* pert. to Prussia or its people. —**Prussian blue,** a dark blue dye or pigment.

pry (prī) *n.* a lever. —*v.t.* 1, raise or move by a lever. 2, extract or move with difficulty. —*v.i.* peer curiously or impertinently.

psalm (säm) *n.* a sacred song or poem. —**psalm′ist,** *n.* —**psal′mo·dy** (sä′mə-dē; sal′-) *n.*

Psal′ter (sâl′tər) *n.* the Book of Psalms.

pseu′do (soo′dō) *adj.* feigned; sham.

pseu·do- *pref.* false; sham.

pseu′do·nym″ (soo′də-nim″) *n.* a false name; pen name.

pshaw (shâ) *interj.* of disdain.

psi (sī) *n.* the twenty-third letter of the Greek alphabet (Ψ, ψ).

psit″ta·co′sis (sit″ə-kō′sis) *n.* a contagious disease of birds, transferable to man: parrot fever.

psy′che (sī′kē) *n.* the human soul.

psy·chi′a·try (sī-kī′ə-trē) *n.* (*Med.*) the science dealing with mental diseases. —**psy″chi·at′ric** (sī″kē-at′rik) *adj.* —**psy·chi′a·trist,** *n.*

psy′chic (sī′kik) *adj.* 1, pert. to the mental or spiritual life. 2, pert. to mysterious mental forces. 3, sensitive to such forces. —**psy′chi·cal·ly,** *adv.*

psy·cho- *pref.* of the mind; by mental processes.

psy″cho·a·nal′y·sis (sī″kō-ə-nal′ə-sis) *n.* a method of relieving mental disorders by a study of the subconscious emotional life of the patient. —**psy″cho·an′a·lyze,** *v.t.* —**psy″cho·an′a·lyst,** *n.*

psy·chol′o·gy (sī-kol′ə-jē) *n.* 1, the science of the mind and mental activities. 2, (*Colloq.*) attitude. 3, (*Colloq.*) the use of stratagems. —**psy″cho·log′i·cal,** *adj.* —**psy″chol′o·gist,** *n.*

psy″cho·pa·thol′o·gy (sī″kō-pə-thol′ə-jē) *n.* the science dealing with mental illness and abnormality.

psy·chop'a·thy (sĭ-kŏp'ə-thē) *n.* mental disease.

psy'cho·path" (sĭ'kō-păth") *n,* one mentally afflicted.

psy"cho·path'ic (-ĭk) *adj.* pert. to any mental disorder, its study or treatment. —**psy"cho·path'i·cal·ly,** *adv.*

psy·cho'sis (sĭ-kō'sĭs) *n.* [*pl.* -ses (sēz)] a mental disease. —**psy·chot'ic** (-kŏt'ĭk) *adj.*

psy"cho·so·mat'ic (sĭ'kō-sō-măt'ĭk) *adj.* of a physical disease, induced by emotional factors.

ptar'mi·gan (tär'mə-gən) *n.* a kind of grouse.

pter"o·dac'tyl (ter"ə-dak'tĭl) *n.* an extinct large flying reptile.

pto'maine (tō'mān) *n.* a chemical compound, often poisonous, found in decaying organic matter.

pub *n.* (*Brit.*) public house.

pu'ber·ty (pū'bər·tē) *n.* the age at which a person first can procreate.

pu·bes'cent (pū-bes'ənt) *adj.* arrived, or arriving, at puberty. —**pu·bes'cence,** *n.*

pu'bic (pū'bĭk) *adj.* pert. to the front of the pelvis.

pub'lic (pŭb'lĭk) *adj.* **1,** pert. to the people at large. **2,** open to, or shared by, the people. **3,** known to all; not secret. **4,** engaged in service to the people. —*n.* the entire community or a specified group. —**public enemy,** a criminal at large. —**public house** (*Brit.*) a bar; pub. —**public relations,** organized publicity. —**public school, 1,** a school paid for by public funds. **2,** (*Brit.*) a private boarding school. —**pub'lic-spir'it·ed,** seeking the best interests of the community.

pub'li·can (pŭb'lə-kən) *n.* **1,** (*Brit.*) an innkeeper. **2,** in ancient Rome, a tax collector.

pub"li·ca'tion (pŭb"lĭ-kā'shən) *n.* **1,** the act or business of publishing. **2,** a book, periodical, etc.

pub'li·cist (pŭb'lĭ-sĭst) *n.* **1,** a writer on current affairs, esp. international. **2,** one who is retained to manage publicity for another.

pub·lic'i·ty (pŭb-lĭs'ə-tē) *n.* **1,** a bringing to public attention. **2,** common knowledge; notoriety.

pub'li·cize" (pŭb'lĭ-sīz") *v.t.* make known by publicity.

pub'lish *v.t.* **1,** make generally known; proclaim. **2,** print and offer for sale, as a book, etc.

puce (pūs) *adj.* of a purple-brown color.

puck (pŭk) *n.* **1,** the sliding disk used in hockey. **2,** (*cap.*) a mischievous sprite.

puck'er (pŭk'ər) *v.i. & t.* draw up into small bulges or wrinkles. —*n.* a furrow.

puck'ish (pŭk'ĭsh) *adj.* mischievous. —**puck'ish·ness,** *n.*

pud'ding (pŭd'ĭng) *n.* a soft, bulky dessert.

pud'dle (pŭd'əl) *n.* **1,** a small pool of muddy water. **2,** a watertight covering of clay mixed with water. —*v.t.* convert (pig iron) into wrought iron. —**pud'dling,** *n.*

pudg'y (pŭj'ē) *adj.* short and fat.

Pueblo

pueb'lo (pwĕb'lō) *n.* [*pl.* -los (lōz)] a Span. Amer. village of adobe houses.

pu'er·ile (pū'ər-ĭl) *adj.* childish; trivial. —**pu'er·il'i·ty,** *n.*

pu·er'per·al (pū-ĕr'pər-əl) *adj.* pert. to childbirth.

puff (pŭf) *n.* **1,** a short blast, as of wind, smoke, etc. **2,** a light, fluffy pad. **3,** (*Colloq.*) undue praise; a plug. —*v.i.* **1,** emit a puff. **2,** breathe hard. —*v.t.* **1,** expel with puffs; smoke with puffs. **2,** (usually with *up* or *out*) distend; inflate. **3,** praise. —**puff'y,** *adj.*

puff'ball" *n.* a ball-shaped mushroom.

puf'fin (pŭf'ĭn) *n.* a bird of the auk family.

pug *n.* **1,** a small dog with a squat, wrinkled face. **2,** a short, tip-tilted nose: pugnose. **3,** (*Slang*) pugilist.

pu'gil·ist (pū'jə-lĭst) *n.* a professional boxer. —**pu'gil·ism,** *n.*

pug·na'cious (pŭg-nā'shəs) *adj.* given to fighting. —**pug·nac'i·ty** (-nas'ə-tē) *n.*

puke (pūk) *v.t. & i.* (*Vulgar*) vomit.

pul'chri·tude" (pŭl'krĭ-tood") *n.* beauty. —**pul'chri·tu'di·nous,** *adj.*

pule (pūl) *v.i.* whine; whimper.

pull (pŭl) *v.t.* **1,** draw with force toward one; tug. **2,** extract, as a tooth. **3,** pluck; gather. **4,** rip; rend. —*v.i.* **1,** draw, drag, tug, etc. **2,** move; be under away. —*n.* **1,** the effort exerted in hauling, drawing, etc. **2,** a device for pulling. **3,** a hard climb. **4,** (*Slang*) influence.

pul'let (pŭl'it) *n.* a young hen.

pul'ley (pŭl'ė) *n.* a wheel, or series of wheels, used with a rope or belt to transmit power.

Pull'man (pŭl'mən) *n.* (*T.N.*) an extra-fare railroad car for sleeping or lounging.

pull'o"ver *n.* a sweater pulled on over the head.

pul'mo·nar"y (pŭl'mə-ner'ė) *adj.* pert. to the lungs.

pul'mo"tor (pŭl'mō"tər) *n.* (*T.N.*) an apparatus for pumping air into the lungs.

pulp *n.* 1, the fleshy part of a fruit. 2, a moist mixture of wood fibers, etc. from which paper is made. 3, a cheap paper; a magazine printed on it. —**pulp'y**, *adj.*

pul'pit (pŭl'pit) *n.* 1, the stand from which a sermon is preached. 2, preachers collectively.

pul'sate (pŭl'sāt) *v.i.* beat; throb. —**pul·sa'tion**, *n.*

pulse (puls) *n.* the throbbing of arteries as blood is pumped along them by the heart.

pul'ver·ize" (pŭl'və-rīz") *v.t.* grind or crush into a fine powder.

pu'ma (pū'mə) *n.* the cougar.

pum'ice (pum'is) *n.* a light spongy volcanic rock used in polishing, etc.

pum'mel (pum'əl) *v.t.* 1, beat with the fists. 2, pommel.

pump *n.* 1, a machine for moving, or compressing, liquids or gases. 2, a shoe without straps or lacings. —*v.t.* 1, move (a fluid) by means of a pump. 2, draw information from.

pum'per·nick"el (pum'pər-nik"əl) *n.* a coarse, dark brown rye bread.

pump'kin *n.* a vine or its large, deep-yellow, gourdlike fruit.

pun *n.* a humorous play on words of similar sound. —**pun'ster**, *n.*

punch *n.* 1, a blow, as with the fist. 2, a tool for stamping holes. 3, a mixed beverage. —*v.t.* 1, strike, as with the fist. 2, poke; prod; hence, herd, as cattle. 3, perforate or impress with a punch. —**punch'-drunk"**, *adj.* having confused or dazed actions, due to head injuries.

pun'cheon (pun'chən) *n.* 1, a large cask. 2, an upright timber. 3, a punching tool.

punc·til'i·o (punk-til'ė-ō) *n.* correct formal behavior.

punc·til'i·ous (punk-til'ė-əs) *adj.* scrupulously careful. —**punc·til'i·ous·ness**, *n.*

punc'tu·al (punk'choo-əl) *adj.* sel-dom late; prompt. —**punc"tu·al'i·ty**, *n.*

punc'tu·ate" (punk'choo-āt") *v.t.* separate into sentences, clauses, and the like, by means of certain marks, as period, comma, dash, etc. —**punc"tu·a'tion**, *n.*

punc'ture (punk'chər) *v.t.* prick; make a small hole in. —*n.* act or effect of puncturing.

pun'dit *n.* a learned man.

pun'gent (pun'jənt) *adj.* 1, sting-ing to the taste or smell. 2, caustic; biting. —**pun'gen·cy**, *n.*

pun'ish *v.t.* inflict a penalty on (a person) or for (an offense). —**pun'ish·a·ble**, *adj.*

pun'ish·ment (-mənt) *n.* act or effect of punishing; penalty.

pu'ni·tive (pū'nə-tiv) *adj.* pert. to, or inflicting, punishment.

punk *n.* 1, dry, crumbly wood, or a fungus, used as a tinder. 2, (*Slang*) a worthless youth. —*adj.* (*Slang*) of low quality.

punt *n.* 1, a flat-bottomed boat. 2, a kick of a football dropped from the hands, before it touches the ground. —*v.t. & i.* 1, propel a punt. 2, kick (a football).

pu'ny (pū'nė) *adj.* feeble; petty. —**pu'ni·ness**, *n.*

pup *n.* 1, [also, **pup'py**] a young dog. 2, the young of various mam-mals. —**pup'tent**, a small tent.

pu'pa (pū'pə) *n.* [*pl.* -**pae** (pė)] the stage in an insect's life between the larval and adult stages.

pu'pil (pū'pəl) *n.* 1, a person re-ceiving instruction. 2, the dark center of the eye.

pup'pet (pup'it) *n.* a doll moved by wires; hence, a person or state con-trolled by another. —**pup'pet·ry**, *n.*

pur'blind" (pẽr'blīnd") *adj.* partly blind; hence, obtuse; dull. —**pur'-blind·ness**, *n.*

pur'chase (pẽr'chəs) *v.t.* buy. —*n.* 1, the act of buying; something bought. 2, a hold or leverage for moving heavy bodies.

pur'dah (pẽr'də) *n.* 1, a curtain. 2, seclusion of women, in India.

pure (pyûr) *adj.* 1, free from pollu-tion. 2, chaste. 3, genuine; sincere. 4, abstract, as sciences. 5, sheer; simple. —**pure'ness**, *n.*

pu·rée' (pyû-rā') *n.* a thick soup of sieved vegetables.

pur'ga·tive (pẽrg'ə-tiv) *n.* that which purges. —*adj.* purging.

pur'ga·to"ry (pẽr'gə-tôr'ė) *n.* (*Rom. Cath.*) a place where penitent souls are purified.

purge (pêrj) *v.t.* **1,** cleanse from impurities, bodily or spiritual. **2,** flush (the bowels) by a physic. **3,** remove disloyal members from a state or party). —*n.* **1,** the act of purging. **2,** a physic; purgative. —pur·ga'tion (-gā'shən) *n.*

pu'ri·fy" (pyŭr'i-fī") *v.t.* make pure. —pu"ri·fi·ca'tion, *n.*

pur'ist (pyūr'ist) *n.* a stickler for exactness.

pu'ri·tan (pyûr'ə-tən) *n.* a religious zealot who frowns on frivolity. —pu"ri·tan'i·cal, *adj.*

pu'ri·ty (pyûr'i-tė) *n.* pureness.

purl (pêrl) *n.* **1,** a knitting stitch. **2,** a ripple; eddy. —*v.i.* make purls.

pur'lieus (pêr'looz) *n. pl.* outskirts, environs.

pur·loin' (pər-loin') *v.t.* steal.

pur'ple (pêr'pəl) *n.* **1,** a bluish-red color. **2,** an emperor's robe of this color; regal power.

pur·port' (pər-pôrt') *v.t.* profess; seem to mean. —*n.* (pêr'pôrt) meaning; import.

pur'pose (pêr'pəs) *v.t.* intend; mean. —*n.* **1,** intention; aim. **2,** intended effect; use.

pur'pose·ful *adj.* **1,** determined; resolved. **2,** serving a purpose. —pur'pose·ful·ness, *n.*

pur'pose·ly *adj.* deliberately; intentionally.

purr (pêr) *v.t.* make a low vibrating sound, as a contented cat. —*n.* this sound.

purse (pêrs) *n.* **1,** any small receptacle for carrying money; hence, means; finances. **2,** a sum of money collected as a gift or offered as a prize. —*v.t.* pucker (the lips). —purse strings, power or control over money or spending.

purs'er (pêr'sər) *n.* a ship's officer in charge of accounts.

pur·su'ant (pər-soo'ənt) *adj.* **1,** following. **2,** (with *to*) according. —pur·su'ance, *n.*

pur·sue' (pər-soo') *v.t.* **1,** follow with intent to catch. **2,** proceed along; continue. **3,** seek after. **4,** be engaged in.

pur·suit' (pər-soot') *n.* **1,** act of following. **2,** an occupation.

pur'sy (pêr'sė) *adj.* fat and short-winded.

pu'ru·lent (pyûr'ə-lənt) *adj.* full of, or discharging, pus. —pur'u·lence, *n.*

pur·vey' (pər-vā') *v.t. & i.* provide (food supplies). —pur·vey'or, *n.*

pur'view (pêr'vū) *n.* **1,** scope; extent of anything. **2,** range of physical or mental vision.

pus *n.* the yellowish-white matter in an inflamed sore.

push (pûsh) *v.t.* **1,** thrust forcibly against, in order to move. **2,** advance or extend by effort. —*v.i.* **1,** exert impelling pressure. **2,** force one's way. —*n.* **1,** a shove. **2,** a crowd of people. **3,** (*Colloq.*) energy; enterprise.

push-'but'ton *adj.* automatic; done by, or as though by, merely pushing an electrical signal.

push'cart" *n.* a cart pushed by hand, used by a vendor, etc.

push'o'ver *n.* (*Slang*) a weak-willed person; an easy task.

pu'sil·lan'i·mous (pū"sə-lan'ə-məs) *adj.* mean-spirited; cowardly. —pu"sil·la·nim'i·ty, *n.*

puss (pûs) *n.* a cat. Also, pus'sy.

puss'y·foot" *v.t.* move warily or fearfully; hedge.

pussy willow a small willow tree.

pus'tule (pus'chūl) *n.* a small, pus-filled pimple.

put (pût) *v.t.* [put, put'ting] **1,** set, lay, or cause to be in any place, position, or condition. **2,** assign; attribute. **3,** propound; propose for attention. **4,** (with *across* or *over*) accomplish; effect the acceptance of. **5,** (with *by*) save, as money. **6,** (with *up*) give lodging to. **7,** (with *up with*) tolerate. —*v.i.* **1,** (with *about*) turn. **2,** (with *on*) pretend. **3,** (with *out*) set forth.

pu'ta·tive (pū'tə-tiv) *adj.* supposed; reputed.

pu'tre·fy" (pū'trə-fī") *v.i. & t.* decay or cause to decay. —pu"tre·fac'tion, *n.*

pu·tres'cence (pū-tres'əns) *n.* process of becoming rotten. —pu·tres'cent, *adj.*

pu'trid (pū'trid) *adj.* rotten; foul.

putt (put) *n.* (*Golf*) a stroke made to send a ball along the ground. —*v.t. & i.* make (the ball) so roll. —putt'er, *n.* a golf club for this purpose.

put'tee (put'ė) *n.* a legging.

put'ter (put'ər) *v.i.* busy oneself in an ineffective manner.

put'ty (put'ė) *n.* a soft, doughy cement for filling cracks, etc.

put-'up' *adj.* fraudulently prearranged.

puz'zle (puz'əl) *n.* a perplexing problem; a device or toy to test one's ingenuity. —*v.t.* perplex. —*v.i.* ponder. —**puz'zle·ment,** *n.*

Pyg'my (pig'mē) *n.* one of a dwarf race of central Africa; hence (*l.c.*) a dwarf.

py·jam'as (pə-jām'əs) *n.pl.* pajamas.

py'lon (pī'lon) *n.* **1,** a gateway of one or two truncated pyramids. **2,** a high tower.

py·lo'rus (pī-lôr'əs) *n.* the opening from the stomach to the intestines. —**py·lor'ic,** *adj.*

py"or·rhe'a (pī"ə-rē'ə) *n.* inflammation of the sockets of the teeth.

pyr'a·mid (pir'ə-mid) *n.* (*Geom.*) a solid whose base is a polygon and whose sides are all triangles meeting in a common point. —*v.i. & t.* reinvest (profits or winnings) for greater profit. —**py·ram'i·dal,** *adj.*

Pyramids

pyre (pīr) *n.* a heap of wood for burning a corpse.

py'rex (pī'reks) *n.* (*T.N.*) a heat-resistant glassware used for cooking utensils.

pyr·ex'i·a (pī-rek'sē-ə) *n.* (*Med.*) fever. —**py·ret'ic,** *adj.*

pyr'i·dine" (pir'ə-dēn") *n.* a colorless liquid, of pungent odor, used as a solvent, germicide, and in medicine.

py"ro·ma'ni·a (pī"rə-mā'nē-ə) *n.* a mania for starting fires. —**py"ro·ma'ni·ac,** *n.*

py"ro·tech'nics (pī"rə-tek'niks) *n.* a display of fireworks.

py·rox'y·lin (pī-rok'sə-lin) *n.* guncotton; nitrocellulose, esp. in solution.

Pyr'rhic victory (pir'ik) a victory gained at too great cost.

py'thon (pī'thon) *n.* a large snake that crushes its prey.

Q

Q, q (kū) *n.* seventeenth letter of the English alphabet.

quack (kwak) *n.* **1,** the cry of a duck; a similar harsh, flat sound. **2,** a false pretender to medical skill. —*v.i.* make a noise as a duck. —*adj.* fraudulent. —**quack'er·y,** *n.* deceptive practice.

quad (kwod) *n.* **1,** the square-shaped court of a college or like group of buildings. **2,** blank metal used to space type.

quadr- *pref.* four; fourth.

quad'ran"gle (kwod'rang"gəl) *n.* **1,** a plane figure with four sides and four angles. **2,** quad. —**quad·ran'gu·lar** (kwə-drang'gyə-lər) *adj.*

quad'rant (kwod'rənt) *n.* **1,** the fourth part. **2,** a quarter of a circle. **3,** an instrument for measuring altitudes.

quad·rat'ic (kwod-rat'ik) *adj.* **1,** belonging to a square. **2,** (*Math.*) concerning the square as the highest power of an unknown quantity.

quad·ren'ni·al (kwod-ren'ē-əl) *adj.* **1,** every four years. **2,** for four years' duration. —*n.* a fourth anniversary.

quad"ri·lat'er·al (kwod"rə-lat'ər-əl) *n.* a plane figure with four straight sides. —*adj.* four-sided.

qua·drille' (kwə-dril') *n.* a dance for four or more couples.

quad·ril'lion (kwod-ril'yən) *n.* a thousand trillions.

quad·roon' (kwod-roon') *n.* a person of one-quarter Negro blood.

quad'ru·ped" (kwod'rū-ped") *n.* a four-footed animal. —*adj.* four-footed.

quad'ru·ple (kwod'rū-pəl) *adj.* four times. —*v.t.* (kwod-rū'pəl) multiply by four. —**quad'ru·plet,** *n.* one of four children born of one birth.

quad·ru'pli·cate (kwod-rūp'li-kət) *n.* four identical copies; the fourth such copy. —*v.t.* (-kāt") make four copies of.

quaff (kwäf) *v.t. & i.* drink freely.

quag'mire" (kwag'mīr") *n.* an area of muddy ground; a marsh.

qua'hog (kwä'hog) *n.* a large, edible clam of the Atlantic coast.

quail (kwāl) *v.i.* cower; shrink away; flinch; lose courage. —*n.* a game bird; the partridge.

Quail

quaint (kwānt) *adj.* pleasingly odd or unusual. —**quaint'ness,** *n.*

quake (kwāk) *v.i.* tremble; shake; shudder. —*n.* a shaking or tremulous agitation, esp. an earthquake.

Quak'er (kwā'kər) *n.* a member of the Society of Friends, a Christian religious sect.

qual"i·fi·ca'tion (kwol'i-fi-kā'shən) *n.* **1,** act or result of qualifying. **2,** a quality that meets some requirement.

qual'i·fied (kwol'i-fīd") *adj.* fit; competent.

qual'i·fy" (kwol'i-fī") *v.t.* **1,** modify; limit; restrict. **2,** establish the authority of; empower; instruct; fit. **3,** soften; assuage. —*v.t.* fill requirements for a place or occupation.

qual'i·ta"tive (kwol'ə-tā"tiv) *adj.* in quality, not quantity.

qual'i·ty (kwol'ə-tē) *n.* **1,** essential nature. **2,** a trait; characteristic. **3,** high birth or rank. **4,** superiority, relatively considered.

qualm (kwäm) *n.* **1,** a twinge of conscience; compunction. **2,** a sudden sensation of nausea.

quan'da·ry (kwon'də-rē) *n.* state of bewilderment or perplexity; a dilemma.

quan'ti·ta"tive (kwon'ti-tā"tiv) *adj.* in quantity, not quality.

quan'ti·ty (kwon'tə-tē) *n.* **1,** amount; weight; bulk. **2,** a portion, esp. a large amount. **3,** a number. **4,** duration (of a sound).

quan'tum (kwon'təm) *n.* [*pl.* **-ta**] **1,** amount. **2,** the smallest unit of radiant energy. —**quantum theory,** a hypothesis in physics that the emission of radiant energy is not continuous.

quar'an·tine" (kwor'ən-tēn") *n.* **1,** time during which an incoming ship is held for inspection for contagious disease. **2,** the place where such ship is held. **3,** a period of enforced seclusion, usually to prevent contagion. —*v.t.* isolate.

quar'rel (kwor'əl) *n.* a squabble; disagreement; dispute; petty fight. —*v.i.* find fault; dispute. —**quar'rel·some,** *adj.* disposed to quarrel.

quar'ry (kwor'ē) *n.* **1,** an open excavation from which building materials, as stone, are taken. **2,** prey; any object of eager pursuit.

quart (kwôrt) *n.* a unit of capacity; in liquid measure equal to two pints or one-fourth gallon, in dry measure, one-eighth peck.

quar'ter (kwôr'tər) *n.* **1,** one-fourth of the whole. **2,** a U.S. silver coin: one-fourth dollar or 25 cents. **3,** three consecutive months. **4,** section; region; locality. **5,** one leg of an animal with bordering parts for use as meat. **6,** mercy. **7,** (*pl.*) a specific dwelling place; station; lodgings. —*v.t.* **1,** divide into four equal parts. **2,** furnish with lodgings.

quar'ter·back" *n.* (*Football*) the back who directs the play of his team.

quar'ter·deck" *n.* (*Naut.*) an upper deck used by officers.

quar'ter·ly (-lē) *n.* a periodical published each three months.

quar'ter·mas"ter *n.* (*Mil.*) a supply officer.

quar·tet' (kwôr-tet') *n.* **1,** a group of four. **2,** (*Music*) a composition in four parts. Also, **quar·tette'.**

quar'to (kwôr'tō) *n.* [*pl.* **-tos**] a book whose pages are about 9½ by 12 inches.

quartz (kwôrts) *n.* a common hard mineral occurring in many varieties, some prized as semiprecious stones.

quash (kwosh) *v.t.* **1,** crush; subdue. **2,** annul.

qua·si- (kwā'sī) *pref.* almost; purportedly but not wholly genuine.

quas'sia (kwosh'ə) *n.* a medicinal bitter extracted from the bark and wood of an Amer. tree.

qua·ter'na·ry (kwə-tẽr'nə-rē) *adj.* consisting of or arranged in fours. —*n.* **1,** the number four. **2,** a group of four.

quat'rain (kwot'rān) *n.* a stanza of four lines, usually rhyming alternately.

qua'ver (kwā'vər) *v.i.* **1,** shake; tremble; vibrate. **2,** sing or speak in a tremulous tone. **3,** (*Music*) trill. **4,** (*Music*) an eighth-note. —*n.* a shaking or trembling, esp. of the voice.

quay (kē) *n.* a dock for landing and loading a ship's cargo.

quea'sy (kwē'zē) *adj.* **1,** sick at the stomach. **2,** easily nauseated; squeamish. —**quea'si·ness,** *n.*

queen (kwēn) *n.* **1,** the wife of a king. **2,** a female sovereign. **3,** the most notable woman in a particular sphere. **4,** the perfect female bee, ant, or termite. **5,** a playing card depicting a queen. **6,** the most valuable piece in chess. —**queen mother,** the widow of a king and mother of a present sovereign.

queer (kwir) *adj.* odd; strange; eccentric. —*v.t.* (*Colloq.*) spoil; upset. —**queer'ness,** *n.*

quell (kwel) *v.t.* **1,** subdue; crush. **2,** allay; quiet.

quench (kwench) *v.t.* **1,** satisfy, as thirst. **2,** extinguish or put out, as a fire. **3,** repress or still, as anger. **4,** cool (hot metal) suddenly.

quer'cine (kwẽr'sin) *adj.* of or pert. to the oak tree.

quer'u·lous (kwer'ə-ləs) *adj.* habitually complaining; fretful.

que'ry (kwir'ē) *n.* a question; an inquiry. —*v.t.* & *i.* question; doubt.

quest (kwest) *n.* a search; pursuit.

ques'tion (kwes'chən) *n.* **1,** an interrogation; inquiry. **2,** doubt; dispute; controversy. **3,** a subject under discussion; a motion to be voted upon. —*v.t.* **1,** inquire of. **2,** doubt; challenge; take exception to. —**ques'tion-a-ble,** *adj.* subject to doubt. —**question mark,** the mark of punctuation (?) denoting inquiry or doubt; the interrogation point.

ques"tion-naire' (-nȧr') *n.* a series of questions to be answered.

queue (kū) *n.* **1,** a waiting line. **2,** hair braided and worn as a pigtail. —*v.i.* (with *up*) get in line.

quib'ble (kwib'əl) *v.i.* equivocate; bring up trifling objections to evade the point. —*n.* an evasive argument.

quick (kwik) *adj.* **1,** fast; speedy; rapid. **2,** perceptive; alert. **3,** hasty; easily aroused. **4,** (*Archaic*) living. —*n.* **1,** living beings. **2,** sensitive flesh. —**quick'ness,** *n.*

quick'en (kwik'ən) *v.t.* & *i.* make or become faster or more active.

quick'-fro'zen *adj.* (of food) frozen rapidly to zero or below, for preservation.

quick'ie (-ē) *n.* (*Slang*) something produced in haste; a drink consumed in haste.

quick'lime" *n.* a caustic substance made from limestone.

quick'sand" *n.* a bog.

quick'sil"ver *n.* metallic mercury.

quick'step" *n.* a fast marching pace, as of soldiers.

quid (kwid) *n.* **1,** a cud; a lump for chewing, as gum or tobacco. **2,** (*Brit. slang*) a pound sterling.

quid'di-ty (kwid'ə-tē) *n.* **1,** essence. **2,** a trifling nicety.

qui-es'cent (kwī-es'ənt) *adj.* still; resting; tranquil. —**qui-es'cence,** *n.*

qui'et (kwī'ət) *adj.* **1,** still; smooth; tranquil. **2,** silent; noiseless. **3,** composed; subdued. **4,** modest; not glaring. —*v.t.* calm; pacify; hush; allay. —*v.i.* become calm; abate. —*n.* **1,** repose; rest; stillness. **2,** peace. **3,** composure; calmness. **4,** silence. —**qui'et-ness,** *n.*

qui'e-tude (kwī'ə-tood) *n.* repose; rest; tranquillity.

qui-e'tus (kwī-ē'təs) *n.* **1,** release, as from debts. **2,** death.

quill (kwil) *n.* **1,** a strong feather from a bird; its stem. **2,** a pen made from a feather. **3,** a sharp spine, as of a porcupine. **4,** a pick used for playing certain string instruments.

quilt (kwilt) *n.* a warm, padded bed cover. —*v.t.* & *i.* make a quilt.

quince (kwins) *n.* a fruit tree or its yellow applelike fruit.

qui'nine (kwī'nīn) *n.* a bitter alkaloid obtained from cinchona bark, used medicinally, esp. for malaria.

quin·que- (kwin'kwe) *pref.* five.

quin'sy (kwin'zē) *n.* severe inflammation of the throat and tonsils accompanied by swelling and pus.

quint (kwint) *n.* **1,** a set or sequence of five. **2,** (*Music*) a fifth.

quin'tal (kwin'təl) *n.* a weight, orig. 100 pounds, now varying in different countries.

quin-tes'sence (kwin-tes'əns) *n.* the concentrated and purest essence of anything; the perfect form.

quin-tet' (kwin-tet') *n.* a group of five. Also, **quin-tette'.**

quin'tu-ple (kwin'tyū-pəl) *adj.* five times. —*v.t.* multiply by five. —**quin'tu-plet,** *n.* one of five children born of one birth.

quip (kwip) *n.* a witty remark.

quire (kwir) *n.* one-twentieth of a ream; 24 (sometimes 25) uniform sheets of paper.

quirk (kwėrk) *n.* **1,** idiosyncrasy; deviation. **2,** a quick turn.

quirt (kwėrt) *n.* a riding whip.

quis'ling (kwiz'ling) *n.* a traitor who helps an enemy invade his country.

quit (kwit) *v.t.* & *i.* [quit'ted, -ting] **1,** leave; abandon; resign; satisfy; clear.

quite (kwīt) *adv.* **1,** wholly; completely. **2,** considerably; very.

quits (kwits) *adj.* (*Colloq.*) on even terms; released from obligation.

quit'tance (kwit'əns) *n.* **1,** a discharge from obligation; receipt. **2,** recompense.

quit'ter (kwit'ər) *n.* one who abandons a task through discouragement or fear.

quiv'er (kwiv'ər) *v.i.* quake; shiver; flutter. —*n.* **1,** a tremor; shiver. **2,** a case for holding arrows.

quix·ot'ic (kwiks-ot'ik) *adj.* absurdly or extravagantly romantic or chivalrous; impractical; visionary.

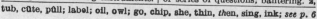

Quiver

quiz (kwiz) *n.* **1,** a puzzling question or series of questions; bantering. **2,**

an examination in school; a question-and-answer program on radio or television. —v.t. [quizzed, quiz'zing] 1, chaff; make sport of. 2, question. 3, peer at.

quiz'zi·cal (kwiz'i-kəl) *adj.* bantering; teasing.

quoin (koin) *n.* 1, an external angle of a building; a stone forming such an angle. 2, a wedgelike device used in printing for locking up type.

quoits (kwoits) *n. sing.* a game of pitching rings, as of iron or rubber, at a peg. —**quoit**, *n.* such a ring.

quon'dam (kwon'dam) *adj.* former; in time past.

Quon'set hut (kwon'sət) a prefabricated metal shelter.

quo'rum (kwôr'əm) *n.* the number of members whose presence validates a meeting.

quo'ta (kwō'tə) *n.* the share or proportion assigned to one of a group.

quo·ta'tion (kwō-tā'shən) *n.* 1, repetition of words previously uttered. 2, a citation of a price. —**quotation mark**, a mark of punctuation: " or ' (*quote*), " or ' (*unquote*).

quote (kwōt) *v.t. & i.* 1, repeat, copy or cite words previously uttered. 2, give the current market price of. 3, enclose within quotation marks. —*n.* (*Colloq.*) quotation.

quoth (kwōth) *v.* (*Archaic*) says.

quo·tid'i·an (kwō-tid'ē-ən) *adj.* daily.

quo'tient (kwō'shənt) *n.* the number produced by dividing a given number by another.

R

R, r (är) the eighteenth letter of the English alphabet.

rab'bi (rab'ī) *n.* master; a Jewish doctor of scriptural law. —**rab·bin'i·cal** (rə-bin'i-kəl) *adj.*

rab'bit (rab'it) *n.* a small rodent related to the hare. —**rabbit punch**, a blow on the back of the neck. —**Welsh rabbit** [or, **rare'bit**] *n.* melted cheese served on toast.

rab'ble (rab'əl) *n.* any confused, disorderly crowd; a mob.

rab'id *adj.* 1, furious; raging. 2, zealous; fanatical. 3, affected with or pert. to rabies. —**ra·bid'i·ty**, *n.*

ra'bies (rā'bēz) *n.* an infectious disease: *hydrophobia*.

rac·coon' (ra-koon') *n.* a small carnivorous No. Amer. mammal.

race (rās) *n.* 1, a contest or effort to reach a goal first; a rush. 2, a rapid current of water. 3, a family, division of people, tribe, or nation. —v.i. & t. engage in a contest of speed; run swiftly; cause to run. —**rac'er**, *n.* a racing car or its driver.

ra'cial (rā'shəl) *adj.* pert. to a race (of people).

rac'ism (rās'iz-əm) *n.* prejudice against certain peoples.

rack (rak) *n.* 1, an open framework or stand for holding articles. 2, a toothed bar engaging a gear. 3, an ancient instrument of torture; hence, pain or distress. —v.t. 1, strain; worry. 2, place on a rack.

rack'et (rak'it) *n.* 1, a disorderly, confused noise; din; hurly-burly. 2, a dishonest enterprise. 3, [also, **rac'quet**] the bat used in tennis, squash, etc. 4, (*pl.*) an indoor ball game.

rack"et·eer' (-ə-tir') *n.* one engaged in a dishonest enterprise; a gangster.

rac"on·teur' (rak"on-tėr') *n.* a skillful narrator of anecdotes.

rac'y (rās'ē) *adj.* 1, piquant; spicy. 2, (*Colloq.*) suggestive; off-color. —**rac'i·ness**, *n.*

ra'dar (rā'där) *n.* a device timing the echo of radio waves to detect objects they strike.

ra'di·al (rā'dē-əl) *n.* pert. to a radius; of or being radii.

ra'di·ant (rā'dē-ənt) *adj.* 1, emitting rays; shining; sparkling. 2, beaming, as with kindness or joy. —**ra'di·ance**, *n.*

ra'di·ate" (rā'dē-āt") *v.t. & t.* 1, issue and proceed in rays from a point, as heat or light. 2, spread in all directions from a central source. —**ra'di·a'tion**, *n.*

ra'di·a"tor (rā'dē-ā"tər) *n.* an apparatus, as a grill, that radiates heat waves, as to warm a room, dispel the heat from an automobile engine, etc.

rad'i·cal (rad'i-kəl) *adj.* 1, (*Math.*) pert. to a root. 2, drastic. —*n.* 1, an extreme liberal in politics. 2, (*Math.*) a root; the sign ($\sqrt{\ }$) expressing it. 3, (*Gram.*) a root.

ra'di·o" (rā'dē-ō") *n.* 1, wireless telephone and telegraph transmission and reception. 2, a receiving set for sounds so transmitted. —v.t. & i. send (a message) by radio. —**radio station**, a place from which radio broadcasts are made.

ra"di·o·ac'tive *adj.* radiating energy in atoms or particles of atoms. —**ra"di·o·ac·tiv'i·ty**, *n.*

ra'di·o·gram' *n.* a message sent by radio.

ra"di·ol'o·gy (rā'dē·ol'ə·jē) *n.* the study or use of x-rays and radioactive substances.

ra"di·o·ther'a·py *n.* treatment by x-rays or radioactive rays.

rad'ish *n.* the crisp, pungent root of a garden plant; the plant.

ra'di·um (rā'dē·əm) *n.* a metallic chemical element, no. 88, symbol Ra.

ra'di·us (rā'dē·əs) *n.* [*pl.* -i (-ī)] 1, a line drawn from the center of a circle or sphere to the circumference or surface. 2, the measure of this line; any limited area.

ra'dix (rā'diks) *n.* [*pl.* rad'i·ces (rad'ə-sēz)] 1, the root of a plant. 2, (*Math.*) the base number of a system, as 10 in the decimal system. 3, a root word.

raf'fi·a (raf'ē-ə) *n.* a species of palm, used for weaving.

raff'ish (raf'ish) *adj.* rowdy.—**raff'ish·ness**, *n.*

raf'fle (raf'əl) *n.* a lottery to dispose of one prize, usually merchandise. —*v.t.* (often with *off*) dispose of by raffle.

raft (râft) *n.* 1, a wooden platform to float in water. 2, (*Colloq.*) an accumulation; a collection.

raft'er (râf'tər) *n.* a sloping beam of a roof.

rag *n.* 1, a worn or worthless piece of cloth. 2, (*pl.*) shabby clothes. 3, (*pl.*) (*Slang*) any clothes, as *glad rags*. 4, (*Colloq.*) jazz music: *ragtime.* —*adj.* made of or with rags, as paper. —*v.t.* [ragged, rag'ging] (*Slang*) badger; tease.

rag'a·muf"fin (rag'ə-muf"in) *n.* a ragged person.

rage (rāj) *n.* 1, violent anger; fury. 2, extreme violence; intensity. 3, enthusiasm; vogue; a fad. —*v.i.* 1, be furious with anger. 2, storm. 3, have furious course or effect.

rag'ged (rag'id) *adj.* 1, tattered; frayed; shaggy; dressed in wornout clothes. 2, slipshod.

rag'lan (rag'lən) *n.* a topcoat with the sleeves extending down from the collar without shoulder seams.

ra·gout' (ra-goo') *n.* a highly seasoned stew of meat and vegetables.

rag'time' *n.* an early form of jazz music.

rag'weed" (rag'wēd") *n.* a herb whose pollen aggravates some asthmatic symptoms.

raid (rād) *n.* a hostile or predatory incursion; a sudden onset. —*v.t. & i.* attack; rob.

rail (rāl) *n.* 1, a bar passing from one support to another, as for a barrier. 2, a metal bar used to form a track for a wheeled vehicle. 3, transportation by railroad. 4, a small wading bird. —*v.i.* speak bitterly; scoff; inveigh. —**rail'ing**, *n.* a barrier made of rails; a fence.

Rail

rail'ler·y (rā'lə-rē) *n.* banter.

rail'road" *n.* [also, **rail'way"**] a common carrier operating trains over permanent tracks of rails; the tracks. —*v.t.* (*Slang*) 1, force and speed to a conclusion. 2, devise false evidence against; frame. —**rail'road"ing**, *n.* work pert. to the operation of a railroad.

rail'way" *n.* railroad.

rai'ment (rā'mənt) *n.* clothing.

rain (rān) *n.* 1, water falling in drops from the clouds. 2, a shower or outpouring of anything. —*v.i.* produce water falling in drops. —*v.t.* shower down; give abundantly. —**rain check**, a baseball ticket for future use; hence, a standing invitation.

rain'bow" *n.* an arc of prismatic colors.

rain'coat" *n.* a light waterproof outer coat.

rain'drop" *n.* a drop of rain.

rain'fall" *n.* rain.

rain'storm" *n.* a heavy rain.

rain'y *adj.* constantly or often raining. —**rain'i·ness**, *n.*

raise (rāz) *v.t.* 1, move to a higher place; hoist; elevate. 2, increase the height of; build up. 3, cause to rise. 4, grow or breed, as crops, cattle; bring up. 5, muster; collect; procure, as an army or money. —*n.* (*Colloq.*) an increase in pay. —**raised**, *adj.* 1, leavened. 2, in relief, as carving.

rai'sin (rā'zən) *n.* a dried grape.

ra'jah (rä'jə) *n.* an East Indian prince.

rake (rāk) *n.* 1, a long-handled toothed implement for scraping loose materials together; a similar implement. 2, an idle, dissolute man; a libertine. —*v.t.* 1, gather or smooth with or as with a rake; (with *up*) glean. 2, ransack. 3, scratch. 4, (*Mil.*) fire upon, lengthwise.

rake-'off" *n.* (*Slang*) a rebate or commission, usually illegal.

rak'ish (rāk'ish) *adj.* **1,** (*Naut.*) inclined, as a mast. **2,** jaunty. **3,** dissolute. —**rak'ish·ness,** *n.*

ral'ly (ral'ē) *v.t.* **1,** draw or call together for a common purpose. **2,** assemble and reconstitute as a disorganized army. **3,** banter; tease. —*v.i.* **1,** reunite. **2,** recover energy or effectiveness. —*n.* **1,** a renewal of energy in joint action. **2,** in tennis, a sustained exchange. **3,** a quick recovery. **4,** a mass meeting. **5,** a race or test among sport cars.

ram *n.* **1,** a male sheep. **2,** (*cap.*) Aries, a sign of the Zodiac. **3,** an instrument of war for battering; the armored prow of a warship. —*v.t.* (**rammed, ram'ming**) **1,** batter. **2,** force or drive down. **3,** stuff; cram.

ram'ble (ram'bəl) *v.i.* **1,** roam or wander about; rove. **2,** digress. —*n.* a sauntering walk. —**ram'bler,** *n.* **1,** a wanderer. **2,** a climbing rose. —**ram'bling,** *adj.* wandering; roundabout.

ram·bunc'tious (ram-bunk'shəs) *adj.* (*Colloq.*) boisterous. —**rambunc'tious·ness,** *n.*

ram'e·kin (ram'ə-kin) *n.* an individual baking dish. Also, **ram'equin.**

ram"i·fi·ca'tion (ram"i-fi-kā'shən) *n.* a branch; subdivision.

ram'i·fy" (ram'ə-fī") *v.i. & t.* form or divide into branches.

ramp *n.* a sloping passageway.

ram'page (ram'pāj) *n.* violent, furious or excited behavior.

ram'pant (ram'pənt) *adj.* raging and unchecked.

ram'part (ram'pärt) *n.* **1,** a mound, usually with a parapet, surrounding a fortified place. **2,** a bulwark; a protective barrier.

ram'rod" *n.* a rod for tamping the charge of a muzzle-loading gun.

ram'shack"le (ram'shak"əl) *adj.* tumble-down; rickety.

ran *v.* pret. of *run.*

ranch *n.* a large farm for raising livestock. —**ranch'er,** *n.* owner of a ranch.

ran'cid (ran'sid) *adj.* having a rank, tainted smell or taste. —**rancid'i·ty,** *n.*

ran'cor (rang'kər) *n.* bitter animosity; spitefulness. Also, **ran'cour.** —**ran'cor·ous,** *adj.*

ran'dom (ran'dəm) *adj.* haphazard; casual. —**at random,** haphazardly.

ra'nee (rä'nē) *n.* the wife of a rajah.

rang *v.* pret. of *ring.*

range (rānj) *v.t.* **1,** make a row or rows of; set in definite order. **2,**

oppose. **3,** rove over or along. —*v.i.* **1,** be in or form a parallel line or direction. **2,** roam; wander. **3,** vary, within specified limits. —*n.* **1,** a series in a lane or row. **2,** scope; extent. **3,** distance from one point to another. **4,** a large tract of land for grazing. **5,** a course for shooting or target practice. **6,** a cooking stove. —**range finder,** an instrument for determining the distance of a target from a gun, etc.

rang'er (rān'jər) *n.* **1,** a trooper patrolling a wide area. **2,** (*cap.*) an Amer. soldier trained for raiding.

rang'y (rān'jē) *adj.* tall and slender.

rank *n.* **1,** a row, esp. one conceived as horizontal; a line; formation. **2,** a class, order. **3,** relative position; standing, as social, ordinal, etc. **4,** (*pl.*) (*Mil.*) enlisted men. —*v.t.* **1,** arrange in lines or formations. **2,** assign to a particular class. **3,** take precedence of or over; rate above. —*v.i.* occupy a relative position. —*adj.* **1,** strong in growth, as weeds; rich and fertile. **2,** offensive; unmitigated. —**rank and file,** the common people; people indiscriminately.

ran'kle (rang'kəl) *v.i.* fester; be irritating.

ran'sack (ran'sak) *v.t.* **1,** search thoroughly. **2,** plunder.

ran'som (ran'səm) *n.* the price or cost of redeeming a hostage. —*v.t.* redeem by paying.

rant *v.i.* declaim violently and with little sense; rave.

rap *v.t. & t.* (**rapped, rap'ping**) **1,** strike (with) a quick sharp blow. **2,** criticize adversely. —*n.* (*Colloq.*) **1,** a cutting remark. **2,** a bit. **3,** (*Slang*) penalty.

ra·pa'cious (rə-pā'shəs) *adj.* greedy; grasping; predatory. —**rapa'cious·ness,** *n.*

ra·pac'i·ty (rə-pas'ə-tē) *n.* rapaciousness.

rape (rāp) *n.* **1,** forcible seizing and violation; ravishing. **2,** a plant grown for fodder and oil. —*v.t.* ravish.

rap'id *adj.* **1,** moving swiftly. **2,** requiring little time. —*n.* (usually *pl.*) a swift current in a river. —**rap'id·ness,** *n.*

ra·pid'i·ty (rə-pid'ə-tē) *n.* rapidness; swiftness; speed.

Rapier

ra'pi·er (rā'pē-ər) *n.* a long, narrow, pointed two-edged sword.

rap'ine (rap'in) *n.* plundering.

rap·port' (ra-pôr') *n.* harmonious relation; accord.

rap"proche"ment' (rȧ-prȧsh'-
mäṅ') *n.* an establishment of harmonious relations.

rap·scal'lion (rap-skal'yən) *n.*
(*Colloq.*) a scamp; a rascal.

rapt *adj.* ecstatically engrossed or
bemused. —**rapt'ness,** *n.*

rap'ture (rap'chər) *n.* ecstatic joy.
—**rap'tur·ous,** *adj.*

rare (râr) *adj.* 1, thin, not dense;
sparse. 2, very uncommon; remarkable; excellent; choice. 3, (of meat)
not thoroughly cooked. —**rare'ness,**
n.

rare'bit (râr'bit) *n.* Welsh rabbit.

rar'e·fy (râr'ə-fī') *v.t. & i.* make
or become thin or less dense. —**rar'-
e·fac'tion,** *n.*

rare'ly (râr'lē) *adv.* seldom; un-
commonly.

rar'i·ty (râr'ə-tē) *n.* 1, state of
being uncommon. 2, something
unusual.

ras'cal (ras'kəl) *n.* 1, a scoundrel.
2, a scamp. —**ras·cal'i·ty,** *n.*

rash *adj.* too hasty in judgment,
speech, or action; reckless; precipitate. —*n.* an eruption on the skin.
—**rash'ness,** *n.*

rash'er (rash'ər) *n.* a slice, or
small serving, of bacon or ham.

rasp *v.t.* grate with a coarse, rough
instrument. —*v.i.* irritate (one's
nerves). —*n.* a coarse file. —**rasp'-
ing,** *adj.* (of a voice, etc.) harsh.

rasp'ber"ry (răz'ber'ē) *n.* 1, a
sweet, red or black, edible berry
from a plant of the rose family.
2, (*Slang*) an expression of derision.

rat *n.* 1, a rodent similar to the
mouse but larger. 2, (*Slang*) a betrayer or informer; a contemptible
person. 3, a bulging roll of hair.
—*v.t.* [rat'ted, -ting] 1, catch or
kill rats. 2, be a betrayer; inform.

ratch'et (rach'it)
n. a toothed bar
or wheel, back-
ward motion of
which is checked
by a stop.

rate (rāt) *n.* 1,
amount, quantity,
range, or degree,
measured accord-
ing to some stand-
ard. 2, a price;
a fixed charge. —*v.t.* 1, appraise;
fix the relative scale, rank, or position of. 2, scold; censure. —*v.i.*
have (a certain) standing.

Ratchet and Wheel

rath'er (răth'ər) *adv.* 1, sooner;
preferably. 2, more correctly. 3, on
the contrary. 4, somewhat; considerably.

raths'kel"ler (rots'kel'ər) *n.* a
barroom in a cellar.

rat'i·fy" (rat'ə-fī") *v.t.* 1, accept
and sanction formally. 2, confirm;
establish. —**rat'i·fi·ca'tion,** *n.*

rat'ing (rā'ting) *n.* 1, relative
standing; appraisal. 2, rank of a
noncommissioned sailor or seaman.
3, a scolding.

ra'tio (rā'shō) *n.* the relation between two quantities; proportion.

ra"ti·oc'i·nate" (rash'ē-os'ə-nāt")
v.i. reason. —**ra"ti·oc'i·na'tion,** *n.*

ra'tion (rā'shən) *n.* 1, an allowance, esp. of a necessity. 2, (*pl.*)
meals. —*v.t.* apportion.

ra'tion·al (rash'ən-əl) *adj.* 1, of,
pert. to, or attributable to, reason
or the power of reasoning; sane. 2,
(*Math.*) designating a number that
can be represented as the quotient
of two integers or polynomials.
—**ra"tion·al'i·ty,** *n.*

ra'tion·al·ism (-iz-əm) *n.* a doctrine that places reason above faith.
—**ra'tion·al·ist,** *n.*

ra'tion·al·ize" (-īz") *v.t. & i.* explain or interpret according to supposed reason. —**ra"tion·al·i·za'tion,**
n.

rat'line (rat'lin) *n.* (*Naut.*) a rope
hung horizontally, used as a step in
climbing. Also, **rat'lin.**

rat·tan' (ra-tan') *n.* 1, a climbing
palm whose stems are used for
wickerwork, canes, etc. 2, a cane.

rat'ter (rat'ər) *n.* a dog or cat that
kills rats.

rat'tle (rat'əl) *v.i. & t.* 1, make or
cause to make a rapid succession of
clicking sounds. 2, talk rapidly. 3,
move with a clatter. 4, (*Colloq.*) confuse. —*n.* 1, the act or effect of
rattling. 2, a toy that produces a
clattering sound. 3, one of the horny
cells at the end of a rattlesnake's
tail.

rat'tle·brain" *n.* a giddy, chattering person.

rat'tle·snake" *n.* a venomous
Amer. snake whose tail rattles when
shaken. Also (*Colloq.*) **rat'tler.**

rat'tle·trap" *n.* a shaky, rickety
object. —*adj.* shaky.

rat'ty (rat'ē) *adj.* seedy. —**rat'ti-
ness,** *n.*

rau'cous (rä'kəs) *adj.* harsh of
voice; hoarse.

rav'age (rav'ij) *v.t. & i.* lay waste;
devastate; pillage. —*n.* devastation.

rave (rāv) *v.i. & t.* talk insanely, extravagantly, or overenthusiasti-
cally. —*n.* (*Colloq.*) unrestrained
praise; the object of it. —*adj.*
(*Colloq.*) extremely enthusiastic.

rav'el (rav'əl) *v.t. & i.* 1, draw
apart thread by thread; fray. 2, disentangle or become disentangled.

tub, cūte, pull; label; oil, owl; go, chip, she, thin, then, sing, ink; see p. 6

ra'ven (rā'vən) *n.* a large glossy, black crow. —*adj.* deep, lustrous black.

rav'en (rav'ən) *v.t. & i.* 1, obtain by violence. 2, swallow greedily. —rav'en·ing, *adj.* eager for prey.

rav'en·ous (rav'ə-nəs) *adj.* furiously hungry.

ra·vine' (rə-vēn') *n.* a deep valley.

ra"vi·o'li (ra"vē-ō'lē) *n.pl.* an Ital. dish of chopped meat wrapped in dough.

rav'ish *v.t.* 1, seize and carry off. 2, enrapture. 3, rape. —rav'ish·ing, *adj.* entrancing. —rav'ish·ment, *n.*

raw (rā) *adj.* 1, uncooked. 2, in a natural state or condition; not processed by manufacture, etc. 3, harsh, sharp, or chilly; bleak, as of weather. 4, without covering, as of skin; naked. 5, untried; untrained; inexperienced. —*n.* 1, a raw article or condition. 2, a sore place. —raw material, a substance of which manufactured goods are made. —raw'ness, *n.*

raw'boned' (-bōnd') *adj.* gaunt.

raw'hide' *n.* 1, untanned leather. 2, a leather whip.

ray (rā) *n.* 1, a line of light; a similar emanation from a central source. 2, a beam of intellectual light. 3, a stripe. 4, one of several lines emanating from a point. 5, a sea fish, as the skate, etc.

ray'on (rā'on) *n.* a silklike cellulose yarn or fabric.

raze (rāz) *v.t.* level to the ground; tear down; demolish.

ra'zor (rā'zər) *n.* a sharp-edged instrument used for shaving. —*adj.* extremely sharp.

ra'zor·back' *n.* 1, a hog whose back resembles intersecting planes. 2, a whale with a similar back.

razz (raz) *v.t. & i.* (*Colloq.*) tease; heckle.

re (rā) *n.* second tone in the scale.

re (rē) *n.* (*Law*) (preceded by *in*) the case of.

re- (rē) *pref.* 1, back: denoting reverse action. 2, (with hyphen when necessary to avoid ambiguity), again; anew. [In addition to words defined in the text, the following words may be defined by adding *again* to the root word.]

re"ad·just'
re"ap·pear'
re"ap·point'
re"ar·range'
re"as·sem'ble
re"as·sert'
re·born'
re·build'
re"com·mence'
re·con'quer
re·con'sti·tute
re·"cre·ate'
re"dis·cov'er
re·ech'o

re"e·lect'
re"em·bark'
re"en·force'
re·en'ter
re"es·tab'lish
re·fit'
re·heat'
re·kin'dle
re·load'
re·mar'ry
re·name'
re·o'pen
re·paid'
re"pub·li·ca'tion
re·pub'lish
re·read'
re·set'
re"u·nite'
re·vis'it

reach (rēch) *v.t. & i.* 1, stretch out; extend outward. 2, attain; arrive at; extend as far as. 3, obtain access to; establish communication with. 4, influence. 5, hand over; deliver. 6, strive. —*n.* 1, the act or capacity of stretching out for something. 2, a continuous stretch or course. 3, the distance one can reach. 4, range of capacity or ability.

re·act' (rē-akt') *v.i.* 1, act in a reverse or opposite direction. 2, act mutually or reciprocally upon each other. 3, respond. 4, return to a former condition. —re·ac'tor, *n.*

re·ac'tion (rē-ak'shən) *n.* 1, an opposed or return action. 2, a response. 3, a tendency to revert as to former customs or ideology. 4, mutual or reciprocal action.

re·ac'tion·ar·y (-er-ē) *adj. & n.* (one) favoring a return to old, esp. conservative, ways and methods.

read (rēd) *v.t. & i.* [*pret. & p.p.* read (red)] 1, understand (something written or printed) by interpretation of the signs used. 2, understand by observation or scrutiny. 3, utter aloud (written words); recite. 4, peruse (a book, etc.); study. 5, infer. 6, solve (a riddle); tell fortunes.

read'a·ble *adj.* 1, legible. 2, interesting.

read'er *n.* 1, a person who reads or likes to read. 2, in some churches, a minor clerical order. 3, a book for the teaching of reading. 4, an interpreter.

read'i·ly (red'ə-lē) *adv.* 1, willingly. 2, easily.

read'ing (rē'ding) *n.* 1, act of reading. 2, a recital; rendition. 3, interpretation; inference. 4, the study of reading. 5, printed matter.

read'y (red'ē) *adj.* 1, prepared for immediate use or action. 2, willing. 3, about (to). 4, immediately available; handy. 5, prompt; facile; quick. —read'i·ness, *n.*

read'y·made' *adj.* manufactured before being offered for sale, as clothes.

re·a'gent (rē-ā'jənt) *n.* a substance that causes chemical reaction.

re'al (rē'əl) *adj.* 1, existing, not imaginary; actual. 2, genuine; true;

authentic. **3**, of property, immovable, as lands.

real estate land, together with any buildings on it.

re·al·ism (rē'ə-liz-əm) *n.* **1**, interest only in the actual or real, not in the ideal or abstract. **2**, fidelity to actual appearance or fact, as in art.

re·al·ist (rē'əl-ist) *n.* one who tries to see or portray things as they are, not idealized. —**re·al·is'tic**, *adj.* —**re'al·is'ti·cal·ly**, *adv.*

re·al'i·ty (rē-al'ə-tē) *n.* **1**, state of actual existence. **2**, fact; truth.

re'al·ize (rē'ə-līz') *v.t.* **1**, recognize the nature or existence of. **2**, comprehend; understand, or feel distinctly. **3**, achieve. **4**, make a profit of or on. **5**, exchange for cash. —*v.i.* convert property into cash; profit. —**re'al·i·za'tion**, *n.*

re'al·ly (rē'ə-lē) *adv.* **1**, as a fact; truly; actually. **2**, indeed.

realm (relm) *n.* a domain; sphere.

Re'al·tor (rē'əl-tôr') *n.* (T.N.) a member of a certain real-estate brokers' organization.

re'al·ty (rē'əl-tē) *n.* real estate.

ream (rēm) *n.* **1**, a quantity of paper, usually 500 sheets. **2**, (*pl.*) (*Colloq.*) a large quantity. —*v.t.* enlarge and smooth (a hole).

Reamer

ream'er (rē'mər) *n.* **1**, a tool for enlarging holes. **2**, a device for extracting juice from an orange, etc.

reap (rēp) *v.t.* **1**, cut with a sickle or other implement and gather; harvest. **2**, garner as the fruit of one's labors. —**reap'er**, *n.* **1**, one who reaps. **2**, a machine for reaping.

rear (rir) *n.* **1**, the back; a position lying backward; the background. **2**, (Mil.) the body of an army or fleet that comes last. —*adj.* hindmost. —*v.t.* **1**, set or hold up; elevate. **2**, build; construct; erect. **3**, foster; nurture; train, as children. **4**, raise, as plants or animals. —*v.i.* **1**, rise on the hind legs, as a horse. **2**, (with *up*) express resentment. —**rear admiral**, a naval officer ranking above captain and commodore. —**rear guard**, a detachment to follow and protect a marching army.

rear'most *adj.* last of all.

rea'son (rē'zən) *n.* **1**, a statement given to create, confirm, or justify a belief, conclusion, or action; a promise; ground; excuse. **2**, intellect; the faculty of understanding, inferring, and deducing, esp. as man does. **3**, sanity. **4**, moderation; right. —*v.i.* exercise the mind; reflect; think. —**rea'son·ing**, *n.*

rea'son·a·ble *adj.* **1**, rational. **2**, amenable to sound sense. **3**, not exceeding the bounds of common sense; sensible. **4**, moderate in amount or price.

re"as·sur'ance (rē'ə-shūr'əns) *n.* **1**, restored confidence. **2**, something that reassures.

re"as·sure' (rē'ə-shūr') *v.t.* instill confidence in.

re·bate' (rē'bāt) *n.* a return of part of a payment. —*v.t.* (rē-bāt') return (part of a payment received).

re·bel' (ri-bel') *v.i.* **1**, make war against one's government; revolt against any authority or order. **2**, refuse or dislike to do something expected. —*n.* (reb'əl) **1**, one who rebels. **2**, an unconventional person.

re·bel'lion (ri-bel'yən) *n.* **1**, an armed revolt. **2**, a spirit of resistance to authority.

re·bel'lious (ri-bel'yəs) *adj.* rebelling; defiant; resisting control. —**re·bel'lious·ness**, *n.*

re'birth' (rē'bėrth) *n.* **1**, a new or second birth. **2**, a revival; renaissance.

re·bound' (rē-bownd') *v.i.* spring back; bounce. —*n.* (rē'bownd) **1**, the act of flying back; recoil. **2**, (*Colloq.*) recovery from an unhappy love affair.

re·buff' (ri-buf') *v.t. & n.* snub.

re·buke' (ri-būk') *v.t.* chide; reprimand. —*n.* reproof.

re'bus (rē'bəs) *n.* a representation of words or phrases by means of figures or pictures.

re·but' (ri-but') *v.t.* disprove by argument or evidence; refute, esp. in a debate. —**re·but'tal**, *n.*

re·cal'ci·trant (ri-kal'si-trənt) *adj.* refusing to submit; refractory.

re·call' (ri-kâl') *v.t.* **1**, remember; recollect. **2**, call back; summon anew. **3**, revoke; countermand. —*n.* **1**, the act of recalling; revocation. **2**, the right to vote an elected official out of office.

re·cant' (ri-kant') *v.t. & i.* contradict formally one's previous assertion; retract. —**re'can·ta'tion** (rē-) *n.*

re'cap' (rē-kap') *v.t.* put a new tread on (a worn tire). —*n.* (rē'kap) a recapped tire.

re"ca·pit'u·late (rē"kə-pich'ə-lāt') *v.t.* **1**, summarize; review. **2**, repeat (past stages of evolution) in development. —**re"ca·pit'u·la'tion**, *n.*

re·cap'ture (rē-kap'chər) *v.t.* seize, remember, or enjoy again. —*n.* **1**, a taking again; recovery. **2**, lawful seizure of property or earnings by a government.

re·cede' (ri-sēd') v.i. 1, withdraw; fall away. 2, turn back or aside. 3, incline or slope backward.

re·ceipt' (ri-sēt') n. 1, the act or state of receiving. 2, something received, esp. (pl.) money taken in. 3, a written acknowledgment of having received something, esp. money. 4, a recipe.

re·ceiv'a·ble adj. owing to oneself. —n. (usually pl.) an account due from another.

re·ceive' (ri-sēv') v.t. 1, get by transfer as from a primary source, as money, a wound, an impression, etc. 2, give admission, recognition, or welcome to. 3, hold; contain. —v.i. 1, come into custody of something by transfer. 2, greet and entertain visitors. 3, deal in stolen goods.

re·ceiv'er n. 1, one who or that which receives (taxes, etc.). 2, a dealer in stolen goods. 3, one appointed to handle the affairs of a bankrupt. 4, an instrument for receiving signals, sounds, etc. 5, a receptacle. —re·ceiv'er·ship, n.

re'cent (rē'sənt) adj. 1, of or pert. to time not long past. 2, of relatively modern date; fresh. —re'cent·ly, adv. not long ago.

re·cep'ta·cle (ri-sep'tə-kəl) n. a container, as a wastebasket.

re·cep'tion (ri-sep'shən) n. 1, the act or manner of receiving; a letting in. 2, a greeting or welcome. 3, a formal entertainment of guests. —re·cep'tion·ist, n. one employed to greet visitors.

re·cep'tive (ri-sep'tiv) adj. 1, willing or ready to receive or accept. 2, able to hold and contain. —re·cep'tive·ness, re·cep·tiv'i·ty, n.

re'cess (rē'ses) n. 1, an interval of relief; a rest period. 2, an alcove; a niche; a nook. 3, (pl.) a place of retirement or seclusion. —v.t. (rē-ses') 1, put in, make, or order a recess. 2, set back. —v.i. adjourn for a short time.

re·ces'sion (rē-sesh'ən) n. 1, act of receding. 2, a recessed place. 3, a brief decline in business prosperity.

re·ces'sion·al (rē-sesh'ən-əl) n. a hymn sung while clergy and choir retire at the end of a church service.

re·ces'sive (rē-ses'iv) adj. 1, tending to recede. 2, tending to yield.

re·cid'i·vism (ri-sid'ə-viz-əm) n. relapse into crime by a convicted criminal. —re·cid'i·vist, n.

rec'i·pe (res'ə-pē) n. directions, as for preparing a specific dish.

re·cip'i·ent (ri-sip'ē-ənt) n. one who receives or accepts something.

re·cip'ro·cal (ri-sip'rə-kəl) adj. in mutual relation; concerning, given, or owed by each with regard to the other. —n. (Math.) 1, the quotient resulting from the division of unity by a quantity, as the reciprocal of 4 is 1/4. 2, a complement.

re·cip'ro·cate" (ri-sip'rə-kāt') v.t. & i. 1, give and return mutually; act in return or response. 2, (Mech.) move backward and forward. —re·cip"ro·ca'tion, n. —reciprocating engine, one in which the pistons move back and forth.

rec"i·proc'i·ty (res"i-pros'ə-tē) n. mutual exchange or aid; coöperation.

re·cit'al (ri-sīt'əl) n. act of reciting; esp., a musical performance.

rec"i·ta'tion (res"i-tā'shən) n. 1, a reciting or recital. 2, a piece recited; a declamation.

rec"i·ta·tive' (res"i-tə-tēv') n. a partly spoken passage in an opera.

re·cite' (ri-sīt') v.t. 1, deliver orally, (something memorized); rehearse. 2, give an account or statement of; tell. 3, enumerate. —v.i. state or perform a lesson, etc.

reck (rek) v.t. & i. heed.

reck'less (rek'ləs) adj. daring; imprudent. —reck'less·ness, n.

reck'on (rek'ən) v.t. 1, count; compute. 2, hold in estimation as; regard. —v.i. 1, figure up. 2, rely; depend. 3, (Colloq.) think; suppose; guess. —reck'on·ing, n. 1, an accounting. 2, a final settlement.

re·claim' (rē-klām') v.t. 1, recover or assert right to (something lost or surrendered). 2, redeem; save (something abandoned or neglected). —rec"la·ma'tion (rek"lə-mā'shən) n.

re·cline' (ri-klīn') v.i. lie down.

re·cluse' (ri-kloos') n. a person who lives in seclusion; a hermit.

rec"og·ni'tion (rek'əg-nish'ən) n. the act of recognizing; acceptance; notice.

re·cog'ni·zance (ri-kog'nə-zəns) n. 1, (Law) a surety bond. 2, recognition.

rec'og·nize" (rek'əg-nīz') v.t. 1, identify or acknowledge something or someone as previously known. 2, acknowledge or accept formally. 3, appreciate. —rec'og·niz'a·ble, adj.

re·coil' (ri-koil') v.i. spring back; react. —n. (rē'koil") the act or extent of recoiling.

rec"ol·lect' (rek"ə-lekt') v.t. bring back to the mind; remember. —rec"ol·lec'tion, n. the act of recalling; something remembered.

rec"om·mend' (rek'ə-mend') *v.t.* 1, put in a favorable light before another; state to be worthy. 2, advise. —**rec"om·men·da'tion,** *n.*

rec'om·pense" (rek'əm-pens") *v.t.* pay, in return for something. —*n.* remuneration; repayment.

rec'on·cile" (rek'ən-sīl") *v.t.* 1, restore to union and friendship after estrangement. 2, adjust; settle. 3, bring to agreement. —**rec"on·cil'i·a'tion** (-sil"ē-ā'shən) *n.*

rec'on·dite' (rek'ən-dīt") *adj.* hard to understand; deep in meaning.

re"con·di'tion (rē"kən-dish'ən) *v.t.* restore to original condition; repair; renovate.

re·con'nais·sance (ri-kon'ə-səns) *n.* act of reconnoitering.

re"con·noi'ter (rē"kə-noi'tər) *v.t. & i.* make a preliminary inspection of (a region, enemy's position, etc.).

re"con·sid'er (rē"kən-sid'ər) *v.t.* think about again, esp. to change a decision. —**re"con·sid·er·a'tion,** *n.*

re"con·struct' (rē"kən-strukt') *v.t.* construct again; rebuild.

re"con·struc'tion (-struk'shən) *n.* 1, act of rebuilding. 2, (*cap.*) the return of the Confederate States to the Union after the Civil War.

re·cord' (ri-kôrd') *v.t.* 1, write down, so as to keep as evidence. 2, register; enroll, as voters or pupils. 3, transcribe for reproduction by phonograph, etc. —*n.* (rek'ərd) 1, the act of recording; an account or report. 2, all the known facts; previous experience. 3, a disk, etc., to reproduce sound on. 4, the highest achievement in a competition. —*adj.* exceeding all others.

re·cord'er *n.* 1, an official who keeps records. 2, a registering instrument. 3, a type of flute.

Recorder

re·count' (ri-kownt') *v.t.* 1, tell; relate; narrate in order or detail. 2, (rē"kownt') count again. —*n.* (rē'kownt') a second enumeration.

re·coup' (ri-koop') *v.t. & i.* recover (one's losses).

re·course' (rē'kôrs) *n.* a source of or appeal for help.

re·cov'er (ri-kuv'ər) *v.t.* get or obtain (something lost) again; regain; save. —*v.i.* 1, grow well again after illness; come back to a former, better state. 2, (*Law*) obtain a judgment, as for damages.

re·cov'er·y (-ə-rē) *n.* act or fact of recovering; what is recovered.

rec're·ant (rek'rē-ənt) *adj.* 1, craven; cowardly. 2, unfaithful to duty. —*n.* a coward or traitor.

rec"re·a'tion (rek"rē-ā'shən) *n.* diversion from toil; play. —**rec"re·a'tion·al,** *adj.* —**rec're·a'tive,** *adj.*

re·crim'i·nate" (ri-krim'ə-nāt") *v.i.* answer an accusation with another. —**re·crim"i·na'tion,** *n.*

re"cru·desce' (rē"kroo-des') *v.i.* 1, become raw or sore again. 2, break out afresh. —**re"cru·des'cence,** *n.* —**re"cru·des'cent,** *adj.*

re·cruit' (ri-kroot') *v.t. & i.* 1, enlist (new men), esp. for an army. 2, gather or recover (strength, provisions, etc.). —*n.* a newly enlisted member, esp. a soldier or sailor.

rec'tal (rek'təl) *adj.* of or pert. to the rectum.

rec'tan'gle (rek'tang"gəl) *n.* a four-sided plane figure having all right angles. —**rec·tan'gu·lar,** *adj.*

rec·ti- *pref.* straight.

rec'ti·fy" (rek'ti-fī") *v.t.* make right or straight; correct; amend. —**rec"ti·fi·ca'tion,** *n.* —**rec'ti·fi"er,** *n.*

rec"ti·lin'e·ar (rek"tə-lin'ē-ər) *adj.* composed of straight lines.

rec'ti·tude" (rek'ti-tūd") *n.* rightness of principle or practice.

rec'to (rek'tō) *n.* [*pl.* **-tos**] the right-hand, odd-numbered page of an open book.

rec'tor (rek'tər) *n.* 1, a priest or clergyman in charge of a parish. 2, the head of a school or college. —**rec'tor·ate** (-ət) *n.*

rec'to·ry (rek'tə-rē) *n.* a parsonage.

rec'tum (rek'təm) *n.* the terminal section of the intestine.

re·cum'bent (ri-kum'bənt) *adj.* leaning, reclining. —**re·cum'ben·cy,** *n.*

re·cu'per·ate" (ri-kū'pə-rāt") *v.i.* recover health. —**re·cu"per·a'tion,** *n.* —**re·cu'per·a·tive,** *adj.*

re·cur' (ri-kėr') *v.i.* [**-curred',** **-cur'ring**] appear again; return. —**re·cur'rence,** *n.* —**re·cur'rent,** *adj.*

rec'u·sant (rek'yə-zənt) *n. & adj.* (one who is) obstinate in refusal to comply.

red *n.* 1, a warm bright color, the color of fresh blood; any dark shade of this color, as crimson, scarlet, etc. 2, a radical; specif. a communist. —*adj.* [red'der, -dest] of this color. —**red'dish,** *adj.* —**red'ness,** *n.*

re·dact' (ri-dakt') *v.t.* edit. —**re·dac'tion,** *n.*

red'cap" *n.* a porter in a railroad station.

red'coat″ *n.* (*Hist.*) a Brit. soldier.

Red Cross an organization that helps victims of war and disaster.

red'den (red'ən) *v.t. & i.* make or become red; blush.

re·deem' (ri-dēm') *v.t.* **1,** buy back; pay off (a loan or debt). **2,** liberate from captivity or obligation by paying ransom. **3,** perform or fulfill a promise. **4,** atone for; compensate for. —**re·deem'a·ble,** *adj.*

re·deem'er *n.* one who ransoms or atones for another; (*cap.*) Jesus Christ.

re·demp'tion (ri-demp'shən) *n.* act or result of redeeming.

red flag a signal of danger.

red'hand″ed *adj.* overtly guilty.

red hat (*Colloq.*) a Rom. Cath. cardinal.

red'head″ *n.* a person with red hair. —**red'head″ed,** *adj.*

red herring a false, diversionary clue.

red-'hot' *adj.* **1,** very hot; intense. **2,** very new; affording unusual opportunity.

red'let″ter *adj.* memorable; auspicious.

red light a signal to stop. —**red-light district,** one where brothels are located.

red'o·lent (red'ə-lənt) *adj.* having or diffusing a sweet scent; fragrant. —**red'o·lence,** *n.*

re·dou'ble *v.t. & i.* **1,** double again. **2,** increase greatly. **3,** echo.

re·doubt' (ri-dowt') *n.* a small fort.

re·doubt'a·ble (ri-dow'tə-bəl) *adj.* causing dread or respect; formidable.

re·dound' (ri-downd') *v.t.* **1,** roll or flow back. **2,** accrue.

re·dress' (ri-dres') *v.t.* set right; remedy. —*n.* (rē'dres″) relief; atonement; compensation.

red'skin″ *n.* an Amer. Indian. Also, **red man.**

red tape excessive and tedious adherence to form and routine.

re·duce' (ri-doos') *v.t.* **1,** bring down; diminish in size, quantity, or value. **2,** weaken; degrade. **3,** bring to any specified state, condition, or form. **4,** subdue; raze. —*v.i.* (*Colloq.*) make oneself less fat, esp. by diet. —**re·duc'tion** (-duk'shən) *n.*

re·dun'dant (ri-dun'dənt) *adj.* superfluous; esp., using more words than are needed. —**re·dun'dan·cy,** *n.*

red'wood″ *n.* a sequoia.

reed (rēd) *n.* **1,** any tall, broad-leaved grass growing near water, or its hollow or pulp-filled stem. **2,** a musical pipe; reed instrument. **3,** (*Music*) a thin, vibratory tongue used in a mouthpiece. —**reed'y,** *adj.*

reef (rēf) *n.* **1,** a low rocky or sandy ridge near the water line; a shoal; a sand bar. **2,** (*Naut.*) a part of a sail that can be rolled up. —*v.t.* roll up.

reef'er *n.* **1,** a short outer coat. **2,** (*Slang*) a marijuana cigarette.

reek (rēk) *v.t.* give off an offensive odor. —*n.* an offensive odor.

reel (rēl) *n.* **1,** any of various revolving devices for winding yarn, fishing lines, etc. **2,** a spool of motion-picture film. **3,** a lively dance. **4,** a staggering motion; a sensation of dizziness. —*v.t.* **1,** wind upon a reel. **2,** (with *off*) utter fluently and rapidly. —*v.i.* **1,** whirl. **2,** stagger.

reeve (rēv) *v.t.* (*Naut.*) pass the end of a rope through a hole, as in a block. —*n.* **1,** a bird, the female of the ruff. **2,** a sheriff, bailiff, or similar officer.

re·fec'tion (ri-fek'shən) *n.* refreshment; a repast.

re·fec'to·ry (ri-fek'tə-rē) *n.* a dining room.

re·fer' (ri-fėr') *v.t.* [**re·ferred'**, **-fer'ring**] **1,** submit (to another person of authority) for consideration and decision. **2,** direct (someone to another person or source). **3,** assign. —*v.i.* **1,** relate. **2,** have recourse; appeal. **3,** allude; direct the attention (to).

ref″er·ee' (ref″ə-rē') *n.* a person deputed to settle a matter in dispute; an umpire. —*v.t. & i.* arbitrate.

ref'er·ence (ref'ə-rəns) *n.* **1,** act of referring; consultation. **2,** a casual mention. **3,** a written recommendation. **4,** a citation. —**reference book,** a book of classified information.

ref″er·en'dum (ref″ə-ren'dəm) *n.* a popular vote; plebiscite.

re·fill' (rē-fil') *v.t.* fill again. —*n.* (rē'fil″) a supply to replace one used or worn out.

re·fine' (ri-fīn') *v.t.* **1,** bring or reduce to a pure state. **2,** give culture to; polish. —**re·fined',** *adj.* cultivated; pure.

re·fine'ment (-mənt) *n.* **1,** act of refining; cultivation. **2,** elegance.

re·fin'er (ri-fīn'ər) *n.* a person or establishment that makes gasoline from petroleum, sugar from cane, etc. —**re·fin'er·y,** *n.* a refiner's factory.

re·flect' (ri-flekt') *v.t.* **1,** throw back, as rays of light or heat after they strike a surface. **2,** present an image of; mirror. **3,** bring about. **4,** ponder. —*v.i.* **1,** throw back rays, etc. **2,** meditate. **3,** (with *on*) bring reproach or blame.

re·flec'tion (ri-flek'shən) *n.* **1,** act or result of reflecting. **2,** an image, as in a mirror. **3,** meditation. **4,** comment. **5,** an unfavorable remark; slur. Also, **re·flex'ion.**

re·flec'tive (ri-flek'tiv) *adj.* **1,** reflecting. **2,** being, or pert. to, reflection.

re·flec'tor (ri-flek'tər) *n.* a part for reflecting light.

re'flex (rē'fleks) *n.* an involuntary action of the nervous system in response to some stimulus.

re·flex'ive (ri-flek'siv) *adj.* (*Gram.*) denoting action upon the subject, as in *he wrongs himself.*

re'flux" (rē'fluks") *n.* a flowing back, as of a tide; ebb.

re·for'est (rē-fôr'əst) *v.t.* replant with trees. —**re"for·es·ta'tion,** *n.*

re·form' (ri-fôrm') *v.t.* make over; change, esp. to a better state; improve. —*v.i.* abandon evil ways. —*n.* **1,** change or improvement, esp. in social institutions. **2,** betterment of conduct. —**reform school,** a reformatory.

re–"form' (rē–"fôrm') *v.t. & i.* **1,** form again; reconstruct. **2,** make different in shape or form.

ref"or·ma'tion (ref"ər-mā'shən) *n.* **1,** a change for the better. **2,** (*cap.*) the 16th-century movement that led to the formation of Protestant churches.

re·form'a·to·ry (ri-fôr'mə-tôr-ē) *n.* a place of detention for juvenile criminals.

re·form'er *n.* one who urges betterment of conditions or morals.

re·fract' (ri-frakt') *v.t.* bend abruptly; esp., deflect a ray of light.

re·frac'tion (ri-frak'shən) *n.* an oblique direction given a ray of heat, light, or sound, passing into a different medium.

Refraction

re·frac'to·ry (ri-frak'tə-rē) *adj.* unmanageable; unyielding.

re·frain' (ri-frān') *v.i.* hold oneself back; abstain; forbear. —*n.* something repeated, esp. a phrase or verse in a poem or song; a chorus.

re·fresh' (ri-fresh') *v.t.* make fresh again; invigorate; stimulate. —*v.i.* become fresh.

re·fresh'ment (-mənt) *n.* **1,** act or result of refreshing. **2,** (*pl.*) a light meal served at a party.

re·frig'er·ant (ri-frij'ər-ənt) *n. & adj.* a substance that causes cooling.

re·frig'er·ate" (ri-frij'ə-rāt") *v.t.* make cold; freeze (food or liquids). —**re·frig"er·a'tion,** *n.*

re·frig'er·a"tor (ri-frij'ə-rā"tər) *n.* a cabinet for cold storage.

re"fu'el (rē-fū'əl) *v.t. & i.* supply or take in fresh fuel.

ref'uge (ref'ūj) *n.* a shelter or protection from danger or distress; an asylum.

ref"u·gee' (ref"ū-jē') *n.* one who flees for safety.

re·ful'gence (rė-ful'jəns) *n.* brilliant light, splendor. —**re·ful'gent,** *adj.*

re·fund' (rė-fund') *v.t.* **1,** pay back. **2,** (rē–") refinance, as by a new bond issue. —*n.* (rē'fund") a repayment.

re·fur'bish (rė-fėr'bish) *v.t.* clean and polish.

re·fus'al (ri-fūz'əl) *n.* **1,** act or result of refusing. **2,** first option.

re·fuse' (ri-fūz') *v.t.* **1,** decline to do or grant; deny. **2,** decline to accept; reject.

ref'use (ref'ūs) *n.* garbage; rubbish.

ref"u·ta'tion (ref"ū-tā'shən) *n.* act or result of refuting; that which refutes.

re·fute' (ri-fūt') *v.t.* defeat by argument or proof; disprove.

re·gain' (ri-gān') *v.t.* **1,** get again; recover. **2,** get back to; reach again.

re'gal (rē'gəl) *adj.* royal; majestic.

re·gale' (ri-gāl') *v.t. & i.* entertain sumptuously; divert; feast. —**re·gale'ment,** *n.*

re·ga'li·a (ri-gā'lē-ə) *n. pl.* **1,** emblems; insignia. **2,** personal finery.

re·gard' (ri-gärd') *v.t.* **1,** look upon; observe; consider. **2,** have a particular attitude toward; esteem. **3,** have relation to; concern. —*n.* **1,** reference; respect. **2,** a particular feeling, esp. of respect. **3,** scrutiny. **4,** concern; interest. —**re·gard'ful,** *adj.* thoughtful; attentive. —**re·gard'ing,** *prep.* in reference to; concerning. —**re·gard'less,** *adj.* indifferent; not caring. —*adv.* notwithstanding.

re·gat'ta (ri-gat'ə) *n.* a boat race, esp. of yachts.

re'gen·cy (rē'jən-sē) *n.* **1,** a board of regents. **2,** state of being a regent. **3,** government by a regent.

re·gen'er·ate" (rė-jen'ər-āt") *v.t.* **1,** make over completely; reform thoroughly. **2**, bring into existence again. **3**, (*Electricity*) amplify the input by part of the output. —*v.i.* be formed again or improved. —*adj.* (-ət) reformed. —**re"gen·er·a'tion,** *n.* —**re·gen'er·a·tive,** *adj.*

re'gent (rē'jənt) *n.* **1**, one who governs when the legitimate ruler cannot. **2**, one of a board of governing education, a college, etc.

reg'i·cide (rej'ə-sīd") *n.* the killing or killer of a king.

re·gime' (rā-zhēm') *n.* the mode, system, style, or rule of management or government.

reg'i·men (rej'ə-mən) *n.* a system of regulation or remedy.

reg'i·ment (rej'ə-mənt) *n.* a body of soldiers, usually two battalions commanded by a colonel. —*v.t.* systematize; bring under strict and uniform control. —**reg"i·men'tal,** *adj.* pert. to a regiment. —**reg"i·men'tals,** *n.pl.* military dress. —**reg"i·men·ta'tion,** *n.* act or effect of regimenting.

re'gion (rē'jən) *n.* **1**, a large area of indefinite extent; a country. **2**, a district, section. —**re'gion·al,** *adj.*

reg'is·ter (rej'is-tər) *n.* **1**, an official written record; a record book; a recording device. **2**, (*Music*) the compass or range of a voice or instrument. **3**, a device for regulating the passage of heat or air. **4**, in printing, exact adjustment of position. **5**, a recording office. —*v.t.* **1**, enter in a register; record. **2**, mark or indicate on a scale. **3**, demonstrate (some kind of emotion). **4**, insure delivery of (a letter). —*v.i.* **1**, cause one's name to be recorded. **2**, place printing type or plates in proper position. **3**, (*Colloq.*) create an impression.

reg'is·trar" (rej'is-trär") *n.* a recording officer.

reg"is·tra'tion (rej"is-trā'shən) *n.* **1**, act of registering or being registered. **2**, the number of persons registered.

reg'is·try (rej'is-trē) *n.* act or place of recording.

reg'nant (reg'nənt) *adj.* reigning.

re·gress' (rē'gres) *n.* passage back; return. —*v.i.* (ri-gres') go back; retrogress. —**re·gres'sion** (ri-gresh'ən) *n.* —**re·gres'sive** (ri-gres'iv) *adj.*

re·gret' (ri-gret') *v.t.* **1**, look back at with sorrow; lament. **2**, be distressed on account of; rue. —*n.* **1**, grief; a painful sense of loss. **2**, (*pl.*) a written note declining an invitation. —**re·gret'ful,** *adj.*

reg'u·lar (reg'yə-lər) *adj.* **1**, conforming to a rule, law, type, prescribed mode, customary form, or design; normal; customary. **2**, steady; rhythmical. **3**, (*Mil.*) professional. **4**, (*Colloq.*) thorough;

sportsmanlike. —**reg"u·lar'i·ty** (-lar'ə-tē) *n.*

reg'u·late" (reg'yə-lāt") *v.t.* **1**, direct or govern by rule. **2**, put or keep in good order. **3**, adjust (an instrument, as a clock). —**reg"u·la'tion,** *n.* —**reg'u·la"tor,** *n.*

re·gur'gi·tate" (rē-gėr'ji-tāt") *v.t. & i.* bring back (specif. food from the stomach). —**re·gur"gi·ta'tion,** *n.*

re"ha·bil'i·tate" (rē"hə-bil'ə-tāt") *v.t.* restore to good condition or respectable position. —**re"ha·bil"i·ta'tion,** *n.*

re'hash (rē'hash) *n.* something made over but with nothing new in substance. —*v.t.* (rē-hash'). **1**, make into a different form. **2**, go over again, as an argument.

re·hearse' (ri-hėrs') *v.t.* **1**, practice (as a play) for a public performance. **2**, repeat. **3**, enumerate. —*v.i.* perform for practice. —**re·hears'al,** *n.*

reign (rān) *n.* **1**, sovereignty; royal or supreme power. **2**, the time during which a sovereign rules. —*v.i.* rule.

re"im·burse' (rē"im-bėrs') *v.t.* pay back; restore; refund. —**re"im·burse'ment,** *n.*

rein (rān) *n.* **1**, a long strap attached to a bridle, by which the rider or driver controls a horse. **2**, (usually *pl.*) any means of restraint or control. —*v.t.* restrain.

re"in·car'nate (rē"in-kär'nāt) *v.t.* endow a spirit with a new or different body.

re"in·car·na'tion (rē"in-kär-nā'shən) *n.* **1**, a rebirth in a new embodiment. **2**, the belief that souls are reborn.

rein'deer" (rān'-dir") *n.* a deer used as a draft animal in Arctic regions.

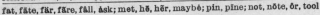
Reindeer

re"in·force' (rē"in-fôrs') *v.t.* strengthen by supplying additional men, materials, support, etc. Also, **re"ën·force'.**

re"in·force'ment (-mənt) *n.* **1**, act or effect of reinforcing. **2**, that which reinforces; (*Mil.*, often *pl.*) new troops, ships, etc.

re"in·state' (rē"in-stāt') *v.t.* restore to a former position. —**re"in·state'ment,** *n.*

re·it'er·ate" (rē-it'ə-rāt") *v.t.* repeat; iterate. —**re·it"er·a'tion,** *n.*

re·ject' (ri-jekt') *v.t.* **1**, throw away as useless; discard. **2**, refuse to accept; decline. **3**, refuse to grant; deny. —*n.* (rē'jekt) an imperfect article. —**re·jec'tion,** *n.*

re·joice' (ri-jois') *v.i. & t.* feel joy and gladness; exult; gladden.

re·join' (ri-join') *v.t. & i.* 1, answer. 2, (rē'join') unite or join again.

re·join'der (-dər) *n.* a reply.

re·ju've·nate' (ri-joo've-nāt") *v.t.* make youthful; renew; refresh. —**re·ju"ve·na'tion,** *n.*

re·lapse' (ri-laps') *v.i.* slip back into a former state, as illness or evil ways. —*n.* a recurrence of illness; a backsliding.

re·late' (ri-lāt') *v.t.* 1, connect with (something else). 2, tell; narrate. 3, ally by kinship. —*v.i.* have reference, kinship, or connection with something. —**re·lat'ed,** *adj.* associated; connected; akin.

re·la'tion (ri-lā'shən) *n.* 1, narration; a narrative. 2, kinship; a kinsman. 3, (*pl.*) affairs; dealings. 4, bearing; close connection. 5, reference. —**re·la'tion·ship,** *n.*

rel'a·tive (rel'ə-tiv) *adj.* 1, having bearing on something; close in connection. 2, belonging to or respecting something else. 3, comparative, not absolute. 4, (*Gram.*) referring to an antecedent. —*n.* a person connected by blood or affinity.

rel"a·tiv'i·ty (rel"ə-tiv'ə-tē) *n.* 1. quality or state of being connected with; interdependence. 2, a theory in physics (the Einstein theory) that motion, time, space, etc. are not absolute; that time is a dimension; etc.

re·lax' (ri-laks') *v.t. & i.* make or become less tense, severe, assiduous, or the like; slacken; ease; unbend. —**re"lax·a'tion** (rē"-) *n.*

re'lay (rē'lā) *n.* 1, a fresh supply of men or animals held in readiness; a shift. 2, a race among teams of successive runners. —*v.t.* send by a series of messengers or media.

re·lease' (ri-lēs') *v.t.* 1, set free; unfasten. 2, free from pain, obligation, penalty, etc. 3, let be shown or sold, as a motion picture or book. —*n.* 1, liberation, as from prison. 2, discharge or freedom from any burden. 3, a news item, motion picture, etc., made available for publication. 4, a surrender of a claim.

rel'e·gate' (rel'ə-gāt') *v.t.* send away or out of the way; consign. —**rel'e·ga'tion,** *n.*

re·lent' (ri-lent') *v.i.* become less obdurate; feel compassion; soften; yield. —**re·lent'less,** *adj.* ever harsh or pressing.

rel'e·vant (rel'ə-vənt) *adj.* concerning the case in question; pertinent; applicable. —**rel'e·vance,** *n.*

re·li'a·ble (ri-lī'ə-bəl) *adj.* dependable; trustworthy. —**re·li"a·bil'i·ty,** *n.*

re·li'ance (ri-lī'əns) *n.* confidence; trust. —**re·li'ant,** *adj.*

rel'ic (rel'ik) *n.* 1, that which remains after decay of the rest. 2, a memento held in religious veneration. 3, (*pl.*) remains.

rel'ict (rel'ikt) *n.* a widower or, esp., a widow.

re·lief' (ri-lēf') *n.* 1, the act of relieving; alleviation; comfort. 2, that which removes or lessens pain, want, etc. 3, assistance given to the poor. 4, release from a post of duty by a substitute; the substitute. 5, the projection of a figure from a plane surface.

re·lieve' (ri-lēv') *v.t.* 1, remove or lessen anything that weighs down or pains; alleviate. 2, free from pain, want, anxiety, etc.; comfort. 3, substitute for. 4, heighten the effect or interest of, by contrast or variety.

re·li'gion (ri-lij'ən) *n.* 1, a system of faith in and worship of a deity. 2, devoutness; dedication to a holy life. 3, a doctrine or custom accepted on faith.

re·li'gious (ri-lij'əs) *adj.* 1, pert. to a religion. 2, devout. 3, conscientious; diligent.

re·lin'quish (ri-ling'kwish) *v.t.* give up; desist from; quit; surrender. —**re·lin'quish·ment,** *n.*

rel'i·quar"y (rel'ə-kwăr"ē) *n.* a repository for relics.

rel'ish *v.t.* be pleased with; enjoy; esp., eat with pleasure. —*n.* 1, a pleasing taste; flavor. 2, appreciation; gusto. 3, an appetizer.

re·luc'tant (ri-luk'tənt) *adj.* acting or doing with positive disinclination; unwilling. —**re·luc'tance,** *n.*

re·ly' (ri-lī') *v.i.* (with *on*) have confidence; trust; depend.

re·main' (ri-mān') *v.i.* 1, continue in a place; stay. 2, continue in a specified state without change. 3, endure; last. 4, be left after something has been taken away. 5, be held in reserve. —*n.* (*pl.*) that which is left; a dead body; relics.

re·main'der (-dər) n. 1, anything left after the removal of a part. 2, a surplus.

re·mand' (ri-mand') v.t. send, call, or order back.

re·mark' (ri-märk') v.t. & i. 1, note in the mind; observe. 2, express by way of comment. —n. a casual statement.

re·mark'a·ble adj. worthy of notice; extraordinary.

re·me'di·al (ri-mē'dē-əl) adj. serving to cure or correct.

rem'e·dy (rem'ə-dē) n. 1, any treatment that cures a disease. 2, anything that corrects or counteracts an evil. 3, (Law) redress. —v.t. 1, cure; heal. 2, remove something evil from; counteract; redress. —**re·me'di·a·ble** (rə-mē'dē-ə-bəl) adj.

re·mem'ber (ri-mem'bər) v.t. 1, retain in the mind; recall; recollect. 2, observe, as an anniversary. 3, acknowledge (some service) with money; tip. 4, convey regards from. —v.i. utilize the memory.

re·mem'brance (ri-mem'brəns) n. 1, act of remembering; something remembered. 2, memory. 3, a souvenir; a greeting card, gift, etc.

re·mind' (ri-mīnd') v.t. put in mind; recall to the memory or notice of. —**re·mind'er**, n. something that serves to remind.

rem'i·nisce' (rem"ə-nis') v.t. recall the past to mind.

rem'i·nis'cence (rem"ə-nis'əns) n. 1, recollection. 2, something remembered. esp. nostalgically. —**rem"i·nis'cent**, adj.

re·mise' (ri-mīz') n. (Law) a surrender or release, as of a claim.

re·miss' (ri-mis') adj. negligent; dilatory. —**re·miss'ness**, n.

re·mis'sion (ri-mish'ən) n. 1, a giving up or discharge, as of a debt. 2, the act of forgiving; pardon. 3, abatement.

re·mit' (ri-mit') v.t. [**re·mit'ted, -ting**] 1, pardon; forgive. 2, refrain from enacting. 3, make less intense or violent; slacken. 4, restore; replace. 5, send in payment for goods received. 6, (Law) transfer (a case) to a lower court. —v.i. 1, abate. 2, send payment. —**re·mit'tal**, n.

re·mit'tance (ri-mit'əns) n. money sent. —**remittance man**, an exile living on remittances from home.

rem'nant (rem'nənt) n. a small remainder; a remainder of a bolt of cloth, ribbon, etc.

re·mod'el (rē-mod'əl) v.t. make over; reform; recondition.

re·mon'strance (ri-mon'strəns) n. an objection; protest.

re·mon'strate (ri-mon'strāt) v.t. present strong reasons against something; object; protest.

rem'o·ra (rem'ə-rə) n. a parasitical marine fish.

Remora

re·morse' (ri-môrs') n. self-accusatory regret. —**re·morse'ful**, adj. regretful and conscious of guilt. —**re·morse'less**, adj. relentless.

re·mote' (ri-mōt') adj. far away; distant; not closely connected. —**re·mote'ness**, n.

re·mount' (rē-mownt') v.t. & i. mount again, as a horse.

re·mov'a·ble (ri-moov'ə-bəl) adj. not fixed. —n. (usually pl.) furniture and loose possessions.

re·move' (ri-moov') v.t. 1, change from one place to another; transfer; move. 2, displace, as from an office. 3, destroy. —v.i. transfer from one residence, place, etc. to another. —**re·mov'al**, n.

re·mu'ner·ate" (ri-mū'nə-rāt') v.t. pay (a person) for any service, loss, or expense; recompense. —**re·mu'ner·a'tion**, n. —**re·mu'ner·a·tive**, adj. profitable.

ren"ais·sance' (ren'ə-säns') n. a new emergence or revival, specif. (cap.) of art and literature after the Dark Ages.

re'nal (rē'nəl) adj. pert. to the kidneys.

re·nas'cence (ri-nas'əns) n. a rebirth; renaissance.—**re·nas'cent**, adj.

rend v.t. & i. [pret. & p.p. rent] tear apart violently; split.

ren'der (ren'dər) v.t. 1, cause to be or become. 2, afford for use or benefit; present. 3, give or pay back; return. 4, translate. 5, reproduce; represent, as a part in a play. 6, reduce; melt; clarify by frying.

ren'dez·vous" (rän'də-voo") n. [pl. -vous" (-vooz")] 1, a place of meeting. 2, an appointment. —v.t. & i. assemble.

ren·di'tion (ren-dish'ən) n. the act of rendering; a translation; interpretation; performance.

ren'e·gade" (ren'ə-gād") n. one who deserts his faith, cause, party, etc.; a turncoat; a traitor.

re·nege' (ri-nig') v.i. 1, in card-playing, deviate from rule, esp. by revoking. 2, (Colloq.) back down.

re·new' (ri-nū') *v.t.* **1,** make fresh or vigorous again. **2,** make again; reaffirm, as a promise. **3,** replenish. **4,** grant again; extend the term of. —**re·new'al,** *n.* act or effect of renewing; extension of a contract.

ren'net (ren'it) *n.* **1,** the fourth stomach of a calf. **2,** a substance derived from this stomach, used to curdle milk; rennin.

ren'nin (ren'in) *n.* a substance that coagulates milk; rennet.

re·nounce' (ri-nowns') *v.t. & i.* refuse to acknowledge; abandon. —**re·nounce'ment,** *n.*

ren'o·vate" (ren'ə-vāt") *v.t.* restore to freshness or new condition. —**ren"o·va'tion,** *n.* —**ren'o·va"tor,** *n.*

re·nown' (ri-nown') *n.* a great reputation for achievements; fame. —**re·nowned',** *adj.* famous.

rent *n.* **1,** payment for the use of property. **2,** an opening made by tearing; a separation. —*adj.* torn. —*v.t.* **1,** let; grant the use of, for payment. **2,** hire. —*v.i.* be leased or let out. —*v.* pret. & p.p. of *rend.*

rent'al (ren'təl) *n.* **1,** the rate paid as rent. **2,** income from rented property. —*adj.* pert. to rent.

re·nun"ci·a'tion (ri-nun"sē-ā'shən) *n.* act of renouncing, esp. as a voluntary sacrifice.

re·or'gan·ize" (rē-ôr'gə-nīz") *v.t. & i.* organize again or in a new way. esp. of a business or corporation, —**re·or"gan·i·za'tion,** *n.*

rep *n.* **1,** a corded fabric. **2,** (*Slang*) reputation.

re·pair' (ri-pär') *v.t.* go to a specified place. —*v.t.* **1,** restore to good condition. **2,** make amends for; make good. —*n.* **1,** act of restoring to good condition. **2,** good condition.

rep'a·ra·ble (rep'ə-rə-bəl) *adj.* capable of being repaired.

rep"a·ra'tion (rep"ə-rā'shən) *n.* the act of making amends; (*pl.*) compensation for damage.

rep"ar·tee' (rep"ər-tē') *n.* a ready, pertinent, and witty reply; an exchange of such replies.

re·past' (ri-pàst') *n.* a meal.

re·pa'tri·ate" (rē-pā'trē-āt") *v.t. & i.* restore to one's own country. —**re·pa"tri·a'tion,** *n.*

re·pay' (rē-pā') *v.t.* **1,** pay back; refund. **2,** requite; return, as a visit. —**re·pay'ment,** *n.*

re·peal' (ri-pēl') *v.t.* recall or annul (a law); revoke; abrogate. —*n.* act of repealing; esp. (U.S., often *cap.*) the 21st Amendment, repealing the 18th (prohibition) Amendment.

re·peat' (rē-pēt') *v.t.* **1,** do, make, or perform again. **2,** say again; reiterate. **3,** say over from memory; recite. —*v.i.* **1,** say or do as before.

2, vote more than once for one candidate at one election. —*n.* (*Music*) a sign (:||:) that a passage is to be repeated.

re·peat'er *n.* **1,** one who repeats. **2,** a watch that strikes. **3,** an automatic firearm.

re·pel' (ri-pel') *v.t.* [**re·pelled',** **-pel'ling**] **1,** drive back; force to return; check the advance of. **2,** resist; oppose; reject. **3,** arouse repulsion in; disgust. —*v.i.* be disgusting. —**re·pel'lent,** *adj.*

re·pent' (ri-pent') *v.i. & t.* regret, grieve for or do penance for (a sin or crime). —**re·pent'ance,** *n.* —**re·pent'ant,** *adj.*

re"per·cus'sion (rē"pər-kush'ən) *n.* **1,** the reaction to, or result of, an action. **2,** a rebounding; echo.

rep'er·toire" (rep'ər-twär") *n.* a list of the works a performer or company can perform.

rep'er·to·ry (rep'ər-tôr-ē) *n.* **1,** repertoire. **2,** an inventory; a stock. —*adj.* designating a theatrical company performing various plays or operas.

rep"e·ti'tion (rep"ə-tish'ən) *n.* the act or result of repeating. —**rep"e·ti'tious,** *adj.* tending to reiterate.

re·pine' (ri-pīn') *v.i.* complain; mourn.

re·place' (ri-plās') *v.t.* **1,** put back; restore; return. **2,** take the place of. **3,** substitute for.

re·place'ment (-mənt) *n.* **1,** act or effect of replacing. **2,** a substitute.

re·plen'ish (ri-plen'ish) *v.t.* fill again. —**re·plen'ish·ment,** *n.*

re·plete' (ri-plēt') *adj.* completely filled; stuffed. —**re·ple'tion,** *n.*

re·plev'in (ri-plev'ən) *n.* (*Law*) the recovery of one's property held by another, subject to later court judgment. —*v.t.* seize by replevin. Also, **re·plev'y.**

rep'li·ca (rep'li-kə) *n.* an exact copy; a duplicate.

re·ply' (ri-plī') *v.t. & i.* say in answer; respond. —*n.* an answer.

re·port' (ri-pôrt') *n.* **1,** a statement of facts or figures ascertained by investigation; an account or accounting. **2,** a rumor. **3,** (*pl.*) a record of court judgments and opinions. **4,** the sound of an explosion. —*v.t.* **1,** serve as a reporter. **2,** present oneself for duty. —*v.t.* **1,** give an account of; relate. **2,** say.

re·port'er *n.* one who reports: a newspaper writer; a court stenographer.

rep"or·tor'i·al (rep"ər-tôr'ē-əl) *adj.* pert. to reporters or their work.

re·pose' (ri-pōz') *n.* **1,** a state of rest; sleep. **2,** tranquillity; composure. —*v.i.* **1,** lie at rest; be tranquil. **2,** be situated. **3,** rely. —*v.t.* **1,** lay; place. **2,** set at rest. —**re·pos'al,** *n.*

re·pos'i·to·ry (ri-poz'i-tôr-ē) *n.* a place where things are situated or stored.

re"pos·sess' (rē"pə-zes') *v.t.* regain possession of, esp. something leased or sold conditionally.

rep"re·hend' (rep"ri-hend') *v.t.* chide sharply; reprove; censure. —**rep"re·hen'sion** (-hen'shən) *n.*

rep"re·hen'si·ble (rep"ri-hens'ə-bəl) *adj.* highly blameworthy.

rep"re·sent' (rep"ri-zent') *v.t.* **1,** portray; depict; describe. **2,** play the rôle of; impersonate. **3,** denote; symbolize; stand for. **4,** speak and act for; be a substitute for. **5,** set forth; assert. **6,** be composed of; consist in.

rep"re·sen·ta'tion (-zen-tā'shən) *n.* **1,** act or result of representing; a portrayal; description. **2,** a statement; a claim; a complaint. **3,** the right to be represented in a governing body. **4,** a delegation.

rep"re·sen'ta·tive (-zen'tə-tiv) *adj.* **1,** serving to represent. **2,** composed of delegates of the people. **3,** typical; characteristic. —*n.* one who or that which represents; an agent, delegate, or substitute; (*cap.*) a U.S. Congressman, member of the House of Representatives.

re·press' (ri-pres') *v.t.* **1,** put down; subdue; crush. **2,** keep under due restraint. —**re·pres'sion** (-presh'ən) *n.* —**re·pres'sive** (-pres'iv) *adj.*

re·prieve' (ri-prēv') *v.t.* **1,** grant a respite to; spare for a time. **2,** suspend or delay the execution of (a criminal). —*n.* a respite.

rep'ri·mand" (rep'rə-mand") *v.t.* reprove severely; censure, esp. publicly. —*n.* a severe reproof.

re·print' (rē-print') *v.t.* print again. —*n.* (rē'print') a reproduction or new edition of something printed.

re·pris'al (ri-prī'zəl) *n.* any act done in retaliation.

re·prise' (ri-prēz') *n.* (*Music*) a repetition of a main theme.

re·proach' (ri-prōch') *v.t.* charge with a fault; upbraid. —*n.* **1,** a severe expression of censure. **2,** shame; disgrace. **3,** a cause or object of disgrace. —**re·proach'ful,** *adj.* accusing; expressing blame.

rep'ro·bate" (rep'rə-bāt") *n.* one who is profligate or unprincipled.

re"pro·duce' (rē"prə-doos') *v.t.* **1,** make a copy of; duplicate. **2,** procreate. **3,** produce again. —*v.i.* **1,**

beget; generate offspring. **2,** be capable of being copied, as by printing.

re"pro·duc'tion (rē"prə-duk'shən) *n.* act, process, or result of reproducing; a copy, picture, etc. —**re"pro·duc'tive,** *adj.*

re·proof' (ri-proof') *n.* an expression of blame; rebuke.

re·prove' (ri-proov') *v.t.* censure; chide. —**re·prov'al,** *n.*

rep'tile (rep'til) *n.* **1,** a creeping animal, as the snake, lizard, crocodile, etc. **2,** a low, mean person. —**rep·til'i·an,** *adj.*

re·pub'lic (ri-pub'lik) *n.* a nation whose government is wholly elected, having no king.

re·pub'li·can (ri-pub'li-kən) *adj.* **1,** being, pert. to or favoring a republic. **2,** (*cap.*) designating one of the two chief political parties in the U.S. —*n.* **1,** one who favors republican government. **2,** (*cap.*) a member or adherent of the Republican party. —**re·pub'li·can·ism,** *n.*

re·pu'di·ate" (ri-pū'dē-āt") *v.t.* **1,** refuse to acknowledge or to pay. **2,** cast away; reject; renounce. —**re·pu'di·a'tion,** *n.*

re·pug'nance (ri-pug'nəns) *n.* **1,** a feeling of distaste or aversion. **2,** state of being repugnant.

re·pug'nant (ri-pug'nənt) *adj.* **1,** highly distasteful; offensive. **2,** contrary in nature.

re·pulse' (ri-puls') *v.t.* **1,** beat or drive back; repel. **2,** refuse; reject. —*n.* **1,** a driving back. **2,** refusal; denial.

re·pul'sion (ri-pul'shən) *n.* **1,** act or effect of repulsing. **2,** repugnance.

re·pul'sive (ri-pul'siv) *adj.* **1,** repelling. **2,** offensive; causing intense aversion. —**re·pul'sive·ness,** *n.*

rep'u·ta·ble (rep'yə-tə-bəl) *adj.* held in esteem; respectable. —**rep'u·ta·bil'i·ty,** *n.*

rep"u·ta'tion (rep"yə-tā'shən) *n.* **1,** the estimation of a person or thing by the community. **2,** fame.

re·pute' (ri-pūt') *n.* reputation; esp., good reputation. —*v.t.* hold in thought; regard; deem; estimate. —**re·put'ed,** *adj.* supposed to be. —**re·put'ed·ly,** *adv.* supposedly.

re·quest' (ri-kwest') *n.* **1,** an asking for something; a petition; demand. **2,** that which is asked for. —*v.t.* express desire for; ask. —*adj.* at someone's request.

re'qui·em (rē'kwē-əm) *n.* a Mass for the dead; music for such a Mass.

re·quire' (ri-kwīr') *v.t.* **1,** ask or claim, as by right; demand; exact. **2,** order to do something; call on. **3,** need; want. —**re·quire'ment,** *n.*

req'ui·site (rek'wə-zit) *adj.* required; indispensable. —*n.* something essential or indispensable.

req"ui·si'tion (rek"wi-zish'ən) *n.* 1, act of demanding. 2, a written order, as for supplies. —*v.t.* order; seize officially.

re·quite' (ri-kwīt') *v.t.* repay (either good or evil); recompense; retaliate. —**re·quit'al,** *n.*

rere'dos (rir'dos) *n.* a screen or background, esp. behind an altar.

Reredos

re·scind' (ri-sind') *v.t.* abrogate; repeal; take back.

re·scis'sion (ri-sizh'ən) *n.* act of rescinding.

re'script (rē'skript) *n.* an edict.

res'cue (res'kū) *v.t.* deliver from danger or evil; liberate. —*n.* an act of rescuing.

re·search' (ri-sêrch') *n.* study or investigation of facts, esp. scientific, not readily available. —**re'search'-er,** *n.* one who does research, esp. in assembling facts for a writer.

re·sem'blance (ri-zem'bləns) *n.* similarity, esp. in appearance.

re·sem'ble (ri-zem'bəl) *v.t.* have similarity to; look alike.

re·sent' (ri-zent') *v.t.* consider to be an injury or an affront. —**re·sent'ful,** *adj.* angry at having been injured. —**re·sent'ment,** *n.*

res"er·va'tion (rez'ər-vā'shən) *n.* 1, the act of keeping back or withholding. 2, anything withheld, as a qualification on a statement or contract. 3, something reserved for future use or occupation. 4, a tract of public land set aside for some special use, as an *Indian reservation.*

re·serve' (ri-zêrv') *v.t.* 1, retain or set apart for future or special use. 2, keep as one's own. —*n.* 1, that which is kept for future or special use, esp. capital retained for future or contingent liabilities. 2, a reservation. 3, self-restraint; a distant manner. 4, fighting men subject to call but not on active duty. —**reserved',** *adj.* reticent; self-restrained.

re·serv'ist (ri-zêrv'ist) *n.* a member of a military reserve force.

res'er·voir (rez'ər-vwär") *n.* a supply stored for future use; a place of such storage, esp. of water.

re·side' (ri-zīd') *v.i.* 1, dwell permanently or for a considerable time. 2, be inherent in, as a quality.

res'i·dence (rez'i-dəns) *n.* 1, act of residing. 2, a dwelling.

res'i·den·cy (rez'i-dən-sē) *n.* 1, residence. 2, an official residence.

res'i·dent (rez'i-dənt) *n.* one who dwells (in a certain place). —**res"i·den'tial** (-den'shəl) *adj.* pert. to or consisting of dwellings.

re·sid'u·al (rə-zij'oo-əl) *adj.* remaining; left over.

re·sid'u·ar·y (rə-zij'oo-er-ē) *adj.* 1, remaining in an estate after deducting specific bequests. 2, inheriting a residuary estate.

res'i·due" (rez'i-dū") *n.* that which is left over; the remainder; the rest.

re·sign' (ri-zīn') *v.i.* 1, submit oneself; be reconciled; endure with patience. 2, give up an office, position, or post. —*v.t.* 1, relinquish. 2, submit. —**re·signed',** *adj.* reconciled (to some ill).

res"ig·na'tion (rez"ig-nā'shən) *n.* 1, act or result of resigning. 2, uncomplaining acceptance of misfortune.

re·sil'i·ent (ri-zil'i-ənt) *adj.* 1, springing back; rebounding; 2, buoyant; not readily discouraged. —**re·sil'i·ence,** *n.*

res'in (rez'in) *n.* 1, a hardened secretion of many plants, esp. trees, used in varnish, medicines, etc. 2, rosin. —**res'in·ous,** *adj.*

re·sist' (ri-zist') *v.t.* 1, oppose, exert physical or moral force against. 2, withstand. —*v.i.* make opposition to. —**re·sist'i·ble,** *adj.* —**re·sis'tor,** *n.*

re·sist'ance (-əns) *n.* 1, the act or power of resisting; the degree of an opposing force. 2, the extent to which an electrical conductor impedes a flow of current. —*adj.* utilizing electrical resistance.

re·sist'ant (-ənt) *adj.* resisting.

re·sole' (rē-sōl') *v.t.* put a new sole on (a shoe).

res'o·lute (rez'ə-loot) *adj.* having a fixed purpose; unwavering.

res"o·lu'tion (rez"ə-loo'shən) *n.* 1, the quality of having a fixed purpose; determination; firmness. 2, something determined upon; a decision of a legislative body. 3, the act of resolving; an analysis; a solution or answer.

re·solve' (ri-zolv') v.t. **1,** determine; decide; express as a resolution. **2,** separate into constituent parts; reduce by mental analysis; solve. —v.i. **1,** establish a purpose; determine in the mind. **2,** become by analysis. —n. **1,** a resolution. **2,** firmness or fixedness of purpose; determination. —re·solved', adj. determined; firm.

res'o·nant (rez'ə-nənt) adj. **1,** resounding; capable of decided sympathetic vibrations. **2,** having a rich, vibrant tone. —res'o·nance, n.

res·or'cin·ol (rez-ôr'si-nōl) n. a derivative of benzene, used in medicines.

re·sort' (ri-zôrt') v.i. **1,** (with to) have recourse; apply. **2,** go customarily or frequently. —n. **1,** a place frequently visited. **2,** the act of having recourse to; a source of aid.

re·sound' (ri-zownd') v.i. **1,** ring with echoing sounds; reverberate; be filled with sound. **2,** give forth a loud sound. —re·sound'ing, adj. **1,** ringing. **2,** thorough.

re·source' (ri-sôrs') n. **1,** any source of aid or support; an expedient to which one may resort. **2,** (pl.) available means; funds or supplies; assets. —re·source'ful, adj. clever in finding and utilizing resources.

re·spect' (ri-spekt') v.t. **1,** treat with special consideration or high regard; heed. **2,** have reference to; relate to. —n. **1,** high esteem; courteous or considerate treatment. **2,** a point; a particular; a feature. **3,** (pl.) compliments.

re·spect'a·ble adj. **1,** worthy of esteem; highly regarded. **2,** decent. **3,** fairly good or large. —re·spect"a·bil'i·ty, n.

re·spect'ful adj. deferent.

re·spect'ing prep. regarding; concerning.

re·spec'tive (-spek'tiv) adj. pertaining individually to each. —re·spec'tive·ly, adv. with each in proper order.

res"pi·ra'tion (res"pə-rā'shən) n. breathing. —re·spir'a·to·ry (ri-spīr'ə-tôr-ē) adj.

res'pi·ra'tor (res'pə-rā'tər) n. **1,** a device to produce involuntary breathing. **2,** a mask to exclude noxious gases or substances.

re·spire' (ri-spīr') v.i. & t. breathe.

res'pite (res'pit) n. **1,** an interval of rest or relief. **2,** a postponement.

re·splend'ent (ri-splen'dənt) adj. shining with brilliant luster; splendid. —re·splend'ence, n.

re·spond' (ri-spond') v.i. **1,** give an answer; make a reply. **2,** show reaction to a force or stimulus.

re·spond'ent (ri-spon'dənt) adj. answering; responsive. —n. (Law) defendant.

re·sponse' (ri-spons') n. **1,** an answer or reply. **2,** a reaction. **3,** a verse said or sung by choir or congregation in reply to one read by the pastor.

re·spon"si·bil'i·ty (ri-spon"sə-bil'ə-tē) n. **1,** the state of being responsible. **2,** a duty; charge.

re·spon'si·ble (ri-spon'sə-bəl) adj. **1,** answerable; accountable. **2,** able to satisfy any reasonable claim. **3,** involving important work or trust.

re·spon'sive (ri-spon'siv) adj. **1,** readily answering or reacting. **2,** constituting an answer or reaction. **3,** pert. to the use of responses.

rest n. **1,** a state of quiet or repose. **2,** freedom from care; peace; quiet. **3,** sleep. **4,** a place of quiet; a shelter. **5,** that on or in which anything leans for support. **6,** (Music) a silence or pause between tones. **7,** that which is left; remainder. —v.i. **1,** cease action or performance; be without motion; pause. **2,** take repose; be tranquil. **3,** have a foundation; be supported. **4,** remain. **5,** lean; trust; rely. —v.t. **1,** place at rest; give repose to. **2,** lay or place, as on a foundation. **3,** leave; allow to remain.

res'tau·rant (res'tə-rənt) n. a place where meals are sold; a public eating house.

res"tau·ra·teur' (res"tə-rə-tēr') n. the proprietor of a restaurant.

rest'ful adj. promoting comfort or tranquillity. —rest'ful·ness, n.

res"ti·tu'tion (res"tə-tū'shən) n. **1,** the act of returning or restoring to someone what is his. **2,** the act of making amends. **3,** restoration.

res'tive (res'tiv) adj. **1,** uneasy; impatient. **2,** refractory.

rest'less (-ləs) adj. unable to rest or sleep; uneasy. —rest'less·ness, n.

res"to·ra'tion (res"tə-rā'shən) n. **1,** the act of restoring or being restored. **2,** (cap.) the reestablishment of the British monarchy in 1660.

re·stor'a·tive (ri-stôr'ə-tiv) adj. healing; stimulating.

re·store' (ri-stôr') v.t. **1,** bring back to a former state; return to a former position. **2,** heal; cure. **3,** renew or reëstablish after interruption. **4,** return (something lost or taken) to the owner.

re·strain' (ri-strān') v.t. hold back; check; repress; restrict; confine.

re·straint' (ri-strānt') n. **1,** the act of holding back; hindrance; confinement. **2,** reserve; self-control. **3,** a limitation.

re·strict′ (ri-strikt′) *v.t.* attach limitations to; limit; restrain. —**re·stric′tion**, *n.* —**re·stric′tive**, *adj.*

re·sult′ (ri-zult′) *v.i.* **1,** proceed or arise as a consequence or effect; be the outcome. **2,** (with *in*) terminate. —*n.* **1,** a consequence; effect; outcome. **2,** (*Math.*) a quantity or value obtained by calculation. —**re·sult′ant**, *adj.*

re·sume′ (ri-zoom′) *v.t.* take up again after interruption; begin again. —*v.i.* proceed after interruption.

ré″su·mé′ (rez″oo-mā′) *n.* a summary.

re·sump′tion (ri-zum′shən) *n.* act or effect of resuming.

re·sur′gent (ri-sèr′jənt) *adj.* rising or apparring again. —**re·sur′gence,** *n.*

res″ur·rect′ (rez″ə-rekt′) *v.t.* **1,** restore to life; reanimate; renew; reconstruct. **2,** take from the grave, as a dead body.

res″ur·rec′tion (rez″ə-rek′shən) *n.* **1,** act or result of resurrecting. **2,** (*cap.*) the rebirth of souls on the judgment day. **3,** (*cap.,* with *the*) the rising of Christ from the dead.

re·sus′ci·tate″ (ri-sus′ə-tāt″) *v.t.* & *i.* revive; bring to life again. —**re·sus″ci·ta′tion,** *n.*

re′tail (rē′tāl) *n.* the sale of commodities in small quantities to the ultimate consumer. —*adj.* pert. to such sales. —*v.t.* **1,** sell to the ultimate consumer. **2,** tell in detail. —**re′tail′er,** *n.* the keeper of a store.

re·tain′ (ri-tān′) *v.t.* **1,** hold or keep in possession, use, or practice. **2,** keep in mind; remember. **3,** engage the services of.

re·tain′er *n.* **1,** that which holds in, as a retaining wall. **2,** a servant long employed. **3,** a preliminary fee for services.

re·take′ (rē-tāk′) *v.t.* **1,** take again; recapture. **2,** photograph again. —*n.* (rē′tāk″) a second photographing, as of a motion picture scene.

re·tal′i·ate″ (ri-tal′ē-āt″) *v.t.* & *i.* return like for like, esp. evil for evil. —**re·tal′i·a′tion,** *n.* —**re·tal′i·a·to·ry,** *adj.*

re·tard′ (ri-tärd′) *v.t.* **1,** make slow or slower; obstruct. **2,** defer; postpone. —**re″tar·da′tion,** *n.*

retch (rech) *v.i.* strain, as in vomiting; try to vomit.

re·ten′tion (ri-ten′shən) *n.* act or result of retaining. —**re·ten′tive,** *adj.* serving or tending to retain.

ret′i·cent (ret′ə-sənt) *adj.* disposed to be silent; reserved. —**ret′i·cence,** *n.*

re·tic′u·late″ (ri-tik′yə-lāt″) *adj.* being or resembling a network.

ret′i·cule″ (ret′ə-kūl″) *n.* a woman's handbag, orig. of network.

ret′i·na (ret′i-nə) *n.* the innermost coating of the back of the eye, extending in to the optic nerve and receiving the images of vision.

ret′i·nue″ (ret′i-nū″) *n.* a body of followers or attendants.

re·tire′ (ri-tīr′) *v.i.* **1,** draw back; retreat. **2,** go into a private place. **3,** withdraw from business or public life. **4,** go to bed. —*v.t.* **1,** take or lead back; withdraw. **2,** make inactive; relieve of duty. **3,** withdraw from circulation, as bonds. —**re·tire′ment,** *n.*

re·tired′ *adj.* **1,** having discontinued work after long service. **2,** sequestered; secluded.

re·tir′ing *adj.* diffident; shy.

re·tort′ (ri-tôrt′) *v.t.* **1,** return or turn back, as an argument upon the originator; retaliate. **2,** reply sharply. —*v.i.* make a sharp reply. —*n.* **1,** a retaliatory remark. **2,** a glass vessel with a long neck, used in chemistry.

Retort and Receiver

re·touch′ (rē-tuch′) *v.t.* alter details of (a photograph, film, or engraving) for improvement.

re·trace′ (rē-trās′) *v.t.* **1,** go back over; trace backward. **2,** trace again, as a drawing.

re·tract′ (ri-trakt′) *v.t.* **1,** draw back or in, as a cat's claws. **2,** take back; undo; recant. —*v.i.* **1,** shrink back; recede. **2,** undo or unsay what has been previously done or said.

re·trac′tile (ri-trak′til) *adj.* capable of being drawn back in.

re·trac′tion (ri-trak′shən) *n.* a disclaimer of, or apology for, an incorrect statement.

re·trac′tive (-tiv) *adj.* drawing back in.

re·trac′tor *n.* **1,** a muscle that draws back a part of the body. **2,** anything that serves to retract.

re·tread′ (rē-tred′) *v.t.* **1,** tread again. **2,** recap or cut grooves in (a tire). —*n.* (rē′-) a retreaded tire.

re·treat′ (ri-trēt′) *n.* **1,** the act of withdrawing; a backward movement under enemy pressure. **2,** a state of seclusion; retirement. **3,** a place of retirement, privacy, or security. **4,** an asylum. **5,** (*Mil.*) the bugle call that signals retirement from action. —*v.i.* go back; run from an enemy.

re·trench′ (ri-trench′) *v.t.* & *i.* cut down; curtail, esp. expenses; economize. —**re·trench′ment,** *n.*

ret″ri·bu′tion (ret″rə-bū′shən) *n.* reward or punishment for past good or evil, esp. punishment for evil. —**re·trib′u·tive** (ri-trib′yū-tiv) *adj.*

re·trieve′ (ri-trēv′) *v.t.* & *i.* **1,** find again; recover; regain. **2,** search for and bring in killed or wounded game.

re·triev′er (ri-trē′vər) *n.* a dog bred or trained to bring in game.

Retriever

ret·ro- *pref.* back; backward; behind.

ret″ro·ac′tive (ret″rō-ak′tiv) *adj.* applicable to past events, as a law. —**ret″ro·ac·tiv′i·ty,** *n.*

ret′ro·grade (ret′rə-grād″) *adj.* **1,** moving or directed backward; retreating. **2,** deteriorating. —*v.i.* go or move backward; lose ground; deteriorate. —**ret″ro·gra·da′tion,** *n.*

ret′ro·gress (ret′rə-gres″) *v.i.* revert to a worse condition; decline. —**ret″ro·gres′sion** (-gresh′ən) backward movement; deterioration.

ret′ro·spect″ (ret′rə-spekt″) *n.* the act of looking backward; contemplation of the past. —**ret″ro·spec′tive,** *adj.*

ret″ro·spec′tion (-spek′shən) *n.* the act of looking backward (in time).

ret″rous·sé′ (ret″roo-sā′) *adj.* (of a nose) turned up.

re·turn′ (ri-tẽrn′) *v.t.* **1,** come or go back to a former place, position, or state. **2,** recur. **3,** make a reply; retort. —*v.t.* **1,** send or give back; restore. **2,** cast back; reflect. **3,** repay; requite. **4,** report. **5,** elect or re-elect to office. **6,** yield (a profit). —*n.* **1,** the act or an act of returning; a recurrence; repayment. **2,** (*pl.*) a result, esp. of an election. **3,** a profit or yield. **4,** a reply.

re·un′ion (rē-ūn′yən) *n.* **1,** the act of uniting again. **2,** a gathering of friends, relatives, etc.

re·vamp′ (rē-vamp′) *v.t.* remodel; renovate.

re·veal′ (ri-vēl′) *v.t.* make known; disclose; divulge.

rev′eil·le (rev′ə-lē) *n.* (*Mil.*) a bugle call sounded at daybreak.

rev′el (rev′əl) *v.i.* **1,** join in merrymaking; carouse. **2,** take great pleasure (in); delight (in). —*n.* a boisterous merrymaking. —**rev′el·ry,** *n.*

rev″e·la′tion (rev″ə-lā′shən) *n.* **1,** the act of revealing; a disclosure, esp. by supernatural means. **2,** a striking accession of information.

re·venge′ (ri-venj′) *v.t.* inflict punishment because of; avenge. —*n.* retaliation of wrongs. —**re·venge′ful,** *adj.* seeking vengeance.

rev′e·nue″ (rev′ə-nū″) *n.* **1,** income from real or personal property. **2,** the income of a state from taxation.

re·ver′ber·ate (ri-vẽr′bə-rāt″) *v.t.* return as sound; reëcho. —**re·ver′ber·a′tion,** *n.* a series of echoes.

re·vere′ (ri-vir′) *v.t.* regard with deepest respect and awe; venerate.

rev′er·ence (rev′ər-əns) *n.* **1,** act of revering; veneration. **2,** title of certain clergymen. **3,** a bow or curtsy.

rev′er·end (rev′ər-ənd) *adj.* deserving of respect: applied to a clergyman. —*n.* (*Colloq.*) a clergyman.

rev′er·ent (rev′ər-ənt) *adj.* **1,** respectful. **2,** devout. —**rev″er·en′tial** (-en′shəl) *adj.* characterized by awe or respect.

rev′er·ie (rev′ə-rē) *n.* a state of fanciful meditation; a daydream.

re·vers′ (rə-vir′) *n. sing.* & *pl.* a part of a garment turned back, as a lapel. Also, **re·vere′.**

re·verse′ (ri-vẽrs′) *adj.* turned backward; opposite; contrary. —*n.* **1,** a change to an opposite form, state, condition, or direction. **2,** a change of fortune, specif. for the worse. **3,** the opposite; the contrary. —*v.t.* **1,** turn about, around, upside down, or in an opposite direction. **2,** set aside; annul, as a legal decree. —*v.i.* change to an opposite position, direction, motion, etc. —**re·ver′sal,** *n.* —**re·vers′i·ble,** *adj.*

re·ver′sion (ri-vẽr′shən) *n.* **1,** act or result of reverting. **2,** the right of future possession of a property. —**re·ver′sion·ar·y,** *adj.*

re·vert′ (ri-vẽrt′) *v.i.* go back to a former place, position, or state.

re·vet′ (ri-vet′) *v.t.* put a facing of masonry on an embankment, etc. —**re·vet′ment,** *n.*

re·view′ (ri-vū′) *n.* **1,** a going over anything again; an examination. **2,** a survey of the past. **3,** a critical report, as of a book or play; a periodical devoted to critical articles. **4,** (*Mil.*) a formal inspection; parade. **5,** (*Law*) a judicial reconsideration by a higher court. —*v.t.* **1,** look back upon. **2,** repeat; examine again. **3,** write about critically. **4,** (*Mil.*) make a formal inspection of. —**re·view′er,** *n.* one who reviews; a critic.

re·vile′ (ri-vīl′) *v.t.* abuse in speech or writing. —**re·vile′ment,** *n.*

re·vise′ (ri-vīz′) *v.t.* make changes or corrections in; amend.

re·vi′sion (ri-vizh′ən) *n.* act or result of revising.

re·viv′al (ri-vīv′əl) *n.* 1, act or effect of reviving; restoration. 2, a meeting to promote religious awakening. 3, the reproduction of a play formerly presented.

re·vive′ (ri-vīv′) *v.i.* come back to life after apparent death; be renewed or refreshed. —*v.t.* 1, bring back to life or use. 2, refresh; recall; reawaken.

rev′o·ca·ble (rev′ə-kə-bəl) *adj.* subject to being revoked.

rev″o·ca′tion (rev″ə-kā′shən) *n.* annulment; recall.

re·voke′ (ri-vōk′) *v.t.* annul by taking back; repeal; cancel. —*v.i.* in card playing, fail to follow suit when able and obliged to do so.

re·volt′ (ri-vōlt′) *n.* an uprising against government or authority; rebellion; insurrection. —*v.i.* break away from established authority; rebel. —*v.t.* repel; shock. —**re·volt′-ing,** *adj.* repulsive.

rev″o·lu′tion (rev″ə-loo′shən) *n.* 1, the act of revolting. 2, a complete rotation. 3, the act of traveling completely around a circuit. 4, a cycle. 5, a total change of conditions, specif. a radical social or political change; a major revolt.

rev″o·lu′tion·ar·y (-er-ē) *adj.* 1, pert. to a revolution. 2, revolving. 3, drastic; radical. —*n.* a revolutionist.

rev″o·lu′tion·ist *n.* one who participates in a revolution.

rev″o·lu′tion·ize (-īz″) *v.t.* effect an extreme change in.

re·volve′ (ri-volv′) *v.i.* 1, turn or roll around on an axis; rotate. 2, move about a center. 3, pass through periodic changes; recur. —*v.t.* turn or cause to roll around, as on an axis —**revolving fund,** one maintained by balanced borrowings and repayments.

Revolver

re·volv′er *n.* a repeating pistol having a revolving cylinder to hold cartridges.

re·vue′ (ri-vū′) *n.* a musical variety show, usually of parodies.

re·vul′sion (ri-vul′shən) *n.* a sudden, violent change of feeling.

re·ward′ (ri-wôrd′) *v.t.* 1, repay, as for good conduct or merit; recompense. 2, make a return for. —*n.* 1, a repayment or prize for merit or accomplishment. 2, profit. 3, a sum of money offered for the finding of a criminal or of a lost article.

re·write′ (rē-rīt′) *v.t.* write again in different words or form. —*n.*

(rē′rīt″) something rewritten, esp. a newspaper story from oral report.

rhap′so·dize″ (rap′sə-dīz″) *v.t. & i.* speak or write rhapsodically.

rhap′so·dy (rap′sə-dē) *n.* an expression of extravagant enthusiasm. —**rhap·sod′ic** (-sod′ik) *adj.* —**rhap·sod′i·cal·ly,** *adv.*

-rhe·a (-rē-ə) *suf.* flow; discharge.

rhe′o·stat″ (rē′ə-stat″) *n.* a resistance coil for regulating or adjusting electric current.

rhet′o·ric (ret′ə-rik) *n.* the art of using language effectively. —**rhet′o·ri′cian** (-rish′ən) *n.*

rhe·tor′i·cal (rə-tôr′i-kəl) *adj.* 1, pert. to rhetoric. 2, for effect only; not intended to be taken literally.

rheum (room) *n.* a cold.

rheu·mat′ic (roo-mat′ik) *adj.* pert. to rheumatism. —*n.* one subject to rheumatism. —**rheumatic fever,** a disease, usually of children, affecting the joints and heart. —**rheu·mat′-i·cal·ly,** *adv.*

rheu′ma·tism (roo′mə-tiz-əm) *n.* a disease characterized by inflammation of the joints.

Rh factor a property of the blood which when present (Rh positive) may cause agglutination of the red cells.

rhi′nal (rī′nəl) *adj.* pert. to the nose; nasal.

rhine′stone″ (rīn′stōn″) *n.* 1, imitation diamond. 2, rock crystal.

rhi·ni′tis (rī-nī′tis) *n.* an inflammation of the nasal mucous membrane.

rhi·noc′er·os (rī-nos′ər-əs) *n.* a huge pachyderm with one or two upright horns on the snout.

rho (rō) *n.* the 17th letter of the Greek alphabet (P, ρ).

rho′di·um (rō′dē-əm) *n.* a metallic chemical element, no. 45, symbol Rh.

rho″do·den′dron (rō″də-den′-drən) *n.* any of various hardy shrubs bearing flowers in clusters.

rhom′boid (rom′boid) *n.* a parallelogram with opposite sides equal and no right angle.

Rhombus   *Rhomboid*

rhom′bus (rom′bəs) *n.* an equilateral parallelogram with no right angle.

rhu'barb (roo'bärb) *n.* 1, a garden plant with tender, pink, acid leaf-stalks, used for sauce, pies, etc. 2, the root of an Oriental rhubarb, used in medicines. 3, (*Slang*) noisy objection to an arbiter's decision.

rhyme (rīm) *n.* 1, agreement in the terminal sounds of words or verses. 2, a couplet or short poem containing rhymes. 3, a word that rhymes with another. —*v.i. & t.* make a rhyme or rhymes. Also, **rime.**

rhythm (rith'əm) *n.* 1, movement characterized by equal or regularly alternating beats. 2, that quality in music or poetry which is produced by a regular succession of accents; cadence. 3, recurrence at regular or uniform intervals. —**rhyth'mic, rhyth'mi·cal,** *adj.*

ri·al'to (rē-al'tō) *n.* 1, a theatrical district, esp. in New York City. 2, a market place, esp. (*cap.*) in Venice.

ri·a'ta (rē-ä'tə) *n.* a lariat.

rib *n.* 1, one of the series of curved bones enclosing the chest of man and animals. 2, something likened to such a bone; a slender elongated member, timber, or ridge. —*v.t.* [**ribbed, rib'bing**] 1, strengthen or support by ribs. 2, (*Colloq.*) tease.

rib'ald (rib'əld) *adj.* coarsely humorous. —**rib'ald·ry,** *n.*

rib'bon (rib'ən) *n.* 1, a narrow strip of fabric, as silk; a similar strip of paper, metal, etc. or of color. 2, a tape for trimming. 3, (*pl.*) shreds. 4, an inked tape for a typewriter. Also, **rib'and** (-ənd).

ri'bo·fla'vin (rī'bō-flā'vin) *n.* a vitamin property, esp. vitamin B₂.

rice (rīs) *n.* the grain from a plant grown in warm climates. —*v.t.* press into shreds. —**ric'er,** *n.* a utensil for ricing potatoes, etc.

rich *adj.* 1, having much money or great possessions; wealthy. 2, abundantly supplied; abounding. 3, productive; fertile. 4, elegant; luxurious; costly. 5, full in tone; strong in color; vivid. 6, containing desirable, nutritious, or fattening ingredients. 7, (*Colloq.*) preposterous. —**rich'es,** *n.pl.* wealth. —**rich'ness,** *n.*

rick (rik) *n.* a heap or pile, as of hay.

rick'ets (rik'its) *n.* a disease characterized by softness of the bones and distortions.

rick'et·y (rik'ə-tē) *adj.* 1, tottering; shaky. 2, affected with rickets.

rick'ey (rik'ē) *n.* a cold drink made of lime juice, carbonated water, and gin: *gin rickey.*

rick'sha (rik'shä) *n.* (*Colloq.*) jin-rikisha.

ric''o·chet' (rik'ə-shā') *n.* a rebounding or a skipping of an object

passing over a flat surface. —*v.i.* rebound and glance off.

rid *v.t.* [**rid, rid'ding**] free from anything superfluous or objectionable. —*adj.* clear or relieved (of).

rid'dance (rid'əns) *n.* the act of ridding; deliverance.

rid'den (rid'ən) *v. p.p.* of *ride.*

rid'dle (rid'əl) *n.* 1, a puzzling question; an enigma; a perplexing person or thing. 2, a coarse sieve. —*v.t.* 1, fill with holes, by or as by shot. 2, sift through a coarse sieve.

ride (rīd) *v.i.* [**rode** (rōd), **rid'den** (rid'ən), **rid'ing**] 1, be carried on an animal's back or in a vehicle, ship, or plane. 2, (of a ship) float. 3, move on or about something. 4, carry passengers. 5, climb up, as an ill-fitting coat. —*v.t.* 1, sit on and manage (a horse) in motion. 2, travel on, through, or over. 3, treat harshly; tease; harass. —*n.* a journey on which one is borne.

rid'er (rīd'ər) *n.* 1, one who or that which rides. 2, a clause added to a document.

ridge (rij) *n.* 1, the crest of two sloping surfaces rising to meet at an angle. 2, a mountain or hill in this form.

ridge'pole'' *n.* the horizontal timber at the top of a roof.

rid'i·cule'' (rid'ə-kūl'') *n.* incitement of contemptuous laughter; derision. —*v.t.* make to appear absurd.

ri·dic'u·lous (ri-dik'yə-ləs) *adj.* laughable; absurd; preposterous. —**ri·dic'u·lous·ness,** *n.*

rid'ing (rīd'ing) *n.* (*Brit.*) a district.

rife (rīf) *adj.* prevalent; current.

riff (rif) *n.* a note or phrase serving to punctuate swing music.

rif'fle (rif'əl) *n.* 1, a ripple, as on water. 2, a method of shuffling cards. 3, grooves on the bottom of a sluice for catching particles of mineral.

riff'raff'' (rif'raf'') *n.* 1, scraps; rubbish; trash. 2, the rabble.

ri'fle (rī'fəl) *v.t.* 1, search, esp. to rob; ransack; plunder. 2, cut spiral grooves in the bore of a gun barrel). —*n.* a portable firearm or a cannon having a rifled bore.

rift *n.* an opening made by splitting; a cleft or crevice; a fissure.

rig *v.t.* [**rigged, rig'ging**] 1, fit with necessary equipment, as a ship with sails. 2, (with *out*) dress, oddly or gaudily. 3, raise or lower (prices) artificially. —*n.* 1, (*Naut.*) arrangement of masts, sails, etc. 2, dress; equipment.

rig'ger (rig'ər) *n.* a mover of heavy objects.

rig'ging (rig'ing) *n.* rig, especially sails, masts, etc.

right (rīt) *adj.* **1,** in conformity with the moral law or standards; just; good. **2,** in conformity with truth, fact, or reason; correct; also orderly. **3,** proper; fitting; convenient. **4,** in good condition. **5,** pert. to the side or direction that is eastward when one faces north. **6,** conservative, in politics. **7,** straight; direct. —*adv.* **1,** directly. **2,** justly. **3,** properly. **4,** correctly; exactly. **5,** very. **6,** toward the right side. —*n.* **1,** conformity to an authoritative standard. **2,** that which conforms to a rule. **3,** a just claim or title. **4,** the right side or direction. **5,** (*cap.*) the Conservative party. —*v.t.* **1,** set straight; adjust or correct. **2,** vindicate. —*v.i.* resume a vertical position. —**right angle,** an angle of 90°. —**right of way, 1,** the right to proceed before another. **2,** land over which a railroad, etc. may pass. —**right triangle,** a triangle with one right angle.

right'a·bout' *adv.* in a half circle.

right'eous (rī'chəs) *adj.* virtuous; devout. —**right'eous·ness,** *n.*

right'ful *adj.* having or based on a just claim. —**right'ful·ness,** *n.*

right-'hand' *adj.* to the right; for the right hand. —**right-hand man,** a chief assistant. —**right'-hand'ed,** *adj.* more adept with the right hand than with the left.

right'ist *n.* a conservative in politics.

rig'id (rij'id) *adj.* **1,** stiff, not pliant or easily bent; inflexible; unyielding. **2,** strict; exacting. —**ri·gid'i·ty,** *n.*

rig'ma·role (rig'mə-rōl') *n.* long, incoherent discourse; nonsense; unnecessary formalities.

rig'or (rig'ər) *n.* **1,** stiffness; inflexibility. **2,** strictness; austerity; sternness. Also, **rig'our.** —**rig'or·ous,** *adj.*

ri''gor mor'tis (rig'ər-môr'tis) *n.* the stiffening of the body after death.

rile (rīl) *v.t.* (*Colloq.*) annoy; vex.

rill (ril) *n.* a small brook.

rim *n.* **1,** the border, edge, or margin of anything. **2,** of a wheel, the outer part.

rime (rīm) *n.* **1,** rhyme. **2,** white frost; hoarfrost. —*v.t. & i.* rhyme.

rind (rīnd) *n.* an outer covering; a thick skin.

ring *v.i.* [**rang, rung, ring'ing**] **1,** resound, as a bell when struck. **2,** give a signal with a bell. **3,** sound loudly and clearly. **4,** have the sensation of a humming or buzzing sound. **5,** reverberate; reëcho. —*v.t.* **1,** cause (a bell, etc.) to sound. **2,** announce; celebrate. **3,** (with *up*) telephone to. **4,** (with *in*) introduce unfairly. **5,** [*pret. & p.p.* **ringed**] encircle; surround with, or as with, a ring. —*n.* **1,** the sound of a bell; a peal or clang; resonance. **2,** a telephone call. **3,** a circular band or hoop; an ornamental band for the finger, etc. **4,** anything circular; arrangement or array in a circle. **5,** a group. **6,** an area for sports, exhibitions, etc.; arena. **7,** prizefighting.

ring'er *n.* **1,** in quoits, a cast that encircles the pin. **2,** (*Slang*) a person who greatly resembles another: *dead ringer.* **3,** (*Slang*) a superior athlete, race horse, etc. rung in under an assumed name.

ring'lead'er *n.* a leader in mischief or objectionable acts.

ring'let *n.* a curl of hair.

ring'side' *n.* the seating space next to a boxing ring.

ring'worm' *n.* a contagious skin disease.

rink *n.* a section of ice, or a floor, for skating.

rinse (rins) *v.t.* wash lightly, esp. wash out (soap) with fresh water. —*n.* a light wash, as for removing soap, dyeing hair, etc.

ri'ot (rī'ət) *n.* **1,** a disturbance arising from disorderly conduct; a brawl. **2,** revelry. **3,** confusion; a haphazard mixture. **4,** (*Slang*) a cause of hearty laughter. —*v.i.* act without restraint. —**ri'ot·ous,** *adj.*

rip *v.t. & i.* [**ripped, rip'ping**] **1,** tear or cut open or off; slit; undo a seam. **2,** saw (wood) with the grain. **3,** (*Colloq.*) utter with violence. —*v.i.* be torn or split open. **2,** (*Colloq.*) rush headlong. —*n.* **1,** a rent or tear made by ripping. **2,** (*Colloq.*) a roué. —**rip'per,** *n.*

ri·par'i·an (ri-pâr'ē-ən) *adj.* pert. to, or situated on, the bank of a river, lake, etc.

rip cord a cord for opening a parachute during descent.

ripe (rīp) *adj.* **1,** ready for harvest; mature. **2,** in the best condition for use. **3,** ready for action or effect. —**ripe'ness,** *n.*

rip'en (rī'pən) *v.t. & i.* make or become ripe.

ri·poste' (ri-pōst') *n.* a return thrust in fencing; a clever retort.

rip'ping (rip'ing) *adj.* splendid.

rip'ple (rip'əl) *n.* **1,** the light ruffling of the surface of the water; a little wave. **2,** a sound of or like that of water running over a stony bottom. —*v.t. & i.* form ripples (in).

tub, cūte, pŭll; label; oil, owl; go, chip, she, thin, *then,* sing, ink; *see p. 6*

rip'roar"ing adj. boisterously exhilarating; hilarious; jolly.

rip'saw" n. a saw with coarse teeth, for sawing with the grain.

rip'tide" n. a strong undertow.

rise (rīz) v.i. [rose (rōz), ris'en (riz'ən), ris'ing] 1, move from a lower to a higher position; move upward. 2, stand up. 3, slope or extend upward; stand in height. 4, swell, as dough. 5, emerge; come into sight or existence. 6, increase in force, value, position, etc. 7, take up arms; rebel. —n. 1, ascent; emergence; appearance. 2, degree of ascent. 3, an elevated place. 4, spring; source; origin. 5, increase.

ris'i·ble (riz'ə-bəl) adj. 1, having the faculty of laughing. 2, exciting laughter.

risk n. 1, exposure to loss or harm; danger; peril. 2, chance; hazard. 3, a contingency covered by insurance. —v.t. 1, expose to injury or loss. 2, take the chance of. —risk'y, adj.

ris·qué' (ris-kā') adj. somewhat indelicate, as a story; daring.

rite (rīt) n. a ceremonial, religious or other solemn service.

rit'u·al (rich'oo-əl) adj. pert. to or consisting of ceremonials. —n. a prescribed form or manner. —rit'u·al·is'tic, adj. —rit'u·al·is'ti·cal·ly, adv.

ri'val (rī'vəl) n. one who is in pursuit of the same object or thing; an opponent. —adj. competing. —v.t. 1, stand in competition with. 2, emulate. —ri'val·ry, n.

riv'en (riv'ən) adj. split; torn apart.

riv'er (riv'ər) n. 1, a large stream of water flowing throughout the year. 2, a copious flow.

riv'et (riv'it) n. a malleable metal pin or bolt used to fasten pieces together. —v.t. fasten with such a pin; fasten firmly.

riv'u·let (riv'yə-lət) n. a small stream or brook.

roach (rōch) n. 1, a common freshwater fish. 2, a cockroach.

road (rōd) n. 1, a public way for passage or travel; a highway. 2, any means or way of approach. 3, an anchorage.

road'bed" n. the foundation of a railroad track or highway.

road'house" n. a restaurant and dance hall by a rural road.

road'ster (-stər) n. 1, a small open automobile. 2, a driving horse.

road'way" n. a road.

roam (rōm) v.i. & t. travel aimlessly; rove; wander over.

roan (rōn) adj. of a horse, having a bay, sorrel, or chestnut color interspersed with gray or white.

roar (rōr) v.i. 1, bellow; cry aloud. 2, make a full, deep sound, as of wind, waves, or a crowd. 3, guffaw. —v.t. shout. —n. a roaring sound, as of a lion.

roar'ing adj. 1, that roars. 2, extremely active; outstanding.

roast (rōst) v.t. 1, cook (as meat) before an open fire, or in an oven. 2, heat to excess. 3, (Slang) ridicule or castigate. —v.i. be heated; be cooked by roasting. —n. a cut of meat suitable for roasting. —roast'er, n. a pan or chamber for roasting.

rob v.t. [robbed, rob'bing] strip or deprive of something by force. —rob'ber, n. —rob'ber·y, n.

robe (rōb) n. 1, a gown or a long, loose outer garment, sometimes symbolizing honor or authority. 2, (pl.) dress; attire. 3, a dressed pelt, blanket, etc. used as a wrap. —v.t. clothe.

rob'in n. a red-breasted, migratory thrush of No. Amer.

Robin

ro'bot (rō'bət) n. an automaton resembling a man. —robot bomb, robot plane, one that guides itself or is controlled by radio.

ro·bust' (rō-bust') adj. 1, strong; vigorous. 2, rough; boisterous; rude. 3, requiring vigor. —ro·bust'ness, n.

roc (rok) n. a fabulous large bird.

rock (rok) n. 1, a mass of stony material; a fragment or piece of it. 2, a foundation; strength. 3, (pl.) (Slang) money; jewels. —v.t. & i. move backward and forward; sway. —rock and rye, rye whiskey flavored with sugar crystals (rock candy). —rock garden, one grown among rocks.

rock'bot'tom adj. lowest possible.

rock'bound" adj. 1, surrounded by rocks. 2, impenetrable.

rock'er n. 1, a curved piece on which a cradle or chair moves backward and forward. 2, a chair so mounted: rocking chair. 3, an oscillating part in a machine.

rock'et (rok'it) n. a tube propelled into the air by self-contained explosives, used in fireworks, warfare, etc. —v.i. rise with great rapidity.

rock'ribbed" (rok'ribd") adj. 1, marked by rocky ridges. 2, inflexible; unyielding.

rock'y (-ē) adj. 1, of or like stone; rough with, or as with, crushed stone. 2, shaky. —rock'i·ness, n.

ro·co·co (rə-kō′kō) *n.* an excessively elaborate style of ornamentation. —*adj.* in this style.

rod *n.* 1, a slender, straight stick. 2, a scepter; fig. authority. 3, a switch used for chastisement. 4, a measure of length, 16½ feet. 5, (*Slang*) a pistol.

rode (rōd) *v.* pret. of *ride.*

ro′dent (rō′dənt) *n.* a member of an order of gnawing mammals with sharp, strong teeth.

ro·de′o (rō-dā′ō) *n.* 1, a roundup of cattle. 2, a public performance of horsemanship, lassoing, etc.

rod″o·mon·tade′(rod″ə-mon-tād′) *n.* vainglorious boasting; bravado.

roe (rō) *n.* 1, a small, agile, very graceful deer of Europe and Asia. 2, the doe of the stag or red deer. 3, the eggs of a fish or of various crustaceans. 4, a mottled appearance in wood, esp. in mahogany.

roe′buck″ *n.* the male of a species of deer, the roe deer.

Roent′gen ray (rent′gən) x-ray.

rog′er (roj′ər) *interj.* (*Slang*) very well; order received.

rogue (rōg) *n.* 1, a dishonest person; a knave. 2, a mischievous or playful person. —**ro′guish** (-gish) *adj.*

ro′guer·y (rō′gə-rē) *n.* knavishness.

roil *v.t.* 1, make turbid by stirring up (water, etc.). 2, annoy; vex.

roist′er (rois′tər) *v.i.* bluster; swagger; bully; be noisy. —**roist′-er·er,** *n.*

rôle (rōl) *n.* an actor's part.

roll (rōl) *v.i.* 1, move along a surface by turning over and over. 2, travel on wheels. 3, revolve. 4, sway. 5, move in ripples, as waves. 6, make a deep prolonged sound. 7, be wound or curled in cylindrical form. 8, turn over and over while lying down; wallow. —*v.t.* 1, cause to roll or rotate; whirl. 2, give expression to a prolonged deep sound. 3, (often with *up*) wrap around an axis. 4, press or level with rollers. 5, trill, esp. the letter R. —*n.* 1, something wound into a cylinder. 2, a small bread; a biscuit. 3, a list of names. 4, the act of rolling. 5, a deep, prolonged or sustained sound. 6, a swell or undulation of the surface. 7, a swagger. —**roll call,** a calling of names, to which those present must answer. —**rolling pin,** a wooden cylinder for rolling dough. —**rolling stock,** railroad cars.

roll′er *n.* 1, a cylinder used as a wheel, bearing, core, pressing surface, etc. 2, a heavy wave. —**roller bearing,** a bearing in which revolving cylinders bear the shaft. —**roller coaster,** a miniature railway used at amusement parks. —**roller skate,** a skate mounted on wheels.

rol′lick (rol′ik) *v.i.* frolic; be gay. —**rol′lick·ing,** *adj.*

roll′top″ desk a desk with a cover that slides upward.

ro′ly·po″ly (rō′lē-pō″lē) *adj.* round; pudgy. —*n.* a kind of dessert.

Ro′man (rō′mən) *adj.* 1, pert. to Rome. 2, (*l.c.*) denoting any printing type not italic. 3, denoting the numerals (as I = 1, V = 5, X = 10, etc.) used in ancient Rome. —*n.* a citizen or inhabitant of Rome. —**Roman nose,** a nose with a prominent bridge.

Roman Catholic a member of the Christian church of which the Pope, or Bishop of Rome, is the pontiff.

ro·mance′ (rō-mans′) *n.* 1, a tale or novel of extraordinary, not real or familiar, life. 2, a fiction; a falsehood. 3, a love affair. —*adj.* (*cap.*) denoting a language almost wholly derived from Latin, as Italian, Spanish, French. —*v.i.* 1, make up fanciful tales. 2, (*Colloq.*) make love.

Ro·ma′ni·an (rō-mā′nē-ən) *n.* & *adj.* Rumanian.

ro·man′tic (rō-man′tik) *adj.* 1, fanciful; fabulous; pert. to romance. 2, given to sentimental or amorous feelings. 3, in art and literature, imaginative and free from classical rule. —**ro·man′ti·cal·ly,** *adv.* —**ro·man′ti·cism,** *n.*

romp *v.i.* leap and frisk about in play. —*n.* boisterous play. —**romp′ers,** *n. pl.* a small child's overalls.

ron′do (ron′dō) *n.* [*pl.* -**dos**] (*Music*) a work in which the principal theme is often repeated.

rood *n.* 1, a crucifix. 2, a varying unit of measurement.

roof *n.* 1, the external upper covering of a building, car, etc. 2, any house. 3, an upper limit. —*v.t.* cover with a roof; shelter. —**roof′ing,** *n.* a material for making a roof.

rook (rûk) *n.* 1, a Europ. crow. 2, a piece used in chess. —*v.i. & t.* cheat. —**rook′-er·y,** *n.* a roost for rooks.

Rook

rook′ie (rûk′ē) *n.* (*Slang*) an inexperienced recruit.

room *n.* 1, extent of space, great or small. 2, space or place unoccupied or unobstructed. 3, freedom; opportunity. 4, an apartment; chamber. —*v.i.* (*Colloq.*) lodge. —**room′er,** *n.* a lodger.

room·ette′ (rū-met′) *n.* a small private compartment in a railroad sleeping car.

room'mate" *n.* one with whom one shares a bedroom.

room'y (rōōm'ē) *adj.* spacious. —**room'i·ness**, *n.*

roost *n.* 1, a pole, a perch, or a place, for fowls to rest at night. 2, (*Colloq.*) a temporary abiding place. —*v.i.* perch, as a bird.

roost'er (rōōs'tər) *n.* the male of the domestic chicken; a cock.

root *n.* 1, the part of a plant that grows downward into the soil. 2, the foundation of anything. 3, a source, origin, or cause. 4, (*Math.*) a quantity that when multiplied by itself a certain number of times will produce a given quantity. 5, the part of a word that conveys its essential meaning. —*v.t.* 1, plant firmly; fix. 2, tear up or out, as by the roots. —*v.i.* 1, take root; be firmly fixed; be established. 2, turn up the earth with the snout. 3, (*Colloq.*) cheer; (with *for*) wish well. —*adj.*—**root'er**, *n.* (*Colloq.*) a supporter; one who applauds. —**root beer,** a beverage flavored with aromatic roots.

rope (rōp) *n.* 1, a thick, strong cord made of several strands twisted together. 2, a row or string of things. 3, a stringy, glutinous formation. —*v.t.* 1, fasten or enclose with a strong cord; catch; lasso. 2, (*Slang*) (with *in*) fool; trick.

Roque'fort (rōk'fərt) *n.* a strong French cheese.

ro'sa·ry (rō'zə·rē) *n.* 1, (*Rom. Cath.*) a string of beads used in counting prayers. 2, a garland or bed of roses. 3, an anthology.

rose (rōz) *n.* 1, a thorny shrub bearing flowers in various colors. 2, a light crimson color. —*adj.* —*v.* pret. of *rise*. —**rose diamond,** one with a faceted top and flat bottom. —**rose fever,** a form of hay fever caused by grass pollen, occurring in the Spring.

ros'e·ate (rō'zē·ət) *adj.* rose-colored; blushing.

rose'bud" *n.* the bud of a rose.

rose'bush" *n.* the bush on which roses grow.

rose'mar"y (rōz'mâr"ē) *n.* a fragrant evergreen shrub.

ro·sette' (rō·zet') *n.* a design or ornament in circular, roselike form.

rose'wa"ter *n.* a water scented with oil of roses.

rose'wood" *n.* a tree, or its reddish, fragrant wood.

ros'in (roz'in) *n.* the solid substance (resin) left after the distillation of the oil of turpentine.

ros'ter (ros'tər) *n.* 1, a list of names. 2, a schedule; a program.

ros'trum (ros'trəm) *n.* a pulpit or platform for a speaker.

ros'y (rō'zē) *adj.* 1, rose-colored. 2, favorable; promising. —**ros'i·ness**, *n.*

rot *v.i.* [**rot'ted, -ting**] 1, undergo natural decomposition; decay. 2, become corrupt; deteriorate. —*n.* 1, the process or result of decaying. 2, a parasitic disease. 3, (*Slang*) nonsense; humbug.

ro'ta·ry (rō'tə·rē) *adj.* turning, as a wheel on its axis.

ro'tate (rō'tāt) *v.i. & t.* 1, revolve or move around a center or axis. 2, alternate serially. —**ro·ta'tion**, *n.*

rote (rōt) *n.* mechanical routine in learning; repetition without attention to meaning.

ro"to·gra·vure' (rō"tə·grə·vyūr') *n.* a process for gravure printing from cylindrical plates.

ro'tor (rō'tər) *n.* a rotating part of a machine.

rot'ten (rot'ən) *adj.* 1, having rotted; decayed. 2, (*Colloq.*) very bad. —**rot'ten·ness**, *n.*

rot'ter (rot'ər) *n.* a scoundrel; cad.

ro·tund' (rō·tund') *adj.* round or rounded out; bulbous; obese. —**ro·tun'di·ty**, *n.*

ro·tun'da (rō·tun'də) *n.* a round building or room, esp. one with a dome.

rou·é' (rōō·ā') *n.* a dissolute man; a rake.

rouge (rōōzh) *n.* 1, a red cosmetic or coloring for the skin. 2, a red powder or paste used for polishing. —*v.t. & i.* apply rouge (to).

rough (ruf) *adj.* 1, not smooth to the touch or to the sight; uneven. 2, left in a natural or incomplete state; crude; approximate. 3, severe; harsh. 4, lacking refinement; uncouth. 5, boisterously violent. —*n.* (with *the*) crudeness; rawness. —*adv.* in a crude, coarse, or harsh manner. —**rough it,** endure hardships. —**rough'ness**, *n.*

rough'age (ruf'ij) *n.* coarse, bulky food.

rough-'and-read'y *adj.* crude but effective.

rough'en (-ən) *v.t.* make rough.

rough'house" *n.* boisterous play. —*v.t.* treat violently but in fun.

rough'neck" *n.* a boor; a rowdy.

rough'shod' *adj.* 1, shod with spiked horseshoes. 2, ruthless.

rou·lade' (rōō·läd') *n.* meat rolled around a filling and cooked.

rou·lette' (rōō·let') *n.* 1, a game of betting on the number at which a revolving wheel will stop. 2, a cutting tool using a rowel.

round (rownd) *adj.* **1,** having the shape, or approximately the shape, of a circle, cylinder, or sphere. **2,** having curved sections, lines or surfaces; convex. **3,** easy, smooth and brisk in motion. **4,** full; liberal. **5,** approximate. —*n.* **1,** a round object. **2,** series; circuit; course or tour of duty. **3,** a period of action between intermissions. **4,** a rung of a ladder or chair. **5,** a cut of beef. **6,** ammunition for a single shot or volley. —*v.t.* **1,** give rotundity to. **2,** (with *out*) complete or perfect. **3,** encircle; encompass. **4,** make a course along or around. —*v.i.* **1,** grow or become rotund. **2,** mature; develop. —*adv.* **1,** on all sides, so as to surround. **2,** with a rotating movement. **3,** in, within, or through a circuit. **4,** in circumference. **5,** from beginning to end. —*prep.* around; about. —**round'ness,** *n.*

round'a·bout' *adj.* circuitous; indirect.

round'er **1,** one who travels a circuit. **2,** a dissolute person; an idler.

round'house' *n.* a circular building where locomotives are repaired.

round robin an act in which all members of a group participate.

round table a group assembled for discussion.

round trip one to a place and back again.

round'up *n.* **1,** an assembly or driving together. **2,** a summation.

rouse (rowz) *v.t.* cause to start up from sleep, inactivity, indifference, etc.; stir up; provoke. —*v.i.* start or rise up; be stirred to action.

roust'a·bout' (rowst'ə-bowt') *n.* **1,** a laborer on a wharf or river boat. **2,** a laborer at odd jobs.

rout (rowt) *n.* **1,** a confused retreat after a defeat. **2,** a disorderly crowd; the rabble. —*v.t.* **1,** disperse by defeating; drive away in disorder. **2,** (with *out*) turn out. **3,** cut away.

route (root) *n.* **1,** a way; road. **2,** a course; line of travel. —*v.t.* send by a certain route.

rou·tine' (roo-tēn') *n.* a customary procedure or course of action. —*adj.* entirely customary; not deviating from routine.

rove (rōv) *v.i. & t.* wander at pleasure; roam; ramble.

row (rō) *n.* a series of persons or things in a straight line. —*v.t. & t.* propel (a boat) by means of oars.

row *n.* a noisy disturbance; a quarrel. —*v.i.* quarrel.

row'boat' (rō'bōt') *n.* a small boat propelled by oars.

row'dy (row'dē) *n.* a rough, quarrelsome person. —*adj.* rough; dis-

reputable. —**row'dy·ish,** *adj.* —**row'dy·ism,** *n.*

row'el (row'əl) *n.* **1,** the wheel of a horseman's spur. **2,** a similar wheel for cutting, perforating, etc.

roy'al (roi'əl) *adj.* **1,** pert. or related to a king or queen. **2,** majestic. **3,** large or superior of its kind. —**roy'al·ist,** *n.* an adherent of a monarchy.

roy'al·ty (-tē) *n.* **1,** the state or condition of being royal; royal persons collectively. **2,** a fee paid for the use of prerogatives such as a patent, copyright, etc.

rub *v.t.* [**rubbed, rub'bing**] **1,** apply pressure and friction by motion over the surface of. **2,** smooth, polish, clean, etc., by rubbing. **3,** affect as if by friction; annoy; disturb. —*v.i.* move or act with friction; rub something. —*n.* **1,** the act of rubbing. **2,** a disturbing factor.

rub'ber (rub'ər) *n.* **1,** one who or that which rubs. **2,** something made of rubber, esp. a pencil eraser. **3,** an elastic, tough, waterproof substance obtained from the sap of various tropical trees. **4,** a series of games, usually three. —*adj.* made of rubber. —**rubber check** (*Slang*) a check that is worthless.

rub'ber·ize' (-īz") *v.t.* waterproof (as cloth) with rubber.

rub'ber·neck' *n.* (*Slang*) **1,** an inquisitive person. **2,** a sight-seeing bus.

rub'ber-stamp' *v.t.* **1,** imprint with inked rubber type. **2,** (*Colloq.*) approve without scrutiny.

rub'ber·y *adj.* tough and elastic. —**rub'ber·i·ness,** *n.*

rub'bish (rub'ish) *n.* waste material; trash; litter.

rub'ble (rub'əl) *n.* **1,** rough broken stones. **2,** trash.

rub'down' *n.* a massage of the body, esp. after exercise.

rube (roob) *n.* (*Slang*) a crude or unwashed countryman.

ru·bel'la (roo-bel'ə) *n.* a mild contagious disease: German measles.

ru'bi·cund' (roo'bə-kund") *adj.* inclining to redness; ruddy.

ru'ble (roo'bəl) *n.* the monetary unit of Russia. Also, **rou'ble.**

ru'bric (roo'brik) *n.* a heading or caption in a book or other writing.

ru'by (roo'bē) *n.* **1,** a clear, red precious stone, a variety of corundum. **2,** a pure crimson red color.

ruche (roosh) *n.* a frill or strip of dress trimming. Also, **ruch'ing.**

ruck (ruk) *n.* **1,** a fold or crease. **2,** the common run of persons or things.

ruck'sack' *n.* a knapsack.

ruc'tion (ruk'shən) *n.* a disturbance; a row; rumpus.

rud'der (rud'ər) *n.* a flat piece hinged vertically, used for directing a ship or airplane.

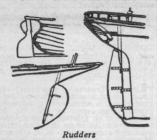

Rudders

rud'dy (rud'ē) *adj.* of a red color. —rud'di·ness, *n.*

rude (rood) *adj.* 1, rough; crude; primitive. 2, ill-bred; discourteous; impolite. 3, sturdy; rugged. —rude'ness, *n.*

ru'di·ment (roo'di-mənt) *n.* 1, an undeveloped state. 2, (usually *pl.*) an element or first principle, as of an art or science. —ru'di·men'ta·ry (-men'tə-rē) *adj.*

rue (roo) *v.t.* repent of; regret; feel sorrow or suffering on account of. —*n.* a garden plant used in medicine. —rue'ful, *adj.* sorrowful.

ruff (ruf) *n.* 1, a large, projecting, frilled collar of fine material. 2, a breed of domestic pigeons. 3, in card playing, an act of trumping.

ruf'fi·an (ruf'ē-ən) *n.* a brutal man; a thug. —ruf'fi·an·ly, *adj.*

ruf'fle (ruf'əl) *v.t.* 1, draw up into gathers, folds, or pleats. 2, disturb the arrangement, orderliness, or composure of; rumple; ripple; agitate. —*n.* 1, a gathered border or trimming. 2, a low beat of a drum.

rug *n.* 1, a thick, heavy floor covering. 2, a lap robe.

Rug'by (rug'bē) *n.* a Brit. form of football.

rug'ged (rug'id) *adj.* 1, having a rough surface; shaggy; hilly; uneven. 2, unpolished; uncultivated. 3, harsh; austere. 4, fierce; tempestuous. 5, (*Colloq.*) robust; strong. —rug'ged·ness, *n.*

ru'in (roo'in) *n.* 1, collapse, moral or physical; downfall; overthrow. 2, that which promotes decay or destruction. 3, (often *pl.*) anything, as a building, in a state of destruction, decay, or wreck. —*v.t.* damage essentially and irreparably. —ru'in·a'tion, *n.* —ru'in·ous, *adj.*

rule (rool) *n.* 1, a regulation for standard procedure; a law. 2, an established method or way of doing anything. 3, government; supreme authority. 4, a scaled strip; ruler. 5, a printed or drawn straight line. —*v.t.* 1, determine; settle. 2, govern; control. 3, mark with lines. —*v.i.* 1, have power or command. 2, prevail; decide. —rule of thumb, a practical method; a rough guide.

rul'er (roo'lər) *n.* 1, one who governs. 2, a scaled strip of wood, or metal with a straight edge, used for measuring and drawing lines.

rul'ing *n.* an authoritative decision. —*adj.* governing; chief; prevalent.

rum *n.* 1, an alcoholic liquor distilled from sugar cane. 2, any strong alcoholic drink. 3, a card game; rummy. —*adj.* (*Slang*) queer; odd; droll. —rum runner, *n.* a ship carrying contraband liquor.

Ru·ma'ni·an (roo-mā'nē-ən) *n.* & *adj.* of or pert. to Rumania, its people, or their language. Also, Ro·ma'ni·an, Rou·ma'ni·an.

rum'ba (rum'bə) *n.* a fast dance, originally Cuban, or the music for it.

rum'ble (rum'bəl) *v.i.* 1, make a deep, heavy, continuous sound. 2, move with such a sound; roll heavily or noisily. —*v.t.* utter, or cause to make, such a sound. —*n.* 1, a rumbling sound. 2, an open seat at the back of a roadster or coupé.

ru'mi·nant (roo'mi-nənt) *n.* a cud-chewing animal. —*adj.* 1, cud-chewing. 2, contemplative.

ru'mi·nate (roo'mə-nāt) *v.i.* 1, chew the cud. 2, meditate; ponder. —*v.t.* 1, chew again. 2, turn over in the mind. —ru'mi·na'tion, *n.*

rum'mage (rum'ij) *v.t.* & *i.* hunt through; ransack. —rummage sale, a sale of miscellaneous articles.

rum'my (rum'ē) *n.* 1, a card game. 2, (*Slang*) an alcoholic.

ru'mor (roo'mər) *n.* 1, popular report. 2, an unconfirmed but widely circulated story; a piece of gossip. Also, ru'mour.

rump *n.* 1, the back parts of an animal; the buttocks. 2, a remnant.

rum'ple (rum'pəl) *v.t.* & *i.* make uneven; wrinkle; become mussed. —*n.* a wrinkle.

rum'pus (rum'pəs) *n.* (*Colloq.*) a noisy or disorderly commotion; a brawl. —rumpus room, a room for games and play.

run *v.i.* [ran, run, run'ning] 1, move swiftly on foot. 2, make haste; rush; flee; steal away; abscond. 3, pursue a course; travel. 4, perform a regular passage from place to place.

5, flow. 6, discharge a fluid, as tears; become fluid. 7, extend from point to point; spread. 8, operate; work. 9, be a candidate for office; compete in a race. 10, go or pass by; elapse, as time. 11, (with *to*) have a proclivity or general tendency. 12, have a certain direction, course, tenor, or form. 13, keep going; continue. —*v.t.* 1, cause (anything) to go or to function; direct; operate. 2, accomplish; undertake. 3, travel past or through successfully. 4, smuggle. 5, sew several stitches at the same time. —*n.* 1, the act of moving at a rapid pace. 2, a passage; journey; trip; distance covered. 3, a current; a flow. 4, course; progress; a continued course. 5, a tendency; general character. 6, a general and extraordinary demand, as on a bank. 7, in baseball, the act of making a score. 8, in certain card games, a sequence. 9, free access to a place. 10, a place where animals may range. 11, a herd or school moving together. 12, a small stream of water; a brook. 13, a ravel, as in hose.

run'a·bout" *n.* a light, open automobile or motor boat.

run'a·round" *n.* 1, (*Colloq.*) an abscess near a finger- or toenail. 2, (*Slang*) an evasion. 3, type set around an illustration.

run'a·way" *adj.* 1, escaped; out of control. 2, eloping. —*n.* 1, a horse, etc. that has escaped. 2, an easy victory, as in a race.

run-"down" *adj.* 1, in poor health or condition. 2, of a clock, etc., not wound.

rune (roon) *n.* a character of an ancient Europ. alphabet. —**ru'nic,** *adj.*

rung *n.* a rounded bar forming the crosspiece of a ladder, a brace on a chair, a spoke, etc. —*v.* p.p. of *ring.*

run'ner (run'ər) *n.* 1, one who runs; a messenger; a racer. 2, the base on which a sled, etc. slides. 3, a shoot from a plant. 4, a narrow rug or table scarf.

run"ner-up" *n.* the contestant finishing in second place.

running board a long step at the side of a vehicle.

running head the heading at the top of each page of a book.

running mate a competitor or candidate allied with another.

run-'off" *n.* 1, water flowing off the land. 2, a deciding contest.

runt *n.* any undersized animal, esp. the smallest of a litter.

run'way" *n.* a channel; course; a level strip for airplanes landing and taking off.

ru·pee' (roo-pē') *n.* a monetary unit of India.

rup'ture (rup'chər) *n.* 1, the act or result of breaking; a breach of peace. 2, hernia, esp. abdominal hernia. —*v.t.* 1, break; burst. 2, cause to suffer from hernia. —*v.i.* suffer a break.

ru'ral (rûr'əl) *adj.* pert. to the country or to country life.

ruse (rooz) *n.* artifice; trickery; a stratagem.

rush *v.i.* 1, move or drive forward with violent haste. 2, move or act with undue eagerness; hurry. —*v.t.* 1, cause to go swiftly or violently. 2, (*Football*) carry (the ball) forward. 3, cause to hasten; push. 4, (*Slang*) entertain, to induce to join a fraternity or sorority. 5, (*Colloq.*) court. —*n.* 1, a driving forward with eagerness and haste. 2, an eager demand; a run. 3, (*Colloq.*) urgent pressure. 4, a scrimmage. 5, (*pl.*) the first prints of a motion picture film, for inspection. 6, any of various hollow-stemmed water plants.

rusk *n.* a sweet, toasted bread or biscuit; zwieback.

rus'set (rus'it) *n.* 1, a reddish-brown color. 2, a kind of winter apple with a brownish skin. —*adj.* reddish-brown.

Rus'sian (rush'ən) *adj.* pert. to Russia, its people, or its language.

rust *n.* 1, the reddish coating that forms on iron exposed to air and moisture. 2, any corrosive formation. 3, an orange-red color. —*v.i.* become rusty.

rus'tic (rus'tik) *adj.* 1, pert. to the country; rural. 2, unsophisticated; simple. 3, rude; simply constructed. —*n.* a country person. —**rus'ti·cal·ly,** *adv.* —**rus·tic'i·ty** (-tis'ə-tē) *n.*

rus'ti·cate" (rus'ti-kāt") *v.t. & i.* send or go to live in the country. —**rus"ti·ca'tion,** *n.*

rus'tle (rus'əl) *v.i. & i.* 1, make a murmuring sound by the rubbing of parts against each other. 2, (*Colloq.*) stir about. 3, (*Slang*) steal (cattle). —*n.* the sound of rustling. —**rus'tler,** *n.* a cattle thief.

rust'y (rus'tē) *adj.* 1, covered with rust. 2, out of practice. 3, reddish. 4, hoarse. —**rust'i·ness,** *n.*

rut *n.* 1, a narrow track worn or cut in the ground. 2, an established habit or mode of procedure. 3, the period of heat in various animals. —**rut'ted,** *adj.* furrowed.

ru'ta·ba"ga (roo"tə-bā'gə) *n.* a variety of nutritious turnip.

ruth'less (rooth'lis) *adj.* having no pity; merciless. —**ruth'less·ness,** *n.*

rye (rī) *n.* 1, a hardy cereal plant or its seeds. 2, whiskey made of rye.

S

S, s (es) the nineteenth letter of the English alphabet.

's (s or z; see p. 8) *suf.* marking the possessive form of nouns. —*contraction* is, as, *he's* (he is).

Sab'bath (sab'əth) *n.* a day of rest and religious dedication.

sab·bat'i·cal (sə-bat'i-kəl) *adj.* pert. to a rest period or (*cap.*) to the Sabbath. —**sabbatical year,** a year's leave of absence (every seventh year).

sa'ber (sā'bər) *r.* a one-edged, curved sword.

Saber

sa'ble (sā'bəl) *n.* 1, an animal of the marten family; its fur. 2, the color black. —*adj.* 1, made of sable fur. 2, black.

sa·bot' (sa-bō') *n.* a wooden shoe.

sab'o·tage' (sab'ə-täzh') *n.* malicious destruction. —*v.t.* wilfully and maliciously destroy or impede.

sab"o·teur' (sab'ə-tėr') *n.* one who commits sabotage.

sac (sak) *n.* a pouch or cavity in an animal.

sac'cha·rin (sak'ə-rin) *n.* a chemical sweetening compound. —**sac'cha·rine',** *adj.* sweet; sugary.

sac"er·do'tal (sas"ər-dō'təl) *adj.* pert. to a priest or to priestly functions.

sa'chem (sā'chəm) *n.* a No. Amer. Indian chief.

sa·chet' (sa-shā') *n.* a small bag of perfuming herbs, etc.

sack (sak) *n.* 1, a bag, esp. a large one. 2, (*Slang*) discharge from employment. 3, pillage. —*v.t.* 1, plunder. 2, (*Colloq.,*) discharge.

sack'cloth' *n.* a coarse cloth, symbol of mourning.

sac'ra·ment (sak'rə-mənt) *n.* a devotional rite or symbol.

sa'cred (sā'krid) *adj.* dedicated to a deity; holy; inviolable. —**sa'cred·ness,** *n.*

sac'ri·fice (sak'rə-fīs") *n.* 1, an offering, as to God or a deity. 2, a voluntary loss. —*v.t.* —**sac'ri·fi'cial** (-fish'əl) *adj.*

sac'ri·lege (sak'rə-lij) *n.* profanation of something sacred. —**sac'ri·le'gious** (-lij'əs) *adj.*

sac'ro·sanct' (sak'rə-sankt") *adj.* exceedingly sacred.

sad *adj.* sorrowful; causing sorrow. —**sad'ness,** *n.* —**sad sack** (*Slang*) a futile or hopeless person.

sad'den (sad'ən) *v.t. & i.* make or become sad.

sad'dle (sad'əl) *n.* 1, a seat for a rider. 2, a cut of meat. —*v.t.* 1, put a saddle on. 2, burden.

sad'i"ron *n.* a flatiron.

sad'ism (sad'iz-əm) *n.* gratification derived from causing pain. —**sad'ist,** *n.* —**sa·dis'tic,** (sə-dis'tik) *adj.* —**sa·dis'ti·cal·ly,** *adv.*

sa·fa'ri (sə-fär'ē) *n.* an expedition, esp. for hunting.

safe (sāf) *adj.* 1, free from danger or injury; secure. 2, unharmed. 3, trustworthy. —*n.* a repository for valuables. —**safe'ness,** *n.*

safe-'de·pos'it box a steel box kept in a bank's vault.

safe'guard' *n.* a means of security or protection. —*v.t.* protect.

safe'keep"ing *n.* care.

safe'ty (-tē) *n.* 1, safeness. 2, protection; safekeeping. 3, a device to prevent injury or accident. 4, in football, a down behind one's own goal line, scoring 2 points for the opponents. —**safety glass,** unshatterable glass. —**safety match,** a match requiring a prepared surface for striking. —**safety pin,** a pin with a sheathed point: see *pin,* illus. —**safety razor,** one with a guarded blade. —**safety valve,** 1, an automatic escape valve. 2, an outlet for the emotions.

saf'fron (saf'rən) *n.* 1, a crocus. 2, a deep orange color.

sag *v.i.* [**sagged, sag'ging**] 1, droop; hang unevenly. 2, decline in price. —*n.* a sinking; a dip.

sa'ga (sä'gə) *n.* a narrative of heroic exploits.

sa·ga'cious (sə-gā'shəs) *adj.* wise. —**sa·gac'i·ty** (sə-gas'ə-tē) *n.*

sag'a·more (sag'ə-môr) *n.* a No. Amer. Indian chief.

sage (sāj) *adj.* profoundly wise. —*n.* 1, a wise man. 2, a herb for seasoning. 3, a bush: *sagebrush.*

Sag"it·ta'ri·us (saj"i-tār'ē-əs) *n.* a constellation, the Archer (see *zodiac*).

sa'hib (sä'ib) *n.* (*Indian*) master.

said (sed) *v. pret. & p.p.* of *say.*

sail (sāl) *n.* 1, a piece of canvas, etc., spread to the wind to propel a ship. 2, a voyage. —*v.i.* move along in or as in a vessel. —*v.t.* 1, manage (a vessel). 2, travel over. —**set sail,** begin a voyage.

sail'boat" *n.* a boat equipped with sails.

sail'fish" *n.* a large sea-fish with a high dorsal fin.

sail'or *n.* 1, a mariner; an enlisted seaman. 2, a flat-brimmed hat, usually of straw.

saint (sānt) *n.* 1, a person who has died and is in heaven. 2, a person of great purity. —**saint'hood,** *n.*

Saint Bernard (bər-närd') one of a breed of large, shaggy dogs.

saint'ed *adj.* 1, canonized. 2, sacred. 3, saintly.

saint'ly *adj.* being or befitting a saint. —**saint'li·ness,** *n.*

saith (seth) *v.* (*Archaic*) says.

sake (sāk) *n.* 1, interest; account. 2, purpose.

sa'ke (sä'kė) *n.* a Jap. rice liquor.

sa·laam' (sə-läm') *n.* an obeisance.

sal'a·ble (sāl'ə-bəl) *adj.* sellable.

sa·la'cious (sə-lā'shəs) *adj.* impure; obscene. —**sa·la'cious·ness,** *n.*

sal'ad (sal'əd) *n.* a dish of uncooked green herbs, fruit, cold vegetables, etc.

sal'a·man"der (sal'ə-man"dər) *n.* 1, a lizardlike amphibian. 2, a mythical animal able to live in fire.

Salamander

sa·la'mi (sə-lä'mė) *n.* a spicy Italian sausage.

sal'a·ry (sal'ə-rė) *n.* compensation for work. —**sal'a·ried,** *adj.*

sale (sāl) *n.* 1, an act of selling. 2, a selling at a reduced price. —**sales tax,** a tax on retail sales.

sales'man (sālz'mən) *n.* [*pl.* -men] one whose profession or specialty is selling. —**sales'girl, sales'la'dy, sales'wom"an,** *n.fem.* —**sales'man·ship,** *n.* ability to sell.

sa'li·ent (sā'lė-ənt) *adj.* conspicuous; projecting. —*n.* a projecting angle. —**sa'li·ence,** *n.*

sa'line (sā'lìn) *adj.* pert. to salt.

sa·li'va (sə-lī'və) *n.* a fluid secreted in the mouth. —**sal'i·va·ry** (sal'ə-ver-ė) *adj.* —**sal'i·vate"** (sal'ə-vāt") *v.t.* secrete saliva.

Salk vaccine (sâk) a vaccine used to combat infantile paralysis.

sal'low (sal'ō) *adj.* of an unhealthy, yellowish complexion. —**sal'lowness,** *n.*

sal'ly (sal'ė) *n.* 1, a rushing forth; a sortie. 2, a witty remark. —*v.i.* set out briskly.

sal"ma·gun'di (sal"mə-gun'dė) *n.* 1, a hash or stew. 2, any mixture.

salm'on (sam'ən) *n.* a marine and fresh-water food fish.

sa·lon' (sə-lon') *n.* 1, a drawing room. 2, a fashionable gathering.

sa·loon' (sə-loon') *n.* 1, a barroom. 2, a public hall. 3, a sedan.

sal'si·fy (sal'sə-fė) *n.* a vegetable, the oyster plant.

salt (sâlt) *n.* 1, a mineral, sodium chloride, found in deposits or in sea water, used as a seasoning. 2, (*pl.*) a medicinal compound. 3, piquancy; spice; wit. 4, (*Colloq.*) a sailor. —*v.t.* season or preserve with salt. —**salt'ed,** *adj.* —**salt'y,** *adj.*

salt'cel"lar *n.* a dish or shaker for salt.

salt lick a natural deposit of salt, which animals come to lick.

salt'pe"ter (sâlt"pē'tər) *n.* niter.

salt water 1, sea water; the sea. 2, a solution of salt in water.

sa·lu'bri·ous (sə-loo'brē-əs) *adj.* favorable to health. —**sa·lu'brious·ness, sa·lu'bri·ty,** *n.*

sal'u·tar·y (sal'yə-ter-ė) *adj.* 1, healthful. 2, beneficial.

sal"u·ta'tion (sal"yû-tā'shən) *n.* 1, act of greeting or saluting. 2, the formal opening of a letter.

sa·lu'ta·to·ry (sə-loo'tə-tôr-ė) *adj.* pert. to a salutation. —*n.* an address of welcome. —**sa·lu"ta·to'ri·an,** *n.*

sa·lute' (sə-loot') *v.t. & i.* 1, greet; kiss. 2, honor formally. —*n.* an act of greeting or tribute.

sal'vage (sal'vij) *n.* the saving of property from danger of loss; the property saved. —*v.t.* save.

sal·va'tion (sal-vā'shən) *n.* 1, deliverance; that which saves. 2, redemption.

Salvation Army a religious and charitable body, organized on military lines.

salve (sàv) *n.* 1, a healing ointment. 2, anything that soothes. —*v.t.* heal; soothe.

sal'ver (sal'vər) *n.* a tray.

sal'vo (sal'vō) *n.* a discharge of artillery.

sam'ba (sàm'bə) *n.* a So. Amer. dance.

same (sām) *adj.* 1, identical; agreeing in kind, degree, or amount. 2, just mentioned. 3, unchanged.

—pron. the same person or thing. **—same'ness,** *n.* **1,** identity. **2,** monotony.

sam'o·var" (sam'ə-vär") *n.* a copper urn for making tea.

Sam"o·yed' (sam"ə-yed') *n.* a white-haired Siberian dog.

sam'pan *n.* a small skifflike boat of China.

sam'ple (sam'pəl) *n.* a representative specimen. **—v.t.** test; taste.

sam'pler *n.* **1,** a piece of embroidery. **2,** one who samples.

sam'u·rai" (sam'ū·rī") *n. sing. & pl.* a member of the Jap. military class.

san"a·to'ri·um (san"ə-tôr'ē-əm) [*pl.* -a (-ə)] *n.* a sanitarium.

sanc'ti·fy" (sank'tə-fī") *v.t.* **1,** make holy; purify. **2,** consecrate. **—sanc"ti·fi·ca'tion,** *n.*

sanc'ti·mo"ny (sank'tə-mō'nē) *n.* hypocritical devoutness. **—sanc"ti·mo'ni·ous,** *adj.*

sanc'tion (sank'shən) *n.* **1,** authorization. **2,** ratification. **3,** a non-military punitive act by one nation against another. **—v.t. 1,** countenance; approve. **2,** ratify.

sanc'ti·ty (sank'tə-tē) *n.* holiness; sacredness.

sanc'tu·ar"y (sank'chū-er"ē) *n.* **1,** a sacred place. **2,** a place of refuge.

sanc'tum (sank'təm) *n.* **1,** a sacred place. **2,** a private retreat.

sand *n.* **1,** the fine debris of rocks, in soil-like particles. **2,** (*pl.*) a desert or beach. **3,** (*Colloq.*) grit; pluck. **—v.t. 1,** sprinkle with sand. **2,** sandpaper. **—sand'er,** *n.*

san'dal (san'dəl) *n.* a low shoe.

san'dal·wood" (san'dəl-wuod") *n.* a fragrant Asiatic tree.

sand'bag" *n.* a sand-filled bag. **—v.t.** (*Slang*) hit or betray unexpectedly.

sand'blast" *v.t.* clean (stone, etc.) with sand driven by air.

sand'hog" *n.* a worker in tunnel construction.

sand'man" *n.* [*pl.* -men"] a fabled spirit that makes children sleepy.

sand'pa"per *n.* paper coated with an abrasive, esp. sand. **—v.t.** rub sandpaper on, to smooth.

sand'pi"per (sand'pī"pər) *n.* a small wading bird.

sand'stone" *n.* soft, crumbly rock.

sand'wich *n.* meat, cheese, etc. between two slices of bread.

sand'y (san'dē) *adj.* **1,** of or like sand. **2,** yellowish, as *sandy hair*. **3,** gritty. **—sand'i·ness,** *n.*

sane (sān) *adj.* **1,** mentally sound. **2,** reasonable. **—sane'ness,** *n.*

San'for·ized" (san-fə-rīzd") (*T.N.*) a process to prevent shrinking.

sang *v.* pret. of *sing.*

san'gui·nar"y (sang'gwi-ner'ē) *adj.* **1,** bloody. **2,** bloodthirsty.

san'guine (sang'gwin) *adj.* **1,** hopeful; confident; cheerful. **2,** ruddy.

san"i·tar'i·um (san"ə-tār'ē-əm) *n.* an establishment for invalids.

san'i·tar"y (san'ə-ter"ē) *adj.* **1,** pert. to conditions affecting health. **2,** hygienic.

san"i·ta'tion (san"ə-tā'shən) *n.* the process of garbage disposal, sewage, etc.

san'i·ty (san'ə-tē) *n.* saneness.

sank *v.* pret. of *sink.*

San'skrit *n.* the ancient literary language of India.

sap *n.* **1,** the fluid that circulates in a plant. **2,** (*Slang*) a fool. **3,** (*Mil.*) a ditch dug to approach an enemy position. **—v.t.** [sapped, sap'ping] undermine. **—sap'per,** *n.* a soldier who digs or fights in saps.

sap'id *adj.* tasty; agreeable. **—sa·pid'i·ty** (sə-pid'ə-tē) *n.*

sa'pi·ent (sā'pē-ənt) *adj.* wise. **—sa'pi·ence,** *n.*

sap'ling *n.* a young tree.

sap'phire (saf'īr) *n.* **1,** a precious stone, a transparent blue variety of corundum. **2,** deep blue.

sap'py (sap'ē) *adj.* **1,** full of sap or vitality. **2,** (*Slang*) foolish. **—sap'pi·ness,** *n.*

sar'a·band" (sar'ə-band") *n.* **1,** a lively Span. castanet dance. **2,** a slow, stately Span. dance.

Sar'a·cen (sar'ə-sən) *n.* (formerly) a Mohammedan.

sar'casm (sär'kaz-əm) *n.* bitter irony; taunting comment.

sar·cas'tic (sär-kas'tik) *adj.* being or using sarcasm. **—sar·cas'ti·cal·ly,** *adv.*

sar·co'ma (sär-kō'mə) *n.* a malignant tumor of the connective tissue.

sar·coph'a·gus (sär-kof'ə-gəs) *n.* an ornamental stone coffin.

sar·dine' (sär-dēn') *n.* a small fish allied to the herring, often canned in oil.

---

sar·don'ic (sär-don'ĭk) *adj.* sneering; sarcastic. —**sar·don'i·cal·ly**, *adv.*

sar·gas'so (sär-gas'ō) *n.* a seaweed. Also, **sar·gas'sum**.

sa'ri (sä'rē) *n.* a single long piece of silk or cotton, the principal garment of a Hindu woman.

sa·rong' (sä-rông') *n.* a Malay woman's one-piece garment.

Sari   Sarong

sar'sa·pa·ril'la (sas"pə-ril'ə) *n.* a tropical Amer. plant; a soft drink made from its root.

sar·to'ri·al (sär-tōr'ē-əl) *adj.* pert. to a tailor or his work.

sash *n.* 1, the framed part of a window. 2, a band worn around the waist.

sa·shay' (sa-shā') *v.i.* (*Colloq.*) move glidingly.

sas'sa·fras' (sas'ə-fras") *n.* a No. Amer. tree; the aromatic bark of the root.

sas'sy (sas'ē) *adj.* (*Colloq.*) saucy; insolent. —**sas'si·ness**, *n.*

sat *v.* pret. & p.p. of *sit*.

Sa'tan (sā'tən) *n.* the chief evil spirit; the devil. —**sa·tan'ic**, *adj.* —**sa·tan'i·cal·ly**, *adv.*

satch'el (sach'əl) *n.* a small bag, used as luggage.

sate (sāt) *v.t.* satisfy; fill.

sa·teen' (sa-tēn') *n.* a cotton fabric resembling satin.

sat'el·lite (sat'ə-līt") *n.* 1, a moon. 2, an attendant; follower. 3, a country supposedly independent but actually controlled by another.

sa'ti·ate' (sā'shē-āt") *v.t.* surfeit; oversatisfy; glut. —**sa'ti·a·ble**, *adj.* —**sa'ti·a'tion**, *n.*

sa·ti'e·ty (sə-tī'ə-tē) *n.* state of being satiated; surfeit.

sat'in (sat'ən) *n.* & *adj.* a lustrous fabric. —**sat'in·y**, *adj.*

sat'in·wood' *n.* an E. Ind. tree or its fine, hard wood.

sat'ire (sat'īr) *n.* the use of irony, ridicule, etc., in writing. —**sa·tir'i·cal** (sə-tir'ə-kəl) *adj.* —**sat'i·rist**, *n.* —**sat'i·rize'** (sat'ə-rīz") *v.t.*

sat"is·fac'tion (sat"is-fak'shən) *n.* act, means or result of satisfying. —**sat"is·fac'to·ry** (-tə-rē) *adj.*

sat'is·fy' (sat'is-fī') *v.t.* 1, gratify completely; supply the needs of. 2,

pay fully. 3, convince. 4, fulfill the conditions of. 5, atone for.

sat'rap (sat'rap) *n.* a subordinate but despotic ruler. —**sat'rap·y**, *n.*

sat'u·rate' (sach'ə-rāt") *v.t.* soak; impregnate fully. —**sat"u·ra'tion**, *n.*

Sat'ur·day (sat'ər-dē) *n.* the seventh day of the week.

sat'ur·nine' (sat'ər-nīn") *adj.* morose; phlegmatic.

sat'yr (sat'ər) *n.* a sylvan deity, half human and half goat.

sauce (sâs) *n.* 1, a relish or appetizer. 2, a compote of fruit. 3, (*Colloq.*) pertness; insolence.

sauce'pan' *n.* a small cooking pan with a handle.

sau'cer (sâ'sər) *n.* a small, round dish.

sau'cy (sâ'sē) *adj.* pert. —**sau'ci·ness**, *n.*

sau'er·kraut' (sow'ər-krowt") *n.* fermented, sour cabbage.

saun'ter (sân'tər) *v.i.* walk in a leisurely way; stroll.

sau'sage (sâ'sij) *n.* minced meat, seasoned, often stuffed into a membranous tube.

sau·té' (sō-tā') *v.t.* pan fry.

sau·terne' (sō-tērn') *n.* a sweet, white French wine.

sav'age (sav'ij) *adj.* 1, uncivilized; uncultivated. 2, ferocious; barbarous. —*n.* a savage person. —**sav'age·ry** (-rē) *n.*

sa·vant' (sa-vänt') *n.* a man of learning.

save (sāv) *v.t.* 1, preserve from danger, injury, or loss; deliver from sin. 2, conserve; set apart; hoard. —*v.i.* 1, put aside money for the future. 2, be frugal. —*prep.* & *conj.* except.

sav'ing *n.* 1, economy. 2, a reduction in expenditure. 3, (*pl.*) money put aside. —*adj.* redeeming. —*prep.* & *conj.* save.

sav'ior (sāv'yər) *n.* 1, a rescuer. 2, (*cap.*) [usually, **Sav'iour**] Jesus Christ.

sa'vor (sā'vər) *n.* taste; flavor. *v.i.* taste; season. Also, **sa'vour**.

sa'vor·y (sā'və-rē) *adj.* tasty; agreeable. —*n.* 1, an appetizing dish. 2, either of two herbs used for seasoning.

sav'vy (sav'ē) (*Slang*) *v.t.* & *i.* understand. —*n.* understanding.

saw (sâ) *n.* 1, a metal blade with teeth, used for cutting. 2, a proverb. —*v.t.* & *i.* 1, cut with or use a saw. 2, pret. of *see*.

saw'buck' *n.* 1, a sawhorse. 2, (*Slang*) a ten-dollar bill.

saw'dust *n.* tiny fragments of wood.

saw'horse *n.* a support for holding wood while it is sawed.

saw'mill *n.* a mill where logs are sawed into planks.

saw'yer (sâ'yer) *n.* one who saws wood.

Sawhorse

Sax'on (sak'sən) *adj.* 1, pert. to an ancient Teutonic people. 2, pert. to Saxony. —*n.* a Saxon person.

sax'o·phone'' (sak'sə-fōn'') *n.* a brass wind instrument.

say (sā) *v.t.* [*pret. & p.p.* said (sed)] 1, utter, express, or declare in words; tell. 2, suppose. 3, decide. —*n.* 1, what one has to say. 2, the opportunity to speak or decide.

say'ing *n.* a proverbial expression.

say-'so'' *n.* (*Colloq.*) 1, a personal assertion. 2, a decision.

scab (skab) *n.* 1, an incrustation formed over a healing sore. 2, a strikebreaker. —**scab'by,** *adj.*

scab'bard (skab'ərd) *n.* a sheath for a sword, etc.

sca'bi·es (skā'bē-ēz') *n.* an infectious parasitic skin disease.

scads (skadz) *n. pl.* (*Slang*) a large amount, as of money.

scaf'fold (skaf'əld) *n.* 1, a temporary supporting platform. 2, a platform for a gallows. —**scaf'fold·ing,** *n.* a scaffold for workmen.

scal'a·wag'' (skal'ə-wag'') *n.* (*Colloq.*) a worthless fellow; a scamp.

scald (skåld) *v.t.* 1, burn with a boiling liquid or steam. 2, cook slightly. 3, cleanse with boiling water. —*n.* 1, a sore caused by scalding. 2, a disease of fruit.

scale (skāl) *n.* 1, a thin, horny piece of cuticle, as on a fish. 2, a flake; a scab. 3, (*sing. or pl.*) a balance for weighing. 4, (*Music*) a series of tones at fixed intervals. 5, a series of marks for measurement or computation. 6, a gradation. 7, a system of proportion. 8, a table of prices, wages, etc. —*v.t.* 1, deprive of scales; clean. 2, skip, as a stone over water. 3, weigh. 4, climb up or over. 5, project or adjust according to scale.

scal'lion (skal'yən) *n.* a variety of onion with a small bulb.

scal'lop (skal'əp) *n.* 1, a bivalve mollusk; its wavy-edged shell. 2, one of a series of small curves cut in the edge of a garment, etc.

scalp (skalp) *n.* the integument of the upper part of the head. —*v.t.* 1, remove the scalp of. 2, (*Colloq.*) buy and sell (tickets) for quick profit. —**scalp'er,** *n.* a ticket broker who charges exorbitantly.

scal'pel (skal'pəl) *n.* a light, straight surgical knife.

scamp (skamp) *n.* a rascal.

scam'per (skam'pər) *v.i.* run quickly.

scan (skan) *v.t.* [**scanned, scan'ning**] 1, examine minutely; scrutinize. 2, glance over hastily. 3, read for metrical structure. —*v.i.* conform to a meter.

scan'dal (skan'dəl) *n.* public disgrace; a cause of disgrace. —**scan'dal·ize''** (-īz'') *v.t.* shock.

scan'dal·mon'ger (skan'dəl-mung'gər) *n.* one who gossips.

scan'dal·ous *adj.* 1, disgraceful. 2, defamatory.

Scan'di·na'vi·an (skan'di-nā'vē-ən) *adj. & n.* pert. to Scandinavia, its people or languages.

scan'sion (skan'shən) *n.* analysis of metrical verse.

scant (skant) *adj.* scarcely sufficient. —**scant'y,** *adj.* small; scant.

scape'goat'' (skāp'gōt'') *n.* one made to bear the blame for others' misdeeds.

scape'grace'' (skāp'grās'') *n.* a graceless fellow; a scamp.

scap'u·la (skap'yə-lə) *n.* the shoulder blade. —**scap'u·lar,** *adj.*

scar (skär) *n.* a mark remaining after a wound has healed. —*v.t. & i.* [**scarred, scar'ring**] mark with a scar; form a scar in healing.

scar'ab (skar'əb) *n.* 1, a beetle. 2, an amulet in the form of a beetle.

scarce (skârs) *adj.* 1, insufficient; not abundant. 2, uncommon; rare. —**scarce'ness,** *n.*

scarce'ly *adv.* hardly; barely; probably not.

scar'ci·ty (skâr'sə-tē) *n.* scarceness; shortage; dearth.

scare (skâr) *v.t.* 1, frighten. 2, (with *up*) get. —*v.i.* become frightened.

scare'crow'' *n.* 1, a semblance of a man, set up to frighten crows. 2, a poorly dressed person. 3, a thin person.

scarf (skärf) *n.* 1, a decorative strip of material; a muffler; a cravat. 2, a joint for uniting two timbers.

scar'i·fy'' (skar'ə-fī') *v.t.* 1, scratch. 2, harass. —**scar'i·fi·ca'tion,** *n.*

scar'let (skär'lit) *n. & adj.* a brilliant red color. —**scarlet fever**, a contagious febrile disease.

scarp (skärp) *n.* 1, a steep slope. 2, an escarpment.

scar'y (skär'ē) *adj.* 1, causing fright. 2, timid. —**scar'i·ness**, *n.*

scat (skat) *v.i.* [scat'ted, -ting] (*Colloq.*) drive off. —*interj.* Go away!

scathe (skāth) *v.t.* 1, criticize severely. 2, injure. —**scath'ing**, *adj.*

scat'ter (skat'ər) *v.t.* 1, throw loosely about. 2, dispose. 3, put to flight. —*v.i.* disperse. —**scat'ter-brain'**, *n.* a giddy person. —**scatter rug**, a small rug used with others.

scav'en·ger (skav'in-jər) *n.* 1, an animal or organism that devours refuse. 2, a street cleaner.

sce·nar'i·o' (si-när'ē-ō') *n.* the outline of a drama or motion picture.

scene (sēn) *n.* 1, the place where anything is done or takes place. 2, a stage setting; a division of a play. 3, a particular incident. 4, a view; a picture. 5, an exhibition of strong feeling.

scen'er·y (sēn'ə-rē) *n.* 1, the aggregate of features in a view. 2, stage settings.

scen'ic (sē'nik) *adj.* pert. to scenery; abounding in fine scenery. —**scen'i·cal·ly**, *adv.* —**scenic railway**, a roller-coaster.

scent (sent) *n.* 1, an odor. 2, the course of an animal. 3, a perfume. 4, the sense of smell. —*v.t.* 1, smell. 2, suspect. 3, perfume.

scep'ter (sep'tər) *n.* a staff emblematic of royalty. Also, **scep'tre**.

scep'tic (skep'tik) *n.* skeptic.

sched'ule (skej'ûl) *n.* 1, a statement of contents, details, etc. 2, agenda. 3, a timetable. —*v.t.* place on a schedule; plan.

sche·mat'ic (skē-mat'ik) *adj.* pert. to a scheme or diagram. —**schemat'i·cal·ly**, *adv.*

scheme (skēm) *n.* 1, a regular or formal plan; a system. 2, a plot; an intrigue. —*v.t. & i.* plan; plot. —**schem'er**, *n.* —**schem'ing**, *adj.* plotting; crafty.

scher'zo (sker'tzō) *n.* (*Music*) a movement of a light or playful nature.

Schick test (shik) a diphtheria immunity test.

schism (siz'əm) *n.* a division or separation. —**schis·mat'ic**, *adj.*

schist (shist) *n.* a crystalline rock formed in parallel layers.

schiz·o- (skiz-ō) *pref.* split.

schiz'o·phre'ni·a (skiz'ə-frē'nē-

ə) *n.* a mental disorder, splitting of the personality. —**schiz'oid, schiz'o·phren'ic** (-fren'ik) *adj.*

schnapps (shnäps) *n.* liquor.

schnau'zer (shnow'zər) *n.* a Ger. breed of terrier.

schol'ar (skol'ər) *n.* 1, a student. 2, a learned man. —**schol'ar·ly**, *adj.*

schol'ar·ship' *n.* 1, learning; erudition. 2, monetary assistance granted to a scholar.

scho·las'tic (skə-las'tik) *adj.* pert. to schools, scholars, or education. —**scho·las'ti·cal·ly**, *adv.*

school (skool) *n.* 1, an educational establishment. 2, a united group or sect. 3, a specific method, etc. 4, a large body of fish, whales, etc. —*v.t.* educate; train. —**school board**, a body governing local schools. —**school'book'**, *n.* textbook. —**school'boy', school'girl', school'house'**, *n.* —**school'ing**, *n.* education; learning. —**school'marm'** (-märm') *n.* a woman schoolteacher, or any prim woman (formerly thought to be typical of schoolteachers). —**school'room', school'teach'er**, *n.*

schoon'er (skoo'nər) *n.* 1, a sailing vessel. 2, a tall glass for beer.

schot'tische (shot'ish) *n.* a Scottish dance, similar to the polka.

schwa (shwä) *n.* the indeterminate vowel sound of most unaccented syllables in English; the symbol (ə) for it.

sci·at'ic (sī-at'ik) *adj.* pert. to or affecting the hip.

sci·at'i·ca (sī-at'i-kə) *n.* pain and tenderness in a sciatic nerve.

sci'ence (sī'əns) *n.* 1, a branch of knowledge; what is known concerning a subject. 2, (*Colloq.*) a natural science, as physics or chemistry. 3, special skill.

sci'en·tif'ic (sī'ən-tif'ik) *adj.* 1, pert. to science. 2, systematic and accurate. —**sci'en·tif'i·cal·ly**, *adv.*

sci'en·tist (sī'ən-tist) *n.* one versed in a science.

scim'i·tar (sim'ə-tər) *n.* a curved, single-edged sword.

scin·til'la (sin-til'ə) *n.* the least particle; a trace.

scin'til·late' (sin'tə-lāt') *v.i.* emit sparks; twinkle; shine. —**scin'til·la'tion**, *n.*

sci'on (sī'ən) *n.* 1, a descendant. 2, a shoot or twig used for grafting.

scis'sors (siz'ərz) *n. pl.* or *sing.* a cutting instrument consisting of two pivoted blades.

scle·ro'sis (skli-rō'sis) *n.* [*pl.* -ses (-sēz)] a hardening of a tissue or part.

scoff (skof) v.i. (with *at*) jeer.

scold (skōld) v.t. & i. chide; find fault. —n. a railing woman.

sconce (skons) n. 1, a wall bracket for candles, etc. 2, a defensive bulwark. 3, (*Archaic*) the head.

scone (skōn) n. a soft cake or biscuit.

scoop (skoop) n. 1, an instrument for hollowing out anything. 2, a hollow. 3, the act of scooping. 4, (*Colloq.*) a journalistic beat. —v.t. 1, (with *out*) remove or hollow with a scoop. 2, publish news earlier than.

scoot (skoot) v.i. go hastily; dart. —v.t. eject.

scoot'er n. 1, a child's foot-propelled vehicle. 2, an iceboat.

scope (skōp) n. 1, outlook; intellectual range. 2, room for free observation or action. 3, extent; length; sweep.

-scope (skōp) suf. a means or instrument for viewing.

sco·pol'a·mine (skō-pol'ə-mēn") n. an alkaloid used as a depressant and as an anesthetic in obstetrics.

scor·bu'tic (skôr-bū'tik) adj. pert. to or affected with scurvy.

scorch (skôrch) v.t. & i. 1, burn superficially; singe. 2, parch. 3, criticize caustically. —n. a superficial burn. —scorched earth policy, total destruction of one's own territory, to impede an invader.

scorch'er n. anything that scorches; (*Colloq.*) a very hot day; a caustic statement.

score (skōr) n. 1, the points made in a game or match. 2, a reckoning; account. 3, a notch; a scratch. 4, reason; ground. 5, twenty; (*pl.*) many. 6, a copy of a musical composition. —v.t. & i. 1, make, record, or write a score. 2, berate.

scorn (skôrn) n. contempt; disdain. —v.t. 1, disdain. 2, reject.

scorn'ful (-fəl) adj. full of or expressing contempt.

Scor'pi·o (skôr'pē-ō) n. a constellation, the Scorpion (see *zodiac*).

scor'pi·on (skôr'pē-ən) n. a venomous arachnid.

Scorpion

Scot (skot) n. a native or inhabitant of Scotland. —Scots, adj. —Scots'man, n.

Scotch (skoch) adj. Scottish. —n. 1, a whiskey distilled in Scotland.

2, (*l.c.*) a cut. 3, (*l.c.*) a block or wedge. —v.t. (*l.c.*) 1, cut; crush. 2, block (a wheel). —Scotch tape (*T. N.*) an adhesive cellulose tape —Scotch terrier [also, Scot'tie (skot'ē)] a short-legged, small terrier.

scot-'free" (skot'frē") adj. safe; clear; without charge or tax.

Scotland Yard the police headquarters in London, England.

Scot'tish (skot'ish) adj. of or pert. to Scotland.

scoun'drel (skown'drəl) n. an unprincipled man; a villain.

scour (skowr) v.t. & i. 1, clean by friction; brighten. 2, cleanse dirt from. 3, search through; range.

scourge (skûrj) n. 1, a whip. 2, an affliction; a cause of affliction. —v.t. whip; afflict.

scout (skowt) n. 1, a soldier, airplane, etc., sent to reconnoiter. 2, an observer. 3, (*cap.*) a Boy Scout or Girl Scout. —v.t. & i. 1, reconnoiter. 2, ridicule.

scout'mas"ter n. adult leader of a troop of Scouts. —scout'mis"tress, n.fem.

scow (skow) n. a large, flat-bottomed boat for freight.

scowl (skowl) v.i. lower the brows; look gloomy, severe, or angry. —n. an angry frown.

scrab'ble (skrab'əl) v.i. 1, scratch. 2, scrawl. 3, scramble. —n. (*cap.*; *T. N.*) a parlor game based on crossword puzzles.

scrag'gly (skrag'lē) adj. irregular; ragged. —scrag'gy, adj. thin; scrawny.

scram (skram) v.i. [scrammed, scram'ming] (*Slang*) go away.

scram'ble (skram'bəl) v.i. 1, struggle along as if on all fours. 2, strive eagerly and rudely. —v.t. mix together. —n. act of scrambling. —scrambled eggs, 1, eggs mixed while frying. 2, (*Slang*) yellow braid worn by a naval officer.

scrap (skrap) n. 1, a detached portion; a fragment. 2, (*pl.*) fragments of food. 3, discarded iron or steel. 4, (*Slang*) a fight or quarrel. —v.t. [scrapped, scrap'ping] 1, break up. 2, discard as useless. 3, (*Slang*) fight.

scrap'book" n. a blank book for pictures, clippings, etc.

scrape (skrāp) v.t. 1, shave or abrade the surface of. 2, (with *out* or *off*) remove; erase. 3, (with *together* or *up*) collect. —v.i. 1, rub lightly. 2, get by with difficulty. 3, save. —n. 1, the act or sound of scraping. 2, an embarrassing predicament. —scrap'er, scrap'ing, n.

scrap'ple (skrap'əl) *n.* a highly spiced hash served at breakfast.

scrap'py (skrap'ē) *adj.* (*Slang*) pugnacious. —**scrap'pi·ness,** *n.*

scratch (skrach) *v.t. & i.* 1, mark or wound slightly. 2, rub, as with the fingernails, to relieve itching. 3, scribble. 4, dig with the claws. 5, rub roughly; grate against. 6, erase. 7, withdraw from a race. —*n.* 1, an act or result of scratching. 2, a position without allowance or penalty. —**scratch pad,** a memorandum pad. —**scratch'y,** *adj.*

scrawl (skrâl) *v.t.* write or draw carelessly. —*n.* a careless script.

scraw'ny (skrâ'nē) *adj.* meager; lean. —**scraw'ni·ness,** *n.*

scream (skrēm) *v.i. & t.* 1, utter a sharp, piercing outcry. 2, emit a shrill sound. 3, (*Colloq.*) laugh immoderately. —*n.* 1, a screaming sound. 2, (*Colloq.*) a joker; something funny. —**scream'er,** *n.* a banner headline in a newspaper.

screech (skrēch) *v.i. & t.* scream harshly. —*n.* a shriek. —**screech'y,** *adj.*

screed (skrēd) *n.* 1, a harangue. 2, a section of plastering.

screen (skrēn) *n.* 1, any partition or curtain that conceals or protects. 2, a protective formation, as of troops. 3, a pretext. 4, a sieve. 5, a surface on which motion pictures are projected; motion pictures collectively. —*v.t. & i.* 1, conceal; protect. 2, sift. 3, film; exhibit.

screw (skroo) *n.* 1, a nail-like device having an external thread, that turns in a nut or is driven into wood. 2, a propeller. 3, coercion. 4, (*Slang*) a prison guard. —*v.t. & i.* 1, turn (a screw); attach by a screw. 2, twist; contort.

screw'ball" *n. & adj.* (*Slang*) an eccentric person.

screw'driv"er *n.* a tool for turning screws.

scrib'ble (skrib'əl) *v.t. & i.* write carelessly. —*n.* a scrawl.

scribe (skrīb) *n.* 1, a penman; a public writer. 2, (*Colloq.*) an author.

scrim'mage (skrim'ij) *n.* 1, a skirmish; a tussle. 2, (*Football*) the clash of opposing lines; a practice game. —*v.i.* engage in a scrimmage.

scrimp (skrimp) *v.t. & i.* be sparing in or of; pinch. —**scrimp'y,** *adj.* meager.

scrip (skrip) *n.* a certificate promising future payment.

script (skript) *n.* 1, handwriting; printing type like handwriting. 2, the manuscript of a play or motion picture.

Scrip'ture (skrip'chər) *n.* 1, the Bible. 2, any sacred writing. —**scrip'tur·al,** *adj.*

scriv'ner (skriv'nər) *n.* scribe.

scrod (skrod) *n.* a young codfish.

scrof'u·la (skrof'yə-lə) *n.* a disorder characterized by glandular swelling. —**scrof'u·lous,** *adj.*

scroll (skrōl) *n.* 1, a roll of paper or parchment, esp. a writing. 2, a spiral or coiled ornament. —**scroll'work",** *n.* spiral decoration.

scro'tum (skrō'təm) *n.* the pouch of skin containing the testicles.

scrouge (skrowj) *v.t.* (*Colloq.*) squeeze; crowd.

scrounge (skrownj) *v.t. & i.* obtain by sponging on or pilfering from another person.

scrub (skrub) *v.t. & i.* [**scrubbed, scrub'bing**] cleanse by rubbing hard. —*n.* 1, underbrush. 2, a worn-out or inferior animal. 3, anything inferior. 4, (*Sports*) a substitute player. 5, a form of baseball. —*adj.* makeshift. —**scrub'by,** *adj.*

scruff (skruf) *n.* the nape of the neck.

scrump'tious (skrump'shəs) *adj.* (*Slang*) very fine; first-rate.

scru'ple (skroo'pəl) *n.* 1, a conscientious reluctance. 2, a small amount. —*v.i.* hesitate.

scru'pu·lous (skroop'yə-ləs) *adj.* 1, upright; moral. 2, exact; punctilious. —**scru'pu·lous·ness,** *n.*

scru'ti·nize" (skroo'tə-nīz") *v.t.* observe or investigate closely.

scru'ti·ny (skroo'tə-nē) *n.* close observation; examination.

scud (skud) *v.i.* [**scud'ded, -ding**] 1, move quickly. 2, run before a gale.

scuff (skuf) *v.t.* 1, spoil the finish by scraping. 2, scrape with the feet. —*v.i.* shuffle. —*n.* a type of slipper.

scuf'fle (skuf'əl) *v.i.* 1, fight or struggle confusedly. 2, shuffle. —*n.* 1, a brief, rough fight. 2, shuffle.

scull (skul) *n.* 1, an oar. 2, a light racing boat for one rower. —*v.t. & i.* propel (a boat) with a scull.

scul'ler·y (skul'ə-rē) *n.* a back kitchen.

scul'lion (skul'yən) *n.* a menial kitchen servant.

sculp'ture (skulp'chər) *n.* 1, the art of carving or shaping figures. 2, a piece of such work. —**sculp'tur·al,** *adj.* —**sculp'tor,** *n.*

scum (skum) *n.* 1, a film of extraneous matter on a liquid. 2, refuse. 3, worthless persons. —**scum'my,** *adj.*

scup'per (skup'ər) *n.* an opening to let water run off the deck of a ship.

scurf (skėrf) *n.* flakes of skin that are shed, as dandruff.

scur'ril·ous (skėr'ə-ləs) *adj.* indecently or grossly abusive; offensive. —**scur·ril'i·ty,** *n.*

scur'ry (skėr'ē) *v.i.* hurry along; scamper.

scur'vy (skėr'vē) *n.* a disease characterized by swelling, hemorrhages, etc., caused by improper diet. —*adj.* low; contemptible.

scut'tle (skut'əl) *n.* 1, a container for coal. 2, a hurried run. 3, a small opening. —*v.i.* hurry. —*v.t.* sink (a ship) by cutting holes in the bottom.

scut'tle-butt' *n.* 1, a cask. 2, (*Slang*) gossip.

scythe (sīth) *n.* an instrument with a long blade for cutting grass.

sea (sē) *n.* 1, the salt waters on the earth's surface; the ocean. 2, a region of the ocean; a large lake. 3, a swell; a large wave. 4, an overwhelming quantity.

Sea'bee' *n.* a member of a U. S. Navy construction battalion.

sea'board' *n.* coast.

sea'coast' *n.* seashore.

sea'far'er (-fär'ər) *n.* a traveler by sea. —**sea'far'ing,** *adj.*

sea'food' *n.* edible marine fish and shellfish.

sea'go'ing *adj.* used for, or suitable for, ocean travel.

sea gull a marine bird; gull.

sea horse a fish with a head suggesting a horse's.

seal (sēl) *n.* 1, an impressed device used to authenticate a document; a stamp for impressing the device. 2, a tight closure; a substance used to effect it. 3, a marine carnivorous mammal; its fur; its skin used for leather. —*v.t.* 1, authenticate, close, or secure, with a seal. 2, determine irrevocably. 3, close; confine.

sea legs ability to walk (as on a ship) without losing balance.

Seal

sea level the mean level of the sea.

sea lion a variety of seal.

Sea'ly·ham' (sē'lē-ham') *n.* a shaggy terrier of Welsh origin.

seam (sēm) *n.* 1, the line formed by joining two edges, as in sewing. 2, a fissure or gap; a ridge. 3, a stratum. —*v.t.* & *i.* sew a seam.

sea'man (-mən) *n.* [*pl.* -men] a sailor. —**sea'man·ship,** *n.* skill in the operation of a ship.

seam'stress (-strəs) *n.* a woman who sews.

seam'y (sē'mē) *adj.* sordid.

sé'ance (sā'äns) *n.* a session or meeting of spiritualists.

sea'plane' *n.* an airplane with pontoons.

sea'port' *n.* a city having a harbor on the sea.

sear (sir) *v.t.* 1, burn or brown the surface of. 2, make callous. 3, dry up.

search (sėrch) *v.t.* 1, go through and examine carefully; explore. 2, probe. 3, penetrate. —*v.i.* seek; investigate. —*n.* process of searching; investigation. —**search warrant,** a legal order authorizing a search.

search'ing *adj.* keen; penetrating.

search'light' *n.* an electric light that sends a concentrated beam.

sea shell the shell of any sea mollusk.

sea'shore' *n.* land by the sea; a beach.

sea'sick' *adj.* nauseated by the rolling of a vessel. —**sea'sick'ness,** *n.*

sea'side' *n.* seashore.

sea'son (sē'zən) *n.* 1, a quarter of the year: spring, summer, autumn, or winter. 2, a particular period as to weather, business activity, fashion, etc. 3, a suitable time. —*v.t.* 1, mature; ripen. 2, render palatable with spices, herbs, etc. 3, give zest to; qualify; imbue. —*v.i.* mature.

sea'son·a·ble *adj.* suitable; opportune.

sea'son·al *adj.* pert. to, or depending upon, the season.

sea'son·ing *n.* spices, etc.

sea'way' *n.* 1, headway, for a ship. 2, a channel provided for seagoing ships.

seat (sēt) *n.* 1, a place or thing to sit on. 2, that part of a chair, garment, etc., on which one sits. 3, a site; location. 4, a right to sit or attend. —*v.t.* 1, place on a seat; locate; fix. 2, furnish with seats or room for sitting.

sea'weed' *n.* any plant growing in the sea.

sea'wor'thy *adj.* in condition for sea travel.

se·ba'ceous (si-bā'shəs) *adj.* being, containing or secreting fat.

se'cant (sē'kant) *n.* 1, (*Geom.*) a line across an arc. 2, a trigonometric ratio.

se·cede' (si-sēd') *v.i.* withdraw, esp. from a political or religious organization.

se·ces'sion (si-sesh'ən) *n.* act of seceding, as (*cap.*) that of the Confederate States in 1861. —**se·ces'sion·ist,** *n.* one who favors secession.

se·clude' (si-klood') *v.t.* shut away; keep in solitude.

se·clu'sion (si-kloo'zhən) *n.* 1, act or effect of secluding. 2, a secluded condition or place; solitude. —**se·clu'sive** (-siv) *adj.*

sec'ond (sek'ənd) *adj.* 1, next after the first in order, time, value, etc.; the ordinal of two. 2, subordinate. 3, another. —*n.* 1, the one next after the first. 2, a supporter; an attendant in a prize fight or duel. 3, an imperfect product. 4, the sixtieth part of a minute. —*v.t.* support; assist. —**second fiddle,** a minor role. —**second nature,** habit. —**second sight,** clairvoyance.

sec·on·dar·y (sek'ən-der-ē) *adj.* 1, of a second class or group. 2, subordinate; derived, not primary. —**secondary school,** a high school.

sec"ond·class' *adj.* 1, in the next-to-highest class. 2, inferior.

sec"ond·hand' *adj.* 1, not original. 2, previously used.

sec'ond·rate' *adj.* inferior.

se'cre·cy (sē'krə-sē) *n.* 1, the state of being secret. 2, secretive manner; strict silence.

se'cret (sē'krit) *adj.* 1, kept private or concealed. 2, not apparent; mysterious. —*n.* something not revealed. —**secret service,** a governmental branch that investigates secretly: in the U. S., a bureau of the Treasury Dept.

sec"re·tar'i·at (sek"rə-ter'ē-ət) *n.* an administrative bureau.

sec're·tar"y (sek're-ter"ē) *n.* 1, a recording or corresponding officer. 2, a stenographer. 3, a cabinet minister. 4, a writing desk. —**sec"re·tar'i·al,** *adj.*

se·crete' (si-krēt') *v.t.* 1, hide. 2, produce by secretion.

se·cre'tion (si-krē'shən) *n.* 1, the process of preparing substances by glandular activity. 2, the product secreted. —**se·cre'to·ry,** *adj.*

se·cre'tive (si-krē'tiv) *adj.* maintaining secrecy; reticent.

sect (sekt) *n.* a religious denomination. —**sec·tar'i·an,** *adj.* & *n.*

sec'tion (sek'shən) *n.* 1, a part cut or separated; a distinct portion. 2,

a region. 3, the act of cutting; a surgical operation.

sec'tion·al *adj.* 1, composed of several sections. 2, local. —**sec'tion·al·ism,** *n.* undue regard for local interests.

sec'tor (sek'tor) *n.* 1, a plane figure enclosed between the arc of a circle and two radii. 2, a mathematical scale. 3, a combat area.

sec'u·lar (sek'yə-lər) *adj.* temporal; worldly; not of the church. —**sec'u·lar·ism,** *n.*

se·cure' (si-kyūr') *adj.* 1, free from danger; safe. 2, firm; stable. 3, certain. —*v.t.* 1, make safe; make certain. 2, obtain. 3, fasten.

se·cur'i·ty (si-kyūr'ə-tē) *n.* 1, safety. 2, a guaranty or pledge. 3, a bond or stock certificate.

se·dan' (si-dan') *n.* a two-seated closed automobile.

se·date' (si-dāt') *adj.* quiet; composed; serious. —**se·date'ness,** *n.*

sed'a·tive (sed'ə-tiv) *adj.* tending to soothe or calm. —*n.* a calming medicine.

sed·en·tar"y (sed'ən-ter"ē) *adj.* characterized by a sitting position.

sedge (sej) *n.* a grasslike plant.

sed'i·ment (sed'ə-mənt) *n.* the matter that settles to the bottom of a liquid; dregs.

se·di'tion (si-dish'ən) *n.* incitement of rebellion. —**se·di'tious,** *adj.*

se·duce' (si-doos') *v.t.* lead astray; entice away from duty, rectitude, or chastity. —**se·duc'er,** *n.*

se·duc'tion (si-duk'shən) *n.* act or effect of seducing.

se·duc'tive (-tiv) *adj.* tending to seduce; enticing.

sed'u·lous (sej'ə-ləs) *adj.* diligent; persevering. —**sed'u·lous·ness,** *n.*

see (sē) *v.t.* [**saw** (sà), **seen** (sēn)] **see'ing**] 1, perceive by the eye; observe; view. 2, comprehend. 3, make sure. 4, escort; attend. 5, visit. 6, in poker, etc., meet or call (a bet). —*v.i.* 1, have the power of sight. 2, understand. 3, consider. —*n.* the seat or jurisdiction of a bishop. —**see'ing,** *conj.* inasmuch as. —**seeing-eye dog,** a dog trained to guide the blind.

seed (sēd) *n.* [*pl.* **seeds** or **seed**] 1, the fertilized and natural ovule of a plant. 2, semen, sperm, etc. 3, offspring; descendants. 4, origin. —*v.t.* 1, plant. 2, distribute (players) evenly in a tournament. —*v.i.* produce seed. —**seed pearl,** a very small pearl.

seed'ling *n.* a young plant.

seed'y (sē'dē) *adj.* 1, gone to

seed; shabby. **2,** (*Colloq.*) not well. —seed'i·ness, *n.*

seek (sēk) *v.t.* [*pret. & p.p.* **sought** (sät)] **1,** go in search or quest of. **2,** resort to. **3,** attempt; endeavor.

seem (sēm) *v.i.* **1,** appear; appear to be. **2,** appear to oneself.

seem'ing *adj.* ostensible; apparent. —*n.* an appearance.

seem'ly (-lē) *adj.* becoming; proper; decent. —seem'li·ness, *n.*

seen (sēn) *v.* p.p. of *see.*

seep (sēp) *v.i.* ooze gently through pores. —seep'age (-ij) *n.*

seer (sir) *n.* a prophet; clairvoyant. —seer'ess, *n.fem.*

seer'suck·er (sir'suk'ər) *n.* a crinkled cotton fabric.

see'saw" (sē'sä") *n.* **1,** a board balanced on a support, on which two children move alternately up and down. **2,** any up-and-down movement. —*v.i.* move like a seesaw.

Seesaw

seethe (sēth) *v.t.* **1,** boil. **2,** be agitated.

seg'ment (seg'mənt) *n.* a part cut off; a section.

seg're·gate" (seg'rə-gāt") *v.t. & i.* separate or detach from others.

seg're·ga'tion (-gā'shən) *n.* act or effect of segregating; esp., separation of Negroes and white persons.

seg'ue (seg'wā) *n.* (*Radio*) a brief musical passage between episodes.

seine (sān) *n.* a large fishing net.

seis'mo·graph (siz'mə-gráf) *n.* a device that records earthquakes.

seize (sēz) *v.t.* **1,** grasp suddenly. **2,** comprehend. **3,** take legal or forcible possession of. **4,** afflict.

sei'zure (sē'zhər) *n.* **1,** the act of seizing. **2,** a sudden attack; a fit.

sel'dom (sel'dəm) *adv.* rarely; infrequently.

se·lect' (si-lekt') *v.t.* choose. —*adj.* **1,** choice. **2,** fastidious; exclusive.

se·lec"tee' (si-lek'tē') *n.* one drafted for military service.

se·lec'tion (si-lek'shən) *n.* act of choosing; a thing or things chosen.

se·lec'tive (-tiv) *adj.* **1,** pert. to or determined by selection. **2,** careful in choosing. —selective service, conscription of selected persons.

se·lec"tiv'i·ty (-tiv'ə-tē) *n.* (*Radio*) precision in tuning qualities.

se·lect'man (-mən) *n.* [*pl.* -men] a member of a town governing board.

self *n.* [*pl.* selves (selvz)] **1,** a person in his relations to his own person. **2,** nature; individuality. **3,** personal interest and benefit. —*pron.* (*Colloq.*) myself, himself, etc. —*adj.* single; uniform; unmixed.

self- *pref.* **1,** expressing reflexive action: on or to oneself or itself. **2,** in or by oneself or itself. [In addition to words defined in the text, the following words formed by prefixing self- may be defined by reference to the root word.]

self-"ad·dressed'	self-"in·dul'gent
self-"as·sur'ance	self-"in·flict'ed
self-"com·mand'	self-"load'ing
self-"com·pla'-cent	self-"love'
	self-"pit'y
self-"con·tained'	self-"pres"er·va'-tion
self-"con·trol'	
self-"de·cep'tion	self-"pro·pelled'
self-"de·ni'al	self-"pro·tec'tion
self-"de·struc'-tion	self-"re·li'ance
	self-"re·proach'
self-"dis"ci·pline	self-"re·straint'
self-"ed'u·cat"ed	self-"sac'ri·fice"
self-"es·teem'	self-"ser'vice
self-"ex·plan'a-to·ry	self-"styled'
	self-"sup·port'
self-"gov'erned	self-"sus·tain'ing
self-"help'	self-"taught'
self-"im·posed'	self-"wind'ing
self-"in·duced'	

self-"cen'tered *adj.* absorbed in oneself.

self-"con'fi·dence *n.* the state of not feeling the need of assistance. —self-"con'fi·dent, *adj.*

self-"con'scious *adj.* ill at ease when with others. —self-"con'-scious·ness, *n.*

self-"de·fense' *n.* protection of oneself when attacked.

self-"de·ter'mi·na'tion *n.* determination of one's own course; autonomy.

self-"ef·fac'ing *adj.* diffident; very modest.—self-"ef·face'ment, *n.*

self-"ev'i·dent *adj.* obvious; requiring no proof.

self-"ex·pres'sion *n.* utilization or pursuit of an outlet for one's personality.

self-"im·por'tant *adj.* pompous. —self-"im·por'tance, *n.*

self-"in'ter·est *n.* personal advantage.

self'ish *adj.* devoted only to oneself. —**self'ish·ness**, *n.*

self'less *adj.* entirely unselfish. —**self'less·ness**, *n.*

self-"made' *adj.* successful wholly by one's own efforts.

self-"pos·sessed' *adj.* composed.

self-"re·li'ance *n.* self-confidence. —**self-"re·li'ant**, *adj.*

self-"re·spect' *n.* becoming pride.

self-"right'eous *adj.* righteous in one's own esteem. —**self-"right'·eous·ness**, *n.*

self'same' *adj.* identical.

self-"sat'is·fied' *adj.* complacent. —**self-"sat'is·fac'tion**, *n.*

self-"seek'ing *adj.* selfish.

self-"start'er *n.* an electric motor that cranks an automobile.

self-"suf·fi'cient *adj.* **1,** requiring no help, companionship, etc. **2,** unduly self-confident.

self-"willed' *adj.* obstinate.

sell (sel) *v.t.* [*pret. & p.p.* sold (sōld)] **1,** transfer to another for money. **2,** keep for sale. **3,** betray. **4,** cause acceptance. —*v.i.* **1,** engage in selling. **2,** be in demand; be sold.

sell'out' *n.* a complete disposal by selling, as of theater seats.

sel'tzer (sel'tsər) *n.* an effervescent mineral water, or carbonated water resembling it.

sel'vage (sel'vij) *n.* the finished edge of a fabric. Also, **sel'vedge.**

se·man'tic (si-man'tik) *adj.* pert. to meaning in language. —**se·man'tics**, *n.* the study of meaning.

sem'a·phore' (sem'ə-fôr") *n.* a signaling device or method.

Semaphores
Left: Railroad Semaphore
Right: Semaphore Flag Signal

sem'blance (sem'bləns) *n.* **1,** a likeness; an image. **2,** outward appearance.

se'men (sē'mən) *n.* the male reproductive fluid.

se·mes'ter (si-mes'tər) *n.* a major division of the academic year, usually one half.

sem·i- *pref.* **1,** half. **2,** partly.

sem"i·an'nu·al *adj.* once every six months.

sem"i·cir"cle *n.* half a circle;

sem"i·co"lon *n.* a mark of punctuation (;) used to separate major sentence elements more distinctly than the comma.

sem"i·fi'nal *adj.* a round or match in a contest, next to the final one. —*n.* [*also,* sem"i·fi'nals] this round, match, or matches.

sem"i·nar" (sem'ə-när") *n.* a small group, or course, for advanced study.

sem"i·nar"y (sem'ə-ner"ē) *n.* a school, esp. one for the ministry or for young women.

sem"i·pre'cious *adj.* of less than the highest (gem) value.

Sem'ite (sem'īt) *n.* a member of any Semitic people.

Se·mit'ic (sə-mit'ik) *adj.* relating to the Semites or their languages, such as Hebrew, Aramaic, Assyrian, and Arabic;

sen *n.* a Jap. coin, 1/100 yen.

sen'ate (sen'it) *n.* a legislative assembly; (*cap.*) the upper legislative house of the U. S.

sen'a·tor (sen'ə-tər) *n.* a member of a senate, as (*cap.*) of the U. S. Senate. —**sen"a·to'ri·al** (-tôr'ē·əl) *adj.*

send *v.t. & i.* [*pret. & p.p.* sent] **1,** cause to go; dispatch. **2,** impel. **3,** (with *out*, etc.) produce or give off. **4,** (*Slang*) stimulate or excite. —**send'er**, *n.* **1,** one who sends. **2,** a transmitter.

send-'off' *n.* **1,** a start. **2,** a farewell demonstration.

se·nes'cent (sə-nes'ənt) *adj.* growing old. —**se·nes'cence**, *n.*

sen'es·chal (sen'ə-shəl) *n.* the manager of a nobleman's estate.

se'nile (sē'nīl) *adj.* pert. to or characterizing old age. —**se·nil'i·ty** (sə-nil'ə·tē) *n.*

sen'ior (sēn'yər) *adj.* **1,** older; elder. **2,** older in office or service. **3,** pert. to the last year of a high school or college course. —*n.* **1,** a person who is older or of higher rank. **2,** a member of the senior class.

sen·ior'i·ty (sē·nyor'ə·tē) *n.* state of being older in years, service, etc.

sen'na (sen'ə) *n.* a cathartic drug derived from cassia.

se·ñor' (sā-nyôr') *n.* (*Span.*) **1,** mister. **2,** sir. —**se·ño'ra** (-nyō'rə) *n.fem.* a married woman; Mrs. —**se·ño·ri'ta** (sā"nyə·rē'tə) *n.fem.* Miss.

sen·sa'tion (sen-sā'shən) *n.* **1,** a mental impression caused by an affection of a bodily organism; sensitive apprehension. **2,** a state of, or the cause of, excited interest or feeling.

sen·sa'tion·al (-əl) *adj.* intended to thrill. —**sen·sa'tion·al·ism,** *n.*

sense (sens) *n.* **1,** a special faculty of sensation: sight, smell, taste; touch, or hearing. **2,** consciousness; understanding; discriminative perception. **3,** practical intelligence. **4,** meaning. **5,** intention. —*v.t.* perceive by the senses.

sense'less (-ləs) *adj.* **1,** unconscious. **2,** stupid. **3,** nonsensical. —**sense'less·ness,** *n.*

sen'si·ble (sen'sə-bəl) *adj.* **1,** reasonable. **2,** aware; cognizant. **3,** perceptible through the senses. **4,** capable of sensation.

sen"si·bil'i·ty (sen"sə-bil'ə-tē) *n.* **1,** mental receptivity. **2,** capacity for the more refined feelings.

sen'si·tive (sen'sə-tiv) *adj.* **1,** pert. to the senses; capable of receiving sensations. **2,** of keen sensibility; easily hurt. **3,** quickly responsive; readily affected. —**sen'si·tive·ness, sen'si·tiv'i·ty,** *n.*

sen'si·tize (-tīz") *v.t.* treat so as to make sensitive.

sen'so·ry (sen'sə-rē) *adj.* pert. to sensation or the senses.

sen'su·al (sen'shū-əl) *adj.* pert. to the senses; not intellectual; carnal; voluptuous. —**sen'su·al·ism,** *n.* —**sen'su·al·ist,** *n.*

sen"su·al'i·ty (sen"shoo-al'ə-tē) *n.* unrestrained self-gratification.

sen'su·ous (sen'shū-əs) *adj.* affecting, or affected through, the senses.

sent *v.* pret. & p.p. of *send.*

sen'tence (sen'təns) *n.* **1,** a number of words constituting a complete statement, inquiry, etc. **2,** the punishment determined for a convicted criminal. **3,** an opinion. —*v.t.* pronounce sentence upon.

sen·ten'tious (sen-ten'shəs) *adj.* given to the use of maxims; didactic.

sen'tient (sen'shənt) *adj.* having the power of feeling or perception. —**sen'tience,** *n.*

sen'ti·ment (sen'tə-mənt) *n.* **1,** higher feeling; emotion. **2,** tender susceptibility. **3,** an opinion; mental attitude. **4,** an expression of feeling.

sen"ti·men'tal (sen"tə-men'təl) *adj.* **1,** of a tender nature. **2,** mawkish. **3,** appealing to the feelings. —**sen'ti·men'tal·ist,** *n.* a sentimental person. —**sen"ti·men·tal'i·ty** (-tal'ə-tē) *n.* state of being sentimental; emotionalism.

sen'ti·nel (sen'tə-nəl) *n.* a soldier stationed as a guard.

sen'try (sen'trē) *n.* a guard; a sentinel.

se'pal (sē'pəl) *n.* a small leaf forming part of a flower.

sep'a·rate" (sep'ə-rāt") *v.t.* **1,** disunite; disconnect. **2,** divide, place, or keep apart. —*v.i.* **1,** part. **2,** come apart; open. —*adj.* (-rət) **1,** divided; apart. **2,** distinct; individual. —**sep'ar·a·ble,** *adj.*

sep"a·ra'tion *n.* **1,** act or effect of separating. **2,** that which separates; a partition, etc. **3,** a limited divorce.

sep'a·ra"tor *n.* an apparatus for separating cream from milk.

se'pi·a (sē'pē-ə) *n.* & *adj.* a dark brown color.

sept- *pref.* seven.

Sep·tem'ber (sep-tem'bər) *n.* the ninth month of the year.

sep'tic (sep'tik) *adj.* pertaining to decay. —**septic tank,** a tank for sewage disposal.

sep'ul·cher (sep'əl-kər) *n.* a tomb; a burial vault. Also, **sep'ul·chre.**

se·pul'chral (sə-pul'krəl) *adj.* **1,** pert. to burial. **2,** deep; hollow in tone. **3,** gloomy.

se'quel (sē'kwəl) *n.* **1,** a continuation. **2,** a consequence.

se'quence (sē'kwəns) *n.* **1,** a succession. **2,** order of succession. **3,** a series.

se·ques'ter (si-kwes'tər) *v.t.* put aside; seclude. —**se"ques·tra'tion,** *n.*

se'quin (sē'kwin) *n.* **1,** a spangle. **2,** a former gold coin.

se·quoi'a (si-kwoi'ə) *n.* either of two very large coniferous trees of California.

se·ragl'io (si-ral'yō) *n.* **1,** a harem. **2,** a Turkish palace.

se·ra'pe (se-rä'pē) *n.* a bright-colored shawl or wrap.

ser'aph (ser'əf) *n.* [*pl.* **ser'a·phim** (-ə-fim) or **ser'aphs**] an angel. —**se·raph'ic** (sə-raf'ik) *adj.*

Serb (sĕrb) *adj.* & *n.* pert to Serbia, its people, language, etc. Also, **Ser'bi·an** (sĕr'bē-ən).

sere (sir) *adj.* withered; dry.

ser"e·nade' (ser"ə-nād') *n.* an evening song of love.

se·rene' (sə-rēn') *adj.* **1,** tranquil; calm. **2,** clear. —**se·rene'ness,** *n.*

se·ren'i·ty (sə-ren'ə-tē) *n.* tranquillity; sereneness.

serf (sĕrf) *n.* a peasant attached to a feudal estate. —**serf'dom,** *n.*

serge (sėrj) *n.* a twilled worsted fabric.

ser'geant (sär'jənt) *n.* **1,** a non-commissioned officer, ranking above a corporal. **2,** a police or court officer. —**sergeant-at-arms,** an official appointed to maintain order, as in a court.

ser'i·al (sir'ė-əl) *adj.* **1,** published in installments. **2,** successive. —*n.* a serial story.

se'ri·al·ize (-īz') *v.t.* publish in installments.

se'ries (sir'ēz) *n.* a continued succession of similar things.

Serif

ser'if *n.* a short cross-line on a letter of type.

se'ri·ous (sir'ē-əs) *adj.* **1,** grave; solemn. **2,** in earnest. **3,** weighty; critical. —**se'ri·ous·ness,** *n.*

ser'mon (sėr'mən) *n.* **1,** a religious discourse. **2,** any admonitory speech. —**ser'mon·ize** (-īz') *v.t.* preach; moralize.

ser'pent (sėr'pənt) *n.* **1,** a snake. **2,** (*cap.*) Satan.

ser'pen·tine" (sėr'pən-tēn") *adj.* winding about; tortuous.

ser'rate (ser'it) *adj.* having sharp teeth. —**ser·ra'tion,** *n.*

se'rum (sir'əm) *n.* **1,** the clear liquid in the blood. **2,** immunized blood serum. —**se'rous,** *adj.*

serv'ant (sėr'vənt) *n.* one who serves, esp. a domestic employee.

serve (sėrv) *v.t.* **1,** attend or wait upon; work for. **2,** aid. **3,** (with *for*) be a substitute for. **4,** avail. **5,** (*Law*) give (a summons, etc.) to. **6,** (*Tennis*) put (the ball) in play. **7,** (of animals) mate with. **8,** supply. —*v.i.* **1,** act as a servant or waiter. **2,** suffice; be convenient. **3,** serve something.

serv'ice (sėr'vis) *n.* **1,** act or result of serving; duty performed or needs supplied. **2,** (often *pl.*) religious worship. **3,** a set of dishes, etc. —**ser'vice·a·ble,** *adj.* useful. —**service man,** a member of an armed force.

ser"vi·ette' (sėr"vė-et') *n.* a napkin.

ser'vile (sėr'vil) *adj.* menial; obsequious. —**ser·vil'i·ty,** *n.*

ser'vi·tor (sėr'vi-tər) *n.* an attendant; a waiter.

ser'vi·tude" (sėr'vi-tood") *n.* slavery.

ses'a·me (ses'ə-mė) *n.* a tropical herbaceous plant; its edible seed.

ses·qui- (ses'kwė) *pref.* one and a half.

ses'sion (sesh'ən) *n.* **1,** the sitting of a court, council, etc. **2,** one period in a series.

set *v.t.* [**set, set'ting**] **1,** put in a certain place or position; fix; establish. **2,** adjust. **3,** start; employ; assign. **4,** mount, as a gem. **5,** adapt to music. **6,** (with *down*) write. **7,** arrange (type) for printing. **8,** (with *forth*) express. —*v.i.* **1,** sink; settle. **2,** become fixed. **3,** (with *out* or *forth*) begin. —*n.* **1,** a related group; a collection. **2,** a number of persons customarily associated. **3,** a hardening. **4,** a tendency. **5,** build; carriage. **6,** a stage setting; scenery. **7,** a scoring unit, as in tennis. —*adj.* **1,** placed; fixed. **2,** obstinate. **3,** prescribed.

set'back" *n.* **1,** a reverse; a recession. **2,** a setting of part of a building behind a lower part.

set·tee' (se-tē') *n.* a small sofa; a bench with a back.

set'ter (set'ər) *n.* a kind of long-haired hunting dog.

set'ting *n.* **1,** environment; scene; scenery. **2,** a mounting, as for a jewel.

set'tle (set'əl) *v.t.* **1,** fix in position or condition; establish; decide. **2,** adjust, as a dispute. **3,** calm. **4,** colonize. **5,** clear of dregs. **6,** pay (a bill). —*v.i.* **1,** become fixed; come to rest. **2,** establish a permanent residence. **3,** become clear. **4,** sink. **5,** decide; arrange; agree. —*n.* a bench.

set'tle·ment *n.* **1,** act or result of settling; an adjustment; payment. **2,** a small colony. **3,** a welfare establishment.

set'tler (-lər) *n.* a colonizer.

set-'to' *n.* (*Colloq.*) a fight.

set'up" *n.* **1,** system. **2,** (*Slang*) a contest easy to win. **3,** ice, etc., for mixing a drink.

sev'en (sev'ən) *n. & adj.* the cardinal number between six and eight, expressed by 7.

sev'en·teen" (-tēn") *n. & adj.* seven plus ten; also expressed by 17. —**sev"en·teenth'** (-tēnth') *n. & adj.*

sev'enth (sev'ənth) *adj. & n.* the ordinal of seven, also written 7th; one of seven equal parts. —**seventh heaven,** bliss.

sev'en·ty (-tė) *n. & adj.* ten times seven; also expressed by 70. —**sev"en·ti·eth** (-tė-əth) *n. & adj.*

sev'er (sev'ər) *v.t.* separate; divide into parts; cut apart. —**sev'er·ance,** *n.*

sev·er·al (sev'ər-əl) *adj.* **1,** three or more, but not many. **2,** various. **3,** individual; separate. **4,** distinct. —*n.* a few.

se·vere' (si-vir') *adj.* **1,** serious or earnest; austere. **2,** rigorous; trying. **3,** harsh. **4,** sharp; distressing; extreme. —**se·ver'i·ty** (-ver'ə-tē) *n.*

sew (sō) *v.t. & i.* join or attach by means of a thread, wire, etc.

sew'age (soo'ij) *n.* waste matter.

sew'er (soo'ər) *n.* a conduit for carrying off waste water and refuse. —**sew'er·age,** *n.* a system of sewers.

sex (seks) *n.* **1,** the anatomical and physiological distinction between male and female. **2,** either males or females, considered collectively. —**sex appeal,** the quality of attracting amatory interest.

sex- *pref.* six.

Sextant

sex'tant (seks'tənt) *n.* **1,** one-sixth of a circle. **2,** an instrument used in navigation.

sex·tet' (seks-tet') *n.* a group of six, esp. musicians. Also, **sex·tette'.**

sex'ton (seks'tən) *n.* a minor official of a church.

sex'u·al (sek'shoo-əl) *adj.* **1,** pert. to sex. **2,** (*Colloq.*) pert. to carnal love. —**sex''u·al'i·ty** (-al'ə-tē) *n.*

sex'y *adj.* (*Slang*) concerned with or suggesting carnal love. —**sex'i·ness,** *n.*

shab'by (shab'ē) *adj.* **1,** seedy; (of *clothes*) much worn. **2,** mean; contemptible. —**shab'bi·ness,** *n.*

shack (shak) *n.* a rough cabin.

shack'le (shak'-əl) *n.* **1,** a fetter; hobble. **2,** a coupling device. **3,** the bar of a padlock. —*v.t.* **1,** chain with shackles. **2,** hamper.

shad *n.* an Amer. food fish.

Shackles

shade (shād) *n.* **1,** darkness caused by interception of rays of light. **2,** a shaded place. **3,** a dark area. **4,** a trace. **5,** a ghost. **6,** a screen against light. **7,** a gradation of color. —*v.t.* **1,** screen from light. **2,** obscure; darken.

shad'ing (shā'ding) *n.* **1,** a slight difference. **2,** application of shade.

shad'ow (shad'ō) *n.* **1,** the dark image of a body intercepting the light. **2,** shade. **3,** an inseparable companion. **4,** a spy. **5,** a phantom. —*v.t.* **1,** shade; cloud. **2,** trail; stay near. —**shad'ow·y,** *adj.*

shad'y (shā'dē) *adj.* **1,** affording shade. **2,** (*Colloq.*) of doubtful character. —**shad'i·ness,** *n.*

shaft (shäft) *n.* **1,** a long, slender, cylindrical body, as an arrow, spear handle, etc. **2,** a bar transmitting motion. **3,** passage, as in a mine, or for an elevator.

shag *v.t.* [**shagged, shag'ging**] roughen. —*n.* a rough surface; a coarse material.

shag'gy (shag'ē) *adj.* having rough hair or nap; unkempt. —**shag'gi·ness,** *n.*

shah (shä) *n.* king: the monarch of Iran.

shake (shāk) *v.t.* [**shook** (shuk), **shak'en, shak'ing**] **1,** cause to vibrate or tremble; agitate. **2,** loosen; weaken; cause to doubt. **3,** (with *down*) (*Slang*) extort money from. —*v.i.* be agitated; tremble; totter. —*n.* **1,** an act of shaking. **2,** (*pl.*) the ague. **3,** (*Colloq.*) an instant. **4,** a shaken drink.

shake'down'' *n.* **1,** preparation or conditioning, as of a new ship. **2,** (*Slang*) extortion. **3,** a makeshift bed, as of straw.

Shak'er *n.* a member of a celibate religious sect.

shake'up'' *n.* a reorganization.

shak'o (shā'kō) *n.* [*pl.* -**os**] a high, plumed, military hat.

shak'y *adj.* **1,** trembling. **2,** insecure; wavering. —**shak'i·ness,** *n.*

shale (shāl) *n.* a rock that splits readily into thin leaves.

shall (shal) *aux. v.* [*pret.* should (shud)] **1,** (first person) expressing the future: am or are going to or sure to. **2,** (second and third persons) must.

shal'lop (shal'əp) *n.* a light open boat.

shal·lot' (shə-lot') *n.* an onionlike vegetable.

shal'low (shal'ō) *adj.* **1,** not deep. **2,** superficial. —*n.* a shoal.

sham *adj.* counterfeit; pretended. —*n.* an imposture; make-believe; an imitation. —*v.i. & t.* [**shammed, sham'ming**] pretend; feign.

sham'ble (sham'bəl) *v.i.* walk awkwardly. —*n.* **1,** a shambling walk. **2,** (*pl.*) a slaughterhouse.

shame (shām) *n.* **1,** a remorseful consciousness of guilt. **2,** disgrace or dishonor; a cause of it. —*v.t.* **1,** make ashamed. **2,** disgrace. **3,** influence by reproach. —**shame'faced"**, *adj.* ashamed; showing shame. —**shame'ful**, *adj.* disgraceful. —**shame'less**, *adj.* overbold; conscienceless.

sham·poo' *v.t.* wash (the hair). —*n.* a washing of the hair; a preparation for it.

sham'rock" (sham'rok") *n.* a three-leaved plant, emblem of Ireland.

sham'us (shom'əs) *n.* (*Slang*) a private detective.

shang'hai (shang'hī) *v.t.* abduct and force to serve as a seaman.

shank *n.* **1,** the leg between the knee and the ankle. **2,** the part of a tool, etc., that connects the acting part with the handle. **3,** (*Colloq.*) the latter part, as, *shank of the evening.*

shan'tung *n.* a silk fabric.

shan'ty (shan'tē) *n.* a rough or flimsy hut or house.

shape (shāp) *n.* **1,** form; outward contour; appearance. **2,** proper form. **3,** condition. —*v.t.* **1,** give form to; create. **2,** adapt. **3,** express. —*v.i.* **1,** take form. **2,** (with *up*) come out; reach proper form. —**shape'ly**, *adj.* pleasingly formed.

share (shār) *n.* **1,** a portion; an allotted part. **2,** a unit of stock in a corporation. **3,** a plow blade. —*v.t.* **1,** divide; apportion. **2,** have jointly. —*v.i.* **1,** partake. **2,** give a portion to others.

share'crop"per *n.* a farmer who divides the crop with his landlord.

share'hold"er *n.* stockholder.

shark (shärk) *n.* **1,** a large and ferocious marine fish. **2,** a predatory person. **3,** (*Slang*) an expert.

shark'skin" *n.* a heavy suiting fabric.

sharp (shärp) *adj.* **1,** having a fine cutting edge or point. **2,** well-defined; distinct. **3,** abrupt; angular. **4,** keenly affecting a sense: pungent, shrill, keenly cold, etc. **5,** acute; keen. **6,** barely honest. **7,** (*Music*) of a note, marked (♯), raised a half tone. **8,** (*Music*) above the intended pitch. —*adv.* sharply; quickly; exactly. —*n.* **1,** (*Music*) a tone raised half a step. **2,** a sharper. **3,** (*Colloq.*) an expert. —**sharp'ness**, *n.*

sharp'en (shär'pən) *v.t. & i.* make or become sharp. —**sharp'en·er**, *n.* a tool or machine for sharpening an edge or point.

sharp'er *n.* a swindler.

sharp'shoot"er *n.* **1,** an expert marksman. **2,** a sharper.

shat'ter (shat'ər) *v.i. & t.* **1,** break in pieces. **2,** disorder; impair.

shave (shāv) *v.t.* **1,** slice with a keen instrument. **2,** make bare. **3,** cut down gradually. **4,** come very close to. —*v.i.* remove hair with a razor. —*n.* **1,** an act of shaving. **2,** (*Colloq.*) a narrow escape.

shav'er *n.* **1,** one who shaves. **2,** (*Colloq.*) a youngster.

shave'tail" *n.* (*Slang*) a newly-appointed second lieutenant.

shav'ing *n.* a thin slice, esp. of wood.

shawl (shâl) *n.* a loose covering for the shoulders.

shay (shā) *n.* a light carriage.

she (shē) *pron.* [*poss.* **her** (hẽr), hers; *obj.* **her**] **1,** the third person, sing., fem., nominative; a female person other than the speaker and the person addressed. **2,** any female.

sheaf (shēf) *n.* [*pl.* **sheaves** (shēvz)] a bundle, as of grain, papers, etc.

shear (shir) *v.t.* **1,** clip or cut. **2,** remove by clipping, as fleece. —**shears**, *n. sing. & pl.* large scissors.

sheath (shēth) *n.* a case or covering; a scabbard.

sheathe (shēth) *v.t.* put into a sheath; enclose; cover.

she·bang' (shə-bang') *n.* (*Slang*) establishment; outfit.

shed *v.t.* [**shed**, **shed'ding**] **1,** throw off, molt, or cause to flow off. **2,** disperse, as light. —*v.i.* cast or let fall a covering, etc. —*n.* a rude structure for shelter or storage.

sheen (shēn) *n.* luster.

sheep (shēp) *n. sing. & pl.* **1,** a ruminant mammal, valued for its flesh, skin, fleece, etc. **2,** a timid person. **3,** ignorant imitators. —**sheep'ish**, *adj.* embarrassed.

sheep'fold" *n.* a pen or shelter for sheep.

sheep'skin" *n.* **1,** sheep's fur; a garment made of it. **2,** parchment; (*Colloq.*) a diploma.

sheer (shir) *adj.* **1,** very thin; diaphanous. **2,** unmixed; absolute. **3,** precipitous. —*adv.* **1,** absolutely; quite. **2,** steeply. —*v.i.* (with *off*) swerve.

sheet (shēt) *n.* **1,** a rectangular piece of cloth bedding. **2,** a broad, flat, very thin piece of anything. **3,** a newspaper. **4,** an expanse or surface. **5,** a rope fastened to a sail. —**sheet'ing**, *n.*

sheik (shēk) *n.* **1,** an Arab chief. **2,** (*Slang*) a bold lover.

shek'el (shek'əl) *n.* a silver coin of the ancient Jews.

shelf *n.* [*pl.* **shelves**] **1,** a horizontal plank for supporting objects. **2,** a ledge. **3,** a reef.

shell (shel) *n.* **1,** a hard outer case or covering. **2,** something flimsy, hollow, or concave. **3,** a light racing boat. **4,** a projectile; a cartridge. —*v.t.* **1,** remove, or take out of, the shell. **2,** bombard. —**shell game,** a swindling game. —**shell out,** hand over; pay. —**shell shock,** a psychoneurosis caused by battle strain.

shel·lac' (shə-lak') *n.* a purified plastic resin; a varnish made from it. —*v.t.* paint with shellac.

Shellfish

shell'fish" *n.* an aquatic animal having a shell, as an oyster, lobster, etc.

shel'ter (shel'tər) *n.* whatever shields or protects; a refuge; a roofed place. —*v.t. & i.* house; protect.

shelve (shelv) *v.t.* **1,** put on a shelf. **2,** put aside; put off.

she·nan'i·gan (shə-nan'ə-gən) *n.* (*Colloq.*) foolery; a prank.

shep'herd (shep'ərd) *n.* **1,** a sheepherder. **2,** a pastor; (*cap.*) Jesus Christ. **3,** a breed of dog. —**shep'herd·ess,** *n.fem.*

sher'bet (shêr'bət) *n.* an ice containing milk.

sher'iff (sher'if) *n.* the chief lawenforcement officer of a county.

sher'ry (sher'ē) *n.* a strong wine of southern Spain.

Shet'land (shet'lənd) *n.* **1,** a small, rough-coated pony. **2,** a soft, loosely-twisted wool.

shew (shō) *v.* (*Brit.*) show.

shib'bo·leth" (shib'ə-leth") *n.* a password; a slogan.

shield (shēld) *n.* **1,** a broad plate of defensive armor. **2,** anything that protects. **3,** an escutcheon. —*v.t.* protect; screen.

shift *v.t.* transfer to another place or person; change; exchange. —*v.i.* **1,** change place, position, direction, etc. **2,** alter. **3,** get along. —*n.* **1,** a change; a turning. **2,** a group of workmen; the time they work. **3,** an expedient; a resource. —**shift'less,** *adj.* lazy. —**shift'y,** *adj.* tricky; evasive.

shil·le'lagh (shə-lā'lē) *n.* (*Ireland*) a cudgel.

shil'ling (shil'ing) *n.* a Brit. monetary unit, 1/20 of a pound sterling.

shil'ly-shal'ly (shil'ē-shal'ē) *v.i.* act in an irresolute manner.

shim'mer (shim'ər) *v.i.* shine with a tremulous light. —**shim'mer·y,** *adj.*

shim'my (shim'ē) *n.* **1,** abnormal vibration; jiggling. **2,** a jazz dance. **3,** (*Colloq.*) a chemise.

shin *n.* **1,** the front of the leg from knee to ankle. **2,** the tibia. —*v.t. & i.* [**shinned, shin'ning**] [Also, **shin'ny**] climb by hugging with arms and legs.

shin'bone" *n.* the tibia.

shin'dig" *n.* (*Slang*) a dance or party.

shine (shīn) *v.t.* **1,** cause to gleam. **2,** polish. —*v.i.* [*pret. & p.p.* **shone** (shōn)] **1,** glow; appear bright; gleam. **2,** excel. —*n.* **1,** light; luster. **2,** fair weather. —**shin'y,** *adj.*

shin'er *n.* **1,** a minnow. **2,** (*Slang*) a black eye.

shin'gle (shing'gəl) *n.* **1,** a thin piece of wood, etc. used as roofing. **2,** closely bobbed hair. **3,** a small signboard. **4,** a gravelly beach. —*v.t.* roof with shingles.

shin'gles (shing'gəlz) *n.* an inflammatory skin disease.

shin'ny (shin'ē) *n.* a game similar to hockey. —*v.i.* (with *up*) climb.

Shin'to (shin'tō) *n.* a Jap. religion; ancestor worship.

ship *n.* **1,** a large vessel, usually seagoing. **2,** an aircraft. —*v.t.* [**shipped, ship'ping**] **1,** put or take on board a ship or boat. **2,** send or transport. —*v.t.* embark.

ship'board" *n.* any deck or interior part of a ship.

ship'build"ing *n.* construction of ships.

ship'load" *n.* a full load for a (particular) ship.

ship'mate" *n.* a fellow sailor.

ship'ment *n.* **1,** act or result of shipping. **2,** a quantity of goods shipped.

ship'per (ship'ər) *n.* one who ships goods; consignor.

ship'ping *n.* **1,** the business of transporting goods. **2,** ships collectively.

ship'shape" *adj.* in good order.

ship'wreck" *n.* **1,** the sinking or destruction of a ship. **2,** ruin. —*v.t.* ruin.

ship'yard *n.* a place where ships are built.

shire (shīr) *n.* a county.

shirk (shĕrk) *v.t. & i.* evade work, responsibility, etc. —**shirk'er,** *n.*

shirr (shĕr) *v.t.* 1, draw up (a fabric). 2, bake (eggs).

shirt (shĕrt) *n.* a garment for the upper body. —**shirt'ing,** *n.*

shiv'a·ree (shiv'ə-rē') *n.* a mock serenade of newlyweds.

shiv'er (shiv'ər) *v.i.* tremble or quiver with cold or fear. —*n.* shake.

shoal (shōl) *n.* 1, a sandbank in the water. 2, a group of fish. 3, a crowd.

shoat (shōt) *n.* a young pig.

shock (shok) *n.* 1, a violent collision. 2, any sudden, violent impact. 3, a condition of prostration; a stroke. 4, the sensory impression caused by an electric current. 5, a group of sheaves of grain in a field. 6, a thick mass, as of hair. —*v.t.* 1, affect with a shock; surprise; outrage; horrify. 2, stack (grain). —**shock absorber,** a device for retarding rebound. —**shock therapy,** treatment of certain diseases by inducing electric or other shock. —**shock troops,** experienced assault troops.

shock'ing *adj.* causing surprise, consternation, or indignation.

shod *v.* pret. & p.p. of **shoe.**

shod'dy (shod'ē) *n.* 1, a low quality fabric; anything inferior. 2, sham. —*adj.* 1, inferior. 2, sham; ungenerous. —**shod'di·ness,** *n.*

shoe (shoo) *n.* 1, a covering for the human foot. 2, a horseshoe. 3, an outer covering or housing, as a tire. —*v.t.* [pret. & p.p. shod] put shoes on.

shoe'bill' *n.* an African wading bird.

shoe'horn' *n.* a device used to slip one's feet into shoes.

shoe'lace' *n.* shoestring.

shoe'mak'er *n.* cobbler.

shoe'string' *n.* 1, a lace for tying a shoe. 2, a very small capital, in business.

shoe'tree' *n.* a form for keeping shoes in shape.

shone (shōn) *v.* pret. & p.p. of **shine.**

shoo *interj.* begone!

shoot *v.t.* [pret. & p.p. shot] 1, hit, wound, or kill with a missile from a weapon. 2, discharge (a weapon). 3, send out or forth. 4, traverse rapidly. 5, take a picture of. —*v.i.* 1, discharge a missile; fire. 2, hunt. 3, dart forth or along. 4, be emitted; sprout. 5, (with *up*) grow rapidly. —*n.* 1, a shooting party. 2, a sprout. —**shooting iron** (*Slang*) a firearm. —**shooting star,** a meteor.

shop *n.* 1, a store. 2, a workroom; a factory; (*Colloq.*) an office. 3, one's own business. —*v.i.* [shopped, shop'ping] visit stores as a customer.

shop'keep'er *n.* a tradesman.

shop'lift'er *n.* one who steals from shop counters.

shop'per (shop'ər) *n.* 1, one who shops. 2, one sent to buy from a competitor, for comparison of goods.

shop'worn' *adj.* deteriorated by display.

shore (shōr) *n.* 1, land adjacent to water. 2, a prop. —*v.t.* (with *up*) prop. —**shor'ing,** *n.* props.

shorn (shōrn) *v.* p.p. of **shear.**

short (shôrt) *adj.* 1, not long; not tall. 2, brief; concise. 3, deficient; (with *of*) insufficiently supplied with. 4, of vowels, not prolonged in utterance. 5, of stocks, not possessed at time of sale. 6, crumbling readily, as pastry. 7, curt. —*adv.* 1, briefly. 2, abruptly. 3, insufficiently. —*n.* 1, whatever is short. 2, (*pl.*) short trousers or drawers. —**short circuit,** a low-resistance electrical connection, usually accidental. —**short cut,** a shorter route or method. —**short shrift,** little delay or mercy. —**short wave,** a radio wave sixty meters or less in length.

short'age (-ij) *n.* deficiency.

short'bread' *n.* a rich cake made short with butter.

short'cake' *n.* a cake or biscuit covered with fruit.

short-"change' *v.t.* (*Colloq.*) give inadequate change to; cheat.

short'com'ing *n.* a failing.

short'en *v.t.* make shorter.

short'en·ing *n.* fat used in baking.

short'hand' *n.* a system of taking notes.

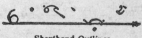

Shorthand Outlines

short'hand'ed *adj.* having too few workers.

short'horn' *n.* one of a breed of cattle.

short'lived' (-līvd') *adj.* of brief life or duration.

short'sight'ed *adj.* 1, nearsighted. 2, lacking foresight; not provident. —**short'sight'ed·ness,** *n.*

short'stop" *n.* (*Baseball*) an infield position.

short-'wind"ed (-win"did) *adj.* tending to be out of breath after little exertion. **—short-'wind"ed-ness,** *n.*

shot *n.* **1,** an act of shooting; range. **2,** small pellets. **3,** one who shoots. **4,** a move or stroke in a game. **5,** (*Slang*) a guess. **6,** (*Slang*) a drink; one injection of a drug. **7,** a photograph. **—v.** pret. & p.p. of *shoot.*

shot'gun" *n.* a gun firing charges of small shot. **—shotgun wedding** (*Jocular*) a wedding forced upon the bridegroom.

shot-'put" *n.* a contest at hurling a heavy metal ball.

should (shd) *aux. v.* **1,** pret. or subjunctive of *shall.* **2,** ought to.

shoul'der (shōl'dər) *n.* **1,** a part of the body from the side of the neck to the upper joint of the arm (or foreleg). **2,** a ledge. **3,** the unpaved side of a road. **—v.t.** & *i.* **1,** carry on, or as on, the shoulder. **2,** push with the shoulder.

shoul'der-blade" *n.* a flat bone in the shoulder; scapula.

shout (showt) *v.i.* & *t.* **1,** cry out. **2,** laugh noisily. **—n.** a loud cry.

shove (shuv) *v.t.* **1,** push along a surface. **2,** jostle. **—v.i. 1,** push. **2,** (with *off*) depart. **—n.** a push.

shov'el (shuv'əl) *n.* a long-handled implement with a broad scoop. *v.t.* & *i.* transfer with a shovel.

show (shō) *v.t.* [*p.p.* **shown** (shōn) or **showed**] **1,** allow to be seen; exhibit; indicate. **2,** instruct; guide. **3,** (with *up*) expose the faults of. **—v.i. 1,** be seen; appear. **2,** finish third in a horse race. **3,** (with *off*) perform ostentatiously. **4,** (with *up*) appear; stand out. **—n. 1,** a theatrical performance. **2,** an exhibition. **3,** ostentatious display. **4,** (*Colloq.*) a chance.

show'boat" *n.* a river boat used as a traveling theater.

show'down" *n.* a final disclosure or test.

show'er (show'ər) *n.* **1,** a light rain; a spray. **2,** a large number. **3,** a bestowal of gifts. **4,** a shower bath. **—v.t. 1,** wet copiously. **2,** bestow or scatter abundantly. **—v.i. 1,** rain. **2,** take a shower bath. **—show'er-y,** *adj.* raining intermittently.

show'man (-mən) *n.* [*pl.* **-men**] one who puts on a show. **—show'-man-ship,** *n.*

shown (shōn) *v.* pret. & p.p. of *show.*

show-'off" *n.* one given to ostentation.

show'room" *n.* a room for exhibition of goods for sale.

show'y *adj.* **1,** imposing. **2,** gaudy. **—show'i-ness,** *n.*

shrank *v.* pret. of *shrink.*

shrap'nel (shrap'nəl) *n.* a bursting projectile that showers missiles.

shred *v.t.* [**shred'ded, -ding**] tear or cut into small pieces or strips. **—n. 1,** a small strip. **2,** a particle.

shrew (shroo) *n.* **1,** a scolding woman. **2,** a small mouselike animal. **—shrew'ish,** *adj.*

shrewd (shrood) *adj.* astute; quickwitted. **—shrewd'ness,** *n.*

shriek (shrēk) *n.* a shrill outcry or utterance. **—v.t.** & *i.* utter such a cry.

shrift *n.* a shriving. **—short shrift,** disposition without delay.

shrike (shrīk) *n.* the butcherbird.

Shrike

shrill (shril) *adj.* sharp, high, and piercing in sound. **—v.t.** & *i.* utter (such a sound). **—shrill'ness,** *n.*

shrimp *n.* **1,** an edible, long-tailed crustacean. **2,** a small person.

shrine (shrīn) *n.* a consecrated or hallowed place.

shrink *v.i.* [**shrank, shrunk, shrink'ing**] **1,** contract spontaneously; diminish; shrivel. **2,** draw back; recoil. **—v.t.** cause to contract; lessen. **—shrink'age,** *n.*

shrive (shrīv) *v.t.* & *i.* [**shrived or shrove, shriv'en**] grant absolution to; impose penance on; confess.

shriv'el (shriv'əl) *v.t.* & *i.* contract; wrinkle; wither.

shroud (shrowd) *n.* **1,** a burial cloth. **2,** something that envelops or conceals. **3,** (*pl.*) (*Naut.*) strong guy ropes. **—v.t.** cover; obscure.

Shrove Tuesday (shrōv) the day before Lent.

shrub *n.* a woody plant smaller than a tree. **—shrub'ber-y,** *n.*

shrug *v.t.* & *i.* [**shrugged, shrug'-ging**] raise and contract the shoulders, expressing doubt, indifference, etc. **—n.** such a gesture.

shrunk *v.* p.p. of *shrink.*

shrunk'en *adj.* having shrunk.

shuck (shuk) *n.* **1,** a husk or pod, as of corn. **2,** a shell. **—v.t.** remove the husk or shell from. **—shucks,** *interj.* expressing deprecation.

shud'der (shud'ər) *n.* a convulsive tremor of the body, as from horror, etc. **—v.i.** tremble violently.

shuf'fle (shuf'əl) *v.t. & i.* 1, move with scraping feet. 2, mix. 3, shift evasively. —*n.* an act of shuffling.

shuf'fle-board" *n.* a game played by pushing disks toward marked squares on a board or court.

shun *v.t.* [**shunned**, **shun'ning**] keep away from; avoid; refrain from.

shunt *v.t.* 1, turn aside. 2, shift (as a train). 3, (with *off*) relegate; foist. —*n.* a shift or shifting.

shut *v.t.* [**shut**, **shut'ting**] 1, close; bring together. 2, (with *in* or *up*) confine; prevent access to. 3, (with *out*) exclude; prevent from scoring. —*v.i.* 1, become closed; close. 2, (with *down*) discontinue. 3, (with *up*) (*Colloq.*) stop talking. —*adj.* closed.

shut'ter (-ər) *n.* one who or that which shuts, esp. a hinged panel for a window, a device for a camera lens, a movable slide, etc.

shut'tle (shut'əl) *n.* 1, a device for passing thread in a loom or sewing machine. 2, a train running back and forth for a short distance. —*v.t. & i.* move to and fro.

shut'tle-cock" *n.* a cork with a tail of feathers, used in *badminton* and *battledore* and *shuttlecock*.

shy (shī) *adj.* 1, timid; bashful. 2, cautious; wary. 3, scant; short. —*v.i.* start back in fear. —*v.t.* throw. —*n.* a start, as in fear. —**shy'ness**, *n.*

Shy'lock (shī'lok) *n.* (often *l.c.*) a usurious moneylender.

shy'ster (shī'stər) *n.* a lawyer without professional honor.

si (sē) *n.* the seventh tone of a musical scale. Also, **ti** (tē).

Si'a·mese' (sī'ə-mēz') *adj. & n.* pert. to Siam (Thailand), its people, language, etc.; Thai. —**Siamese twins**, twins born with joined bodies.

sib *n.* a kinsman.

sib'i·lant (sib'ə-lənt) *adj.* having a hissing sound. —*n.* s or z. —**sib'i·lance**, *n.*

sib'ling *n.* a full brother or sister.

sib'yl (sib'il) *n.* a prophetess.

sic (sik) *adv.* (quoted) exactly as written, even though incorrect.

sick (sik) *adj.* 1, ill. 2, nauseated. 3, depressed. 4, disgusted. 5, (with *of*) satiated. —*n.* sick people. —*v.t.* set upon, esp. of a dog. —**sick bay**, a ship's hospital. —**sick'ness**, *n.*

sick'en (-ən) *v.t. & i.* make or become sick. —**sick'en·ing**, *adj.* causing nausea or disgust.

sick'le (sik'əl) *n.* a short-handled scythe with a curved blade.

sick'ly *adj.* 1, unhealthy in fact

or appearance. 2, mawkish. 3, feeble. —**sick'li·ness**, *n.*

side (sīd) *n.* 1, a terminal surface or line. 2, either half, as of the body, right or left. 3, an aspect; a point of view. 4, a position in a lawsuit, game, etc. —*adj.* being on, coming from, or aimed toward, one side. —*v.i.* (with *with*) ally oneself.

side'board" *n.* a piece of dining-room furniture.

side'burns" *n.pl.* short side whiskers.

side'car" *n.* 1, a car attached to a motorcycle. 2, a cocktail made with brandy and Cointreau.

side'light" *n.* 1, an incidental aspect of anything. 2, a narrow window beside a door.

side line *n.* an additional business or line of merchandise. 2, (*Sports*) a side boundary.

side'long" *adj.* to the side; sidewise. —*adv.* sidewise.

si·de're·al (sī-dir'ē-əl) *adj.* pert. to the stars; based on fixed stars.

side show an incidental attraction, as at a circus.

side'slip" *n.* of a banked airplane, a sliding sideways and down.

side'split"ting *adj.* uproariously funny.

side'step" *v.t. & i.* evade.

side'swipe" *v.t.* strike glancingly.

side'track" *v.t.* 1, move to a siding. 2, divert

side'walk" *n.* the paved path for foot traffic beside a street.

side'ways" *adj. & adv.* to the side; from one side. Also, **side'wise"**.

sid'ing (sī'ding) *n.* 1, a track for idle railroad cars. 2, boards for the sides of a frame house.

si'dle (sī'dəl) *v.i.* move obliquely; edge along. —*n.* this movement.

siege (sēj) *n.* 1, a prolonged surrounding of a place by an enemy. 2, a long illness. —**siege guns**, artillery used to bombard a fortress.

si·en'na (sē-en'ə) *n.* a brown pigment or color.

si·er'ra (sē-er'ə) *n.* mountains in a succession of peaks.

si·es'ta (sē-es'tə) *n.* a midday nap.

sieve (siv) *n.* 1, a straining pan. 2, a leakage of information.

sift *v.t.* 1, separate the large from the small. 2, scrutinize.

sigh (sī) *v.i. & t.* breathe out audibly, expressing disappointment. —*n.* an act or sound of sighing.

sight (sīt) *n.* **1,** the faculty of vision; visual perception. **2,** point of view. **3,** a coming into view. **4,** something seen; something unusual (interesting, distressing) to see. **5,** (*Colloq.*) a surprising number. **6,** an aid to aiming. **7,** aim. —*v.t.* get sight of; aim at. —*v.t.* get sight of; aim at. —**sight'ly,** *adj.* pleasing to the eye.

sight'see'ing *n.* brief visiting of places of interest. —**sight'see'** (*Colloq.*) *v.i.* —**sight'se'er,** *n.*

sig'ma (sig'mə) *n.* the eighteenth letter of the Greek alphabet (Σ, σ, s).

sign (sīn) *n.* **1,** a mark or symbol. **2,** a display board. **3,** a gesture. **4,** a symptom. **5,** a trace. —*v.t.* **1,** affix a signature to; write (one's name). **2,** indicate by sign. —*v.i.* **1,** write one's signature. **2,** (with *off*) end.

sig'nal (sig'nəl) *n.* **1,** a sign carrying a message, often in code. **2,** a radio wave. —*adj.* **1,** serving as a signal. **2,** eminent; conspicuous. —*v.t. & i.* make a signal (to). —**sig'nal·ize"** (-īz") *v.t.* indicate distinctly.

sig'na·to·ry (sig'nə-tôr-ē) *n.* one who signs. —*adj.* signing.

sig'na·ture (sig'nə-tyûr) *n.* **1,** a person's name in his own handwriting. **2,** any distinguishing sign. **3,** a folded, printed sheet.

sign'board" *n.* a large mounting for advertising signs.

sig'net (sig'nət) *n.* a small seal.

sig·nif'i·cance (sig-nif'i-kəns) *n.* **1,** the real or implied meaning. **2,** consequence. **3,** expressiveness. —**sig·nif'i·cant,** *adj.*

sig'ni·fy" (sig'ni-fī") *v.t.* mean; suggest. —**sig"ni·fi·ca'tion,** *n.*

si'gnor (sē'nyôr) *n.* (*Ital.*) a gentleman; Mr.; sir. Also, **si·gno're** [*pl.* -ri]. —**si·gno'ra, si"gno·ri'na** (-rē'nä) *n. fem.*

sign'post" *n.* a post bearing a sign or signs.

si'lage (sī'lij) *n.* fodder stored in a silo.

si'lence (sī'ləns) *n.* **1,** the absence of sound. **2,** abstention from speech or noise. **3,** absence of mention. **4,** secrecy. —*v.t.* restrain from making sound or speech. —**si'lenc·er,** *n.* a device to silence a firearm.

si'lent (sī'lənt) *adj.* **1,** making no sound. **2,** tacit. —**silent partner,** an inactive partner.

sil"hou·ette' (sil"ō-et') *n.* **1,** an outline drawing. **2,** a two-dimensional outline, as of a ship.

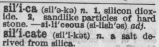

Silhouette

sil'i·ca (sil'ə-kə) *n.* **1,** silicon dioxide. **2,** sandlike particles of hard stone. —**si·li'ceous** (si-lish'əs) *adj.*

sil'i·cate (sil'i-kət) *n.* a salt derived from silica.

sil'i·con (sil'i-kən) *n.* a crystalline chemical element, no. 14, symbol Si.

sil'i·co'sis (sil'i-kō'sis) *n.* a disease caused by inhaling stone dust.

silk *n.* a fine soft fiber, produced by the silkworm; a thread or fabrics made from it. —**silk'en, silk'y,** *adj.* —**silk-"stock'ing,** *adj.* aristocratic.

silk'worm" *n.* a moth larva from whose cocoon silk is spun.

sill (sil) *n.* a horizontal foundation, as of a door.

sil'ly (sil'ē) *adj.* **1,** foolish; witless. **2,** ridiculous. —**sil'li·ness,** *n.*

si'lo (sī'lō) *n.* an airtight storehouse for grain, etc.

silt *n.* earthy sediment.

sil'ver (sil'vər) *n. & adj.* **1,** a precious metallic chemical element, no. 47, symbol Ag. **2,** silver coin; money. **3,** silver tableware. **4,** a lustrous, grayish-white color. —**sil'ver·y,** *adj.*

silver fox a fox with black, silver-gray tipped fur; the fur.

sil'ver·smith" *n.* a craftsman who makes articles of silver.

sil'ver·ware" *n.* tableware and dishes of silver.

sim'i·an (sim'ē-ən) *adj.* pert. to an ape or monkey. —*n.* monkey or ape.

sim'i·lar (sim'ə-lər) *adj.* resembling. —**sim"i·lar'i·ty** (-lar'ē-tē) *n.*

sim'i·le" (sim'ə-lē") *n.* a comparison, as a figure of speech.

si·mil'i·tude" (si-mil'i-tood") *n.* **1,** resemblance. **2,** a comparison.

sim'mer (sim'ər) *v.i. & t.* continue in a state just below the boiling point. —*n.* this state of heat.

si"mon-pure' (sī"mən-pyûr') *adj.* genuine.

si'mo·ny (sī'mə-nē) *n.* the selling of ecclesiastical offices, indulgences, etc.

si·moom' *n.* a hot wind.

simp *n.* (*Slang*) a fool.

sim'per (sim'pər) *v.i. & t.* smile or say in a silly manner.

sim'ple (sim'pəl) *adj.* **1,** elementary; not complicated. **2,** plain; not elaborate. **3,** pure; absolute. **4,** unaffected; unassuming. **5,** insignificant. **6,** humble. **7,** easily deceived; silly.

sim'ple-mind'ed *adj.* foolish.

sim'ple·ton (-tən) *n.* a fool.

---

sim·plic'i·ty (sim-plis'ə-tē) *n.* condition of being simple.

sim'pli·fy' (sim'pli-fī") *v.t.* make easier or less complex. —**sim"pli·fi·ca'tion,** *n.*

sim'u·late' (sim'yə-lāt") *v.t.* 1, pretend. 2, imitate; resemble. —**sim"u·la'tion,** *n.*

si"mul·ta·ne·ous (sī"məl-tā'nē-əs) *adj.* existing, occurring, or operating at the same time. —**si"mul·ta'ne·ous·ness,** *n.*

sin *n.* 1, a transgression of the law of God. 2, a serious fault; an error. —*v.i.* [**sinned, sin'ning**] commit a sin. —**sin'ful,** *adj.* —**sin'ner,** *n.*

since (sins) *adv.* 1, from then till now. 2, subsequently. 3, before now; ago. —*prep.* throughout all the time, or at some time, following. —*conj.* 1, from the time when; during the time after. 2, because.

sin·cere' (sin-sir') *adj.* free from falsehood, pretense, or deceit. —**sin·cer'i·ty** (-sĕr'ə-tē) *n.*

si'ne·cure" (sī'nə-kyūr") *n.* an easy job.

sin'ew (sin'ū) *n.* 1, a tendon. 2, strength; vigor. 3, a mainstay. —**sin'ew·y,** *adj.* 1, strong. 2, vigorous. 3, stringy.

sing *v.i.* [**sang, sung, sing'ing**] 1, utter words or sounds musically. 2, murmur, whistle, etc. —*v.t.* utter musically; chant.

singe (sinj) *v.t.* burn superficially.

sin'gle (sing'gəl) *adj.* 1, pert. to one person or thing; individual. 2, alone; detached. 3, unmarried. —*v.t.* (with *out*) select individually. —*n.* 1, that which is single. 2, (*Baseball*) a one-base hit. 3, (*pl.*) (*Tennis*) a contest between two players. —**sin'gle·ness,** *n.*

sin'gle-breast'ed (-bres'tid) *adj.* (of a coat or vest) overlapping only enough to allow fastening.

single file a line of people or things, one behind the other.

sin'gle-hand'ed *adj. & adv.* 1, unaided. 2, done with one hand.

sin'gle-mind'ed *adj.* undeviating. —**sin'gle-mind'ed·ness,** *n.*

sin'gle·ton (-tən) *n.* (*Card Games*) a holding of one card in a suit.

sin'gly (sing'glē) *adv.* 1, separately; individually. 2, one at a time.

sing'song" *adj.* monotonously rhythmical.

sin'gu·lar (sing'gū-lər) *adj.* 1, unusual. 2, eccentric. 3, (*Gram.*) denoting or relating to one person or thing. —**sin'gu·lar'i·ty** (-lar'ə-tē) *n.*

sin'is·ter (sin'is-tər) *adj.* 1, malicious; harmful; ominous. 2, on the left side.

sink *v.i.* [**sank, sunk, sink'ing**] 1, fall or decline; settle. 2, become submerged. 3, incline downward. 4, decrease. —*v.t.* 1, force downward. 2, place by excavation. 3, diminish. 4, suppress; overwhelm. —*n.* 1, a basin, esp. in a kitchen; a drain. 2, a low area. —**sink'a·ble,** *adj.*

sink'er *n.* 1, a weight on a fishing line. 2, (*Slang*) a doughnut.

Si·no- (sī-nō-) *pref.* Chinese.

sin'u·ous (sin'ū-əs) *adj.* 1, full of curves; winding. 2, devious. —**sin"u·os'i·ty, sin'u·ous·ness,** *n.*

si'nus (sī'nəs) *n.* a cavity or recess, esp. in the skull. —**si"nus·i'tis,** *n.* inflammation of the sinuses.

Sioux (soo) *adj. & n.sing. & pl.* pert. to a tribe of No. Amer. Indians.

sip *v.t. & i.* [**sipped, sip'ping**] drink little by little. —*n.* a small quantity sipped.

si'phon (sī'fən) *n.* 1, a bent tube used to draw a liquid over an elevation. 2, a bottle for aerated water. —*v.t.* draw off with a siphon.

Siphon

sip'per (sip'ər) *n.* a tube for sipping.

sir (sĕr) *n.* 1, a respectful term of address to a man. 2, (*cap.*) the title of a knight or baronet.

sire (sīr) *n.* 1, a father; a male parent. 2, a term of address to a sovereign. —*v.t.* beget.

si'ren (sī'rən) *n.* 1, a mythical alluring sea nymph. 2, an alluring and dangerous woman. 3, a device for producing a whistle; its sound.

sir'loin (sĕr'loin) *n.* a cut of beef.

si·roc'co (sə-rok'ō) *n.* a hot southeast wind from N. Afr.

sir'up *n.* syrup.

si'sal (sī'səl) *n.* a hemplike fiber taken from the agave.

sis'sy (sis'ē) *n.* (*Colloq.*) an effeminate boy.

sis'ter (sis'tər) *n.* 1, a female relative having the same parents as another. 2, a fellow person, female.

sis'ter·hood" *n.* 1, state of being a sister or sisters. 2, an association of women.

sis'ter-in-law" *n.* [*pl.* **sis'ters-**] 1, the sister of one's spouse. 2, the wife of one's brother.

sis'ter·ly *adj.* befitting a sister. —**sis'ter·li·ness,** *n.*

sit *v.i.* [**sat, sit'ting**] 1, take a posture with back erect, body bent

at the hips; be seated. **2,** perch. **3,** remain. **4,** be located; be in office; convene. —**sit′ter,** n. a part-time nurse for children. —**sit′ting,** n. the act or period of sitting; session. —**sit-down strike,** occupation of an employer's premises by strikers.

site (sīt) n. location.

sit′u·ate″ (sich′ū-āt″) v.t. place in a particular place. —adj. located.

sit″u·a′tion (sich″ū-ā′shən) n. **1,** location. **2,** condition. **3,** a job.

six (siks) n. & adj. the cardinal number between five and seven, expressed by 6.

six′pence (-pens) n. a Brit. coin worth six pennies. —**six′pen″ny,** adj.

six-′shoot″er n. (Colloq.) a revolver, esp. of .45 caliber.

six·teen′ (-tēn′) n. & adj. ten plus six, also expressed by 16. —**six·teenth′** (-tēnth′) adj. & n.

sixth (siksth) adj. & n. the ordinal of six, also written 6th; one of six equal parts. —**sixth sense,** intuition.

six′ty (-tē) n. & adj. ten times six, also expressed by 60. —**six′ti·eth** (-tē-əth) adj. & n.

size (sīz) n. **1,** bulk; volume; extent. **2,** a standard measure for clothes, etc. **3,** a gluey substance for bonding or glazing, as starch. —v.t. **1,** (with up) estimate. **2,** starch, glaze, etc. —**siz′a·ble,** adj. fairly large. —**siz′ing,** n. material for glazing, etc.

siz′zle (siz′əl) [**siz′zled, siz′zling**] v.i. **1,** sputter. **2,** (Colloq.) be very hot. —n. a sputtering sound.

skate (skāt) n. **1,** a steel runner for gliding; a shoe or attachment with small wheels (roller skate). **3,** a fish of the ray family. —v.i. glide or roll on skates.

ske·dad′dle (ski-dad′əl) v.i.(Slang) run away.

skein (skān) n. a coiled length of yarn or thread.

skel′e·ton (skel′ə-tən) n. **1,** the assemblage of bones of the body. **2,** an inner framework. **3,** an outline. —adj. —**skel′e·tal,** adj.

skep′tic (skep′tik) n. one inclined to doubt. Also, **scep′tic.** —**skep′ti·cal,** adj. doubting; incredulous.

skep′ti·cism (skep′ti-siz-əm) n. inclination to doubt; questioning nature. Also, **scep′ti·cism.**

sketch (skech) n. **1,** a rough drawing. **2,** an outline; synopsis. **3,** a short humorous act; skit. —v.t. delineate or describe roughly. —**sketch′y,** adj. not detailed.

skew (skū) v.i. swerve.

skew′er (skū′ər) n. a long pin; a spit used in roasting meat.

ski (skē) n. a long wooden runner for gliding on snow. —v.i. [**skied, ski′ing**] travel on skis. —**ski′er,** n.

skid n. **1,** a timber or metal band forming a track. **2,** a supporting runner. **3,** a friction brake. **4,** a framework. **5,** an act of skidding. —v.i. & i. [**skid′ded, -ding**] **1,** slide without rotating. **2,** swerve. —**skid row** or **road,** a street or section where vagrants and alcoholics live.

skid-doo′ (ski-doo′) interj. (Slang) go away!

skiff (skif) n. a small boat.

skill (skil) n. technical ability or knowledge; expertness. —**skill′ful, skil′ful, skilled,** adj.

skil′let (skil′it) n. **1,** a frying pan. **2,** a long-handled saucepan.

skim v.t. & i. [**skimmed, skim′ming**] **1,** lift or scrape off the top of (a liquid). **2,** read superficially. **3,** glide lightly (over). —**skim milk,** milk without its natural cream.

skimp v.t. & i. provide meagerly; scrimp. —**skimp′y,** adj. meager.

skin n. **1,** the outer covering of a body. **2,** a pelt. **3,** a rind or peel. —v.t. [**skinned, skin′ning**] **1,** remove the skin from; peel. **2,** (Slang) swindle. —v.i. (Slang) abscond.

skin′div″er n. a diver who penetrates deep water carrying a supply of oxygen but not wearing a diver's suit. —**skin′div″ing,** n.

skin′flint″ n. a stingy, grasping person; tightwad.

skin′ner n. **1,** one who skins. **2,** a driver of teams of mules.

skin′ny (skin′ē) adj. lean; underweight; thin. —**skin′ni·ness,** n.

skip v.i. [**skipped, skip′ping**] **1,** jump lightly. **2,** bounce; ricochet. **3,** pass over something. **4,** (Colloq.) flee. —v.t. **1,** jump over. **2,** cause to ricochet. **3,** (Colloq.) evade. —n. act of skipping. —**skip tracer,** a detective who seeks debt-evaders.

skip′per (skip′ər) n. captain of a ship; chief; master.

skir′mish (skẽr′mish) n. a minor battle. —v.i. engage in a skirmish.

skirt (skẽrt) n. **1,** a garment, or part of it, hanging down from the waist. **2,** an apron. **3,** (Slang) a woman. —v.t. lie or pass along the border of.

skit n. a short, comic play.

skit′tish (skit′ish) adj. **1,** apt to shy. **2,** restless. **3,** coy.

skive (skīv) v.t. slice (leather) thinly. —**skiv′er,** n. **1,** a thin slice of leather. **2,** a knife for skiving.

skul·dug′ger·y (skul-dug′ə-rē) n. dishonest trickery.

skulk v.i. **1,** sneak away. **2,** slink.

skull (skul) *n.* the bony framework of the head. —**skull and crossbones**, a human skull above two crossed bones, used to label poisons (formerly, on pirates' flags).

skull'cap" *n.* a brimless, close-fitting cap.

skunk *n.* 1, a small fur-bearing animal of the weasel family that ejects a fetid fluid. 2, (*Colloq.*) a contemptible person. —*v.t.* (*Slang*) keep scoreless. —**skunk cabbage**, a foul-smelling plant.

Skunk

sky (skī) *n.* the surrounding space as seen from the earth.

Skye terrier a small, short-legged, usually white terrier.

sky'lark" *n.* a lark that sings as it flies.

sky'light" *n.* a window in a ceiling.

sky'line" *n.* 1, tall buildings seen outlined against the sky. 2, the visible horizon.

sky'rock"et *n.* a small rocket used in fireworks. —*v.i.* achieve wealth, fame, etc. rapidly.

sky'scrap"er *n.* a tall building.

sky'writ"ing *n.* writing trailed in smoke from an airplane.

slab *n.* a flat, thick piece.

slack (slak) *adj.* 1, loose, not taut. 2, slow; sluggish. 3, negligent. —*n.* 1, a slack condition or part. 2, a decrease in activity. —**slack'en**, *v.t. & i.* make or become more slack. —**slack'er**, *n.* a shirker, esp. of military service. —**slacks**, *n. pl.* loose trousers.

slag *n.* 1, the waste matter from smelting. 2, lava.

slain (slān) *v.* p.p. of *slay*.

slake (slāk) *v.t.* 1, appease, as thirst, wrath, etc. 2, abate. 3, treat (lime) with water.

sla'lom (slä'lōm) *n.* a skiing race.

slam *v.t. & i.* [**slammed, slam'ming**] 1, shut or strike with violence or noise. 2, (*Slang*) criticize adversely. —*n.* 1, a bang. 2, (*Slang*) criticism. 3, in card playing, the winning of all the tricks.

slan'der (slan'dər) *n.* 1, aspersion. 2, (*Law*) defamation by oral utterance. —*v.t.* defame. —**slan'der·ous**, *adj.*

slang *n.* 1, language of coarse, familiar or jocular character, regarded as below the level of written or colloquial speech. 2, jargon; cant.

slant (slänt) *v.i. & t.* 1, lie obliquely. 2, have a bias; incline. —*n.* 1, an oblique direction or position. 2, bias. 3, point of view.

slap *v.t.* [**slapped, slap'ping**] 1, strike with the open hand or with something flat. 2, strike with. 3, rebuke. —*n.* act of slapping; a slapping blow. —**slap'dash"**, *adv.* hastily and carelessly. —**slap'stick"**, *n. & adj.* rough comedy.

slash *v.t.* 1, hack violently. 2, make slits in. —*v.i.* make a wide cutting stroke. —*n.* 1, a slashing stroke; a wound. 2, an ornamental slit. 3, debris of felled trees. 4, (usually *pl.*) a swampy tract.

slat *n.* a strip of wood, etc.; a lath.

slate (slāt) *n.* 1, a fine-grained rock, easily split. 2, a plate of this rock, as for writing upon. 3, a written record. 4, a dull bluish-gray color. 5, a list of candidates. —*v.t.* 1, cover with slate. 2, destine.

slat'tern (slat'ərn) *n.* a slovenly woman. —**slat'tern·ly**, *adj.*

slaugh'ter (slâ'tər) *n.* 1, the killing of domestic animals for food. 2, massacre; carnage. —*v.t.* kill; massacre. —**slaugh'ter·house"**, *n.*

Slav (släv) *n. & adj.* a member of one of the peoples dominant in eastern Europe.

slave (slāv) *n.* 1, a person who is the property of another. 2, an addict. 3, a drudge. —*v.i.* drudge. —**slave driver**, a hard taskmaster. —**slav'ish**, *adj.*

slav'er (slā'vər) *n.* 1, a trader in slaves. 2, a ship carrying slaves.

slav'er (slav'ər) *v.i.* 1, let saliva dribble from the mouth. 2, show inordinate desire. —*n.* 1, saliva. 2, drivel.

slav'er·y (slā'və-rē) *n.* 1, the condition of a slave; bondage. 2, the practice of enslaving humans. 3, drudgery.

slav'ey (slā'vē) *n.* (*Colloq.*) a maid of all work.

Slav'ic (släv'ik) *adj.* pert. to the Slavs, as Russians, Poles, etc., and their languages.

slaw (slâ) *n.* chopped cabbage served as a salad: *coleslaw*.

slay (slā) *v.t.* [**slew, slain** (slān), **slay'ing**] 1, kill by violence. 2, (*Slang*) affect powerfully.

slea'zy (slē'zē; slā'-) *adj.* flimsy, unsubstantial. —**slea'zi·ness**, *n.*

sled *n.* a vehicle mounted on runners for moving on snow or ice. —**sled'ding**, *n.* (*Colloq.*) going.

sledge (slej) *n.* 1, a large sled. 2, a large, heavy hammer: *sledgehammer*.

sleek (slēk) *adj.* 1, smooth and glossy. 2, well groomed. 3, suave. —*v.t.* preen. —**sleek'ness**, *n.*

sleep (slēp) *n.* 1, the natural state of bodily rest, marked by suspension of consciousness. 2, inactivity; repose. —*v.i.* [*pret. & p.p.* **slept**] 1, go to sleep. 2, lie in death. 3, (with *away, off,* etc.) pass, as time, a condition, etc. —**sleeping bag,** a lined bag in which to sleep on the ground. —**sleeping sickness,** a disease that causes extreme lethargy.

sleep'er *n.* 1, one who sleeps. 2, a railroad car with berths. 3, a railroad tie. 4, (*Colloq.*) an unexpected success.

sleep'walk'er *n.* a somnambulist.

sleep'y (-ē) *adj.* 1, anxious to sleep; drowsy. 2, tranquil; quiet. —**sleep'i·ness,** *n.*

sleet (slēt) *n.* partly frozen rain.

sleeve (slēv) *n.* 1, the part of a garment that covers the arm. 2, a tubular covering or jacket.

sleigh (slā) *n.* a horse-drawn sled.

sleight (slīt) *n.* an artful feat, esp. of conjuring: *sleight-of-hand.*

slen'der (slen'dər) *adj.* 1, small in width or diameter. 2, scanty. 3, weak. —**slen'der·ness,** *n.*

slen'der·ize' (-īz') *v.t.* (*Colloq.*) make, or make to seem, more slender.

sleuth (slooth) *n.* 1, (*Colloq.*) a detective. 2, a bloodhound.

slew (sloo) *v.* pret. of *slay.* —*v.i.* veer; twist. —*n.* [also, **slue**] 1, a twist. 2, (*Colloq.*) a great number.

slice (slīs) *n.* 1, a thin broad piece. 2, an act of cutting. 3, a slicer. 4, (*Golf*) an oblique stroke. —*v.t. & i.* cut into slices. —**slic'er,** *n.*

slick (slik) *adj.* 1, sleek. 2, ingenious; sly. —*n.* 1, a smooth patch. 2, a magazine printed on coated paper. —*v.t.* (often with *up*) make smooth, sleek or elegant.

slick'er *n.* 1, an oilskin coat. 2, (*Colloq.*) a sly fellow; a swindler.

slide (slīd) *v.i.* [*pret. & p.p.* **slid**] 1, slip over a smooth surface. 2, go smoothly. 3, deteriorate. —*v.t.* cause to glide. —*n.* 1, an act of sliding; a place for sliding; an

Slide Rule

avalanche. 3, a sliding part; 4, a picture on glass, for projection on a screen. —**slide fastener,** a zipper. —**slide rule,** a device for calculat-

ing, by the relative position of two graduated rulers. —**sliding scale,** a basis for varying prices, wages, etc., according to conditions.

slight (slīt) *adj.* 1, small. 2, of little importance. 3, slender; frail. —*v.t.* 1, disdain; ignore. 2, do negligently. —*n.* discourteous neglect.

slim *adj.* [**slim'mer, -mest**] 1, slender; thin. 2, meager. —**slim'ness,** *n.*

slime (slīm) *n.* an offensive viscous liquid. —**slim'y,** *adj.*

sling *n.* 1, a device for hurling a missile by hand: *slingshot.* 2, a loop for suspending a load. —*v.t.* [*pret. & p.p.* **slung**] 1, fling. 2, suspend, etc. by a sling.

slink *v.i.* [*pret. & p.p.* **slunk**] go in a furtive manner.

slip *v.i.* [**slipped, slip'ping**] 1, lose hold; slide back. 2, err. 3, slide. 4, move quietly. —*v.t.* 1, put or move quietly. 2, cast off. —*n.* 1, an act of slipping. 2, a woman's undergarment. 3, a pillowcase. 4, the space between two wharves. 5, a strip, as of paper. 6, a slender person. —**slip cover,** a removable cloth cover for a piece of furniture. —**slip stream,** the air forced back by an aircraft propeller.

slip'o'ver *n.* a sweater, etc., to be pulled over the head.

slip'page (-ij) *n.* act, result or extent of slipping.

slip'per (-ər) *n.* a low shoe.

slip'per·y *adj.* 1, offering little friction, as though greasy. 2, sly; insecure. —**slip'per·i·ness,** *n.*

slip'shod' *adj.* negligent; careless; slovenly.

slip-'up' *n.* a careless error.

slit *v.t.* **slit'ted** or **slit, slit'ting**] 1, make a long narrow cut in. 2, cut into strips. —*n.* a long, narrow, straight cut or aperture.

slith'er (slith'ər) *v.i.* slide; go unsteadily; slip. —**slith'er·y,** *adj.*

sliv'er (sliv'ər) *n.* a fragment broken off; a splinter.

slob *n.* (*Slang*) a slovenly or uncultivated person.

slob'ber (slob'ər) *v.i. & t., & n.* slaver; drool. —**slob'ber·y,** *adj.*

sloe (slō) *n.* a small, black plum. —**sloe-'eyed',** *adj.* dark-eyed. —**sloe gin,** an alcoholic beverage flavored with sloes.

slog *v.i.* [**slogged, slog'ging**] plod.

slo'gan (slō'gən) *n.* a distinctive phrase or cry, used as a rallying cry, motto, catch-phrase in advertising, etc.

sloop *n.* a one-masted sailboat.

slop *n.* **1,** a puddle. **2,** an unappetizing mess. **3,** (*pl.*) waste liquid; sewage. —*v.t.* & *i.* [slopped, slop′ping] **1,** spill, splash. **2,** (*Colloq.*) be effusive.

slope (slōp) *n.* a slanting surface; slant. —*v.i.* be slanting or oblique. —*v.t.* cause to slant.

slop′py (-ē) *adj.* **1,** untidy. **2,** splashing. —**slop′pi·ness,** *n.*

slosh *n.* **1,** slush. **2,** nonsense. —*v.t.* & *i.* muddle; mix; splash.

slot *n.* a long narrow aperture or recess. —**slot machine,** a device for vending, etc., activated by dropping a coin in a slot. —**slot′ted,** *adj.*

sloth (slâth) *n.* **1,** laziness; indolence. **2,** a small arboreal mammal of So. America. —**sloth′ful,** *adj.*

slouch (slowch) *v.i.* bend downward; droop. —*n.* **1,** a drooping posture. **2,** an inept person.

slough (sluf) *n.* **1,** a molted part, as the skin of a snake. **2,** (slow) a marsh. —*v.t.* **1,** molt; cast off; shed. **2,** discard. Also, **sluff.**

slov′en (sluv′ən) *n.* one who is habitually untidy. —**slov′en·ly,** *adj.*

slow (slō) *adj.* **1,** taking a relatively long time. **2,** dull-witted. **3,** tardy; sluggish. **4,** slack. **5,** tedious. —*v.t.* & *i.* make or become slow. —*adv.* (*Colloq.*) slowly. —**slow′ness,** *n.*

sludge (sluj) *n.* slush; ooze.

slug *n.* **1,** a billet or ingot; a lead weight or bullet; a counterfeit coin; a bar of metal. **2,** a snail-like terrestrial mollusk. **3,** a heavy blow. —*v.t.* [slugged, slug′ging] strike heavily. —**slug′ger,** *n.*

slug′gard (slug′ərd) *n.* one habitually lazy or slow.

slug′gish (slug′ish) *adj.* lazy; torpid.

sluice (sloos) *n.* a channel for carrying off surplus water; the stream of water. —*v.t.* drench.

slum *n.* (often *pl.*) a squalid residential section. —*v.i.* [slummed, slum′ming] visit the slums, esp. as a sightseer.

slum′ber (slum′bər) *v.i.* & *t.,* & *n.* sleep.

slump *v.i.* sink heavily. —*n.* a sudden sinking or decline.

slung *v.* pret. & p.p. of *sling.*

slunk *v.* pret. & p.p. of *slink.*

slur (slêr) [slurred, slur′ring] *v.t.* **1,** run together (as separate words or notes). **2,** (usually with *over*) treat slightingly; ignore. **3,** disparage. —*n.* **1,** a slurred utterance; (*Music*) a curved line indicating a slur. **2,** a disparaging remark. **3,** a blot or stain.

slush *n.* **1,** watery snow. **2,** a watery mixture of mud, etc. **3,** drivel. **4,** bribery. —*v.t.* splash; flush.

slut *n.* **1,** a slovenly woman. **2,** a female dog. —**slut′tish,** *adj.*

sly (slī) *adj.* [sly′er, sly′est] **1,** meanly artful; cunning; shrewd. **2,** stealthy; insidious. **3,** roguish. —**sly′ness,** *n.*

smack (smak) *v.t.* **1,** separate (the lips) with a sharp sound. **2,** slap. **3,** kiss noisily. —*v.i.* **1,** make a sharp sound; slap. **2,** (with *of*) suggest. —*n.* **1,** a smacking noise. **2,** a resounding blow. **3,** a trace; suggestion. **4,** a small fishing vessel. —*adv.* squarely and abruptly.

small (smâl) *adj.* **1,** little; of limited scope; restricted. **2,** humble. **3,** mean; petty. —**small fry,** youngsters. —**small hours,** late hours. —**small potatoes** (*Colloq.*) of little consequence. —**small talk,** chatter.

small′pox″ *n.* an acute contagious disease often leaving pockmarks on its survivors.

smart (smärt) *v.i.* **1,** sting. **2,** feel physical or mental distress. —*v.t.* cause to smart. —*n.* **1,** a sting. **2,** mental distress. —*adj.* **1,** keen; acute; severe. **2,** brisk. **3,** clever; shrewd. **4,** vivacious; witty. **5,** neat; fashionably groomed. —**smart′en,** *v.t.* make neat, spruce, etc. —**smart′ness,** *n.*

smash *v.t.* **1,** break to pieces. **2,** defeat utterly. **3,** strike against something. —*v.i.* **1,** break to pieces; be ruined, bankrupt, etc. **2,** dash against something. —*n.* **1,** a violent blow. **2,** destruction. **3,** a sweet drink. —**smash-′up″,** *n.* a collision.

smat′ter·ing (smat′ər-ing) *n.* a slight or superficial knowledge or assortment.

smear (smir) *v.t.* **1,** overspread with grease, dirt, paint, etc.; daub. **2,** soil; sully. —*n.* a smudge.

smell (smel) *v.t.* **1,** perceive through the nose. **2,** inhale the odor of. **3,** detect or discover as though by smell. —*v.i.* inhale or give out an odor, esp. an offensive odor. —*n.* **1,** the sense of smell. **2,** odor; scent; aroma. **3,** the act of smelling. **4,** a trace. —**smelling salts,** a pungent restorative. —**smell′y,** *adj.* having a strong or offensive odor.

smelt *v.t.* melt (ore). —*n.* a small food fish.

smelt′er (smel′tər) *n.* a place where ore is melted, to yield metal.

smi′lax (smī′laks) *n.* any of various woody vines.

smile (smīl) *n.* 1, a widening of the mouth, with parted lips, indicating pleasure, amusement, or favor. 2, a favoring aspect. —*v.t. & i.* assume, or express by, a smile.

smirch (smėrch) *v.t.* soil; discolor; sully. —*n.* a stain; smear.

smirk (smėrk) *n.* an affected or knowing smile. —*v.i.* so smile.

smite (smīt) *v.t.* [smote (smōt), smit'ten (smit'ən)] 1, strike with a hard blow; afflict. 2, affect; captivate.

smith *n.* a worker in metal; a blacksmith. —**smith'y**, *n.* his workshop.

smith'er·eens" (smith'ər-ēnz") *n. pl.* (*Colloq.*) fragments.

smock (smok) *n.* a thin, loose outer robe.

smock'ing (-ing) *n.* embroidery stitches that gather material into folds.

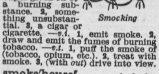

Smocking

smog *n.* (*Colloq.*) smoke and fog.

smoke (smōk) *n.* 1, the visible vapor given off by a burning substance. 2, something unsubstantial. 3, a cigar or cigarette. —*v.i.* 1, emit smoke. 2, draw and emit the fumes of burning tobacco. —*v.t.* 1, puff the smoke of (tobacco, opium, etc.). 2, treat with smoke. 3, (with *out*) drive into view.

smoke'house" *n.* a shed for smoking meat.

smokeless powder white gunpowder, which burns with little smoke.

smok'er *n.* 1, one who smokes. 2, a car in which smoking is permitted. 3, a meeting at which smoking is permitted.

smoke screen an obscuring cloud of, or as of, smoke.

smoke'stack" *n.* an upright pipe carrying off smoke.

smok'y (smō'kē) *adj.* 1, smoking; visibly vaporous. 2, dark; cloudy; grayish-blue. —**smok'i·ness,** *n.*

smol'der (smōl'dər) *v.i.* 1, burn and smoke without flame. 2, exist in a suppressed state.

smooth (smooth) *adj.* 1, having an even surface; not obstructed. 2, without sudden jolts or breaks; uniform. 3, not lumpy. 4, bland. 5, harmonious. 6, tranquil. 7, mild. 8, flowing, as speech. —*v.t.* 1, make smoother. 2, calm; allay; mollify; palliate. —**smooth'ness,** *n.*

smor'gas·bord" (smôr'gəs-bôrd") *n.* Swedish hors d'oeuvres.

smoth'er (smuth'ər) *v.t.* 1, suffocate; cover so as to deprive of air. 2, stifle; repress or suppress. —*v.i.* be smothered.

smoul'der (smōl'dər) *v.i.* smolder.

smudge (smuj) *n.* 1, a dirty mark; a blot or smear. 2, a smoky fire. —*v.t. & i.* stain; blacken. —**smudg'y,** *adj.*

smug *adj.* [smug'ger, -gest] self-satisfied. —**smug'ness,** *n.*

smug'gle (smug'əl) *v.t. & i.* transport (goods) secretly, esp. to avoid payment of duties. —**smug'gler,** *n.*

smut *n.* 1, sooty matter. 2, obscenity. —**smut'ty,** *adj.*

snack (snak) *n.* a small portion, esp. of food.

sna"fu' (sna"foo') *adj.* (*Slang*) in disorder: *Situation Normal—All Fouled Up.*

snag *n.* an obstruction; an obstacle. —*v.t.* [snagged, snag'ging] 1, impede; entangle. 2, trap, as with a snag. —**snag-'toothed",** **snag'gle-toothed",** *adj.* with teeth projecting awry.

snail (snāl) *n.* 1, a mollusk with a spiral shell. 2, a slow mover.

Snail

snail'paced" *adj.* sluggish.

snake (snāk) *n.* 1, any of an order of reptiles with elongated, tubular, limbless bodies: serpent. 2, a treacherous person.

snak'y *adj.* 1, pert. to snakes. 2, flexible; sinuous. 3, treacherous.

snap *v.t.* [snapped, snap'ping] 1, make a sudden sharp sound; click. 2, break suddenly. 3, move suddenly. 4, (with *at*) bite suddenly. 5, speak sharply. —*v.t.* 1, make a clicking sound. 2, break. 3, retort. 4, (with *up*) grab. 5, take an instantaneous photograph of. —*n.* 1, a sharp sound; a click. 2, a quick motion. 3, something that snaps. 4, a thin, brittle cake. 5, briskness; vigor. 6, a brief spell. 7, (*Slang*) an easy task. —*adj.* 1, offhand. 2, easy. 3, operated by a device that snaps.

snap'drag"on (snap'drag"ən) *n.* a flowering plant.

snap'per (-ər) *n.* 1, a large marine fish. 2, a snapping turtle.

snap'pish (-ish) *adj.* apt to bite or snap. —**snap'pish·ness,** *n.*

snap'py (-ē) *adj.* 1, snapping; crackling. 2, brisk; cold and stimulating, as weather. 3, (*Colloq.*) smart, as dress; lively and clever, as repartee; quick. 4, snappish. —**snap'pi·ness,** *n.*

snap'shot" *n.* a photograph.

snare (snâr) *n.* **1,** a trap. **2,** a cord, as one stretched across a head of a drum. —*v.t.* catch, entangle.

snarl (snärl) *v.t. & i.* **1,** utter an angry cry, as a dog; speak angrily. **2,** entangle; become entangled. —*n.* **1,** act of snarling; a surly tone. **2,** a tangled mass.

snatch (snach) *v.t.* seize abruptly or violently. —*v.i.* grab hastily. —*n.* **1,** the act of snatching; (*Slang*) a kidnaping. **2,** a fragment or bit.

sneak (snēk) *v.i.* go or act in a stealthy, furtive manner; slink; skulk. —*v.t.* **1,** do furtively. **2,** (*Colloq.*) steal. —*n.* **1,** one who sneaks. **2,** (*pl.*) [also, **sneak'ers**] soft-soled low shoes. —**sneak thief,** a thief who does not break his way in. —**sneak'y,** *adj.*

sneer (snir) *v.i.* express scorn, as by a grimace. —*v.t.* utter with a sneer. —*n.* a contemptuous expression or utterance.

sneeze (snēz) *n.* a sudden, involuntary, spasmodic expulsion of air through the nose and mouth. —*v.i.* make a sneeze. —**sneeze at** (*Colloq.*) treat with scorn.

snick'er (snik'ər) *v.i. & t.* laugh in a suppressed manner. —*n.* giggle.

snide (snīd) *adj.* mean; invidious.

sniff (snif) *v.i. & t.* **1,** draw in air audibly. **2,** (with *at*) show scorn or disdain (of). —*n.* a sniffing.

snif'fle (-əl) *v.i.* sniff repeatedly.

snif'ter (snif'tər) *n.* **1,** a pear-shaped brandy glass. **2,** (*Slang*) a small drink.

snip *v.t. & i.* cut off with one light stroke. —*n.* **1,** the act or result of snipping. **2,** (*Colloq.*) an insignificant person. **3,** (*pl.*) shears.

snipe (snīp) *n.* a long-billed wading bird. —*v.i.* hunt snipe; shoot. —**snip'er,** *n.* a sharpshooter.

snip'py (-ē) *adj.* snappish; curt. —**snip'pi-ness,** *n.*

snitch (snich) (*Slang*) *v.t.* steal. —*v.i.* turn informer.

sniv'el (sniv'əl) *v.i.* **1,** weep and sniffle. **2,** pretend contrition; whine.

snob *n.* one who unduly esteems social position. —**snob'bish,** *adj.* —**snob'bish-ness, snob'ber-y,** *n.*

snood *n.* a band or fillet to confine the hair.

snook'er (snŭk'ər) *n.* a form of pocket billiards.

snoop *v.i.* (*Colloq.*) prowl and spy.

snoot'y (snoo'tē) *adj.* (*Slang*) snobbish. —**snoot'i-ness,** *n.*

snooze (snooz) *n. & v.i.* (*Colloq.*) sleep.

snore (snôr) *v.i.* breathe with a hoarse noise during sleep. —*n.* a snoring sound.

snor'kel (snôr'kəl) *n.* a device to supply air to the engine of a submarine.

snort (snôrt) *v.i.* **1,** force air audibly through the nose. **2,** scoff. —*n.* a snorting sound or act.

snot *n.* (*Vulgar*) mucus from the nose.

snot'ty *adj.* (*Colloq.*) snobbish; impudent. —**snot'ti-ness,** *n.*

snout (snowt) *n.* the forepart of an animal's head, esp. the nose.

snow (snō) *n.* **1,** water vapor frozen into crystals, falling to earth in flakes; a fall of snow; fallen snow. **2,** something very white. **3,** (*Slang*) cocaine or heroin. —*v.i.* send down or fall as snow. —**snow under,** bury.

snow'ball'' *n.* snow, pressed into a ball.

snow'bank'' *n.* a heap of snow.

snow'bird'' *n.* (*Slang*) a drug addict.

snow'bound'' *adj.* confined by impassable snow.

snow'clad'' *adj.* topped with snow, as a mountain.

snow'drift'' *n.* drifted snow.

snow'fall'' *n.* a fall of snow.

snow'flake'' *n.* a snow crystal.

snow'man'' *n.* **1,** a crude statue of a human figure, made of snow. **2,** a humanoid beast, by some supposed to exist in Tibet, also called *abominable snowman* or *yeti* (yet'ē).

snow'plow'' *n.* a blade for pushing aside snow.

snow'shoe'' *n.* a network in a frame, worn for walking on snow.

snow'storm'' *n.* a heavy snowfall; blizzard.

snub *v.t.* [**snubbed, snub'bing**] **1,** check or stop suddenly. **2,** slight; ignore. —*adj.* (of the nose) turned up at the tip. —**snub'by,** *adj.*

snuff (snuf) *v.t. & i.* sniff. —*v.t.* extinguish, as a candle. —*n.* **1,** sniff. **2,** powdered tobacco.

snuff'box'' *n.* a pocket container for snuff.

snuf'fle (snuf'əl) *v.i. & t., & n.* sniff or sniffle.

snug *adj.* [**snug'ger, -gest**] **1,** comfortable; cozy. **2,** fitting closely. **3,** compact; neat. —**snug'ness,** *n.*

snug'gle (snug'əl) *v.i. & t.* cuddle; nestle.

so (sō) *adv.* **1,** in the degree, amount, manner, etc. expressed or implied. **2,** very; extremely. **3,** such being the case. **4,** consequently. —*interj.* expressing mild surprise.

soak (sōk) *v.i.* be permeated by a liquid; become thoroughly wet; permeate. —*v.t.* **1,** drench; saturate. **2,** absorb. **3,** (*Slang*) beat hard; charge exorbitantly. —*n.* (*Slang*) an immoderate drinker.

so-'and-so *pron.* someone whose name is not known or specified.

soap (sōp) *n.* 1, a substance used for cleansing. 2, (*Slang*) flattery: *soft soap.* —*v.t.* cover or treat with soap. —**soap opera,** a sentimental radio drama.

soap'box *n.* the podium of an unauthorized orator.

soap'stone *n.* a soft stone, a variety of talc.

soap'suds *n.* suds.

soap'y (-ē) *adj.* 1, containing soap. 2, flattering. —**soap'i-ness,** *n.*

soar (sôr) *v.i.* 1, fly upward; glide in air: 2, rise higher, or to great height.

sob *v.i.* & *t.* [**sobbed, sob'bing**] weep convulsively. —*n.* a convulsive catching of the breath in weeping.

so'ber (sō'bər) *adj.* 1, not intoxicated. 2, sedate; serious; solemn. 3, subdued, as in color. —*v.t.* & *i.* make or become sober. —**so'ber-ly,** *adv.* seriously. —**so'ber-ness,** *n.*

so-bri'e-ty (sō-brī'ə-tē) *n.* soberness, not drunkenness.

so'bri-quet (sō'brī-kā') *n.* a nickname. Also, **sou'bri-quet.**

so-"called' *adj.* thus (perhaps unjustifiably) designated.

Soccer

soc'cer (sok'ər) *n.* a form of football.

so'cia-ble (sō'shə-bəl) *adj.* gregarious; friendly; amiable. —*n.* a social gathering. —**so"cia-bil'i-ty,** *n.*

so'cial (sō'shəl) *adj.* 1, pert. to communal activities; gregarious; friendly. 2, pert. to or tending to advance human society. 3, fashionable. —*n.* a social gathering. —**social register,** a book listing members of fashionable society. —**social security,** a general insurance and old-age-pension plan.

so'cial-ism (-iz-əm) *n.* ownership of exploitable capital and means of production by the government, not by individuals or by private enterprise. —**so'cial-ist,** *n.* —**so"cial-ist'-ic** (-is'tik) *adj.*

so'cial-ite (sō'shə-līt') *n.* (*Colloq.*) a member of fashionable society.

so'cial-ize (-īz") *v.t.* make social or socialistic. —**socialized medicine,** medical care provided by the state. —**so"cial-i-za'tion,** *n.*

so-ci'e-ty (sō-sī'ə-tē) *n.* 1, human beings collectively. 2, the fashionable world. 3, a community. 4, an association. 5, companionship.

so'ci-ol'o-gy (sō"shē-ol'ə-jē) *n.* the science of human society. —**so"ci-o-log'i-cal** (-ə-loj'i-kəl) *adj.* —**so"ci-ol'o-gist,** *n.*

sock (sok) *n.* 1, a short stocking. 2, (*Slang*) a hard blow. —*v.t.* (*Slang*) hit hard.

sock'et (sok'it) *n.* a hollow into which something is fitted.

sod *n.* 1, the upper layer of grassy land. 2, a piece of turf.

so'da (sō'da) *n.* 1, sodium or one of its oxides. 2, water charged with carbon dioxide; any drink prepared with it: *soda water.* —**soda fountain,** a counter at which ice cream and drinks are served.

so-dal'i-ty (sō-dal'ə-tē) *n.* an association.

sod'den (sod'ən) *adj.* soaked; bloated.

so'di-um (sō'dē-əm) *n.* a metallic chemical element, no. 11, symbol Na. —**sodium chloride,** salt. —**sodium silicate,** waterglass.

so'fa (sō'fə) *n.* a long, upholstered seat with a back and arms.

soft (sâft) *adj.* 1, yielding readily to pressure; not hard or stiff. 2, agreeable to the touch; mild, bland, delicate, melodious, etc. 3, kind, lenient, etc. 4, not robust. 5, easy. 6, (of water) relatively free of mineral salts. —*adv.* in a soft manner. —**soft'ness,** *n.*

soft'ball" *n.* baseball played with a larger, softer ball; the ball used.

soft drink a sweet beverage containing no alcohol.

sof'ten (sâf'ən) *v.t.* & *i.* make or become softer. —**sof'ten-er,** *n.*

soft'heart"ed *adj.* very sympathetic.

soft-'ped"al *v.t.* suppress.

soft soap (*Colloq.*) flattery.

soft-'spo"ken *adj.* beguiling; persuasive.

soft'y (sâf'tē) *n.* (*Colloq.*) 1, a weak-willed or softhearted person. 2, a person of scant endurance.

sog'gy (sog'ē) *adj.* sodden. —**sog'gi-ness,** *n.*

soil *n.* 1, the portion of the earth's surface in which plants grow. 2, land. 3, filth. —*v.t.* stain; defile; make dirty or foul. —*v.i.* become soiled.

soi-rée' (swä-rā') *n.* a social gathering in the evening.

so'journ (sō'jẽrn) *v.i.* dwell temporarily. —*n.* a temporary stay.

---

fat, fāte, fär, fāre, fäll, ásk; met, hē, hẽr, maybė; pin, pīne; not, nōte, ôr, tool

sol n. 1, (sōl) (*Music*) the fifth tone of a scale. 2, (sol) (*cap.*) the sun.

sol'ace (sol'is) n. comfort in sorrow. —v.t. comfort.

so'lar (sō'lər) adj. pert. to the sun. —solar plex'us (plek'səs), the system of nerves behind the stomach. —solar system, the sun and the planets revolving around it.

so·lar'i·um (sō-lâr'ē-əm) n. [pl. -a (-ə)] a glass-enclosed room; sunroom.

sold (sōld) v. pret. & p.p. of *sell*.

sol'der (sod'ər) n. a fusible metal. —v.t. join with solder. —soldering iron, a tool for melting solder.

sol'dier (sōl'jər) n. a man engaged in military service; one of an army. —v.i. (*Colloq.*) malinger. —sol'dier·ly, adj. —soldier of fortune, a mercenary or adventurer. —sol'dier·y, n. soldiers collectively.

sole (sōl) n. 1, the under surface of the foot, or of a shoe. 2, any of several flatfishes. —adj. unique; only; alone.

sol'e·cism (sol'ə-siz-əm) n. a formal error, as in grammar.

sol'emn (sol'əm) adj. 1, sober in manner or aspect. 2, gravely impressive. —so·lem'ni·ty (sə-lem'nə-tē) n. —sol'em·nize' (-nīz') v.t.

so·lic'it (sə-lis'it) v.t. 1, seek to obtain; request. 2, address entreaties to; petition. —v.i. seek to obtain something. —so·lic'i·ta'tion, n.

so·lic'i·tor (sə-lis'ə-tər) n. 1, one who solicits. 2, (*Brit.*) a lawyer who prepares cases for barristers.

so·lic'i·tous (sə-lis'ə-təs) adj. anxious.

so·lic'i·tude (sə-lis'ə-tood) n. anxiety or concern for the welfare of others.

sol'id adj. 1, existing in three-dimensional space. 2, compact; undivided; dense. 3, firm; hard; strong. 4, united; unanimous. 5, reliable; financially sound. —n. a solid substance. —so·lid'i·ty, n.

sol'i·dar'i·ty (sol'i-dar'ə-tē) n. union; community of interests.

so·lid'i·fy' (sə-lid'ə-fī') v.t. & i. make or become solid. —so·lid'i·fi·ca'tion, n.

so·lil'o·quy (sə-lil'ə-kwē) n. the act of talking to oneself. —so·lil'o·quize' (-kwīz') v.i. & t.

sol'i·taire' (sol'ə-tār') n. 1, a puzzle or game played by one person alone. 2, a precious stone, esp. a diamond, set alone.

sol'i·tar'y (sol'ə-ter'ē) adj. 1, alone. 2, single; sole. 3, characterized by solitude; not social.

sol'i·tude (sol'ə-tood') n. the state of being alone or remote.

so'lo (sō'lō) n. [pl. -los] a performance by one person alone. —adj. alone; performed alone. —so'lo·ist, n.

so'lon (sō'lon) n. a lawmaker.

sol'stice (sol'stis) n. either of the two times when the sun is at its greatest distance from the celestial equator, about June 21 and Dec. 21.

sol'u·ble (sol'yə-bəl) adj. 1, capable of being dissolved. 2, capable of being solved. —sol''u·bil'i·ty, n.

so·lu'tion (sə-loo'shən) n. 1, an explanation or answer. 2, a fluid containing something dissolved.

solve (solv) v.t. find the answer to (a problem, puzzle, etc.); clear up.

sol'ven·cy (sol'vən-sē) n. ability to pay all just debts.

sol'vent (sol'vənt) adj. 1, able to pay all just debts. 2, having the power of dissolving. —n. a fluid that dissolves a specified substance.

so·mat'ic (sō-mat'ik) adj. pert. to the body.

som'ber (som'bər) adj. 1, dark in color; dull. 2, gloomy; dismal. Also, som'bre. —som'ber·ness, n.

som·bre·ro (som-brâr'ō) n. [pl. -ros] a broad-brimmed Mexican hat.

Sombrero

some (sum) adj. 1, of an unspecified but considerable number or quantity. 2, certain (one or ones) not specified. 3, (*Slang*) considerable; notable. —pron. an unspecified number or portion. —adv. (*Slang*) somewhat or considerably.

-some (-səm) suf. showing a tendency (to), as *meddlesome*.

some'bod"y pron. a person unspecified. —n. a person of consequence.

some'day" adv. on some indefinite day.

some'how" adv. in an unspecified way.

some'one" pron. somebody.

some'place" adv. & n. somewhere.

som'er·sault" (sum'ər-sâlt") n. an acrobatic turning over of the body.

some'thing" n. an unspecified thing.

some'time" adv. at some indefinite time. —adj. former.

some'times" adv. occasionally.

some'what" adv. to some extent. —n. some part.

some'where" *adv.* in, at, or to some unspecified place. —*n.* an unspecified place.

som·nam'bu·late" (som-nam'-byə-lāt") *v.i. & t.* walk, etc., in one's sleep. —**som·nam'bu·list,** *n.*

som'no·lent (som'nə-lənt) *adj.* 1, sleepy. 2, causing sleep. —**som'no·lence,** *n.*

son (sun) *n.* a male in relation to his parents.

so'nar (sō'när) *n.* a device to time the echo of sound waves in water, used in detecting submarines or obstructions and measuring depths.

so·na'ta (sə-nä'ta) *n.* a musical composition in contrasted movements.

song (sâng) *n.* 1, a short poem set to music. 2, poetry. 3, the act or sound of singing. —**song'ster,** *n.* singer. —**song'stress,** *n.fem.*

song'bird" *n.* a bird that sings.

son'ic (son'ik) *adj.* 1, of or pert. to sound. 2, of the speed of sound.

son-'in-law" *n.* [*pl.* **sons-'-**] the husband of one's daughter.

son'net (son'it) *n.* a fourteen-line poem.

son'ny (sun'ē) *n.* a term of address to a boy.

so·no'rous (sə-nôr'əs) *adj.* richly resonant in sound; deep; full. —**so·nor'i·ty** (sə-nôr'ə-tē) *n.*

soon *adv.* 1, in a short time; before long. 2 promptly; quickly.

soot (sût) *n.* a black substance, chiefly carbon, produced by faulty combustion. —**soot'y,** *adj.*

sooth *n.* (*Archaic*) truth. —**sooth'-say"er,** *n.* a fortune-teller.

soothe (sooth) *v.t.* 1, calm; mollify. 2, allay (pain, etc.).

sop *n.* 1, something dipped in a liquid, as bread. 2, something that pacifies; a bribe. —*v.t. & i.* [**sopped, sop'ping**] 1, dip; soak. 2, (with *up*) absorb. —**sop'ping,** *adj.* drenched. —**sop'py,** *adj.* 1, soaked. 2, rainy.

soph'ism (sof'iz-əm) *n.* an adroit but fallacious argument. —**soph'ist,** *n.* —**so·phis'tic** (sə-fis'tik) *adj.* —**so·phis'ti·cal·ly,** *adv.*

so·phis'ti·cate" (sə-fis'ti-kāt") *v.t.* make less natural, more worldly. —*n.* a sophisticated person. —**so·phis'ti·cat"ed,** *adj.* experienced and worldly-wise; artificial. —**so·phis"ti·ca'tion,** *n.*

soph'ist·ry *n.* use of sophisms.

soph'o·more" (sof'ə-môr") *n.* a second-year student. —**soph"o·mor'ic,** *adj.* immature; superficial.

so'po·rif'ic (sop"ə-rif'ik) *adj.* 1, causing sleep. 2, sleepy. —*n.* something that causes sleep.

so·pran'o (sə-pran'ō) *n.* [*pl.* -os] the highest singing voice in women; the singer; the voice part.

sor'cer·y (sôr'sə-rē) *n.* witchcraft; magic. —**sor'cer·er,** *n.* —**sor'cer·ess,** *n.fem.*

sor'did (sôr'did) *adj.* 1, mercenary. 2, ignoble; base. 3, squalid. —**sor'did·ness,** *n.*

sore (sōr) *adj.* 1, sensitive; painful. 2, suffering pain. 3, (*Colloq.*) offended; angry. —*n.* an inflamed or infected spot. —**sore'head",** *n.* (*Slang*) a disgruntled person. —**sore'ness,** *n.*

sor'ghum (sôr'gəm) *n.* a cereal grass; a syrup made from it.

so·ror'i·ty (sə-rôr'ə-tē) *n.* a women's society, esp. in college.

sor'rel (sor'əl) *n.* 1, any of various plants. 2, a light reddish-brown color; a horse of this color.

sor'row (sor'ō) *n.* 1, distress of mind; sadness; grief. 2, a cause of grief. —*v.i.* grieve. —**sor'row·ful,** *adj.*

sor'ry (sor'ē) *adj.* 1, feeling sorrow, regret, or pity. 2, deplorable. 3, worthless; mean; poor.

sort (sôrt) *n.* 1, a class, kind, variety, species, etc. 2, character. 3, way; fashion. —*v.t.* 1, classify. 2, separate from others that differ.

sor'tie (sôr'tē) *n.* 1, a sally of troops. 2, a combat mission of aircraft.

S O S (es"ō"es') a call for help.

so-'so" *adj. & adv.* fair; mediocre; indifferently.

sot *n.* a habitual drunkard. —**sot'tish,** *adj.*

sou (soo) *n.* a French coin of low value.

sou·brette' (soo-bret') *n.* an actress who plays a pert young woman.

souf·flé' (soo-flā') *n.* a fluffy baked dish.

sought (sât) *v.* pret. & p.p. of *seek.*

soul (sōl) *n.* 1, the spiritual part of man. 2, emotional feeling. 3, nobility; courage. 4, the essential part of anything; a leader. 5, the personification of a quality. 6, a human being. —**soul'ful,** *adj.* expressing deep feeling.

sound (sownd) *n.* 1, the sensation produced in the organs of hearing by certain vibrations in the air. 2, these vibrations; any auditory effect. 3, the general effect or tone. 4, a narrow passage of water; an inlet. —*v.i.* 1, make a sound. 2, make a particular sound or impression. 3, measure depth at sea. 4, seek information. —*v.t.* 1, cause to make a sound. 2, utter. 3, measure the depth of water. 4, investigate.

—*adj.* **1**, in good condition; healthy. **2**, reliable; substantial. **3**, honorable. —**sound'ness**, *n.* —**sound track**, that part of a movie film carrying the sound record.

sound'proof" *adj.* insulating against or resisting the passage of sound.

soup (soop) *n.* **1**, a cooked liquid food. **2**, (*Slang*) nitroglycerin. —**soup up** (*Slang*) speed up (an automobile engine).

soup'y (soo'pē) *adj.* like soup; (of fog) thick —**soup'i-ness**, *n.*

sour (sowr) *adj.* **1**, having an acid or tart taste. **2**, fermented. **3**, unpleasant. **4**, morose in disposition. **5**, excessively acid, as soil. —*v.t. & i.* make or become sour; spoil. —**sour grapes**, a pretense of not wanting something unobtainable. — **sour'ness**, *n.*

source (sôrs) *n.* a place from which something comes; origin.

sour'dough" *n.* a seasoned prospector.

souse (sows) *v.t. & i.* **1**, drench; soak. **2**, pickle. **3**, (*Slang*) intoxicate. —*n.* (*Slang*) a drunkard.

south (sowth) *n.* **1**, the point of the compass opposite north. **2**, (often *cap.*) a region in this direction, esp. the former Confederate States. —*adj. & adv.* toward, in or from the south.

south"east' *n., adj., & adv.* midway between south and east. —**south"east'er·ly**, *adj. & adv.* —**south"east'ern**, *adj.*

south'er·ly (suth'ər-lē) *adj. & adv.* toward or from the south.

south'ern (suth'ərn) *adj.* in or pert. to the south. —**south'ern·er**, *n.*

south paw" *n. & adj.* (*Slang*) a left-handed person.

south"west' *n., adj., & adv.* midway between south and west. —**south"west'er·ly**, *adj.* —**south"-west'ern**, *adj.*

south"west'er *n.* **1**, a storm from the southwest. **2**, a waterproof hat.

sou"ve·nir' (soo"və-nir') *n.* **1**, a memento or keepsake. **2**, a memory.

sov'er·eign (sov'rin) *n.* **1**, one having supreme power; a monarch. **2**, a Brit. gold coin worth one pound. —*adj.* **1**, having supreme power. **2**, supreme; greatest. —**sov'er·eign·ty**, *n.*

so'vi·et' (sō'vē-et") *n.* **1**, in Russia, a council, esp. a town meeting. **2**, (*cap.*) (often *pl.*) the U.S.S.R.

sow (sō) *v.t. & i.* **1**, scatter or plant (seed). **2**, scatter seed over (land). **3**, disseminate.

sow (sow) *n.* a female hog.

soy (soi) *n.* a plant or its edible seed: the *soybean*. Also, soy'a (-ə).

spa (spä) *n.* a mineral spring.

space (spās) *n.* **1**, the unlimited expanse in all directions in which material objects exist. **2**, a particular portion of this expanse. **3**, enough room. **4**, a blank area. —*v.t.* place a certain distance apart. —**space ship**, an aircraft that could travel beyond the atmosphere of the earth.

spa'cious (spā'shəs) *adj.* roomy; broad. —**spa'cious·ness**, *n.*

spade (spād) *n.* **1**, a long-handled tool for digging. **2**, the symbol (♠); a playing card so marked. —*v.t.* dig with a spade.

spa'dix (spā'diks) *n.* a spikelike flower head.

spa·ghet'ti (spə-get'ē) *n.* a cordlike, solid food paste of Ital. origin.

span *n.* **1**, the full extent or stretch of anything; a space of time. **2**, the distance between two supports of a bridge; a bridge. **3**, the distance between thumb and little finger when extended: about 9 inches. **4**, a pair (of horses). —*v.t.* [**spanned, span'ning**] **1**, measure. **2**, extend or reach over.

span'gle (spang'gəl) *n.* a small glittering piece. —*v.t.* decorate with spangles.

span'iel (span'yəl) *n.* any of various hunting or pet dogs.

Span'ish *adj.* of or pert. to Spain, its people, or their language. —*n.* **1**, the language of Spain. **2**, the Spanish people.

Spaniel

spank *v.t.* strike with the open hand; punish. —*n.* a slap. —**spank'ing**, *adj.* brisk.

spar (spär) *n.* **1**, a pole on a mast; a mast. **2**, a part of the frame of an airplane. **3**, any of various lustrous minerals. **4**, (*cap.*) a member of the women's reserve of the U. S. Coast Guard. —*v.i.* [**sparred, spar'ring**] **1**, box cautiously or for practice. **2**, wrangle; dispute. **3**, fight with spurs, as cocks do.

spare (spâr) *v.t. & i.* **1**, show mercy to. **2**, refrain from injuring, using, saying, etc. **3**, dispense with. —*adj.* **1**, in excess; in reserve. **2**, meager. **3**, lean. **4**, frugal. —*n.* an extra or reserve thing. as a tire.

spare'rib" *n.* an upper pork rib.

spar'ing (spâr'ing) *adj.* economical; scanty; restricted.

spark (spärk) *n.* **1**, a fiery particle. **2**, an electrical discharge or arc. **3**, (*Colloq.*) a suitor. —*v.i. & t.* **1**, produce or issue as sparks. **2**, (*Colloq.*) court; woo.

spar'kle (spär'kəl) *v.i.* **1**, emit

little sparks. **2**, glitter. **3**, effervesce. **4**, be vivacious. —*n.* scintillation.

spar′kler (spär′klər) *n.* something that sparkles: a gem; a kind of firework.

spark plug **1**, the sparking device in an engine **2**, (*Slang*) one who encourages or inspires others.

spar′row (spar′ō) *n.* any of various small birds.

sparse (spärs) *adj.* **1**, thinly distributed. **2**, thin; scanty. —**sparse′ness**, spar′si·ty, *n.*

Spar′tan (spär′tən) *adj.* strictly disciplined and courageous. —*n.* a person of enduring courage.

spasm (spaz′əm) *n.* **1**, a sudden, involuntary contraction of the muscles. **2**, a brief burst of activity or feeling.

spas·mod′ic (spaz-mod′ik) *adj.* **1**, pert. to or like a spasm. **2**, violent but intermittent. —**spas·mod′i·cal·ly**, *adv.*

spas′tic (spas′tik) *adj.* characterized by spasms. —*n.* one afflicted with a spastic disease. —**spas′ti·cal·ly**, *adv.*

spat *n.* **1**, a petty dispute. **2**, a light blow. **3**, a splash, as of rain. **4**, (*pl.*) short cloth gaiters. **5**, a young oyster. —*v.i. & t.* [**spat′ted**, **-ting**] quarrel; strike lightly.

spate (spāt) *n.* a freshet; storm.

spa′tial (spā′shəl) *adj.* pert. to, being or existing in space.

spat′ter (spat′ər) *v.t. & i.* **1**, scatter or sprinkle in small drops. **2**, a splash. —*n.* a sprinkling.

spat′u·la (spach′ə-lə) *n.* a flat-bladed implement for mixing or spreading. —**spat′u·late** (-lət) *adj.* shaped like a spatula.

spav′in *n.* a diseased condition of the hock of a horse. —**spav′ined**, *adj.*

spawn (spân) *n.* **1**, the eggs of fishes, etc. **2**, offspring. —*v.i. & t.* (esp. of fishes) produce offspring.

spay (spā) *v.t.* remove the ovaries of a female animal.

speak (spēk) *v.i. & t.* [**spoke**, **spo′ken**, **speak′ing**] **1**, utter words; express. **2**, talk; converse. **3**, deliver a public address.

speak′eas″y *n.* (*Slang*) an illegal barroom.

speak′er (-ər) *n.* **1**, one who speaks. **2**, an orator. **3**, a presiding officer, as (*cap.*) of the U.S House of Representatives. **4**, loudspeaker.

speak′ing *adj.* **1**, talking. **2**, lifelike.

spear (spir) *n.* **1**, a long-handled, sharp-headed weapon; any similar instrument. **2**, a blade of grass; a shoot. —*v.t.* **1**, pierce with a spear. **2**, capture.

spear′head″ *n.* **1**, the sharp point of a spear. **2**, a leader or leading force.

spear′mint″ *n.* the common mint used for flavoring.

spe′cial (spesh′əl) *adj.* **1**, of a particular kind; being a particular one. **2**, peculiar to a particular person, thing, or purpose. **3**, unusual; exceptional.

spe′cial·ist *n.* one who specializes, esp. in a medical field.

spe′cial·ize″ (-īz″) *v.i.* pursue a particular course of study or work. —**spe″cial·i·za′tion**, *n.*

spe′cial·ty (-tē) *n.* **1**, a particular or preferred item, subject, skill, etc. **2**, a novelty.

spe′cie (spē′shē) *n.* coin.

spe′cies (spē′shēz) *n. sing. & pl.* **1**, a category of biological classification, lower than a genus. **2**, any class of persons or things.

spe·cif′ic (spə-sif′ik) *adj.* **1**, explicit; definite. **2**, of a particular kind. —*n.* **1**, something specific. **2**, a medicinal remedy. —**spe·cif′i·cal·ly**, *adv.* —**specific gravity**, the density of a substance relative to that of water.

spec″i·fi·ca′tion (spes′ə-fi-kā′-shən) *n.* **1**, a statement of particulars, as of dimensions, materials, etc. **2**, act or result of specifying.

spec′i·fy″ (spes′ə-fī″) *v.t.* **1**, name expressly. **2**, state as a condition.

spec′i·men (spes′ə-mən) *n.* an individual or part used as a typical example of the whole.

spe′cious (spē′shəs) *adj.* apparently but not actually, sound; deceptive. —**spe″ci·os′i·ty** (-os′i-tē) *n.*

speck (spek) *n.* a tiny particle; a spot. —*v.t.* spot.

speck′le (spek′əl) *v.t.* mark with small spots.

spec′ta·cle (spek′tə-kəl) *n.* **1**, a striking sight or view. **2**, a large public display. **3**, (*pl.*) eyeglasses.

spec·tac′u·lar (spek-tak′yə-lər) *adj.* impressive; thrilling.

spec′ta·tor (spek′tā-tər) *n.* an onlooker; a witness.

spec′ter (spek′tər) *n.* **1**, a ghost. **2**, a source of terror. Also, **spec′tre**. —**spec′tral**, *adj.*

spec′tro·scope″ (spek′trə-skōp″) *n.* an instrument for producing the spectrum of any light. —**spec″tro·scop′ic** (-skop′ik) *adj.* —**spec″tro·scop′i·cal·ly**, *adv.*

spec'trum (spek'trəm) *n.* the band of colors formed by dispersed light.

spec'u·late (spek'yə-lāt″) *v.i.* 1, meditate or ponder; reflect. 2, theorize; conjecture. 3, make a risky investment. —**spec·u·la'tion,** *n.* —**spec'u·la'tive,** *adj.* —**spec'u·la'tor,** *n.*

speech (spēch) *n.* 1, the power of speaking. 2, a particular utterance; an address. 3, a language. 4, a manner of speaking. —**speech'less,** *adj.* deprived of speech by emotion, as surprise.

speed (spēd) *n.* 1, rapidity of motion or performance. 2, rate of progress or motion. —*v.i.* [*pret. & p.p.* **speed'ed** or **sped**] 1, expedite. 2, (with *up*) increase the speed of. —*v.i.* 1, move, etc. with rapidity. 2, (with *up*) increase speed. —**speed'er,** *n.* one who drives at an illegally high speed.

speed·om'e·ter (spē-dom'i-tər) *n.* a device that indicates the rate of speed of an automobile, etc.

speed'way″ *n.* a road designed for fast automobile travel or for races.

speed'y *adj.* 1, rapid. 2, prompt; not delayed. —**speed'i·ness,** *n.*

spell (spel) *v.i.* 1, form or express by or in letters. 2, (of letters) form or constitute (a word). 3, replace temporarily; relieve. —*v.i.* form words with the proper letters. —*n.* 1, a charm; an enchantment. 2, a turn of work. 3, a short period. 4, (*Colloq.*) an ailment.

spell'bind″er *n.* a fascinating speaker.

spell'bound″ *adj.* enchanted; fascinated.

spell'er *n.* 1, one who spells. 2, an elementary spelling textbook.

spell'ing *n.* the process of forming words from letters; orthography.

spend *v.i.* [*pret. & p.p.* **spent**] 1, pay or give out (money, etc.). 2, consume; use up. 3, employ or while away (time). —*v.i.* pay out money, etc.

spend'thrift' *n. & adj.* an extravagant person; a prodigal.

spent *adj.* exhausted. —*v.* pret. & p.p. of *spend.*

sperm (spėrm) *n.* the male reproductive cell: *spermatozoön.*

spew (spū) *v.i. & i., & n.* vomit.

sphere (sfir) *n.* 1, a round solid body; a globe. 2, a field of knowledge, influence, or activity. —**spher'i·cal** (sfer'i-kəl) *adj.*

sphe'roid (sfir'oid) *n.* the solid generated by rotation of an ellipse. —**sphe·roid'al,** *adj.*

sphinx (sfinks) *n.* 1, a mythical creature, usually half human and half lion. 2, an enigmatic or inscrutable person.

Sphinx

spice (spīs) *n.* 1, an aromatic or pungent vegetable substance used for seasoning food. 2, anything that gives zest or piquancy. —*v.t.* add spice to. —**spic'y,** *adj.*

spick-'and-span' (spik'ən-span″) *adj.* 1, neat. 2, new and fresh.

spi'der (spī'dər) *n.* 1, an eight-legged arachnid, esp. one that spins a web. 2, something resembling a spider, esp. a frying pan.

spiel (spēl) (*Slang*) *n.* a persuasive talk. —**spiel'er,** *n.* a barker.

spig'ot (spig'ət) *n.* a faucet.

spike (spīk) *n.* 1, a large metal nail. 2, a sharp-pointed projection. 3, an ear, as of wheat. —*v.t.* 1, pierce with a spike; furnish with spikes. 2, make useless; frustrate. 3, add alcohol or liquor to (a drink).

spill (spil) *v.t.* 1, cause or allow to run or fall out. 2, shed (blood). 3, let the wind out (of a sail). 4, divulge. —*v.i.* run or fall out; overflow. —*n.* 1, a running out. 2, (*Colloq.*) a fall.

spill'way″ *n.* an outlet for surplus water.

spilt *adj.* spilled.

spin *v.t.* [**spun, spin'ning**] 1, draw out and twist into threads, as wool, etc. 2, make with threads; fabricate. 3, cause to revolve rapidly. 4, (with *out*) prolong. —*v.i.* 1, revolve rapidly. 2, move, ride, etc., rapidly. —*n.* 1, a spinning motion; a spiral course. 2, a rapid ride. —**spin'ner,** *n.* —**spinning wheel,** a machine once used in the home to make thread or yarn.

spin'ach (spin'ich) *n.* a vegetable having edible green leaves.

spi'nal (spī'nəl) *adj.* of, in or pert. to the spine. —**spinal column,** the series of vertebrae.

spin'dle (spin'dəl) *n.* a slender pointed rod or pin, esp. one used in spinning. —**spin'dling, spin'dly,** *adj.* tall and slender.

spin'drift' *n.* a windswept spray.

spine (spīn) *n.* 1, the backbone. 2, any bony part, as a quill. 3, a thorn. —**spine'less,** *adj.* feeble; irresolute.

spin'et (spin'it) *n.* a small piano.

spin′ster (spin′stər) *n.* an un-married woman.

spi·rae′a (spi-rē′ə) *n.* any of various flower-bearing shrubs.

spi′ral (spi′rəl) *n.* 1, a curve winding around a fixed point and continually receding from it. 2, a coil; a helix. —*adj.* coiled.

spire (spīr) *n.* 1, an upright structure tapering to a point, as a steeple. 2, the top. 3, the shoot of a plant.

spir′it *n.* 1, the inspiring principle or dominant influence. 2, soul. 3, the nature of a person; disposition; attitude. 4, (often *pl.*) vivacity; optimism. 5, (*cap.*) in the Trinity, the Holy Spirit. 6, the essence or real meaning. 7, a supernatural being; an angel; a fairy; a ghost. 8, a chemical distillation; (*pl.*) strong distilled alcoholic liquor. —*v.t.* (with *away*) carry off secretly. —spir′it·ed, *adj.* full of courage, vigor, etc. —spir′it·u·ous, *adj.* alcoholic.

spir′it·u·al (spir′i-choo-əl) *adj.* 1, pert. to the soul or spirit. 2, relating to sacred things. —*n.* a religious song, esp. of Negro origin. —spir′it·u·al′i·ty, *n.*

spir′it·u·al·ism *n.* belief in communication with the spirits of the dead. —spir′it·u·al·ist, *n.*

spit *v.t. & t.* [spat or spit, spit′ting] 1, eject saliva from the mouth. 2, spew out. 3, [*pret. & p.p.* spit′ted] impale on a sharp stick, etc. —*n.* 1, saliva. 2, the image of a person. 3, a sharp stick or bar. 4, a narrow point of land.

spite (spīt) *n.* ill will; malevolence. —*v.t.* thwart. —in spite of, notwithstanding. —spite′ful, *adj.* malicious.

spit′tle (-əl) *n.* saliva.

spit·toon′ (-toon′) *n.* a cuspidor.

spitz (spits) *n.* a kind of Pomeranian dog.

splash *v.t.* 1, spatter, as with water or mud. 2, dash or throw about (water, etc.). —*v.i.* spatter water, or in water. —*n.* 1, the act or sound of splashing. 2, a quantity splashed. 3, an ostentatious display. —splash′y, *adj.*

splat *n.* the center upright member of the back of a chair.

splat′ter (splat′ər) *v.t. & t.* splash.

Splat

splay (splā) *v.t. & t.* spread out. —*adj.* spread out; turned outward; awkward. —splay′foot″, *n.*

spleen (splēn) *n.* 1, an organ in the abdomen in which the blood is modified. 2, ill humor; melancholy.

3, anger; malice. —sple·net′ic (spli-net′ik) *adj.*

splen′did *adj.* excellent; admirable; grand. Also, (*Colloq.*) splendif′er·ous (-dif′ə-rəs).

splen′dor (splen′dər) *n.* brilliant luster; magnificence; grandeur. Also, splen′dour. —splen′dor·ous, *adj.*

splice (splīs) *v.t.* join together, as two ropes. —*n.* a joint of ropes.

spline (splīn) *n.* a thin strip of wood.

splint *n.* 1, a thin piece of wood, etc., used to immobilize a fractured bone. 2, a thin strip for weaving a basket, etc.

splin′ter (splin′tər) *n.* a sharp, thin, split-off piece of wood, bone. etc. —*v.t. & t.* break into splinters.

split *v.t. & t.* [split, split′ting] 1, rend or cleave lengthwise. 2, burst asunder. 3, divide; disunite. —*n.* 1, a crack or rent. 2, a division; a schism. 3, a split willow twig. 4, (*Colloq.*) a bottle of half the usual size. —*adj.* divided; cleft. —split′ting, *adj.* extreme; severe, as a headache.

splotch (sploch) *n.* a large, ill-defined spot. —*v.t.* blot.

splurge (splērj) *n.* an extravagant display or expenditure. —*v.i.* spend extravagantly or ostentatiously.

splut′ter (splut′ər) *v.i. & t.* talk or utter incoherently; sputter.

spoil *v.t.* 1, seriously impair. 2, overindulge, as a child. 3, plunder; despoil. —*v.i.* decay; become tainted. —*n.* (*pl.*) plunder. —spoil′age, *n.*

spoke (spōk) *n.* one of the bars joining the hub and rim of a wheel. —*v.* pret. of *speak.*

spo′ken (spō′kən) *v.* p.p. of *speak.* —*adj.* oral, not written.

spokes′man (spōks′mən) *n.* [*pl.* -men] one who speaks for others.

spo″li·a′tion (spō″lē-ā′shən) *n.* a despoiling or illegal spoiling.

sponge (spunj) *n.* 1, a marine invertebrate; its dried, absorbent framework. 2, any similar absorbent substance. 3, (*Colloq.*) a parasitical person. —*v.t. & t.* 1, wipe with a sponge. 2, (*Colloq.*) live at the expense of another. —spon′gy, *adj.*

spon′sor (spon′sər) *n.* 1, one who vouches for another; a godparent. 2, a buyer of radio or television time. —*v.t.* vouch for; be a patron of. —spon′sor·ship, *n.*

spon″ta·ne′i·ty (spon″tə-nē′ə-tē) *n.* natural, impulsive action; spontaneousness.

spon·ta′ne·ous (spon-tā′nē-əs) *adj.* 1, proceeding from internal impulse. 2, arising naturally; instinctive. —spon·ta′ne·ous·ness, *n.*

spoof *v.t. & i.* (*Slang*) hoax; tease.

spook (spūk) *n.* (*Colloq.*) a ghost. —**spook'y,** *adj.* —**spook'i·ness,** *n.*

spool *n.* a small cylinder on which thread, wire, etc. are wound.

spoon *n.* 1, a utensil consisting of a concave bowl and a handle. 2, any implement or object resembling this. 3, a wooden-faced golf club. —*v.t. & i.* 1, convey in a spoon. 2, (*Colloq.*) pet; make love. —**spoon'ful** (-fŭl) *n.* [*pl.* -fuls].

spoor (spŭr) *n.* the track or trail of a wild animal.

spo·rad'ic (spō-rad'ik) *adj.* appearing at irregular intervals; occasional. —**spo·rad'i·cal·ly,** *adv.*

spore (spōr) *n.* a germ; a seed; a source of being.

sport (spōrt) *n.* 1, an outdoor or athletic pastime. 2, fun; diversion. 3, jesting; a subject of diversion. 4, (*Colloq.*) a sportsmanlike person; a sporting man. —*v.i.* play; frolic.

sport'ing *adj.* 1, relating to outdoor pastimes. 2, sportsmanlike. 3, pert. to gambling. —**sporting house,** house of prostitution.

spor'tive (spōr'tiv) *adj.* frolicsome; jesting. —**spor'tive·ness.** *n.*

sports'man (spōrts'mən) *n.* [*pl.* -men] 1, one who engages in field sports. 2, a fair contestant. —**sports'man·like',** *adj.* —**sports'man·ship',** *n.*

sport'y (spōr'tē) *adj.* 1, sporting. 2, flashy. —**sport'i·ness,** *n.*

spot *n.* 1, a stain; a blemish. 2, a small mark; a speck. 3, a place; a site. —*v.t.* [**spot'ted, -ting**] 1, stain; mark with spots. 2, note; recognize. 3, place. 4, (*Colloq.*) give a handicap of or to. —*v.i.* become spotted. —**on the spot,** 1, handy. 2, in an embarrassing position.

spot'less *adj.* unsullied; clean.

spot'light' *n.* 1, a strong movable light. 2, the center of attraction.

spot'ter (-ər) *n.* one who watches and locates.

spot'ty (-ē) *adj.* occurring in spots; irregular. —**spot'ti·ness,** *n.*

spouse (spows) *n.* one's husband or wife.

spout (spowt) *v.t. & i.* 1, discharge, or issue forth, in a stream. 2, utter or declaim volubly. —*n.* a tube or opening that guides a flow.

sprain (sprān) *n.* a violent straining of muscles and ligaments.

sprang *v.* pret. of *spring.*

sprawl (sprâl) *v.i. & t.* 1, be stretched out carelessly; be spread out aimlessly. 2, scramble.

spray (sprā) *n.* 1, finely divided water or other liquid blown by air. 2, an atomizer. 3, a branch of a tree or of a flowering plant; a similar ornament or design. —*v.t. & i.* scatter or apply as a spray. —**spray gun,** a pistol-shaped device for spraying paint.

spread (spred) *v.t. & i.* [*pret. & p.p.* **spread**] 1, stretch out; unfold. 2, flatten out in a sheet; distribute evenly. 3, set out; display. 4, disperse; scatter; disseminate. 5, extend. 6, push apart. —*n.* 1, extension or expansion. 2, an expanse. 3, a feast; a spread food, as jam. 4, a coverlet. —**spread'er,** *n.*

spree (sprē) *n.* a lively frolic.

sprig *n.* a small branch; a shoot.

spright'ly (sprīt'lē) *adj. & adv.* lively; animated. —**spright'li·ness,** *n.*

spring *v.i.* [**sprang, sprung, spring'ing**] 1, leap. 2, rise up or issue forth suddenly. 3, recoil; warp. —*v.t.* 1, cause to leap or rise. 2, disclose or produce suddenly. 3, release the spring of, as a trap; (*Slang*) provide bail for. —*n.* 1, a leap. 2, the vernal season, in No. Amer. approx. March 21 to June 21. 3, the beginning or freshest time of anything. 4, water rising to the surface of the earth. 5, any source of supply. 6, an elastic strip of steel or spiral wire. 7, elasticity; motive power. 8, a split; a warp. —**spring fever,** a lazy feeling that comes with spring weather.

spring'board' *n.* a diving board.

spring'er *n.* a spaniel used in hunting.

spring'time' *n.* the spring.

spring'y *adj.* resilient; elastic; agile. —**spring'i·ness,** *n.*

sprin'kle (spring'kəl) *v.t.* 1, scatter in drops or particles. 2, bespatter. 3, distribute; diversify. —*v.i.* rain slightly. —*n.* a light rain; a spray.

sprin'kler (spring'klər) *n.* a device for sprinkling water.

sprin'kling (spring'kling) *n.* a small scattered amount.

sprint *n.* a short run at full speed. —*v.i.* run at full speed.

sprit *n.* a small spar that crosses a sail diagonally.

sprite (sprīt) *n.* an elf; a fairy.

sprock'et (sprok'it) *n.* a projection on a wheel that engages a chain.

sprout (sprowt) *v.i. & t.* 1, begin to grow. 2, put forth shoots. —*n.* a shoot or bud.

spruce (sproos) *adj.* trim and neat in appearance. —*v.t. & i.* (with *up*) make neat. —*n.* a coniferous evergreen tree; its wood.

sprung v. p.p. of *spring*.

spry (sprī) adj. nimble; lively. — **spry'ness**, n.

spud n. 1, a small-bladed spade or chisel. 2, (*Colloq.*) a potato.

spume (spūm) v.t. & i., & n. foam; froth.

spun v. pret. & p.p. of *spin*.

spunk n. (*Colloq.*) mettle; pluck. — **spunk'y**, adj. bold; courageous.

spur (spẽr) n. 1, a pointed instrument worn on the heel, to goad a horse; any similar projection. 2, an incentive. — v.t. [spurred, spur'ring] goad; incite. — v.i. press forward; hasten.

Spur

spu'ri·ous (spyūr'ē-əs) adj. not genuine or authentic; counterfeit. — **spu'ri·ous·ness**, n.

spurn (spẽrn) v.t. 1, reject with disdain. 2, kick.

spurt (spẽrt) n. 1, a forcible gush of liquid. 2, a short, sudden effort. — v.i. & t. gush or advance suddenly.

sput'nik n. artificial satellite, esp. one launched by the U.S.S.R.

sput'ter (sput'ər) v.i. & t. 1, spit out or emit small particles explosively. 2, speak or utter explosively and incoherently. — n. an act or result of sputtering.

spu'tum (spū'təm) n. [pl. -ta (-tə)] spittle, esp. when mixed with mucus.

spy (spī) n. 1, a secret watcher. 2, a secret agent in enemy territory. — v.t. 1, observe secretly. — v.t. 1, (with *on*) observe secretly. 2, (with *out*) discover by observation. 3, catch sight of; see.

spy'glass n. a hand telescope.

squab (skwob) n. a young, unfledged pigeon. — **squab'by**, adj. short and stout.

squab'ble (skwob'əl) n. a petty quarrel. — v.i. bicker.

squad (skwod) n. a small party or group, esp. of soldiers. — **squad car**, a crusing police car.

squad'ron (skwod'rən) n. an operating unit of warships, cavalry, aircraft, etc.

squal'id (skwol'id) adj. dirty; filthy; degraded. — **squal'id·ness**, n.

squall (skwâl) n. 1, a sudden, violent gust of wind. 2, (*Colloq.*) a commotion. 3, a scream or cry. — v.i. cry violently. — **squall'y**, n.

squal'or (skwol'ər; skwā'lər) n. filthy and depressed condition.

squan'der (skwon'dər) v.t. spend wastefully; dissipate.

square (skwār) n. 1, a plane figure having four equal sides and four right angles. 2, an open area in a city. 3, a city block. 4, an instrument for determining right angles. 5, the result obtained by multiplying a number by itself. — adj. 1, like a square; at right angles. 2, straight, level, or even. 3, equitable; honest. 4, unequivocal. 5, satisfying, as a meal. — v.t. 1, make square. 2, adjust; true. 3, settle (a debt). — v.i. 1, agree (with). 2, (with *off*) prepare to box. — **square dance**, one for four or more couples. — **square deal** (*Colloq.*) a mutually honest transaction. — **square root**, the number of which a given number is the square. — **square shooter**, (*Colloq.*) an honest person.

square-'rigged adj. see *rig*.

squash (skwosh) v.t. 1, press into pulp; crush. 2, (*Colloq.*) suppress; silence. — v.i. 1, be crushed. 2, make a splashing sound. — n. 1, the act or sound of squashing. 2, a game played with rackets in a walled court: *squash rackets*. 3, a trailing plant of the melon family; its green or yellow fruit, used as a vegetable. — **squash'y**, adj. soft and wet; easily crushed.

squat (skwot) v.i. [squat'ted, -ting] 1, sit close to the ground; crouch. 2, settle on public land. — adj. [squat'ter, -test] short and thick. — n. a squatting posture. — **squat'ter**, n.

squaw (skwâ) n. a No. Amer. Indian woman, esp. a wife.

squawk (skwâk) v.i. 1, make a loud, harsh outcry. 2, (*Colloq.*) complain loudly. — n. act of squawking.

squaw'man n. [pl. -men] a white man living with a squaw.

squeak (skwēk) n. 1, a short, sharp, shrill sound. 2, (*Colloq.*) a narrow escape; a close thing. — v.t. & i. make a squeaking sound.

squeal (skwēl) n. 1, a prolonged shrill cry. 2, (*Slang*) the act of an informer. — v.t. & i. utter a squeal.

squeam'ish (skwē'mish) adj. easily nauseated; fastidious; prudish.

squee'gee (skwē'jē) n. a rubber blade for wiping water from panes.

squeeze (skwēz) v.t. 1, exert pressure upon; compress; force; cram. 2, express; extract. — v.i. press; push. — n. 1, the act of squeezing. 2, a handshake; a hug; an embrace. 3, (*Colloq.*) a predicament.

squelch (skwelch) v.t. suppress. — n. (*Colloq.*) a crushing remark.

squib (skwib) n. 1, a short, satirical writing. 2, a firecracker.

squid (skwid) n. any of various members of the octopus family.

squint (skwint) v.i. look askance, obliquely, or with narrowed eyes.

squire (skwīr) n. 1, a landed proprietor. 2, a lady's escort. 3, an attendant. 4, a justice of the peace. —v.t. attend; escort.

squirm (skwẽrm) v.i. 1, wriggle. 2, writhe mentally. —n. a wriggle.

squir'rel (skwẽr'əl) n. a bushy-tailed, arboreal rodent.

squirt (skwẽrt) v.t. & i. eject or issue suddenly in a thin stream. —n. 1, a thin stream of water, etc. 2, (Colloq.) a small, insignificant fellow.

stab v.t. & i. [stabbed, stab'bing] 1, pierce with, or thrust with, pointed weapon. 2, betray. —n. act of stabbing; a thrust or wound.

sta·bil'i·ty (stə-bil'ə-tē) n. firmness; permanence.

sta'bi·lize (stā'bə-līz") v.t. make stable; steady. —**sta"bi·li·za'tion,** n.

sta'ble (stā'bəl) n. 1, a building for horses, cattle, etc. 2, a collection of racing horses. —adj. 1, firmly fixed; steady. 2, not changing or wavering. —v.t. lodge in a stable.

stac·ca'to (stə-kä'tō) adj. (Music) 1, abrupt. 2, separated by slight pauses.

stack (stak) n. 1, an orderly pile or heap. 2, a chimney or funnel. 3, (pl.) bookshelves. —v.t. 1, pile in a stack. 2, prearrange dishonestly.

sta'di·um (stā'dē·əm) n. a structure of tiers of seats enclosing an athletic field.

staff (staf) n. 1, a stick or pole; a cane. 2, a body of workers or assistants. 3, the lines and spaces on which musical notes are written.

stag n. 1, an adult male deer. 2, (Colloq.) a man not accompanied by a woman. —adj. (Colloq.) for men only.

stage (stāj) n. 1, a single time, period, or step of a gradual process. 2, a raised platform, esp. in a theater. 3, the theatrical profession; drama. 4, a station for changing horses. —v.t. exhibit on a stage.

stage'coach" n. a horse-drawn public passenger coach.

stage fright nervousness caused by public appearance.

stage'hand" n. a worker who handles the sets, etc. in a theater.

stage-'struck" adj. obsessed with a desire to act.

stage whisper a whisper intended to be overheard.

stag'ger (stag'ər) v.i. move unsteadily; falter. —v.t. 1, cause to falter; shock. 2, arrange in a zigzag

order. —n. 1, an unsteady movement. 2, (pl.) a cerebral and spinal disease of horses, etc.

stag'nant (stag'nənt) adj. not moving; stagnating. —**stag'nan·cy,** n.

stag'nate (stag'nāt) v.i. 1, cease to run or flow; lose freshness. 2, be or become inactive. —**stag·na'tion,** n.

stag'y (stā'jē) adj. theatrical. —**stag'i·ness,** n.

staid (stād) adj. sober and sedate; not flighty. —**staid'ness,** n.

stain (stān) n. 1, a discoloration. 2, a blot; a taint. 3, a liquid for coloring wood. —v.t. & i. discolor.

stainless steel an alloy of steel with chrome, nickel, etc. to inhibit rusting.

stair (stãr) n. 1, a step, or series of steps, rising to a higher level. 2, (pl.) such steps collectively.

stair'case" n. a flight of stairs. Also, **stair'way".**

stake (stāk) n. 1, a pointed stick or post. 2, money wagered; (Colloq.) capital. 3, that which is risked or to be gained. —v.t. 1, mark, support, etc., with stakes. 2, hazard or wager.

Stak·han'o·vite" (stə-kän'ə-vīt") adj. pert. to an incentive system for increasing workers' productiveness, in the U.S. S. R.

sta·lac'tite (stə-lak'tīt) n. a calcium deposit hanging from the roof of a cave.

stal'ag n. a German prisoner-of-war camp.

Stalactite and Stalagmite

sta·lag'mite (stə-lag'mīt) n. a formation similar to a stalactite, but rising from the floor.

stale (stāl) adj. 1, not fresh. 2, trite. 3, physically overtrained. —v.t. & i. make or become stale. —**stale'ness,** n.

stale'mate" n. a deadlocked situation. —v.t. deadlock; thwart.

stalk (stäk) v.i. 1, walk with slow, dignified strides. 2, approach game stealthily. —v.t. approach stealthily. —n. 1, an act of stalking. 2, the principal stem or support, esp. of a plant. —**stalk'y,** adj. tall and thin.

stall (stäl) n. 1, a compartment, esp. one for an animal in a stable; a booth; a seat or pew. 2, a state of arrested operation or motion. 3, (Colloq.) a delaying pretext. —v.t. & i. 1, cause to stick or stop. 2, (Colloq.) evade; delay.

stal'lion (stal'yən) n. a male horse kept for breeding.

stal′wart (stål′wərt) *adj.* strong and brave. —*n.* a stalwart person.

sta′men (stā′mən) *n.* the pollen-bearing organ of a plant.

stam′i·na (stam′ə-nə) *n.* lasting strength; endurance.

stam′mer (stam′ər) *v.t. & t.* speak or utter with involuntary breaks and repetitions. —*n.* a stammering.

stamp *v.t.* 1, crush or pound; strike the foot down on. 2, impress; seal. 3, characterize. 4, affix a stamp on. —*v.i.* strike the foot down; walk heavily. —*n.* 1, a downward thrust of the foot. 2, a device for stamping; a die. 3, a mark; a seal; a piece of adhesive paper, as postage. —**stamp′ing ground,** a place one frequents.

stam·pede′ (stam-pēd′) *n.* a concerted, panic-stricken rush. —*v.i. & t.* move in a stampede.

stance (stans) *n.* posture; in golf, the position of the feet.

stanch (stånch) *v.t.* stop the flow of a liquid, esp. blood. —*adj.* 1, firm. 2, trustworthy; loyal. 3, watertight, as a ship. Also, **staunch.** —**stanch′ness,** *n.*

stan′chion (stan′shən) *n.* a post or pillar.

stand *v.i.* [*pret. & p.p.* **stood** (stud)] 1, be in or assume an upright position. 2, be stagnant; stop. 3, be situated. 4, continue. 5, (with *for*) be representative. 6, move (back, aside, etc.). —*v.t.* 1, set upright. 2, (with *for*) tolerate. 3, endure. 4, (with *by*) support; abide by. —*n.* 1, an act of standing. 2, a determined position. 3, a structure, platform, or piece of furniture; a grandstand, etc. 4, a growth, as of grain. —**stand pat,** decline to change.

stand′ard (stan′dərd) *n.* 1, a basis of comparison; a criterion; measure. 2, a flag or emblem. 3, something upright or standing. —*adj.* serving as a basis of comparison.

stand′ard·ize″ (-īz″) *v.t.* make uniform. —**stand″ard·i·za′tion,** *n.*

stand-′by″ *n.* a reliable supporter or resource.

stand-′in″ *n.* a temporary substitute for a motion-picture actor.

stand′ing *n.* 1, rank; reputation. 2, length of experience, etc. —*adj.* 1, upright. 2, continuing; permanent.

stand-′off″ *n.* 1, a state of being evenly matched. 2, a tie. —**stand-off′ish,** *adj.* aloof.

stand-′out″ *n.* something conspicuous, esp. for excellence.

stand′pipe″ *n.* a large vertical pipe or water tower.

stand′point″ *n.* point of view.

stand′still″ *n.* a halt.

stan′za (stan′zə) *n.* a unit, several lines, of a poem or song.

sta′ple (stā′pəl) *n.* 1, a loop of wire, driven as a nail or fastener. 2, a principal commodity. 3, a raw material. —*adj.* chief or principal, as commodities; basic. —*v.t.* fasten with staples. —**sta′pler,** *n.* a device for driving staples.

star (stär) *n.* 1, a body in space, esp. one outside the solar system; a sun. 2, a figure (★) representing this. 3, an asterisk (*). 4, a distinguished or leading performer. —*v.t. & t.* [**starred, star′ring**] 1, mark with a star. 2, feature. —*adj.* brilliant; leading. —**star′dom,** *n.*

star′board″ (stär′bôrd″) *n., adj. & adv.* (Naut.) the right side, as one faces the bow of a vessel.

starch (stärch) *n.* a carbohydrate occurring in cereals, potatoes, etc.; this substance prepared for stiffening, etc. —*v.t.* stiffen with starch.

star chamber a severe and arbitrary court.

starch′y (stär′chē) *adj.* 1, full of starch. 2, (Colloq.) formal in manner. —**starch′i·ness,** *n.*

stare (stär) *v.i. & t.* gaze steadily and fixedly. —*n.* a steady gaze.

star′fish″ *n.* a star-shaped fish.

star′gaz″er *n.* an idle dreamer.

stark (stärk) *adj.* 1, sheer; downright. 2, rigid. 3, desolate; naked. —*adv.* entirely; absolutely. —**stark′-ness,** *n.*

star′light″ *n.* light from the stars, or a time when stars can be seen.

star′ling (stär′ling) *n.* any of various birds.

star′ry (-ē) *adj.* sparkling with, or as with, stars. —**star′ri·ness,** *n.*

Stars and Stripes the flag of the U.S.A.

star-′span′gled *adj.* dotted with stars. —**the Star-Spangled Banner,** the U.S. flag or the U.S. national anthem.

start (stärt) *v.i.* 1, begin or enter upon an action, etc.; set out. 2, make a sudden involuntary move; jerk. —*v.t.* originate; set in motion; establish; begin. —*n.* 1, a beginning; the outset. 2, a lead. 3, a twitch; a jerk.

star′tle (stär′təl) *v.t.* surprise; alarm; shock. —**star′tling,** *adj.*

star·va′tion (stär-va′shən) *n.* act or process of starving; famishment.

starve (stärv) v.i. 1, die of hunger. 2, suffer from hunger or want. —v.t. cause to starve.

stash v.t. (Slang) put away; hide.

state (stāt) n. 1, mode or form of existence; position; situation; condition; structure. 2, dignity; ceremony; great style. 3, the whole people; a nation; a civil community, esp. (often cap.) one of the states of the U. S. —adj. 1, pert. to civil government. 2, pert. to a state of the U. S. ceremonious. —v.t. declare. —state'hood, n.

stat'ed (stā'tid) adj. 1, settled. 2, explicit.

state'ly (-lè) adj. majestic; dignified. —state'li.ness, n.

state'ment (-mənt) n. 1, a spoken or written declaration. 2, an accounting.

state'room" n. a private room on a train or ship.

state'side" adj. & adv. in or toward the United States.

states'man (-mən) n. [pl. -men] a leader in government. —states'man.ship, n.

stat'ic (stat'ik) adj. 1, fixed; stationary; stagnant. 2, pert. to a stationary charge of electricity. 3, (Radio) pert. to atmospheric electrical interference. —n. (Radio) static interference. —stat'i.cal.ly, adv.

sta'tion (stā'shən) n. 1, an assigned place or position. 2, a headquarters. 3, standing. —v.t. assign; place. —station house, a police station. —station wagon, an automobile to carry both passengers and baggage.

sta'tion.ar"y (stā'shə-ner"è) adj. not moving; fixed; not changing.

sta'tion.er (stā'shə-nər) n. a dealer in stationery.

sta'tion.er.y (stā'shə-ner"è) n. writing materials, esp. paper.

sta'tion.mas"ter n. a person in charge of a railroad station.

sta.tis'tics (stə-tis'tiks) n. 1, the science of collecting and interpreting numerical data. 2, (constr. as pl.) the data. —sta.tis'ti.cal, adj. —stat'is.ti'cian (stat'is-tish'ən) n.

stat'u.ar.y (stach'oo-er-è) n. statues collectively.

stat'ue (stach'oo) n. a carved or molded figure, esp. of a person.

stat'u.esque" (stach"oo-esk') adj. of dignified bodily form and posture.

stat'u.ette" (stach'oo-et'ⁿ n. a small statue.

stat'ure (stach'ər) n. 1, a person's natural height. 2, elevation; standing.

sta'tus (stā'təs) n. 1, relative standing. 2, position; condition.

sta'tus quo (-kwō) (Lat.) the existing state or condition.

stat'ute (stach'ùt) n. an ordinance or law. —stat'u.to.ry, adj.

staunch (stänch) adj. stanch.

stave (stāv) n. 1, a pale or piece of wood, esp. for the side of a barrel. 2, a stanza. 3, (Music) a staff. —v.t. 1, (with in) crush in; break. 2, (with off) avert; keep off.

stay (stā) v.i. 1, remain. 2, hold out; persevere. 3, stop; pause; linger. —v.t. 1, halt; restrain. 2, suspend; delay. 3, prop up; support. —n. 1, a pause or halt; an indefinite sojourn. 2, a stoppage or suspension. 3, a prop. 4, (pl.) a corset. 5, (Naut.) a guy rope or wire.

stead (sted) n. place.

stead'fast" adj. firm; resolute. —stead'fast.ness, n.

stead'y (sted'è) adj. 1, firmly fixed; 2, regular; uniform. 3, resolute. 4, industrious. —v.t. & i. make or become steady. —n. (Colloq.) a regular sweetheart. —stead'i.ness, n.

steak (stāk) n. a thick slice of meat, esp. beef.

steal (stēl) v.t. [stole (stōl) sto'len, steal'ing] 1, take dishonestly and secretly. 2, obtain surreptitiously or by surprise. —v.i. 1, practice theft. 2, move stealthily. —n. (Colloq.) a great bargain.

stealth (stelth) n. a secret or furtive procedure. —stealth'y, adj.

steam (stēm) n. 1, water in a gaseous state, esp. when produced by boiling. 2, (Colloq.) energy; enthusiasm. —v.t. give out, or move by, steam. —v.t. 1, treat with steam. 2, (Colloq.) (with up) arouse enthusiasm in.

steam'boat" n. steamship.

steam engine an engine in which steam supplies the power.

steam'er n. 1, a device for steaming. 2, a steamship.

steam'fit"ter n. a skilled worker who installs pipes, etc. that carry steam at high pressure.

steam roller 1, a steam-driven engine for leveling roads. 2, (Colloq.) any agency that ruthlessly overrides and crushes. —steam'roll"er, v.t.

steam'ship" n. a ship propelled by a steam engine.

steam shovel a steam-powered machine for excavating.

steed (stēd) n. a horse.

steel (stēl) n. 1, iron modified to increase its hardness, toughness, etc. 2, something made of steel. —v.t. instill with courage or resolution.

steel'y (stē'lē) *adj.* hard; unflinching. —**steel'i·ness**, *n.*

steel'yard *n.* a balance scale.

steep (stēp) *adj.* 1, almost perpendicular; precipitous. 2, (*Colloq.*) excessive, as a price. —*v.t.* & *t.* soak; saturate.—**steep'ness**, *n.*

Steelyard

stee'ple (stē'pəl) *n.* a lofty tower, esp. on a church; a spire.

stee'ple·chase' *n.* a horse race over obstacles.

stee'ple·jack' *n.* a man who repairs steeples, etc.

steer (stir) *v.t.* & *t.* 1, direct and govern; guide; pilot. 2, follow (a course). —*n.* a castrated male bovine, raised for beef. —**steering wheel,** a wheel used to guide a ship, automobile, etc.

steer'age (-ij) *n.* third, or lowest, class in a passenger ship.

steers'man (stirz'mən) *n.* [*pl.* -men] a pilot.

stein (stīn) *n.* a mug for beer.

stel'lar (stel'ər) *adj.* starlike; pert. to stars.

stem *n.* 1, the main body of a plant, the supporting stalk. 2, a stemlike part, as of a goblet. 3, ancestry. 4, (*Gram.*) the unchanged part in a series of inflectional forms. 5, (*Slang*) a street. —*v.t.* [**stemmed, stem'ming**] stop; check; stanch.

stench *n.* an offensive odor.

sten'cil (sten'səl) *n.* a form cut so that a design or letters can be rubbed through it; such a design or letters.

ste·nog'ra·phy (stə-nog'rə-fē) *n.* the art of writing in shorthand. —**ste·nog'ra·pher,** *n.* —**sten'o·graph'ic** (sten'ə-graf'ik) *adj.* —**sten'o·graph'i·cal·ly,** *adv.*

sten'o·type' (sten'ə-tīp") *n.* (*T.N.*) a keyboard instrument for writing phonetic shorthand.

sten·to'ri·an (sten-tôr'ē-ən) *adj.* loud and powerful in sound.

step *n.* 1, one completed movement in walking, running, or dancing. 2, the distance of a step; a short distance. 3, gait; pace. 4, a support for the foot. 5, gradation; degree; interval. 6, an expedient; a measure. —*v.t.* [**stepped, step'ping**] 1, walk; go. 2, dance. 3, press with the foot. —*v.t.* 1, (with *off*) measure by steps. 2, perform, as a dance. 3, grade; vary. —**stepping stone,** something to step and pause on briefly.

step- *pref.* indicating relationship through the marriage of a parent, as *stepfather, stepson,* etc.

step-'ins" *n.pl.* a woman's under garment.

step'lad"der *n.* a short ladder held erect by a frame.

steppe (step) *n.* an extensive, treeless plain.

stere (stir) *n.* a cubic meter.

ster'e·o·scope" (ster'ē·ə-skōp") *n.* an optical instrument that makes photographs appear three-dimensional. —**ster'e·o·scop'ic** (-skop'ik) *adj.*

ster'e·o·type" (ster'ē-ə-tīp") *n.* a type plate cast from a mold. —*adj.* hackneyed; unoriginal.

ster'ile (ster'il) *adj.* 1, free from living germs. 2, barren; unproductive. —**ste·ril'i·ty,** *n.* —**ster'i·lize'** (-līz") *v.t.* cause to be sterile.

ster'ling (stėr'ling) *adj.* 1, (of silver) of standard pureness, 92½%. 2, (of money) in Brit. money, measured by the pound sterling. 3, of great excellence.

stern (stėrn) *adj.* harsh; austere; severe. —*n.* the hinder part, esp. of a ship. —**stern'ness,** *n.*

ster'num (stėr'nəm) *n.* [*pl.* -nums; -na (-nə)] the breastbone.

ster'to·rous (stėr'tə-rəs) *adj.* characterized by noisy breathing.

stet (*Lat.*) let it stand.

steth'o·scope" (steth'ə-skōp") *n.* (*Med.*) an instrument for listening to sounds in the chest.

ste've·dore" (stē'və-dôr") *n.* one who loads or unloads vessels.

stew (stoo) *v.t.* & *t.* 1, cook by simmering or slowly boiling. 2, (*Colloq.*) fret; worry. —*n.* 1, a dish of stewed meat, etc. 2, (*Colloq.*) a state of agitation; a predicament. —**stewed,** *adj.* (*Colloq.*) drunk.

stew'ard (stoo'ərd) *n.* 1, a manager or trustee; a chief servant. 2, a servant, esp. in a club or ship. —*v.t.* & *t.* guard; conserve. —**stew'ard·ess,** *n.fem.* —**stew'ard·ship,** *n.*

stick (stik) *n.* 1, a piece of wood, generally small and slender. 2, a club; a rod; a cane. 3, any slender piece. 4, (*pl.*) (*Colloq.*) rural regions. 5, a stab. —*v.t.* [*pret.* & *p.p.* **stuck** (stuk)] 1, stab; pierce; prod. 2, thrust (a pin, etc.) 3, put. 4, attach; fasten. 5, (*Colloq.*) nonplus; puzzle. 6, (*Slang*) impose upon. —*v.i.* 1, remain; adhere; cling; abide. 2, extend or protrude. 3, (with *at*) scruple. 4, be held fast; stall.

stick'er *n.* 1, a persistent person. 2, an adhesive label. 3, (*Colloq.*) a puzzling problem.

stick'ler (stik'lər) *n.* one who is insistently precise. —**stick'le,** *v.t.*

stick·-up" n. (Slang) a hold-up robbery.

stick'y (-ĭ) adj. 1, adhesive. 2, humid. —**stick'i·ness,** n.

stiff (stif) adj. 1, rigid; not easily bent. 2, moving with difficulty. 3, formal; unbending. 4, awkward. 5, strong; hard; severe. 6, expensive. —n. (Slang) a corpse. —**stiff'ness,** n.

stiff'en (stif'ən) v.t. & i. make or become stiff. —**stiff'en·ing,** n.

stiff'-necked" (-nekt") adj. 1, suffering from stiffness of the neck. 2, (Colloq.) obstinate. 3, (Colloq.) haughty.

sti'fle (stī'fəl) v.t. 1, smother; suffocate. 2, extinguish. 3, suppress. —v.i. suffocate.

stig'ma (stig'mə) n. 1, a brand or mark of infamy; a disgrace. 2, [pl. **stig'ma·ta** (-mə-tə)] wounds corresponding to those of Christ crucified. 3, (Bot.) the part of the pistil that receives the pollen. —**stig·mat'ic** (-mat'ik) adj. —**stig·mat'i·cal·ly,** adv. —**stig'ma·tize"** (-mə-tīz") v.t.

stile (stīl) n. a series of steps over a fence or wall.

sti·let'to (sti-let'ō) n. [pl. -tos] a slender, triangular-bladed dagger.

still (stil) adj. 1, motionless; tranquil; silent. 2, not sparkling, as wine. —v.t. silence. —n. 1, silence. 2, a distilling apparatus. 3, a single photograph from a motion picture film. —adv. 1, now as previously. 2, nevertheless. —conj. nevertheless. —**still'ness,** n. —**still'ly,** adj. quiet.

still'born" adj. dead when born.

still life a painting of inanimate objects.

stilt n. 1, a high post. 2, (pl.) two poles to extend the length of the legs, for walking above ground level. —**stilt'ed,** adj. stiffly formal.

stim'u·lant (stim'yə-lənt) n. that which stimulates.

stim'u·late" (stim'yə-lāt") v.t. 1, excite to action; invigorate. 2, quicken. —**stim"u·la'tion,** n.

stim'u·lus (stim'yə-ləs) n. [pl. -li" (-lī")] 1, an excitation of a sense organ; what excites it. 2, an incentive; any prod to action.

sting v.t. & i. [pret. & p.p. stung] 1, pain by pricking. 2, distress. 3, goad into action. —n. 1, the venomous organ of a bee, etc. 2, a sharp pain.

sting'er n. 1, that which stings or astounds. 2, a sting of a bee, etc. 3, a cocktail of brandy and liqueur.

sting'ray" n. a flat fish.

stin'gy (stin'jĭ) adj. 1, niggardly. 2, scanty. —**stin'gi·ness,** n.

stink v.i. [stank, stunk, stink'ing] 1, emit a strong offensive smell. 2, have a bad reputation. —n. a bad smell. —**stink'er,** n. (Slang) a mean or dishonorable person.

stint v.t. & i. be stingy toward; restrict. —n. 1, limitation. 2, an allotted task.

sti'pend (stī'pend) n. fixed pay.

stip'ple (stip'əl) v.t. mark with dots or a grained pattern.

stip'u·late" (stip'yə-lāt") v.t. & i. 1, settle by agreement. 2, make a condition of; require. —**stip"u·la'tion,** n. a condition; requirement.

stir (stėr) v.t. & i. [stirred, stir'ring] 1, set in motion; arouse; awake. 2, circulate; agitate. 3, move; move briskly. —n. 1, activity; bustle; commotion. 2, emotion. 3, (Slang) a prison.

stir'ring (stėr'ing) adj. 1, moving; affecting. 2, rousing; thrilling.

stir'rup (stėr'əp) n. a loop to support a rider's foot. —**stirrup cup,** a farewell drink.

stitch (stich) n. 1, in sewing, knitting, etc., one whole movement of the needle; its result. 2, (Colloq.) a bit of clothing. 3, a sudden muscular pain. 4, (pl.) (Colloq.) unrestrained laughter. —v.t. & i. 1, make stitches; sew. 2, staple.

stoat (stōt) n. an ermine.

stock (stok) n. 1, a stem; a race or line of descent; a breed. 2, a family of languages. 3, livestock. 4, a principal supporting part. 5, a supply of merchandise for sale. 6, a reserve supply. 7, the shares of a corporation: capital stock. 8, the broth from boiling meat. 9, a flowering garden plant. 10, a wide necktie reaching to the chin. 11, (pl.) a framework for confining petty offenders. 12, the shoulder support of a gun; butt. —adj. 1, kept on hand; staple; commonplace. 2, pert. to a repertory theatrical company. —v.t. 1, furnish with stock. 2, keep on hand. —v.i. (with up) lay in a supply. —**take stock in,** attach importance to.

Stocks

stock·ade' (stok-ād') n. an enclosure of upright posts.

stock'brok"er n. a broker in corporate stocks.

stock exchange an association of stockbrokers. Also, **stock market.**

stock'hold"er n. an owner of corporate stock.

stock'ing (stok'ing) n. a knitted covering for the foot and lower leg.

stock market stock exchange.

stock'pile" *n.* a reserve supply.

stock-'still' *adj.* motionless.

stock'y (-ē) *adj.* short and thick. —**stock'i·ness,** *n.*

stock'yard" *n.* **1,** an enclosure for livestock. **2,** a slaughter house.

stodg'y (stoj'ē) *adj.* heavy and dull. —**stodg'i·ness,** *n.*

sto'gy (stō'gē) *n.* **1,** a long, coarse cigar. **2,** a heavy shoe.

sto'ic (stō'ik) *n.* one indifferent to pain or pleasure. —**sto'i·cal,** *adj.* —**sto'i·cal·ly,** *adv.* —**sto'i·cism** (-sizəm) *n.*

stoke (stōk) *v.t. & i.* supply with fuel. —**stok'er,** *n.*

stole (stōl) *n.* **1,** an ecclesiastical vestment. **2,** a woman's long neckpiece of fur, etc. —*v.* pret. of *steal.*

sto'len (stō'lən) *v.* p.p. of *steal.*

stol'id *adj.* impassive. —**sto·lid'i·ty** (stə-lid'i-tē) *n.*

stom'ach (stum'ək) *n.* **1,** the digestive organ. **2,** the abdomen or belly. **3,** appetite for food. **4,** inclination; liking. —*v.t.* put up with; endure.

Stomach

D—diaphragm;   L—liver;   H—heart;
S—stomach;   I—intestines.

stom'ach-ache" *n.* indigestion.

stom'ach·er (-ər) *n.* a garment covering the stomach.

sto·mach'ic (stō-mak'ik) *adj.* aiding digestions. —*n.* a tonic.

stone (stōn) *n.* **1,** the substance of rock; a piece of rock; something made of rocks. **2,** a gem. **3,** a hard, rounded object, as a *hailstone.* **4,** a unit of weight, 14 lbs. —*adj.* of stone. —*adv.* (in compounds) completely, as *stone-deaf.* —*v.t.* throw stones at. —**Stone Age,** the era when stone implements were first used. —**stone'ware",** *n.* a coarse pottery.

ston'y (stō'nē) *adj.* **1,** pert. to, or abounding in, stone. **2,** unfeeling; merciless. —**ston'i·ness,** *n.*

stood (stud) *v.* pret. & p.p. of *stand.*

stooge (stooj) *n.* (*Colloq.*) the foil for a comedian; a compliant dupe.

stool *n.* **1,** a single seat or rest without arms or back. **2,** an evacuation of the bowels. **3,** a decoy. —**stool pigeon** (*Slang*) a spy; an informer.

stoop *v.i.* **1,** bend the body forward and downward. **2,** descend; condescend; lower oneself (to). —*n.* **1,** a stooping movement or position. **2,** a small porch and the steps to it.

stop *v.t.* [stopped, stop'ping] **1,** close up or block up, as a hole. **2,** check; impede; restrain. **3,** cease from; discontinue. —*v.i.* **1,** halt. **2,** cease; desist. **3,** tarry; make a stay. —*n.* **1,** the act or result of stopping. **2,** a place where trains, etc. stop. **3,** an obstacle. **4,** (*Music*) a hole, fret, organ control, etc. —**stop'page** (-ij) *n.*

stop'gap" *n. & adj.* a temporary expedient.

stop'light" *n.* **1,** a red light displayed as a signal to traffic to stop; **2,** a warning light at the rear of an automobile.

stop·o'ver *n.* a brief stay.

stop'per (stop'ər) *n.* one who or that which stops, esp. a closure for a bottle.

stop'watch" *n.* a watch whose movement can be stopped, as for timing races.

stor'age (stôr'ij) *n.* act or fact of storing; safekeeping.

store (stôr) *n.* **1,** a place where goods are stored or kept for sale. **2,** a supply for future use. —*v.t.* **1,** stock. **2,** put away. —**store'room",** **store'house",** *n.* a repository.

sto'ried (stôr'ēd) *adj.* **1,** celebrated in story. **2,** having stories.

stork (stôrk) *n.* a wading bird.

storm (stôrm) *n.* **1,** an atmospheric disturbance, with high wind, rain, or snow, etc. **2,** a vehement outbreak; a tumult. **3,** a violent assault. —*v.i.* **1,** blow, rain, etc. **2,** fume; rage. **3,** move with violence. —*v.t.* attack. —**storm'y,** *adj.* —**storm window,** a window outside a window.

sto'ry (stôr'ē) *n.* **1,** a literary narrative; an account. **2,** the plot of a novel, drama, etc. **3,** (*Colloq.*) a lie. **4,** [also, **sto'rey**] a floor of a building.

sto'ry·tell"er *n.* **1,** one who tells stories. **2,** a liar.

stoup (stoop) *n.* a basin for holy water.

stout (stowt) *adj.* **1,** bulky in figure; corpulent. **2,** bold and brave;

firm. —*n.* strong ale, beer, or porter. —stout'ness, *n.*

stout'heart"ed *adj.* courageous; resolute.

stove (stōv) *n.* an apparatus for furnishing heat or for cooking. —*v.* pret. of *stave* (*in*). —**stove'pipe"**, *n.* a pipe for carrying off smoke from a stove. —stovepipe hat (*Colloq.*) a tall silk hat.

stow (stō) *v.t.* pack (cargo, etc.); put away. —stow'age, *n.*

stow'a·way" *n.* one who hides aboard a ship.

stra·bis'mus (strə-biz'məs) *n.* an ailment of the eye; cross-eyes.

strad'dle (străd'əl) *v.i.* & *t.* **1,** sit or stand astride. **2,** (*Colloq.*) favor both sides. —*n.* a straddling.

Strad"i·var'i·us (strad"ə-vār'ē-əs) *n.* a fine violin made by one of the Stradivari family.

strafe (strāf) *v.t.* fire at (ground troops) from an airplane.

strag'gle (strag'əl) *v.i.* **1,** wander away; stray. **2,** spread irregularly or untidily. —strag'gly, *adj.*

straight (strāt) *adj.* **1,** without bend or deviation. **2,** upright; honorable. **3,** regular; unmodified; undiluted. —*adv.* directly; at once. —**straight man**, the foil for a comedian. —straight'ness, *n.*

straight'a·way" *adj.* & *n.* without a curve, as a race course.

straight'en *v.t.* & *i.* make or become straight.

straight'for"ward *adj.* **1,** direct. **2,** honest; open.

straight'way" *adv.* at once.

strain (strān) *v.t.* **1,** stretch to the utmost or beyond the proper limit. **2,** sprain. **3,** press through a filter. —*v.i.* exert oneself. —*n.* **1,** a stretching or deforming force or effect. **2,** great effort. **3,** a passage of music. **4,** streak or trace. —strained, *adj.* affected; forced. —strain'er, *n.* a filter or sieve.

strait (strāt) *n.* [Also, **straits**] **1,** a narrow connecting passage of water. **2,** a position of difficulty or need. —*adj.* narrow; confined; strict.

strait'en (strā'tən) *v.t.* impoverish; confine.

strait jacket a restraining coat.

strait-'laced" *adj.* strict; puritanical.

Strait Jacket

strand *v.t.* & *i.* **1,** drive or run aground. **2,** leave in a helpless posi-

tion. —*n.* **1,** a piece of twisted yarn; a filament; a tress of hair; a string, as of pearls. **2,** a beach.

strange (strānj) *adj.* **1,** unfamiliar; new; unusual; surprising. **2,** alien; foreign. **3,** reserved; distant. —strange'ness, *n.*

stran'ger (strān'jər) *n.* **1,** a person not known. **2,** a newcomer.

stran'gle (strang'gəl) *v.t.* & *i.* kill by choking.

stran'gu·late" (strang'gū-lāt") *v.t.* obstruct; compress. —stran'gu·la'tion, *n.*

strap *n.* a narrow strip of leather, etc. —*v.t.* [**strapped, strap'ping**] fasten, sharpen, or chastise with a strap. —strapped, *adj.* (*Colloq.*) without funds. —strap'ping, *adj.* (*Colloq.*) tall and robust.

stra'ta (strā'tə; strat'ə) *n.* pl. of *stratum.*

strat'a·gem (strat'ə-jəm) *n.* a means of deception; a trick.

stra·te'gic (strə-tē'jik) *adj.* **1,** pert. to strategy. **2,** of vital importance. Also, stra·te'gi·cal.

strat'e·gy (strat'ə-jē) *n.* **1,** the skillful employment and coördination of tactics. **2,** artful planning and management. —strat'e·gist, *n.*

strat'i·fy" (strat'ə-fī") *v.t.* form in layers. —strat"i·fi·ca'tion, *n.*

strat'o·sphere" (strat'ə-sfīr") *n.* the region of the earth's atmosphere 6 to 60 miles above ground.

stra'tum (strā'təm) *n.* [*pl.* **stra'ta**, **stra'tums**] a layer, as of the earth's crust, of the atmosphere, etc.

straw (strä) *n.* **1,** a single stalk of grain; such stalks when dried. **2,** a paper tube. **3,** a trifle. —*adj.* **1,** of straw. **2,** ineffective. **3,** pale yellow. —straw boss (*Colloq.*) a subforeman. —straw vote, an unofficial test vote.

straw'ber"ry *n.* a low herb, its red fruit, or the color of the fruit.

stray (strā) *v.i.* wander; deviate. —*n.* **1,** a lost domestic animal. **2,** a homeless person. —*adj.* **1,** wandering. **2,** isolated; casual.

streak (strēk) *n.* **1,** a line, stripe, or mark. **2,** a stratum or vein. **3,** a disposition; a trait. —*v.t.* mark with streaks. —*v.i.* **1,** move rapidly. **2,** become streaked. —streak'y, *adj.*

stream (strēm) *n.* **1,** a course of running water. **2,** any continuous flow. —*v.t.* & *i.* flow in a stream.

stream'er *n.* **1,** a pennant. **2,** a headline across five or more newspaper columns.

stream'line" *v.t.* **1,** shape so as to offer little wind resistance, like a drop of water. **2,** modernize by eliminating superfluities.

street (strēt) n. 1, a passageway for vehicles and pedestrians in a town or city. 2, the part of such a passageway used by vehicles. 3, such passageway and its abutting properties. 4, a stock exchange.

street'car'' n. a trolley car.

street'walk''er n. a prostitute.

strength (strength) n. the power of exerting muscular force; power; vigor. —**strength'en**, v.t. & i. make or grow stronger.

stren'u·ous (stren'ū-əs) adj. energetic; vigorous. —**stren'u·ous·ness**, n.

strep''to·coc'cus (strep''tə-kok'əs) n. [pl. -coc'ci' (-kok'sī')] a microorganism that forms chains, causing certain diseases.

strep''to·my'cin (strep''tə-mī'sin) n. an antibiotic effective against certain diseases.

stress (stres) n. 1, importance; emphasis; accent on a word or syllable. 2, a strain. —v.t. 1, emphasize; accent. 2, subject to strain.

stretch (strech) v.t. 1, draw out or extend to full length or extent. 2, extend too far. 3, (Colloq.) exaggerate. —v.i. 1, extend over a distance, period of time, etc. 2, be elastic. 3, reach. 4, (with out) recline; be prolonged. 5, extend one's limbs. —n. 1, an extent of distance, area, or time. 2, the act of stretching. 3, a straightaway. 4, (Slang) a term of imprisonment.

stretch'er (-ər) n. 1, a litter. 2, a device for stretching.

strew (stroo) v.t. [p.p. **strewed** or **strewn** (stroon)] 1, scatter. 2, overspread by scattering.

stri'a (strī'ə) n. [pl. -ae (ē)] a groove or ridge. —**stri'ate** (-āt) adj.

strick'en (strik'ən) adj. strongly affected or afflicted; struck; wounded.

strict (strikt) adj. 1, precise. 2, exacting; severe. —**strict'ness**, n.

stric'ture (strik'chər) n. 1, a sharp criticism; censure. 2, a morbid contraction of a canal in the body.

stride (strīd) v.i. [**strode** (strōd), **strid'den** (strid'ən), **strid'ing**] walk with long steps. —n. a long step or its distance; a striding gait.

stri'dent (strī'dənt) adj. creaking; harsh; grating. —**stri'den·cy**, n.

strife (strīf) n. conflict; discord; a quarrel.

strike (strīk) v.t. [**struck** (struk), **strik'ing**] 1, give a blow to; hit; attack. 2, inflict (a blow, etc.). 3, cause to ignite. 4, stamp out; print. 5, effect. 6, come upon suddenly. 7, appear to. 8, lower; pull down. —v.i. 1, inflict a blow. 2, run aground. 3, grab at bait. 4, (Naut.) yield. 5, (with out) go; proceed. 6,

(with upon) discover. 7, (with out) in baseball, have three strikes; (Colloq.) fail. 8, engage in a strike. —n. 1, a refusal by employees to work. 2, (Baseball) a suitable pitch not hit. 3, (Bowling) a knocking down of all pins with the first bowl. 4, a discovery; an accession. —**strik'er**, n.

strike'break''er n. a worker who replaces striking employees.

strik'ing adj. impressive.

string n. 1, a line, thread, cord, or thong; a tendril. 2, (pl.) stringed musical instruments; a series; a chain. 4, (Colloq.) a limitation or condition. —v.t. [pret. & p.p. **strung**] 1, make a string of. 2, (with up) hang. 3, (Slang) hoax. —**string bean**, 1, a leguminous garden vegetable. 2, (Slang) a tall, thin person. —**string'y**, adj.

strin'gent (strin'jənt) adj. 1, vigorous; exacting; urgent. 2, straitened. —**strin'gen·cy**, n.

strip v.t. [**stripped**, **strip'ping**] 1, (with of) take away; deprive; divest. 2, deprive of clothing. 3, tear off (the thread of a screw, the teeth of a gear, etc.). —v.i. 1, remove one's clothes. 2, (with off) separate. —n. 1, a narrow piece, as of cloth or territory. 2, a continuous series. 3, a runway. —**strip'per**, n. —**strip tease**, a dance in which the dancer gradually disrobes.

stripe (strīp) n. 1, a streak or band of a different color or nature. 2, a kind; character. 3, (pl.) insignia.

strip'ling n. a youth.

strive (strīv) v.i. [**strove** (strōv), **striv'en** (striv'ən), **striv'ing**] 1, make strenuous effort; endeavor. 2, struggle; fight.

strob'o·scope'' (strob'ə-skōp'') n. an instrument for studying rapid revolution or motion.

strode (strōd) v. pret. of **stride**.

stroke (strōk) n. 1, a sweeping movement. 2, a mark, as of a pen. 3, an act of striking; a blow; a sudden affliction. 4, a coup. 5, a caress. —v.t. rub gently.

stroll (strōl) v.i. walk leisurely; saunter. —v.t. saunter through. —n. a walk for pleasure. —**stroll'er**, n. a baby carriage.

strong (strông) adj. 1, possessing or exerting great physical or moral power. 2, powerful. 3, extreme in kind; intense. 4, rancid. —**strong'ness**, n.

strong-'arm'' adj. violent. —v.t. coerce by violence.

strong'hold'' n. a fortress.

strop n. a strap to sharpen razors;

strove (strōv) v. pret. of **strive**.

struck v. pret. & p.p. of **strike**.

struc'ture (struk'chər) *n.* **1,** that which is built. **2,** form; the mode of construction or organization. —**struc'tur·al,** *adj.*

strug'gle (strug'əl) *v.i. & t.* labor or contend urgently or strenuously.

strum *v.i. & t.* [**strummed, strum'ming**] play carelessly on a stringed instrument.

strum'pet (strum'pət) *n.* a harlot.

strung *v.* pret. & p.p. of *string.*

strut *v.i.* [**strut'ted, -ting**] walk pompously. —*n.* **1,** a strutting walk. **2,** a brace or support.

strych'nine (strik'nin) *n.* a colorless, odorless crystalline poison.

stub *n.* **1,** a projection; a short remaining piece. **2,** a space for memoranda, as in a checkbook. —*v.t.* [**stubbed, stub'bing**] strike (the toe).

stub'ble (-əl) *n.* **1,** stubs of grain. **2,** rough growth, as of beard.

stub'born (stub'ərn) *adj.* **1,** obstinately determined or perverse. **2,** tough. —**stub'born·ness,** *n.*

stub'by (-ē) *adj.* thickset; bristly. —**stub'bi·ness,** *n.*

stuc'co (stuk'ō) *n.* daubed plaster or cement on walls.

stuck (stuk) *v.* pret. & p.p. of *stick.* —**stuck-'up',** *adj.* haughty.

stud *n.* **1,** a protuberance, as a knob. **2,** an upright support. **3,** a buttonlike fastener. **4,** an establishment for breeding, as horses or dogs. —*v.i.* [**stud'ded, -ding**] **1,** set with studs. **2,** scatter over at intervals.

stu'dent (stoo'dənt) *n.* one who studies; a pupil; a scholar.

stud'ied (stud'ēd) *adj.* **1,** deliberate. **2,** carefully considered.

stu'di·o" (stoo'dē-ō") *n.* an artist's workroom; a place for painting, broadcasting, etc.

stu'di·ous (stoo'dē-əs) *adj.* **1,** diligent in study. **2,** thoughtfully attentive. —**stu'di·ous·ness,** *n.*

stud'y (stud'ē) *n.* **1,** the mental effort of understanding. **2,** an exercise. **3,** a branch of learning. **4,** deep meditation. **5,** deliberate contrivance. **6,** a portrait or sketch. **7,** a room for study. —*v.i.* try to learn; ponder; plan. —*v.t.* examine thoughtfully.

stuff (stuf) *n.* **1,** material. **2,** rubbish. —*v.t.* **1,** cram full. **2,** pack tightly. —*v.t.* eat greedily. —**stuffed shirt** (*Slang*) a pompous person. —**stuff'ing,** *n.* filling.

stuff'y (-ē) *adj.* **1,** poorly ventilated. **2,** dull; prudish. —**stuff'i·ness,** *n.*

stul'ti·fy" (stul'tə-fī") *v.t.* make absurd or ineffectual. —**stul'ti·fi·ca'tion,** *n.*

stum'ble (stum'bəl) *v.i.* **1,** strike the foot; trip. **2,** stagger. **3,** blunder. **4,** (with *on* or *across*) discover accidentally. —*n.* a false step; a blunder. —**stumbling block,** an obstacle; a cause of downfall.

stump *n.* **1,** the truncated lower part of a tree. **2,** any remaining part or stub. **3,** (*pl.*) (*Colloq.*) legs. **4,** a political rostrum. —*v.t.* **1,** nonplus. **2,** (*Colloq.*) make political speeches in. —*v.i.* **1,** walk heavily. **2,** make political speeches. —**stump'y,** *adj.* **1,** stocky. **2,** abounding in stumps.

stun *v.t.* [**stunned, stun'ning**] **1,** deprive of consciousness by a blow, etc. **2,** astound; bewilder; stupefy. —**stun'ner,** *n.* —**stun'ning,** *adj.* (*Colloq.*) strikingly beautiful.

stung *v.* pret. & p.p. of *sting.*

stunk *v.* p.p. of *stink.*

stunt *v.t.* check or hinder the growth or development of. —*v.i.* (*Colloq.*) perform a stunt. —*n.* an athletic or other feat done to impress an audience.

stu'pe·fy" (stū'pə-fī") *v.t.* deprive of sensibility; shock. —**stu'pe·fac'tion** (-fak'shən) *n.*

stu·pen'dous (stū-pen'dəs) *adj.* astounding; prodigious.

stu'pid (stū'pid) *adj.* **1,** lacking ordinary activity of mind. **2,** inane. —**stu·pid'i·ty** (stoo-pid'ə-tē) *n.*

stu'por (stoo'pər) *n.* insensibility.

stur'dy (stėr'dē) *adj.* strong; robust; unyielding. —**stur'di·ness,** *n.*

stur'geon (stėr'jən) *n.* any of various large fishes.

Sturgeon

stut'ter (stut'ər) *v.t. & i.* utter or speak with breaks and repetitions; stammer. —*n.* a stuttering.

sty (stī) *n.* **1,** a pen for swine. **2,** any filthy place. **3,** an inflammation of the eyelid.

styg'i·an (stij'ē-ən) *adj.* dark; infernal.

style (stīl) *n.* **1,** a characteristic mode of expression or action. **2,** the prevalent fashion. **3,** a stylus; the pointer on a sundial; any pen, pin, or peg. **4,** a trade name. —*v.t.* **1,** de-

sign. 2, name. —**styl'ish,** *adj.* fashionably elegant. —**styl'ist,** *n.* one whose style is distinctive.

sty'lus (stī'ləs) *n.* a pointed instrument, as for writing on wax.

sty'mie (stī'mē) *n.* in golf, obstruction by the opponent's ball; hence, any minor but insurmountable obstacle. —**sty'mied,** *adj.*

styp'tic (stip'tik) *adj.* checking bleeding.

sty'rene (stī'rēn) *n.* a thermoplastic substance.

sua'sion (swā'zhən) *n.* a persuasive effort.

suave (swäv) *adj.* urbane; bland. —**suav'i·ty,** *n.*

sub *n.* (*Colloq.*) substitute, submarine, etc.

sub- *pref.* **1,** under. **2,** inferior.

sub·al'tern (sub-âl'tərn) *n.* a junior officer.

sub·com·mit'tee *n.* a committee acting for a larger committee.

sub·con'scious (sub-kon'shəs)*adj.* present in the mind but beyond consciousness.

sub"cu·ta'ne·ous (sub"kū-tā'nē-əs) *adj.* beneath the skin.

sub'deb" *n.* a teen-age girl, usually under 18, not yet a debutante. Also, **sub"deb·u·tante'.**

sub"di·vide' *v.t.* divide (esp. real estate) into smaller parts. —**sub'di·vi"sion,** *n.*

sub·due' (səb-doo') *v.t.* **1,** overcome by force; conquer. **2,** prevail over. **3,** repress. **4,** soften; allay.

sub·ject (sub'jikt) *n.* **1,** a topic; a theme; a person or idea being discussed. **2,** one under the authority of another, esp. a king. **3,** a recipient of treatment. **4,** (*Gram.*) the word representing the person or thing acting. —*adj.* **1,** under the power of another. **2,** (with *to*) exposed or liable to; conditioned upon. —*v.t.* (sub-jekt') **1,** treat. **2,** expose. —**subject matter,** substance (of a book, etc.).

sub"jec'tion (-jek'shən) *n.*

sub"jec'tive (sub-jek'tiv) *adj.* **1,** pert. to the thinking subject. **2,** introspective. —**sub"jec·tiv'i·ty,** *n.*

sub"join' *v.t.* add below.

sub·ju·gate" (sub'jə-gāt") *v.t.* **1,** vanquish. **2,** make subservient. —**sub"ju·ga'tion,** *n.*

sub·junc'tive (səb-junk'tiv) *adj.* (*Gram.*) expressing contingency, doubt, or supposition, not reality.

sub"lease" *n.* a lease granted by a lessee. —*v.t.* [*also,* **sub·let'**] grant or receive a sublease.

sub'li·mate" (sub'lə-māt") *v.t.* **1,** elevate; purify. **2,** turn into, or replace with, more wholesome interests or activities. **3,** vaporize by heat and allow to solidify again. —**sub"li·ma'tion,** *n.*

sub·lime' (sə-blīm') *adj.* exalted; lofty. —**sub·lim'i·ty** (-lim'ə-tē) *n.*

sub"ma·chine' gun a portable machine gun.

Submarine

sub"ma·rine' *adj.* under water. —*n.* a boat able to submerge.

sub·merge' (səb-mĕrj') *v.t. & i.* sink below the surface, as of water. —**sub·mer'gence,** *n.*

sub·mers'i·ble (sub-mĕr'sə-bəl) *adj.* capable of being submerged. —*n.* a submarine.

sub·mis'sion (-mish'ən) *n.* act or effect of submitting.

sub·mis'sive (-mis'iv) *adj.* yielding; obedient.

sub·mit' (səb-mit') *v.t. & i.* [**submit'ted, -ting**] **1,** yield. **2,** refer to another. **3,** propose.

sub·nor'mal *adj.* below average, esp. in intelligence.

sub·or'di·nate (sə-bôr'di-nət) *adj. & n.* secondary; inferior. —**subor"di·na'tion,** *n.*

sub·orn' (sə-bôrn') *v.t.* bribe to perform an unlawful act. —**sub"orna'tion** (sub"ər-nā'shən) *n.*

sub·poe'na (sə-pē'nə) *n.* a writ summoning a witness. —*n.* serve a subpoena on. Also, **sub·pe'na.**

sub·ro·gate" (sub'rō-gāt") *v.t.* transfer (a claim, etc.). —**sub"roga'tion,** *n.*

sub·scribe' (səb-skrīb') *v.t. & i.* **1,** give consent to. **2,** endorse. **3,** engage to receive a magazine, etc. periodically.

sub·scrip'tion (-skrip'shən) *n.* **1,** a signature; assent. **2,** agreement to pay, contribute, etc. **3,** an order for a periodical.

sub·se·quent (sub'sə-kwənt) *adj.* following in time; later; succeeding.

sub·ser'vi·ent (səb-sĕr'vē-ənt) *adj.* **1,** subordinate. **2,** servile. —**subser'vi·ence,** *n.*

sub·side' (səb-sīd') *v.t.* **1,** abate. **2,** sink lower. —**sub·sid'ence,** *n.*

sub·sid'i·ar"y (səb-sid'ē-er"ē) *adj.* lending assistance; supplementary; secondary. —*n.* **1,** a subsidiary thing or person. **2,** a company owned or controlled by a larger company.

sub'si·dize' (sub'si-dīz") *v.t.* support financially.

sub'si·dy (sub'sə-dē) *n.* pecuniary aid.

sub·sist' (səb-sist') *v.i.* **1,** exist; have the means to live. **2,** continue. —**sub·sist'ence,** *n.*

sub'soil' *n.* the soil next below the topsoil.

sub'stance (sub'stəns) *n.* **1,** any particular kind of corporeal matter; material. **2,** subject matter. **3,** wealth.

sub·stan'tial (-stan'shəl) *adj.* **1,** real; actual. **2,** genuine.

sub·stan'ti·ate' (-stan'shē-āt') *v.t.* establish by evidence. —**sub·stan'ti·a'tion,** *n.*

sub·stan'tive (-stən-tiv) *n.* (*Gram.*) a noun or pronoun; something that exists. —*adj.* **1,** pert. to a noun, etc. **2,** real; existing independently; essential.

sub'sti·tute" (sub'stə-tūt") *n.* a person or thing serving in place of another. —*v.t. & i.* supply or serve as a substitute. —**sub"sti·tu'tion,** *n.*

sub'ter·fuge" (sub'tər-fūj") *n.* an artifice; an evasion.

sub"ter·ra'ne·an (sub"tə-rā'nē-ən) *adj.* underground; hidden.

sub'ti"tle *n.* **1,** a secondary title. **2,** printed words shown in the course of a motion picture.

sub'tle (sut'əl) *adj.* **1,** delicate; refined. **2,** artful; crafty. **3,** discerning; discriminating; shrewd. Also, **sub'tile.** —**sub'tle·ness, sub'tle·ty,** *n.*

sub·tract' (səb-trakt') *v.t. & i.* take away; deduct. —**sub·trac'tion,** *n.*

sub'tra·hend (sub'trə-hend) *n.* a quantity to be subtracted.

sub'urb (sub'ərb) *n.* a district outside of, but adjoining, a city. —**sub·ur'ban** (sə-bėr'bən) *adj.*

sub·ver'sive (-vėr'siv) *adj.* tending or intended to overthrow (a government, etc.).

sub·vert' (səb-vėrt') *v.t.* overthrow; destroy. —**sub·ver'sion,** *n.*

sub'way" *n.* an underground railway.

suc·ceed' (sək-sēd') *v.i.* **1,** accomplish what is attempted; terminate, usually well. **2,** follow; come next. —*v.t.* come after; be heir to.

suc·cess' (sək-ses') *n.* **1,** a favorable termination. **2,** a person or thing that prospers. —**suc·cess'ful,** *adj.*

suc·ces'sion (-sesh'ən) *n.* **1,** a following in order; descent. **2,** the act or right of succeeding.

suc·ces'sive (-ses'iv) *adj.* following in order.

suc·ces'sor (-ses'ər) *n.* one who follows or replaces another.

suc·cinct' (sək-sinkt') *adj.* concise; brief. —**suc·cinct'ness,** *n.*

suc'cor (suk'ər) *n.* help. Also, **suc'-cour.**

suc'co·tash" (suk'ə-tash") *n.* a dish of lima beans and corn.

suc'cu·lent (suk'yə-lənt) *adj.* **1,** juicy. **2,** interesting. —**suc'cu·lence, suc'cu·len·cy,** *n.*

suc·cumb' (sə-kum') *v.i.* **1,** give way under pressure; yield. **2,** die.

such *adj.* **1,** of that kind, character, or extent; like; similar. **2,** the same as previously specified or mentioned. **3,** of that class or character. —*pron.* **1,** such a person or thing; such persons or things. **2,** the same.

suck (suk) *v.t. & i.* **1,** draw into the mouth by creating a partial vacuum with the lips and tongue. **2,** absorb; inhale.

suck'er *n.* **1,** one who or that which sucks. **2,** any of various fishes. **3,** (*Colloq.*) a lollipop. **4,** (*Colloq.*) a dupe; a gull.

suck'le (suk'əl) *v.i. & t.* nurse at the breast. —**suck'ling,** *n.* a baby at the breast.

su'crose (soo'krōs) *n.* cane sugar.

suc'tion (suk'shən) *n.* the process or condition of sucking; sucking force.

sud'den (sud'ən) *adj.* happening or done unexpectedly; abrupt. —**sud'den·ness,** *n.*

suds (sudz) *n. pl.* **1,** water foaming with soap. **2,** (*Slang*) beer.

sue (soo) *v.t. & i.* **1,** institute process in law against. **2,** make a petition; woo.

suede (swād) *n.* undressed leather, esp. kid.

su'et (soo'it) *n.* fatty tissue.

suf'fer (suf'ər) *v.t. & i.* **1,** feel or undergo pain; sustain damage or loss. **2,** allow; permit; tolerate.

suf'fer·ance (suf'ər-əns) *n.* **1,** tacit consent. **2,** endurance.

suf·fice' (sə-fīs') *v.i.* be enough or adequate. —*v.t.* satisfy.

suf·fi'cien·cy (sə-fish'ən-sē) *n.* **1,** adequacy. **2,** a sufficient income.

suf·fi'cient (sə-fish'ənt) *adj.* adequate; enough.

suf'fix (suf'iks) *n.* a terminal formative element added to a word or root to make a derivative word. —*v.t.* (sə-fiks') attach at the end.

suf'fo-cate (suf'ə-kāt") *v.t. & i.* 1, kill by impeding respiration. 2, stifle; smother. —**suf'fo-ca'tion**, *n.*

suf'fra-gan (suf'rə-gan) *adj. & n.* assistant (bishop).

suf'frage (suf'rij) *n.* the political right or act of voting.

suf'fra-gist (suf'rə-jist) *n.* a person advocating female suffrage. Also, *(Colloq.)* **suf'fra-gette'**, *n.fem.*

suf·fuse' (sə-fūz') *v.t.* overspread, as with a liquid or tincture. —**suf-fu'sion**, *n.*

sug'ar (shŭg'ər) *n.* a sweet crystalline substance. —*v.t.* 1, sweeten. 2, make agreeable. —*v.i.* form sugar. —**sug'ar·y**, *adj.*

sugar beet a white beet yielding sugar.

sugar cane a tall grass yielding sugar.

sug'ar·plum" *n.* a candy.

sug·gest' (səg-jest') *v.t.* 1, propose for consideration. 2, intimate. 3, call to mind by association.

sug·ges'tion (-jes'chən) *n.* act or result of suggesting; a proposal; hint.

sug·ges'tive (-jes'tiv) *adj.* 1, tending to suggest. 2, suggesting something improper.

su'i·cide" (soo'ə-sīd") *n.* 1, intentional self-destruction. 2, one who takes his own life. —**su'i·ci'dal** (-sī'dəl) *adj.*

suit (soot) *n.* 1, a set of garments. 2, a suing in a court of law. 3, a petition or appeal. 4, a courtship. 5, a division of the pack of playing cards: spades, hearts, diamonds, or clubs. —*v.t. & i.* 1, adapt. 2, be appropriate. 3, satisfy.

suit'a·ble *adj.* appropriate; becoming. —**suit'a·bil'i·ty**, *n.*

suit'case" *n.* a rectangular traveling bag.

suite (swēt) *n.* 1, a series or set. 2, a retinue.

suit'ing *n.* cloth for making a suit.

suit'or *n.* one who courts a woman.

sul'fa (sul'fə) *n. & adj.* designating certain antibacterial compounds, as **sul'fa·nil'a·mide"** (-nil'ə-mīd") and its derivatives, as **sul'fa·di'a·zine"** (-dī'ə-zēn"), **sul'fa·pyr'i·dine"** (-pir'ə-dēn"), **sul'fa·thi'a·zole"** (-thī'ə-zōl").

sul'fur (sul'fər) *n.* a nonmetallic chemical element, no. 16, symbol S, used in medicine, gunpowder, etc. Also, **sul'phur**. —**sul'fur'ic** (-fyūr'ik) *adj.* —**sul'fur·ous**, *adj.*

sulk *v.i.* be silently resentful. —*n.* a sullen mood.

sulk'y (sul'kē) *adj.* morose. —*n.* a light two-wheeled carriage used in trotting races. —**sulk'i·ness**, *n.*

sul'len (sul'ən) *adj.* morose; gloomy. —**sul'len·ness**, *n.*

sul'ly (sul'ē) *v.t.* stain; defile.

sul'phur (sul'fər) *n.* sulfur.

sul'tan (sul'tən) *n.* the sovereign of a Mohammedan country. —**sul·tan'a** (-tă'nə) *n.fem.* —**sul'tan·ate** (-tə-nāt) *n.*

sul'try (sul'trē) *adj.* 1, very hot and moist. 2, passionate. —**sul'tri·ness**, *n.*

sum *n.* 1, the aggregate; total. 2, a quantity of money. —*v.t.* [**summed**, **sum'ming**] 1, add together. 2, (with *up*) condense; recapitulate.

su'mac (shoo'mak) *n.* a shrub; its leaves, used in tanning.

sum'ma·ry (sum'ə-rē) *n.* a condensed statement. —*adj.* 1, brief; concise. 2, (*Law*) immediately judged. —**sum·mar'i·ly** (sə-mâr'ə-lē) *adv.* —**sum'ma·rize"** (-rīz") *v.t.*

sum·ma'tion (sə-mā'shən) *n.* a summing up; total.

sum'mer (sum'ər) *n. & adj.* the warm season; in the No. hemisphere, approx. June 21 to Sept. 21.

sum'mer·house" *n.* a small shelter in a garden.

sum'mer·time *n.* summer.

sum'mit (sum'it) *n.* the top; the highest point or degree.

sum'mon (sum'ən) *v.t.* 1, call or send for, with authority; call together. 2, (with *up*) rouse. —**sum'mons**, *n.* an order to appear.

sump'tu·ous (sump'choo-əs) *adj.* lavish; luxurious; grand. —**sump'tu·ous·ness**, *n.*

sun *n.* 1, the central body of the solar system. 2, the sunshine. 3, anything splendid or luminous. —*v.t. & i.* [**sunned**, **sun'ning**] expose to the sun. —**sun lamp**, a lamp casting ultraviolet rays.

sun'beam" *n.* a beam of sunlight.

sun'bon'net *n.* a bonnet shading the face.

sun'burn" *n.* a burning of the skin from exposure to the sun.

sun'dae (sun'dē) *n.* ice cream with syrup, fruit, etc.

Sun'day (sun'dē) *n.* the first day of the week, observed by most Christians as the Sabbath.

sun'der (sun'dər) *v.t. & i.* part; sever.

sun'di'al *n.* a device on which a shadow indicates the time.

sun'down" *n.* dusk; nightfall.

sun'dry (sun'drĕ) *adj.* several; various. —**sun'dries,** *n.pl.* miscellaneous articles.

sun'fish" *n.* a large seafish.

sun'flow"er *n.* a tall plant bearing showy yellow flowers.

sung *v.* p.p. of *sing.*

sunk *v.* p.p. of *sink.*

sunk'en (sunk'ən) *adj.* **1,** submerged. **2,** on a lower level. **3,** concave; hollow.

sun'light" *n.* light from the sun. —**sun'lit,** *adj.*

sun'ny (-ĕ) *adj.* **1,** bright with sunshine. **2,** cheerful. —**sun'niness,** *n.*

sun'rise" *n.* appearance of the sun above the horizon.

sun'set" *n.* disappearance of the sun below the horizon.

sun'shade" *n.* a shield from the sun, as a parasol.

sun'shine" *n.* **1,** bright sunlight. **2,** cheer.

sun'spot" *n.* a dark patch appearing on the sun.

sun'stroke" *n.* prostration from the sun's rays or heat.

sun'up" *n.* sunrise.

sup *v.i.* [supped, sup'ping] eat the evening meal.

su'per (soo'pər) *n.* (*Colloq.*) superintendent, supernumerary, etc.

su·per- (soo-pər) *pref.* over, above, or beyond; superior; superlative; transcending.

su"per·an'nu·at"ed (-an'ū-ā"tid) *adj* too old; past retirement age.

su·perb' (sû-pėrb') *adj.* magnificent; elegant; excellent.

su"per·car'go *n.* a person in charge of a cargo in transit.

su"per·charg"er *n.* a mechanism to force air into an engine.

su"per·cil'i·ous (soo"pər-sil'ĕ-əs) *adj.* haughtily contemptuous. —**su"per·cil'i·ous·ness,** *n.*

su"per·e'go *n.* (*Psychoanal.*) a moral conscience that regulates the ego.

su"per·er'o·gate" (soo"pər-er'ə-gāt") *v.i.* do more than duty requires. —**su"per·e·rog'a·to'ry,** *adj.*

su"per·fi'cial (soo"pər-fish'əl) *adj.* **1,** lying on the surface; external. **2,** not deep or thorough. —**su"per·fi'ci·al'i·ty** (-fish"ē-al'ə-tē) *n.*

su·per'flu·ous (soo-pėr'floo-əs) *adj.* more than is needed. —**su"per·flu'i·ty** (-floo'ə-tē) *n.*

su"per·for'tress *n.* a large bombing plane, the U.S. B-29.

su"per·het'er·o·dyne" (soo"pər-het'ər-ə-dīn") *adj.* pert. to a radio receiver that changes the frequency of the incoming wave.

su"per·hu'man *adj.* surpassing ordinary human power.

su"per·im·pose' *v.t.* lay (something) over something else.

su"per·in·tend' (soo"pər-in-tend') *v.t.* have charge of; manage. —**su"per·in·tend'ent,** *n.*

su·pe'ri·or (sə-pir'ē-ər) *adj.* **1,** higher in rank or office. **2,** more excellent; greater; higher. **3,** proud. —*n.* **1,** one superior to another. **2,** the head of a convent, etc. —**su·pe"ri·or'i·ty** (-ôr'ə-tē) *n.*

su·per'la·tive (sə-pėr'lə-tiv) *adj.* **1,** surpassing all others; supreme. **2,** excessive. **3,** (*Gram.*) expressing the highest degree by being, or as though, modified by *most.*

su'per·man" *n.* [*pl.* -men] a man of extraordinary powers.

su·per'nal (soo-pėr'nəl) *adj.* **1,** lofty. **2,** celestial.

su"per·nat'ur·al *adj.* beyond the normal; not to be explained rationally.

su"per·nu'mer·ar"y (soo"pər-nū'mə-rer"ē) *n.* an extra person or thing; a theatrical extra.

su'per·scribe' *v.t.* write on or over. —**su"per·scrip'tion,** *n.*

su"per·sede' (soo"pər-sēd') *v.t.* **1,** replace; supplant. **2,** set aside.

su"per·son'ic (soo"pər-son'ik) *adj.* **1,** above the audible limit. **2,** exceeding the speed of sound.

su"per·sti'tion (soo"pər-stish'ən) *n.* an unreasoning belief in an omen, supernatural agency, etc. —**su"per·sti'tious,** *adj.*

su"per·struc"ture *n.* something erected on a foundation.

su"per·vene' (soo"pər-vēn') *v.i.* be added; occur unexpectedly. —**su"per·ven'tion,** *n.*

su'per·vise' (soo"pər-vīz") *v.t.* oversee; have charge of. —**su"per·vi'sion** (-vizh'ən) *n.* —**su"per·vi'sor,** *n.* —**su"per·vi'so·ry,** *adj.*

su·pine' (soo-pīn') *adj.* lying on the back. —**su·pine'ness,** *n.*

sup'per (sup'ər) *n.* a light evening meal.

sup·plant' (sə-plänt') *v.t.* displace and take the place of.

sup'ple (sup'əl) *adj.* pliant; flexible; limber. —**sup'ple·ness,** *n.*

sup'ple·ment (sup'lə-mənt) *n.* an addition to something substantially completed. —*v.t.* (-ment") add to.

sup'pli·ant (sup'lĕ-ənt) *n.* a petitioner. —*adj.* supplicating. Also, **sup'pli·cant.**

sup·pli·cate (sup'li-kāt") v.i. & t. entreat; petition.—**sup"pli·ca'tion,** n.

sup·ply' (sə-plī') v.t. furnish; provide.—n. 1, the act of providing. 2, a store or stock. 3, the quantity available.—**sup·pli'er,** n.

sup·port' (sə-pôrt') v.t. 1, bear; hold up. 2, uphold; back; speak for; encourage; aid. 3, provide for; maintain. 4, act with or accompany (a performer).—n. 1, maintenance. 2, a base; something that supports.—**sup·port'a·ble,** adj. endurable; tenable.

sup·pose' (sə-pōz') v.t. make a hypothesis; assume.—**sup·pos'ed·ly** adv.

sup"po·si'tion (sup'ə-zish'ən) n. act or result of supposing.

sup·pos"i·ti'tious (sə-poz"i-tish'əs) adj. 1, pretended; spurious. 2, supposed. Also, **sup"po·si'tious.**

sup·press' (sə-pres') v.t. 1, restrain; abolish. 2, repress. 3, withhold from publication.—**sup·pres'sion** (-presh'ən) n.

sup'pu·rate" (sup'yə-rāt") v.i. produce pus.—**sup"pu·ra'tion,** n.

su·pra- pref. above.

su·prem'a·cy (soo-prem'ə-sē) n. state of being supreme; highest power.

su·preme' (sə-prēm') adj. highest; utmost.—**Supreme Being,** God.

sur·cease' (sĕr-sēs') n. cessation; end.

sur·charge" (sĕr'chärj) n. an extra charge.

sur'cin"gle (sĕr'sing"gəl) n. 1, a girth for a horse. 2, a girdle.

sure (shŭr) adj. 1, confident; undoubting. 2, certain. 3, stable; unfailing; infallible.—adv. (Colloq.) surely.—**sure'ly,** adv. securely; certainly; doubtless.—**sure'ness,** n.

sure'ty (shŭr'ə-tē) n. 1, security against loss or damage; a pledge. 2, a guarantor; a sponsor.

surf (sĕrf) n. the swell of the sea that breaks on the shore.

sur'face (sĕr'fis) n. 1, the outside; an outer face. 2, external appearance.—adj. pert. to the surface; superficial.

surf'board" n. a board on which one stands in the sport of riding crests of waves.

Surfboard

sur'feit (sĕr'fit) n. excess, esp. in eating or drinking; satiety.

surge (sĕrj) n. a large wave or billow; swell.—v.i. & t. swell.

sur'geon (sĕr'jən) n. a physician who practices surgery.

sur'ger·y (sĕr'jə-rē) n. 1, the treatment of disease, injury, etc., by manual or instrumental operations. 2, an operating room.

sur'gi·cal (sĕr'ji-kəl) adj. pert. to surgery.

sur'ly (sĕr'lē) adj. ill-humored; ill-tempered.—**sur'li·ness,** n.

sur·mise' (sĕr-mīz') n. a conjecture; a guess.—v.t. & i. guess.

sur·mount' (sĕr-mownt') v.t. 1, pass over. 2, overcome; prevail over.—**sur·mount'a·ble,** adj.

sur'name" (sĕr'nām") n. a family name.

sur·pass' (sĕr-pàs') v.t. be greater than; exceed; transcend.—**sur·pass'ing,** adj. greatly excelling; extraordinary.

sur'plice (sĕr'plis) n. a white, loose-fitting clerical vestment.

sur'plus (sĕr'pləs) n. 1, what is left over. 2, the excess of assets over liabilities.—adj. left over; excess.—**sur'plus·age,** n.

sur·prise' (sər-prīz') v.t. 1, come upon unexpectedly. 2, strike with astonishment.—n. 1, a surprising act or event. 2, astonishment.

sur·re'al·ism (sə-rē'ə-liz-əm) n. art interpreting the workings of the subconscious mind.—**sur·re'al·ist,** n. & adj.

sur·ren'der (sə-ren'dər) v.t. give up; relinquish.—v.i. give oneself up; yield.—n. a yielding.

sur"rep·ti'tious (sĕr'əp-tish'əs) adj. 1, done by stealth; clandestine. 2, acting in a stealthy way.—**sur"rep·ti'tious·ness,** n.

sur'rey (sĕr'ē) n. a light, four-wheeled carriage.

sur'ro·gate" (sĕr'ə-gāt") n. 1, a deputy; a substitute. 2, a judge having jurisdiction over the probate of wills, estates, etc.

sur·round' (sə-rownd') v.t. enclose on all sides; encompass; encircle.—**sur·round'ings,** n.pl. environment.

sur'tax" (sĕr'taks") n. an additional tax, esp. on income.

sur·veil'lance (sĕr-vā'ləns) n. 1, a careful watch. 2, supervision.

sur·vey' (sĕr-vā') v.t. 1, view; scrutinize. 2, determine the boundaries, extent, position, etc. of a piece of land.—n. (sĕr'vā) 1, a general view. 2, a statistical study. 3, a surveying.—**sur·vey'or,** n.

sur·viv'al (sĕr-vīv'əl) n. 1, fact of surviving. 2, something that has survived.

sur·vive' (sẽr-vīv') v.i. continue to live. —v.t. outlive; outlast. —**sur·vi'vor**, n.

sus·cep'ti·ble (sə-sep'tə-bəl) adj. 1, (with of or to) capable of being affected. 2, (with to) liable. 3, impressionable. —**sus·cep''ti·bil'i·ty**, n.

sus·pect' (sə-spekt') v.t. 1, imagine to be guilty, without proof. 2, distrust; doubt; mistrust. 3, surmise. —n. (sus'pekt) a suspected person. —adj. (sus'pekt) open to suspicion; doubtful.

sus·pend' (sə-spend') v.t. 1, hold from above and keep from falling; cause to hang. 2, interrupt; delay. 3, defer; postpone. 4, debar temporarily. —v.i. cease; stay.

sus·pend'er n. 1, (pl.) straps to hold up the trousers. 2, a garter.

sus·pense' (sə-spens') n. anxious expectancy or indecision.

sus·pen'sion (sə-spen'shən) n. 1, act or result of suspending. 2, temporary stoppage; stay. —**suspension bridge**, a bridge held up by cables hung between towers.

sus·pen'so·ry (sə-spen'sə-rē) adj. suspending. —n. a bandage or appliance that holds something up.

sus·pi'cion (sə-spish'ən) n. 1, the act of suspecting. 2, a slight trace.

sus·pi'cious (sə-spish'əs) adj. exciting or feeling suspicion. —**sus·pi'cious·ness**, n.

sus·pire' (sə-spīr') v.i. sigh; breathe.

sus·tain' (sə-stān') v.t. 1, maintain; support; keep alive. 2, assist. 3, endure; undergo. 4, corroborate; affirm. 5, of a tone, prolong. —**sustaining program**, a radio or television program that is not sponsored.

sus'te·nance (sus'tə-nəns) n. 1, act of sustaining. 2, nourishment; means of living.

sut'ler (sut'lər) n. a peddler who follows an army.

su'ture (soo'chər) n. 1, a sewing together of a wound, etc. 2, the thread used. —v.t. sew (a wound).

svelte (svelt) adj. slender.

swab (swob) n. 1, a mop. 2, a bit of cotton for cleansing or medicating. —v.t. [swabbed, swab'bing] mop; wipe with a swab.

swad'dle (swod'əl) v.t. wrap (a newborn child).

swag n. (Slang) loot.

swag'ger (swag'ər) v.i. 1, strut. 2, bluster. —n. a gait suggesting arrogance.

swain (swān) n. a male escort; a lover.

swal'low (swol'ō) v.t. 1, take into the stomach through the throat. 2, accept credulously; take patiently. 3, suppress; retract. —v.i.

perform the motions of swallowing. —n. 1, the act of swallowing. 2, a mouthful. 3, any of various longwinged, graceful birds. —**swal''low-tail'**, n. a cutaway dress coat.

swam v. pret. of swim.

swamp (swomp) n. 1, a marsh; a bog. —v.t. & i. 1, flood; fill (a boat) with water. 2, overwhelm.

swan (swon) n. a large, white swimming bird with a gracefully curved neck. —**swan song**, the last work or performance.

swank n. (Slang) pretentious smartness. —**swank'y**, adj.

swans-'down' n. 1, very soft down from a swan. 2, a fabric of similar softness.

swap (swop) v.t. & i. [swapped, swap'ping] barter; exchange.

sward (swôrd) n. turf.

swarm (swôrm) n. 1, a colony of honeybees. 2, a mob. —v.i. throng.

swarth'y (swôr'thē) adj. dark in complexion. Also, swart. —**swarth'i·ness**, n.

swash (swosh) v.t. & i. splash.

swash'buck''ler (-buk''lər) n. a swaggering bully.

swas'ti·ka (swos'ti-kə) n. a form of cross adopted as the emblem of the Nazi party. Also **swas'ti·ca**.

Swastikas

swat (swot) v.t. [swat'ted, -ting] (Colloq.) hit sharply. —n. a blow.

swatch (swoch) n. a sample strip of cloth.

swath (swoth) n. 1, a mowed path. 2, the sweep of a scythe.

swathe (swāth) v.t. bind with a bandage; wrap.

sway (swā) v.t. & i. 1, bend back and forth. 2, rule. 3, prejudice; influence. 4, vacillate. —n. rule.

swear (swâr) v.i. & t. [swore (swôr), sworn, swear'ing] 1, affirm something on oath. 2, promise on oath; vow. 3, curse. 4, (Colloq.) (with off) give up (a habit, etc.).

sweat (swet) v.i. 1, perspire heavily. 2, exude or condense moisture. 3, (Colloq.) drudge; suffer; wait impatiently. —v.i. 1, excrete or exude. 2, cause to sweat. —n. the process or product of sweating. —**sweat'y**, adj. perspiring.

sweat'er (swet'ər) n. a knitted garment for the upper body.

sweat'shirt'' n. a warm pullover shirt, worn by athletes.

sweat'shop" *n.* a factory where workers are oppressed.

Swed'ish (swē'dish) *adj. & n.* of or pert. to Sweden, its people, language, etc.

sweep (swēp) *v.t.* [*pret. & p.p.* swept] 1, move by, or as by, a long brushing stroke. 2, brush over with a broom; clear. 3, pass over. 4, drag over; trail. —*v.i.* 1, clear with a broom. 2, move steadily. 3, extend. 4, move ceremoniously. —*n.* 1, an act of sweeping. 2, reach; range; an extent; a curve. 3, one who sweeps. —**sweep'ing,** *adj.* of wide range; overwhelming.

sweep'stakes" *n.* a gambling transaction; a lottery.

sweet (swēt) *adj.* 1, having the taste of sugar or honey. 2, pleasing. 3, amiable. 4, dear; precious. 5, nonacid; fresh. 6, fragrant. —*n.* a candy, dessert, etc. —**sweet'ness,** *n.*

sweet'bread" *n.* the pancreas of an animal, used as meat.

sweet'bri'er *n.* a long-stemmed rose; the eglantine.

sweet'heart" *n.* a person beloved.

sweet'meat" *n.* a candy.

sweet pea a climbing plant or its fragrant flower.

sweet potato a climbing plant or its edible yellow root.

sweet tooth (*Colloq.*) a liking for candy, etc.

sweet William a plant of the pink family.

swell (swel) *v.i. & t.* [*p.p.* swelled or swol'len (swō'lən)] 1, grow in bulk; bulge; expand. 2, rise, as a wave. 3, show elation. —*n.* 1, an increase; a bulge. 2, a wave. 3, (*Slang*) a socially prominent person. —*adj.* (*Slang*) 1, elegant. 2, excellent.

swel'ter (swel'tər) *v.i. & t.* suffer from heat. —**swel'ter·ing,** *adj.* sultry.

swept *v.* pret. & p.p. of *sweep.*

swerve (swẽrv) *v.i. & t.* turn aside suddenly. —*n.* a sudden veering.

swift *adj.* 1, moving with great speed; rapid. 2, prompt. —*n.* a long-winged bird. —**swift'ness,** *n.*

swig *v.t. & i.* [swigged, swig'ging] (*Colloq.*) drink by large drafts. —*n.* a drink; a deep draft.

swill (swil) *n.* garbage; hogwash. —*v.t. & i.* drink greedily.

swim *v.i.* [swam, swum, swim'-ming] 1, propel oneself through the water. 2, be immersed. 3, be dizzy. —*v.t.* swim across. —**swim'mer,** *n.* —**swim'ming·ly,** *adv.* easily; prosperously.

swin'dle (swin'dəl) *v.t. & i.* cheat; defraud. —*n.* —**swin'dler,** *n.*

swine (swīn) *n. sing. & pl.* 1, the domestic hog. 2, any animal of the hog family. 3, a contemptible person. —**swin'ish,** *adj.*

swing *v.i. & t.* [*pret. & p.p.* swung] 1, move to and fro, while suspended; sway. 2, (*Colloq.*) be hanged. 3, (*Colloq.*) manage. —*n.* 1, a seat suspended by ropes. 2, steady rhythm. 3, (*Colloq.*) a style of dance music. —**swing shift,** (*Colloq.*) a shift of work from 4 p.m. to midnight.

swipe (swīp) *v.t. & i.* 1, strike with a long, sweeping blow. 2, (*Colloq.*) steal. —*n.* a sweeping blow.

swirl (swẽrl) *v.i. & t.* whirl; eddy. —*n.* a twist; a curl. —**swirl'y,** *adj.*

swish *v.i. & t.* 1, whisk; flourish. 2, rustle. —*n.* a swishing sound or act.

Swiss (swis) *adj.* pert. to Switzerland, its people, etc. —*n.* a Swiss citizen.

switch (swich) *n.* 1, a flexible twig or rod. 2, a device for making or breaking an electric current. 3, a change; a device for changing, as a *railroad switch.* 4, a tress of hair. —*v.t.* 1, whip. 2 shift; divert. —*v.i.* change course.

switch'board" *n.* a device for making telephone connections.

switch'man (-mən) *n.* [*pl.* -men] a tender of a railroad switch.

Swivel Joint

swiv'el (swiv'əl) *n.* a pivoted support. —*v.t. & i.* pivot.

swiz'zle stick (swiz'əl) a stick for stirring drinks.

swol'len (swō'lən) *adj.* swelled.

swoon *v.i. & n.* faint.

swoop *v.i.* sweep down. —*n.* a sudden sweeping down.

sword (sõrd) *n.* 1, a weapon with a long edged blade. 2, (*Fig.*) warfare.

sword'fish" *n.* a large fish with a hard, pointed nose.

swords'man (sõrdz'mən) *n.* [*pl.* -men] a skilled fencer.

swore (swõr) *v.* pret. of *swear.*

sworn (swõrn) *v.* p.p. of *swear.*

swum *v.* p.p.p. of *swim.*

swung *v.* pret. & p.p. of *swing.*

syb'a·rite" (sib'ə-rīt") *n.* a self-indulgent, luxury-loving person. —**syb"a·rit'ic** (rit'ik) *adj.* —**syb"a·rit'i·cal·ly,** *adv.*

syc'a·more" (sik'ə-môr") *n.* 1, (*U.S.*) the buttonwood or any plane tree. 2, (*Eng.*) the maple.

syc'o·phant (sik'ə-fənt) *n.* a servile flatterer. —**syc'o·phan·cy,** *n.*

syl·lab′i·cate″ (si-lab′i-kāt″) *v.t.* form or divide into syllables. Also, **syl·lab′i·fy″** (-fī″). —**syl·lab′i·ca′tion**, **syl·lab″i·fi·ca′tion**, *n.*

syl′la·ble (sil′ə-bəl) *n.* the smallest separately articulated element in human utterance; one of the parts into which a word is divided. —**syl·lab′ic** (si-lab′ik) *adj.* —**syl·lab′i·cal·ly**, *adv.*

syl′la·bus (sil′ə-bəs) *n.* a compendium; an abstract.

syl′lo·gism (sil′ə-jiz-əm) *n.* two premises and a conclusion.

sylph (silf) *n.* a slender woman.

syl′van (sil′vən) *adj.* 1, pert. to the woods. 2, wooded; woody.

sym′bol (sim′bəl) *n.* 1, an object standing for or representing something else; an emblem. 2, a letter, figure, or character. —**sym·bol′ic** (-bol′ik) *adj.* —**sym·bol′i·cal·ly**, *adv.* —**sym′bol·ize″** (-līz″) *v.t.*

sym′bol·ism (-iz-əm) *n.* 1, a set of symbols. 2, symbolic meaning.

sym′me·try (sim′ə-trē) *n.* 1, regularity or accordance of form. 2, excellence of proportion. —**sym·met′ri·cal** (si-met′ri·kəl) *adj.*

sym″pa·thet′ic (sim″pə-thet′ik) *adj.* 1, feeling sympathy; compassionate. 2, sharing a feeling. —**sym″pa·thet′i·cal·ly**, *adv.*

sym′pa·thize″ (-thīz″) *v.i.* feel or express sympathy.

sym′pa·thy (sim′pə-thē) *n.* 1, fellow-feeling; compassion. 2, condolence. 3, agreement; approval; accord.

sym′pho·ny (sim′fə-nē) *n.* 1, an elaborate musical composition for an orchestra. 2, any harmony of sounds, words, or colors. —**sym·phon′ic** (-fon′ik) *adj.* —**sym·phon′i·cal·ly**, *adv.*

sym·po′si·um (sim-pō′zē-əm) *n.* 1, a meeting for discussion. 2, a collection of writings on one subject.

symp′tom (simp′təm) *n.* a sign or indication, esp. of a particular disease. —**symp″to·mat′ic**, *adj.* —**symp″to·mat′i·cal·ly**, *adv.*

syn- *pref.* with; together.

syn′a·gogue″ (sin′ə-gog″) *n.* an organization or assembly of the Jews for religious instruction and worship; the building where this is held.

syn′chro·nize″ (sing′krə-nīz″) *v.i.* agree in time; occur at the same time. —*v.t.* cause to agree in time. —**syn″chro·ni·za′tion**, *n.* —**syn′chro·nous** (-nəs) *adj.*

syn′co·pate″ (sing′kə-pāt″) *v.t.* (*Music*) accent beats normally unaccented. —**syn″co·pa′tion**, *n.*

syn′di·cate (sin′di-kət) *n.* 1, an association of persons or corpora-

tions in a particular enterprise. 2, an agency that supplies features for simultaneous publication in different newspapers. —*v.t.* (-kāt″) 1, combine. 2, distribute (newspaper features). —**syn″di·ca′tion**, *n.*

syn′od (sin′əd) *n.* an ecclesiastical council. —**syn′od·al**, *adj.*

syn′o·nym (sin′ə-nim) *n.* a word having the same, or nearly the same, meaning as another. —**syn·on′y·mous** (si-non′ə-məs) *adj.*

syn·op′sis (si-nop′sis) *n.* [*pl.* **-ses** (-sēz)] a summary; outline. —**syn·op′tic**, *adj.* —**syn·op′ti·cal·ly**, *adv.*

syn′tax (sin′taks) *n.* the due arrangement of words and phrases in a sentence. —**syn·tac′ti·cal**, *adj.*

syn′the·sis (sin′thə-sis) *n.* [*pl.* **-ses** (-sēz)] the combination of separate elements into a complex whole; the product. —**syn′the·size″** (-sīz″) *v.t.*

syn·thet′ic (sin-thet′ik) *adj.* 1, pert. to or based on synthesis. 2, artificial. —**syn·thet′i·cal·ly**, *adv.*

syph′i·lis (sif′ə-lis) *n.* a chronic, infectious venereal disease. —**syph″i·lit′ic**, *adj. & n.*

sy·rin′ga (sə-ring′gə) *n.* a flowering shrub, esp. the mock orange.

sy·ringe′ (sə-rinj′) *n.* a device used to draw in and eject a liquid.

syr′up (sir′əp) *n.* any concentrated solution of sugar, flavored or medicated. Also, **sirup**. —**syr′up·y**, *adj.*

sys′tem (sis′təm) *n.* 1, a number of things adjusted as a connected whole; a scheme, plan, or method. 2, regular method or order. 3, a concurrence of bodily parts. 4, the entire body.

sys″te·mat′ic (-at′ik) *adj.* following a system; methodical. —**sys″te·mat′i·cal·ly**, *adv.*

sys′tem·a·tize″ (-ə-tīz″) *v.t.* make systematic.

sys·tem′ic (sis-tem′ik) *adj.* pert. to a system, esp. the body. —**sys·tem′i·cal·ly**, *adv.*

sys′to·le (sis′tə-lē) *n.* the normal contraction of the heart.

T

T, t (tē) the twentieth letter of the English alphabet. —**to a T**, exactly.

-′t contraction of *it*.

tab *n.* 1, a flap or strap. 2, a tag; label. 3, a bill; accounting.

Ta·bas′co (tə-bas′kō) *n.* (*T.N.*) a seasoning made from pepper.

tab'by (tab'ė) *n.* **1,** a female cat. **2,** an old maid. **3,** any watered silk fabric. —*adj.* striped or brindled.

tab'er·nac"le (tab'ėr-nak"әl) *n.* **1,** a place or house of worship. **2,** a receptacle for the Eucharist.

ta'ble (tā'bәl) *n.* **1,** an article of furniture having a flat top supported on legs. **2,** a plane surface; a level tract of ground; a plateau. **3,** food served; fare. **4,** persons gathered at a table. **5,** an arrangement of written or printed information for classification in small space. **6,** a list. —*v.t.* **1,** place on a table. **2,** postpone discussion of. —**table tennis,** a game like tennis, usually played indoors on a large table; ping-pong.

tab'leau (tab'lō) *n.* [*pl.* -leaux (-lō; -lōz)] **1,** a picture. **2,** a striking scene. **3,** an arrangement or array.

ta'ble·cloth" *n.* a cloth cover for, a table.

table d'hôte (tä'bәl dōt') (*Fr.*) a method used by restaurants, whereby a complete meal is served for a fixed price.

ta'ble·land" *n.* a plateau.

ta'ble·spoon" *n.* a spoon holding 1/2 fluid ounce. —**ta'ble·spoon"ful** *n.* [*pl.* -fuls].

tab'let (tab'lit) *n.* **1,** a small flat slab or piece, esp. one intended to receive an inscription. **2,** a number of sheets of paper bound together. **3,** a flattish cake, as of soap; a pill.

tab'loid *n.* a newspaper printed on sheets about 15" x 11" in size. —*adj.* smaller than the usual size.

ta·boo' *n.* a ban or prohibition. —*adj.* prohibited; ostracized. Also, **ta·bu'.**

ta'bor (tā'bәr) *n.* a small drum.

tab"o·ret' (tab'ә-ret') *n.* **1,** a low stand. **2,** a frame for embroidery. **3,** a stool.

tab'u·lar (tab'yә-lәr) *adj.* pert. to, or in the form of, a table.

tab'u·late" (tab'yә-lāt") *v.t.* enter in a table or list; put in the form of a table. —**tab"u·la'tion,** *n.* —**tab'u·la"tor,** *n.*

ta·chom'e·ter (tә-kom'ә-tәr) *n.* an instrument for measuring velocity.

tac'it (tas'it) *adj.* **1,** implied or understood, not expressed. **2,** silent. —**tac'it·ness,** *n.*

tac'i·turn" (tas'ә-tērn") *adj.* saying little; reserved in speech. —**tac'i·turn"i·ty,** *n.*

tack (tak) *n.* **1,** a small, short nail with a large head. **2,** any temporary fastening; a basting stitch. **3,** a course in sailing, esp. one obliquely toward the wind; a leg of a zigzag course. **4,** a course in general; a line of procedure. **5,** food; fare. —*v.t.* **1,** nail with tacks; attach, esp. temporarily. **2,** steer (a sailing vessel) on a tack. —*v.i.* change course.

tack'le (tak'әl) *n.* **1,** an apparatus for moving heavy loads. **2,** equipment or gear, as for fishing. **3,** the act of seizing or tackling. **4,** a position on a football team. —*v.t.* **1,** grasp. **2,** undertake to deal with.

tack'y (tak'ė) *adj.* **1,** sticky; adhesive. **2,** (*Colloq.*) dowdy. —**tack'i·ness,** *n.*

tact (takt) *n.* good judgment in dealing with persons; diplomacy. —**tact'ful,** *adj.* —**tact'less,** *adj.*

tac'tic (tak'tik) *n.* a particular expedient. —**tac'ti·cal,** *adj.* —**tac·ti'cian** (-tish'әn) *n.*

tac'tics (tak'tiks) *n.sing.* the art of maneuvering forces in battle.

tac'tile (tak'til) *adj.* pert. to the sense of touch. —**tac·til'i·ty,** *n.*

tad'pole" (tad'pōl") *n.* a frog or toad in the larval stage.

Tadpole

tael (tāl) *n.* a Chinese unit of weight; a money based on this weight.

taf'fe·ta (taf'i-tә) *n. & adj.* a lustrous silk or rayon fabric.

taf'fy (taf'ė) *n.* a candy made of molasses and sugar. Also, **tof'fee.**

tag *n.* **1,** a label tied or attached to something. **2,** a tatter. **3,** a binding on the end of a cord, ribbon, etc. **4,** something added, or at the end; a refrain, a moral, etc. **5,** a children's game in which one must pursue and touch another. —*v.t.* [**tagged, tag'ging**] **1,** furnish with a tag. **2,** (*Colloq.*) follow closely. —*v.i.* (with *along*) go as a follower. —**tag day,** a day on which contributions are solicited in exchange for tags.

tail (tāl) *n.* **1,** the posterior extremity of an animal, esp. a projecting appendage. **2,** any flexible appendage. **3,** the rear, bottom, concluding, or inferior part of anything. **4,** (*pl.*) the reverse of a coin. —*v.t. & i.* follow after.

tail'board" *n.* the hinged platform at the rear of a truck. Also, **tail gate.**

tail'coat" *n.* a man's coat with a long tail, for formal dress.

tail'light" *n.* a warning light at the rear of a vehicle.

tai'lor (tā'lәr) *n.* one whose business is to make and mend outer garments. —*v.t.* **1,** shape (a garment) to fit the body. **2,** outfit with clothing. —**tai'lor-made"**, *adj.* made to exact order.

tail spin a spiral, nearly vertical descent by an airplane.

tail wind a wind blowing in the direction of travel of an airplane.

taint (tānt) *n.* 1, a stain or blemish. 2, contamination. —*v.t.* tinge with something deleterious; corrupt.

take (tāk) *v.t.* [**took** (tûk), **tak'en**] 1, get by one's own action. 2, seize; capture. 3, accept willingly; receive; swallow, absorb, etc. 4, understand; construe. 5, be affected by or infected with. 6, attack and surmount. 7, deceive; trick. 8, carry; carry off; remove. 9, conduct; escort. 10, choose; select. 11, be the subject of; experience. 12, need; require. 13, subtract. 14, (with *up*) enter into or upon. 15, attract; please. 16, (with *on*) undertake to do; employ; consume; acquire. 17, ascertain, as by measurement. 18, (often with *down*) write down; record. 19, do; make; perform; execute, etc. 20, (with *after*) resemble. —*v.i.* 1, have effect; operate; develop. 2, be successful; win favor. 3, apply oneself. 4, make one's way; proceed. 5, admit of being taken. —*n.* 1, the act of taking; what is taken. 2, (*Slang*) gross income or net profit.

take-"home" pay net wages received after deduction of taxes, etc.

take-'off" *n.* 1, a beginning, as of an airplane flight. 2, (*Colloq.*) a burlesque; an imitation.

tak'ing *adj.* captivating.

talc (talk) *n.* a soft mineral, magnesium silicate.

tal'cum (tal'kəm) *n.* pulverized talc used as a powder.

tale (tāl) *n.* 1, a narrative of events, real or imaginary. 2, rumor. —**tale'-bear'er**, *n.* informer.

tal'ent (tal'ənt) *n.* 1, an inborn ability or aptitude. 2, persons of ability. 3, performers, as in radio shows. 4, an ancient, widely variable unit of weight. —**tal'ent-ed**, *adj.*

ta'les (tā'lēz) *n.* a number of persons summoned to serve on a jury panel. —**tales'man** (tālz'mən) *n.* a person so summoned.

tal'is-man (tal'is-mən) *n.* [*pl.* **-mans**] an inscribed amulet or charm.

talk (tâk) *v.i.* 1, utter words by the voice; speak. 2, interchange thoughts; converse. 3, chatter; prate; gossip. —*v.t.* 1, say; speak. 2, discuss. —*n.* 1, the act of talking; speech; conversation. 2, a conference or discussion. 3, report; rumor. 4, a subject of talk. 5, manner of talking; language; dialect. —**taling machine**, a phonograph.

talk'a-tive (-ə-tiv) *adj.* inclined to talk much. —**talk'a-tive-ness**, *n.*

talk'ie (tâk'ē) *n.* (*Colloq.*) a motion picture with vocal sound: *talking picture.*

talk'ing-to" *n.* (*Colloq.*) a scolding.

tall (tâl) *adj.* 1, having relatively great stature; high. 2, having a specified height. 3, (*Colloq.*) difficult to believe; extraordinary. —**tall'-ness**, *n.*

tal'low (tal'ō) *n.* an oily substance used for making candles, soap, etc.

tal'ly (tal'ē) *n.* 1, an account kept of items; a reckoning or score. 2, a tag or label. —*v.t.* 1, record; register; score. 2, count; enumerate. 3, furnish with a tally; tag. —*v.i.* be in correspondence; accord.

tal'ly-ho" (tal'ē-hō") *n.* a coach drawn by four horses. —*interj.* used by hunters on sighting a fox.

Tal'mud *n.* a collection of authoritative dicta on the Jewish religious law and life.

tal'on (tal'ən) *n.* a claw, esp. of a bird of prey.

ta'lus (tā'ləs) *n.* 1, [*pl.* **-li (-lī)**] the anklebone. 2, a slope.

tam *n.* tam o'shanter.

ta-ma'le (tə-mä'lē) *n.* a Mexican dish of corn and minced meat.

tam'a-rack" (tam'ə-rak") *n.* an American larch tree.

tam'a-rind (tam'ə-rind) *n.* a tropical tree or its sweet fruit.

tam"bou-rine' (tam"bə-rēn') *n.* a small single-headed drum with jingling metal disks set in its frame.

Tambourine

tame (tām) *adj.* 1, changed from the wild state; domesticated. 2, gentle; tractable; docile. 3, dull; insipid. —*v.t.* make tame. —**tam'a-ble**, *adj.* —**tame'ness**, *n.*

tam"o'shan'ter (tam"ə-shan'tər) *n.* [also, **tam**] a Scottish flat cap or hat.

tamp *v.t.* press down by repeated strokes; pound lightly. —**tamp'er**, *n.*

tam'per (tam'pər) *v.i.* meddle; touch improperly or harmfully.

tam'pon *n.* an absorbent plug to stop hemorrhage.

tan *v.t.* [**tanned, tan'ning**] 1, convert (a hide) into leather. 2, make brown by exposure to the sun. 3, (*Colloq.*) thrash. —*v.i.* become tanned. —*n. & adj.* a yellowish-brown color.

tan'a-ger (tan'ə-jər) *n.* a small songbird.

tan'dem (tan'dəm) *adv.* one behind another.

tang *n.* **1,** a strong or distinctive taste or flavor. **2,** a sharp sound; a twang. **3,** a slender projecting part of an object. —*v.i.* clang; twang.

tan'gent (tan'jənt) *n.* **1,** a straight line marking the direction of motion of a point at any instant in generating a plane curve. **2,** a sudden divergence from one course to another. —*adj.* **1,** touching. **2,** being a tangent. —**tan·gen'tial** (-jen'shəl) *adj.*

tan"ge·rine' (tan'jə-rēn') *n.* **1,** a small, loose-skinned variety of orange. **2,** a reddish-orange color.

tan'gi·ble (tan'jə-bəl) *adj.* **1,** capable of being touched; having corporeal existence. **2,** definite or concrete; capable of being realized. —**tan'gi·bil'i·ty,** *n.*

tan'gle (tang'gəl) *v.t.* **1,** unite confusedly; snarl. **2,** catch, as in a trap; perplex. —*v.i.* be or become tangled. —*n.* a mass of tangled fibers; a confused jumble.

tan'go (tang'gō) *n.* a So. Amer. round dance for couples.

tank *n.* **1,** a large receptacle for storing fluids. **2,** a pool of water. **3** an armored self-propelled combat vehicle. —**tank'age,** *n.*

tank'ard (tank'ərd) *n.* a large drinking cup with a hinged lid.

tank'er *n.* a ship for transporting oil.

tan'ner (tan'ər) *n.* one who tans hides. —**tan'ner·y,** *n.* a tanner's place of business.

tan'nin *n.* a substance used in tanning hides: *tannic acid.*

tan'sy (tan'zē) *n.* a flowering weed.

tan'ta·lize" (tan'tə-līz") *v.t.* tease by arousing and disappointing expectation.

tan'ta·mount" (tan'tə-mownt") *adj.* equivalent, as in value, force, or effect.

tan'trum (tan'trəm) *n.* (*often used in pl.*) a fit of temper.

tap *v.t.* [tapped, tap'ping] **1,** strike lightly; pat. **2,** pierce or unplug (a container) to draw off liquid. **3,** provide outlets for (an electric wire, etc.). **4,** cut an internal screw thread in. —*v.i.* strike light blows; rap audibly. —*n.* **1,** a gentle blow; an audible rap. **2,** (*pl.*) a military signal on a bugle or drum: *lights out.* **3,** a piece of leather or metal fastened to the bottom of a shoe. **4,** a plug, faucet, or spigot in a hole. **5,** an outlet. **6,** an instrument for cutting internal screw threads. —**tap dance,** one in which the rhythm is tapped with the feet.

tape (tāp) *n.* a long, narrow band of flexible material. —*v.t.* bind or fasten with tape. —**tape measure,** a tape marked for measuring distance. —**tape recording,** a recording of sound on magnetized plastic tape, by means of an electronic device called a *tape recorder.*

ta'per (tā'pər) *v.i.* **1,** become gradually slenderer at one end. **2,** become gradually less; diminish. —*v.t.* make in tapered form; cause to diminish. —*v.i.* (with *off*) gradually reduce consumption of something. —*n.* **1,** gradual diminution of width. **2,** a slender candle.

tap'es·try (tap'is-trē) *n.* a woven fabric reproducing elaborate designs, often pictorial.

tape'worm" *n.* a parasitic worm that lives in the intestines of humans and animals.

tap"i·o'ca (tap'ē-ō'kə) *n.* a starchy food substance.

ta'pir (tā'pər) *n.* a tropical hoofed mammal resembling swine.

tap'pet (tap'it) *n.* a cam.

tap'room" *n.* a barroom.

tap'root" *n.* a main root.

taps *n.sing.* see *tap, n.,* def. 2.

tar (tär) *n.* **1,** any of various dark, viscid products obtained from organic substances, as wood, coal, etc.; pitch. **2,** a sailor. —*v.t.* [tarred, tar'ring] smear with, or as with, tar. —**tar'ry** (tär'ē) *adj.*

tar"an·tel'la (tar'ən-tel'ə) *n.* a whirling Ital. dance.

ta·ran'tu·la (tə-ran'chə-lə) *n.* any of various large spiders.

tar'dy (tär'dē) *adj.* **1,** not punctual; late. **2,** moving slowly; sluggish. —**tar'di·ness,** *n.*

tare (tār) *n.* **1,** a weed; vetch. **2,** the weight of a container or vehicle without contents.

tar'get (tär'git) *n.* **1,** a design of concentric circles, aimed at in a shooting contest. **2,** anything aimed or shot at. **3,** a goal or objective.

tar'iff (tar'if) *n.* **1,** the duties levied on imports; customs. **2,** any table or system of charges; a price list.

tar'nish (tär'nish) *v.t.* **1,** dull the luster of; discolor. **2,** cast a stain upon; sully. —*v.i.* become tarnished. —*n.* discoloration or impurity.

ta'ro (tä'rō) *n.* a starchy, tuberous plant of tropical regions.

tar·pau'lin (tär-pâ'lin) *n.* a cloth cover of waterproofed canvas.

tar'pon (tär'pon) *n.* a large game fish of warm Atlantic regions.

tar'ra·gon" (tar'ə-gon") *n.* a plant whose leaves are used in seasoning.

tar'ry (tar'ė) v.i. 1, remain in a place; stay; sojourn. 2, delay or be tardy; linger.

tar'sus (tär'səs) n. [pl. -si (-sī)] a bone structure joining ankle and foot. —tar'sal, adj.

tart (tärt) adj. 1, acid or sour to the taste. 2, sharp in character or expression; biting; sarcastic, etc. —n. 1, a small fruit pie. 2, (Slang) a woman of low character. —tart'ness, n.

tar'tan (tär'tən) n. a woolen or worsted cloth with a pattern of crossing varicolored stripes; a plaid.

Tar'tar (tär'tər) n. Tatar.

tar'tar (tär'tər) n. 1, an earthy substance deposited on the teeth by the saliva. 2, potassium tartrate as used in various drugs. 3, an adversary hard to overcome. —cream of tartar, purified tartar, used in baking. —tartar steak, chopped beef, eaten raw. —tar-tar'ic (-tar'-ik) adj.

task (task) n. 1, a definite amount of work to be done; a job or stint. 2, a burdensome piece of work. —v.t. put a strain upon. —task force, a naval force acting as a unit.

task'mas"ter n. one who assigns tasks (esp., hard tasks) to others.

tas'sel (tas'əl) n. a pendent fringe of threads.

taste (tāst) v.t. & i. 1, try or perceive the flavor of by taking into the mouth. 2, eat or drink a little of. —v.i. have a specified flavor. —n. 1, the sense by which flavor or savor is perceived, operating through organs in the mouth. 2, flavor or quality as perceived by these organs. 3, the act of tasting. 4, a portion tasted; a morsel. 5, a liking; predilection; relish. 6, particular preference. 7, good judgment in aesthetic matters. —taste bud, a group of cells on the tongue. —taste'ful, adj. showing good taste. —tast'y, adj. palatable.

tat v.t. & i. [tat'ted, -ting] knot thread with a shuttle, to make lace.

Ta'tar (tä'tər) n. one of an Asiatic people related to the Turks.

tat'ter (tat'ər) n. 1, a torn piece of cloth hanging from a garment. 2, (pl.) ragged or torn clothing.

tat'ting (tat'ing) n. a kind of knotted lace made of thread.

tat'tle (tat'əl) v.i. 1, gossip; divulge secrets. 2, talk idly; chatter. —v.t. disclose by tattling. —n. idle talk; gossip. —tat'tler, tat'tle-tale", n. a gossip; an informer.

tat-too' (ta-too') n. 1, a picture, etc. inscribed on the skin by the

insertion of pigments. 2, a drumming signal calling soldiers to their quarters. —v.t. mark with tattoos.

tau (tow) n. the nineteenth letter of the Greek alphabet (T, τ).

taught (tât) v. pret. & p.p. of teach.

taunt (tânt) v.t. 1, reproach scornfully; ridicule. 2, twit; provoke. —n. a gibe; taunting statement.

taupe (tōp) n. & adj. mole-colored; gray-brown.

tau'rine (tâ'rīn) adj. pert. to, or resembling, a bull.

Tau'rus (tôr'əs) n. a constellation, the Bull (see zodiac).

taut (tât) adj. 1, stretched or drawn tight; tense, not slack. 2, tidy; neat. —taut'en, v.t. & i. make or become taut. —taut'ness, n.

tau-tol'o-gy (tâ-tol'ə-jē) n. needless repetition of the same idea in other words. —tau"to-log'i-cal, adj.

tav'ern (tav'ərn) n. 1, a house in which liquor is sold to be drunk on the premises. 2, an inn.

taw (tä) n. a game played with marbles; a marble; a line from which the players shoot.

taw'dry (tâ'drē) adj. showy but tasteless; gaudy; cheap. —taw'dri-ness, n.

taw'ny (tâ'nē) adj. & n. of a yellowish-brown color; tan. —taw'ni-ness, n.

tax (taks) n. 1, an enforced contribution to the public funds, levied on persons, property, or income by governmental authority. 2, a burdensome charge, obligation, or task. 3, (Colloq.) any charge. —v.t. & i. 1, levy a tax (on); 2, lay a burden on. 3, accuse; blame.

tax·a'tion (tak-sā'shən) n. act or effect of levying a tax.

tax'i (tak'sē) n. [also, tax'i-cab"] an automobile for public hire for short trips. —v.i. 1, go by taxicab. 2, (of an airplane) move on land or water. —taxi dancer, a girl who acts as dancing partner for pay.

tax'i-der"my (tak'sə-dėr"mē) n. the art of preserving and stuffing the skins of animals. —tax"i-der'-mist, n.

tax-on'o-my (taks-on'ə-mē) n. the science of classification. —tax"o-nom'i-cal, adj. —tax-on'o-mist, n.

tax'pay"er n. one who pays taxes, esp. as a landowner.

tea (tē) n. 1, an oriental plant whose dried leaves, infused with hot water, make a beverage; the beverage; a similar beverage made of other plants. 2, a light evening meal. 3, an afternoon reception.

tea ball a small porous bag or container of tea leaves.

teach (tēch) *v.t.* [*pret.* & *p.p.* taught (tât)] **1**, impart knowledge or practical skill to; educate; instruct. **2**, impart knowledge of. —*v.i.* give lessons.

teach′er (-ər) *n.* one who teaches, esp. in a school.

tea′cup″ *n.* a cup in which tea or another hot beverage is served. —**tea′cup·ful,** *n.*

teak (tēk) *n.* a large Indian tree; its hard, durable wood.

tea′ket″tle *n.* a kettle with a spout, in which water is boiled.

teal (tēl) *n.* a wild duck.

team (tēm) *n.* **1**, a group of persons joined together in an action, esp. in a game. **2**, two or more horses, oxen, etc., harnessed together. —*v.t.* & *i.* join together in a team.

team′mate″ *n.* a member of the same team.

team′ster (-stər) *n.* a driver of a team or truck.

team′work″ *n.* coördination of effort.

tea′pot″ *n.* a pot with a spout, in which tea is steeped.

tear (tir) *n.* **1**, a drop of the liquid flowing from the eye. **2**, (*pl.*) sorrow; grief. **3**, a drop of any liquid.

tear (târ) *v.t.* [tore (tōr), torn (tōrn), tear′ing] **1**, pull apart or into pieces. **2**, make (holes, etc.) by rending forcibly. **3**, lacerate. **4**, (with *off, out, down,* etc.) drag violently; remove; raze; wrench; etc. **5**, affect with grief or pity. —*v.i.* **1**, become torn. **2**, move or act with haste or violence. —*n.* **1**, a rip, rent, or fissure. **2**, turbulent motion; violent haste; an outburst of emotion. **3**, (*Slang*) a spree.

tear′drop″ (tir′-) *n.* a tear.

tear′ful (tir′fəl) *adj.* weeping; sorrowful. —**tear′ful·ness,** *n.*

tear gas (tir) a gas that temporarily blinds, used as a weapon.

tea′room″ *n.* a small restaurant.

tea rose a small, yellowish-pink rose; its color.

tear′y (tir′ē) *adj.* nearly weeping. —**tear′i·ness,** *n.*

tease (tēz) *v.t.* **1**, worry or plague with persistent requests, insinuations, etc.; chaff with good-humored jests. **2**, separate the fibers of (wool, etc.) —*n.* one who teases.

tea′sel (tē′zəl) *n.* **1**, a plant with thorny leaves or blooms. **2**, a device for raising the nap of cloth.

tea′spoon″ *n.* a small spoon for table use, 1/3 tablespoon in capacity. —**tea′spoon·ful** (-fûl) *n.* [*pl.* -fuls].

teat (tēt) *n.* a nipple of the mammary gland.

tea wagon a small serving table on wheels.

tech′ni·cal (tek′ni-kəl) *adj.* **1**, pert. to the methods or technique of an art, science, etc. **2**, peculiar to a particular art, etc.; esoteric. **3**, insistent on exact details or construction.

tech″ni·cal′i·ty (tek″ni-kal′ə-tē) *n.* **1**, technical character. **2**, detail of technique; a technical term or point.

tech·ni′cian (tek-nish′ən) *n.* **1**, a skilled worker in a technical field. **2**, one skilled in technique.

tech′ni·col″or (tek′nə-kul″ər) *n.* (*T.N.*) a method of making motion pictures in color.

tech·nique′ (tek-nēk′) *n.* **1**, method of performance. **2**, technical skill.

tech·noc′ra·cy (tek-nok′rə-sē) *n.* a plan of social reform based on greater control and utilization of industrial power. —**tech′no·crat″,** *n.*

tech·nol′o·gy (tek-nol′ə-jē) *n.* industrial arts collectively; the systematic knowledge of a particular art. —**tech″no·log′i·cal,** *adj.*

tec·ton′ics (tek-ton′iks) *n.* **1**, constructive arts. **2**, structural geology. —**tec·ton′ic,** *adj.*

te′di·ous (tē′dē-əs) *adj.* long, slow, and tiresome. —**te′di·ous·ness,** *n.*

te′di·um (tē′dē-əm) *n.* boresomeness.

tee (tē) *n.* **1**, the letter *T*; something shaped like it. **2**, the starting place in the play of a hole of golf. **3**, a small heap or peg to elevate a golf ball. —**tee off**, drive a golf ball.

teem (tēm) *v.i.* be full, prolific, or abundant.

-teen (tēn) *suf.* plus ten, as in *fourteen.*

teen′age″ *adj.* 13 to 19 years old. —**teen′a″ger,** *n.*

teens (tēnz) *n.pl.* the ages 13 to 19 inclusive.

tee′ny (tē′nē) *adj.* (*Colloq.*) tiny.

tee′pee (tē′pē) *n.* a tent of No. Amer. Indians. Also, te′pee.

Teepee

tee′ter (tē′tər) *v.i.* & *t.* move back and forth; seesaw; move unsteadily. —*n.* a seesaw; a seesaw motion.

teeth (tēth) *n.* pl. of *tooth.*

teethe (tēth) *v.i.* grow teeth.

tee·to'tal (tē-tō'təl) *adj.* **1,** pert. to total abstinence from intoxicating liquor. **2,** absolute; entire. —**tee·to'tal·er,** *n.*

tee·to'tum (tē-tō'təm) *n.* a top spun with the fingers.

teg'u·ment (teg'yə-mənt) *n.* a natural covering; integument.

tel·au'to·graph" (tel-â'tə-gràf") *n.* an apparatus and system for transmitting handwriting electrically.

tel·e- *pref.* distant.

tel·e- *pref.* far off.

tel'e·cast" (tel'ə-kàst") *n.* & *v.* broadcast by television.

tel'e·gram" *n.* a message sent by telegraph.

tel'e·graph" (tel'ə-gràf") *n.* an apparatus and system for transmitting code messages by electric currents in wires. —*v.t.* & *i.* **1,** send a telegram (to or about). **2,** (*Colloq.*) give advance notice (of). —**te·leg'ra·pher** (tə-leg'rə-fər) *n.*

te·leg'ra·phy (tə-leg'rə-fē) *n.* transmission by telegraph.

te·lep'a·thy (tə-lep'ə-thē) *n.* communication between minds by means other than the ordinary and normal. —**tel'e·path'ic,** *adj.* —**tel"e·path'i·cal·ly,** *adv.*

tel'e·phone" (tel'ə-fōn") *n.* an apparatus and system for transmitting speech and sounds by electric currents in wires. —*v.t.* & *i.* speak to or call by telephone. —**tel"e·phon'ic** (-fon'ik) *adj.* —**tel"e·phon'i·cal·ly,** *adv.* —**te·leph'o·ny** (tə-lef'ə-nē) *n.*

tel'e·pho'to (tel'ə-fō'tō) *adj.* (of a lens) permitting photography at a distance. —*n.* a picture transmitted by electric wire: *telephotograph.* —**tel"e·pho'to·graph'ic,** *adj.* —**tel"e·pho·tog'ra·phy** (-tog'rə-fē) *n.*

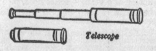
Telescope

tel'e·scope" (tel'ə-skōp") *n.* an optical instrument by means of which distant objects are made to appear nearer and larger. —*v.t.* & *i.* slide, fit, or come together like a collapsing telescope; shorten.

tel"e·scop'ic (-skop'ik) *adj.* **1,** pert. to a telescope; visible only through a telescope. **2,** farseeing. —**tel"e·scop'i·cal·ly,** *adv.*

Tel'e·type" (tel'ə-tīp") *n.* an apparatus and system for transmitting typewritten messages electrically.

tel'e·vise" (tel'ə-vīz") *v.t.* send (a picture, show, etc.) by television.

tel'e·vi"sion (tel'ə-vizh"ən) *n.* an apparatus and system for transmitting visual images by wireless electrical or electronic means.

tell (tel) *v.t.* [*pret.* & *p.p.* told (tōld)] **1,** make known; disclose; communicate. **2,** give an account of; narrate; relate. **3,** express in words; say. **4,** explain. **5,** inform. **6,** discern; recognize. **7,** command; bid. **8,** assert positively. **9,** count; enumerate. —*v.i.* **1,** give an account; make a report. **2,** be an indication or evidence of something. **3,** have force or effect; produce a severe effect. —**tell off,** rebuke. —**tell on,** inform against.

tell'er *n.* one who tells or counts; esp., a bank teller.

tell'ing *adj.* effective; striking.

tell'tale" *n.* **1,** a tattler. **2,** an indicator or gauge. —*adj.* that reveals or betrays; significant.

tel·lu'ri·um (tə-lûr'ē-əm) *n.* a chemical element, symbol Te, No. 52.

tem·blor" (tem-blôr') *n.* an earthquake; one tremor of an earthquake.

te·mer'i·ty (tə-mer'ə-tē) *n.* boldness; rashness. —**te·mer'i·tous,** *adj.*

tem'per (tem'pər) *n.* **1,** state of mind or feelings; mood; disposition. **2,** irritability. **3,** calmness of mind; self-restraint. **4,** the state of a metal as to hardness and elasticity. **5,** a modifying substance. —*v.t.* **1,** moderate; mitigate. **2,** bring to a desired condition. **3,** modify by admixture.

tem'per·a (tem'pər-ə) *n.* in painting, distemper.

tem'per·a·ment (tem'pər-ə-mənt) *n.* **1,** the tendencies peculiar to an individual; natural disposition. **2,** tendency to act without self-restraint. **3,** the plan of tuning for a musical instrument.

tem"per·a·men'tal (-men'təl) *adj.* **1,** having a strongly marked temperament; irritable or sensitive. **2,** constitutional; innate.

tem'per·ance (tem'pər-əns) *n.* moderation, esp. in the use of intoxicating liquors.

tem'per·ate (tem'pər-ət) *adj.* moderate. —**tem'per·ate·ness,** *n.*

tem'per·a·ture (tem'pər-ə-chûr) *n.* condition with respect to hotness or coldness.

tem'pered (tem'pərd) *adj.* **1,** moderated; made less violent. **2,** having a specified disposition, as *good-tempered.* **3,** of metals, modified by heat treatment.

tem'pest (tem'pist) *n.* a violent windstorm; any great commotion or tumult.

tem·pes'tu·ous (tem-pes'choo-əs)

adj. stormy; tumultuous. **—tem·pes'tu·ous·ness,** *n.*

tem'ple (tem'pəl) *n.* **1,** an edifice dedicated to the service of a deity; a church. **2,** a revered headquarters. **3,** the flattened area at the side of the head above the cheek. Also, **tem'plate.**

tem'plet (tem'plit) *n.* a pattern or guide used in shaping a piece of work. Also, **tem'plate.**

tem'po (tem'pō) *n.* **1,** rate of movement, as in music. **2,** a favorable movement for action.

tem'po·ral (tem'pə-rəl) *adj.* **1,** pert. to time. **2,** of the present life or this world; worldly; secular.

tem'po·rar''y (tem'pə-rer'ē) *adj.* lasting for a time only.

tem'po·rize'' (tem'pə-rīz'') *v.i.* **1,** defer action or decision to gain time; delay. **2,** yield temporarily.

tempt *v.t.* **1,** induce or incite; entice; dispose to evil. **2,** be attractive to; allure; invite. **3,** risk provoking; defy. **—tempt'er,** *n.* **—tempt'ress,** *n.fem.*

temp·ta'tion (temp-tā'shən) *n.* act or effect of tempting; an inducement; enticement.

ten *n. & adj.* the cardinal number between 9 and 11, expressed by 10.

ten'a·ble (ten'ə-bəl) *adj.* capable of being held or maintained. **—ten·a·bil'i·ty, ten'a·ble·ness,** *n.*

ten'ace (ten'is) *n.* in card playing, a holding of two cards near but not adjacent in rank.

te·na'cious (tə-nā'shəs) *adj.* **1,** holding fast; retentive. **2,** persistent in an opinion or view; stubborn. **3,** sticky or viscous. **4,** highly cohesive; tough.

te·nac'i·ty (tə-nas'ə-tē) *n.* quality of being tenacious.

ten'ant (ten'ənt) *n.* one who holds property by lease or rent. **—v.t. & i.** inhabit. **—ten'an·cy,** *n.* **—ten'ant·ry,** *n.* tenants collectively.

Ten Commandments a series of rules for moral behavior, given by God to Moses (Ex. 20).

tend *v.i.* **1,** be inclined or disposed. **2,** lead in a particular direction. **3,** attend. **—v.t.** take care of; wait upon; attend.

ten'den·cy (ten'dən-sē) *n.* **1,** disposition to act in a particular way. **2,** a particular inclination; a mode, direction, or outcome.

ten·den'tious (ten-den'shəs) *adj.* serving or written as propaganda. **—ten·den'tious·ness,** *n.*

ten'der (ten'dər) *adj.* **1,** soft in substance, not hard or tough. **2,** delicate in constitution, health, etc.; gentle; sensitive. **3,** affectionate; sentimental; considerate. **4,** immature. **5,** requiring careful handling; critical. **—n. 1,** one who

tends; an attendant. **2,** an auxiliary boat or railroad car. **3,** an offer; the act of tendering. **4,** something offered; money that must be accepted in payment of a debt: *legal tender.* **—v.t.** offer; present for acceptance. **—ten'der·ness,** *n.*

ten'der·foot'' *n.* a soft or inexperienced person; a novice.

ten'der·heart''ed *adj.* kind; sympathetic. **—ten''der·heart'ed·ness,** *n.*

ten'der·ize'' (-īz'') *v.t.* make tender.

ten'der·loin'' *n.* **1,** a cut of tender meat. **2,** the underworld section of a city.

ten'don (ten'dən) *n.* a band of tough, fibrous tissue; a sinew.

ten'dril *n.* a threadlike growth from the stem of a vine.

ten'e·ment (ten'ə-mənt) *n.* **1,** a multiple dwelling, esp. of inferior class. **2,** any dwelling occupied by a tenant. **3,** an apartment in a multiple dwelling. **4,** any place of abode.

ten'et (ten'ət) *n.* any opinion, principle, or doctrine held to be true.

ten'nis (ten'is) *n.* a game of propelling a ball, struck by a racket, across a net.

ten'on (ten'ən) *n.* a projecting end for insertion into a mortise. **—v.t.** make or join by a tenon.

ten'or (ten'ər) *n.* **1,** the general course of a thought, saying, discourse, etc.; purport; drift. **2,** a male singing voice of highest range.

ten'pen''ny *adj.* **1,** [also, ten'pence] 10 Brit. pennies in value. **2,** of a nail, 3 in. long.

ten'pins'' *n.sing.* a bowling game.

tense (tens) *adj.* **1,** stretched tight; strained to stiffness; taut. **2,** in a state of mental strain or nervous tension. **—v.t. & i.** make or become tense. **—n.** (*Gram.*) time, of the action of a verb. **—tense'ness,** *n.*

ten'sile (ten'sil) *adj.* **1,** pert. to tension. **2,** ductile.

ten'sion (ten'shən) *n.* **1,** the act of stretching; the state of being strained or tense. **2,** mental strain; excitement. **3,** an opposition of physical or electrical forces; pressure. **—ten'sion·al,** *adj.*

ten'si·ty (ten'sə-tē) *n.* a state of tension.

ten'sor (ten'sər) *n.* **1,** a muscle that tightens or stretches a part. **2,** a set of equations describing the properties of space.

tent *n.* a portable shelter of cloth, skins, etc. supported by one or more poles. **—v.i.** live in a tent.

ten'ta·cle (ten'tə-kəl) *n.* **1,** a slender appendage of an animal; a feeler. **2,** any sensitive filament.

---

fat, fāte, fär, fāre, fåll, àsk; met, hē, hèr, maybē; pin, pīne; not, nōte, ôr, tool

ten·ta·tive (ten'tə-tiv) *adj.* based on or done as a trial; experimental. —**ten·ta·tive·ness,** *n.*

ten'ter·hook" (ten'tər-hŭk") *n.* a hook used to hold cloth stretched on a drying frame. —**on tenterhooks,** in a state of suspense; apprehensive.

tenth *adj.* the ordinal of ten, also written 10th. —*n.* one of ten equal parts.

ten'u·ous (ten'ū-əs) *adj.* 1, thin in consistency; rarefied. 2, slender or small. 3, of slight significance. —**ten'u·ous·ness,** *n.*

ten'ure (ten'yər) *n.* 1, the holding of something, as property, office, etc. 2, the period of such holding.

te'pee (tē'pē) *n.* teepee.

tep'id *adj.* moderately warm; lukewarm. —**te·pid'i·ty,** *n.*

ter'bi·um (tẽr·bē·əm) *n.* a metallic chemical element, symbol Tb, No. 65.

ter·cen'te·nar"y (tẽr·sen'tə·nâr"ē) *adj.* pert. to or comprising 300 years. —*n.* the 300th anniversary.

term (tẽrm) *n.* 1, a word or phrase, esp. one particular to some branch of knowledge. 2, the period of time through which something lasts, as a course of instruction in a school or college. 3, (*pl.*) conditions offered for acceptance; rates. 4, (*pl.*) relative position; circumstances. 5, a mathematical expression treated as a unit. —*v.t.* apply a term to; name; call; designate. —**term insurance,** life insurance effective for a limited number of years.

ter'ma·gant (tẽr'mə·gənt) *n.* a quarrelsome or shrewish woman.

ter'mi·na·ble (tẽr'mə-nə-bəl) *adj.* that may be terminated.

ter'mi·nal (tẽr'mə-nəl) *adj.* 1, situated at or forming the extremity, boundary, or limit of something. 2, final. 3, pert. to a terminus. —*n.* 1, a terminal part or structure. 2, a principal railroad station. 3, an electrical connection. —**terminal leave,** leave with pay (accumulated unused leave) given to a member of the armed forces before discharge.

ter'mi·nate" (tẽr'mə-nāt") *v.t.* 1, bring to an end; finish; conclude. 2, form the end, boundary, or limit of. —*v.i.* 1, come to an end; cease. 2, result. —**ter'mi·na'tion,** *n.*

ter"mi·nol'o·gy (tẽr"mə-nol'ə-jē) *n.* the vocabulary of terms peculiar to a science or art.

ter'mi·nus (tẽr'mə-nəs) *n.* [*pl.* -ni" (-nī")] an end, extremity, boundary, or limit.

ter'mite (tẽr'mīt) *n.* a social insect that burrows into and undermines wooden structures; white ant.

tern (tẽrn) *n.* an aquatic bird of the gull family.

terp"si·cho·re'an (tẽrp"si-kə-rē'ən) *adj.* pert. to dancing. —*n.* a dancer.

ter'race (ter'əs) *n.* 1, an elevated tract of flat ground; one of a series of tracts at different levels. 2, an outdoor promenade; a balcony. 3, a street cut in a slope. —*v.t.* cut in a series of terraces.

ter'ra cot'ta (ter'ə kot'ə) *n.* 1, a hard earthenware; something made of it. 2, an orange-brown color.

ter'ra fir'ma (ter'ə-fẽr'mə) (*Lat.*) solid ground.

ter·rain' (te-rān') *n.* a tract of land with regard to its suitability for a particular purpose.

ter"ra·my'cin (ter'ə-mī'sin) *n.* an antibiotic drug.

ter'ra·pin (ter'ə-pin) *n.* any of several fresh-water and tidewater turtles.

ter·raz'zo (ter-rät'tsō) *n.* a flooring of cemented stone.

ter·res'tri·al (tə-res'trē-əl) *adj.* 1, pert. to the earth or dry land. 2, worldly; mundane. 3, living on land.

ter'ri·ble (ter'ə-bəl) *adj.* 1, such as to excite terror; dreadful; fearsome. 2, excessive; severe. 3, (*Colloq.*) unpleasant; unskillful. —**ter'ri·ble·ness,** *n.*

ter'ri·er (ter'ē-ər) *n.* any of several breeds of small dog.

Terriers
Cairn
Boston
Smooth Fox
Scottish

ter·rif'ic (tə-rif'ik) *adj.* 1, causing terror. 2, (*Colloq.*) extraordinary; extreme. —**ter·rif'i·cal·ly,** *adv.* —**ter·rif'ic·ness,** *n.*

ter'ri·fy" (ter'i-fī") *v.t.* fill with terror; frighten.

ter'ri·to·ry (ter'i-tôr'ē) *n.* 1, a tract of land; a region or district. 2, a domain; realm. 3, (*cap.*) a region belonging to the U. S., not a state. —**ter"ri·to'ri·al,** *adj.*

ter'ror (ter'ər) *n.* 1, intense fear, fright, or dread; a cause of fear. 2, the use of violence as a political instrument; (*cap.*) a period of such violence; a terrorist group.

ter'ror·ist (ter'ər) *n.* one who employs violence politically.

ter'ror·ize" (-īz") *v.t. & t.* dominate by intimidation; fill with dread.

tŭb, cūte, pŭll; label; oil, owl; go, chip, she, thin, *then*, sing, ink; *see p. 6*

ter'ry (ter'ê) n. [also, terry cloth] a fabric with a pile of loops.

terse (têrs) adj. saying much in few words; brief and pithy; concise. —**terse'ness,** n.

ter'ti-ar''y (têr'shē-er''ē) adj. third in order or rank.

tes'sel-late'' (tes'ə-lāt'') v.t. form into a variegated pattern of small squares.

test n. a critical trial or examination; a trial. —v.t. subject to a test; try; assay. —**test tube,** a glass vial used in laboratory work.

tes'ta-ment (tes'tə-mənt) n. 1, a document directing disposition of property after death of the owner; a will. 2, an agreement; a covenant between God and man. 3, (cap.) either of the two major parts of the Bible; the Mosaic dispensation (Old Testament) or Christian dispensation (New Testament). —**tes''-ta-men'ta-ry,** adj.

tes'tate (tes'tāt') adj. having made a valid will.

tes'ta''tor (tes'tā''tər) n. one who makes a will. —**tes-ta'trix** (tes-tā'-triks) n.fem.

tes'ter (tes'tər) n. a canopy.

tes'ti-cle (tes'tə-kəl) n. the male sex gland. Also, **tes'tis** [pl. -tes (-tēz)].

tes'ti-fy'' (tes'ti-fī'') v.i. give testimony, esp. under oath; attest to facts. —v.t. give evidence of.

tes''ti-mo'ni-al (tes''tə-mō'nē-əl) n. 1, a written recommendation or certificate. 2, an expression of esteem or appreciation. —adj. pert. to testimony or a testimonial.

tes'ti-mo''ny (tes'tə-mō''nē) n. 1, a statement made under oath by a witness. 2, evidence; proof. 3, open declaration, as of faith.

tes-tos'ter-one'' (tes-tos'tə-rōn'') n. the hormone secreted by the testicles, used medicinally.

test tube a hollow glass cylinder, closed at one end, used in chemical experiments.

tes'ty (tes'tē) adj. ill-tempered; irascible; petulant. —**tes'ti-ness,** n.

tet'a-nus (tet'ə-nəs) n. an infectious, often fatal, bacillic disease, marked by rigid spasm of voluntary muscles, as lockjaw.

tête-'a-tête' (tāt'ə-tāt') n. a private conversation, esp. between two persons. —adj. & adv. (in) private.

teth'er (teth'ər) n. a rope to restrain a grazing animal; a halter or leash. —v.t. restrain with a tether.

tet-ra- pref. four.

tet''ra-eth'yl (tet''rə-eth'əl) adj. pert. to tetraethyl lead; see ethyl.

Tet''ra-gram'ma-ton'' (tet'rə-gram'ə-ton'') n. the letters JHVH (or YHWH, etc.), representing the name of God, rendered in English as Jehovah (or Yahweh, etc.).

te'trarch (tē'trärk) n. one of four joint rulers. —**te'trar-chy** (-kē) n.

Teu-ton'ic (tū-ton'ik) adj. pert. to the Teutons, or Germanic peoples.

text (tekst) n. 1, the main body of a book; the actual wording of anything written or printed; the author's words. 2, the subject of a discourse; a theme or topic. 3, a passage of Scripture taken as a theme. 4, the words of a song, oratorio, etc. 5, a style of printing type (A, a); Old English.

text'book'' n. a book used for instruction.

tex'tile (teks'til) adj. pert. to weaving or fabrics. —n. cloth.

tex'tu-al (teks'chû-əl) adj. being or pert. to a text.

tex'ture (teks'chər) n. 1, the particular arrangement of the constituent parts of any body; structure. 2, surface characteristics.

-th suf. 1, condition of being, as warmth. 2, denoting ordinal numbers, as fourth.

tha-las'sic (thə-las'ik) adj. pert. to the sea; marine.

than (than) conj. a particle used to introduce the second member of a comparison.

thank v.t. express gratitude to. —n. (pl.) an expression of gratitude. —**thanks to,** as a result of; due to. —**thank you, thanks,** interj. expressing gratitude.

thank'ful (-fəl) adj. grateful. —**thank'ful-ness,** n.

thank'less (-ləs) adj. 1, unappreciated. 2, ungrateful. —**thank'-less-ness,** n.

thanks''giv'ing n. 1, the act or occasion of giving thanks, esp. to God. 2, (cap.) a U. S. holiday, the 4th or last Thursday in November.

that (that) adj. & pron. [pl. those] 1, (demonstrative) indicating or emphasizing a person or thing. 2, (relative) as a subject or object in a relative clause, usually one defining or restricting its antecedent. —adv. to such an extent or degree. —conj. 1, the following; namely. 2, for this purpose.

thatch (thach) n. 1, a covering, as for a roof, of straw, rushes, leaves, etc. 2, the hair covering the head. —v.t. cover with a thatch.

thaw (thâ) v.i. 1, of ice, melt. 2, become so warm as to melt ice. 3, become less formal or reserved. —v.t. cause to thaw. —n. the act or process of thawing.

the (thə; emphatic or isolated, thē) *def. art.* used before a noun or pronoun to particularize it, indicate an individual, mark a generic term, emphasize preëminence, etc.

the·a·ter (thē'ə-tər) *n.* 1, a building or room fitted with a stage or screen and tiers of seats for spectators. 2, dramatic works or performances collectively. 3, a field of operations. Also, **the'a·tre**.

the·at·ri·cal (thē-at'ri-kəl) *adj.* 1, pert. to the theater. 2, affected; histrionic. —*n.* (*pl.*) dramatic productions.

the·at'rics (thē-at'riks) *n.* 1, the art of staging dramatic performances. 2, histrionics.

thee (thē) *pron.* 1, (*Archaic or poetic*) obj. sing. of *thou.* 2, (*Dial. and among Quakers*) you.

theft *n.* the act or an instance of stealing; larceny.

their (thâr) *pron. poss.* of *they;* in the predicate, **theirs** (thârz).

the'ism (thē'iz-əm) *n.* the belief in the existence of a God. —**the'ist,** *n.* —**the·is'tic,** *adj.* —**the·is'ti·cal·ly,** *adv.*

them (them) *pron. obj.* of *they.*

theme (thēm) *n.* 1, a subject of discourse or discussion; a topic. 2, a brief essay. 3, a principal subject in a musical composition.

them·selves' (-selvz') *pron.* emphatic form of *them;* reflexive form of *they.*

then (then) *adv.* 1, at that time. 2, afterward; next in order. 3, at another time. 4, in that case; for this reason; therefore. 5, on the other hand. —*adj.* being at that time.

thence (thens) *adv.* 1, from that place. 2, from that time; afterward. 3, from that source; for that reason. —**thence'forth',** *adv.* from that time or place onward.

the·oc'ra·cy (thē-ok'rə-sē) *n.* government by priests.

the·ol'o·gy (thē-ol'ə-jē) *n.* the systematic study of God and His divinity. —**the'o·log'i·cal,** *adj.* —**the'o·lo'gi·an** (-lō'jē-ən) *n.*

the'o·rem (thē'ə-rəm) *n.* 1, a statement of something to be proved; a theoretical proposition. 2, a formula or equation expressing a natural law.

the'o·ret'i·cal (thē'ə-ret'i-kəl) *adj.* 1, in accordance with a theory. 2, impractical.

the'o·rist (thē'ə-rist) *n.* one who studies or draws conclusions from theory.

the'o·ry (thē'ə-rē) *n.* 1, a set of propositions describing the operation and causes of natural phenomena. 2, a proposed but unverified explanation. 3, the principles of

an art, as distinguished from its practice. —**the'o·rize''** (-rīz'') *v.i.*

the·os'o·phy (thē-os'ə-fē) *n.* any philosophical or religious system based on a claim of special insight into the divine nature; specif. Brahmanism or metempsychosis. —**the·o·soph'i·cal** (-sof'i-kəl) *adj.* —**the·os'o·phist,** *n.*

ther''a·peu'tic (ther'ə-pū'tik) *adj.* pert. to the curing of disease; having remedial effect. —**ther''a·peu'ti·cal·ly,** *adv.* —**ther''a·peu'tics,** *n.* the branch of medicine concerned with this.

ther'a·py (ther'ə-pē) *n.* the treatment of a disease; a remedial process. —**ther'a·pist,** *n.*

there (thâr) *adv.* 1, in, at, or to that place. 2, at that point in time, action, etc. 3, in that respect; in those circumstances. 4, an introductory word before the verb *be* when the subject is placed after it, as in *there is hope.* —*interj.* see!

there- *pref.* adding a sense of time, place, direction or agency, as in:

there'a·bout''	there·in'
there'a·bouts'	there·in·af'ter
there·af'ter	there·in'to
there·at'	there·un'der
there·by'	there·with'
there·from'	

there'for'' *adv.* for that person or thing.

there'fore'' *adv.* for that reason; as a result; consequently.

there''up·on' *adv.* then; after that.

there''with·al' *adv.* in addition to that; following that.

therm- *pref.* heat.

ther'mal (thêr'məl) *adj.* pert. to heat or temperature.

ther''mo·dy·nam'ics (thêr''mō-dī-nam'iks) *n.* the science concerned with the conversion of heat to energy, the control of temperature, etc. —**ther''mo·dy·nam'ic,** *adj.*

ther·mom'e·ter (thêr-mom'i-tər) *n.* an instrument for measuring temperature. —**ther''mo·met'ric,** *adj.*

ther''mo·plas'tic (thêr''mə-plas'-tik) *n. & adj.* a plastic that may be heated and molded more than once.

ther'mos (thêr'məs) *n.* (*T.N.*) a *thermos bottle,* insulated so as to maintain the temperature of its contents; a vacuum bottle.

ther''mo·set'ting (thêr''mə-set'-ing) *adj.* pert. to a plastic that can be molded only once.

ther'mo·stat'' (thêr'mə-stat'') *n.* an instrument for maintaining a desired temperature.

-ther·my (thêr-mē) *suf.* heat.

the·sau'rus (thē-sôr'əs) *n.* [*pl.* **-ri** (-rī)] 1, a collection of words classified by meaning. **2,** any repository; treasury.

these (*thēz*) *pron. & adj.* pl. of *this.*

the′sis (*thē′sis*) *n.* [*pl.* -ses (sēs)] **1,** a proposition advanced for discussion, proof, etc. **2,** the subject of a composition. **3,** an essay or dissertation, esp. by a candidate for a degree.

Thes′pi·an (*thes′pē-ən*) *adj.* of the drama. —*n.* an actor.

the′ta (*thā′tə*) *n.* the eighth letter of the Greek alphabet (Θ, θ).

thew (*thū*) *n.* muscle; sinew.

they (*thā*) *pl. pron.* [*poss.* **their** or **theirs;** *obj.* **them**] nominative plural of *he, she,* and *it.*

thi′a·mine (*thī′ə-min*) *n.* vitamin B₁.

thick (*thik*) *adj.* **1,** having relatively great extent between opposite sides. **2,** having a specified measure between opposite sides. **3,** compactly arranged; dense. **4,** abundant; abounding with something. **5,** heavy; profound; obscure; intense, etc. **6,** mentally dull. **7,** (*Colloq.*) close in friendship; intimate. **8,** (*Colloq.*) disagreeable; unacceptable. —*n.* the thickest part. —**thick′en,** *v.t. & i.* make or become thick. —**thick′ness,** *n.*

thick′et (*thik′it*) *n.* a concentration of shrubs, trees, etc.

thick′set″ *adj.* **1,** growing or occurring close together. **2,** heavily built; stout.

thick-′skinned″ *adj.* not sensitive.

thief (*thēf*) *n.* [*pl.* **thieves** (*thēvz*)] **1,** one who steals; one who commits larceny or robbery. **2,** any lawless wrongdoer.

thieve (*thēv*) *v.i.* be a thief; steal. —**thiev′er·y,** *n.* —**thiev′ing, thiev′ish,** *adj.*

thigh (*thī*) *n.* the part of the leg between the hip and the knee in man; a corresponding part.

thim′ble (*thim′bəl*) *n.* **1,** a metal cap worn on the finger to push a needle in sewing. **2,** a sleeve; bushing.

thim′ble-rig″ *v.t.* [-rigged″, -rig″-ging] swindle.

thin *adj.* [**thin′ner, -nest**] **1,** having relatively little extent between opposite sides; very narrow. **2,** having the constituent parts loose or sparse; not dense. **3,** lacking richness or strength; flimsy; transparent; weak, etc. —*v.t. & i.* make to become thin or thinner. —**thin′ness,** *n.*

thine (*thīn*) *pron. poss.* of *thou.*

thing *n.* **1,** a material object without life. **2,** a matter, affair, fact, circumstance, action, deed, etc.

3, (*pl.*) personal possessions. **4,** a living being. —**the thing,** that which is proper or fashionable.

think *v.t.* [*pret. & p.p.* **thought** (*thôt*)] **1,** hold as a belief or opinion; judge; consider. **2,** form a mental concept of; imagine. **3,** hold or bear in mind; recollect. **4,** reflect upon; meditate; ponder. **5,** expect. —*v.i.* **1,** exercise the mind; cogitate; reflect. **2,** have an opinion or belief. **3,** (with *of*) bring something to mind; remember; make a discovery or invention; have expectation; show consideration.

thin′ner (-ər) *n.* a solvent.

thin′-skinned″ *adj.* very sensitive; touchy.

third (*thėrd*) *n. & adj.* the member of a series next after the second. —*n.* one of 3 equal parts. —**third degree,** an examination accompanied by torture or intimidation. —**third person** (*Gram.*) one other than the speaker and person spoken to. —**third rail,** a live rail supplying power to an electric locomotive. —**third-rate′,** *adj.* inferior.

thirst (*thėrst*) *n.* **1,** bodily need of drink. **2,** an ardent desire or craving for anything. —*v.i.* feel thirst. —**thirst′y,** *adj.* feeling thirst.

thir·teen′ (*thėr-tēn′*) *n. & adj.* three plus ten, also expressed by 13. —**thir·teenth′,** *adj. & n.*

thir′ty (*thėr′tē*) *n. & adj.* three times ten, also expressed by 30. —**thir′ti·eth,** *adj. & n.*

this (*this*) *pron.* [*pl.* **these** (*thēz*)] *& adj.* a demonstrative term indicating a person or thing immediately present, nearby, nearer than another, or previously referred to. —*adv.* to the specified extent or degree.

this′tle (*this′əl*) *n.* any of several plants having prickly stems and leaves.

thith′er (*thith′-ər*) *adv.* to or toward that place.

tho (*thō*) *adv.* though.

thong (*thâng*) *n.* a narrow strip of leather.

tho′rax (*thôr′aks*) *n.* the part of the body between the neck and abdomen. —**tho·rac′ic** (*thə-ras′ik*) *adj.*

tho′ri·um (*thôr′ē-əm*) *n.* a radioactive chemical element, symbol Th, No. 90.

thorn (*thôrn*) *n.* **1,** a sharp excrescence on a plant; a spine or prickle. **2,** any of various thorny shrubs. **3,** something that wounds or annoys. —**thorn′y,** *adj.*

Thistle

thor'ough (thẽr'ə) *adj.* **1,** done completely or perfectly; fully executed. **2,** leaving nothing undone; exhaustive in action or operation. **3,** being completely such. —**thor'ough-ness,** *n.*

thor'ough-bred" *adj.* **1,** bred from the best stock. **2,** superior. —*n.* a thoroughbred person or animal, esp. a racehorse.

thor'ough-fare" *n.* a main road.

thor'ough-go"ing *adj.* complete; consummate.

those (thōz) *pron.* pl. of *that.*

thou (thow) *pron.* [*poss.* **thy** (thī), **thine** (thīn)] (*Archaic*) sing. pron. of the second person.

though (thō) *conj.* **1,** in spite of the fact that. **2,** even if. **3,** nevertheless; yet. **4,** if. —*adv.* however.

thought (thât) *n.* **1,** the act or product of thinking; mental activity; an idea, opinion, etc. **2,** attention; regard or care. —*v.* pret. & p.p. of *think.*

thought'ful (-fəl) *adj.* **1,** pensive. **2,** considerate. —**thought'ful-ness,** *n.*

thought'less (-ləs) *adj.* inconsiderate; careless. —**thought'less-ness,** *n.*

thou'sand (thow'zənd) *n.* & *adj.* ten times one hundred, expressed by 1,000. —**thou'sandth,** *adj.* & *n.* the ordinal of this number, also written 1,000th; one of 1,000 equal parts, esp. of 1 inch.

thrall (thrâl) *n.* **1,** one in bondage; a serf or slave. **2,** slavery. —**thrall'dom, thrall'dom.**

thrash *v.t.* **1,** beat or whip, as for punishment. **2,** defeat thoroughly. **3,** thresh. —*v.i.* toss about violently.

thrash'er (thrash'ər) *n.* a thrush-like songbird.

thread (thred) *n.* **1,** a fine cord made of twisted fibers, used in weaving or sewing. **2,** any fine filament. **3,** something thin and long. **4,** the spiral groove or ridge of a screw. **5,** a theme; sequence. —*v.t.* **1,** pass a thread through the eye of (a needle). **2,** string, as beads. **3,** form a screwthread on or in. **4,** pervade; steer through (something narrow or intricate). —*v.i.* move in a winding course.

thread'bare" *adj.* **1,** shabby; scanty. **2,** trite; hackneyed.

threat (thret) *n.* **1,** a declaration of intention or determination to harm another. **2,** an indication of impending danger or evil.

threat'en (thret'ən) *v.t.* & *i.* utter or be a threat (against).

three (thrē) *n.* & *adj.* the cardinal number between 2 and 4, expressed by 3 (ordinal, *third*).

three-"deck'er *n.* something with three layers, esp. a sandwich made with three slices of bread.

three'fold" *adj.* times three; in three parts.

three'pence (thrip'əns) *n.* a Brit. coin worth three pennies. —**three'pen"ny** (thrip'ə-nē) *adj.*

thren'o-dy (thren'ə-dē) *n.* a song of lamentation; a dirge.

thresh *v.t.* **1,** beat (a cereal plant) with a flail, to separate the grain or seeds. **2,** discuss (a matter) exhaustively.

thresh'old (thresh'ōld) *n.* **1,** a doorsill. **2,** a point of beginning.

threw (throo) *v.* pret. of *throw.*

thrice (thrīs) *adj.* three times.

thrift *n.* economical management; the saving of money. —**thrift'y,** *adj.*

thrill (thril) *v.t.* **1,** affect with a sudden wave of emotion or sensation, esp. of pleasure. **2,** cause to vibrate or quiver. —*v.i.* **1,** be thrilled. **2,** produce a thrill. —*n.* **1,** a sudden keen emotion. **2,** a tremor, or tingling; vibration. —**thrill'er,** *n.* an exciting story, play, etc., esp. when of small artistic value.

thrive (thrīv) *v.i.* be fortunate or successful; prosper; flourish.

throat (thrōt) *n.* **1,** the passage from the mouth to the stomach or lungs. **2,** the front of the neck. **3,** any narrowed part or passage.

throat'y (-ē) *adj.* (of sounds) produced or modified in the throat. —**throat'i-ness,** *n.*

throb *v.i.* [**throbbed, throb'bing**] **1,** beat, as the heart, with increased force or rapidity. **2,** pulsate; vibrate. **3,** feel emotion. —*n.* a strong pulsation.

throe (thrō) *n.* **1,** a violent pang; a spasm or paroxysm. **2,** (*pl.*) convulsive pain.

throm-bo'sis (throm-bō'sis) *n.* clotting of the blood in any part of the circulatory system.

throne (thrōn) *n.* **1,** the ceremonial chair of a sovereign, bishop, etc. **2,** sovereign power.

throng (thrâng) *n.* a large crowd or multitude. —*v.i.* assemble in large numbers. —*v.t.* fill with a crowd.

thros'tle (thros'əl) *n.* a Europ. thrush.

throt'tle (throt'əl) *n.* a valve regulating the admission of fuel to an engine. —*v.t.* **1,** strangle; suffocate. **2,** silence. **3,** check.

through (throo) *prep.* **1,** from one side or end of to the other; completely across or over. **2,** between or among the parts of. **3,** within the limits of; during the period of. **4,** to the end of. **5,** by agency of. **6,** by reason or in consequence of. —*adv.* **1,** from one side or end to the other. **2,** from beginning to end; all the way. **3,** thoroughly. **4,** to the end or completion. —*adj.* passing or extending to a destination with little or no interruption.

through·out' *prep. & adv.* in every part (of).

throw (thrō) *v.t.* [**threw** (throo), **thrown** (thrōn), **throw'ing**] **1,** toss or fling through the air with a jerk of the arm; propel in any way; cast; hurl. **2,** put carelessly. **3,** bring to the ground. **4,** shape, as on a lathe. **5,** lose (a contest) intentionally. —*v.i.* make a cast, etc. —*n.* **1,** the act or a result of throwing. **2,** the distance traveled or displacement of a moving part. **3,** a scarf or blanket.

throw'a·way" *n.* an advertising circular.

throw'back" *n.* an instance of atavism.

thrown (thrōn) *v.* p.p. of *throw.* —thrown in, added without extra charge.

thrum *v.t. & i.* [**thrummed, thrum'ming**] play (a stringed instrument) by plucking; drum or tap idly (on).

thrush *n.* **1,** any of numerous songbirds. **2,** a disease caused by a fungus.

thrust *v.t.* [*pret. & p.p.* **thrust**] **1,** push forcibly; shove. **2,** compel; drive; force. **3,** stab. —*v.i.* make a thrust; lunge. —*n.* **1,** a push, lunge, or stab. **2,** force exerted linearly.

thud *n.* a dull, blunt, or hollow sound. —*v.i. & t.* [**thud'ded, -ding**] make a thud.

thug *n.* a professional cutthroat.

thumb (thum) *n.* the shortest and thickest finger of the hand. —*v.t.* **1,** run through with the thumb; handle. **2,** solicit (a ride) by pointing with the thumb. —all thumbs, awkward. —under one's thumb, **1,** readily available. **2,** controlled by.

Thumbscrew

thumb'nail" *n.* the nail on the thumb. —*adj.* very small.

thumb'screw" *n.* a screw that may be turned by hand.

thumb'tack" *n.* a tack that may be driven by the thumb.

thump *n.* **1,** a heavy blow. **2,** the dull sound of a blow. —*v.t. & i.* pound.

thun'der (thun'dər) *n.* **1,** the loud atmospheric noise that often follows lightning. **2,** any loud noise. **3,** vehement and threatening utter-

ance. —*v.i.* **1,** give forth a resounding noise. **2,** utter denunciation. —*v.t.* utter or move with great noise. —thun'der·ous, *adj.*

thun'der·bolt" *n.* **1,** a flash of lightning. **2,** a sudden, violent or astonishing event.

thun'der·show"er *n.* a brief rain and electrical storm.

thun'der·storm" *n.* a storm of lightning and thunder and, usually, heavy but brief rain.

thun'der·struck" *adj.* very astonished; thrown into consternation.

Thurs'day (thẽrz'dė) *n.* the fifth day of the week.

thus (thus) *adv.* **1,** in this way. **2,** in consequence; accordingly. **3,** so.

thwack (thwak) *v.t.* strike with something flat. —*n.* a whack.

thwart (thwôrt) *v.t.* prevent from accomplishing a purpose; frustrate; baffle. —*n.* a transverse part.

thy (thī) *pron.* poss. of *thou.* —thy'-self", *pron.* reflexive and emphatic form of *thou.*

thyme (tīm) *n.* a plant of the mint family; a seasoning.

thy'mus (thī'məs) *n.* a ductless gland near the neck.

thy'roid (thī'roid) *n.* a ductless gland near the neck, which regulates metabolism.

ti (tē) *n.* the seventh note in the diatonic scale. Also, **si** (sē).

ti·ar'a (tī-âr'ə) *n.* **1,** an ornament worn on the head by women. **2,** a diadem worn by the Pope.

tib'i·a (tib'ė-ə) *n.* [*pl.* -**ae** (-ē)] the shinbone.

tic (tik) *n.* a twitching of the face.

tick (tik) *n.* **1,** a slight, sharp sound, as of a clock. **2,** a small mark; a dot. **3,** a small quantity; an instant of time. **4,** any of various parasitic insects or arachnids. **5,** the cloth case of a mattress, pillow, etc. made of *ticking.* **6,** (*Colloq.*) score or account; credit. —*v.i.* make a slight, esp. a recurrent, sound. —*v.t.* mark with a tick.

tick'er *n.* **1,** something that ticks; (*Slang*) a watch; the heart. **2,** a telegraph instrument that prints on a tape.

tick'et (tik'it) *n.* **1,** a slip of paper entitling one to admission, service, etc. **2,** a label or tag. **3,** a party's list of candidates. **4,** a license. **5,** (*Colloq.*) proper procedure. **6,** a police summons. —*v.t.* **1,** furnish with a ticket; label. **2,** schedule.

tick'ing *n.* tick, def. 5.

tick'le (tik'əl) *v.t.* **1,** touch so as to produce a tingling sensation. **2,**

amuse; gratify. —*v.i.* produce or feel a tingling sensation. —**tick'ler,** *n.* a reminder.

tick'lish *adj.* **1,** sensitive to tickling. **2,** requiring careful handling; risky. —**tick'lish·ness,** *n.*

tick"tack-toe' (tĭk"tak-tō') *n.* a game of placing three naughts or crosses in a row. Also, **tit"tat-toe'.**

tick'tock' (-tok") *n.* the sound of a clock ticking.

tid'al (tī'dəl) *adj.* pert. to or being a tide. —**tidal wave,** a very large ocean wave.

tid'bit" *n.* a savory bit, esp. of food.

tid'dly·winks" (tĭd'lē-winks") *n.* a table game of snapping small disks into a cup.

tide (tīd) *n.* **1,** the periodic rise and fall of terrestrial water. **2,** a movement; a flow, current or stream. *v.t.* bear; carry.

tide'wa"ter *n.* water that rises and falls with the tides.

tid'ings (tī'dingz) *n.pl.* news.

ti'dy (tī'dē) *adj.* **1,** kept in good order; neat. **2,** (*Colloq.*) fairly large; apt. —*v.t. & i.* make neat. —**tid'i·ness,** *n.*

tie (tī) *v.t.* **[tied, ty'ing] 1,** attach or make fast by a knotted cord, etc.; bind; fasten or join in any way. **2,** restrict; constrain. **3,** make the same score as, in a contest. —*v.i.* **1,** make equal scores. **2,** join. —*n.* **1,** anything that binds or unites. **2,** a cravat; necktie. **3,** a connecting beam; a transverse timber. **4,** equality of scores.

tier (tir) *n.* a row or rank, esp. one of several at different levels.

tie-'up" *n.* a stoppage.

tiff (tif) *n.* **1,** a petty quarrel. **2,** a peevish mood. —*v.i.* quarrel.

ti'ger (tī'gər) *n.* **1,** a large, carnivorous feline of Asia. **2,** a person of great fierceness. —**ti'gress,** *n.fem.*

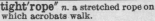

Tiger

tiger lily a variety of lily bearing showy yellow flowers with black spots.

tight (tīt) *adj.* **1,** firmly fixed in place. **2,** fitting closely, esp. too closely. **3,** stretched taut; tense. **4,** compact in texture; dense. **5,** hard to obtain. **6,** (*Colloq.*) stingy. **7,** (*Slang*) drunk; tipsy. —*adv.* securely; tensely. —**tight'en,** *v.t. & i.* —**tight'ness,** *n.*

tight-'fist"ed *adj.* parsimonious.

tight-'lipped" *adj.* secretive.

tight'rope" *n.* a stretched rope on which acrobats walk.

tights *n.pl.* close-fitting trousers worn by acrobats, etc.

tight'wad" *n.* (*Slang*) a stingy person.

tilde (til'də) *n.* a diacritical mark ("), as on ñ to indicate a nasal sound.

tile (tīl) *n.* **1,** a thin slab or plate of baked clay, etc. used as building material. **2,** a block used in masonry construction. **3,** a pottery tube or pipe. **4,** tiles collectively. —*v.t.* construct, cover, or drain with tiles.

till (til) *n.* a drawer, tray, or box for keeping money or valuables. —*v.t. & i.* cultivate (land); plow. —*prep. & conj.* until.

till'age (-ij) *n.* cultivation of land; tilled land.

till'er (-ər) *n.* **1,** a farmer. **2,** a lever that controls a rudder.

tilt *v.i. & t.* **1,** lean or incline away from a vertical or normal position; slant. **2,** engage in a joust or combat; make thrusts (at); charge. **3,** forge (steel). —*n.* **1,** a sloping position. **2,** a joust, contest, or dispute; a thrust. **3,** an awning.

tim'bale (tĭm'bəl) *n.* a small pastry cup filled with cooked food.

tim'ber (tĭm'bər) *n.* **1,** growing trees. **2,** wood; a wooden member or beam. **3,** personal character; quality. —*v.t.* furnish with timber. —**timber line,** the height or line, on mountains or in polar regions, beyond which trees do not grow.

tim'bre (tĭm'bər) *n.* the quality or tone color of a sound.

time (tīm) *n.* **1,** the relationship of any event to any other, as being before, simultaneous, or after; continuous duration. **2,** the measurement of duration, as by a clock. **3,** an epoch, era, period, season, etc. **4,** an extent of duration, as an hour, day, etc.; hours worked, or the pay therefor; a prison term. **5,** a point of time; a particular occasion. **6,** (often *pl.*) a historical period; a state of affairs. **7,** leisure; opportunity. **8,** one of several recurrent instances. **9,** (*pl.*) a term denoting multiplication, as in *two times six.* **10,** rhythm; tempo; meter; rate. —*adj.* **1,** pert. to time. **2,** equipped with a timing device. **3,** pert. to installment buying. —*v.t.* **1,** determine the moment, duration, or rate of. **2,** choose the time or occasion for. **3,** regulate as to time. —**at times,** occasionally. —**on time, 1,** punctual. **2,** by installment payments. —**time clock,** one that records hours worked. —**time exposure,** exposure of film for more than one-half second; a picture so taken. —**time out,** a rest period.

time- hon"ored *adj.* respected by reason of age.

time'keep"er *n.* **1,** one who records a worker's hours worked and wages due. **2,** one who watches the time, as in a contest.

time'less (-ləs) *adj.* unending. —**time'less-ness,** *n.*

time'ly *adj.* opportune. —**time'li-ness,** *n.*

time'piece" *n.* a clock, watch, etc.

tim'er (tī'mər) *n.* **1,** one who or that which measures or records time. **2,** a device for supplying the spark in an internal combustion engine.

time'ta"ble *n.* a schedule of the times of planned occurrences, esp. a railroad schedule.

time zone an area throughout which standard time is the same.

tim'id *adj.* **1,** easily alarmed; fearful; shy. **2,** characterized by fear. —**ti·mid'i·ty, tim'id·ness,** *n.*

tim'ing (tī'ming) *n.* synchronization; effective choice of a time.

tim'or·ous (tim'ə-rəs) *adj.* timid. —**tim'or·ous·ness,** *n.*

tim'o·thy (tim'ə-thē) *n.* a grass grown for hay.

tim"pa·ni (tim'pə-nē) *n.* tympani.

tin (tin) *n.* **1,** a metallic chemical element, no. 50, symbol Sn. **2,** sheet iron or steel coated with tin: *tin plate.* **3,** a container made of tin plate: *tin can.* —*adj.* **1,** made of tin, or tin plate. **2,** worthless; counterfeit. —*v.t.* [**tinned, tin'ning**] **1,** coat with tin. **2,** preserve in tin cans.

tinc'ture (tink'chər) *n.* **1,** a solution of a medicinal substance in alcohol. **2,** a tinge. —*v.t.* tinge.

tin'der (tin'dər) *n.* any easily-ignited material.

tine (tīn) *n.* a slender projection; a prong, as of a fork.

tin foil a thin sheet of tin, used to wrap various merchandise.

ting *n.* a high-pitched metallic sound. —*v.t. & i.* make this sound.

tinge (tinj) *v.t.* **1,** color slightly; tint. **2,** imbue slightly with something, as flavor. —*n.* **1,** a moderate degree of coloration. **2,** a slight admixture of anything.

tin'gle (ting'gəl) *v.i.* have a prickling or stinging sensation. —*n.* this sensation.

tink'er (tink'ər) *n.* **1,** a mender of metal household utensils. **2,** a bungler. **3,** a handyman. —*v.i. & t.* work as a tinker; meddle (with). —**tinker's dam,** something worthless.

tin'kle (ting'kəl) *v.i.* give forth short, light, metallic sounds. —*n.* such a sound.

tin'ny (tin'ē) *adj.* like tin: flimsy; metallic in sound; sour in taste. —**tin'ni·ness,** *n.*

tin'sel (tin'səl) *n.* **1,** a glittering material of metal in sheets or strips. **2,** false show. —*v.t.* decorate.

tint *n.* **1,** a variety of a color; a hue. **2,** a pale color. —*v.t.* color slightly.

tin"tin·nab"u·la'tion (tin"ti-nab"yə-lā'shən) *n.* the sound of bells ringing.

tin'type" *n.* a photograph on a metal plate.

ti'ny (tī'nē) *adj.* very small.

-tion (shən) *suf.* see *-ation.*

tip *n.* **1,** the extremity of something long and slender; an outermost point; the top or apex. **2,** a small piece attached to an extremity. **3,** a light blow; a tap. **4,** the state of being tilted. **5,** a small present of money. **6,** a bit of information or advice. —*v.t.* [**tipped, tip'ping**] **1,** form the tip of. **2,** strike lightly or obliquely. **3,** tilt; overturn. **4,** give a tip to. —*v.i.* **1,** tilt; incline; be overturned; topple. **2,** give tips.

tip'off" *n.* a warning or hint.

tip'pet (tip'it) *n.* a covering for the neck and shoulders, esp. a scarf or muffler wound around the neck.

tip'ple (tip'əl) *v.i. & t.* drink (intoxicating liquor) habitually. —**tip'pler,** *n.* a habitual drinker.

tip'staff" *n.* a minor police or court officer.

tip'ster (-stər) *n.* (*Colloq.*) one who furnishes private information.

tip'sy (-sē) *adj.* slightly intoxicated. —**tip'si·ness,** *n.*

tip'toe" *n.* a movement or posture on the toes. —*adj.* standing or moving on tiptoe, to reach high or walk quietly. —*v.i.* move on tiptoe.

tip'top" *n. & adj.* the highest point or quality.

ti'rade (tī'rād) *n.* a long speech or writing of censure or denunciation.

tire (tīr) *v.i.* become weary or jaded. —*v.t.* make weary; fatigue. —*n.* [also, *Brit.,* **tyre**] a rubber or iron hoop around a wheel. —**tired,** *adj.* weary; impatient; dissatisfied. —**tire'less,** *adj.* diligent; untiring. —**tire'some,** *adj.* tedious.

tis'sue (tish'oo) *n.* **1,** the cellular substance of which living bodies are composed. **2,** a woven fabric, esp. one very light and thin. **3,** thin, translucent paper: *tissue paper.*

tit *n.* **1,** a small bird, esp. the titmouse. **2,** (*Vulgar*) teat.

ti'tan (tī'tən) *n.* a person or thing of enormous size and power. —**ti-tan'ic,** *adj.* —**ti-tan'i·cal·ly,** *adv.*

ti·ta'ni·um (tī-tā'nē·əm) *n.* a metallic chemical element, no. 22, symbol Ti.

tit'bit" n. tidbit.

tithe (tīth) n. a tenth part; a tax; a contribution to a church, etc.

ti'tian (tish'ən) n. & adj. a yellow-red color.

tit'il·late (tit'ə-lāt") v.t. excite agreeably; tickle. —**tit"il·la'tion,** n.

tit'i·vate (tit'i-vāt) v.t. (Colloq.) dress smartly; spruce up. —**tit"i·va'tion,** n.

ti'tle (tī'təl) n. 1, a name assigned to distinguish an individual thing. 2, a descriptive heading or caption. 3, a word or phrase denoting rank, honors, etc. 4, the rank of champion. 5, right to the possession of property. 6, a division of a statute or law. —v.t. give a name or appellation to. —**title rôle,** the rôle from which the name of a play is derived.

tit'mouse" (tit'mows") n. [pl. -mice"] a small bird.

tit'ter (tit'ər) v.i. & n. laugh in a restrained manner; giggle; snicker.

tit'u·lar (tit'yə-lər) adj. of, being, or pert. to a title; by virtue of one's title. —**tit"u·lar'i·ty,** n.

tiz'zy (tiz'ē) n. dither.

TNT (tē'en-tē') n. trinitrotoluene, a powerful explosive.

to (too) prep. 1, indicating motion or purpose toward something. 2, indicating a destination, result, outcome, limit, or point of space, time, or degree. 3, indicating relations, as comparison, opposition, agreement, accompaniment, contiguity. 4, a particle used before the infinitive of a verb. —adv. toward someone or something, usually implied; in an inward direction. —**to and ro,** alternately toward and away from a point.

toad (tōd) n. a terrestrial member of the frog family.

toad'stool" (tōd'stool") n. a fungus having an umbrellalike cap on a stalk.

toad'y (tō'dē) n. a servile, fawning person; a sycophant. —v.i. fawn.

toast (tōst) n. 1, sliced bread browned by heat. 2, a complimentary sentiment endorsed by drinking; the person complimented. —v.t. 1, expose to heat. 2, compliment by a toast. —**toast'er,** n. a device for making toast.

toast'mas"ter n. a master of ceremonies at a dinner.

to·bac'co (tə-bak'ō) n. a plant whose large leaves, containing nicotine, are prepared for smoking and chewing, and snuff. —**to·bac'co·nist** (-ə-nist) n. a dealer in tobacco.

to·bog'gan (tə-bog'ən) n. a board-like sled with low or no runners.

—v.i. 1, coast on snow. 2, fall rapidly or abruptly.

toc'sin (tok'sin) n. a warning bell or signal.

to·day' (tə-dā') n. & adj. 1, the present day. 2, the present period.

tod'dle (tod'əl) v.i. walk with short, unsteady steps. —n. a toddling walk.

tod'dy (tod'ē) n. a hot drink of whiskey diluted and sweetened.

to-do' (tə-doo') n. commotion; fuss.

toe (tō) n. 1, a digit of the foot. 2, the forepart of a foot. 3, the part of a stocking or shoe that covers the toes. 4, a part resembling a toe; a projection, stud, etc. —v.t. & i. touch, reach, strike, etc. with the toes. —**toe the mark,** behave as instructed. —**toe hold,** 1, a slight or precarious grip, with or as with the toes. 2, a wrestling grip upon an opponent's foot. —**toe'nail",** n.

tof'fee (tof'ē) n. taffy. Also, **tof'fy.**

tog n. (Colloq.) (usually pl.) a garment. —**togged out,** dressed.

to'ga (tō'gə) n. a loose outer garment, as that of the ancient Romans; a robe.

to·geth'er (tū-geth'ər) adv. 1, in conjunction; in one gathering, mass, or body. 2, simultaneously; contemporaneously. 3, with each other; in common; mutually. 4, in or into junction or union. 5, without intermission or interruption.

tog'gle (tog'əl) n. 1, a transverse pin or bar. 2, a linkage of levers to produce motion at right angles to a thrust.

toil v.i. 1, work hard; labor. 2, move or travel with difficulty or weariness. —n. 1, fatiguing labor. 2, a laborious task. 3, (pl.) a net for trapping game.

Toggle Joint

toile (twäl) n. a thin linen fabric.

toi'let (toi'lit) n. 1, a water closet, bathroom, or dressing room. 2, the process of dressing, including bathing, make-up, etc.; personal appearance as a result of this. 3, a dressing table. —**toilet set,** articles as comb, brush, etc. —**toilet water,** a light perfume.

toi'let·ry (-rē) n. an article or preparation used in dressing, as a cosmetic.

toil'worn" adj. affected by much toil or use.

to'ken (tō'kən) n. 1, something regarded as representing something else; a sign or symbol; a keepsake or memento. **2,** an indication, symptom, or evidence. **3,** a special coin issued as a ticket. —*adj.* serving only as an expression of good faith.

told (tōld) *v.* pret. & p.p. of *tell.*

tol·er·a·ble (tol'ər-ə-bəl) *adj.* **1,** endurable. **2,** somewhat good; not bad. —**tol'er·a·ble·ness,** *n.*

tol·er·ance (tol'ər-əns) *n.* **1,** disposition to be patient and fair; freedom from bigotry. **2,** power of enduring or resisting the action of a drug. **3,** allowed variation from standard dimensions. —**tol'er·ant,** *adj.*

tol·er·ate″ (tol'ə-rāt″) *v.t.* **1,** allow to be, be done or practiced; permit. **2,** bear with patience; endure without complaint or ill effect. —**tol′er·a′tion,** *n.*

toll (tōl) *n.* **1,** a fee or tax collected for a particular service. **2,** a succession of slow single strokes of a bell; one such stroke. —*v.t.* **1,** cause (a bell) to toll. **2,** announce, signal, etc. by a bell. —*v.i.* give forth slow repeated sounds. —**toll call,** a long-distance telephone call. —**toll gate,** a point at which tolls are collected for the use of a bridge, highway, etc.

tol'u·ene″ (tol'yū-ēn″) *n.* a liquid derivative of coal tar, used as a solvent, detonator, etc. Also, **tol'u·ol.**

tom *n.* the male of various animals, as the cat.

tom'a·hawk″ (tom'ə-hâk″) *n.* an Amer. Ind. stone-headed hatchet.

to·ma'to (tə-mā'tō) *n.* a plant bearing a pulpy fruit, usually red.

tomb (toom) *n.* **1,** an excavation made to receive a dead body; a grave. **2,** a monument to one dead: *tombstone.* **3,** death.

tom'boy″ *n.* an athletic, boylike girl.

tomb'stone″ *n.* a stone marker for a grave.

tom'cat″ *n.* a male cat.

tome (tōm) *n.* a large book.

tom'fool'er·y *n.* silly or prankish behavior.

tom'my·rot″ (tom'ē-rot″) *n.* (*Slang*) nonsense.

to·mor'row (tə-mor'ō) *n.* & *adj.* **1,** the day after this day. **2,** the future; a future day.

tom'tit″ *n.* a small bird.

tom-'tom″ *n.* a primitive drum.

-to·my *suf.* cutting, denoting a surgical operation.

ton (tun) *n.* **1,** a unit of weight: 2,000 lbs. avoirdupois (*short ton*), or 2,240 lbs. (*long ton*), or 1,000 kilograms (*metric ton*). **2,** a variable unit of volume or capacity, as 40 cubic feet (*shipping ton*) or 35 cubic feet of salt water (*displacement ton*). **3,** (*Colloq.*) any large amount.

ton'al (tōn'əl) *adj.* pert. to a tone or to tonality.

to·nal'i·ty (tō-nal'ə-tē) *n.* **1,** (*Music*) a system of tones; key. **2,** a color scheme.

tone (tōn) *n.* **1,** any resonant sound. **2,** a sound of definite pitch; a musical note. **3,** a sound with respect to its pitch, volume, and timbre. **4,** accent, inflection, or modulation, esp. of the voice. **5,** a color; a shade or tint. **6,** the state of tension or firmness proper to bodily tissues. **7,** prevailing character; style; temper; spirit; tenor. **8,** elegance; stylishness. —*v.t.* give a proper or desired tone to. —**tone color,** timbre. —**tone deaf,** unable to perceive differences in musical tones by hearing. —**tone down,** reduce, in intensity of sound, color, etc.; subdue. —**tone poem,** a musical composition.

tong (tong) *n.* a Chinese political party or private society.

tongs (tângz) *n. pl.* an implement for grasping and lifting something.

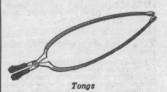

Tongs

tongue (tung) *n.* **1,** a fleshy, freely movable organ in the mouth, the principal organ of taste (in man, also of speech). **2,** an animal's tongue as meat. **3,** speech or talk; a language or dialect. **4,** a tongue-like part, as the clapper of a bell, a strip of leather in a shoe, a small strip of land projecting into water, etc. —*v.t.* **1,** sound with the tongue. **2,** put a tongue on. —**tongue and groove,** a joint formed by a projecting strip on one piece of wood which fits into a groove in another. —**tongue in cheek,** facetiously.

tongue-'lash″ing *n.* a scolding.

tongue-'tied' *adj.* **1,** having an impediment of the speech. **2,** speechless from shyness or astonishment.

ton'ic (ton'ik) *n.* **1,** a medicine that improves the bodily tone. **2,** anything that imparts strength or vigor. **3,** the first degree of a musical scale; the keynote. —*adj.* **1,** invigorating. **2,** pert. to a musical tone or tones. **3,** pert. to muscular tension. —**ton·ic'i·ty** (-is'ə-tē) *n.*

to·night' (tə-nīt') *n.* & *adj.* the present or coming night.

ton'nage (tun'ij) *n.* **1,** capacity or displacement in tons. **2,** ships collectively.

ton·neau' (tə-nō') *n.* the interior of a closed automobile body.

ton'sil (ton'səl) *n.* either of two masses of lymphoid tissue at the back of the mouth.

ton"sil·lec'to·my (-lek'tə-mē) *n.* removal of the tonsils.

ton"sil·li'tis (-lī'tis) *n.* inflammation of the tonsils.

ton·sor'i·al (ton-sôr'ē-əl) *adj.* pert. to a barber.

ton'sure (ton'shər) *n.* **1**, the cutting or shaving of hair from the head. **2**, a shaved spot on the head of a priest or monk.

ton'y (tōn'ē) *adj.* (*Colloq.*) stylish. —**ton'i·ness,** *n.*

too *adv.* **1**, in addition; also; furthermore. **2**, more than enough; beyond what is normal or proper. **3**, exceedingly; extremely.

took (tûk) *v. pret. of* take.

tool *n.* **1**, any implement for working, cutting, shaping, etc. **2**, an unwitting or compliant agent of another. —*v.t. & i.* shape, etc. with a tool; ornament (the cover of a book, etc.).

toot *n.* **1**, the sound of a horn. **2**, (*Slang*) drunken revelry. —*v.t. & i.* blow or make the sound of a horn.

tooth *n.* [*pl.* **teeth** (tēth)] **1**, one of the hard bodies set in a row in the jaw. **2**, any toothlike projection, as on a comb; a cog on a wheel. **3**, something sharp, distressing, or destructive. **4**, taste; relish. —**in the teeth of,** in defiance of; straight against.

tooth'ache" *n.* pain in a tooth.

tooth'brush" *n.* a small, long-handled brush for cleaning the teeth.

tooth'paste" *n.* a paste used for cleaning the teeth.

tooth'pick" *n.* a small pointed piece for cleaning the teeth.

tooth'some (-səm) *adj.* palatable. —**tooth'some·ness,** *n.*

top *n.* **1**, the highest point or part of anything; the summit or apex. **2**, the highest position in rank, etc. **3**, the most perfect example or type; the best. **4**, a lid or cover; a roof. **5**, a toy, made to spin on its point. —*adj.* highest; uppermost; foremost; chief; principal. —*v.t.* [**topped, top'ping**] **1**, be the top of. **2**, furnish with a top. **3**, reach the top of. **4**, rise above; surpass. **5**, get over; vault; cross. **6**, complete; perfect. **7**, remove the top of; prune. **8**, hit (a ball) above the center.

to'paz (tō'paz) *n.* **1**, a gem, silicate of aluminum. **2**, a yellow variety of sapphire or quartz. —*adj.* yellow.

top'coat" *n.* a light overcoat.

tope (tōp) *v.i.* drink intoxicating liquor habitually. —**top'er,** *n.*

top'flight" *adj.* of highest class.

top-'heav"y *adj.* likely to topple; structurally unsound. —**top-'heav"i·ness,** *n.*

top-'hole' *adj.* (*Brit.*) excellent.

top'ic (top'ik) *n.* a subject or theme of a discourse, etc.

top'i·cal (top'i-kəl) *adj.* **1**, pert. to matters of current interest. **2**, pert. to the topic. **3**, local.

top kick (*Colloq.*) a first sergeant; a boss.

top'knot" *n.* a tuft of hair on top of the head; a crest.

top'mast" *n.* (*Naut.*) a mast on top of a lower mast.

top'most" *adj.* highest.

top'notch" *adj.* (*Colloq.*) excellent.

to·pog'ra·phy (tə-pog'rə-fē) *n.* the relief features of a land area; the surface configuration of anything. —**top"o·graph'i·cal,** *adj.*

top'per *n.* **1**, a high silk hat: top hat. **2**, a woman's topcoat.

top'ping *n.* a top layer or covering. —*adj.* (*Colloq.*) excellent.

top'ple (top'əl) *v.i.* fall down with the top or head foremost; tumble as from being too heavy at the top.

tops *adj.* (*Slang*) the very best.

top'sail (top'səl) *n.* a sail above a lower sail.

top secret the highest classification of secrecy in the U.S. government.

top'soil" *n.* surface soil, essential to agriculture.

top'sy-tur'vy (top'sē-tēr'vē) *adj. & adv.* upside down; in reverse of normal position or order; disorderly. —**top'sy-tur'vi·ness,** *n.*

toque (tōk) *n.* a woman's hat with little or no brim.

To'rah (tō'rə) *n.* **1**, the Pentateuch. **2**, the Scriptures of Judaism.

torch (tôrch) *n.* **1**, something burning carried in the hand to give light; (*Brit.*) a flashlight. **2**, a portable instrument producing a jet of flame. **3**, any source of illumination or enlightenment.

torch'bear"er *n.* a leader; (*Colloq.*) a zealous adherent.

torch'light" *n.* light given by a torch.

tore (tōr) *v. pret. of* tear.

tor'e·a·dor" (tôr'ē·ə-dôr") *n.* in bullfighting, an assistant of the matador.

tor·ment' (tôr-ment') *v.t.* **1**, afflict with pain or misery; distress, worry, or annoy. **2**, stir up; disturb. —*n.* (tôr'ment) suffering; something that torments. —**tor·men'tor,** *n.*

torn (tôrn) v. p.p. of *tear*.

tor·na·do (tôr-nā'dō) n. a destructive whirlwind.

tor·pe·do (tôr-pē'dō) n. 1, a self-propelled missile containing an explosive charge, launched in water. 2, a submarine mine. 3, a charge of explosive. 4, (*Slang*) a hired ruffian.

tor'pid (tôr'pid) adj. sluggish; slow; inactive. —**tor·pid'i·ty**, n.

tor'por (tôr'pər) n. 1, sluggishness in bodily functioning; stupor. 2, stupidity. 3, inactivity; lethargy.

torque (tôrk) n. a force that tends to cause torsion or rotation.

tor'rent (tor'ent) n. 1, an abundant and violent flow of water; a heavy rain. 2, an overwhelming flow of anything. —**tor·ren'tial** (-shəl) adj.

tor'rid (tor'id) adj. 1, hot, dry, and arid in climate. 2, ardent; passionate. —**Torrid Zone**, the zone centered on the Equator.

tor'sion (tôr'shən) n. the act or result of twisting. —**tor'sion·al**, adj.

tor'so (tôr'sō) n. [pl. -sos] the trunk of the human body.

tort (tôrt) n. (*Law*) a civil wrong calling for compensation in damages.

tor·til'la (tôr-tē'yə) n. a Mexican cake of unleavened corn meal.

tor'toise (tôr'təs) n. a turtle of a terrestrial variety.—**tor'toise-shell"**, adj. of tortoise shell, or its yellow-and-brown coloring.

tor'tu·ous (tôr'choo-əs) adj. full of twists and turns; winding; crooked. —**tor'tu·ous·ness**, n.

tor'ture (tôr'chər) n. 1, the act of willfully inflicting severe pain. 2, excruciating pain or anguish. 3, a cause of anguish. —v.t. 1, subject to torture. 2, distort. —**tor'tur·er**, n.

to'ry (tôr'ē) n. & adj. one who is conservative in political views, esp. a supporter of an established monarchy or aristocracy.

toss (tâs) v.t. 1, throw or fling, esp. with little effort. 2, tumble about; agitate. 3, jerk. —v.i. 1, be pitched or rocked about; sway. 2, move restlessly. 3, decide something by the way a tossed coin falls. —n. a throw, fling, jerk, or pitch.

toss-'up" n. 1, the tossing of a coin. 2, (*Colloq.*) an even chance.

tot n. 1, a small child. 2, a small quantity.—v.t. [tot'ted, -ting] (usually with *up*) add.

to'tal (tō'tal) adj. 1, pert. to the whole; taking all together. 2, being or comprising the whole. 3, complete; absolute. —n. 1, the sum; the whole or aggregate. —v.t. & i. 1, ascertain the sum of; add up. 2,

amount to. —**total war**, war waged with greatest possible effort.

to·tal"i·tar'i·an (tō-tal"i-târ'ē-ən) adj. pert. to a government that suppresses opposition. —n. an adherent of such government. —**to·tal"i·tar'i·an·ism**, n.

to·tal'i·ty (tō-tal'ə-tē) n. an entirety; a whole.

to·tal·i·za'tor (tō'təl-i-zā'tər) n. (*T.N.*) a device for registering pari-mutuel ticket sales. Also, **to'tal·iz"er**.

tote (tōt) v.t. (*Colloq.*) carry.

to'tem (tō'təm) n. an emblem of a clan or family. —**to'tem·ism**, n.

totem pole a post carved or painted with totems, erected by certain American Indians.

Totem Pole

tot'ter (tot'ər) v.i. 1, walk unsteadily. 2, sway or shake as if about to fall. —n. an act of tottering.

tou·can' (too-kän') n. a tropical Amer. bird with an enormous beak and brilliant plumage.

touch (tuch) v.t. 1, perceive by physical contact; feel by tactile sense. 2, be or come in contact with. 3, reach; stop at; equal; attain. 4, put the hand on; handle. 5, refer or allude to; deal with. 6, pertain or relate to. 7, (with *up*) modify; improve. 8, affect, as with pity. 9, tinge; imbue. 10, (*Slang*) borrow or beg money from. —v.i. 1, come or be in contact. 2, (with *on* or *upon*) allude to something briefly. —n. 1, the sense of feeling. 2, the act of touching; adjacency. 3, communication. 4, a quality perceptible to the touch. 5, a small quantity or degree. 6, a detail of handiwork. 7, skill or style in execution. —**touch and go**, a precarious state of affairs.

touch'down" n. a scoring play in football.

touched (tucht) adj. 1, affected with emotion. 2, mentally feeble; eccentric.

touch'ing prep. in reference to; —adj. emotionally affecting.

touch'stone" n. a test or criterion.

touch'y adj. 1, irritable. 2, risky; delicate. —**touch'i·ness**, n.

tough (tuf) adj. 1, not easily broken or cut. 2, flexible without brittleness; hardy. 3, stiff in consistency; difficult to chew. 4, unyielding; hardened; incorrigible. 5, troublesome; hard to do or bear.

6, violent; severe. **7**, rowdy; vicious. —*n.* a ruffian or bully. —**tough'en,** *v.t.* make tougher. —**tough'ness,** *n.*

tou·pee' (too-pā') *n.* a patch of false hair.

tour (tŭr) *n.* **1**, a journey to several places in succession. **2**, a period of work or duty. —*v.i. & t.* travel about. —**tour'ist,** *n.* a traveler for pleasure.

tour'ma·line (tŭr'mə-lēn) *n.* a mineral, a gem when transparent.

tour'na·ment (tŭr'nə-mənt) *n.* a meeting for contests.

tour'ney (tŭr'nē) *n.* tournament.

tour'ni·quet (tŭr'ni-ket) *n.* a tight bandage to stop bleeding.

tou'sle (tow'zəl) *v.t.* rumple.

tout (towt) *v.t.* **1**, sell horse-race betting information. **2**, solicit business, votes, etc. **3**, spy. —*v.t.* **1**, praise highly. **2**, sell a betting tip to. —*n.* one who touts.

tow (tō) *v.t.* drag by a rope or chain. —*n.* **1**, the act of towing; a rope or chain. **2**, the fiber of flax, hemp, or jute. —**tow'age,** *n.*

to·ward' (tôrd, twôrd) *prep.* **1**, in the direction of. **2**, in furtherance of. **3**, with respect to; concerning. **4**, near. Also, **to·wards'.**

tow'el (tow'əl) *n.* a cloth or paper for wiping. —**tow'el·ing,** *n.*

tow'er (tow'ər) *n.* a high, slender building or structure. —*v.i.* rise aloft; stand high. —**tow'er·ing,** *adj.*

tow'head''ed *adj.* having flax-colored hair.

town *n.* **1**, an inhabited place, larger than a village. **2**, [also, **town'ship**] a division of a county. **3**, a city or borough. —**town hall**, headquarters of a town's government. —**town meeting**, a meeting of the citizens of a town.

town'ship'' *n.* **1**, a unit of territory, varying in size and function in different states and countries, in the U.S. usually 6 miles square. **2**, a town.

towns'man (townz'mən) *n.* [*pl.* -men] an inhabitant of a town or of the same town. —**towns'peo'ple,** *n.pl.*

tox·e'mi·a (tok-sē'mē-ə) *n.* the presence of toxins in the blood. —**tox·e'mic,** *adj.*

tox'ic (tok'sik) *adj.* **1**, poisonous. **2**, pert. to a toxin. —**tox·ic'i·ty** (toks-is'ə-tē) *n.*

tox''i·col'o·gy (tok'si-kol'ə-jē) *n.* the science of poisons. —**tox''i·co·log'i·cal,** *adj.* —**tox''i·col'o·gist,** *n.*

tox'in (tok'sin) *n.* a poisonous product of microörganisms.

toy (toi) *n.* **1**, any article played with by a child; a plaything. **2**, a trinket; a trifle. **3**, a dog of small size. —*adj.* **1**, made as a plaything.

2, diminutive. —*v.i.* **1**, play. **2**, act idly; trifle.

trace (trās) *n.* **1**, a mark, track, or any evidence of someone or something formerly present or existent. **2**, a very small quantity of something. **3**, a line or sketch. **4**, a strap, rope, or chain for hitching a draft animal. **5**, a bar or lever for transferring motion. —*v.t.* **1**, follow the footprints or track of. **2**, determine the course, development, or history of. **3**, find evidence of; investigate. **4**, copy (a drawing, etc.) by marking the lines on superimposed transparent paper. **5**, make a plan of.

trac'er (trās'ər) *n.* one who or that which traces. —*adj.* that traces. —**skip tracer**, one who traces debtors. —**tracer bullet**, one that blazes in flight, to indicate its course.

tra·che·a (trā'kē-ə) *n.* [*pl.* -ae' (-ē')] the tube that conveys air from the larynx to the lungs; the windpipe. —**tra'che·al,** *adj.*

trac'ing (trās'ing) *n.* a traced copy.

track (trak) *n.* **1**, marks left in the ground, as footprints, a rut, etc. **2**, a system of rails to support and guide a moving vehicle, esp. a railroad. **3**, a path laid out for a race; running and field sports. **4**, a path or trail. **5**, a course of motion, travel, action, etc. —*v.t.* **1**, pursue; trace. **2**, make a track on; make footprints with (mud, etc.). **3**, traverse; explore. —**track meet**, a series of track contests.

tract (trakt) *n.* **1**, an expanse of land or water; a region. **2**, a particular system in the body. **3**, a brief printed treatise.

trac'ta·ble (trak'tə-bəl) *adj.* **1**, easily led; docile; compliant. **2**, easily managed, worked, or wrought. —**trac''ta·bil'i·ty,** *n.*

trac'tion (trak'shən) *n.* **1**, the act of dragging or hauling; the state of being drawn. **2**, power of pulling or attracting. **3**, adhesive friction. —**trac'tive,** *adj.*

trac'tor (trak'tər) *n.* a self-propelled vehicle that pulls heavy loads.

trade (trād) *n.* **1**, the business of buying and selling; commerce. **2**, a sale or exchange. **3**, an occupation, esp. skilled mechanical work. **4**, the persons engaged in the same occupation. **5**, customers. —*v.t.* buy, sell, barter, or exchange. —*v.i.* engage in commerce. —**trad'er,** *n.*

trade-'in'' *n.* property given in part payment of a purchase.

trade-'last'' a compliment reported to another on condition of receiving one oneself.

trade'mark'' *n.* a patented name or visual mark attached to a product.

trade name a name coined to identify a product; trademark.

trades'man (trādz'mən) *n.* [*pl.* -men] a shopkeeper; merchant.

trade union an organization of workers in a skilled trade.

trade wind a prevailing wind relied upon by ships.

tra·di·tion (trə-dish'ən) *n.* the handing down of customs, practices, doctrines, etc.; something so handed down. —**tra·di'tion·al,** *adj.*

tra·duce' (trə-dūs') *v.t.* defame; slander.

traf'fic (traf'ik) *n.* **1,** the coming and going of persons, vehicles, etc. **2,** commercial dealings; the transportation of goods. —*v.t.* [-ficked, -fick·ing] carry on traffic; deal. —**traffic circle,** a road intersection designed to avoid cross traffic. —**traf'fick·er,** *n.*

tra·ge'di·an (trə-jē'dē-ən) *n.* an actor in a tragedy. —**tra·ge'di·enne'** (-en') *n. fem.*

trag'e·dy (traj'-ə-dē) *n.* **1,** a lamentable event or state of affairs; a disaster or calamity. **2,** a drama with an unhappy ending.

Traffic Circle

trag'ic (traj'ik) *adj.* being or suggesting a tragedy; very unhappy. Also, **trag'i·cal.**

trail (trāl) *v.t.* **1,** drag loosely, as along the ground; draw along behind. **2,** follow the trail of; track. **3,** (*Colloq.*) follow behind, as in a race. **4,** make a path through; mark out. —*v.i.* **1,** hang down or be dragged loosely behind something. **2,** proceed idly or lazily; loiter or straggle. **3,** be dispersed. —*n.* **1,** a rough path. **2,** a track or scent. **3,** something that trails behind. **trail'blaz"er,** *n.* one who goes first, a pioneer or originator.

trail'er (trāl'ər) *n.* **1,** a vehicle drawn by another. **2,** a kind of mobile house drawn by an automobile. **3,** a trailing plant. **4,** brief excerpts from a motion picture to advertise it.

train (trān) *n.* **1,** a railroad locomotive and the cars connected to it. **2,** a procession of persons, vehicles, etc. traveling together. **3,** a body of attendants; a retinue. **4,** something that trails along behind; a trailing skirt. **5,** a series of events, ideas, etc. —*v.t.* **1,** subject to discipline and instruction; make proficient or fit. **2,** aim or direct, as a gun. —*v.i.* undergo or impart training.

train·ee' (trā-nē') *n.* one who receives training, esp. military.

train'er *n.* **1,** one who trains others. **2,** in some sports, one who gives rubdowns, applies bandages, etc.

train'man (-mən) *n.* [*pl.* -men] a member of a railroad conductor's crew.

trait (trāt) *n.* a distinguishing feature or quality.

trai'tor (trā'tər) *n.* one who betrays; one guilty of treason. —**trai'tor·ous,** *adj.*

tra·jec'to·ry (trə-jek'tə-rē) *n.* the curve described by a projectile in flight.

tram *n.* a wheeled car; (*Brit.*) a streetcar. —**tram'way",** *n.*

tram'mel (tram'əl) *n.* **1,** an impediment. **2,** an instrument for drawing ellipses. **3,** a shackle. —*v.t.* shackle; hamper.

tramp *v.i.* **1,** walk with a heavy step. **2,** walk steadily or resolutely; trudge. **3,** travel about as a vagabond. —*v.t.* **1,** traverse on foot. **2,** trample underfoot. —*n.* **1,** a heavy tread. **2,** the sound of a heavy footstep. **3,** a long walk. **4,** a vagabond who lives by begging or stealing. **5,** a freight ship without fixed ports of call.

tram'ple (tram'pəl) *v.t.* **1,** step heavily upon; crush with the feet. **2,** suppress by force.

trance (trāns) *n.* **1,** a state of partial unconsciousness. **2,** a daze.

tran'quil (trang'kwil) *adj.* calm; serene; undisturbed. —**tran·quil'li·ty,** *n.* —**tran'quil·ize"** (-īz") *v.t.*

trans- *pref.* across; beyond.

trans·act' (trans-akt') *v.t. & i.* carry through (dealings, etc.) to a conclusion; perform; do. —**trans·ac'tion,** *n.* performance; a deal.

trans"at·lan'tic *adj.* **1,** crossing the Atlantic Ocean. **2,** situated across the Atlantic.

tran·scend' (tran-send') *v.t.* go or be beyond (a limit, etc.); surpass; excel. —**tran·scend'ence,** *n.* —**tran·scend'ent,** *adj.*

tran"scen·den'tal (tran"sen-den'təl) *adj.* beyond ordinary experience.

tran"scen·den'tal·ism (-iz-əm) *n.* a philosophy based on reasoning or intuition, not empiricism.

trans"con·ti·nen'tal *adj.* crossing, or situated across, a continent; (*U.S.*) coast-to-coast.

tran·scribe' (tran-skrīb') *v.t.* **1,** make a written copy of. **2,** put into writing; write in other characters; transliterate. **3,** make a phonograph recording of. **4,** arrange (a musical composition) for other instruments.

tran'script (tran'skript) *n.* a written copy.

tran·scrip'tion (-skrip'shən) *n.* **1,** act or result of transcribing. **2,** a transcript. **3,** a record for broadcasting.

---

fat, fāte, fär, fâre, fâll, ásk; met, hē, hēr, maybē; pin, pīne; not, nŏte, ôr, tool

tran'sept n. that part of a cross-shaped church at right angles to the nave.

trans·fer' (trans-fer') v.t. [transferred', -fer'ring] 1, move or convey from one place to another. 2, make over custody or ownership of. 3, copy or impress (a design, etc.) from one surface to another. —n. (trans'fer) 1. the act or means of transferring. 2, a ticket valid as fare on another car of a transit system. 3, something to be transferred, as a design. —trans"fer·ee', n. —trans·fer'ence, n. —trans·fer'or, n.

trans·fig"u·ra'tion (trans-fig"yə-rā'shən) n. 1, transfiguration. 2, (cap.) the change in appearance of Christ on the Mount.

trans·fig'ure (trans-fig'yər) v.t. 1, change the outward form or appearance of; transform. 2, give a glorified appearance to; exalt. —trans·fig'ure·ment, n.

trans·fix' v.t. 1, pierce through: fasten by pinning down. 2, make motionless with amazement, etc. —trans·fix'ion, n.

trans·form' (trans-fôrm') v.t. change in form, appearance, or condition.

trans"for·ma'tion n. 1, act or effect of transforming. 2, a wig.

trans·form'er n. an apparatus for changing electric current.

trans·fuse' (trans-fūz') v.t. transfer (liquid) by or as by pouring; inject; infuse. —trans·fu'sion, n. a transfer of blood from one person to another.

trans·gress' (trans-gres') v.t. & i. 1, go beyond (a limit, etc.). 2, break or violate (a law or rule). —transgres'sion (-gresh'ən) n. —transgres'sor (-gres'ər) n.

tran'sient (tran'shənt) adj. passing with time; not enduring; temporary; momentary. —n. one who stays briefly, as a guest. —tran'sience, n.

tran·sis'tor (tran-sis'tər) n. a small electronic device used instead of a tube, to amplify the signal.

tran'sit n. 1, passage or conveyance from one place to another. 2, a surveying instrument for measuring angles.

tran·si'tion (-zish'ən) n. a change from one place or state to another. —tran·si'tion·al, adj.

tran'si·tive (tran'sə-tiv) adj. 1, (of a verb) taking a direct object.

2, making, or having power to make, a transition.

tran'si·to"ry (tran'sə-tôr'ē) adj. lasting only for a time; fleeting.

trans·late' (trans-lāt') v.t. 1, express the sense of in words of another language. 2, explain by using other words. 3, transfer. —trans·la'tion, n. —trans·la'tor, n.

trans·lit'er·ate (trans-lit'ər-āt') v.t. spell in another alphabet or language. —trans"lit·er·a'tion, n.

trans·lu'cent (trans-loo'sənt) adj. transmitting light without being transparent. —trans·lu'cence, n.

trans"mi·gra'tion (trans"mī-grā'shən) n. passage, esp. of a soul reborn in another body. —trans·mi'grate, v.i.

trans·mis'si·ble adj. capable of being transmitted. —trans·mis'si·bil'i·ty, n.

trans·mis'sion (trans-mish'ən) n. 1, the act or result of transmitting. 2, a system of gears for transmitting power in an automobile.

trans·mit' v.t. [trans·mit'ted, -ting] 1, send onward or along; hand over, or down to, a recipient or destination. 2, communicate; emit. —trans·mit'tal, n.

trans·mit'ter (-ər) n. the sending part of a radio or telephone apparatus.

trans·mute' (trans-mūt') v.t. & i. change from one nature, form, or substance to another. —trans"mu·ta'tion, n.

tran'som (tran'səm) n. 1, a beam above a door separating it from a window. 2, a hinged window or panel above a door. 3, any crossbeam.

trans·par'ent (trans-par'ənt) adj. 1, permitting distinct vision through a solid substance. 2, easily understood; manifest. —trans·par'ence, trans·par'en·cy, n.

tran·spire' (tran-spīr') v.i. 1, emit a vapor; exhale or perspire. 2, escape through pores. 3, become known. 4, happen; occur. —tran"spi·ra'tion, n.

trans·plant' (trans-plänt') v.t. remove from one place and plant, fix or establish in another.

trans·port' (trans-pôrt') v.t. 1, carry from one place to another; convey. 2, imbue with strong emotion. 3, carry into banishment. —n. (trans'pôrt) 1, the act or business of transporting. 2, a means of transport, esp. a ship for carrying troops. 3, rapture.

trans"por·ta'tion (trans"pôr-tā'shən) n. 1, act or result, or a means, of conveying. 2, traveling expenses.

trans·pose' (trans-pōz') v.t. 1, alter the position or order of. 2, exchange the places of. 3, [also v.i.] arrange or perform (music) in a different key. —trans"po·si'tion, n.

trans·ship' *v.t. & i.* ship by more than one carrier.

trans·ver'sal (trans-vẽrs'əl) *n.* a line intersecting two or more other lines.

trans·verse' (trans-vẽrs') *adj.* lying across something; extending from side to side.

trans·vest'ism (tranz-vest'iz-əm) *n.* desire to wear the clothes of the opposite sex. Also, **trans·ves'ti·tism.** —trans·vest'ite, *n.*

trap *n.* **1,** any contrivance for catching animals; a pitfall or snare; a stratagem. **2,** a U-bend in a pipe. **3,** (*pl.*) baggage; equipment; the percussion instruments of a band. **4,** a door in a floor, ceiling, or roof; trap door. **5,** a light two-wheeled carriage. —*v.t.* [trapped, trap'ping] catch in a trap; ensnare in any way. —*v.i.* trap animals. —trap door, a door in a ceiling.

tra·peze' (trə-pēz') *n.* a horizontal bar suspended by two ropes, used for gymnastic exercises.

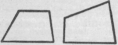

Trapezoid & Trapezium

tra·pe'zi·um (trə-pē'zē-əm) *n.* a quadrilateral plane figure having no two sides parallel.

trap'e·zoid" (trap'i-zoid") *n.* a quadrilateral figure with two sides parallel.

trap'per (-ər) *n.* one who traps animals.

trap'pings (-ingz) *n.pl.* equipment.

Trap'pist (trap'ist) *adj.* pert. to a Rom. Cath. order of monks.

trap'rock" *n.* an igneous rock, as basalt.

trap'shoot"ing *n.* the sport of shooting at flying targets.

trash *n.* anything worthless or useless; waste material; rubbish. —trash'y, *adj.*

trau'ma (trâ'mə) *n.* **1,** a bodily injury. **2,** a mental shock. —trau·mat'ic, *adj.* —trau·mat'i·cal·ly, *adv.*

trav'ail (trav'āl) *n.* painful labor.

trav'el (trav'əl) *v.i.* **1,** go from place to place; make a journey. **2,** move on a fixed track, as a mechanical part. **3,** advance; proceed. **4,** (*Colloq.*) move speedily. —*v.t.* pass over or through. —*n.* the act of traveling. —trav'el·er, *n.*

trav'e·logue" (trav'ə-lâg") *n.* a lecture or motion picture describing a journey.

trav'erse (trav'ərs) *v.t.* **1,** pass across, over, or through. **2,** contradict; obstruct. **3,** turn and aim (a gun). —*n.* something that lies or moves crosswise; a crosswise barrier. —*adj.* transverse.

trav'es·ty (trav'is-tē) *n.* a burlesque of a literary or dramatic composition; any debased likeness. —*v.t.* imitate grotesquely.

trawl (trâl) *n.* a fishing net or line dragged by a boat. —*v.i.* fish with a trawl. —trawl'er, *n.* a fishing boat.

tray (trā) *n.* a flat vessel or shallow box for holding something.

treach'er·ous (trech'ə-rəs) *adj.* **1,** committing treachery. **2,** deceptive; unreliable. —treach'er·ous·ness, *n.*

treach'er·y (trech'ə-rē) *n.* violation of allegiance or faith; betrayal of trust; treason or perfidy.

trea'cle (trē'kəl) *n.* molasses.

tread (tred) *v.i.* [trod, trod'den (-dən), tread'ing] set the foot down; step; walk. —*v.i.* **1,** walk on, in, or along. **2,** trample. **3,** execute by walking or dancing. —*n.* **1,** a stepping; the sound of a step; a single step. **2,** the outermost surface, as of a shoe, tire, etc., that touches the ground or road. **3,** a bearing surface, as of a rail or stair.

trea'dle (tred'əl) *n.* a lever operated by the foot.

tread'mill" *n.* a mill powered by animals walking on a wheel, etc.

trea'son (trē'zən) *n.* violation of the allegiance due a state. —trea'son·a·ble, *adj.* constituting treason. —trea'son·ous, *adj.*

treas'ure (trezh'ər) *n.* **1,** an accumulation of money or jewels. **2,** anything prized highly. —*v.t.* **1,** collect and save; retain carefully. **2,** regard as precious; prize. —treasure trove (trōv) money or valuables (of an unknown owner) found in the earth.

treas'ur·er (trezh'ər-ər) *n.* the officer in charge of funds.

treas'ur·y (trezh'ə-rē) *n.* **1,** the funds of a government, corporation, etc.; the department administering them. **2,** a place where money or valuables are kept.

treat (trēt) *v.t.* **1,** regard, behave toward, or deal with; discuss. **2,** apply methods of relief or cure to (a patient or disease). **3,** subject to a process. **4,** entertain by paying for food, drink, amusement, etc. —*v.i.* **1,** discuss something. **2,** carry on negotiations. **3,** bear the expense of regalement. —*n.* **1,** entertainment paid for; one's turn to pay. **2,** (*Colloq.*) anything enjoyable.

trea'tise (trē'tis) *n.* a book treating of a particular subject.

treat'ment (-mənt) *n.* **1,** act or manner of dealing with something. **2,** therapy.

trea'ty (trē'tē) n. a written agreement between nations.

tre'ble (treb'əl) adj. **1**, threefold. **2**, high in pitch; soprano. —n. a high-pitched part, tone, etc. —v.t. & i. triple.

tree (trē) n. **1**, a large perennial plant with a single permanent woody trunk. **2**, any of various devices or parts in the form of a pole, bar, etc. **3**, a genealogical diagram: *family tree.* —v.t. drive into a tree.

tre'foil" (trē'foil") n. a three-leaved plant, esp. the clover.

trek v.i. [**trekked, trek'king**] travel; migrate. —n. a journey.

trel'lis (trel'is) n. a framework of crossbars; a lattice.

trem'ble (trem'bəl) v.i. **1**, shake or vibrate with continued movement; shiver; quake. **2**, be agitated by fear. **3**, vacillate. —n. a shivering or vibratory motion. —trem'bly, adj.

tre·men'dous (tri-men'dəs) adj. **1**, very great in size, amount, degree, etc.; huge; gigantic. **2**, (*Colloq.*) excellent. —tre·men'dous·ness, n.

trem'o·lo" (trem'ə-lō") n. [pl. **-los"**] rapid reiteration of a musical tone.

trem'or (trem'ər) n. a shake, quiver, or vibration; a trembling or vibratory movement.

trem'u·lous (trem'yə-ləs) adj. **1**, trembling; unsteady. **2**, fearful; timid; irresolute. **3**, wavy, as a line. —trem'u·lous·ness, n.

trench n. a long, narrow excavation in the ground, esp. as a shelter in warfare; a ditch or furrow. —v.t. & i. dig a trench (in); fortify. —**trench coat**, a heavy raincoat.

trench'ant (tren'chənt) adj. **1**, keenly effective; incisive. **2**, thoroughgoing. —trench'an·cy, n.

trench'er·man (tren'chər-mən) n. [pl. **-men**] a heavy eater.

trench mouth an infectious disease of the mucous membranes of the throat and mouth.

trend n. tendency to go in a particular direction or course; drift, bent, or inclination.

tre·pan' (tre-pan') n. a cylindrical saw; a boring instrument. —v.t. [**-panned', -pan'ning**] cut with a trepan.

tre·phine' (tri-fīn') n. a cylindrical saw used in brain surgery.

Trephine

trep"i·da'tion (trep'ə-dā'shən) n. tremulous agitation, as from alarm.

tres'pass (tres'pəs) v.i. **1**, enter without right upon another's land; encroach. **2**, commit a wrong; transgress; sin. —n. an offense; sin.

tress (tres) n. **1**, a lock or braid of hair. **2**, (pl.) the hair of the head.

tres'tle (tres'əl) n. **1**, a short horizontal bar supported by legs; a sawhorse. **2**, a bridge supported by framework.

trey (trā) n. a playing card, die, domino, etc. with three spots.

tri- pref. three.

tri'ad (trī'ad) n. a group of three closely-related things.

tri'al (trī'əl) n. **1**, an action in a judicial court to determine a cause. **2**, a test; an examination. **3**, a try or attempt. **4**, the state of being tried or tested; probation. **5**, a hardship. —adj. **1**, pert. to a trial. **2**, done as a test or experiment. —**trial balance**, a statement of the current totals in a ledger. —**trial balloon**, an act or statement to test public reaction. —**trial and error**, a method of solving a problem by a series of guesses.

tri'an"gle (trī'ang"gəl) n. **1**, a plane figure formed by three straight lines. **2**, a drawing instrument in this shape. **3**, a steel bar bent into a triangle used as a musical percussion instrument. **4**, two men and a woman, or two women and a man involved in emotional conflict. —tri·an'gu·lar (trī-ang'gyū-lər) adj.

tri·an"gu·la'tion (trī-ang"gyū-lā'shən) n. a measuring by inferring unknown sides or angles of a triangle. —tri·ang'u·late" (-lāt") v.t.

tribe (trīb) n. **1**, an aggregate of people united by common ancestry, intermarriage, or allegiance. **2**, any class or body of individuals. —trib'al, adj. —tribes'man, n.

trib"u·la'tion (trib'yə-lā'shən) n. a state, cause, or instance of affliction or suffering.

tri·bu'nal (trī-bū'nəl) n. a court of justice.

trib'une (trib'ūn) n. **1**, a person who upholds or defends popular rights. **2**, a dais or pulpit.

trib'u·tar"y (trib'yə-ter"ē) n. **1**, a river, brook, etc. that flows into another body of water. **2**, one who pays tribute. —adj. contributory.

trib'ute (trib'ūt) n. **1**, a gift or compliment as a mark of gratitude or respect. **2**, any forced payment.

trice (trīs) n. an instant; moment.

trich"i·no'sis (trik"ə-nō'sis) n. a disease caused by a parasitic worm.

trick (trik) n. **1**, any method of deceiving; a stratagem, ruse, or wile. **2**, a practical joke, prank, or hoax. **3**, a peculiar habit or mannerism. **4**, a batch of playing cards, one played from each hand. **5**, (*Colloq.*) a girl. **6**, a turn of work or duty. —adj. fraudulent; crafty; unreliable; unusual. —v.t. & i. **1**, dupe; swindle. **2**, (with *out*) dress; array.

trick′er·y (-ə-rė) *n.* deception.

trick′le (trik′əl) *v.i.* flow slowly, irregularly, or by drops. —*v.t.* cause to trickle. —*n.* a trickling flow.

trick′ster (-stər) *n.* a deceiver; a joker.

trick′y *adj.* **1,** crafty. **2,** unreliable; ticklish. —**trick′i·ness,** *n.*

tri·col′or (trī′kul′ər) *n.* the flag of the Fr. republic.

tri′cot (trē′kō) *n.* a knitted fabric.

tri′cy·cle (trī′sik·əl) *n.* a three-wheeled vehicle for a child; a velocipede.

tri′dent (trī′dənt) *n. & adj.* a spear or fork having three prongs.

tried (trīd) *v.* pret. & p.p. of *try.*

tri′fle (trī′fəl) *n.* something trivial or insignificant. —*v.i.* **1,** deal with something lightly or idly. **2,** waste time; dally. —**tri′fler,** *n.* —**tri′fling,** *adj.* insignificant.

trig *adj.* [**trig′ger, -gest**] **1,** neat; spruce. **2,** in good condition. —*n.* a block used to check the motion of a wheel, cask, etc.

trig′ger (trig′ər) *n.* a lever for releasing a spring, esp. on a firearm.

trig″o·nom′e·try (trig″ə-nom′ə-trė) *n.* the branch of mathematics that deals with measurement of and by means of triangles.

trill (tril) *n.* **1,** a rapid alternation of two adjacent musical tones. **2,** any quavering, tremulous sound. **3,** a warbling, as of a bird. —*v.i. & t.* sound vibrantly.

tril′lion (tril′yən) *n. & adj.* the cardinal number represented by 1 followed by 12 zeros (U.S. & Fr.) or 18 zeros (Brit. & Ger.).

tril′o·gy (tril′ə-jė) *n.* a group of three related things, as plays.

trim *v.t.* [**trimmed, trim′ming**] **1,** make neat or orderly. **2,** remove by clipping or pruning. **3,** deck with ornaments. **4,** (*Colloq.*) defeat. —*v.i.* come to a desired adjustment or position. —*n.* **1,** position, condition, or order. **2,** dress, equipment, or decoration; ornamental borders or furnishings. —*adj.* [**trim′mer, -mest**] **1,** neat; spruce; smart. **2,** in good order or condition. —**trim′mer,** *n.* —**trim′ming,** *n.* —**trim′ness,** *n.*

tri·mes′ter (trī-mes′tər) *n.* a period of three months.

trin′i·ty (trin′ə-tė) *n.* a group of three, esp. (*cap.*) Father, Son and Holy Ghost or Spirit.

trin′ket (tring′kit) *n.* a trifling ornament or keepsake.

tri′o (trē′ō) *n.* a group of three.

trip *n.* **1,** a journey or voyage. **2,** a catching of the foot against an obstacle; a stumble. **3,** a slip or error. **4,** a light, short step. **5,** a catch or

trigger; a sudden release, as by a trigger. —*v.i.* [**tripped, trip′ping**] **1,** stumble. **2,** make a mistake. **3,** run or step lightly; skip. —*v.t.* **1,** cause to stumble, fall, or err. **2,** perform with a tripping step. **3,** release suddenly. —**trip′per,** *n.*

tri·par′tite (trī-pär′tīt) *adj.* embracing three parties, as a treaty.

tripe (trīp) *n.* **1,** the stomach of a cow or ox, prepared as food. **2,** (*Slang*) anything worthless.

trip′ham″mer *n.* a heavy hammer allowed to fall by a tripping device.

tri′ple (trip′əl) *adj.* consisting of three parts; threefold; of three kinds. —*n.* a threefold object or amount; (*Baseball*) a three-base hit. —*v.t. & i.* multiply by three.

trip′let *n.* one of three children born at one birth; one of a group of three; (*pl.*) the three collectively.

tri′plex (trip′leks) *adj.* threefold. —*n.* something triple; an apartment having three stories.

trip′li·cate″ (trip′li-kāt″) *v.t.* make in three copies. —*adj.* (-kət) made in three copies. —*n.* (-kət) the third copy. —**trip″li·ca′tion,** *n.*

tri′pod (trī′pod) *n.* a stand having three legs. —**trip′o·dal** (trip′ə-dəl) *adj.*

trip′ping *adj.* light and lively.

trip′tych (trip′tik) *n.* three pictures, etc., esp. in hinged frames.

tri·sect′ (trī-sekt′) *v.t.* divide in three parts. —**tri·sec′tion,** *n.*

trite (trīt) *adj.* stale; hackneyed. —**trite′ness,** *n.*

tri′tium (trish′yəm) *n.* an isotope of hydrogen.

trit′u·rate″ (trich′ə-rāt″) *v.t.* grind to powder. —**trit″u·ra′tion,** *n.*

tri′umph (trī′umf) *n.* **1,** the winning of a war or contest; success. **2,** exultation over victory or success. —*v.i.* win; succeed.

tri·um′phal (trī-um′fəl) *adj.* pert. to or commemorating a victory.

tri·um′phant (trī-um′fənt) *adj.* victorious; exulting in victory.

tri·um′vir (trī-um′vər) *n.* a member of a triumvirate.

tri·um′vi·rate (trī-um′və-rit) *n.* three joint rulers; their government.

triv′et (triv′it) *n.* a three-legged stool or stand.

triv′i·a (triv′ė-ə) *n.pl.* trivial matters or things.

triv′i·al (triv′ė-əl) *adj.* of little importance or significance. —**triv″i·al′i·ty,** *n.*

-trix *suf.* denoting a feminine agent, as *executrix.*

tro′che (trō′kė) *n.* a medicinal tablet or pill.

tro'chee (trō'kē) n. (*Prosody*) a metrical foot of two syllables, long then short. —**tro·cha·ic** (-kā'ik) *adj. & n.*

trod v. pret. of *tread*.

trod'den (trod'ən) v. p.p. of *tread*.

trog'lo·dyte" (trog'lə-dīt") n. 1, a dweller in a cave. 2, one who lives in seclusion. —**trog"lo·dyt'ic** (-dit'-ik) *adj.*

troi'ka (troi'kə) n. a team of three horses; the carriage they draw.

Tro'jan horse (trō'jən) an ostensible gift intended as a trap.

troll (trōl) v.i. & t. 1, sing in a full, jovial tone; sing a round. 2, fish with a moving line. 3, turn around; roll. —n. 1, a round song. 2, equipment for trolling. 3, a fairy dwarf.

trol'ley (trol'ē) n. 1, a pulley or block moving on an overhead wire, to convey loads or feed electric current. 2, a streetcar.

trol'lop (trol'əp) n. 1, a slovenly woman. 2, a prostitute.

trom'bone (trom'bōn) n. a musical wind instrument having a sliding U-shaped section. —**trom'bon·ist,** *n.*

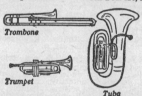

Trombone

Trumpet

Tuba

troop n. 1, an assemblage of people; a herd or flock; a multitude. 2, a unit of armed forces; (*pl.*) a body of soldiers. —v.i. & t. flock together; march or maneuver. — **troop'er,** n. a policeman or soldier.

tro'phy (trō'fē) n. 1, something captured in war, hunting, etc. 2, a prize or medal, etc.

-tro·phy (trə-fē) *suf.* denoting nourishment.

trop'ic (trop'ik) n. 1, either of the two parallels of latitude 23½° distant from the equator, north (tropic of Cancer) or south (tropic of Capricorn). 2, (*pl.*) the region lying between these two parallels; the Torrid Zone. —**trop'i·cal,** *adj.* pert. to the torrid zone.

trop'o·sphere" (trop'ə-sfir") n. the layer of atmosphere about 6 to 12 miles above the earth's surface.

-tro·py *suf.* growth. Also, **-tro·pism.**

trot v.i. [**trot'ted, -ting**] go at a pace between a walk and a run.

—v.t. 1, cause (a horse) to trot. 2, (with *out*) produce for inspection. —n. 1, a trotting gait. 2, (*Colloq.*) an illicit translation used by students; a crib. 3, a long fishing line with numerous hooks.

troth (trâth) n. 1, a promise to marry. 2, *Archaic,* truth.

trot'ter (trot'ər) n. 1, a trotting horse. 2, pig's foot, as food.

trou'ba·dour" (troo'bə-dôr") n. an itinerant lyric poet or singer.

trou'ble (trub'əl) v.t. 1, disturb in the mind; annoy; worry. 2, put to inconvenience. —n. 1, discomfort; distress; inconvenience. 2, a cause or source of trouble. —**trou'ble·some,** *adj.* causing trouble. —**trou'blous,** *adj.*

trou'ble·shoot"er n. one who locates and eliminates sources of trouble.

trough (trâf) n. 1, a long narrow container for water, food for animals, etc. 2, a shallow open ditch; a deep groove.

trounce (trowns) v.t. defeat decisively; thrash.

troupe (troop) n. a traveling theatrical company. —v.i. travel as member of a troupe. —**troup'er,** n.

trou'sers (trow'zərz) n. pl. a garment for men, extending downward from the waist, covering each leg separately. —**trou'ser,** *adj.*

trous·seau' (troo-sō') n. a bride's clothes and other outfit.

trout (trowt) n. [*pl.* **trout**] a freshwater game fish.

Trout

trow (trō) v.i. (*Archaic*) believe.

trow'el (trow'əl) n. a short-handled tool with a flat or concave blade, for digging, spreading, etc.

troy (troi) *adj.* pert. to a system of weights used for gold, silver, etc.

tru'ant (troo'ənt) n. & adj. one who is absent without leave, esp. a student. —**tru'an·cy,** n.

truce (troos) n. 1, a negotiated suspension of hostilities. 2, a respite.

truck (truk) n. 1, an automotive vehicle for carrying heavy loads. 2, a frame on wheels for carrying loads; such a frame supporting a railway car or locomotive. 3, the top of a mast. 4, vegetables raised for marketing. 5, miscellaneous articles. 6, dealings; barter. —v.t. 1, transport by truck. **2,** barter; peddle. —*v.i.* **1,** use or drive a truck. **2,** deal; bargain. —**truck'age,** *n.* —**truck'er,** *n.* truckman. —**truck farm,** a farm raising garden vegetables for sale.

truck'le (truk'əl) *n.* a small wheel, pulley, or caster. —*v.i.* be tamely submissive or obsequious. —**truckle bed,** a bed that can be pushed under another bed when not in use.

truck'man (-mən) *n.* [*pl.* -**men**] the owner or operator of a motor truck used as a common carrier.

truc'u·lent (truk'yə-lənt) *adj.* overbearing; cruel. —**truc'u·lence,** *n.*

trudge (truj) *v.i.* walk, esp. laboriously or wearily.

true (troo) *adj.* **1,** being in accordance with fact; not false. **2,** correct; accurate. **3,** genuine. **4,** firm in adherence to principles; faithful; loyal; truthful. **5,** sure; reliable. **6,** rightful; legitimate. —*n.* that which is true. —*v.t.* make true; shape or adjust exactly. —*adv.* in a true or truthful manner. —**true bill,** an indictment by a grand jury. —**true blue,** loyal. —**true'ness,** *n.* —**tru'ly,** *adv.*

truf'fle (truf'əl) *n.* a subterranean edible fungus.

tru'ism (troo'iz-əm) *n.* an obvious truth.

trump *n.* **1,** a playing card or suit given temporary rank higher than all cards of other suits. **2,** (*Colloq.*) a delightful person. —*v.t.* **1,** take with a trump card. **2,** (with *up*) fabricate deceitfully. —*v.i.* play a trump card.

trump'er·y (-ə-rē) *n. & adj.* something showy but of little value.

trum'pet (trum'pit) *n.* **1,** a musical wind instrument (see *trombone*). **2,** a noise-making toy. **3,** a loud cry, as of an elephant. **4,** a hearing aid: *ear trumpet.* —*v.i. & t.* **1,** make a trumpet's sound. **2,** proclaim. —**trum'pet·er,** *n.*

trun'cate (trung'kāt) *v.t.* reduce in size by cutting off a part. —**trunca'tion,** *n.*

trun'cheon (trun'chən) *n.* a baton or staff of office; a policeman's club.

trun'dle (trun'dəl) *n.* a small wheel, roller, or caster. —*v.t. & i.* **1,** move on trundles. **2,** roll along; whirl; rotate. —**trundle bed,** truckle bed.

trunk *n.* **1,** the main stem of a tree. **2,** the human or animal body without the head and limbs. **3,** the proboscis of an elephant. **4,** a large box or chest for carrying clothes in traveling. **5,** the main part or line of something having branches. **6,** (*pl.*) short trousers or breeches. —*adj.* pert. to a main line. —**trunk'ful,** *n.*

truss (trus) *v.t.* fasten; bind securely; confine closely. —*n.* **1,** a rigid framework, as to support a bridge. **2,** a belt worn for support, as of a hernia. **3,** a bundle or pack.

trust *n.* **1,** reliance on the integrity, veracity, etc. of a person; confidence. **2,** confident expectation. **3,** expectation of future payment; credit. **4,** management of property by one party (trustee) for the benefit of another (beneficiary); property given or held in trust. **5,** a group or company controlling a number of other companies. **6,** any monopolistic organization. —*adj.* pert. to a trust. —*v.t.* rely on; believe; give credit to. —*v.i.* have confidence; be trustful. —**trust company,** a bank that administers trusts.

trus·tee' (trus-tē') *n.* one to whom property is entrusted for management. —**trus·tee'ship,** *n.*

trust'ful *adj.* confiding. —**trust'-ful·ness,** *n.*

trust'wor·thy *adj.* reliable. —**trust'wor'thi·ness,** *n.*

trust'y *adj.* reliable. —*n.* a convict trusted not to escape. —**trust'i·ness,** *n.*

truth (trooth) *n.* **1,** conformity of assertion to fact or reality; the state of being true. **2,** that which is true; a fact; reality.

truth'ful *adj.* **1,** speaking the truth, esp. habitually. **2,** correct; true. —**truth'ful·ness,** *n.*

try (trī) *v.t.* [*pret. & p.p.* **tried** (trīd)] **1,** attempt to do or accomplish; essay; undertake. **2,** test. **3,** examine judicially; subject to trial. **4,** subject to strain, trouble, or affliction. **5,** (with *out*) refine; render. —*v.i.* make an attempt or trial. —*n.* an attempt or effort. —**try'ing,** *adj.* annoying; tiring.

try'out *n.* a trial to determine fitness.

tryst (trist) *n.* an appointed meeting, esp. between lovers.

tsar (tsär) *n.* czar. —**tsar'e·vitch,** *n.* son of a czar. —**tsa·ri'na,** *n.fem.*

tset'se (tset'sē) *n.* an Afr. bloodsucking fly that transmits diseases.

T square *n.* a T-shaped ruler for drawing parallel lines.

tub *n.* **1,** a tanklike vessel for bathing: *bathtub.* **2,** a shallow cylindrical vessel. **3,** (*Colloq.*) a slow or clumsy boat. **4,** (*Colloq.*) a bath.

tu'ba (too'bə) *n.* a musical wind instrument (see *trombone*).

tub'by (tub'ē) *adj.* **1,** short and fat. **2,** having a dull sound. —**tub'-bi·ness,** *n.*

tube (toob) *n.* **1,** a long, hollow cylinder of metal, glass, etc. **2,** a duct, canal, pipe, etc., for containing or conveying fluid. **3,** a bulb of glass fitted with electrodes. **4,** a tunnel; a subway

tu′ber (too′bər) *n.* a plant having an enlarged fleshy rootlike part, as the potato. —**tu′ber·ous,** *adj.*

tu′ber·cle (too′bər-kəl) *n.* a small, rounded protuberance or excrescence, as on a bone. —**tubercle bacillus,** the organism causing tuberculosis.

tu·ber′cu·lin (tu-bėr′kyə-lin) *n.* a preparation used in treating and testing for tuberculosis.

tu·ber″cu·lo′sis (too-bėr″kyū-lō′sis) *n.* **1,** an infectious disease marked by the formation of tubercles. **2,** this disease affecting the lungs; consumption. —**tu·ber′cu·lar, tu·ber′cu·lous,** *adj.*

tube′rose″ *n.* a bulbous plant bearing white flowers.

tu′bu·lar (too′byû-lər) *adj.* being or pert. to a tube or tubes.

tuck (tuk) *v.t.* **1,** press into a narrow space; cram. **2,** cover snugly with wrappings. **3,** make tucks in. —*v.i.* draw together; contract. —*n.* a flat fold in cloth.

tuck′er (-ər) *n.* **1,** one who tucks. **2,** a neckcloth. —**tuckered out** (*Colloq.*) fatigued.

Tu′dor (too′dər) *adj.* pert. to an Eng. dynasty or its period, 1485–1603.

Tues′day (tūz′dè) *n.* the third day of the week.

tuft *n.* a small bunch of fibrous material, as hair, feathers, grass, etc. bound at one end.

tug *v.t.* [**tugged, tug′ging**] pull with force or effort; drag; haul; tow. —*v.i.* exert effort in pulling or otherwise. —*n.* **1,** a strong pull; a sudden jerk. **2,** a boat for towing: *tugboat.* **3,** a strenuous contest or struggle. **4,** a strap; trace. —**tug of war,** a pulling contest.

tu·i′tion (too-ish′ən) *n.* **1,** a fee for instruction. **2,** the act or business of teaching. —**tu·i′tion·al,** *adj.*

tu′lip (too′lip) *n.* a bulbous plant bearing cup-shaped flowers.

tulle (tool) *n.* a fine fabric; silk or rayon net.

tum′ble (tum′bəl) *v.i.* **1,** lose footing or support; fall down. **2,** descend rapidly, as prices. **3,** roll about; toss; pitch. **4,** perform gymnastic exercises. **5,** (*Slang*) (often with *to*) become suddenly aware of something. —*v.t.* **1,** cast down; upset. **2,** throw or move about; put in disorder. **3,** rotate in a box of abrasive material, for cleaning. —*n.* **1,** an act of tumbling; a fall or turn. **2,** a state of confusion. **3,** (*Slang*) a sign of recognition.

tum′bler (tum′blər) *n.* **1,** a drinking glass. **2,** a gymnast; an acrobat. **3,** a lever, pin, etc. that holds the bolt of a lock. **4,** a cog or rotating part.

tum′ble·weed″ *n.* a U.S. weed that breaks off at the roots in the fall.

tum′brel (tum′brəl) *n.* a dump cart. Also, **tum′bril.**

tu′mid (too′mid) *adj.* **1,** swollen; protuberant. **2,** pompous. —**tu-mid′i·ty,** *n.*

tu′mor (too′mər) *n.* an abnormal swelling in the body. Also, **tu′mour.**

tu′mult (too′mult) *n.* **1,** the commotion and uproar of a multitude. **2,** violent disturbance; high excitement. —**tu·mul′tu·ous,** *adj.*

tun *n.* a large cask.

tu′na (too′nə) *n.* a large, oceanic food and game fish.

tun′dra (tun′drə) *n.* a level, treeless plain of arctic regions.

tune (toon) *n.* **1,** a succession of tones having musical coherence; an air or melody. **2,** adjustment to proper pitch or frequency. **3,** harmony; accord. **4,** good condition. —*v.t.* & *i.* adjust to a proper pitch or frequency; bring or come into harmony. —**tune′ful,** *adj.* melodious. —**tuning fork,** a pronged instrument that vibrates at an exact tone.

tung′sten (tung′stən) *n.* a metallic chemical element, no. 74, symbol W.

tu′nic (too′nik) *n.* a short coat or shirt; a blouse.

tun′nel (tun′əl) *n.* **1,** an underground roadway or passage. **2,** the burrow of an animal. —*v.t.* & *i.* penetrate by digging.

tun′ny (tun′è) *n.* a large food fish of the mackerel family.

tur′ban (tėr′bən) *n.* **1,** a headdress formed by winding a long scarf around the head. **2,** a brimless hat.

tur′bid (tėr′bid) *adj.* **1,** clouded, opaque, or muddy, as a liquid. **2,** confused; muddled. —**tur·bid′i·ty,** *n.*

Turban

tur′bine (tėr′bin) *n.* a motor in which a vaned wheel is made to revolve by a flow of liquid or gas.

tur·bo- *pref.* turbine-driven.

tur′bo·jet″ (tèr′bō-jet″) *n.* a jet-propulsion engine supercharged by a turbine.

tur'bot (tẽr'bət) *n.* a variety of flatfish.

tur'bu·lent (tẽr'byû-lənt) *adj.* disturbed; tumultuous; riotous. —**tur'bu·lence**, *n.*

tu·reen' (tû-rēn') *n.* a deep dish with a cover, for holding soup.

turf (tẽrf) *n.* 1, the matted grass, roots, earth, mold, etc. covering grassland. 2, a section of this cut out; a sod. 3, a racetrack for horses; horse-racing. 4, peat. —*v.t.* cover with turf. —**turf'y**, *adj.*

tur'gid (tẽr'jid) *adj.* tumid;

tur'key (tẽr'kē) *n.* a large American fowl.

Turk'ish (tẽr'kish) *adj.* pert. to Turkey, its people, language, etc. —**Turkish bath**, a steam bath with bodily massage.

Turkey

tur'mer·ic (tẽr'mər-ik) *n.* an E. Indian plant, used for making a condiment, a yellow dye, etc;

tur'moil (tẽr'moil) *n.* commotion; tumult; agitation.

turn (tẽrn) *v.t.* 1, move to or from a position; shift or twist. 2, move to a new direction, course, or purpose. 3, reverse; fold back. 4, revolve or rotate; shape or perform by rotating. 5, alter or change in a specified way. 6, make sour or fermented. 7, meditate on. 8, go around; pass beyond. —*v.i.* 1, rotate or revolve. 2, assume a new direction, course, position, etc. 3, change; become different. 4, (with *on*) be dependent. 5, become sour; ferment. 6, be or become curved; bend. —*n.* 1, movement about a center; a rotation or revolution; a twist. 2, a change of direction, course, or position. 3, a bend, curve, angle, fold, etc. 4, one's occasion to act; a spell of work, duty, etc. 5, a change in appearance, condition, or character. 6, trend; tendency; bent. 7, (*Colloq.*) a nervous shock.

turn'a·bout" *n.* 1, a turning to the opposite direction. 2, alternation of privileges.

turn'coat" *n.* a renegade;

turn'er *n.* 1, a woodworker. 2, a gymnast.

turn'ing *n.* 1, act or result of turning. 2, place of turning; a bend; curve. —**turning point**, 1, a critical point. 2, a change for the better.

tur'nip (tẽr'nəp) *n.* a plant whose root and leaves are used as vegetables.

turn'key" *n.* a jailer.

turn'out" *n.* 1, those who attend a meeting, etc. 2, output. 3, costume; outfit.

turn'o'ver *n.* 1, rate or volume of business. 2, rate of change in personnel employed. 3, a small semicircular pie.

turn'pike" *n.* a toll highway;

turn'stile" *n.* a device of revolving arms to bar passage or count those passing through.

turn'ta"ble *n.* 1, a revolving platform to change the direction of a locomotive. 2, the rotating disk of a phonograph.

tur'pen·tine" (tẽr'pən-tīn") *n.* an oily substance extracted from several trees, used in making paint.

tur'pi·tude" (tẽr'pi-tood") *n.* wickedness; depravity. —**tur'pi·tud'i·nous**, *adj.*

tur'quoise (tẽr'kwoiz) *n.* an opaque precious stone; its blue-green color.

tur'ret (tẽr'it) *n.* 1, a small tower rising from a larger building. 2, an attachment on a lathe for holding and applying several tools. 3, a gun tower on a fort or battleship.

tur'tle (tẽr'təl) *n.* any of an order of reptiles having two surfaces of strong shell, from between which the head and limbs protrude. —**turn turtle**, capsize; upset.

tur'tle·dove" (tẽr'təl-duv") *n;* a variety of dove.

tush *interj.* of disapproval.

tusk *n.* 1, a long pointed tooth. 2, a toothlike part, as a prong. —**tusk'er**, *n.* a tusked animal.

tus'sle (tus'əl) *n.* scuffle.

tut *interj.* of mild reproach.

tu'te·lage (too'tə-lij) *n.* guardianship; instruction. —**tu'te·lar·y**, *adj.*

tu'tor (too'tər) *n.* a teacher, esp. one engaged for private instruction. —*v.t. & i.* 1, instruct, esp. privately. 2, study under a tutor. —**tu'tor·age**, *n.* —**tu·tor'i·al** (-tôr'ē-əl) *adj.*

tut'ti-frut'ti (too'tē-froo'tē) *n.* a preserve of mixed fruits.

tu·whit', tu·whoo' (tû-hwit' tû-hwoo') the cry of the owl.

tux (tuks) *n.* (*Colloq.*) tuxedo;

tux·e'do (tuk-sē'dō) *n.* a man's tailless evening coat; dinner jacket.

twad'dle (twod'əl) *v.i. & t.* talk in a trivial and tedious manner. —*n.* idle, senseless talk or writing.

twain (twān) *n.* (*Archaic*) two;

twang *n.* 1, the sharp sound of a tense string when plucked. 2, a nasal tone of voice. —*v.i. & t.* make such a sound.

tweak (twēk) *v.t.* pinch and pull or twist. —*n.* a jerk or twist.

tweed (twēd) *n.* a coarse wool cloth; (*pl.*) garments of this fabric.

tweet (twēt) *n. & v.* chirp.

tweez'ers (twē'zərz) *n.pl.* a small two-pronged gripping tool.

Twelfth night the evening preceding the twelfth day after Christmas.

twelve (twelv) *n.* the cardinal number, 10 plus 2, expressed by 12. —**twelfth**, *adj. & n.*

twelve'month *n.* a year.

twen'ty (twen'tē) *n.* a cardinal number, twice ten, expressed by 20. —**twen'ti-eth**, *adj. & n.*

twen'ty-one' *n.* 1, twenty plus one. 2, a card game, blackjack.

twice (twīs) *adv.* 1, two times. 2, doubly.

twid'dle (twid'əl) *v.t.* twirl, esp. with the fingers. —*v.i.* play idly.

twig *n.* a small shoot of a tree or other plant.

twi'light' (twī'līt') *n.* 1, light from the sky when the sun is below the horizon. 2, early evening. —**twilight sleep**, relief from the pain of childbirth, given by scopolamine.

twill (twil) *n.* a fabric woven so as to show parallel diagonal lines.

twin *n.* 1, one of two children brought forth at a birth. 2, one of two persons or things closely alike. —*adj.* 1, being one of twins. 2, occurring in pairs.

twine (twīn) *n.* 1, a strong cord or string. 2, something twisted. —*v.t. & i.* twist together; interweave.

twinge (twinj) *n.* a sudden sharp pain.

twin'kle (twing'kəl) *v.i.* 1, shine with quick, irregular gleams. 2, (of the eyes) sparkle with amusement or kindliness. —*n.* a gleam; gleams of light.

twin'kling *n.* 1, intermittent shining. 2, an instant.

twirl (twêrl) *v.t.* cause to revolve rapidly; spin; whirl. —*v.i.* 1, rotate; be whirled about. 2, wind; coil. —*n.* 1, a rapid spin; a gyration. 2, a curl or convolution. —**twirl'er**, *n.* (*Baseball*) a pitcher.

twist *v.t.* 1, wrap (something flexible) around and around; combine by winding. 2, wring out of shape; distort; warp. 3, cause to rotate; turn. 4, form by bending, curving, etc. 5, pervert in meaning; misinterpret; misapply. —*v.i.* 1, be bent or coiled; wind; twine. 2, rotate or revolve; move in a spiral course. 3, change direction. 4, be or become distorted in shape. —*n.* 1, a bend, curve, knot, etc. 2, a tangle, kink,

crook, etc. 3, a twisting motion or course. 4, spin imparted to a ball. 5, something formed by twisting. 6, a dance in which one contorts the torso. —**twist'er**, *n.* a tornado.

twit *v.t.* taunt; reproach. —*n.* a gibe or reproach.

twitch (twich) *v.t.* 1, pull or move with a quick jerk. 2, pinch; squeeze. —*v.i.* jerk suddenly, as from muscular spasm. —*n.* 1, a sudden muscular contraction; a twinge. 2, a slight, sudden movement. 3, a tug or jerk.

twit'ter (twit'ər) *v.i.* 1, chirp rapidly or excitedly. 2, giggle.

two (too) *n.* the cardinal number, one plus one, expressed by 2.

two-'by-four' *n.* a timber 2 inches thick and 4 inches wide.

two-'edged' *adj.* 1, having two sharp edges. 2, doubly effective.

two-'faced' *adj.* deceitful; hypocritical.

two-'fist'ed *adj.* strong in a fight.

two'fold' *adj.* times two; double.

two'pence (tup'əns) *n.* (*Brit.*) two pennies. —**two'pen'ny** (tup'nē) *adj.*

two'some *n.* two persons; a duo.

two-'step' *n.* a dance.

ty-coon' (tī-koon') *n.* a wealthy and powerful businessman.

tyke (tīk) *n.* 1, a dog. 2, a child.

tym'pa-ni (tim'pə-nē) *n.pl.* [*sing.* -no (-nō)] orchestral kettledrums. —**tym'pa-nist**, *n.*

tym'pa-num (tim'pə-nəm) *n.* 1, a stretched membrane; a drum or tambourine. 2, the eardrum or middle ear. 3, a vibrating device, as the diaphragm of a telephone.

Tympanum

type (tīp) *n.* 1, a kind or class. 2, a typical person or thing. 3, a model or pattern. 4, a rectangular block bearing a letter or character in relief, used in printing; such printing blocks collectively. —*v.t. & i.* 1, ascertain the type of. 2, symbolize. 3, typewrite.

type'script' *n.* typewritten copy.

type'set'ter *n.* compositor.

type'writ'er (tīp'rī'tər) *n.* a machine for writing letters and characters like those produced by printing type. —**type'write''**, *v.t. & i.* —**type'writ'ing**, *n.*

ty'phoid fever (tī'foid') *n.* an infectious bacillic disease marked by inflammation and ulceration of the intestines.

ty-phoon' (tī-foon') *n.* a cyclone of the W. Pacific ocean.

tub, cûte, pûll; label; oil, owl; go, chip, she, thin, *then*, sing, ink; *see p. 6*

ty'phus (tī'fəs) *n.* an acute infectious disease carried by lice.

typ'i·cal (tip'ĭ-kəl) *adj.* **1,** pert. to a type. **2,** conforming to a type; being a representative specimen.

typ'i·fy" (tip'ĭ-fī") *v.t.* **1,** exemplify. **2,** represent by a type of symbol.

typ'ist (tīp'ist) *n.* one who operates a typewriter.

ty·pog'ra·phy (tī-pog'rə-fē) *n.* **1,** the art or work of setting type. **2,** the style of printed matter. —**ty·pog'ra·pher,** *n.* —**ty"po·graph'i·cal,** *adj.*

tyr'an·nize" (tir'ə-nīz") *v.i. & t.* dominate tyrannically.

tyr'an·ny (tir'ə-nē) *n.* unrestrained exercise of power; unmerciful rule. —**ty·ran'ni·cal** (tĭ-ran'ĭ-kəl), **tyr'an·nous** (tir'ə-nəs) *adj.*

ty'rant (tī'rənt) *n.* a despot; an absolute ruler.

ty'ro (tī'ro) *n.* a beginner in learning something; a novice.

tzar (tsär) *n.* czar.

tzet'ze (tset'sē) *n.* tsetse.

U

U, u (ū) the 21st letter of the English alphabet.

u·biq'ui·tous (ū-bik'wə-təs) *adj.* existing everywhere; inescapable. —**u·biq'ui·tous·ness,** *n.* —**u·biq'ui·ty,** *n.*

U-'boat" (ū'bōt") *n.* a German submarine.

ud'der (ud'ər) *n.* the baggy mammary gland of a cow.

ug'ly (ug'lē) *adj.* **1,** unpleasing or repulsive in appearance. **2,** disagreeable; inclement; threatening. —**ugly duckling,** an unpromising child who becomes beautiful as an adult. —**ug'li·ness,** *n.*

u'kase (ū'kās) *n.* an edict; decree.

U·krain'i·an (ū-krā'nē-ən) *n. & adj.* of or pert. to the Ukraine, a large region and republic in the Soviet Union, its people, language, etc.

u"ku·le'le (oo"kə-lā'lē) *n.* a small stringed musical instrument.

ul'cer (ul'sər) *n.* **1,** an infected sore. **2,** a moral blemish. —**ul'cer·ous,** *adj.*

ul'cer·ate" (-āt") *v.t. & i.* (cause to) become ulcerous. —**ul'cer·a'tion,** *n.*

Ukulele

ul'na (ul'nə) *n.* [*pl.* -**nae** (-nē)] the large bone of the forearm. —**ul'nar,** *adj.*

ul'ster (ul'stər) *n.* an overcoat.

ul·te'ri·or (ul-tir'ē-ər) *adj.* kept concealed.

ul'ti·mate (ul'tə-mət) *adj.* **1,** being the last, as of a series; most remote. **2,** eventual; final; decisive. —*n.* the final stage or degree.

ul"ti·ma'tum (ul"tə-mā'təm) *n.* a final statement of conditions.

ul'tra (ul'trə) *adj.* beyond the ordinary; extreme; superlative; excessive.

ul·tra- *pref.* beyond; excessive; superlative. [In the following compounds, the prefix adds merely the sense of "overmuch" to the adjective.] **ul"tra·con·serv'a·tive,** *adj.* —**ul"tra·fash'ion·a·ble,** *adj.* —**ul"tra·mod'ern,** *adj.* —**ul"tra·re·li'gious,** *adj.*

ul"tra·ma·rine' (ul"trə-mə-rēn') *n.* a deep blue color.

ul"tra·mon'tane (ul"trə-mon'tān) *adj.* **1,** south of the Alps; in Italy. **2,** recognizing the Pope as head of all Christianity.

ul"tra·vi'o·let (ul"trə-vī'ə-lit) *adj.* pert. to invisible rays lying beyond violet in the spectrum.

ul'u·late" (ūl'yə-lāt") *v.i.* howl like a wolf; wail. —**ul'u·la'tion,** *n.*

um'ber (um'bər) *n.* a reddish-brown pigment.

um·bil'i·cal (um-bil'ĭ-kəl) *adj.* pert. to the umbilicus. —**umbilical cord,** the tube through which a mother nourishes a fetus.

um·bil'i·cus (um-bil'ĭ-kəs) *n.* [*pl.* -**i·ci** (-sī)] the depression in the middle of the abdomen.

um'bra (um'brə) *n.* [*pl.* -**brae** (-brē)] shadow; a dark spot.

um'brage (um'brij) *n.* **1,** resentment. **2,** foliage. —**um·bra'geous** (-brā'jəs) *adj.*

um·brel'la (um-brel'ə) *n.* **1,** a portable screen from rain or the sun. **2,** aerial protection given by fighter planes to troops or ships below.

u'mi·ak (oo'mē-ak) *n.* an open boat used by Eskimos.

um'laut (ûm'lowt) *n.* (*Ger.*) modification of a vowel sound, or the diacritical mark (¨) as in ä, ö, ü, in transliteration indicated by *e* following the vowel.

um'pire (um'pīr) *n.* an arbiter; referee.

un- *pref.* not; signifying the converse, reversal, or absence of some quality, action, or condition.

un·a·bridged' (un″ə-brijd′) *adj.* **1,** not shortened; not restricted. **2,** (of a dictionary) not a condensation or shorter version of a larger dictionary; omitting no applicable material.

un-"A·mer'i·can *adj.* **1,** not befitting a loyal U.S. citizen. **2,** not consistent with American beliefs, customs, etc.

u·nan'i·mous (ū-nan′ə-məs) *adj.* being of one mind; all agreeing; without exception. **—u"na·nim'i·ty** (ū″nə-nim′ə-tē) *n.*

un"a·ware' (un″ə-wâr′) *adj.* not conscious (of something); not knowing or realizing. **—un"a·wares',** *adv.*

un"be·lief' (un″bi-lēf′) *n.* lack of belief, esp. in religious dogma. **—un″- be·liev'er,** *n.*

un·bend' *v.t.* [-bent', -bend'ing] **1,** release from strain or tension. **2,** straighten; untie. **—v.i. 1,** relax; become less formal, etc. **2,** become unbent. **—un·bend'ing,** *adj.*

un·blush'ing *adj.* shameless.

un·bos'om (un-bûz′əm) *v.t. & i.* disclose (thoughts, feelings).

un·bound'ed *adj.* without boundaries or limits; vast.

un·break'a·ble *adj.* **1,** incapable of being broken. **2,** resistant to breaking.

un·bri'dled (un-brī′dəld) *adj.* unrestrained; uncontrolled.

un·called'-for' (un-kâld′fôr′) *adj.* **1,** unwarranted; impertinent; improper. **2,** not claimed, as merchandise.

un·can'ny (un-kan′ē) *adj.* eerie; weird; mysterious. **—un·can'ni-ness,** *n.*

un·cap' *v.t.* [-capped', -cap'ping] remove the cap or cover from.

un·cer'tain *adj.* **1,** not certain; doubtful. **2,** unsteady or hesitant; not firm. **—un·cer'tain-ty,** *n.*

un·chal'lenged (un-chal′ənjd) *adj.* unquestioned; acknowledged; agreed.

un'cle (ung′kəl) *n.* **1,** a brother of one's father or mother. **2** the husband of one's aunt. **3,** any elderly man, regarded familiarly. **4,** (*Slang*) a pawnbroker. **—Uncle Sam,** the U.S., its government or people.

un·com'mon (un-kom′ən) *adj.* not common or usual; out of the ordinary; exceptional. **—un·com'mon·ness,** *n.*

un·con·cern' (un″kən-sērn′) *n.* lack of anxiety; indifference. **—un″- con·cerned',** *adj.*

un·con'scion·a·ble (un-kon′shən-ə-bəl) *adj.* **1,** not in accord with conscience; unscrupulous. **2,** unduly excessive.

un·con'scious (un-kon′shəs) *adj.* **1,** not aware (of something). **2,** having lost consciousness; being in a stupor, faint, etc. **3,** not endowed with awareness of one's own existence. **4,** pert. to mental processes not consciously perceived. **—un·con'scious·ness,** *n.*

un·couth' (un-kooth′) *adj.* **1,** ill-mannered; clumsy. **2,** strange; unusual. **—un·couth'ness,** *n.*

unc'tion (unk′shən) *n.* **1,** the act of anointing with oil. **2,** anything soothing; a divine or spiritual influence.

unc'tu·ous (unk′choo-əs) *adj.* oily; suave. **—unc'tu·ous·ness,** *n.*

un·cut' *adj.* **1,** (of a stone) not cut or polished. **2,** (of a book) not separated into leaves.

un"de·ceive' (un″di-sēv′) *v.t.* free from a mistaken idea or belief.

un'der (un′dər) *prep.* **1,** beneath and covered by; below the surface of. **2,** in a lower place or position. **3,** receiving; bearing; undergoing. **4,** less than. **5,** inferior to. **6,** subject to. **7,** in accordance with. **8,** in. **9,** during the existence of. *—adv.*

[In the following words, formed of words defined elsewhere in the dictionary, the prefixed *un-* forms an antonym of the root word.]

un"a·bashed'	un"ap·proach'a·ble	un"be·liev'a·ble
un"a·bat'ed	un·apt'	un"be·liev'ing
un·a'ble	un"arm'	un·bi'ased
un·ac'cent·ed	un"a·shamed'	un·bid'den
un"ac·cept'a·ble	un·asked'	un·bind'
un"ac·com'pa·nied	un"as·sail'a·ble	un·bleached'
un"ac·count'a·ble	un"as·sist'ed	un·blink'ing
un"ac·cus'tomed	un"as·sum'ing	un·bolt'
un"ac·quaint'ed	un"at·tached'	un·born'
un"a·dorned'	un"at·tain'a·ble	un·bound'
un"a·dul'ter·at"ed	un"at·tend'ed	un·bowed'
un"ad·vised'	un·au'thor·ized	un·brace'
un"af·fect'ed	un"a·vail'a·ble	un·braid'
un"a·fraid'	un"a·vail'ing	un·bro'ken
un·aid'ed	un"a·void'a·ble	un·buck'le
un"al·loyed'	un·bal'ance	un·bur'den
un·al'ter·a·ble	un·bar'	un·busi'ness-like"
un"am·bi'tious	un·bear'a·ble	un·but'ton
un"an·nounced'	un·beat'en	un·caused'
un·an'swer·a·ble	un"be·com'ing	un·ceas'ing
un"ap·pre'ci·a"tive		

---

lower. —*adj.* **1,** beneath. **2,** lower; subordinate.

un·der- *pref.* **1,** below; lower in place or rank. **2,** lesser in degree, esp. less than a proper or usual degree.

[In the following words, the prefix *under-* implies sense 1.]

un"der·arm'	un"der·pass"
un"der·bod'ice	un"der·pin'
un"der·car'riage	un"der·prop'
un"der·class'man	un"der·sea"
un"der·clothes"	un"der·shirt"
un"der·cov'er	un"der·side"
un"der·cur'rent	un"der·sign'
un"der·gar'ment	un"der·skirt"
un"der·grad'u·ate	un"der·slung"
un"der·growth"	un"der·soil'
un"der·hung'	un"der·waist"
un"der·laid'	un"der·wa'ter

[In the following words, the prefix *under-* implies sense 2.]

un"der·act'	un"der·pay'
un"der·armed'	un"der·play'
un"der·bid'	un"der·priv'-
un"der·bred'	i·leged
un"der·charge'	un"der·sized'
un"der·de·vel'op	un"der·stock'
un"der·do'	un"der·tone'
un"der·ex·pose'	un"der·trump'
un"der·feed'	un"der·val'ue
un"der·nour'ish	un"der·weight'

un"der·age' (un"dər-āj') *adj.* of less than legal or suitable age.

un"der·brush' (un"dər-brush') *n.* shrubs, etc. growing under trees.

un"der·cut' *v.t.* **1,** cut so as to leave an overhanging edge. **2,** undersell. **3,** strike (a ball) on the underside.

un"der·dog" (un"dər-dâg") *n.* one who gets the worst of it, or is at a disadvantage, in a struggle.

un"der·es'ti·mate (un"dər-es'-ti-māt") *v.t.* estimate at too low a value, amount, rate, etc. —*n.* (-mət) too low an estimate. —**un"-der·es'ti·ma'tion,** *n.*

un"der·fed' (un"dər-fed') *adj.* very thin, as from malnutrition.

un"der·foot' (un"dər-fût') *adj.* & *adv.* **1,** under the foot; lying on the ground. **2,** in the way.

un"der·go' (un"dər-gō') *v.t.* [-went', -gone', -go'ing] be subjected to; experience; sustain.

un"der·ground" *adj.* **1,** sunken, buried. **2,** in secrecy. —*n.* **1,** (*Brit.*) subway. **2,** a secret organization opposing government or occupation forces.

un"der·hand' *adj.* & *adv.* **1,** secret and mean; sly; deceitful. **2,** with the hand below the shoulder or under the object.

un"der·hand'ed *adj.* underhand.

un"der·lie' (un"dər-lī') *v.t.* [-lay', -ly'ing] **1,** be situated under. **2,** be the basis or foundation of.

un"der·line" (un"dər-līn") *v.t.* & *n.* underscore.

un"der·ling (un'dər-ling) *n.* one in a subordinate or inferior position (usually in disparagement).

un"der·mine' (un"dər-mīn') *v.t.* **1,** dig a hole or passage under. **2,** weaken or injure by secret or underhand means.

un"der·most' *adj.* lowest.

un"der·neath' (un"dər-nēth') *prep.* & *adv.* beneath; under; below.

un"der·rate' (un"dər-rāt') *v.t.* rate too low; underestimate.

un"der·score" (un"dər-skôr") *v.t.*

[In the following words, formed of words defined elsewhere in the dictionary, the prefixed *un-* forms an antonym of the root word.]

un"cer·e·mo'ni·ous	un·com'fort·a·ble	un·cured'
un·chain'	un"com·mu'ni·ca"tive	un·curl'
un·change'a·ble	un·com·plain'ing	un·dam'aged
un·changed'	un"com·pli·men'ta·ry	un·daunt'ed
un·chang'ing	un"com·pro·mis'ing	un"de·cid'ed
un·char'i·ta·ble	un"con·di'tion·al	un"de·feat'ed
un·chart'ed	un·con·di'tioned	un"de·fend'ed
un·chaste'	un"con·form'i·ty	un"de·filed'
un·checked'	un·con·nect'ed	un"de·fined'
un·Chris'tian	un"con'quer·a·ble	un"dem·o·crat'ic
un·cir'cum·cised	un"con·sti·tu'tion·al	un·de·ni'a·ble
un·civ'il	un"con·trol'la·ble	un"de·nom"i·na'tion·al
un·civ'i·lized"	un"con·ven'tion·al	un"de·served'
un·clad'	un·cooked'	un"de·sign'ing
un·claimed'	un·cork'	un"de·sir'a·ble
un·clasp'	un"cor·rupt'ed	un"de·vel'oped
un·clean'	un·count'ed	un·dig'ni·fied"
un·clench'	un·cou'ple	un"di·min'ished
un·cloak'	un·cov'er	un"dip·lo·mat'ic
un·clog'	un·crit'i·cal	un"di·rect'ed
un·close'	un·crossed'	un"dis·cov'ered
un·clothe'	un·crowned'	un"dis·mayed'
un·cloud'ed	un·cul'ti·vat"ed	un"dis·patched'
un·coil'	un·cul'tured	un"dis·put'ed

fat, fāte, fär, fâre, fâll, ȧsk; met, hē, hêr, maybē; pin, pīne; not, nōte, ôr, tool

print or draw a line under; empha-size. —*n.* such a line.

un'der·sec're·tar·y *n.* a deputy to a secretary, in a U. S. government department ranking next under the head.

un'der·sell' *v.t.* [-sold', -sell'ing] **1,** sell for a lower price than. **2,** understate the virtues of.

un'der·shot' *adj.* **1,** driven by water underneath. **2,** (of the lower jaw) protruding.

un'der·stand' *v.t. & i.* **1,** grasp the meaning (of); comprehend. **2,** have full knowledge (of). **3,** be told (of); realize; believe. **4,** sympathize (with).

un'der·stand'ing *n.* **1,** intelli-gence; mental apprehension and ap-preciation. **2,** good relations. **3,** a private or unexpressed agreement. **4,** sympathy. —*adj.* intelligent; sympathetic.

un'der·state' (un″dər-stāt′) *v.t.* state with less than due emphasis; represent in lesser degree than the reality. —**un'der·state'ment,** *n.*

un'der·stood' (un″dər-stůd′) *adj.* **1,** inferred. **2,** agreed.

un'der·stud'y (un′dər-stud″ė) *n.* one trained to substitute for an actor or actress. —*v.t.* act as an understudy to.

un'der·take' *v.t.* **1,** try to do; attempt. **2,** engage to perform or execute. —**un'der·tak'er,** *n.* a funeral director.

un'der·tak'ing *n.* **1,** a project, esp. a business venture. **2,** the business of preparing the dead for burial and arranging funerals.

un'der·tone' *n.* **1,** a tone of less than normal loudness, in speaking. **2,** a tone, hue, etc. lying under an-other.

un'der·tow' (un'dər-tō′) *n.* a strong current below the surface of water, as the backflow from a beach.

un'der·wear' (un'dər-wâr″) *n.* gar-ments worn beneath the outer clothing; underclothes.

un'der·world' *n.* **1,** the com-munity of criminal or degraded persons. **2,** Hades or hell.

un'der·write' *v.t.* **1,** subscribe to; endorse; guarantee; indemnify. **2,** insure against loss.

un'der·writ'er *n.* **1,** one in the insurance business. **2,** one who subscribes to bonds, etc., for resale.

un·dis'ci·plined (un-dis′ə-plĭnd) *adj.* unruly; not controllable.

un'dis·guised' (un″dis-gīzd′) *adj.* lacking disguise or pretense; candid; open.

un·do' (un-doo′) *v.t.* [-done' -do'-ing] **1,** annul; reverse (the effect of). **2,** spoil; ruin. **3,** unfasten. —**un·do'ing,** *n.*

un·doubt'ed (un-dow′tĭd) *adj.* not questioned; obviously true. —**un-doubt'ed·ly,** *adv.* surely.

un·due' (un-doo′; -dū′) *adj.* **1,** un-warranted; disproportionate; ex-cessive. **2,** not yet payable.

un'du·lant (un′dyə-lənt) *adj.* waving; wavy. —**undulant fever,** a recurrent disease usually contracted from bacteria in raw milk.

un'du·late' (un′dyə-lāt″) *v.i. & t.* move or be formed in waves; rise and fall. —*adj.* (-lət) wavy. —**un″-du·la'tion,** *n.*

un·du'ly (un-doo′lė; -dū′lė) *adv.* **1,** without warrant or right. **2,** ex-cessively.

un·earth' (un-ėrth′) *v.t.* **1,** discover; bring to light. **2,** dig up; disinter.

un·earth'ly *adj.* **1,** supernatural; weird. **2,** (*Colloq.*) extraordinary.

un·eas'y (un-ē'zē) *adj.* **1,** not comfortable in mind or body; disturbed; restless. **2,** not easy in manner; constrained. —**un·eas'i·ly,** *adv.* —**un·eas'i·ness,** *n.*

un"em·ployed' (un"em-ploid') *adj.* **1,** without a job; out of work. **2,** not in use. —**un"em·ploy'ment,** *n.*

un·end'ing *adj.* without end, or seemingly so.

un"ex·am'pled (un"eg-zam'pəld) *adj.* without precedent.

un·feel'ing (un-fē'ling) *adj.* **1,** hardhearted; unsympathetic. **2,** insensitive; devoid of feeling. —**un·feel'ing·ness,** *n.*

un·for'tu·nate *adj.* **1,** not lucky. **2,** regrettable. —*n.* a pitiable person.

un·found'ed (un-fown'did) *adj.* without foundation; not based on fact; unwarranted.

un·frock' (un-frok') *v.t.* deprive of ecclesiastical rank or status.

un·furl' (un-fẽrl') *v.t.* spread out, as a flag; display.

un·fur'nished (un-fẽr'nisht) *adj.* without furniture.

un·gain'ly (un-gān'lē) *adj.* clumsy; awkward; uncouth. —*adv.* awkwardly.

un"gram·mat'i·cal (un"grə-mat'i-kəl) *adj.* not in conformity to rules of grammar.

un'guent (ung'gwənt) *n.* an ointment; salve.

un'gu·late (ung'gyə-lət) *adj.* **1,** having hoofs. **2,** hooflike. —*n.* a hoofed mammal.

un·hand' *v.t.* take the hand from; let go; release.

un·hap'py *adj.* **1,** sad. **2,** unfortunate. —**un·hap'pi·ness,** *n.*

un·health'y (un-hel'thē) *adj.* **1,** in poor health. **2,** unwholesome; likely to turn out badly. —**un·health'i·ness,** *n.*

un·heard-'of" (un-hẽrd'uv") *adj.* not hitherto known or existent; unprecedented.

un·hinge' (un-hinj') *v.t.* **1,** remove the hinges of; take off of hinges. **2,** detach; derange. **3,** unbalance mentally; discompose; craze. —**un·hinged',** *adj.*

un·hol'y (un-hō'lē) *adj.* **1,** sinful; impious. **2,** (*Colloq.*) extreme; unseemly. —**un·ho'li·ness,** *n.*

un·horse' (un-hôrs') *v.t.* **1,** throw down from a horse. **2,** dislodge.

u·ni- *pref.* one; having only one; single.

u"ni·cam'er·al (ū'nə-kam'ə-rəl) *adj.* (of a legislature) having only one chamber.

u'ni·corn" (ū'nə-kôrn") *n.* a fabulous animal with a single long horn and usually the body of a horse.

u'ni·form' (ū'nə-fôrm') *adj.* **1,** unchanging; even; regular. **2,** the same as others. —*n.* a distinctive dress worn by all the members of a military force, a society, etc. —**u"ni·form'i·ty,** *n.*

u'ni·fy' (ū'nə-fī') *v.t.* collect, class, or form into a single whole; make uniform. —**u"ni·fi·ca'tion,** *n.*

u"ni·lat'er·al (ū"nə-lat'ər-əl) *adj.* **1,** affecting or done by only one party (of two or more). **2,** having or pert. to only one side.

un"im·por'tant *adj.* not important; insignificant. —**un"im·por'tance,** *n.*

[In the following words, formed of words defined elsewhere in the dictionary, the prefixed *un-* forms an antonym of the root word.]

un·hes'i·tat"ing	un"in·vit'ed	un·man'ner·ly
un·hitch'	un·is'sued	un·marked'
un·hook'	un·just'	un·mar'ried
un·hur'ried	un·kind'	un·mask'
un·hurt'	un·knot'	un·matched'
un"i·den'ti·fied	un·lace'	un·meas'ured
un"im·ag'i·na·ble	un"la·ment'ed	un·mer'ci·ful
un"im·ag'i·na"tive	un·lash'	un·mer'it·ed
un"im·paired'	un·latch'	un·mind'ful
un"im·peach'a·ble	un·leash'	un"mis·tak'a·ble
un"im·proved'	un·li'censed	un·mit'i·gat·ed
un"in·flect'ed	un·lim'ber	un·mixed'
un"in·formed'	un·lim'it·ed	un·mo·lest'ed
un"in·hab'it·a·ble	un·link'	un·moved'
un"in·hab'it·ed	un·list'ed	un·mov'ing
un"in·i'ti·at"ed	un·lit'	un·mus'i·cal
un·in'jured	un·load'	un·muz'zle
un"in·spired'	un·lock'	un·named'
un"in·tel'li·gent	un·love'ly	un·nat'u·ral
un"in·tel'li·gi·ble	un·luck'y	un·nec'es·sar"y
un"in·ten'tion·al	un·make'	un·neigh'bor·ly
un·in'ter·est·ed	un·man'age·a·ble	un·no'ticed
un·in'ter·est·ing		un"ob·served'
un"in·ter·rupt'ed		un"ob·struct'ed

un'ion (ūn'yən) *n.* **1,** the act of joining two or more things into one. **2,** something made by uniting; a league, combination, compound, etc. **3,** marriage. **4,** an organization of workers: a labor or trade union. **5,** a flag symbolizing union; a jack: *union jack.* **6,** a coupling device. —**union shop,** a shop where labor relations are controlled by fixed contract between employer and labor union. —**un'ion·ism,** *n.* —**un'ion·ize″** (-īz″) *v.t. & i.* organize in a labor union.

u·nique' (ū-nēk') *adj.* **1,** being the only one of its kind. **2,** unusual; rare. —**u·nique'ness,** *n.*

u'ni·son (ū'nə-sən) *n.* **1,** coincidence in pitch of two or more tones. **2,** accord in sentiment or action.

u'nit (ū'nit) *n.* **1,** a single thing or person. **2,** a group of things or persons regarded as a single entity. **3,** a component part. **4,** any standard quantity used as a measure. **5,** the quantity and integer 1. —**u'ni·tar″y** (ū'ni-ter″ē) *adj.*

U″ni·ta'ri·an (ū″ni-tār'ē-ən) *adj & n.* of a sect that believes God exists in one person, not the Trinity.

u·nite' (ū-nīt') *v.t. & i.* **1,** combine so as to form one; make a union (of); connect. **2,** join in feeling or sympathy; agree. —**u·nit'ed,** *adj.*

u'ni·ty (ū'nə-tē) *n.* **1,** the state of being united or uniform. **2,** the quantity and integer 1. **3,** harmony among elements.

u'ni·valve″ (ū'ni-valv″) *n.* a mollusk having only one shell.

u″ni·ver'sal (ū″nə-vėr'səl) *adj.* **1,** pert. to the, or a, universe; generally applicable. **2,** comprehensive; wide in scope. **3,** widely adaptable or effective in different directions, as of a mechanical contrivance. —**u″ni·ver·sal'i·ty,** *n.* —**universal joint,**

universal coupling, a coupling of two shafts, so designed that one of them can change direction.

U″ni·ver'sal·ist *adj. & n.* pert. to a Christian denomination or its doctrine of universal salvation.

u·ni·verse″ (ū′nə-vėrs″) *n.* **1,** the totality of all existing things. **2,** the whole world; all mankind. **3,** an individual's own sphere or ken. —**island universe,** any of the collections of stars in space; a galaxy.

u″ni·ver'si·ty (ū″nə-vėr'sə-tē) *n.* an institution of higher learning, embracing both colleges and postgraduate schools.

un·kempt' *adj.* not combed, as hair; untidy. —**un·kempt'ness,** *n.*

un·known' (un-nōn') *adj.* **1,** not known, discovered, determined, or identified. **2,** unfamiliar. —*n.* something unknown; (*Math.*) a symbol for an unknown quantity. —**un·know'a·ble,** *adj.* beyond the range of human knowledge. —**un·know'ing,** *adj.* ignorant; unsophisticated.

un·law'ful *adj.* against the law. —**un·law'ful·ness,** *n.*

un·learn' (un-lėrn') *v.t.* put out of the mind or memory; forget.

un·leav'ened (un-lev'ənd) *adj.* (of bread) not raised with yeast, etc.

un·less' (un-les') *conj.* if it be not that; if not; except in case that. —*prep.* except.

un·let'tered (un-let'ərd) *adj.* lacking book knowledge; uneducated.

un·like' (un-līk') *adj.* not like; different; dissimilar. —*prep.* differently from. —**un·like'ness,** *n.*

un·like'ly *adj. & adv.* **1,** not probable. **2,** having little prospect of success; unpromising. —**un·like'li·ness,** *n.*

un·oc'cu·pied″
un″of·fend'ing
un·o'pened
un·or'gan·ized″
un·or'tho·dox
un·pack'
un·paid'
un·pal'at·a·ble
un·par'don·a·ble
un″par·lia·men'ta·ry
un·pen'
un·peo'pled
un″per·turbed'
un·prej'u·diced
un″pre·med'i·tat″ed
un″pre·pared'
un″pre·tend'ing
un·print'a·ble
un″pro·duc'tive
un″pro·fes'sion·al
un·prof'it·a·ble
un·prom'is·ing
un″pro·nounce'a·ble
un″pro·tect'ed
un″pro·voked'
un·pub'lished

un·pun'ished
un·qual'i·fied″
un·quench'a·ble
un·ques'tion·a·ble
un·ques'tioned
un·qui'et
un·read'
un·read'a·ble
un·read'y
un·real'
un·rea'son·a·ble
un·rea'son·ing
un·pin'
un·planned'
un·pleas'ing
un·plowed'
un·plug'
un·pol'ished
un″pol·lut'ed
un″prec'e·dent·ed
un″pre·dict'a·ble
un″rec·og·niz'a·ble
un·rec'og·nized″
un″re·cord'ed
un·reel'
un″re·fined'

un″re·flect'ing
un″re·gen'er·ate
un″re·lat'ed
un″re·lent'ing
un″re·li'a·ble
un″re·lieved'
un″re·li'gious
un″re·mem'bered
un″re·mit'ting
un″re·quit'ed
un″re·served'
un″re·sist'ing
un″re·strained'
un″re·strict'ed
un·rig'
un·right'eous
un·ripe'
un·ri'valed
un·robe'
un·roll'
un·ruf'fled
un·sad'dle
un·safe'

un·looked-'for (un-lŭkt'fôr) *adj.* unexpected.

un·loose' (un-loos') *v.t.* loosen; untie; release.

un·luck'y *adj.* **1,** having bad luck. **2,** regrettable. —**un·luck'i-ness,** *n.*

un·make' (un-māk') *v.t.* **1,** take apart; reduce to original components. **2,** ruin; destroy; depose.

un·man' *v.t.* **1,** deprive of manly spirit; dishearten. **2,** emasculate. **3,** deprive of men, as a ship. —**un·man'ly,** *adj.* weak; womanish.

un·mean'ing (un-mē'ning) *adj.* **1,** without meaning or significance. **2,** expressionless, as a face.

un·men'tion·a·ble (un-men'shən-ə-bəl) *adj.* not fit to be mentioned. —*n.* (usually *pl.*) any undergarment.

un·mor'al (un-mor'əl) *adj.* **1,** having no moral aspect. **2,** neither moral nor immoral.

un·nerve' *v.t.* cause to lose courage or resolution.

un·num'bered (un-num'bərd) *adj.* **1,** innumerable; very many. **2,** not numbered.

un''of·fi'cial *adj.* **1,** lacking official sanction. **2,** tentative.

un·pack' *v.t.* & *i.* remove a packing, or something that has been packed (from).

un·par'al·leled'' (un-par'ə-leld'') *adj.* having no parallel or equal; unmatched.

un·pleas'ant *adj.* **1,** displeasing. **2,** disagreeable in manner, disposition, etc. —**un·pleas'ant·ness,** *n.*

un·pop'u·lar *adj.* disliked by a majority of persons. —**un·pop'u-lar'i·ty,** *n.*

un·prac'ticed (un-prak'tist) *adj.* **1,** not done usually or at all. **2,** not trained; unskillful.

un·prin'ci·pled (un-prin'sə-pəld) *adj.* lacking moral principles; unscrupulous; wicked.

un·quote' *v.t.* close a quotation. —*n.* a mark (as '') so signifying.

un·rav'el (un-rav'əl) *v.t.* **1,** separate the threads or fibers of; disentangle. **2,** free from perplexity; solve.

un·rest' *n.* lack of rest or quiet; a state of agitation.

un·rid'dle (un-rid'əl) *v.t.* solve, as a riddle; interpret; fathom.

un·rip' *v.t.* [**-ripped'**, **-rip'ping**] rip; tear apart.

un·rul'y (un-roo'lē) *adj.* not submissive; balky; ungovernable. —**un·ru'li·ness,** *n.*

un·say' *v.t.* retract or recant (something said).

un·scathed' (un-skā*th*d') *adj.* not injured; unharmed.

un·scram'ble (un-skram'bəl) *v.t.* make orderly; disentangle.

un·scru'pu·lous *adj.* not honest, ethical, etc. —**un·scru'pu·lous·ness,** *n.*

un·self'ish *adj.* not putting one's own interests first. —**un·self'ish-ness,** *n.*

un·sex' (un-seks') *v.t.* deprive (a woman) of womanly qualities.

un·shake'a·ble (un-shāk'ə-bəl) *adj.* determined; not open to persuasion.

un·shak'en *adj.* having lost no faith, resolution, force, etc.

un·smil'ing (un-smī'ling) *adj.* serious in demeanor; dour.

un·sound' (un-sownd') *adj.* **1,** not sound; diseased, decayed, or defective. **2,** not well-founded; invalid. **3,** financially insecure; unreliable.

un·speak'a·ble (un-spē'kə-bəl) *adj.* inexpressible; very bad.

un·stead'y *adj.* **1,** not steady; shaky. **2,** not reliable or resolute. —**un·stead'i·ness,** *n.*

un·stop' *v.t.* open; release.

[In the following words, formed of words defined elsewhere in the dictionary, the prefixed *un-* forms an antonym of the root word.]

un·said'	un·set'tled	un·sought'
un·sal'a·ble	un·shack'le	un·spar'ing
un·san'i·tar·y	un·shad'ed	un·spoiled'
un''sat·is·fac'to·ry	un·shaped'	un·spo'ken
un·sat'is·fied	un·shape'ly	un''sports'man·like''
un·sa'vo·ry	un·shav'en	un·spot'ted
un·schooled'	un·sheathe'	un·sta'ble
un''sci·en·tif'ic	un·shod'	un·stained'
un·screw'	un·sight'ly	un''states'man·like''
un·seal'	un·skilled'	un·strained'
un·sea'son·a·ble	un·skill'ful	un·strap'
un·sea'soned	un·sling'	un·string'
un·seat'	un·snap'	un''sub·dued'
un''se·cured'	un·snarl'	un''sub·stan'tial
un·see'ing	un·so'ber	un''suc·cess'ful
un·seem'ly	un·so'cia·ble	un·suit'a·ble
un·seen'	un·sold'	un·suit'ed
un·set'	un·sol'dier·ly	un·sul'lied
un·set'tle	un''so·phis'ti·cat''ed	un''sup·port'ed
		un''sur·passed'

un·strung' *adj.* **1.** removed from a string; with strings relaxed. **2.** nervously upset; distraught.

un·stud'ied (un-stud'ĕd) *adj.* not affected in manner; artless; natural.

un·sung' *adj.* not duly honored.

un·sure' *adj.* **1.** not sure. **2.** not confident; hesitant.

un·think'a·ble (un-think'ə-bəl) *adj.* **1.** unworthy of consideration. **2.** inconceivable. **—un·think'ing,** *adj.* showing lack of thought; heedless.

un·tie' (un-tī') *v.t.* undo (a knot); release the fastenings of; set free.

un·til' *conj. & prep.* up to the time that; when or before.

un·time'ly (un-tīm'lē) *adj.* **1.** premature. **2.** inopportune; inconvenient. **—un·time'li·ness,** *n.*

un·tir'ing (un-tīr'ing) *adj.* unceasing in effort; not yielding to fatigue. **—un·tir'ing·ness,** *n.*

un'to *prep.* (*Archaic*) to; until.

un·told' (un-tōld') *adj.* **1.** not told or revealed. **2.** not counted; too vast to be measured.

un·touch'a·ble (un-tuch'ə-bəl) *adj.* **1.** loathsome to the touch. **2.** that cannot be reached. **3.** impalpable; intangible. **—n.** a member of the lowest caste in India, whose touch is thought to pollute.

un·to·ward' (un-tôrd') *adj.* unfavorable; troublesome.

un·truth' *n.* a falsehood; lie. **—un·truth'ful,** *adj.*

un·u'su·al *adj.* strange; uncommon. **—un·u'su·al·ness,** *n.*

un·var'nished (un-vär'nisht) *adj.* **1.** not varnished **2.** not embellished or disguised; stark.

un·war'rant·a·ble (-ə-bəl) *adj.* lacking justification; without authority; unjust. Also, **un·war'rant·ed.**

un·washed' (un-wosht') *adj.* not washed; (of persons) unclean and vulgar.

un·whole'some *adj.* not healthful; unhealthy. **—un·whole'some·ness,** *n.*

un·wield'y (un-wēl'dē) *adj.* too large or bulky to be easily handled. **—un·wield'i·ness,** *n.*

un·wit'ting (un-wit'ing) *adj.* not knowing or realizing; unaware.

un·wont'ed (un-won'tid) *adj.* not usual or customary.

un·writ'ten (un-rit'ən) *adj.* not written. **—unwritten law,** a custom that is observed as though it were formal law; esp., that crimes in defense of honor should not be punished.

up *adv.* **1.** in, toward, or to a more elevated position; to an erect position; higher. **2.** at or to a source or point of importance. **3.** to an equally advanced point or extent. **4.** well prepared or equipped. **5.** into activity. **6.** in process of happening. **7.** ended. **8.** together or close. **—prep.** **1.** to a higher position on or in; near the top of. **2.** toward the source, center, interior, etc. of. **—adj.** going or tending to higher position. **—n.** an upward movement; improvement. **—v.t.** [upped, up'ping] (*Colloq.*) make larger; bid or bet higher than.

up·braid' *v.t.* blame; rebuke.

up'bring'ing *n.* childhood training; rearing.

up'coun'try *n.* a region away from the seacoast or lowlands. **—adj. & adv.** in or toward such a region.

up'grade" *n.* an upward slope; rising grade. **—adj. & adv.** upward. **—v.t.** put in a higher grade or classification than previously.

up·heav'al (up-hēv'əl) *n.* **1.** a bursting upward, as in an earthquake. **2.** a violent disturbance, as a revolution.

un"sus·pect'ed	un·thread'	un·warped'
un"sus·pect'ing	un·throne'	un·war'y
un"sus·pi'cious	un·ti'dy	un·wa'ver·ing
un"sus·tained'	un·touched'	un·wea'ried
un·sweet'ened	un·trained'	un·weave'
un·swept'	un·tram'meled	un·wed'
un·swerv'ing	un·tried'	un·wel'come
un"sym·pa·thet'ic	un·trimmed'	un·well'
un·tack'	un·trou'bled	un·wept'
un·taint'ed	un·true'	un·wil'ling
un·tak'en	un·tu'tored	un·wind'
un·tamed'	un·twist'	un·wise'
un·tan'gle	un·used'	un·wom'an·ly
un·tar'nished	un·ut'ter·a·ble	un·work'a·ble
un·tast'ed	un·var'y·ing	un·world'ly
un·taught'	un·veil'	un·wor'thy
un·ten'a·ble	un·ver'i·fied	un·wound'ed
un·ten'ant·ed	un·vexed'	un·wrap'
un·teth'er	un·vis'it·ed	un·yoke'
un·thank'ful	un·voiced'	un·youth'ful
	un·want'ed	

up·hill adj. & adv. on or toward the top of a hill.

up·hold' v.t. [-held', -hold'ing] support; advocate; confirm.

up·hol·ster (up-hōl'stər) v.t. provide (the framework of furniture) with cushions, covering, etc. —up·hol'ster·er, n. —up·hol'ster·y, n.

up'keep" n. maintenance.

up'land (-lənd) n. & adj. 1, up-country. 2, high land.

up·lift' v.t. elevate. —n. (up'lift) 1, elevation. 2, moral advancement; inspiration.

up·on' (ə-pon') prep., 1, up and on; 2, on.

up'per (up'ər) adj. 1, higher in place or position. 2, superior in rank, station, etc. —n. an upper part or section; the part of a shoe above the sole. —on one's uppers, poverty-stricken. —upper house, the senior or smaller of two legislative bodies, as the U.S. Senate. —the upper hand, mastery.

up"per·case' adj. & n. capital (of a letter)

up"per·cut" n. an upward blow.

up"per·most" adj. & adv. highest in place, position, rank, power, etc.

up'pish (up'ish) adj. insolent; haughty. —up'pish·ness, n.

up'right' adj. 1, vertical or erect. 2, honest; righteous. —n. something standing erect or vertical, as a supporting post. —adv. vertically. —up'right'ness, n. —upright piano, one in which the strings and sounding board are placed vertically.

up'ris·ing (up"rīz'ing) n. rebellion; insurrection.

up'roar" n. violent disturbance and noise; bustle and clamor.

up·roar'i·ous (-rôr'ē-əs) adj. 1, clamorous. 2, hilarious. —up·roar'i·ous·ness, n.

up·root' v.t. tear out by the roots; remove forcibly.

up·set' v.t. 1, knock down from an erect or normal posture; overturn; throw into confusion. 2, overthrow; spoil. 3, perturb. —n. (up'set) 1, a fall; an overturning. 2, an unexpected result. —adj. overturned; disordered; disturbed.

up'shot" n. result.

up·side-"down' adj. & adv. 1, having on top the side that should be on the bottom. 2, in total disorder.

up'si·lon" (ūp'sə-lon") n. the twentieth letter of the Greek alphabet (Υ, υ).

up·stage" adj. & adv. (Theater) at or to the back of the stage; (Colloq.) haughty. —v.t. get between (an actor) and the audience.

up'stairs" adj., adv. & n. (in, to, etc.) the second or a higher story.

up·stand'ing adj. highly respectable; upright.

up'start" n. a presumptuous person.

up'stream" adj. & adv. to or toward the source of a river, etc.; against the current.

up'take" n. 1, a ventilating pipe or shaft. 2, comprehension; awareness.

up-'to-date' adj. 1, in accordance with, or conforming to, the latest ideas or fashions; modern. 2, extending to the present time.

up'town" adj., adv. & n. (in or to) a section away from the main business district.

up'turn" n. 1, a turning over or up. 2, a change for the better.

up'ward (up'wərd) adv. 1, toward a higher position, degree, etc. 2, toward the source, interior, etc. 3, in the upper part. 4, more. —adj. moving or directed upward.

up'wards (-wərdz) adv. in an upward direction. —upwards of, somewhat more than.

u·ra'ni·um (yū-rā'nē-əm) n. a radioactive chemical element, no. 92, symbol U.

ur'ban (ėr'bən) adj. pert. to, comprising, living in, or characteristic of a city.

ur·bane' (ėr-bān') adj. affable; suave. —ur·ban'i·ty (-ban'ə-tē) n.

ur'chin (ėr'chin) n. a mischievous boy; any small boy.

u·re'a (yū-rē'ə) n. a substance found in urine, used in plastics.

u·re'mi·a (yū-rē'mē-ə) n. a morbid bodily condition due to retention of waste products. —u·re'mic, adj.

u·re'ter (yū-rē'tər) n. the tube carrying urine from kidney to bladder.

u·re'thra (yū-rē'thrə) n. the tube through which urine is discharged from the bladder.

urge (ėrj) v.t. 1, push onward; drive vigorously. 2, exhort. 3, advocate earnestly. —n. an impelling force; an impulse.

ur'gen·cy (ėr'jən-sē) n. 1, insistence. 2, imperative necessity.

ur'gent (ėr'jənt) adj. 1, imperative; needed at once. 2, insistent.

u'ric (yūr'ik) adj. of or pert. to urine or urea.

u'rin·al (yūr'i-nəl) n. a receptacle to receive urine.

u"ri·nal'y·sis (yūr'i-nal'ə-sis) n. an analysis of a specimen of urine, made for medical purposes.

u'ri·na·ry (-ner-ē) adj. pert. to the organs that excrete urine.

u'ri·nate" (-nāt") v.t. discharge urine. —u"ri·na'tion, n.

u'rine (yūr'in) *n.* a fluid secretion of the kidneys, excreting waste products.

urn (ẽrn) *n.* **1,** a vase with a base. **2,** a vessel for making tea, coffee, etc.

u·rol'o·gy (yūr-ol'ə-jē) *n.* the study and treatment of organs that excrete urine. —**u'ro·log'i·cal,** *adj.* —u.rol'o·gist, *n.*

ur'sine (ẽr'sīn) *adj.* pert. to a bear; bearlike.

us *pron.* obj. pl. of *I.*

us'age (ū'sij) *n.* **1,** customary practice or way of acting or doing; an established way of using words or phrases. **2,** the use or enjoyment of something.

use (ūz) *v.t.* **1,** employ for a purpose; put to service. **2,** consume or expend. **3,** treat. —*n.* (ūs) **1,** the act of using, employing, or putting to service; the state of being used. **2,** utility; service. **3,** an instance or way of using something. —us'a·ble (ū'zə-bəl) *adj.* —us'er (ū'zər) *n.* —used to (ūs'tū) accustomed to (with a noun); in past time use.

use'ful (ūs'fəl) *adj.* having a practical function, purpose, or effect; worthwhile. —use'ful·ness, *n.*

use'less (ūs'ləs) *adj.* without function or effect; not useful. —use'less·ness, *n.*

ush'er (ush'ər) *n.* **1,** one who escorts persons to seats in a church, theater, etc. **2,** one in charge of a door. —*v.t.* **1,** escort. **2,** (with *in*) introduce; contribute to the beginning of.

u'su·al (ū'zhū-əl) *adj.* **1,** ordinary; normal. **2,** customary; habitual. —u'su·al·ly, *adv.* on most occasions.

u'su·fruct (ū'zū-frukt) *n.* the right to use; the yield from use.

u·surp' (ū-sẽrp') *v.t.* seize and hold (office, power, etc.) by force and without right. —u"sur·pa'tion, *n.*

u'su·ry (ū'zhə-rē) *n.* exorbitant interest paid or charged. —u'su·rer, *n.* —u·su'ri·ous (ū-zhūr'ē-əs) *adj.*

u·ten'sil (ū-ten'səl) *n.* an implement, instrument, or vessel, esp. one used in preparing food.

u'ter·us (ū'tər-əs) *n.* [*pl.* -i (-ī)] the organ in which the fetus rests and grows; the womb. —u'ter·ine (-in) *adj.*

u·til"i·tar'i·an (ū-til"-ə-târ'ē-ən) *adj.* useful rather than ornamental.

u·til'i·ty (ū-til'ə-tē) *n.* **1,** the state of being useful; something useful. **2,** a public service, as an agency supplying electricity, water, etc. —utility man, one who does any odd jobs.

u'ti·lize" (ū'tə-līz") *v.t.* make use of; put to service. —u"ti·li·za'tion, *n.*

ut'most" (ut'mōst") *adj.* **1,** of the greatest degree, quantity, etc. **2,** at the farthest or outermost point. —*n.* the limit. Also, **ut'ter·most.**

U·to'pi·an (ū-tō'pē-ən) *adj.* relating to an imaginary ideal state (Utopia) or condition; hence, idealistic but not practical.

ut'ter (ut'ər) *v.t.* **1,** give audible expression to; say. **2,** issue; emit. —*adj.* complete; absolute; unconditional.

ut'ter·ance *n.* **1,** act of uttering; issuance; something said. **2,** manner of speaking.

ut'ter·most" *adj. & n.* utmost.

u'vu·la (ū'vyə-lə) *n.* the fleshy conical body hanging down from the soft palate in the back of the mouth. —u'vu·lar, *adj.*

ux·o'ri·ous (uk-sôr'ē-əs) *adj.* excessively fond of one's wife. —ux·o'ri·ous·ness, *n.*

V

V, v (vē) **1,** the 22nd letter of the English alphabet. **2,** (*cap.*) five, 5, the Rom. numeral.

va'can·cy (vā'kən-sē) *n.* **1,** state of being vacant; a vacant space. **2,** an available job, space, etc.

va'cant (vā'kənt) *adj.* **1,** having no contents; empty; devoid of something. **2,** having no occupant; untenanted. **3,** idle; disengaged. **4,** vacuous; stupid.

va'cate" (vā'kāt") *v.t.* **1,** make vacant; quit; empty. **2,** make void; annul.

va·ca'tion (vā-kā'shən) *n.* **1,** a period of release from work; holiday. **2,** act of vacating. —va·ca'tion·ist, *n.*

vac'ci·nate" (vak'sə-nāt") *v.t.* inoculate with a vaccine, esp. to immunize against smallpox. —vac"ci·na'tion, *n.*

vac'cine (vak'sēn) *n.* a weakened virus introduced into a healthy body to induce immunity against the disease.

vac'il·late" (vas'ə-lāt") *v.i.* **1,** waver in opinion, sentiment, determination, etc.; be irresolute. **2,** sway; stagger. —vac"il·la'tion, *n.*

vac'u·ous (vak'ū-əs) *adj.* **1,** showing no intelligence; blank. **2,** empty; unfilled. —va·cu'i·ty (-kū'ə-tē) *n.*

vac'u·um (vak'ū-əm) *n.* **1,** space void of matter. **2,** a space largely exhausted of air or gas. —vacuum bottle, thermos. —vacuum cleaner, a device that sucks in dust, etc., for housecleaning. —vacuum tube, a sealed tube of glass or metal, used in electronic devices, as radio.

vag'a·bond" (vag'ə-bond") *adj.* having no settled habitation; wandering; nomadic. —*n.* 1, a wanderer; esp. a worthless vagrant; a tramp.

va·gar'y (və-gâr'ē) *n.* a capricious or extravagant thought or action.

va·gi'na (və-jī'nə) *n.* the passage from vulva to uterus in a female animal. —**vag'i·nal** (vaj'i-nəl) *adj.*

va'grant (vā'grənt) *adj.* 1, vagabond. 2, uncertain; erratic (as ideas). —*n.* 1, a vagabond. 2, one without visible or reputable means of support. —**va'gran·cy,** *n*

vague (vāg) *adj.* 1, not definite, precise, or clear. 2, mentally confused. 3, indistinct to sight or other sense. —**vague'ness,** *n.*

vain (vān) *adj.* 1, ineffective; futile. 2, of no real value; trivial. 3, excessively proud of oneself; conceited. —**vain'ness,** *n.*

vain·glo'ri·ous *adj.* inordinately proud, boasting, or pretentious. —**vain·glo'ri·ous·ness,** *n.* —**vain'glo'ry,** *n.*

val'ance (val'əns) *n.* a short drape or curtain used as an ornamental border.

vale (vāl) *n.* valley.

val"e·dic'to·ry (val"ə-dik'tə-rē) *adj.* bidding farewell; farewell. —*n.* an oration of farewell, esp. by a member of a graduating class. —**val"e·dic·to'ri·an,** *n.* one who delivers a valedictory.

Valance

va'lence (vā'ləns) *n.* (*Chem.*) the relative combining capacity of an atom compared with the hydrogen atom. Also, **va'len·cy.**

-va·lent (vā'lənt) *suf.* having a valency of, as *univalent.*

val'en·tine (val'ən-tīn") *n.* 1, a sentimental missive sent on St. Valentine's day, Feb. 14. 2, a sweetheart chosen on this day.

val'et (val'ət, va-lā') *n.* 1, a personal manservant to a man. 2, one whose business is pressing and cleaning clothes.

val"e·tu"di·nar'i·an (val"ə-tū"də-nâr'ē-ən) *n. & adj.* (one) in poor health; invalid.

val'iant (val'yənt) *adj.* 1, brave; courageous. 2, showing valor. —**val'ian·cy,** *n.*

val'id *adj.* 1, well supported by fact; sound; just. 2, legally effective or binding. —**va·lid'i·ty,** *n.*

val'i·date" (val'i-dāt") *v.t.* make valid. —**val"i·da'tion,** *n.*

va·lise' (və-lēs') *n.* a small leather traveling bag.

val'ley (val'ē) *n.* 1, a relatively low tract of land between hills. 2, the lowlands along the course of a river. 3, any hollow, depression, or dip.

val'or (val'ər) *n.* strength of mind in braving danger. Also, **val'our.** —**val'or·ous,** *adj.*

val'u·a·ble (val'ū-ə-bəl) *adj.* of great value or price. —*n.* (usually *pl.*) an expensive personal possession, as a jewel. —**val'u·a·ble·ness,** *n.*

val"u·a'tion (val"ū-ā'shən) *n.* 1, act of appraising or estimating value. 2, estimated worth.

val'ue (val'ū) *n.* 1, that for which something is regarded as useful or desirable; utility, merit, or worth. 2, price. 3, import. 4, degree; number; amount; duration, etc. —*v.t.* 1, regard as desirable or useful. 2, estimate the value of. —**val'ued,** *adj.* highly regarded. —**val'ue·less,** *adj.* worthless.

valve (valv) *n.* 1, any device used to control the flow of a fluid through a pipe, vent, etc. 2, a hinged lid or flap, as of the shell of a clam, etc. 3, an electron tube. —**val'vu·lar** (val'vyə-lar) *adj.*

va·moose' (va-moos') *v.i.* depart rapidly; run away.

vamp *n.* 1, the front part of the upper of a shoe or boot. 2, a patch added to something old. 3, an improvised musical accompaniment. 4, (*Slang*) a flirtatious woman. —*v.t.* 1, repair; patch; renovate. 2, (*Slang*) use feminine wiles on.

Vampire Bat

vam'pire (vam'pīr) *n.* 1, a supposed bloodsucking monster. 2, any of various bloodsucking or similar bats. 3, an extortionist, esp. a flirtatious or predatory woman. —**vampire bat,** a bloodsucking bat.

van *n.* 1, a large covered wagon or truck. 2, (*Brit.*) a light delivery truck; a baggage or freight car. 3, vanguard.

va·na'di·um (və-nā'dē-əm) *n.* a rare element, no. 23, symbol V, used to harden steel.

van'dal *n.* one who willfully destroys things of beauty. —**van'dal·ism,** *n.* wanton destruction.

van·dyke' (-dīke') *n.* (often *cap.*) a short pointed beard.

vane (vān) *n.* **1,** a device that turns with the wind and shows its direction: *weathervane.* **2,** blade, plate, fin, etc. moved by a fluid stream.

van'guard' (van'gärd') *n.* the foremost units, as of an advancing army; the leaders, as of a social movement.

va·nil'la (və-nil'ə) *n.* a tropical orchid; a flavoring extract made from its bean.

va·nil'lin (və-nil'ən) *n.* an artificial compound giving a vanilla flavor.

van'ish *v.i.* **1,** fade from sight; disappear. **2,** pass away; cease to exist. **3,** (*Math.*) become zero.

van'i·ty (van'ə-tē) *n.* **1,** excessive pride; excessive attention to one's appearance. **2,** futility; worthlessness. **3,** a thing or trait regarded as vain. **4,** a small cosmetic case carried by a woman. **5,** a woman's dressing table.

van'quish (vang'kwish) *v.t.* defeat in battle or contest.

van'tage (van'tij) *n.* a position affording superior power or opportunity.

vap'id *adj.* lacking animation or flavor. —**va·pid'i·ty** (və-pid'ə-tē), **vap'id·ness,** *n.*

va'por (vā'pər) *n.* **1,** a gas made visible by particles of liquid or dust, as steam, fog, smoke. **2,** any matter in gaseous state. —*v.t. & i.* change to vapor. Also, **va'pour.**

va'por·ize' (-īz') *v.t. & i.* make or become vapor. —**va''por·i·za'tion,** *n.*

va'por·ous (-əs) *adj.* **1,** pert. to or of vapor. **2,** unsubstantial; vague. —**va'por·ous·ness,** *n.*

var'i·a·ble (vâr'ē-ə-bəl) *adj.* **1,** tending to change; not constant. **2,** capable of being varied. —*n.* that which varies. —**var''i·a·bil'i·ty,** *n.*

var'i·ance (vâr'ē-əns) *n.* act or effect of varying; difference. —**at variance,** in disagreement.

var'i·ant (vâr'ē-ənt) *adj.* tending to change; different; diverse. —*n.* an altered form of something.

var''i·a'tion (ver''ē-ā'shən) *n.* **1,** the act or process of varying; change; modification. **2,** a point or aspect of difference. **3,** the amount of change; variance. **4,** a different form.

var'i·col'ored (vâr'ē-kul''ərd) *adj.* variegated; motley.

var'i·cose' (var'i-kōs'') *adj.* dilated; abnormally swollen, esp. of veins. —**var''i·cos'i·ty** (-kos'ə-tē) *n.*

var'ied (vâr'ēd) *adj.* **1,** assorted; differing. **2,** altered.

var'i·e·gat''ed (vâr'ē-ə-gāt''ed) *adj.*

marked with different colors. —**var'·i·e·gate'',** *v.t.* —**var''i·e·ga'tion,** *n.*

va·ri'e·ty (və-rī'ə-tē) *n.* **1,** a mixture of different things. **2,** difference or discrepancy. **3,** a variant; a subdivision. **4,** vaudeville.

va·ri'o·la (və-rī'ə-lə) *n.* smallpox: —**va·ri'o·lous,** *adj.*

var''i·om'e·ter (vâr''ē-om'ə-tər) *n.* an instrument for regulating or measuring electrical variations.

var''i·o'rum (vâr''ē-ôr'əm) *adj.* presenting several versions (of a text).

var'i·ous (vâr'ē-əs) *adj.* **1,** differing; having diverse features; not uniform. **2,** some; several; many. —**var'i·ous·ness,** *n.*

var'let (vär'lit) *n.* (*Archaic*) a rascal.

var'mint (vär'mənt) *n.* (*Dial.*) **1,** an insect; bug; any undesirable creature. **2,** a low or rascally person.

var'nish (vär'nish) *n.* **1,** a resinous coating material that produces a glossy surface. **2,** superficial social polish. —*v.t.* finish with, or as with, varnish.

var'si·ty (vär'sə-tē) *n.* (*Slang*) the principal team of a school or college in a given sport.

var'y (vâr'ē) *v.t.* **1,** make different; alter. **2,** make of different kinds; diversify. —*v.i.* **1,** be different or diverse. **2,** undergo change. **3,** be variable.

vas'cu·lar (vas'kyə-lər) *adj.* pert. to bodily ducts that convey fluid, as blood and lymph. —**vas''cu·lar'·i·ty** (-lar'ə-tē) *n.*

vase (vās) *n.* a hollow vessel, as for holding cut flowers, etc.

vas'e·line (vas'ə-lēn'') *n.* (*T.N.*) a greasy petroleum product used as an ointment and lubricant.

vas''o·mo'tor (vas''ə-mō'tər) *adj.* regulating the blood vessels.

vas'sal (vas'əl) *n.* **1,** a feudal tenant. **2,** a subject, follower, or retainer. —**vas'sal·age,** *n.*

vast (våst) *adj.* very great in extent, quantity, etc. —**vast'ness,** *n.*

vat *n.* a large container for liquids.

Vat'i·can (vat'i-kən) *n.* the palace of the Pope, at Rome.

vaude'ville (vōd'vil) *n.* a theatrical show comprising separate acts of different kinds. —**vaude·vil'lian** (-yən) *n.*

vault (vålt) *n.* **1,** a chamber with an arched or concave roof, esp. one underground; any underground room. **2,** a chamber used as a safe. **3,** a jump; the act of vaulting. —*v.i. & t.* jump or leap, esp. with

---

tŭb, cūte, pŭll; label; oil, owl; go, chip, she, thin, *then,* sing, ink; *see p. 6*

aid of the hands resting on something.

vaunt (vânt) *v.t.* speak of boastfully.

V-'Day' day of victory (in World War II): in Europe (*V-E Day*), May 8, and over Japan (*V-J Day*), Sept. 2, 1945.

veal (vēl) *n.* the meat of a calf.

vec'tor (vek'tər) *n.* & *adj.* a line graphically representing both magnitude and direction; a quantity which may be represented by such a line.

Ve'da (vā'də) *n.* one of the Hindu scriptures. —**Ve'dic,** *adj.*

Ve-dan'ta (vā-dän'tə) *n.* a Hindu philosophy, a derivation of the Vedas.

ve-dette' (və-det') *n.* (*Naval*) a small scouting boat.

veep (vēp) *n.* (*Slang*) vice-president.

veer (vir) *v.t.* change direction, as wind. —*n.* a change of direction.

veg'e-ta-ble (vej'ə-bəl) *n.* **1,** any herbaceous plant used wholly or in part for food. **2,** any plant. —*adj.* **1,** being an edible plant. **2,** belonging to the plant kingdom. —**veg'e-tal,** *adj.*

veg"e-tar'i-an (vej'ə-tãr'ē-ən) *n.* & *adj.* one who eats no meat.

veg'e-tate" (vej'ə-tāt") *v.i.* **1,** grow or live like a plant. **2,** be mentally inactive. —**veg'e-ta-tive,** *adj.*

veg"e-ta'tion (vej'ə-tā'shən) *n.* **1,** plants collectively. **2,** the act of vegetating.

ve'he-ment (vē'ə-mənt) *adj.* showing strength or impetuosity in feeling; eager, fervent, or passionate. —**ve'he-mence,** *n.*

ve'hi-cle (vē'ə-kəl) *n.* **1,** any carriage or conveyance on wheels or runners. **2,** any medium for producing effects. —**ve-hic'u-lar** (və-hik'yū-lər) *adj.*

veil (vāl) *n.* **1,** a piece of light fabric worn over the face or head. **2,** anything that screens or conceals. —*v.t.* **1,** cover with a veil. **2,** hide; disguise. —**take the veil,** become a nun.

Veil

vein (vān) *n.* **1,** one of the tubes that convey blood to the heart. **2,** a riblike part supporting a membrane, as a leaf. **3,** a stratum or deposit; a lode. **4,** a fissure or cavity; a small natural watercourse. **5,** a streak or stripe. —*v.t.* furnish or mark with veins. —**vein'y,** *adj.*

veldt (velt) *n.* the open, scrubby country of So. Afr. Also, **veld.**

vel'lum (vel'əm) *n.* **1,** parchment made from calfskin. **2,** a paper of similar texture.

ve-loc'i-pede" (və-los'ə-pēd") *n.* a light vehicle with three wheels propelled by foot power; a tricycle.

ve-loc'i-ty (və-los'ə-tē) *n.* quickness or rate of motion; speed.

ve-lours' (və-lūr') *n.* (*Fr.*) velvet.

ve-lure' (və-lūr') *n.* a velvet.

vel'vet (vel'vit) *n.* **1,** a fabric with a thick, soft pile. **2,** something of similar texture. **3,** (*Slang*) net profit. —**vel'vet-y,** *adj.*

vel"ve-teen' (vel"və-tēn') *n.* a cotton fabric woven like velvet.

ve'nal (vē'nəl) *adj.* open to bribery; corrupt. —**ve-nal'i-ty** (vē-nal'ə-tē) *n.*

vend *v.t.* & *i.* sell; purvey. —**vendee',** *n.* buyer. —**vend'i-ble,** *adj.* —**vending machine,** a coin-slot machine for selling merchandise.

ven-det'ta (ven-det'ə) *n.* a feud.

ven'dor (ven'dər) *n.* **1,** a seller; a peddler. **2,** a machine for dispensing merchandise on insertion of coins: *vending machine.* Also, **vend'er.**

ve-neer' (və-nir') *n.* **1,** a thin layer of fine wood or other material applied as an outer coating. **2,** one of the layers in plywood. **3,** outward show to give a fair appearance; superficial ornamentation. —*v.t.* **1,** cover with a veneer. **2,** make into plywood.

ven'er-a-ble (ven'ər-ə-bəl) *adj.* **1,** worthy of veneration. **2,** old and dignified; ancient. —**ven"er-a-bil'i-ty, ven'er-a-ble-ness,** *n.*

ven'er-ate" (ven'ə-rāt") *v.t.* regard with reverence. —**ven"er-a'tion,** *n.*

ve-ne're-al (və-nir'ē-əl) *adj.* pert. to diseases arising from copulation.

ven'er-y (ven'ə-rē) *n.* hunting; the chase.

Ve-ne'tian (və-nē'shən) *adj.* & *n.* of or pert. to Venice. —**Venetian blind,** a screen for a window, having adjustable slats.

venge'ance (ven'jəns) *n.* retributive punishment; revenge.

venge'ful (venj'fəl) *adj.* seeking revenge. —**venge'ful-ness,** *n.*

ve'ni-al (vē'nē-əl) *adj.* pardonable; excusable. —**ve-ni-al'i-ty,** *n.*

ve-ni're-man (vi-nī'rē-mən) *n.* [*pl.* -**men**] one summoned to be a juror.

ven'i-son (ven'ə-zən) *n.* the flesh of a deer or like animal.

ven'om (ven'əm) *n.* **1,** poison secreted by snakes, spiders, etc. **2,**

spite; malice; virulence. —**ven'om·ous,** *adj.*

ve'nous (vē'nəs) *adj.* of or pert. to the veins.

vent *n:* 1, a small aperture or passage; an outlet. 2, an emission or discharge. 3, utterance. —*v.t.* 1, let out; discharge. 2, utter.

ven'ti·late" (ven'tə-lāt") *v.t.* let fresh air into; expose to the action of air. —**ven"ti·la'tion,** *n.* —**ven'ti·la·tor,** *n.* a device, as an opening, shaft, fan, etc. for ventilating.

ven'tral (ven'trəl) *adj.* pert. to the abdominal side of the body.

ven'tri·cle (ven'tri-kəl) *n.* a small cavity or hollow organ of the body; a chamber of the heart. —**ven·tric'u·lar** (-yū-lər) *adj.*

ven·tril'o·quism (ven-tril'ə-kwiz-əm) *n.* the art of uttering sounds so that they seem to come from a source other than the speaker. —**ven·tril'o·quist,** *n.*

ven'ture (ven'chər) *n.* a hazardous enterprise. —*v.t.* 1, expose to risk; stake. 2, expose oneself to the risk of; utter daringly. —*v.t.* risk. —**ven'tur·ous, ven'ture·some,** *adj.*

ven'ue (ven'ū) *n.* the scene of a crime or the jurisdiction of a court.

ve·ra'cious (və-rā'shəs) *n.* 1, disposed to tell the truth. 2, true. —**ve·ra'cious·ness,** *n.*

ve·rac'i·ty (və-ras'ə-tē) *n.* truthfulness; accuracy.

ve·ran'da (və-ran'də) *n.* an open porch or gallery, usually roofed.

verb (vėrb) *n.* a word that expresses action or existence; a part of speech that predicates and combines with a subject to form a sentence.

verb'al (vėr'bəl) *adj.* 1, expressed in words. 2, oral, not written. 3, pert. to a verb.

ver·ba'tim (vər-bā'təm) *adj.* in exactly the same words.

ver·be'na (vər-bē'nə) *n.* a plant with showy flowers.

ver'bi·age (vėr'bē-ij) *n.* wordiness; verbosity.

ver·bose' (vər-bōs') *adj.* using more words than are necessary; wordy. —**ver·bos'i·ty** (-bos'ə-tē) *n.*

ver'dant (vėr'dənt) *adj.* 1, green with vegetation. 2, inexperienced. —**ver'dan·cy,** *n.*

ver'dict (vėr'dikt) *n.* 1, the finding of a jury. 2, any judgment or decision.

ver'di·gris" (vėr'də-grēs") *n.* a greenish patina that forms on copper, etc.

ver'dure (vėr'jər) *n.* 1, green vegetation. 2, greenness, esp. of growing plants. 3, fresh or healthy condition.

verge (vėrj) *n.* 1, brink; edge; rim. 2, a point or limit beyond which something begins. —*v.i.* be at a border; approach.

ver'ger (vėr'jər) *n.* a minor church officer, as an usher or sexton.

ver'i·fy" (ver'ə-fī") *v.t.* ascertain or prove to be true. —**ver"i·fi·ca'tion,** *n.*

ver'i·ly (ver'ə-lē) *adv.* (*Archaic*) truly; really.

ver"i·si·mil'i·tude" (ver"i-si-mil'ə-tūd") *n.* an appearance of truth.

ver'i·ta·ble (ver'i-tə-bəl) *adj.* true; genuine. —**ver"i·ta·bil'i·ty,** *n.*

ver'i·ty (ver'ə-tē) *n.* 1, the quality of being true or real. 2, a truth; a reality.

ver'juice" (vėr'joos") *n.* the juice of a sour fruit.

ver·mi- *pref.* wormlike.

ver"mi·cel'li (vėr"mə-sel'ē) *n.* a thin spaghetti.

ver·mic'u·late (vėr-mik'yū-lət) *adj.* 1, marked with wavy lines. 2, infested with worms.

ver'mi·form" (vėr'mə-fôrm") *adj.* long and slender, resembling a worm.

ver·mil'ion (vər-mil'yən) *n.* & *adj.* a bright yellow-red color.

ver'min (vėr'min) *n. pl.* or *sing.* 1, small noxious animals collectively, esp. insects that infest the body, houses, etc. 2, an obnoxious person or persons. —**ver'min·ous,** *adj.*

ver·mouth' (vər-mooth') *n.* a spiced wine. Also, **ver·muth'.**

ver·nac'u·lar (vər-nak'yə-lər) *adj.* & *n.* pert. to the native or common language of a place or group.

ver'nal (vėr'nəl) *adj.* 1, pert. to spring. 2, pert. to early age; youthful.

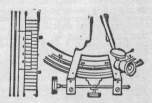

Vernier

ver'ni·er (vėr'nē-ər) *n.* an auxiliary device to measure fractional parts of subdivisions of a graduated scale.

ver·sa·tile (vĕr'sə-til) *adj.* 1, having ability in many different fields. 2, pivoted so as to swing or turn freely. —**ver·sa·til'i·ty,** *n.*

verse (vĕrs) *n.* 1, metrical composition; poetry. 2, a line of poetry or prose. 3, a poem. 4, a stanza.

versed (vĕrsd) *adj.* experienced; practiced; skilled.

ver'si·fy (vĕr'sə-fī') *v.t. & i.* write in poetry. —**ver'si·fi·ca'tion,** *n.*

ver'sion (vĕr'zhən) *n.* 1, a particular form or variant of something; a particular translation. 2, a narration from a particular point of view.

ver'so (vĕr'sō) *n.* 1, a left-hand page of a book. 2, the reverse side.

ver'sus (vĕr'səs) *prep.* against, as opposing parties in a lawsuit or contest.

ver·te·bra (vĕr'tə-brə) *n.* [*pl.* -brae (-brē) or -bras] any of the bone segments forming the spinal column. —**ver'te·bral,** *adj.*

ver·te·brate (vĕr'tə-brāt') *adj.* having a spine or backbone. —*n.* a vertebrate animal.

ver'tex (vĕr'teks) *n.* [*pl.* -es or ver'ti·ces" (-sēz")] the highest point; a point where two lines intersect.

ver'ti·cal (vĕr'tə-kəl) *adj.* being perpendicular to the horizon; upright. —*n.* 1, something vertical, as a line, supporting post, etc. 2, an upright position. —**ver'ti·cal·ness,** *n.*

ver·tig'i·nous (vĕr-tij'ə-nəs) *adj.* 1, turning around; whirling. 2, unstable.

ver'ti·go" (vĕr'tə-gō") *n.* a disordered condition marked by dizziness.

verve (vĕrv) *n.* enthusiasm; dash.

ver'y (ver'ē) *adv.* to a high degree; greatly; extremely. —*adj.* 1, [*superl.* ver'i·est] true; actual; genuine. 2, exact; innermost.

ves'i·cle (ves'ə-kəl) *n.* a bladder-like structure, cavity, sac, or cyst.

ve·sic'u·lar (ve-sik'yû-lər) *adj.* pert. to or like a vesicle. —**ve·sic'u·late** (-lət) *adj.* having vesicles.

ves'per (ves'pər) *n.* 1, evening; the evening star. 2, (*pl.*) a religious service held in late afternoon.

ves'sel (ves'əl) *n.* 1, a ship or other craft for traveling on water. 2, a hollow container. 3, a tube or duct.

vest *n.* a short sleeveless garment worn by men under the coat; any similar garment. —*v.t.* 1, clothe; cover or adorn with fabric. 2, endow with something, as authority. 3, put (rights, property, etc.) in possession of someone.

ves'tal (ves'təl) *adj.* virginal; chaste. —*n.* 1, a virgin. 2, a nun.

vest'ed (ves'tid) *adj.* 1, owned securely. 2, clothed; robed.

ves'ti·bule" (ves'tə-būl") *n.* a hall or antechamber between an outer door and inner room.

ves'tige (ves'tij) *n.* a remainder or evidence of something no longer present; a trace. —**ves·tig'i·al,** *adj.*

vest'ment (-mənt) *n.* a garment, esp. an official or ceremonial dress.

ves'try (ves'trē) *n.* 1, a room in a church where vestments are kept. 2, a chapel. —**ves'try·man,** *n.*

vet *n.* 1, veteran (of a war). 2, veterinarian.

vetch (vech) *n.* any of several leguminous plants used for forage.

vet'er·an (vet'ər-ən) *n.* 1, one who has had long experience. 2, a former soldier or other serviceman. —*adj.* having long experience.

vet'er·in·ar"y (vet'ər-ə-ner"ē) *adj.* pert. to medical and surgical care of domestic animals. —*n.* [also, vet"-er·i·nar'i·an] one who practices veterinary medicine.

ve'to (vē'tō) *n.* 1, rejection by one branch of government of measures proposed by another. 2, the right to reject. 3, any ban or prohibition. —*v.t.* reject; prohibit; refuse to endorse.

vex (veks) *v.t.* 1, make angry or displeased. 2, annoy; worry; harass.

vex·a'tion (veks-ā'shən) *n.* annoyance; irritation. —**vex·a'tious,** *adj.*

vi'a (vī'ə) *prep.* by way of; by a route through.

vi'a·ble (vī'ə-bəl) *adj.* capable of living, esp., able to live outside the womb. —**vi"a·bil'i·ty,** *n.*

vi'a·duct" (vī'ə-dukt") *n.* a bridge for carrying a road, railroad, waterway, etc. over a depression.

vi'al (vī'əl) *n.* a small bottle or flask.

vi'and (vī'ənd) *n.* an article of food.

vi·at'i·cum (vī-at'ə-kəm) *n.* 1, communion given to a dying person. 2, an allowance for traveling expenses.

vi'brant (vī'brənt) *adj.* 1, vibrating; resonant. 2, full of vigorous enthusiasm. —**vi'bran·cy,** *n.*

vi'brate (vī'brāt) *v.i.* 1, swing to and fro, as a pendulum; oscillate. 2, move rapidly to and fro, as a plucked string; quiver; resound; thrill. —**vi·bra'tion,** *n.* —**vi'bra·tor,** *n.* —**vi'bra·to·ry,** *adj.*

vic'ar (vik'ər) *n.* 1, an assistant clergyman. 2, one in charge of a dependent parish or chapel. 3, a deputy. —**Vicar of Christ,** the Pope.

vic′ar·age (-ij) *n.* the residence or office of a vicar.

vi·car′i·ous (vī-kãr′ė-əs) *adj.* substituting for or, feeling in place of, another. —**vi·car′i·ous·ness**, *n.*

vice (vīs) *n.* **1,** any immoral or evil practice. **2,** prostitution. **3,** a defect; a bad habit. **4,** vise. —*prep.* instead of; in place of.

vice- (vīs) *pref.* denoting a deputy or subordinate.

vice″ge′rent (-jir′ənt) *n.* a deputy.

vi·cen′ni·al (vī-sen′ė-əl) *n.* & *adj.* **1,** 20 years. **2,** the 20th anniversary.

vice-″pres′i·dent *n.* an officer of a government, corporation, etc. ranking next below the president. —**vice-″pres′i·den·cy,** *n.*

vice″re′gal *adj.* being or pert. to a viceroy.

vice′roy (-roi) *n.* a deputy king. —**vice′roy·ship,** *n.*

vi′ce ver′sa (vī′sə vėr′sə) conversely: denoting reciprocal relationship or reversal of order.

vi′chy (vish′ė) *n.* **1,** a carbonated, naturally effervescent water; soda. **2,** (*cap.*) an alkaline, still water from Vichy, France.

vi·cin′i·ty (vi-sin′ə-tė) *n.* the region surrounding or near a place; the neighborhood.

vi′cious (vish′əs) *adj.* **1,** addicted to vice; wicked; depraved. **2,** evil; pernicious. **3,** faulty; defective. **4,** malicious; spiteful. —**vicious circle**, a series of successively consequent effects in which the last affects the first. —**vi′cious·ness,** *n.*

vi·cis′si·tude″ (vi-sis′i-tūd″) *n.* **1,** change of condition; succession of one set of circumstances by another. **2,** (*pl.*) good or bad fortune.

vic′tim (vik′tim) *n.* **1,** one who suffers from a harmful agency. **2,** one who is cheated or duped. —**vic′tim·ize″** (-mīz″) *v.t.*

vic′tor (vik′tər) *n.* one who wins.

Victoria

Vic·to′ri·a (vik-tôr′ė-ə) *n.* a kind of horse-drawn carriage.

Vic·to′ri·an (vik-tôr′ė-ən) *adj.* **1,** pert. to the time of Queen Victoria of England, 1837–1901. **2,** prudish; smug.

vic′to·ry (vik′tə-rė) *n.* **1,** the winning of a contest or battle. **2,** any successful performance. —**vic·to′ri·ous** (-tôr′ė-əs) *adj.*

vic·tro′la (vik-trō′lə) *n.* (*T.N.*) a phonograph.

vict′ual (vit′əl) *n.* (*pl.*) food or provisions, esp. for human beings. —*v.t.* & *i.* supply with or obtain provisions. —**vict′ual·er,** *n.* a supplier of food; a restaurateur.

vid′e·o (vid′ė-ō) *adj.* pert. to television. —*n.* television.

vie (vī) *v.i.* [**vied, vy′ing**] strive for superiority; compete.

Vi″en·nese′ (vē″ə-nēz′) *adj.* & *n.* of or pert. to Vienna.

view (vū) *n.* **1,** examination by eye; inspection; survey. **2,** range of vision. **3,** what is seen; scene, prospect, etc. **4,** mental contemplation; visualization. **5,** a particular aspect or mental attitude; an opinion, judgment, theory, etc. **6,** purpose; aim. —*v.t.* **1,** look at. **2,** consider; regard in a particular way.

view′point″ *n.* **1,** a place from which something may be seen. **2,** attitude of mind: *point of view.*

vi·ges′i·mal (vi-jes′i-məl) *adj.* twentieth; by twenties.

vig′il (vij′əl) *n.* **1,** a keeping awake; a watch kept at night. **2,** watchful attention at any time.

vig′i·lant (vij′ə-lənt) *adj.* alert to detect danger. —**vig′i·lance,** *n.*

vig″i·lan′te (vij″ə-lan′tė) *n.* one of a group of self-appointed citizens acting to maintain order.

vi·gnette′ (vin-yet′) *n.* **1,** a photograph shaded at the edges so as to have no clear border. **2,** a descriptive literary sketch. **3,** a decorative illustration in a book. —*v.t.* **1,** outline; describe. **2,** make a (photographic) vignette of.

vig′or (vig′ər) *n.* **1,** active strength of body; good physical condition. **2,** mental energy. **3,** strength or force in general; powerful action; potency. Also, **vig′our.** —**vig′or·ous,** *adj.*

vi′king (vī′king) *n.* a Scandinavian mariner.

vile (vīl) *adj.* **1,** morally base; depraved; villainous. **2,** repulsive; obnoxious; disgusting. **3,** low in station; mean. **4,** of small value; paltry. —**vile′ness,** *n.*

vil′i·fy″ (vil′ə-fī″) *v.t.* defame. —**vil″i·fi·ca′tion,** *n.*

vil′la (vil′ə) *n.* a rural residence.

vil′lage (vil′ij) *n.* a small assemblage of houses, less than a town. —**vil′lag·er,** *n.*

vil′lain (vil′ən) *n.* **1,** the chief antagonist of the hero in a play or novel. **2,** a wicked person; rascal; scoundrel. —**vil′lain·ess,** *n.fem.* —**vil′lain·ous,** *adj.* —**vil′lain·y,** *n.*

vim *n.* energy; impetuosity.

vin′di·cate″ (vin′də-kāt″) *v.t.* **1,** clear, as from an accusation or imputation. **2,** maintain as true or correct. **3,** regain possession of (property) by legal procedure. —**vin″-di·ca′tion,** *n.*

vin·dic′tive (vin-dik′tiv) *adj.* disposed to seek revenge; bitter. —**vin-dic′tive·ness,** *n.*

vine (vīn) *n.* **1,** any plant with a long slender stem that trails on the ground or climbs upright objects. **2,** the grape plant. **3,** wine.

vin′e·gar (vin′ə-gər) *n.* **1,** a sour liquid obtained by fermentation of fruit juices. **2,** sourness of speech, temper, etc. —**vin′e·gar·y,** *adj.*

vine′yard″ (vin′yərd) *n.* a plantation for grapes, esp. for wine-making.

vi′nous (vī′nəs) *adj.* pert. to wine or vines.

vin′tage (vin′tij) *n.* **1,** the wine from a particular crop of grapes; the crop or output of anything. **2,** the gathering of grapes; the harvest season. **3,** wine-making. —*adj.* exceptionally fine.

vint′ner (vint′nər) *n.* a dealer in wines.

vi′nyl (vī′nil) *n.* pert. to certain compounds used in plastics (*vinyl resins,* as styrene, vinylite, koroseal, etc.)

vi′ol (vī′əl) *n.* a stringed musical instrument similar in shape to a violin but with more than four strings. —**vi′ol·ist,** *n.*

vi·o′la (vē-ō′lə) *n.* the alto instrument of the violin class. —**vi·o′list,** *n.*

vi′o·late″ (vī′ə-lāt″) *v.t.* **1,** break or infringe, as a contract. **2,** break in upon; do violence to. **3,** treat with irreverence; desecrate; profane. **4,** ravish (a woman). —**vi′o·la·ble,** *adj.* —**vi″o·la′tion,** *n.* —**vi′o·la·tor,** *n.*

vi′o·lent (vī′ə-lənt) *adj.* **1,** acting with, or characterized by, strong physical force. **2,** vehement; passionate; furious. —**vi′o·lence,** *n.*

vi′o·let (vī′ə-lit) *n.* **1,** any of numerous herbs bearing small short-stemmed flowers; the flower. **2,** a blue or reddish-blue color; the spectrum color of highest frequency visible to the eye.

vi″o·lin′ (vī′ə-lin′) *n.* a stringed musical instrument played with a bow; the treble member of the modern family of such instruments. —**vi′o·lin′ist,** *n.*

Violin

Viola

Violoncello

vi″o·lon·cel′lo (vē′ə-lon-chel′ō) *n.* cello.

vi·os′ter·ol (vī-os′tər-ol″) *n.* a prepared oil that supplies vitamin D.

VIP (vē′ī′pē′) *n.* (*Slang*) very important personage.

vi′per (vī′pər) *n.* **1,** a venomous snake. **2,** a malignant or treacherous person. —**vi′per·ous, vi′per·ish,** *adj.*

vi·ra′go (vi-rā′gō) *n.* an ill-tempered or violent woman.

vir′gin (vẽr′jin) *n.* **1,** a person, esp. a woman, who has not had sexual intercourse. **2,** (*cap.*) Mary, mother of Jesus. —*adj.* **1,** being a virgin; pure. **2,** fresh; new; unused. —**vir-gin′i·ty,** *n.*

vir′gin·al (-əl) *adj.* pure; fresh. —*n.* a kind of spinet.

virgin birth the doctrine that Jesus was miraculously born of a virgin mother.

Virginia reel a type of square dance.

Vir′go (vẽr′gō) *n.* a constellation, the Virgin (see *zodiac*).

vir′ile (vir′əl) *adj.* **1,** of or like a man; masculine; manly. **2,** capable of procreating. **3,** forceful. —**vi-ril′i·ty** (və-ril′ə-tē) *n.*

vir′tu·al (vẽr′choo-əl) *adj.* equivalent to, though somewhat different or deficient. —**vir·tu·al′i·ty,** *n.*

vir′tue (vẽr′choo) *n.* **1,** conformity to moral law; uprightness; rectitude. **2,** a commendable quality. **3,** chastity. **4,** inherent power; effect.

vir″tu·os′i·ty (vẽr″choo-os′ə-tē) *n.* great individual skill.

vir″tu·o′so (vẽr″choo-ō′sō) *n.* [*pl.* -sos, -si (-sē)] **1,** one who has great skill in a fine art, as music. **2,** a connoisseur.

vir·tu·ous (vẽr'choo-əs) *adj.* moral; upright; chaste. —**vir'tu·ous·ness**, *n.*

vir'u·lent (vir'yə-lənt) *adj.* **1**, like a poison; deadly; malignant. **2**, bitterly hostile; acrimonious. —**vir'u·lence**, *n.*

vi'rus (vī'rəs) *n.* **1**, an agent of infection, esp. one smaller than common bacteria. **2**, a pernicious influence.

vi'sa (vē'zə) *n.* an endorsement making a passport valid for entry into a particular country. Also, **vi·sé'** (-zā').

vis'age (viz'ij) *n.* **1**, the face, esp. of a human being. **2**, countenance; appearance; aspect.

vis'cer·a (vis'ər-ə) *n.* *pl.* [*sing.* **vis'cus** (-kəs)] **1**, the soft interior parts of the body. **2**, the bowels. —**vis'cer·al**, *adj.*

vis'cid (vis'id) *adj.* having a glutinous consistency; sticky. —**vis·cid'i·ty**, **vis'cid·ness**, *n.*

vis'cose (vis'kōs) *n. & adj.* a solution of cellulose used in making rayon.

vis·cos'i·ty (vis-kos'ə-tē) *n.* thickness of consistency of a liquid; resistance to flow.

vis'count (vī'kownt) *n.* a nobleman ranking next below a count (or earl).

vis'cous (vis'kəs) *adj.* **1**, viscid. **2**, having high viscosity.

vise (vīs) *n.* an apparatus for gripping and holding an object while work is performed on it. Also, **vice**.

vis'i·ble (viz'ə-bəl) *adj.* **1**, capable of being seen. **2**, open to view; conspicuous. **3**, perceptible to the mind. —**vis"i·bil'i·ty**, *n.*

vi'sion (vizh'ən) *n.* **1**, the sense of sight; ability to see. **2**, the ability to visualize; foresight. **3**, a pleasing or vivid scene. **4**, a supernatural or prophetic presentiment, as in a dream or trance. **5**, a fanciful or unpractical view.

vi'sion·ar·y (-er-ē) *adj.* **1**, unpractical. **2**, given to idealistic theorizing. —*n.* a dreamer; theorizer.

vis'it (viz'it) *v.t.* **1**, go to see (a person, place, etc.); call upon. **2**, stay with, as a guest. **3**, afflict, as with suffering; assail. —*v.i.* make calls. —*n.* a friendly or official call; a stay as a guest. —**vis'i·tor**, *n.*

vis'it·ant (viz'i-tənt) *n.* one visiting for a short period.

vis"i·ta'tion (viz"i-tā'shən) *n.* **1**, an official visit. **2**, a boon or affliction regarded as an act of God.

vi'sor (vī'zər) *n.* a part projecting above the eyes, as on a cap, to shade or protect them. Also, **vi'zor**.

vis'ta (vis'tə) *n.* a view or prospect, esp. one of great depth.

vis'u·al (vizh'ū-əl) *adj.* **1**, pert. to vision; used in seeing; optical. **2**, visible to the eye or mind.

vis'u·al·ize" (vizh'ū-ə-līz") *v.t.* **1**, form a mental image of. **2**, make perceptible. —*v.i.* form mental images. —**vis"u·al·i·za'tion**, *n.*

vi'tal (vī'təl) *adj.* **1**, pert. to life; alive. **2**, essential to existence or well-being. **3**, critically important. **4**, invigorating. **5**, fatal. —**vital statistics**, birth and death records. —**vi'tal·ness**, *n.*

vi·tal'i·ty (vī-tal'ə-tē) *n.* **1**, the power to live; the principle of life. **2**, vigor; energy.

vi'ta·min (vī'tə-min) *n.* a food constituent essential to the proper functioning of the body. Also, **vi'ta·mine**.

vi'ti·ate" (vish'ē-āt") *v.t.* make faulty or imperfect; contaminate; spoil; invalidate. —**vi"ti·a'tion**, *n.*

vit're·ous (vit'rē-əs) *adj.* **1**, pert. to or consisting of glass. **2**, resembling glass, as in hardness, finish, etc. —**vit're·ous·ness**, *n.*

vit'ri·fy" (vit'ri-fī") *v.t. & i.* change to a glassy state by heat. —**vit"ri·fi·ca'tion**, **vit'ri·fac'tion**, *n.*

vit'ri·ol (vit'rē-əl) *n.* **1**, sulfuric acid. **2**, any metallic sulfate of glassy appearance. **3**, something extremely caustic, as criticism. —**vit"ri·ol'ic**, *adj.* —**vit"ri·ol'i·cal·ly**, *adv.*

vi·tu'per·ate" (vī-tū'pə-rāt") *v.t.* address or find fault with abusively. —**vi·tu"per·a'tion**, *n.*

vi·va'cious (vī-vā'shəs) *adj.* animated; lively; sprightly. —**vi·va'cious·ness**, *n.*

vi·vac'i·ty (vi-vas'ə-tē) *n.* high spirits; vivaciousness.

viv'id (viv'id) *adj.* **1**, lifelike; animated; bright. **2**, clearly perceptible. **3**, vigorous or lively in action. —**viv'id·ness**, *n.*

viv'i·fy" (viv'ə-fī") *v.t.* enliven; give life to.

vi·vip'a·rous (vī-vip'ə-rəs) *adj.* bearing young alive, not in eggs. —**vi·vip'a·rous·ness**, *n.*

viv'i·sect" (viv'ə-sekt") *v.t.* dissect the living body of (an animal), for experimental purposes. —**viv"i·sec'tion**, *n.*

vix'en (vik'sən) *n. fem.* **1**, a female fox. **2**, an ill-tempered woman. —**vix'en·ish**, *adj.*

vi·zier' (vi-zir') *n.* a chief minister of a Mohammedan sovereign.

vi'zor (vī'zər) *n.* visor.

vo'ca·ble (vō'kə-bəl) *n.* any word, regarded as a group of letters or sounds, without reference to meaning. —*adj.* that may be spoken.

vo·cab'u·lar"y (vō-kab'yû-ler"ê) *n.* 1, the words of a language collectively. 2, the stock of words used by a particular person, group, etc. 3, a written list of words, as a dictionary.

vo'cal (vō'kəl) *adj.* 1, pert. to the voice, speech, or singing. 2, pert. to expression in speech; able or insistent in speaking. —*n.* 1, a vocal sound, esp. a vowel. 2, (*Colloq.*) the singing part of a musical performance. —**vocal cords**, membranes in the larynx that vibrate to produce sound. —**vo'cal·ist**, *n.* a singer. —**vo'cal·ize**" (-īz") *v.t. & i.* utter; sing.

vo·ca'tion (vō-kā'shən) *n.* 1, a particular profession, business, or occupation; calling. 2, a summons or feeling of being called to a particular activity, esp. religious. —**vo·ca'tion·al**, *adj.* pert. to an occupation; giving training for a trade.

voc'a·tive (vok'ə-tiv) *adj. & n.* calling by name; (*Gram.*) designating the case of one directly addressed.

vo·cif'er·ate" (vō-sif'ə-rāt") *v.i. & t.* cry out noisily; shout. —**vo·cif"er·a'tion**, *n.*

vo·cif'er·ous (vō-sif'ə-rəs) *adj.* exclaiming; clamorous; noisy. —**vo·cif'er·ous·ness**, *n.*

vod'ka (vod'kə) *n.* a Russian alcoholic liquor distilled from cereals or potatoes.

vogue (vōg) *n.* prevalent fashion; popularity.

voice (vois) *n.* 1, sound uttered by the mouth of a living creature, esp. human. 2, the vocal sounds characteristic of a particular person. 3, expression by, or as though by, speaking, singing, etc. 4, the right to speak, vote, etc. 5, a person or agency by which something is revealed. 6, a singer; his rôle or part. 7, (*Gram.*) a relative verb inflection, active (as, *I do it*) or passive (as, *it is done by me*). —*v.t.* give utterance to. —**voice'less**, *n.*

-voiced *suf.* having a specified kind of voice, as *soft-voiced.*

void *adj.* 1, not legally binding; invalid; null. 2, having no contents; vacant. 3, ineffectual. —*v.t.* 1, nullify. 2, empty; evacuate. —*n.* a vacuum; empty place. —**void'ness**, *n.*

voile (voil) *n.* a thinly-woven dress fabric.

vol'a·tile (vol'ə-til) *adj.* 1, changing to vapor readily or rapidly. 2, fickle; frivolous. 3, transient; unstable; —**vol"a·til'i·ty**, *n.*

vol·can'ic (vol-kan'ik) *adj.* 1, pert. to a volcano. 2, violently eruptive. —**vol·can'i·cal·ly**, *adv.*

vol·ca'no (vol-kā'nō) *n.* a vent in the earth's surface, commonly at the top of a mountain, from which molten rock and heated gases issue or have issued.

vole (vōl) *n.* a small rodent of the rat family.

vo·li'tion (vō-lish'ən) *n.* the act or power of willing; voluntary action. —**vo·li'tion·al**, *adj.*

vol'i·tive (vol'ə-tiv) *adj.* expressing a wish.

vol'ley (vol'ê) *n.* 1, a flight or discharge of a number of missiles at one time. 2, the sound of concerted explosions. 3, (in games) the striking of a ball before it touches the ground. —*v.t. & i.* send or fly in a volley.

vol'plane (vol'plān) *v.i.* glide in an airplane without motor power. —*n.* a glide without motor power.

volt (vōlt) *n.* 1, a unit of electrical force. 2, a sideward step.

volt'age (vōl'tij) *n.* the force of an electric current, expressed in volts.

vol·ta'ic (vol-tā'ik) *adj.* pert. to electric current.

vol'u·ble (vol'yə-bəl) *adj.* speaking fluently; glib. —**vol"u·bil'i·ty**, *n.*

vol'ume (vol'ūm) *n.* 1, a book, esp. one of a set. 2, amount or capacity measured in three dimensions; cubic magnitude. 4, mass or quantity, esp. a large amount. 5, loudness or softness; roundness of tone.

vo·lu'mi·nous (və-loo'mi-nəs) *adj.* 1, having many volumes; copious; prolix. 2, large in bulk. —**vo·lu'mi·nous·ness**, *n.*

vol'un·tar"y (vol'ən-ter"ê) *adj.* 1, done of one's own accord or free choice. 2, controlled by the will. 3, having the power of making free choice. —*n.* a piece of organ music interpolated in a church service. —**vol'un·tar"i·ness**, *n.*

vol"un·teer' (vol"ən-tir') *n. & adj.* one who enters into any service of his own free will. —*v.i.* offer or undertake to do something. —*v.t.* offer or state voluntarily.

vo·lup'tu·ar·y (və-lup'choo-er-ê) *n.* a sensualist.

vo·lup'tu·ous (və-lup'choo-əs) *adj.* seeking, affording, or suggestive of pleasure. —**vo·lup'tu·ous·ness**, *n.*

vo·lute' (və-loot') *n. & adj.* a spiral or whorled formation.

vom'it *v.i.* 1, eject the contents of the stomach through the mouth; throw up. 2, be emitted; come out with force or violence. —*v.t.* throw up; emit. —*n.* the act of vomiting; what is thrown up.

vom'i.to.ry (vom'i-tôr-ē) *n.* **1,** an emetic. **2,** a doorway for entrance and exit.

voo'doo *n. & adj.* **1,** a form of witchcraft or conjuration. **2,** a fetish of voodoo worship. —**voo'doo.ism,** *n.*

vo.ra'cious (vō-rā'shəs) *adj.* greedily devouring; ravenous. —**vo.ra'cious.ness, vo.rac'i.ty** (vō-ras'ə-tē) *n.*

vor'tex (vôr'teks) *n.* **1,** a whirling motion or mass; a whirlpool or eddy. **2,** destructive force that draws one in. —**vor'ti.cal,** *adj.*

vo'ta.ry (vō'tə-rē) *n. & adj.* **1,** one bound by a vow, as a monk or nun. **2,** a devotee.

vote (vōt) *n.* **1,** a formal expression of choice. **2,** the right to choose or elect; franchise; suffrage. **3,** votes collectively; a decision made by voting. **4,** a ballot. —*v.i.* indicate a choice. —*v.t.* enact, establish, grant, declare, etc. by voting. —**vot'er,** *n.*

vo'tive (vō'tiv) *adj.* **1,** in accordance with a vow. **2,** optional, not prescribed. —**vo'tive.ness,** *n.*

vouch (vowch) *v.t.* assert; attest. —*v.i.* (with *for*) attest or warrant to be true, reliable, etc.

vouch'er (-ər) *n.* a receipt or authorization for an expenditure.

vouch"safe' *v.t.* bestow or grant condescendingly.

vow *n.* a solemn promise or pledge. —*v.t.* promise solemnly; swear. —**take vows,** enter a religious order.

vow'el (vow'əl) *n. & adj.* **1,** a speech sound uttered without friction and with more or less open mouth. **2,** a letter standing for such a sound; in English, *a, e, i, o, u,* sometimes *y.*

voy'age (voi'ij) *n.* a journey to a distant place, esp. by water. —*v.i. & t.* travel (to). —**voy'ag.er,** *n.*

vul'can.ite" (vul'kən-īt") *n.* hard rubber, used for making combs, etc.

vul'can.ize" (vul'kə-nīz") *v.t.* **1,** treat (rubber) with sulfur and heat. **2,** patch (as a tire) with rubber fused by heat. —**vul"can.i.za'tion,** *n.*

vul'gar (vul'gər) *adj.* **1,** ignorant or deficient of good taste; coarse; unrefined. **2,** plebeian. **3,** ordinary; common. —**vul'gar.ness,** *n.*

vul.gar'i.an (vul-gâr'ē-ən) *n.* a vulgar person.

vul'gar.ism (vul'gə-riz-əm) *n.* a word or expression not in good usage.

vul.gar'i.ty (vul-gâr'ə-tē) *n.* **1,** the state of being vulgar. **2,** something vulgar.

Vul'gate (vul'gāt) *n.* a Latin version of the Bible, the authorized version of the Rom. Cath. Church. —*adj.* (*l.c.*) common; in popular use.

vul'ner.a.ble (vul'nər-ə-bəl) *adj.* **1,** susceptible of being wounded, assaulted, or conquered. **2,** open to reproof. **3,** not resistant to evil influence. —**vul'ner.a.bil'i.ty,** *n.*

vul'pine (vul'pīn) *adj.* pert. to a fox; foxlike.

vul'ture (vul'chər) *n.* **1,** a large carrion-eating bird. **2,** a rapacious or ruthless person. —**vul'tur.ine** (-rīn), **vul'tur.ous,** *adj.*

Vulture

vul'va (vul'və) *n.* the external parts of the female genital organs.

W

W, w (dub'əl-yū) the twenty-third letter of the English alphabet.

wab'ble (wob'əl) *v.i.* wobble.

wack'y (wak'ē) *adj.* (*Slang*) **1,** slightly demented. **2,** odd. —**wack,** *n.* an eccentric person. —**wack'i.ness,** *n.*

wad (wod) *n.* **1,** a small mass of soft material; a packing or filling. **2,** (*Slang*) a roll of money. —*v.t.* [**wad'ded, -ding**] form into or pack with a wad.

wad'ding (wod'ing) *n.* material for stuffing; wads collectively.

wad'dle (wod'əl) *v.i.* rock from side to side in walking. —*n.* a rocking gait. —**wad'dler,** *n.*

wade (wād) *v.i.* **1,** walk through a substance that impedes, as water, sand, etc. **2,** make progress against obstacles. **3,** (with *in*) begin vigorously. —*v.t.* pass or cross by wading.

wad'er (wād'ər) *n.* **1,** one who wades. **2,** a long-legged bird. **3,** (*pl.*) high boots.

wa'di (wä'dē) *n.* in North Africa, a river channel, usually dry.

wa'fer (wā'fər) *n.* **1,** a thin, usually sweetened, delicate cake. **2,** any similar disk. —**wa'fer.y,** *adj.*

waf'fle (wof'əl) *n.* a flat batter-cake baked in a mold. —**waffle iron,** a griddle with a hinged cover, both having indented surfaces.

waft (wàft) *v.t.* bear or convey through, or as through, a buoyant medium, as water or air. —*n.* something wafted; a gust.

wag *v.i. & t.* [**wagged, wag'ging**] move or cause to move from side to side. —*n.* **1**, a shake; an oscillation. **2**, one who jokes; a wit. —**wag the tongue** (*Colloq.*) talk.

wage (wāj) *v.t.* engage in; carry on, as a war. —*n.* rate of payment for work; (*pl.*) recompense; pay.

wa'ger (wā'jər) *n.* a bet. —*v.t. & i.* bet.

wag'gish (wag'ish) *adj.* jocular. —**wag'gish.ness,** *n.*

wag'gle (wag'əl) *v.t. & i.* wag.

wag'on (wag'ən) *n.* **1**, a wheeled vehicle, esp. a four-wheeled freight vehicle. **2**, a railroad freight car Also, (*Brit.*) **wag'gon.** —**wag'on-er,** *n.* —**on the wagon,** abstaining from liquor.

wa·hoo' (wä-hoo') *n.* **1**, any of several trees or shrubs. **2**, a food fish.

waif (wāf) *n.* **1**, a homeless person, esp. a child. **2**, a stray animal or thing.

wail (wāl) *v.i. & t.* express sorrow by a mournful sound; lament. —*n.* a plaintive cry or sound.

wain'scot (wān'skət) *n.* a wooden lining, usually paneled, of the walls of a room. —**wain'scot'ing,** *n.*

wain'wright" (wān'rīt") *n.* a wagon maker.

waist (wāst) *n.* **1**, the part of the human body between the ribs and the hips. **2**, a middle part. **3**, an undergarment. **4**, a bodice; a blouse.

waist'coat" (wāst'kōt; (*Brit.*) wes'-kət) *n.* a man's vest.

waist'line" *n.* the body between ribs and hips.

wait (wāt) *v.i.* **1**, remain, expecting something. **2**, (with *on*) attend as a servant. **3**, (*Archaic*) call (upon); visit. —*n.* a stay; a delay.

wait'er (-ər) *n.* **1**, a server at the table. **2**, a tray. —**wait'ress,** *n.fem.*

waive (wāv) *v.t.* relinquish; forgo; defer for the present.

waiv'er (wāv'ər) *n.* (*Law*) the intentional relinquishment of a right or claim.

wake (wāk) *v.i.* [*pret.* **waked** or **woke** (wōk)] **1**, stop sleeping; be unable to sleep. **2**, become active. —*v.t.* **1**, rouse from sleep. **2**, arouse; reanimate. —*n.* **1**, an all-night watch over a corpse; a vigil. **2**, the track left by a boat in the water.

wake'ful (-fəl) *adj.* unable to sleep. —**wake'ful.ness,** *n.*

wak'en (wāk'ən) *v.t.* wake.

wale (wāl) *n.* **1**, a streak or stripe produced by a blow; a welt. **2**, a ridge or plank along the edge of a ship. **3**, a ridge in cloth.

walk (wâk) *v.i.* **1**, move by steps with a moderate gait; go or travel on foot. **2**, wander about. **3**, behave in any particular manner. **4**, in baseball, achieve first base on balls. —*v.t.* **1**, move on foot at a moderate gait. **2**, lead or drive at a moderate speed; carry. **3**, take for a stroll. —*n.* **1**, a stroll; a distance covered by walking. **2**, way of living. **3**, range or sphere of action. **4**, gait; carriage. **5**, a path. **6**, a slow pace or gait. **7**, in baseball, a base on balls. —**walking papers** (*Slang*) notice of dismissal. —**walking stick,** a cane.

walk'a·way" *n.* an easy victory. Also, **walk'o"ver.**

walk'ie-talk'ie (-ē) *n.* (*Slang*) a portable radio receiving and transmitting set.

walk'up" *n.* (*Colloq.*) an apartment not served by an elevator.

wall (wâl) *n.* **1**, a structure of stone, brick, or other materials serving to enclose, divide, support, or defend. **2**, a solid fence. **3**, any enclosing part or shell. —*v.t.* enclose or seal with, or as with, a wall; fortify.

wal'la·by (wol'ə-bē) *n.* any of the smaller kangaroos of Australia.

wall'board" *n.* fibers, minerals, etc. pressed into thick sheets.

wal'let (wol'it) *n.* **1**, a pocketbook, esp. one in which bank notes, papers, etc. lie flat. **2**, a bag or kit.

wall'eyed" *adj.* having a large staring eye showing much white.

wall'flow"er *n.* **1**, a Europ. perennial plant. **2**, (*Colloq.*) a person unable to attract a partner at a dance

wal'lop (wol'əp) *v.t.* **1**, beat soundly. **2**, defeat conclusively. —*n.* a heavy blow.

wal'low (wol'ō) *v.i.* **1**, roll the body in sand, mire, etc. **2**, dwell with satisfaction in. —*n.* **1**, the act of wallowing. **2**, a place where animals, as hogs, wallow.

wall'pa"per *n.* paper for covering the walls of a room.

wal'nut (wâl'nut) *n.* any of various trees bearing edible, hard-shelled nuts; the wood or nut of such a tree.

wal'rus (wol'rəs) *n.* a large, carnivorous Arctic sea mammal related to the seal.

waltz (wâlts) *n.* **1**, a dance for couples, in ¾ time; music for such a dance. **2**, (*Slang*) easy or effortless progress. —*v.t. & i.* dance (a waltz). *Walrus*

wam'pum (wom'pəm) *n.* small shell beads used for money by No. Amer. Indians.

---

fat, fāte, fär, fâre, fâll, àsk; met, hē, hêr, maybē; pin, pīne; not, nōte, ôr, tool

wan (won) *adj.* [wan'ner, -nest] of a sickly hue; pale; colorless. —wan'ness, *n.*

wand (wond) *n.* a slender stick; a rod, esp. one used by a conjurer.

wan'der (won'dər) *v.i.* 1, roam; ramble; stroll. 2, go astray; err. 3, be delirious. —*v.t.* travel aimlessly about. —wan'der·er, *n.*

wan'der.lust *n.* restless desire to roam.

wane (wān) *v.i.* decrease, as in size; decline. —*n.* decreasing.

wan'gle (wang'gəl) *v.i. & t.* (*Colloq.*) contrive; accomplish or obtain by shrewdness.

want (wont) *v.t.* 1, feel a desire for. 2, be without; lack. 3, require; need. —*v.i.* be lacking or deficient; be in need. —*n.* 1, lack or scarcity of what is needed or desired; poverty. 2, a desire. —want ad (*Colloq.*) a short advertisement for something desired. —want'ing, *adj.* lacking; needed.

wan'ton (won'tən) *adj.* 1, unrestrained; wild; reckless. 2, heartless; malicious. 3, dissolute. —*n.* an unrestrained or dissolute person. —*v.i.* revel. —*v.t.* squander. —wan'ton·ness, *n.*

wap'i·ti (wop'ə-tē) *n.* the No. Amer. stag or elk.

war (wôr) *n.* 1, armed conflict among nations; such conflict between parties in the same state (civil war). 2, any strife or conflict. 3, the profession of arms. —*v.i.* [warred, war'ring] carry on a war. —at war, engaged in warfare; warring. —war dance, war paint, war whoop, respectively a dance, a facial paint worn, or a cry, used by primitive peoples to arouse warlike emotions or frighten an enemy. —war horse, a horse trained for battle; hence, an experienced campaigner of any sort.

war'ble (wôr'bəl) *v.i. & t.* 1, carol or sing. 2, sound vibratingly; quaver. —*n.* a song, esp. of a bird. —war'bler, *n.* any of various songbirds.

ward (wôrd) *v.t.* (with *off*) fend off; turn aside; repel. —*n.* 1, the act of keeping guard. 2, one under guardianship, esp. a minor. 3, a political division of a city. 4, one of the sections of a hospital. 5, a curved ridge of metal inside a lock; a notch on a key that fits it. —ward heeler (*Colloq.*) a minor political worker.

-ward (wərd) *suf.* forming adjectives and adverbs: in the direction of. Also, -wards (wərdz) *suf.* forming adverbs.

ward'en (wôr'dən) *n.* 1, a guard or guardian. 2, the chief officer of a prison. 3, the title of various chief officers. 4, a kind of pear.

ward'er (wôr'dər) *n.* a keeper; a guard.

ward'robe" (wôrd'rōb") *n.* 1, a cabinet for clothes. 2, one's supply of clothing.

ward'room" (wôrd'room") *n.* the quarters of officers, except the captain, on a war vessel.

ward'ship" *n.* custody.

ware (wār) *n.* 1, (usually *pl.*) articles of merchandise. 2, a term used in compound, denoting articles, as *chinaware.*

ware'house" *n.* a place for storage.

war'fare" *n.* the waging of war.

war'head" *n.* a compartment containing an explosive charge, at the forward part of a torpedo or other missile.

war'like" *adj.* disposed to make war.

warm (wôrm) *adj.* 1, having a moderate degree of heat; communicating or causing heat. 2, having the sensation of heat. 3, hearty; earnest; affectionate; intimate. 4, new; fresh. 5, close, in a guessing game. —*v.t. & i.* make or become warm. —warm'ness, *n.*

warm'blood"ed *adj.* 1, denoting animals, esp. mammals, with warm blood. 2, ardent; impulsive. —warm'blood"ed·ness, *n.*

warm'heart"ed *adj.* kindly; generous; sympathetic. —warm'heart"ed·ness, *n.*

war'mong"er (-mong'gər) *n.* one who incites to warfare.

warmth (wôrmth) *n.* warmness; ardor.

warn (wôrn) *v.t.* 1, put on guard; caution. 2, advise; notify.

warn'ing *n.* 1, a caution; admonition. 2, (*Brit.*) notice of dis. missal or resignation from a job. —*adj.* that warns.

warp (wôrp) *v.t.* 1, turn or twist out of shape; distort; pervert. 2, pull (a ship) with a rope. 3, twist (the wings of an airplane) to maintain balance. —*v.i.* 1, be twisted out of proper shape. 2, swerve. —*n.* 1, a twist; distortion. 2, the lengthwise threads on a loom.

war'path" *n.* among Amer. Indians, a warring campaign. —on the warpath, bellicose; wrathful.

war'plane" *n.* a plane designed for fighting.

war'rant (wor'ənt) *n.* 1, that which attests or proves; a guaranty. 2, sanction; justification. 3, (*Law*) a writ authorizing an arrest, search, or seizure. —*v.t.* 1, guarantee; indemnify. 2, authorize; justify. 3, affirm. —war'ran·tor, *n.* —warrant officer, an Army or Navy officer below commissioned but above noncommissioned rank.

war'ran·ty (wor'ən-tė) *n.* a guarantee; assurance.

war'ren (wor'ən) *n.* 1, a shelter or pen for rabbits or game. 2, any crowded section.

war'rior (wôr'yər) *n.* a fighting man.

war'ship' *n.* a ship designed for fighting.

wart (wôrt) *n.* a small, hard growth on the skin. —**wart'y,** *adj.*

wart'hog' *n.* a large, ugly, African wild swine.

war'y (wâr'ė) *adj.* cautious of danger; alert. —**war'i·ness,** *n.*

was (wuz) *v.* pret. of *be.* —**was'n't** (wuz'ənt) contraction of *was not.*

wash (wosh) *v.t.* 1, cleanse in or with a liquid, esp. water. 2, flow over or against; wet. 3, (with *away*) remove; absolve. 4, sweep. 5, process by immersing in a liquid. —*v.i.* 1, cleanse oneself, etc., in or with water. 2, stand cleansing by water without injury. 3, flow. —*n.* 1, a cleansing by water; articles to be cleansed. 2, the flow, sweep, or sound of a body of water. 3, the wake of a vessel. 4, waste articles or liquid; alluvia. 5, a liquid for washing. 6, a body of water. —**wash'a·ble,** *adj.* that can safely be washed in water.

wash'board' *n.* a corrugated board for scrubbing clothes.

wash'bowl' *n.* a basin.

wash'cloth' *n.* a cloth for use in washing oneself. Also, **wash'rag'**.

washed out 1, faded. 2, fatigued. 3, expelled after failure.

washed up (*Colloq.*) spent; finished.

wash'er (-ər) *n.* 1, one who or that which washes; a washing machine. 2, a small metal gasket.

wash'er·wom''an *n.* [*pl.* -wom''en] a laundress.

wash'ing *n.* clothes to be washed.

wash'out' *n.* 1, a place where soil or a foundation has been eroded. 2, (*Slang*) a failure.

wash'rag' *n.* washcloth.

wash'room' *n.* a lavatory and toilet.

wash'stand' *n.* a cabinet or fixture for holding a washbowl.

wash'tub' *n.* a tub for washing clothes.

wash'wom''an *n.* [*pl.* -wom''en] a laundress.

wasp (wosp) *n.* an insect allied to the bee.

wasp'ish *adj.* 1, peevish. 2, slender-waisted. —**wasp'ish·ness,** *n.*

was'sail (wos'əl) *n.* 1, a toast. 2, a drink of spiced ale. 3, a drinking party. —*v.i.* carouse.

waste (wāst) *adj.* 1, desolate; uninhabited; untilled; unproductive. 2, rejected as unfit for use; unused. —*v.t.* 1, devastate; ruin. 2, consume or wear away the strength and substance of. 3, squander; throw away. —*v.i.* decay or diminish in strength, substance, or value; wear or pine away. —*n.* 1, a desolate place or region. 2, gradual loss or decay. 3, broken, spoiled, useless, or superfluous material; refuse. 4, useless expenditure. 5, a drain pipe. —**wast'age,** *n.*

waste'bas''ket *n.* a receptacle for unwanted papers.

waste'ful (-fəl) *adj.* needlessly spending or spent. —**waste'ful·ness,** *n.*

wast'rel (wās'trəl) *n.* a spendthrift; a profligate.

watch (woch) *v.i.* 1, be attentive, circumspect, or closely observant. 2, keep vigil. 3, keep guard. 4, wait. —*v.t.* 1, look at attentively. 2, take care of; tend; guard. —*n.* 1, a keeping awake for the purpose of attending, guarding, or preserving; vigil. 2, close, constant observation; supervision. 3, a force on duty, esp. for guarding; a sentinel. 4, a period of duty, on a ship, four hours. 5, a timepiece carried in the pocket or worn on the wrist.

watch'dog' *n.* 1, a dog trained to bark a warning. 2, a guardian.

watch'ful (-fəl) *adj.* alert. —**watch'ful·ness,** *n.*

watch'man (-mən) *n.* [*pl.* -men] a guard.

watch'tow''er *n.* a tower in which to post a lookout.

watch'word' *n.* 1, a secret password. 2, a slogan; a rallying cry.

wa'ter (wot'ər, wä'-) *n.* 1, the transparent, odorless, tasteless fluid, H_2O, that falls in rain. 2, a body of water; (*pl.*) a flood. 3, any liquid secretion of an animal body. 4, transparency denoting the fine properties of a precious stone. —*v.t.* 1, moisten; irrigate. 2, supply with water. 3, dilute; assign unjustified value to (a stock). 4, produce a gleaming, wavy pattern upon (a fabric). —*v.i.* 1, give off or fill up with liquid. 2, get or take in water.

water buffalo a carabao.

water closet 1, a device, with a seat, for disposing of excrement. 2, a toilet room.

water color 1, a paint soluble in water. 2, a picture painted with such paint.

wa'ter·course' *n.* a stream or river, or its bed.

wa'ter·cress' *n.* a salad herb.

wa'ter·fall' *n.* a cascade; a cataract.

wa'ter·front" *n.* docks etc. at the water's edge.

wa'ter·glass" *n.* a substance that forms a protective coating.

water ice a frozen desert like ice cream, made without milk.

watering place a spa.

watering pot a can with a perforated spout, for spraying water on flowers.

water lily a plant with floating leaves and showy flowers, that grows in water.

wa'ter·line" *n.* the line at which a floating body is out of the water.

wa'ter·logged" (-lăgd") *adj.* saturated so as to sink in water.

Wa'ter·loo *n.* a final defeat.

wa'ter·mark" *n.* a design impressed in paper during its manufacture.

wa'ter·mel"on *n.* a large edible melon.

water polo a ball game played by swimmers.

water power power derived from a flow or fall of water.

wa'ter·proof" *adj.* impervious or resistant to water.

water rat an aquatic rodent, as the muskrat.

wa'ter·shed" *n.* **1,** a ridge off which water flows or drains. **2,** the area drained by a river.

wa'ter·side" *n.* a shore or bank.

wa'ter·spout" *n.* a gyrating column of rising moisture, caused by a whirlwind at sea.

water table the level below which the soil is saturated with water.

wa'ter·tight" *adj.* **1,** impenetrable by water. **2,** that cannot be evaded or controverted.

wa'ter·way" *n.* a course navigable by water.

water wheel a wheel turned by water power.

water wings inflated bags to support a person in water.

wa'ter·works" *n.* a system for supplying water to a city.

wa'ter·y (-ė) *adj.* **1,** pert. to or consisting of water; wet; dripping. **2,** thin, as a liquid. —**wa'ter·i·ness,** *n.*

watt (wot) *n.* a unit of electrical activity or power. —**watt'age,** *n.*

wat'tle (wot'ǝl) *n.* **1,** a framework of poles. **2,** a rod; a twig. **3,** a fleshy lobe hanging from the throat or firmness of a bird or the mouth of a fish. —*v.t.* interweave.

wave (wāv) *v.i.* **1,** move up and down or to and fro; undulate; flutter. **2,** have a curved form or direction. **3,** give a signal by waving the hands. —*v.t.* **1,** move to and fro; brandish. **2,** shape in undulations or curves. —*n.* **1,** a ridge in the surface of a liquid. **2,** (*pl.*) the sea. **3,** an influx of anything. **4,** a gesture or signal made by moving the hand. **5,** a curl in the hair. **6,** (*cap.*) a woman serving in the U. S. Navy. —**wave length,** the distance between two particles in the same phase of a wave: now applied chiefly to the band assigned to a radio transmitting station.

wave'let *n.* a ripple.

wa'ver (wā'vǝr) *v.i.* **1,** sway; falter. **2,** be irresolute; vacillate. —*n.* a wavering motion.

wav'y (wāv'ė) *adj.* **1,** abounding in waves. **2,** curly. —**wav'i·ness,** *n.*

wax (waks) *v.i.* increase in size; grow, specif. of the moon. —*n.* a thick, sticky substance secreted by bees; any similar oily substance. —**wax'works",** *n.* an exhibit of forms modeled in wax.

wax'en (wak'sǝn) *adj.* **1,** yellowish, as wax. **2,** of the consistency of wax.

wax'wing" *n.* a passerine bird.

wax'y (-ė) *adj.* like wax. —**wax'i·ness,** *n.*

way (wā) *n.* **1,** a course leading from one place to another; a road, passage, route, etc. **2,** room for passage. **3,** a journey. **4,** distance. **5,** direction. **6,** a respect; a particular. **7,** condition or state. **8,** a plan; mode; method. **9,** progress; headway. **10,** (*pl.*) the timbers on which a ship is built and launched. —**way station,** a minor railroad station.

way'far"er *n.* a traveler, esp. on foot.

way'lay" *v.t.* ambush.

way'side" *n.* the side of a road; a secluded place.

way'ward" (-wǝrd) *adj.* **1,** rebellious; perverse. **2,** irregular; accidental. —**way'ward·ness,** *n.*

we (wē) *pron. pl.* of I (*poss.* our, ours; *obj.* us) the first person, nominative, pl.; used as sing. by monarchs and editors.

weak (wēk) *adj.* **1,** lacking physical strength or endurance. **2,** lacking moral or mental strength or firmness. **3,** inadequate or unsatisfactory; faulty. **4,** (*Com.*) tending downward in price. —**weak'ly,** *adj.* & *adv.* —**weak'ness,** *n.*

weak'en (-ǝn) *v.t.* & *i.* make or become weaker.

weak'fish" *n.* an edible sea fish.

weak-'kneed" *adj.* irresolute; easily controlled.

weak′ling n. a weak person.

wealth (welth) n. 1, valuable and large material possessions; riches. 2, profusion; abundance. 3, all property. —**wealth′i·ness,** n. —**wealth′y,** adj.

wean (wēn) v.t. 1, accustom (a child or young animal) to food other than mother's milk. 2, alienate.

weap′on (wep′ən) n. any instrument used in fighting.

wear (wâr) v.t. [wore (wōr), worn (wôrn), **wear′ing**] 1, carry or bear on the body, as clothing. 2, consume or deteriorate by friction or frequent use. 3, make weary. 4, bear; show. —v.i. 1, last or hold out. 2, waste; diminish. —n. 1, use; deterioration. 2, garments. —**wear′a·ble,** adj. —**wear′ing,** adj. tiring.

wea′ry (wir′ē) adj. 1, exhausted either physically or mentally; tired. 2, discontented. 3, causing fatigue. —v.t. & i. tire. —**wea′ri·ness,** n. —**wea′ri·some,** adj. tiresome.

wea′sel (wē′zəl) n. a small carnivorous mammal. **weasel words,** evasive language.

weath′er (weth′-ər) n. the state of the atmosphere in regard to heat, cold, wetness, dryness, humidity, storm, etc. —v.t. 1, bear up against and survive. 2, condition by exposure. 3, (Naut.) sail to windward of. —adj. (Naut.) windward.

Weasel

weath′er·beat″en adj. marked or hardened by exposure.

weath′er·board″ n. clapboard.

weath′er·cock″ n. a figure of a bird, on top of a weather vane.

weath′er·proof″ adj. resistant to rain, wind, etc.

weather strip a strip to seal a crack around a window, etc.

weather vane a device that turns with the wind, to show its direction.

weave (wēv) v.t. [wove (wōv), wo′ven, weav′ing] 1, form by interlacing flexible parts, as threads; produce (a fabric) on a loom. 2, contrive or construct. —v.i. 1, become interlaced. 2, wind in and out. —n. a pattern produced by weaving.

web n. 1, that which is woven. 2, a trap, plot, or scheme. 3, the membrane of skin connecting the toes of a bird or animal, as a duck. —**webbed,** adj. —**web′bing,** n. —**web′foot″ed,** adj.

wed v.t. & i. [**wed′ded** or **wed,** **wed′ding**] take for husband or wife; marry; unite closely.

wed′ding (wed′ing) n. an occasion or anniversary of marriage.

wedge (wej) n. 1, a triangular-shaped solid, used to separate, split, or raise objects. 2, an act that serves to introduce or divide. —v.t. 1, use a wedge on. 2, compress closely. —v.i. force one's way.

wedg′ie (wej′ē) n. a woman's shoe giving elevation as with a high heel but with the sole almost flat.

wed′lock″ n. matrimony.

Wednes′day (wenz′dē) n. the fourth day of the week.

wee (wē) adj. [we′er, we′est] tiny.

weed (wēd) n. 1, a useless or characteristically unwanted plant. 2, (Colloq.) tobacco. 3, (pl.) a widow's mourning attire. —v.t. free from obnoxious plants. —v.i. root up weeds. —**weed out,** remove weeds or other undesirable elements (from).

weed′y (-ē) adj. 1, like a weed; lanky. 2, being or like widow's weeds. 3, abounding in weeds. —**weed′i·ness,** n.

week (wēk) n. 1, a period of seven consecutive days. 2, the working days of the week. —**week′day″,** n. any day but Sunday. —**week end,** the period from the end of the working week through Sunday. —**week′ly,** adj. & adv. occurring once each week.

weep (wēp) v.i. [pret. & p.p. wept] 1, shed tears; lament. 2, drip; give out moisture. 3, droop. —v.t. shed, as tears. —**weep′ing,** adj. drooping, as the branches of a tree: as, weeping willow.

wee′vil (wē′vəl) n. any of various beetles.

weft n. the woof.

weigh (wā) v.t. 1, determine the heaviness of. 2, consider; ponder. 3, (Naut.) raise or lift up. 4, (with down) burden; oppress. —v.i. have weight or influence.

weight (wāt) n. 1, the downward force of a body; heaviness. 2, mass. 3, something used on account of its heaviness. 4, a system of units for expressing the heaviness of bodies. 5, pressure; care; burden. 6, importance; influence. —v.t. 1, add to the heaviness of. 2, adjust the proportions of.

weight′y (-ē) adj. 1, momentous; influential. 2, burdensome. —**weight′i·ness,** n.

weird (wird) adj. unearthly; uncanny. —**weird′ness,** n. —**Weird Sisters,** the Fates.

welch v.i. welsh.

wel′come (wel′kəm) adj. gladly received or permitted. —n. a kindly, warm greeting; hospitable reception. —v.t. receive gladly.

weld v.t. unite (pieces of metal); join. —n. a solid union; a welt where union was made.

wel'fare" (wel'fār") *n.* **1,** prosperous or healthy condition. **2,** charity.

wel'kin *n.* (*Archaic*) the sky; the firmament.

well (wel) *n.* **1,** an excavation in the ground as a source of water, oil, gas, etc.; a spring. **2,** any source of origin or supply; a fount. **3,** a dangerous depression; a whirlpool. —*v.i.* issue; pour forth. —*adv.* [bet'ter, best] **1,** in a good, right, or worthy manner; abundantly. **2,** favorably. **3,** conveniently. —*adj.* in good health. —as well (as), also.

well-"bal'anced *adj.* **1,** properly adjusted or proportioned. **2,** sensible.

well-"be'ing *n.* good health; welfare.

well"born' *adj.* of gentle or noble birth.

well"bred' *adj.* having good manners.

well-"de-fined' *adj.* leaving no room for doubt; clear.

well-"dis-posed' *adj.* favorable.

well-"fed' *adj.* prosperous-looking.

well'head' *n.* a source.

well-"heeled' *adj.* wealthy.

well-"in-formed' *adj.* abreast of current events.

well-"mean'ing *adj.* having good intentions. —**well-"meant'**, *adj.*

well-"nigh' *adv.* very nearly.

well-"off' *adj.* wealthy or fortunate.

well-"read' (-red') *adj.* having read many books; educated.

well-"round'ed *adj.* complete.

well'spring" *n.* a constant source.

well-"to-do' *adj.* prosperous; wealthy.

welsh *v.i.* fail to pay a gambling loss. Also, **welch.**

Welsh *adj.* & *n.* of or pert. to Wales, its people, language, etc. —**Welsh'man,** *n.*

welt *n.* **1,** a strip of material, esp. leather, standing out. **2,** a wale.

wel'ter (wel'tər) *v.i.* **1,** wallow (in something). **2,** roll or toss; be tossed. —*n.* **1,** rolling or wallowing motion. **2,** turmoil; ferment.

wel'ter-weight" (wel'tər-wāt") *n.* a boxer weighing 136 to 147 pounds.

wen *n.* a small, benign tumor.

wench *n.* a girl or young woman.

wend *v.i.* proceed; go. —*v.t.* direct (one's way or course).

went *v.* pret. of *go.*

wept *v.* pret. & p.p. of *weep.*

were (wēr) *v.* pret. & subjunctive of *be.*

were'wolf" (wēr'wûlf") *n.* [*pl.* -wolves] in folklore, a human being turned into a wolf.

west *n.* **1,** the direction lying on the left hand when one faces the north; the point where the sun sets at the equinox. **2,** any place to the west; (*cap.*) Europe and the Americas. —*adj.* & *adv.* toward the sunset. —**west'er-ly,** *adj.* toward the west. —**west'ward,** *adj.*

west'ern (wes'tərn) *adj.* pert. to the west. —*n.* (*Colloq.*) a story or motion picture depicting cowboy life in the western U.S. —**west'ern-er,** *n.* —**west'ern-most",** *adj.*

wet *adj.* [wet'ter, -test] **1,** covered with or permeated by a moist or fluid substance. **2,** rainy. **3,** (*Colloq.*) opposed to Prohibition. —*n.* **1,** moisture, specif. rain. **2,** a person opposed to Prohibition. —*v.t.* & *i.* [wet'ted, -ting] drench with water or other fluid; urinate. —**wet'ness,** *n.* —wet blanket (*Slang*) a depressing person. —wet nurse, a woman employed to suckle the infant of another.

wet'back" *n.* a person who enters the U.S. illegally, usually from Mexico, to take a temporary job.

whack (hwak) *v.t.* & *i.* strike a smart resounding blow. —*n.* **1,** a heavy blow. **2,** (*Colloq.*) an attempt. —**whack'ing,** *adj.* (*Slang*) enormous.

whale (hwāl) *n.* **1,** any of an order of marine mammals; the largest known animals. **2,** (*Colloq.*) anything huge. —*v.i.* pursue the business of whale fishing. —*v.t.* (*Colloq.*) thrash; castigate.

Whale

whale'boat" *n.* a large rowboat originally used by whale fishermen.

whale'bone" *n.* baleen; a flexible strip of it, used to stiffen a corset.

whal'er (hwāl'ər) *n.* a whaling ship.

wharf (wôrf) *n.* [*pl.* wharves (wôrvz)] a mooring platform for ships; a dock; a pier. —**wharf'age,** *n.*

what (hwot) *pron. sing.* & *pl.* **1,** which thing or things. **2,** that which. —*adj.* **1,** (*interrogative*) which. **2,** any; whatever. **3,** (*exclamatory*) how extraordinary!; how large! **4,** in part; partly. —*conj.* but that.

what'ev'er *pron.* **1,** anything which; all that. **2,** no matter what. —*adj.* **1,** any or all that. **2,** of any kind.

what'not" *n.* **1,** a stand to display small ornaments. **2,** anything indiscriminately.

what'so·ev"er *adj. & pron.* of whatever nature or kind.

wheat (hwēt) *n.* any of various cereal plants whose grain is ground into flour and makes bread. —**wheat'-en,** *adj.* of wheat.

whee'dle (hwē'dəl) *v.t. & i.* cajole; gain by flattery; coax.

wheel (hwēl) *n.* **1,** a circular frame or disk capable of turning on an axis. **2,** a bicycle. **3,** a firework that revolves while burning. **4,** the office of pilot or driver. **5,** a turning maneuver; a circular course. **6,** (*pl.*) machinery. **7,** (*Slang*) an important person. —*v.t.* cause to turn; cause to move on or as on wheels. —*v.i.* **1,** turn; rotate. **2,** move on wheels or on a bicycle.

wheel'bar"row *n.* a vehicle for pushing small loads.

wheel'base" *n.* the distance between centers of axles on a vehicle.

wheel chair a conveyance for an invalid.

wheeled *adj.* having (such, or so many) wheels.

wheel horse 1, the horse at the pivot of a team. **2,** an essential worker.

wheel housing the space reserved from an automobile seat or body to give play to the wheels.

wheel'wright" *n.* a maker of wheels.

wheeze (hwēz) *v.i.* breathe with difficulty and audibly. —*n.* **1,** the sound of such a breath. **2,** a joke.

whelk (hwelk) *n.* an edible, spiral-shelled mollusk.

whelp (hwelp) *n.* the young of certain animals, as the dog. —*v.i. & t.* bring forth young.

when (hwen) *adv.* **1,** at what or which time. —*conj.* **1,** as soon as. **2,** at which time. —*n.* a time specified.

whence (hwens) *adv.* from that or which place.

when"ev'er *adv. & conj.* at whatever time.

where (hwâr) *adv.* **1,** at or in what place. **2,** to which place? whither? —*conj.* **1,** at, in, or to the place in which. **2,** whereas. **3,** whence.

where'a·bouts" *n.* location.

where·as' *conj.* this being the case.

where·at' *adv.* at which.

where'by" *adv.* for which reason; how.

where'fore" *adv. & conj.* **1,** why? **2,** consequently. —*n.* a reason.

where·in' *adv.* in which.

where"of' *conj.* of what, which, or whom.

where'up·on" *adv.* at which juncture.

wher·ev'er *conj.* in, at, or to whatever place. Also, **where"so·ev'er.**

where·with' *adv.* with which.

where'with·al" *n.* the means; money.

wher'ry (hwer'ē) *n.* a light boat.

whet (hwet) *v.t.* [**whet'ted, -ting**] **1,** sharpen. **2,** excite.

wheth'er (hwet͟h'ər) *conj.* **1,** introducing the first of two or more alternatives, the second being introduced by *or.* **2,** introducing a single alternative, the other being implied.

whet'stone" *n.* a stone for sharpening knives, etc.

whey (hwā) *n.* the watery part of milk. —**whey'ey** (hwā'ē) *adj.*

which (hwich) *pron.* **1,** (*interrogative*) what one? (of several). **2,** (*relative*) the one that. **3,** (*relative*) that (with additional information). —*adj.* indicating one of a number of known or specified things.

which·ev'er *pron. & adj.* any one; Also, **which"so·ev'er.**

whiff (hwif) *n.* a puff; a slight current or gust of air, smoke, etc. —*v.i. & t.* blow; puff.

whif'fle-tree" (hwif'əl-trē") *n.* a crossbar to which a horse's harness is attached.

Whig (hwig) *n.* (*Hist.*) a member of: **1,** an English political party, later known as Liberals. **2,** a 19th-century U.S. political party.

while (hwīl) *n.* a space of time, esp. a short time. —*conj.* [also, **whilst**] **1,** during or in the time that; as long as. **2,** though; whereas.

whim (hwim) *n.* a fancy; a capricious desire.

whim'per (hwim'pər) *v.i. & t.* cry with a low, whining voice; utter plaintively. —*n.* a low, peevish cry.

whim'si·cal (hwim'zi-kəl) *adj.* quaintly humorous; odd. —**whim"-si·cal'i·ty, whim'si·cal·ness,** *n.*

whim'sy (hwim'zē) *n.* a fanciful notion.

whine (hwīn) *v.i. & t.* **1,** utter a plaintive, prolonged nasal sound. **2,** complain in a feeble way. —*n.* a whining utterance or tone.

whin'ny (hwin'ē) *n.* the cry of a horse; a low or gentle neigh. —*v.i.* utter this sound.

whip (hwip) *v.t.* [**whipped, whip'ping**] **1,** punish with a scourge, rod, etc.; flog; beat. **2,** move or pull with a sudden quick motion; jerk; snatch. **3,** overlay or wrap with cord. **4,**

bring or keep together. **5**, sew with an over-and-over stitch. **6**, beat into a froth. —*v.i.* **1**, move suddenly and nimbly; thrash around. **2**, in fishing, cast. —*n.* **1**, an instrument for lashing; a scourge. **2**, a driver. **3**, a swishing or whipping motion. **4**, a conveyance for hoisting. **5**, a preparation of beaten eggs, cream, etc. **6**, a party disciplinarian in a legislature. —**whip hand**, control. —**whipping boy**, a scapegoat.

whip′cord″ *n.* a ribbed fabric.

whip′lash″ *n.* the flexible striking end of a whip.

whip′per·snap″per (hwip′ər-snap″ər) *n.* an insignificant person.

whip′pet (hwip′it) *n.* **1**, a kind of dog, a cross between a greyhound and a terrier. **2**, something slight and speedy; a small, fast tank.

whip′ple·tree″ (hwip′əl-trē″) *n.* a crossbar at the front of a horse-drawn vehicle.

whip′poor·will″ (hwip′ər-wil″) *n.* an Amer. nocturnal bird; its cry.

whip′saw″ *n.* a narrow saw in a frame. —*v.t.* (*Slang*) defeat doubly.

whir (hwėr) *v.i.* [**whirred, whir′ring**] fly, dart, revolve, or move quickly with a buzzing sound. —*n.* a buzzing sound.

whirl (hwėrl) *v.t.* **1**, cause to revolve rapidly; rotate. **2**, carry swiftly away. —*v.i.* **1**, revolve swiftly. **2**, reel. —*n.* **1**, a spinning movement or sensation. **2**, a round of parties, events, etc.

whirl′i·gig (hwėrl′ə-gig) *n.* something that revolves.

whirl′pool″ *n.* a circular eddy in a body of water.

whirl′wind″ *n.* **1**, a destructive wind moving in a vortical path. **2**, a rushing force.

whisk (hwisk) *v.t.* **1**, sweep or brush with a light, rapid motion. **2**, move quickly. —*v.i.* move nimbly and swiftly. —*n.* **1**, a small brush; *whiskbroom.* **2**, a rapid, light, sweeping motion.

whisk′er (hwisk′ər) *n.* a hair on the face, esp. (*pl.*) those on a man's face. —**whisk′ered**, *adj.*

whis′key (hwis′kē) *n.* a strong alcoholic liquor, made chiefly from grain. Also, **whis′ky.**

whis′per (hwis′pər) *v.i.* **1**, speak softly with the breath, without vibration of the vocal cords. **2**, gossip; plot. **3**, make a low rustling sound. —*v.t.* say under the breath; say secretly. —*n.* **1**, a whispering voice or utterance. **2**, a hint or insinuation. **3**, a low, rustling sound.

whist (hwist) *n.* a game of cards, the forerunner of bridge. —*interj.* hush!

whis′tle (hwis′əl) *v.i.* **1**, make shrill or musical sound by forcing the breath through pursed lips or air through a pipe. **2**, move with a whizzing sound. **3**, (*Colloq.*) desire in vain. —*v.t.* **1**, sound by whistling. **2**, signal to, by whistling. —*n.* **1**, a whistling sound; a device for producing it. **2**, (*Colloq.*) the throat. —**whis′tler**, *n.*

whit (hwit) *n.* a little; a jot.

white (hwīt) *adj.* **1**, of the color of pure snow. **2**, of a light color; gray. **3**, fair-skinned. **4**, pale. **5**, pure. **6**, blank; unprinted. **7**, (*Colloq.*) sportsmanlike; honorable. —*n.* a white color; something of this color, as: the albumen of an egg; a member of the Caucasian race; a part of the eyeball. —*v.t.* make white. —**white′ness**, *n.* —**whit′ish**, *adj.*

white′cap″ *n.* a wave.

white-′col″lar *adj.* pert. to clerical or professional workers.

white elephant an embarrassing possession.

whit′en (hwīt′ən) *v.t. & i.* make or become whiter.

white feather a symbol of cowardice.

white flag a symbol of surrender or peaceful intent.

white heat intense heat, excitement, etc. —**white-′hot″**, *adj.*

white lead lead carbonate, used in paints; a paint containing it.

white lie a harmless falsehood.

white-′liv″ered *adj.* cowardly.

white plague tuberculosis.

white slave a woman forced into prostitution.

white′wash″ *v.t.* **1**, paint with whitewash. **2**, exculpate; vindicate (one who is guilty). **3**, (*Colloq.*) defeat, when the loser fails to score. —*n.* **1**, a white paint, usually of quicklime and water. **2**, vindication. **3**, (*Colloq.*) a victory over a scoreless opponent.

whith′er (hwith′ər) *adv.* wherever: to which place.

whit′ing (hwīt′ing) *n.* any of various edible fish.

Whit′sun·tide″ *n.* the 8th week after Easter, beginning with *Whitsunday.* —**Whit′sun**, *adj.*

whit′tle (hwit′əl) *v.t. & i.* cut or form with a knife; pare. —**whit′tler**, *n.*

whiz *v.i.* [**whizzed, whiz′zing**] **1**, make a humming or hissing sound. **2**, move rapidly; rush. —*n.* **1**, a sound made by rapid motion through the air. **2**, (*Slang*) someone very capable. —**whiz′zer**, *n.*

who (hoo) *pron. sing. & pl.* [*poss.* whose (hooz) *obj.* whom (hoom)] 1, what or which person or persons? 2, that person; those persons.

whoa (hwō) *interj.* stop!

who·dun'it (hoo-dun'it) *n.* (*Slang*) a detective story or motion picture.

who·ev'er *pron.* no matter who·ever.

whole (hōl) *adj.* 1, not broken or injured; intact; unimpaired. 2, entire; complete. 3, having full blood relationship. —*n.* 1, the complete thing; the total. 2, an organic unity. —**whole hog** (*Slang*) all the way. —**whole'ness**, *n.* —**whol'ly**, *adv.*

whole'heart"ed *adj.* sincere; enthusiastic. —**whole'heart"ed·ness**, *n.*

whole'sale" (hōl'sāl") *n.* sale of goods in quantity to retailers. —*adj.* 1, pert. to trade with dealers. 2, in great quantities; extensive; indiscriminate. —*v.t.* sell by wholesale. —**whole'sal"er**, *n.*

whole'some (hōl'səm) *adj.* 1, contributing to health of body, mind, or character. 2, healthy or sound-looking. —**whole'some·ness** *n.*

whom (hoom) *pron.* objective of *who.*

whoop (hwoop) *v.i.* 1, shout; halloo; hoot. 2, gasp after coughing, as in the disease *whooping cough.* —*n.* 1, a loud call or shout. 2, a gasp.

whoo'pee (hwoo'pē) *n.* (*Slang*) hilarity.

whoops (hwoops) *interj.* expressing enthusiasm.

whop'per (hwop'ər) *n.* (*Colloq.*) anything unusually large, esp. a lie. —**whop'ping**, *adj.* (*Colloq.*) very large.

whore (hōr) *n.* an unchaste woman; a prostitute. —**whor'ish**, *adj.*

whorl (hwêrl) *n.* a spiral or coil-shaped part or pattern.

whose (hooz) *pron.* poss. of *who* or *which.*

why (hwī) *adv.* 1, used interrogatively, for what cause, reason, or purpose? 2, on account of which. —*n.* the reason or cause. —*interj.* used as an expletive.

wick (wik) *n.* a strip or cord that draws up the fuel that burns in a lamp or candle.

wick'ed (wik'id) *adj.* 1, evil; sinful. 2, harmful; pernicious. 3, difficult; disagreeable. 4, (*Colloq.*) mischievous. —**wick'ed·ness**, *n.*

wick'er (wik'ər) *n. & adj.* a small pliant twig. —**wick'er·work"**, *n.* anything made of wicker.

wick'et (wik'it) *n.* 1, a small gate or window. 2, in croquet, an arch. 3, in cricket, one of the goals.

wide (wīd) *adj.* 1, having considerable extension from side to side; broad. 2, having a specified width. 3, vast; spacious. 4, embracing many subjects. 5, spread apart; open. 6, deviating or far from a point. —*adv.* 1, a long way; afar. 2, extensively; far apart. 3, astray. —**wide'ness**, *n.*

wide-'a·wake' *adj.* fully awake.

wide-'eyed" (īd) *adj. & adv.* having the eyes widely open, as with astonishment.

wid'en (wīd'ən) *v.t. & i.* make or become wider.

wide'spread" *adj.* covering a great area, or known to many persons.

widg'eon (wij'ən) *n.* a duck, the baldpate. Also, **wi'geon**.

wid'ow (wid'ō) *n.* 1, a woman who has not remarried since the death of her husband. 2, in some card games, additional cards dealt to the table. —*v.t.* bereave of a spouse. —**wid'ow·er**, *n. masc.* —**wid'ow·hood"**, *n.*

width *n.* linear extent from side to side.

wield (wēld) *v.t.* 1, use or exert (power, etc.) 2, handle; brandish.

wie'ner (wē'nər) *n.* a kind of small sausage. Also, **wie'ner·wurst"**.

wife (wīf) *n.* [*pl.* wives (wīvz)] a woman wedded to a man; a man's spouse. —**wife'hood**, *n.* —**wife'ly**, *adj.* befitting a wife.

wig *n.* an artificial covering of hair for the head. —**wigged**, *adj.*

wig'gle (wig'əl) *v.t. & i.* wobble; wriggle. —*n.* —**wig'gly**, *adj.*

wight (wīt) *n.* (*Archaic*) a person.

wig'wag" *v.i. & t.* [**wig'wagged"**, -**wag"ging**] 1, move or cause to move to and fro. 2, signal by waving flags. —*n.* a system of signaling with two flags.

wig'wam (wig'wom) *n.* the hut of a No. Amer. Indian.

Wigwag

wild (wīld) *adj.* 1, living or growing in a natural state; not domesticated; not cultivated. 2, stormy; violent. 3, savage; ferocious. 4, extravagant; fantastic. 5, reckless; rash. 6, wide of the mark. 7, disorderly; boisterous. 8, (*Colloq.*) ardent; enthusiastic. —*n.* (often *pl.*) an uninhabited or uncultivated region. —wild fowl, ducks, geese, etc. —wild'ness, n.

wild'cat" (wīld'kat") n. 1, any of various small, untamed cats, as the lynx. 2, a quick-tempered person. —adj. 1, speculative; unsound. 2, of a strike, unsanctioned. —v.t. [-cat"ted, -ting] drill wells experimentally for oil or gas.

wil'der·ness (wil'dər-nəs) n. an uninhabited tract of land; a desert.

wild'fire" n. a spreading, uncontrollable fire.

wile (wīl) n. a sly trick; a stratagem. —v.t. 1, lure; entice. 2, (with away) pass (time) pleasantly. —wil'y, adj.

will (wil) n. 1, the faculty of conscious and deliberate action; volition. 2, desire; choice; pleasure. 3, purpose; determination. 4, a legal document to dispose of property after the owner's death. —aux. v. [pret. would] 1, expressing the future: am, is, are, etc. about to, sure to; determined to, etc. 2, expressing desire; wish, want. 3, is able to; can. —v.t. [pret. & p.p. willed] 1, determine; decide. 2, bequeath. 3, influence.

will'ful (-fəl) adj. 1, deliberate; intentional. 2, obstinate; headstrong. Also, wil'ful. —will'ful·ness, n.

will'ing adj. 1, favorably disposed; amenable. 2, voluntary. 3, eager to serve or comply. —will'ing·ness, n.

will-o'-the-wisp' (wil'ə-thə-wisp') n. 1, a light (from burning gas) that flits over marshes. 2, an elusive or misleading hope.

wil'low (wil'ō) n. 1, any of a genus of trees or shrubs with slender flexible twigs, valuable for wickerwork; its wood. 2, in baseball and cricket, the bat. —wil'low·y, adj. supple.

wil'ly-nil'ly (wil'ē-nil'ē) adv. regardless of one's wishes.

wilt v.i. & t. 1, become or make limp or drooping. 2, weaken.

Wil'ton (wil'tən) a heavy carpet, orig. made at Wilton, Eng.

wim'ple (wim'pəl) n. a woman's head covering, as worn by nuns.

win v.t. [won (wun), win'ning] 1, acquire by effort; gain. 2, be victorious in. 3, gain the favor of. 4, prevail on; induce. 5, reach; attain. —v.i. gain one's end; be successful or victorious. —n. (Colloq.) a victory. —win'ner, n.

wince (wins) v.i. shrink, as in pain or from a blow; start back. —n. a flinch.

winch n. hoisting machine.

wind n. 1, a natural current of air. 2, air artificially put in motion. 3, breath; the power of respiration. 4, idle talk; bombast. 5, scent. 6, flatulence. 7, (pl.) wind instruments. —v.t. put out of breath. —wind'ed, adj. out of breath. —wind instrument, any musical instrument sounded by air.

wind (wīnd) v.t. [wound (wownd), wind'ing] 1, go in a devious course; twist. 2, entwine itself round something. 3, (Colloq.) (with up) come to a conclusion; end. —v.i. 1, turn; coil; twist. 2, entwine; enfold. 3, insinuate; worm. 4, (Colloq.) (with up) bring to a conclusion. —n. a turn; a bend.

wind'bag" (wind'-) n. (Slang) a chatterer; a braggart.

wind'blown" (wind'-) adj. made disorderly by the wind, as hair.

wind'break"er (wind'-) n. an outer jacket.

wind'bro"ken (wind'-) adj. of a horse, having the heaves.

wind'fall" (wind'-) n. an unexpected and fortunate acquisition

wind'jam"mer (wind'jam"ər) n. a sailing ship.

wind'lass (wind'ləs) n. a machine for hoisting.

Windmill

wind'mill" (wind'-) n. a mill driven by blades turned by the wind.

win'dow (win'dō) n. 1, an opening in the wall of a building to let in light and air. 2, any similar opening. —window box, a box of soil in which to grow plants, placed below a window. —window dressing, a display in a store's window; any display designed to impress. —window envelope, an envelope with a transparent panel.

win'dow·pane" n. a glass pane in a window.

win'dow·shop" v.i. [-shopped" -shop"ping] look at display windows without intending to buy.

window sill a sill under a window.

wind'pipe" (wind'-) n. the trachea.

wind'row" (wind'rō") n. a ridge of hay, etc. arranged for drying.

wind'shield" (wind'-) n. a glass shield before a driver of an automobile.

wind'up" (wīnd'-) n. (Colloq.) 1 a conclusion. 2, a baseball pitcher's preparatory movements.

wind'ward (wind'wərd) adv. & adj. toward the wind.

wind'y (win'dē) *adj.* **1,** marked by much blowing of wind. **2,** voluble; wordy. —**wind'i·ness,** *n.*

wine (wīn) *n.* the fermented juice of fruit or plants, specif. of the grape. —*v.t.* regale with alcoholic liquors. —*v.i.* drink wine. —*adj.* a dark red color. —**wine'bib"ber,** *n.* a heavy drinker. —**win'er·y,** *n.* a place where wine is made.

wine'sap" *n.* a red apple.

wing *n.* **1,** a limb, usually occurring in pairs, by which certain animals fly; any similar appendage. **2,** flight. **3,** one of the chief supporting planes of an airplane. **4,** a part of a building projecting from the main part. **5,** one of the sides of a stage of a theater. **6,** anything projecting to the side. **7,** (*pl.*) an emblem worn by a military flier. **8,** protection. —*v.t.* **1,** equip with wings. **2,** traverse in flight. **3,** accomplish by means of flight. **4,** shoot; wound; disable. —*v.i.* fly; soar.

wing chair an upholstered chair with winglike projections of the back.

wing'spread" *n.* the distance, tip to tip, of outstretched wings.

wink *v.i.* **1,** close and open the eye quickly, as a signal. **2,** (with *at*) condone. —*n.* an act of winking. —**wink at,** overlook; condone. —**forty winks,** a short nap.

win'ning (win'ing) *adj.* **1,** that wins. **2,** attractive. —*n.pl.* gains.

win'now (win'ō) *v.t.* **1,** drive off chaff from (grain) by a current of air. **2,** sift; weed out; test. —*v.i.* **1,** winnow grain. **2,** flutter.

win'some (-səm) *adj.* charming. —**win'some·ness,** *n.*

win'ter (win'tər) *n. & adj.* **1,** the cold season; in the No. hemisphere, approximately Dec. 22 to March 21. **2,** a period of dreariness or adversity. —*v.i.* spend or pass the winter. —*v.t.* keep or shelter during the winter. —**win'ter·ize"** (-īz") *v.t.* prepare for winter.

win'ter·green" (win'tər-grēn") *n.* an evergreen plant bearing aromatic leaves and berries.

win'ter·time" *n.* winter.

winter wheat wheat planted in the fall.

win'try (win'trē) *adj.* of or like winter; cold; forbidding. —**win'tri·ness,** *n.*

wipe (wīp) *v.t.* **1,** clean or dry by gently rubbing, as with a soft cloth. **2,** remove, as dirt. **3,** cleanse. —*n.* an act of wiping. —**wipe out,** destroy.

wire (wīr) *n.* **1,** a pliable thread or slender rod of metal; a piece of this

material. **2,** a telegram. —*v.t.* **1,** provide with wire. **2,** snare. **3,** send a telegram; telegraph to. —*v.i.* telegraph. —**wire recording,** recording of sound on magnetized wire.

wire'hair" *n.* a type of fox terrier: *wirehaired terrier.*

wire'less (-ləs) *n.* a telegraph or telephone not requiring connection by wires; radio.

wire'pull"ing *n.* the use of influence to gain unfair advantage.

wir'ing *n.* a system of connected wires.

wir'y (wīr'ē) *adj.* lean but muscular. —**wir'i·ness,** *n.*

wis'dom (wiz'dəm) *n.* **1,** the power or faculty of forming a sound judgment in any matter; sagacity; experience. **2,** erudition. —**wisdom tooth,** the third molar, in the back of the jaw.

wise (wīz) *adj.* **1,** having the power of discerning and judging rightly. **2,** having knowledge; learned. **3,** experienced; cunning. **4,** judicious. **5,** (*Slang*) too smart; aware. —*n.* **1,** wise persons collectively. **2,** manner; way; mode.

-wise *suf.* forming adverbs: in the manner of, as *likewise*; in the direction of, as *sidewise.*

wise'a"cre *n.* one who affects wit or cleverness.

wise'crack" *n.* (*Slang*) a quip. —**wise'crack"er,** *n.*

wish *v.t.* **1,** long for; desire; crave. **2,** (*Colloq.*) (with *on*) shunt off. —*v.i.* form or express a desire. —*n.* **1,** eager desire or longing. **2,** a request. **3,** the thing desired.

wish'bone" *n.* the forked bone in front of the breast of a fowl.

wish'ful (-fəl) *adj.* based on desire; desirous. —**wish'ful·ness,** *n.*

wish'y-wash'y (wish'ē-wash'ē) *adj.* (*Colloq.*) **1,** feeble. **2,** vacillating.

wisp *n.* **1,** a tuft of hay or straw, hair, etc. **2,** a fragment. —**wisp'y,** *adj.*

wist *v.* knew.

wis·ta'ri·a (wis-tār'ē-ə) *n.* a climbing shrub bearing clusters of purplish or white flowers. Also, **wis·te'ri·a.**

wist'ful (wist'fəl) *adj.* longing, but with little hope. —**wist'ful·ness,** *n.*

wit *n.* **1,** cleverness; intelligence; sense; (often *pl.*) power to reason. **2,** clever, amusing sayings and writings; one apt at making them. —**to wit,** namely.

witch (wich) *n.* **1,** a woman with magic powers derived from evil spirits; a sorceress. **2,** a hag; a crone. **3,** (*Colloq.*) a fascinating woman. —**witch'er·y,** *n.* —**witch'ing,** *adj.* bewitching; fascinating.

witch'craft" *n.* magic.

witch hazel a shrub bearing yellow flowers; a soothing lotion prepared from its bark.

with *prep.* **1,** accompanying; beside; carrying. **2,** possessing; holding. **3,** opposed to; against; compared to. **4,** using. **5,** having in association or connection, or as a reason. **6,** away from.

with·al' (with-âl') *adv. & prep.* considering everything; besides.

with·draw' (with-drâ') *v.t.* take back; recall; retract. —*v.i.* retire; retreat. **with·draw'al,** *n.*

withe (with) *n.* a tough, flexible twig, esp. of willow.

with'er (with'ər) *v.i. & t.* **1,** shrivel up; dry out; decay. **2,** languish. **3,** abash.

with'ers (with'ərz) *n. pl.* the highest part of the back of a horse.

with·hold' (with-hōld') *v.t.* [-**held'** -**hold'ing**] **1,** restrain. **2,** refuse to grant or release. —**withholding tax,** a deduction from wages for payment of Federal income tax.

with·in' (with-in') *adv.* **1,** pert. to the inside; indoors; internally; inwardly. —*prep.* in; inside of; not exceeding.

with·out' (with-owt') *adv.* on or as to the outside; outdoors; externally. —*prep.* **1,** outside of; beyond. **2,** lacking; independent of.

with·stand' *v.t.* [*pret. & p.p.* **with·stood'**] resist successfully; oppose.

wit'less (-ləs) *adj.* stupid; foolish. —**wit'less·ness,** *n.*

wit'ness (wit'nəs) *v.t.* **1,** see or know by personal presence. **2,** attest to (a document) by one's signature. **3,** testify. —*n.* **1,** one who sees personally. **2,** one who gives evidence or witnesses a document. **3,** testimony.

wit'ti·cism (wit'i-siz-əm) *n.* a witty remark.

wit'ting·ly (wit'ing-lē) *adv.* knowingly.

wit'ty (wit'ē) *adj.* characterized by, or apt at making, original and clever remarks. —**wit'ti·ness,** *n.*

wive (wīv) *v.t. & i.* marry.

wives (wīvz) *n.* pl. of *wife.*

wiz'ard (wiz'ərd) *n.* **1,** one supposed to have magic powers; a sorcerer. **2,** an unusually skilled person. —*adj.* **1,** enchanting. **2,** (*Brit. slang*) superb. —**wiz'ard·ry,** *n.* **1,** sorcery. **2,** admirable skill.

wiz'ened (wiz'ənd) *adj.* dried up; shriveled.

wob'ble (wob'əl) *v.i.* **1,** move from side to side; rock. **2,** tremble. —*n.* a rocking motion. —**wob'bly,** *adj.*

woe (wō) *n.* **1,** intense unhappiness; grief; sorrow. **2,** an affliction.

woe'be·gone" *adj.* sorrowful.

woe'ful (-fəl) *adj.* **1,** sorrowful. **2,** causing or expressing woe. —**woe'-ful·ness,** *n.*

woke (wōk) *v.* pret. of *wake.*

wolf (wûlf) *n.* [*pl.* **wolves** (wûlvz)] **1,** a wild, carnivorous animal of the dog family. **2,** a cruel, cunning, greedy person. **3,** (*Slang*) a man who makes advances to many women. —*v.t.* devour ravenously. —**wolf'-ish,** *adj.*

wolf'hound" *n.* a large hound used to hunt wolves.

wolf pack a group of submarines hunting together for enemy shipping.

wol'fram (wûl'frəm) *n.* a mineral, a source of tungsten. Also, **wolf'-ram·ite"** (-īt").

wol"ver·ine' (wûl"və-rēn') *n.* **1,** a small, ferocious, carnivorous animal, related to the marten. **2,** (*cap.*) (*Colloq.*) an inhabitant of Michigan.

wom'an (wûm'ən) *n.* [*pl.* **wom'en** (wim'ən)] **1,** an adult human female; a wife; a female attendant. **2,** the female sex. **3,** feminine nature. —**wom'an·hood",** *n.* the state of being a woman; women collectively. —**wom'an·ish,** *adj.* unbecomingly feminine. —**wom'an·kind",** *n.* —**wom'an·like",** *adj.* —**wom'an·ly,** *adj.* befitting a woman.

womb (woom) *n.* the uterus.

wom'bat *n.* an Australian marsupial resembling a small bear.

wom'en (wim'ən) *n.* pl. of *woman.* —**wom'en·folk",** *n.*

won (wun) *v.* pret. & p.p. of *win.*

won'der (wun'dər) *n.* **1,** a strange thing; a cause of surprise or admiration; a marvel; a prodigy. **2,** astonishment. —*v.i.* **1,** entertain doubt or curiosity; speculate. **2,** marvel. —**won'der·ment,** *n.* —**won'drous,** *adj.*

won'der·ful (-fəl) *adj.* **1,** extraordinary; marvelous. **2,** delightful. —**won'der·ful·ness,** *n.*

won'der·land" *n.* a wonderful place.

wont *adj.* accustomed; in the habit. —*n.* custom; habit; practice. —**wont'ed,** *adj.*

woo *v.t. & i.* seek the favor or love of; court. —**woo'er,** *n.*

wood (wûd) *n.* **1,** the hard, fibrous substance of the body of a tree. **2,** (often *pl.*) a forest. **3,** timber. —**wood alcohol,** methyl alcohol. —**wood pulp,** wood fibers, prepared for use in manufacturing paper.

wood'bine" (wŭd'bīn") *n.* **1,** honeysuckle. **2,** the Virginia creeper.

wood'chuck" (wŭd'chuk") *n.* a burrowing, hibernating marmot; the ground hog.

wood'cock" *n.* a game bird.

wood'craft" *n.* the art of living on nature.

wood'cut" *n.* a printing block of wood; a print made from one.

wood'ed *adj.* thick with trees.

wood'en (-ən) *adj.* **1,** made of wood. **2,** inflexible; unimaginative. **3,** not sensitive; expressionless. —**wood'en·head"ed,** *adj.* stupid; obstinate.

wood'land (-lənd) *n.* a forest.

wood'peck"er *n.* a bird that bores into trees with its bill.

wood'shed" *n.* a shed for storing cut firewood.

woods'man (wŭdz'mən) *n.* [*pl.* -men] a forester.

wood'wind" *n.* a musical wind instrument, as the flute, clarinet, etc.

wood'work" *n.* interior trim and fixtures made of wood.

wood'y (-ē) *adj.* **1,** wooded. **2,** of or resembling wood. —**wood'i·ness,** *n.*

woof *n.* the crosswise threads in weaving.

wool (wŭl) *n.* **1,** the fleece of the sheep; any fabric or yarn made of it. **2,** kinky hair.

wool'en (-ən) *adj. & n.* made of wool. Also, **wool'len.**

wool'gath"er·ing *n.* desultory thought causing inattention.

wool'ly (-ē) *adj.* of or like wool. —**wool'lies,** *n.pl.* woolen clothes. —**wool'li·ness,** *n.*

wool'sack" *n.* the wool-stuffed seat of the Lord Chancellor, in the Eng. House of Lords.

wooz'y (woo'zē) *adj.* (*Slang*) **1,** confused; befuddled. **2,** shaky. —**wooz'i·ness,** *n.*

word (wẽrd) *n.* **1,** a sound or combination of sounds, or its graphic representation, expressing an idea; a term. **2,** (*pl.*) speech; written words; a song lyric; a quarrel. **3,** information; a report; a command; a signal or password; a motto. **4,** a promise. **5,** (*cap.*) Holy Scripture. —*v.t.* express in words; phrase. —**word'ing,** *n.* phrasing. —**word'less,** *adj.* silent; tacit.

word'y (-ē) *adj.* verbose. —**word'i·ness,** *n.*

wore (wôr) *v.* pret. of **wear.**

work (wẽrk) *v.i.* **1,** put forth effort; labor; toil; strive. **2,** act; operate, esp. effectively. **3,** ferment; seethe. **4,** make way slowly. **5,** be employed; perform labor. —*v.t.* **1,** prepare or fashion by labor; operate; employ. **2,** sew; embroider. **3,** do; accomplish. **4,** (often with *on*, etc.) affect; influence; persuade; provoke. **5,** exact labor or service from. **6,** solve. —*n.* **1,** effort or exertion; toil; labor. **2,** employment; a job; an undertaking; a project. **3,** a product of effort; deed; performance. **4,** (*pl.*) a factory. **5,** (*pl.*) a mechanism, as of a watch. **6,** (*pl.*) the entire output of an artist, writer, etc. **7,** (*pl.*) engineering structures, esp. public ones.

-work *suf.* product of (what is specified).

work'a·ble (-ə-bəl) *adj.* **1,** feasible; practicable. **2,** tractable. —**work"a·bil'i·ty,** *n.*

work'a·day" *adj.* commonplace; matter-of-fact.

work'bench" *n.* a table on which to do work.

work'book" *n.* an instructive manual or drill book.

work'day" *n.* hours worked in a day. Also, **working day.**

work'er (-ər) *n.* one who works; esp., a laborer.

work'house" *n.* a poorhouse or small prison.

work'ing *adj.* **1,** that works. **2,** effective; in operation. —**work'ing·man",** *n.* a laborer.

work'man (-mən) *n.* [*pl.* -men] a skilled worker. —**work'man·like",** *adj.* competently executed. —**work'-man·ship",** *n.*

work'out" *n.* **1,** a performance for practice or exercise. **2,** (*Colloq.*) a trying experience.

world (wẽrld) *n.* **1,** the whole creation; the universe; the earth. **2,** the human race; mankind. **3,** a class or society of persons; a sphere; realm. **4,** material concerns. **5,** public or social life. **6,** a particular part of the earth. **7,** a great number or quantity.

world'ly (-lē) *adj.* **1,** mundane; material; not spiritual. **2,** sophisticated. —**world'li·ness,** *n.* —**world'ly-wise",** *adj.* experienced; knowing; shrewd.

world'wide" *adj.* throughout the earth.

worm (wẽrm) *n.* **1,** any small, creeping tube-shaped animal. **2,** a contemptible person; an unfortunate person. **3,** something that silently harasses. **4,** any device resembling a worm, as a spiral part. **5,** (*pl.*) any disease caused by parasitic worms. —*v.i.* work or act slowly, stealthily, or secretly. —*v.t.* free from worms. —**worm gear,** a wheel driven by a screw. —**worm'y,** *adj.*

worm'wood" (wẽrm'wŭd") *n.* **1,** a bitter herb used in tonics and in absinthe. **2,** bitterness.

worn (wôrn) *v.* pret. & p.p. of *wear.* —*adj.* weary. —**worn'ness,** *n.*

worn-'out' *adj.* **1,** unfit for use. **2,** exhausted.

wor'ry (wûr'ė) *v.t.* **1,** cause to feel anxious; harass; bother. **2,** grasp with the teeth and shake. —*v.i.* **1,** be anxious; fret. **2,** (*Colloq.*) manage somehow. —*n.* anxiety; trouble. —**wor'ri·er,** *n.* —**wor'ri·some** (-səm) *adj.* causing worry.

worse (wẽrs) *adj. & adv.* comp. of *bad, ill, badly.* —**wors'en,** *v.t. & i.*

wor'ship (wẽr'ship) *n.* **1,** reverence and homage, esp. to God. **2,** religious services. **3,** a title of honor. —*v.t.* **1,** pay divine honors to; adore (God). **2,** love or admire inordinately. —*v.i.* perform or attend religious services. —**wor'ship·er,** *n.* —**wor'ship·ful,** *adj.*

worst (wẽrst) *adj. & adv.* superl. of *bad, ill, badly.* —*v.t.* defeat. —*n.* that which is worst.

wor'sted (wûs'tid) *n.* **1,** a tight-twisted woolen yarn; fabric made of it. **2,** a woolen yarn for knitting.

wort (wẽrt) *n.* **1,** a plant, herb, or vegetable: used in old plant names, as *colewort.* **2,** the infusion of malt which, after fermentation, becomes beer.

worth (wẽrth) *adj.* **1,** meriting; deserving. **2,** having a specified value. **3,** equivalent in value to. **4,** possessing. —*n.* **1,** value, esp. in money. **2,** excellence; merit.

worth'less (-ləs) *adj.* useless; worth nothing; undeserving. —**worth'less·ness,** *n.*

worth'while' *adj.* serving a useful purpose. —**worth'while'ness,** *n.*

wor'thy (wẽr'thė) *adj.* deserving respect. —**wor'thi·ness,** *n.*

would (wûd) *v.* pret. of *will.*

would-'be' *adj.* hoping or pretending to be.

wound (woond) *n.* **1,** an injury to flesh or tissue, esp. one caused by violence. **2,** any injury; something that hurts. —*v.t. & i.* **1,** hurt by violence. **2,** hurt the feelings (of).

wound (wownd) *v.* pret. & p.p. of *wind.*

wove (wōv) *v.* pret. of *weave.*

wo'ven (wō'vən) *v.* p.p. of *weave.*

wow *interj.* expressing admiration or wonder. —*v.t.* (*Slang*) captivate. —*n.* (*Slang*) a wonderful person, thing, or performance.

wrack (rak) *n.* wreck.

wraith (rāth) *n.* an apparition; a specter; a ghost. —**wraith'y,** *adj.*

wran'gle (rang'gəl) *v.i.* argue noisily; dispute. —*v.t.* round up (livestock). —*n.* a noisy quarrel. —**wran'gler,** *n.*

wrap (rap) *v.t.* [wrapped, wrap'ping] **1,** cover with (paper, etc.); envelop; make into a bundle. **2,** roll or fold (paper, etc.) around. —*n.* a cloak or shawl; (*Colloq.*) an overcoat.

wrap'per (-ər) *n.* **1,** any covering. **2,** a dressing gown.

wrap'ping (rap'ing) *n.* that which wraps; material for wrapping.

wrath (rāth) *n.* **1,** fierce anger; rage. **2,** vengeance. —**wrath'ful,** *adj.*

wreak (rēk) *v.t.* inflict.

wreath (rēth) *n.* something twisted or formed into a circular band; a garland.

wreathe (rēth) *v.t.* form by twisting; intertwine; encircle.

wreck (rek) *n.* **1,** destruction, disruption, or ruin. **2,** one who or that which is in a state of ruin; remains; a shipwrecked vessel. —*v.t.* cause the ruin or demolition of. —**wreck'age,** *n.*

wreck'er (-ər) *n.* **1,** one who wrecks. **2,** a car for removing or towing wrecked cars.

wren (ren) *n.* any of a family of small, migratory songbirds.

wrench (rench) *n.* **1,** a violent, sudden twist or jerk; a sprain. **2,** a grasping tool. —*v.t.* **1,** give a sudden twist to; distort. **2,** sprain. **3,** wrest forcibly.

Wrenches

Open-end

Ratchet

Pipe

wrest (rest) *v.t.* remove or seize by, or as if by, violent twisting; wring; wrench.

wres'tle (res'əl) *v.i.* **1,** struggle, as two persons each trying to throw the other to the mat in a contest. **2,** contend; grapple; strive. —*v.t.* contest with in wrestling. —*n.* a wrestling match. —**wres'tler,** *n.* —**wres'tling,** *n.*

wretch (rech) *n.* **1,** one who is very unhappy or unfortunate. **2,** a contemptible person.

wretch'ed *adj.* **1,** miserable. **2,** mean; lowly. —**wretch'ed·ness,** *n.*

wrig'gle (rig'əl) *v.i.* **1,** move along sinuously; writhe; squirm. **2,** make way by opportunism and shrewdness. —*n.* a squirming motion. —**wrig'gler,** *n.* —**wrig'gly,** *adj.*

wright (rīt) *n.* a workman.

wring (ring) *v.t.* [wrung (rung), wring'ing] 1, twist or flex forcibly. 2, distress. 3, squeeze out; extort. —*v i.* writhe. —*n.* a twist. —**wring'er**, *n.* a device for pressing water from washed clothes. —**wringing wet**, drenched.

wrin'kle (ring'kəl) *n.* 1, a slight ridge or furrow in a surface; a crease in the skin, esp. one caused by old age. 2, (*Colloq.*) a good or new idea. —*v.t. & i.* crease; pucker.

wrist (rist) *n.* 1, the joint between the hand and the forearm. 2, a connecting stud or pin: *wrist pin.*

wrist'let *n.* a band around the wrist.

wrist watch a watch strapped to the wrist.

writ (rit) *n.* 1, (*Law*) a written order or document. 2, Scripture.

write (rīt) *v.t.* [wrote (rōt), writ'-en (rit'ən) writ'ing] 1, form (letters or characters) on a surface by hand. 2, set down for re-ding. as with a pen or typewriter cause to be written, as by dictation. 3, cover with writing. 4, (with *off*) treat as a loss; forget about. —*v.i* 1, write words or characters 2, work as an author. 3, conduct a correspondence.

write-'up' *n.* a written account, esp. a laudatory description.

writhe (rīth) *v.i.* twist one's body, as from pain.

writ'ing (rīt'ing) *n.* 1, written matter; a literary work; 2, handwriting.

writ'ten (rit'ən) *v. p.p. of write.*

wrong (râng) *adj.* 1, deviating from right, truth, or morals. 2, not correct in fact; mistaken. 3, unsuitable; improper. —*adv.* not rightly; incorrectly; amiss. —*n.* evil; harm; injury. —*v.t.* 1, do harm to; treat unfairly. 2, unjustly blame or disapprove of.

wrong'do'er (-doo″ər) *n.* a sinner. —**wrong'do'ing,** *n.*

wrong'ful (-fəl) *adj.* injurious; unlawful. —**wrong'ful-ness,** *n.*

wrote (rōt) *v. pret. of write.*

wroth (roth) *adj.* very angry.

wrought (rât) *v. & adj.* worked; formed, fashioned, or hammered. —**wrought iron,** iron purified of carbon. —**wrought-'up',** *adj.* disturbed; excited.

wrung (rung) *v.* pret. & p.p. of *wring.*

wry (rī) *adj.* 1, twisted to one side; askew; distorted. 2, ironic. —**wry'-ness,** *n.*

wy'an-dotte" (wī'ən-dot″) *n.* a breed of domestic fowl.

X

X, x (eks) the twenty-fourth letter of the English alphabet.

xan-tho- *pref.* yellow.

xan'thous (zan'thəs) *adj.* yellow; yellow-skinned.

xe'bec (zē'bek) *n.* a small Mediterranean three-masted vessel. Also, **ze'bec.**

xe'ni-a (zē'nē-ə) *n.* (*Bot.*) the effect of pollen on a seed or fruit, other than on the embryo.

xen-o- *pref.* alien.

xe'non (zē'non) *n.* an inert gaseous chemical element, no. 54, symbol Xe.

xen"o-pho'bi-a (zen″ə-fō'bē-ə) *n.* fear or hatred of foreigners.

xe-ro- *pref.* dry.

xe'ro-phyte (zē'rə-fīt) *n.* a plant that grows in arid regions, as the cactus. —**xe"ro-phyt'ic** (-fit'ik) *adj.* —**xe"ro-phyt'i-cal-ly,** *adv.*

X'mas *abbr.* Christmas.

x-'ray" (eks'rā″) *n.* 1, (*pl.*) electromagnetic radiations of extremely short wave length and high penetrating power, commonly used to photograph the interior of solids and for the treatment of skin or cancerous diseases. 2, a photograph made by x-rays. —*v.t.* examine, photograph, or treat by x-rays.

xy'lem (zī'lem) *n.* the woody tissue of plants.

xy-lo- *pref.* wood; wooden.

xy-log'ra-phy (zī-log'rə-fē) *n.* wood engraving. —**xy"lo-graph'ic,** *adj.* —**xy"lo-graph'i-cal-ly,** *adv.*

xy'loid (zī'loid) *adj.* resembling wood.

xy'lo-phone" (zī'lə-fōn″) *n.* a musical instrument comprising a series of wooden bars processed to sound musical tones when struck with wooden hammers. —**xy'lo-phon"ist,** *n.*

Y

Y, y (wī) the twenty-fifth letter of the English alphabet.

-y (ē; i) *suf.* forming adjectives; 1, of the nature of, as *misty.* 2, being; as *guilty.*

yacht (yot) *n.* a pleasure ship used solely for its owner's personal purposes. —*v.i.* travel in a yacht. —**yacht'ing,** *n.* —**yachts'man** (-mən) *n.* the owner of a yacht.

ya'hoo (yä'hoo) *n.* a coarse, uncouth person.

Yah'weh (yä'we) *n.* variant transliteration of Jehovah.

yak *n.* a long-haired Asiatic ox.

yam *n.* 1, a tuberous root cultivated as food. 2, the sweet potato.

yank *v.t. & i.* pull suddenly; jerk. —*n.* 1, a jerk. 2, (*cap.*), (*Slang*) Yankee.

Yan'kee (yang'kē) *n.* 1, a citizen of the U. S. 2, a native of the N. E. states. 3, in the southern U. S., any native of the northern states. —*adj.* pert. to Yankees.

yap *v.i.* [yapped, yap'ping] 1, yelp. 2, talk foolishly, or in a barking manner. —*n.* a yelp.

yard (yärd) *n.* 1, the ground adjoining a building. 2, an enclosure or area in which any work is carried on. 3, a unit of linear measure, equal to 3 ft. 4, a rod or spar, esp. a crosswise piece on a mast.

yard'age (-ij) *n.* distance or area in yards.

yard'arm" *n.* (*Naut.*) an end of a yard.

yard'stick" (yärd'stik") *n.* 1, a calibrated stick one yard long. 2, any standard of measurement.

yarn (yärn) *n.* 1, fibers of cotton, wool, etc. twisted together. 2, a tale, esp. a fabricated one. —*v.i.* tell or exchange stories.

yaw (yä) *v.i.* turn to one side, heading off course. —*n.* a deviation.

yawl (yäl) *n.* a small two-masted sailing vessel.

yawn (yän) *v.i.* 1, open the mouth involuntarily in reaction from fatigue or sleepiness. 2, open wide; extend far. —*n.* a yawning.

yaws (yäz) *n.pl.* a skin disease.

y·clept' (i-klept') *v.* (*Archaic*) named.

ye (yē) *pl. pron.* (*Obs.*) you.

yea (yā) *adv.* 1, yes. 2, truly; indeed. —*n.* an affirmative vote.

year (yir) *n.* 1, the period of one revolution of the earth about the sun, about 365 days. 2, the period from Jan. 1 to the next Dec. 31 inclusive (calendar year); any period of 365 or 366 consecutive calendar days. 3, the period of an annually-recurring activity, as a school year. 4, (*pl.*) age; old age; time. —**year'ly**, *adj. & adv.*

year'book" *n.* an annual publication, usually dealing with events of the past year.

year'ling (yir'ling) *n.* an animal one year old, or in its second year.

yearn (yẽrn) *v.i.* desire strongly; long for something. —**yearn'ing**, *n.*

yeast (yēst) *n.* 1, a yellowish substance, an aggregate of minute fungi, used to leaven bread and ferment liquors. 2, any froth or spume. —*v.i.* ferment.

yeast'y (-ē) *adj.* frothy; light. —**yeast'i·ness**, *n.*

yegg (yeg) *n.* (*Slang*) a robber, esp. one who cracks safes.

yell (yel) *v.i.* cry out; shout. —*v.t.* utter in a loud, piercing tone. —*n.* 1, a shout or scream. 2, a cry or slogan uttered in concert by a crowd.

yel'low (yel'ō) *n.* the color of lemons, the yolk of an egg, etc.; a hue between orange and green in the spectrum. —*adj.* 1, of this color. 2, yellow-skinned; belonging to the Mongolian race. 3, (*Colloq.*) cowardly; contemptible. 4, offensively sensational (of newspapers). —**yellow fever**, an infectious febrile disease, also called *yellow jack.* —**yellow peril**, Oriental peoples, when viewed as dangerous because so numerous.

yellow jacket a variety of wasp.

yelp (yelp) *v.i.* give a quick, shrill cry, like a dog. —*n.* a sharp cry; a bark.

yen *n.* 1, the monetary unit of Japan, formerly worth about .50 dollar. 2, (*Colloq.*) yearning.

yeo'man (yō'mən) *n.* [*pl.* -men] 1, a petty officer of the U. S. Navy whose duties are clerical. 2, (*Brit.*) an independent farmer; (*Archaic*) an attendant or servant. —**yeo'man·ry**, *n.* yeomen collectively. —**yeoman service**, vigorous and effective work.

yes *adv.* a word expressing affirmation, agreement, consent. —**yes'man"**, *n.* one who always agrees with a superior.

yes'ter- (yes'tər) *adj.* past, as *yester year*, a past year. —**yes"ter·eve'**, **yes"ter·night'**, **yes"ter·year'**, *n.*

yes'ter·day (yes'tər-dā) *n.* 1, the day preceding the present day. 2, time of the immediate past. —*adv.* on yesterday.

yet *adv.* 1, at or up to the present or some future time; hitherto; already. 2, as formerly; still; in continuation. 3, in addition; besides; moreover. —*conj.* nevertheless; notwithstanding.

yew (ū) *n.* an evergreen coniferous tree; its wood.

Yid'dish (yid'ish) *n.* a language of the Jews, incorporating Hebrew, German, and other words.

yield (yēld) v.t. & i. 1, produce in payment. 2, bring forth by natural process; bear (as fruit); produce. 3, surrender; relinquish. —v.i. give way; assent; comply. —n. what is produced. —yield'ing, adj. compliant; tractable.

yo'del (yō'dəl) v.t. & t. sing with alternation between ordinary voice and falsetto.

yo'ga (yō'gə) n. a Hindu ascetic philosophy.

yo'gi (yō'gē) n. a practitioner of yoga, a Hindu philosophical system.

yo'gurt (yō'gûrt) n. a curdled milk food.

yoicks (yoiks) interj. a cry of fox hunters.

yoke (yōk) n. 1, a contrivance for fastening together the necks of two draft animals, as oxen. 2, anything resembling a yoke in form or use, as the collar-piece of a garment. 3, something that binds or holds parts together. 4, servitude; slavery. —v.t. put a yoke on; couple; link.

yo'kel (yō'kəl) n. a rustic or countryman; an awkward person.

yolk (yōk) n. 1, the yellow substance of an egg. 2, the vital or essential part of anything.

Yom Kip'pur (yom kip'ər) a fast day, the Day of Atonement, in Judaism.

yon adj. (Poetic) yonder.

yon'der (yon'dər) adv. & adj. in that (distant or more distant) place.

yore (yōr) adv. (Archaic) long ago.

Yorkshire pudding a batter pudding baked in roast-meat drippings.

you (ū) pron. sing. & pl. [poss. your (yûr), yours] the personal pronoun of the second person; in nominative it always takes a plural verb.

young (yung) adj. 1, being in an early stage of life or growth; not yet mature. 2, recent; not fully developed. 3, having the appearance and vigor of youth. 4, inexperienced. —n. offspring. —young'ish, adj. —young'ness, n.

young'ster (-stər) n. a young person.

your (yûr) pron. poss. of you. —yours, poss. of you, used predicatively. —your-self', emphatic and reflexive form of you.

youth (ūth) n. 1, the period of life from puberty to maturity; adolescence. 2, the earliest stage. 3, the condition of being young. 4, the qualities of early age, as vigor. 5, a young person, esp. male; young persons collectively. —youth'ful, adj. —youth'ful-ness, n.

yowl v.i. utter a long wailing cry; howl. —n. such a cry.

yt·ter'bi·um (i-tẽr'bē-əm) n. a metallic chemical element, no. 70, symbol Yb.

yt'tri·um (it'rē-əm) n. a metallic chemical element, no. 39, symbol yt.

yu·an' (ū-än') n. sing. & pl. the monetary unit of China, formerly worth about .50 dollar.

yuc'ca (yuk'ə) n. a plant of the lily family.

Yu'go·slav'' (ū'gō-släv'') adj. & n. of or pert. to Yugoslavia, its people, language, etc.

yule (ūl) n. Christmas or the Christmas season. Also, yule'tide''.

Z

Z, z (zē) the twenty-sixth letter of the English alphabet.

za'ny (zā'nē) n. 1, a clownish person; an amusing fool. 2, a simpleton.

zeal (zēl) n. fervent ardor; eagerness; enthusiasm; diligence.

zeal'ot (zel'ət) n. one who is fanatically earnest.

zeal'ous (zel'əs) adj. diligent. —zeal'ous-ness, n.

ze'bec (zē'bek) n. xebec.

ze'bra (zē'brə) n. an Afr. mammal related to the horse, marked with alternate light and dark stripes.

ze'bu (zē'bū) n. a bovine animal having a hump over the shoulders, domesticated in the Orient.

zed n. (Brit.) the letter z.

ze'nith (zē'nith) n. 1, the point in the sky directly above an observer or place on the earth. 2, the highest point of anything; culmination.

zeph'yr (zef'ər) n. a mild, gentle breeze.

Zep'pe·lin (zep'ə-lin) n. a type of dirigible balloon with a cigar-shaped bag.

ze'ro (zir'ō) [pl. -ros] n. 1, the symbol 0, meaning the absence of quantity; the cipher. 2, the first or lowest point on a scale of measurement, as a thermometer. 3, naught; nothing. —zero hour, a time set for the commencement of action.

zest n. 1, keen relish; hearty enjoyment; gusto. 2, piquant or appealing flavor; an enjoyable quality. —zest'ful, adj. —zest'y, adj.

ze'ta (zā'tə) n. the sixth letter of the Greek alphabet (Z, ζ).

zig'zag'' n. a sharp angle or series of such angles; a line or course that turns abruptly from side to side —adj. having sharp turnings or angles. —v.i. & t. [-zagged'', -zag''-ging] advance or form in zigzags.

zinc (zink) *n.* a metallic chemical element, no. 30, symbol Zn. —**zinc ointment**, a salve containing zinc oxide. —**zinc oxide**, an oxide of zinc, an antiseptic.

zin'ni·a (zin'ē·ə) *n.* a plant having showy yellow or red flowers.

Zi'on (zī'ən) *n.* **1**, a hill in Jerusalem, designated as holy. **2**, heaven.

Zi'on·ism (zī'ə-niz-əm) *n.* advocacy of the establishment of a Jewish nation (now Israel) in Palestine. —**Zi'on·ist**, *n.*

zip *n.* **1**, the sound of a bullet in flight. **2**, (*Colloq.*) energy; vim. —*v.t.* [zipped], zip'ping] sound or move with a zip. —*v.t.* fasten with a zipper.

zip'per (zip'ər) *n.* a fastening device that causes two strips of metal studs to interlock.

zip'py (-ē) *adj.* pert; lively. —**zip'pi·ness**, *n.*

zir'con (zėr'kon) *n.* a common silicate mineral used as a gem.

zir·co'ni·um (zėr-kō'nē-əm) *n.* a metallic element, no. 40, symbol Zr.

zith'er (zith'ər) *n.* a musical instrument comprising a number of strings stretched over a flat sounding board, played with the fingers or a plectrum.

zlo'ty (zlä'tē) *n.* [*pl.* **-tys**] the monetary unit of Poland, formerly worth about .20 dollar.

zo'di·ac' (zō'dē-ak") *n.* the imaginary belt in the sky in which lie the apparent paths of the sun, moon, and principal planets. There are twelve signs of the zodiac:

Aquarius (*Water Bearer*)	Virgo (*Virgin*)
Pisces (*Fishes*)	Libra (*Balance*)
Aries (*Ram*)	Scorpio (*Scorpion*)
Taurus (*Bull*)	Sagittarius (*Archer*)
Gemini (*Twins*)	
Cancer (*Crab*)	Capricornus (*Goat*)
Leo (*Lion*)	

Signs of the Zodiac

zo·di'a·cal (zō-dī'ə-kəl) *adj.* pert; to the zodiac.

zo'ic (zō'ik) *adj.* pert. to animal life;

zom'bi (zom'bē) *n.* **1**, a snake deity worshiped by certain tribes of Afr. and the W.I. **2**, a dead body brought to life. Also, **zom'bie**.

zone (zōn) *n.* **1**, a part of the surface of a sphere lying between two parallel planes. **2**, any of the five arbitrary divisions of the surface of the earth: North Frigid, North Temperate, Torrid, South Temperate, South Frigid. **3**, region; district; any distinct, defined, or delimited area. —*v.t.* **1**, encircle like a belt. **2**, divide into or mark with zones. —**zon'al**, *adj.*

zoo *n.* an enclosure where live animals are kept for public exhibition;

zo-ō- *pref.* pert. to living animals.

zo'ö·log'i·cal (zō'ə-loj'i-kəl) *adj.* pert. to zoology. —**zoölogical garden**, a **zoo;**

zo·öl'o·gy (zō-ol'ə-jē) *n.* the general science of animal life. —**zo·öl'o·gist**, *n.*

zoom *v.i. & t.* fly (an aircraft) on a sudden upward course.

zoot suit (*Slang*) an extreme costume popular during the 1940's among young male jitterbugs.

zor'il (zôr'il) *n.* a South African animal resembling the skunk.

Zo"ro·as'tri·an (zō"rə-as'tre-ən) *adj.* pert. to Zoroaster, Persian prophet of 1000 B.C., his religion or philosophy.

Zou·ave' (zoo-äv') *n.* formerly, a brightly-dressed French infantryman.

zounds (zowndz) *interj.* of surprise;

Zu'lu (zoo'loo) *adj. & n.* of or pert. to a So. African people, their language, etc.

zwie'back" (tswē'bäk") *n.* a kind of toasted bread prepared in small pieces.

Zwing'li·an (zwing'lē-ən) *adj.* pert. to Ulrich Zwingli, 1484–1531, Swiss Protestant reformer.

zyme (zīm) *n.* the specific principle regarded as the cause of a zymotic disease.

zy·mo- *pref.* pert. to leaven.

zy·mo'sis (zī-mō'sis) *n.* **1**, an infectious or contagious disease. **2**, fermentation as a supposed cause of disease. —**zy·mot'ic** (-mot'ik) *adj.*

zy'mur·gy (zī'mər-jē) *n.* (*Chem.*) the science and study of fermentation, as in brewing.

ABBREVIATIONS

A.A., Alcoholics Anonymous.
A. & M., Agricultural and Mechanical.
A.A.U., Amateur Athletic Union.
A.B., Bachelor of Arts.
abbr., abbreviation.
ABC, American Broadcasting Company; Argentina, Brazil, and Chile.
A.C., alternating current.
A/C, account.
acct., account; accountant.
A.D., Anno Domini.
A.D.A., Americans for Democratic Action.
adj., adjective; (cap.) Adjutant.
Adm., Admiral.
adv., adverb.
advt., advertisement.
ae., aet., aetat., aetatis (Lat.) aged.
AEC, Atomic Energy Commission.
AEF, American Expeditionary Force.
aero., aeronautical; aeronautics.
A.F. & A.M., Ancient Free and Accepted Masons.
A.F.L., A.F. of L., American Federation of Labor.
Afr., Africa, African.
AID, Agency for International Development.
Ak., Alaska.
Al., Ala., Alabama.
Alas., Alaska.
A.L.P., American Labor Party.
Alta., Alberta.
AM, amplitude modulation. A.M., Master of Arts. A.M., a.m., ante meridiem.
A.M.A., American Medical Association.
Amer., America; American.
AMG, Allied Military Government.
amp., ampere; amperage.
AMVETS, American Veterans of World War II.
anat., anatomical; anatomy.
anon., anonymous.
AP, Associated Press.
APO, Army Post Office.
Apr., April.
apt(s)., apartment(s).
Ar., Arkansas.
A.R.C., American (National) Red Cross.
Arch., Archbishop; (l.c.) architect.
archit., architect; architecture.
arith., arithmetic; arithmetical.
Ariz., Az., Arizona.
Ark., Arkansas.
art., article.
A-S., A.S., Anglo-Saxon.
ASCAP, American Society of Composers, Authors, and Publishers.
assn., association.
asst., assistant.

Assyr., Assyrian.
Atl., Atlantic.
att., atty., attorney.
Aug., August.
Aus., Austl., Australia.
Aust., Austria; Austrian.
aux., auxiliary.
A.V., Authorized Version (of the Bible).
av., average.
Ave., Av., Avenue.
AWOL, absent without official leave.

B.A., Bachelor of Arts; Buenos Aires.
Bart., Bt., Baronet.
B.B.A., Bachelor of Business Administration.
B.B.C., British Broadcasting Corporation.
bbl., barrel; barrels.
B.C., British Columbia; before Christ.
bd., board.
BEF, British Expeditionary Force or Forces.
Belg., Belgian; Belgium.
Benj., Benjamin.
b.f., boldface (type).
Bib., Bible; Biblical.
biol., biology.
B/L, bill of lading.
bldg., blg., building.
Blvd., Boulevard.
BMI, Broadcast Music, Inc.
bn., battalion.
bot., botany.
B.P.O.E., Benevolent and Protective Order of Elks.
Braz., Brazil; Brazilian.
Brig., Brigadier.
Brit., British.
bro., bros., brother(s).
B.S., Bachelor of Science.
B. S. A., Boy Scouts of America.
B/S, bill of sale.
B.T.U., British thermal unit(s).
Bulg., Bulgaria; Bulgarian.
B. W. I., British West Indies.

C., centigrade.
C.A., Central America; Coast Artillery.
ca., circ., circa (about).
CAA, Civil Aeronautics Authority.
CAB, Civil Aeronautics Board.
Cal., Calif., Ca., California.
Can., Canada; Canadian.
cap., capital(ized).
Capt., Captain.
CARE, Coöperative for American Remittances to Europe.
CATV, Community Antenna Television.
C.B., Companion of the Bath.

C. B. I., China, Burma, India.
CBS, Columbia Broadcasting System.
c.c., carbon copy; cubic centimeters.
CCC, Civilian Conservation Corps; Commodity Credit Corporation.
cd., cord.
C.E., Civil Engineer.
cent., centigrade; centimeter; century.
CENTO, Central Treaty Organization.
C.G., Coast Guard.
Ch., China; Chinese; (l.c.) chapter.
Chas., Charles.
Ch.E., Chemical Engineer.
chem., chemistry; chemical; chemist.
chm., chairman.
Chr., Christian.
Chron., Chronicles.
CIA, Central Intelligence Agency.
CID, Criminal Investigation Department.
C. in C., Commander in Chief.
C.I.O., Congress of Industrial Organizations.
cm., centimeters.
CO, conscientious objector.
C.O., Commanding Officer.
Co., company; county; Colorado.
c/o, care of.
C.O.D., cash on delivery; collect on delivery.
Col., Colonel; Columbia.
colloq., colloquial.
Colo., Colorado.
Com., Commander; Commodore; commerce.
comp., comparative.
Comr., Commissioner.
Cong., Congregational; Congress; Congressional.
conj., conjunction.
Conn., Ct., Connecticut.
cont., continued.
Cor., Corinthians.
CORE, Congress of Racial Equality.
Corp., Corporal; Corporation.
C.P.A., Certified Public Accountant.
Cpl., Corporal.
C.P.O., Chief Petty Officer.
C. R., Costa Rica.
cr., credit; creditor.
C.S.A., Confederate States of America.
C.S.T., Central Standard Time.
ct., cent(s).
cu., cubic.
cwt., hundredweight.
C. Z., Canal Zone (Panama).
Czech., Czechoslovakia.

D. A., District Attorney.
D.A.R., Daughters of the American Revolution.
DAV, Disabled American Veterans.
dB, decibel.
D. C., District of Columbia.
D.C., direct current.
D.D., Doctor of Divinity.
D.D.S., Doctor of Dental Surgery.

DDT, dichloro-diphenyl-trichloro-ethane (an insecticide).
Dec., December.
Del., De., Delaware.
Dem., Democratic.
Den., Denmark.
dept., department.
Deut., Deuteronomy.
DEW, distant early warning.
DFC, Distinguished Flying Cross.
dial., dialect(ical).
dir., director.
D.Litt., Doctor of Letters.
DMZ, demilitarized zone.
DNA, deoxyribonucleic acid.
do., ditto.
DOA, dead on arrival.
doz., dozen; dozens.
DP, displaced person.
Dr., Doctor; (l.c.) debit; debtor; dram.
D.Sc., Doctor of Science.
DSC, Distinguished Service Cross.
DSO, Distinguished Service Order.
DST, Daylight Saving Time.
d.t., delirium tremens.
D.V.M., Doctor of Veterinary Medicine.
dwt., pennyweight.

E., east.
ECA, Economic Coöperation Administration.
Eccl., Ecclesiastes.
econ., economics.
Ecua., Ecuador.
ed., editor(ial).
Edw., Edward.
E.E., Electrical Engineer.
EFTA, European Free Trade Association.
Eg., Egypt; Egyptian.
e.g., for example.
Eliz., Elizabeth; Elizabethan.
ENE, east-northeast.
Eng., England; English.
engr., engineer.
Ens., Ensign.
ERA, earned-run average.
ESE, east-southeast.
ESP, extrasensory perception.
Esq., Esqr., Esquire.
E.S.T., Eastern Standard Time.
Est., Estonia; established.
Esth., Esther.
et al., and others.
etc., et cetera.
Eth., Ethiopia.
ETO, European Theater of Operations.
et seq., and the following.
Eu., Europ., European.
EVA, extravehicular activity.
Ex., Exodus.
Ez., Esr., Ezra.
Ezek., Ezekiel.

F., Fahrenheit; Fellow.
F. & A. M., Free and Accepted Masons.
FAO, Food and Agriculture Organization.
FBI, Federal Bureau of Investigation.

FCA, Farm Credit Administration.
FCC, Federal Communications Commission.
FDA, Food and Drug Administration.
Feb., February.
Fed., Federal.
fem., feminine.
ff., following pages.
F.F.V., First Families of Virginia.
FHA, Federal Housing Administration.
fig., figuratively.
Fin., Finland; Finnish.
Fl., Fla., Florida.
Flem., Flemish.
FM, frequency modulation.
fn., footnote.
f.o.b., free on board.
F.O.E., Fraternal Order of Eagles.
FPO, Fleet Post Office.
Fr., Father; French.
Fri., Friday.
ft., feet; foot; fort.
FTC, Federal Trade Commission.
fwd., forward.

Ga., Georgia.
Gal., Galatians.
gal., gallon; gallons.
G. B., Great Britain.
gent., gentleman.
Geo., George.
geom., geometrical; geometry.
Ger., German; Germany.
GHQ, General Headquarters.
GI, General (or Government) Issue; a private soldier.
Gk., Greek.
gm., gram; grams.
G T, Greenwich mean time.
GNP, gross national product.
G.O.P., Grand Old Party (Republican party).
Gov., governor.
Govt., government.
G.P., general practitioner.
G.P.O., Government Printing Office.
GPU, (formerly) Soviet Secret Police.
gr., grain; gross.
gram., grammar.
Gr. Br., Gr. Brit., Great Britain.
G.S.A., Girl Scouts of America.

Hag., Haggai.
Heb., Hebrew(s).
H. I., Hawaiian Islands.
hist., historical.
H. J., here lies.
H. M., His (Her) Majesty.
H.M.S., His (Her) Majesty's Ship.
Hon., Honorable.
h.p., horsepower.
HQ, headquarters.
H.R., House of Representatives.
hr., hour; hours.
H.R.H., His (Her) Royal Highness.
ht., height.
Hz, hertz.

I., Island(s); Isle(s).
Ia., Iowa.

ibid., in the same place.
ICBM, Intercontinental Ballistic Missile.
ICC, Interstate Commerce Commission.
I.D., identification.
Ida., Idaho.
i.e., that is.
Il., Ill., Illinois.
I.L.O., International Labor Organization.
in., inch; inches; (*cap.*) Indiana.
inc., inclosure; (*cap.*) incorporated.
incl., inclusive.
Ind., Indiana.
inf., infinitive.
I.N.R.I., Jesus of Nazareth, King of the Jews.
INS, International News Service.
inst., the present month.
interj., interjection.
I.O.O.F., Independent Order of Odd Fellows.
I.O.U., I owe you.
I.Q., intelligence quotient.
Ire., Ireland.
IRO, International Refugee Organization.
IRBM, Intermediate Range Ballistic Missile.
Is., is., island; islands; (*cap.*) Isaiah.
Ital., Italian; (*l.c.*) italic (type).
ITO, International Trade Organization.
IUD, intrauterine device.
IWW, Industrial Workers of the World.

Jan., January.
Jap., Japan; Japanese.
Jas., James.
jct., junction.
j.g., junior grade.
Jno., John.
Jos., Joseph; Josiah.
Josh., Joshua.
J.P., Justice of the Peace.
jr., junior.
Judg., Judges.

K, king (Chess).
Kan., Kans., Kas., Kansas.
K.C., King's Counsel; Knights of Columbus.
kc., kilocycle(s).
K.G., Knight (of the Order) of the Garter.
keg(s): kilogram(s).
kilo., kilogram(s); kilometer(s).
K. K. K., Ku Klux Klan.
K.O., knockout.
K. of P., Knights of Pythias.
KP, kitchen police.
K.T., Knight Templar.
Kt., knight.
kw., kilowatt(s).
Ky., Kentucky.

La., Louisiana.
Lab., Labrador.
Lam., Lamentations.
Lat., Latin.
lb., pound(s).

LC, landing craft; **LS**, landing ship; **LCI**, landing craft, infantry; **LCP**, landing craft, personnel; **LST**, landing ship, tank; etc.

l. c., lower case (type).

LM, **LEM**, lunar module.

L. I., Long Island.

Lieut., **Lt.**, Lieutenant.

Litt.D., Doctor of Letters.

LL.B., Bachelor of Laws.

LL.D., Doctor of Laws.

L.O.O.M., Loyal Order of Moose.

LSD, lysergic acid diethylamide (a hallucinogenic drug).

Ltd., Limited.

M., Monsieur.

m., meter(s); noon.

M.A., Master of Arts.

Macc., Maccabees.

Maj., Major.

Man., Manitoba.

Mar., March.

masc., masculine.

Mass., **Ma.**, Massachusetts.

math., mathematics.

M.C., Master of Ceremonies; Member of Congress.

M.D., Doctor of Medicine.

Md., Maryland.

mdse., merchandise.

Me., Maine.

M.E., Methodist Episcopal; Mechanical Engineer.

mech., mechanics.

med., medicine.

Medit., Mediterranean.

memo., memorandum.

Messrs., Messieurs.

Mex., Mexican.

mfg., manufacturing.

mfr., manufacturer.

Mgr., Manager; Monsignor.

Mic., Micah.

Mich., **Mi.**, Michigan.

mil., military.

min., mineral; mineralogy.

Minn., **Mn.**, Minnesota.

MIRV, multiple independent re-entry vehicle.

misc., miscellaneous.

Miss., **Ms.**, Mississippi.

Mlle., Mademoiselle.

MM., Messieurs.

mm., millimeter(s).

Mme., Madame.

Mo., Missouri.

M.O., money order.

mo., month(s).

Mon., Monday.

Mont., Montana.

M.P., military police; Member of Parliament.

m.p.h., miles per hour.

Mr., Mister.

Mrs., Mistress.

ms, manuscript.

Msgr., Monsignor.

M/Sgt., Master Sergeant.

M.S.T., Mountain Standard Time.

Mt., mountain; Montana.

MVD, the Soviet Ministry of Internal Affairs.

myth., mythology.

n., noun.

N., north.

N.A.A.C.P., National Association for the Advancement of Colored People.

NAB, National Association of Broadcasters.

N.A.M, National Association of Manufacturers.

NASA, National Aeronautics and Space Administration.

natl., national.

NATO, North Atlantic Treaty Organization.

naut., nautical.

N. B., New Brunswick; note well.

NBC, National Broadcasting Company.

N. C., North Carolina.

N.C.A.A., National Collegiate Athletic Association.

NCO, non-commissioned officer.

N. D., North Dakota.

NE, northeast.

N. E., New England.

Nebr., **Neb.**, **Nb.**, Nebraska.

Neh., Nehemiah.

Neth., Netherlands.

Nev., **Nv.**, Nevada.

N. F., **Newf.**, Newfoundland.

NG, no good.

N. H., New Hampshire.

N. J., New Jersey.

NKVD, the Soviet Secret Police.

NLRB, National Labor Relations Board.

N. M., New Mexico.

NNE, north-northeast.

NNW, north-northwest.

No., north; northern; number.

nom., nominative.

Nor., Norwegian; Norway.

Nov., November.

N.P., no protest.

NRA, National Recovery Administration.

N. S., New Style; Nova Scotia.

NSA, National Student Association.

N. T., New Testament.

NTA, sodiumnitrilotriacetate, used in some detergents as a substitute for phosphates.

Num., Numbers.

NW, northwest.

N. Y., New York.

N. Y. C., New York City.

N. Z., New Zealand.

O., **Oh.**, Ohio.

OAS, Organization of American States.

OAU, Organization of African Unity.

ob., he (she) died.

Obad., Obadiah.

O.B.E., Officer (of the Order) of the British Empire.

obj., objective; object.

OCS, Officer Candidate School.

Oct., October.

O.D., Officer of the Day; overdraft; olive drab (uniforms).

O.E.D., Oxford English Dictionary.

OEO, Office of Economic Opportunity.

O. E. S., Order of the Eastern Star.
Ogpu, (formerly) Soviet Secret Police.
Ok., Okla., Oklahoma.
Ont., Ontario.
OPA, Office of Price Administration.
Or., Ore., Oreg., Oregon.
orch., orchestra.
orig., original(ly).
O.S., Old Style; ordinary seaman.
OSS, Office of Strategic Services.
O. T., Old Testament.
OTS, Officers' Training School.
OWI, Office of War Information.
Ox., Oxford.
oz., ounce(s).

Pa., Pennsylvania.
PA, public address.
P.A., Purchasing Agent.
Pac., Pacif., Pacific.
p. adj., participial adjective.
Pan., Panama.
par., paragraph; parallel.
Para., Paraguay.
paren., parentheses.
pathol., pathology.
PBX, private branch (telephone) exchange.
pc., piece.
p. c., per cent; post card.
P.D., Police Department.
pd., paid.
P.E.N., (International Association of) Poets, Playwrights, Editors, Essayists and Novelists.
Penn., Penna., Pennsylvania.
Pers., Persia; Persian.
pert., pertaining.
Peruv., Peruvian.
Pfc., Private, First Class.
PGA, Professional Golfers' Association.
phar., pharm., pharmaceutical; pharmacopoeia; pharmacy.
Ph.B., Bachelor of Philosophy.
Ph.D., Doctor of Philosophy.
Phil., Philemon; Philip; Philippians; Philippine.
Phila., Philadelphia.
photog., photography.
P. I., Philippine Islands.
pkg., package(s).
pl., plural.
plupf., pluperfect.
P.M., p.m., post meridiem; postmortem; (cap.) Postmaster.
P.O., post office.
Pol., Poland; Polish.
Port., Portugal; Portuguese.
po, possessive.
POW, prisoner of war.
p.p., parcel post; past participle; postpaid.
P.P.S., post postscriptum.
P. R., Puerto Rico; public relations.
pr., pair.
pref., prefix.
prep., preposition.
pret., preterit.
Prof., professor.
pron., pronoun.
Prot., Protestant.

pro tem., for the time being.
prox., (Lat.) proximo; next (month).
P.S., postscript.
Ps., Psalm(s).
P.S.T., Pacific Standard Time.
pt., point.
P.T.A., Parent-Teacher Association.
PT boat, patrol torpedo boat.
p.t.o., please turn over (the page).
Pvt., Private.
PWA, Public Works Administration.
PX, Post Exchange.

Q., Quebec.
Q.E.D., which was to be demonstrated.
QMC, Quartermaster Corps.
qt., quart.
Que., Quebec.
q.v., which see.

RAF, Royal Air Force.
R.C., Red Cross; Reserve Corps; Roman Catholic.
R.D., Rural Delivery.
Rep., Republican; Representative.
Rev., Revelation; Reverend.
R.F.D., Rural Free Delivery.
R. I., Rhode Island.
R.I.P., rest in peace.
rm., ream (paper); room.
R.N., Registered Nurse.
RNA, ribonucleic acid.
Robt., Robert.
Rom., Roman; Romans.
Rom. Cath., Roman Catholic.
ROTC, Reserve Officers' Training Corps.
r.p.m., revolutions per minute.
R.R., railroad; Right Reverend.
R.S.V., Revised Standard Version (of the Bible).
R.S.V.P., please reply.
rt., right.
Rum., Rumania; Rumanian.
Rus., Russ., Russia; Russian.
Ry., Railway.

S., south.
S. A., South Africa; South America; corporation; (Slang) sex appeal.
SAC, Strategic Air Command.
Salv., Salvador; Salvator.
Sam., Saml., Samuel.
S.A.R., Sons of the American Revolution.
Sask., Saskatchewan.
Sat., Saturday; Saturn.
sc., science.
S. C., South Carolina.
Scot., Scottish; Scotland.
S. D., South Dakota.
SDS, Students for a Democratic Society.
SE, southeast.
SEATO, Southeast Asia Treaty Organization.
SEC, Securities and Exchange Commission.
Sept., September.
sgd., signed.
Sgt., Sergeant.

SHAEF, Supreme Headquarters, Allied Expeditionary Forces.
Shak., Shakespeare.
S. I., Staten Island.
Sib., Siberia; Siberian.
Sic., Sicily; Sicilian.
Sig., sig., signor.
sing., singular.
S. J., Society of Jesus.
Slav., Slavic; Slavonian.
So., south; southern.
SP, shore patrol.
Span., Sp., Spain; Spaniard; Spanish.
SPAR, Women's Coast Guard Reserves.
S.P.C.A., Society for Prevention of Cruelty to Animals.
S.P.C.C., Society for Prevention of Cruelty to Children.
sq., square.
Sr., Senior; Señor; Sister.
Sra., Señora.
SRO, standing room only.
SS., Saints.
S.S., steamship.
SSE, south-southeast.
S.S.R., Soviet Socialist Republic.
S/Sgt., Staff Sergeant.
SST, supersonic transport.
SSW, south-southwest.
St., Saint (fem. Ste.); Strait; Street
suf., suff., suffix.
Sun., Sund., Sunday.
superl., superlative.
supt., superintendent.
S.W., southwest.
Swed., Sweden; Swedish.
Swtz., Swit., Switz., Switzerland.
Syr., Syria.

t.b., tuberculosis.
tbsp., tablespoon.
TD, touchdown.
Tenn., Tn., Tennessee.
Tex., Tx., Texas.
Theo., Theodore; Theodosia.
Thos., Thomas.
Thurs., Thursday.
Tim., Timothy.
TKO, technical knockout.
T.N., trade name.
tp., twp., township.
Tr., Troop.
treas., treasurer; treasury.
tsp., teaspoon.
Tues., Tuesday.
TV, television.
TVA, Tennessee Valley Authority.

U.A.W., United Auto, Aircraft, or Agricultural Implements Workers.
u.c., upper case (type).
U.D.C., United Daughters of the Confederacy.
UFO, unidentified flying object.
UHF, ultrahigh frequency.
U. K., United Kingdom.
Ukr., Ukraine.
ult., last month.
U.M.W., United Mine Workers.
U.N., United Nations.

UNESCO, United Nations Educational, Scientific and Cultural Organisation.
UNICEF, United Nations Children's Fund.
UNRRA, United Nations Relief and Rehabilitation Administration.
UP, United Press.
Uru., Uruguay.
U. S., United States (of America).
U. S. A., Union of South Africa; United States Army; United States of America.
USES, United States Employment Service.
USIA, United States Information Agency.
U.S.M.A., United States Military Academy.
USMC, United States Marine Corps.
USN, United States Navy.
U.S.N.A., United States Naval Academy.
USNR, United States Naval Reserve.
USO, United Service Organizations.
U.S.P., United States Pharmacopoeia.
U.S.S., United States Ship, or Steamer.
U.S.S.R., Union of Soviet Socialist Republics.
Ut., Utah.

v., verb.
VA, Veterans' Administration.
Va., Virginia.
V.C., Victoria Cross.
V.D., venereal disease.
Venez., Venezuela.
vet., veteran; veterinarian.
V.F.W., Veterans of Foreign Wars.
VHF, very high frequency.
V. I., Virgin Islands.
v.i., verb intransitive.
V.I.P., very important personage.
viz., namely.
vol., volume.
V.P., Vice-President.
V.S., Veterinary Surgeon.
vs., versus.
Vt., Vermont.
v.t., verb transitive.
VTOL, vertical takeoff and landing.

W., west.
WAAC, Women's Auxiliary Army Corps.
WAAF, Women's Auxiliary Air Force.
WAC, Women's Army Corps.
WAF, Women in the Air Force.
Wash., Wa., Washington.
WASP, Women's Air Force Service Pilots.
WAVES, Women Appointed for Volunteer Emergency Service (U. S. Navy).
W. C. T. U., Women's Christian Temperance Union.
Wed., Wednesday.
WHO, World Health Organization.

W. I., West Indies.
Wi., Wis., Wisc., Wisconsin.
wk., week; work.
Wm., William.
WNW, west-northwest.
W.O., Warrant Officer.
WPA, Works Progress Administration.
WPB, War Production Board.
w.p.m., words per minute.
WRENS, Women's Royal Naval Service.
WSW, west-southwest.
Wv., W. Va., West Virginia.
Wyo., Wy., Wyoming.

Xmas, Christmas.

Y., Young Men's Christian Association.
yd., yard(s).
Y.M.C.A., Young Men's Christian Association.
Y.M.H.A., Young Men's Hebrew Association.
yr., year(s).
Yuc., Yucatan.
Y.W.C.A., Young Women's Christian Association.
Y.W.H.A., Young Women's Hebrew Association.

Zech., Zechariah.
Zeph., Zephaniah.
ZIP, Zone Improvement Plan.

GAZETTEER

An otherwise unidentified entry in the Gazetteer denotes an independent or self-governing country. A dependency is indicated by the name of the mother country, in parentheses. The following special abbreviations are used: *Mand.*, mandate; *Protect.*, protectorate; *Terr.*, territory; *Trust.*, trusteeship; *Fr. C.*, French Community; *Br. C. of N.*, (British) Commonwealth of Nations. Population figures for the United States and the U.S.S.R. are based on the 1970 census; the United Nations reports or estimates of 1969 have been followed for most other countries.

Abidjan (ä″bi-jän′) City (cap. of Ivory Coast) pop. 282,000.

Abyssinia, see *Ethiopia*.

Accra (e-krä′) City (cap. of Ghana) pop. 615,800.

Addis Ababa (ad′is ab′e-be) City (cap. of Ethiopia) pop. 644,120.

Adelaide (ad′e-lād) City (Australia) pop. 742,300.

Aden (ä′den) City (cap. of So. Yemen) pop. 150,000.

Admiralty Is. (Australia) 820 sq. mi., pop. 13,000.

Adriatic Sea (ä″drē-at′ik) between Italy & Yugoslavia, 50,000 sq. mi.

Aegean Sea (ē-jē′on) between Greece & Turkey, 40,000 sq. mi.

Afars & the Issas (ä′färs; is′es) Fr. Terr., 9,000 sq. mi., pop. 81,200, cap. Djibouti.

Afghanistan (af-gan′is-tan″) 250,-000 sq. mi., pop. 16,516,000, cap. Kabul.

Africa (af′ri-ke) Continent, 11,-530,000 sq. mi., pop. 345,000,000.

Ahmedabad (ä″med-ä-bäd′) City (India) pop. 1,507,921.

Akron (ak′ren) City (Ohio) pop. 273,266, urban area 542,775.

Alabama (al″-e-ba′me) State (U.S.) 51,078 sq. mi., pop. 3,444,165, cap. Montgomery.

Alaska (e-las′ke) State (U.S.) 577,-065 sq. mi., pop. 300,382, cap. Juneau.

Albania (al-bān′ye) 11,096 sq. mi., pop. 2,075,000, cap. Tiranë (Ti-rana).

Albany (âl′be-nē) City (cap. of N.Y.) pop. 114,873, urban area 486,525.

Alberta (al-bẽr′te) Prov. (Canada) 248,800 sq. mi., pop. 1,463,203, cap. Edmonton (ed′men-ten).

Albuquerque (al″boo-kẽr′kê) City (N.M.) pop. 243,751, urban area 297,451.

Aleutian Is. (e-loo′shen) (U.S.) 6,800 sq. mi., pop. 6,000.

Alexandria (al″ig-zan′drē-e) City (Egypt) pop. 1,803,900.

Algeria (al-jir′ē-e) 851,284 sq. mi., pop. 13,349,000, cap. Algiers.

Algiers [*Fr.* Alger] (al-jirz′, al-zhe′) City (cap. of Algeria) pop. 903,530.

Amazon River (am′e-zon) (Brazil) 4,000 miles.

Amman (äm′män) City (cap. of Jordan) pop. 330,220.

Amsterdam (am′ster-dam″) City (cap. of Netherlands) pop. 852,-479, urban area 1,047,588.

Andaman Is. (an′de-man) (India) 2,508 sq. mi., pop. 21,316, cap. Port Blair (blâr).

Andaman Sea (an′de-man) part of Bay of Bengal, 218,100 sq. mi.

Andorra (an-dôr′e) 191 sq. mi., pop. 19,000, cap. Andorra la Vella (Andorra la Vieja) (lä vä′yä, lä vē-ā′hä).

Angola (ang-gō′le) (Port.) 481,351 sq. mi., pop. 5,430,000, cap. Luanda.

Ankara (ang′ke-re) City (cap. of Turkey) pop. 905,660.

Annapolis (e-nap′e-lis) City (cap. of Md.) pop. 29,592.

Antarctica (ant-ärk′ti-ke) Continent, 5,000,000 sq. mi.

Antigua (an-tē′gwe) I. (Br.) 108 sq. mi., pop. 63,000, cap. St. Johns.

Antilles, Greater, Lesser (an-til′lēz) two groups of Caribbean islands.

Antilles, Netherlands (an-til′lēz) (Neth.) 390 sq. mi., pop. 218,000, cap. Willemstad.

Antwerp (ant′werp) City (Belgium) pop. 234,099, urban area 673,259.

Apia (ä-pē′ä) City (cap. of W. Samoa) pop. 25,480.

Arabia (e-rā′bē-e) Peninsula, SW Asia; includes Saudi Arabia, Yemen, Southern Yemen, Muscat and Oman, Trucial Oman, Kuwait, Qatar, and the Bahrain Is.

Aral, Lake (ar′el) (U.S.S.R.) 26,-233 sq. mi.

Arctic Ocean (ärk′tik) 5,450,000 sq. mi.

Argentina (är-jen-tē′ne) 1,078,266 sq. mi., pop. 23,983,000, cap. Buenos Aires.

Arizona (ar-i-zō′ne) State (U.S.) 113,580 sq. mi., pop. 1,770,900, cap. Phoenix.

Arkansas (är′ken-sâ) State (U.S.) 52,725 sq. mi., pop. 1,923,295, cap. Little Rock.

Armenia (är-mē′nē-e) (U.S.S.R.) 11,544 sq. mi., pop. 2,493,000, cap. Yerevan.

---

fat, fāte, fär, fâre, fâll, ásk; met, hē, hẽr, maybê; pin, pīne; not, nōte, ôr, tool tub, cūte, pûll; label; oil, owl; go, chip, she, thin, *then*, sing, ink; *see p. 6*

533

Ascension I. (ə-sen'shən) (Br.) 34 sq. mi., pop. 1,486, cap. George-town.

Asia (ā'zhə) Continent, 17,000,000 sq. mi., pop. (without U.S.S.R.) 1,988,000,000.

Asunción (ä-soon-syän') City (cap. of Paraguay) pop. 411,500.

Athens (ath'ənz) City (cap. of Greece) pop. 627,564, urban area 1,852,709.

Atlanta (at-lan'tə) City (cap. of Ga.) pop. 496,973, urban area 1,172,778.

Atlantic Ocean (at-lan'tik) 41,-000,000 sq. mi., inc. Arctic Ocean.

Augusta (ə-gus'tə) City (cap. of Me.) pop. 21,945.

Austin (ås'tin) City (cap. of Tex.) pop. 251,808.

Australia (ås-trāl'yə) 1, Common-wealth of (Br. C. of N.) 2,974,581 sq. mi., pop. 12,296,000, cap. Canberra. 2, Continent, 2,948,366 sq. mi., pop. 11,000,000.

Austria (ås'trē-ə) 32,369 sq. mi., pop. 7,271,000, cap. Vienna.

Azerbaijan (ä″zər-bī-jän') (U.S.S.R.) 33,011 sq. mi., pop. 5,111,000, cap. Baku.

Azores Is. (ə-zōrz') (Port.) 890 sq. mi., pop. 333,400, cap. Ponta Delgada (pon'tə del-gä'də).

Azov, Sea of (ā'zof) No. of the Black Sea, 14,000 sq. mi.

Baffin Bay (baf'in) between Green-land & Baffin Island, approx. 180,000 sq. mi.

Baghdad (bag'dad) City (cap. of Iraq) pop. 1,745,328.

Bahama Is. (bə-hä'mə; -hä'-) (Br.) 4,375 sq. mi., pop. 195,000, cap. Nassau.

Bahrain Is. (bä'rān) Br. Protect., 213 sq. mi., pop. 207,000, cap. Manama.

Baikal, Lake (bī-kal') (U.S.S.R.) 11,780 sq. mi.

Baku (bä-koo') City (cap. of Azerbaijan, U.S.S.R.) pop. 1,261,-000.

Balearic Is. (bal″ē-a'rik) (Sp.) 1,936 sq. mi., pop. 404,497, cap. Palma (päl'mä).

Balkan States (bål'kən) Albania, Bulgaria, Greece, Rumania, Tur-key & Yugoslavia.

Baltic Sea (bål'tik) between Ger-many & Scandinavia, 163,000 sq. mi.

Baltimore (bål'ti-môr) City (Md.) pop. 905,759, urban area 1,579,-781.

Bamako (bä-mä-kä') City (cap. of Mali) pop. 182,000.

Bangkok (bang'kok) City (cap. of Thailand) pop. 1,608,805.

Bangladesh [formerly East Pakis-tan] (bang'glə-desh″) 54,501 sq. mi., pop. 55,243,000, cap. Dacca.

Bangui (bäng'gē) City (cap. of C.

African Republic) pop. 150,000.

Barbados (bär-bā'dōz) I. (Br. C. of N.) 166 sq. mi., pop. 254,000, cap. Bridgetown.

Barcelona (bär-sə-lō'nə) City (Spain) pop. 1,794,381.

Barents Sea (bar'ents) No. of Scandinavia & U.S.S.R., 529,096 sq. mi.

Basse-Terre (bäs-tår') 1, City (cap. of St. Kitts) pop. 15,726. 2, City (cap. of Guadeloupe) pop. 14,000.

Basutoland (bə-soo'tō-land) see *Lesotho.*

Bathurst (bath'ĕrst) City (cap. of Gambia) pop. 31,800.

Baton Rouge (bat'ən roozh) City (cap. of La.) pop. 165,963.

Bechuanaland (bech″û-ä'nə-land) see *Botswana.*

Beirut [*Fr.* Beyrouth] (bā-root') City (cap. of Lebanon) pop. 700,000.

Belfast (bel'fast) City (cap. of No. Ireland) pop. 390,700.

Belgium (bel'jəm) 11,775 sq. mi., pop. 9,646,000, cap. Brussels.

Belgrade [*Serb.* Beograd] (bel'-grād, be′ə-grād) City (cap. of Yugoslavia) pop. 585,234.

Belize (be-lēz') City (cap. of Br. Honduras) pop. 48,421.

Belo Horizonte (be″lō-rē-zon'te) City (Brazil) pop. 1,167,026.

Bengal, Bay of (ben-gäl') between India and Indo-China, approx. 650,000 sq. mi.

Benghazi (ben-gä'zē) City (cap. of Libya) pop. 137,295.

Bering Sea (bir'ing) between Alas-ka & Siberia, 878,000 sq. mi.

Berlin (bər-lin') City, pop. 3,221,-000: East Berlin (cap. of East Germany) 1,086,000; West Berlin (West Germany) 2,135,000.

Bermuda (bər-mūd'ə) I. (Br.) 21 sq. mi., pop. 52,000, cap. Hamilton.

Bern (bĕrn) City (cap. of Switzer-land) pop. 166,800.

Bhutan (boo″tän') 18,000 sq. mi., pop. 770,000, cap. Thimphu (tim″-foo').

Birmingham 1, (bĕr'ming-əm) City (England) pop. 1,074,900, urban area 2,446,400. 2, (bĕr'ming-ham″) City (Ala.) pop. 300,910, urban area 558,099.

Biscay, Bay of (bis'kā) bay off coasts of France & Spain, 160,000 sq. mi.

Bismarck (biz'märk) City (cap. of N.D.) pop. 34,703.

Bismarck Archipelago (biz'märk) Austl. Trust., 19,660 sq. mi., pop. 225,100, including New Britain, New Ireland, New Hanover, and the Admiralty Is.

Bissau (bi-sow') City (cap. of Port. Guinea) pop. 18,309.

Black Sea, between Europe & Asia, 170,000 sq. mi.

Bogotá (bō″as-tä') City (cap. of

Colombia) pop. 2,037,904.

Boise (boi′zĕ) City (cap. of Ida.) pop. 74,990.

Bolivia (bə-liv′ē-ə) 412,777 sq. mi., pop. 4,804,000, cap. La Paz, also Sucre.

Bombay (bom-bā′) City (India) pop. 5,534,358.

Bonn (bŏn) City (cap. of West Germany) pop. 138,090.

Bordeaux (bôr-dō′) City (France) pop. 266,662.

Borneo (bôr′nē-ō) I. (Indonesia & Malaysia) 289,000 sq. mi., pop. 3,800,000.

Boston (bâs′tən) City (cap. of Mass.) pop. 641,071, urban area 2,652,575.

Bothnia, Gulf of (both′nē-ə) between Sweden & Finland, 43,000 sq. mi.

Botswana (bot-swä′nə) [formerly Bechuanaland] (Br. C. of N.) 238,605 sq. mi., pop. 629,000, cap. Gaborone.

Brazil (brə-zil′) 3,286,170 sq. mi., pop. 90,840,000, cap. Brasilia (brə-zil′ē-ə) (pop. 379,699).

Brazzaville (brä′zä-vēl′) City (cap. of People′s Republic of Congo) pop. 99,002.

Brisbane (bris′băn) City (Australia) pop. 680,000.

British Columbia (kə-lum′bē-ə) Prov. (Canada) 359,279 sq. mi., pop. 1,873,674, cap. Victoria.

Brunei (Brü-nī′) Br. Protect. (Borneo) 2,226 sq. mi., pop. 116,-000, cap. Brunei (pop. 9,702).

Brussels [Fr. Bruxelles] (brus′əls, brook-sel′) City (cap. of Belgium) pop. 166,920, urban area 1,077,035.

Bucharest [Rum. Bucuresti] (boo′kə-rest″, boo″koo-resht′) City (cap. of Rumania) pop. 1,431,993.

Budapest (boo′də-pest″) City (cap. of Hungary) pop. 2,000,000.

Buenos Aires (bwā′nes ī′res) City (cap. of Argentina) pop. 3,549,-000, urban area 9,070,000.

Buffalo (buf′ə-lō) City (N.Y.) pop. 462,768, urban area 1,086,594.

Bujumbura (boo″jam-bûr′ə) City (cap. of Burundi) pop. 71,000.

Bulgaria (bul-ger′ē-ə) 42,796 sq. mi., pop. 8,436,000, cap. Sofia.

Burma (bûr′mə) 261,610 sq. mi., pop. 26,980,000, cap. Rangoon.

Burundi (bū-rŭn′dē) 10,744 sq. mi., pop. 3,475,000, cap. Bujumbura.

Byelorussian S.S.R. (bye′lā-roo′-sē-ən) (U.S.S.R.) 83,012 sq. mi., pop. 9,003,000, cap. Minsk (mēnsk).

Cairo (kī′rō) City (cap. of U.A.R.) pop. 4,225,700.

Calcutta (kal-kut′ə) City (India) pop. 3,134,161, urban area 5,074,-668.

California (kal-i-fôr′nē-ə) State (U.S.) 156,803 sq. mi., pop. 19,-

953,134, cap. Sacramento.

Cambodia (kam-bō′dē-ə) 69,884 sq. mi., pop. 6,701,000, cap. Pnompenh.

Cameroun (kăm-roon′) 161,787 sq. mi., pop. 5,562,000, cap. Yaoundé.

Canada (kan′ə-də) (Br. C. of N.) 3,621,616 sq. mi., pop. 21,089,000, cap. Ottawa.

Canal Zone (U.S.) 362 sq. mi., pop. 44,650, cap. Balboa Heights (bal-bō′ə).

Canary Is. (kə-ner′ē) (Sp.) 2,894 sq. mi., pop. 944,448, cap. Las Palmas, Santa Cruz (läs päl′mäs, san′tə krooz).

Canberra (kăn′ber-ə) City (cap. of Australia) pop. 119,235.

Canton [Chinese Kwangchow] (kan-ton′, gwäng-jō′) City (China) pop. 1,840,000.

Cape Town, City (cap. of Union of South Africa) pop. 508,341, urban area 807,211.

Cape Verde Is. (kāp vêrd) (Port.) 1,557 sq. mi., pop. 250,000, cap. Praia (prī′ə).

Caracas (kə-rä′kəs) City (cap. of Venezuela) pop. 786,710, urban area 2,064,033.

Caribbean Sea (kar′ə-bē′ən) between So. America & West Indies, 750,000 sq. mi.

Caroline Is. (kar′ə-līn) U.S. Trust., 525 sq. mi., pop. 35,301, cap. Truk (trŭk).

Carson City (kär′sən) City (cap. of Nev.) pop. 15,468.

Casablanca (kas′ə-blang′kə) City (Morocco) pop. 1,320,000.

Caspian Sea (kas′pē-ən) between Europe & Asia, 169,383 sq. mi.

Cayenne (kī-en′) City (cap. of Fr. Guinea) pop. 18,010.

Cayman Is. (kī-măn′) (Br.) 104 sq. mi., pop. 12,000, cap. Georgetown.

Celebes (sel′ə-bēz) (Indonesia) 72,-986 sq. mi., pop. 8,700,000, cap. Makassar (mə-kas′ər) (pop. 384,-159).

Central African Republic (af′ri-kən) (Fr. C.) 238,000 sq. mi., pop. 1,518,000, cap. Bangui.

Central America (ə-mer′i-kə) district comprising Guatemala, Honduras, El Salvador, Nicaragua, Costa Rica, and Panama.

Ceylon (sē-lon′) (Br. C. of N.) 25,332 sq. mi., pop. 12,240,000, cap. Colombo.

Chad (chăd) (Fr. C.) 455,598 sq. mi., pop. 3,510,000, cap. Fort-Lamy.

Changsha (chăng′shä) City (cap. of Hunan, China) pop. 703,000.

Channel Is. (chan′əl) (Br.) 75 sq. mi., pop. 117,000.

Charleston (chärls′tən) 1, City (cap. of W. Va.) pop. 71,505, urban area 157,662. 2, City (S.C.) pop. 66,945, urban area 228,399.

tub, cūte, pŭll; label; oil, owl; go, chip, she, thin, then, sing, ink; see p. 6

Charlotte (shär'lət) City (N.C.) pop. 241,178.

Chengtu (chung-doo') City (China) pop. 1,107,000.

Cheyenne (shī-en') City (cap. of Wyo.) pop. 40,914.

Chicago (shi-kä'gō) City (Ill.) pop. 3,366,957, urban area 6,714,578.

Chile (chil'ē) 286,396 sq. mi., pop. 9,566,000, cap. Santiago.

China (chī'nə) 1, [People's Republic of China] 3,768,727 sq. mi., pop. 740,000,000, cap. Peking (Peiping). 2, [The Republic of China] see Taiwan.

Chosen (chō'sen') see Korea.

Christmas (kris'məs) 1, I. (Australia) 64 sq. mi., pop. 3,524. 2, Is. (U.S., Br.) 184 sq. mi.

Chungking [Chinese Pahsien] (chung'king', bä-shyen') City (China) pop. 2,121,000.

Cincinnati (sin-si-na'tē) City (Ohio) pop. 452,524, urban area 1,110,514.

Ciudad Trujillo (thyoo'thäth troo-hē'yō) former name of capital of Dominican Republic.

Cleveland (klēv'lənd) City (Ohio) pop. 750,903, urban area 1,959,-880.

Cocos Is. (ko'kəs) (Australia) 5 sq. mi., pop. 1,000.

Cologne [Ger. Köln] (kə-lōn', kůln) City (West Germany) pop. 853,-864.

Colombia (kə-lum'bē-ə) 439,828 sq. mi., pop 20,463,000, cap. Bogota.

Colombo (kə-lum'bō) City (cap. of Ceylon) pop. 551,200.

Colorado (kol-ə-rad'ō) State (U.S.) 103,967 sq. mi., pop. 2,207,259, cap. Denver.

Columbia (kə-lum'bē-ə) City (cap. of S.C.) pop. 113,542, urban area 241,781.

Columbus (kə-lum'bəs) City (cap. of Ohio) pop. 539,677, urban area 790,019.

Comoro Is. (ko-mō'rō) Fr. Terr., 863 sq. mi., pop. 270,000, cap. Moroni (mō-rō'nē).

Conakry (kon'ə-krē") City (cap. of Guinea) pop. 197,267.

Concord (kon'kôrd) City (cap. of N.H.) pop. 30,022.

Congo (kon'gō) region in C. Africa, now: Democratic Republic of Congo [formerly Belgian Congo] 902,-274 sq. mi., pop. 17,100,000, cap. Kinshasa; and People's Republic of Congo [formerly Moyen Congo] (Fr. C.) 175,676 sq. mi., pop. 880,000, cap. Brazzaville.

Connecticut (kə-net'i-kət) State (U.S.) 4,899 sq. mi., pop. 3,031,-709, cap. Hartford.

Constantinople, see Istanbul.

Cook Is. (kůk) (New Zeal.) 90 sq. mi., pop. 20,000, cap. Avarua.

Copenhagen (kō"pən-hä'gən) City

(cap. of Denmark) pop. 863,691, urban area 1,377,890.

Coral Sea, part of Pacific Ocean NE of Australia.

Corsica (kôr'si-kə) I. (Fr.) 3,367 sq. mi., pop. 269,831, cap. Ajaccio (ä-yät'chō).

Costa Rica (kos'tə-rē'kə) 19,239 sq. mi., pop. 1,695,000, cap. San José (sän hä-se').

Crete (krēt) I. (Greece) 3,232 sq. mi., pop. 483,075, cap. Canea (kə-nē'ə).

Cuba (kū'bə) 42,857 sq. mi., pop. 8,250,000, cap. Havana.

Curaçao (kûr'ə-sow) see Netherlands Antilles.

Cyprus (sī'prəs) (Br. C. of N.) 3,572 sq. mi., pop. 630,000, cap. Nicosia (ni'kä-zē'ə).

Czechoslovakia (chek'ō-slō-väk"-yə) 49,356 sq. mi., pop. 14,418,000, cap. Prague.

Dacca (dak'ə) City (cap. of Bangladesh) pop. 829,000.

Dahomey (də-hō'mē) 42,471 sq. mi., pop. 2,640,000, cap. Porto Novo.

Dakar (dä-kär') City (cap. of Senegal) pop. 581,000.

Dallas (dal'əs) City (Tex.) pop. 844,401, urban area 1,338,684.

Damascus [Arabic Esh Shâm] (də-mas'kəs, ash-sham') City (cap. of Syria) pop. 789,840.

Danzig [Pol. Gdansk] (dan'tsig, gə-däny'sk) City (Poland) pop. 364,000.

Dar es Salaam (där'es-sə-läm') City (cap. of Tanzania) pop. 272,821.

Davis Strait (dā'vis) between Greenland & Baffin Island.

Dayton (dā'tən) City (Ohio) pop. 243,601, urban area 685,942.

Dead Sea, between Palestine & Jordan, 340 sq. mi.

Delaware (del'ə-wâr) State (U.S.) 1,978 sq. mi., pop. 548,104, cap. Dover.

Delhi (del'ē) City (India) pop. 3,621,101.

Denmark (den'märk) 16,556 sq. mi., pop. 4,910,000, cap. Copenhagen.

Denver (den'vər) City (cap. of Colo.) pop. 514,678, urban area 1,047,311.

Des Moines (di-moin') City (cap. of Iowa) pop. 200,587.

Detroit (dē-troit') City (Mich.) pop. 1,511,482, urban area 3,970,-584.

Dili (dil'ē) City (cap. of Port. Timor) pop. 52,158.

District of Columbia (kə-lum'bē-ə) (U.S.) 61 sq. mi., pop. 756,510.

Djakarta (jə-kär'tə) City (cap. of Indonesia) pop. 2,906,533.

Djibouti (ji-boo'tē) City (cap. of

Afars) pop. 61,500.

Dodecanese Is. (dō-dek'ə-nēz) (Greece) 1,030 sq. mi., pop. 123,-021.

Doha (dō'hə) City (cap. of Qatar) pop. 45,000.

Dominica (dō-min'i-kə) (Br.) 290 sq. mi., pop. 74,000, cap. Roseau.

Dominican Republic (də-min'ə-kən) 19,129 sq. mi., pop. 4,174,000, cap. Santo Domingo.

Douglas (dug'ləs) City (cap. of Isle of Man) pop. 19,517.

Dover (dō'vər) City (cap. of Del.) pop. 17,488.

Dresden (drez'dən) City (East Germany) pop. 499,848.

Dublin [*Gaelic* **Baile Atha Cliath**] (dub'lin, blä-klē'ə) cap. of Republic of Ireland, pop. 568,772, urban area 650,153.

Durban (dĕr'bən) City (So. Africa) pop. 560,010.

Ecuador (ek'wə-dôr) 115,000 sq. mi., pop. 5,890,000, cap. Quito.

Edinburgh (ed'ən-bĕr'ə) City (cap. of Scotland) pop. 470,404.

Egypt (ē'jipt) see *United Arab Republic.*

Eire (er'ə) former name for the *Republic of Ireland.*

Ellesmere I. (elz'mĕr) (Canada) 82,119 sq. mi., pop. 150.

El Paso (el pas'ō) City (Tex.) pop. 322,261.

England and Wales (ing'glənd, wālz) 58,340 sq. mi., pop. 48,827,-000, cap. London.

Erie, Lake (ir'ē) (Great Lakes) 9,940 sq. mi.

Eritrea (er-i-trē'ə) (Ethiopia) 15,-754 sq. mi., pop. 1,589,400, cap. Asmara (äs-mä'rä).

Erivan, see *Yerevan.*

Estonia or Estonian S.S.R. (es-tō'nyə) (U.S.S.R.) 17,838 sq. mi., pop. 1,357,000, cap. Tallinn (täl'-lin).

Ethiopia (ē'thē-ō'pē-ə) 350,000 sq. mi., pop. 24,769,000, cap. Addis Ababa.

Europe (ū'rəp) Continent, 1,920,-000 sq. mi., pop. 460,000,000 (without U.S.S.R.).

Faeroe Is. (fer'ō) (Den.) 540 sq. mi., pop. 38,000, cap. Thorshavn (tôrs-hown').

Falkland Is. (fåk'lənd) (Br.) incl. S. Georgia, 5,618 sq. mi., pop. 2,721, cap. Stanley.

Fernando Poo (fer-nän'dō pō'ō) I. (Equatorial Guinea) 800 sq. mi., pop. 80,000, cap. Santa Isabel (sän'tä ē-sä-bel').

Fiji (fē'jē) Is. (Br.) 7,055 sq. mi., pop. 519,000, cap. Suva.

Finland (fin'lənd) 130,500 sq. mi., pop. 4,703,000, cap. Helsinki.

Florida (flor'idə) State (U.S.) 54,-262 sq. mi., pop. 6,789,443, cap. Tallahassee.

Formosa, see *Taiwan.*

Fort-de-France (fôr'dĕ-fräns") City (cap. of Martinique) pop. 40,380.

Fort-Lamy (lä-mē') City (cap. of Chad) pop. 99,000.

Fort Lauderdale (lâ'dər-dāl") City (Florida) pop. 139,122, urban area 613,797.

Fort Worth (wĕrth) City (Tex.) pop. 393,476, urban area 676,944.

France (frans) 212,736 sq. mi., pop. 50,320,000, cap. Paris.

Frankfort (frank'fərt) City (cap. of Ky.) pop. 21,356.

Franz Josef Land (fränts' yō'zef-länt") Arctic archipelago (U.S.S.R.) 8,000 sq. mi.

Freetown (frē'town) City (cap. of Sierra Leone) pop. 170,600.

French Indo-China (in'dō-chī'nə) former Fr. terr., now: Cambodia, Laos, Vietnam.

French Sudan (soo-dan') see *Mali.*

Friendly Is., see *Tonga.*

Fundy, Bay of (fun'dē) between Nova Scotia & New Brunswick, 6,300 sq. mi.

Gabon (gä-bân') (Fr. C.) 103,088 sq. mi., pop. 485,000, cap. Libreville.

Galapagos Is. (gä-lä'pä-gås) (Ecuador) 3,042 sq. mi., pop. 2,391, cap. San Cristobal (san krəs-tō'bəl).

Galilee, Sea of (gal'ə-lē") (Israel) 64 sq. mi.

Gambia (gam'bē-ə) (Br. C. of N.) 3,999 sq. mi., pop. 357,000, cap. Bathurst.

Gdansk, see *Danzig.*

Geneva (jə-nē'və) City (Switzerland) pop. 169,500, urban area 307,500.

Genoa [*Ital.* **Genova**] (jen'ō-ə, je-nō'və) City (Italy) pop. 843,632.

Georgetown (jôrj'town) 1. City (cap. of Cayman) pop. 2,573. 2. City (cap. of Guyana) pop. 97,160.

Georgia (jôr'jə) State (U.S.) 58,518 sq. mi., pop. 4,589,575, cap. Atlanta.

Georgian S.S.R. (jôr'jyən) (U.S.S.R.) 28,687 sq. mi., pop. 4,688,000, cap. Tiflis (Tbilisi) (tif"-lis, tbi'lē-se).

Germany (jĕr'mə-nē) former German Empire, now: Democratic Republic of Germany (East Germany), 41,479 sq. mi., pop. 16,-010,000, cap. East Berlin; and Federal Republic of Germany (West Germany), 95,737 sq. mi., pop. 58,707,000, cap. Bonn.

Ghana (gä'nə) (Br. C. of N.) 88,802 sq. mi., pop. 8,600,000, cap. Accra.

Gibraltar (ji-brâl'tər) (Br.) 2 sq.

mi., pop. 27,000.

Gibraltar, Strait of, between Spain & Africa.

Gilbert and Ellice Is. (gil'bərt; el'is) (Br.) 349 sq. mi., pop. 54,000, cap. Tarawa (tar'ə-wä').

Glasgow (glas'kō) City (Scotland) pop. 927,948.

Goa (gō'ə) (India) 1,313 sq. mi., pop. 626,978, cap. Pangim (bän-zhēn').

Gold Coast, former name of *Ghana.*

Gorky (gôr'kē) City (U.S.S.R.) pop. 1,170,000.

Great Bear Lake (Canada) 12,275 sq. mi.

Great Britain, see *United Kingdom.*

Great Lakes, chain of 5 lakes between U.S. & Canada: Erie, Huron, Michigan, Ontario, Superior.

Great Salt Lake (Utah) 2,560 sq. mi.

Great Slave Lake (Canada) 10,980 sq. mi.

Greece (grēs) 51,182 sq. mi.; pop. 8,835,000, cap. Athens.

Greenland (grēn'lənd) (Den.) 839,-999 sq. mi., pop. 47,000, cap. Godthaab (gät'häp).

Grenada (gre-nä'de) (Br.) 133 sq. mi., pop. 105,000, cap. St. George's.

Guadalajara (gwä'thä-lä-hä'rä) City (Mexico) pop. 1,352,109.

Guadeloupe and Dependencies (gwä'de-loop') (Fr.) 688 sq. mi.; pop. 323,000, cap. Basse-Terre.

Guam (gwäm) U.S. Terr., 206 sq. mi., pop. 89,626, cap. Agaña (ä-gä'nye).

Guatemala (gwät'e-mä-le) 45,452 sq. mi., pop. 5,014,000, cap. Guatemala City (pop. 577,120).

Guiana (gē-ä'ne) see *Guyana.*

Guiana, Dutch (gē-ä'ne) see *Surinam.*

Guiana, French (gē-ä'ne) (Fr.) 35,135 sq. mi., pop. 40,000, cap. Cayenne (kī-en').

Guinea (gin'ē) 96,525 sq. mi., pop. 3,890,000, cap. Conakry.

Guinea, Portuguese (gin'ē) (Port.) 13,948 sq. mi., pop. 530,000, cap. Bissau.

Guinea, Equatorial (gin'ē) (Sp.) 10,830 sq. mi., pop. 281,000, cap. Santa Isabel.

Guyana (gē-ä'ne) (Br. C. of N.) 89,480 sq. mi., pop. 742,000, cap. Georgetown.

Hague, The [*Dutch* 's Gravenhage] (hāg, skrä'vən-hä'ks) City (Netherlands) pop. 570,765.

Haiti (hā'tē) 10,714 sq. mi., pop. 4,768,000, cap. Port-au-Prince.

Hamburg (ham'bûrg) City (West Germany) pop. 1,826,411.

Hamilton (ham'il-tən) 1, City (cap. of Bermuda) pop. 3,000, 2, City (Canada) pop. 298,121, urban area 471,000.

Hanoi (ha-noi') City (cap. of North Vietnam) pop. 414,620, urban area 643,576.

Harbin (här'bin) City (Manchuria) pop. 1,552,000.

Harrisburg (har'ris-bûrg) City (cap. of Pa.) pop. 68,061, urban area 240,751.

Hartford (härt'fərd) City (cap. of Conn.) pop. 158,017, urban area 465,001.

Havana [*Span.* La Habana] (he-van'e, lä ä-vä'ne) City (cap. of Cuba) pop. 990,000, urban area 1,565,700.

Hawaii (hä-wī'ē) State (U.S.) 6,420 sq. mi., pop. 768,561, cap. Honolulu.

Helena (hel'e-ne) City (cap. of Mont.) pop. 22,730.

Helsinki (hel'sing-kē) City (cap. of Finland) pop. 523,051.

Hiroshima (hī'rō-shē'me, *Jap.* hē-räsh'mä) City (Japan) pop. 542,-000.

Hispaniola (his-pan'e-ō'le) I.; includes Haiti and Dominican Republic.

Holland, see *Netherlands.*

Honduras (hon-door'es) 43,277 sq. mi., pop. 2,495,000, cap. Tegucigalpa.

Honduras, British (hon-door'es) (Br.) 8,766 sq. mi., pop. 120,000, cap. Belize.

Hong Kong (hong'kong') (Br.) 391 sq. mi., pop. 3,990,000, cap. Victoria.

Honolulu (ho'ne-loo'loo) City (cap. of Hawaii) pop. 319,784, urban area 442,397.

Honshu (hon'shoo) I. (Jap.) 88,-000 sq. mi., pop. 48,681,000, cap. Tokyo.

Houston (hūs'tən) City (Tex.) pop. 1,232,802, urban area 1,677,-863.

Huang or Yellow River (hwäng) (China) 3,000 miles.

Hudson Bay, bay of No. Canada, 281,900 sq. mi.

Hungary (hung'ge-rē) 35,875 sq. mi., pop. 10,295,000, cap. Budapest.

Huron, Lake (hyū'rən) (Great Lakes) 23,010 sq. mi.

Hyderabad (hī'dēr-e-bàd') City (India) pop. 1,294,800.

Iceland (īs'lənd) 39,709 sq. mi., pop. 203,000, cap. Reykjavik.

Idaho (ī'de-hō) State (U.S.) 82,808 sq. mi., pop. 712,567, cap. Boise.

Ifni (ēf'nē) (Morocco) 579 sq. mi., pop. 52,000.

Illinois (il-e-noi') State (U.S.) 55,-947 sq. mi., pop. 11,113,976, cap. Springfield.

India (in'dē-e) (Br. C. of N.) 1,059,342 sq. mi., pop. 536,984,-000, cap. New Delhi.

Indiana (in'dē-an'e) State (U.S.)

36,205 sq. mi., pop. 5,193,669, cap. Indianapolis (in″dē-ən-ap′ə-lis) (pop. 743,155).

Indian Ocean, between Africa & Australia, 28,350,000 sq. mi.

Indo-China (in′dō chī′nə) Peninsula comprising Burma, Thailand, Cambodia, Laos, Vietnam, and Malaya.

Indonesia (in″dō-nē′zhə) 575,892 sq. mi., pop. 116,000,000, cap. Djakarta.

Iowa (ī′ə-wə) State (U.S.) 55,986 sq. mi., pop. 2,824,376, cap. Des Moines.

Iran [formerly Persia] (ī-ran′, pēr′zhə) 628,000 sq. mi., pop. 27,892,000, cap. Teheran.

Iraq [formerly Mesopotamia] (ī-rak′, mes″ō-pō-tā′mē-ə) 116,600 sq. mi., pop. 8,840,000, cap. Baghdad.

Ireland, Northern (īr′lənd) (U.K.) 5,238 sq. mi., pop. 1,513, 000, cap. Belfast.

Ireland, Republic of (īr′lənd) 26,601 sq. mi., pop. 2,921,000, cap. Dublin.

Irish Sea, between Ireland & Great Britain, 75,000 sq. mi.

Islamabad (is-läm′ə-bäd″) City under construction (cap. of Pakistan).

Isle of Man (Br.) 221 sq. mi., pop. 50,000, cap. Douglas.

Israel (iz′rē-əl) 7,992 sq. mi., pop. 2,822,000, cap. Jerusalem.

Istanbul [formerly Constantinople] (is″tan-bool′, kon″stan-ti-nō′pəl) City (Turkey) pop. 1,742,978.

Italy (it′ə-lē) 116,000 sq. mi., pop. 53,170,000, cap. Rome.

Ivory Coast 124,503 sq. mi., pop. 4,195,000, cap. Abidjan.

Jackson (jak′sən) City (cap. of Miss.) pop. 153,968.

Jacksonville (jak′sən-vil) City (Fla.) pop 518,131.

Jakarta (jə-kär′tə) see Djakarta.

Jamaica (jə-mā′kə) I. (Br. C. of N.) 4,450 sq. mi., pop. 1,959,000, cap. Kingston.

Japan (jə-pan′) 144,550 sq. mi., pop. 102,321,000, cap. Tokyo.

Japan, Sea of (jə-pan′) between Japan and Korea, 391,100 sq. mi.

Java and Madura (jä′və, mä-doo′rä) (Indonesia) 51,032 sq. mi., pop. 72,600,000.

Jefferson City (jef′ər-sən) City (cap. of Mo.) pop. 32,407.

Jersey City (jēr′zē) City (N.J.) pop. 260,545.

Jerusalem (jə-roo′sə-lem) City (cap. of Israel) pop. 275,000.

Jesselton (jes′əl-tən) City (cap. of Sabah, E. Malaysia) pop. 21,719.

Johannesburg (jō-han′is-bērg″) City (Union of So. Africa) pop. 595,083, urban area 1,125,525.

Jordan [formerly Transjordan]

(jôr′dən) 37,300 sq. mi., pop. 2,160,000, cap. Amman.

Juneau (joo′nō) City (cap. of Alaska) pop. 6,050.

Kabul (kä′bûl) City (cap. of Afghanistan) pop. 289,703.

Kampala (käm-pä′lä) City (cap. of Uganda) pop. 46,735.

Kanpur (kän′pûr) City (India) pop. 1,163,524.

Kansas (kan′zəs) State (U.S.) 82,-113 sq. mi., pop. 2,246,578, cap. Topeka.

Kansas City (kan′zəs) City (Mo.) pop. 501,859, urban area 1,101,-787.

Karachi (ke-rä′chē) City (former cap. of Pakistan) pop. 3,060,000.

Katmandu (kät-män-doo′) City (cap. of Nepal) pop. 121,019.

Kazakh S.S.R. (kä-zäk′) (U.S.S.R.) 1,064,092 sq. mi., pop. 12,850,000, cap. Alma-Ata.

Keeling Is. (kē′ling) see Cocos Is.

Kentucky (kən-tuk′ē) State (U.S.) 40,109 sq. mi., pop. 3,218,706, cap. Frankfort.

Kenya (kēn′yə) (Br. C. of N.) 224,960 sq. mi., pop. 10,506,000, cap. Nairobi.

Kharkov (kär′kof) City (Russia) pop. 1,223,000.

Khartoum (kär-toom′) City (cap. of Sudan) pop. 194,000.

Kiev (kē′yef) City (Russia) pop. 1,632,000.

Kingston (kings′tən) City (cap. of Jamaica) pop. 123,403.

Kinshasa [formerly Leopoldville] (kin-shä′sä) City (cap. of Democratic Republic of Congo) pop. 901,520.

Kirghis S.S.R. (kir-gēz′) (U.S.S.R.) 77,838 sq. mi., pop. 2,933,000, cap. Frunze (froon′ze).

Kitakyushu (kē″tä-kyoo′shoo) City (Japan) pop. 1,050,000.

Kiubyshev (kyoo′bi-shef″) City (U.S.S.R.) pop. 1,047,000.

Kobe (kō′be) City (Japan) pop. 1,253,000.

Korea (kō-rē′ə) 1, Democratic People's Republic of Korea (North Korea) 47,862 sq. mi., pop. 13,-300,000, cap. Pyongyang (pyung′-yäng). 2, Republic of Korea (South Korea) 37,424 sq. mi., pop. 31,139,000, cap. Seoul.

Kuala Lumpur (kwä′lä lûm′pûr) City (cap. of Malaysia) pop. 316,230.

Kuching (koo′ching) City (cap. of Sarawak, E. Malaysia) pop. 50,-579.

Kuril Is. or Chishima (koo-rēl′, chē-shē′mä) (U.S.S.R.) 3,944 sq. mi., pop. 15,000.

Kuwait (kû-wāt′) 5,991 sq. mi., pop. 570,000, cap. Al Kuwait (pop. 99,609, urban area 295,273).

Kwangchow, see Canton.

tub, cūte, pûll; label; oil, owl; go, chip, she, thin, then, sing, ink; see p. 6

Kyoto (kyō'tō) City (Japan) pop. 1,410,000.

Labrador (lab'rə-dôr') (Newfoundland) 112,000 sq. mi., pop. 21,300, cap. Battle Harbour.

Lagos (lā'gäs) City (cap. of Nigeria) pop. 841,749.

Lahore (lə'hôr) City (Pakistan) pop. 1,823,000.

Lansing (lan'sing) City (cap. of Mich.) pop. 131,546, urban area 229,518.

Laos (lā'ōs) 89,343 sq. mi., pop. 2,893,000, cap. Vientiane.

La Paz (lä-päz') City (cap. of Bolivia) pop. 525,000.

Latvia or Latvian S.S.R. (lat'vē-ə) (U.S.S.R.) 24,954 sq. mi., pop. 2,365,000, cap. Riga (rē'gä).

Lebanon (leb'ə-nən) 3,475 sq. mi., pop. 2,645,000, cap. Beirut.

Leeds (lēdz) City (England) pop. 506,100, urban area 1,730,210.

Leeward Is. (lē'wərd) (Br.) 423 sq. mi., pop. 382,000, cap. St. John's.

Leipsig (līp'sig) City (East Germany) pop. 590,291.

Leningrad (len'in-grad') City (Russia) pop. 3,513,000.

Leopoldville (lē'ə-pōld-vil) see Kinshasa.

Lesotho [formerly Basutoland] (lə-sō'tō) (Br. C. of N.) 11,716 sq. mi., pop. 930,000, cap. Maseru.

Liberia (lī-bir'ē-ə) 43,000 sq. mi., pop. 1,150,000, cap. Monrovia.

Libreville (lē'brə-vēl') City (cap. of Gabon) pop. 57,000.

Libya (lib'ē-ə) 679,358 sq. mi., pop. 1,869,000, cap. Tripoli, also, Benghazi.

Liechtenstein (lik'tən-stīn) 65 sq. mi., pop. 21,000, cap. Vaduz (vä'dūts).

Lima (lē'mə) City (cap. of Peru) pop. 2,415,700.

Lincoln (link'ən) City (cap. of Neb.) pop. 149,518.

Lisbon [Port. Lisboa] (liz'bən, lēzh-bō'ə) City (cap. of Portugal) pop. 828,000.

Lithuania or Lithuanian S.S.R. (lith'ū-ā'nyə) (U.S.S.R.) 24,151 sq. mi., pop. 3,129,000, cap. Vilnyus (Vilna) (vil'nē-ūs, vil'nə).

Little Rock (lit'əl-rok") City (cap. of Ark.) pop. 132,483.

Liverpool (liv'ər-pool) City (England) pop. 688,000, urban area 1,368,630.

Lome (lō-mā') City (cap. of Togo) pop. 90,600.

London (lun'dən) City (cap. of England) pop. 7,763,800.

Long Beach (lông'bēch') City (Calif.) pop. 358,633.

Los Angeles (los an'je-les) City (Calif.) pop. 2,816,061, urban area 8,351,266.

Louisiana (lū-ēz'ē-an'ə) State (U.S.) 45,177 sq. mi., pop. 3,643,-

180, cap. Baton Rouge.

Louisville (loo'i-vil) City (Ky.) pop. 361,472, urban area 739,396.

Lourenço Marques (lä-ren'sō mär"kes, (' p. of Mozambique) pop. 178,565.

Loyalty . . . . . . -tē) (Fr.) 800 sq. mi., pop. 11,500, cap. Lifou (lē-foo').

Luanda (lū-än'də) City (cap. of Angola) pop. 224,540.

Lusaka (loo-sä'kə) City (cap. of Zambia) pop. 238,200.

Lüshun [formerly Port Arthur] (lyoo'shūn) City (People's Republic of China) pop. 126,000, urban area 1,508,000.

Luxembourg (luk'səm-bêrg) 999 sq. mi., pop. 337,000, cap. Luxembourg (pop. 77,458).

Lyon (lē-ōn', City (France) pop. 527,800, urban area 1,074,823.

Macao (mə-kow') (Port.) 6 sq. mi., pop. 161,252, cap. Macao.

Madagascar, see Malagasy Republic.

Madeira Is. (mə-dir'ə) (Port.) 308 sq. mi., pop. 268,600, cap. Funchal (fūn-shäl').

Madison (mad'i-sən) City (cap. of Wis.) pop. 173,258, urban area 205,457.

Madras (mə-dräs') City (India) pop. 2,047,735.

Madrid (mə-drid') City (cap. of Spain) pop. 2,850,361.

Madura (mä-doo'rə) I. (Indonesia) 1,725 sq. mi., pop. 11,585, cap. Pamekasar (pä"mä-kə-sän').

Magellan Straits of (mə-jel'ən) at so. tip of So. America.

Maine (mān) State (U.S.) 31,040 sq. mi., pop. 992,048, cap. Augusta.

Malacca, Straits of (mə-lak'ə) between Sumatra & Malaya.

Malagasy Republic [formerly Madagascar] (mä-lä-gä'sē, mad-ə-gas'kər, (Fr. C.) 241,094 sq. mi., pop. 6,643,000 cap. Tananarive.

Malawi [formerly Nyasaland] (mä-lä'wē, (Br. C. of N.) 48,442 sq. mi., pop. 4,394,000, cap. Zomba.

Malaysia [formerly Federation of Malaya] (mə-lä'zhə, (Br. C. of N.) 128,430 sq. mi., pop. 10,583,000, cap. Kuala Lumpur.

Maldive Is. (mal'dīv) 115 sq. mi., pop. 108,000 cap. Male (mä-lā') (pop. 11,760).

Mali Republic [formerly French Sudan] (mä'lē 584,942 sq. mi., pop. 4,881,000, cap. Bamako.

Malta (mâl'tə) (Br. C. of N.) 122 sq. mi., pop. 328,000 cap. Valletta.

Managua (mə-nä'gwä) City (cap. of Nicaragua) pop. 262,047.

Manama (mə-nä'mə) City (cap. of Bahrain) pop. 79,098.

Manchester (man'ches-tər) City (England) pop. 602,800, urban area 2,451,660.

Manchuria (man-chŭr'ē-ə) (People's Republic of China) 412,801 sq. mi., pop. 53,000,000, cap. Shenyang.

Manila (mə-nil'ə) City (The Philippines) pop. 1,499,000.

Manitoba (man-i-tō'bə) Prov. (Canada) 219,723 sq. mi., pop. 963,066, cap. Winnipeg.

Marianas Is. (mar'ē-an'əs) U.S. Trust., 247 sq. mi., pop. 31,284, cap. Saipan (sī-pan').

Marquesas Is. (mär-kā-səs) (Fr.) 480 sq. mi., pop. 4,838, cap. Atuana (ä"tū-ä'nä).

Marseille (mär-sā') City (France) pop. 889,029.

Marshall Is. (mär'shəl) U.S. Trust., 74 sq. mi., pop. 17,363, cap. Kwajalein (kwä'jə-lān).

Martinique (mär-ti-nēk') (Fr.) 425 sq. mi., pop. 332,000, cap. Fort-de-France.

Maryland (mer'i-lənd) State (U.S.) 9,887 sq. mi., pop. 3,922,399, cap. Annapolis.

Maseru (maz'ə-roo") City (cap. of Lesotho) pop. 14,000.

Masqat, see *Muscat.*

Massachusetts (mas-ə-choo'səts) State (U.S.) 7,907 sq. mi., pop. 5,689,170, cap. Boston.

Mauritania (mâ-rə-tā'nē-ə) 328,-185 sq. mi., pop. 1,140,000, cap. Nouakchott.

Mauritius (mâ-rish'əs) I. (Br. C. of N.) 720 sq. mi., pop. 823,000, cap. Port Louis.

Medellin (mā"thä-yēn') City (Colombia) pop. 967,825.

Mediterranean Sea (med"i-tə-rā'-nē-ən) between Europe & Africa, 1,145,000 sq. mi.

Melbourne (mel'bərn) City (Australia) pop. 76,200, urban area 2,108,499.

Memphis (mem'fis) City (Tenn.) pop. 623,530.

Mesopotamia, see *Iraq.*

Mexico (mek'si-kō) 760,373 sq. mi., pop. 48,933,000, cap. Mexico City (pop. 3,483,649).

Mexico, Gulf of, off so. U.S. and east Mexico, 700,000 sq. mi.

Miami (mī-am'ē) City (Fla.) pop. 334,859, urban area 1,219,661.

Michigan (mish'i-gən) State (U.S.) 57,022 sq. mi., pop. 8,875,083, cap. Lansing.

Michigan, Lake (Great Lakes) 22,400 sq. mi.

Micronesia (mī"krə-nē'zhə) see *Pacific Islands.*

Midway I. (U.S.) 2 sq. mi., pop. 2,000.

Milan [*Ital.* **Milano**] (mi-lan', mē-lä'nō) City (Italy) pop. 1,687,264.

Milwaukee (mil-wâ'kē) City (Wis.) pop. 717,099, urban area 1,252,457.

Minneapolis (min-ē-ap'ə-lis) City (Minn.) pop. 431,977, urban area 1,704,423.

Minnesota (min-i-sō'tə) State (U.S.) 80,009 sq. mi., pop. 3,804,-971, cap. St. Paul.

Mississippi (mis'i-sip'ē) State (U.S.) 47,420 sq. mi., pop. 2,216,-912, cap. Jackson.

Mississippi-Missouri River (U.S.) 3,710 miles.

Missouri (mə-zûr'ē) State (U.S.) 69,270 sq. mi., pop. 4,676,501, cap. Jefferson City.

Mobile (mō'bēl) City (Ala.) pop. 190,026.

Mogadishu (mog"ə-dish'oo) City (cap. of Somalia) pop. 172,671.

Moldavian S.S.R. (mol-dā'vē-ən) (U.S.S.R.) 13,012 sq. mi., pop. 3,572,000, cap. Kishinev.

Monaco (mon'ə-ko) 370 acres, pop. 23,000, cap. Monaco.

Mongolian Republic (mon-gō'lē-ən) 625,946 sq. mi., pop. 1,240,-000, cap. Ulan Bator.

Monrovia (mən-rō'vē-ə) City (cap. of Liberia) pop. 80,992.

Montana (mon-tan'ə) State (U.S.) 146,316 sq. mi., pop. 694,409, cap. Helena.

Monterrey (mon"tə-rā') City (Mexico) pop. 1,011,887.

Montevideo (mon"ti-vi-dā'ō) City (cap. of Uruguay) pop. 1,154,465.

Montgomery (mont-gum'ə-rē) City (cap. of Ala.) pop. 133,386.

Montpelier (mont-pēl'yər) City (cap. of Vt.) pop. 8,609.

Montreal (mon"trē-âl') City (Que.) pop. 2,527,000.

Montserrat Is. (mont-sə-rat') (Br.) 32 sq. mi., pop. 15,000, cap. Plymouth (plim'əth).

Morocco (mə-rok'ō) 171,031 sq. mi., pop. 15,050,000, cap. Rabat (rä-bät').

Moscow [*Russ.* **Moskva**] (mos'kō, mus-kvä') City (cap. of U.S.S.R.) pop. 6,942,000, urban area 7,061,-000.

Mozambique (mō"zəm-bēk') (Port.) 297,731 sq. mi., pop. 7,376,000, cap. Lourenço Marques.

Mukden, see *Shenyang.*

Munich [*Ger.* **München**] (mū'nik, myün'chen) City (W. Germany) pop. 1,260,553.

Muscat and Oman (mus'kat, ō'man) 82,000 sq. mi., pop. 565,-000, cap. Muscat (pop. 5,080).

Nagoya (nə-goi'ə) City (Japan) pop. 1,996,000.

Naha (nä-hä) City (cap. of Ryukyu) pop. 284,000.

Nairobi (nī-rō'bē) City (cap. of Kenya) pop. 478,000.

Namibia (nä-mē'bē-ə) (in dispute) 318,261 sq. mi., pop. 615,000, cap. Windhoek.

Nanking (nan'king') City (China) pop. 1,419,000.

Naples [*Ital.* **Napoli**] (nā'pəlz, nä'-pō-lē) City (Italy) pop. 1,267,073.

Nashville (nash'vil) City (cap. of Tenn.) pop. (Nashville-Davidson City) 447,877.

Nassau (nas'â) City (cap. of Bahamas) pop. 100,000.

Nauru [formerly Pleasant Island] (nä-oo'roo) 8.22 sq. mi., pop. 7,000, cap. Nauru.

Nebraska (ne-bras'ke) State (U.S.) 76,653 sq. mi., pop. 1,483,493, cap. Lincoln.

Nepal (ni-pâl') 54,000 sq. mi., pop. 10,845,000, cap. Katmandu.

Netherlands or Holland (neth'ər-lendz, hol'end) 12,883 sq. mi., pop. 12,873,000, cap. Amsterdam (seat of government, The Hague).

Nevada (ni-vä'de) State (U.S.) 109,802 sq. mi., pop. 488,738, cap. Carson City.

Newark (noo'erk) City (N.J.) pop. 382,417.

New Britain Is. (brit'en) Austl. Trust. 14,600 sq. mi., pop. 154,000, cap. Kokopo (kä'kä-pä).

New Brunswick (bruns'wik) Prov. (Canada) 27,473 sq. mi., pop. 616,788, cap. Fredericton (fred'rik-tən).

New Caledonia (kal'e-dō'nē-e) (Fr.) 7,201 sq. mi., pop. 98,000, cap. Nouméa.

New Delhi (del'ē) City (cap. of India) pop. 324,233.

Newfoundland (noo'fend-lend) Prov. (Canada) 152,734 sq. mi., pop. 493,396, cap. St. John's.

New Guinea, NE (gin'ē) Austl. Trust., 93,000 sq. mi., pop. 1,695,-000, cap. Port Moresby (môrz'bē).

New Guinea, Netherlands (gin'ē) see Indonesia.

New Hampshire (hamp'sher) State (U.S.) 9,024 sq. mi., pop. 737,681, cap. Concord.

New Hebrides Is. (heb'ri-dēz) (Br. & Fr.) 5,700 sq. mi., pop. 80,000, cap. Vila (vē'lä).

New Ireland (īr'lend) I., Austl. Trust., 3,800 sq. mi., pop. 50,129, cap. Kavieng (ka-vē-eng').

New Jersey (jûr'zē) State (U.S.) 7,522 sq. mi., pop. 7,168,164, cap. Trenton.

New Mexico (mek'si-kō) State (U.S.) 121,511 sq. mi., pop. 1,016,-000, cap. Santa Fe.

New Orleans (ôr'lē-enz) City (La.) pop. 593,471, urban area 961,728.

New York (yôrk) 1, State (U.S.) 47,929 sq. mi., pop. 18,190,740, cap. Albany. 2, City (N.Y.) pop. 7,867,760, urban area 16,206,841.

New Zealand, Dominion of (zē'-lend) (Br. C. of N.) 103,934 sq. mi., pop. 2,777,000, cap. Wellington.

Niamey (nē-e-mā') City (cap. of Niger) pop. 78,991.

Nicaragua (nik'e-rä'gwe) 57,143 sq. mi., pop. 1,915,000, cap. Managua.

Nicobar Is. (nik-ō-bär') (India) 635 sq. mi., pop. 12,452, cap. Car Nicobar (kär nik-ō-bär').

Nicosia (nik'ō-sē'e) City (cap. of Cyprus) pop. 112,000.

Niger (nī'jer) 501,930 sq. mi., pop. 3,909,000, cap. Niamey.

Nigeria (ni-jir'ē-e) (Br. C. of N.) 372,674 sq. mi., pop. 63,870,000, cap. Lagos.

Nile River (nīl) (U.A.R.) 4,145 miles.

Norfolk (nôr'fek) 1, City (Va.) pop. 307,951, urban area 668,259. 2, I. (Austl.) 13 sq. mi., pop. 1,000.

North America (e-mer'i-ke) Continent, 8,500,000 sq. mi., pop. 314,000,000.

North Carolina (kar-e-lī'ne) State (U.S.) 49,142 sq. mi., pop. 5,082,-059, cap. Raleigh.

North Dakota (de-kō'te) State (U.S.) 70,054 sq. mi., pop. 617,-761, cap. Bismarck.

Northern Rhodesia (rō-dē'zhe) see Zambia.

North Sea, off NW Europe, 222,-000 sq. mi.

Northwest Territories (Canada) 1,258,217 sq. mi., pop. 28,738.

Norway (nôr'wā) 124,560 sq. mi., pop. 3,851,000, cap. Oslo.

Nouméa (noo-mā'e) City (cap. of New Caledonia) pop. 41,853.

Nova Scotia (nō've skō'she) Prov. (Canada) 20,743 sq. mi., pop. 756,039, cap. Halifax (hal'i-faks).

Novosibirsk (nō'vō-si-birsk') City (U.S.S.R.) pop. 1,161,000.

Nukualofa (noo-koo"e-lō'fe) City (cap. of Tonga) pop. 15,545.

Nyasa, Lake (nī-as'e) (Africa) 11,430 sq. mi.

Nyasaland (nī-as'e-land) see Malawi.

Oakland (ōk'lend) City (Calif.) pop. 361,561.

Ob-Irtysh River (ōb'-ir-tish') (U.S.S.R.) 3,460 miles.

Ohio (ō-hī'ō) State (U.S.) 41,122 sq. mi., pop. 10,652,017, cap. Columbus.

Okhotsk, Sea of (ō-kotsk') (U.S.-S.R.) 587,500 sq. mi.

Oklahoma (ōk-le-hō'me) State (U.S.) 69,283 sq. mi., pop. 2,559,-229, cap. Oklahoma City (pop. 356,661, urban area 579,788).

Olympia (ō-lim'pye) City (cap. of Wash.) pop. 23,111.

Omaha (ō'me-hâ) City (Nebr.) pop. 347,328, urban area 491,776.

Oman, see Muscat and Oman.

Ontario (on-târ'ē-ō) Prov. (Canada) 363,282 sq. mi., pop. 6,960,870, cap. Toronto.

Ontario, Lake (Great Lakes) 7,540 sq. mi.

Oregon (or'e-gon) State (U.S.)

96,350 sq. mi., pop. 2,091,385, cap. Salem.

Orkney Is. (ôrk′nè) (Scotland) 376 sq. mi., pop. 17,300, cap. Kirkwall (kêrk′wâl).

Osaka (ō-sä′kə) City (Japan) pop. 3,078,000.

Oslo (oz′lō) City (cap. of Norway) pop. 487,916.

Ottawa (ot′ə-wə) City (cap. of Canada) pop. 290,741, urban area 518,000.

Ouagadougou (wä″gä-doo′goo) City (cap. of Upper Volta) pop. 77,500.

Pacific Is. (pə-sif′ik) U.N. Trust., 8,484 sq. mi., pop. 98,000, cap. Saipan.

Pacific Ocean, 70,000,000 sq. mi.

Pakistan [formerly West Pakistan] (pak′is-tan) (Br. C. of N.) 310,-236 sq. mi., pop. 47,633,000, cap. Islamabad.

Palau Is. (pä-low′) U.S. Trust., 175 sq. mi., pop. 10,280, cap. Korror (kä-rôr′).

Palestine (pal′əs-tīn″) see Israel.

Panama (excluding Canal Zone) (pan′ə-mä) 28,575 sq. mi., pop. 1,417,000, cap. Panama (pop. 389,000).

Panama Canal, between Pacific Ocean & Gulf of Mexico, 50 mi.

Papeete (pä-pē-ā′te) City (cap. of Fr. Polynesia) pop. 22,278.

Papua Territory (pap′yoo-ə) (Austl.) 90,540 sq. mi., pop. 620,-000, cap. Port Moresby.

Paraguay (par′ə-gwā) 150,518 sq. mi., pop. 2,303,000, cap. Asunción.

Paramaribo (par″ə-mar′i-bō) City (cap. of Surinam) pop. 110,867.

Paris (par′is) City (cap. of France) pop. 2,590,771, urban area 8,196,-746.

Peking [formerly Peiping] (pe-king′, bā′ping) City (cap. of People's Republic of China) pop. 4,010,000.

Pennsylvania (pen″sil-vā′ni-ə) State (U.S.) 45,045 sq. mi., pop. 11,793,909, cap. Harrisburg.

Pernambuco, see Recife.

Persia, see Iran.

Persian Gulf, between Iran & Arabia, 88,800 sq. mi.

Peru (pə-roo′) 513,000 sq. mi., pop. 13,172,000, cap. Lima.

Philadelphia (fil-ə-del′fè-ə) City (Pa.) pop. 1,948,609, urban area 4,021,066.

Philippines, Republic of the (fil′ə-pēnz″) 115,600 sq. mi., pop. 37,158,000, cap. Quezon City.

Phoenix (fē′niks) City (cap. of Ariz.) pop. 581,562, urban area 863,357.

Phoenix Is. (fē′niks) (U.S. & Br.) 16 sq. mi., pop. 850.

Pierre (pir) City (cap. of S.D.) pop. 9,699.

Pitcairn I. (pit′kârn) (Br.) 2 sq. mi., pop. 97.

Pittsburgh (pits′bêrg) City (Pa.) pop. 520,117, urban area 1,846,-042.

Pnompenh (nom-pen′) City (cap. of Cambodia) pop. 393,995.

Poland (pō′lend) 119,734 sq. mi., pop. 32,555,000, cap. Warsaw.

Polynesia, French (pol″i-nē′zhə) Fr. Terr., 1,544 sq. mi., pop. 103,000, cap. Papeete.

Port Arthur and Dairen (dī′ren) see Lūshun, Talien.

Port-au-Prince (por″tō-prins′) City (cap. of Haiti) pop. 240,000.

Portland (pôrt′lənd) City (Ore.) pop. 382,619, urban area 824,926.

Port-Louis (pôr″lwē′) City (cap. of Mauritius) pop. 134,900.

Port Moresby (môrz′bē) City (cap. of Papua) pop. 41,848.

Port-of-Spain, City (cap. of Trinidad) pop. 93,954.

Porto-Novo (pôr″tō-nō′vō) City (cap. of Dahomey) pop. 74,500.

Portugal (pôr′chə-gəl) 35,413 sq. mi., pop. 9,560,000, cap. Lisbon.

Prague [Czech Praha] (präg, prä′hä) City (cap. of Czechoslovakia) pop. 1,031,870.

Fretoria (pri-tōr′ē-ə) City (cap. of Republic of South Africa) pop. 303,684.

Prince Edward I., Prov. (Canada) 2,184 sq. mi., pop. 108,535, cap. Charlottetown.

Providence (prov′i-dəns) City (cap. of R.I.) pop. 176,920, urban area 795,311.

Puerto Rico (pwer″tō-rē′kō) (U.S.) 3,423 sq. mi., pop. 2,689,932, cap. San Juan.

Pusan (pū-sän) City (So. Korea) pop. 1,425,703.

Pyong Yang (pyûng′yäng′) City (cap. of No. Korea) pop. 653,100.

Qatar (kä′tär) (Br.) 4,000 sq. mi., pop. 100,000, cap. Doha.

Québec (kwi-bek′; Fr. kä-) Prov. (Canada) 523,860 sq. mi., pop. 5,780,845, cap. Québec (pop. 166,-984, urban area 424,000).

Queen Elizabeth Is. (i-liz′ə-bəth) (Canada) 134,920 sq. mi., pop. 310.

Quezon City (kā′zon) City (cap. of Philippines) pop. 545,600.

Quito (kē′tō) City (cap. of Ecuador) pop. 496,410.

Rabat (rə-bät′) City (cap. of Morocco) pop. 435,000.

Raleigh (râ′lē) City (cap. of N.C.) pop. 121,577.

Rangoon (rang-goon′) City (cap. of Burma) pop. 821,800.

Recife or Pernambuco (re-sē′fə, pêr″nəm-boo′kō) City (Brazil) pop. 1,100,464.

Red Sea, between Asia & Africa, 178,000 sq. mi.

Réunion (rä-û-nyon′) I. (Fr.) 970

sq. mi., pop. 436,000, cap. St. Denis.

Reykjavik (rā'kyə-vēk") City (cap. of Iceland) pop. 81,026.

Rhode Island (rōd-ī'lənd) State (U.S.) 1,058 sq. mi., pop. 949,723, cap. Providence.

Rhodesia (rō-dē'zhə) [formerly **Southern Rhodesia**] 150,333 sq. mi., pop. 5,090,000, cap. Salisbury.

Richmond (rich'mənd) City (cap. of Va.) pop. 249,621, urban area 416,563.

Rio de Janeiro (rē'ō-dā-jə-nā'rō) City (Brazil) pop. 4,207,322.

Rio de Oro (rē'ō-dā-ō'rō) (Sp.) 71,533 sq. mi., pop. 24,000, cap. Villa Cisneros (vē'lyä sēs-nṳ'ros).

Rio Muni or Continental Spanish Guinea (rē'ō moo'nē) see *Equatorial Guinea*.

Riyadh (ri-yäd') City (cap. of Saudi Arabia) pop. 225,000.

Rochester (ro'ches-tər) City (N.Y.) pop. 296,233, urban area 601,361.

Romania, see *Rumania*.

Rome [*Ital.* **Roma**] (rōm, rō'mä) City (cap. of Italy) pop. 2,656,104.

Rotterdam (rot'ər-dam") City (Netherlands) pop. 704,853, urban area 1,057,842.

Ruanda-Urundi (roo-än'dä-û-rūn'dē) see *Rwanda* and *Burundi*.

Rumania (roo-mān'yə) 91,671 sq. mi., pop. 20,010,000, cap. Bucharest.

Russia (rush'ə) see *Union of Soviet Socialist Republics*.

Russian S.F.S.R. (rush'ən) (U.S.S.R.) 6,593,391 sq. mi., pop. 130,090,000, cap. Moscow.

Rwanda (rwän'dä) 10,170 sq. mi., pop. 3,500,000, cap. Kigali.

Ryukyu Is. (ryoo'kyoo) (U.S. Admin.) 921 sq. mi., pop. 982,000, cap. Naha (nä'hä).

Sabah (sä'bə) State (Malaysia) pop. 633,000, cap. Jesselton.

Sacramento (sak-rə-men'tō) City (cap. of Calif.) pop. 254,413, urban area 633,732.

Saigon (sī-gon') City (cap. of So. Vietnam) pop. 1,682,000.

St. Croix (sānt kroi) (Virgin Is., U.S.) 80 sq. mi., pop. 214,000, cap. Christiansted (kris'tyän-sted).

St. Denis (san de-nē') City (cap. of Réunion) pop. 65,614.

St. Helena (sānt he-lē'nə) I. (Br.) 47 sq. mi., pop. 4,613, cap. Jamestown.

St. John (sānt jon) (Virgin Is., U.S.) 20 sq. mi., pop. 928.

St. Johns, City (cap. of Antigua) pop. 21,595.

St. Kitts-Nevis-Anguilla (kits; ne'vis; ang-gwil'ə) (Br.) 155 sq. mi., pop. 56,000, cap. Basse-Terre.

St. Louis (sānt lū'əs) City (Mo.) pop. 622,236, urban area 1,882,-944.

St. Lucia (sānt loo'shē-ə) I. (Br.)

233 sq. mi., pop. 110,000, cap. Castries (käs'trēs).

St. Paul (sānt pâl) City (cap. of Minn.) pop. 309,980.

St. Petersburg (sānt pē'tərz-bərg) City (Florida) pop. 213,189, urban area 495,159.

St. Thomas (sānt tom'əs) (Virgin Is., U.S.) 32 sq. mi., pop. 17,932, cap. Charlotte Amalie (am'ə-lē).

St. Vincent (sānt vin'sənt) (Br.) 150 sq. mi., pop. 91,000, cap. Kingston.

Sakhalin (sä-kä-lēn') I. (U.S.S.R.) 29,000 sq. mi., pop. 700,000, cap. Yuzhno-Sakhalinsk (yoo'zhnə-suk"-hel-yēnsk').

Salem (sā'ləm) City (cap. of Ore.) pop. 68,296.

Salisbury (sôlz'bĕr-ē) City (cap. of So. Rhodesia) pop. 180,000, urban area 380,000.

Salt Lake City (sâlt lāk) City (cap. of Utah) pop. 175,885, urban area 479,342.

Salvador, El (säl-vä-dôr') 13,176 sq. mi., pop. 3,390,000, cap. San Salvador.

Samoa, American (sä-mō'ə) Is. (U.S.) 76 sq. mi., pop. 27,769, cap. Pago Pago (päng'gō päng'gō).

Samoa, Western (sä-mō'ə) Is. (Br. C. of N.) 1,133 sq. mi., pop. 141,000, cap. Apia.

San'a (sä-nä') City (cap. of Yemen) pop. 60,000.

San Antonio (san an-tō'nē-ō) City (Tex.) pop. 654,153.

San Diego (san dē-ā'gō) City (Calif.) pop. 696,769, urban area 1,198,323.

San Francisco (san fran-sis'kō) City (Calif.) pop. 715,674, urban area 2,987,850.

San Jose (sän" hō-zā') 1, City (cap. of Costa Rica) pop. 182,961. 2, City (Calif.) pop. 436,965, urban area 1,025,273.

San Juan (sän hwän) City (cap. of Puerto Rico) pop. 444,952.

San Marino (san mə-rē'nō) 38 sq. mi., pop. 19,000, cap. San Marino (pop. 2,621).

San Salvador (sän säl-vä-dôr') City (cap. of El Salvador) pop. 340,544.

Santa Fe (san"tə fā') City (cap. of N.M.) pop. 41,167.

Santa Isabel (sän'tä ē-sä-bel') City (cap. of Equatorial Guinea) pop. 37,237.

Santiago (sän"tē-ä'gō) City (cap. of Chile) pop. 2,447,741.

Santo Domingo (sän'tō dō-ming'-gō) City (cap. of Dominican Republic) pop. 654,757.

São Paulo (sow pow'lō) City (Brazil) pop. 5,684,706.

São Tomé and Principe (sow tō-mä'; prēn'sē-pe) (Port.) 372 sq. mi., pop. 66,000, cap. São Tomé (pop. 5,714).

Sarawak (sə-rä'wäk) (Malaysia) 50,000 sq. mi., pop. 950,000, cap. Kuching.

Sardinia (sär-din'yə) I. (Ital.) 9,301 sq. mi., pop. 1,419,362, cap. Cagliari (kä'lyē-rē).

Saskatchewan (sas-kach'ə-wàn) Prov. (Canada) 251,700 sq. mi., pop. 955,344, cap. Regina (rē-jī'nə).

Saudi Arabia Kingdom of (sä-oo'dē) 353,000 sq. mi., pop. 7,200,-000, cap. Riyadh.

Scotland (skot'lənd) (U.K.) 30,405 sq. mi., pop. 5,195,000, cap. Edinburgh.

Seattle (sē-at'əl) City (Wash.) pop. 530,831, urban area 1,238,-107.

Senegal (sen-ə-gäl') (Fr. C.) 77,401 sq. mi., pop. 3,780,000, cap. Dakar.

Seoul [Jap. **Keijo**] (sōl su'ool, kā'jō", City (cap. of South Korea) pop. 3,794,959.

Seychelles (sā-shel') Is. (Br.) 156 sq. mi., pop. 51,000, cap. Victoria.

Shanghai (shang'hī) City (China) pop. 6,900,000.

Shenyang [formerly **Mukden**] (shun-yäng, muk'den City (cap. of Manchuria) pop. 2,411,000.

Shetland Is (shet'lənd) (Scotland) 550 sq. mi., pop. 17,812, cap. Lerwick (lār'wik).

Siam, see *Thailand.*

Sian (shē'än) City (China) pop. 1,310,000.

Sicily (sis'ə-lē) I. (Ital.) 9,926 sq. mi., pop. 4,721,000, cap. Palermo (pə-ler'mō).

Sierra Leone (sē-er'ə lē-ō'nē) (Br. C. of N.) 27,925 sq. mi., pop. 2,512,000, cap. Freetown.

Sikkim (sik'im) (India) 2,818 sq. mi., pop. 191,000, cap. Gangtok.

Singapore (sing-ə-pōr') (Br. C. of N.) 220 sq. mi., pop. 2,017,000, cap. Singapore (pop. 1,987,900).

Society Is (sō-sī'ə-tē) (Fr.) 650 sq. mi., pop. 68,245, cap. Papeete.

Socotra (sō-kō'trə) I. (Southern Yemen) 1,400 sq. mi., pop. 12,000, cap. Tamridah.

Sofia (sō'fē-ə) City (cap. of Bulgaria) pop. 840,113.

Solomon Is. (sol'ə-mən) Austl. Trust., 4,070 sq. mi., pop. 72,500, cap. Kieta (kē-ā'tə).

Solomon Is., British (sol'ə-mən) Br. Protect., 11,000 sq. mi., pop. 150,000, cap. Honiara (hō-nē-ä'rä).

Somalia (sō-mä'lē-ə) 262,000 sq. mi., pop. 2,730,000, cap. Mogadishu.

Somaliland, French (sō-mä'li-land) see *Afars.*

South Africa, Republic of 472,-494 sq. mi., pop. 19,618,000, cap. Cape Town also, Pretoria.

South America (ə-mer'i-kə) Continent, 6,814,000 sq. mi., pop. 186,000,000.

South Carolina (kar-ə-lī'nə) State (U.S.) 30,594 sq. mi., pop. 2,590,-516, cap. Columbia.

South China Sea between China, Vietnam & the Philippines, 1,148,-500 sq. mi.

South Dakota (də-kō'tə) State (U.S.) 76,536 sq. mi., pop. 665,-507, cap. Pierre.

Southern Yemen (yem'ən) 111,-080 sq. mi., pop. 1,220,000, cap. Madina ash-Shaab (mə-dē'nət-ash-shäb", and Aden.

South-West Africa, see *Namibia.*

Spain (spān) 194,295 sq. mi., pop. 32,946,000, cap. Madrid.

Spanish Saha a (sᵖ-hä'ᵉ- -här'ə) (Sp.) 102,700 sq. mi., pop. 63,000, cap. El Aaiín (el-ä-ē-oon').

Spitsbergen [Nor. **Svalbard**] (spits'berg-ə svàl'bㄹ Is. (Norway) 24,29 s . mi., pop. 3,431.

Springfield (spring'fēld) City (cap. of Ill.) pop. 91,753.

Stockholm (stok'hōm") City (cap. of Sweden) pop. 756,697, urban area 1,288,769.

Sucre (soo'krā) City (cap. of Bolivia) pop. 58,359.

Sudan (soo-dän') 967,500 sq. mi., pop. 15,186,000, cap. Khartoum.

Sudanese Republic, see *Mali Republic.*

Suez Canal (soo'ez) between Mediterranean & Red Seas, 107 mi.

Sulu Sea (soo'loo) between Philippine Is. & Borneo.

Sumatra (sū-mä'trə) I. (Indonesia) 164,148 sq. mi., pop. 15,439,000, cap. Padang (pä'däng').

Superior, Lake (Great Lakes) 31,-810 sq. mi.

Surabaja (sūr'ə-bä'yə) City (Indonesia) pop. 1,007,945.

Suva (soo'vä) City (cap. of Fiji) pop. 54,157.

Sverdlovsk (svûrd-lōvsk') City (U.S.S.R.) pop. 1,026,000.

Swan Is. (swän) (U.S.) 1 sq. mi., pop. 28.

Swaziland (swä'zi-land) (Br. C. of N.) 6,704 sq. mi., pop. 410,000, cap. Mbabane (m-hä-bä'nə).

Sweden (swē'd n) 173,394 sq. mi., pop. 7,978,000, cap. Stockholm.

Switzerland (swit'zər-lənd) 15,944 sq. mi., pop. 6,280,000, cap. Bern.

Sydney (sid'nē) City (Australia) pop. 155,480, urban area 2,444,-735.

Syracuse (sir'ə-kyoos) City (N.Y.) pop. 197,201, urban area 376,169.

Syria (sir'ē-ə) (U.A.R.) 71,227 sq. mi., pop. 5,866,000, cap. Damascus.

Tadzhik S.S.R. (tä-jik') (U.S.S.R.) 54,019 sq. mi., pop. 2,900,000, cap. Dushanbe.

Tahiti (tä-hē'tē) see *French Polynesia.*

Taipei (tī-pā') City (cap. of Taiwan) pop. 1,604,543.

Taiwan or **Formosa** (tī-wän', fôr-mō'sə) [The Republic of China] 13,885 sq. mi., pop. 13,800,000, cap. Taipei.

Taiyuan (tī'yü-än') City (China) pop. 1,020,000.

Talien [formerly **Dairen**] (dä'lēen') City (People's Republic of China) pop. 595,000, urban area 1,508,000.

Tallahassee (tal-ə-has'ē) City (cap. of Fla.) pop. 71,763.

Tampa (tam'pə) City (Fla.) pop. 277,767, urban area 368,742.

Tananarive (tä-nä-nä-rēv') City (cap. of Malagasy Republic) pop. 332,885.

Tanganyika (tan-gən-yē'kə) see *Tansania.*

Tanganyika, Lake (Africa) 12,700 sq. mi.

Tangier (tan-jir') City (Morocco) pop. 160,000.

Tansania (tan''zə-nē'ə; tan-zä'nē-ə) (Br. C. of N.) 362,820 sq. mi., pop. 12,926,000, cap. Dar es Salaam.

Tashkent (tash-kent') City (cap. of Uzbek S.S.R.) pop. 1,385,000.

Tasmania (taz-mä'nē-ə) I. (Austl.) 26,215 sq. mi., pop. 389,500, cap. Hobart (hō'bərt).

Tegucigalpa (te-goo''sē-gäl'pä) City (cap. of Honduras) pop. 253,283.

Teheran (te-ə-rän') City (cap. of Iran) pop. 2,719,730.

Tel Aviv-Jaffa (tel a-vēv', jaf'ə) City (Israel) pop. 384,700, urban area 838,000.

Tennessee (ten-ə-sē') State (U.S.) 41,961 sq. mi., pop. 3,924,164, cap. Nashville.

Texas (tek'səs) State (U.S.) 263,644 sq. mi., pop. 11,196,730, cap. Austin.

Thailand [formerly **Siam**] (tī'land, sī-am') 200,148 sq. mi., pop. 34,738,000, cap. Bangkok.

Tibet (ti-bet') (People's Republic of China) 469,413 sq. mi., pop. 1,300,000, cap. Lhasa (lä'sə).

Tientsin (tin'sin) City (China) pop. 3,220,000.

Timor (tē'môr) I. (Indonesia & Port.) 13,071 sq. mi., pop. 850,000.

Timor, Portuguese (tē'môr) e. part of Timor (Port.) 7,330 sq. mi., pop. 465,000, cap. Dili.

Tiranë (tē-rä'nə) City (cap. of Albania) pop. 169,300.

Tobago, see *Trinidad and Tobago.*

Togo (tō'gō) 20,733 sq. mi., pop. 1,815,000, cap. Lomé.

Togoland (tō'gō-land) former Br. Trust., now part of Ghana.

Tokelau Is. (tō'kə-low') (New Zeal.) 4 sq. mi., pop. 2,000.

Tokyo (tō'kē-ō) City (cap. of Japan) pop. 9,012,000, Greater Tokyo, 11,350,000.

Toledo (tə-lē'dō) City (Ohio) pop. 383,818, urban area 487,789.

Tonga (Friendly) Is. (tong'gə) (Br. C. of N.) 269 sq. mi., pop. 83,000, cap. Nukualofa.

Topeka (tə-pē'kə) City (cap. of Kan.) pop. 125,011.

Toronto (tə-ron'tō) City (Ont.) pop. 664,584, urban area 2,280,000.

Transjordan, see *Jordan.*

Trenton (tren'tən) City (cap. of N.J.) pop. 104,638.

Trieste (trē-est') (Italy, Yugoslavia) 287 sq. mi., pop. 280,017.

Trinidad and Tobago (trin'ə-dad, tə-bä'gō) Is. (Br. C. of N.) 1,980 sq. mi., pop. 1,040,000, cap. Port of Spain.

Tripoli (trip'ə-lē) City (cap. of Libya) pop. 247,365.

Tristan da Cunha (tris'tan dä koon'yə) I. (Br.) 40 sq. mi., pop. 262.

Trucial Oman (troo'shəl ō-män') 82,278 sq. mi., pop. 135,000.

Tsingtao (ching'dow') City (China) pop. 1,121,000.

Tucson (too'son) City (Ariz.) pop. 262,933.

Tulsa (tul'sə) City (Okla.) pop. 330,409.

Tunis (too'nis) City (cap. of Tunisia) pop. 468,997.

Tunisia (too-nizh'ə) 48,300 sq. mi., pop. 5,027,000, cap. Tunis.

Turin [*Ital.* **Torino**] (tūr'in, tō-rē'nō) City (Italy) pop. 1,142,210.

Turkey (tẽr'kē) 296,185 sq. mi., pop. 34,375,000, cap. Ankara.

Turkmen S.S.R. (tûrk'men) (U.S.S.R.) 188,417 sq. mi., pop. 2,158,000, cap. Ashkhabad.

Turks and Caicos Is. (Jamaica) (tẽrks, ki'kōs) (Br.) 166 sq. mi., pop. 6,148, cap. Grand Turk.

Uganda (yoo-gan'də) (Br. C. of N.) 80,292 sq. mi., pop. 9,526,000, cap. Kampala.

Ukrainian S.S.R. (yū-krän'yən) (U.S.S.R.) 226,687 sq. mi., pop. 47,136,000, cap. Kiev.

Ulan Bator (oo'län bä'tôr) City (cap. of Mongolia) pop. 195,300.

Union of South Africa, see *South Africa, Republic of.*

Union of Soviet Socialist Republics 8,649,798 sq. mi., pop. 241,748,000, cap. Moscow.

United Arab Republic [formerly **Egypt**] 457,327 sq. mi., pop. 32,501,000, cap. Cairo.

United Kingdom (of Great Britain and Northern Ireland) 94,279 sq. mi., pop. 55,534,000, cap. London.

United States of America 3,554,613 sq. mi., pop. 203,184,772 (50 states), cap. Washington.

Upper Volta (vōl'tə) (Fr. C.) 105,538 sq. mi., pop. 5,278,000, cap. Ouagadougou.

fat, fäte, fär, fåre, fåll, åsk; met, hē, hẽr, maybē; pin, pīne; not, nōte, ôr, tool

Uruguay (yûr'ə-gwā) 72,172 sq. mi., pop. 2,852,000, cap. Montevideo.

Utah (yoo'tâ", -tä") State (U.S.) 82,346 sq. mi., pop. 1,059,273, cap. Salt Lake City.

Uzbek S.S.R. (ûz'bek) (U.S.S.R.) 158,069 sq. mi., pop. 11,963,000, cap. Tashkent.

Valencia (və-len'shē-ə) City (Spain) pop. 499,131.

Valletta (və-let'ə) City (cap. of Malta) pop. 15,432.

Vancouver (van-koo'vər) City (B.C.) pop. 410,375, urban area 955,000.

Vatican City (vat'i-kən) 109 acres, pop. 1,025.

Venezuela (ven-i-zwā'lə) 325,143 sq. mi., pop. 10,035,000, cap. Caracas.

Venice [*Ital.* **Venezia**] (ven'is, vä-nā'tsyə) City (Italy) pop. 367,327.

Vermont (vər-mont') State (U.S.) 9,278 sq. mi., pop. 444,330, cap. Montpelier.

Versailles (ver-sī') City (France) pop. 84,445.

Victoria (vik-tôr'ē-ə) City (cap. of Hong Kong) pop. 674,962. 633,-138.

Victoria I. (vik-tôr'ē-ə) (Canada) 81,930 sq. mi., pop. 50,000.

Victoria, Lake (vik-tôr'ē-ə) (Africa) 26,000 sq. mi.

Vienna [*Ger.* **Wien**] (vē-en'ə, vēn) City (cap. of Austria) pop. 1,642,-072.

Vientiane (ven-tyen') City (cap. of Laos) pop. 132,253.

Viet-Nam or **Vietnam** (vēt'näm; vyet-näm') 1, Democratic Republic of Viet-Nam (North Viet-Nam) 59,934 sq. mi., pop. 21,340,-000, cap. Hanoi. 2, Republic of Viet-Nam (South Viet-Nam) 65,-948 sq. mi., pop. 17,867,000, cap. Saigon.

Virgin Is. (vēr'jin) 1, (U.S.) 132 sq. mi., pop. 63,200, cap. Charlotte Amalie. 2, (Br.) 58 sq. mi., pop. 9,000, cap. Road Town.

Virginia (vər-jin'yə) State (U.S.) 39,899 sq. mi., pop. 4,648,494, cap. Richmond.

Vladivostok (vlad"i-və-stok') City (Asian U.S.S.R.) pop. 442,000.

Wake (wāk) I. (U.S.) 3 sq. mi., pop. 1,000.

Wales (wālz) (U.K.) 7,466 sq. mi., pop. 2,724,000, cap. Cardiff (kär'-dif).

Wallis and Futuna Is. (wol'is; foo-too'nə) Fr. Terr., 106 sq. mi., pop. 9,000, cap. Mata-Utu.

Warsaw [*Pol.* **Warszawa**] (wôr'sâ, vär-shä'və) City (cap. of Poland) pop. 1,273,600.

Washington (wosh'ing-tən) 1, City (cap. of U.S.) pop. 756,510, urban

area 2,481,489. 2, State (U.S.) 66,927 sq. mi., pop. 3,409,169, cap. Olympia.

Wellington (wel'ing-tən) City (cap. of New Zealand) pop. 134,-400.

West Indies (in'dēz) Archipelago, 100,000 sq. mi., pop. 9,000,000.

West Virginia (vər-jin'yə) State (U.S.) 24,090 sq. mi., pop. 1,744,-237, cap. Charleston.

White Russian S.S.R., see *Byelorussian S.S.R.*

White Sea, off no. U.S.S.R. (Eur.), 36,680 sq. mi.

Wichita (wich'i-tâ) City (Kan.) pop. 276,554.

Willemstad (vil'əm-stät) City (cap. of Netherlands Antilles) pop. 43,-547.

Wilmington (wil'ming-tən) City (Delaware) pop. 79,978, urban area 371,267.

Windhoek (vint'hŭk) City (cap. of Namibia) pop. 36,051.

Windward Is. (wind'wərd) (Br.) 821 sq. mi., pop. 367,416, cap. St. George's.

Winnipeg (win'ə-peg) City (Manitoba) pop. 257,005, urban area 523,000.

Winnipeg, Lake (Canada) 9,398 sq. mi.

Wisconsin (wis-kon'sin) State (U.S.) 54,715 sq. mi., pop. 4,417,-731, cap. Madison.

Wuhan (woo'hän') City (China) pop. 2,146,000.

Wyoming (wī-o'ming) State (U.S.) 97,506 sq. mi., pop. 332,416, cap. Cheyenne.

Yangtze River (yang'tsē") (China) 3,400 miles.

Yaoundé (yä-oon-dā') City (cap. of Cameroon) pop. 101,000.

Yellow Sea, between Korea & China.

Yemen (yem'ən) 75,000 sq. mi., pop. 5,000,000, cap. San'a.

Yerevan [*Russ.* **Erivan**] (ye-rə-vän', er"ə-vän'yə) City (cap. of Armenian S.S.R.) pop. 767,000.

Yokohama (yō"kə-hä'mə) City (Japan) pop. 2,047,000.

Yugoslavia (yoo-gō-slä'vē-ə) 99,-079 sq. mi., pop. 20,351,000, cap. Belgrade.

Yukon Territory (yoo'kon) (Canada) 205,346 sq. mi., pop. 14,382, cap. Dawson.

Zambia (zam'bē-ə) (Br. C. of N.) 290,586 sq. mi., pop. 4,208,000, cap. Lusaka.

Zanzibar (zan-zi-bär') see *Tanzania.*

Zetland (zet'lənd) see *Shetland Is.*

Zomba (zom'bə) City (cap. of Malawi) pop. 19,666.

Zurich (zūr'ik) City (Switzerland) pop. 432,400, urban area 671,500.

An effort has been made to adapt the pronunciations of foreign words to the sounds that English-speaking persons are accustomed to use. The following sounds, however, have no near equivalents in English:

ü—the French *u*, German *ü*: *ē* with the lips rounded as though to say *oo*.

ö—the French *eu*, German *ö*: *ā* with the lips rounded as though to say *ō*.

ñ—as in French *bon*: a nasal sound given to the preceding vowel; it is not completed by the touch of the tongue, as is the English *n*.

kh—as in German *ach*: an *h* (breathing) sound with the tongue in position for *k*.

ab in·i'ti·o (ab i-nish'ē-ō) (*Lat.*) from the beginning.

ad in"fi·ni'tum (ad in"fə-nī'təm) (*Lat.*) to infinity; without end.

ad va·lo'rem (ad və-lōr'em) (*Lat.*) according to value.

af·faire' d'a·mour' (ă-fâr' dă-moor') (*Fr.*) a love affair. —**af·faire' d'hon·neur'** (dă-nōr') a duel.- **af·faire' de coeur'** (də kōr') a love affair.

a·gent' pro·vo·ca·teur' (ă-zhăñ' prä-vă-kă-tör') (*Fr.*) a professional agitator.

Ag'nus De'i (ag'nəs dē'ī; ăn'yoos de'ē) (*Lat.*) Lamb of God.

à la carte (ă lä kärt') (*Fr.*) by the card; from the bill of fare.

al fres'co (al-fres'kō) (*Ital.*) in the open air.

al'ter e'go (al'tər ē'gō) (*Lat.*) another I; an intimate friend.

a·mi'cus cu'ri·ae (a-mī'kəs kū'rē-ē) (*Lat.*) a friend of the court.

a·mour'-pro'pre (ă-moor' prä'pr) (*Fr.*) self-esteem.

an·cien' ré·gime' (äñ-syäñ' rā-zhēm') (*Fr.*) the old order.

an'no Do'mi·ni (an'ō dom'ə-nī) (*Lat.*) in the year of our Lord.

an'nu·it coep'tis (an'ū-it sep'tis) (*Lat.*) He (God) approves our undertakings: motto on the reverse of the great seal of the U.S.

An'schluss (än'shlŭs) (*Ger.*) an alliance; union.

an'te bel'lum (an'tē bel'əm) (*Lat.*) before the war.

an'te me·ri'di·em (an'tē mə-rid'-ē-əm) (*Lat.*) before noon.

a pos·te·ri·o'ri (ä pos-tir"i-ôr'ē) (*Lat.*) from what follows after.

a·près' moi le dé·luge' (ä-pre mwä' lə dā-lūzh') (*Fr.*) after me, the deluge.

a pri·o'ri (ä prē-ôr'ē, ā"prī-ō'rī) (*Lat.*) from previous (assumptions).

a·ri've·der'ci (ä rē"vä-dăr'chē) (*Ital.*) until we meet again.

ars lon'ga, vi'ta bre'vis (ärz lăng'gə vī'tə brē'vis) (*Lat.*) art is long, life is short.

au con·traire' (ō käñ-trâr') (*Fr.*) on the contrary.

au cou·rant' (ō koo-räñ') (*Fr.*) up-to-date.

au fait (ō fe') (*Fr.*) well-informed; sophisticated.

auf Wie'der·seh"en (owf vē'dər-zā"ən) (*Ger.*) till we meet again; goodbye.

au na·tu·rel' (ō nä-tū-rel') (*Fr.*) in the natural state; nude.

au re·voir' (ō rə-vwär') (*Fr.*) till we meet again goodbye.

a've at'que va'le (ă'vē at'kwē vä'-lē) (*Lat.*) hail and farewell.

à vo"tre san·té (ä vätr" säñ-tā') (*Fr.*) to your health.

beau monde (bō° mōñd') (*Fr.*) fashionable society.

beaux-arts' (bō-zär') (*Fr.*) the fine arts.

belles-let'tres (bel-let'r) (*Fr.*) fine literature.

bête noire (bet nwär') (*Fr.*) an aversion; object of dislike.

bil'let-doux' (bil'ē-doo', bē"yä-doo') (*Fr.*) love letter.

bon mot (bōñ' mō')(*Fr.*) a witty saying.

bon vi·vant' (bōñ vē-väñ') (*Fr.*) an epicure; a good companion.

bon vo·yage' (bōñ vwä-yäzh') (*Fr.*) happy trip; farewell.

ca"ba·lle'ro (kab'əl-yär'ō) (*Span.*) cavalier.

car'pe di'em (kär'pē dī'əm) (*Lat.*) make use of the day.

carte blanche (kärt' blänsh') (*Fr.*) unlimited authority.

ca've ca'nem (kā'vē kä'nəm) (*Lat.*) beware the dog.

cha·cun à son goût' (shä-kuñ' nä sōñ goo') (*Fr.*) each to his own taste.

chef-d'oeu'vre (she-dövr') (*Fr.*) a masterpiece.

cher·chez' la femme' (sher-shā' lä fäm') (*Fr.*) look for the woman.

cir'ca (sûr'kə) (*Lat.*) about.

com·bien' (käñ-byeñ') (*Fr.*) how much?

com·ment"al·lez-vous'? (kə-mäñ"-tä-lā-voo') (*Fr.*) how are you?

com·ment' vous por·tez-vous'? (kə-mäñ'voo"pōr-tā-voo') (*Fr.*) how are you?

comme il faut' (ku-mēl-fō')(*Fr.*) as it should be.

cor'pus de·lic'ti (kôr'pəs di-lik'tī)

(*Lat.*) the facts connected with a crime.

coup de grâce' (koo"də gräs') (*Fr.*) a merciful finishing blow.

coup d'é•tat' (koo" dā-tä') (*Fr.*) a political stroke; a revolution.

cum lau'de (kûm low'dē) (*Lat.*) with praise.

de fac'to (dē fak'tō) (*Lat.*) in fact; actual.

De'i gra'ti•a (dē'ī grä'shē-ə; de'ē grä'tsē-ə) (*Lat.*) by the grace of God.

de gus'ti•bus non est dis"pu•tan'dum (dē gus'ti-bəs non est dis"pū-tan'dəm) (*Lat.*) there is no disputing about tastes.

de ju're (dē jūr'e) (*Lat.*) by right or lawful title.

de mor'tu•is nil ni'si bo'num (dē môr'tū-is nil ni'sī bō'nəm) (*Lat.*) of the dead speak nothing but good.

de no'vo (dē nō'vō) (*Lat.*) from the beginning.

De'o gra'ti•as (dē'ō grä'shē-əs; de'ō grä'tsē-əs) (*Lat.*) thanks be to God.

De'o vo•len'te (dē'ō vō-len'tē; de'ō) (*Lat.*) God being willing.

de pro•fun'dis (dē prō-fun'dis) (*Lat.*) out of the depths.

de ri•gueur' (də-rē"gör') (*Fr.*) obligatory.

der•nier' cri (der-nyä" krē') (*Fr.*) the last word.

de trop' (də trō') (*Fr.*) too much.

de'us ex ma'chi•na (dē'əs eks mak'i-nə) (*Lat.*) a god from a machine; (*fig.*) a person, event, or object unexpectedly introduced into a story to resolve the plot.

Di'es ir'ae (dē"ās ir'ī) (*Lat.*) day of wrath; Judgment Day.

Dieu et mon droit (dyö' ā môṅ drwä') (*Fr.*) God and my right: motto on British royal arms.

di'tat De'us (dī'tat dē'əs) (*Lat.*) God enriches: motto of Arizona.

dol'ce far nien'te (dōl'che fär nyen'te) (*Ital.*) sweet to do nothing; (*fig.*) sweet idleness.

dra'ma•tis per•so'nae (dram'ə-tis pər-sō'nē) (*Lat.*) the characters in a play.

ec'ce ho'mo (ek'sē hō'mō) (*Lat.*) behold the man.

en fa•mille' (äṅ"fȧ-mē'ə) (*Fr.*) at home; informally.

en•fant ter•ri'ble (äṅ-fäṅ te-rēbl') (*Fr.*) an unruly child.

en•fin' (äṅ-fäṅ') (*Fr.*) finally.

en masse' (äṅ-mäs') (*Fr.*) all together; collectively.

en pass•ant' (äṅ"pä-säṅ') (*Fr.*) in passing; by the way.

en rap•port' (äṅ rä-pōr') (*Fr.*) in harmony.

en route' (äṅ root') (*Fr.*) on the way.

en•tr'acte' (äṅ-träkt') (*Fr.*) an interval or brief entertainment between acts.

en•tre nous (äṅ-trə-noo') (*Fr.*) between us.

e plu'ri•bus u'num (ē plûr'i-bəs ū'nəm) (*Lat.*) one out of many: motto of the U.S.

ex•em'pli gra'ti•a (eg-zem'plī grä'-shē-ə) (*Lat.*) for example.

ex'e•unt (ek'sē-ənt) (*Lat.*) they go out.

ex li'bris (eks lē'bris) (*Lat.*) from the books (of).

ex of•fi'ci•o' (eks ə-fish'ē-ō') (*Lat.*) by right of office.

ex post fac'to (eks pōst fak'tō) (*Lat.*) after the deed (is done).

fait ac•com•pli' (fe"tä-käṅ-plē') (*Fr.*) an accomplished fact.

faux pas (fō pä') (*Fr.*) a false step.

fin de siè'cle (faṅ də sye'kl) (*Fr.*) end of the century.

fla•gran'te de•lic'to (flə-gran'tē dē-lik'tō) (*Lat.*) during the commission of the crime.

Ge•sund'heit (gə-zûnt'hīt) (*Ger.*) good health.

hic ja'cet (hik jā'set) (*Lat.*) here lies.

ho•ni soit' qui mal y pense' (ō"nē swä' kē mäl ē päns') (*Fr.*) shamed be he who thinks evil of it.

hors de com•bat' (ôr"də-käṅ-bä') (*Fr.*) out of the fight; disabled.

i•bi'dem (i-bī'dəm; ib'ə-dem) (*Lat.*) in the same place.

i•dée' fixe (è-dā' fēks') (*Fr.*) a fixed idea; obsession.

i'dem (ī'dem) (*Lat.*) the same.

id est (id est) (*Lat.*) that is.

in ex•tre'mis (in eks-trē'mis) (*Lat.*) at the very end; near death.

in'fra dig'ni•ta'tem (in"frə dig'ni-tā'təm) (*Lat.*) beneath one's dignity.

in lo'co pa•ren'tis (in lō'kō pə-ren'tis) (*Lat.*) in the place of a parent.

in me•mo'ri•am" (in mə-môr'ē-am") (*Lat.*) in memory (of).

in sta'tu quo (in stā'tū kwō') (*Lat.*) in the same condition.

in'ter nos' (in'tər nōs') (*Lat.*) between us.

in to'to (in tō'tō) (*Lat.*) in full; wholly.

ip'se dix'it (ip'sē dik'sit) (*Lat.*) he himself has said it.

ip'so fac'to (ip'sō fak'tō) (*Lat.*) by virtue of the same fact.

je ne sais quoi (zhə nə sā kwä') (*Fr.*) I don't know what.

jeu•nesse' do•rée' (zhö-nes' dä-rā') (*Fr.*) gilded youth.

Kul•tur' (kûl-tûr') (*Ger.*) culture, esp. that of the Germans.

lais'sez faire' (le"sā fär') (*Fr.*) let alone; noninterference.

lap'sus lin'guae (lap'səs ling'gwė) (*Lat.*) a slip of the tongue.

la'res et pe•na'tes (lâr'ėz et pė-nā'tēz) (*Lat.*) household gods.

le roi est mort (lə rwä' ā môr') (*Fr.*) the king is dead.

l'é•tat', c'est moi (lā-tä' sā mwä') (*Fr.*) I am the state.

let'tre de ca•chet' (let'r də kä-she') (*Fr.*) a sealed letter (ordering arrest).

lo'co ci•ta'to (lō'kō sĭ-tā'tō) (*Lat.*) in the place cited.

lo'cum te'nens (lō'kəm tē'nenz) (*Lat.*) a substitute.

lo'cus si•gil'li (lō'kəs si-jil'ī) (*Lat.*) the place of the seal.

mag'num o'pus (mag'nəm ō'pəs) (*Lat.*) major work; great work.

mal de mer (mäl'də mâr') (*Fr.*) seasickness.

ma•ña'na (mä-nyä'nä) (*Span.*) tomorrow; sometime in the future.

man sagt (män zäkt) (*Ger.*) they say.

ma're nos'trum (mā'rė nos'trəm) (*Lat.*) our sea.

ma'ter (mā'tər) (*Lat.*) mother.

me'a cul'pa (me'a-kŭl'pa) (*Lat.*) I am to blame.

mens sa'na in cor'por•e sa'no (menz sā'nə in kôr'pôr-ė sā'nō) (*Lat.*) a sound mind in a sound body.

mi•ra'bi•le dic'tu (mi-rab'ə-lė dik'too) (*Lat.*) marvelous to relate.

mise en scène (mē'zän-sen') (*Fr.*) stage setting.

mo'dus op'e•ran'di (mō'dəs op'ə-ran'dī) (*Lat.*) method of working.

mo'dus vi•ven'di (mō'dəs vi-ven'dī) (*Lat.*) way of living or getting along.

mo•ri•tu'ri te sa'lu•ta'mus (môr"ė-tyūr-ė te sal"ū-tā'məs) (*Lat.*) we about to die salute thee.

ne plus ul'tra (nē"plus ul'trə) (*Lat.*) no more beyond; the ultimate.

n'est-ce pas? (nes-pä') (*Fr.*) is it not?

nicht wahr? (nikht vär') (*Ger.*) not true?

nil des'pe•ran'dum (nil des"pə-ran'dəm) (*Lat.*) despair of nothing.

ni'si (nī'sī) (*Lat.*) unless.

no•blesse' o•blige' (nä-bles' ȧ-blēzh') (*Fr.*) nobility obligates.

nol'le pros'e•qui (nol'ė pros'ė-kwi) (*Lat.*) to be unwilling to prosecute.

no'lo con•ten'de•re (nō'lō kon-ten'-də-re) (*Lat.*) I am unwilling to contest.

nom de plume (nom'də-ploom') (*Fr.*) pen name.

non com'pos men'tis (non kom'-pos men'tis) (*Lat.*) not of sound mind.

non se'qui•tur (non sek'wi-tėr) (*Lat.*) it does not follow.

nou'veau riche' (noo"vō rēsh') (*Fr.*) newly rich.

ob'i•it (ob'ė-it) (*Lat.*) he (she) died.

ob'i•ter dic'tum (ob'i-tər dik'təm) (*Lat.*) a passing remark; an incidental opinion.

on dit' (ôn dē') (*Fr.*) they say.

par ex'cel•lence" (pär ek'sə-läns') (*Fr.*) above all others.

par'ti•ceps cri'mi•nis (pär'ti-seps krim'in-is) (*Lat.*) an accomplice.

pas'sim (pas'im) (*Lat.*) at different places; here and there.

pa'ter (pä'tər) (*Lat.*) father.

pa'ter nos'ter (pä'tər nä'stər) (*Lat.*) our father; the Lord's prayer.

pec•ca'vi (pe-kä'vė) (*Lat.*) I have sinned.

per an'num (pər an'əm) (*Lat.*) by the year.

per cap'i•ta (pər kap'i-tə) (*Lat.*) by the head; by individuals.

per di'em (pər dī'em) (*Lat.*) by the day.

per se (pər sē'; sā') (*Lat.*) by itself.

per•so'na non gra'ta (pər-sō'nə non grä'tə) (*Lat.*) an unacceptable person.

pièce de ré"sis'tance (pyes də räz"ēs"täns') (*Fr.*) the main dish, event, etc.

porte"-co•chère' (pôrt'kō-shâr') (*Fr.*) a covered carriage entrance.

pour•boire' (pūr-bwär') (*Fr.*) a tip to a servant.

pre•si'dio (prä-sē'dyō) (*Span.*) a fort.

prie-dieu' (prē-dyö') (*Fr.*) a kneeling desk for prayer.

pri'ma fa'cie (prī'mə fā'shė) (*Lat.*) at first sight.

pro tem'po•re (prō tem'pə-rė) (*Lat.*) for the time being.

quid pro quo (kwid' prō kwō) (*Lat.*) something in return; an exchange.

¿quién sa'be? (kyen sä'bė) (*Span.*) who knows?

qui va là? (kē"vä-lä') (*Fr.*) who goes there?

qui vive' (kē-vēv') (*Fr.*) 1, who goes there? 2, alertness.

quod e'rat de"mon•stran'dum (kwod e'rat dem"ən-stran'dəm) (*Lat.*) which was to be proved.

quod vi'de (kwod vī'dē) (*Lat.*) which see.

ra'ra a'vis (rär'ə ā'vis) (*Lat.*) a rare bird; an unusual thing.

re•cher•ché' (rə-sher-shā') (*Fr.*) sought with care; rare.

re•duc'ti•o ad ab•sur'dum (ri-duk'shē-ō ad ab-sėr'dəm) (*Lat.*) reduction to absurdity.

re"qui•es'cat in pa'ce (rek"wė-es'-kat in pä'che) (*Lat.*) may he (she) rest in peace.

res ges'tae (räs ges'tė) (*Lat.*) things done.

ri'gor mor'tis (ri'gər môr'tis) (*Lat.*) the stiffness of death.

sanc'tum sanc•to'rum (sank'təm

sank-tôr'əm) (*Lat.*) Holy of Holies.

sang-froid' (sän-frwä') (*Fr.*) calmness; indifference.

sa'voir faire' (sav'wär-fâr') (*Fr.*) to know what to do; poise.

se hab'la Es'pa·ñol' (sā ä'blä es"pä-nyōl') (*Span.*) Spanish is spoken here.

sem'per fi·de'lis (sem'pər fi-dē'lis) (*Lat.*) ever faithful.

sem'per pa·ra'tus (sem'pər pə-rā'təs) (*Lat.*) ever ready.

sha·lom' (shä-lōm') (*Hebrew*) peace. -shalom a·lei'chem (a-lā'kəm) peace be with you.

sic (sik) (*Lat.*) so; thus.

sic tran'sit glo'ri·a mun'di (sik tran'sit glôr'ē-ə mun'dē) (*Lat.*) so passes away the glory of the world.

s'il vous plaît (sēl voo plā') (*Fr.*) if you please; please.

si'ne di'e (sē'ne dī'ē) (*Lat.*) without (setting) a day (to meet again).

si'ne qua non' (sē'ne kwä nōn') (*Lat.*) an absolute necessity.

soi·gné' (swä-nyā') (*Fr.*) well-groomed.

sot'to vo'ce (sot'tō vō'che) (*Ital.*) under the breath.

sta'tus quo (stā'təs kwō) (*Lat.*) the existing condition.

sub ro'sa (sub rō'zə) (*Lat.*) secretly.

su'i gen'e·ris (soo'ē jen'ər-is) (*Lat.*) of its own kind; unique.

tem'pus fu'git (tem'pəs fū'jit) (*Lat.*) time flies.

ter'ra fir'ma (ter'ə fēr'mə) (*Lat.*) solid earth.

tour de force (tûr' də fôrs') (*Fr.*) a feat of skill or strength.

tout à fait (too' tä-fe') (*Fr.*) entirely.

tout de suite (toot'swēt') (*Fr.*) at once; immediately.

va'de me'cum (vä'dē mē'kəm) (*Lat.*) go with me.

vae vic'tis (vē vik'tis) (*Lat.*) woe to the vanquished.

ve'ni, vi'di, vi'ci (vā'nē vē'dē vē'sē) (*Lat.*) I came, I saw, I conquered.

ver'bum sa'pi·en'ti (vēr'bəm sä"pē-en'tē) (*Lat.*) a word to the wise.

vi'de (vī'dē) (*Lat.*) see.

vi·de'li·cet (vi-del'i-set) (*Lat.*) to wit; namely.

vis-à-vis' (vē"zä-vē') (*Fr.*) face to face.

vi'va vo'ce (vī'vä vō'che) (*Lat.*) orally.

vive (vēv) (*Fr.*) long live: vive le roi (lə rwä) long live the king.

vox pop'u·li vox De'i (voks pop'ū-li voks dē'ī) (*Lat.*) the voice of the people (is) the voice of God.

wie geht's? (vē gāts) (*Ger.*) how goes it?; how are you?

NEW WORDS

a·bort' (ə-bôrt') *v.i.* end prematurely, as a mission or a pregnancy.

a·bor'tion (ə-bôr'shən) *n.* premature termination, as of a mission or a pregnancy.

ac'a·deme" (ak'ə-dēm") *n.* academic environment.

Ach"ro·my'cin (ak"rə-mī'sin) *n.* (*T.N.*) an antibiotic drug.

ac'id (as'id) (*Slang*) LSD, a drug producing hallucinations.

acid test a severe test of genuineness or effectiveness.

ac·tiv·ism (ak'tiv-iz-əm) *n.* a doctrine advocating the use of force. —**ac'ti·vist,** *n.*

ad'man *n.* a person who writes advertisements.

aer'o- (âr'ō-) *pref.* pert. to aircraft or aviation.

Af"ri·kaans' (af"ri-käns'; -kans') *n.* one of the two official languages of the Union of South Africa, developed from Dutch.

Af"ri·ka'ner (af"rə-kä'nĕr) *n.* a South African native of European descent.

Af"ro-A·mer'i·can (af"rō-ə-mer'-i-kən) *adj.* & *n.* pert. to American Negroes.

air'bus" *n.* a very large, luxurious airliner.

a'le·a·tor"y (a'lē-ə-tôr'ē) *adj.* pert. to or governed by chance.

al'go·rism (al'gə-riz-əm) *n.* 1, the system of Arabic numbers. 2, calculation; arithmetic. *Also,* **al'go·rithm** (-rith-əm).

al'ler·gen (al'ər-jən) *n.* substance that causes an allergic reaction. —**al'ler·gen'ic,** *adj.*

al'pha particle (al'fə) (*Physics*) a positively-charged particle consisting of four protons and two neutrons.

alpha ray (*Physics*) a stream of alpha particles.

A·mer'i·ca'na (ə-mer"i-ka'nə; -kä'nə) *n. pl.* materials (documents, antiques, etc.) bearing on American history.

am"er·i'ci·um (am"ə-ris(h)'ē-əm) *n.* (*Chem.*) a radioactive chemical element, no. 95, symbol Am, produced artificially from plutonium.

Am'er·ind (am'ər-ind) *n.* an American Indian or Eskimo.

a·mi'no acid (ə-mē'nō; am'i-no)

(*Chem.*) any of a large group of organic compounds which are basic constituents of proteins.

a·mor'al (a-môr'əl; ā"-) *adj.* 1, neither moral nor immoral; nonmoral. 2, having no sense of moral responsibility. —**a" mo·ral'i·ty,** *n.*

am·poule' (am-pool') *also,* **am'-pule** (-pūl) *n.* a sealed glass bulb holding one or more doses of a hypodermic injection.

an'a·log" (an'ə-lâg") *adj.* employing measurement along scales rather than by numerical counting. —**analog computer,** a computer that expresses inter-relationships between variables.

an'dro·gen (an'drə-jən) *n.* a substance, such as male sex hormones, that enhances masculinity.

an'droid *n.* an automaton in human form.

an'thro·po- (an'thrə-pō-) *pref.* pert. to a human being; man.

an'ti·gen (an'ti-jən) *n.* any substance or organism, such as bacteria, that stimulates the production of an antibody.

an"ti-Sem'i·tism (an"tē-sem'i-tiz-əm) *n.* prejudice against the Jewish people. —**an"ti-Se·mit'ic** (-sə-mit'ik) *adj.*

aq'ua·cade' (ak'wə-kād") *n.* a spectacular musical entertainment, with feats performed in the water.

Aq'ua-Lung" (ak'wə-lung") *n.* (*T.N.*) an underwater breathing apparatus using compressed air cylinders.

ar"chi·tec·ton'ics (ar"ki-tek-tän'iks) *n.* 1, the science of construction or structure. 2, the science of systematizing knowledge. —**ar"-chi·tec·ton'ic,** *adj.*

area code any of a series of 3-digit call numbers used to designate various telephone calling areas in the U.S. and Canada.

ar'ti·fact" (ar'ti-fakt") *n.* a man-made object, esp. from prehistoric times.

art'y (är'tē) *also,* **art'sy** (ärt'sē) *adj.* (*Colloq.*) affectedly or superficially interested in the fine arts.

as'ta·tine" (as'tə-tēn") *n.* an unstable radioactive chemical element, one of the halogens, no. 85, symbol At, a product of radioactive decay.

as"tro·nau'tics (as"trə-nâ'tiks)

553

n. the science of space travel.

as·tro·phys·ics (as″trō-fiz′iks) *n.* the branch of astronomy dealing with the physical properties of heavenly bodies; astronomical physics. —**as″tro·phys′i·cal,** *adj.*

a·to′nal (ā-tō′nəl) *adj.* (*Music*) having no tonality or key. —**a″to·nal′i·ty** (ā″tō-nal′ə-tē) *n.*

au·di·o·phile″ (ā′dē-ō-fīl″) *n.* one interested in sound and sound reproduction.

au′tism (ā′tiz-əm) *n.* excessive involvement in oneself. —**au·tis′tic,** *adj.*

au″to·ma′tion (ā″tə-mā′shən) *n.* the handling and fabrication of materials by automatic machinery, esp. when no part of the process of manufacture is done by hand.

a″vi·on′ics (ā″vē-än′iks) *n.* the use of electronic devices in aviation. —**a″vi·on′ic,** *adj.*

ba·bush′ka (bə-boosh′kə) *n.* a woman's scarf worn over the head and tied under the chin.

back′log″ (bak′lôg″) *n.* something in reserve; unfilled orders on hand.

bac·ter″i·cide″ (bak-tir′ə-sīd″) *n.* a substance that destroys bacteria.

bac·ter″i·ol′o·gy (bak-tir′ē-ol′ə-jē) *n.* the science dealing with bacteria.

bag *n.* (*Slang*) function or purpose in life, as, "That's my bag."

Ba′ke·lite″ (bā′kə-līt″) *n.* (*T.N.*) a thermosetting plastic made of phenol and formaldehyde.

balance of payments the difference in value between a country's exports and imports of goods and services.

balance of power an equilibrium of power (between states) that discourages hostile acts of one state against another by minimizing the chances of a successful outcome.

Ban′tu (ban′too) *n. & adj.* pert. to a large family of Negro tribes of Africa.

bar′ba·rism (bar′bə-riz-əm) *n.* 1, lack of civilization. 2, something barbarous. 3, a word, phrase, form, etc., alien to accepted usage.

bar mitz′vah (bär-mits′və) *n.* 1, a Jewish boy who has attained his 13th birthday. 2, the synagogue ceremony recognizing that attainment.

Basic English a select vocabulary of English words (originally 750) intended as a teaching aid and an international language.

beat generation a youth culture characterized by rock music and the use of drugs.

beat′nik (bēt′nik) *n.* a member of the beat generation, usually adopting unconventional dress and behavior.

Bed′ou·in (bed′u-win) *n.* 1, one of the Arabs of the Asian and African desert. 2, any nomad or wanderer.

ben′ny (ben′nē) *n.* (*Slang*) a Benzedrine pill or capsule.

Ben′ze·drine″ (ben′zə-drēn″) *n.* (*T.N.*) a drug used to combat fatigue and to relieve nasal congestion; amphetamine.

Ber′ber (bär′bər) *n. & adj.* pert. to a North African people inhabiting Barbary and the Sahara, or their language.

ber·kel′i·um (bər-kēl′ē-əm) *n.* an unstable, radioactive, metallic element, no. 97, symbol Bk, produced artificially from americium.

be′ta particle (bā′tə) an electron emitted by a radioactive substance.

be′ta·tron″ (bā′tə-tron″) *n.* a device for accelerating electrons to high velocity by varying a magnetic field.

bhang (bang) *n.* 1, an East Indian hemp plant. 2, a narcotic obtained from it.

bi·ki′ni (bi-kē′nē) *n.* a woman's scanty two-piece bathing suit.

bi·lin′gual (bī-ling′gwəl) *adj.* 1, able to speak two languages. 2, expressed in two languages.

bi″o·chem′is·try (bī″ō-kem′is-trē) *n.* the chemistry of life and living things.

bi″o·de·grad′a·ble (bī″ō-dē-grā′də-bəl) *adj.* able to be decomposed by bacterial action.

bi″o·phy′sics (bī″ō-fiz′iks) *n.* the physics of life and living things.

bi′op·sy (bī′äp-sē) *n.* the removal of tissue or fluids from the body for examination.

bi′o·tin (bī′ə-tin) *n.* vitamin H, found in liver, egg yolk, etc.

bit *n.* 1, a unit of memory capacity, as of a digital computer. 2, a unit of information, the result of a choice between two alternatives; in a binary computer, either 0 or 1.

black (blak) *n. & adj.* pert. to dark-skinned peoples; by many in the U.S. this term is now preferred to Negro.

black light invisible ultraviolet or infrared light.

Black Mus′lim (mus′ləm) a member of a Negro religious organization following the tenets of Islam.

Black Nationalism a Negro movement advocating political separation of Negroes and whites by formation of a Negro nation either within the boundaries of the U.S. or abroad.

Black Power a movement among American Blacks to achieve political and economic power without integration.

blast off *v.i.* take off (said of rockets).—**blast-off**, *n.* action of blasting off.

blip *n.* an image on a radar screen.

Bloody Mary a beverage made of vodka and tomato juice, often with seasonings added.

Bool'e·an algebra (bool'ē-ən) *n.* a system of algebra that proceeds deductively from a set of unproved axioms concerning the use of certain undefined symbols.

boot camp a military basic training station.

box office 1, a booth where tickets are sold. 2, (*Slang*) receipts from sale of tickets.

buffer state a small neutral nation situated between larger, potentially hostile nations.

bust *v.t.* (*Slang*) arrest.

cab'by *also*, **cab'bie** (kab'ē) *n.* (*Colloq.*) taxicab driver.

ca·boo'dle (kə-boo'dəl) *n.* (*Colloq.*) the whole crowd or collection.

caf'tan *also*, **kaf'tan** (kaf'tən) *n.* a long garment with long sleeves, tied at the waist, worn in the Near East.

cal'i·for'ni·um (kal'ə-fôr'nē-əm) *n.* an unstable, radioactive chemical element, no. 98, symbol Cf, produced artificially from curium.

camp *n.* (*Art*) something interesting or entertaining because of its banality or archaism.

can'dle·pin' (kan'dəl-pin') *n.* a nearly cylindrical bowling pin, tapering in at top and bottom.—**can'dle·pins'**, *n. sing.* a bowling game using candlepins and a small round ball.

capital goods facilities or goods used to produce other goods.

capital punishment the death penalty.

carbon 14 a radioactive isotope of carbon used in dating archaeological and geological samples.

carbon mon·ox'ide (mon-oks'-īd) a colorless, poisonous gas, CO, formed in combustion.

car jockey (*Slang*) garage attendant.

car'o·tene' (kăr'ə-tēn') *n.* a pigment found in various plants (such as carrots) and converted to vitamin A in the body.

cas·sette' (kə-set') *n.* 1, a light-proof case for holding photographic or X-ray film. 2, a compact container of recording tape, incorporating both supply and take-up reels, used in a machine specially designed for it.

ca've·at'' (ka'vē-at'') *n.* 1, a warning. 2, (*Law*) notice to suspend action until further hearing.

ce'si·um (sē'zē-əm) *n.* a rare, monovalent metallic element, no. 55, symbol Cs.

charge account an established line of credit with a retail store.

cha·ris'ma (kə-riz'mə) *n.* a supernatural power for eliciting enthusiastic popular support; attributed to a person or a position.—**char''is·mat'ic** (kăr''is-mat'ik) *adj.*

cheese'burg''er (chēz'bėr''gėr) *n.* a hamburger grilled with cheese on top.

chem'ur·gy (kĕm'ėr-jē) *n.* a branch of applied chemistry dealing with industrial uses of agricultural products.

chicken feed (*Slang*) 1, a paltry sum of money; meager pay. 2, small change.

chi'no (chē'nō) *n.* 1, a cotton fabric. 2, an article of clothing made from this fabric.

chlor'i·nate'' (klôr'ə-nāt'') *v.t.* combine or treat with chlorine.—**chlor''in·a'tion**, *n.*

cho·les'ter·ol (kə-les'tə-rōl; -rol) *n.* a fatty alcohol, $C_{27}H_{45}OH$, found in bile, gallstones, etc., used in the preparation of certain hormones, and a possible cause of arteriosclerosis.

chop'stick'' *n.* a pencil-sized stick, two of which are used together by many Asian peoples as an eating utensil.

Christian Science the religious system of the Church of Christ, Scientist, that emphasizes the treatment of disease by mental and spiritual means.

chron'o·graph'' (kron'ə-graf'') *n.* a stopwatch used for measuring speeds, distances, etc.

Cin'e·ma·scope'' (sin'ə-mə-skōp') *n.* (*T.N.*) a wide-screen motion-picture system utilizing a special wide-angle lens.

Cin''e·ra'ma (sin'ə-rä'mə) *n.* (*T.N.*) a motion-picture system featuring a wide field of view, formed by projecting on a curved screen three films taken simultaneously from different angles.

civil rights the personal rights,

as freedom of speech and freedom of assembly.

civ'vies also, **civ'ies** (sĭv'ēz) n. pl. (Colloq.) civilian clothes (as opposed to military uniform).

closed circuit television transmission by wire to a limited number of receivers.

coffee house 1, a public room where coffee and other refreshments are served and where guests assemble, as in a club for conversation and games. 2, café; nightclub.

coffee shop a restaurant in which simple meals are served either at a counter or at tables.

col·lage' (kə-lazh'; kō-) n. (Art) a composition made of fragments of different materials stuck together.

col'loid (kol'oid) n. (Chem.) a substance that, when dispersed in another medium, forms particles larger than molecules but smaller than particles of suspension.

col·lo'qui·um (kə-lō'kwē-əm) n. conference; discussion.

color line systematic segregation by races; exclusion of, or discrimination against, nonwhite (esp. black) peoples.

Common Market a customs union established in 1958, orig. including Belgium, Luxembourg, France, West Germany, Italy, and the Netherlands.

complex number a number expressed as the sum of a real number and an imaginary number.

con·do·min'i·um (kon''də-min'ē-əm) n. 1, joint sovereignty over a territory by several nations. 2, a coöperative apartment building in which the tenants own their own apartments.

con·glom'er·ate (kən-glom'ər-ət) n. a company that operates businesses in a wide variety of mutually unrelated fields.

con·sor'ti·um (kən-sôr'tē-əm; -shē-əm; -shəm) n. 1, international business agreement; cartel. 2, society; association. 3, a meeting; colloquium.

con·spec'tus (kən-spek'təs) n. an outline or summary of a subject.

contact lens a thin plastic shell fitted to the front of the eyeball under the eyelids to correct vision.

con·tain'er·i·za'tion (kən-tān'-ər-i-zā'shən) n. the use in shipping of large containers that are transported as units in specially equipped transports.

con·tin'u·um (kən-tin'ū-əm) n. [pl. -a (-ə)] 1, a whole that is continuous in every part or aspect. 2, (Math.) an aggregate having at least one member between any two

given members, like the set of all real numbers.

con'trail (kon'trāl) n. streaks of vapor created by rockets and airplanes, esp. at high altitudes. Also, **vapor trail.**

con·vec'tion (kən-vek'shən) n. 1, the transfer of heat by the circulation of heated masses in a fluid. 2, the transfer of electricity through change in position of the particles.

co'öp (kō'op) n. coöperative.

Cor'fam (kôr'fam) n. (T.N.) a synthetic leather substitute, used in making shoes, etc.

cos·mol'o·gy (koz-mol'ə-jē) n. the branch of philosophy concerned with the origin and attributes of the universe, such as space, time, and causality. —**cos''mo·log'i·cal,** adj. —**cos·mol'o·gist,** n.

cos·mog'o·ny (koz-mog'ə-nē) n. a theory or story of the origin of the universe.

cos'mo·naut (kos'mə-nât') n. a Russian astronaut.

cov'en (kuv'ən) n. band of witches, esp. thirteen.

credibility gap lack of confidence or trust between two entities (as between a government and its public).

cry''o·gen'ics (krī'ə-jen'iks) n. (Physics) the study of very low temperatures.

cu'ri·a (kyūr'ē-ə) n. [pl. -ae'' (-ē'')] 1, the administrative bodies through which the Pope governs the Roman Catholic Church (Curia Romana). 2, the senate house of ancient Rome. 3, the senate of other Italian cities.

cu'ri·um (kyûr'ē-əm) n. an unstable, radioactive, metallic element, no. 96, symbol Cm.

cy''ber·net'ics (sī''bər-net'iks) n. sing. the comparative study of calculating machines and the human nervous system.

cy'borg (sī'bôrg) n. a human being, modified by the provision of artificial organs.

da·shi'ki (da-shē'kē) n. a brightly colored African robe or tunic.

de''brief' (dē''brēf') v.t. interrogate about a mission just completed.

dec're·ment (dek'rə-mənt) n. 1, the act of becoming less; decrease. 2, (Math.) negative increment.

de-es'ca·late (dē-es'kə-lāt) v.t. & i. to reduce the scope or intensity of. —**de·es''ca·la'tion,** n.

de·gauss' (dē-gâs') v.t. to make nonmagnetic.

delft n. 1, a kind of pottery decorated in colors. Also, **delf,**

delft'ware". 2, a shade of blue often found in delft.

de·mog'ra·phy (di-mog'rə-fè) *n.* the science of vital statistics relating to deaths, births, population, etc.

de"mon·ol'o·gy (dē"mən-ol'ə-jè) *n.* 1, the study of demons or the belief in them. 2, the doctrines of demon worshipers. —**de"mon·ol'o·gist,** *n.*

de·mot'ic (dè-mot'ik) *adj.* of the common people; popular.

des·truct' (des-trukt') *v.i.* be destroyed by a built-in device. *Also,* **self"-des·truct'.**

de·ten'tion (di-ten'shən) *n.* 1, act of detaining. 2, state of being detained. 3, the act of withholding something that belongs to or is claimed by another.

Di·lan'tin (dī-lan'tin) *n.* (*T.N.*) diphenylhydantoin sodium, a drug used in treating epilepsy.

diploma mill (*Slang*) an educational institution granting diplomas fraudulently or without proper standards.

dis"ad·van'taged (dis"əd-van'təjd) *adj.* deprived of the basic conditions for normal development (as education, adequate health care, civil rights) and hence predestined to inequality in society; underprivileged.

dis"com·bob'u·late (dis"kəm-bob'ū-lāt) *v.t.* confuse; disconcert.

dis·in"te·gra'tion (dis-in"tə-grā'shən) *n.* a change in the composition of an atomic nucleus, either through bombardment or through radioactive ejection of particles.

dock *v.i.* join in space (as two spacecraft).

dol'men (dol'mən) *n.* (*Archaeol.*) one of a number of ancient structures, believed to be tombs, formed by a horizontal slab of rock set atop two or more upright stones.

domino theory the theory that if one country is taken over by a Communist regime, the neighboring countries will soon be overrun in turn.

Dopp'ler effect (däp'lər) an apparent change in the frequency of sound, light, or radio waves reaching an observer when the wave source and the observer are in motion relative to one another.

dorm (dôrm) *n.* (*Colloq.*) dormitory.

do·sim'e·ter" (dō-sim'ə-tər") *n.* a device for measuring doses, as of X-rays.

drag *v.t. & i.* (*Colloq.*) race, esp. in automobiles. —*n.* (*Slang*) 1, something boring or tiresome. 2, a puff, as on a cigarette. —**in drag** (of a man) dressed in women's clothing.

Dram'a·mine (dram'ə-mēn) *n.* (*T.N.*) dimenhydrinate, a drug used to prevent motion sickness.

dra·mat'ics (drə-mat'iks) *n. pl.* stage plays. —*n. sing.* 1, the art or study of acting in, writing, and producing plays. 2, histrionics.

dum'dum *n.* a soft-nosed bullet designed to spread on impact.

Dy'nel (dī'nel) *n.* (*T.N.*) a synthetic, flame-resistant fiber; the yarn or fabric made from it.

dys·lex'i·a (dis-leks'è-ə) *n.* an impairment of the ability to read. —**dys·lex'i·ac,** *adj.*

dys·pro'si·um (dis-prō'zè-əm) *n.* a metallic element of the rare-earth group, no. 66, symbol Dy.

dys'tro·phy (dis'trə-fè) *n.* faulty nutrition.

earth science a science, such as geography, geology, etc., that deals with the earth.

eb'on·ite (eb'ə-nīt) *n.* hard rubber, esp. when black.

e·col'o·gy (i-kol'ə-jè) *n.* 1, (*Biol.*) the study of the relations between organisms and their environment. 2, (*Sociol.*) the study of the causes and effects of the spatial distribution of population.

egg'head" *n.* (*usu. contemptuous*) intellectual; highbrow.

e"go·cen'tric (ē"gō-sen'trik) *adj.* self-centered; selfish; individualistic. —*n.* an egocentric person.

ei·det'ic (ī-det'ik) *adj.* based on intuition.

ein'stein"i·um (īn'stīn"è-əm) *n.* an unstable, radioactive chemical element, no. 99, symbol E, produced artificially.

electoral college a body of persons (electors) chosen by the voters of the several states to elect the president and vice-president of the U.S.

electric eye a photoelectric cell.

e·lec"tro·mag'net (ē-lek"trō-mag'nət) *n.* a device consisting of an iron core that becomes magnetized by electric current passing through a wire coiled around it.

elementary school a school giving six to eight years of instruction to children beginning usually at the age of six.

e·mote' (è-mōt') *v.i.* to express emotion.

English horn the alto instrument of the oboe family.

en·plane' (en-plān') *v.i.* board an airplane.

en"ter·i'tis (en"tə-rī'tis) n. inflammation of the intestines.

en·thuse' (en-thooz'; -thūz') v. (Colloq.) —v.i. make enthusiastic. —v.i. become enthusiastic; show enthusiasm.

en·train' (en-trān') v.i. board a train. —v.t. put on a train.

ep'i·cen"ter (ep'ə-sen"tər) n. 1, the part of the earth immediately above the focus of an earthquake. 2, focus; center.

e·pig'ra·phy (i-pig'rə-fē) n. 1, the science of deciphering and explaining inscriptions. 2, inscriptions collectively.

e·pox'y resin (e-päks'ē) n. a thermosetting resin used as an adhesive or a protective coating. Also, epoxy.

Ep'som salts (ep'səm) hydrated magnesium sulphate, used as a cathartic.

es·ca·late" (es'kə-lāt") v.t. & i. increase the scope or intensity of.

es·pres'so (es-pres'sō) n. (Ital.) coffee brewed with forced steam.

-esque (-esk) suf. like; having the style or manner of, as picturesque, arabesque.

eu·phen'ics (ū-fen'iks) n. the science of improving the human species by modifying biological development.

Eu'ro·dol"lar (yū'rō-dol"ər) n. U.S. dollars circulating among European banks.

eu·then'ics (ū-then'iks) n. 1, the science of adjusting living conditions to improve the human race. 2, the science of improving growth conditions of plants and animals.

ex"is·ten'tial·ism (eks"is-ten'-shəl-iz-əm) n. a humanistic philosophy stating that each man is responsible for forming his self and must with his free will oppose his uncertain, purposeless, and seemingly hostile environment.

ex"per·tise' (eks"pər-tēz') n. specialized skill; know-how.

ex·pres'sion·ism (eks-presh'ən-iz-əm) n. (Art) 1, the effort to convey the artist's inner feelings rather than to represent external reality. 2, free expression of one's individuality in writing, painting, etc.

ex·press'way" (eks-pres'wā") n. a high-speed, usually divided, limited-access highway.

ex·trem'ism (eks-trēm'-iz-əm) n. a disposition or tendency to go to extremes in one's beliefs or actions.

ex'urb (eks'ərb) n. region beyond the city and suburbs, usually inhabited by the wealthy. —ex-

ur'ban·ite (eks-ər'bən-īt) n. one who lives in the exurbs.

ex·ur'bi·a (eks-ər'bē-ə) n. the exurbs collectively.

fail-safe adj. 1, automatically compensating for a mistake or failure. 2, irreversibly reacting (as to launch a counterattack) on the occurrence of certain predetermined conditions.

fair-trade agreement an agreement under which a retailer must not undersell minimum price levels set by a manufacturer.

falling star a meteorite.

fall'out n. 1, the falling of radioactive debris after a nuclear explosion. 2, the debris itself.

Far East a part of Asia including Japan, China, Vietnam, Korea, etc.

favorite son at a U.S. presidential convention, a person favored as a nominee by the delegates from his state.

feath'er·bed" n. 1, a mattress or thick quilt stuffed with feathers. 2, (Slang) an easy job. —v.i. be paid for work not actually done by holding an unnecessary job that a labor union requires an employer to provide.

feed'back" n. a return of part of the output of a system to the input.

fellow traveler one who supports the Communist Party but is not a member of it.

fer'mi·um (fėr'mē-əm) n. an unstable, radioactive metallic element, no. 100, symbol Fm, produced artificially.

fi'ber·glass n. glass drawn into a strong, pliable filament, used as a cord in automobile tires, in masses for insulation, or spun and woven into fabrics.

film'dom n. the motion picture industry.

fire'ball" n. 1, an early type of bomb. 2, something like a ball of fire, as a luminous meteor. 3, the cloud of hot, luminous gases produced by a nuclear explosion. 4, (Colloq.) an extremely energetic person.

first lady (often cap.) the wife of the U.S. president or of a state governor.

fis'sile (fis'īl; -əl) adj. capable of being split; fissionable.

flashbulb (Photog.) a glass bulb containing magnesium foil and oxygen, giving a brief, brilliant flash of light when ignited.

flash cube (Photog.) a plastic cube containing four small flashbulbs arranged to fire in sequence

flu·o'ri·date'' (floor'ə-dāt*) *v.t.* & *i.* add a fluoride (to a water supply) in order to prevent tooth decay.

flu'o·ride'' (floo'ə-rīd*) *n.* a chemical compound of fluorine with another element.

flying saucer an unidentified flying object resembling a luminous dish.

folk-rock *n.* & *adj.* (*Music*) pert. to music combining a rock beat with folk-song lyrics.

For·mi'ca (fôr-mī'kə) *n.* (*T.N.*) any of various laminated plastic products used in construction and in making furniture.

fran'ci·um (fran'sē-əm) *n.* an unstable radioactive chemical element, no. 87, symbol Fr.

freak out (*Slang*) **1,** lose control of oneself under the influence of drugs; have a bad "trip." **2,** experience similar reaction without drugs.

free trade commercial trading between countries without government-imposed duties, tariffs, etc.

free university an informally organized forum offering classes in subject matter not usually available in regular university courses.

frog'man *n.* a specially trained underwater swimmer.

fuss'bud·get *n.* one who fusses about insignificant things.

g (gē) *n.* **1,** gravity; acceleration of gravity. **2,** a unit of force equal to the force of gravity.

gad''o·lin'i·um (gad'*ə-lin'ē-əm) *n.* a metallic element of the rare-earth group, no. 64, symbol Gd.

ga·lac'tic (gə-lak'tik) *adj.* (*Astron.*) pert. to the galaxy or Milky Way.

game theory the application of the mathematical laws of probability to finding the best strategy for winning at games, war, politics, etc.

gam'y (gā'mē) *adj.* [-i·er, -i·est] **1,** having the flavor of game. **2,** spirited; plucky. **3,** racy; off-color.

ga·ze'bo (gə-zē'bō) *n.* [*pl.*-bos *or* -boes] a summerhouse or garden pavilion.

gel (jel) *n.* (*Chem.*) a jellylike or solid material formed by the coagulation of a colloidal solution. —*v.t.* [**gelled, gelling**] form or become a gel.

General Assembly an organ of the United Nations composed of all member nations, each of which has one vote.

ge''o·des'ic dome (jē''ə-dez'ik) a dome or vault constructed with lightweight, straight elements under tension, usu. producing polygonal designs.

ge''o·met'ric progression *or* **series** (jē''ə-met'rik) a series of numbers or terms, each of which is a constant multiple of the one preceding it: as, 1, 2, 4, 8, 16, 32, etc.

ge''o·phys'ics (jē''ō-fiz'iks) *n.* the study of the structure of the earth and the physical forces that affect it.

ger''i·at'rics (jer'ē-at'riks) *n. sing.* the study and treatment of diseases attendant on old age.

German measles a contagious disease resembling measles that can cause congenital defects in infants born to mothers infected during the first 3 mos. of pregnancy; rubella.

ger''on·tol'o·gy (jer''ən-tol'ə-jē) *n.* the science that deals with the phenomena of old age.

ge·stalt' (gə-shtält') *n.* a structure (psychological, physical, or biological) having properties not derivable from the sum of its parts.

gig *n.* **1,** any fancy, unusual hairdo. **2,** (*Music*) a playing engagement, as a concert.

glitch (glich) *n.* a sudden, brief surge of electrical power.

gob'ble·dy·gook'' (gob'əl-dē-gūk*) *n.* **1,** obscure, inflated language; officialese. **2,** meaningless confusion of words; nonsense. **3,** specialized, technical language; jargon.

go'cart'' (gō'kärt*) *n.* **1,** a child's walker. **2,** a small baby carriage or stroller. **3,** a small-scale, often motorized, open racing car for children.

go'-go'' (gō'gō*) *adj.* (*Slang*) modern; fashionable. *Also,* **à go-go.**

graf·fi'to (grə-fē'tō) *n.* [*pl.* -ti (-tē)] an inscription or design written or scratched on a wall, stone, etc.

graphic arts the pictorial arts: drawing, painting, engraving, etc.; sometimes also printing, process engraving, etc.

grass (gras) *n.* (*Slang*) marijuana.

grind'er (grīn'dər) *n.* (*Slang*) a large sandwich; a hero.

groove (groov) *v.t.* (*Slang*) react intuitively to one's environment (situations, people, etc.).

gu'ru (goo'roo) *n.* a personal teacher and intellectual (and usually spiritual or mystical) guide.

gut *adj.* (*Slang*) **1,** easy, simple: *a gut course.* **2,** basic; fundamental. **3,** intuitive, nonintellectual: *a gut reaction.*

gy'ro·com''pass (ji'rō-kum''pəs) *n.* a motor-driven gyroscope placed with its axis parallel to that of the earth and thus indicating true north regardless of rotation of the earth and the movement of a ship.

haf'ni·um (haf'ne-əm) n. a metallic element no. 72, symbol Hf.

half'-life" n. the time required for half the atoms of a radioactive substance to undergo radioactive decay.

hal·lu'cin·o·gen" (hə-loo'sə-nə-jən") n. a drug that causes hallucinations.

hap'pen·ing (hap'ən-ing) n. 1. a theatrical event usually partially or wholly spontaneous often involving audience participation. 2. any spontaneous social occurrence.

hash n. (Slang) hashish.

have (hav) n. (Colloq.) a person or nation that has material wealth.

have-not n. (Colloq.) a person or nation lacking in material wealth.

head'phone" n. a radio telephone, or high-fidelity receiver held against the ear(s) by a clamp over the head. Also, **head'set"**.

hel'i·port" (hel'ə-pôrt") n. an airport for helicopters.

he"ma·tol'o·gy (hē"mə-tol'ə-jē) n. a branch of biology dealing with the blood.

hep"a·ti'tis (hep"ə-tī'tis) n. inflammation of the liver.

hep'cat" (hep'kat") n. (Slang) a performer or admirer of jazz music.

he'ro (hi'rō) n. a large sandwich made with a long, narrow loaf of bread.

hertz (herts) n. a unit equaling one cycle (of a periodic process) per second.

het"er·o·sex'u·al (het"ər-ə-sek'-shoo-əl) adj. 1. pert. to different sexes. 2. manifesting sexual desire toward a member of the opposite sex. —n. a heterosexual person.

hex"a·chlor'o·phene (heks"ə-klôr'ə-fēn) n. an antibacterial agent used esp. in soaps.

hi·ba'chi (hi-bä'chē) n. a small charcoal-burning brazier.

hig'gle·dy-pig'gle·dy (hig'əl-dē-pig'əl-dē) adj. & adv. in disorder or confusion; topsy-turvy. —n. a jumble, confusion.

high adj. (Slang) under the influence of alcohol or drugs, esp. stimulants or psychedelic drugs. —n. (Slang) the effects of a stimulant or psychedelic drug; a "trip."

high fidelity the reproduction of audio signals through their full frequency range with a minimum of distortion.

high-rise adj. & n. pert. to a building with many stories.

high-tension adj. (Electricity) involving high voltage, usu. 1,000 volts or more.

hip'pie also **hip'py** (hip'ē) n. a nonconformist person, usu. one who rejects conventional social behavior and dress and often a user of drugs.

holding company 1. a company whose chief or sole business is to acquire the securities of other companies. 2. an operating company that owns a controlling interest in the stock of another.

hol'mi·um (hōl'mē-əm) n. a rare-earth metallic element, no. 67, symbol Ho.

hol'o·gram" (hol'ə-gram") n. an image produced on a sensitized surface by holography.

hol'o·graph" (hol'ə-graf") v. produce an image (of an object) using holography. – n. a hologram.

ho·log'ra·phy (hō-log'rə-fē) n. a kind of three-dimensional lensless photography using lasers.

hoo'kah also **hoo'ka** (hûk'ə) n. an Oriental tobacco pipe having a vase of water through which the smoke is drawn to be cooled.

hopped'-up" (hopt'up") adj. 1. under the influence of drugs; doped. 2. (Slang) very excited; enthusiastic.

hot pants pants with very short legs, usu. worn by women.

hov'er·craft" (huv'ər-kraft") n. a motorized vehicle that travels over the surface of land or water supported on a cushion of air created by large fans in the body of the vehicle.

hu'man·oid" (hū'mə-noid") adj. having human characters. —n. a humanoid being.

hunger strike refusal to eat in an effort to force compliance with one's demands.

hung-up adj. (Slang) 1. disturbed; depressed. 2. obsessed; addicted.

hush'pup"py (hush'pup"ē) n. 1. a cornmeal fritter. 2. (cap., T.N.) a lightweight rubber-soled shoe.

hy'dro·foil" (hī'drə-foil") n. a fin attached to a speedboat that lifts the hull above the water when a certain speed is reached.

hy·dro'gen·ate" (hī-dro'jən-āt") v.t. combine with hydrogen.

hy"per·gol'ic (hī"pər-gol'ik) adj. self-igniting upon interaction of components without external aid; said of fuels.

imaginary number (Math.) imaginary part.

imaginary part (Math.) the part

of a complex number containing the imaginary unit (as "3i" in 5 + 3i).

imaginary unit (*Math.*) the positive square root of minus 1, symbol i.

im·pe'dance (im-pē'dəns) *n.* (*Electricity*) the apparent resistance to the flow of an alternating current that corresponds to the actual resistance to the flow of a direct current.

im·plode (im-plōd') *v.t. & i.* burst inward. —**im·plo'sion** (im-plō'zhən) *n.*

in'board (in'bōrd) *adj. & adv.* 1, inside a ship's hull. 2, toward the inside.

income tax a tax levied on annual income, usu. on a graduated percentage basis.

in'di·um (in'dē-əm) *n.* a rare, silver-white metallic element, no. 49, symbol In.

in·duc'tance (in-duk'təns) *n.* the property of an electric circuit by which a varying current in it creates a varying magnetic field that in turn induces an electromotive force in it or a neighboring circuit; measured in henrys. *Also,* self-inductance.

industrial park an area zoned for industrial and business use and characterized by coordinated plant design.

in'fa·my (in'fə-mē) *n.* notoriety; dishonor.

in'fight"ing (in'fīt"ing) *n.* rivalry within an organization or group.

in·jec'tion (in-jek'shən) *n.* process of boosting a spacecraft into the desired trajectory.

in·sem'i·nate" (in-sem'ə-nāt") *v.t.* sow seeds in; impregnate.

in·ser'tion (in-sûr'shən) *n.* process of putting a spacecraft into orbit.

integrated circuit a complete circuit, comprising transistors, resistors and other components, inseparably associated in a single miniature unit.

internal medicine a branch of medicine dealing with the diagnosis and nonsurgical treatment of the internal organs.

i"so·met'ric (ī"sō-met'rik) *adj.* (*of muscle contraction*) taking place against resistance but without lengthening or shortening of the muscle fibers.

i"so·ton'ic (ī"sō-tän'ik) *adj.* (*of muscle contraction*) taking place without resistance but with lengthening or shortening of the muscle fibers.

jab'ber·wock"y (jab'ər-wok"ē) *n.*

gibberish; nonsensical speech.

jal'ou·sie (jal'oo-zē; -ə-sē) *n.* a blind or shutter made of slats set at an angle to admit air but exclude sun and rain.

jazz'y (jaz'ē) *adj.* (*Slang*) [-i·er, -i·est] 1, containing or in the style of jazz. 2, wildly exciting or energetic.

jer'ry·built" (jer'ē-bilt") *adj.* constructed hastily and with flimsy materials. —**jer'ry·build"** (-bild") *v.t.*

jet engine an engine producing motion by exhaust of hot air and gases from combustion.

jet'li"·ner (jet'lī"nər) *n.* a jet-propelled passenger airplane.

joint *n.* (*Slang*) a marijuana cigarette.

jour"nal·ese' (jûr"nə-lēz') *n.* the style of writing characteristic of newspapers.

joy ride (*Colloq.*) 1, a ride for pleasure in an automobile, esp. when the car is used surreptitiously or driven recklessly. 2, a trip (usu. on drugs).

jun'kie (jung'kē) *n.* (*Slang*) a dope addict.

ka·ra'te (kə-rä'tē) *n.* a Japanese system of self-defense.

kar'ma (kär'mə) *n.* 1, in Hinduism and Buddhism, the ethical consequences of the totality of one's actions that determine the destiny of one's subsequent existence or existences until one has achieved spiritual liberation. 2, fate; destiny. —**kar'mic** (kär'mik) *adj.*

ka·zoo' (kə-zoo') *n.* a musical instrument or toy consisting of a tube containing a membrane that vibrates sympathetically when the player hums into the tube.

key'punch" *n.* a machine, operated from a keyboard, that punches holes or notches in cards for use in data-processing machines.

kib·buts' (ki-būts') *n.* [*pl.* **kib'-but·sim'** (ki'būt-sēm')] in Israel, a communally owned, operated, and organized collective farm or settlement.

kick'shaw" (kik'shä") *n.* 1, something fantastic and trifling. 2, an unsubstantial dish or food.

kin"e·mat'ics (kin"ə-mat'iks) *n. sing.* a branch of dynamics dealing with motion considered apart from mass and force. *Also,* cin"e-mat'ics (sin"-).

kin"es·the'sia (kin"əs-thē'zhə) *n.* the sensation of bodily tension or movement perceived through nerve ends in the muscles, tendons, and joints.

Ko'dak (kō'dak) *n.* (*T.N.*) a small portable camera, esp. one with a universal lens.

K' ra"tion *n.* a concentrated food product used as an emergency field ration by the U.S. Army.

land'ed (lan'did) *adj.* **1.** consisting of land, as *landed property.* **2.** owning land.

land-poor *adj.* owning much land but lacking capital because the land is unproductive or encumbered.

lan'tha·nide" (lan'thə-nīd") *n.* any of the rare-earth elements. *Also,* **lan'tha·non"** (-nän").

lan'tha·num (lan'thə-nəm) *n.* a metallic element, usu. included with the rare-earth elements, no. 57, symbol La.

la'ser (lā'zər) *n.* a device producing an intense, highly directional beam of light through **L**ight **A**mplification by **S**timulated **E**mission of (electromagnetic) **R**adiation.

Las'tex (las'teks) *n.* (*T.N.*) elastic yarn consisting of silk, cotton, etc., wound around a latex rubber core.

launch vehicle a rocket used to launch a satellite, capsule, etc., into space.

law·ren'ci·um (lä-ren'sē-əm) *n.* a radioactive chemical element, no. 103, symbol Lw, produced artificially.

lay off *v.t. & t.* **1.** measure off; mark off the boundaries of. **2.** discharge an employee, usu. temporarily. **3.** (*Slang*) stop; cease (criticizing, etc.).

lay-off *n.* discharging of an employee, usu. temporary.

lazy Su'san (soo'zən) a revolving tray for food.

leit'mo·tif" *also,* **leit'mo·tiv"** (līt'mō-tēf") *n.* **1.** (*Music*) a theme recurring in a musical drama and associated with a particular idea, situation, or person. **2.** a dominant motive or emotion.

le'o·tard" (lē'ə-tärd") *n.* a close-fitting sleeveless garment worn by acrobats and dancers; (*also pl.*) tights.

liberal arts studies (as language, history, philosophy) providing general knowledge rather than professional or vocational training.

lie detector a polygraph used to detect certain bodily changes believed to accompany the telling of lies under interrogation.

life-style *n.* a person's particular way of living.

lin'gua fran'ca (ling'gwə-frang'kə) *n.* **1.** a spoken language consisting mainly of Italian, French, Greek, and Arabic elements; employed in some Mediterranean ports. **2.** any mixed language (as Swahili, pidgin English) used for commercial or other purposes among speakers of mutually unintelligible languages.

lit'ter-bug" (lit'ər-bug") *n.* (*Slang*) one who litters, esp. in public places.

log'roll"ing (lăg'rō"ling) *n.* the trading of votes by legislators to obtain support for measures of interest to each one.

lox (loks) *n.* smoked salmon.

lun"cheon·ette' (-et') *n.* a restaurant at which sandwiches and light meals are served, often at a counter.

lu·te'ti·um (loo-tē'shē-əm) *n.* a rare-earth metallic element, no. 71, symbol Lu.

ly·ser'gic acid di·eth'yl·a·mide" (lī-sər'jik; dī-eth'əl-ə-mīd") a crystalline compound causing psychotic symptoms similar to schizophrenia; LSD.

Mace (mās) *n.* (*T.N.*) a chemical compound, combining the effects of tear gas and nerve gas used to control riots, etc.

magnetic field a space in which magnetic force is present, as around a magnet or a conductor carrying an electric current.

ma·ña'na (mä-nyä'nə) *adv. & n.* tomorrow; (*fig.*) (at) an indefinite time in the future.

ma'ser (mā'sər) *n.* a device that amplifies or produces electromagnetic waves through **M**icrowave **A**mplification by **S**timulated **E**mission of **R**adiation.

mass production production of goods in large quantities, usu. by machine.

max'i·dress" (maks'ē-) *n.* a woman's ankle-length dress. **—max'i·skirt"**, *n.* a woman's ankle-length skirt. *Also, colloq.,* **max'i.**

Med'i·caid" (med'i-kād") *n.* a government program of medical aid for the financially underprivileged.

Med'i·care" (med'i-kār") *n.* a government program of medical aid for the aged.

meg"a·lop'o·lis (meg"ə-läp'ə-ləs) *n.* **1.** a very large city. **2.** the heavily populated region around a large city; urban area.

men"de·le'vi·um (men"də-lē'vē-əm) *n.* a radioactive chemical element, no. 101, symbol Md.

mental deficiency subnormal intellectual development, often caused by a defect in the central nervous system. *Also,* **mental re-tardation.**

me·per'i·dine" (mə-per'ə-dēn")
n. a synthetic, morphine-like narcotic drug.

Mer·ca'tor projection (mər-kā'tər) a map in which all meridians and parallels of latitude are straight lines, with distances between the parallels lengthening near the poles.

mercy killing *n.* the painless putting to death of persons suffering from incurable diseases; euthanasia.

mes'ca·line" *also,* **mes'ca·line"** (mes'kə-lēn") *n.* a crystalline, hallucinogenic compound.

me'son (mā'sän) *n.* an unstable nuclear particle of variable charge, first found in cosmic rays. *Also,* **me'so·tron"** (mā'sə-trän")

me'te·or·oid" (mē'tē-ə-roid") *n.* (*Astron.*) a small body in space that becomes a meteor upon encountering the earth's atmosphere.

meth'a·done" (meth'ə-dōn") *n.* a synthetic, morphine-like narcotic drug.

meth'e·drine" (meth'ə-drēn") *n.* an amphetamine drug; "speed."

meth"od·ol'o·gy (meth'ə-dol'ə-jē) *n.* 1, a system of methods. 2, the branch of logic dealing with the principles of reasoning in scientific inquiry.

Met'ra·zol" (met'rə-zol") *n.* (*T.N.*) a drug, $C_6H_{10}N_4$, a heart and lung stimulant.

mi'cro·groove" (mī'krə-groov") *n.* 1, an extremely narrow groove in a long-playing phonograph record. 2, such a record.

mi'cro·wave" (mī'krə-wāv") *n.* (*Radio*) a very small electromagnetic wave having a wavelength less than 10 meters.

Middle East 1, a region including Iran, Iraq, and Afghanistan, and sometimes Burma, Tibet, and India. 2, (*Brit.*) the Near East (sense 1).

mid'i·dress" (mid'ē-) *n.* a woman's dress of mid-calf length. — **mid'i·skirt"**, *n.* a woman's skirt of mid-calf length. *Also, colloq.,* **mid'i.**

milk of magnesia a watery suspension of magnesium hydroxide, $Mg(OH)_2$, used as a mild laxative.

Milky Way (*Astron.*) a luminous band in the heavens composed of innumerable stars.

min'i·dress" (min'ē-) *n.* a very short dress for women. — **min'i·skirt"**, *n.* a very short skirt for women. *Also, colloq.,* **min'i.**

minimal art (*Art*) a movement,

esp. in painting and sculpture, rejecting complexity and tradition.

mis·pri'sion (mis-prizh'ən) *n.* 1, concealment of the crime of another, esp. of treason. 2, any serious offense, esp. in a position of trust.

mixed media the combining of several media, as drama, film, music, etc., in a theatrical production.

mob'ster (mob'stər) *n.* (*Slang*) one of a criminal mob; gangster.

mod'u·lar (moj'oo-lər) *adj.* 1, pert. to modulation. 2, of a module.

mon'aur·al (män'ôr-əl) *adj.* 1, pert. to or for use with one ear. 2, monophonic.

mon"o·nu·cle·o'sis (män"ō-noo-clē-ō'sis) *n.* an infectious disease characterized by an abnormal increase in the number of white blood cells with one nucleus in the bloodstream.

mon"o·phon'ic (män"ə-fän'ik) *adj.* 1, consisting of a solo voice with accompaniment. 2, having only one part. 3, pert. to sound transmission on a single channel.

mon'o·rail" (män'ə-rāl") 1, a single rail serving as the track for a train that either hangs from it or straddles it. 2, a train that uses a monorail.

motor scooter a two-wheeled motorized vehicle less powerful than a motorcycle and having a seat that the driver does not straddle.

mystery play a medieval religious drama based on the Scriptures.

mys·tique' (mis-tēk') *n.* semi-mystical beliefs and attitudes surrounding a person, institution, etc., and endowing him or it with a special aura and significance.

na'no- (na'nō) *pref.* one billionth.

natural gas a mixture of gaseous hydrocarbons found in deposits in the earth often associated with petroleum, used as a fuel.

natural science 1, any of the sciences dealing directly with the physical world, as biology, chemistry, physics, etc. 2, these sciences collectively.

nautical mile a unit of linear measure used in navigation, 1/60 of a degree or about 6,080 feet.

Near East 1, a region including southwestern Asia (Syria, Turkey, Jordan, etc.) and sometimes the Balkans and Egypt. 2, (*Brit.*) the Balkans.

Ne'groid (nē'groid) *adj.* resembling or akin to the Negroes. —*n.* a Negroid person; a Black.

ne"o·dym'i·um (nē"ō-dim'ē-əm) *n.* a rare-earth metallic element, no. 60, symbol Nd.

New Left a loosely organized political movement composed largely of young people seeking radical social and economic change.

nit"ty-grit'ty (nit'ē-grit'ē) *n.* (*Slang*) the essential facts, issues, elements, etc.

no·bel'i·um (nō-bel'ē-əm) *n.* a radioactive chemical element, no. 102, symbol No, produced artificially.

non"co·öp·er·a'tion (nän"kō-op-ər-ā'shən) *n.* 1, failure to work together harmoniously. 2, refusal to perform civic duties in protest against an unpopular administration.

non·met'al (nän-met'əl) *n.* any element not distinctly a metal, esp. an electronegative element that forms stable compounds with hydrogen and whose oxides are not basic, as carbon, nitrogen, oxygen, the halogens, etc.

non"vi'o·lence (nän"vī'ə-ləns) *n.* 1, abstention on principle from all forms of violence. 2, the doctrine of such abstention in the effort to achieve one's objectives.

nose cone the part of a space vehicle that contains the instrumentation and that returns to earth at the end of a mission; the forward end of a rocket or missile.

nuclear physics the branch of physics that deals with the structure and transformations of nuclei.

nu·cle'ic acid (noo-klā'ik) any of several complex acids found in all living cells.

nu'cle·on (noo'klē-än) *n.* a proton or neutron, esp. in a nucleus.

numbers game *or* **racket** an illegal lottery in which the participants bet on certain digits of a statistical number tabulated and published daily. *Also,* **policy game.**

nursery school a school for children under 5 years of age.

o'bit (ō'bit) *n.* (*Slang*) an obituary.

ob·struc'tion·ist (äb-struk'-shən-ist) *n.* one who willfully impedes progress, esp. in a legislative body.

oc·cult'ism (ō-kul'tiz-əm) *n.* the study or practice of the occult sciences.

occupational therapy the treatment of mental and physical disorders by suitable work.

o"cean·og'ra·phy (ō"shən-äg'rə-fē) *n.* a branch of geography dealing with the ocean and its phenomena.

od'ys·sey (äd'ə-sē) *n.* a long wandering; an intellectual or spiritual quest.

om'buds·man (äm'buds-mən) *n.* a government official who investigates complaints from the public.

op art a movement, esp. in painting and sculpture, specializing in geometric construction, optical illusion, and mechanical devices.

oral contraceptive any of several hormone compounds in pill form taken to prevent conception and pregnancy.

o"ri·ga'mi (ôr"ə-gä'mē) *n.* the art of Japanese paper folding.

or"tho·don'tics (ôr"thə-dän'tiks) *n. sing.* a branch of dentistry dealing with irregularities of the teeth and the correction of them, esp. by mechanical means.

or"tho·pe'dics (-pē'diks) *n.* prevention or correction of physical deformities, esp. in children.

os·cil'lo·scope" (ə-sil'ə-skōp") *n.* an instrument for tracing a graphic picture of an electric wave on a fluorescent screen.

o'ver·kill" *n.* the nuclear capacity to destroy many times the total population of an enemy nation or of the world.

oxygen mask a mask worn over the nose and kept supplied with oxygen, for protection against poison gas, etc.

oxygen tent an enclosure supplied with oxygen in which a patient is kept for aid in breathing.

pad'dy wagon (pad'ē) *n.* an enclosed police truck used to carry prisoners. *Also,* **Black Maria** (mə-rī'ə).

pan·dem'ic (pan-dem'ik) *adj.* 1, common to or characteristic of a whole people. 2, affecting a very high proportion of the population (of a country or an area), as a disease.

panty-hose *n.* stockings and panties combined in one garment worn by women.

pap'er·back" *adj.* bound with paper, instead of cardboard, etc. —*n.* a paperback book.

Pap test a test to detect cancer in smears of various bodily secretions, esp. from the cervix and the vagina.

par'a·troops" (par'ə-troops") *n. pl.* troops trained and equipped to parachute from an airplane.

par'sec (pär'sek) *n.* a unit of measure equal to 3.26 light years.

Passion play 1, a dramatic representation of scenes from the Passion of Jesus. 2, similar dramatic treatment of the suffering and death of a famous religious or spiritual leader.

pay dirt 1, (*Mining*) earth containing a remunerative quantity of gold. 2, (*Colloq.*) something profitable.

pay station a public coin-operated telephone. *Also*, pay telephone *or* 'phone.

per·cen'tile (per-sen'tīl; -til) *n.* one of 100 equal consecutive groups arranged in order of magnitude, or the points dividing them. —*adj.* pert. to a percentile or to a division by percentiles.

per"i·cyn'thi·on (per"ə-sin'thē-on) *n.* the point nearest the moon in the lunar orbit of a satellite.

pest'i·cide" (pest'ə-sīd") *n.* an agent (as a chemical) used to kill pests.

pe·yo'te (pā-yō'tē) *n.* a stimulant drug derived from mescal.

pho'to·cop"y *n.* a photographic reproduction of printing, drawing, etc. —*v.t. & i.* make a photocopy (of). *Also*, photoduplicate, *n. & v.i.*

phys"i·at'rics (fis"ē-at'riks) *n.* a system of medicine founded on the healing powers of nature.

physical science one of the sciences of physical laws and facts, as chemistry, physics, etc.

pig'gy·back" *adv.* 1, on the back and shoulders. 2, on a railroad flatcar. —*n.* a system of freight transporting utilizing special railroad flatcars to transport truck trailers.

piz'za (pēt'tsə) *n.* an Italian baked dish resembling a pie, made of leavened bread dough rolled out into a thin sheet (usu. round) and topped with a tomato and cheese sauce and other seasonings.

plac'ard (plak'erd) *n.* a notice posted in a public place; a poster. —*v.t.* (plak'ərd; plə-kärd') 1, place posters on. 2, make known by placards.

pla·ce'bo (plə-sē'bō) *n.* 1, (*Med.*) an inert medicine prescribed to humor or pacify a patient. 2, (*Rom. Cath. Ch.*) the vespers for the dead. 3, a control dose given to one of two groups in a medical experiment.

plank'ton (plank'tən) *n.* the microscopic animals and plants that drift freely in natural bodies of water and on which most marine life feeds.

plate glass a superior kind of thick glass, rolled and polished,

used for mirrors, shop windows, etc.

pliss (plis) *n.* a portable life-support system (PLSS) containing oxygen supply, air conditioning, communications equipment, etc. (worn by astronauts while on the surface of the moon).

ploy (ploi) *n.* 1, a game; an escapade or trick. 2, a stratagem or remark that subtly puts an antagonist at a disadvantage in a game or in argument or conversation.

po·lit'i·co (pə-lit'i-kō) *n.* a politician.

poll tax a capitation tax; sometimes a prerequisite to the exercise of the right to vote.

pol"y·es'ter (päl'ē-es'tər) *n.* 1, an ester used in making fibers, resins, and plastics. 2, a polyester fiber, often blended with other fibers (as cotton or wool). 3, a polyester resin used for making packaging or backing films or for molding and laminating.

pol'y·graph" (päl'ē-graf") a device that records tracings of several different signals at once (as of blood pressure, pulse, respiration, etc.).

po·lyph'o·ny (pə-lif'ə-nē) *n.* 1, (*Music*) a combining of two or more individual but harmonizing melodies. 2, a multiplicity of sounds (as in an echo). —**pol'y·phon'ic** (päl'ə-fän'ik) *adj.*

pol"y·un·sat'u·rat·ed (päl'ē-un-sat'yū-rā-ted) *adj.* of animal or vegetable fats, having molecules with many double or triple bonds (associated with lower concentration of cholesterol in the blood). —**pol'y·un·sat'u·rate** (-rit) *n.*

pol"y·ur'e·thane" (päl'ē-yūr'ə-thān") *n.* any of various polymers used in making resins, flexible and rigid foams, and elastic, rubberlike substances.

pop art a movement, esp. in painting and sculpture, dealing with objects from everyday life and borrowing the techniques of commercial art.

pot *n.* (*Slang*) marijuana. —**pot'ted** (pät'id) *adj.* (*Slang*) intoxicated with marijuana or alcohol.

pra"se·o·dym'i·um (prā"zē-ō-dim'ē-əm) *n.* a rare-earth metallic element, no. 59, symbol Pr.

primary school a school offering the first three grades of elementary school and sometimes kindergarten.

pro'gram (prō'gram) *n.* a sequence of coded instructions for a digital computer. —**pro'gram·mer** (-ər) *n.*

pro·me'thi·um (prə-mē'thē-əm)

n. a rare-earth metallic element, no. 61, symbol Pm.

pro'pane (prō'pān) *n.* (*Chem.*) a saturated hydrocarbon, C_3H_8, found in petroleum.

pro·pel'lant (prə-pel'ənt) *n.* a propelling agent, as a fuel or an explosive.

pro"phy·lax'is (prō"fə-lak'sis; prof'ə-) *n.* 1, protection from or prevention of disease. 2, preventive treatment. *Also*, pro'phy·lax"y. —pro"phy·lac'tic (-lak'tik) *adj.* & *n.*

prop'jet engine a turbo-propeller engine.

pro"tac·tin'i·um (prō"tak-tin'ĕ-əm) *n.* a short-lived radioactive chemical element formed from uranium 235, no. 91, symbol Pa. *Also*, pro"to·ac·tin'i·um (prō"tō-).

psy"che·del'ic (sī"kə-del'ik) *adj.* pert. to or causing a state of extreme calm, heightened senses, esthetic perception, and frequently hallucination and distortion of perception.

psych out (*Slang*) 1, figure out (the motives or behavior of); outwit. 2, talk oneself out of or into; lose one's nerve.

pul'sar (pul'sär) *n.* a rapidly pulsating radio source from space of very short but gradually lengthening period.

punch'card" *n.* a card having holes or notches punched in particular positions with assigned meaning for use in automatic data-processing machines.

putsch (pŭch) *n.* a secret, rapidly executed attempt to overthrow a government; a coup.

qua'sar (kwā'zär) *n.* 1, a quasi-stellar radio source, one of the brightest and most distant bodies in the universe, emitter of very intense radio and visible radiation. 2, [*also*, quasi-stellar object *or* QSO] a quasar not emitting any radio signals but producing very intense visible radiation.

rab'ble-rou"ser (rab'əl-row"zər) *n.* one who stirs up the masses; demagogue.

radiation sickness *or* **syndrome** sickness caused by exposure to radiation (as from nuclear explosion or from X-rays) characterized by loss of hair, nausea, bleeding, etc.

radio astronomy a branch of astronomy dealing with radio signals received from outer space or with the use of radar for celestial observation.

ra'di·o·graph" *n.* an image produced on a sensitized surface by radiation other than light, as X-rays or gamma rays.

ra'di·o·phone" *n.* 1, a device for communication by radio waves rather than by wires. 2, an apparatus for the production of sound by means of radiant energy.

radio-telephone *n.* a radiophone.

radio telescope a combination of radio receiver and antenna used for celestial observations.

ra'ga (rä'gä) *n.* (*Music*) any of the traditional modal patterns of Hindu music.

ram'jet engine the simplest type of jet engine, in which air forced into the narrow front end of the engine is compressed and combined with hot gases from combustion to provide thrust; efficient only at high speeds.

rare-earth element *or* **metal** any of a series of metallic elements, nos. 58-71, whose oxides are found in relatively scarce minerals and are very difficult to separate.

ra"tion·ale' (ra"shə-nal') *n.* the rational basis for something; justification.

re·act'ant (rē-ak'tənt) *n.* an initial factor in a chemical reaction.

re·ac'tor (rē-ak'tər) *n.* 1, a chemical reagent. 2, a device in which a nuclear chain reaction may be initiated and controlled to produce heat or for production of other fissionable materials. *Also*, atomic reactor *or* pile, nuclear reactor.

Ré'a·mur scale (rā'ə-myûr) a temperature calibration scale on which the freezing and boiling points of water are 0°R and 80°R, respectively.

red shift a shift in the spectrum toward longer wavelengths, sometimes (as in radiation from celestial bodies) caused by the Doppler effect.

re-en'try *n.* the return of a spacecraft into the earth's atmosphere.

ret'ro·rock"et *n.* an auxiliary rocket or jet engine on a spacecraft or satellite used to slow down its speed, as for landing on a celestial body.

revolving charge account a charge account that charges a fixed rate of interest each month on the balance remaining due at the beginning or end of that month or on the average balance due during that month.

rhe'ni·um (rē'nē-əm) *n.* a rare heavy metallic element, symbol Re, no. 75.

rhe·o·stat (rē'ə-stat") n. a variable resistor used for regulating current. *Also,* **resistance box.**

rhythm method a method of birth control based on abstention from sexual intercourse during ovulation.

ri·bo·nucle"ic acid (rī'bō-noo-klā"ik) molecules of nucleic acid, found in all living cells, used by the body in the production of proteins.

rock'a·bil"ly (rok'ə-bil"ē) n. a combination of country-Western and rock music.

Ror'schach test (rōr'shäk) a personality and intelligence test consisting of 10 inkblot designs to be described by the subject in his own terms.

ru·bid'i·um (roo-bid'ē-əm) n. a metallic element, no. 37, symbol Rb.

ru·the'ni·um (roo-thē'nē-əm) n. a rare metallic element, no. 44, symbol Ru.

Sa'bin vaccine (sā'bin) a live attenuated virus taken orally to combat infantile paralysis.

sa·mar'i·um (sə-mar'ē-əm) n. a rare-earth metallic element, no. 62, symbol Sm.

sat'u·rat"ed (sat'yū-rā"tid) adj. (*Chem.*) of animal or vegetable fats, having no double or triple bonds (associated with higher concentration of cholesterol in the blood).

sau'na (sâ'nə) n. 1, a Finnish steam bath using water thrown on heated rocks. 2, a similar bath using dry heat from heated rocks.

scan'di·um (skan'dē-əm) n. a white metallic element, sometimes included with the rare-earth elements, no. 21, symbol Sc.

scu'ba (skoo'bə) n. a Self-Contained Underwater Breathing Apparatus used for extended periods of underwater swimming. *Also,* **SCUBA.**

seat belt a protective belt worn in automobiles and aircraft.

se·le'ni·um (sə-lē'nē-əm) n. a nonmetallic toxic chemical element, no. 34 symbol Se.

sem"i·con·duc'tor n. a solid (such as silicon or germanium) having more conductivity than an insulator but less than good conductors; used in transistors, diodes, etc.

sen'sor (sen'sər) n. a device that responds to a physical stimulus (as heat or light) by emitting a signal for measurement, operating a control, etc.

ser"en·dip'i·ty (ser"ən-dip'ə-tē) n. an assumed talent for making discoveries by accident.

service module the part of a spacecraft containing fuel cells, the engines, and propellant tanks.

ser"vo·mech'a·nism (sẽr"vō-mek'ə-niz-əm) n. an automatic control device, triggered by mechanical or electrical impulses that operates a machine or maintains performance of a machine at a desired standard.

ser'vo·mo"tor n. a motor that supplements a control device (such as a servomechanism).

shock wave 1, the blast caused by an explosion. **2,** a small region of very abrupt pressure and velocity changes caused when the speed of an object in a medium exceeds the speed at which the medium can transmit sound (as when an aircraft in the air exceeds the speed of sound).

si·tar' (sē-tär') n. an Indian plucked-string instrument with a long neck and sympathetic strings.

sit'-in n. a nonviolent demonstration usu. involving the obstruction of a public place by sitting there and refusing to move unless carried away.

soda pop a carbonated soft drink.

solid-state adj. using only semiconductors, such as transistors and diodes (i.e., no vacuum tubes).

sonic boom (sän'ik) a sound like the blast of an explosion produced by a shock wave when it reaches the ground.

soul (sōl) adj. (*Slang*) pert. to the usages, customs, and traditions of U.S. Negroes: applied to food, music, etc. —n. (*Slang*) a unique quality attributed to U.S. Negroes, resulting from a combination of racial pride, tradition, and social customs.

soul brother (*Slang*) a Negro; occasionally applied to a person not a Negro who is known to be sympathetic to the Negro cause.

sound spec'tro·graph" (spek'-trə-graf") n. an instrument that analyzes a complex sound into its component elements.

space'craft" (spās'kraft") n. a vehicle built for travel in space.

space'-time" n. the four-dimensional order combining the three physical coordinates (height, width, and depth) with the temporal coordinate.

speed n. (*Slang*) any amphetamine, esp. methedrine.

spin'-off" n. 1, the transfer of a branch of a corporation's activities to a smaller corporation controlled by it in return for all of the securities of the smaller corporation.

2, any product derived from a larger, usu. unrelated enterprise.

splash'-down" n. the return landing of a spacecraft or missile on the water.

ster'e·o (ster'ē-ō) n. (*Colloq.*) **1,** a stereoscopic photograph. **2,** stereophonic reproduction. **3,** a stereophonic sound system. —*adj.* (*Colloq.*) **1,** stereoscopic. **2,** stereophonic.

ster"e·o·phon'ic (ster"ē-ə-făn'ik) *adj.* pert. to or rendering the illusion of true auditory perspective, usu. through the use of two or more microphones for recording and speakers for playback.

stoned (stōnd) *adj.* (*Slang*) intoxicated with alcohol or drugs.

strep throat sore throat with fever caused by infection.

stron'ti·um (strän'tē-əm; -chəm) n. a metallic element, no. 38, symbol Sr. —**strontium 90,** a heavy radioactive isotope of strontium found in nuclear fallout and dangerous because assimilated by humans and animals.

sty'ro·foam" (stī'rə-fōm") n. a rigid plastic foam made from polystyrene.

sub"a·tom'ic *adj.* pert. to particles smaller than the atom or to phenomena occurring within the atom.

submarine n. (*Colloq.*) a large sandwich; a hero.

sub"son'ic *adj.* **1,** pert. to speed less than that of sound in air. **2,** moving or capable of moving at subsonic speed.

sub·urb'i·a (sə-bĕr'bē-ə) n. the suburbs collectively.

sul'fa drug (sul'fə) any of a group of synthetic antibacterial drugs used to combat infection, as of pneumonia or strep throat.

su"per·con·duc·tiv'i·ty n. unusually high conductivity, esp. in metals at very low temperatures.

supermarket n. a self-service retail market, usu. one of a chain, that sells food and other convenience items.

sup·pos'i·tor"y (sə-päz'ə-tôr"ē) n. a small capsule of medication, usu. cylindrical or oval, introduced into the rectum, vagina, etc., where it is melted by body temperature.

swa'mi (swä'mē) n. **1,** lord; master: used of a Hindu religious teacher or monk. **2,** seer; prophet.

swing'er n. (*Slang*) one who adopts in his life-style the permissive moral and intellectual attitudes of present-day youth; said esp. of members of the older generations.

syn'chro·mesh" (sin'krə-mesh") adj. designed to produce synchronized, smooth shifting of gears: *a synchromesh transmission.*

syn'drome (sin'drōm) n. a set of symptoms that characterize a certain disease or condition.

syn'er·gism (sin'ər-jiz-əm) n. the combined effect of two or more agents (as drugs) that is greater than the effect of either of the agents used alone.

syn'the·si'zer (sin'thə-sī"zər) n. someone or something that synthesizes; esp., a machine that reconstructs a given sound by recreating and combining its component frequencies.

tan'ta·lum (tan'tə-ləm) a corrosion-resistant metallic element with high melting point, no. 73, symbol Ta.

tape recorder a machine that records sound in the form of electrical impulses on a special magnetic tape.

ta'rot (ta'rō) n. **1,** any of a set of 22 pictorial playing cards used for fortunetelling. **2,** a card game played with the 22 tarots added to 56 cards of the usual suits.

tech·ne'ti·um (tek-nē'shē-əm) n. a radioactive metallic element, no. 43, symbol Tc, produced artificially.

tee'ny-bop"per (tē'nē-bäp"ər) n. (*Slang*) a young teenage girl who follows the latest fads; used esp. in the 1960s.

tel"e·com·mu"ni·ca'tion (tel"ə-) n. the science of communication at a distance (by radio, cable, wire, etc.).

te·lem'e·try (tə-lem'ə-trē) n. transmission of radio signals and coded data from a space vehicle or satellite to a station on the earth, or vice versa.

tel'e·port" (tel'ə-pôrt") v.t. move (a person or object) without physical contact either by mystical means or by conversion of matter to energy for transmission. —**tel'e·por·ta'tion,** n.

tem'plate (tem'plāt) n. a pattern or guide used by hand or by machine to reproduce accurately a certain outline or placement.

ter'mi·na"tor (tĕr'mə-nā"tər) n. the line between the light and dark portions of the moon's or a planet's disk.

ter'ror·ism (ter'ər-iz-əm) n. the use of terror and intimidation to gain one's political objectives.

thal'li·um (thal'ē-əm) n. a metallic chemical element, no. 81, symbol Tl.

ther'mo·cou"ple (thẽr"mō-kup'-əl) n. a device for measuring temperature.

ther"mo·nu'cle·ar (thẽr"mō-noo'klē-ər) adj. 1, pert. to the extremely high temperatures required to initiate nuclear fusion, as in a hydrogen bomb. 2, pert. to the intense heat energy released as a result of nuclear fission, as in the bombardment of uranium.

thing n. (Colloq.) what one is most comfortable or most adept at doing: *do one's own thing.*

think tank (Colloq.) a group of experts engaged in research and problem-solving.

third world the underdeveloped countries of the world, esp. in Asia and Africa.

three-dimensional also, **3-D** adj. 1, having three dimensions, i.e., height, width, and depth. 2, lifelike; realistic. 3, having an illusion of depth, often achieved through stereoscopic means.

thru'way (throo'wā) n. a high-speed divided highway, sometimes having a toll.

thu'li·um (thoo'lē-əm) n. a rare-earth metallic element, no. 69, symbol Tm.

ti·sane' (ti-zän') n. an infusion of dried leaves or flowers used medicinally or as a beverage.

tour'ism (tûr'iz-əm) n. 1, travel for pleasure. 2, the economic activities related to and dependent on tourism.

trans"ves'tite (tranz"ves'tīt) n. one who adopts the dress and manner of the opposite sex.

trip n. (Slang) the hallucinations, heightened perceptions, etc., experienced under the influence of a hallucinogenic drug. —v.i. to have a psychedelic experience.

trunk line 1, a transportation or supply route for long distance through traffic; main line. 2, a direct link between two telephone offices or switchboards.

tube n. (Slang) a television receiver.

tur'bo·pro·pel'ler engine also, **tur'bo·prop"** (tûr'bō-) an engine combining the thrust of a turbine-powered propeller with the additional thrust of hot exhaust gases.

tur'bo·jet" engine a ramjet engine provided with a turbine-powered compressor.

turn on (Slang) 1, use or cause to use a hallucinogenic drug. 2, experience or cause to experience without drugs the sense stimulation usually associated with their use.

3, make or become elated, excited, etc.

tweet'er (twē'tər) n. a loudspeaker responsive only to the higher frequencies and used only for reproducing high-pitched sounds.

twist n. a dance involving vigorous arm and hip movement.

ultra-high frequency also, **UHF** designating frequencies from 300 to 3000 megacycles.

ul'tra·son"ic adj. supersonic.

un"der·a·chieve' v.i. not produce results (as in school) commensurate with one's assumed potential. —un"der·a·chiev'er, n.

un'der·ground" adj. pert. to anything (as movies, publications, literature, etc.) that is experimental, radical, unconventional, etc.

under-the-counter adj. illegal; illicit; unlawful.

up'pi·ty (up'ə-tē) adj. arrogant; presumptuous.

up-tight adj. (Slang) 1, tense; nervous. 2, conventional in attitude.

Van Allen radiation belt a belt of ionizing radiation surrounding the earth and extending from approx. 500 miles to approx. 30,000 miles into space.

var'i·fo"cal lens (var'ə-fō'kəl) zoom lens.

very high frequency also, **VHF** designating radio frequencies from 30 to 300 megacycles.

vi·bra'to (vi-brä'tō) n. a tremulous effect or tremolo produced in singing and on various instruments to impart warmth and expressiveness to the tone.

vi·cu'ña (vi-kyoo'nyə) n. 1, a wild ruminant of the Andes, related to the llama. 2, a fabric made from the wool of this animal.

voice'print n. the distinctive pattern of wavy lines made by an individual's voice on a sound spectrograph: used for identification.

weed (wēd) n. (Slang) marijuana.

weight'less adj. having no weight, esp. as a result of a lack of gravitational pull, as in space. —weight'less·ness, n.

welfare state 1, a social system under which the state assumes primary responsibility for the physical, mental, and social well-being of its citizens. 2, a nation, state, etc., in which the system of the welfare state is adopted.

wheat germ the embryo of the wheat kernel, used as a source of vitamins.

wire'tap"per (wī'ər-tap"ər) *n.* one who gets information messages, etc., by electronically listening to someone's telephone conversations. —wire'tap", *n. & v.t. & i.*

woof'er (wûf'ər) *n.* a loudspeaker responsive only to the lower frequencies and used only for reproducing low-pitched sounds.

wrap up 1, conclude, work out the details of. 2, summarize. —wrap'up², *n.* summary; précis.

X'-chro"mo•some *n.* a female sex chromosome.

xe•rog'ra•phy (zi-rāg'rə-fē) *n.* copying by use of light action on an electrically charged photo conductive insulating surface that transfers a special printing powder only from those areas that remain electrically charged, thereby reproducing the image to be copied.

Xe'rox (zī'-rŏks) *n.* 1, (*T.N.*) a machine that copies by xerography. 2,

a copy made by xerography. —*v.t.* to copy by xerography.

Y'-chro"mo•some *n.* a male sex chromosome.

yip'pie (yip'ē) *n.* a radical hippie activist.

ZIP code 1, [*also,* ZIP code number] a special 5-digit number assigned by the U.S. Postal Service to each of the many postal districts throughout the U.S. to speed the distribution of mail. 2, the entire system of ZIP code numbers.

zip gun a homemade gun using .22 caliber bullets.

zonked (zănkt) *adj.* (*Slang*) under or as if under the influence of a hallucinogenic drug.

zoom lens a motion-picture or television camera lens permitting change in the image size without loss of focus. *Also,* varifocal lens.

TABLES OF WEIGHTS AND MEASURES

U.S. SYSTEM

Linear Measure

		1 inch (in)	= 2.54 centimeters (cm)
12	inches	= 1 foot (ft)	0.3048 meter (m)
3	feet	1 yard (yd)	0.9144 meter
5½	yards	1 rod (rd)	5.029 meters
40	rods	1 furlong (fur)	201.168 meters
8	furlongs	1 (statute) mile (mi)	1609.344 meters
3	(statute) miles	1 (land) league	4.828 kilometers
6	feet	1 fathom	1.828 meters
1000 fathoms or 1.1508 statute miles		1 nautical mile (knot)	1.852 kilometers

Area or Square Measure

		1 square inch (sq in)	= 6.452 square centimeters
144	square inches	= 1 square foot (sq ft)	929.030 square centimeters
9	square feet	1 square yard (sq yd)	0.836 square meter
30¼	square yards	1 square rod (sq rd)	25.293 square meters
160	square rods	1 acre	0.405 hectare
640	acres	1 square mile (sq mi)	258.999 hectares
1	square mile	1 section (of land)	
36	square miles	1 township	

Volume or Cubic Measure

		1 cubic inch (cu in)	= 16.387 cubic centimeters
1,728	cubic inches	= 1 cubic foot (cu ft)	0.028 cubic meter
27	cubic feet	1 cubic yard (cu yd)	0.765 cubic meter
16	cubic feet	1 cord foot	
8	cord feet	1 cord	3.625 cubic meters

Capacity Measures

Dry Measure

1 pint (pt)	=	(33.60 cubic inches)	= 0.551 liter
2 pints		1 quart (qt)	1.101 liters
8 quarts		1 peck (pk)	8.810 liters
4 pecks		1 bushel (bu)	35.238 liters

Liquid Measure

1 minim	=	(0.004 cubic inch)	= 0.062 milliliter
60 minims		1 fluid dram (fl dr)	3.697 milliliters
8 fluid drams		1 fluid ounce (fl oz)	0.030 liter
4 fluid ounces		1 gill	0.118 liter
8 fluid ounces		1 cup	0.236 liter
2 cups		1 pint (pt)	0.473 liter
2 pints		1 quart (qt)	0.946 liter
4 quarts		1 gallon	3.785 liters

1 teaspoon (tsp)	1⅓ fluid drams
1 tablespoon (tsb)	3 teaspoons

Weights
Avoirdupois Weight

		1 grain (gr)	= 0.065 gram
27.34 grains	=	1 dram (dr)	1.772 grams
16 drams		1 ounce (oz)	28.350 grams
16 ounces		1 pound (lb)	453.592 grams
100 pounds		1 hundredweight (cwt)	45.359 kilograms
2000 pounds		1 ton (tn)	907.18 kilograms
14 pounds (Great Britain)		1 stone	6.35 kilograms

Troy Weight

		1 grain	= 0.065 gram
3.086 grains	=	1 carat (c)	200. milligrams
24 grains		1 pennyweight (dwt)	1.555 grams
20 pennyweights		1 ounce (oz)	31.104 grams
12 ounces		1 pound (lb)	373.242 grams

METRIC SYSTEM

Linear Measure

	1 millimeter (mm) =	0.039 inch
10 millimeters =	1 centimeter (cm)	0.394 inch
10 centimeters	1 decimeter (dm)	3.937 inches
10 decimeters	1 meter (m)	39.37 inches
10 meters	1 decameter (dam)	32.8 feet
10 decameters	1 hectometer (hm)	328. feet
10 hectometers	1 kilometer (km)	0.621 mile

Square Measure

	1 square millimeter = (sq mm)	0.002 square inch
100 square millimeters =	1 square centimeter (cm^2)	0.155 square inch
100 square centimeters	1 square decimeter (dm^2)	15.499 square inches
100 square decimeters	1 square meter (m^2)	1549. square inches
1 square meter	1 centaire	10.76 square feet
100 centiares	1 are (a)	119.6 square yards
100 ares	1 hectare (ha)	2.471 acres
100 hectares	1 square kilometer (km^2)	0.386 square mile

Volume Measure

	1 cubic centimeter (cm^3) =	.061 cubic inch
1000 cubic centimeters =	1 cubic decimeter (dm^3)	61.02 cubic inches
1000 cubic decimeters	1 cubic meter (cm^3)	35.314 cubic feet

Capacity Measure

	1 milliliter (ml)	=	.027 fluid drams
1 milliliters	= 1 centiliter (cl)		.338 fluid ounce
10 centiliters	1 deciliter (dl)		3.38 fluid ounces
10 deciliters	1 liter (l)		1.057 liquid quarts or 0.908 dry quart
10 liters	1 decaliter (dal)		2.64 gallons or 0.284 bushel
10 decaliters	1 hectoliter (hl)		26.418 gallons or 2.838 bushels
10 hectoliters	1 kiloliter (kl)		264.18 gallons or 28.38 bushels

Weights

	1 milligram (mg)	0.015 grain
10 milligrams	= 1 centigram (cg)	0.154 grain
10 centigrams	1 decigram (dg)	1.543 grains
10 decigrams	1 gram (g)	15.432 grains
10 grams	1 decagram (dag)	0.353 ounce
10 decagrams	1 hectogram (hg)	3.527 ounces
10 hectograms	1 kilogram (kg)	2.205 pounds
100 kilograms	1 quintal	220.46 pounds
10 quintals	1 metric ton (t)	2204.6 pounds

SIGNET and MENTOR Books for Your Reference Shelf